AA

365

Pub Walks
& Cycle Rides
in Britain

A PUB ON THE WAY

Produced by AA Publishing
© Automobile Association Developments Limited 2005

Published by AA Publishing (a trading name of Automobile Association Developments Limited, whose registered office is Fanum House, Basing View, Basingstoke, Hampshire RG21 4EA; registered number 1878835)

Ordnance Survey® This product includes mapping data licensed from Ordnance Survey® with the permission of the Controller of Her Majesty's Stationery Office.
© Crown copyright 2005. All rights reserved. Licence number 399221

ISBN-10: 0-7495-4625-5
ISBN-13: 978-0-7495-4625-0
A02014

A CIP catalogue record for this book is available from the British Library.

The contents of this book are believed correct at the time of printing. Nevertheless, the publishers cannot be held responsible for any errors or omissions or for changes in the details given in this book or for the consequences of any reliance on the information it provides. We have tried to ensure accuracy, but things do change and we would be grateful if readers would advise us of any inaccuracies they encounter. This does not affect your statutory rights.

Please write to: 365 Pub Walks and Cycle Rides in Britain
AA Publishing, Fanum House, Basing View, Basingstoke RG21 4EA

We have taken all reasonable steps to ensure that these walks and cycle rides are safe and achievable by walkers and cyclists with a realistic level of fitness. However, all outdoor activities involve a degree of risk and the publishers accept no responsibility for any injuries caused to readers whilst following these routes. For more advice on using this book and walking and cycling in safety, see page 6.

Versions of these routes appear in the AA 50 and 100 Local Walks series and in 1,001 Walks in Britain.

Visit AA Publishing at www.theAA.com/bookshop

Page layout by Andrew Milne Design, West Sussex
Colour reproduction by kdp, Newbury, Berkshire
Printed and bound in China by Leo Paper Group

AA Publishing would like to thank Chartech for supplying aqua3 OS maps for this book. For more information or to order maps visit their website at www.aqua3.com

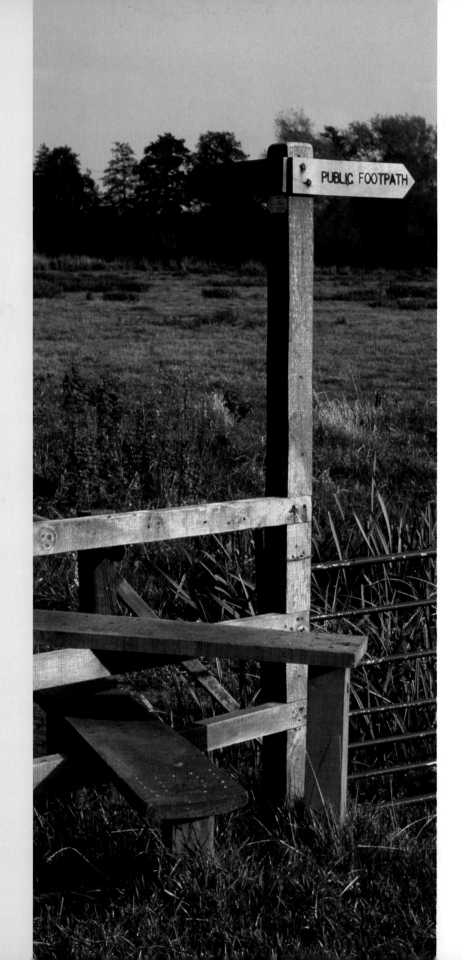

Contents

page

SOUTHWEST ENGLAND   7 – 60
Cornwall, Devon, Somerset, Dorset, Bath & NE Somerset, Wiltshire

SOUTHEAST ENGLAND   61 – 114
Hampshire, Isle of Wight, West Sussex, East Sussex, Surrey, London, Berkshire, Buckinghamshire, Kent

WALES & THE MARCHES   115 – 146
Pembrokeshire, Vale of Glamorgan, Cardiff, Isle of Anglesey, Conwy, Denbighshire, Powys, Herefordshire, Shropshire, Swansea, Gwynedd, Wrexham

CENTRAL ENGLAND (SOUTH)   147 – 202
Gloucestershire, Oxfordshire, Worcestershire, Warwickshire, Birmingham, West Midlands

CENTRAL ENGLAND (NORTH)   203 – 252
Staffordshire, Derbyshire

EASTERN ENGLAND   253 – 290
Northamptonshire, Leicestershire, Rutland, Essex, Suffolk, Norfolk, Hertfordshire, Bedfordshire, Cambridgeshire, Nottinghamshire, Lincolnshire

NORTHWEST ENGLAND   291 – 344
Cheshire, Lancashire, Cumbria, Merseyside

NORTHEAST ENGLAND   345 – 398
South Yorkshire, West Yorkshire, East Riding of Yorkshire, South Yorkshire, Durham, Tyne & Wear, Northumberland

SCOTLAND   399 – 413
Stirling, City of Edinburgh, Scottish Borders, Perth & Kinross, Dumfries & Galloway, Highlands

Using this book

Each main walk and cycle ride has a coloured panel giving essential information, including the distance, terrain, nature of the paths, and where to park your car.

MAPPED WALK AND CYCLE ROUTES

1 MINIMUM TIME: The time stated for each route is the estimated minimum time that a reasonably fit family group would take to complete the circuit. This does not include rest or refreshment stops.

2 MAPS: Each main route is shown on a detailed map. However, some detail is lost because of the scale. For this reason, we always recommend that you use the maps along with the suggested OS map.

3 START/FINISH: Indicates the start and finish point and parking. The six-figure grid reference prefixed by two letters refers to a 100km square of the National Grid. You'll find more information on grid references on most Ordnance Survey maps.

4 LEVEL OF DIFFICULTY: The illustrated walks and cycle rides have been graded from 1 to 3. Easier routes, such as those with little total ascent, on easy footpaths or level trails, or those covering shorter distances are graded 1. The hardest routes, either because they include a lot of ascent, greater distances, or are in hilly, more demanding terrains, are graded 3.

5 TOURIST INFORMATION: A contact number for the nearest tourist information office is given for further local information, in particular opening details for the

attractions listed in the 'Where to go from here' section.

6 CYCLE HIRE: We list, within reason, the nearest cycle hire shop/centre.

7 ⬤ Here we highlight at a glance any potential difficulties or hazards along the route. If a particular route is suitable for older, fitter children we say so here.

TEXT-ONLY WALKS

Each chapter finishes with a number of text-only walk routes. All have comprehensive, note-form directions. For each route we suggest a pub, either on the route or as close as possible.

About the pub

Generally, all the pubs featured are on the walk or cycle route. Some are close to the start/finish point, others are at the midway point, and occasionally, the recommended pub is a short drive from the start/finish We have included a cross-section of pubs, from homely village locals and isolated rural gems to traditional inns and upmarket country pubs that specialise in food. What they all have in common is that they serve food and welcome children.

The description of the pub is intended to convey its history and character and in the 'food' section we list a selection of dishes served. Under 'family facilities', we say if the pub offers a children's menu or smaller portions of adult dishes, and whether the pub has a family room, highchairs, baby-changing facilities, or toys. There is detail on the garden, terrace, and any play area.

DIRECTIONS: If the pub is close to the start point we state 'see Getting to the start'. If the pub is on the route we indicate where, in addition to general directions. If the pub is a short drive away from the finish point, we give detailed directions.

PARKING: The number of parking spaces is given. All but a few of the walks and

rides start away from the pub. If the pub car park is the parking/start point, then we have been given permission by the landlord to print the fact. You should always let the landlord or a member of staff know that you are using the car park before setting off.

OPEN: If the pub is open all week we state 'daily' and if it's open throughout the day we say 'all day', otherwise we just give the days/sessions the pub is closed.

FOOD: If the pub serves food all week we state 'daily' and if food is served throughout the day we say 'all day', otherwise we just give the days/sessions when food is not served.

BREWERY/COMPANY: This is the name of the brewery to which the pub is tied or the pub company that owns it. 'Free house' means that the pub is independently owned and run.

REAL ALE: We list the regular real ales available on handpump. 'Guest beers' indicates that the pub rotates beers from a number of microbreweries.

DOGS: On the mapped walk routes, we say if dogs are allowed into the pub or not, and detail any restrictions.

ROOMS: We list the number of bedrooms and how many are en suite. For prices please contact the pub.

Please note that pubs change hands frequently and new chefs are employed, so menu details and facilities may change at short notice. Not all the pubs featured in this guide are listed in the *AA Pub Guide*. For information on those that are, including AA-rated accommodation, and for a comprehensive selection of pubs across Britain, please refer to the *AA Pub Guide* or visit www.theAA.com

Alternative refreshment stops

We suggest other pubs or cafés along the route. If there are no other places on the route, we list the nearest village or town where you can find somewhere else to eat and drink.

☞ Where to go from here

Many of the routes are short and may only take a few hours. You may wish to explore the surrounding area after lunch or before tackling the route, so we have selected a few attractions with children in mind.

000

1
3h00 | 8.5 MILES | 13.7 KM | LEVEL 123 | **4**
SHORTER ALTERNATIVE ROUTE
1h30 | 4 MILES | 6.4 KM | LEVEL 123

2 MAP: OS Explorer OL24 White Peak

3 START/FINISH: Rudyard Old Station, grid ref SJ 955579

TRAILS/TRACKS: old railway trackbed

LANDSCAPE: wooded lake shore, peaceful pastures and meadows

PUBLIC TOILETS: Rudyard village

5 TOURIST INFORMATION: Leek, tel 01538 483741

6 CYCLE HIRE: none near by

THE PUB: The Abbey Inn, Leek, see Directions to the pub, page 27

7 ⬤ Take care along the banks of the lake – keep well away from the shore line

Walking and cycling in safety

WALKING

All the walks are suitable for families, but less experienced family groups, especially those with younger children, should try the shorter or easier walks first. Route finding is usually straightforward, but the maps are for guidance only and we recommend that you always take the suggested Ordnance Survey map with you.

Risks

Although each walk has been researched with a view to minimising any risks, no walk in the countryside can be considered to be completely free from risk. Walking in the outdoors will always require a degree of common sense and judgement to ensure safety, especially for young children.

- Be particularly careful on cliff paths and in upland terrain, where the consequences of a slip can be serious.
- Remember to check tidal conditions before walking on the seashore.
- Some sections of routes are by, or cross, busy roads. Remember traffic is a danger even on minor country lanes.
- Be careful around farmyard machinery and livestock.
- Be aware of the consequences of changes in the weather and check the forecast before you set out. Ensure the whole family is properly equipped, wearing appropriate clothing and a good pair of boots or sturdy walking shoes. Take waterproof clothing with you and carry spare clothing and a torch if you are walking in the winter months. Remember the weather can change quickly at any time of the year, and in moorland and heathland areas, mist and fog can make route finding much harder. In summer, take account of the heat and sun by wearing a hat and carrying enough water.
- On walks away from centres of population you should carry a whistle and survival bag. If you do have an accident requiring emergency services, make a note of your position as accurately as possible and dial 999.

CYCLING

Cycling is a fun activity which children love, and teaching your child to ride a bike, and going on family cycling trips, are rewarding experiences. Not only is cycling a great way to travel, but as a regular form of exercise it can make an invaluable contribution to a child's health and fitness, and increase their confidence and independence.

The growth of motor traffic has made Britain's roads increasingly dangerous and unattractive to cyclists. Cycling with children is an added responsibility and, as with everything, there is a risk when taking them out cycling. However, in recent years measures have been taken to address this, including the on-going development of the National Cycle Network (8,000 miles utilising quiet lanes and traffic-free paths) and local designated off-road routes for families, such as converted railway lines, canal tow paths and forest tracks.

In devising the cycle rides in this guide, every effort has been made to use these designated cycle paths, or to link them with quiet country lanes and waymarked byways and bridleways. Unavoidably, in a few cases, some relatively busy B-roads link the quieter, more attractive routes.

Rules of the road

- Ride in single file on narrow and busy roads.
- Be alert, look and listen for traffic, especially on narrow lanes and blind bends and be extra careful when descending steep hills, as loose gravel can lead to an accident.
- In wet weather make sure you keep a good distance between you and other riders.
- Make sure you indicate your intentions clearly.
- Brush up on *The Highway Code* before venturing out on to the road.

Off-road safety code of conduct

- Only ride where you know it is legal to do so. It is forbidden to cycle on public footpaths, marked in yellow. The only 'rights of way' open to cyclists are bridleways (blue markers) and unsurfaced tracks, known as byways, which are open to all traffic and waymarked in red.
- Canal tow paths: you need a permit to cycle on some stretches of tow path (www.waterscape.com). Remember that access paths can be steep and slippery and always get off and push your bike under low bridges and by locks.
- Always yield to walkers and horses, giving adequate warning of your approach.

- Don't expect to cycle at high speeds.
- Keep to the main trail to avoid any unnecessary erosion to the area beside the trail and to prevent skidding, especially if it is wet.
- Remember the Country Code.

Cycling with children

Children can use a child seat from the age of eight months, or from the time they can hold themselves upright. A number of child seats fit on the front or rear of a bike, and it's worth investigating towable two-seat trailers. 'Trailer bicycles', suitable for five-to ten-year-olds, can be attached to the rear of an adult's bike, so that the adult has control, allowing the child to pedal if he/she wishes. Family cycling can be made easier by using a tandem, as it can carry a child seat and tow trailers. 'Kiddy-cranks' for shorter legs can be fitted to the rear seat tube, enabling either parent to take their child out cycling. For older children it is better to purchase the right size bike: an oversized bike will be difficult to control, and potentially dangerous.

Preparing your bicycle

Basic routine includes checking the wheels for broken spokes or excess play in the bearings, and checking for punctures, undue tyre wear and the correct tyre pressures. Ensure that the brake blocks are firmly in place and not worn, and that cables are not frayed or too slack. Lubricate hubs, pedals, gear mechanisms and cables. Make sure you have a pump, a bell, a rear rack to carry panniers and, if cycling at night, a set of working lights.

Preparing yourself

Equipping the family with cycling clothing need not be expensive; comfort is the key. Essential items for cycling are padded cycling shorts, warm stretch leggings (avoid tight-fitting and seamed trousers like jeans or baggy tracksuit trousers that may become caught in the chain), stiff-soled training shoes, and a wind/waterproof jacket. Fingerless gloves are comfortable.

A cycling helmet provides essential protection and are essential for young children learning to cycle.

Wrap your child up with several layers in colder weather. Make sure you and those with you are easily visible by all road users, by wearing light-coloured or luminous clothing in daylight and reflective strips or sashes in failing light and when it is dark.

What to take with you

Invest in a pair of medium-sized panniers (rucksacks can affect balance) to carry the necessary gear for the day. Take extra clothes with you, the amount depending on the season, and always pack a light wind/waterproof jacket. Carry a basic tool kit (tyre levers, adjustable spanner, a small screwdriver, puncture repair kit, a set of Allen keys) and practical spares, such as an inner tube, a universal brake/gear cable, and a selection of nuts and bolts. Also, always take a pump and a strong lock.

Cycling, especially in hilly terrain and off-road, saps energy, so take enough food and drink. Always carry plenty of water, especially in hot and humid weather. Consume high-energy snacks like cereal bars, cake or fruits, eating little and often to combat feeling weak and tired. Remember that children get thirsty (and hungry) much more quickly than adults so always have food and diluted juices available for them.

And finally, the most important advice of all—enjoy yourselves!

Useful cycling websites

- National Cycle Network: www.sustrans.org.uk www.nationalcyclenetwork.org.uk
- British Waterways (tow path cycling): www.waterscape.com
- Forestry Commission (for cycling on Forestory Commission woodland): www.forestry.gov.uk/recreation
- Cyclists Touring Club: www.ctc.org.uk

Southwest

ENGLAND

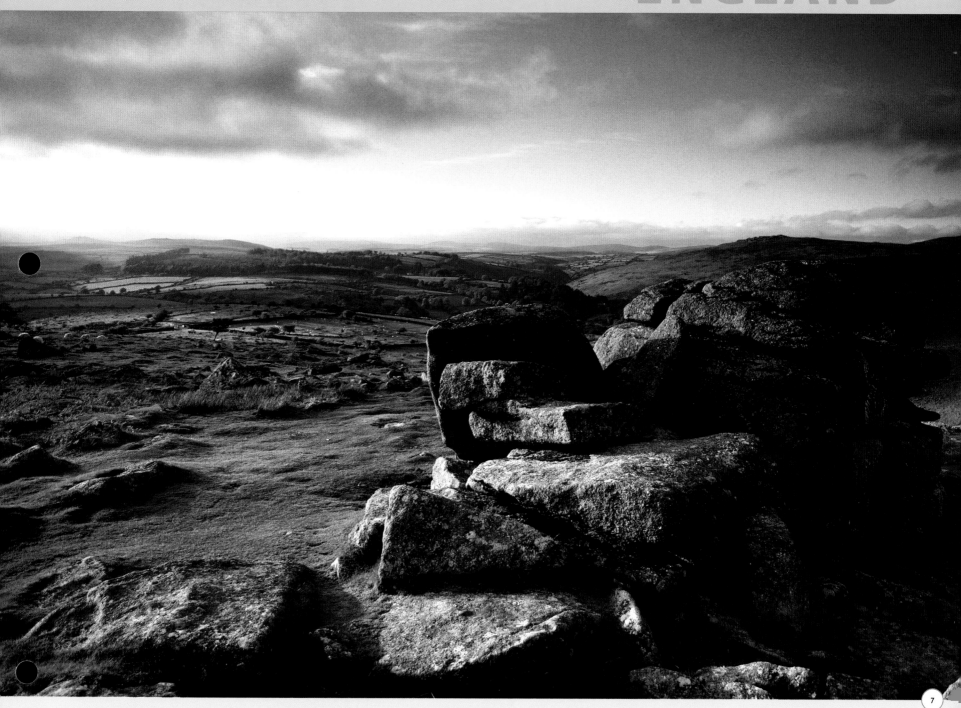

Contents

		page
1	Lamorna, Cornwall	9
2	Marazion, Cornwall	11
3	Cadgwith, Cornwall	13
4	St Agnes, Cornwall	15
5	Nare Head, Cornwall	17
6	Pentewan Valley, Cornwall	19
7	Padstow, Cornwall	21
8	Bude Bay, Cornwall	23
9	Braunton, Devon	25
10	Torrington, Devon	27
11	Cremyll, Cornwall	29
12	Brent Tor, Devon	31
13	Plym Valley, Devon	33
14	Burgh Island, Devon	35
15	Dartington, Devon	37
16	Teign Valley, Devon	39
17	Exmouth, Devon	41
18	Broadhembury, Devon	43
19	Seatown, Dorset	45
20	Osmington, Dorset	47
21	Corfe Castle, Dorset	49
22	Bristol & Bath, Bath & NE Somerset	51
23	Bradford on Avon, Wiltshire	53
24	Corsham, Wiltshire	55
25 to 27	Cornwall	57
28 to 30	Devon	57
31 to 36	Somerset	58
37 to 42	Dorset	59
43 to 48	Wiltshire	60

SOUTHWEST ENGLAND

KEY

- ■ Walk route
- ● Cycle route
- ■ Unmapped walk

The lapwing (Vanellus vanellus)

The Merry Maidens. Legend has it that 19 girls were turned to stone here

A circular walk to Lamorna

A coastal and inland walk from Lamorna Cove, passing an ancient stone circle.

Quarries and standing stones

The walk starts from popular, picturesque Lamorna Cove, once the scene of granite quarrying. The quay at Lamorna was built so that ships could load up with the quarried stone, but the tidal regimen made berthing difficult. Much of the stone was carried overland.

The coast path west from Lamorna winds its sinuous way through tumbled granite boulders, then climbs steeply to the cliff tops. Soon the path descends steeply to the delightful St Loy's Cove, a secluded boulder beach. Spring comes early at St Loy; the subtropical vegetation through which the walk leads reflects the area's mild and moist micro-climate. From St Loy's

woods you climb inland to reach two enthralling monuments. The first is the Tregiffian burial chamber, a late Bronze Age entrance grave.

Just along the road from Tregiffian is the Merry Maidens stone circle. This late Neolithic/Bronze Age structure is an ancient ceremonial and ritual site of major importance. The final part of the walk leads to a wonderful old trackway that leads over water-worn stones into the Lamorna Valley along a route that may well have originated in the time of the stone circles themselves.

the walk

1 From the far end of the seaward car park in the cove, at the end of the terrace above **Lamorna Harbour**, follow the coast path through some short rocky sections. Continue along the coast path past the tops of Tregurnow Cliff and Rosemodress Cliff.

2 Pass the **nature reserve** (open access) set up by author Derek Tangye, who lived along this coast, then pass above the entrance ramp and steps to **Tater du Lighthouse**. Pass a large residence on the right and then, where the track bends right, keep left along the narrow coast path, at a signpost.

3 Descend steeply (take great care when the ground is muddy) from Boscawen Cliff to **St Loy's Cove**. Cross a section of sea-smoothed boulders that may be slippery when wet. Follow the path inland through dense vegetation and by the stream. Cross a private drive then climb steeply uphill. Go over a stile onto a track, turn right over a stile and follow the path through trees.

4 By a **wooden signpost** and three trees, go sharply down right and cross the stream on large boulders, then follow a hedged-in path round left. In about 50yds (46m), by a wooden signpost, go sharp right and up to a surfaced lane. Turn left and follow the lane uphill. At a junction with a bend on another track, keep ahead and uphill. At **Boskenna Farm** buildings follow the surfaced lane round left and keep ahead.

5 From the lane, at the entrance drive to a bungalow on the right, the right-of-way goes through a field gate (not signed), then cuts across the field corner to a wooden stile in a wire fence. Beyond this, the way (there's no path) leads diagonally across the field to its top right-hand corner, where a stile leads into a large roadside lay-by with a **granite cross** at its edge.

A striking variety of rocks around the shore at Lamorna Cove

| 3h30 | 6 MILES | 9.7 KM | LEVEL 1 2 3 |

MAP: OS Explorer 102 Land's End

START/FINISH: Lamorna Cove; parking at the Quay; grid ref: SW 450241

PATHS: good coastal footpaths, field paths and rocky tracks

LANDSCAPE: picturesque coastline, fields and wooded valleys, 7 stiles

PUBLIC TOILETS: Lamorna Cove

TOURIST INFORMATION: Penzance, tel 01736 362207

THE PUB: Lamorna Wink, Lamorna

❶ Undulating, rugged and stony coast path; a few steep ascents and descents; suitable for older, more experienced children

Getting to the start

Lamorna Cove is signposted off the B3315 between Penzance and Land's End, 4 miles (6.4km) west of Penzance via Newlyn. Drive through Lamorna village, passing the Lamorna Wink to the cove and parking area.

Researched and written by:
David Hancock, Des Hannigan

The Tregiffian burial chamber

while you're there

The Tregiffian burial chamber is a late Bronze Age entrance grave which was uncovered in the 1960s. The cup-marked stone is a reproduction; the valuable original is in the county museum at Truro.

One of Cornwall's most famous monuments, the Merry Maidens stone circle, refers to a myth of young girls turned to stone for dancing on a Sunday. The standing stones near by, called the Pipers, were reputedly the guilty musicians.

Lamorna Wink

This oddly named pub was one of the original Kiddleywinks, a product of the 1830 Beer Act that enabled any householder to buy a liquor licence. Popular with walkers and tourists exploring the rugged Penwith Peninsula, the Wink is an unspoilt, no-frills country local decorated with warship mementoes, sea photographs and nautical brassware. One of the simply furnished rooms has a pool table and books for sale, while the homely main bar is warmed in winter by a glowing coal fire. You'll find tip-top Cornish beer on tap, best enjoyed in summer at one of the picnic benches to the front or in the side garden.

Food

Expect a limited lunchtime menu offering sandwiches, filled jacket potatoes, fresh local crab, salads and ploughman's lunches.

Family facilities

Children are welcome in the eating areas of the bar.

Alternative refreshment stops

There is a shop and a café at Lamorna Cove by the car park.

☛ Where to go from here

Combine a visit to one of Cornwall's finest beaches at Porthcurno with a tour of the Museum of Submarine Telegraphy, housed in underground tunnels that were the centre of the British communications system during World War Two (www.porthcurno.org.uk). Don't miss the Minack Theatre built high on the cliffs above Porthcurno by one remarkable woman: Rowena Cade. There are few better backdrops for plays than the one at this famous little theatre – dramatic cliffs and blue sea stretching into the distance. Time your visit to one of the summer season plays (www.minack.com).

about the pub

Lamorna Wink
Lamorna, Penzance
Cornwall TR19 6XH
Tel 01736 731566

DIRECTIONS: see Getting to the start

PARKING: 40

OPEN: daily; all day in summer

FOOD: lunchtimes only (check in winter)

BREWERY/COMPANY: free house

REAL ALE: Sharp's Doom Bar, Skinner's Cornish Knocker

DOGS: allowed inside

6 Follow the road right to the **Tregiffian burial chamber** on the right and then to the **Merry Maidens stone circle**. From the stone circle continue to a field corner, then cross over a steep wall stile by a gate. Follow a path diagonally right across the next field towards buildings. Go over a stone stile onto a road, then go down the left-hand of two lanes, a surfaced lane with a 'No Through Road' sign.

7 Where the lane ends keep ahead onto a **public bridleway**. Follow a shady and very rocky track downhill to the public road. Turn right and walk down the road, with care, passing the **Lamorna Wink pub**, to the car park.

what to look for

If you do this walk in spring you will be treated to a genuine 'host of golden daffodils'. The cliffside paths are flanked by hundreds of daffodils that have spread from cultivated meadows. Until recent years, flower-growing was an important element in the small-scale market gardening carried out along this western coast of Mount's Bay. Another marvellous floral display is offered by the swathes of bluebells, found on the open cliffs and in the lush woodland behind St Loy's Cove.

did you know?

The Botallack tin mine on the edge of the cliffs had a shaft extending 0.5 mile (800m) under the sea. A by-product of tin smelting was arsenic, commonly used in the production of dyes and cosmetics.

Mine buildings perched on the tin-mining coast of St Just and Botallack

Marazion to Penzance

St Michael's Mount seen from across the river

Enjoy an easy ride along one of south Cornwall's most beautiful bays.

St Michael's Mount

Marazion – and the whole of Mount's Bay – is dominated by the rocky bulk of St Michael's Mount, accessible by foot via the 600yd (549m) causeway at low tide, and by ferry from the beach when the tide is up (weather permitting). This extraordinary granite outcrop is topped by a medieval castle, dating from the 12th century and now mainly in the care of the National Trust. Originally the site of a Benedictine priory, it has been the home of the St Aubyn family for over 300 years. There is also a 14th-century church on the rock, as well as a pub, restaurant and shops round the little harbour, and a private garden with limited opening times. Marazion Marsh, passed on the right of the road near the start of the ride, is the largest reedbed in Cornwall. An RSPB nature reserve, this area of reedbeds, open water and willow carr attracts overwintering bitterns, sedge, Cetti's and reed warblers, butterflies and damselflies. There is a hide from which the birds can be watched (including the rare, spotted crake) and good access via boardwalks.

the ride

1 This ride is part of the First and Last Trail, the first stretch of the Cornish Way long-distance cycle route, which starts at Land's End and runs for 180 miles (288km) through the county. Marazion, where this ride starts, is Cornwall's oldest charter town, dating from 1257. Its unusual name comes from the Cornish 'marghas yow' – Thursday market. Marazion was the main trading port in Mount's Bay until Penzance overtook it in the 16th century. It's worth having a look around this attractive village before you set off.

From the pub car park cycle uphill (away from the beach) onto West End. (The Godolphin Arms can be found by turning right.) Turn left along **West End** and cycle out of the village. There is a parking area on the left along much of this road, so look out for people opening their car doors suddenly. **Marazion Marsh** lies to the right.

2 Where the road bears right to cross the Penzance to Exeter main railway line, keep straight ahead through a **parking area**, with the Pizza Shack (and toilets behind) on the right. Again, take care cycling through the car park.

3 Keep ahead and leave the car park to the left of the old station (now the **Station pub**), to join a level track that runs along the back of the beach. Follow this track, passing more public toilets on the right.

St Michael's Mount, seen from Marazion

1h30 · **5 MILES** · **8 KM** · **LEVEL 123**

(2)

MAP: OS Explorer 102 Land's End

START/FINISH: The Godolphin Arms car park, Marazion, grid ref: SW 516306

TRAILS/TRACKS: short stretch of road, track generally level, rough and bumpy in places

LANDSCAPE: village, beach, seaside, townscape

PUBLIC TOILETS: on Points **2** and **3** of the route, and in the car park at Penzance

TOURIST INFORMATION: Penzance, tel 01736 362207

CYCLE HIRE: The Cycle Centre, Penzance, tel 01736 351671

THE PUB: The Godolphin Arms, Marazion

🅛 Short stretch of road at start and finish, one car park to be negotiated

Getting to the start

From Penzance, take the A30 past the heliport. At the second roundabout turn right, signed Marazion. The Godolphin Arms car park is signed right (towards the beach).

Why do this cycle ride?

This level, easy, there-and-back route along the edge of Mount's Bay, with spectacular views over St Michael's Mount, is an ideal option for families with young children. With just a short road stretch at the start and finish, the ride runs along the back of the huge expanse of sands between Marazion and Penzance, originally a tiny fishing community, today popular with tourists.

Researched and written by: Sue Viccars

did you know?

During the 18th century Penzance had the largest tin smelter in Cornwall, a crucial source of wealth and jobs for the local community. After smelting, the high-quality tin was poured from a kettle into moulds to form ingots.

Each company had its own sign to stamp on the ingots; in Cornwall a lamb with a flag, a holy symbol representing purity, was much favoured.

*Cetti's warbler
(Cettia cetti)*

The Godolphin Arms

Located right at the water's edge opposite St Michael's Mount, The Godolphin Arms affords superb views across the bay. It's so close that the sea splashes at the windows in the winter and you can watch the movement of seals, dolphins, ferries and fishing boats. From the traditional wood-floored bar and beer terrace to the light and airy restaurant and most of the bedrooms, the Mount is clearly visible.

Food

The bar menu offers a choice of salads, sandwiches, light bites such as pan-fried sardines and spicy meatballs, and seafood tagliatelle, or ham, egg and chips. Seafood features prominently on the dinner menu, perhaps line-caught whole sea bass stuffed with thyme and lemon.

Family facilities

Children of all ages are allowed in the pub. There's an area set aside for families, and high chairs and baby-changing facilities for young children. Smaller portions from the main menu, a children's menu and two family bedrooms are also available. The beach is just below the pub's rear terrace.

about the pub

The Godolphin Arms
West End, Marazion
Penzance, Cornwall TR17 0EN
Tel 01736 710202
www.godolphinarms.co.uk

DIRECTIONS: see Getting to the start

PARKING: 70

OPEN: daily; all day

FOOD: daily; all day in summer

BREWERY/COMPANY: free house

REAL ALE: Sharp's Special and Eden Ale, Skinner's Spriggan

ROOMS: 10 en suite

Alternative refreshment stops
There are plenty of pubs, cafés and restaurants in both Marazion and Penzance.

☛ Where to go from here
Head for Newlyn where you will find Britain's only working salt pilchard factory, the Pilchard Works, where you can experience at first hand a Cornish factory that has continued producing salt pilchards for over 90 years (www.pilchardworks.co.uk). Art lovers should visit the Penlee House Gallery and Museum in Penzance (www.penleehouse.org.uk) to learn more about the Newlyn School of Artists and view one of the regular exhibitions. Kids will enjoy a visit to the Lighthouse Centre in Penzance or to the Wild Bird Hospital and Sanctuary in Mousehole. For information about St Michael's Mount see www.nationaltrust.org.uk.

4 Take care where the track drops to meet an entrance road to a **beachside car park** (there are warning notices 'Give way to traffic'). Pass through the parking area and continue along the track, with the railway close by on the right.

5 Pass the **heliport**, from which helicopters fly regularly to the Isles of Scilly, which lie more than 17 miles (28 km) southwest of Land's End (day trips are available). Good views open up ahead towards Penzance.

6 On approaching the station the track narrows into a concrete walkway and becomes busier, so look out for pedestrians. Follow the track into the car park by Penzance railway and bus station, with the **tourist information centre** to the right. This is where you should turn round and return to Marazion. The First and Last

Trail actually runs along the road to Newlyn and beyond, but is pretty busy in terms of traffic and is not recommended for families with young children.

There is a lot to see in Penzance, however, which developed as in important pilchard fishing centre in medieval times. Penzance, Newlyn and Mousehole (along the coast to the west) were all destroyed by Spanish raiders in 1595, but by the early 17th century Penzance's fortunes had revived on account of the export of tin from local mines, and it became a fashionable place to live. The coming of the Great Western Railway in Victorian times gave the town another boost and it is now the main centre in Penwith (the far western part of Cornwall). The harbour is always full of interest, and it is from here that the RMV *Scillonian* makes regular sailings to the Isles of Scilly.

did you know?

Local crabs are brought ashore by fishermen who work from small coves such as Cadgwith and Carleon. As well as crabs, lobsters and crawfish are also caught – the latter usually in tangle nets.

Traps for lobster and crab

Around Cadgwith

A wandering route between coast and countryside through the landscape of the Lizard Peninsula.

Serpentine rock

The serpentine rock of the Lizard Peninsula is fascinating. Its geological label, serpentinite fails to slither quite so easily off the tongue as does its popular usage 'serpentine'. The name derives from the sinuous veins of green, red, yellow and white that wriggle across the dark green or brownish red surface of the rock. The best serpentine is easily carved and shaped and can be polished to a beautiful sheen. In the 19th century serpentine furnishings were the height of fashion but the industry declined during the 1890s. Serpentine became less popular for use in shop fronts and monuments as cheaper, more resilient marble from Italy and Spain began to dominate the market. Today serpentine craftsmen still operate in little workshops on The Lizard and you can buy serpentine souvenirs at Lizard Village. Throughout this walk are stiles built of serpentine whose surfaces are mirror-smooth and slippery. Admire, but take care when they are wet.

The walk first takes a fittingly wandering route inland to the sleepy village of Ruan Minor from where a narrow lane leads down to the Poltesco Valley. At the mouth of the valley is Carleon Cove, once the site of waterwheels, steam engines, machine shops, storehouses and a factory where serpentine was processed. Only a few ruins remain. A narrow harbour pool, almost stagnant now, is dammed on the seaward side by a deep shingle bank where once there was an outlet to the sea.

From Carleon Cove the coast path is followed pleasantly to Cadgwith, an archetypal Cornish fishing village. Cadgwith has a number of thatched cottages, a rare sight in windy Cornwall, although coverings of wire-mesh on most of them indicate wise precaution against storm damage.

Cadgwith still supports a fleet of small fishing boats and is given an enduring identity because of it. Beyond the village the coast path leads to the Devil's Frying Pan, a vast gulf in the cliffs caused by the collapse of a section of coast. From here the path leads on for a short distance along the edge of the cliffs before the route turns inland to the Church of the Holy Cross at Grade. Two fields beyond the church you find the ancient St Ruan's Well and the road that leads back to the start of this ramble.

the walk

1 Go left along a grassy ride below the **car park**, to a stile. Cross a field, then branch right through a gate to join a

The sea bubbles and fizzes at the Devil's Frying Pan at Cadgwith

---

2h00	4.5 MILES	7.2 KM	LEVEL 1 2 3

MAP: OS Explorer 103 The Lizard

START/FINISH: Cadgwith car park, about 350yds (320m) from Cadgwith. Busy in summer; grid ref: SW 719146

PATHS: very good, coast path occasionally rocky in places, field paths

LANDSCAPE: landlocked lanes and woodland tracks, coastal footpaths high above the sea

PUBLIC TOILETS: Ruan Minor and Cadgwith

TOURIST INFORMATION: Helston, tel 01326 565431

THE PUB: Cadgwith Cove Inn, Cadgwith Cove

❶ There are two moderate climbs along the coast path and the cliff path can be slippery when wet

Getting to the start

From the A394 at Helston take the A3083 south, signposted 'The Lizard'. After 8 miles (12.9km) turn left for Cadgwith and follow signs for the car park. Avoid entering the village as the lanes are very steep and narrow.

Researched and written by: David Hancock, Des Hannigan

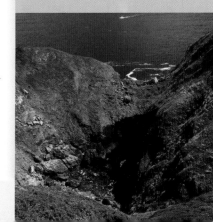

while you're there

Water is slow to drain from the soil of the Cadgwith and Lizard areas, due to the impermeable nature of the underlying rock. This results in the development of many marshy areas, known as wet flushes, which support moisture-loving plants.

There are several places where you should see the greater horsetail, an attractive, exotic-looking plant that has long feathery branches and segmented flower stalks. On the coast proper look for the sturdy tree mallow, a tall plant with hairy stem and purple flowers.

wooded path. Turn right at a lane, cross a bridge then, on the corner by the **postbox**, go up the track ahead. Turn right at an unsigned junction and continue to the main road at **Ruan Minor**.

2 Go left and, just beyond the shop, turn left down a surfaced path. Rejoin the main road by a **thatched cottage** (there are toilets just before the road). Cross diagonally right, then go down a lane past the Church of St Ruan.

3 Just past an **old mill** and a bridge, go right at a T-junction to reach the car park at **Poltesco**. From the far end of the car park follow a track, signposted 'Carleon Cove'. Go right at a junction.

4 Turn left at a T-junction just above the cove and again turn left where the path branches in about 0.25 mile (400m). Continue along the cliff-edge path to **Cadgwith**.

5 Follow a narrow path, signposted 'Coast Path'. By a house gateway, go left up a surfaced path, signposted '**Devil's Frying Pan**'. At an open area turn left, pass Townplace Cottage, cross a meadow and reach the Devil's Frying Pan itself.

6 At a junction, just past a chalet studio, follow a path inland to a T-junction with a rough track. Turn left and, at a public lane, go left again to reach the entrance to **Grade church**, after 1 mile (1.6km). Go through the gate to the church.

7 Follow the field edge behind the church, then cross the next field to reach a lane. **St Ruan's Well** is opposite diagonally left. Turn right for 200yds (183m), then branch off right between **stone pillars** to return to the car park.

Above: The village of Cadgwith perches on steep slopes. Thatched buildings are of local serpentine rock

what to look for

The Church of St Ruan is a small, endearing building built mainly of local serpentine stone. It has a low tower, as if bitten off by the notorious Lizard wind. The east window is dedicated to Thomas Richard Collinson Harrison, a 16 year old who died in a cliff fall in 1909. Grade Church stands on raised ground above flood-prone fields. It is a raw, but atmospheric building that can be satisfyingly gloomy and primeval on dull days and at dusk.

Cadgwith Cove Inn

Whitewashed 300-year-old smugglers' inn set right on the Lizard coastal path overlooking the old pilchard cellars and the colourful fishing vessels on the steep shingle beach in this attractive cove. Virtually unchanged since the old smuggling days, the two rustic bars are simply furnished and each has a warming winter fire. Relics of bygone seafaring days adorn the walls, including prints and photographs of old fishermen and scenes of Cadgwith many years ago. The half-panelled lounge bar opens out onto a sun-trap patio with wooden benches, the ideal meeting place for walkers seeking a pint of Sharp's ale and the best crab sandwich for miles.

Food

Seafood is a speciality, with crab landed on the beach appearing in sandwiches, soups and salads, as well as local fish and chips, fish casserole and lobster in season. Alternatives include ploughman's lunches, lasagne, meat pies and steaks.

Family facilities

There's a specified family area where children are welcome. Smaller portions of some of the main menu dishes are available, while younger family members can choose from the children's menu.

about the pub

Cadgwith Cove Inn
Cadgwith, Helston
Cornwall TR12 7JX
Tel 01326 290513
www.cadgwithcoveinn.com

DIRECTIONS: see Getting to the start; pub in village above cove

PARKING: use village car park

OPEN: daily; all day Saturday and Sunday, and July and August

FOOD: daily

BREWERY/COMPANY: Punch Taverns

REAL ALE: Flowers IPA, Sharp's Doom Bar, guest beer

DOGS: allowed inside

ROOMS: 7 bedrooms, 2 en suite

Alternative refreshment stops

The Old Cellars Restaurant in Cadgwith is licensed and features the courtyard of old pilchard processing 'cellars' right opposite Cadgwith harbour beach.

☛ Where to go from here

Visit the Goonhilly Satellite Earth Station Experience near Helston. Here you can journey through the history of international satellite and radio communications in the Connected Earth Gallery, discover the interactive exhibition area and take a guided tour of the site, getting closer to the massive satellite dishes (www.goonhilly.bt.com).

Red hot poker Kniphofia uvaria

while you're there

A few miles to the north and east of St Agnes Head is Goonhavern's World in Miniature theme park. Here you can stroll amongst smaller versions of famous world sites such as the Taj Mahal and the Statue of Liberty. Other attractions include Tombstone, a Wild West town complete with saloon, bank, shops, stable and jail. The Adventure Dome is the original 180-degree cinema direct from the US, with two exciting films showing. The 12-acre (5ha) gardens are beautifully landscaped with over 70,000 plants and shrubs.

St Agnes Head to St Agnes Beacon

A bracing walk along the cliffs at St Agnes, followed by an inland climb to the top of St Agnes Beacon and an optional coast path walk to the pub.

Cliffs and mines

The awesome sea cliffs of St Agnes Head are well hidden from above. There is no easy view, unless you are a very skilled rock climber. On St Agnes Head and on Carn Gowla, the cliff that runs south from the headland, vast 300ft (91m) high walls of rock soar from an ever restless sea. They do not end at clear-cut edges, however. Instead they merge with gentle slopes of grass and heather that in turn rise gently to the cliff top. Yet you are always aware of the exhilarating exposure of these great gulfs as you stroll safely by.

This walk takes you along the flat cliff top tracks and past the little promontory of Tubby's Head, once an Iron Age settlement fortified by an earth embankment across its neck. From here you pass through what was once an industrious mining landscape, signposted by the remains of mine buildings such as the mighty Towanroath Shaft, a granite castle-keep of a building standing directly above the sea amidst swathes of pink thrift and cream-coloured bladder campion in summer. Built in 1872, this was the pumping house for the Wheal Coates mine whose buildings, further uphill, you see from the coast path. Flooding of the deeper Cornish mines was always a major problem and separate pumping houses were built to draw up water and eject it through tunnels, known as adits, in the cliff face below. The buildings of Towanroath

Trevaunance Cove, north of St Agnes Head, is one of Cornwall's best beaches

Shaft were skilfully restored by the National Trust in the early 1970s.

Beyond Towanroath the path descends into Chapel Porth where you can enjoy the delights of a typical Cornish beach. During the 19th century the entire valley floor that leads down to the cove was given over to the processing of the mineral ore that came from dozens of tin and copper mines, scattered across the surrounding landscape. As you walk up the valley, you pick your way through a landscape now overgrown by nature, but that was once subdued by industry. From the valley floor the route leads up a delightful valley,

protected from the harsh onshore weather by high ground. Soon, you climb onto the bare, rounded summit of St Agnes Beacon, 629ft (192m) high and a superb viewpoint. As the name makes clear, this prominent hilltop was used traditionally for the lighting of signal fires and for celebratory bonfires. From the Beacon's airy heights you drop down effortlessly to the coast once more.

the walk

1 Join the coastal footpath from wherever you park along the cliff top. Follow the stony track across **Tubby's Head**. Branch off right onto a narrower path about 100yds (91m) before old mine buildings (these are the remains of Wheal Coates mine). Cross a stone stile and continue to **Towanroath mine engine house**.

2 About 50yds (46m) beyond Towanroath branch off right at a signpost and descend to **Chapel Porth Beach**.

3 Cross the stream at the back corner of the car park and follow a path up **Chapel Coombe** next to the stream. Pass below a mine building and where the path forks among trees, go left through a wooden kissing gate.

4 Cross a **bridge** then turn right onto a track. After a gate and a sharp left-hand bend, bear off right along a grassy track. Pass a house on the left, walk parallel with the **stream**, pass beside a gate and keep alongside a field before turning left over a wooden stile by a gate onto a track. After 50yds (46m), reach a junction with a wide track. Turn left and continue to a public road.

STIPPY STAPPY

3h30	7 MILES	11.3 KM	LEVEL 1 2 3

SHORTER ALTERNATIVE ROUTE

3h00	5 MILES	8 KM	LEVEL 1 2 3

MAP: OS Explorer 104 Redruth & St Agnes

START/FINISH: St Agnes Head. Number of parking places along the clifftop track, grid ref: SW 699512

PATHS: good coastal footpaths and inland tracks

LANDSCAPE: dramatic coastal cliffs and a high heath-covered hill

PUBLIC TOILETS: Chapel Porth

TOURIST INFORMATION: Newquay, tel 01637 854020

THE PUB: Driftwood Spars Hotel, Trevaunance Cove

❶ Narrow cliff-edge paths, old mine workings and one steady climb to the top of St Agnes Beacon

Getting to the start

St Agnes is on the B3277 and signposted off the A30, 5 miles (8km) north of Redruth at the junction with the A390. In the village centre, turn left opposite the church, then take the third road right in a mile (1.6km) to reach the cliff parking at St Agnes Head.

Researched and written by: David Hancock, Des Hannigan

while you're there

Spend some time in St Agnes, a highly individual village with some fascinating features including a picturesque stepped terrace of houses known famously as Stippy Stappy; they are one of the most photographed subjects in Cornwall. St Agnes' beach is at Trevaunance Cove to the north of the village.

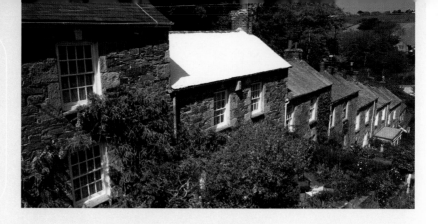

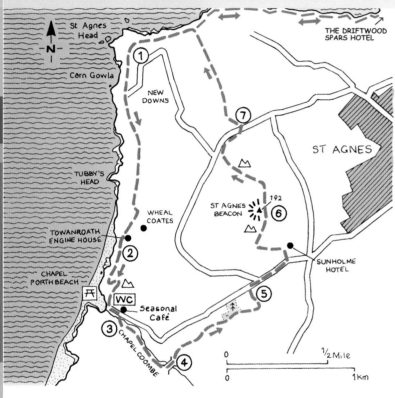

5 Turn right along the public road and keep ahead at a junction. In 200yds (183m), next to the entrance to the **Sunholme Hotel**, continue up a stony track on the left. After 50yds (46m), at a junction, go left and follow a path rising to the obvious summit of **St Agnes Beacon**.

6 From the summit of the Beacon follow the lower of two tracks, heading north west, down towards a road. Just before you reach the road turn right along a narrow path, skirting the base of the hill. Look out for a narrow path left leading downhill, eventually emerging at the road by a seat.

7 Cross over and follow the track opposite, across **New Downs**, directly to the edge of the cliffs, then turn left at a junction with the coast path and return to

the car park. To walk to the **Driftwood Spars Hotel** at Trevaunance Cove, turn right along the coast path for a mile (1.6km). Return along the coast back to the car.

what to look for

In summer the heathery vegetation of the St Agnes cliff tops and the inland hill of the Beacon attract a wealth of butterflies such as the grayling, a brown-coloured butterfly distinguished by the black edges to its wings and the two white-pupilled spots on its fore wings. It feeds on wild thyme and heather and often perches on the rocks. Another butterfly to look out for here is the green hairstreak. It is golden-brown on its upper wings and distinctively green on its under side.

Driftwood Spars Hotel

Constructed in the 17th century of huge ship's timbers and spars (hence the name), with stone and slate, the inn – once a marine chandlery, sail loft and tin miners trading post – is just 100yds (91m) from one of Cornwall's best beaches, making it an ideal family destination. An old smugglers' tunnel completes the picture, while fine views, home-brewed beers and roaring log fires in the atmospheric bars add to the appeal.

Food
Wide-ranging menus take in traditional bar snacks, fresh local fish and seafood and an assortment of Italian, Indian and Greek dishes.

Family facilities
Children of all ages are welcome throughout the inn. Expect to find a children's menu, smaller portions of adult dishes, high chairs and five family bedrooms.

Alternative refreshment stops
There is a seasonal café at Chapel Porth, at the midway point of the walk. St Agnes village has a couple of good pubs where you can get bar meals.

☛ **Where to go from here**
Take the ultimate undersea safari at the Blue Reef Aquarium in Newquay. Enjoy close encounters with graceful sharks and rays and stroll among the colourful inhabitants of a coral reef in a spectacular underwater tunnel (www.bluereefaquarium.co.uk). Newquay Zoo is set in exotic lakeside gardens, where monkeys and wallabies roam freely along with otters in the oriental garden. Highlights include feeding time talks, animal encounters, the tropical house and the penguin pool (www.newquayzoo.co.uk).

about the pub

Driftwood Spars Hotel
Trevaunance Cove, St Agnes
Cornwall TR5 0RT
Tel 01872 552428
www.driftwoodspars.com

DIRECTIONS: return to the village centre and turn left along the B3277, then right at the junction with the B3285 and follow signs left for Trevaunance Cove.

PARKING: 80

OPEN: daily; all day

FOOD: daily

BREWERY/COMPANY: free house

REAL ALE: Tetley, Sharp's Own and Doom Bar, St Austell HSD, Cuckoo Ale

DOGS: allowed inside

ROOMS: 15 en suite

while you're there

King Harry Ferry is one of only seven chain ferries operating in England. It provides a vital and picturesque link between the Roseland peninsula and Feock, saving up to 30 miles (48km) on a round trip to Truro. The ferry's name is shrouded in mystery, but is possibly linked with Henry VIII. One story is that the king spent his honeymoon with Anne Boleyn at St Mawes Castle, and signed a charter for the ferry during his visit.

St Mawes Castle defended the Fal Estuary

To Nare Head and Veryan

A coastal and field walk through some of South Cornwall's more remote and endearing landscapes.

Remote Cornish coast

There are parts of the Cornish coast that seem especially remote, where main roads have been kept at arms' length and where human development has not gone beyond farming and small scale sea-going. The lonely stretch of South Cornish coast between Gerrans Bay and Veryan Bay,

with Nare Head at its centre, is one such place, a landscape where people seem to have lived always at a healthy distance from too much intrusion.

The walk begins at the seasonally popular Carne Beach. A steady hike along the coast path from here soon brings you to a steep descent into the narrow Paradoe, pronounced 'Perada', Cove. On a spur of land above the sea is the ruin of a small cottage. This was the home of a 19th-century fisherman called Mallet, who lived during the week in this lonely spot, fishing from 'Mallet's Cove' below. He then

returned at weekends to his wife at the village of Veryan, a few miles inland. Eventually Mallet emigrated to Australia – without his wife. Weekends had become non-negotiable, perhaps. The little ruined cottage above the restless sea still speaks of a life of extraordinary detachment.

From Paradoe it is a long, punishing climb to the flat top of Nare Head. Beyond the Head a pleasant ramble takes you along the coast past the steep Rosen Cliff and by lonely coves. Offshore lies the formidable Gull Rock. You soon head inland from this into a lost world of little fields and meadows that straggle across country to Veryan.

From Veryan the route wanders back towards the sea, past the ancient landmark of Carne Beacon, a Bronze Age burial site that saw later service as a signal station, as a triangulation point and as a Second World War observation post. Before these later uses, the bones beneath had been disturbed by curious Victorians. A few fields away lies 'Veryan Castle', known also as 'The Ringarounds', the site of a late Iron Age farming settlement. These ancient sites prove that this absorbing landscape has given refuge to people for thousands of years. From the high ground the route leads down to the coast once more.

the walk

1 Turn left out of the car park and walk up the road, with care. Just past the steep bend, turn off right and go up steps and onto the coast path. Follow the coast path to **Paradoe Cove** and then begin the long climb up to Nare Head. Continue to **Rosen Cliff** with good views of Gull Rock.

3h00 | **5 MILES** | **8 KM** | **LEVEL 1 2 3**

MAP: OS Explorer 105 Falmouth & Mevagissey

START/FINISH: Carne Beach National Trust car park; grid ref: SW 906384

PATHS: good coastal footpath, field paths, quiet lanes, 18 stiles (field stiles are often overgrown)

LANDSCAPE: vegetated coast with some cliffs, mainly flat fields on inland section

PUBLIC TOILETS: Carne Beach, Veryan

TOURIST INFORMATION: Truro, tel 01872 274555

THE PUB: The New Inn, Veryan

❶ The coast path can be slippery after rain. Steep sections of coast/cliff path make the early stages of this walk suitable only for older, fitter children

Getting to the start

From the A39 east of Truro take the A3078 for Tregony and St Mawes. Pass through Tregony then, at a junction by a petrol station, turn left for Veryan. Follow signs into the village, pass the church and the New Inn, following signs for the Nare Hotel. Continue for 2 miles (3.2km), pass the hotel and drop down to Carne Beach and the car park.

Researched and written by:
David Hancock, Des Hannigan

5

WALK

Wild yellow gorse in Cornwall

A summer adult black-headed gull (Larus ridibundus)

what to look for

Veryan is one of South Cornwall's most fascinating villages. It is famous for its five whitewashed round houses with thatched conical roofs. They date from the early 19th century and were the inspiration of the Revd Jeremiah Trist, a local landowner. Various fanciful myths attach to these houses but they seem to have simply reflected a contemporary fashion for ornamental architecture. Gull Rock, the steep-sided island that lies a short distance offshore from Nare Head is a seabird colony and it has belonged to the National Trust since 1989. The rock's seabirds were exploited for centuries, their eggs were harvested for food, a precarious exercise because the bulk of seabirds nest on the sheer, land-facing cliff. The birds themselves were also trapped and shot for food. In its time Gull Rock even featured as a location for the 1950s film Treasure Island. Gull Rock is now a secure nesting site for guillemots, kittiwakes, herring gulls, cormorants and shags.

2 Above **Kiberick Cove** go through a gap in a wall and turn sharply left to follow a path uphill through scrub and round to the right to reach a stile by a gate into a lane end. Turn right and follow the lane inland to reach a right-hand bend just past a house.

3 Go left and over a **wall stile** here, follow the left edge of a field, then go over another stile on the left. Bear half-right across the next field to reach a gate, then turn right and follow the right-hand field edge to cross two stiles to reach a road. Turn left.

4 Just past **Tregamenna Manor Farm**, on a bend, go over a stile by a gate. Cut across the corner of the field, then go right over a stile. Cross the next field towards houses to a stile and then continue to a T-junction with a lane. Turn right to visit Veryan and **The New Inn**.

5 Return back up the lane, between the two thatched round houses then, just past **Churchtown Farm**, go left again over a stile. Follow the edge of the field to a stile into a lane. (To visit Veryan Castle, turn right along the lane to reach the access path to the castle on the left.) Go immediately left over two stiles, then follow a path, past **Carne Beacon**, to a lane.

6 At a corner junction keep ahead down the lane, signposted 'Carne Village Only'. Bear right down a driveway past **Beacon Cottage**. Go through the gate signposted 'Defined Footpaths Nos 44 & 45'. Follow the track round to the right past a garage, then follow a grassy track, keeping ahead at a junction signposted '**Carne Beach**'. Go through a gate (put dogs on leads here please) and follow a path alongside a grassy bank and fence.

7 Abreast of an old wooden gate up on the right, bear away left and downhill through the scrub, (the path isn't evident at first), and soon pick up a path that leads through gorse to join the coast path back to Carne Beach and the **car park**.

Veryan is known for its round houses

The New Inn

Set in a sleepy village in the heart of the unspoilt Roseland Peninsula, close to safe sandy beaches and St Mawes, the New Inn was formerly two early 18th-century cottages before being converted into a pub. Inside the whitewashed stone exterior is a single carpeted bar, which is delightfully simple, with stone fireplaces, one with a wood-burning stove, warming either end of the long beamed room. Polished brasses and tankards adorn the bar and old photographs of the village line the walls. Upstairs there are three en suite bedrooms.

Food
Simple, satisfying dishes range from lunchtime pasta meals, ham, egg and chips, cottage pie, home-made pizzas, ploughman's lunches and filled rolls. Evening additions include sea bass with pesto, lamb shank, fillet steak with Stilton sauce and specials like whole lemon sole.

Family facilities
Children of all ages are allowed in the pub and smaller portions of the main menu dishes are served. Secluded rear garden.

Alternative refreshment stops
The Tregarthen Coffee Shop, part of the Elerkey Guest House, is in Veryan.

☞ Where to go from here
St Mawes has a very pretty harbourside and estuary views, a long waterfront to stroll along and a remarkably well preserved 16th-century castle to visit (www.english-heritage.org.uk). Take the King Harry Ferry across the Fal estuary to see the beautifully kept gardens at Trelissick, set in 500 acres (202ha) of riverside parkland (www.nationaltrust.org.uk), or head east to explore the fully restored Lost Gardens of Heligan near Mevagissey (www.heligan.com).

about the pub

The New Inn
Veryan, Truro
Cornwall TR2 5QA
Tel 01872 501362
www.veryan44.freeserve.co.uk

DIRECTIONS:	see Getting to the start
PARKING:	roadside parking
OPEN:	daily
FOOD:	daily
BREWERY/COMPANY:	St Austell Brewery
REAL ALE:	St Austell Tinner's Ale, HSD and Tribute
DOGS:	not allowed inside
ROOMS:	3 bedrooms; 2 en suite

while you're there

St Austell grew around the local quarrying and mining industries, especially china clay which was discovered here in 1748. The waste tips, known as the Alps, are being reclaimed and the older ones, planted with trees, look like natural hills.

China clay works at St Austell

Through the Pentewan Valley

The sundial garden at the Lost Gardens of Heligan

A gentle ride along the banks of the St Austell River, with an optional extension to Heligan Gardens.

The Lost Gardens and Pentewan
Even if you don't get as far as the Lost Gardens of Heligan on your bike, you should somehow include it in your itinerary. Home of the Tremayne family for over 400 years, the story of the 'uncovering' of the gardens during the 1990s by Tim Smit (latterly of Eden Project fame) and his team is well known. But this is so much more than just a 'garden' – for a start it covers 200 acres – there's also a subtropical

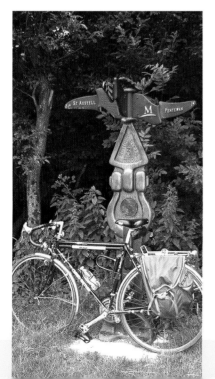

jungle, farm walks, fabulous vegetable gardens, various wildlife projects, and the romantic 'Lost Valley', as well as a farm shop, attractive restaurant, plants sales and shop.

It's worth taking some time to have a look around Pentewan village, with its narrow streets and attractive square. The glorious sandy beach, popular with holidaymakers, is featured in the Lloyds Bank 'Black Horse' advertisements. The old harbour opposite the Ship Inn is now silted up, a recurring problem during the life of the railway due to clay waste being washed downriver from the mines. This, and the growing importance of the ports at Par and Fowey, contributed to the closure of the Pentewan railway, which never reached the Cornwall Railway's main line, in 1918.

the ride

1 From the village car park return towards the B3273 and pass through the **parking area** for Pentewan Valley Cycle Hire, and round a staggered barrier onto the trail, which initially runs levelly through marshy woodland. The trail emerges from woodland onto the banks of the **St Austell River**, with a caravan site opposite.

2 Turn right and follow the trail along the riverbank. Watch out for pedestrians as this is a popular stretch. Along part of the trail walkers have the option of taking a narrow parallel route on a bank.

Top right: The Lost Gardens of Heligan
Left: Millennium signpost

3 Note the turn-off left across the river to the Lost Gardens of Heligan. Pass round the edge of a small parking area into **King's Wood** (owned by the Woodland Trust), and follow the trail as signed left back onto the riverbank. Dip into woodland again, then bear right, away from the river onto a **lane**, with a small parking area a little uphill to the right.

4 Turn left; pass a small parking area to meet a tarmac lane on a bend. Bear right as signed. Turn left opposite 'Brooklea' and continue on a narrow wooded path, with a caravan site left. The track bears left at **Molingey** – with the London Apprentice on the other side of the river – then right to run along the right bank of the river again. Follow this tarmac way as it bears right through fields, then left along the edge of the **water treatment works**. Turn left for 50yds (46m) to meet the B3273. Turn right along the pavement.

5 Cross the lane to **Tregorrick**, and take the **second lane** on the left (Sawles Road – unsigned). Follow this quiet country lane to its end. For St Austell (and a possible extension to the Eden Project) turn left uphill to cross the A390. For Pentewan either turn around here, or for a more pleasant alternative, turn right and cycle steeply uphill through pleasant countryside. Drop to a T-junction and turn right, steeply downhill, through Tregorrick. On meeting the B3273 turn left to return to **Pentewan**.

6 **Heligan extension**: just after passing Point 2 above, turn right to cross the river on the **footbridge** (you must dismount). On reaching the B3273, turn left.

| 2h30 | 10 MILES | 16.1 KM | LEVEL 123 |

SHORTER ALTERNATIVE ROUTE

| 1h30 | 7 MILES | 11.3 KM | LEVEL 123 |

MAP: OS Explorer 105 Falmouth & Mevagissey

START/FINISH: Pentewan Valley Cycle Hire; grid ref: SX 017473

TRAILS/TRACKS: mainly well-surfaced track, some woodland paths, little roadwork

LANDSCAPE: woodland and fields, riverside, roadwork on extension

PUBLIC TOILETS: in centre of Pentewan

TOURIST INFORMATION: St Austell, tel 01726 879500

CYCLE HIRE: Pentewan Valley Cycle Hire, tel 01726 844242

THE PUB: The Ship, Pentewan

🚴 Busy roads (in season) and steep ascent/descent on Heligan extension

Getting to the start
Pentewan lies just off the B3273, about 1.5 miles (2.4km) north of Mevagissey. Lane-side parking in Pentewan is limited, but there is a free car park. Start at the cycle hire shop.

Why do this cycle ride?
This pleasant route, which opened in 1995, follows the line of the old Pentewan railway along the tranquil St Austell river. A loop through quiet lanes provides a convenient 'turnaround', and an optional, steep extension to the Lost Gardens of Heligan for those seeking more strenuous exercise.

Researched and written by: Sue Viccars

6

CYCLE

Displays in St Austell's Wheal Martin Museum

Pass the touring park left, then turn right to cross the road as signed. Turn left with the pavement, then continue on a track. This bears right, away from the road into **Tremayne Estate woodland**. Climb steadily uphill for 0.75 mile (1.2km), levelling off as the track passes beneath a road. Bear left to a fork; Mevagissey may be found via the right fork. Keep left to meet the road (note that this can be busy); turn left for 0.5 mile (0.8km) to find **Heligan** on the left.

7 On leaving Heligan, turn right along the road. Cycle gently downhill, with great views over St Austell Bay. Turn left on the **first narrow lane**, steeply downhill. On meeting the next minor road, turn left, even more steeply, to meet the B3273 opposite **Pentewan Sands Holiday Park**. Turn left towards the Esso garage, then right into Pentewan village.

The Ship

about the pub

The Ship
West End, Pentewan
St Austell, Cornwall PL26 6BX
Tel: 01726 842855
www.staustellbrewery.co.uk

DIRECTIONS: see Getting to the start; pub on the main village street

PARKING: none

OPEN: daily; all day May to October

FOOD: daily

BREWERY/COMPANY: St Austell Brewery

REAL ALE: St Austell Tinner's Ale, Tribute and HSD

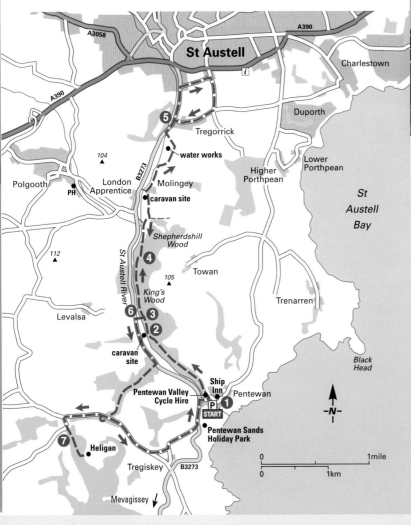

Festooned with colourful hanging baskets, the attractive Ship Inn fronts on to the main village street and is a real picture in summer, drawing in passing visitors, coast path walkers and cyclists fresh from the Pentewan Valley Trail. Tables fill early in the garden on fine days as they make the most of the pub's view across the village and the old harbour. The interior is equally appealing, with beams, shipwreck and maritime memorabilia, comfortable furnishings and a welcoming atmosphere filling the two bars, and there's the added attraction of the full complement of St Austell ales on hand-pump.

Food

Expect a traditional choice of pub meals that includes sandwiches, crusty baguettes, fisherman's lunch (smoked mackerel), steak and kidney pudding, and ham, egg and chips at lunch. Evening additions take in various grills and fresh local fish.

Family facilities

Children are allowed in the lounge bar where under 11s have a children's menu to choose from. Food is not served outside due to pestering crows and seagulls.

Alternative refreshment stops

There are cafés at the Lost Gardens of Heligan and a choice of pubs and cafés in Pentewan.

☞ Where to go from here

For an unforgettable experience in a breathtaking location, visit the Eden Project (www.edenproject.com) north of St Austell. It is the gateway into a fascinating world of plants and human society – space age technology meets the lost world in the biggest greenhouse ever built. There are two gigantic geodesic conservatories: the Humid Tropics Biome and the Warm Temperate Biome. To view the largest display of shipwreck artefacts in Britain, head for the Charlestown Shipwreck and Heritage Centre (www.shipwreckcharlestown.com), and for more information on the Lost Gardens of Heligan visit www.heligan.com.

Prideaux Place was used as a location for Trevor Nunn's film version of Twelfth Night, *and has often featured in film and television productions based on the work of Rosamunde Pilcher.*

A tour boat at Padstow

The ferry across the Camel estuary linking Padstow with Rock is one of the oldest ferry routes in the country. There has been some form of crossing here since 1337.

The Camel Trail – Edmonton to Padstow

Right: Padstow Harbour

2h00 · 10 MILES · 16.1 KM · LEVEL 123

Fabulous views and wonderful birdlife make this section of the Camel Trail a delight at any time of year.

Padstow and Prideaux Place
Although Padstow is frequently almost overrun with visitors – especially so since chef Rick Stein took up residence – it is still an attractive little town with an interesting maritime history. St Petroc is said to have come here from Wales in the 6th century AD and founded a monastery which was later sacked by the Vikings in the 10th century. The name Padstow comes from 'Petroc stow' (Petroc's church). Being the only decent harbour on the north coast between Bude and St Ives, Padstow was once the fourth most important port in the country, exporting copper and tin, slate and farm produce. Padstow's famous ancient and pagan Obby Oss ceremony takes place every year on May Day. Rumour has it that it even deterred a party of raiding Frenchmen during the Hundred Years' War!

The Prideaux family – whose origins date back to the 11th century – built their home, Prideaux Place, above the town in the 16th century, and their descendants still live there. This beautiful Elizabethan mansion – now open to the public – is surrounded by gardens laid out in Georgian and Victorian times. A tunnel, giving the family private access, leads from the grounds to St Petroc's Church.

the ride

1 The Quarryman Inn is a fascinating place. Behind the pub are two terraces of stone cottages, originally homes for workers at the quarries (Point 3); when these fell into disuse in the early 20th century the building became a TB isolation hospital. Today it is a very welcoming pub. From the **car park** turn right. At the crossroads turn left and enjoy a lovely downhill run, with increasingly good views over the River Camel and rolling farmland beyond. The Camel was known as the Allen river until 1870, thought to derive from the Irish word alain, for beautiful: it's clear to see why. Pass through the hamlet at **Tregunna** and follow the lane over a bridge to its end. Turn right down a narrow earthy path to reach the trail.

2 Turn right and follow the trail along the edge of the **estuary**. At low tide it's almost like cycling along the edge of a beach as the river is flanked by broad expanses of sand and the views are superb. The creeks and sandbanks attract wintering wildfowl – widgeon, goldeneye, long tailed duck – as well as many divers and waders, spring and autumn migrants. Look out for curlew, oystercatcher, shelduck and little egret. One of the main reasons for constructing the railway was to transport sea sand, rich in lime, from the estuary, to fertilise farmland away from the coast. Granite, slate, tin, iron and copper from mines on Bodmin Moor were exported.

MAP: OS Explorer 106 Newquay & Padstow
START/FINISH: The Quarryman Inn, Edmonton; grid ref: SW 964727
TRAILS/TRACKS: well-surfaced former railway track
LANDSCAPE: river estuary, rolling farmland
PUBLIC TOILETS: Padstow
TOURIST INFORMATION: Padstow, tel 01841 533449
CYCLE HIRE: Camel Trail Cycle Hire, Wadebridge, tel 01208 814104
THE PUB: The Quarryman Inn, Edmonton
❗ Padstow is very busy at holiday times – leave your bikes at the secure lock-up on the quay and go into town on foot

Getting to the start
Edmonton is west of Wadebridge. Bypass Wadebridge on the A39 signed 'St Columb Major/Padstow'. About 1 mile (1.6km) after crossing the Camel turn right, before Whitecross, on a lane signed 'Edmonton'.

Why do this cycle ride?
If you prefer to avoid Wadebridge, try this route to access the lower part of the Camel Trail. It is busier than the Dunmere to Wadebridge stretch, but the views make it worthwhile, and starting from the Quarryman's Arms is a bonus. If you want to keep away from crowds of people, turn round on the edge of Padstow, or just dive in quickly for an ice cream. If you like birdlife don't forget your binoculars.

Researched and written by: Sue Viccars

did you know?

Although the mysteries of Tintagel Castle have never been satisfactorily explained, recent excavations have revealed Dark Age (AD 500–1000) connections between Spain and Cornwall. Additionally, the discovery of 'Arthnou' stone suggests that this was a royal place for the Dark Age rulers of Cornwall.

Looking down on the ruins of Tintagel Castle

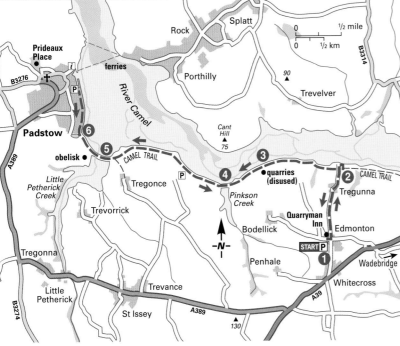

The Quarryman Inn

You can expect a genuine warm welcome at this 18th-century village inn that evolved around a carefully reconstructed slate-built courtyard of old quarrymen's cottages. Gas heaters warm this area on cooler days and it is a lovely sheltered spot to enjoy a drink or evening meal. Among the features at this unusual pub are several bow windows – one is a delightful stained-glass quarryman panel – and interesting old brass optics above the fireplace in the beamed bar. Tip-top ale comes from local small breweries and the menu includes fresh local fish.

Food

At lunch tuck into roast ham sandwiches or filled Italian bread (smoked bacon, Brie and cranberry), Cornish fish pie or the curry of the day. Evening additions include tempura prawns with sweet chilli sauce, oven-roasted lamb shank, roast duck with cherry sauce and local fish such as whole bass stuffed with bacon.

Family facilities

Children of all ages are welcome in the pub. Smaller portions of adult meals are available and younger family members have their own menu to choose from.

Alternative refreshment stops

You'll be spoilt for choice in Padstow as there are some good pubs and cafés and a few excellent restaurants.

☛ Where to go from here

Visit the Delabole Slate Quarry near Camelford, the oldest and largest working slate quarry in England. There are tours every weekday (www.delaboleslate.com).

Camelford is also the location for the nation's foremost museum of cycling history, from 1818 to the present day, with over 400 cycles and cycling medals. Overlooking the wild Cornish coast are the 13th-century ruins of Tintagel Castle, the legendary birthplace of King Arthur and home to Merlin the magician (www.english-heritage.org.uk). Close to Padstow is the Crealy Adventure Park where kids can scare themselves on the Haunted Castle ride, the Raging River Watercoaster and the Thunder Falls (www.crealy.co.uk).

about the pub

The Quarryman Inn
Edmonton, Wadebridge
Cornwall PL27 7JA
Tel 01208 816444

DIRECTIONS: see Getting to the start

PARKING: 100

OPEN: daily; all day

FOOD: daily

BREWERY/COMPANY: free house

REAL ALE: Skinner's & Sharp's beers, Timothy Taylor Landlord, guest beers

---

3 A long cutting ends at the spoil heaps of the old slate quarries, with rounded, wooded **Cant Hill** opposite. The estuary is widening as it approaches the sea; there's a glimpse of **Padstow** ahead on the left bank. The mouth of the Camel Estuary is marred by the notorious Doom Bar, a shifting sandbank responsible for more than 300 shipwrecks from 1760 to 1920. If you're cycling the Camel Trail on a sunny day it's hard to imagine such disasters.

4 Continue past **Pinkson Creek** – you may see herons – and continue on to pass the parking area at **Oldtown Cove**. Once through the next cutting you'll get fantastic views towards Rock, on the other side of the estuary, with Brea Hill and Daymer Bay beyond, and out to the open sea. The trail bears away from the estuary through a cutting.

5 Cross the bridge over **Little Petherick Creek**. The Saints' Way, a 30-mile (48km) walking route, links Fowey on the south coast with Padstow's St Petroc's Church. It runs along the edge of the creek and past the **obelisk** (commemorating Queen Victoria's jubilee in 1887) on Dennis Hill, seen ahead. The creek is also an important habitat for little egret and a good range of wading birds.

6 Follow the trail past a lake on the left and then past houses on the edge of Padstow, with moored boats on the water right. **Rock**, opposite, is a popular sailing and watersports venue, and there's always masses to watch on the water. The trail ends at the **quay** and car park; you should dismount at this point to explore the town. Retrace your tracks along the Camel Trail to Edmonton.

Maer Lake Nature Reserve

The snipe has one of the longest bills in relation to its overall size of any bird. It probes soft mud with erratic jerky movements. Snipe are cryptically marked and usually keep well hidden until they are flushed, when they rise explosively, uttering their distinctive hoarse calls.

Teal, our smallest duck, winters here. The drakes display a bright chestnut head banded with deep green, a horizontal white line along the grey body and a yellow triangle under the tail.

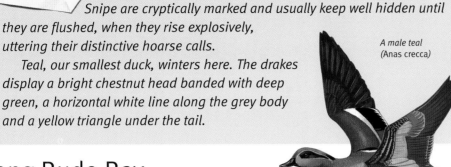

A male teal (Anas crecca)

Along Bude Bay

2h30 **5 MILES** **8 KM** **LEVEL 123**

8

WALK

A pleasant stroll through coastal heathland where the cliff edges provide a refuge for masses of wild flowers.

Coastal flora and fauna

The windswept coastal grasslands of North Cornwall seem unlikely havens for plant life, but, around Bude, the cliff edges especially, provide a unique refuge for wild flowers. This walk follows the flat cliff land north of Bude with an inland section on the return. Along the way you'll find numerous wild flowers that turn the cliff top into a riot of colour in spring and early summer.

The walk starts from the northern outskirts of Bude at Crooklets Beach and quickly you're on cropped grasslands of the National Trust's Maer Cliff and Maer Down. In spring the dominant flower here is the spring squill. Other early plants which flourish here are the lilac-coloured early scurvy grass, the pink thrift and white sea-campion. At Northcott Mouth the cliffs give way to a wide stony beach. Here the route of the walk turns inland and climbs uphill to follow the line of an old bridleway, often choked with grass and brambles, but with typical hedgerow plants such as foxglove and red valerian poking through.

Soon you reach the road to Sandy Mouth Beach and the cliff path back to Crooklets. Once more there are many wild flowers here. The grass is laced with the yellow and orange flowers of kidney vetch and the yellow heads of hawkweed and, by July, is scattered with the pink and white florets of the aromatic wild carrot. From Crooklets the walk angles inland to a final stroll through an area of typically dense woodland, a dramatic contrast in habitat to the open cliff top. Here primroses and daffodils appear in early spring. Sycamore, beech, alder, cypress, Scots pine and Corsican pine create a sheltered and moist environment within which plants like the tall yellow flag iris and the lilac-coloured water mint thrive.

The last section of the walk leads you past the Maer Lake Nature Reserve, which is flooded in winter. There is no public access to the area from the roadside but you can get an excellent view of the many birds through binoculars.

the walk

1 Go towards the beach, cross a bridge and head for some steps. Pass in front of **beach huts**, then turn left along a stony track between walls. Go up some steps and onto the **coast path**, signed 'Maer Cliff'.

2 Go through a gate and along a track behind a white building, called **Northcott House**. Bear off to the left, by a signpost, down a path to the sea at **Northcott Mouth beach**. From here, bear right along a track that will take you back inland, past a group of houses on the left, and continue uphill to pass some more houses.

3 Where the track bends round to the right, leave it and keep straight ahead to a gate. Keep outside the left edge of the overgrown **bridle path** ahead.

4 Reach a field gate and follow a track through fields. Keep left at a junction with another track, then continue to a T-junction with a public road. Turn left and walk down the road, with care, to **Sandy Mouth**.

5 Pass the National Trust **information kiosk** and descend towards the beach, then go left and uphill and follow the coast path back to Northcott Mouth beach, and a **red lifeguard hut** passed earlier.

Bude harbour on Cornwall's north coast

MAP: OS Explorer 111 Bude, Boscastle & Tintagel and 126 Clovelly & Hartland

START/FINISH: Crooklets Beach Car Park (pay-and-display); grid ref: SS 204071

PATHS: excellent throughout, grassy coast path, field path, metalled lanes

LANDSCAPE: coastal cliffs

PUBLIC TOILETS: Crooklets Beach and Sandy Mouth

TOURIST INFORMATION: Bude, tel 01288 354240

THE PUB: The Inn on the Green, Bude

❗ Keep well back from the cliff edges

Getting to the start

Follow signs off the A39 for Bude. Go through the town centre and follow signs to Crooklets and Poughill. Turn left at Flexbury on the northern edge of Bude for Crooklets Beach. Large pay-and-display car park by the beach.

Researched and written by: David Hancock, Des Hannigan

8

WALK

while you're there

Bude is the only port on the harsh North Cornwall coast. It developed quickly after the Bude to Launceston canal was built in the 1820s; the impressive sea-lock survives, and a couple of miles of canal. The arrival of the railway in the 1880s (now closed) put the canal out of business, but introduced the holidaymakers upon which the town still largely depends.

6 Follow the roadside path just past the lifeguard hut and retrace your steps to the **white bungalow** passed earlier. Go along the track behind the building and then keep ahead along a broad track along the edge of **three fields**.

7 At a field corner by a **footpath sign** go through the open gateway ahead then turn left and follow the field edge into a hedged-in path. Continue between trees to a lane by a house at **Rosemerrin**. Continue to a road.

8 Turn right along the road, with **Maer Lake Nature Reserve** down to your left. Cross at a junction with Maer Down Road, go left, then right, passing **The Inn on the Green**, and return to the car park.

what to look for

Butterflies that are likely to be seen along the cliffs in summer include the meadow brown, probably Britain's commonest butterfly, its name a perfect description of its dusky colour. Look also for the common blue, a small butterfly with an almost lilac tinge, and for the glamorous painted lady with its tawny-orange wings and black and white markings. The painted lady's main habitat is Southern Spain and North Africa from where large swarms often migrate north in April and May, finding no difficulty in crossings of the English Channel.

The Inn on the Green

Imposing, blue-painted inn/hotel built in 1900 and located just a stone's throw from Crooklets Beach and overlooking the broad expanse of Summerleaze Down and Bude golf course. Beyond the front summer terrace you will find a comfortable lounge bar furnished with sofas and easy chairs and decorated with beach-scene prints. The adjoining bar has chunky wooden tables and chairs and pool table.

Food
Lunchtime bar meals range from filled baguettes and sandwiches to ploughman's, beefburgers and jacket potatoes filled with chilli or tuna and mayonnaise. The more extensive evening menu includes pasta meals, fisherman's pie, beef stroganoff, pan-fried steaks with pepper, Stilton or mushroom sauce. Sunday roast lunches.

Family facilities
Children are welcome away from the bar and in the restaurant. There is a basic children's menu and smaller portions of the Sunday roast lunches are available.

Alternative refreshment stops
There is a National Trust seasonal café above Sandy Mouth Beach at the halfway point of the walk and there are a number of beachside cafés at Crooklets Beach.

☛ Where to go from here
Enjoy a drive north along the A39, visiting the village of Morwenstow, Cornwall's most northerly parish, along the way. The Church of St John Baptist contains the graves of over 40 shipwrecked sailors, buried by the eccentric Parson Hawker who spent 40

years here serving 'a mulititude of smugglers, wreckers and dissenters'. The church is fascinating and there are some beautiful clifftop views and walks. Venture further, into Devon, and you should visit Hartland Quay, once a thriving port for over 250 years before storms destroyed the harbour. The former harbour buildings comprise a hotel, shop and a small museum illustrating the history of this remarkable place.

about the pub

The Inn on the Green
Crooklets Beach, Bude
Cornwall EX23 8NF
Tel 01288 356013
www.innonthegreen.info

DIRECTIONS: see Getting to the start

PARKING: Crooklets Beach Car Park

OPEN: daily; all day

FOOD: daily

BREWERY/COMPANY: free house

REAL ALE: Sharp's Doom Bar, St Austell Tinner's Ale

DOGS: allowed in the bar

ROOMS: 26 bedrooms, 17 en suite

Map labels

Seasonal Café
WC
SANDY MOUTH
⑤ ④
Overgrown bridleway
③
-N-
BUDE BAY
NORTHCOTT MOUTH BEACH
THE BUNGALOW
⑥
②
⑧ ROSEMERRIN
MAER LAKE NATURE RESERVE
⑦
MAER DOWN
0 ½ Mile
0 1 Km
Crooklets Beach
The Inn on the Green
Café
WC
P
FLEXBURY
①

did you know?

An air-sea rescue Sea King helicopter from Chivenor was the first to arrive at Boscastle when the village was hit by floods in 2004. It helped rescue 55 people in the UK's largest peacetime emergency operation, and the crew were decorated for bravery.

did you know?

Barnstaple Fair could be as old as the town itself. Starting in mid-September, it once followed a market. Today the fair is purely for ceremony and entertainment; dignitaries toast proclamations with traditional spiced ale and a carnival procession raises money for charity.

Barnstaple Fair

The Tarka Trail – Braunton to Barnstaple

A gentle ride along the Taw estuary from historic Braunton to Barnstaple's old quayside.

9

CYCLE

Braunton

DEVON

Braunton Burrows

As you set off along the Tarka Trail from Braunton look right and in the distance you'll see a ridge of sand dunes (dating from the last Ice Age) – those nearest the sea are around 100ft (over 30m) high. This is Braunton Burrows, the second largest dune system in the UK, designated as an UNESCO International Biosphere Reserve in November 2002. The whole dune system is moving gradually inland, in some places as much as 10ft (3m) per year, and is well worth exploring. There are areas of managed meadowland, grassland, marsh and sandy habitats. Almost 500 different species of flowering plant have been identified, including 11 orchids. Sustainable tourism is the keyword here, and access for visitors is managed carefully so that fragile parts of the site are protected. The area is easily accessible by road or bike.

Braunton has a fascinating agricultural history, too. Between the village and the Burrows lies Braunton Great Field, a rare example of medieval strip farming. This area once lay beneath the sea and is extremely fertile. There's also an area of tidal saltmarsh, enclosed in the early 19th century for grazing cattle.

the ride

1 The car park marks the site of the old Braunton railway station, closed in 1965. The line – Barnstaple to Ilfracombe – was opened in 1874, and the last train ran in 1970. Cycle to the far end of the **car park** and turn right into the overflow area. Bear left and leave the car park by the police station (right). Bear right onto Station Road and cycle down it, passing the cycle hire on the left. Turn right into **Station Close** and then immediately left down a tarmac way. At the end cross the lane; keep ahead through black bollards to cross another lane, with a roundabout right.

2 Follow signs left to pick up the **old railway line**. Pass a wetland conservation area (left) and pass round a staggered barrier to cross a lane (the wire fences right mark the boundary of RAF Chivenor).

3 (Note: For The Williams Arms turn left here; at the end of the lane cross the A361 with care; the pub is on the other side.) Cycle on to reach a roundabout at the entrance to **RAF Chivenor**. The church ahead left is St Augustine's at Heanton Punchardon, built by Richard Punchardon (owner of Heanton estate) after his return from the Crusades in 1290. The village, formerly Heanton (Saxon Hantona – High Town) took on his name from that time. Cross the road by the roundabout and keep ahead through a wooded section.

4 Emerge suddenly from woodland onto the **Taw Estuary**, with far-reaching views. Listen for the oystercatcher's piping call, and watch out for curlew, easily identified by its curving bill. In winter thousands of migrant birds feed on the broad sandbanks here. Pass castellated **Heanton Court** on the left, a refuge for Royalists in the Civil War. The then owner of the Heanton estate, Colonel Albert Basset, fought for Barnstaple, which eventually fell to the Parliamentarians. Continue along the banks of the Taw to pass the **football club** (left).

5 Cross arched **Yeo Bridge**, a swing bridge over a tributary of the Taw, and pass the **Civic Centre** on the left (cyclists and pedestrians separate here). Bear left away from the river to meet the road. Turn right

1h30 | **11 MILES** | **17.7 KM** | **LEVEL 123**

MAP: OS Explorer 139 Bideford, Ilfracombe & Barnstaple

START/FINISH: Braunton car park (contributions), grid ref: SS 486365

TRAILS/TRACKS: level tarmac and gritty former railway track

LANDSCAPE: townscape, estuary

PUBLIC TOILETS: at start and in Barnstaple

TOURIST INFORMATION: Barnstaple, tel 01271 375000

CYCLE HIRE: Otter Cycle Hire, tel 01271 813339; Tarka Trail Cycle Hire, Barnstaple, tel 01271 324202

THE PUB: The Williams Arms, Wrafton

❶ Busy crossing of A361 on route to the Williams Arms

Getting to the start

Braunton lies on the A361 Barnstaple to Ilfracombe road in north Devon. The car park is signed from the traffic lights in the centre of the village. If approaching from Barnstaple, turn left, and 100yds (91m) later turn left into the car park.

Why do this cycle ride?

Visiting Barnstaple by car at the height of the tourist season can be something of a trial as this north Devon market town, the oldest borough in the country, can get pretty choked by traffic. So what better way to get into the heart of Barnstaple than by cycling from Braunton via the Tarka Trail along the edge of the Taw estuary?

Researched and written by: Sue Viccars

while you're there

The 18-acre (7ha) Marwood Hill Gardens contain three small lakes and rare trees and shrubs. There are bog gardens, a walled garden, collections of clematis, camellias, and eucalyptus. Alpine plants are also a feature, and there is a plant shop.

Marwood Hill Gardens in Barnstaple

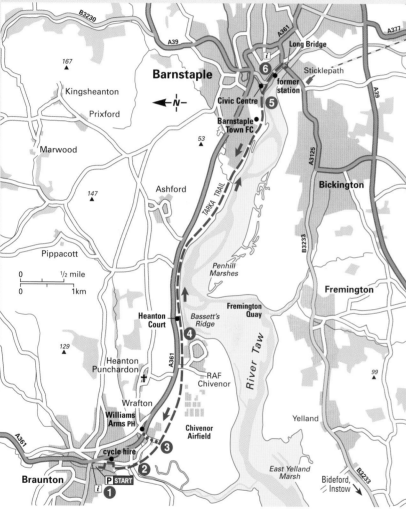

The Williams Arms

A modernised thatched village pub that is well worth the short diversion off the trail as it is really geared up to family dining and has the added attractions of a play area and aviary in its spacious garden. Popular with both holidaymakers and locals, the two huge bars have been smartly refurbished with plush red carpets, a mix of modern furnishings and a self-service carvery, yet they retain some character in the form of low-beamed ceilings and open fires. Separate games area with pool table, darts and TV.

Food

The lounge bar menu offers a good choice of filled rolls and paninis, ploughman's lunches with home-cooked ham or local cheddar, steaks from the grill, and specialities like steak and venison pie, Exmoor venison braised in red wine and brandy, roast duck with orange sauce, and roast meats from the daily carvery.

Family facilities

Children are welcome throughout the pub. It is really geared to family dining and you'll find a games/TV room, a basic kid's menu, smaller portions for older children, high chairs, and a play fort and aviary in the large garden.

about the pub

The Williams Arms
Wrafton, Braunton
Devon EX33 2DE
Tel 01271 812360
www.williams-arms.co.uk

DIRECTIONS: the pub is beside the A361 Braunton to Barnstaple road, 1 mile (1.6km) south east of Braunton. See Point 3

PARKING: 100

OPEN: daily; all day

FOOD: daily

BREWERY/COMPANY: free house

REAL ALE: Bass

Alternative refreshment stops

There are plenty of pubs and cafés in Braunton and Barnstaple, and en route you'll find Heanton Court, another family-friendly pub.

☞ Where to go from here

On the edge of Exmoor at Blackmoor Gate is the Exmoor Zoological Park, which specializes in smaller animals, many endangered, such as the golden headed lion tamarins. There are contact pens and children are encouraged to participate (www.exmoorzoo.co.uk).
Combe Martin Wildlife Park and Dinosaur Park is a subtropical paradise with hundreds of birds and animals and animatronic dinosaurs, plus there are sea lion shows, falconry displays and animal handling sessions (www.dinosaur-park.com).

along the cycle path past **old Barnstaple Town Station** on the right (the railway reached the south side of the river in 1854, and this side in the early 1870s). Bear right as signed, then left along the **quay** (note: there is no wall along the edge).

6 Continue on to pass **Barnstaple Heritage Centre** (left), with its elaborate statue of Queen Anne. The Riverside Café (with cycle racks) lies a few yards along on

the left, just before Barnstaple's Long Bridge over the Taw (there has been a bridge here since the 13th century). There is evidence of a settlement at Barnstaple from early Saxon times; trade via the Taw was vital to the town's prosperity for centuries. Queen Anne's Walk marks the site of the Great and Little Quays, once bustling with ocean-going ships, including five bound for Sir Francis Drake's Armada fleet in 1588.

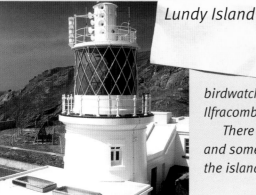

Lundy Island

Lundy Island out in the Bristol Channel is 3 miles (4.8km) by 0.5 mile (800m). Steep cliffs rise on all sides, offering spectacular views and excellent birdwatching for trippers who come by boat from Bideford or Ilfracombe (subject to weather and tide).

There are three lighthouses, the remains of a medieval castle, and some cottages available as holiday lets; no cars are allowed on the island.

The Tarka Trail – Great Torrington to Bideford

A lighthouse near Lametry Bay on Lundy Island

2h30 | 11 MILES | 17.7 KM | LEVEL 123

MAP: OS Explorer 126 Clovelly & Hartland

START/FINISH: car park on Great Torrington Common, grid ref: SS 485193

TRAILS/TRACKS: level former railway track, now smooth tarmac

LANDSCAPE: woodland, river and estuary, saltmarsh, townscape

PUBLIC TOILETS: near Bideford station

TOURIST INFORMATION: Bideford, tel 01237 477676

CYCLE HIRE: Torridge Cycle Hire, Station Yard, tel 01805 622633; Bideford Cycle Hire, East-the-Water, tel 01237 4241123

THE PUB: The Puffing Billy, Great Torrington

Getting to the start

From Great Torrington take the A386 Bideford road across Great Torrington Common. Use the car park on the common opposite the junction with the B3227.

Why do this cycle ride?

The Tarka Trail, a 180-mile (290km) cycleway and footpath, offers great opportunities for exploring north Devon. The trail opened in May 1992, and those sections along former railway lines make great cycling routes. This ride from Great Torrington to Bideford, along the broad banks of the River Torridge, is one of three options, and can easily be linked to the route from Instow to Barnstaple.

Researched and written by: Sue Viccars

Tarka the Otter

The Tarka Trail is named after the hero of north Devon, author Henry Williamson's famous novel *Tarka the Otter*, published in 1927. Williamson moved to Georgeham, near Braunton in 1921, having visited the area in 1914, at which time he became captivated by this remote part of north Devon. He came here both to recover from the horrors of active service in World War One and also to write, and between 1921 and 1972 almost 50 works were published. His best known is the tale of Tarka the Otter,

much of which is based around the River Torridge, which flows northwest for 9 miles (14.5km) from its source to its junction with the River Taw just beyond Appledore. Tarka was born just below Canal Bridge, downstream from Torrington, and met his end on the River Torridge too. The story was made into a film and, by strange coincidence, Williamson died on the same day as the filming of Tarka's death scene, in 1977. It seems fitting that today, after many years of decline, otters are returning to Devon's rivers as a result of deliberate policy to improve habitat and water quality.

the ride

1 Turn right along the A386 and descend to pick up the Tarka Trail on the right before **Rolle Bridge**. It runs between The Puffing Billy – the old station building – and cycle hire in the goods yard opposite. Turn left along the trail to pass the pub and garden (cycle racks) on the left. The railway reached Bideford (from Barnstaple) in 1855; the extension (under the London and South Western Railway) from Bideford to Torrington opened July 1872, and closed in the mid 1960s. The 'Atlantic Coast Express' ran from here all the way to London Waterloo. Cycle over the **River Torridge** as it loops its way towards the sea.

2 Pause at the next river crossing to look at **Beam Weir**; as you cross the river for the third time look left towards Beam Aqueduct. Part of the railway utilised the bed of the former Rolle Canal, involved in a

A fisherman on the River Torridge where Henry Williamson set his novel Tarka the Otter

scheme to link with the Bude Canal in north Cornwall; only a 6-mile (9.7km) section was completed, in 1827. Lime and coal were carried inland from the coast to Torrington, and agricultural produce exported. Pass a **picnic area** left, and continue between the A386 and the Torridge (right). Look right through the trees towards Weare Giffard, with its 14th-century church and 15th-century manor house. Pass **Weare Giffard Cross** (left).

3 Where the Torridge takes a wide loop east cycle through **Landcross Tunnel** (lit), then through a cutting by Landcross Bridge. Now with the River Yeo on the left, cycle on to meet the **old iron railway bridge** over the Torridge.

4 The whole feel of the route changes here: the river is wide and slow, with large expanses of saltmarsh and reedbed – home to sedge warbler and reed bunting – and beautiful views. The bridge overlooks the 'Pool of the Six Herons' (mentioned in *Tarka*) – look out for herons, lapwing, redshank and curlew. Saltmarsh plants (specially adapted to seawater inundations) and reedbeds protect the river banks from erosion, and the mudflats support millions of invertebrates, food for wading birds. Limestone was shipped in from south Wales for burning in the limekiln left of the bridge; local woodland supplied timber for charcoal.

5 Continue along the right bank of the Torridge, with increasingly good views of **Bideford**, a significant port in medieval times, today a busy market town and working port. Its 24-arched stone bridge

A perfectly posed puffin

Have a look at the charming cove at Buck's Mill. When herring and mackerel fishing declined in the 19th century, local men travelled daily over to Lundy Island to work in the quarry there. The surname Braund is common in this area; it is thought to result from seven Spanish sailors who were wrecked and washed up here at the time of the Spanish Armada.

recalls the town's early prosperity – it is said that each arch was funded by a local parish, and the size of the arch reflects their respective wealth! The 19th-century novelist Charles Kingsley (who lived at Clovelly during his childhood) described Bideford as 'the Little White Town that slopes upward from its broad river tide': little has changed.

6 Turn-around is **old Bideford Station** – 220.5 miles (355km) from Waterloo! The Tarka Trail goes on to Instow. Refreshments are available from the **Railway Carriage Visitor Centre**. If you have time when you finish the ride, take a look around Great Torrington, noted for the Battle of Great Torrington in 1646, the end of Royalist resistance in the West Country in the Civil War.

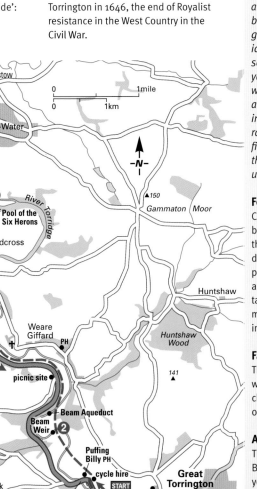

The Puffing Billy

Smack beside the former railway route and looking every inch the old station building it once was, the Puffing Billy is gradually being restored and makes the ideal post-ride refreshment stop on this section of the Tarka Trail. On fine days you can relax in the trail-side garden with a pint of locally-brewed Cavalier ale. There's a real sense of history inside due to the mass of authentic railway and station memorabilia that fills the atmospheric bars, including the original signs and platform notices used at the station.

Food
Call in during the morning for coffee, bacon sandwiches and croissants from the Early Morning Shunters menu. On the daytime menu you'll find baguettes and ploughman's lunches, ham, egg and chips and steak and kidney pie. Specials may take in lasagne, spaghetti carbonara and mixed grills, and a separate menu is served in the Station Restaurant.

Family facilities
The pub is very child friendly; they are welcome everywhere and there's a children's menu and a big play area outside in the garden.

Alternative refreshment stops
There's a good choice of pubs and cafés in Bideford, including at Bideford old station, your turn-around point.

☞ Where to go from here
Take a fascinating factory tour at Dartington Crystal in Great Torrington and watch craftsmen transform hot molten crystal

into elegant glassware from the safety of elevated viewing galleries. Children can have fun in the glass activity area and you can discover the story of glass and the history of Dartington at the Visitor Centre (www.dartington.co.uk). Stroll down the steep cobbled street of Clovelly, one of Devon's most famous coastal villages, or visit the Milky Way Adventure Park to experience some exhilarating rides and shows (www.themilkyway.co.uk). Another family attraction – The Big Sheep (www.thebigsheep.co.uk) – is close to Bideford.

about the pub

The Puffing Billy
Station Hill, Great Torrington
Devon EX38 8JD
Tel 01805 623050

DIRECTIONS: right off the A386 1 mile (1.6km) west of Great Torrington, just before Rolle Bridge over the River Torridge

PARKING: 30

OPEN: daily; all day Easter to October; closed Wednesdays November to Easter

FOOD: daily

BREWERY/COMPANY: free house

REAL ALE: Clearwater Cavalier and 1646, guest beers

Mount Edgcumbe House was built in the mid-16th century and subsequently enlarged. It was heavily damaged by German incendiary bombs in 1941 and rebuilt in the 1960s. In 1971 the country park was established and the house opened to the public. It has a fine collection of mainly modern furnishings and Victorian artefacts. Paintings are by such artists as Sir Joshua Reynolds. The surrounding gardens include the Earl's Garden, an 18th-century formal design.

Although rebuilt, Mount Edgcumbe House, retains its grandeur

Mount Edgcumbe Country Park

A walk round the Mount Edgcumbe estate on the shores of Plymouth Sound.

Mount Edgcumbe

The Mount Edgcumbe Country Park is a green oasis that flies in the face of Plymouth's crowded waterfront opposite. The two are separated by The Narrows, a few hundred yards of the 'Hamoaze', the estuary formed by the rivers Tavy, Lynher and Tamar. Mount Edgcumbe stands on the Cornish side of the river, although it was not always 'Cornish'. In Anglo Saxon times, Devon extended across the estuary as far as Kingsand. Today, however, Mount Edgcumbe and its waterfront settlement of Cremyll are emphatically Cornish. They stand on the most easterly extension of the Rame Peninsula, known with ironic pride by local people as the 'Forgotten Corner'. In truth Rame is one of the loveliest parts of the South West, let alone of Cornwall, and this walk takes you round the shores of the inner estuary, and then over the spine of the eastern peninsula, before returning to Cremyll along the open of Plymouth Sound.

The first section of the route takes you to peaceful Empacombe, where there is a tiny harbour contained within a crescent-shaped quay. It was here, during 1706-9, that workshops servicing the building of the famous Eddystone Lighthouse were located. Behind the harbour is the Gothic façade of Empacombe House.

The path follows the wooded shoreline of the tidal basin known as Millbrook Lake, then climbs steeply inland to reach Maker Church on the highest point of the peninsula, with views up the Tamar to the Saltash bridges. From here you wander through tiny fields to reach a track that descends to the coast path on the southern side of the peninsula and the more bracing sea shore of Plymouth Sound. Finally you reach the delightful park environment that surrounds Mount Edgcumbe House where you can explore the lovely gardens.

the walk

1 From the car park go left along the footway opposite the entrance. Where the footway ends at an **old fountain** and horse trough, cross back left and go through a gap by a telephone kiosk, signposted '**Empacombe**'. Alternatively, from the ferry slipway, turn left to the old fountain, then cross to the right. Keep left past the **Old School Rooms**. Turn right at a junction then pass an obelisk and follow the path alongside the tree-hidden creek to Empacombe.

2 At a surfaced lane, by a house, keep ahead and go down to **Empacombe Quay**. Turn left beyond the low wall (dogs under control please) and skirt the edge of the small harbour to reach a stone stile onto a wooded path. Continue round **Palmer Point** and on to a public road.

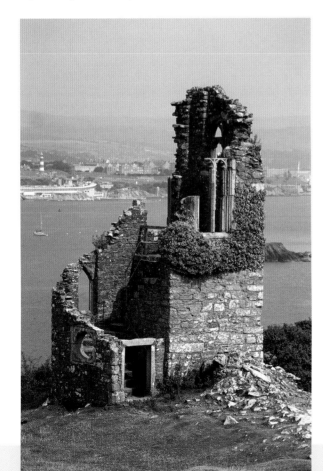

The folly (left) and gardens (above) in Mount Edgcumbe Country Park

---

3h00 | **6 MILES** | **9.7 KM** | **LEVEL 123**

MAP: OS Explorer 108 Lower Tamar Valley & Plymouth

START/FINISH: Cremyll car park, grid ref: SX 453534. Alternatively reach Cremyll by ferry from the Plymouth side. Daily service between Admiral's Hard, Stonehouse, Plymouth and Cremyll

PATHS: good throughout, muddy in places in wet weather, 5 stiles

LANDSCAPE: wooded shoreline of tidal creek, fields, woods and coast

PUBLIC TOILETS: Cremyll

TOURIST INFORMATION: Plymouth, tel 01752 304849

THE PUB: Edgcumbe Arms, Cremyll

⚠ Waterside paths – keep children supervised

Getting to the start

On the Cornish side Cremyll is best approached from the A38 between Saltash and Liskeard, taking the A374 towards Torpoint, then the B3247 following signs for Mount Edgcumbe Country Park. The car park is on the left as you enter Cremyll. For most it is simplest to take the ferry from Plymouth. From the city centre, follow signs for Torpoint and the Torpoint ferry, for 'Mount Edgcumbe via Cremyll ferry'. When facing the ferry slipway there is a left turn for the free car park.

Researched and written by:
Des Hannigan, Brian Pearse

Plymouth Hoe

Hoe means 'high place' or hill. For even better views over Plymouth Sound, climb to the top of Smeaton's Tower, the archetypal red-and-white lighthouse. It was built in 1789 on the treacherous Eddystone Rocks 14 miles (22km) out to sea, and was reassembled on the Hoe when it was replaced by a larger lighthouse in 1882.

Smeaton's Tower on Plymouth Hoe

3 Go through the kissing gate opposite, signposted '**Maker Church, Kingsand**'. Follow the track ahead for 55yds (50m), then bear right, up the open field (no obvious path) heading between telegraph poles, to find a faint path leading to a kissing gate into into **Pigshill Wood**. Bear right along a track, go left at signposts and climb uphill following footpath signs. Cross a track, then go up some stone steps to reach more steps onto a public road. Cross, with care, and follow a path to **Maker Church**.

4 Turn sharp right in front of the church, follow the field edge, then go over a stile on the left. Follow the next field edge and cross a stile on the left, then follow the path past a **house** and across a lane into a field. Cross two fields to a lane. Turn left down the lane.

5 Pass **Hooe Lake Cottage** at the bottom and turn left to join the **coast path**, signposted just a few paces along the lane. Keep to the upper path at a junction, then merge with another track from the left and continue through the **woods**.

6 After a **folly shelter** the path zig-zags steeply up through the woods to the left to avoid a landslip. At the **ruined stone shelter** at the top turn right and drop back down through the woods. Cross the main track again and take a path zig-zagging steeply downhill to the coast. Follow the coast path signs back to **Mount Edgcumbe** and **Cremyll**.

Edgcumbe Arms

The inn dates from the 15th century and is on the Tamar Estuary, next to Mount Edgcumbe Country Park, and close to the foot ferry from Plymouth. Views from the bow window seats and waterside terrace are glorious, taking in Drake's Island, the Royal William Yard and the marina. Real ales from St Austell and home-cooked food are served in a series of rooms, which are full of character with American oak panelling, deep leather sofas, log fires and stone flagged floors.

Food

Fresh local seafood and Cornish steaks are a feature of the menus alongside a daily curry and steak and ale pie. A good choice of bar snacks is also available.

Family facilities

Families will find a genuine welcome to children. There are two family bedrooms, a specified family area in the bar, high chairs and a children's menu.

Alternative refreshment stops

The Orangery Restaurant and Tea Room is in the Old Orangery in Mount Edgcumbe estate's Italian garden.

☞ Where to go from here

Catch the ferry across to Plymouth and follow the Waterfront Walkway to The Hoe and the Plymouth Dome, a high-tech visitor centre that lets you explore the sounds and smells of an Elizabethan Street, walk the gun-deck of a galleon, dodge the press gang, and witness the devastation of the Blitz (www.plymouthdome.info). In Cornwall, head for Anthony House near Torpoint to view a fine, largely unaltered 18th-century mansion, which contains contemporary furniture and family portraits (www.nationaltrust.org.uk). Children will love the Monkey Sanctuary near Looe, where they can see a colony of Amazonian woolly monkeys in extensive indoor and outdoor territory (www.monkeysanctuary.org).

about the pub

Edgcumbe Arms
Cremyll, Torpoint
Cornwall PL10 1HX
Tel 01752 822294
www.smallandfriendlyinns.co.uk

DIRECTIONS: see Getting to the start

PARKING: use public car park

OPEN: daily; all day (except early Jan to end Feb)

FOOD: daily

BREWERY/COMPANY: St Austell Brewery

REAL ALE: St Austell Tribute, Tinner's Ale and HSD

DOGS: allowed in the bars

ROOMS: 6 en suite

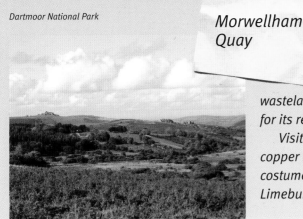

Morwellham Quay

Morwellham was the greatest copper port in Queen Victoria's empire. Once the mines were exhausted the port area disintegrated into wasteland, until 1970 when a charitable trust was set up for its restoration.

Visitors can ride by electric tramway underground into a copper mine, last worked in 1869. The staff wear Victorian costumes, and replica costumes can be tried on in the Limeburner's Cottage.

A miniature railway at Morwellham

Around Brent Tor

A climb up to the Church of St Michael de Rupe at Brent Tor in West Devon.

Brent Tor

Anyone exploring western Dartmoor cannot fail to notice a conical peak, topped with a tower, protruding high above the rolling fields and woodlands towards the Cornish border. This strange natural formation is Brent Tor and, surprisingly, has nothing to do with the granite tors of Dartmoor. It is a remnant of the mass of lava that poured out onto the seabed here over 300 million years ago, when the area was a shallow sea. The softer rocks around have been eroded away over the millennia, leaving behind this extraordinary landmark 1,100ft (334m) above sea level. The name is thought to derive either from Ango-Saxon *brene* meaning 'beacon' or the Celtic *bryn* (hill or mound). Lying just inside the National Park boundary, it provides the perfect focus for a relaxing exploration of this quiet corner of West Devon.

The 13th-century Church of St Michael de Rupe ('of the rock') was originally built in around 1130. Rebuilt towards the end of the 13th century, the tower was added during the 15th century. Services are held on Sunday evenings from Easter to September, and the views from here are breathtaking.

North Brentor was added to the parish in 1880, and all burials then took place at Christ Church in the village, since the soil on top of Brent Tor was too thin to accommodate a decent grave.

the walk

1 Walk straight ahead from your car towards **Brent Tor**, which positively invites you to visit it. Where the lane veers right turn left along an unfenced lane (dead end and weak bridge signs). Go gently downhill and over a **cattle grid**. The tarmac lane becomes a gravelly track and passes **Blacknor Park** (left), to cross the old railway line.

2 The stony track runs steeply uphill, levels off and runs into a green lane. At the next T-junction of tracks turn left to pass **South Brentor Farm** and a lane (right), and keep straight on slightly uphill – under beech trees – to pass 'Hillside' on the left.

3 Just past two **cottages** on the left the lane bends sharp left. Turn right through a metal gate following the bridleway marker along the bottom of the field, keeping the hedge left. Brent Tor is above to the right. Pass through **double metal gates** to meet the Tavistock to Lydford road – take care, there is fast traffic on this road.

The Church of St Michael, on the hill of Brent Tor

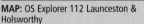

2h00 | **4 MILES** | **6.4 KM** | **LEVEL 1**23

MAP: OS Explorer 112 Launceston & Holsworthy

START/FINISH: lay-by past cattle grid outside Mary Tavy on moorland road to North Brentor village, grid ref: SX 495800

PATHS: tracks and green lanes, open fields and lanes

LANDSCAPE: open moorland and rolling farmland

PUBLIC TOILETS: at car park, Brent Tor

TOURIST INFORMATION: Tavistock, tel 01822 612938

THE PUB: Brentor Inn, North Brentor

❶ One steep climb up Brent Tor

Getting to the start

The walk starts near Mary Tavy, which is about 5 miles north of Tavistock on the A386. Turn left at the garage in Mary Tavy, following the Brentor signs. In 0.5 mile (800m), cross a cattle grid onto open moorland. Park on the moorland to the right or in the small lay-by a little down the road on the left.

Researched and written by:
Brian Pearse, Sue Viccars

12

The straight lines of the church contrast with rugged Brent Tor

Looking south east from Brent Tor

4 Turn right to reach the car park, toilets and **information board** for Brent Tor on the left.

5 Turn right and take the steep path up to the **church** – it's always windy up here – then retrace your steps to the road and turn right to pass **Brentor Inn** on your left.

6 When you reach **two white cottages** on either side of the road, turn right down a tarmac lane signposted '**Brentor and Mary Tavy**'. The lane runs gently downhill, with the moor rising steeply up behind the village ahead. This western edge of the moor is very different from the eastern side, where there is usually a long drive-in along wooded river valleys.

7 At the edge of the houses go straight on, keeping the old chapel right, until you reach the 1914–18 **war memorial**. Turn right slightly downhill to pass the phone box, church and village hall. Follow the lane

what to look for

Just south west of Brent Tor is an enclosed area of mounds and depressions, all that remains of a 19th-century manganese mine, a major source of employment from 1815 to 1856. The manganese was used in the production of glass, bleach and steel, and was shipped out down the River Tamar from Morwellham Quay.

as it veers right to cross the **old railway line**. You can see the old station complete with platform canopy below you to the right.

8 Pass over the cattle grid onto the open moor, and up the lane. Where the lane bends right and you see two big **granite gateposts** in the beech-lined wall right, cut left diagonally over the edge of **Gibbet Hill** on an indistinct grassy track. The lane leads back to the car, but this is a more pleasant route. At the crest of the hill you will see your route back to your car on the lane below to the right.

did you know?

Mary Tavy and Peter Tavy are two villages on the west edge of Dartmoor. Mary Tavy claimed the world's largest copper mine in the 19th century, while Peter Tavy was more of an agricultural area. The surrounding moor is thickly sprinkled with Bronze Age remains. On Standon Down, more than 70 hut circles represent an unenclosed Bronze Age village.

Brentor Inn

Set beside the lonely and windswept road between Lydford and Tavistock, this white-painted inn dates from the early 1800s and enjoys wonderful, far-reaching views across Dartmoor, up to Brent Tor (the focus of this walk), and into Cornwall from its beer garden. Spruced up following a period of neglect and then closure, the pub's single bar sports old flagstones, thick stone walls, dark wood pub furnishings and two warming winter fires.

Food
Hearty walking appetites will be satisfied by the range of traditional bar meals on offer, namely home-cooked pies, fresh fish and chips and lunchtime sandwiches.

Family facilities
Children are welcome in the conservatory dining area where they can order smaller portions of the main menu dishes

about the pub

Brentor Inn
North Brentor, Tavistock
Devon PL19 0NF
Tel 01822 811001
www.brentorinn.com

DIRECTIONS: just after Point **5**, before the turning to North Brentor

PARKING: 60

OPEN: all day; closed Monday

FOOD: daily

BREWERY/COMPANY: free house

REAL ALE: St Austell Tinner's Ale, guest beers

DOGS: allowed inside

Alternative refreshment stops
If you drive north to Lydford go to the 16th-century Castle Inn (hotel and restaurant). There is also a National Trust restaurant at Lydford Gorge.

☛ Where to go from here
Visit Lydford, signposted off the A386 to the north. It was a Saxon fortress town, with its own mint in the 9th century. Lydford Castle, actually the moor's infamous stannery prison, is worth a visit. Just down the road is the National Trust's Lydford Gorge, where the crashing waterfalls and whirlpools of the River Lyd – the most impressive being the Devil's Cauldron – can be seen from a number of woodland walks. The 98ft (30m) White Lady waterfall is spectacular (www.nationaltrust.org.uk).

The Plym Valley trail

A pleasant ride along the line of the old Plym Valley railway, with an optional extension to the National Trust's magnificent house and parkland at Saltram.

Plym Bridge Woods and Blaxton Meadow

This railway line opened in 1859 under the South Devon and Tavistock Railway, and ran for 16 miles (25.7km) from Plymouth to Tavistock. The cycle route through Plym Bridge Woods is one of the best bits. The woods became popular with daytrippers who alighted at Plym Bridge Halt, built in 1906 (on the site of the car park mentioned in Point 5). You'll also see evidence of industrial activity: there were several quarries here, workers' cottages, a small lead/silver mine, a canal and three railway lines. The remains of 18th-century Rumple Quarry – from which slate was extracted – and engine house are passed on the right, soon after entering the woods. Plym Bridge Woods are particularly lovely in spring, thick with wood anenomes, primroses, bluebells and ransoms.

Once in the Saltram estate you soon pass Blaxton Meadow on your right, an area of managed saltmarsh on the Plym Estuary. It was enclosed in 1886 and developed as agricultural land, and around the time of World War Two supported a cricket ground! Plans to regenerate the saltmarsh started in 1995, and today it provides suitable habitats for a wide range of flora and fauna, with large numbers of migrant waders; look out for flocks of curlews in winter, and deep red samphire beds in autumn.

the ride

1 Return to the lane, turn right and descend into Clearbrook and continue past **The Skylark Inn** for about 500yds (457m). Turn right opposite the village hall on a track. After 100yds (91m) turn right up a steep, narrow path; at the top by the **pylon** bear left downhill (cyclists should dismount). This turns sharp left, then right through a gate onto the rough, gritty, old railway line. Follow this for about 0.5 mile (0.8km) to **Goodameavy**, where tarmac takes over. (Note: to avoid this initial rough section turn left at the fork by the parking area, signed 'Goodameavy', and cycle steeply downhill to join the railway.)

2 Soon after Goodameavy the track passes through **Shaugh Tunnel** (note: there are lights, but these are turned off between dusk and dawn – there's a colony of roosting bats in the tunnel), and then under an aqueduct. Pass Shaugh Bridge Halt and cross **Ham Green viaduct**; look back left and you'll catch sight of the Dewerstone Rock above the wooded Plym Valley just above its junction with the River Meavy.

3 At **Ham Bridge** the route meets a lane; turn right uphill towards **Bickleigh**. At the T-junction turn left and proceed very steeply downhill (young children should dismount). Turn right on a narrow wooded path back onto the railway line and continue through deciduous woodland. Pass over Bickleigh viaduct and into the National Trust's **Plym Bridge Woods**. Continue over Cann viaduct – look over the left side to see the remains of Rumple wheelpit by the river below, and the face of **Cann Quarry** beyond.

4 At Plym Bridge follow signs sharp left to leave the track. For a picnic by the river, turn left under the railway towards the 18th-century bridge; the meadow is on the right (leave your bikes on the lane). For **Saltram House** – created in the 18th century with 500 acres (202ha) of parkland – cross the car park entrance and turn right on a level woodland track. Cycle towards Plymouth (note that Plymouth is one end of the Devon Coast to Coast route, which runs for 102 miles/163km to Ilfracombe – watch out for serious and speedy cyclists!) to emerge by **Coypool Park-and-Ride** on the right.

5 Cross the road at the T-junction and follow the narrow path ahead (barrier); cross the next road and take the rough track opposite. Just past the **playing field gates** (right) bear right on a narrow path to emerge under the A38. Bear diagonally right to find a railed tarmac path uphill left. Follow that up and down, then along the edge of the Plym Estuary to reach the National Trust's **Saltram Estate**.

6 At the edge of parkland keep right, and follow the estuary to **Point Cottage**. Turn left inland on an estate lane to cross the parking area, with the house and **shop** left. At the signpost bear left, signed '**Riverside walk and bird hide**' and cycle carefully downhill, avoiding pedestrians, keeping straight on where the tarmac way bears left towards offices. Re-enter the **parkland** and keep ahead to rejoin the outward route.

SOUTHWEST ENGLAND · CYCLE · 13 · Plym Valley · DEVON

3h00 · **13.5 MILES** · **21.7 KM** · **LEVEL 123**
SHORTER ALTERNATIVE ROUTE
2h15 · **10.5 MILES** · **16.9 KM** · **LEVEL 123**

MAP: OS Explorer OL20 South Devon

START/FINISH: Clearbrook parking area above village, grid ref SX 518650

TRAILS/TRACKS: mix of bumpy and well-surfaced track

LANDSCAPE: wooded valley, townscape, estuary and parkland on extension

PUBLIC TOILETS: Coypool (Point 5)

TOURIST INFORMATION: Plymouth, tel 01752 304849

CYCLE HIRE: Tavistock Cycles, Tavistock, tel 01822 617630

THE PUB: The Skylark Inn, Clearbrook

⚠ First 0.75 mile (1.2km) rough and bumpy (alternative lane access given), steep hills at Bickleigh and busy roads on extension

Getting to the start
Clearbrook lies on Dartmoor's western edge, clearly signposted off the A386 Tavistock to Plymouth road, 2.5 miles (4km) south of Yelverton. Follow the lane across the down and park at the furthest parking area on the right where the road forks.

Why do this cycle ride?
This ride – particularly if the extension to Saltram House is included – covers an impressive range of landscapes: moorland, woodland, river estuary and parkland. The views at both the northern (Dartmoor) and southern (Plym Estuary) ends are impressive, and the outskirts of Plymouth, for Saltram House, passed quickly.

Researched and written by: Sue Viccars

did you know?

The Shaugh Tunnel is built on a curve, so the far end cannot be seen from the entrance. A resident bat colony adds to the frisson of excitement experienced by cyclists entering the tunnel, but some bat-friendly lights have now been installed.

Saltram House

The original building was a Tudor mansion, but this was replaced in 1743 by Sir John and Lady Catherine Parker. In 1768 their son commissioned Robert Adam to design the staterooms and the salon, and the house represents one of Adam's finest surviving works.

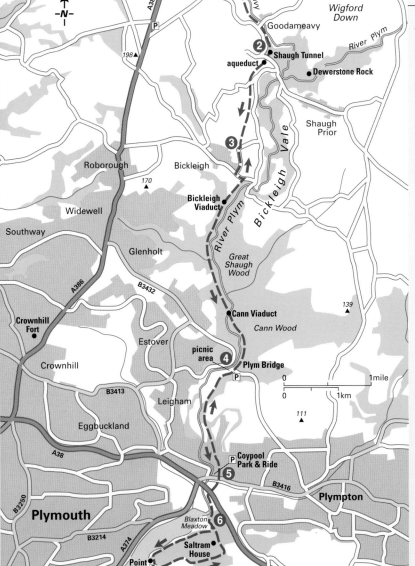

The Skylark Inn

Although only minutes from Plymouth, you will find the Skylark tucked away in a pretty row of cottages in a sleepy village on the southern flanks of Dartmoor. It's a welcoming two-room pub, the beamed main bar is simply furnished and boasts a big fireplace with wood-burning stove. Although very much a lively local the pub also bustles with passing walkers and cyclists exploring the National Park. Large back garden for summer alfresco eating and drinking.

Food

Good wholesome food is served from an extensive menu that features hot pasties, beef sandwiches, battered cod with chips, pasta meals, short-crust pastry pies, lamb tagine and vegetable stew with dumplings. Sunday roast lunches.

Family facilities

Children are welcome in the rear family room (no under 14s in the bar). There's a children's menu and an adventure play area in the garden.

Alternative refreshment stops

There is a licensed café at Saltram House.

☞ Where to go from here

At Buckland Monachorum you'll find Buckland Abbey, formerly a 13th-century Cistercian Abbey, which was sold to Sir Francis Drake in 1581. He lived here until his death in 1596. Restored buildings house a fascinating exhibition about the abbey's history, including Drake's drum (www.nationaltrust.org.uk). At the National Marine Aquarium in Plymouth, Britain's biggest aquarium, you can see 15 species of shark and ray, walk through an underwater tunnel and enter the Twilight Zone (www.national-aquarium.co.uk). Discover Plymouth's past and much more at the Plymouth Dome, a high-tech visitor centre with audio-visual commentaries and observation galleries (www.plymouthdome.gov.uk). If you visit Saltram House by bike, your entry fee is refunded (www.nationaltrust.org.uk).

about the pub

The Skylark Inn

Clearbrook, Yelverton
Devon PL20 6JD
Tel 01822 853258
www.theskylarkinn.co.uk

DIRECTIONS: see Getting to the start; descend into Clearbrook and the Skylark Inn is on the left

PARKING: 16

OPEN: daily; all day Saturday and Sunday

FOOD: daily; all day Saturday and Sunday

BREWERY/COMPANY: Unique Inns

REAL ALE: Courage Best, Sharp's Special, Bass, Clearbrook Ale

Burgh Island

Take a ride on the lumbering sea tractor over to Burgh Island. It's great fun and saves getting your feet wet as the tide rushes in. The tractor runs year-round, every half hour in summer, every hour in winter.

The tractor was designed specifically for the purpose; it can operate in 10ft (33m) of seawater and in gale conditions up to force 9 – which makes it an experience to equal the best of fairground rides.

The tractor that takes visitors to Burgh Island

Bigbury-on-Sea and Burgh Island

A chance to mingle with the stars in an art deco dream and have a drink in Devon's oldest inn.

Bigbury and Burgh Island

The broad, sandy beaches and dunes at Bigbury-on-Sea and Bantham, at the mouth of the River Avon south of Kingsbridge, attract hundreds of holidaymakers every summer, drawn by the appeal of sun, sand and sea. There's no doubt that this is a perfect spot for a family day out. Gone are the days of the 16th or 17th centuries when Bigbury was merely famous for its catches of pilchards! But there's something else appealing about this part of the South Devon coast. Just off Bigbury beach, 307yds (282m) from shore, lies craggy Burgh Island, with its famous hotel gazing at the mainland. This extraordinary island is completely surrounded by the sea at high tide but is accessible via the weird and wonderful sea tractor that ploughs its way through the waters.

The island was known as la Burgh in the 15th century, and later Borough Island. There was a chapel dedicated to St Michael on its summit in 1411, and it has been likened to the much larger St Michael's Mount in Cornwall. The remains of a 'huer's hut' at the top of the island – a fisherman's lookout – is evidence of the times when pilchard fishing was a mainstay of life here too, hence the building of the Pilchard Inn, housed in one of the original fisherman's cottages. But it is the island's more recent history that is so fascinating. It was bought in 1929 by wealthy industrialist Archibald Nettlefold, who built the Burgh Island Hotel, much as we see it today. He ran it as

a guest house for friends and celebrities, and it became a highly fashionable venue for the jet-set in the 1930s. Noel Coward was among the famous who visited, and it is thought that Edward, Prince of Wales and Wallis Simpson escaped from the limelight here; but the island's most famous connection has to be with Agatha Christie.

Two of her books, *Evil Under the Sun* and *And Then There Were None*, were written here, and the influence of the hotel and its location on her writing is clear. By the mid 1980s the hotel had fallen into disrepair, and two London fashion consultants, Beatrice and Tony Porter, bought the island and restored the hotel to its original 1930s Art Deco glory, complete with the famous Palm Court and authentic Twenties cocktail bar. For a bit of escapism Burgh Island is hard to beat – but take your cheque book!

the walk

1 Leave the car park through the entrance. Follow **coast path signs** right (for the low tide route to the seasonal ferry to Bantham), then left towards the road,

then left again up a grassy area. Turn left before the **bungalow**, then left (unmarked path) to reach the road. Turn right and walk steeply uphill to **Mount Folly Farm**.

2 Turn left along a gravelly track (signed '**Ringmore**'). At the top of the field is a junction of paths; go through the gate, then through the metal gate ahead, keeping downhill by the hedge on your right. Walk downhill through a kissing gate. Cross the **farm track** and up the field, to reach a high stile, then descend steps into a narrow lane.

3 Cross over, following signs for **Ringmore**, through the left of the two gates. Walk down into the next combe, keeping the hedgebank right. Cross the stream at the bottom on a **concrete walkway**, and over a stile. Ignore the path left, but go straight ahead, uphill, through a **plantation** and gate onto a narrow path between a fence and hedge.

4 Pass through a kissing gate, then turn right. Turn immediately left uphill though a **metal gate/kissing gate** to join a track that leads to Ringmore. Turn right at

Left: Burgh Island is connected to the mainland by sands

| 1h45 | 3 MILES | 4.8 KM | LEVEL 123 |

MAP: OS Explorer OL20 South Devon

START/FINISH: huge car park at Bigbury-on-Sea, grid ref: SX 651442

PATHS: fields, tracks (muddy in winter), coast path, 2 stiles

LANDSCAPE: rolling coastal farmland and cliff top

PUBLIC TOILETS: at car park

TOURIST INFORMATION: Kingsbridge, tel 01548 853195

THE PUB: Pilchard Inn, Burgh Island

❶ Steep sections of narrow coast path close to the cliff edge

Getting to the start

Bigbury-on-Sea is signposted off the A379 between Plymouth and Kingsbridge. A mile (1.6km) east of Modbury, turn right on the B3392 towards Bigbury and Bigbury-on-Sea. On entering Bigbury-on-Sea there is a large pay-and-display car park by the beach on the left.

Researched and written by: Brian Pearse, Sue Viccars

while you're there

In addition to reconstructed rooms, a walled garden and farm gallery are features of the Cookworthy Museum of Rural Life, founded to commemorate William Cookworthy, 'father' of the English china clay industry.

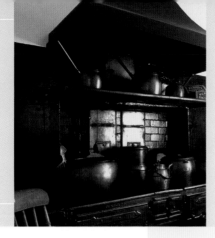

A re-created kitchen in Cookworthy Museum of Rural Life

First winter black-headed gull (Larus ridibundus)

the lane, then left at the **church** to find the **Journey's End pub** on the right.

5 From the pub turn right down the narrow lane which gives way to a footpath. It winds round to meet a tarmac lane. Turn left downhill. Walk straight on down the track (signed to '**Lower Manor Farm**') and keep going down past the '**National Trust Ayrmer Cove**' notice. After a small gate the track splits; keep left (unsigned) and straight on.

6 Turn left through a kissing gate and walk towards the cove on a grassy path above the combe (left). Pass through a gate and over two stiles to gain the **beach**.

7 Follow coast path signs ('**Challaborough**') left over a small footbridge then climb very steeply uphill to the cliff top and great views over Burgh Island. The cliffs are crumbly here – take care. The path is narrow, with a wire fence left, and leads to **Challaborough** – basically one huge holiday camp.

8 Turn right along the beach road and follow the track that leads uphill along the coast towards **Bigbury**. Go straight on to meet the tarmac road, then right on a narrow gravel path to the **car park**.

Pilchard Inn

Atmospheric 14th-century white-walled pub located on a tiny tidal island reached only by giant sea tractor when the tide is in – stroll across the sand when to tide is out. Once frequented by pirates and smugglers, the island is still said to be haunted by the notorious Tom Crocker who was shot outside the pub. Two rustic bars with a seafaring atmosphere, ancient exposed timbers, stone walls, blazing log fires and slate floors are furnished with old wooden settles. The main catch off the island was pilchard – hence the name.

Food

Unsurprisingly, seafood figures on the simple menu, which takes in fish soup, crab sandwiches, seafood risotto, and other sandwiches filled with beef and horseradish or chicken and avocado.

Family facilities

Children are welcome in the non-smoking bar and kid-sized sandwiches are available. When the tide is out, children can play on the sandy beach while mum and dad enjoy a drink on the beach-edge terrace.

Alternative refreshment stops

The wonderful Bay Café at Bigbury has great views over Burgh Island. There's Venus Café and a beach café at Challaborough. The Journey's End at Ringmore is full of atmosphere and has great food.

☛ Where to go from here

In the Old Grammar School in Kingsbridge is the Cookworthy Museum of Rural Life. Reconstructed room-sets of a Victorian kitchen, an Edwardian pharmacy, a costume room and an extensive collection of local historical items are gathered here to illustrate South Devon life. Explore Totnes and its castle, one of the best surviving examples of a Norman motte and bailey castle with spectacular views, and take a steam train ride through the Dart Valley on the South Devon Railway (www.southdevonrailway.org).

about the pub

Pilchard Inn
Burgh Island, Bigbury-on-Sea
Devon TQ7 4BG
Tel: 01548 810514
www.burghisland.com

DIRECTIONS: see Getting to the start (use tractor at high tide)

PARKING: start point car park

OPEN: daily; all day

FOOD: lunchtimes only (except summer evening barbeques Thursday to Saturday)

BREWERY/COMPANY: free house

REAL ALE: Teignworthy beers, Greene King Old Speckled Hen, Pilchard Bitter, guest beers

DOGS: allowed inside

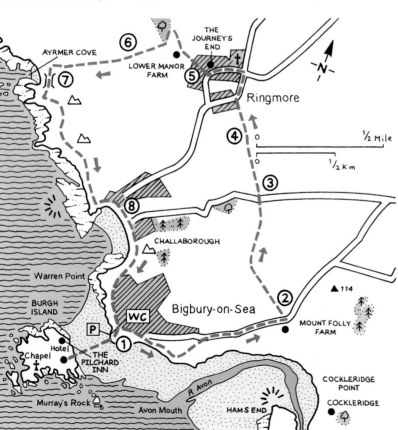

AYRMER COVE
THE JOURNEY'S END
⑥
LOWER MANOR FARM
⑤
⑦
Ringmore
N
④
½ Mile
½ Km
③
⑧
CHALLABOROUGH
Warren Point
▲ 114
BURGH ISLAND
WC
Bigbury-on-Sea
②
MOUNT FOLLY FARM
P
①
Hotel
Chapel
THE PILCHARD INN
COCKLERIDGE POINT
R Avon
Murray's Rock
Avon Mouth
HAM S END
COCKLERIDGE

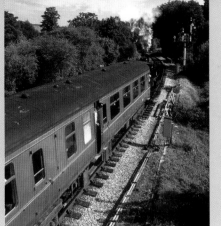

Staverton

Staverton station has featured in many television programmes, and films such as The Railway Children. *In 1999 the passing loop beyond Bishops Bridge signal box was completed and passed fit to carry passenger traffic. This has enabled a more frequent service between Buckfastleigh and Totnes, resulting in two trains at peak season instead of just one.*

Dart Valley Railway runs from Buckfastleigh to Staverton

A peregrine falcon (Falco peregrinus) *in flight*

Around Dartington Hall Estate

A gentle walk around the Dartington Hall Estate, with a pretty pub loop along the steam railway.

Dartington Estate

You could be forgiven for thinking that Dartington is really nothing more than what you see as you cross the roundabout on the A384 leading south from the A38 to Totnes – just somewhere you pass en route to the South Hams. But there's so much more to Dartington than that, and the story behind 'the vision' of Leonard and Dorothy Elmhirst, who bought the estate in 1925, is a fascinating one. This walk circles the estate and you should allow time at the end to visit its central buildings.

Dartington Hall was described by Nikolaus Pevsner in his classic book on the buildings of Devon as 'the most spectacular medieval mansion' in Devon. The great hall and main courtyard were built for John Holand, Duke of Exeter, at the end of the 14th century, and although all the buildings have since been carefully restored, to walk through the gateway into the courtyard today, with the superb Great Hall with its hammerbeam roof opposite, is to step back in time. Arthur Champernowne came to own the manor in 1554, and made various alterations, and the estate stayed in the hands of the Champernowne family until 1925. Further restoration work was carried out in Georgian times, but by the time the Elmhirsts came on the scene the Hall was derelict. Modern visitors can explore the Great Hall, courtyard and gardens, providing they are not in use, in return for a moderate fee.

St Mary's Church can be found on the northern edge of the estate just off the Totnes road. You'll pass the site of the original estate church just to the north of the Hall. It was demolished in 1873, leaving only the tower, which can be seen today. The new church, which is wonderfully light and spacious, was built in 1880, following the exact dimensions of the original building, and re-using various items from it, such as the south porch with its lovely star vault, the chancel screen, font, pulpit and roof. A tablet in the outer east wall records the rebuilding and subsequent consecration of the church by Frederick, Bishop of Exeter. The Dartington Hall Trust, a registered charity, was set up in 1935, and evolved from the vision of Leonard Elmhirst and his American wife Dorothy Whitney Straight, who bought the derelict hall and 1,000 acres (405ha) of the estate and set about making their dream reality. He was interested in farming and forestry, and in increasing employment opportunities in rural areas. She believed passionately in the arts as a way of promoting personal and social improvement. Their joint aim was to provide a foundation where both dreams could be realised simultaneously, and Dartington Hall today, home to Dartington College of Arts and a whole range of other educational facilities, provides the perfect setting.

the walk

1 From the car park turn left downhill. Follow the pavement until you reach the **River Dart**.

2 Turn left through a kissing gate (no footpath sign) and follow the river northwards. This part of the walk is likely to be very muddy after rainfall. The Dart here is broad, tree-lined and slow-moving. Pass through a **kissing gate**, through a strip of woodland and over another stile into the next meadow. At the end of that pass through another kissing gate onto a short **wooded track**.

3 Walk along the river edge of the next field (with **Park Copse** to your left). At the end of that field go through a kissing gate into **Staverton Ford Plantation**. Where the track veers sharply left go through the gate in the wall ahead, then right to follow a narrow, wooded path back towards the

Top: Steam train at Staverton station
Below: The stone Staverton Bridge

| 2h30 | 5 MILES | 8 KM | LEVEL 1 2 3 |

MAP: OS Explorer 110 Torquay & Dawlish

START/FINISH: opposite entrance to Dartington Hall, grid ref: SX 799628

PATHS: fields, woodland tracks and country lanes

LANDSCAPE: river meadows, parkland and mixed woodland

PUBLIC TOILETS: outside entrance to Dartington Hall and Staverton village

TOURIST INFORMATION: Totnes, tel 01803 863168

THE PUB: The Sea Trout Inn, Staverton

❶ Dogs not allowed within Dartington Hall grounds

Getting to the start

Dartington is about 2 miles (3.2km) north west of Totnes on the A384. Follow signs for Dartington Hall. There are car parks on the left opposite the main entrance.

Researched and written by: Brian Pearse, Sue Viccars

while you're there

The Woodlands Leisure Park at Blackawton outside Totnes offers 60 acres (23ha) of indoor and outdoor attractions including three watercoasters, a 545-yard (500m) toboggan run, arctic gliders, a mystic maze, and 15 massive play zones. The rock'n'roll tugboat is definitely an unusual ride. There is also a wide selection of birds and animals to see, and the indoor falconry centre gives flying displays.

Woodlands Leisure Park

river. Keep on this path as it runs parallel with the Dart, becoming a broad woodland track through **North Wood**. When you see buildings through the trees on the right, leave the track and walk downhill to a metal gate and a lane.

4 Turn right to cross **Staverton Bridge**. Before the level crossing turn right to pass through **Staverton Station yard** into a park-like area between the railway and river. Follow the path across the single-track railway and walk on to meet a lane by **Sweet William Cottage**.

5 Turn right and follow the lane to its end. Go straight ahead on a small gritty path to pass the **Church of St Paul de Leon**, who was a 9th-century travelling preacher. Turn left at the lane to pass the public toilets,

and left at the junction to **The Sea Trout Inn**. After your break retrace your steps to the metal gate past **Staverton Bridge**.

6 Turn immediately right to rejoin the track. Follow this until it runs downhill and bends left. Walk towards the gate on the right, then turn left on the narrow concrete path. The houses of **Huxham's Cross** can be seen right. Keep on the concrete path, which leaves the woodland to run between wire fences to meet a concrete drive at the **Dartington Crafts Education Centre**. Follow the drive to meet the road.

7 Turn left to pass **Old Parsonage Farm**. Keep on the road and pavements back to **Dartington Hall**, passing the gardens and ruins of the original church (right), until you see the **car park** on the left.

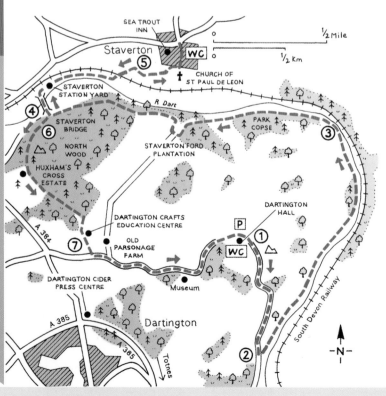

The Sea Trout Inn

Situated in the tranquil rural surroundings of the Dart Valley, this attractive 15th-century inn has a loyal local following. It's a rambling, whitewashed building with a relaxed atmosphere and a good combination of comfortable hotel, elegant restaurant and village pub serving cracking Palmer's beers. A fishing theme runs through the pub, some specimens mounted in showcases, others depicted in paintings or on plates. From the open-plan and plushly furnished main bar there's access to a sheltered, patio-style garden complete with pond and fountain. Separate public bar with pool table. Eleven comfortably furnished en suite bedrooms makes this an ideal base for touring Dartmoor and the South Devon coast.

Food
An interesting bar menu features sausage, kidney and bacon casserole with parsnip purée or rump steak with lyonnaise potatoes and béarnaise sauce, plus classics such as bangers and mash and gammon and egg.

Family facilities
Children are welcome in the eating area of the bar and restaurant and overnight in two family bedrooms. There's a children's menu and smaller portions are available.

Alternative refreshment stops
There are two excellent eateries at Dartington Cider Press Centre – Cranks vegetarian restaurant and Muffins, which provides light lunches in the open air. Within the grounds of Dartington Hall there is the White Hart restaurant and bar, where you can enjoy a drink in atmospheric surroundings.

about the pub

The Sea Trout Inn
Staverton, Totnes
Devon TQ9 6PA
Tel 01803 762274
www.seatroutinn.com

DIRECTIONS: village signposted off the A384 between Dartington and the A38 at Buckfastleigh, see Point 5 of walk

PARKING: 80

OPEN: daily

FOOD: daily

BREWERY/COMPANY: Palmer's Brewery

REAL ALE: Palmer's IPA, Gold and Copper Ale

DOGS: allowed inside

ROOMS: 11 en suite

☞ Where to go from here
Spend some time at the Cider Press Centre. There's farm food, a bookshop, woodturning, great refreshments, a cookshop, Dartington pottery shop, toy shop and plant centre. You can't fail to notice the steam trains running along the opposite side of the river. This is the South Devon Railway, which runs from Buckfastleigh to Totnes. The station at Buckfastleigh has old locomotives and rolling stock on display, a museum and café, riverside walks and a picnic area (www.southdevonrailway.org). Nearby is Buckfast Butterflies and Otter Sanctuary (www.ottersandbutterflies.co.uk), and Buckfast Abbey, a Benedictine monastery by the River Dart (www.buckfast.org).

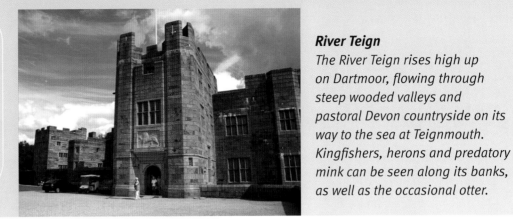

Castle Drogo in Dartmoor National Park

River Teign

The River Teign rises high up on Dartmoor, flowing through steep wooded valleys and pastoral Devon countryside on its way to the sea at Teignmouth. Kingfishers, herons and predatory mink can be seen along its banks, as well as the occasional otter.

Bridford and the Teign Valley

Daffodils at Steps Bridge, a climb up Heltor Rock on route for Bridford and a very special church.

Teign Valley

In early springtime many people travel out to Steps Bridge (built in 1816) to stroll along the River Teign, enjoying the sight of thousands of tiny wild daffodils crowding the riverbanks. But there's a better way to explore this valley, which includes a close look at an example of that most characteristic Dartmoor feature, a tor, and a pint at one of the Teign Valley's best pubs as an added bonus!

Much of the ancient semi-natural woodland and valley meadows around Steps Bridge is a Site of Special Scientific Interest (SSSI), and many acres are owned by the National Trust. Dunsford Wood (on the opposite bank of the Teign from the car park) is managed as a nature reserve by the Devon Wildlife Trust. These woodlands are glorious all year round: there are snowdrops in February, daffodils in early spring, wood anenomes and ransoms; then foxgloves, woodrush and cow-wheat in summer. Look out for the nests of the wood ant by the side of the path, which can be as much as a metre high. If you place your cheek or hand near to a nest you'll get a shock – the ants squirt formic acid from their abdomens in a defensive move, and it stings!

Blackingstone Rock is another outlying tor, 1 mile (1.6km) south west of Heltor Rock. Turn right rather than left at Point 4 and you will soon be aware of its huge, granite mass rising above the lane on the left. You can get to the top by climbing up an almost vertical

flight of steps which was added in the 19th century for that purpose. The views of the surrounding countryside are worth the effort.

While you're in Bridford, part way round the walk, it's well worthwhile going inside the church. The original chapel on this site was dedicated by Bishop Bronescombe in 1259, to the murdered Archbishop Thomas á Becket, who died at Canterbury Cathedral in 1170. This was still a common practice in many West Country churches during the century following his death. The present building dates from the 15th century, and its most famous feature is the superb eight-bay rood screen, thought to date from 1508. The faces of the richly carved and coloured figures were mutilated by Puritan soldiers during the Civil War, but what survives is still impressive. The doors are also unusual in that they are made in one piece rather than being divided in the middle. These details are often overlooked by the Steps Bridge hordes.

the walk

1 Cross the road, following the signs to the **youth hostel**. Turn right up the concrete track, then left. When you reach the youth hostel turn right again, this time following signs for **Heltor Farm**. The steep path leads uphill through delightful oak, then beech woodland. At a fork of paths turn left and up over some wooden steps by the gate into a field.

2 Follow wooden footpath posts straight up the field. Go through the metal gate, then between granite gateposts; look right to see **Heltor Rock**. Pass signs for **Lower Heltor Farm**. Before a metal gate onto a green lane, turn left through a wooden

gate following permissive footpath signs through a new woodland. With a dog you may need to continue on the Right of Way around the farmhouse.

3 Follow the signs down wooden steps, across **ponds** and through a gate. Turn left up the tarmac lane.

4 At the top of the lane turn left (signs for **Bridford**). After 200yds (183m) turn left over a stile up the narrow fenced permissive path to **Heltor**, from where you can enjoy an amazing panorama. Retrace your steps to the road and turn left.

5 The lane eventually bends left, then right, to reach the edge of **Bridford**. Turn right down a small steep lane signed 'Parish Hall and Church'. Follow the path round the churchyard, down steps and right to find **The Bridford Inn**.

The River Teign at Steps Bridge in Bridford Woods

2h45   **5 MILES**   **8 KM**   **LEVEL 123**

16

 WALK

MAP: OS Explorer 110 Torquay & Dawlish

START/FINISH: free car park at Steps Bridge, grid ref: SX 804883

PATHS: woodland paths, open fields and country lanes, 7 stiles

LANDSCAPE: steeply wooded valleys and undulating farmland

PUBLIC TOILETS: at car park

TOURIST INFORMATION: Moretonhampstead, tel 01647 440043

THE PUB: The Bridford Inn, Bridford

⚠ Some steep woodland paths

Getting to the start

Steps Bridge is on the B3212 between Exeter and Moretonhampstead, 9 miles (14.4km) west of Exeter. Steps Bridge is not long after the signs for Dunsford and is well signposted itself. Cross the bridge and go a little up the hill, past the Steps Bridge Café and turn right into the car park.

Researched and written by:
Brian Pearse, Sue Viccars

Grey heron

6 Turn left from the pub and follow the road through the centre of the village. Take the fourth lane (**Neadon Lane**) on the right, by a telephone box. Just past where a bridleway joins (from the left) the lane dips to the right, downhill; take the left fork ahead to pass **Birch Down Farm**. Take the path up to the left, beside the field behind the farm. Take the stile and cross the field, keeping the wire fence to your right. Continue up the right-hand edge of the next field to a stile in the top corner. Then cross over a **tumbledown granite wall** and carry straight on through an area of prickly gorse bushes, heading towards a footpath signpost. Cross a stile by some beech trees.

7 Continue along the top of the field and down a green lane towards **Lower**

Lowton Farm. At a wooden gate turn right along the permissive bridleway to avoid the farm. At the next T-junction turn right, towards **Steps Bridge**, then through a small wooden gate. Continue down the deeply banked green lane until you reach a gate onto a surfaced lane.

8 Turn left through the middle gate, signed '**Byway to Steps Bridge**'. At the edge of **Bridford Wood** (by the National Trust sign) turn right following the footpath signposts. The path is fairly narrow and quite steep. Go left, then right, to cross a sandy track, keeping downhill. The path then runs to the left, now high above the river to **Steps Bridge** where it meets the road opposite the café. Turn left here to return to your car.

The Bridford Inn

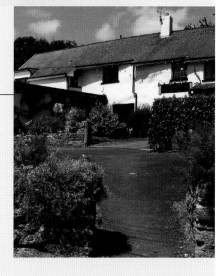

Deep down twisting narrow lanes on the edge of the Dartmoor National Park, the Bridford Inn appropriately advertises itself as being 'the middle of nowhere, the centre of the universe'. It can be found at the end of the village and is a cracking community local with a popular games room replete with dart board and pool table. Speciality evenings, great bar food and locally-brewed beers draw locals and walkers into the big bar with its blazing winter log fire and warm welcome.

Food

Expect traditional pub meals in the form of lunchtime sandwiches, lasagne, cod and chips, various basket meals, and home-made soups, steak and ale pie, ham, egg and chips, and Sunday roast lunches.

Family facilities

Children are welcome inside and youngsters have their own menu to choose from. The beer garden has a play area.

Alternative refreshment stops

Another good pub just down the road is the Royal Oak at Dunsford. The Steps Bridge Café is open 10am–6pm and offers accommodation.

☞ Where to go from here

Go and have a look at the three reservoirs near Hennock, on the ridge between the Teign and Wray valleys – Tottiford, Kennick and Trenchford. These beautiful expanses of fresh water, surrounded by coniferous woodland and rhododendron-covered slopes, provide plentiful opportunities for easy walks and peaceful picnics. Head

south through the Teign Valley to view the Canonteign Falls, a magical combination of waterfalls, woodlands and lakes. To the north is the impressive Castle Drogo, a granite castle built between 1910 and 1930 by Sir Edwin Lutyens, and which combines the grandeur of a medieval castle with the comfort of a 20th-century home (www.nationaltrust.org.uk).

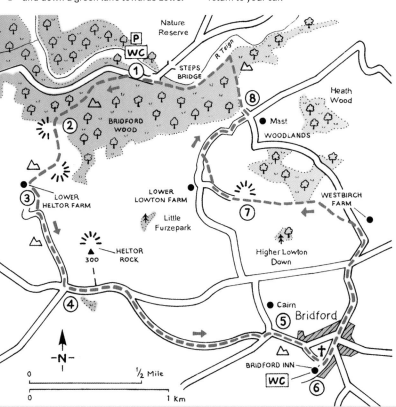

Dawlish Warren Nature Reserve

This Nature Reserve (open to the public) is located on a long sand spit at the mouth of the River Exe. Habitats include grassland, dunes, salt marsh and mudflats, and the site is the main roost for the wildfowl and wading birds of the Exe estuary. Nearly 600 different types of flowering plant have been recorded, including the Warren crocus, and orchids.

Budleigh Salterton Nature Reserve

while you're there

Budleigh Salterton has a small but interesting museum on local history, including the Budleigh Salterton railway, and the natural history of the River Otter. There is a fine costume collection and a beautiful display of Devon lace.

Exmouth to Knowle

Explore the old Exmouth to Budleigh Salterton railway line with the chance of a stop at the pub in Knowle.

The Jurassic Coast

No visit to this part of Devon would be complete without a visit to the coast, and that's one thing that's missing from this cycle ride. Go down to Exmouth's sea front and have a drink at The Grove, which has fabulous views across Exmouth's 2 mile (3.2km) long sandy beach both out to sea and across the Exe estuary to the sandspit and nature reserve at Dawlish Warren.

The coastline from Exmouth all the way to Old Harry Rocks on the Isle of Purbeck in Dorset – 95 miles (155km) away – was awarded World Heritage Site status in 2001, the first in England. It's hard to imagine, but the red rocks of this part of east Devon date back 200 to 250 million years, the Triassic period, when hot desert conditions prevailed. The red colouring comes from the weathering of iron minerals (similar to the Namib Desert in Africa today). The Geoneedle on the red cliffs at Orcombe Point, just east of Exmouth, marks the inauguration of the World Heritage Site. You can take a boat trip along the coast from Exmouth past Budleigh Salterton's famous pebble beds, deposited by one of the huge rivers that flowed through the desert over 200 million years ago, and today piled up to form a large part of the beach.

the ride

1 From the car park cycle back downhill to the entrance to the park. Turn left on the road and cycle up **Marpool Hill** for about 200yds (183m). Turn left where signed on the cycleway/path (note that cyclists should keep on the left). Follow this tarmac way – watch out for pedestrians – along the top of the park, then between houses, to meet a road.

One of the information boards on the cycle trail

2 Turn right on the pavement up to the traffic lights. Dismount to cross the B3178; turn left, then right after 20yds (18m). Follow this narrow winding tarmac way between fences – take care – to reach another road at **Littleham Cross** (Exmoor Motor Spares, 20yds/18m, left, sells cycle repair kits etc). Cross the road and cycle along Jarvis Close. Keep ahead on a tarmac way, which bears left downhill, then right to reach **Littleham Road**.

3 Cross over. You can push your bike straight ahead on a narrow way between bungalows, or turn right down the road for 100yds (91m), then left into **Bidmead Close**. After 20yds (18m) bear right uphill on a tarmac path – John Hudson Close – to rejoin the old **railway line**.

4 Follow the track under a bridge (Capel Lane – access to the route, and also to the Clinton Arms in Littleham) and on into open countryside. Pass a picnic table on the right with views towards **Dawlish Warren**, and over the 15th-century tower of Littleham's Church of St Margaret and St Andrew, where Lady Nelson is buried. The track becomes gritty and runs pleasantly through farmland, then through **Knowle Hill plantations** (access to Castle Lane). When the line opened in 1903 it was said that it ran through 'beautiful hills and beautiful meadows, with bright colours of earth and field and woodland and gay flowers beside the line'. Sadly it never realised its full potential, and fell to Beeching's axe; the last train ran on 4 March 1967. The cycle route was opened in 1998, and has become a haven for wildlife and flowers.

17

CYCLE

| 2h00 | 11 MILES | 17.6 KM | LEVEL 123 |

SHORTER ALTERNATIVE ROUTE

| 1h45 | 10 MILES | 16 KM | LEVEL 123 |

MAP: OS Explorer 115 Exmouth & Sidmouth

START/FINISH: Phear Park, Exmouth, grid ref: SY 008815

TRAILS/TRACKS: mainly well-surfaced track, short stretches on broad pavements

LANDSCAPE: townscape, woodland and farmland

PUBLIC TOILETS: Phear Park, and just off the route at Littleham Cross (Point 2)

TOURIST INFORMATION: Exmouth, tel 01395 222299

THE PUB: The Grove, Exmouth

⚠ Busy B3178 to pub at Knowle (pavement)

Getting to the start

Exmouth lies east of the mouth of the Exe on the south Devon coast. From the A376 turn left at traffic lights into Gipsy Lane. At the roundabout turn right, then left into Phear Park. From the B3178 Salterton Road turn right. Descend Marpool Hill, bear right at the roundabout, and right into Phear Park.

Why do this cycle ride?

The route follows part of 'The Buzzard', an 80-mile (129km) circular ride through east Devon. It's an easy, quiet ride, mainly along the old Exmouth to Budleigh railway line. There's an optional 1 mile (1.6km) extension at the end for refreshments at the child-friendly Dog and Donkey in Knowle.

Researched and written by: Sue Viccars

while you're there

Spanning nearly 300 years of horticultural history, the magnificent gardens of Bicton Park are set in East Devon's picturesque Otter Valley. The 63 acres (25ha) of grounds include an historic formal garden inspired by Versailles, a beautiful glass palm house, specimen trees and a woodland railway.

Avocet
(Recurvirostra avosetta)

5 Pass under another bridge on the top of **Knowle Hill** – the deep cutting here was mainly dug out by hand, with the help of two 'steam navvies' (early steam-driven shovels) – then enjoy a long gentle downhill run under beech trees. Leave the track on a tarmac way that bears right uphill to reach **Bear Lane**, from where there is a glimpse ahead of the wooded top of **High Peak** (515ft/157m) on the coast, site of an Iron Age fort.

6 For a break at the pub, turn right down Bear Lane to the B3178. Turn right downhill (take care – fortunately there is a pavement) to find the Dog and Donkey at the bottom of the hill on the left. To return to **Exmouth**, retrace the route. It is possible to cycle on to **Budleigh Salterton** – named after salt pans that used to be sited at the mouth of the River Otter, the estuary of which is now a nature reserve – but the roads tend to be busy and so this is not recommended for families.

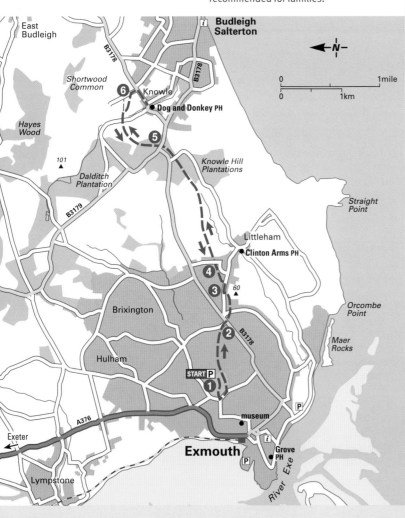

The Grove

A smartly refurbished Young's pub set back from the beach, with a first-floor dining room and balcony enjoying spectacular views across the mouth of the River Exe and along the coast to Torbay. The sheltered rear garden is a super spot for rest and refreshment after time spent on the bike or beach. Inside, the roomy panelled bars are comfortably furnished and feature open fires, well-kept beers, decent wines by the glass, and local prints on the walls.

Food
A menu listing traditional British dishes highlights steak and Young's ale pie, Cumberland sausages and mash, fish pie, beer battered fish and chips, and ham, egg and chips. Lighter meals include ploughman's lunches, Caesar salad and smoked salmon and cream cheese panini.

Family facilities
Children of all ages are welcome inside and there's a family dining area and a children's menu. There's a play area in the garden.

Alternative refreshment stops
Exmouth has an extensive range of pubs and cafés to choose from. There's a café in Phear Park, the Dog and Donkey pub at the suggested turn-around point, or plenty of pubs and cafés in Budleigh Salterton if you choose to cycle on.

☛ Where to go from here
The World of Country Life at Sandy Bay is an all-weather family attraction where kids can meet friendly farm animals, view working models and exhibits from a bygone age, including steam and vintage vehicles, and enjoy a safari train ride through a 40-acre deer park (www.worldofcountrylife.co.uk). For exhilarating rides and huge indoor and outdoor play areas head for Crealy Adventure Park at Clyst St Mary (www.crealy.co.uk). See wholemeal flour being ground at an historic water-powered mill and various pottery, weaving and spinning studios at Otterton Mill (www.ottertonmill.com).

about the pub

The Grove
The Esplanade, Exmouth
Devon EX8 1BJ
Tel 01395 272101
www.youngs.co.uk

DIRECTIONS: from the car park follow signs through the town centre to the Esplanade

PARKING: none – on-street meter parking

OPEN: daily; all day

FOOD: daily; all day

BREWERY/COMPANY: Young's Brewery

REAL ALE: Young's Bitter, Special, Smiles IPA, seasonal beers

Broadhembury   DEVON

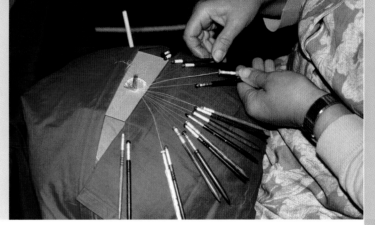

A woman making lace in Honiton's All Hallow's Museum

Broadhembury

Beech woods and rolling farmland around an unspoilt thatched village.

The Drewe family

Broadhembury is one of those unspoilt showpiece Devon villages that gives you the impression that nothing has changed for centuries and that you've entered a time warp. The picturesque main street is lined with well-preserved cob and thatched cottages and pretty flower-filled gardens. Much of Broadhembury as you see it today developed as an estate village under the patronage of the Drewe family in the early 17th century, and you get the feeling that this village is not struggling for survival.

St Andrew's Church holds many memorials to members of the family who were highly influential in the development of the village. In 1603 Edward Drewe, Sergeant-at-Law to Queen Elizabeth I, bought Abbey Farm and created The Grange, which remained the family seat for nearly 300 years. Edward Drewe was a successful lawyer, who already owned Sharpham and Killerton. The oak drawing room at The Grange is said to be one of the most beautiful in the country. The house is private, but you can see it from the south east approach road to the village.

The church was consecrated in 1259, but the building dates mainly from the 15th century, constructed of local flint and chalky limestone from Beer. It's set at the end of a cul-de-sac of chestnut trees and has been much restored. The 1480 tower is almost 100ft (30m) high and the timbers of the roof were painted in the late 15th century and were only discovered in 1930 when repair work was carried out. There is also an unusual 15th-century font, which is damaged (probably during the Civil War) and decorated with primitive figures of apostles and clergy, and an 18th-century memorial to Augustus Toplady, who wrote the hymn *Rock of Ages*.

Just a mile (1.6km) to the south east of the village lies Hembury hillfort, on a spur of the Blackdown Hills at 883ft (269m) above sea level. There was a causewayed camp here around 2500 BC, and the site was inhabited until around AD 75.

the walk

1 Return to the road and turn left uphill. Very shortly, just before another 20% sign, a **bridleway sign** points right through a parking area under beech trees. After a few minutes this narrow, level path reaches a signpost and metal gate (left), indicating that you have reached the **Devon and**

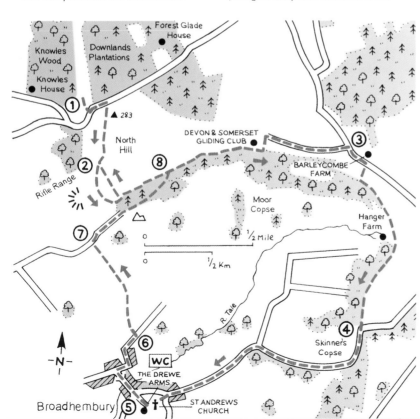

2h30   **5.5 MILES**   **8.8 KM**   **LEVEL 123**

MAP: OS Explorer 115 Exeter & Sidmouth

START/FINISH: unsurfaced car park at Knowles Wood, grid ref: SY 095068

PATHS: country lanes, pastures and woodland paths, 7 stiles

LANDSCAPE: rolling farmland and beech woods

PUBLIC TOILETS: by the Drewe Arms in the centre of Broadhembury

TOURIST INFORMATION: Honiton, tel 01404 43716

THE PUB: The Drewe Arms, Broadhembury

Getting to the start

Broadhembury is off the A373, 6 miles (9.7km) north west of Honiton. From the M5 Junction 28 at Cullompton take the A373 towards Honiton. After about 3 miles (4.8km), pass the Keeper's Cottage pub on the right and take the next turn left, signposted to Sheldon. Continue following the Sheldon signs straight ahead for about 2 miles (3.2km) until the hill steepens and approaches woodland. Soon turn left under the barrier into the car park.

Researched and written by: Brian Pearse, Sue Viccars

while you're there

The quiet and genteel resort of Sidmouth is an architectural gem, with over 500 listed structures. Regency buildings have elegant wrought-iron balconies and white-painted facades, all prettily enhanced by beautiful gardens and floral displays. Smaller cottages were built for servants, and many retain their original thatched roofing, stone foundations and cob walls.

The town's peaceful existence is disturbed only by an international folk festival held during the first week of August every year.

The seafront at Sidmouth

Somerset Gliding Club. Ignore the gate, continuing on the bridleway.

2 Pass through the next two gates and onto the **airfield**. Turn right along the edge, keeping to the right of the clubhouse. Follow the tarmac drive left over a cattle grid and down the lane to join a road.

3 Turn right; pass **Barleycombe Farm** (on the left), then follow bridleway signs right through a gate, left through another and into a field. Follow the track along the bottom of the field. The path curves right through a stand of beech trees and a metal gate, then runs straight across the next field towards a big beech tree and gate. Take the stony track through the gate. After 100yds (91m) bear right along a grassy path (ignore the gate straight ahead) and through two gates, with a **coniferous plantation** to the right.

4 The path ends at a lane; turn right downhill into **Broadhembury**. At **St Andrew's Church** cross the road and go through the churchyard, then under the lychgate and downhill to find **The Drewe Arms** (left) for a welcome break.

5 To continue the walk, from the pub, turn left down the main street to reach the bridge and **ford**. Turn right up the lane, past the playground and up the hill.

6 Just past a group of **thatched cottages** go left over the stile in the hedge and up the field, aiming for a stile in the top left corner. Go over that and straight ahead, keeping the **old farmhouse** and barn conversions to your right. Continue over the next stile, then another, then right, round the edge of the field, and over a small stile ahead into a small copse. Another stile leads into the next field; look straight across to locate the next stile in the beech hedge opposite, which takes you into a green lane.

7 Turn right and walk uphill between conifers, on the left, and fields until a metal gate leads on to another and back on to the **airfield**.

8 Turn left along the edge of the field. Go left over the second gate to rejoin the **bridleway**, which leads back to the road. Turn left downhill to find your car.

what to look for

The Devon and Somerset Gliding Club is near the start of the walk at North Hill, over 900ft (280m) above sea level – a popular spot with skylarks, too. The return leg skirts along the edge of the airfield; the gliders are launched using a steel cable, so it's wise to keep well out of the way. There's something quite magical – and tempting – about watching the gliders drift silently through the air above you, often reaching heights of over 2,000ft (600m).

The Drewe Arms

Set in an archetypal thatched Devon village and dating back to the 15th century, the small, thatched Drewe Arms has a charmingly rustic feel with dado-boarded walls, a pile of magazines next to the inglenook fireplace (with blazing log fire in winter), various rural artefacts and a warm, convivial atmosphere. Striking mullioned windows, carved ceiling beams and quaint old furniture lend the pub its particular tasteful character. The best available West Country produce form the basis of the daily blackboard menus that major in fresh fish. In addition to locally brewed Otter beers there are well chosen house wines, all offered by the glass.

Food
Expect on any one day to feast on pollack baked with Cheddar and cream or sea bream with orange and chilli. Steamed mussels with garlic and herbs, griddled sardines and smoked haddock and Stilton

Top: The pretty villge of Broadhembury

about the pub

The Drewe Arms
Broadhembury, Honiton
Devon EX14 3NF
Tel 01404 841267

DIRECTIONS: village is off the A373 north of Honiton; pub is in the village centre

PARKING: 20

OPEN: closed Sunday evening

FOOD: daily

BREWERY/COMPANY: free house

REAL ALE: Otter Ale, Bitter, Head and Bright

DOGS: not allowed inside

rarebit are all offered in two portion sizes – large and very large. For more dedicated meat-eaters are rare beef and hot chicken baguettes and a Bookmaker's fillet steak with anchovy butter.

Family facilities
Well-behaved children are welcome in the eating area and all dishes can be served as half portions. There is a lawned garden with views of the church for alfresco meals.

Alternative refreshment stops
Café serving tea, coffee and light snacks at Broadhembury Craft Centre.

☞ Where to go from here
At Uffculme (off M5 Junction 27) is the Coldharbour Mill Working Wool Museum (www.coldharbourmill.org.uk). It has been producing textiles since 1790 and is now a working museum, still making knitting wools and fabrics on period machinery. South west of Honiton is Cadhay Manor, a classic Tudor manor. Crealy Adventure Park at Clyst St Mary offers a fun experience for the whole family through rides and indoor and outdoor play areas (www.crealy.co.uk).

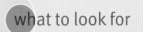

*Pied flycatcher
(Ficedula hypoleuca)*

From Seatown to Golden Cap

what to look for

The National Trust owns the ruined church of St Gabriel's (little more than a low shell with a porch to one side) and the neighbouring row of thatched cottages that have been smartly refurbished and are let out as visitor accommodation. They are all that remains of the fishing village of Stanton, sheltering in the valley behind the cliffs, which was largely abandoned after the coast road was rerouted inland in 1824.

Climb a fine top, owned by one of the country's most popular charities.

Golden Cap

Golden Cap is the rather obvious name for a high, flat-topped hill of deep orange sandstone on the cliffs between Charmouth and Bridport. It represents the tail end of a vein of the warm-coloured sandstone that stretches down from the Cotswolds. The Cap is the highest point on the south coast, at 627ft (191m), with views along the shore to the tip of Portland Bill in one direction and to Start Point in the other. Inland, you can see Pilsdon Pen and as far as the heights of Dartmoor.

Climbing towards the top, you pass from neat fields, through a line of wind-scoured oak trees, into an area of high heathland, walking up through bracken, heather, bilberry and blackberry, alive with songbirds. The loose undercliff on the seaward side creates a different habitat. In botanical and wildlife terms, Golden Cap is one of the richest properties in the National Trust's portfolio. Today we tend to associate the National Trust with the upkeep of grand houses but, in fact, its first acquisition, way back in 1896, was a stretch of coast in Wales. Today the charity is one of Britain's biggest private landowners.

On the very top of Golden Cap itself is a simple memorial to the Earl of Antrim, chairman of the Trust in the 1960s and 1970s. It was he who spearheaded its 1965 appeal campaign, named 'Enterprise Neptune', to purchase sections of unspoiled coastline before the developers moved in and it was all too late. Golden Cap was part of this and over the years the Trust has continued to buy up pockets of land all around, with the aim of preserving the traditional field pattern that exists in the area between Eype and Lyme Regis.

the walk

1 Walk back up through Seatown. Cross a stile on the left, on to the footpath, signposted **'Coast Path Diversion'**. Cross a stile at the end, bear left to cross a stile and footbridge into **woodland**. Cross a stile at the other side, go through a gate and bear right up the hill, signposted **'Golden Cap'**.

2 Where the track forks by a **seat** keep left. Go through some trees and over a stile. Bear left, straight across the open hillside, with Golden Cap ahead of you. Pass through a line of trees and walk steeply uphill beside the **fence**. Go up some steps, cross a stile and continue ahead. At the **fingerpost** go left through a gate to follow the path of **shallow steps** up through bracken, heather, bilberry and bramble to the top of Golden Cap.

3 For a short cut, return back down the steps and through the gate. Proceed straight ahead to a stile in the hedge, then follow the field edge to a gate and Point 6. For the longer walk, pass the **trig point** and turn right along the top. Pass the stone memorial to the Earl of Antrim. At a **marker stone** turn right and follow the zig-zag path steeply downhill, enjoying great views along the bay to Charmouth and Lyme Regis. Go through a gate and bear right

MAP: OS Explorer 116 Lyme Regis & Bridport

START/FINISH: car park (fee) above gravel beach, Seatown – beware, can flood in stormy weather; grid ref: SY 420917

PATHS: field tracks, country lanes, steep zig-zag gravel path, 7 stiles

LANDSCAPE: windswept coastline of lumps and bumps

PUBLIC TOILETS: at end of road, Seatown

TOURIST INFORMATION: Bridport, tel: 01308 424901

THE PUB: The Anchor Inn, Seatown

❶ Long, steep ascent to the top of Golden Cap; steep descent on longer loop; suitable for fit, older children

Getting to the start

To reach Seatown, take the signed lane opposite the church in Chideock, a small village on the A35 between Bridport and Lyme Regis, 3 miles (4.8km) west of Bridport. Arrive early in summertime to ensure a spave in the car park.

Researched and written by:
David Hancock, Ann F Stonehouse

19

WALK

Seatown DORSET

did you know?

The postscript for the story of the wrecked Hope was that the crew escaped drowning by being washed up on the beach, but the ship broke up and lost its cargo of gold, silver and other valuables. A mini gold-rush ensued.

Boats moored in the harbour of West Bay

while you're there

The quay at West Bay in Bridport was the setting for the television series Harbour Lights. It has the genuine, slightly seedy air of a working harbour, and remains refreshingly unsophisticated.

The Anchor Inn

The Anchor has a spectacular setting in a little cove surrounded by National Trust land, beneath Golden Cap and with lovely cliff and sea views. It is right on the Dorset coastal path (ideal for walkers), and the inn makes the most of its position with a large sun terrace and cliff-side beer garden overlooking the beach. On winter weekdays it is blissfully quiet, while the summer sees it thronging with holidaymakers. The rusted anchor outside belonged to the Hope, which was wrecked on Chesil Beach during a storm in January 1748, while returning from Curaçao to Amsterdam. Inside are two homely bars with open fires and old photos of the pub and cove, and tip-top real ale from Palmers Brewery in nearby Bridport.

Food

A wide-ranging menu offers something for everyone, from sandwiches (try the excellent crab), burgers and jacket potatoes to prime rump steak. There's plenty of freshly caught seafood, including crab and lobster, and game in season. Typical dishes are monkfish in Thai sauce, game

about the pub

The Anchor Inn
Seatown, Chideock
Bridport, Dorset DT6 6JU
Tel: 01297 489215

DIRECTIONS: above the car park at the start of the walk

PARKING: 20

OPEN: daily, all day Easter–September, and Friday, Saturday and Sunday in winter

FOOD: daily, all day Easter–September and winter weekends

BREWERY/COMPANY: Palmers Brewery

REAL ALE: Palmers IPA, 200 and Copper Ale

DOGS: welcome on a lead

casserole, carbonade of beef, and vegetable and spinach pancakes.

Family facilities
Children are welcome in the family room away from the bar.

☛ Where to go from here
Lyme Regis is a pretty old harbour town, with a landmark breakwater, the Cobb, and crumbling cliffs famous for their fossils – learn more at Dinosaurland fossil museum in the town.

over the field towards the ruined **St Gabriel's Church**. In the bottom corner turn down through a gate, passing the ruins on your right, then go through a second gate. Go down the track, passing **cottages** on the left, and bear right towards the access lane.

4 Ignore the Coast Path sign left, and turn right before crossing the stream to follow a waymarked path parallel with the **stream** and beside **St Gabriel's Wood**. The path steepens beyond the wood as you follow the edge of two fields towards farm buildings. Soon cross a stile and turn right along the concrete lane to **Filcombe Farm**.

5 Follow **blue markers** through the farmyard, bearing left through two gates. Walk up the track, go through two more gates and bear left over the top of the green saddle between Langdon Hill and Golden Cap.

6 Go left through a gate in the corner and down a gravel lane (**Pettycrate Lane**) beside the woods, signed 'Seatown'. Ignore a footpath off to the right. At a junction of tracks keep right, downhill, with a delectable green patchwork of fields on the hillside ahead. Pass **Seahill House** on the left and turn right, on to a road. Continue down the road into Seatown to return to your car.

Portland Museum and Shipwreck Centre

Portland's museum was founded in 1930 by Dr Marie Stopes, the museum's first curator and famous birth control pioneer. Today her 17th-century cottage houses not only displays of her life and work, but also a shipwreck and smuggling exhibition, with models, catalogues, data and maps of shipwrecks over the centuries on this rugged Portland coast.

Weymouth's beach is extremely popular on warm summer days

while you're there

Weymouth has a long beach and a lovely old seafront promenade, complete with wrought-iron balustrades. Apart from the usual amusements, attractions include historic Nothe Fort, and a fascinating timewalk through a Victorian brewery – combined with craft outlets – at Brewers Quay.

The White Horse at Osmington

Stone-cut cottages beside the River Jordan in Sutton Poyntz

2h00 | **4 MILES** | **6.4 KM** | **LEVEL 1 2 3**

MAP: OS Explorer OL 15 Purbeck & South Dorset

START/FINISH: Church Lane in Osmington, just off the A353; grid ref: SY 724829

PATHS: farm and village lanes, woodland paths, field paths, 8 stiles

LANDSCAPE: sheltered green valley behind coastline and chalky ridge of White Horse Hill

PUBLIC TOILETS: none on route

TOURIST INFORMATION: Weymouth, tel: 01305 785747

THE PUB: The Springhead, Sutton Poyntz

❶ One steady downland climb

Getting to the start

Osmington village is located north of the A353, 4 miles (6.4km) north of Weymouth. Limited roadside parking by the church.

Researched and written by:
David Hancock, Ann F Stonehouse

Where a sane King George III took a well-earned break.

King George III

Weymouth is a trading port with a patchy history. In the 18th century it was a base for trade with the Americas and the shipping of convicts to Australia. The 1780s saw the emergence of sea bathing (and even seawater drinking) – Weymouth joined in. A royal visit in 1789 rocketed the little town into the top rank of seaside resorts.

Rumours of George III's mental instability threatened to destabilise the country. It was decided that the King should go on a short, highly visible tour to Weymouth, to demonstrate how much better he was. The royal party consisted of the King, the Queen and the three princesses. By the time they reached Weymouth the crowds were ecstatic, with bunting, receptions and gunships firing salutes in the bay. The King

responded to their warmth with a short walk-about on his first evening. He declared that he 'never saw a sight so pleasing'.

George III spent ten weeks here on his first visit, enjoying day trips to Lulworth, Milton Abbey and St Adhelm's Head, and sailing off Portland. The royal family returned two years later for a holiday and then returned every year until 1805.

In 1808 John Rainier (brother of the heroic Rear Admiral Peter Rainier, whose name was given to Mount Rainier near Seattle) arranged for a symbol of the town's undying loyalty and gratitude to be carved into the chalk downs above Osmington. And so an elegant silhouette of the King on horseback was created, around 324ft (99m) high, riding away from the town – presumably in a much healthier condition after his vacation. Once clearly visible from Weymouth, Portland and ships out at sea, today the chalk figure is weathered and

grey, but you can still pick out the graceful lines of the horse's legs and tail, and the King's distinctive cocked hat.

the walk

1 From Osmington church walk down the village street of pretty thatched cottages. At the junction keep on down **Church Lane**. Opposite **The Cartshed**, at the end of a wall, look carefully for and turn left up a long, steep flight of steps, signed **'Sutton Poyntz'**. The path rises through woodland. After a second set of steps bear right on the path which undulates through the trees. Cross a stile and continue straight on to the end of a field.

2 Cross a stile and turn immediately right to cross a second stile and walk down the field. Turn left through a gate and head straight across the field. Cross a **farm track**

did you know?

The harbours at Portland and Weymouth played a critical role in the embarkation of US troops and equipment for the Normandy landings of 6th June 1944. Between then and 7th May 1945, 517,816 troops and 144,093 vehicles were moved through the ports and landed on Omaha Beach.

Portland Harbour as seen from Portland Heights

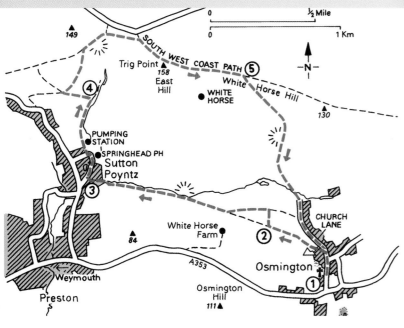

The Springhead

and bear ahead and right. Cross a pair of stiles and continue along the bottom of the field, looking to your right to see the **White Horse**. Continue though a gap. At the end of the next field bear left, through a gateway, then go straight on (**yellow marker**), towards Sutton Poyntz. Soon veer right, cross a **stream** and bear left by a gate. Follow the path to a stile and continue to the road.

3 Turn right, pass the **Mill House** and the tall, red brick mill on the left. Pass the **village pond** and **The Springhead** pub on the right. Bear left and right up a lane by

Springfield Cottage. Go through a gate and follow the track straight ahead. Cross a stile by another gate, with a **pumping station** on the right, below the bottom of the steep combe where the spring emerges.

4 Cross a stile by a gate and turn left up the **grassy lane**. About half-way up the hill turn right, up a track (the upper of two) that leads to the top above the combe, with great views along the valley and down to Weymouth Bay and Portland. Keep right on the green track, go through a gate and keep left along the field edge. Follow the path round to the right and walk up the field (a lane soon joins from the left). Stay on this track past the **trig point**. Go through a gate and keep straight on, with a good view to strip lynchets on the hillside ahead.

5 Go through a gate and bear down to the right, signed '**Osmington**'. The track leads down the hill, through a gate – look back to see the White Horse again. Follow the lane back up through the village to your car.

what to look for

As you walk along White Horse Hill there is a clear view of terracing on the grassy slopes of the combe ahead. These are strip lynchets, relics of a farming system introduced in the 12th and 13th centuries in Dorset, to maximise the land available for cultivation.

about the pub

The Springhead
Sutton Poyntz,
Weymouth
Dorset DT3 6LW
Tel: 01305 832117

DIRECTIONS: in the centre of the village, which is signed off the A353 north east of Weymouth

PARKING: 30

OPEN: daily, all day in summer

FOOD: no food Sunday evening

BREWERY/COMPANY: free house

REAL ALE: Flowers IPA, Greene King Old Speckled Hen

DOGS: welcome in the bar

The Victorian stone pub takes its name from the nearby spring and waterworks, which actually incorporates one of the funnels from Brunel's steamship, the Great Eastern. It stands in a grand location in a sleepy village beside the duck-pond and enjoys splendid views of the Dorset Downs – it's hard to imagine you are so close to bustling Weymouth. It is much modernised inside, and the open-plan carpeted bar and dining room have leather sofas and armchairs in cosy nooks and crannies, and old photos of the pub and village adorn the walls. The pub fairly buzzes on summer weekends, when the garden fills with families and the shady front benches that overlook the village pond and stream become much sought after, so arrive early on sunny days.

Food

The seasonal lunch menu takes in home-made soups, chicken liver parfait, baked chicken supreme, Thai vegetable curry, Caesar salad, and freshly battered fish and chips. Additional dishes may include rack of lamb, lemon sole and Lyme Bay plaice. Separate evening menu.

Family facilities

Families are made very welcome. Children are allowed inside and there's a play area at the far end of the garden.

☛ Where to go from here

The seaside resort of Weymouth has a number of good family attractions, including the Sea Life Park in Lodmoor Country Park, and the Deep Sea Adventure Centre, which tells of underwater exploration, shipwrecks and harbour life, with play areas for all ages (www.deepsea-adventure.co.uk).

The tiny rectangular building was partly rebuilt in brick after a fire in 1780, and is the smallest town hall building in England. It has village relics, and dinosaur footprints 130 million years old. The Ancient Order of Marblers meets here on each Shrove Tuesday.

did you know?

The Isle of Purbeck is not really an island, but is almost cut off from the rest of Dorset by rivers and a long hill. The coastline is famous for its dramatic cliffs, and is best accessed on foot. Purbeck stone has been quarried since Roman times.

Corfe Castle circuit

The town hall and museum in Corfe Castle village

A loop to Kingston from a romantic ruined castle.

A castle condemned

The huge and toothy ruin of Corfe Castle seems to fill the gap in the wall of the Purbeck Hills. It stands on a high mound, and must have been massively imposing when whole. The castle has a grim history. In AD 978 a youthful King Edward was murdered here while visiting his stepmother. His body was buried without ceremony at Wareham, while his half-brother took the throne as Ethelred II. However, stories of miracles resulted in Edward's body being exhumed and transported to Shaftesbury, where an abbey grew up in his honour.

The Normans realised the commanding role a castle could play in defence at Corfe. In around 1106, the big square keep was built. King John used it as a lifelong prison for his niece Eleanor, a potential threat to his throne. The unfortunate Edward II, deposed by his wife Isabella and Roger de Mortimer, was also imprisoned here briefly. The castle again came to the fore during the Civil War. Its owner, Sir John Bankes sided with the King. However, it was his spirited wife Mary who was left, with a handful of women and just five men, to fight off a siege in 1642.

It is said that the Roundheads took the lead from the church roof to make their bullets, and stored their powder and shot in the organ pipes. Despite reinforcements, they failed to take the castle. After a second, more sustained siege, the castle was betrayed in 1646 by one of its defenders and Lady Bankes was forced to give it up. The castle was deliberately destroyed, to prevent its further use.

the walk

1 From the car park bear right then right again on to **West Street**. At the end, go straight on over a cattle grid. Bear left on a path across the heath, the line being **Kingston church tower**. Cross duckboards and go uphill, forking right by a **tumulus**, and walk to the right of a stone block. Continue over the brow of the hill and descend in line with the church tower. The path gradually veers right and leaves the Common by way of a kissing gate, stiles and footbridges.

2 Bear half-left across a field, and across the next, regaining the line of the tower. Go over a **bridge** and ascend a wooded path. Cross a stile and continue up the left edge of a field. Maintain direction after the next stile. Go through a thick hedge and head straight across the next field (the **flag pole** on the church tower being the line) to a kissing gate and turn right up a track. On the ascent fork left, taking the path up through the **woods**.

3 At the top, turn left to the road and walk down through the village. At the junction by the **Scott Arms** turn right. After the **converted church**, go over a stile on the left and bear half-right, signposted to **Afflington**. Pass through a gate at the bottom corner of the field and continue along the left boundary of the next field to a stile in the corner. Shortly, bear left down through scrubland, then turn left on to a **stony track**. As this bears right take the path left (**Purbeck Way**) over a stile and go down the track left into a field.

4 Turn right, go through a **gate** and soon go right over a stile. Cross a narrow wooded strip to a stile and turn left beside the woods. Go over a further stile and proceed straight on, soon to bear left through a gate and around the left edge of a field. Turn left over a stile and **footbridge**, then another stile and turn sharp right. Cross a metalled drive, a stile, a causeway and bridge on to the **Common**.

5 Go straight on over Corfe Common towards the **castle**. Bear left at a **concrete marker**, and go right to a gate. Cross the B3069, go through a gate and straight on, later bearing right behind **houses**. Go through a kissing gate and follow the path (still signed Purbeck Way) towards the centre of Corfe. After it winds through housing go across fields into a **playground**. Turn left then right into West Street to reach the **square**.

Corfe Castle

2h00 **4.25 MILES** **6.8 KM** **LEVEL 1 2 3**

MAP: OS Explorer OL 15 Purbeck & South Dorset

START/FINISH: Corfe Castle; village pay car park; grid ref: SY 958818

PATHS: village lanes, rocky lanes (slippery after rain), moorland tracks, grassy paths

LANDSCAPE: downland, heathland, village streets

PUBLIC TOILETS: car park, Corfe Castle

TOURIST INFORMATION: Wareham, tel: 01929 552740

THE PUB: The Greyhound Inn, Corfe Castle

❗ The main A351 through Corfe is often busy and dangerous.

Getting to the start

The small township of Corfe Castle stands on the A351, midway between Wareham and Swanage, 5 miles (8km) south east of Wareham. The car park is off West Street, close to the village centre.

Researched and written by:
Ann F Stonehouse, Peter Toms

did you know?

One of the most remarkable of Dorset's coastal features is the symmetrical bay of Lulworth Cove. It has been formed by the sea breaching the harder limestone of the outer cliff, and then carving out a circular basin from the softer inner core.

Mupe Bay is a World Heritage Site

21

WALK

6 Turn left by the castle on the path below the **walls**. Go left up the road and soon left again by a gate and over a stile (by a sign to **The Rings**). Cross the fields via series of gates to return to the car park.

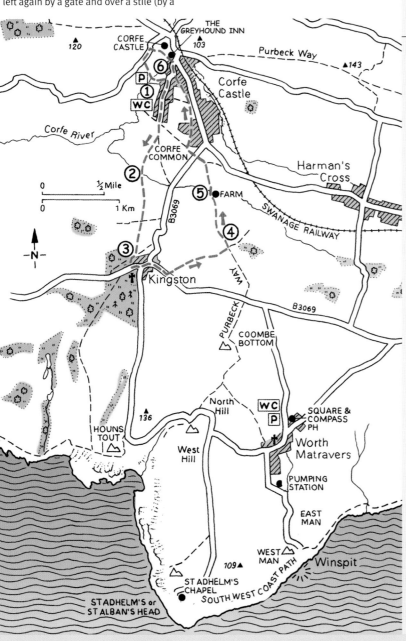

The Greyhound Inn

Lulworth Cove

The battlements of Corfe Castle, once one of England's five royal castles, not only form the dramatic backdrop, but probably furnished the stones to build the Greyhound – originally two cottages with stables – in the 16th century. The pub's garden borders the moat of the castle, and there over super views of the Purbeck Hills, making it a popular place to retreat to after this walk, or following a stroll around the castle ruins. Inside, three pleasant and small low-beamed areas off the main bar have oak panelling, lots of paintings, brass artefacts, and old photos of the village and castle. If you're lucky your visit may coincide with one of Greyhound's three annual beer festivals, when you can join in the fun of sampling 50 real ales and tucking in to the giant hog roast in the garden.

Food

In addition to the weekend carvery and a deli bar where you can create your own sandwich, the regular menu lists soups, salads, ploughman's lunches, farmhouse chicken pie, and beefburgers. Try the chargrilled meat baskets, or order fresh fish or seafood from the daily chalkboard, perhaps whole sea bass, cold lobster salad or monkfish medallions.

Family facilities

Children will love it here. There's a cosy family room kitted out with toys and games, a children's menu, high chairs for youngsters, baby food can be warmed up, and the garden is safe to play in.

Alternative refreshment stops

At the half-way point in Kingston you will find the Scott Arms. There's also a good range of pubs and tea rooms in Corfe Castle.

☞ Where to go from here

Catch the steam train to the coastal resort of Swanage, for the Studland Heritage Centre, the restored Victorian Pier, amusements and the sandy beach (www.swanagerailway.co.uk).

about the pub

The Greyhound Inn

The Square, Corfe Castle
Wareham, Dorset BH20 5EZ
Tel: 01929 480205

DIRECTIONS: in the centre of Corfe Castle

PARKING: use car park on West Street

OPEN: daily, all day in summer, and all day Saturday and Sunday in winter

FOOD: daily, all day in summer

BREWERY/COMPANY: Enterprise Inns

REAL ALE: Ringwood Fortyniner, Gales Best, Hampshire Bohemian Rhapsody

DOGS: welcome indoors

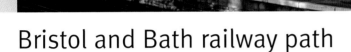

while you're there

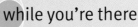

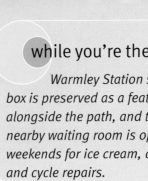

Warmley Station signal box is preserved as a feature alongside the path, and the nearby waiting room is open at weekends for ice cream, drinks and cycle repairs.

Far left: Bitton Station is on the Bristol and Bath railway path

Bristol and Bath railway path

Pulteney Bridge over the River Avon in Bath

3h30 | **18.25 MILES** | **29.4 KM** | **LEVEL 1** 2 3

22

🚲 **CYCLE**

MAP: OS Explorer 155 Bristol & Bath

START/FINISH: car park beside the A420 at Warmley, Kingswood; grid ref: ST 670735

TRAILS/TRACKS: former railway line

LANDSCAPE: wooded cuttings and embankments with occasional views across riverside path into Bath

PUBLIC TOILETS: at car park at start

TOURIST INFORMATION: Bath, tel 01225 477101

CYCLE HIRE: Webbs of Warmley, High Street, Warmley, Bristol, tel 01179 673676

THE PUB: Bird in Hand, Saltford

❗ Traffic lights control major road crossings; dismount when crossing the restored railway line; care when riding alongside the River Avon; route shared with pedestrians.

Getting to the start
Warmley is on the A420 to the east of Bristol. The car park lies 0.25 mile (400m) east of the roundabout junction with the A4174.

Why do this cycle ride
Bath is notorious for its traffic problems. For the cyclist, however, there is a splendid route along the track bed of the former Avon Valley Railway. It penetrates the heart of the city and has attractions of its own along the way: you can visit a brass mill, or ride along a section of the line, pulled by a vintage steam or diesel engine. The cycling is not strenuous, but for a shorter ride, turn around at Saltford.

Researched and written by: Dennis Kelsall

Park and ride with a difference, an easy ride to explore Bath's fine 18th-century architecture

Avon Valley Railway
The first section of the Avon Valley Railway opened in 1835, between Mangotsfield, just north of Warmley and Bristol. Originally a horse-drawn tramway, it transported local coal to Bristol. With growing industrialisation, the track was upgraded for steam and by 1869 had been extended all the way to Bath, following the course of the River Avon as it neared the city. After publication of the Beeching Report, passenger trains were withdrawn in March 1966, although goods traffic continued for a further five years, supplying coal to the gasworks in Bath. In 1972 the track was finally dismantled, but even as British Rail was removing the rails, the Bristol Suburban Railway Society was planning to reopen the line. A 2.5 mile (4km) section is now operational with extensions planned.

Known the world over for its Roman baths and elegant Cotswold-stone Georgian architecture, Bath simply demands exploration. Dedicated to the goddess Sulis, the baths were begun in the 1st century, the focus of a sophisticated city that thrived for

nearly 400 years. After the Romans left, the baths were gradually forgotten and when Nash created his fashionable spa town, nobody even dreamed of their existence. The former complex was only rediscovered in 1880 when sewer works broke into the subterranean ruin, and subsequent excavation revealed the finest Roman remains in the country.

the ride

1 Leaving the car park adjacent to the former Warmley Station, go left to cross the main road at a traffic light controlled crossing and follow the path away beside the old signal box. Hidden behind the trees lining the path are small units, occupying the sites of the former industries that once supported the town. After passing beneath **St Ivel Way**, look for a sculpture that represents a Roman centurion quaffing wine from a flask: it recalls that a Roman road passed nearby. A little further along is a controlled crossing at **Victoria Road**.

2 Pedalling on brings you to **Oldland Common**, the northern terminus of the restored section of the Avon Valley Railway. The path continues beside the track, passing beneath North Street to enter a shallow cutting. The stone here, known as Pennant sandstone, is particularly hard and proved an excellent construction material. The excavated stone was used for several buildings in the vicinity. There are also coal deposits in the area, laid down during the same carboniferous period and these

fuelled local brass foundries and other industries. Later on, at **Cherry Gardens**, the way enters a second cutting, exposing much younger rocks containing fossils of graptolites, belemnites and ammonites, creatures that lived in the Jurassic seas covering the region 200 million years ago. Before long, the **railway yard** at Bitton appears ahead, the cycle track swinging across the line through a gate (look out for passing trains) to reach the station.

3 Even if the trains are not running, there is always something of interest to see in the goods yard, with an assortment of engines and rolling stock either awaiting refurbishment or dismantling for spares. The buffet is generally open and for a small donation you are welcome to wander onto the platform. Go through the car park, over a small level crossing and continue beside the railway. Carry on along an embankment overlooking the Avon's flood meadows, crossing the river to reach **Avon Riverside Station**, where a path on the right drops to a picnic area by the water's edge.

4 At **Saltford**, the Bird in Hand below the embankment invites a break for refreshment. You can also wander into the village and have a look at the restored **Saltford Brass Mill**, which is open on some Saturdays during the summer months. Re-crossing the river the way continues towards Bath, the Avon winding below you twice more before you reach the outskirts of the city.

5 Eventually you emerge on **Brassmill Lane**. Follow the road to the right, keeping ahead on a short cycle lane further

Left: The former Warmley Station

William Champion

Warmley Gardens and Grotto occupy the site of William Champion's mid-18th-century brassworks, which pioneered the commercial production of zinc. The area is open to the public at all times, but the Grotto, a mysterious collection of vaulted chambers made of clinker and mortar, is only open on spring and autumn bank holiday weekends. Also made of clinker is a huge statue of Neptune which, although restored, is still missing a trident. The main entrance is about 545 yards (500m) from the railway path.

Warmley Gardens

on past a 'no entry' sign for motorised traffic. Where the cycle lane ends, turn right (watch for oncoming traffic) to gain a riverside path behind a tool hire shop. Signed towards **Bath city centre**, keep going past the 19th-century industrial quarter of Bath, where more brass and other mills took advantage of the water for both power and transport. The factories have now gone, replaced by modern light industry, but some of the old riverside warehouses remain. The path finally ends near **Churchill Bridge** in the centre of Bath.

6 Although cyclists are common on Bath's streets, the traffic is busy and it is perhaps a good idea to find a convenient spot to secure your bikes whilst you explore on foot. When you are ready to head back, retrace your outward route to **Warmley** along the riverside path and cycleway.

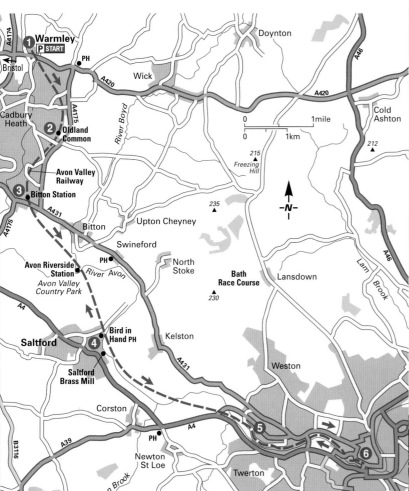

Bird in Hand

Converted in 1869 from two cottages in the original village close to the River Avon, the Bird in Hand first served the workers building the railway through the valley between Bath and Bristol. Now that the railway has gone, this homely village local, which is smack beside the old route, is a favoured resting and refuelling stop for cyclists pedalling the peaceful cycle path between the two cities. There's a comfortable bar area adorned with old pictures of the pub and village, a light and airy conservatory and plenty of outdoor seating for fine-weather eating and drinking.

Food

Lunchtime food ranges from Stilton ploughman's and salad platters to steak and ale pies, omelettes and ham, egg and chips. Evening additions include a mixed grill and daily specials such as salmon fishcakes, sea bass with prawn and lemon butter sauce, dressed crab and rack of lamb with redcurrant and port sauce.

Family facilities

Children are very welcome inside. There's a family area with a box of toys to keep youngsters amused, and a basic children's menu.

Alternative refreshment stops

Range of pubs and cafés in Bath; café at Bitton Station.

☛ Where to go from here

Spend time in Bath visiting the Abbey, the Roman Baths and Pump Rooms (www.romanbaths.co.uk) or the excellent museums (www.bath-preservation-trust.org.uk). In Bristol head for the superb Zoo Gardens (www.bristolzoo.org.uk) or savour the unique sights, sounds and smells of steam trains along the Avon Valley Railway at Bitton (www.avonvalleyrailway.co.uk).

about the pub

Bird in Hand
58 High Street
Saltford, Bristol
BS31 3EN
Tel: 01225 873335

DIRECTIONS: 3 miles (4.8km) along the cycle track from Bitton railway station

PARKING: 36

OPEN: daily

FOOD: daily

BREWERY/COMPANY: free house

REAL ALE: Abbey Bellringer, Butcombe, Courage Best, guest beers

The Roman Baths

From Bradford-on-Avon along the Kennet & Avon Canal

Discover one of Brindley's great canal masterpieces.

Kennet & Avon Canal

John Rennie began the construction of the Kennet and Avon Canal in 1794 to link the Avon and Kennet Navigations between Bath and Bristol and thus create a continuous waterway between Bristol and London. The 57 mile (92km) canal took 16 years to complete and was quite an achievement, requiring two great aqueducts and a spectacular flight of 29 locks at Caen Hill outside Devizes to lift the waterway over 240ft (73m) onto the summit level. It proved a highly profitable venture and was soon carrying over 350,000 tons a year between the two great cities. By the middle of the 19th century, competition from railways foreshadowed its decline, and in 1846 was taken over by the Great Western Railway Company. GWR signs remain on some of its bridges, ominously mounted on the instrument of its ruin, an upended length of railway track. Re-opened in 1990, many of the canal's original features still excite the imagination, none more so than the two splendid stone aqueducts carrying the canal across the Avon Valley, one of them named after the canal company's founding chairman, Charles Dundas. They presented major technical difficulties for Rennie as they had not only to carry a great weight but remain watertight, yet his

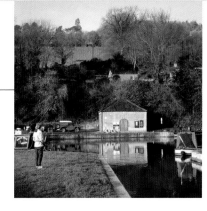

creations combined both aesthetic quality and practicality in the best tradition of the great architects.

the ride

1 Leaving the station car park, turn right along the main road in the direction of Frome. Continue past a mini-roundabout to the Canal Tavern and Lock Inn Café. Go between them to join the towpath and follow it past **Grange Farm** with its massive 600-year-old tithe barn. The River Avon runs below to the right, containing Barton Farm Country Park's picnic and wildlife areas within the intervening spit of land. Beyond a gate, continue beside the canal to **Avoncliff**.

2 The canal now makes an abrupt turn across the Avon Valley, carried above both the river and railway on an imposing aqueduct. Do not cross, but at a sign to Dundas just before, drop steeply right towards the **Cross Guns** pub, then double back left underneath the bridge, climbing left to gain the opposite towpath. Tacked along the wooded valley, the waterway runs pleasantly on, harbouring an assortment of ducks, coots and moorhens. Turning a corner opposite **Limpley Stoke**, pass beneath a road bridge, then look out on the left for a glimpse of a viaduct taking the A36 across the Midford Brook valley.

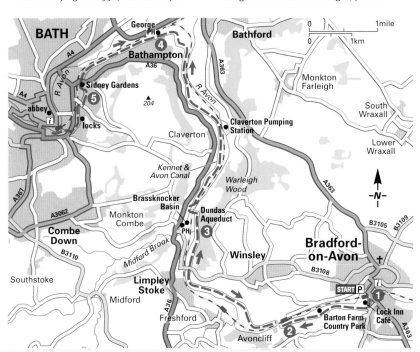

Dundas Aqueduct where the Kennet and Avon Canal turns sharply

| 4h00 | 20 MILES | 32.2 KM | LEVEL 123 |

SHORTER ALTERNATIVE ROUTE

| 3h00 | 15 MILES | 24.1 KM | LEVEL 123 |

MAP: OS Explorer 155 Bristol & Bath & 156 Chippenham & Bradford-on-Avon

START/FINISH: Bradford-on-Avon railway station (pay car park); grid ref: ST 825606

TRAILS/TRACKS: gravel tow path, short section on road

LANDSCAPE: canal tow path through the wooded and pastoral Avon Valley

PUBLIC TOILETS: at start

TOURIST INFORMATION: Bradford-on-Avon, tel 01225 865797

CYCLE HIRE: The Lock Inn Café, 48 Frome Road, Bradford-on-Avon tel: 01225 868068

THE PUB: The George, Bathampton

❗ Care through town; unguarded canal tow paths shared with pedestrians; blind approaches to bridges; dismount in tunnels; flight of steps on approaching Bath

Getting to the start

Bradford-on-Avon is only 5 miles (8km) south east of Bath and lies on the A363 to Trowbridge. Park at the railway station, from where the ride begins.

Why do this cycle ride?

The Kennet and Avon Canal passes through picturesque countryside. An attractive riverside pub at Bathampton offers a turning point although the locks passed into Bath on the longer ride are worth seeing.

Researched and written by: Dennis Kelsall

The window of Sally Lunn's Bun Shop in Bath

The George

The pub's enviable position by the parish church and a bridge over the Kennet and Avon Canal is one of its attractions. The creeper-clad building is so close to the water that the entrance to the upper dining room is from the tow path. When the weather is fine, the tables on the canalside terrace fill quickly with walkers, cyclists and barge visitors, and you can watch the many activities on the canal. Inside, there's a warren of wood-beamed rooms radiating out from the flagstoned central bar, with plenty of space away from the bar for families. The George oozes history, dating back to the 13th century when it was originally a monastery. The last official duel in England was fought on nearby Claverton Down in 1778 following a quarrel over a game of cards at The George. The fatally wounded Viscount du Barré was buried in the churchyard opposite.

Taking life at a leisurely pace along the canal

3 Another sharp turn heralds the **Dundas Aqueduct**, immediately beyond which is the last remnant of the Somerset Coal Canal, completed in 1805 to transport coal from Radstock and Paulton to Bristol. The track just before it leads to **Brassknocker Basin**, where a small exhibition (open daily in summer) describes its history. The route, however, continues ahead, signed 'Bath and Claverton', winding behind a **derrick** and maintenance building and onto the opposite bank. A mile (1.2km) further on, immediately beyond a bridge, a track drops across the railway to the river where there is a restored pump house (**Claverton Pumping Station**), built in 1813 to replenish the water drained by the locks descending to Bath. There are views to Bathford and Batheaston as you pedal the last 1.75 miles (2.8km) to **Bathampton** and The George.

4 To extend the ride, continue beside the canal, the eastern suburbs of Bath rising on the opposite side of the valley. Eventually the city itself comes into view with a glimpse of the abbey at its heart. There are a couple of short tunnels to pass through at **Sidney Gardens**, where you should dismount. Between them, two **ornate cast-iron bridges** span the canal, which, together with the elaborate façade of the second tunnel beneath Cleveland House, were added to placate the owners of Sidney Park, who rather disapproved of common cargo barges passing through their land.

5 Emerging below **Cleveland House**, the towpath doubles back onto the opposite bank, passes former warehouses, now a **marina**, and rises to a road. Taking care, diagonally cross and drop back to the tow path, here having to negotiate a flight of steps. Beyond, the canal falls impressively through a succession of locks, the path periodically rising to cross a couple of roads and a track before meeting the River Avon. To explore Bath, carry on a little further by the river to emerge on the road beside **Churchill Bridge** in the city centre. As the city is busy, it is perhaps preferable to secure your bikes whilst you wander around. The return is back the way you came, but remember you have to climb steps to the road at Bathwick Hill and dismount through the tunnels at Sidney Gardens, or you could return by train.

Food
Expect traditional pub food – sandwiches and filled rolls (roast beef and horseradish), salads, ploughman's lunches, and changing blackboard specials, perhaps roast monkfish, steak and kidney pudding or Tuscan-style swordfish.

Family facilities
Children are welcome away from the bar and a children's menu is available. Keep an eye on children on the canalside terrace.

Alternative refreshment stops
Plenty of eating places in Bradford-on-Avon and Bath. The Lock Inn Café near the start, the Cross Guns at Avoncliff, the Hop Pole and a canalside tea room at Limpley Stoke.

☛ Where to go from here
Take a closer look at the tithe barn and seek out the unspoiled Saxon church in Bradford-on-Avon. Visit the Claverton Pumping Station (www.claverton.org) or explore Bath's famous buildings and museums (www.bath-preservation-trust.org.uk). Peto Gardens at Iford Manor (www.ifordarts.co.uk) are worth seeing.

about the pub

The George
Mill Lane
Bathampton, Bath
Bath & NE Somerset BA2 6TR
Tel: 01225 425079

DIRECTIONS: at Bathampton on the A36 east of Bath, take minor road left downhill to village centre, crossing the canal to the church. The George is beside the canal near the church

PARKING: 50

OPEN: daily; all day

FOOD: daily; all day

BREWERY/COMPANY: Chef & Brewer

REAL ALE: Wadworth 6X, Courage Best & Directors, Greene King Old Speckled Hen

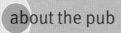

while you're there

Lacock Abbey, home of the pioneer photographer William Fox Talbot, is a magnificent late Victorian country house with extensive servants' quarters, gardens and wooded estate. Lacock village, one of the most beautiful in England, was given to the National Trust by Matilda Talbot in 1944.

Lacock Abbey

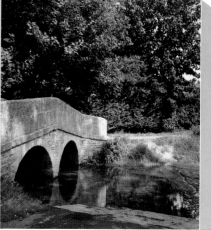

A packhorse bridge over the River Avon at Lacock

Corsham and Corsham Park

Explore this architectural treasure of a town and the adjacent Corsham Park.

Architectural delights

Bath stone characterises this handsome little market town. An air of prosperity pervades the streets where the 15th-century Flemish gabled cottages and baroque-pedimented 17th-century Hungerford Almshouses mix with larger Georgian residences. Architectural historian Nikolaus Pevsner wrote: 'Corsham has no match in Wiltshire for the wealth of good houses'.

Spend time exploring the heart of the town as many of the fine stone buildings along the High Street, Church Street and Priory Street have been well preserved. The Heritage Centre in the High Street has lively exhibits. The Town Hall was formerly the market hall with one storey and open arches before conversion in 1882. North of the post office the unspoiled line of 17th-century weavers' cottages are known as the Flemish Buildings. This was the centre of the cloth industry where the Flemish weavers settled following religious persecution in their homeland. In Church Street, note the gabled cottages of the 18th-

century weavers, with their ornate porches and a door on the first floor for taking in the raw wool.

The finest of the houses is Corsham Court, a splendid Elizabethan mansion built in 1582. It was bought in 1745 by Paul Methuen to house the family's collection of 16th- and 17th-century Italian and Flemish Master paintings and statuary. The house and park you see today are principally the work of 'Capability' Brown, John Nash and Thomas Bellamy. Do take a tour of the house. You will see the outstanding collection of over 140 paintings, including pictures by Rubens, Turner, Reynolds and Van Dyck, fine statuary and bronzes, and the famous collection of English furniture, notably pieces by Robert Adam and Thomas Chippendale.

the walk

1 Turn left out of the long stay car park, then left again along Post Office Lane to reach the High Street. Turn left, pass the **tourist information centre** and turn right into Church Street opposite The Flemish Weaver. Pass the impressive entrance to Corsham Court and enter **St Bartholomew's churchyard.**

2 Bear right across the churchyard, leaving through a gate and walk ahead to join the main path across **Corsham Park**. Turn left and walk along the south side of the park, passing **Corsham Lake**, to reach a stile and gate. Keep ahead to follow a fenced path beside a track to a kissing gate and proceed across a field to a stile and lane.

1h45   **4 MILES**   **6.4 KM**   **LEVEL 1 2 3**

MAP: OS Explorer 156 Chippenham & Bradford on Avon

START/FINISH: Corsham: long stay car park in Newlands Lane; grid ref: ST 871704

PATHS: field paths and country lanes, 10 stiles

LANDSCAPE: town streets, gently undulating parkland, farmland

PUBLIC TOILETS: short stay car park by shopping precinct

TOURIST INFORMATION: Corsham, tel 01249 714660

THE PUB: The Flemish Weaver, Corsham

❶ An easy walk although care should be taken along the road section

Getting to the start

Corsham is just 4 miles (6.4km) south west of Chippenham, where the B3353 meets the A4. The walk begins from the town's long stay car park on Newland's Road, signposted from the main road.

Researched and written by:
David Hancock, Dennis Kelsall

Eighteenth-century houses on Corsham High Street

did you know?

Corsham is an ancient settlement. Its name, probably Saxon in origin, means 'home of Cossa'. The Roman road from Bath to Silchester ran along Corsham's boundary, as did part of the Wansdyke, a ditch between the kingdoms of Wessex and Mercia.

Ethelred the Unready (978–1017) stayed at Corsham Manor when hunting near by. William the Conqueror became Lord of the Manor after the Conquest in 1066, and Corsham's people, livestock, mills and land are recorded in the Domesday Book of 1087.

Corsham's honey-coloured stone houses

Corsham Court, framed by an arched gateway, is filled with fine artwork and furniture

3 Turn left, pass **Park Farm**, a splendid stone farmhouse on your left, and shortly take the waymarked footpath right along a drive to pass **Rose and Unicorn House**. At its end on the right, cross a stile and follow the right-hand field-edge to a stile, then bear half left to a stone stile in the field corner. Ignore the path arrowed right and head straight across the field to a further stile and **metalled farm track**.

4 Through a gap diagonally opposite, bear half left to a stone stile to the left of a **cottage**. Maintain direction across the next field and pass through a gap in the far left corner. Continue along the left-hand side of a field to a stile in the corner. Turn left along the lane for 0.5 mile (800m) to the A4.

5 Go through the gate in the wall on your left and walk along the centre of parkland pasture. Through a metal kissing gate, maintain your direction, gradually closing with the left boundary to reach another kissing gate on the edge of **Myrtle Wood**. Follow the wide path to a further gate and bear half right to a stile.

6 Keep the same direction on a vague trod across the parkland beyond, joining the far boundary and following it left to a kissing gate hidden in a thicket in the corner. Continue by the perimeter to a further gate in the next corner, where there are fine views right to **Corsham Court**. Follow the field-edge as it bends right, but when it then curves right again, keep ahead to join the churchyard wall. Pass the stile by which you entered the park to another stile ahead.

7 Turn left down an avenue of trees to emerge onto Lacock Road, noting the **stone almshouses** opposite. Turn right, and then go right again along the pedestrianised High Street. Turn left back along Post Office Lane to the **car park**.

what to look for

Note the Folly along Church Street, an artificial ruin, set with church windows, built by Nash in 1800 to hide Ethelred House from Corsham Court. Seek out the grave of Sarah Jarvis behind St Bartholomew's Church; she died in 1703 aged 107 having grown a new set of teeth! Look for the plaque at 38 High Street informing you that Sir Michael Tippett, one of Britain's greatest 20th-century composers, lived there between 1960 and 1970.

The Flemish Weaver

Formerly a run-down drinking pub called the Pack Horse, the fortunes of this beautifully positioned town pub, opposite a charming row of old weavers' cottages, have recently been restored. The name refers to the Flemish weavers brought over to the town to help establish the wool trade. The atmosphere is now more continental bistro than town centre pub, with a bright and cheerful interior and pavement seating. You can relax and enjoy quality real ales, good wines by the glass, and freshly prepared food using local and organic produce. Add efficient and very helpful staff and a warm welcome to children and you have a great post-walk refreshment stop.

Food

For lunch, order filled baguettes, ploughman's lunches or, perhaps, ham, egg and chips, spaghetti with stir-fried vegetables, or braised steak and vegetables from the daily menu. Evening additions may take in organic rump steak with peppercorn sauce and pan-fried tuna with oriental sauce.

Family facilities

Although there are no special facilities children of all ages are made to feel very welcome. Smaller portions of adult dishes are readily available and there's a safe garden that families can use on sunny days.

Alternative refreshment stops

Corsham is well served by pubs, cafés and restaurants.

☛ Where to go from here

Visit Sheldon Manor (3 miles/4.7km north), Wiltshire's oldest inhabited manor house. Dating from 1282, this well-preserved Plantaganet house features a 15th-century chapel, authentic furnishings and beautiful informal terraced gardens. Near by is the preserved National Trust village of Lacock with its fine abbey and photography museum (www.nationaltrust.org.uk).

about the pub

The Flemish Weaver
63 High Street, Corsham
Wiltshire SN13 0EZ
Tel: 01249 701929

DIRECTIONS: on High Street next to the Town Hall

PARKING: use town car parks

OPEN: daily

FOOD: no food Tuesday & Sunday evenings

BREWERY/COMPANY: Unique Pub Company

REAL ALE: Banks's Original, Moles Best, 2 guest beers

DOGS: allowed in the garden only

24

WALK

25 PORT QUIN
CORNWALL

6 MILES (9.7KM) 4hrs

PATHS: Good coastal and field paths. Several sections of coast path run very close to unguarded cliff edges. May not be suitable for children and dogs. 14 stiles

SUGGESTED MAP: aqua3 OS Explorer 106 Newquay & Padstow

GRID REFERENCE: SW 999809

PARKING: Port Isaac. Large car park on outskirts of village, can be busy in summer. Allowed on Port Isaac's stony beach, but this is tidal so check tides! Small car park at Port Quin

PUB: Golden Lion, Port Isaac

❶ Exit car park by lower terrace; turn **L** along track, keeping **R** where it branches ('Coast Path'). At road, keep ahead and down Fore Street to The Platt at entry to **harbour**. Just past Port Isaac Fishermen Ltd, turn **R** up Roscarrock Hill Lane ('Coast Path').

❷ At top of lane, pass footpath sign on L; shortly, keep to

R of gateway to terrace of houses; bear **R** ('Coastal Footpath'). Follow path round **Lobber Point**.

❸ Descend to Pine Haven Cove; cross stile. (Wooden fence skirts along inside edge of path from here.) Climb uphill and round edge of enormous gulf. Cross stile at end of fenced section and cross **Varley Head**. (Path ahead runs close to cliff edge and is fenced on inside.)

❹ Beyond bench descend steep steps (hand rail) into **Downgate Cove** and **Reedy Cliff**. Follow coast path up to seaward edge of **Kellan Head** (steep). Continue along path to **Port Quin**.

❺ Turn **L** at Port Quin; go up road past car park entrance. At bend in road bear **L** ('Public Footpath to Port Isaac'). Pass cottages and keep up slope to gate with stone stile (dogs under strict control). Follow path alongside hedge; climb to stile between 2 gates. Keep alongside **R-H** edge of next fields.

❻ Cross stile beside gate; turn **L** and follow **L** field edge to stile. Go **L** over stile; descend into wooded valley bottom. Cross footbridge over stream, then go over stile. Proceed and climb (steeply) through gorse to open field slope. Continue across field (no obvious path), aiming to **L** of pole that comes into view.

❼ Cross stone stile; follow hedged-in path downhill to junction with lane at Point ❷. Turn **R** and retrace steps to **Port Isaac** and on to car park.

26 PENDEEN
CORNWALL

5 MILES (8KM) 4hrs

PATHS: Coastal footpath, field paths and moorland tracks

SUGGESTED MAP: aqua3 OS Explorer 102 Land's End

GRID REFERENCE: SW 383344

PARKING: Free car park in centre of Pendeen village, opposite Boscaswell Stores, on the B3306

PUB: Star Inn, St Just

❶ Turn **L** out of car park and follow road to entrance of Geevor Tin Mine. Go down drive to reception building and keep to its **L** down road between buildings, signposted 'Levant'.

❷ Just beyond buildings, turn **L** along narrow path that soon bears **R** and becomes unsurfaced track between walls. Turn **L** at huge boulder and head towards very tall chimney stack ahead. Continue across broken ground to National Trust's **Levant Engine House**.

❸ Follow bottom edge of Levant car park and then rough track to reach **Botallack Count House**. Keep on past **Manor Farm** and reach public road at **Botallack**. Turn **L**.

❹ Go **L** at main road (watch out for fast traffic) then turn **L** along Cresswell Terrace to stile. Follow field paths to old mining village of **Carnyorth**. Cross main road, then follow lane opposite, turning **R** at junction, to reach solitary house.

❺ Keep **L** of house, go over stile and cross field to opposite hedge to reach hidden stile. Follow path through small fields towards radio mast. Cross final stile on to rough track.

❻ Go **L**, then immediately **R** at junction. Keep on past **radio mast**, then follow path through gorse and heather to rocky outcrop of **Carn Kenidjack** (not always visible when misty).

❼ At junction abreast of **Carn Kenidjack**, go back **L** along path past small granite parish boundary stone, eventually emerging on road. Turn **R** and in about 140yds (128m), go **L** along obvious broad track opposite house.

❽ Keep **L** at junction. By 2 large stones on L, bear off **R** along grassy track. Go **L** over big stone stile directly above **Church of St John**, built by mining community in 1850s, and descend to main road. Turn **R** to car park.

27 PORTHCURNO
CORNWALL

3.5 MILES (5.7KM) 2hrs 30min

PATHS: Coastal footpath

SUGGESTED MAP: aqua3 OS Explorer 107 St Austell & Liskeard

GRID REFERENCE: SW 384224

PARKING: Porthcurno, St Levan and Porthgwarra

PUB: Logan Rock, Treen

❶ From car park, walk back up approach road; just beyond Porthcurno Hotel, turn **L** along track and follow to cottages. Pass to their **R** and go through kissing gate. Follow field path past granite cross.

❷ Enter **St Levan churchyard** by granite stile. Go round far side of church to entrance gate and on to surfaced lane; cross and follow path opposite ('**Porthgwarra Cove**'). Cross footbridge over stream; shortly, at junction, take **R** fork and follow path to merge with main coast path and keep ahead.

❸ After path begins to descend towards **Porthgwarra**

Cove, branch **R** up wooden steps. Reach track and turn up **R**, then at road, **L**.

❹ Go round sharp **L-H** bend; at footpath signpost, go **R** down path and cross stone footbridge. Continue uphill to reach bend on track, just up from granite houses.

❺ Turn **L**, cross stile beside gate, then down surfaced lane to **Porthgwarra Cove**. Opposite shop and café, go **R** down track ('Coast Path'); follow path **L** in front of house. Go **R** at junction and climb steps.

❻ Continue along coast path, partly reversing previous route past Point ❸. Keep **R** at junctions; eventually descend past **St Levan's Well** to just above **Porth Chapel Beach**. (Control dogs on beach.) Follow coast path steeply over **Pedn-mên-an-mere**; continue to **Minack Theatre** car park.

❼ For surefooted walkers, cross car park and go down track to **L** of Minack compound; descend steep cliff steps (take care). When path levels off, continue to junction. **R** fork leads to Porthcurno Beach and back to car park. Continuation leads to road opposite Beach Café, where **R** turn leads to car park. For less challenging alternative, turn **L** out of Minack car park. Follow approach road to T-junction with public road. Turn **R** and walk down road, watching out for traffic.

28 CADOVER BRIDGE
DEVON

3.5 MILES (5.7KM) 1hr 45min

PATHS: Woodland paths, some rocky, and rough moorland, 4 stiles

SUGGESTED MAP: aqua3 OS Outdoor Leisure 28 Dartmoor

GRID REFERENCE: SX 555646

PARKING: Free car park at Cadover Bridge

PUB: Royal Oak, Meavy

❶ Walk through car park, cross bridge at traffic lights and follow roadside pavement towards **Pyrford** village. Pavement begins on **R-H** side and crosses water-meadows on several small bridges. Enjoy views of **Newark Priory** and, in wet weather, flooded fields attract swans and other waterfowl. Now pavement switches to **L-H** side, and cross **Bourne stream** bridge; then, as road swings hard **R** at Church Hill, keep straight on up steep woodland path to **St Nicholas Church**.

❷ Bear **R** past **church**, cross road, and take stone-

flagged path through churchyard. Nip over 2 stiles at far side and follow signposted path past **Lady Place**. Bear **L** under 1st set of power lines, following field edge on **R**. Carry straight on past footpath turnings, **R** and **L**, as you approach 2nd set of power lines. Cross 2 stiles, and continue for 60yds (55m) to public footpath signpost directly under wires. Turn **R** and head towards corner of garden that juts out into field. Bear slightly **L** here, keeping fence on **L-H** side. Continue over stile at Pyrford Green House and down gravelled drive to **Warren Lane**.

❸ Zig-zag **R** and then **L** across road, then take signposted public footpath up side of open field. Carry on over small footbridge straight ahead and follow waymarked route across Pyrford Golf Course. Watch out for flying golf balls. You'll come out on to Lock Lane, just by **Pyrford Lock**. Turn **R** here and walk across bridge by **Anchor** pub.

❹ Turn **R** again, to join easy-to-follow **River Wey** tow path. Just past **Walsham Lock**, tow path zig-zags **L** and **R** across weir. Continue walking with river on your **R**. Cross little footbridge at **Newark Lock**. From here continue along tow path; you're now on north side of river. Beyond lock, you'll come to **Newark Lane**, take **L** turn here, and cross over **Newark Bridge** to return to car park where walk began.

29 HEDDON GATE
DEVON

5 MILES (8KM) 2hrs

PATHS: Wooded tracks, exposed coast path and quiet lanes, 2 stiles

SUGGESTED MAP: aqua3 OS Outdoor Leisure 9 Exmoor

GRID REFERENCE: SS 655481

PARKING: National Trust car park at Heddon Gate

THE PUB: Hunter's Inn

❶ Walk towards **Hunter's Inn**. To **R** is wooded track ('**Heddon's Mouth**') through gate. Walk down track, which splits; keep **L** ('Heddon's Mouth beach'). Keep to path nearest river. Coast path (unsigned) joins from **R**.

❷ Turn **L** over footbridge, then **R** and walk towards coast to 19th-century lime kiln above rocky beach. Retrace steps, keeping river to **L**, to pass 2 footbridges. Keep going until coast path sign ('Combe Martin') directs you **R**, sharply uphill.

❸ Steep zig-zag climb is rewarded with amazing views across valley and inland. Keep going along narrow path,

running parallel to valley to coast above **Heddon's Mouth**, then turn **L** towards **Peter Rock**. Cliffs here are over 650ft (200m) high and sheer; path is narrow and exposed – take care. Continue along path, which runs inland to meet wall.

❹ Turn **R** ('Combe Martin'). Follow coast path signs through gate, then **R**, along short wire-fenced section and over stile to rejoin cliff edge. Cross stile above **Neck Wood**, then leave National Trust lands via stile and kissing gate. Coast path continues ahead.

❺ Turn **L** and walk uphill, then **L** again where path meets grassy path. Proceed uphill, following fence, to parking area and lane at **Holdstone Down Cross**, on edge of Trentishoe Down.

❻ Turn **L** along narrow lane, following signs for **Trentishoe church** (signpost misleadingly points back way you have come). Walk along lane until you see church above you on L (good place for break).

❼ Continue downhill below **Sevenash Cottage** to pass place where 'Access to coast path' sign points L. Walk down **Trentishoe Hill** (unsuitable for vehicles) which runs through wooded Trentishoe Cleave.

❽ Turn **L** at valley bottom by 2 pretty white cottages. Walk along lane past footpath sign to **Heddon Valley** on L, cross small river, then Heddon river just before **Hunter's Inn**. Turn **R** to find car.

30 HARTLAND QUAY
DEVON

8.75 MILES (14.1KM) 5hrs 30min

PATHS: Coast path through fields; country lanes, 35 stiles

SUGGESTED MAP: aqua3 OS Explorer 126 Clovelly & Hartland

GRID REFERENCE: SS 259245

PARKING: Car park in centre of Hartland village

PUB: Hart Inn

❶ Leave car park past **Hart Inn** (R); turn **R** (North Street). Turn **L** down narrow lane ('Hartland Point'). Pass **Pattard Bridge**; follow lane **R**. Past lane to R, take footpath sign **R** up steps and over stile. Walk up field; cross bank to rejoin lane.

❷ Turn **R** and **R** again at **Youltree Cross**. Turn **L** at Moor Cross ('Exmansworthy'). Lane veers **R**; take next lane **L**. Pass Exmansworthy Farm; turn **R** through car park on to path; cross stile following signs ('Coast Path') to lane (ends at stile into open fields). Follow sign **L**; go ahead to coast path.

❸ Go **L** over stile, cross 6 more, then **R** downhill. Keep to

field edge; cross stile. Go downhill; cross another stile. Cross 2 more to **Shipload Bay**.

❹ Follow coast path through gate and past signs L ('Titchberry'). Cross 6 more stiles. Turn **R** towards sea, pass round gate then between fence and cliff, **R** of radar tower, to **Barley Bay**.

❺ Follow coast path signs (Hartland Quay). Take path **L**, then **L** again along field edge (**Blagdon Cliff**) and over stile. Walk round next stile and on above **Upright Cliff**. Cross stile; descend into combe then round stile. Cross stream. Steps lead up other side to stile. Turn **R**; follow coast path signs **R** over stile into **Smoothlands valley**.

❻ Climb out of **Smoothlands** on to **Blegberry Cliff**. Descend steps into combe; cross stream via kissing gate and up other side and over stile. Cross next stile; descend to combe at **Blackpool Mill**. Pass cottage (R).

❼ Turn **R**; cross stream on bridge. Cross stile; turn **R** on to **Warren Cliff** through gate. Pass **ruined tower**; at gate turn **R** for Hartland Quay.

❽ Turn **L** inside hedge. At field end cross stile; go ahead. Leave field over stile; pass cottages. Go through kissing gate, stile, then another, to **St Nectan's churchyard**. Leave via lychgate; go ahead following road back to **Hartland** village.

31 TARR STEPS
SOMERSET

5.25 MILES (8.4KM) 2hrs 30min

PATHS: Riverside paths and field tracks, some open moor, no stiles

SUGGESTED MAP: aqua3 OS Outdoor Leisure 9 Exmoor

GRID REFERENCE: SS 872323

PARKING: Just over 0.25 mile (400m) east of Tarr Steps – can be full in summer. (Parking at Tarr Steps for disabled people only)

THE PUB: Royal Oak, Withypool

❶ Leave bottom of car park by footpath on **L-H** side ('Scenic Path'). This leads down to **L** of road to Little River, crossing 2 footbridges to **Tarr Steps**, over River Barle, ahead.
❷ Cross Steps, turning upstream at far side ('Circular Walk'). Follow river bank path past wire footbridge. After 0.75 mile (1.2km) cross side-stream on stepping stones, then reach footbridge over river.
❸ Cross, and continue upstream (river now L). After 0.75 mile (1.2km) path crosses wooden footbridge, then divides at signpost.
❹ Turn **R**, uphill ('**Winsford Hill**'). Wide path goes up through woods with stream on R. Where it meets track turn briefly **R** to ford stream; continue uphill on narrower signed path. At low bank with beech trees turn **R** to gate; follow foot of field to tarred lane. Go up to cattle grid on to open moor. Bear **R** on faint track heading up between gorse bushes. After 250yds (229m) reach 4-way signpost.
❺ Turn **R** ('Knaplock') and slant down to hedge corner. Follow hedge briefly, then take path that slants gradually up into moor. After 170yds (155m) sign points back down towards moor-foot banking. Beech bank crosses ahead: aim for lower end, where soft track leads forward, with occasional blue paint-spots. After 0.25 mile (400m) track turns downhill, then back to **L** (becomes firmer as it reaches **Knaplock Farm**).
❻ At farm buildings turn downhill ('Tarr Steps'), on to muddy farm track. Where this turns off into field, continue ahead on stony track, **Watery Lane**. After initial descent this becomes smooth path down to River Barle. Turn **L**, downstream. When path rises above river, look for fork on **R** ('Footpath'). This rejoins river to pass through open field. Cross road and turn **L** up scenic path to return to car.**L** and return to **Chackmore**.

32 PORLOCK
SOMERSET

6 MILES (9.7KM) 3hrs 15min

PATHS: Initial stiff climb then smooth, well-marked paths, no stiles

SUGGESTED MAP: aqua3 OS Outdoor Leisure 9 Exmoor

GRID REFERENCE: SS 885468

PARKING: Pay-and-display at Porlock Central car park; free parking at Whitstone Post, Point E

THE PUB: Ship Inn, Porlock

❶ From car park follow signs for public library; turn **L**. Before church turn **R** (Parsons Street). At parking area with toilets, bridleway sign for Hawkcombe points upstream to footbridge.
❷ Path climbs through bamboo and laurel, to join bridleway from below, up through wood, passing below wall with bench. At top of low wall paths divide.
❸ Turn **L**, still climbing; immediately bear **R** on to sunken path. Emerge at white house ('**Halsecombe**'), keep ahead to field gate marked with blue spot. Follow **L** edge of field, to L-H of 2 gates, leading back into woodland. Take bridleway ahead (occasional blue waymarkers). Track becomes terraced path, running near top edge of wood for 1 mile (1.6km) to reach track.
❹ Turn **L** down track, then **R** into narrow path ('**Whitstone Post**', which runs through bracken and heather into head of Hawk Combe. As path enters hawthorn thicket bear **R** to road signpost at Whitstone Post.
❺ Cross main A39 into parking area; turn **R** on wide path. After 110yds (100m) turn **L** down track. Where it turns L, turn **R** into smaller track. This contours through gorse and heather (superb views over Porlock Bay), then rejoins A39 at cattle grid.
❻ Turn **L**, then **R** into track (bridleway to Porlock). Cross 2 cattle grids to Point ❹ of upward route. Keep on down track for 125yds (114m); turn **L** on to terraced path which runs downhill for 0.25 mile (400m), to wider path. Turn **R** down to stream.
❼ Path runs downstream. On reaching houses it becomes tarred lane and descends through wood. At high wall on **R** sign points to footbridge. Over this, path ascends through woods. Bear **L** on path ('No Horses') and descend to join street at parking area. Turn **L** to cross stream; turn **R** into Mill Lane and Porlock.

33 KILVE
SOMERSET

3 MILES (4.8KM) 1hr 30min

PATHS: Tracks, field paths, and grassy cliff top, 7 stiles

SUGGESTED MAP: aqua3 OS Explorer 140 Quantock Hills & Bridgwater

GRID REFERENCE: ST 144442

PARKING: Pay-and-display at sea end of Sea Lane

THE PUB: Hood Arms, Kilve

❶ From car park head back along lane to ruined **chantry**. Turn into churchyard through lychgate. Pass to **L** of church, to kissing gate.
❷ Signposted track crosses field to gate with stile; bear **R** to another gate with stile and pass along foot of **East Wood**. (At far end, stile allows wandering into wood, April to August only.) Ignoring stile on L, keep ahead to field gate with stile and track crossing stream.
❸ Track bends **L** past gardens and ponds of **East Quantoxhead** to tarred lane. Turn **R**, towards Tudor **Court House**, but before gateway bear **L** into car park. Pass through to tarred path beyond 2 kissing gates. In open field path bears **R**, to **St Mary's Church**.
❹ Return to 1st kissing gate but don't go through; instead bear **R** to field gate, and cross field beyond to lane. Turn **R** and, where lane bends L, keep ahead on to green track. At top, turn **R** at 'Permissive path' notice-board.
❺ Follow field edges down to cliff top, and turn **R**. Clifftop path leads to stile before sharp dip, with ruined **limekiln** opposite, built around 1770 to process limestone from Wales. Most of rest of Somerset is limestone, but it was easier to bring it by sea across Bristol Channel.
❻ Turn round head of dip, and back **L** to cliff top. Here iron ladder descends to foreshore: you can see alternating layers of blue-grey lias (type of limestone) and grey shale. Fossils can be found here, but note that cliffs are unstable – hard hats are now standard wear for geologists. Alternatively, given suitably trained dog and right sort of spear, you could pursue traditional sport of 'glatting' – hunting conger eels in rock pools. Continue along wide clifftop path until tarred path bears **R**, crossing stream into car park.

34 EAST LAMBROOK
SOMERSET

4.75 MILES (7.7KM) 2hrs 30min

PATHS: Little-used field paths (some possibly overgrown by late summer), 24 stiles

SUGGESTED MAP: aqua3 OS Explorer 129 Yeovil & Sherborne

GRID REFERENCE: ST 431190

PARKING: Street parking in East Lambrook village

THE PUB: Rusty Ax, Stembridge

❶ Head into village, eventually turning **L** on to track. After 1 field, track leads **L** to lane (**Hawthorn Hill**). Turn **R** to **The Cottage**, where gate with stile leads into orchard on your **L**. Follow **L** edge and next field. Cross following field, keeping 70yds (64m) from L edge, to gate. Bear **R** to stile-with-footbridge and orchard. At far end gate leads on to **Stockditch Road**.
❷ Turn **L** for 40yds (37m), into overgrown track. Edge of another orchard leads to 2 stiles and footbridge. Follow **L** edges of 2 fields to road; turn **R** to **Rusty Axe pub**.
❸ Keep ahead, on to track, past houses. On crossing crest turn **L** on green track. At next field follow hedge on **L** (ignoring waymarker for different path). Two stiles lead into long field with stumps of former orchard. Keep to **L** of house to join quiet country lane.
❹ Cross into tarred driveway of **Lower Burrow Farm**; follow waymarkers between farm buildings. Bear **L**, slanting uphill, to gateway. Cross next field to double stile. In next field bear **R** to gate and stile. **Burrow Hill Farm** is 1 field ahead. Turn **L**, up side of field and across top to gate. Go up field to poplars and summit of **Burrow Hill**.
❺ Drop to lane at **Pass Vale Farm** and then turn **L** for 0.25 mile (400m) to waymarked field gate on **R**. Follow **L** edges of 2 fields to footbridge with brambly stile. Turn **L** beside stream to another brambly stile and turn **R** to lane.
❻ Turn **L** to gate on **R** ('**East Lambrook**'). Follow **L** edges of 3 fields, then bear **L** over stile and footbridge to 2nd bridge beyond. In next large field, follow waymarkers down **R-H** side and across far end to orchard. Do not cross obvious stile out of orchard but turn **R**, to its far end, where lane leads back into East Lambrook.

35 POLDEN HILLS
SOMERSET

4.5 MILES (7.2KM) 2hrs 15min

PATHS: Initially steep then easy tracks and paths, 3 stiles

SUGGESTED MAP: aqua3 OS Explorer 141 Cheddar Gorge

GRID REFERENCE: ST 480345

PARKING: Car park (free) at Street Youth Hostel, just off B3151; another car park on south side of road

THE PUB: Castlebrook Inn, Compton Dundon

❶ From parking area on youth hostel side, cross and turn **R** on woodland path. Shortly smaller path descends on **L** by steps. At foot of wood turn **R**; at field corner go down short way to track which runs along base of wood to lane.
❷ Go down to **Lower Ivythorn Farm** entrance; turn **L** into track. After 0.5 mile (800m) this reaches corner of unsurfaced road; turn **R**. After 0.25 mile (400m) track turns **L** into field. Follow edge, with ditch and fence L, to gate. In next field continue alongside ditch to corner. Former footbridge is derelict. Take gate on **L**, then turn **R** on field track, passing **L** of Hurst Farm, to tarred lane.
❸ Turn **R** to bridleway sign on **L**. Follow green track to Ham Lane. This leads to crossroads of **B3151** in **Compton Dundon** (**Castlebrook Inn** to R).
❹ Cross busy **B3151** and pass between ancient market cross (R) and Victorian obelisk (L) into Compton Street. At 1st junction keep to **L**, towards **Hood Monument** above. As street climbs, turn **R** and **L** up lane beyond. Where it reaches woodland turn off through waymarked gate ('Reynolds Way'). Path slants up into wood. Shortly before it arrives at road, turn **L** along top of steep ground, to **Hood Monument.**
❺ Continue down through wood to minor road, with main road 50yds (46m) away on R. Ignore path descending opposite but turn **R** for few steps to footpath sign and kissing gate. Grass path heads up crest of **Collard Hill**, (wide views to L).
❻ From summit go straight on down to stile and signposted crossroads of **B3151**. Cross both roads. Ridge road signposted for youth hostel; path is just to **R**, crossing glade into woodland. Keep to **R** of hummocky ground to wood's edge; follow this path to car park.

36 EBBOR GORGE
SOMERSET

4.75 MILES (7.7KM) 2hrs 30min

PATHS: Small paths and field edges, with a rugged descent, 9 stiles

SUGGESTED MAP: aqua3 OS Explorer 141 Cheddar Gorge

GRID REFERENCE: ST 521484

PARKING: Lane above Wookey Hole (optional, small fee)

THE PUB: Wookey Hole Inn, Wookey Hole

❶ From notice-board at top end of car park descend stepped path. After clearing, turn **L** ('The Gorge'). Wide path crosses stream to another junction.
❷ Turn **R**, away from gorge; follow valley down to road. Turn **L**, passing through village of **Wookey Hole**. At end of village, road bends R; take kissing gate on **L** ('West Mendip Way' waymarker post). After 2 more kissing gates turn **L** up spur to stile and top of **Arthur's Point**.
❸ Bear **R** into woods again. Beware: hidden in brambles ahead is top of quarry crag; turn **R**, down to stile. Go down field edge to kissing gate; bear **L** between boulders back into wood. After sharp rise bear **R**, to join Lime Kiln Lane below, which bends L with path on **L** diverting through bottom of wood. This emerges at end of short field track; follow down to footpath signpost.
❹ Turn sharp **L**, on track that passes through **Model Farm**, to Tynings Lane. Turn **L** to signposted stile on your **R**. Go up with fence R, then bear **L** to gate with stile. Go straight up next, large field, aiming for gateway with tractor ruts. Track leads up through wood and field to gate. Slant upwards in same direction to another gate next to stile 100yds (91m) below field's top L corner.
❺ Small path runs along tops of 3 fields with long view across Levels to L. With stile on R and gate and horse trough in front, turn downhill with fence on R; follow fence to stile leading into **Ebbor Gorge** Nature Reserve.
❻ 2nd gate leads into wood. At junction with red arrow and sign ('Car Park') pointing forward, turn **R** into valley and go down – it narrows to rocky gully. At foot of gorge turn **R** ('Car Park'). You are now back at Point ❷ of outward walk. Cross stream, turn **L** at T-junction to wood edge and back **R** to car park.

37 BADBURY RINGS
DORSET

7.5 MILES (12.1KM) 4hrs

PATHS: Farm tracks, roads, grassy lanes and fields, 15 stiles

SUGGESTED MAP: aqua3 OS Explorer 118 Shaftesbury & Cranborne Chase

GRID REFERENCE: ST 959031

PARKING: Car park (donation) at Badbury Rings, signposted off B3082 from Wimborne to Blandford

THE PUB: Anchor, Shapwick

❶ Walk up hill to **Badbury Rings**, then head down track by which you drove in. Cross **B3082** and go down road towards **Shapwick** – its straightness gives away its Roman origins. Pass **Crab Farm**, with Charborough Tower on distant horizon.

❷ At junction with Park Lane turn **R**, then **R** again by Elm Tree Cottage to go up Swan Lane (grassy track). Turn **L** over stile before gate. Go over field, cross stile, and along edge of next field. Cross stile into yard of **Bishops Court Dairy**; turn **R** past 1st barn. At gates bear **L** over stile, then **R**

across field, heading for stile half-way along hedge. Cross and bear **R** to top corner of field.

❸ Cross stile and turn **L** down broad bridleway. After about 0.5 mile (800m) pass line of trees. Turn **R**, up track between high hedges (following blue public bridleway marker). Continue downhill. Follow track to **L**, by side of stream.

❹ Go through gate and reach church on your **L**. Continue towards **Tarrant Abbey Farm** barns. Go **L** through gate and continue diagonally across field to track between fences. Follow uphill, passing above farmhouse. At top of track cross stile and go over next field. Cross road and walk down edge of field. Cross another road into green lane. Bear **L** across stile, then diagonally across field. Go through gate on to road and turn **R**.

❺ Walk on to old **Crawford Bridge**, just to admire it. Retrace steps and turn **R** at footpath sign. Cross stile and walk straight across meadows for 1 mile (1.6km). Reach fence on **L**; walk around it to gate. Go through and follow track to **R**. Cross stile behind farm and walk along road into village.

❻ Pass **Anchor pub** and turn **L**, passing Piccadilly Lane (R-H side). Go straight up road, now retracing route back to car park at **Badbury Rings**.

38 HAMMOON
DORSET

4.25 MILES (6.8KM) 2hrs

PATHS: Field boundaries, grassy tracks, firm road, grassy bridleways, 15 stiles

SUGGESTED MAP: aqua3 OS Explorer 129 Yeovil & Sherborne

GRID REFERENCE: ST 822120

PARKING: Lay-by on Hayward Lane by old brick railway bridge

THE PUB: Saxon Inn, Child Okeford

❶ Go through gate and follow blue markers up farm road, passing **Bere Marsh Farm**. Pass house on L; go straight on through gate.

❷ Where road swings L stay ahead. Bear **R** of **burial ground**, down broad ride. Follow bridleway (blue markers) across fields for 1 mile (1.6km) to **Hammoon**, passing **Diggers Copse** (R). Initially, bridleway is parallel with route of **former railway** on L. After 6th gate pass **Downs Farmhouse**. Track becomes road. Bend **L** then **R** to emerge opposite stump of ancient cross. Cross over to look

at Hammoon's church; walk up lane to admire **Manor Farm** (private).

❸ Return to main road and turn **L**. After crossing weir climb stile on **R**. Head across field bearing **R**, away from tree line, to river. Cross footbridge; look L to see red brick **Fontmell Parva House**. Go diagonally up field to gateway (yellow marker); bear **R** along edge of field, above river. Go through another gateway and straight on, to line of trees. Walk up **R** side of trees, past **chicken farm** (L).

❹ Turn **L** at corner of field across stile; go down lane. At road turn **R** into **Child Okeford** (Saxon Inn is further down, on L). Turn **R** through gateway and immediately go **L** across stile. Walk down beside fence, behind houses, to cross pair of stiles into field. Continue along top, cross another stile and go along path behind hedges.

❺ Emerge at lane; turn **R**. Turn **L** at stile into field. Cross it and 2nd stile; follow edge of field to **R**. Cross pair of stiles, go over muddy track, cross 2 more stiles and bear **L** beside stream. Walk along edge of field, cross stile and keep straight on. Cross another pair of stiles then bear diagonally **L** across field to raised footbridge. Cross and keep straight on across concrete bridge; bear **R** towards bridge in hedge. Cross and bear **L** to corner of field, to return to start.

39 IBBERTON
DORSET

4.25 MILES (6.8KM) 2hrs

PATHS: Quiet roads, muddy bridleways, field paths, 2 stiles

SUGGESTED MAP: aqua3 OS Explorer 117 Cerne Abbas & Bere Regis

GRID REFERENCE: ST 791071

PARKING: Car park at Ibberton Hill picnic site

THE PUB: Crown Inn

❶ Turn **L** along road, following route of **Wessex Ridgeway**, with Ibberton below R. Road climbs gradually, with masts on Bulbarrow Hill ahead.

❷ After 1 mile (1.6km) pass car park on L. At junction bear **R** and immediately **R** again ('**Stoke Wake**'). Pass another car park on R (woods of **Woolland Hill** on R). Pass **radio masts** to L and reach small gate into field on **R**, near end of wood. Before taking it, go extra few steps to road junction ahead for view of escarpment to west.

❸ Go through gate and follow uneven bridleway down. Glimpse spring-fed lake through trees on R. At bottom path

swings **L** to gate. Go through, on to road. Turn **R**, continuing downhill. Follow road into **Woolland**, passing **Manor House** (L) and Old Schoolhouse (R).

❹ Just beyond entrance to **Woolland House** turn **R** into lane and immediately **L** through kissing gate. Path immediately forks. Take **L-H** track, down through marshy patches and young sycamores. Posts with yellow footpath waymarkers lead straight on across meadow, with **Chitcombe Down** up to R. Cross footbridge over stream. Go straight on to cross road. Keeping straight on, go through kissing gate in hedge. Bear **L** down field, cross stile and continue down. Cross footbridge and stile to bear **L** across next field. Go through gate to road junction. Walk straight up road ahead and follow it **R**, into Ibberton. Bear **R** to **Crown Inn**.

❺ Continue up road through village. Path becomes steep. Steps lead up to **church**. Continue up steep path. Cross road and go straight ahead through gate. Keep straight on along fence, climbing steadily. Cross under power lines; bear **L** up next field, to small gate in hedge. Turn **L** up field edge, then go through gate at top on to road, finally turning **L** to return to car park.

40 MARNHULL
DORSET

4 MILES (6.4KM) 2hrs 30min

PATHS: Village roads, pasture (wellies advised in winter), 14 stiles

SUGGESTED MAP: aqua3 OS Explorer 129 Yeovil & Sherborne

GRID REFERENCE: ST 774193

PARKING: Small car park (free) in Marnhull village, opposite butcher

THE PUB: Blackmoor Vale

❶ Turn **L** out of car park and walk along Burton Street. Pass **Blackmoor Vale pub**; keep straight on, down **Ham Lane**. Follow footpath sign straight ahead down field, with trees on L.

❷ At bottom of field track curves L and disappears – turn **R** here to walk down field edge. Cross stile and bear **L** to cross footbridge over **River Stour**. Continue straight ahead. Cross stile in hedge, then footbridge and another stile; bear **L** across field towards **Hamwood Farm**.

❸ Keep to **R** of biggest barn, to pass through farmyard with farmhouse to L-H side. Cross lane, go through gate and head diagonally **R** towards stile, passing close to telegraph pole. Cross bridge and head **R**, across field, towards **Crib House Farm**. Cross over pair of stiles then go **L**, around field edge. Climb stile in corner and turn **L** down road. Just before farmyard turn **R**, through 1st gate. Bear **R** across field. Cross another bridge and make for **Gomershay Farm**. Turn **R** past 1st byre, then turn **L** and **R** through farmyard. At other side of barns turn **L** and pass farmhouse itself. Continue up lane, passing small barn. By old truck bear **R** over brow of field, then cross bridge over river.

❹ At other side of footbridge keep to **R**, past curve of stream; head straight up through gate. Walk up next field and cross stile on to lane. Follow to junction by **Chantry Farm**. Cross road and go into field. Head diagonally **L**, cross stile in bottom corner; walk along edge of next field.

❺ Cross stile into road and turn **R** back into Marnhull village. Go past school to parish church. Turn **L** down **Church Hill**. Follow road as it winds through village, eventually becoming Burton Street by Methodist church. Walk past post office and return to car park.

41 SHERBORNE
DORSET

6.5 MILES (10.4KM) 3hrs

PATHS: Country lanes, green lane, field paths, estate tracks, 9 stiles

SUGGESTED MAP: aqua3 OS Explorer 129 Yeovil & Sherborne

GRID REFERENCE: ST 670157

PARKING: On road by church, Haydon village, 2 miles (3.2km) southeast of Sherborne

THE PUB: Three Elms, North Wootton

❶ Turn **R** and walk up road through village. Where it curls L, turn **R** through gate on to bridleway and go up hill. At top go through gate and bear **L**. Follow blue marker diagonally up to **R**. Go through gate, walk on past trees, then bend up, round field towards trees.

❷ Go through gap and take track down diagonally **L** through woods. At bottom turn **L** along road. After bend take footpath **R**, across field. After trees veer **L**, towards white gate. Cross road, pass **R** of gate, and continue down

field. Pass another white gate then continue ahead on road. At end bear **R** on to A352.

❸ Cross to car park for best view of **Giant hill carving**. Take road down to village; turn **L** signposted 'Pottery'. Turn **R** by stream ('Village Centre'). Continue over slab bridge and pass old mill. Bear **L**, to high street. Turn **L**, and **L** again in front of **Royal Oak**, to church. Walk up Old Pitch Market to Abbey. Turn **R** into churchyard and bear **L**. Go through gate signposted 'Giant's Hill'; bear **L**.

❹ Cross stile, then turn **R** up steps. Follow path to **L**, round contour of hill, below fence. As path divides, keep **R**, up hill, towards top. Bear **L** along ridge, cross stile by fingerpost and head diagonally R, towards barn.

❺ At barn turn **L** and go down through gate. Turn **R** and follow bridleway along hillside with great views to wards Minterne Parva. Keep ahead at junction of tracks; dip down through gateway above woods. Keep straight on; go through gate near road. Turn **L** along grassy track. At gateway turn **L** on to gravel lane.

❻ Directly above **Minterne House**, turn **L** through gate and bear **L**. Go through gate and turn **L**, downhill. Continue down through several gates and keep **R** at fingerpost down broad track. Cross stream, then walk up past **church** to return to car park.

42 WINYARD'S GAP
DORSET

3.25 MILES (5.3KM) 1hr 30min

PATHS: Field paths, some roads, 1 stile

SUGGESTED MAP: aqua3 OS Explorer 117 Cerne Abbas & Bere Regis

GRID REFERENCE: ST 491060

PARKING: Lay-by north of Chedington, opposite Court Farm

THE PUB: Winyard's Gap Inn

❶ Go through gate at back of lay-by; bear **R** on path up through woods. At top of ridge turn **L** for **memorial**. Turn **L** down steps, go back through gate and turn **R** along road. Pass **Winyard's Gap Inn** on R; at junction, cross over and walk up road ahead. Keep **R**, following lane over top of ridge between high banks (**Crook Hill** ahead). After about 0.5 mile (800m) bear **L** through gate ('**Monarch's Way**').

❷ Bear **R** along top of field, with **Chedington Woods** falling away on L, and **Crook Hill** ahead and R. Go through gate at foot of hill; bear **R** through woods, round base.

Cross stile and bear **L** down field. At farm road near trees, turn **R**. Follow up to lane and turn **R**.

❸ Shortly, on corner, go **L** through gate and hook back down fence on bridleway. Go through 2 gates at bottom and continue down field, parallel with top hedge. **Twelve Acre Coppice** (R) is a lovely stretch of mixed woodland. At bottom cross stream via bridge, then go through gate and ahead up track. Go through gate to **L** of barn (blue marker) and turn **R** on farm road, through farmyard. At lane go straight ahead, passing **Home Farm** on L, into **Weston**.

❹ Just before **Weston Manor Farm** detour **R** through gate (blue marker). Turn **L** through gate; turn **R** to resume track straight up hill, with radio mast topping ridge ahead. After short tunnel of trees bear **R** through gate along track, part of **Monarch's Way** commemorating Charles II's flight from Cromwell's army. Go through gate and stay on track. Go through another gate with ponds to R. Pass through 2nd gate to **L** of barn, walk past **Hunter's Lodge Farm** and up drive to road. Turn **R** on main road; follow back down to inn, with care. Turn **L** to return to lay-by and your car.

43 GREAT BEDWYN
WILTSHIRE

5.5 MILES (8.8KM) 2hrs

PATHS: Field paths, woodland tracks, tow path, roads, 1 stile

SUGGESTED MAP: aqua3 OS Explorer 157 Marlborough & Savernake Forest

GRID REFERENCE: SU 279645

PARKING: Great Bedwyn Station

THE PUB: Three Tuns

❶ Walk back to main road in **Great Bedwyn** and turn **R**, then **L** down Church Street. Pass **Lloyd's Stone Museum** and church; take footpath **L** between 2 graveyards. Climb stile, cross field to kissing gate; carefully cross railway line to further kissing gate. Cross footbridge, then bridge over **Kennet and Avon Canal** and descend to tow path.

❷ Turn **R**, pass beneath bridge and continue along tow path for 1.5 miles (2.4km), passing 3 locks, to Lock 60. Cross canal here, turn **L**, then follow wooded path **R** and through tunnel beneath railway. Ascend steps to **Crofton Pumping Station**.

❸ Retrace steps to tow path and Lock 60. Take footpath **R**, waymarked to **Wilton Windmill**; walk by **Wilton Water** along edge of fields. Eventually, turn **R** down short track to lane by village pond in **Wilton**.

❹ Turn **L**, then just past **Swan Inn**, follow lane **L** ('**Great Bedwyn**'). Climb out of village and fork **R** to pass **Wilton Windmill**. Continue along lane and turn **L** on to track, opposite lane to Marten. Just before wooded track snakes downhill, turn **R** along bridle path (unsigned) beside woodland.

❺ At staggered crossing of paths, turn **R**; in 50yds (46m), turn **L** ('**Great Bedwyn**'). Proceed down well-surfaced track; go through gate into **Bedwyn Brail**. Continue through woods, following signs ('**Great Bedwyn**'). Go straight across clearing before forking **L** to re-enter woods in **L-H** corner of clearing.

❻ On emerging in field corner, keep **L** along field boundary, go through gap in hedge and descend along **L-H** side of next field (**Great Bedwyn** visible ahead). Near bottom of field, bear half **R**, downhill to canal.

❼ Pass through gate by bridge and Lock 64 and turn **R** along tow path. Go through car park to road, then turn **L** over canal and rail bridges before turning **R** back to Great Bedwyn Station.

44 OLD SARUM
WILTSHIRE

6 MILES (9.7KM) 2hrs

PATHS: Footpaths, tracks, bridle paths, stretches of road, 12 stiles

SUGGESTED MAP: aqua3 OS Explorer 130 Salisbury & Stonehenge

GRID REFERENCE: SU 139326

PARKING: English Heritage car park (closes 6pm; 4pm winter)

THE PUB: Wheatsheaf, Lower Woodford

❶ Walk back to junction by **Stag**, turn **R** and pass one of **Mentmore Towers**' entrances. Follow road round to **L**, then **R** by Church of St Mary the Virgin. Continue along road; bear **R** at stile, just beyond **Vicarage Cottage**. Go down field, keeping fence to R; look for stile in bottom boundary.

❷ Veer **R** briefly to plank bridge; swing **L** to skirt field, keeping ditch on R. On reaching next plank bridge and waymark, look for pond. Follow path alongside it into next field and pass under telegraph wires to next plank bridge in boundary. Keep ahead and pass under electricity cables. Houses of **Ledburn** can be seen ahead. Make for footbridge; in next field aim slightly **L**, towards house. Keep to L of it, turning **R** at road.

❸ Walk through **Ledburn**, making for **L** bend. On **L** is **Cornfield Cottage**. Cross road to kissing gate and follow track running across farmland. As it curves L, keep ahead, following path across field. On reaching track, turn **R** and follow it to **Sears Crossing**. Cross **railway bridge**, follow track down to road. Turn **L**.

❹ Bear **R** at sign for Grove Church and Farm and down to **Grand Union Canal** at **Church Lock**. Pass Church Lock Cottage before turning **R** to join tow path. Follow **Grand Union** for about 1 mile (1.6km) and, about 140yds (128m) before bridge, with **weir** on the L, leave tow path at plank bridge and bear **R** for few paces to field corner.

❺ Swing **L** and keep boundary on R. Make for 2 gates leading out to road, turn **R**, then **L** at turning for Wing and **Ledburn**. Follow road to **Bridego Bridge**, pass beneath **railway**; keep ahead to **Rowden Farm**.

❻ Bear **L** at next junction for **Mentmore**. Pass Mentmore Courts and **Stud House** before turning **L** at end of stretch of pavement. Opposite junction are 2 wooden gates leading into field. Follow road round to **R** and return to playground and parking area.

45 AVEBURY
WILTSHIRE

5 MILES (8KM) 2hrs 30min

PATHS: Tracks, field paths, some road walking, 3 stiles

SUGGESTED MAP: aqua3 OS Explorer 157 Marlborough & Savernake Forest

GRID REFERENCE: SU 099696

PARKING: Large National Trust car park in Avebury

THE PUB: Red Lion Inn

❶ From car park, walk back to main road and turn **R**. In 50yds (46m), cross and go through gate ('**West Kennett Long Barrow**'). Pass through another gate; follow path alongside **River Kennet**. Go through 2 more gates and cross 2 stiles, your route passing **Silbury Hill**, Europe's largest artificial prehistoric mound.

❷ Beyond gate, walk down **R-H** field edge to gate and **A4**. Cross straight over (carefully) and turn **L**, then almost immediately **R** through gate. Walk down gravel track and cross bridge over stream, track soon narrowing to footpath. Go through kissing gate and turn sharp **L**.

❸ To visit **West Kennett Long Barrow**, 2nd largest barrow in Britain at 300ft (91m) in length, shortly turn **R**. Otherwise go straight on around **L-H** field edge to gate and continue along track. At staggered junction, keep ahead across stile and walk along **R-H** field boundary. Keep **R** in corner by redundant stile and cross stile on your **R** in next corner and proceed up narrow footpath.

❹ At T-junction, turn **L** and descend to road. Turn **L**, then just beyond bridge, take bridle path sharp **R**. Follow **R-H** field edge to gap in corner and keep **L** through next field. At top you'll see **tumuli** (R) and **The Sanctuary**, site of major wooden buildings, possibly used for religious and burial rites (L). Continue to **A4**.

❺ Cross A4 (care) and head up **Ridgeway**. After 500yds (457m), turn **L** off Ridgeway on to byway. Bear half **R** by clump of trees on **tumuli** and keep to established track, eventually reaching T-junction by series of farm buildings (**Manor Farm**).

❻ Turn **L** ('**Avebury**'), and follow metalled track through earthwork and straight over staggered crossroads by **Red Lion Inn**. Turn **L** opposite National Trust signpost and walk back to car park.

46 BREMHILL
WILTSHIRE

4 MILES (6.4KM) 1hr 30min

PATHS: Field paths, bridle paths, metalled roads, 13 stiles

SUGGESTED MAP: aqua3 OS Explorer 156 Chippenham & Bradford-on-Avon

GRID REFERENCE: ST 980730

PARKING: Bremhill church

THE PUB: Dumb Post Inn, Bremhill

❶ Follow drive away from **Farnham Common**, keeping car parking area on your L. Pass refreshment kiosk and veer **R** at fork just beyond. Soon reach gate where you enter National Nature Reserve's car-free zone. Follow **Halse Drive** as it curves **L** and down between trees. When you reach bottom of hill swing **L** into **Victoria Drive**.

❷ Follow broad stony drive between beeches, avoiding turnings either side of route; eventually reach major junction with wide path on L and R. On R is large beech tree with 'Andy 6.9.97' carved on trunk. If you miss path, you shortly reach road. Bear **R** and go up slope, keep **L** at fork and cross several clearings to reach road at junction with Green Lane and **Park Lane**.

❸ Cross road to stile and waymark and go straight ahead, keeping boundary on L. Make for stile and descend into field dip, quickly climbing again to pass alongside grounds of **Dorney Wood**. Walk ahead to field corner, cross stile and turn **R** at road. Head for waymarked footpath on **L** and cross field to gap in trees and hedgerow. Turn **R** and skirt fields, making for belt of trees and banks of undergrowth. Path cuts between 2 oak trees in next field before reaching gap in hedgerow.

❹ Cross stile out to road; turn **L**. Pass Common Lane and Horseshoe Hill; turn **R** at next bridleway. Follow track through wood to next road at **Littleworth Common**. Cross stile to **R** of **Blackwood Arms** and follow Beeches Way. Beyond next stile continue ahead alongside wood, crossing 2 stiles before following fenced path. Go through gate and take path between trees of **Dorney Wood**.

❺ On reaching stile, cross over to road and continue on Beeches Way. Make for next major intersection and keep **R** along **Halse Drive**. Pass **Victoria Drive** and retrace your steps back to car park.

47 EAST KNOYLE
WILTSHIRE

5 MILES (8KM) 2hrs 30min

PATHS: Field paths, woodland bridle paths, metalled lanes

SUGGESTED MAP: aqua3 OS Explorer 143 Warminster & Trowbridge

GRID REFERENCE: ST 879305

PARKING: East Knoyle village hall, adjacent to church

THE PUB: Fox & Hounds, The Green

❶ Turn **L** out of car park; **L** up Wise Lane. Bear **L**; take drive **R**. Continue on track where drive veers L.

❷ Keep ahead uphill; bear **L** along metalled drive. At **Clouds House** stable buildings, take unmarked path **R**, downhill, passing garage to lane in **Milton**. Cross and bear **L** along lower lane.

❸ Pass thatched cottage on **R**; climb bank to stile. Turn **R** behind cottage to gate; climb through woodland edge. At top, bear half-**L** on path then descend to bridle path. Turn **L**, then **R** at next junction; follow path downhill to lane.

❹ Turn **L**, then **R** at T-junction. Take bridle path **L** beyond **Chapel Farm**, forking **R** along track to gate. Continue along field edge, following **L** to gate in field corner. Descend off **Cleeve Hill**, through 2 gates and **Manor Farm** to lane in **West Knoyle**.

❺ Keep ahead. Continue through village, passing **village hall**; beyond 'The Willows', turn **L** to gate beside **Puckwell Coppice**. Follow track ahead to information board. Take footpath to **R**, through gate.

❻ Proceed ahead, cross footbridge and keep **R** at fork of paths. Bear **L** with footpath that exits wood to **R**; descend through trees to footbridge. Bear **L** and follow grassy swathe to gap in field corner. Continue then turn **R** along 1st swathe to gate.

❼ Bear slightly **R** to kissing gate, cross footbridge and keep on to fence stile. Turn **R** along track, then **L** through gate; bear diagonally **R**, then descend to fence stile and copse. Cross footbridge and wire fence; keep ahead, uphill through trees to field. Continue beside woodland to gate in top **L-H** corner.

❽ Follow bridleway uphill through woodland. At junction, turn **L**; at top, bear **R** into cul-de-sac to lane. Turn **L** for **Fox and Hounds**. Turn **R** to **Windmill Hill**, ahead at crossroads and descend into **East Knoyle**. Take footpath by **Wren's Cottage**, cross lane and steps into churchyard. At road, turn **R**; return to start.

48 BRADFORD-ON-AVON
WILTSHIRE

3.5 MILES (5.7KM) 1hr 45min

PATHS: Tow path, field and woodland paths, metalled lanes

SUGGESTED MAP: aqua3 OS Explorers 142 Shepton Mallet;156 Chippenham & Bradford-on-Avon

GRID REFERENCE: ST 824606 (on Explorer 156)

PARKING: Bradford-on-Avon Station car park (charge)

THE PUB: Cross Guns

❶ Walk to end of car park, away from station, and follow path **L** beneath railway and beside River Avon. Enter **Barton Farm Country Park** and keep to path across grassy area to information board. Here you can visit craft shops in former medieval farm buildings and marvel at great beams and rafters of Bradford-on-Avon's magnificent tithe barn, 2nd largest in Britain. With packhorse bridge R, keep ahead to **R** of **tithe barn** to **Kennet and Avon Canal**.

❷ Turn **R** along tow path. Cross bridge over canal in 0.5 mile (800m) and follow path **R** to footbridge and stile. Proceed along **R-H** field edge to further stile, then bear diagonally **L** uphill away from canal to kissing gate.

❸ Follow path through edge of woodland. Keep to path as it bears **L** uphill through trees to reach metalled lane. Turn **R** and walk steeply downhill to **Avoncliff** and **canal**.

❹ Don't cross aqueduct, instead pass Mad Hatter Tea Rooms, descend steps on your **R** and pass beneath canal. Keep **R** by **Cross Guns** and join tow path towards Bradford-on-Avon. Continue for 0.75 mile (1.2km) to bridge passed on your outward route.

❺ Bear off **L** downhill along metalled track and follow it beside River Avon back into **Barton Farm Country Park**. Cross packhorse bridge and railway to Barton Orchard.

❻ Follow alleyway to Church Street and continue ahead to pass **Holy Trinity Church** and **Saxon Church of St Laurence**, jewel in Bradford-on-Avon's crown and not to be missed. Founded by St Aldhelm, Abbot of Malmesbury in AD 700, this building dates back to 10th century. Cross footbridge and walk through St Margaret's car park to road. Turn **R**, then **R** again back into station car park.

Southeast
ENGLAND

Contents

		page
49	Linwood, Hampshire	63
50	New Forest, Hampshire	65
51	New Forest, Hampshire	67
52	Yarmouth, Isle of Wight	69
53	Cowes, Isle of Wight	71
54	Ports Down, Hampshire	73
55	Meon Valley, Hampshire	75
56	Stoughton, West Sussex	77
57	Chichester, West Sussex	79

		page
58	Goodwood, West Sussex	81
59	Amberley, West Sussex	83
60	Amberley, West Sussex	85
61	Seatown, East Sussex	87
62	Ditchling Beacon, East Sussex	89
63	West Firle, East Sussex	91
64	Cuckmere Haven, East Sussex	93
65	Wilmington, East Sussex	95
66	Friston Forest, East Sussex	97

		page
67	Kingston-upon-Thames, Surrey	99
68	Richmond Park, Surrey	101
69	Richmond Park, Surrey	103
70	Barnes, London	105
71	Hyde Park, London	107
72	Holborn, London	109
73 to 74	Hampshire	111
75 to 78	Berkshire	111

		page
79 to 82	Buckinghamshire	112
83	East Sussex	112
84	Surrey	112
85 to 89	Surrey	113
90	London	113
91 to 96	Kent	114

SOUTHEAST ENGLAND

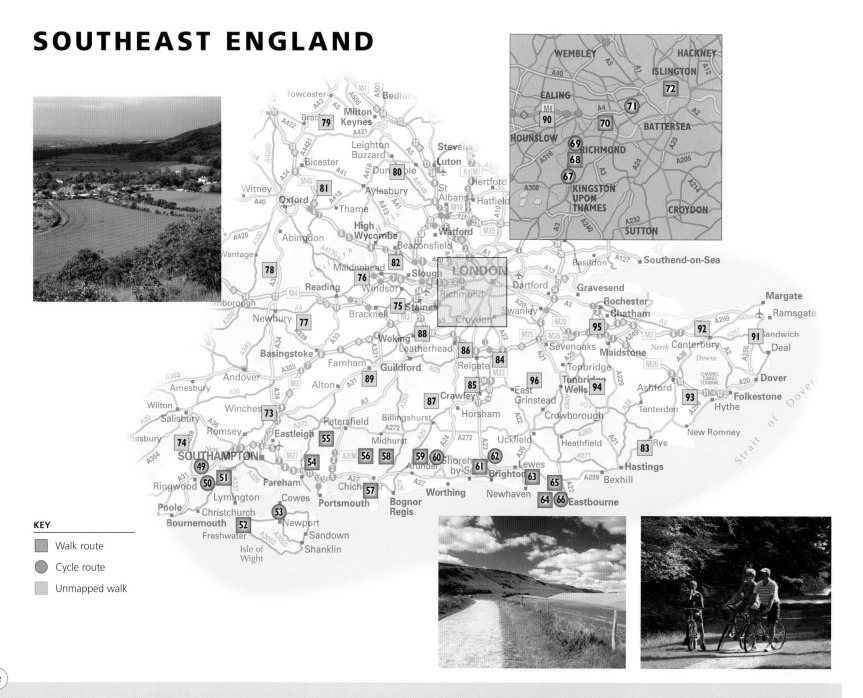

KEY

- ▪ Walk route
- ● Cycle route
- ▪ Unmapped walk

Lyndhurst in the New Forest

A circuit around Linwood

Venture off the beaten track and mix with wildlife in the heart of the New Forest.

New Forest deer
You'll often see deer along this trail, especially early in the morning or around dusk – go quietly for the best chance of seeing these timid woodland residents in their natural habitat. Keep an eye out for roe deer in the cultivated fields close to Dockens Water, between the start of the ride and the point where you join the tarred lane leading up to the Red Shoot Inn. These graceful creatures are 24–28 inches

(61–71cm) high at the shoulder and the males have short, forked antlers. Roe deer have rich reddish-brown coats from May to September, but turn greyer in winter and develop a white patch on the rump.

You'll occasionally spot red deer in the same area, especially on the open heath near Black Barrow. These are our largest native species, and a fully-grown male with his splendid russet coat and impressive antlers may stand nearly 4ft (1.2m) tall at the shoulder. The males are at their boldest when competing for females during the mating season in early autumn.

Fallow deer may pop up almost anywhere on the ride, but a favourite haunt

is in Broomy Bottom, off to your right as you cross Broomy Plain. With their reddish-fawn coats dappled with white spots, these appealing animals have white rumps and a black line running up the tail. The males have broad antlers and stand up to 3ft (0.9m) tall at the shoulder.

the ride

1 Turn right out of the car park and pass the end of the gravel track which leads up to the **High Corner Inn**.

2 At Woodford Bottom bear left at the wooden barrier on your right and pass the ford across the Dockens Water stream, also on your right. Keep to the waymarked cycle route as it follows the gravelled track that winds across the open heath, past a few scattered houses and the tree-capped mound of **Black Barrow**. A few smaller tracks lead off to left and right, but the main gravelled trail is easy enough to follow. Keep straight on as a similar track leads in from your left near the thatched Bogmyrtle Cottage, until you join a tarred lane. Almost at once the lane turns sharp left through a tiny ford and climbs gently up to the road junction at the **Red Shoot Inn**.

3 Turn left opposite the post-box, still following the waymarked cycle route, and continue to climb until the road levels off and swings to the left at **Amie's Corner**. Fork right here, sticking with the waymarked cycle route as it joins a gravelled forest track. The trail dives into Milkham Inclosure through wooden gates beside an attractive whitewashed cottage, then drops to a bridge over the Linford Brook.

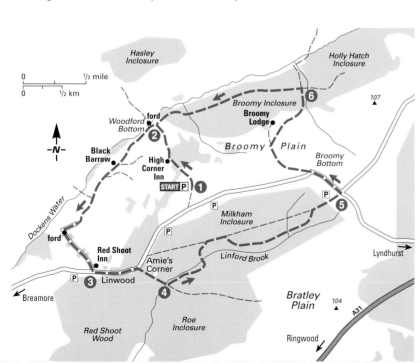

1h45 | **7 MILES** | **11.3 KM** | **LEVEL 123**

MAP: OS Explorer OL22 New Forest

START/FINISH: Spring Bushes car park, Linwood; grid ref: SU 196107

TRAILS/TRACKS: gravelled forest tracks, two short sections on rural lanes

LANDSCAPE: broadleaf and coniferous woodland interspersed with open heathland

PUBLIC TOILETS: none on route

TOURIST INFORMATION: Lyndhurst, tel: 023 8028 2269

CYCLE HIRE: Country Lanes, 9 Shaftesbury Street, Fordingbridge, tel: 01425 655022

THE PUB: The High Corner Inn, Linwood

❶ Moderate hills, some uneven and stony tracks. Suitable for older children, off-road riding experience useful.

Getting to the start
Linwood is a village on a minor road north east of Ringwood. Spring Bushes car park is on the road that runs west from Emery Down, near Lyndhurst, to Rockford, just north of Ringwood.

Why do this cycle ride?
This relatively remote ride offers peace and quiet, and the opportunity to see the New Forest at its best. You'll follow waymarked Forestry Commission off-road cycle tracks deep into the heart of the Forest, with two short sections on tarred roads where you will need to watch out for the occasional car. There are plenty of opportunities for birdwatching or studying the other wildlife.

Researched and written by: David Foster

Dartford warbler
(Sylvia undata)

while you're there

More common in Spain and Portugal than in England, the Dartford warbler is not a frequent sight. The best time to spot one is on a fine sunny morning, when the male will perch singing on a bush.

A serious-looking badger (Meles meles)

49

CYCLE

A family cycles through the countryside at Linwood

The High Corner Inn

The High Corner is an early 18th-century inn, much extended and modernised. It is set in 7 acres (2.8ha) of the New Forest and hidden down an old drovers' track off a narrow Forest lane. A quiet hideaway in winter, mobbed in high summer due to its heart-of-the-Forest location, it is a popular retreat for families, offering numerous bar-free rooms, an outdoor adventure playground and miles of easy New Forest walks. Although extensively refurbished, this rambling old building retains a wealth of beams, wooden and flagstone floors, and a blazing winter log fire in the cosy main bar. There's a separate food servery, plus top-notch Wadworth ales on tap and overnight accommodation in eight well-equipped rooms.

about the pub

The High Corner Inn
Linwood, Ringwood
Hampshire BH24 3QY
Tel: 01425 473973

DIRECTIONS: a gravel track to the High Corner Inn branches off the road, 400yds (366m) west of the start point

PARKING: 200

OPEN: daily, all day in summer, and all day Sunday in winter

FOOD: daily, all day July and August

BREWERY/COMPANY: Wadworth Brewery

REAL ALE: Wadworth Henry's IPA, 6X and JCB

ROOMS: 7 en suite

Food
An extensive printed menu includes sandwiches, ploughman's lunches and salads, as well as freshly battered haddock and chips, beef and 6X pie and sizzling steak platters. Look to the blackboard for daily soups, daily roasts or the likes of baked trout with pine nuts and chargrilled pork loin with spiced apple cream.

Family facilities
This is a great family pub – there's a children's menu, family areas, high chairs and a woodland garden with adventure playground.

Alternative refreshment stops
Also owned by Wadworth Brewery, the Red Shoot Inn offers home-cooked meals and brews its own beer behind the pub.

☛ Where to go from here
Breamore House, north of here off the A338, is a handsome old manor house which dates back to 1583. It has a fine collection of paintings and china, and a countryside museum which includes steam engines (www.breamorehouse.com).

4 A few yards further on turn left at the numbered waymark post 5, then follow the track as it winds through open mixed woodland and re-crosses the **Linford Brook**. Continue as the track bears right at the next **waymark post**, then right again in front of a pair of wooden gates where you enter an area of mainly coniferous woodland. A pair of wooden gates punctuates your progress to the top of the hill, where further gates lead you out into the Forestry Commission's **Milkham car park**. Go through here, cross the car park, and stop at the road junction.

5 Turn left towards **Linwood** and follow the narrow tarred lane for 500yds (457m) until it bears away to the left. Fork right here on to the waymarked cycle trail that follows the gravel track towards **Broomy Lodge** and **Holly Hatch**. Here your route crosses the high heathland plateau of **Broomy Plain**. This is a good spot to see Dartford warblers, meadow pipits and stonechats, and you'll also enjoy long views towards Cranborne Chase and the Wiltshire Downs. Bear right at the next fork and follow the trail down into **Holly Hatch Inclosure**.

6 At the foot of the hill, numbered **waymark post 3** stands at the forest crossroads. Turn left here, on to a lovely tree-shaded track with soft green verges that leads you through the **oak woods**. Two pairs of wooden gates mark your progress through the inclosure, and at length the oaks give way to conifers. Follow the waymarked trail until you rejoin your outward route at a low wooden barrier. Turn left here, and climb the short hill back to the **High Corner Inn**.

did you know?

A more accurate name for the New Forest could have been Old Heathland. This swath of scrubland, fields and woods was earmarked as perfect hunting land by William the Conqueror in 1079. The boundaries were extended, and more trees planted. Locals caught stealing the king's deer were threatened with gruesome punishments but, in return for good behaviour the commoners could collect firewood and peat, and graze their animals.

Deer roaming in Boldrewood Deer Sanctuary

A New Forest loop from Burley

A varied ride from a popular village via 'Castleman's Corkscrew'.

The Castleman Trail
Railway interest is all around you on the mid-section of this ride, which reaches its climax at Holmsley's old station. The Castleman Trail follows the broad, level trackbed of the original main line to Dorchester. The railway was promoted by Charles Castleman, a Wimborne solicitor, who planned the line through his home town. This wasn't exactly the most direct route, and critics quickly dubbed it 'Castleman's Corkscrew'.

The railway opened in 1847, but was swallowed up by the larger and more powerful London & South Western Railway in the following year. At this time Bournemouth was little more than a sleepy village, but passengers for Christchurch could catch a linking coach service from Holmsley station, which was originally known as 'Christchurch Road'. After Bournemouth and Christchurch were linked to the national rail network, Holmsley's traffic evaporated. The station continued to serve its small local community, and handled timber from the nearby inclosures. Its rural seclusion was interrupted for a few years during the Second World War, when the little station became the gateway for a new RAF airfield at Plain Heath. After the war, the railway fell victim to the growing popularity of road transport. Passenger traffic dwindled again and, in 1964,

'Castleman's Corkscrew' was finally axed in the notorious cuts made by Dr Beeching.

the ride

1 Turn right out of the car park, stop at the road junction, and continue straight ahead. Fork left at the **war memorial** into Pound Lane, signed to Bransgore. Pass the Forest Teahouse and cider shop, then follow the lane out over the heath to **Burbush Hill**.

2 Fork left just before the old railway bridge, following the waymarked off-road cycle track through the Forestry Commission's car park and down on to the **old railway line**. The Castleman Trail begins in a lovely sandy cutting, which is smothered with brilliant purple heather in late summer. Soon the old line emerges from the cutting onto a low embankment, with good views out over the boggy heath. You'll often see horse riders in the area and birdwatchers should look out for green woodpeckers, as well as for lapwings, curlews and redshanks, which nest on the heath in early summer. The trail rises briefly to the broken brickwork of **Greenberry Bridge**, which survived the closure of the

Above: The war memorial in Burley
Left: An open path though woodland

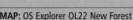

1h00 | **6 MILES** | **9.7 KM** | **LEVEL 123**

MAP: OS Explorer OL22 New Forest

START/FINISH: public fee-paying car park, Burley; grid ref: SU 211030

TRAILS/TRACKS: busy village centre, quiet lanes and an old railway route

LANDSCAPE: bare open heathland contrasts with pretty cottages and wooded village lanes

PUBLIC TOILETS: opposite car park, Burley

TOURIST INFORMATION: Lyndhurst, tel: 023 8028 2269

CYCLE HIRE: Forest Leisure Cycling, The Cross, Burley, tel: 01425 403584

THE PUB: The Queens Head, Burley

🛑 Burley's streets get busy at weekends and during holiday periods. Good traffic sense required.

Getting to the start
Burley village is on a minor road south east of Ringwood, between the A31 and the A35. Leave the A31 at Picket Post, 1 mile (1.6km) east of Ringwood, and follow the signposted route through Burley Street to Burley. Keep left at the war memorial in the centre of the village, and you'll find The Queens Head immediately on your left, with the public car park entrance just beyond the pub's own car park.

Why do this cycle ride?
This route takes you through the heart of the bustling New Forest village of Burley, with its antique shops, tea rooms and horse-drawn wagon rides. In complete contrast, the Castleman cycle trail is the perfect way to experience the surrounding heathland from a level stretch of old railway line. There are good opportunities for birdwatching, and you can visit the Old Station tea rooms at Holmsley.

Researched and written by: David Foster

Lapwing
(Vanellus vanellus)

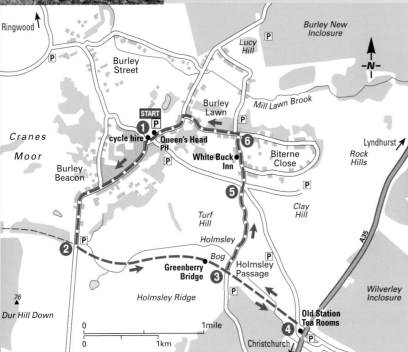

The Queens Head

Family facilities

Children are very welcome in the pub and there's a separate family area and children's menu. Youngsters will love to see the New Forest ponies that often congregate outside the pub.

Alternative refreshment stops

Tea rooms and the Burley Inn in Burley, the White Buck Inn at Burley Lawn, and the Old Station tea rooms at Holmsley are all good alternatives.

☞ Where to go from here

For more information about the New Forest area and its varied wildlife, visit the New Forest Museum and Visitor Centre in nearby Lyndhurst, with exhibitions and an audio-visual show (www.newforestmuseum.org.uk).

The Queen's Head was built in 1633, which makes it one of the oldest buildings in the New Forest. It became a smugglers' haunt in the 17th century, when contraband rum, brandy and tobacco was stored in the spacious cellars, well away from the coast. The main bar is named after Jack Warnes, an infamous local smuggler. The pub has been well modernised over the years and retains plenty of old timbers and panelling, wooden, flagstone and carpeted floors, and a fine Jacobean fireplace where a log fires blazes in winter. You'll find local beers from Ringwood Brewery on handpump and, for sunny summer days, a shaded courtyard garden with picnic tables.

Food

Food is traditional and the lunch and dinner menus are extensive. At lunch expect 'light bites' – seasonal soups, ploughman's and risotto, pasta, salads and sandwiches, alongside beer battered cod, steak and ale pie and specials such as lasagne and cottage pie. Dinner adds potted crab, rack of lamb, venison pie and roast duck with orange and shallot sauce. Sunday roast lunches.

railway, only to be demolished in 1995 when it became unsafe. Continue to the low **wooden barriers** that guard the minor road crossing at **Holmsley Passage**, where you can still see short sections of the original railway lines embedded in the road surface.

3 If you wish, you can shorten the ride by turning left here. To complete the full route, cross the road and continue along the **old railway line**. The trail becomes more shaded as it runs perfectly straight through an avenue of young oak trees. The track crosses **two small bridges** that herald the approach to Holmsley Station. Look out for the **old brick platform** on your right before dismounting at the wooden gate that marks the end of the cycle track.

4 Beyond the gate and across the road, the **Old Station tea rooms** are well worth a visit for morning coffee, home-cooked lunches and cream teas. There's a pleasant garden, as well as a gift shop where you can buy a souvenir of your visit to this unusual refreshment stop. Turn here and retrace your outward route to **Holmsley Passage** (Point 3). Turn right on to the quiet lane, follow it up the hill and stop at the 5-way junction.

5 Cross straight over towards **Burley Lawn** and zig-zag left, then right, past the **White Buck Inn** into Bennetts Lane.

6 Bear left at the next junction into Beechwood Lane and keep straight on through **Lester Square** until you reach a T-junction. Turn left here towards Burley, and continue past the little brick-built **church** of St John the Baptist for the final 400yds (366m) back to the car park.

about the pub

The Queens Head
The Cross, Burley
Ringwood, Hampshire BN24 4AB
Tel: 01425 403423

DIRECTIONS: in the centre of the village

PARKING: 30

OPEN: daily, all day

FOOD: daily, all day

BREWERY/COMPANY: Greene King

REAL ALE: Ringwood Best and Fortyniner, Greene King IPA

Map labels

Ringwood
Burley New Inclosure
Lucy Hill
Burley Street
P
Burley Lawn
Mill Lawn Brook
START
Queen's Head PH
cycle hire
White Buck Inn
Biterne Close
Lyndhurst
Rock Hills
Cranes Moor
Burley Beacon
Turf Hill
Clay Hill
Holmsley
Bog
Greenberry Bridge
Holmsley Passage
Wilverley Inclosure
76
Dur Hill Down
Holmsley Ridge
Old Station Tea Rooms
Christchurch
A35
0 1mile
0 1km
-N-

A pair of New Forest ponies

did you know?

Charcoal-burning is one of the oldest industries in England, and was one of the commoners' rights. Elizabeth I encouraged the use of coal and passed an act that forbade felling timber for burning, so helping to bring about the industry's decline.

Charcoal-burning at Butser Ancient Farm

New Forest trails around Bank

Ancient oaks, towering conifers and historic inclosures are on the route.

Detail of a walk marker post at the New Forest Reptile Centre

Woodland relics

Unenclosed woodlands such as Brinken Wood and Gritnam Wood are among the finest relics of unspoiled deciduous forest in Western Europe. Hummocky green lawns and paths meander beneath giant beech trees and beside stands of ancient holly and contorted oaks, and through peaceful, sunny glades edged with elegant silver birch. 'Inclosures' are areas of managed woodlands where young trees are protected from deer and ponies. Areas of oak trees were first inclosed in the late 17th century to provide the timber needed for the shipbuilding and construction industries. Holidays Hill Inclosure dates from 1676.

Soon after beginning the longer walk you'll pass the most famous and probably the oldest tree in the forest, the Knightwood Oak. It is thought to be at least 350 years old and owes its great age to pollarding (cutting back) its limbs to encourage new branches for fuel and charcoal.

Marvel at this fine tree before walking through Holiday Hills Inclosure to view the New Forest reptillary. Set up to breed rarer species for the wild, including the smooth snake and sand lizard, it offers the opportunity to view some of the forest's more elusive inhabitants.

At the end of Rhinefield Ornamental Drive is the Rhinefield House Hotel, a flamboyant Jacobean-style house, of 1890.

the walk

1 Take the gravel path at the top end of the car park (to the right of 'The Tall Trees Trail' sign), parallel with the road. In 100yds (91m) turn right and descend to a gravel track. Cross straight over then, where it curves left, keep ahead to a gate and the A35. Cross over, go through a gate and keep to the track, uphill to a junction. Turn right and follow the path to a road. Cross into Knightwood Oak car park and follow the signs to the **Knightwood Oak** itself.

2 From the oak bear right down a wide ride. Go through a gate and walk along

| 3h00 | 5 MILES | 8 KM | LEVEL 1 2 3 |

SHORTER ALTERNATIVE ROUTE

| 1h00 | 2 MILES | 3.2 KM | LEVEL 1 2 3 |

MAP: OS Outdoor Leisure 22 New Forest

START/FINISH: Brock Hill Forestry Commission car park; grid ref: SU 266057

PATHS: grass and gravel forest tracks, heathland paths, some roads

LANDSCAPE: Ornamental Drive, ancient forest inclosures and heathland

PUBLIC TOILETS: Blackwater car park, near start of walk

TOURIST INFORMATION: Lyndhurst, tel: 023 8028 2269

THE PUB: The Oak Inn, Bank

❶ Extreme caution needed when crossing the busy A35 (twice). Blind bends on the lane through Bank. Follow directions carefully – unsigned paths, tracks and forest rides

Getting to the start

Look for signs to the Rhinefield Ornamental Drive, off the A35 Lyndhurst-to-Christchurch road, 3 miles (4.8km) south west of Lyndhurst. Parking is signposted on the right, a short distance off the A35.

Researched and written by:
David Hancock, Peter Toms

Map

N

Dark Hat — PORTUGUESE FIREPLACE — Buckhill Mole

HOLIDAYS HILL INCLOSURE — **3** — NEW FOREST REPTILE CENTRE

Historic Oak — ALLUM GREEN — **5**

Knightwood Inclosure — KNIGHTWOOD OAK — **2** — **4** — Bramble Hill — OAK INN — Bank

A35 — **7**

BROCK HILL — **1** — **8** — JESSAMINE COTTAGE GRITNAM — **6**

WARWICKSLADE — Gritnam Wood

P — BRINKEN WOOD — Great Huntley Bank

CUTTING

BLACKWATER ARBORETUM — RHINEFIELD ORNAMENTAL DRIVE — Camel Green — Hurtshill Inclosure

Poundhill Inclosure — WC

0 — ½ Mile
0 — 1 Km

while you're there

Join in the quiz trails, printing, mask making and games at the New Forest Reptile Centre and learn all about the animals that live there. A day of fun for the whole family.

Forestry Commission events

The Forestry Commission organises a diary of events, including a special evening in July when you can enjoy the company of a Forest Ranger in discovering the New Forest deer. It is a pleasant walk to an exclusive deer hide, and during the return the twilight world of other forest creatures is explored.

Filtered sunlight at Knightwood oak and beech glade

the path through more open woodland and bear right towards the A35. Just before a gate and the A35 take the narrow path left. Cross a **footbridge** and turn left along the line of a **drainage ditch**. Maintain this direction to a cottage and turn left to reach the **New Forest Reptile Centre**.

3 Walk back along the access drive, passing **Holiday Hills Cottage**. After 300yds (274m), at a barrier on your left, drop down on to a path and follow it across a **bridge**.

4 Keep to the main path across several clearings, and at the top of a rise fork right. In 25yds (23m) turn right, ultimately descending to and skirting left around cottages and **Allum Green**. Gently climb through trees to a defined crossing of paths and turn right. Shortly, bear half-right across a clearing and **concrete footbridge**, then continue through the woodland edge to a **telegraph pole**. Bear right for 50yds (46m), then left through a gate to the A35.

5 Turn left, then almost immediately right across the road to a gate. Walk ahead to a garden boundary and turn right, the narrow path leading to a lane in Bank. Turn right, pass the **Oak Inn** and walk through and up out of the hamlet. Just before a sharp left-hand bend (by a **cattle-grid**), bear off right beside a barrier and walk straight ahead on a wide path.

6 Go through trees and scrub to a fork on the edge of a clearing. Keep right to follow the path between an oak and a holly tree. Follow the path down past **Dell Cottage** and along the drive to a metalled lane at **Gritnam**.

7 Turn left, and after 100yds (91m), before a bridge, turn right to a **telegraph pole**. Follow the path and turn left along the gravel track to the **water treatment works**. Keep to

its left and continue into thicker woodland (mainly birch). The woods soon become more open. Cross a **footbridge** and immediately turn left. In 25yds (23m) fork right.

8 Walk through **Brinken Wood** and across a clearing to a bridge over **Warwickslade Cutting**. Bear right, go through a gate and turn sharp right at the gravel track. Swing left back to **Brock Hill car park**.

Short walk option

From Point 1, locate the **Tall Trees Trail post** at the top end of the car park and follow the gravel path to the road and cross straight over. Keep to the gravel trail (marked by **red-banded posts**) as it curves right and runs parallel with the road. Pass through an impressive mixed wooded area, the path meandering gently downhill to **Blackwater car park**. Make for the car park entrance and cross the road, signposted '**Blackwater Arboretum**. Shortly, turn right to explore the Tall Trees Trail further and return to the track, or go straight on through a gate into the arboretum. It is well worth exploring the various paths that criss-cross this small area, passing labelled trees and welcome benches. Exit by the far gate and keep to the gravel track to a **crossing of tracks**. Turn right and remain on this track to a second crossing of paths. Turn right, then on reaching the gravel path of the **Tall Trees Trail**, turn left back to the car park.

what to look for

You should see New Forest ponies grazing the lawns and trees as you cross the heath and scrub near Allum Green. They are descendants of a wild breed peculiar to the New Forest and belong to local commoners. Around 3,500 ponies graze the open forest. On the Tall Tree Trail look for the 150ft (46m) tall Douglas fir and the giant Wellingtonias, one of which is 160ft (50m) tall.

The Oak Inn

Ponies graze and pigs run free outside this 18th-century New Forest inn, formerly a cider house, tucked away in a sleepy hamlet. Despite being off the beaten track, The Oak bustles with a welcoming mix of customers, in particular walkers exploring the Forest trails, and the pub remains a true, old-fashioned community local, complete with darts and cricket teams. Inside there are bay windows, antique pine stripped old tables, bare floorboards, ancient beams, and a host of intriguing bric-a-brac – fishing rods, stuffed fish, old ski poles – adorn ceilings and walls. In winter you'll find an effective wood-burning stove to warm your toes by, and the whole pub is blissfully free of modern electronic intrusions. Idyllically set in the Heritage Area, and with a super beer garden for summer drinking, it specialises in freshly prepared food and an ever-changing range of beer, all tapped straight from the barrel.

Food
You'll find lunchtime sandwiches, ploughman's and soups alongside home-cooked ham, egg and chips, cod

about the pub

The Oak Inn
Pinkney Lane, Bank
Lyndhurst, Hampshire SO43 7FE
Tel: 023 8028 2350

DIRECTIONS: village and pub are signposted off the A35, south west of Lyndhurst

PARKING: 25

OPEN: daily, all day

FOOD: daily, all day Sunday

BREWERY/COMPANY: free house

REAL ALE: Ringwood Best, Hop Back Summer Lightning, Bass, guest beers

DOGS: welcome inside

and chips, sausage and mash and daily specials – whole sea bass and grilled lemon sole, for example.

Family facilities
Children are welcome in the eating area of the bar until 6pm. There are no special facilities for them, but they will love the beer garden and the ponies grazing outside.

Alternative refreshment stops
Pubs and cafés in Lyndhurst.

☞ Where to go from here
Take a trip up the Bolderwood Ornamental Drive and visit the deer sanctuary near Bolderwood car park. Specially constructed platforms offer an intimate view of deer roaming the forest. The best time to see them is early morning or late afternoon.

The brent goose (Branta bernicla)

In winter flocks of black-necked brent geese return from their breeding grounds in the High Arctic and fill the mudflats and flood meadows. They feed almost exclusively on eel grass, which grows in the muddy shallows between the high- and low-water marks. Occasionally the snowy white plumage of a wintering egret is also seen here. In summer the saltmarshes are rainbow-bright with pink cushions of thrift, purple sea-lavender and the spikes of golden samphire.

From Yarmouth to Freshwater

An exhilarating three-stage ramble in the footsteps of Alfred, Lord Tennyson.

Tennyson country

Away from the hustle and bustle of the traditional resort towns in the east of the island, West Wight is a quieter, less populated area of great natural beauty, offering areas of open countryside, rugged cliffs, wonderful views and fascinating wildlife. This three-part ramble encapsulates the contrasting landscapes of the area, from the wildlife-rich tidal estuary of the River Yar and the natural wetland habitat of freshwater marshes, to rolling farmland and the magnificent chalk headlands and hills with their breathtaking coastal views.

The poet Alfred, Lord Tennyson (1809–92) and his wife Emily first came to Farringford House (now a hotel) set in parkland beneath Tennyson Down, in 1853. The island inspired some of his greatest poems. 'The Charge of the Light Brigade' was written on the down that now bears his name, and 'Maud', 'Enoch Arden' and 'The Idylls of the King' were all composed at Farringford. The Tennysons later bought a house on the mainland and only returned to Farringford for the winter, where they would be undisturbed.

Memories of the great man and his family are dotted along this walk. On Tennyson Down, where he rambled, you will find the monument erected in his honour in 1897. You can take lunch or afternoon tea at Farringford Hotel. In Freshwater, view the memorials to the family in All Saints Church, while in the peaceful churchyard you will find Emily's grave.

the walk

1 From the car park in Yarmouth make for the town square. Head for the **church** and walk along St James' Street. Cross Tennyson Road into Mill Road and continue straight on towards and past the **old Tide Mill** (built in 1793 to harness the tidal flow of the estuary). Continue through the gate and turn right along the **old railway line**, following it for 1.5 miles (2.4 km) to **The Causeway**.

2 For the short walk back to Yarmouth, turn right, cross The Causeway to the Red Lion and Point 9. To continue the second stage of the walk, turn left at Point 2 and follow the lane to the **B3399**. Turn left

On Tennyson Down you may see rare chalk-loving flowers and grasses, including bee orchids and nettle-leaved bellflowers, and hundred of small butterflies, such as common, chalkhill, small and Adonis blues, skippers and dark green fritillaries.

and soon cross into the unsurfaced **Manor Road**. In 50yds (46m) bear off left, signposted '**Freshwater Way**', and ascend across grassland towards **Afton Down**.

3 Proceed ahead at a junction of paths beside the **golf course**, and follow the gravel track right to the **clubhouse**. Go through a gate by the building and walk down the access track, keeping left to reach the **A3055**. Turn right downhill into **Freshwater Bay**.

4 For the second loop option, walk past the **Albion Hotel** and continue, turning right at Blackbridge Road, at Point 8. For the third section of the long walk, turn left instead by the **bus shelter** and public toilets, along a metalled track signposted '**Coastal Footpath**'. As it bears left, keep ahead through kissing gates and soon begin a steep ascent up a concrete path on to **Tennyson Down**. Keep to the well trodden path to reach the **memorial cross** at its summit.

5 Continue down the wide grassy swathe, which narrows between gorse bushes, to reach the replica of **Old Nodes Beacon**.

White cliffs, the bay and beach at Freshwater

4h30	9.5 MILES	15.3 KM	LEVEL 123

SHORTER ALTERNATIVE ROUTE 1

3h00	6.5 MILES	10.4 KM	LEVEL 123

SHORTER ALTERNATIVE ROUTE 2

1h30	3.5 MILES	5.7 KM	LEVEL 123

MAP: OS Outdoor Leisure 29 Isle of Wight

START/FINISH: ferry terminal or pay-and-display car park opposite, Yarmouth; grid ref: SZ 354897

PATHS: disused railway, woodland and downland paths, some road walking, 4 stiles

LANDSCAPE: freshwater marsh and salt marsh, farmland, downland

PUBLIC TOILETS: at Yarmouth and Freshwater Bay

THE PUB: The Red Lion, Freshwater

❶ Care needed crossing main roads in Yarmouth and Freshwater. Nature reserve can be wet and muddy. Long ascent up Tennyson Down on longest walk. The full 9.5-mile (15.3km) route is recommended only for more experienced older children. Only children over 10 allowed in the pub

Getting to the start

Yarmouth is 10 miles (16.1km) west of Newport on the A3054, on the north west coast of the Isle of Wight. The car park is opposite the ferry terminal. Park at the ferry terminal in Lymington and cross to Yarmouth as a foot passenger on the Wightlink ferry (www.wightlink.co.uk).

Researched and written by: David Hancock, Peter Toms

Pretty wild flowers

did you know?

Every May the Isle of Wight hosts the UK's largest walking festival, which includes over 100 guided walks tailored to suit all ages and abilities, from seasoned ramblers to leisurely strollers.

Striding out on a family walk

(Turn left to visit the hotel.) Turn right, pass the **thatched church**, and turn left down Blackbridge Road.

8 Just before Black Bridge, turn left into **Afton Marshes Nature Reserve**. Join the nature trail, go over the footbridge and turn left following the path beside the stream (this can be very wet) to the **A3055**. Turn left and almost immediately cross over to join **footpath F61** along the course of the old railway. After 0.5 mile (800m) reach **The Causeway**.

9 Turn left and follow the lane to All Saints Church and **The Red Lion** pub. Take the waymarked path (**Freshwater Way F1**) between a cottage and the churchyard wall. Cross two stiles and continue along the farm road. At the farmyard entrance cross the double stile on the left and bear right along the field edge to a stile.

10 At a track and the entrance to **Kings Manor Farm**, cross the stile ahead (by double gates) and follow the wide track to a gate and a junction of paths. Climb the stile on the right, pass through a copse, over another stile and bear left, uphill along the field edge. Cross a stile and maintain direction to another stile and descend into **woodland**, emerging onto a metalled track. Turn left to the **A3054** and turn right to the bridge over the River Yar, back into Yarmouth.

Here, turn very sharp right down a **chalk track**. Turn right into a car park and almost immediately ascend sharp left.

6 The path descends to a gate. Proceed along the **woodland fringe** and continue into more open countryside, then fork left at disused **excavations** on the right. Cross a stile, then keep left and after 50yds (46m) turn sharp left and descend to another stile. Cross the next field to a stile and turn right along the field edge to a stile.

7 After the next stile cross a **farm track**, go through a gate and walk along the track (F47) beside **Farringford Manor Hotel**. Pass beneath a **wooden footbridge** and continue downhill to a gate and the road.

The Red Lion

A husband-and-wife team run this pub, in a picturesque setting beside All Saints Church. It's just a short stroll from the tidal River Yar, which makes it popular with the sailing set from nearby Yarmouth. The Red Lion's origins date from the 11th century, though the current red-brick building is much newer. The open-plan bar is comfortably furnished with country kitchen-style tables and chairs, plus relaxing sofas and antique pine. In addition to the pub's four real ales, including the island's Goddards Best, and a good wine selection (with 16 available by the glass), the pub is renowned for its daily blackboard menu of interesting food.

Food
Everything is freshly made from tried and tested recipes. Typical dishes are whole crab salad, braised half-shoulder of lamb with minted gravy, fresh cod and chips, halibut with chilli and coriander sauce, steak and kidney pie, and apple pie with custard. Lunchtime snacks include baguettes and ploughman's.

about the pub

The Red Lion
Church Place, Freshwater
Isle of Wight PO40 9BP
Tel: 01983 754925
www.redlion-wight.co.uk

DIRECTIONS: from the A3055 east of Freshwater by mini-roundabout and garage follow Yarmouth signs, then turn left for the church

PARKING: 15

OPEN: daily

FOOD: daily

BREWERY/COMPANY: Enterprise Inns

REAL ALE: Fuller's London Pride, Flowers Original, Wadworth 6X, Goddards

DOGS: welcome in the bar

Family facilities
Children under 10 are not permitted in the bar, but there is a fascinating dome structure in the pretty side garden where families can eat, also a gravelled area with tables and chairs beyond the herb garden.

Alternative refreshment stops
Choice of pubs and cafés in Yarmouth. Freshwater Bay has a family-friendly pub and café, and lunch or teas can be found at Farringford Manor Hotel.

☞ **Where to go from here**
Visit the Needles Pleasure Park. Take a boat trip to view the Needles and explore the Old Battery, with its viewing platform and exhibition (www.theneedles.co.uk).

while you're there

The cycle route passes close to HM Prison Parkhurst, which accommodates more than 500 prisoners. It was first built as a military hospital in 1805, then later transformed to a prison for boys awaiting deportation, mainly to Australia, as part of the Parkhurst Act of 1835. It became such a success that the Home Office decided to increase its size, and by 1847 a new wing was built by the prisoners who actually dug the clay and baked the bricks. This wing is still in use today.

A linear ride from Cowes to Newport

Take a return trip down this scenic old railway trail beside the River Medina, on the Isle of Wight.

The Ryde

Half way up the river you'll see a sad relic of former glory stuck in the mud. It's the *Ryde*, a paddle steamer built on Clydeside for the Southern Railway Company's Portsmouth-to-Ryde ferry services, and launched in 1937. Soon after the outbreak of the Second World War in 1939, the ship was requisitioned and converted for use as a Royal Navy minesweeper. Later *Ryde* was refitted with anti-aircraft weapons, and saw service defending the Normandy beaches during the D-Day invasion of Europe.

After the war *Ryde* returned to her work as an Isle of Wight ferry, but within a few years she was eclipsed by the more modern motor vessels built to replace wartime casualties. The old paddle ship found herself downgraded to summer relief duties, excursions and charters around the Solent, before she was finally withdrawn from active duty in 1968. After a couple of years moored on the River Thames as

a tourist attraction, *Ryde* returned to the Isle of Wight and was converted for use as a nightclub at the Island Harbour Marina, on the east bank of the River Medina. In 1977 she was seriously damaged by fire and, by the mid-1990s, *Ryde* lay derelict and neglected in her mud berth. Following a recent survey, there are hopes that funds might be raised to restore the old paddle steamer as a passenger-carrying vessel.

the ride

1 From Medina Road turn into Bridge Road, signposted **'Newport via cycleway'**. Follow the road all the way to the mini-roundabout at the top of the hill and turn left into **Arctic Road**, still following the signposted cycle route. Pass the **UK Sailing Academy** on your left and continue to the very end of the road.

2 Zig-zag right and left as the cycle route joins the **old railway line**, which edges its way clear of industrial Cowes through a tunnel of oak, birch and ash trees. Pass the signposted footpath to **Northwood** on your right and, a little further on, look out for the broken remains of an **old iron and timber bridge**.

3 Beyond the bridge, look out for a distinctive spire and pinnacles poking above the trees across the river. Standing little more than 0.5 mile (800m) from the gates of Osborne House, **St Mildred's church** at Whippingham was remodelled in the mid-18th century for use by the royal family. Queen Victoria gave many of the furnishings, and a permanent exhibition in the churchyard recounts the story of this extraordinary building. Continue ahead along the track.

4 Now the views begin to open up, and between Pinkmead and Stag Lane you'll spot the **old Ryde paddle steamer** slowly rusting in her mud berth at **Island Harbour Marina** on the opposite bank. This is a good area for wildlife – the hedges are thick with blackthorn, dog rose and crab apple, and in summer you'll see dragonflies and red admiral butterflies fluttering above the path. Listen, too, for the plaintive call of curlews, which use their long curved beaks to probe the mudflats for worms.

5 Now the trail crosses the **old trestle viaduct** that once carried the railway over Dodnor Creek. This area of open water, marsh and woodland was created in the 1790s when the creek was dammed to provide power for a proposed tide mill. The creek is protected as a local nature reserve and you may see reed warblers, coots, moorhens and grey herons. Beyond the creek the cycleway climbs briefly across **Dodnor Lane** and approaches the modern **industrial buildings** on the outskirts of

The harbour at Cowes

1h45 · **8 MILES** · **12.9 KM** · **LEVEL 123**

MAP: OS Explorer OL29 Isle of Wight

START/FINISH: Medina Road pay-and-display car park, West Cowes; grid ref: SZ 499956

TRAILS/TRACKS: back streets of Cowes, tarred and level cycle track

LANDSCAPE: wooded, riverside trail

PUBLIC TOILETS: Medina Road, Cowes, also The Quay, Newport

TOURIST INFORMATION: Cowes tel: 01983 813818

CYCLE HIRE: Funation Cycle Hire, Cowes, tel: 01983 200300 (www.funation.co.uk)

THE PUB: The Bargeman's Rest, Newport

❗ One short hill at the start and two sections of public road. Ideal for beginners and children aged eight and over

Getting to the start
On the island, take the A3020 from Newport to West Cowes and follow signs to the floating bridge. Passengers arriving with their bikes on the Red Funnel car ferry from Southampton should follow the one-way system around to the right, and cross the floating bridge to begin the ride in Medina Road, West Cowes.

Why do this cycle ride?
This ride makes a relaxed day out, with easy access from the mainland, too. There's a lot to see from the safe, level trail, which follows the National Cycle Network route along the former Cowes-to-Newport railway line. Route finding is straightforward, and you'll enjoy some lovely views across the River Medina, with plenty of opportunities for birdwatching.

Researched and written by: David Foster

As well as cycle routes, the Isle of Wight has over 500 miles (805km) of well-maintained and signposted footpaths and around 30 miles (48km) of Heritage Coastline. More than half the island is a designated Area of Outstanding Natural Beauty.

Cowes Week is a major event on the Isle of Wight

The Bargeman's Rest

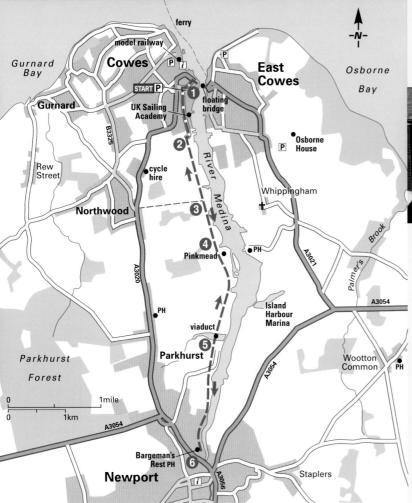

There's a distinct nautical flavour to this large pub, just a short stroll from Newport's town centre. Formerly a warehouse, the building was cleverly converted in 1999 and features pine floors, open fires and a plethora of nautical bric-a-brac, from old pictures and prints, oars and ship's wheels to lanterns, cannons and divers' helmets. The attractive paved terrace that overlooks the yachts moored beside the quay is an equally appealing spot for a relaxing pint of locally brewed Ventnor Golden. Live music is a regular feature, with jazz at lunchtime on Sundays. There are four cycle racks on the patio.

Food

The extensive menu lists the usual pub favourites, from burgers and ploughman's lunches to fish and chips, Cajun chicken and rib-eye steak – there's something for everyone here. Home-made dishes appear on the blackboard – perhaps steak and kidney pie, coq au vin or lamb rogan josh with rice and poppadoms.

Family facilities

Children are very welcome in the large family room and on the patio, which is fenced and safe for kids. You will also find a children's menu, high chairs and baby-changing facilities.

Alternative refreshment stops

Pubs and cafés in Newport.

☛ Where to go from here

Across the river, just beyond East Cowes, is Queen Victoria's seaside retreat, Osborne House, with apartments full of treasured family mementoes. The Swiss Cottage in the garden is a particular delight (www.english-heritage.org.uk).

about the pub

The Bargeman's Rest
Little London Quay, Newport
Isle of Wight PO30 5BS
Tel: 01983 525828
www.bargemansrest.com

DIRECTIONS: on the quay beside the cycleway, north east of the town centre

PARKING: 14

OPEN: daily, all day

FOOD: daily, all day

BREWERY/COMPANY: free house

REAL ALE: Ventnor Golden and Undercliff, Badger Best and Tanglefoot, guest beers

Newport. Look out, here, for a pair of concrete tracks that cross the trail and lead to a pair of slim **concrete jettie**s built out into the river. NEG Micon is one of the world's leading manufacturers of wind turbines, and here a huge rolling gantry loads their products onto waiting barges. The facility was specially designed to minimise disturbance to the birds that feed on the mudflats of this internationally protected wildlife site. Soon, reach the

white gate at the end of the traffic-free route. Stop here, then continue straight ahead as far as the **post-box** on the corner of Hurstake Road. Turn left, signed to **The Bargeman's Rest**, and bear right at the bottom of the hill for the final 300yds (274m) to the pub.

6 Here you can take a well-earned break before retracing your outward route back to Cowes.

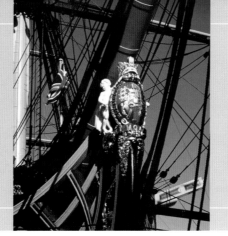

did you know?

HMS Victory is maintained in immaculate condition

The 200th anniversary of the Battle of Trafalgar was celebrated in 2005. Nelson's flagship, Victory, was launched in 1765 at Chatham Dockyard and commissioned in 1778. After 32 years of active service, she was retired to her Portsmouth mooring, where she spent the next 110 years fulfilling a combination of practical and ceremonial roles. In 1922 she was moved into the Royal Naval Dockyard's No. 2 Dry Dock where work began on restoring her to her 'fighting' condition of 1805. Today she is open to the public all year round.

Ports Down and Southwick

A rural ramble from the D-Day village of Southwick to Fort Nelson.

Below: A 19th-century cannon in the grounds of Fort Nelson

Ports Down and Palmerston's Follies

Ports Down rises 381ft (116m) above the coastal plain and extends for some 6.25 miles (10.1km) from Bedhampton to Fareham. It commands impressive views over Portsmouth and Langstone Harbours. This route climbs the backslope of the hill to Nelson's Monument. During the mid-19th century Britain faced the threat of a French invasion under Napoleon III. Fortifications were built around Portsmouth to protect the naval base. Sea forts to the south of the city were bolstered by five more on Ports Down, built between 1860 and 1872. Soon after the completion of Fort Nelson in 1871 the French threat disappeared and the forts became known as Palmerston's Follies.

Hundreds of boats and thousands of men were assembled along Hampshire's low coastline and natural harbours ready for the D-Day invasion of France in June 1944. The planning of Operation Overlord was undertaken in great secrecy from the sleepy village of Southwick. On your return walk you will see a complex of modern buildings surrounding an early 19th-century mansion. The Ministry of Defence acquired Southwick House during the Second World War. Just before D-Day it became the headquarters for General Eisenhower and the Chiefs of Staff. Winston Churchill and Eisenhower supervised the landing from a special train at nearby Droxford Station.

the walk

1 From the village car park turn right to a junction and bear left to a roundabout. Go straight over taking **Crooked Walk Lane** towards Portchester. Climb steeply, bearing right by a **quarry**.

2 Where the road veers sharp left, briefly take Portchester Lane right. Almost immediately turn left through a gap in the verge and follow the footpath across a field, heading for the corner of a **copse**. Skirt the copse and cross a stile. Maintain direction towards **Nelson's Monument** across a further field to a stile and lane. Turn left, pass Nelson's Monument and turn right at the crossroads, signed to **Fort Nelson**.

 54

 WALK

3h00 | **6 MILES** | **9.7 KM** | **LEVEL 1 2 3**

MAPS: OS Explorer 119 Meon Valley

START/FINISH: free car park by the village hall, Southwick, close to HMS Dryad; grid ref: SU 627085

PATHS: field, woodland paths and stretches of road, 15 stiles

LANDSCAPE: open downland and gently rolling farmland

PUBLIC TOILETS: at Fort Nelson, only if visiting the museum

TOURIST INFORMATION: Portsmouth, tel: 023 9282 6722

THE PUB: The Red Lion, Southwick

⚠ Two fairly busy sections of lane with no pavement. Suitable for older, more experienced family groups

Getting to the start

Southwick is a village north of Portsmouth. It lies just north off the B2177 between Wickham and Purbrook. In the village follow signs for HMS Dryad, to find the village hall car park.

Researched and written by: David Halford, David Hancock

54

WALK

did you know?

HMS Dryad, *on the edge of Southwick, is one of three maritime warfare training colleges all sited on the south coast near Portsmouth. The other two are HMS* Collingwood *and* HMS Excellent.

Battleships moored at Portsmouth for the Festival of the Sea

what to look for

While strolling around Southwick look out for the plaque on the Red Lion which records that Generals Montgomery and Eisenhower drank there during D-Day preparations in 1944.

At the Royal Armouries Museum in Fort Nelson, imaginative scenes and hands-on exhibits, together with video presentations, describe the development of artillery over the last 500 years. There are guns from around the world.

3 Having visited the fort, retrace your steps back to the **Monument** and continue down the lane for 50yds (46m). Take the footpath left over a stile. Follow the path indicated by the official diversion sign to the right corner of the **fort**, cross a stile and skirt the edge of the fort to a further stile. Bear half-right across the field, between a **house and pylon**, to a road.

4 Turn right downhill, then right again at the next junction. After 200yds (183m) bear left through **St Nicholas's churchyard**. Rejoin the road and continue past **barns** and a pond. Shortly, beside a lay-by, bear left over a stile and follow the footpath along the left-hand field edge. Continue on between fields, then by **Grub Coppice** to cross a bridge.

5 Climb a stile, and keep to the right-hand field edge to a stile on the right. Cross a further stile and walk along the left-hand field edge. Turn left across a stile by the **stream** and bear right, around the edge of the field to a stile and road. Cross the stile opposite and walk along the right-hand field edge close to a stream. Follow the **field boundary** as it swings left, pass a gate to the next field, and shortly bear right across a stile and **bridge** to join a track.

6 Pass between **farm buildings**, go through a gate and bear left down to the **B2177**. Cross over and take the footpath right along a track. It becomes grassy and bears right into **woodland**. Take the second footpath left, emerge from the trees and head across a narrow field. Cross a bridge, bear right, then half-left making for a **large oak**. Descend steps to a lane.

7 Cross over and bear half-right across the field towards the **church tower**. Cross a bridge and continue through a **plantation**. Beyond another bridge, walk up a drive to the road. Turn left, then right into **Southwick**. Keep left at the junction and left again to the car park.

The Nelson Monument rising above Fort Nelson

The Red Lion

The pretty estate village of Southwick stands on the Pilgrim's Trail from Winchester to Portsmouth, and the low-beamed Red Lion in the heart of the village is the favoured refuelling stop before the final haul up Ports Down Hill. Today, Hampshire brewer Gales owns the pub, offering tip-top pints of Butser bitter and the heady HSB to parched walkers. It is also a popular dining pub with a good, honestly priced menu. Enjoy alfresco eating and drinking on the sunny front terrace, or on the sheltered rear patio.

about the pub

The Red Lion
High Street, Southwick Portsmouth,
Hampshire
PO17 6EF
Tel: 023 9237 7223

DIRECTIONS: see Getting to the start

PARKING: 40

OPEN: closed Monday

FOOD: daily

BREWERY/COMPANY: Gales Brewery

REAL ALE: Gales HSB and Butser, guest beer

DOGS: allowed in garden only

Food

Firm favourites include ham, egg and chips, lambs' liver and bacon with onion gravy, and decent filling snacks such as sandwiches (smoked salmon and cream cheese), ploughman's lunches with crusty bread, salad and pickles, and filled jacket potatoes. More imaginative meals range from salmon, cod and smoked haddock fishcakes and dressed crab, to saddle of lamb stuffed with black pudding, and fillet steak with pink peppercorn sauce.

Family facilities

Although there are no specific facilities for children they are welcome inside, and smaller portions from the main menu are available.

Alternative refreshment stops

In Southwick you have the choice of two pubs – the second one is the Golden Lion. If you visit Fort Nelson, the Powder Keg Café is open all day.

☞ Where to go from here

Learn more about the events leading up to the liberation of France at Portsmouth's D-Day Museum and Overlord Embroidery (www.ddaymuseum.co.uk). The city's Historic Dockyard is home to three fabulous ships, including Nelson's flagship Victory, and the Royal Navy Museum (www.historicdockyard.co.uk).

Meonstoke's parish church

Meon Valley meander

Old Winchester Hill is a favoured haunt of historians and naturalists.

Old Winchester Hill

The hill dominates the Meon Valley. From its summit, some 646ft (197m) above sea level, you have magnificent views. It attracted early settlers and the remains of the fort on the summit date back to the Iron Age. Its defences comprise a massive single bank and ditch enclosing about 14 acres (4 ha), with entrances to east and west. The oval-shaped fort overlies a pattern of prehistoric fields and you will notice some large Bronze Age burial mounds, erected on the crest of the hill between 4,500 and 3,500 years ago.

Old Winchester Hill is now a National Nature Reserve, cared for by English Nature. The sheep-grazed chalk down, with its mix of open grassland, scrub and woodland, is home to rare butterflies and chalk-loving flowers. Walk here in early summer and the hill fort is dotted with fragrant orchids, while in July look out for the rare bright blue round-headed rampion.

On a warm August day the grassland is a sea of colour with hundreds of flowers, plants and wild herbs while the air shimmers with chalkhill blue butterflies. Longer grass attracts hedge and meadow browns and marbled white butterflies.

Bird-lovers should bring binoculars – you may see a peregrine falcon, buzzards soaring high, and summer migrants like the redstart and pied flycatcher. In winter fieldfares and redwings feed in numbers on the abundant berries on the stunted juniper bushes, while the yew woods provide shelter to titmice and goldcrests.

the walk

1 From the car park go through the gate onto the open down and turn left by the nature reserve's **information boards**. Follow the path around the perimeter of the reserve. Merge with a track and bear right towards the **hill fort**. Go through a gate, bear left, then right across the centre of the hill fort.

2 Fork left as you leave the ramparts and head downhill to a **stile**. Walk down a woodland path and emerge beside a gate. Continue downhill, then turn right around the edge of two fields and bear left on to a track. At a junction turn left along a **track**.

3 Where this enters a field, keep ahead along the **stony path** (parallel path if wet). Pass under the **disused railway** (or use the steps to cross the old track bed), and continue to a T-junction.

4 Bear right and cross the **footbridge** over the River Meon to the A32. Cross straight over into Church Lane and continue into **Exton**. Turn left along Shoe Lane. Go right at the junction beyond **The Shoe Inn**, and then bear left along **Allens Farm Lane**.

what to look for

Take a close look at Corhampton Church. Built on an artificial mound, it is remarkable in having no dedication, and has remained almost unaltered since it was built in the early 11th century. Many Saxon details can be seen, including characteristic 'long and short' stonework at the corners. Note too the sundial on the south wall (divided into eight sections not twelve), the 12th-century wall paintings in the chancel, the yew tree, said to be 1,000 years old, and the Romano-British coffin in the churchyard.

5 At a sharp right-hand bend keep ahead along the path beside **Exton Farm**. Go through a kissing gate and bear left along the right-hand edge of **paddocks** to a stile. Pass beside **Corhampton Farm** and church to the **A32**.

6 Cross over, walk left along the pavement and turn right by the **shop**. Take the metalled path beside the last house on your right and enter **Meonstoke churchyard**. Turn left along the lane to a T-junction beside the **Bucks Head**. Turn left, then left again at the junction. Follow the lane right (Pound Lane) and cross the **old railway**.

Left: The view from Old Winchester Hill
Below: Walking in Exton village

55

2h15 · **5.5 MILES** · **8.8 KM** · **LEVEL 123**

WALK

MAP: OS Explorer 119 Meon Valley

START/FINISH: English Nature car park off Old Winchester Hill Lane; grid ref: SU 645214

PATHS: field paths, footpaths, tracks and sections of road, 9 stiles

LANDSCAPE: chalk downland, gently rolling farmland and river valley

PUBLIC TOILETS: none on route

TOURIST INFORMATION: Petersfield, tel: 01730 260446

THE PUB: The Shoe, Exton

❗ Great care needed when crossing the A32 (twice). Very stony and uneven path down to Exton and a long steady climb to the finish. Suitable for more experienced children

Getting to the start

Meonstoke lies between Winchester and Havant. North of Meonstoke, take a minor lane east off the A32 near the George & Falcon at Warnford, to reach Old Winchester Hill in 2 miles (3.2km). The parking area is well signed on the right.

Researched and written by: David Hancock, Peter Toms

Meon Valley · HAMPSHIRE

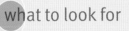

did you know?

Corhampton was called Quedementune in the Domesday Book. Its church is one of the best-preserved late-Saxon churches in the county, two of its architectural features being the chancel arch, and the Saxon sundial to the east of the south doorway.

Corhampton's Saxon church

7 At a crossroads climb the stile on your left. Proceed ahead across the field and pass behind **gardens**, eventually reaching a stile and a lane. Climb the stile opposite and keep to the right-hand field edge to reach a stile. Maintain direction to another stile, then bear diagonally left towards a **house** and road.

8 Turn right and take the track left beside **Harvestgate Farm**. At the top of the track bear left uphill along the field edge, then first right, following the path along the hedge into the next field. Go through the kissing gate on your left into the **Nature Reserve** and ascend steeply to the hill fort ramparts.

9 Pass through a gate and go right to join the outward route by the **fort entrance**. Opposite the information board, follow a path just beneath the downland rim. Bear right over a **stile**, then turn left and retrace your steps to the car park.

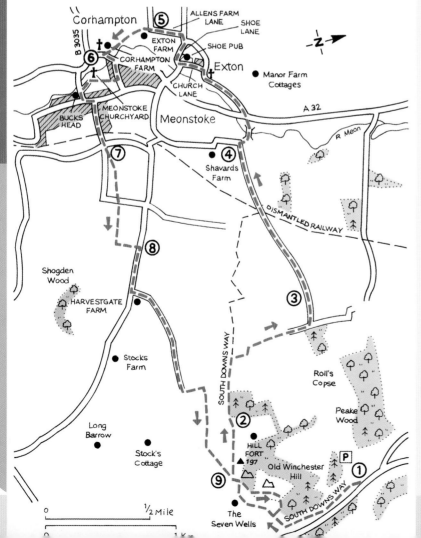

The Shoe Inn

about the pub

The Shoe Inn
Shoe Lane, Exton
Bishop's Waltham, Hampshire
SO32 3NT
Tel: 01489 877526

DIRECTIONS: Exton is just off the A32, 2 miles (3.6km) south of West Meon

PARKING: 18

OPEN: daily

FOOD: daily

BREWERY/COMPANY: Wadworth Brewery

REAL ALE: Wadworth 6X and Henry's IPA, guest beer

DOGS: welcome on leads in the bar and garden

Food
Expect a good range of sandwiches, hot filled ciabattas and a choice of ploughman's, served with home-made chutney. Look to the changing chalkboard menu for salmon fishcakes with sweet pepper salsa, vegetable and herb risotto, red bream with prawns, avocado and tomato butter, or pork fillet with black pudding and a grain mustard sauce.

Family facilities
Children are very welcome in the pub and garden. There's an extensive children's menu, high chairs are available and the toilets have baby-changing facilities.

Alternative refreshment stops
The Bucks Head in Meonstoke (open all day weekends) offers an extensive menu and has a charming riverside garden.

Exton's village pub used to be located in the riverside garden of today's modern-style building, but was rebuilt and relocated across the road following severe flooding in 1938. The pub's unusual name is thought to derive from being next to a former smithy. It's ablaze with colourful flowers during the summer. The interior comprises a rustic main bar and an adjacent, light oak-panelled dining area with a cosy log fire for cooler days. The real attraction in summer is the sun-trap front patio and the delightful garden across the lane beside the crystal-clear River Meon. Wiltshire brewer Wadworth owns the pub and offers its 6X and Henry's IPA on handpump, alongside a changing guest ale.

☞ Where to go from here
Visit St John's churchyard in nearby West Meon. Here you'll find the graves of Thomas Lord, the founder of Lord's cricket ground, who retired to the village in 1830, and Guy Burgess, the former Russian agent.

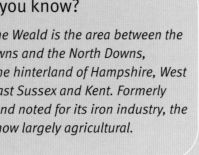

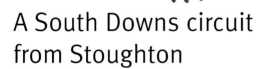

Green woodpecker (Picus viridis)

The magnificent view across the Weald from Devil's Dyke

A South Downs circuit from Stoughton

Discover a magical ancient forest.

An ancient yew forest

You might not expect to find the largest yew forest in Europe at the western extremity of the South Downs, but that's exactly where it is. This remote downland landscape, covering more than 200 acres (81ha), is cloaked with 30,000 yew trees. Once a wartime artillery range, Kingley Vale became one of Britain's first nature reserves in 1952. Today, it is managed by English Nature.

Silent, isolated and inaccessible by car, the grove is a haven for ramblers and naturalists. Our walk skirts the forest, but if you have the time to explore this enchanting place, study the map closely and make up your own route.

The yew is one of our finest trees and can live up to 2,000 years. It is usually a large but squat tree, its branches and dark green needles create a dense evergreen canopy which allows little light to filter to the forest floor. With their deep red trunks, branches and shallow roots twisted into monstrous shapes, some of the yews at Kingley Vale are thought to be at least 500 years old. Even on the sunniest summer's day, the scene is eerily dark, strange and mystical, like something from the pages of a fairy story. The yew has always featured strongly in folklore, and according to legend this place was a meeting point for witches who engaged in pagan rites and wove magical spells here.

Various theories about the origin of the forest have been put forward. Some sources suggest the trees were planted to guide pilgrims travelling across the South Downs to Canterbury. Earlier, Bronze Age kings were buried here, confirmed by various tumuli on the map.

The grove teems with wildlife, and green woodpeckers are just one of 57 species of bird that breed here. The bee orchid blooms in June, and sheep and wild fallow deer keep the turf short for 200 further species of wild flower.

the walk

1 From the car park take the gravel track left (signposted '**bridleway**') and follow it away from the road, skirting dense **beech woodland**. There are striking views on the left over pastoral, well-wooded countryside. Keep right at a fork and follow the track as it curves to the right. Proceed straight on at a major junction of tracks and begin a gradual ascent beneath the boughs of beech trees.

2 Eventually you break cover from the trees at a major junction of waymarked tracks. Go straight on, looking to the right for spectacular views. Continue to the next bridleway sign, and fork left, joining a **path** running roughly parallel to the track. Cut between trees and keep going until, at a gap by a **marker post**, you descend the path on the right. Rejoin the enclosed track, turning left to follow it up the slope towards **The Devil's Humps**.

3 On reaching these tumuli take time to wander off the track and enjoy the magnificent vistas across the Downs. The view to the north, over remote **woodland** and downland, is impressive enough, but the panorama to the south is particularly outstanding. Immediately below you are the trees of **Kingley Vale**. Rejoin and continue along the track, passing the **nature reserve** on your left. Continue between lines of beech trees and more mixed woodland.

Left: View from Bow Hill towards Stoughton
Below: Yew trees on a trail in Kingley Vale

2h00 · **4.5 MILES** · **7.2 KM** · **LEVEL 123**

MAP: OS Explorer 120 Chichester, South Harting & Selsey

START/FINISH: free car park at Stoughton Down; grid ref: SZ 814126

PATHS: mostly woodland paths and downland tracks

LANDSCAPE: dense woodland and rolling downs

PUBLIC TOILETS: none on route

TOURIST INFORMATION: Chichester, tel: 01243 775888

THE PUB: Hare & Hounds, Stoughton

❶ Care needed on the country lane out of Stoughton. Ascents and descents gentle but long

Getting to the start

Stoughton is situated between Petersfield and Chichester, signed 2 miles (3.2km) east off the B2146. Pass through Walderton and Stoughton village, and the car park at Stoughton Down is 1 mile (1.6km) further on.

Researched and written by:
Nick Channer, Peter Toms

did you know?

Walk along the South Downs Way and you will probably see sheep. The downland has been prime sheep-rearing country for many centuries, although grazing has been much reduced in recent years to protect the quality of water as it filters down through the chalk.

Southdown, thickset, stocky and short-legged, is one of the oldest English breeds; it is valued for the quality of its meat and the fine quality and length of its wool. Southdown sheep have been used to improve other breeds, and are found all over the world.

4 Turn right at the next main junction and follow the **bridle track**. On the left are glimpses of **Chichester harbour**, with its complex network of watery channels and sprawling mudflats, distantly visible on a clear day. Descend through an area of beech woods past a **memorial stone**, and keep going until you reach the road. Turn right and walk through the village of **Stoughton**.

5 Pass the entrance to **St Mary's Church** on the left, followed by the **Hare & Hounds** pub. Continue through the village and out of Stoughton. At a left-hand bend look for the entrance to the car park on **Stoughton Down** on the right, where the walk began.

what to look for

Bronze-Age barrows, known as the Devil's Humps, can be seen on Bow Hill. There are several legends on the South Downs concerning the Devil. This one suggests that anyone who runs round the humps six times will experience a sighting!

As you approach Stoughton village, look for a memorial stone on the right of the path. It was in this field, in November 1940, that a Polish pilot officer based at nearby RAF Tangmere died when his Hurricane crashed following aerial combat with a German ME109.

Take a closer look at Stoughton's 11th-century Church of St Mary. The exterior is barn-like, bulky even, and inside it is unexpectedly spacious. The south transept was converted into a tower in the 14th century, the nave is over 30ft (9m) high and there is a striking Norman arch with a triple layer of roll mouldings.

Hare & Hounds

about the pub

Hare & Hounds
Stoughton, Chichester
West Sussex PO18 9JQ
Tel: 023 9263 1433

DIRECTIONS: in the centre of the village, east of the church

PARKING: 6

OPEN: daily

FOOD: daily

BREWERY/COMPANY: free house

REAL ALE: Fuller's London Pride, Timothy Taylor Landlord, Young's Bitter, Hampshire Rose

DOGS: well behaved dogs welcome inside

Food

Choose from a good snack menu, which includes sandwiches and baguettes, or go for something more substantial such as roast beef salad, lasagne or steak and mushroom pie. Everything is cooked on the premises and there are various game dishes in season, perhaps venison steak or saddle of hare. Summer specials may include fresh dressed crab and whole sea bass.

Family facilities

Although there are no special facilities for children, they are welcome inside the pub.

☞ Where to go from here

Historic West Dean Gardens lie to the east of Singleton on the A286, covering 35 acres (14ha), with a pergola by Harold Peto, mixed borders and a superb walled kitchen garden (www.westdean.org.uk).

Stoughton is set in an extremely quiet and very beautiful spot on the lower slopes of the South Downs, and the Hare & Hounds, a striking, creeper-covered building of brick and flint, dates back to the 17th century, when it was two cottages. A pub for some 100 years, it is today a comfortably rustic village local, with each of its three interconnecting beamed rooms sporting old pews, pine tables and chairs and warming winter log fires. In summer the sun-trap front terrace is the favoured spot for weary South Downs walkers to relax and refuel. There's an equally pleasant rear garden with rural views.

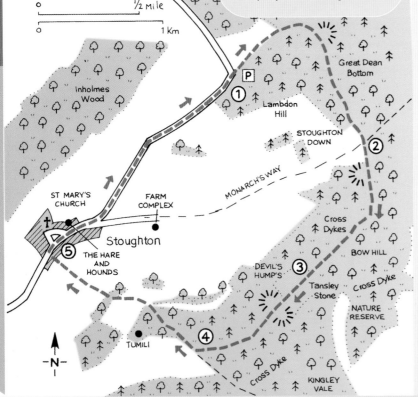

Chichester has established itself as one of the cultural hotspots of southern England, thanks to its summer theatre festival. Plays are staged in the six-sided Festival Theatre, built in 1962. Its first artistic director was Sir Laurence Olivier, who later founded the National Theatre in London using actors from the Chichester company. The theatre now mounts about 750 performances a year, many of them transferring to London's West End or touring the rest of the country and abroad.

From Chichester to Hunston

A fascinating walk combining the ancient treasures of a cathedral city with the delights of the adjacent countryside.

Historic Chichester

A stroll through the quaint streets of Chichester is the best way to appreciate this beautiful city. Chichester's origins date back as far as the late Iron Age, and settled by the Romans in about AD 200. They built the walls and laid out the city plan, which can still be clearly identified.

From the car park you soon find yourself at the heart of Chichester. Make the cathedral your first port of call. This magnificent building includes the site of a shrine to St Richard, Bishop of Chichester in the 13th century, modern tapestries by John Piper and Romanesque stone carvings. Another memorable feature is Graham Sutherland's painting, which depicts Christ appearing to St Mary Magdalen on the first Easter morning.

From the cathedral the walk heads down West Street to the intricately decorated Market Cross, built at the beginning of the 16th century. Situated at the hub of the Roman street plan and distinguished by its flying buttresses, the cross provided shelter for traders. Head up North Street to the Council House, built in 1731 and famous for its huge stone lion and Roman stone. The Latin inscription records the dedication of a temple to Neptune and Minerva. From here it's an easy stroll south to the Pallants.

You then leave the city, by following the Chichester section of the Portsmouth and Arundel Canal out into the countryside and south to Hunston.

the walk

1 Leave the car park, cross the **footbridge** over the Avenue de Chartres and head towards the city centre. Turn right at the city map and then left into South Street. Bear left into **Canon Lane**, just beyond the tourist information centre. Turn right into St Richard's Walk and approach elegant **Chichester Cathedral**.

what to look for

In addition to the remains of the Roman city walls, there is St Mary's Hospital of the Blessed Virgin Mary in St Martin's Square, founded between 1158 and 1170. Originally a hospital, it later became almshouses. Visitors can make an appointment with the guide.

In the nearby Pallants is Pallant House, built by Henry Peckham, a Chichester wine merchant, in 1712. The house is Queen Anne style and each room reflects a particular period of its history.

2 Swing left at the **cloisters**, then left again to keep the stone wall on your left. Make for the West Door and pass the **Bell Tower** to reach West Street. Bear right here. Across the road is a converted church, now a bar. The north face of Chichester Cathedral is clearly seen as you head along West Street. On reaching the **Market Cross**, turn left into North Street and bear right immediately beyond the historic **Council House** into Lion Street.

3 Walk along to **St Martin's Square**, and opposite you at this point is **St Mary's Hospital**. Turn right and pass the Hole in the Wall pub to reach East Street. Glance to the left and you can pick out the **Corn Exchange**. Go straight over into North Pallant and walk along to **Pallant House**. Head straight on into South Pallant and follow the road round to the right, passing **Christ Church** on the left. Turn left at the next junction, make for the traffic lights and continue south into **Southgate**.

4 Cross the railway at **Chichester Station** and then swing left to reach the **canal basin**. Follow the tow path to Poyntz Bridge, dated 1820, and continue to the next bridge which carries the **A27 Chichester bypass**.

Left: Chichester Cathedral
Right: A tapestry and altar inside Chichester Cathedral

2h00   **4.5 MILES**   **7.2 KM**   **LEVEL 1**23

MAP: OS Explorer 120 Chichester, South Harting & Selsey

START/FINISH: fee-car park in Avenue de Chartres, Chichester; grid ref: SZ 857044

PATHS: urban walkways, towpath and field paths, 3 stiles

LANDSCAPE: mixture of city streets and open countryside

PUBLIC TOILETS: at car park and elsewhere in Chichester

TOURIST INFORMATION: Chichester tel: 01243 775888

THE PUB: The Spotted Cow, Hunston

❶ Great care needed when crossing the A27. Suitable for children of all ages.

Getting to the start

Chichester is a city on the south coast between Portsmouth and Bognor Regis. Leave the A27 city bypass at the roundabout where the Witterings are signed to the south and the city centre and railway station to the north. Follow the city centre signs, cross over the railway, then in 200 yards (183m) take the first major turning left – Avenue de Chartres. Pass under the footbridge and exit off the next roundabout into the car park.

Researched and written by:
Nick Channer, David Halford

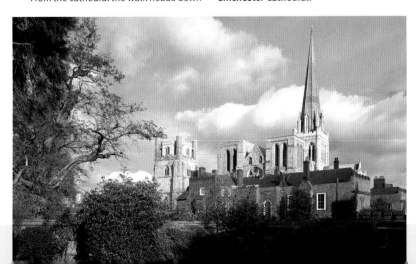

The 1501 Market Cross in Chichester

Chichester Canal

In 1817 an Act of Parliament was passed that permitted the construction of the canal from Chichester harbour to the city, a distance of about 1.5 miles (2.5km). The harbour quay could accommodate vessels of 150–180 tons; however the canal was never profitable because the costs were no less than simply moving goods overland to the coast.

Chichester Cathedral's spire is a replica, built between 1861 and 1866

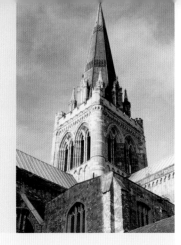

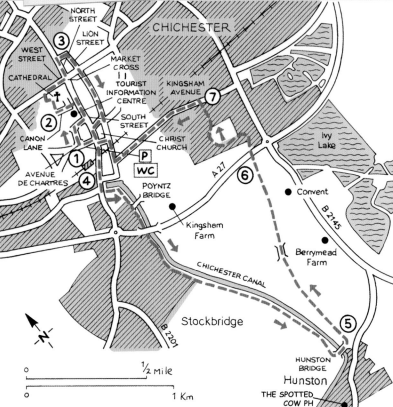

CHICHESTER

NORTH STREET
LION STREET
WEST STREET
CATHEDRAL
MARKET CROSS
TOURIST INFORMATION CENTRE
KINGSHAM AVENUE
SOUTH STREET
CANON LANE
CHRIST CHURCH
AVENUE DE CHARTRES
POYNTZ BRIDGE
Kingsham Farm
Ivy Lake
Convent
B 2145
Berrymead Farm
CHICHESTER CANAL
A 27
B 2201
Stockbridge
HUNSTON BRIDGE
Hunston
THE SPOTTED COW PH

½ mile
1 Km

The Spotted Cow

The Spotted Cow was originally a dairy farm before being converted into a pub in 1955. It's close to the attractions of Chichester harbour and an easy stroll from the city centre via the towpath beside the old canal. Refurbishment in 2000 saw the pub carefully extended to incorporate an old barn, and today it successfully combines the charm and character of a classic country pub (flagstones, heavy beams, open fires) with a modern Mediterranean theme. Upgrading included developing the shaded patio and the sun-trap garden area to the front of the pub. Expect an informal atmosphere, good wines by the glass and local Gales ales on tap.

Food

From an extensive menu you can order snacks and starters such as roast beef and horseradish sandwiches, hearty ploughman's lunches with salad, pickles and crusty bread, fishcakes or scrambled egg and smoked salmon. Main courses include Lancashire hotpot, home-made venison meatballs, fish pie and steak and kidney pie, a range of hand-made sausages, and fresh fish dishes – perhaps sea bass with lemon and coriander.

Family facilities

Families are very welcome and youngsters will find a play area in the garden, a children's menu and reduced price dishes from the blackboard menu. There are baby-changing facilities in the disabled person's toilet.

Alternative refreshment stops

As well as inns and hotels, of which there are many in Chichester, there is Platters restaurant near the Avenue de Chartres car park, and Bishop Bell Rooms close to the cathedral.

☞ Where to go from here

There's plenty to see and do in Chichester, including harbour tours, or head just west of the city to the Roman palace at Fishbourne, with its stunning collection of mosaic floors (www.sussexpast.co.uk).

about the pub

The Spotted Cow
Selsey Road, Hunston
Chichester, West Sussex PO20 6PD
Tel: 01243 486718
www.thespottedcow.net

DIRECTIONS: village and pub are on the B2145 Selsey road south of Chichester

PARKING: 40

OPEN: daily, all day Friday, Saturday and Sunday

FOOD: daily

BREWERY/COMPANY: free house

REAL ALE: Gales BB and HSB, guest beer

DOGS: welcome on a lead

ROOMS: 2 bedrooms

Keep going as far as the next footbridge and follow the path to the road. Confusingly this bridge is labelled Poyntz Bridge on OS maps. (Turn right here to reach **The Spotted Cow** pub, about 250 yards/229m along the road on the right.)

5 Bear left for a few steps to a stile by the entrance to a **car park**. Cross into the field. The cathedral's spire can be seen above the city. Keep the **field boundary** on your immediate right and make for a stile. Continue ahead, with a field on your left and follow the path to a small **footbridge** over a ditch and a stile. Follow the edge of the next field, keeping the same direction. Pass by a **broken stile** in the wooded corner and a few steps beyond you reach the **A27**.

6 Cross over with extreme care to join a footpath opposite. Turn left between **two terraces** of houses and follow the tarmac path to the **recreation ground**. Cross to the far side of the green, keeping the cathedral spire more or less straight ahead. Look for **Cherry Orchard Road**, with a post-box and a phone-box on the corner.

7 Turn left at the crossroads into Kingsham Avenue and follow it into Kingsham Road. Turn right at the T-junction, cross the **railway line** and, on reaching the one-way system, bear left to cross over at the lights. Bear right into Southgate, then left into **Avenue de Chartres**. The car park is on the left.

did you know?

The Goodwood estate hosts the world's largest festival of historic motorsport – the Festival of Speed. The event, run annually since 1993, is motor racing's equivalent of Ascot, where the public can mix with drivers of yesteryear and their machines, today's Formula 1 heroes and their supercars.

A Bugatti at the Goodwood Festival of Speed

From Goodwood to Charlton and beyond

One of Britain's top racecourses lies beside this woodland walk, which includes an optional spur to the Weald and Downland Open Air Museum.

Glorious Goodwood

Think of horse racing on the South Downs and you immediately think of Goodwood, one of Britain's loveliest and most famous racecourses. The course rises and falls around a natural amphitheatre, with the horses dashing along the ridge to create one of the greatest spectacles in the racing world. For one week every summer it becomes 'Glorious Goodwood' when thousands of racegoers travel to Sussex to attend one of the most prestigious events of the sporting and social calendar. According to *The Times*, Goodwood is 'the place to be and to be seen'.

The course opened in 1801 after the Duke of Richmond donated Goodwood Park

to establish a track where members of the Goodwood Hunt Club and officers of the Sussex Militia could attend meetings.

The walk begins at Goodwood Country Park, a popular amenity area characterised by woodland and grassy downland, and initially follows part of the Monarch's Way through extensive woodland, down to the village of East Dean. Along the road is neighbouring Charlton, famous for the Charlton Hunt, established in the 18th century. The hunt's most memorable chase took place on 28th January 1738, beginning before eight that morning and not finishing until nearly six that evening.

Many of those taking part were from the elite upper ranks of society and for ten hours a fox led them a merry dance in the surrounding fields and woods.

If time allows (allow at least 3 hours – 2 miles/3.2km there and back plus plenty to see on site), you can extend the walk at this point and visit the outstanding Weald & Downland Open Air Museum, with its unusual collection of traditional country homes and workplaces.

The grand ivy-covered façade of 18th-century Goodwood House

the walk

1. Make for the western end of Counter's Gate car park and look for a **footpath sign** by an opening leading out to the road. Cross over to a junction of two clear tracks, with a path on the right. Follow the right-hand track, signposted 'public footpath' and part of the **Monarch's Way**, to a gate and stile. Continue past hazel thickets to the next gate and stile, then cross a clearing in the woods.

2. Follow the gently curving path to the right over the grassy, plant-strewn ground and down between trees to reach a **gateway**. The village of **East Dean** can be seen nestling down below. Head diagonally right down the steep field slope to a stile in the corner.

3. Cross into the adjacent field and keep to the right of the boundary fence to a **second stile** leading out to the road. Bear left and walk down into East Dean, passing **Manor Farm**.

4. Turn left at the junction, signed to Singleton (or right, signed to Petworth, to visit the **Star & Garter Inn**), and follow the road towards Charlton. On reaching the village, walk on past **The Fox Goes Free** pub and the Woodstock House Hotel, then take the road left, signed to **Goodwood**.

Titchfield's 16th-century Market Hall and two 15th-century buildings at the Weald and Downland Open Air Museum

| 1h30 | 5 MILES | 8 KM | LEVEL 123 |

SHORTER ALTERNATIVE ROUTE

| 1h30 | 3.5 MILES | 5.7 KM | LEVEL 123 |

MAP: OS Explorers 120 Chichester, South Harting & Selsey, 121 Arundel & Pulborough

START/FINISH: Counter's Gate free car park and picnic area, Goodwood Country Park; or large free car park opposite racecourse; grid ref: TQ 897113 (on Explorer 120)

PATHS: woodland tracks and field paths, section of Monarch's Way and one lengthy stretch of quiet road, 4 stiles

LANDSCAPE: mixture of dense woodland and scenic downland

PUBLIC TOILETS: only if visiting the Weald & Downland Museum

TOURIST INFORMATION: Chichester, tel: 01243 775888

THE PUB: The Fox Goes Free, Charlton

● Take extra care on the road linking East Dean and Charlton. One steep climb back to the Country Park

Getting to the start

Goodwood Racecourse and Country Park lie between Midhurst and Chichester, clearly signed on a minor road between the A286 and the A185.

Researched and written by: Nick Channer, Peter Toms

did you know?

Glorious Goodwood

Set 500ft (152m) high on its green hill in the heart of the South Downs, Goodwood racecourse holds 18 flat-racing days per year. But the major event by far is the Glorious Goodwood meeting over five days in late July or early August. This is when the county set and London's élite gather to see and be seen, having recovered from the exertions of Ascot in June.

Horses at full stretch during the Goodwood races

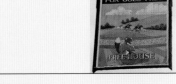

The Fox Goes Free

Built in 1558, the pub was a favoured hunting lodge of William III. More recently, it hosted the first Women's Institute meeting in 1915. The lovely old brick-and-flint building nestles in unspoilt rolling South Downs countryside and has a splendid flint-walled rear garden with apple trees, rustic benches, a barbecue area, and views across sheep-grazed pastures. Inside, the pub exudes charm and character with two huge fireplaces, a low-beamed ceiling, high-backed wooden settles and worn brick floors. On handpump you'll find local ale from Ballards and Arundel breweries, and there are eight wines available by the glass. Comfortable overnight accommodation is offered – very handy for Goodwood Races.

Food

The menu marries traditional and modern styles, and typical dishes include ham, egg and chips, rump of lamb, calf's liver and bacon, steak and kidney pie, local game and fresh fish. Sandwiches, filled baguettes and ploughman's lunches are available at lunchtime.

Family facilities

Children are welcome inside, and families can enjoy the spacious garden on fine summer days. Smaller portions of main dishes are available for children.

about the pub

The Fox Goes Free
Charlton, Goodwood, Chichester
West Sussex PO18 0HU
Tel: 01243 811461

DIRECTIONS: Charlton and the pub are signposted 1 mile (1.6km) off the A286 Chichester to Midhurst road at Singleton

PARKING: 6

OPEN: daily, all day

FOOD: daily, all day Saturday and Sunday

BREWERY/COMPANY: free house

REAL ALE: Ballards Best, Timothy Taylor Landlord, Arundel Best, Fox Bitter, guest beer

DOGS: welcome in the bar and garden

ROOMS: 5 en suite

Alternative refreshment stops

The Star and Garter at East Dean also offers a good range of meals and snacks. There is a café at the Weald & Downland Museum.

☛ Where to go from here

Goodwood House (www.goodwood.co.uk) has State Apartments and paintings by Van Dyck, Reynolds, Stubbs and Canaletto.

5 In 100yds (91m) take the lane left (or the footpath right and straight across fields to visit the **Weald & Downland Museum** at Singleton, returning to this stile by the same route). In a further 100yds (91m), fork left and turn right by the **war memorial**, dedicated to fallen comrades of the Sussex Yeomanry in both world wars. Follow **Chalk Road**, which dwindles to a track on the outskirts of Charlton. Once clear of the village, go through a gate, the track climbing steadily between the trees. On the left are glimpses of a glorious rolling landscape, while to the right Goodwood's superbly set **racecourse** edges into view between the trees. Follow the track all the way to the road and cross over to **Counter's Gate car park**.

what to look for

The village of East Dean, with its pond and ancient cottages of Sussex flint, is one of the prettiest in the area. For many years it was a thriving centre for hurdlemaking, and before World War One seven craftsmen operated here. The Weald and Downland Open Air Museum is set in 50 acres (20ha) of lovely Sussex countryside and offers a fascinating collection of over 40 regional historic buildings which have been saved from destruction, painstakingly restored and rebuilt in their original form. You can discover Victorian labourers' cottages, visit a recreated Tudor farmstead and explore ancient building techniques in the museum's hands-on gallery (www.wealddown.co.uk).

Sloe berries, *fruit of the blackthorn* (Prunus spinosa)

A downland ramble at Amberley

Old traction engines at Amberley Working Museum

2h00 · **5.5 MILES** · **8.8 KM** · **LEVEL 1 2 3**

MAP: OS Explorer 121 Arundel & Pulborough

START/FINISH: Amberley Working Museum car park, by Amberley Station. Visit the museum, then leave your car here while on the walk, by kind permission of the museum management; grid ref: TQ 026117

PATHS: riverside paths, downland tracks and some roads, 5 stiles

LANDSCAPE: Arun Valley and downland

PUBLIC TOILETS: Amberley Museum

TOURIST INFORMATION: Arundel, tel: 01903 882268

THE PUB: The Bridge Inn, Houghton Bridge

❶ Short section beside and crossing busy road; suitable for children of all ages.

Getting to the start

Amberley Working Museum is signed off the B2139, between Arundel and Storrington. Note that the car park is not available on days when special events are taking place at the museum, and also that it is locked at around 6pm.

Researched and written by:
Nick Channer, David Halford

Re-create the past with a visit to a working museum before climbing high on to the Downs.

Amberley Working Museum

Amberley is a charming, tranquil village with a history going back to medieval times and was the summer residence of the Bishops of Chichester. It may sound strange, but this invigorating downland walk begins where reality meets nostalgia. By visiting an old chalk quarry at the start of the route, you have the chance to forget – however briefly – the hurly-burly of the modern world, step into the past and recall a cherished way of life that has long vanished.

Amberley Working Museum is well worth a visit (www.amberleymuseum.co.uk). The open-air museum, which covers 36 acres (15ha) of a long-disused chalk pit in the Arun Valley, opened in 1979. Originally called the Chalk Pits Museum, its objective is to illustrate how the traditional industries of south east England evolved and developed during the 19th and 20th centuries. And it is very successful – few museums thrill and excite adults and children alike as much as this one does. To prove it, there are almost 100,000 visitors a year.

Visit the bus garage and the signwriter's workshop, the locomotive shed, the village blacksmith's, stop at the telephone exchange or discover the wheelwright's shop. You may meet craftspeople from the museum's resident team exercising ancient skills. Using traditional materials and tools, they produce a choice of fine wares which enables them to earn a living and keep their trade thriving. Elsewhere, exhibits are conserved and demonstrated by volunteers, many of whom have acquired a lifetime's experience in their trade.

One of the highlights of a visit to the Amberley Working Museum is a trip around the site on board a vintage bus, or perhaps a tour on the narrow gauge railway. The train ride takes visitors between Amberley and Brockham stations and yet never leaves the museum site! When you finally leave the museum follow the River Arun and begin the gradual climb into the hills. Up here, with its wide open skies and far-ranging views, you can feel the bracing wind in your face as you explore some of the loneliest tracts of downland in Sussex.

the walk

1 Turn left out of the car park and pass under the **railway bridge**. Begin to cross the road bridge spanning the River Arun and then bear left at the **footpath sign** to a stile by a galvanised gate. Once over it, cross the **watermeadows** to the next stile, and a few paces beyond it you reach a footpath sign. Bear left here.

2 Follow the path between trees, turn right on reaching a lane and pass **Sloe Cottage**. Turn left just beyond a caravan site to join a bridleway. Follow the path as it runs above the **camping ground** until it meets a track with a bridleway sign. Cross the track here and join a rough lane.

3 Stay on the lane as it climbs gradually. The Arun can be seen below, threading its way through the valley. Pass some **ruined farm outbuildings** and keep ahead, the lane dwindling to a track along this stretch. Veer left at the fork and follow the **waymarked public right of way**. Head for a signposted crossroads and take the left-hand **public bridleway**.

4 Walk down the **chalk track**, pass through a gate and continue the steep descent. Look for two gates down below, set some distance apart. Cross to the right-hand gate and a reassuring bridleway sign is seen here. Follow the bridleway as it bends left, climbing steeply towards **Downs Farm**. Keep a fence on the left and follow the bridleway as it merges with a wide track.

5 Keep left at the next junction and follow the **South Downs Way** towards the entrance to **Downs Farm**. Veer to the right of the gateway and join a narrow footpath which begins a steep descent. Drop down

*Bewick's swan
(Cygnus columbianus)*

while you're there

Amberley Castle was built on the watermeadows of the River Arun by the Normans. It was strengthened in 1380 and repairs have been made throughout its 900 years of history. Thus it survives in superb condition, to continue enjoying the unsurpassed views, flora and fauna of its riverside location. Today it is a top-class hotel, and only open to guests.

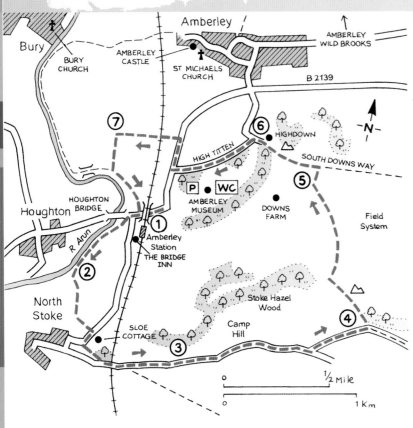

The Bridge Inn

Just two minutes walk from Amberley Working Museum and the start/finish of the walk, the Bridge Inn dates from 1650 and enjoys a super position close to the River Arun. Make the most of the sunny terrace and the lovely views in summer, while on cooler days you can retreat inside the Grade II listed building and relax in the attractive and comfortable open-plan bar and adjoining dining areas. Open log fires, Harveys Sussex Bitter on handpump and a welcoming atmosphere enhance the charm of The Bridge.

about the pub

The Bridge Inn
Houghton Bridge, Amberley
West Sussex BN18 9LR
Tel: 01798 831619

DIRECTIONS: Houghton lies west of Amberley on the B2139

PARKING: 16

OPEN: daily, all day Friday, Saturday and Sunday

FOOD: no food Monday evening

BREWERY/COMPANY: Enterprise Inns

REAL ALE: Harveys Sussex, Fuller's London Pride, guest beer

DOGS: welcome in the bar and garden

Family facilities
Families are welcome inside, and young children have their own menu.

Alternative refreshment stops
There is also a tea room at Houghton Bridge, and a restaurant at the Amberley Working Museum.

☛ Where to go from here
Head west for a few miles to visit Bignor Roman Villa and Museum, the remains of a grand house with the longest Roman mosaic (82ft/25m) in Britain (www.romansinsussex.co.uk).

---

the slope until you reach a tarmac lane and turn right. On the right-hand side is a prominent house called **Highdown**.

6 Veer left at the fork and follow a lane called **High Titten** between trees and hedgerows. The attractions of **Amberley Working Museum** can be spotted at intervals along this stretch. On reaching the road junction, turn right and follow the tarmac path parallel to the road. Turn left at the **South Downs Way sign** and follow the concrete track over the railway line to a **galvanised gate**.

7 Turn left here and follow the bridleway to the bank of the River Arun. Swing left, veering slightly away from the

riverbank, to join a drive and then turn left at the road. Cross over and turn right to return to Amberley Working Museum and its car park.

what to look for

A church at North Stoke, just off the route, is mentioned in the Domesday Book, though nothing here is earlier than the 13th century. The windows in both transepts have some of the most striking early tracery in southern England. From the higher ground, above North Stoke, look across the Arun Valley to the 'Alpine' spire of the church at South Stoke. On a good day you might pick out distant Arundel Castle.

Food
Among the popular dishes are steak, Stilton and mushroom pie, loin of pork with creamed horseradish and parsnip, sea bass grilled with rosemary, Sussex sausages and mash, fresh tuna with mango and ginger chutney, and traditional roast beef on Sunday. Snacks include ploughman's lunches and mussels cooked in garlic, herbs, cream and white wine, served with crusty bread.

60

did you know?

The River Arun is a major West Sussex watercourse, and is the second-fastest-flowing river in the country. It rises 390ft (120m) above sea level at St Leonard's Forest near Horsham and flows for over 25 miles (40km) before reaching the sea at Littlehampton.

The River Arun flowing past houses

Amberley and Bignor Roman Villa

A tour of sandy forests and heathland, and thatched villages snuggling below the South Downs.

Amberley and Bignor

The little knot of streets in Amberley is worth exploring house by house: an extraordinary number of them are thatched or half-timbered. At the start or finish of the ride, follow the no-through road past the church to reach the outer wall of the medieval castle. It is now a hotel and not open to the public, but is worth a look for its marvellous position, brooding over the

marshy meadow known as Amberley Wild Brooks, a rich haunt of birdlife, including teal and Bewick swans.

As you approach Bignor Roman Villa, all you see is a series of strange thatched huts. These shelter what is one of the finest Roman villas ever discovered in Britain. It was found in 1811 by Joseph Tupper who was ploughing the land here when he unearthed a magnificent mosaic floor depicting Ganymede's abduction by an eagle. It was soon realised how important this mostly 4th century AD building was, and the farmer made it a tourist attraction, erecting these shelters. Many Roman villas were built in locations with a beautiful view, and Bignor is no exception.

the ride

1 With The Black Horse on your right and the White House on your left follow the road out of Amberley. Past the **Sportsman pub**, turn left at a T-junction (signposted Greatham). By a building on the left you will see some **sandstone crags** away to the left, an inviting feature for children to clamber up. Turn left at the next junction, signposted Greatham. (If you carry on a short way towards Wiggonholt you will reach the lodge on the right at the edge of Parham Park; from here a ten-minute walk into the estate gives you a good distant view of the grand Elizabethan house.)

2 At the next junction, turn left to **Coldwaltham**, but first detour ahead along a track to **Greatham church** (soon reached via a gate on the right). This is a lovely, unspoilt church with no electricity – it's lit by oil lamps – and with ancient beam structures known as kingposts supporting the roof. The route soon crosses **Greatham Bridge**, with its ten rather wonky arches (a footpath on the near side gives access to the river bank and a lovely view). Wheel across the A29 carefully and take the road ahead signposted **Fittleworth**.

3 After **Coldwaltham Farm** on the right, turn left on a farm road towards **Waltham Park Farm** (if you prefer to avoid the off-road section, do not turn off here;

Above: Detail from a mosaic found at the Roman Villa at Bignor

---

3h00 15 MILES 24.1 KM LEVEL 123

SHORTER ALTERNATIVE ROUTE

2h15 11 MILES 17.7 KM LEVEL 123

MAP: OS Explorer 121 Arundel and Pulborough

START/FINISH: The Black Horse, Amberley village centre; grid ref: TQ 030132

TRAILS/TRACKS: nearly all on quiet roads, with a short section over fields and along well-drained but very sandy tracks; a road alternative is provided

LANDSCAPE: woodland, wetland, parkland, farmland and views of the South Downs

PUBLIC TOILETS: none on route

TOURIST INFORMATION: Arundel, tel: 01903 882268

CYCLE HIRE: City Cycles, 44 Bognor Road, Chichester, West Sussex, tel: 01243 539992

THE PUB: The Black Horse, Amberley

❶ Dismount to cross the A29. The off-road section at Point **3** avoids the B2138, which can be busy, but you will have to push your bike along a soft, sandy path. The full ride has two steep hills

Getting to the start

Turn off the B2139 between Storrington and the A29 at a sign for Amberley and the Black Horse. Park on roadside.

Why do this cycle ride?

From the thatched village of Amberley, the route heads along quiet lanes looking up to the South Downs, before passing silent country estates, timber-framed cottages and the entrance to Bignor Roman Villa. You might spot birds over the wetland of Amberley Wild Brooks.

Researched and written by: Tim Locke

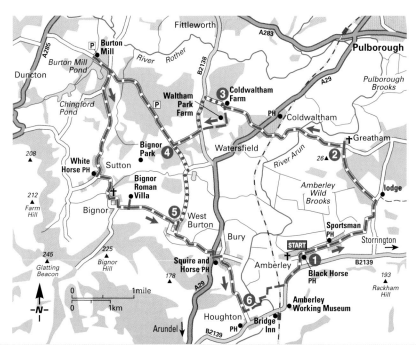

did you know?

The field cricket (Gryllus campestris) is now sadly extremely rare. With a body length of about 1 inch (24mm), it favours short grassland and lives in burrows. The adult may be seen from May to June, with the male singing from the burrow entrance in warm weather.

The bittern (Botaurus stellaris)

Bees swarm above the honeycombs inside a tree hollow

did you know?

Once upon a time Amberley produced large amounts of honey. So important was this crop that the villagers 'wassailed' their bees – that is, they were feted with singing, dancing and drinking of mead.

Above: A large cottage in Amberley

instead carry on to the B2138, turn left then take the first right, signposted Bignor). Fork left at the farm, down an eroded **rocky track**, and turn right at the bottom on a **signposted bridleway** (avoiding the signposted footpath just before). The route is sandy and you will have to push most of the way. Cross the B2138, taking the road ahead signposted Bignor.

4 For the short route turn left in front of the gates to **Bignor Park** to follow signs for **Bignor Roman Villa**; keep right at the first junction and rejoin the main route in West Burton. For the full route, turn right at the gates. Pass a large heath – **Lord's Piece** – grazed by ponies on the left; this is the last site in Britain where you can find field crickets. At the top, keep left towards **Duncton**. At the next junction go straight ahead to **Burton Pond**, which was created for the long-vanished iron industry and which once powered Burton Mill (occasionally open in summer). Here you may spot kingfishers, bitterns and great crested grebes, and there's a nature trail

that skirts the pond. Return to the junction and turn right towards **Sutton**. Turn left in Sutton, by the **White Horse pub**, following signs to Bignor, and pass a wonderful thatched, half-timbered 15th-century house called Yeoman's House. After Bignor church continue to Bignor Roman Villa, then carry on to West Burton.

5 In West Burton take the road signposted to Bury, crossing the **A29** by the traffic island and taking the road opposite and to the right to **Bury**. Turn right in the village, towards **Houghton**.

6 After 1 mile (1.6km) turn left on the **South Downs Way** (marked with blue arrows) and follow the waymarkers across two fields, turning right on the river bank, over the **river bridge** and right on the other side, then left. At the **B2139**, turn left and take the first road on the left back into **Amberley**.

The Black Horse

The Black Horse is a lovely old pub at the heart of this beautiful South Downs village, often called the 'Pearl of Sussex'. One of several knocked-through cottages, it has been nicely revamped, with flagstones, dark red walls, log fires, old pictures and prints on the walls, and heavy beams hung with sheep bells and shepherds tools, donated by the last shepherd to have a flock on the South Downs.

Food

Good traditional bar food is served throughout the pub. Choices include sandwiches (with salad and chips), ploughman's lunches, lasagne, steak and ale pie and home-made curries. Evening dishes may include rack of lamb and fillet steak with tiger prawns.

Family facilities

Children over the age of six are allowed in the bar and restaurant if they are well behaved and eating with their parents. On fine days head for the lovely walled garden.

Alternative refreshment stops

Try the Sportsman, just east of Amberley, the White Horse in Sutton or the Squire and Horse on the A29 at Bury. Burton Mill sometimes serves teas in high summer (tel: 01798 869575 to check first). There is also Houghton Bridge Riverside Tea Garden and Restaurant and The Bridge Inn just off the route near Amberley Working Museum and by the B2139 river bridge.

☛ Where to go from here

Set in a disused chalk pit Amberley Working Museum (www.amberleymuseum.co.uk) is an open-air museum giving an absorbing look at the industrial heritage of the south east, and featuring transport, electricity, telecommunications, industries such as printing, a wheelwright's and resident craftspeople – among them a blacksmith and a clay-pipe maker. Visit the Roman Villa at Bignor along the route (www.romansinsussex.co.uk).

about the pub

The Black Horse
High Street, Amberley
West Sussex BN18 9LR
Tel: 01798 831552

DIRECTIONS: at the north end of the village: from the B2139, drive into Amberley keeping right at the junction; the pub is on the next corner

PARKING: street parking only

OPEN: daily; all day

FOOD: daily; all day Sunday

BREWERY/COMPANY: Pubmaster

REAL ALE: Greene King IPA, Charles Wells Bombardier

Conditions are good for hang-gliders at Devil's Dyke

did you know?

The round-headed rampion, whose local name is Pride of Sussex, is the county's adopted wild flower. It was once quite common, but is now being edged out by hardier scrub and coarse grasses which have thrived since grazing on the South Downs has declined.

A circuit of Devil's Dyke by Poynings

A fine walk with glimpses over the most famous of all the dry chalk valleys.

Devil's Dyke

Sussex is rich in legend and folklore, and the Devil and his fiendish works crop up all over the county. The local landmark of Devil's Dyke blends the natural beauty of the South Downs with the mystery and originality of ancient mythology.

Devil's Dyke is a geological quirk – a spectacular, steep-sided downland combe or cleft 300ft (91m) deep and half a mile (800m) long. It was probably cut by glacial meltwaters in the Ice Age. Rising to over 600ft (180m), views from this beauty spot stretch for miles in all directions. Artist John Constable described this view as the grandest in the world.

Devil's Dyke has long been a tourist honey pot. During the Victorian era and in the early part of the 20th century, the place was akin to a bustling theme park, with a cable car crossing the valley and a steam railway coming up from Brighton. On Whit Monday 1893 a staggering 30,000 people

visited the area. In 1928 HRH the Duke of York dedicated the Dyke Estate for the use of the public forever, and in fine weather it can seem just as crowded as it was in Queen Victoria's day. With the car park full and the surrounding slopes busy with people, Devil's Dyke assumes the feel of a seaside resort at the height of the season. Hang gliders swoop over the grassy downland like pterodactyls, and kite flyers spill from their cars. The views more than make up for all the visitors, and away from the chalk slopes and the car park the walk heads for more peaceful surroundings.

the walk

1 From the Summer Down car park go through the kissing gate and veer right. Join the **South Downs Way** and follow it alongside lines of trees. Soon the path curves left and drops down to the road. Part company with the South Downs Way at this point, as it crosses over to join the **private road** to Saddlescombe, and follow the verge for about 75yds (69m). Bear left at the footpath sign and drop down the bank to a stile.

2 Follow the line of the tarmac lane as it curves right to reach a **waymark**. Leave the lane and walk ahead alongside **power lines**, keeping the line of trees and bushes on the right. Look for a narrow path disappearing into the vegetation and make for a stile. Drop down some steps into the woods and turn right at a **junction** with a bridleway. Take the path running off half-left and follow it between fields and a wooded dell. Pass over a stile and continue to a stile in the left boundary. Cross a footbridge to a further stile and now turn right towards **Poynings**.

3 Head for a gate and footpath sign and turn left at the road. Follow the parallel path along to the **Royal Oak** and then continue to **Dyke Lane** on the left. There is a **memorial stone** here to George Stephen Cave Cuttress, a resident of Poynings for over 50 years, erected by his widow. Follow the tarmac bridleway and soon it narrows to a path. On reaching the fork, by a National Trust sign for **Devil's Dyke**, veer right and begin climbing the steps.

The South Downs seen from Devil's Dyke

1h30	3 MILES	4.8 KM	LEVEL 1 2 3

MAP: OS Explorer 122 South Downs Way: Steyning to Newhaven

START/FINISH: free car park, Summer Down; grid ref: TQ 268112

PATHS: field and woodland paths, 6 stiles

LANDSCAPE: chalk grassland, steep escarpment and woodland

PUBLIC TOILETS: by Devil's Dyke pub

TOURIST INFORMATION: Brighton, tel: 0906 711 2255

THE PUB: Royal Oak, Poynings

❶ Steep steps up the South Downs. Suitable for fitter, older children.

Getting to the start

Poynings is north of Brighton, west of the A23. Take the A281 for Henfield, then turn left for Poynings. Turn left in front of the church, then at the next T-junction, turn right. Follow this road for about 1 mile (1.6km) and turn right, signposted 'Dyke'. The car park is on the right after about 500yds (457m).

Researched and written by: Nick Channer, David Halford

61

WALK

The view west from Devil's Dyke

did you know?

Devil's Dyke was so named because it was said to have been scooped out by the Devil. His dastardly plan was to fill it with water and then release a flood on the surrounding villages, and thus stem the growth of Christianity. Views northwards from Devil's Dyke over the Weald are extensive. On a clear day you can see the North Downs, the Surrey Hills and Ashdown Forest.

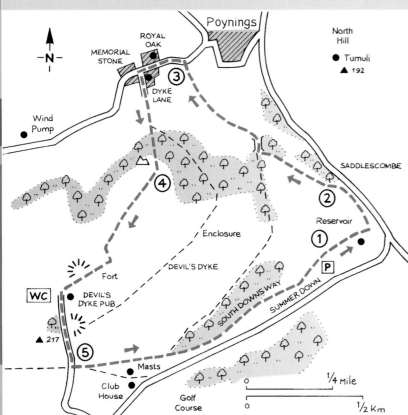

Royal Oak

Nestling at the foot of the South Downs, close to the famous Devil's Dyke, this white-painted pub is popular in summer for its excellent barbecues. So, if walking this way on a fine summer Sunday, time your walk to coincide with the sizzling barbecue and relax with the family in the large garden, which has a huge marquee for a play area. The Royal Oak is a great community pub and you might happen upon their jazz lunches, charity bungee jumps and dancing Morris Men in the garden – it's that sort of place. The unpretentious and comfortably furnished bars are equally welcoming on less clement days, and you'll find Sussex-brewed Harveys Bitter on tap.

about the pub

Royal Oak
The Street, Poynings
Brighton, East Sussex BN45 7AQ
Tel: 01273 857389
www.royaloakpoynings.biz

DIRECTIONS: west of the village centre

PARKING: 50

OPEN: daily, all day

FOOD: daily, all day Saturday and Sunday

BREWERY/COMPANY: free house

REAL ALE: Harveys Best, Greene King Abbot Ale and Old Speckled Hen

DOGS: very welcome inside (biscuits offered)

British' meals – perhaps steak and kidney pie, beer-battered cod and local sausages and mash. Fresh dressed Selsey crab with crusty bread is a popular daily special.

Family facilities
Children are very welcome and their menu is better than most, offering a child's portion of a roast on Sunday. There's a safe, large garden for summer days.

Alternative refreshment stops
The Devil's Dyke pub, three quarters of the way round the walk, has a family dining area and garden patio. Fish and chips, mixed grills and salads feature on the menu.

☛ Where to go from here
Explore the pair of windmills known as Jack and Jill at nearby Clayton. Jill Windmill is a restored post mill, originally constructed in Brighton in 1821 and moved to this location in 1852. She is still open for corn grinding demonstrations on summer Sundays, while her more solid, black-painted companion remains silent.

what to look for

Devil's Dyke consists of 183 acres (74ha) of open downland which is home to all manner of flora and fauna, including horseshoe vetch, the Pride of Sussex flower and the common spotted orchid. The adonis blue butterfly also inhabits the area. The Dyke lies within the South Downs Area of Outstanding Natural Beauty and is a designated Site of Special Scientific Interest (SSSI).

Take a stroll through the village of Poynings, pronounced 'Punnings' locally. The village takes its name from the Poynages family, which held the manor here during the Middle Ages. Michael de Poynages, a 14th-century lord of the manor, left two hundred marcs (£2,400) in his will towards the building of the Church of Holy Trinity.

4 Follow the path up to a gate and continue up the **stairs**. From the higher ground there are breathtaking views to the north and west. Make for a **kissing gate** and head up the slope towards the inn. Keep the **Devil's Dyke pub** on your left and take the road round to the left, passing a bridleway on the left. Follow the path parallel to the road and look to the left for a definitive view of **Devil's Dyke**.

5 Head for the **South Downs Way** and turn left by a National Trust sign for **Summer Down** to a stile and gate. Follow the trail, keeping Devil's Dyke down to your left, and eventually you reach a stile leading into **Summer Down car park**.

Food
Expect a varied menu that includes some good, hearty lunchtime snacks – thick-cut sandwiches, excellent cheese ploughman's (see the blackboard for the day's cheese selection), filled 'jackets', and 'best of

Ditchling Beacon · EAST SUSSEX

did you know?

Ditchling has a strong association with the arts: Eric Gill, sculptor and typographer, and Frank Brangwyn, the Newlyn artist, both lived here. And Dame Vera Lynn still does.

did you know?

Beacons were built from 16th century until the late 19th century. Mounted on high points throughout the southern counties, they were lit as a means of warning the local militias when invasion threatened.

Sheep on a chalky path in the Sussex countryside

Ditchling Beacon and the Chattri War Memorial

One of the most spectacular sections of the South Downs, with views all the way.

Jack and Jill windmills

A hundred years ago the South Downs were dotted with windmills. These two are among the last to survive. Jill Windmill (www.jillwindmill.org.uk) is a wooden corn mill, restored to working order and open free of charge in the afternoon on most summer Sundays and bank holidays. Built in Brighton in 1821, it was originally called Lashmar's Mill. Neighbouring Jack Windmill is a brick tower mill, built in 1866 and now a private house, but you can see it from the car park. They both fell into disuse around 1906 and were probably first nicknamed Jack and Jill in the 1920s.

Chattri War Memorial

The white, Sicilian marble war memorial, inscribed in English and Hindi, is a strangely exotic feature in the Sussex countryside. Erected in 1921, it is dedicated to Indian servicemen who lost their lives in World War One. Some 4,000 were taken to a temporary hospital in Brighton's Royal Pavilion (which must have seemed a very strange place to find themselves in). The Hindus and Sikhs who did not survive were cremated here in funeral pyres sprinkled with symbolic, fruits, flowers and spices in accordance with their religious customs.

the ride

1 Turn left out of the car park, signposted **'public bridleway to Ditchling Beacon'**

and immediately ignore a private driveway on the left to Jack Windmill and another track to the left. Soon fork left uphill at a junction, signposted **South Downs Way** (the right turn goes to a farm). Blue arrow markers with acorn motifs denote the South Downs Way, which you follow for most of the ride. The track rises quite steeply at first and is stony, but it soon levels out and becomes less rough. There are huge views northwards over the Weald and you can see the Surrey hills in the distance. The escarpment is too steep for ploughing, and the wildlife is relatively undisturbed. Nine types of orchid, including the bee orchid (named for obvious reasons) grow hereabouts, and you may spot a pale blue chalkhill butterfly.

2 From **Ditchling Beacon car park** cross the road carefully and take the **South Downs Way** opposite. You will pass one of two dew ponds on the route: this is a man-made feature, created for livestock to drink from, and has a clay lining to stop water draining into the porous chalk. The route climbs up two grassy rises and drops slightly to cross a narrow farm road. From here it becomes clay rather than chalk on the surface, and can be sticky after rain.

3 After the next left, a descending fork (which you avoid), look for a **track** on the right, marked with a blue arrow which leads to a group of trees at the end of the field. This is the site of **Plumpton Plain**, a Bronze Age settlement. Carry on along the South Downs Way.

4 Just beyond a gate is a National Trust sign for **Black Cap**. Walk up to the summit by forking left to the **trig point**.

Enjoy the view which stretches to Seaford Head, a prominent, square-looking sea cliff, and to the Downs near Lewes. Return the same way, to **Ditchling Beacon**.

5 Unless you want to return along the South Downs Way, turn left at the very top of the main ascent after Ditchling Beacon (where **Jack Windmill** comes into view ahead). It's marked with a blue arrow and a sign for '**Chattri and the windmills**' (just after another junction by a signpost on the right marked as the 'Keymer Post', while left is signposted to Brighton). Carry on down, with Brighton in view ahead, and at the second gate (with a waymarker symbol marked 'Chattri and the windmills' and with the number 13 on it), detour ahead to see the **Chattri war memorial**.

6 After the next gate, you'll see the memorial just down on your left. Leave your bike at the top and walk down. Return to the junction at the previous gate and turn left, following signs: the route bends right (number 44) on a fenced path slightly uphill, left (number 45), then downhill and turns right leaving the indicated route to 'Chattri and the windmills' (at number 46), which continues ahead. The track drops and rises, crossing the South Downs Way. passing through a farm to reach Jack and Jill windmills.

3h00 | **11 MILES** | **17.7 KM** | **LEVEL 123**

MAP: OS Explorer 122 South Downs Way: Steyning to Newhaven

START/FINISH: free car park by Jack and Jill windmills; grid ref: TQ 304134. Alternative start: Ditchling Beacon car park, south of Ditchling; grid ref: TQ 333131

TRAILS/TRACKS: quite bumpy chalk and grass tracks, with some sections along clay

LANDSCAPE: chalk downland

PUBLIC TOILETS: none on route

TOURIST INFORMATION: Brighton, tel: 0906 711 2255

CYCLE HIRE: Lifecycle, The Tile House, Preston Park, Preston Road, Brighton tel: 01273 542425 (www.lifecyclebrighton.com)

THE PUB: The Bull, Ditchling

! An energetic ride, with several ascents and descents – not suitable for young children

Getting to the start

Jack and Jill windmills: follow the A273 south from Hassocks, past junctions on the left with the B2112 and turning to Clayton, then turn left just before Pyecombe up Mill Lane. Ditchling Beacon: follow the B2112 south, then fork left on the road leading up to Ditchling Beacon. The car park is on the right at the very top (begin at Point 2).

Why do this cycle ride?

This is a challenging ride, but don't be too put off by the beginning. After that there are some lovely sections on the grassy Downs on either side of Ditchling Beacon. You can either ride from Jack and Jill to Ditchling Beacon and back, continue to Black Cap, or go along tracks to the Chattri Indian war memorial and back to Jack and Jill.

Researched and written by: Tim Locke

did you know?

Anne of Cleves House is a 16th-century timber-framed Wealden hall house. The house is possibly built on the site of King Alfred's royal manor, but Anne didn't ever live here; it was part of her settlement when her marriage to Henry VIII was annulled in 1541. She stayed in England and ironically regularly visited the court. The house hosts civil weddings.

The timber-framed Anne of Cleves House

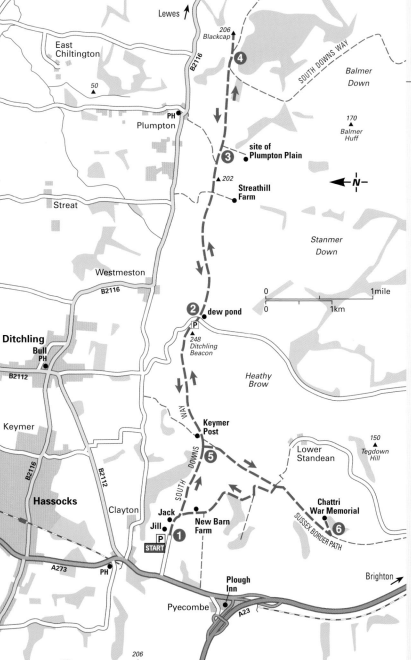

The Bull

Standing in a picturesque street in Ditchling, at the base of the South Downs, The Bull is a welcoming 14th-century beamed inn that has been comfortably refurbished. In the Inglenook Bar is an enormous fireplace with a roaring log fire in winter, low ceilings, old settles and dark wooden furnishings that give the room an ancient, time-worn feeling. Step into the Poacher's Bar and the décor is more modern, with large dining tables, Shaker-style chairs, an open fire and modern art lining the walls. Expect home-cooked food and four handpumped real ales.

about the pub

The Bull
2 High Street, Ditchling
Brighton, East Sussex BN6 8TZ
Tel: 01273 843147

DIRECTIONS: drive down to the A273, turn right towards Hassocks, then first right to Ditchling; the Bull is in the centre of the village, by the crossroads (park in the pub car park or the free public car park opposite). From Ditchling Beacon, turn left out of the car park and follow the road down to Ditchling

PARKING: 25

OPEN: daily; all day

FOOD: daily

BREWERY/COMPANY: free house

REAL ALE: Harveys Best, Greene King Old Speckled Hen, guest beers

ROOMS: 4 en suite

Food
The interesting menu includes sandwiches, dishes of marinated olives, home-made soups and main meals such as medallions of pork fillet with roasted vegetables, sausages and mash, and marinated halloumi, feta and vegetable brochette.

Family facilities
Children are welcome throughout the pub and smaller portions of adult dishes are available. Lovely sun-trap side terrace with views of the village and South Downs.

Alternative refreshment stops
There may be an ice-cream van in the car park at Ditchling Beacon.

☛ Where to go from here
Brighton (www.visitbrighton.com) is in view for much of this ride. It lies some 5 miles (8km) south and is an easy drive via the A23. In warmer months there's a lot happening along the waterfront, including beach volleyball, craft and books stalls and fortune tellers. The Royal Pavilion is a fantastically lavish seaside palace built by George IV, an Indian fantasy that becomes rather more Chinese inside. Just across the little park, there's the free Brighton Museum and Art Gallery which has something for everyone.

From Firle Place to Charleston Farmhouse

Alfriston, where people can meet at the foot of a Saxon market cross

Climb high above a sprawling estate and look towards distant horizons on this superb downland walk.

Feudal Firle and decorated Charleston

Stroll along the South Downs Way between Alfriston and the River Ouse and you can look down towards the sleepy village of Firle, nestling amid a patchwork of fields and hedgerows below the escarpment. There is something that sets this place apart from most other communities. Firle is an estate village with a tangible feudal atmosphere.

At the centre of the village is Firle Place, home to the Gage family for over 500 years and now open to the public. The 18th-century house is magnificent, though it hardly looks classically English. It's built of a pale stone specially imported from Caen in Normandy, with hipped roof, dormers and a splendid Venetian window surmounting the rusticated central archway in the east front. Firle Place is surrounded by glorious parkland and set against a magnificent backdrop of hanging woods. No house could occupy a finer location. A tour of the house reveals some fascinating treasures. The paintings include a collection of old masters with works by Van Dyck, Gainsborough, Reynolds and Rubens and there are also collections of Sèvres porcelain and English and French furniture.

Charleston Farmhouse is also open to the public, and provides a complete contrast to Firle. It was the rustic home in the early 20th century to artists Duncan Grant and Clive and Vanessa Bell, members of the Bloomsbury Set. They personalised the house by painting murals and decorating the furniture.

Above: 18th-century Firle Place

the walk

1 Turn left out of the car park, pass **The Ram Inn** and follow the road round to the right, through the village of **Firle**. Pass the village stores, a footpath to Charleston, and a path to Firle's **Church of St Peter**, all on the left, and continue heading southwards out of the village.

2 Turn right at a junction of concrete tracks and make for the road. Turn left, head for the downland escarpment and begin the long climb, steep in places. On reaching the car park at the top, swing left to a **gate** and join the **South Downs Way**.

3 Head eastwards on the long distance trail and to **Firle Beacon**, passing a **trig point**. Look out for a bridleway crossing over the South Downs Way and bear left.

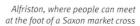

what to look for

In Firle's main street is the quaint old village stores. Until the time when cars began to make shopping in towns and cities easier, Firle benefitted from a tailor, a bootmaker, a butcher and a baker. A blacksmith, a miller and a harness maker also operated in the village.

It's always pleasing to find a church open to visitors, and the sign at the entrance to Firle's church states that the door is open from dawn to dusk. The parish refuses 'to be deterred by occasional thefts, believing it must be available to the people of the village.' The church includes a window dedicated to Henry Rainald Gage KCVO, the 6th Viscount who succeeded to the title in his 17th year in 1912 and died in 1982. The window was designed by John Piper and is possibly his last work in stained glass.

3h30	6.5 MILES	10.4 KM	LEVEL 123

MAP: OS Explorer 123 South Down Ways: Newhaven to Eastbourne

START/FINISH: free car park, Firle; grid ref: TQ 468075

PATHS: tracks, paths and roads

LANDSCAPE: downland and farmland

PUBLIC TOILETS: Firle Place and Charleston Farmhouse

TOURIST INFORMATION: Lewes tel: 01273 483448

THE PUB: The Ram Inn, Firle

❶ Long, occasionally steep ascent and descent of the South Downs escarpment. Best tackled by older family groups as the walk is quite long

Getting to the start

West Firle is signposted south off the A27 between Lewes and Eastbourne, 5 miles (8km) east of Lewes. Pass the entrance to Firle Place on the left, bearing slightly right. The entrance to the village car park is about 50yds (46m) further on, on the left.

Researched and written by:
Nick Channer, David Halford

A field of wheat dotted with red poppies

did you know?

The story of Firle and of the Gage family would not be complete without an account of the greengage. In the 18th century Thomas Gage, a botanist and traveller, introduced a small green plum-like fruit to England, which he first grew at Firle Place. The fruit was named the greengage in Thomas' honour.

The Gage Chapel in the Church of St Peter, Firle

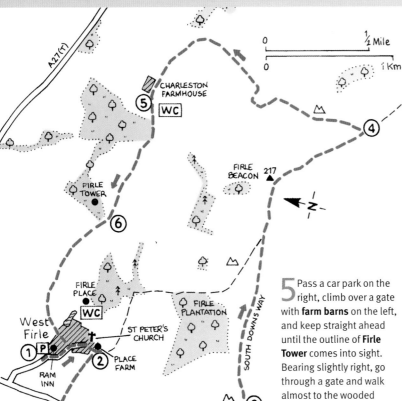

The Ram Inn

5 Pass a car park on the right, climb over a gate with **farm barns** on the left, and keep straight ahead until the outline of **Firle Tower** comes into sight. Bearing slightly right, go through a gate and walk almost to the wooded corner of the field, then bear left to another gate. Swing right to the next gate and continue ahead, with a close-up view of the **tower**. It was built in 1819 to house the gamekeeper.

4 Make for a gate and head diagonally down the escarpment. Aim for a gate and skirt a belt of **woodland** before continuing straight on at a junction of tracks. Pass a house called **Tilton Meadow** and bear left at the next junction, after a large hay barn. Follow the concrete bridleway to a right-angled bend, then swing immediately left towards **Charleston Farmhouse**, once home to members of the Bloomsbury Set.

6 Make for a line of trees and briefly pick your way between them to the edge of a field. Keep to the right-hand edge of the field and make for a gap by some **houses**. Go through a wrought-iron gate by the side of a **brick and flint cottage** and cross the lane to a footpath and gate. Follow the waymarked path across the parkland, cross the main drive and follow the sign for the **church**. Look for a kissing gate and track and follow it to the road. Turn right and return to the car park at Firle.

Family facilities
Children are truly spoilt here – there are toddler, child and hungry small adult menus, and a huge play/family room with microwave and toys. The safe rear garden has play equipment, and the added attractions of a tame goose and cat.

Alternative refreshment stops
Firle Place has a licensed restaurant serving lunches and cream teas. There's also a tea room at Charleston Farmhouse.

☛ Where to go from here
The attractive medieval town of Lewes has many quaint corners to explore, a splendid castle dating back to Norman times, and an intriguing museum in a lovely timber-framed house that once belonged to Anne of Cleves (www.sussexpast.co.uk).

Built of brick and flint and partly tile-hung, The Ram displays a fascinating mixture of periods. The Georgian part was once the local courthouse. Other parts are older – the kitchen dates back nearly 500 years – and there are 14 staircases in this rambling former coach stop. The main bar is a simple, unpretentious affair with a motley collection of tables and chairs and old photos, huge log fires and a comfortably worn and very relaxed atmosphere. Expect few modern-day intrusions here, but all the time-honoured amusements – traditional darts, dominoes, shove halfpenny and toad-in-the-hole. It's not smart, but the Harveys beer is tip-top, the welcome to booted walkers and families is genuinely warm and friendly. A charming flint-walled garden with rustic tables makes an idyllic spot for summer drinking.

Food
Menu choices range through burgers, pasta and varieties of ploughman's to fish and chips, turkey and ham pie, and beef stew and dumplings. Afternoon cream teas.

about the pub

The Ram Inn
Firle, Lewes
East Sussex BN8 6NS
Tel: 01273 858222

DIRECTIONS: on the road into the village, near the car park at the start of the walk

PARKING: use village car park

OPEN: daily, all day

FOOD: daily, all day Friday, Saturday and Sunday

BREWERY/COMPANY: free house

REAL ALE: Harveys Sussex

DOGS: welcome inside on a lead

did you know?

The Sussex coast was notorious for smuggling. The remote shingle beach at Cuckmere saw many a successful smuggling run, although this is difficult to confirm as only the unsuccessful attempts were recorded.

One of the earliest of these was when a French ship was captured in the process of picking up a cargo of wool; the crew of six was imprisoned. Wool was smuggled out of the country to avoid paying tax.

The chalk cliffs that characterise England's south coast

Cuckmere Haven and the Seven Sisters Country Park

Follow a breezy trail beside the Cuckmere River.

Cuckmere Haven

Cuckmere Haven is one of the few undeveloped river mouths in the south east. It was used by smugglers in the 18th century to bring ashore brandy and lace. The scene has changed little, with the eternal surge of waves breaking on the isolated shore. Cuckmere River joins the English Channel here but not before it makes a series of extraordinarily wide loops through water-meadows – earning it the occasional epithet 'Snake River'. Winding ever closer to the sea, the Cuckmere emerges beside the white chalk cliffs known as the Seven Sisters. There are, in fact, eight of these, with the highest, Haven Brow (253ft/77m), closest to the river mouth. On the other side of the estuary rise Seaford Head cliffs, now a nature reserve.

The focal point of the lower valley is Seven Sisters Country Park, 692 acres (280ha) imaginatively planned to blend with the coastal beauty of this area. There are artificial lakes and park trails, and a visitor centre with many interesting exhibits and displays. Wildlife plays a key role, providing naturalists with many hours of enjoyment. The flowers and insects here are at their best in early to mid-summer, while spring and autumn are a good time for views of migrant birds.

Early migrant wheatears may be spotted in the vicinity of the river mouth from late February onwards, and are followed later by martins, swallows, whinchats and warblers. Keep a careful eye out for whitethroats, terns and waders, too. The lakes and lagoons tend to attract waders such as curlews, sandpipers and little stints. Grey phalaropes have also been seen in the park, usually after severe autumn storms. These elusive birds spend most of their lives far out to sea, usually off South America or western Africa.

The walk explores this part of the Cuckmere Valley and begins by heading for the beach. As you make your way there, you might wonder why the river meanders the way it does. The meltwaters of the last Ice Age shaped the landscape and over the centuries rising sea levels and a freshwater peat swamp influenced the river's route to the Channel. Around the start of the 19th century the sea rose to today's level, and a new straight cut with raised banks shortened the Cuckmere's journey. This unnatural waterway controls the river and helps prevent flooding in the valley.

the walk

1 Make for the gate near the entrance to the **Seven Sisters Country Park** and follow the wide, grassy path towards the beach. The path gradually curves to the right, running alongside a **concrete track**. The Cuckmere River meanders beside you, heading for the open sea. Continue ahead between the track and the river and make for a **South Downs Way sign**.

what to look for

Shingle plants thrive on the sheltered parts of beaches, and a stroll at Cuckmere Haven reveals the yellow horned-poppy and the fleshy leaved sea kale. Sea beet, curled dock and scentless camomile also grow here. If you have the time, take a look at the Seaford Head Nature Reserve, which lies on the west side of Cuckmere Haven. This chalk headland, which rises 282ft (85m) above the sea, is a popular local attraction and from here the coastal views are magnificent.

1h30 | **3 MILES** | **4.8 KM** | **LEVEL 123**

MAP: OS Explorer 123 South Downs Way: Newhaven to Eastbourne

START/FINISH: fee-paying car park opposite the Seven Sisters Country Park visitor centre, at Exceat; grid ref: TV 518995

PATHS: grassy trails and well-used paths; mostly beside the Cuckmere or canalised branch of river

LANDSCAPE: exposed and isolated valley and river mouth

PUBLIC TOILETS: opposite car park, by visitor centre

TOURIST INFORMATION: Seaford, tel: 01323 897426

THE PUB: Golden Galleon, Exceat Bridge

🛈 Suitable for children of all ages

Getting to the start
The visitor centre for the Seven Sisters Country Park is just east of the turning at Exceat on the A259 which is signed to Westdean and Alfriston. Park on the south side of the A259, by the green phone-box.

Researched and written by:
Nick Channer, David Halford

Whitethroat
(Sylvia communis)

did you know?

Sea kale (Crambe maritime) is a seashore plant from the mustard family which has edible cabbage-like leaves. It is also known as scurvy grass. Sea beet (Beta vulgaris maritime) is a sprawling perennial that clings to cliffs, shingle beaches and other coastal habitats. Spikes of green flowers appear from July to September.

The red-rumped swallow
(Hirundo daurica)

2 Avoid the long distance trail as it runs in from the left, pass it and the **Foxhole campsite** and keep ahead, through the gate towards the beach. Veer left at the **beach** and South Downs Way sign. On reaching the next gate, don't go through it. Instead, keep right and follow the beach sign. Pass a couple of **wartime pill-boxes** on the left, an evocative reminder of less peaceful times, and go through a gate. Join a stony path and walk ahead to the beach, with the white cliff walls of the **Seven Sisters** rearing up beside you.

3 Turn right and cross the shore, approaching a **Cuckmere Haven Emergency Point sign**. Branch off to the

right to join another track here. Follow this for about 50yds (46m) until you come to a junction and keep left, following the **Habitat Trail** and **Park Trail** (not signed). Keep beside the **Cuckmere** – the landscape here is characterised by a network of meandering channels and waterways, all feeding into the river. Pass a turning for Foxhole campsite and follow the footpath as it veers left, in line with the Cuckmere. Make for a kissing gate and continue on the straight path by the side of the river.

4 Keep ahead to the road at **Exceat Bridge** and on the left is the **Golden Galleon** pub. Turn right and follow the A259 to return to the car park at the country park.

Golden Galleon

This 18th-century inn is a popular refreshment stop for walkers tackling the South Downs Way, and enjoys magnificent views down the Cuckmere estuary to the sea. Formerly a shepherd's bothy, it has grown enough to comfortably accommodate TV crews making an episode of Eastenders, *a Gary Rhodes commercial and a Dickens costume drama. The pub is also thought to have inspired Rudyard Kipling's poem 'Song of the Smugglers'. High-trussed and pitched rafters create an airy feel to the spacious and smartly modernised main bar. But the place to be after this walk is out in the sloping garden, soaking up the views and refreshing pints of Harveys Sussex Bitter.*

Food
Printed menus list a broad range of traditional pub food. Typically, choose from an imaginative range of sandwiches (chicken, mozzarella, tomato and pesto – served until 5pm), 'small plates' like soups, salads and fishcakes, and 'large plates', such as sausages and mash, beef, mushroom and ale pie, and sirloin steak with peppercorn sauce.

Family facilities
Children are welcome in the pub, and families will find a range of children's dishes chalked up on a blackboard, and baby-changing facilities in the toilets.

Alternative refreshment stops
The visitor centre at the Seven Sisters Country Park has a restaurant and tea rooms.

☛ Where to go from here
Paradise Park and Gardens at Newhaven (www.paradisepark.co.uk) has gardens to explore, plus interactive displays and dinosaurs which move at Planet Earth, and rides and amusements for youngsters.

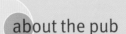

about the pub

Golden Galleon
Exceat Bridge, Seaford
East Sussex BN25 4AB
Tel: 01323 892247
www.mbplc.com

DIRECTIONS: immediately west of Exceat Bridge on the A259

PARKING: 100

OPEN: daily, all day

FOOD: daily, all day

BREWERY/COMPANY: Mitchells & Butler

REAL ALE: Bass, Harveys Sussex, Adnams Bitter

DOGS: allowed in a designated area in the pub and the garden

Lullington Heath National Nature Reserve was established to conserve one of the largest areas of chalk heath remaining in Britain. The fine, slightly acid soil has allowed the development of an intimately mixed chalk and heath community. Species of acid soil plants such as heathers and tormentil grow alongside others that have adapted to the chalk, such as thyme, salad burnet and dropwort.

Purple heather (Calluna vulgaris)

A circuit from Wilmington

Below: The Long Man at Wilmington, of unknown age, was renovated with white bricks in 1874

This downland walk visits a legendary chalk figure which has baffled archaeologists and historians for hundreds of years.

The Long Man of Wilmington

One of Britain's most impressive and enduring mysteries is the focal point of this glorious walk high on the Downs. Cut into the turf below Windover Hill, the chalk figure of the Long Man of Wilmington is the largest representation of the human figure in western Europe and yet it remains an enigma, its origins shrouded in mystery. For centuries experts have been trying to solve this ancient puzzle but no one has been able to prove who he is or what he symbolises.

The earliest drawing, made in 1710 by John Rowley, a surveyor, suggests that the original figure was a shadow or indentation in the grass rather than a bold line. It seems there were distinguishing facial features which may have long faded; the staves being held were not a rake and a scythe as once described and the head was originally a helmet shape, indicating that the Long Man may have been a helmeted war-god. Until the 19th century the figure was only visible in a certain light, particularly when there was a dusting of snow or frost on the ground. The Long Man's ghostly aura, the chill, wintry conditions and the remoteness of these surroundings would surely have been enough to send a shiver down the spine. In 1874, a public subscription was raised through *The Times* and the figure re-cut. To help define the outline of the Long Man, the site was marked out in yellow bricks, though

this restoration work may have incorrectly positioned the feet. In 1969 further restoration work began and the yellow bricks were replaced with pre-cast concrete blocks. These are frequently painted now, so that the shape of the Long Man stands out from a considerable distance away.

Photographed from the air, the figure is elongated, but when viewed from ground level, by an optical illusion he assumes normal human proportions. The walk passes as close as it can to the Long Man before heading out into isolated downland country.

the walk

1 Make for the car park exit and follow the path parallel to the road, heading towards the **Long Man**. Bear left at the next gate and take the Wealdway to the chalk figure. Climb quite steeply, curving to the right. Go through a gate, avoid the Wealdway arrow and go straight ahead towards the escarpment, veering right just below the Long Man.

2 Go through the next gate, cross a **track** and bear left on reaching a fence. A few paces brings you to a gate and a sign for the **South Downs Way**. Pass a small reservoir and follow the track to the road.

3 Turn left and walk down to a signpost for **Lullington church**, following the path beside several cottages. After visiting the church, retrace your steps to the road and turn right. Head down the lane and look for **Alfriston church** on the right. Pass a turning to the village on the right and continue ahead towards Seaford. Look out for a **postbox** and swing left here, signposted '**Jevington**'.

4 Follow the **bridleway** as it climbs steadily between tracts of remote downland. Keep left at the next main junction and there is a moderate climb. Avoid the bridle track branching off to the left and continue ahead towards Jevington. **Lullington Heath National Nature Reserve** is on the right now. Pass a bridleway to

3h00 | **6.25 MILES** | **10.1 KM** | **LEVEL 1 2 3**

MAP: OS Explorer 123 South Downs Way: Newhaven to Eastbourne

START/FINISH: long-stay car park, Wilmington; grid ref: TQ 543041

PATHS: downland paths and tracks, stretch of country road, 1 stile

LANDSCAPE: dramatic downland on east side of Cuckmere Valley

PUBLIC TOILETS: at car park

TOURIST INFORMATION: Eastbourne, tel: 01323 411400

THE PUB: The Giants Rest, Wilmington

🛈 Although quite long, this walk is generally easy and suitable for experienced children of all ages

Getting to the start

Wilmington is signposted south off the A27 between Lewes and Eastbourne, 2 miles (3.2km) west of Polegate. Drive through the village to locate the car park on the right at the top of the hill.

Researched and written by:
Nick Channer, David Halford

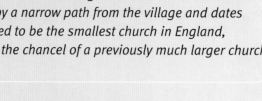

while you're there

The actor Dirk Bogarde mentioned Lullington church in his childhood autobiographies. It is accessed by a narrow path from the village and dates from the 12th century. It is reputed to be the smallest church in England, although all that remains is only the chancel of a previously much larger church.

Left: Lullington church
Right: Skylark (Alauda arvensis)

Charleston Bottom on the right and keep on the track as it climbs quite steeply. Pass a second **sign and map** for the nature reserve and make for a junction with the **South Downs Way**.

5 Turn left and follow the enclosed path to a gate. Go straight ahead alongside **woodland** and pass through a second gate. The path begins a gradual curve to the left and eventually passes along the rim of a spectacular dry valley known as **Tenantry Ground**. Keep the fence on your left and look for a gate ahead. Swing right as you approach it to a stile and then follow the path beside the fence, crossing the top of the **Long Man**.

what to look for

Wilmington Priory, by the car park, was founded for the Benedictine abbey of Grestain in Normandy, and much of the present building dates from the 14th century. As few as two or three monks resided here and they used the parish church in Wilmington rather than build their own place of worship. The monks were engaged in managing the abbey's English estates. The priory is in the care of the Landmark Trust and used as a holiday let. It is not open to the public.

6 Glance to your right and you can just make out the head and body of the chalk figure down below. It's an intriguing view. Continue, keeping the fence on the right, and descend to a **gate**. Turn right here and retrace your steps to the car park at Wilmington.

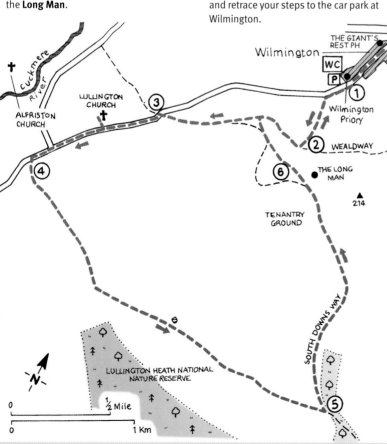

The Giant's Rest

The Giants Rest is a tall Victorian building with a comfortably worn interior. It has an informal atmosphere and offers a friendly welcome to walkers. It takes its name from the giant 240ft (73m) Long Man of Wilmington carved into the chalk downland above the village. On cooler days you can relax in the long wood-floored bar on old pews and benches at rustic pine tables. If you're early and lucky, make sure you bag the fireside seats. There are plenty of newspapers to peruse and traditional games to play (there's usually a puzzle or bar game on each table) while you savour an excellent pint – try the award-winning Timothy Taylor Landlord.

Food

Using fresh produce from local suppliers, the menu lists a good selection of home-cooked food. Typically, tuck into warm salads (smoked duck and bacon), whole grilled plaice with herb butter, local sausage ploughman's, home-cooked ham with bubble-and-squeak and home-made chutney, or daily dishes such as wild rabbit and bacon pie or salmon fishcakes with lemon mayonnaise.

Family facilities

Children of all ages are welcome indoors if well behaved. Good summer alfresco seating on the front lawn and rear terrace with super Downland views.

Alternative refreshment stops

Nearby Alfriston offers a good choice of pubs and tea rooms.

about the pub

The Giant's Rest
The Street, Wilmington, Polegate
East Sussex BN26 5SQ
Tel: 01323 870207

DIRECTIONS: at the north end of the village, near the junction with the A27

PARKING: 12

OPEN: daily, all day Saturday and Sunday and summer school holidays

FOOD: daily

BREWERY/COMPANY: free house

REAL ALE: Timothy Taylor Landlord, Harveys Sussex, Hop Back Summer Lightning

DOGS: welcome on leads

☛ Where to go from here

Just west of here, visit Drusillas Park, one of the very best small zoos in England (www.drusillas.co.uk). Admire the meerkats, bats, penguins, monkeys and reptiles in naturalistic environments, and take part in activities from gold panning to a train ride through the llama paddock.

did you know?

The village of Jevington is named after a Saxon settlement of which Jeva was the local tribal chief. Winston Churchill visited the village in 1940 to watch the final proving of the newly developed Churchill tank on the hills above the village.

Winston Churchill

Friston Forest and Cuckmere Haven

| 4h00 | 12 MILES | 19.3 KM | LEVEL 123 |

SHORTER ALTERNATIVE ROUTE

| 2h00 | 7 MILES | 11.3 KM | LEVEL 123 |

66

CYCLE

Three wonderful contrasts: the Cuckmere river, as it meanders its way to the sea, the tranquil greenery of Friston Forest, and the sweeping views from the top of the South Downs.

Cuckmere Haven
The winding Cuckmere River ends at Cuckmere Haven, the only undeveloped estuary in Sussex, where there is a glorious view along the bottom of the Seven Sisters to the left and the cottages on Seaford Head to the right. The beach is shingle and shelves quite steeply, so this is for stronger swimmers only. During the war, a mock town with lights was built here to mislead enemy bombers into raiding this instead of Newhaven; there are still fortifications here, including concrete 'dragon teeth' tank traps seen to the right, just before the beach. The meadows, reed beds and ponds are important habitats for wildlife. As you approach the beach you will pass an artificial lagoon, made in 1975, and a nesting and feeding area for birds.

Above: A family day out along safe paths

Friston Forest and Westdean village
The forest was planted in the early 20th century over an underground reservoir: at some points on the route you can see the waterworks and water tower. Westdean is a secluded village surrounded by the forest. Next to the church stands a rectory dating from the late 13th century.

the ride

1 From the car park go down towards the vehicular entrance, and just before the road turn right on a track signposted '**public bridleway to Westdean**'. Look out for the bicycle symbols in green, which denote the bike trail you will be following for the first part of the ride.

2 At the first house at Westdean keep forward on the track (signposted **Exceat Hill**), following the green bike symbols. After 1 mile (1.6km) reach a junction marked with five tall red-and-white posts.

3 For a short return to **Westdean**, fork left almost immediately after, and continue following the **green bike symbols**, turning right at the hard forest road (to the left you can see the tall **red and white posts**), then soon left at another bike symbol. The track rises (at the top a short path leads up right to a **viewpoint** over the forest and to the sea) and then falls. Leave the waymarked

trail at a three-way fork, keeping right downhill, past a barrier and houses, then turn right at a road junction into Westdean. Pass the **church** and rectory and drop to a T-junction by **Pond Cottage**, then go ahead towards the flight of steps, where you turn right along the track you were following earlier and retrace to the start.

For the main route, continue ahead at Point 3 and fork left near some **power lines**. Go past a barrier, and forward again on joining a metalled road, which becomes less surfaced (ignore side turns). On reaching a road, turn left along it to **Jevington**. Note the blue plaque on the Hungry Monk restaurant, informing you this was the birthplace of banoffee pie in 1972.

4 Turn left at Jevington and take the track signposted **South Downs Way** and church: inside there is a 1,000-year-old stone carving of Christ stabbing a beast (AD 950), the triumph of Good over Evil. Continue uphill on the South Downs Way, which steepens through the woods (too steep for cycling). Ignore side turns.

5 At the top, emerge from the **woodland**, ignore the South Downs Way to the right and keep forward. There are wonderful views inland and towards the sea from this track, and just to the left is **Lullington Heath Nature Reserve**, where there is an unusual combination of plants because of the acidic conditions on the chalky soil. The track later drops steeply and then rises up to a junction by a small **flint pillar** on the left. Slightly hidden to the right is **Winchester's Pond**, a small pond that is the haunt of dragonflies. Carry on ahead and downhill, forking left

MAP: OS Explorer 123, South Downs Way: Newhaven to Eastbourne

START/FINISH: Seven Sisters Country Park pay car park (on north side of A259; grid ref: TV 518995

TRAILS/TRACKS: well drained, compacted earth and forest tracks, level concrete track to Cuckmere Haven; short downhill road section, steep rough tracks and two stony descents on the long ride

LANDSCAPE: forest, riverside, shingle beach, open chalk downland

PUBLIC TOILETS: at the start

TOURIST INFORMATION: Eastbourne, tel: 01323 411400

CYCLE HIRE: The Cuckmere Cycle Company (by Visitor Centre), tel: 01323 870310; www.cuckmere-cycle.co.uk

THE PUB: The Plough and Harrow, Litlington

❶ Cycle carefully and give pedestrians on the track to Cuckmere Haven priority at busy times. The full ride on the South Downs Way is unsuitable for younger children

Getting to the start
From the A259 between Eastbourne and Seaford, turn off at Seven Sisters Country Park, behind the visitor centre, and immediately turn right for the car park.

Why do this cycle ride?
On this route you will find deep, varied forest laced with cycle paths, and a level, easy ride to the shingle beach at Cuckmere Haven for a famous view of the Seven Sisters.

Researched and written by: Tim Locke

66

CYCLE

while you're there

The Seven Sisters Sheep Centre is actually a working farm based around a 17th-century flint barn – there are lots of other animals including pigs, goats, rabbits and chicks to be fed and cuddled.

Lambing time in March/April is a good time to go, or watch the sheep being milked from July to September. You can ride on a tractor trailer, or retire to the Hayrack Tea Room for a real Sussex cream tea when exhaustion sets in.

The Plough and Harrow

Gloriously situated on the edge of the South Downs, this extended 15th-century brick-and-flint pub stands in sleepy Litlington in a secluded spot in the Cuckmere Valley. Original wattle-and-daub walls and a large open fireplace in the small original building hint at the pub's old age, while the carpeted, low beamed lounge and 'railway dining-car' restaurant in the more modern extension are tastefully furnished. There is a sun-trap front garden and an attractive rear lawn with smart benches and umbrellas for summer drinking.

Food
Good, wholesome pub fare includes ploughman's lunches, home-made pies (steak and Harveys stout), fresh battered cod, dressed Cromer crab with chilli and lemon oil, and Sussex smokies – smoked haddock, cream and potatoes with cheese topping.

Family facilities
Children are very welcome inside and there's a children's menu available.

about the pub

The Plough and Harrow
Litlington, Alfriston
East Sussex BN26 5RE
Tel: 01323 870632

DIRECTIONS: the pub is on the full ride; if you are following the short ride, load up your bikes and turn right out of the car park to get there, or cycle there (an easy 1.6 miles/2.5km each way). It is on the left of the road, near the church

PARKING: 50

OPEN: daily; all day Saturday and Sunday

FOOD: daily

BREWERY/COMPANY: free house

REAL ALE: Harveys Bitter, Badger Tanglefoot, Greene King Old Speckled Hen, guest beer

Alternative refreshment stops
Exceat Farmhouse Restaurant (by the visitor centre) serves meals and snacks. You can also try Litlington Tea Garden in Litlington, the Eight Bells, Jevington, just off route, or the Golden Galleon at Exceat, just west of the start, via the A259.

☛ Where to go from here
South east from Exceat is the Seven Sisters Sheep Centre (www.sheepcentre.co.uk), one of the world's largest collections of sheep, with many rare breeds and other farm animals. Visit the Clergy House in Alfriston (www.nationaltrust.org.uk), or visit Drusillas Park (www.drusillas.co.uk), one of the best small zoos in the country.

---

later to **Litlington**, where the track twists left and then right by **farm buildings**.

6 At the road, turn left through Litlington, past the tea gardens and **The Plough and Harrow** pub. As you continue along the road you can see the figure of a **white horse** etched into the hillside across the valley. The road leads back to the turning to

Westdean and the car park at Exceat. To extend the ride, wheel your bike between the restaurant and **visitor centre** on a brick path to the main road. Cross very carefully and take the gate opposite, near the bus stop. The concrete track leads towards the **sea**. Keep right at two forks, following a bicycle route to the **beach**. Return the same way.

Map labels:

Drusillas Park
Folkington
Polegate
Alfriston
Windover Hill
188
214
SOUTH DOWNS WAY
Eight Bells PH
Winchester's Pond
Plough and Harrow PH
Litlington
134
5
Jevington
Lullington Heath Nature Reserve
Hungry Monk
4
white horse
133
Charleston Bottom
Friston Forest
West Dean
START
visitor centre
Seaford
Exceat
A259
108
Golden Galleon PH
3
water works
Friston
Seven Sisters Country Park
East Dean
A259
Eastbourne
Cuckmere Haven
Seven Sisters
Seven Sisters Sheep Centre
Cuckmere River
-N-

0 ——— 1mile
0 ——— 1km

Hampton Court Workshops

Hampton Court is home to the prestigious Royal School of Needlework, established 1872 to promote embroidery skills. A notable recent piece was the Commonwealth Balcony Hanging for Buckingham Palace, for the Golden Jubilee celebrations.

while you're there

In Kingston look beside the Guildhall on the High Street for the Coronation Stone, a modest lump of greywether sandstone which played a part in the coronations of 10 Saxon kings, including Athelstan, Edward the Martyr and Ethelred. It later found a practical function as a mounting block for horse-riders in the Market Place, and was moved to this spot in 1935. In London Road, look out for David Mach's sculpture of 12 leaning phone boxes, called Out of Order.

Kingston-upon-Thames to Hampton Court

2h00 · 7 MILES · 11.3 KM · LEVEL 123

Above: Kingston Bridge
Left: Traffic-free cycling

MAP: OS Explorer 161 London South

START/FINISH: The Boaters Inn, Canbury Gardens, Kingston-upon-Thames; grid ref: TQ 179702

TRAILS/TRACKS: largely compacted gravel, with some surfaced sections

LANDSCAPE: riverside

PUBLIC TOILETS: Kingston-upon-Thames

TOURIST INFORMATION: Kingston-upon-Thames, tel 020 8547 5592

CYCLE HIRE: none available locally

THE PUB: The Boaters Inn, Kingston-upon-Thames

❗ Give way to pedestrians on the shared riverside path

Getting to the start

From Seven Kings car park in Skerne Road go up Down Hall Road, alongside the railway, and head north to the Boaters Inn via the riverside path. The Boaters Inn is in Canbury Gardens, 0.5 mile (800m) north of Kingston Bridge on the eastern bank of the river. Lower Ham Road runs parallel to the A307 Richmond Road. There are pay-and-display car parks in Kingston-upon-Thames town centre.

Why do this cycle ride?

This is a straightforward ride suitable for all ages and links the pleasant market town of Kingston-upon-Thames with the familiar landmark of Hampton Court Palace via the excellent riverside path.

Researched and written by: James Hatts

A traffic-free riverside ride to one of Britain's most famous royal palaces.

Hampton Court Palace

The palace is often associated with Henry VIII, who in just ten years spent more than £62,000 (equivalent to £18 million today) rebuilding and extending Hampton Court. At the time of his death, Henry had more than 60 houses and Hampton Court was his fourth favourite; he spent 811 days here during his 38-year reign, and all of his six wives came to the palace. The story of Hampton Court goes back to the early 1200s, when the site was first occupied by the Knights Hospitallers of St John of Jerusalem. For another royal occupant of the palace, however, it was later to become a prison – Charles I was held here for three months. George II was the last monarch to use the palace fully; his heir George III didn't much care for Hampton Court, remarking after a fire in some outbuildings that he 'should not have been sorry if it had burnt down'. The palace was opened to the public by Queen Victoria in 1838. Today, besides the palace itself, the world-famous maze and the Great Vine (planted in 1768) continue to delight thousands of visitors every year.

the ride

1 From **The Boaters Inn** turn south along the shady riverside path. Just before the railway bridge follow the **signed cycle route** to the left along Down Hall Road. Turn right at Skerne Road and follow the cycle track under the railway bridge. Use the cycle crossing provided to cross **Wood Street**. Take the buses-and-cyclists-only section of Wood Street round the side of the Bentall Centre, following round to reach the crossroads with Clarence Street. Turn right to approach **Kingston Bridge** using the clearly marked cycle lane.

2 Cross the bridge on the segregated **cycle path** and turn left along the riverside. Keep to the surfaced track known as **Barge Walk**.

did you know?

The little island of Ravens Ait has a history that dates back to the 16th century, and is now a popular venue for civil weddings. It also marks the starting point for the annual Kingston Amateur Regatta, a nautical race to Kingston Bridge.

The River Thames at Hampton Court

An immaculate sunken garden at Hampton Court

3 Soon the watersports centre and yacht club of **Raven's Ait** (an island in the river) is reached. Remain on the riverside path.

4 **Thames Ditton Island**, with its 48 houses, is the next major landmark on the river. **The Pavilion**, designed by Sir Christopher Wren, is on the tow path here. When the surfaced track resumes you are now on **Pavilion Terrace**. Follow the brick wall of Hampton Court Park; soon views of the Broad Walk will emerge. Closer to the palace the path gets wider and will be busy on a fine summer's day.

5 The ride ends at **Hampton Court Bridge**; you may wish to explore the Palace and grounds before returning to Kingston retracing your outward route.

The Boaters Inn

The key to this modern pub's appeal lies in its splendid riverside location, with fine views of the busy Thames. There are moorings provided for those arriving by boat and the 10 per cent discount for rowers demonstrates that this waterside pub takes its river connections seriously. Colourful hanging baskets brighten the façade in summer, and the popular outdoor tables benefit from the shade of large trees in the adjacent Canbury Gardens. The Boaters is known locally for its live jazz and blues nights.

Food

Instead of conventional starters and main courses, the menu is divided into 'small plates' and 'big plates'. From the former you can order Cajun potato wedges and dip or deep-fried brie with fruit sauce; from the latter sausages with wholegrain mustard mash, and various fish, pasta and burger meals. Puddings include spotted dick and custard and blueberry cheesecake.

Family facilities

Children are welcome inside the bar. Facilities include a children's menu and baby-changing facilities.

Alternative refreshment stops

Choose from the pubs and cafés at Hampton Court.

☛ Where to go from here

Spend time exploring Henry VIII's magnificent Tudor palace at Hampton Court. Costumed and audio tours bring 500 years of history alive (www.hrp.org.uk). Visit Ham House, a fine Stuart house built in 1610 in beautiful gardens beside the

about the pub

The Boaters Inn
Canbury Gardens, Lower Ham Road
Kingston Upon Thames, Surrey
KT2 5AU
Tel: 020 8541 4672

DIRECTIONS: see Getting to the start; the pub is beside the Thames

PARKING: pay-and-display in Kingston town centre

OPEN: daily; all day

FOOD: daily; all day

BREWERY/COMPANY: free house

REAL ALE: Greene King IPA, Shepherd Neame Spitfire

Thames, containing an original collection of fine 17th-century furniture (www.nationaltrust.org.uk). Alternatively, stay local and discover more about the history of the town at the Kingston Museum (www.kingston.gov.uk/museums).

Map

Scale: 0 – ½ mile / 0 – 1km

Key locations and roads: Sandy Lane, Chestnut Avenue, A310, B358, **Bushy Park**, Hampton Wick, A308, **Boaters Inn START**, **Bentall Centre**, **Kingston upon Thames**, Lwr Ham Rd, Richmond Road, A307, Hampton Court Road, A308, Hampton Court Way, A309, **Hampton Court Palace**, **Hampton Court Park**, golf course, Pavilion Terrace, **pavilion**, **Thames Ditton Island**, *River Thames*, Barge Walk, Raven's Ait, A240, B3363, Portsmouth Road, A243, Upper Brighton Road, B364, Thames Ditton, A307, **Surbiton**

—N—

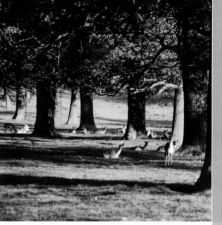

Maids of Honour

The four houses in nearby Maids of Honour Row were built in 1724 for the ladies-in-waiting of the Princess of Wales. Maids of Honour is also the name of a small almond-flavoured tart associated with Richmond, which originated in kitchens of Hampton Court.

did you know?

Richmond Park was named after the town of Richmond, in Yorkshire, by the Earl of Richmond – who became better known as King Henry VII. Welsh-born Henry (1457–1509), the first in a succession of Tudor monarchs, built a palace on Richmond Hill and set out the boundaries of his royal hunting park.

A circuit in Richmond Park

A walking safari through Europe's largest city park, Richmond Park.

Richmond Park

Richmond Park was once a royal hunting ground and, even today, it retains this upper crust image. Covering 2,500 acres (1,013ha), it is a wonderful mix of panoramic views, wildlife havens and landscaped plantations, which are worth seeing in all seasons. For the most part, the walk follows the Tamsin Trail, a 7.5-mile (12.1km) leisure path that runs around the perimeter of the park and that is for the sole use of walkers and cyclists.

The 750 or so deer are free to wander in the parkland, much of which has remained unchanged for centuries. Cars are allowed in certain areas of the park – it's not unusual for drivers to have to wait for a few minutes while a herd of deer crosses the road in front of them – but the best way to observe these beautiful creatures is on foot.

There are two types of deer in the park – red and fallow. The males and females of red deer are stags and hinds, and of fallow deer are bucks and roes. Red deer are indigenous to Britain, but fallow deer were introduced about 1,000 years ago.

Although there are enough plants to provide a nutritional diet for deer, acorns, horse chestnuts and sweet chestnuts also help to build up fat reserves during the winter months. During the rut (from September to November) the stags can often be seen fighting and herding the hinds into small breeding groups. Give them a wide berth if you pass them during the walk and keep your dog on a lead, to avoid alarming them.

If you see a bird that would look more at home in the subtropics than London, it's probably a ring-necked parakeet. These colourful birds, which have very long, pointed wings, were brought to Britain from Africa and India in the 1960s and sold as pets. Those that managed to escape began to breed successfully in the wild, and, despite the colder climate in Britain, their numbers are increasing, Noise from groups can sometimes be heard from the treetops in Richmond Park. They love to eat crab apples in summer and sycamore seeds during the rest of the year. Although they do not represent a problem to other birds, fruit growers may not be so fond of them.

the walk

1 Facing the road from the car park at **Pembroke Lodge** take the path at the far right to follow the **Tamsin Trail** in the general direction of **Ham Gate**. The path veers to the right and later runs close to the road.

2 At a crossroads leading to Ham Gate, turn left past the **Hamcross Plantation**. At the next crossroads turn right to visit the **Isabella Plantation**, otherwise continue and turn left at the next main junction, before another plantation, and circle the wood clockwise along a wide track. Bear right at the next junction and follow the path to the end of the pond.

3 Turn right along a path between the **two ponds** and continue ahead, ignoring paths branching off that would lead you to a car park. After this, turn right and follow the road that swings to the left towards

Top and right: Deer in Richmond Park

Richmond Park

2h30 **6.75 MILES** **10.9 KM** **LEVEL 123**

68

WALK

Richmond Park

SURREY

MAP: OS Explorer 161 London South

START/FINISH: car park at Pembroke Lodge in Richmond Park; grid ref: TQ 189728; Richmond Station (tube and rail) 1.5 miles (2.4km)

PATHS: mainly tarmac paths

LANDSCAPE: parkland and deer

PUBLIC TOILETS: Pembroke Lodge

TOURIST INFORMATION: Richmond, tel 020 8940 9125

THE PUB: The White Cross, Richmond

❶ Do not go close to the deer, particularly in May, June, July and October, and keep dogs on leads at this time

Getting to the start

Richmond Gate is close to the junction of the B321 and B353, a short distance off the A307 between Richmond and Kingston-upon-Thames. From Richmond station turn left into Richmond. Keep bearing left, past shops and the bridge over the river to your right. Continue up Richmond Hill to the Royal Star and Garter Home for ex-servicemen; Richmond Gate is ahead of you, leading into Richmond Park.

Researched and written by:
Rebecca Harris, Deborah King

while you're there

Richmond Palace was one of 14 royal palaces used by Henry's granddaughter, Elizabeth I – she liked to spend Christmas there as the small rooms kept it warmer. The palace itself was destroyed by Parliamentarians during the Civil War, but the brick-built gatehouse can still be seen in the town.

The Isabella Plantation woodland gardens, Richmond Park

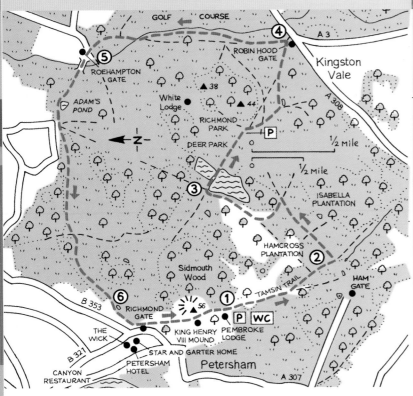

The White Cross

Set right beside the Thames, the view from this Grade II-listed pub is spectacular and much admired, especially from the glorious riverside terrace on long summer evenings. Dating from 1835, it stands on the site of a former convent of Observant Friars, whose insignia was a white cross, and cleverly escapes regular flooding thanks to the monks' design of the earlier building. Inside, a central bar serves several small and cosy rooms, each filled with dark furnishings, local prints and photographs, and open fires – one fitted under a window is still lit on winter evenings. Sash windows give it an airy feel, and the views! It serves tip-top ale from Young's and a good range of wines by the glass.

Food

All food is home cooked and may include leek and potato soup, steak pie, roast pheasant with red wine sauce, lamb shanks, chilli con carne, various pastas, sausages and fish dishes. Puddings include jam sponge and apple and rhubarb crumble. Traditional Sunday roast lunches are available.

Family facilities

Children are only allowed on the terrace, where there are large umbrellas and heaters for cool evenings.

Alternative refreshment stops

The tea room at Pembroke Lodge offers hot dishes and snacks and has seating outside on the terrace in fine weather.

☛ Where to go from here

Take the tube one stop to Kew Gardens (www.kew.org) where you can lose yourself in the magnificent conservatories and discover plants from the world's deserts, mountains and oceans. Wide-open spaces, stunning vistas, wildlife and listed buildings contribute to the Gardens' unique atmosphere.

Robin Hood Gate. Deer are often spotted here but their coats give them good camouflage, especially against a background of bracken.

4 Turn left at Robin Hood Gate. Follow the gravel path of the Tamsin Trail past the Richmond Park Golf Course and on to **Roehampton Gate**.

5 Continue over a footbridge and after a further 500yds (457m), the path winds to the right of **Adam's Pond**, which is one of the watering holes used by the deer. Follow the path across the upper end of the park, past Sheen Gate, to **Richmond Gate**.

6 Turn left at **Richmond Gate** and continue along the path to reach **Pembroke Lodge** and the start of the walk.

what to look for

In the formal garden of Pembroke Lodge is the highest point in the park, Henry VIII Mound. This prehistoric burial ground is not easy to find (take the higher path past the cottage), but well worth the effort, for here is a view of the dome of St Paul's Cathedral through a keyhole of holly. The cathedral may be 10 miles (16.1km) away from the avenue of sweet chestnuts in the park, but this is better than any optical illusion, and the view is also conserved. The King was said to have stood on this mound while his second wife, Anne Boleyn, was being beheaded at the Tower of London.

about the pub

The White Cross

Water Lane, Richmond
Surrey TW9 1TH
Tel: 020 8940 6844

DIRECTIONS: from Richmond Gate head down Richmond Hill on the left-hand side. Cross the road by Richmond Bridge and take the second left, Water Lane, to find the pub by the Thames

PARKING: none

OPEN: daily; all day

FOOD: daily; lunchtimes only

BREWERY/COMPANY: Young's Brewery

REAL ALE: Young's Bitter, Special & seasonal beers

DOGS: welcome inside

The bridge over the River Thames at Richmond

while you're there

George Vancouver (1757–98), the navigator, is buried in the churchyard of 16th-century St Peter's, in Richmond. Vancouver sailed twice with the explorer Captain James Cook, and his surveys in the 1790s of the western coastline of North America are celebrated in the city and the island named after him.

Around Richmond Park

1h30	7 MILES	11.3 KM	LEVEL 1 2 3

Discover the capital's largest open space and enjoy amazing views of the city.

Richmond Park

At 2,500 acres (1,012ha) Richmond Park is Europe's largest urban walled park, which has an abundance of wildlife in its varied landscape of hills, woodland gardens and grasslands. Charles I brought his court to Richmond Palace in 1625 to escape the plague in London and turned it into a park for red and fallow deer. There are more than 750 deer in the park today. Pembroke Lodge was the home of Lord Russell, prime minister in the mid-1800s. His grandson Bertrand Russell grew up here. The restaurant that now occupies the building enjoys spectacular views of the Thames Valley. The Isabella Plantation is a stunning woodland garden that was created in the early 1950s from an existing woodland and is organically run, resulting in a rich flora and fauna. Over 1,000 species of beetle have been recorded in the park. The ancient oaks provide a rich habitat for many types of insect. The park enjoys the status of a Site of Special Scientific Interest and a National Nature Reserve.

the ride

1 On entering the park at Richmond Gate look for the path on the left-hand side. (From Pembroke Lodge car park return to Richmond gate and turn right.) The path skirts **Bishops Pond**. Keep straight on past Cambrian Gate. Adam's Pond is to your right just beyond **East Sheen Gate**. The bridge over Beverley Brook means you are nearly at **Roehampton Gate**.

2 At Roehampton Gate cross the road. The path continues past the café and car park, where cycle hire is available. The **golf course** is to your left. Soon the path crosses Beverley Brook once again, then it remains between the brook and the park road as far as **Robin Hood Gate**.

3 At **Broomfield Hill** the steepest ascent of the ride awaits; signs advise cyclists to dismount. There is a bench at the top where you can recover, and a **refreshment kiosk** is just beyond. The Isabella Plantation is to your right. At **Kingston Gate** the route starts heading north.

4 At **Ham Gate** the path crosses the road and turns right, ascending

A busy stretch of the Tamsin Trail at Roeh

MAP: OS Explorer 161 London South

START/FINISH: Richmond Gate at Richmond Park; grid ref: TQ 184737

TRAILS/TRACKS: largely compacted gravel

LANDSCAPE: parkland and woodland

PUBLIC TOILETS: around the park

TOURIST INFORMATION: Richmond, tel 020 8940 9125

CYCLE HIRE: Roehampton Gate, tel 07050 209249

THE PUB: Lass O'Richmond Hill, Richmond

🛈 Some short, steep climbs and a couple of longer ascents through woodland

Getting to the start

Richmond Gate is at the top of Richmond Hill (B321). You can approach from Richmond town centre or if you are coming from the south leave the A307 at Star and Garter Hill. There's parking at Pembroke Lodge in the park.

Why do this cycle ride?

This is an enjoyable circuit on an easy traffic-free trail shared with pedestrians. The stunning views of St Paul's Cathedral and other London landmarks are the only reminders that you are just 10 miles (16.1km) from the centre of the capital.

Researched and written by: James Hatts

Messing About on the River

A great way to enjoy the scenery and avoid the hassle of London traffic is to catch the ferry down the Thames from Richmond to Westminster Bridge. The mini-cruise takes about 3 hours; call 020 7930 2062 for timetables and information.

The Thames surrounded by greenery at Richmond

parallel to the road. At the T-junction turn left, remaining parallel to the road. Soon the path leaves the road and opens on to a wide tree-lined avenue. As you approach **Pembroke Lodge**, glorious views of the Thames Valley unfold to the left.

5 At Pembroke Lodge the path is sometimes congested with pedestrians. Just beyond Pembroke Lodge, with the

barrow known as **King Henry VIII's mound** on your left, the cycle path unexpectedly moves to the right. At this point a marker beside the path draws attention to the incredible view of **St Paul's Cathedral**, 10 miles (16.1km) away.

6 As you ride on, a panoramic view of other London landmarks opens out. Before long you will be back at **Richmond Gate**.

Lass O'Richmond Hill

Perched high on the steep Richmond Hill this pub is ideally placed for a cycle ride around the park. The sign outside promises 'home cooked food all day, every day, 8 days a week'. The fully air-conditioned interior means that this is a pleasant place to spend time in all weathers, and the main bar is spacious and airy. Abundant window boxes and hanging baskets add a colourful touch to the exterior. There are a few tables on the pavement, but the small garden terrace to the rear is a quieter and more pleasant place to eat and drink on sunny days.

Food

The printed menu has starters such as Wexford-style Stilton and pepper mushrooms and a duo of chicken satay and tiger prawn skewers. Main courses include roast duck with a ginger and scallion sauce and asparagus, pea and mint risotto. Banana toffee crumble and strawberry shortcake are among the puddings. There are also daily chalkboard specials.

about the pub

Lass O'Richmond Hill
8 Queens Road, Richmond
Surrey TW10 6JJ
Tel: 020 8940 1306

DIRECTIONS: on Queen's Road (B353), just to the northeast of Richmond Gate

PARKING: 25 spaces

OPEN: daily; all day

FOOD: daily; all day

BREWERY/COMPANY: Chef & Brewer

REAL ALE: Courage Best, Fuller's London Pride

Family facilities

Children are made welcome and there's a children's menu for younger family members.

Alternative refreshment stops

There are various cafés in the park and at Pembroke Lodge.

☛ Where to go from here

You're spoilt for choice for places to visit after your ride. Head off to Kew Gardens and explore some of the 3,000 acres (1,215ha) and the magnificent conservatories filled with exotic plants (www.kew.org). Take the children to Twickenham Stadium for a behind-the-scenes look at the home of England rugby and Britain's top sporting museum, the Museum of Rugby (www.rfu.com).

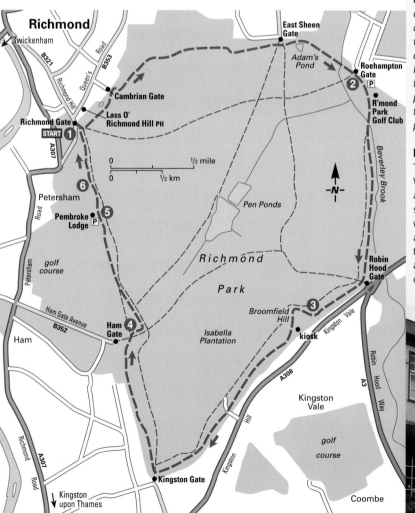

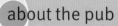

did you know?

More than 150 Boat Races have been held since the first one, in 1829, with Cambridge still just in the lead over Oxford. The first race, between Charles Merivale and Charles Wordsworth, took place at Henley. The following year the event moved to Westminster, and in 1845 to Putney/Mortlake, its present venue. The course record time of 16.19 minutes is held by Cambridge. There have been six sinkings in the course of the race, with two in 1912.

A contemporary illustration of the 1863 Boat Race

The wetlands of Barnes

Explore the award-winning London Wetland Centre and join the course of the Oxford and Cambridge Boat Race.

London Wetland Centre

Rowing boats, like birds, glide gracefully through water and also, like birds, you'll see plenty of them during this easy walk. Barnes has long been associated with the Oxford and Cambridge Boat Race. Indeed, the footbridge, added in 1895, was specifically designed to hold the crowds watching the last stage of the 4.33 mile (7km) race to Mortlake.

The riverside functions rather like a wildlife highway, providing a natural habitat for birds. There are plenty of them to see without having to put a foot inside the London Wetland Centre (LWC) – but to omit it would be to miss out on a very rewarding experience. So why not extend the walk and visit the LWC? There are more than 2 miles (3.2km) of paths and 650yds (594m) of boardwalk to explore once you have paid the admission charge.

The Wildfowl and Wetlands Trust at Slimbridge in Gloucestershire was founded by Sir Peter Scott, son of the great explorer, Scott of the Antarctic. One of his father's diaries carries the words: 'teach the boy nature' and this was indeed achieved, for Peter Scott became a renowned painter and naturalist. In recognition of his achievements, a larger-than-life sculpture of him stands on a raised gravel island at the entrance to the LWC, the only inner city wetland reserve in the world. There are now nine wetland centres in the UK. This one began with four redundant reservoirs owned by Thames Water. They formed a partnership with the housing developer, Berkeley Homes, and donated £11 million

Left: London Wetlands Centre
Below: Hammersmith Bridge

to help construct the centre. The 105 acre (43ha) project took five years to complete.

Once inside, there are three main sections: world wetlands, reserve habitats and waterlife. The first contains captive birds from around the world – North America is accessed via a log cabin complete with authentic furniture. There are information panels too. One of them contradicts the popular belief that swans mate for life. Another tells us about meadowsweet, which is found in damp woods and marshes and used in herbal teas, mead flavouring and even air fresheners.

the walk

1. Turn left out of the London Wetland Centre and follow the path, initially to the left of the **Barnes Sports Centre** and then beside some sports fields. At a T-junction turn left along the well-signposted **Thames Path**, alongside the river in the direction of Hammersmith Bridge.

2. About 100yds (91m) along the path on the left is a **stone post**, denoting the 1-mile (1.6km) marker of the Oxford and Cambridge University Boat Race. Steve Fairbairn, who was born in 1862, founded the Head of the River Race and this was the start of the world-famous, annual boat race that traditionally takes place in March.

3. The landscaped area of smart flats on the left is called **Waterside** and, a few paces further, a red-brick building bears the name **Harrods Village**. Once past this, as if replicating the trademark Harrods colours

 70

WALK

1h30 · **3.75 MILES** · **6 KM** · **LEVEL 123**

MAP: OS Explorer 161 London South

START/FINISH: London Wetland Centre; grid ref: TQ 227767

PATHS: riverside tow path, muddy after rain

LANDSCAPE: views across Thames

PUBLIC TOILETS: at London Wetland Centre

TOURIST INFORMATION: Richmond, tel 020 8940 9125

THE PUB: The Bull's Head, Barnes, SW13

❶ Much of the route is alongside the River Thames, so take extra care with young children

Getting to the start

London Wetland Centre is off the A306 between Hammersmith Bridge and the A3003 in Barnes. There is a car park (free if visiting the Centre). Alternatively, you can access the walk (near Point 5) at Barnes Bridge railway station, or reach the Wetland Centre via bus 283 (known as 'the Duck Bus') from Hammersmith tube.

Researched and written by:
Rebecca Harris, Deborah King

The Boat Race
in progress

while you're there

Barn Elms Park, on Rocks Lane in Barnes, is a modern sports field built on the site of a manor house of that name, long since demolished. Look out for a 17th-century plane tree, which has been declared one of the Great Trees of London (with 40 others) – it takes six people to reach round the trunk.

of green and gold, is **Hammersmith Bridge**. Follow the path past **St Paul's School**, where *Planets* composer Gustav Holst was a music teacher. On the opposite side of the river, Chiswick Church's green roof is visible.

4 Continue along the riverside path to the end as it reaches **Barnes Bridge**.

5 Just past **The Bull's Head** pub by the bridge, turn left into Barnes High Street. At the next junction, by the little pond, bear left into Church Road. Past the **Sun Inn** is a row of village shops and 100yds (91m) further on, the lychgate to St Mary's Church. At the traffic lights continue ahead to return to the **London Wetland Centre** and the start of the walk.

what to look for

The development, Waterside, was constructed by Berkeley Homes after the company purchased 25 acres (10ha) and built the luxury homes that have a unique, bird's-eye view of the centre and its wildlife. Adjacent, the Harrods Village building was once used to store furniture by those taking up posts in the British Empire. Derelict, it was also sold to Berkeley Homes and it now contains 250 flats with green window frames. Even the security guard wears a Harrods green and gold uniform. At the rear of the Sun Inn is Barnes Bowling Club, where Sir Francis Drake is said to have taught Elizabeth I the game of bowls.

The Bull's Head

The imposing Bull's Head overlooking the Thames was established in 1684, and has made its reputation over the last 40 years as a top venue for mainstream, modern jazz and blues. Nightly concerts in the large back room draw music lovers from miles around, encouraged by some fine cask-conditioned ales from Young's, more than 200 wines (30 by the glass) and over 80 malt whiskies. The large, open-plan and bustling bar has a central island servery, plenty of cosy alcoves, a big fireplace stacked with bottles, and a lovely old mirror. The small rear patio is ideal for summer eating and drinking.

Food
Home-cooked meals such as soups, ciabatta sandwiches, roast of the day and steak and kidney pie are on offer in the bar, while fine Thai cooking from the Nuay Thai Bistro in the converted stable is available throughout the pub in the evening.

Family facilities
Children are very welcome in the pub during the day.

Alternative refreshment stops
Unlike many on-site cafés, the Water's Edge Café at the London Wetland Centre is a delight. It's bright and spacious, serves good-quality soups, sandwiches, salads and cakes, and has outdoor seating on large, wooden tables with umbrellas. The south-facing Sun Inn on Church Road, opposite Barnes duck pond, lives up to its name – it's quite a suntrap in summer.

☛ Where to go from here
A visit to the London Wetland Centre before or after your walk is a must (www.wwt.org.uk). Chiswick Church could once be reached by a ferry across the Thames, but since 1934 the only way is by bridge. The artist William Hogarth (from whom the Hogarth Roundabout takes its name) is buried in the churchyard. Also across the bridge is Chiswick House (www.english-heritage.org.uk), a fine English Palladian villa with a magnificent Blue Velvet Room and 18th-century classical gardens.

about the pub

The Bull's Head
373 Lonsdale Road
Barnes, London SW13 9PY
Tel: 020 8876 5241
www.thebullshead.com

DIRECTIONS:	just before you turn left into Barnes High Road (on walk at Point **5**)
PARKING:	none
OPEN:	daily; all day
FOOD:	daily
BREWERY/COMPANY:	Young's Brewery
REAL ALE:	Young's Bitter, Special and Winter Warmer
DOGS:	welcome inside

Map

CHISWICK
CHISWICK CHURCH
A 316
A 4
HOGARTH ROUNDABOUT
RIVER THAMES
THAMES PATH
ST PAUL'S SCHOOL
B 350
HAMMERSMITH BRIDGE
A 4
HARRODS VILLAGE
LEG OF MUTTON NATURE RESERVE
WATERSIDE
A 306
RESERVOIR (DISUSED)
P WC
LONDON WETLAND CENTRE
MARKER STONE
BARNES
ST MARY'S CHURCH
A 3003
A 306
BARNES SPORTS CENTRE
BULL'S HEAD PH
SUN INN
BARNES BRIDGE
BARNES POND
N
½ Mile
½ Km

while you're there

You can't miss the Albert Memorial since it was restored to gilded splendour in 2000. Set on the southern edge of Kensington Gardens, it was designed as a Gothic reliquary by architect George Gilbert Scott in 1876, with a statue by J H Foley beneath the canopy of Queen Victoria's beloved Prince Consort.

Around Hyde Park

Left: Free speech is ecouraged at Speaker's Corner, Hyde Park

Safe, traffic-free cycling in Hyde Park in the heart of London

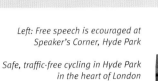

71

CYCLE

| 1h00 | 2.5 MILES | 4 KM | LEVEL 123 |

MAP: OS Explorer 173 London North

START/FINISH: West Carriage Drive car park; grid ref: TQ 269800

TRAILS/TRACKS: well-surfaced paths

LANDSCAPE: urban parkland

PUBLIC TOILETS: in the park

TOURIST INFORMATION: London Line, tel 09068 663344

CYCLE HIRE: London Bicycle Tour Company, 1a Gabriels Wharf, 56 Upper Ground, SE1, tel 020 7928 6838

THE PUB: The Wilton Arms, Kinnerton Street

❗ Be sure to give priority to pedestrians on shared-use paths. Beware of unpredictable rollerbladers!

Getting to the start
The West Carriage Drive car park is south of the bridge over the Serpentine. It can be approached from the A402 Bayswater Road to the north or the A315 Kensington Gore/Kensington Road to the south. The pay-and-display car park is open 8.30am-6.30pm.

Why do this cycle ride?
An ideal ride for families with very young children, this is a chance to make the most of a huge expanse of green space that Londoners often forget they have on their doorstep. Glance to your left as you cross the Serpentine Bridge and you'd never guess that you were in the heart of the capital. Yet elsewhere there are surprising views of familiar London landmarks.

Researched and written by: James Hatts

Discover a green oasis in the heart of the capital.

Hyde Park
Henry VIII and his court once hunted deer in Hyde Park; the Tudor monarch acquired the land from the monks of Westminster Abbey in 1536. Public access was first permitted under James I, but it was Charles I who opened the park fully to the general public in 1637. During the Great Plague in 1665 many Londoners set up camp in the park, hoping to escape the disease. The Serpentine – the vast ornamental lake dominating the park – was created in the 1730s by Queen Caroline, wife of George II.

The latest in Hyde Park's long line of royal connections is the controversial £3.6 million Diana, Princess of Wales Memorial Fountain, unveiled by the Queen in 2004. The fountain was designed by US architect Kathryn Gustafson, and is based on an oval stone ring. Water enters the fountain at its highest point, then bounces down steps. It picks up momentum and is invigorated by jets. As it flows westwards it resembles a babbling brook. Air bubbles are added as it approaches a waterfall before entering a water feature. Water from east and west meets at the reflecting pool, before being pumped out to restart the cycle.

the ride

1 From the West Carriage Drive car park, opposite the **Serpentine Gallery**, cross the road and join the cycle track on the pavement on the west side of West Carriage Drive. The Diana, Princess of Wales **Memorial Fountain** is on your right.

2 The track drops down on to the road to cross the **Serpentine bridge**. Once across be sure to look out for the point where the path resumes on the pavement, as the cycle lane on the road surface stops abruptly.

3 At Victoria Gate cross the road and follow the cycle path along **The Ring**. The path here is on the road, but it is often traffic-free.

4 As you approach Cumberland Gate and Marble Arch, look for the **cycle route sign** for Chelsea Bridge and cross the road to pick up the cycle path on **Broad Walk**. You may need to reduce speed here

Marble Arch, in the northeast corner of Hyde Park, was designed by John Nash in the 1820s as a grand gateway to Buckingham Palace. According to legend, by 1851 state coaches were too broad to fit through it; a more prosaic problem was a desire to remodel the palace frontage. The solution was to remove the arch and rebuild it in the park.

The Wilton Arms

Exuberant hanging baskets and window boxes decorate this early 19th-century pub, and a tasteful conservatory occupies the garden, so arrive early to ensure a seat in summer. Inside, high settles and bookcases create cosy individual seating areas, all fully air-conditioned. Owned by Shepherd Neame, Britain's oldest brewer, it was named after the 1st Earl Wilton and is known locally as the 'Village Pub'.

Food

The chalkboard menu lists the house speciality – a doorstep sandwich of salt roast beef with horseradish and mustard dressing. There's also beef and Guinness pie, fish and chips, lamb hotpot and a choice of curries, alongside staples such as burgers and ploughman's meals.

Family facilities

Children are welcome inside the bar if they are eating, and smaller portions of main menu dishes can be ordered.

Alternative refreshment stops

You will find various cafés and kiosks in Hyde Park.

☛ Where to go from here

Along the ride, stop off at Apsley House, The Wellington Museum at Hyde Park Corner, the 19th-century home of the first Duke of Wellington. From West Carriage Drive you are within walking distance of the South Kensington museums. Spend some time at the Victoria and Albert Museum (www.vam.ac.uk), the Natural History Museum (www.nhm.ac.uk) or the Science Museum (www.sciencemuseum.org.uk). Explore Kensington Gardens and visit the restored Kings Apartments in Kensington Palace (www.hrp.org.uk). The Serpentine Gallery has fascinating changing exhibitions of contemporary art (www.serpentinegallery.org).

as the cycle lane can be obstructed by crowds milling around at **Speakers' Corner**. It then heads south on Broad Walk, a pleasant, wide, tree-lined boulevard.

5 On the approach to **Queen Elizabeth Gate** at Hyde Park Corner, follow signs to the right for **Rotten Row** to return to the car park at West Carriage Drive. If heading for **The Wilton Arms** pub, you will need to leave the park through this gate. On Rotten Row, keep to the left on this fairly narrow path shared with pedestrians and rollerbladers. At West Carriage Drive, use the pedestrian crossing and pick up the cycle track again on the west side in front of the **Serpentine Gallery**. (This simple circular ride can be easily extended eastwards with a foray along **Constitution Hill**'s excellent parallel cycle track to see Buckingham Palace, or to the west to explore Kensington Gardens. Notices at the park entrances show where cycling is currently permitted.)

about the pub

The Wilton Arms
71 Kinnerton Street
London SW1X 8ER
Tel: 020 7235 4854

DIRECTIONS: tucked away behind Knightsbridge and best accessed from Wilton Place. From the Queen Elizabeth Gate of Hyde Park, leave the park and cross to the other side of Knightsbridge. Turn right, and continue until you reach Wilton Place, Turn left here, and take the next right. You will soon spot the pub

PARKING: none

OPEN: daily; all day

FOOD: all day; no food Sunday

BREWERY/COMPANY: Shepherd Neame

REAL ALE: Shepherd Neame Goldings, Spitfire and Master Brew

The Serpentine in Hyde Park

did you know?

There are four Inns of Court: Middle Temple, Inner Temple, Gray's Inn and Lincoln's Inn. Together they lie at the heart of London's legal profession, in a tradition that dates back to the 14th century. Back in medieval times they were hostels where lawyers stayed; now they are a prestigious institution, and while many of the buildings are private, some are open to the public, and exploring the cobbled lanes, narrow alleyways and pretty courtyards gives an insight into another aspect of this great city.

The Inns of Court

Above left: Lincoln's Inn, established in the 14th century

Soak up the atmosphere of these hidden valleys and squares that featured in many of Dickens' novels.

Dickens in legal London

The compact area highlighted here between Temple and Fleet Street is home to some fine buildings that survived the Great Fire of London. Not only that, but to walk through this great legal institution is to take a step back in time. Charles Dickens, who was a keen walker, was a frequent visitor to the area and used it as the setting for some of his novels.

Dickens first saw the darker side of life when his father was imprisoned for debt. He went to work in a shoe-blacking factory and it was this experience that formed the basis of his views on the injustice of poverty and that broadened his scope and insight. At the age of 15 he spent a year as a solicitor's clerk in Gray's Inn. Later he mastered the art of shorthand and took a job as a reporter on the *Morning Herald* before producing a series of articles for monthly and weekly publications, writing these under the pseudonym of 'Boz'. Dickens used these to highlight social issues and the plight of the poor. His novels were initially serialised, and Victorian readers, especially the lower middle classes, couldn't get enough of him – they would eagerly await the next instalment.

You'll see when you reach Fountain Court how little it can have changed in more than 150 years. The place is particularly atmospheric at dusk when the Victorian street lamps are alight. It is here that Tom meets his sister Ruth, in the novel *Martin Chuzzlewit* (1843). Further on, the Middle Temple, with its winding alleys and gardens, feels like a village. Based on his time as a solicitor's clerk, Dickens wrote: 'There is yet, in the Temple, something of a clerkly monkish atmosphere which public offices of law have not disturbed and even legal firms have failed to scare away...'

In *Martin Chuzzlewit*, Dickens describes how Tom felt about going to work in the Temple: '...he turned his face towards an atmosphere of unaccountable fascination, as surely as he turned it to the London smoke – until the time arrived for going home again and leaving it, like a motionless cloud behind'. Although the smoke is no longer around, you'll see what Dickens meant as you explore this calm little areaaway from the busy City streets.

the walk

1 Turn left at the exit to **Temple Station** and up a set of steps. Turn right into Temple Place. At the end go left into Milford Lane then, after a few more paces, go up another series of steps, into Essex Street. Turn right by the **Edgar Wallace pub** into

72

WALK

Holborn LONDON

1h30	1.5 MILES	2.4 KM	LEVEL 123

MAP: AA Street by Street london

START: Temple tube station

FINISH: Holborn tube station

PATHS: paved streets and alleyways

LANDSCAPE: alleyways and buildings of architectural interest

PUBLIC TOILETS: opposite the Law Courts in the Strand

TOURIST INFORMATION: City of London, tel 020 7332 1456

THE PUB: Cittie of Yorke, 22 High Holborn, WC1

Getting to the start

Temple tube station is alongside the Embankment on the Circle and District lines. Parking is severely limited.

Researched and written by:
Leigh Hatts, Deborah King

while you're there

The circular Temple Church is a curiosity which dates from 1185. It had links with the Knights Templar, an order of soldier monks who protected pilgrims travelling to the Holy Land, and effigies of their patrons lie within. A key scene of Dan Brown's internationally popular novel The Da Vinci Code *(2004) is set in the church.*

Temple Church

Cittie of Yorke

A pub has stood on this site since 1430. In 1695, it was rebuilt as the Gray's Inn Coffee House and the large, low-vaulted cellar bar dates from this period. Easily identified from a distance by the large black-and-gold clock that hangs outside, it is a fine piece of Victorian architecture, deceptively large inside, with ornate ceilings and an impressive back room featuring a coal-burning stove dating back to the year of the Battle of Waterloo (1815), and intimate little booths across the very long bar. The gantry above is stacked with thousand-gallon wine vats. The panelled front bar features an original chandelier and portraits of illustrious locals, including Dickens and Sir Thomas More.

Food
In addition to a variety of sandwiches, salads and soups, six hot dishes are freshly prepared each day, often including steak and ale pie and braised lamb shank.

Family facilities
Children are welcome in the eating area of the bar before 6pm.

Alternative refreshment stops
The Old Bank of England pub was a subsidiary branch of the Bank of England until the mid-1970s, when it became the flagship pub for Fuller's. It's a grand affair with chandeliers and high ceilings, and some surprisingly cosy corners. The Bunghole Cellars is a Davy's Wine Bar with sawdust on the floor, where ale is served by the half-gallon.

☞ Where to go from here
North of Holborn tube station, on Doughty Street near Russell Square tube, is the Charles Dickens Museum. The author lived in Doughty Street in his 20s and here you can see pages of his original manuscripts, together with valuable first editions and many personal mementoes (www.dickensmuseum.com). The Elizabethan Hall in the Middle Temple dates from the 16th century. It has a fine example of a double hammerbeam roof. Visitors are allowed in the hall and gallery from 10am to noon and from 3pm to 4pm.

Devreux Court, walk through the gateway into The Temple and go down the steps to **Fountain Court**. (At weekends The Temple Inn of Court is often closed and you should go past the pub front to Fleet Street and turn right. Go left at the Old Bank of England to rejoin the route.)

2 Bear left under an archway into **Middle Temple**, past a small fountain and garden and up the steps, then bear right through some cloisters to reach the **Temple Church** (open for Sunday services). Go through an archway to the right of the church, then left through another archway and along a partly cobbled road to **Fleet Street**.

3 Turn left along Fleet Street and cross at the pedestrian lights. After the Old Bank of England pub turn right into **Bell Yard** and continue ahead on the path that runs alongside the **Royal Courts of Justice**. Turn left and then right into New Square and keep ahead.

4 Take the path on the far right along **Stone Buildings** and, ahead, go through the gates that lead to Chancery Lane. Cross this road and turn right to go

left into the street called Southampton Buildings. After just 20yds (18m) this veers sharply left, past the **London Silver Vaults**. Cross High Holborn and pass through a gateway to Gray's Inn on the right of the **Cittie of Yorke pub**. A few paces further, after Gray's Inn Hall, turn left into **Field Court**.

5 Continue to the end, then turn right and go up the steps into Jockeys Fields. Bear left along Bedford Row and take the second road on the left, **Hand Court**. Just past the Bunghole Cellars at the end, turn right along High Holborn to reach Holborn tube station.

what to look for

If you pop into the Old Bank of England pub, spare a thought for those whose lives were cut short. The vaults and tunnels below the Old Bank and the nearby buildings are where Sweeney Todd is reputed to have butchered clients, the remains of whom were served as fillings in the nearby pie shop of his mistress, Mrs Lovett.

about the pub

Cittie of Yorke
22 High Holborn
London WC1
Tel: 020 7242 7670

DIRECTIONS: beside the gateway to Gray's Inn on High Holborn (on walk just before Point **5**). Nearest tube: Chancery Lane

PARKING: none

OPEN: all day; closed Sunday

FOOD: all day

BREWERY/COMPANY: Samuel Smith Brewery

REAL ALE: Old Brewery Bitter

DOGS: not allowed inside

73 WINCHESTER
HAMPSHIRE

3.5 MILES (5.7KM) 1hr 30min

PATHS: Established riverside paths through water-meadows, 3 stiles

SUGGESTED MAP: aqua3 OS Explorer 132 Winchester

GRID REFERENCE: SU 486294

PARKING: Pay-and-display car parks in city centre

THE PUB: Wykeham Arms

1 From King Alfred's statue on **Broadway**, walk towards city centre, passing **Guildhall** (tourist information centre) on L. Join High Street, then in 100yds (91m), turn **L** along Market Street. Continue ahead into Cathedral Close to pass cathedral main door.

2 Turn **L** down cloister, then **R** through Close ('**Wolvesey Castle**'), to Cheyney Court and exit via Prior's Gate. Turn **L** though Kingsgate, with tiny **Church of St Swithun** above, then bear **L** down **College Street** and shortly pass entrance to **Winchester College**. Beyond road barrier, bear **R** along College Walk then turn **R** at end of wall, along track.

3 Go **L** through gate by private entrance to **College**. Follow path beside **River Itchen** fo 0.5 mile (800m) to gate and road. Cross over and follow gravel path, alongside tributary, to gate and cross open meadow towards **Hospital of St Cross**.

4 Keep **L** alongside wall and through avenue of trees to stile. Proceed ahead along gravel path to 2 further stiles and join farm track leading to road. Turn **L** and walk length of now gated road (traffic-free), crossing **River Itchen** to reach junction of paths by **M3**.

5 Turn **L** along path. Pass gate on R (access to **St Catherine's Hill**). Keep **L** at fork and drop down to follow narrow path by **Itchen Navigation**. Go through car park to road.

6 Turn **L** across bridge and take footpath immediately **R**. Keep to path beside water, disregarding path L (College nature reserve). Soon cross bridge by rowing sheds to join metalled track.

7 Turn **L**, then **L** again at road. Follow road **L** along College Walk then bear **R** at end ('**Riverside Walk**'). Pass Old Bishops Palace (**Wolvesey Castle**) and follow metalled path beside Itchen and up steps to Bridge Street, opposite **City Mill** (National Trust). Turn **L** back to King Alfred's statue.

74 ROCKBOURNE
HAMPSHIRE

4.5 MILES (7.2KM) 1hr 45min

PATHS: Field paths, woodland bridleways and tracks, 9 stiles

SUGGESTED MAP: aqua3 OS Outdoor Leisure 22 New Forest or OS Explorer 130 Salisbury & Stonehenge

GRID REFERENCE: SU 113184

PARKING: Rockbourne village hall car park

THE PUB: Rose & Thistle, Rockbourne

1 Turn **L** out of car park. Take lane **R** towards **Manor Farm**. Turn **R**, signed to church. Cross drive to path to **St Andrew's Church**. Keep by **R-H** edge of churchyard to junction of paths. Proceed behind houses, ignoring 2 paths R. Cross stile. Go **R** through gate.

2 Follow field edge to junction of paths. Keep on **L** to gate. Maintain direction over 2 stiles and by field edge to stile in corner. Climb stile immediately **R**. Bear **L** by edge of meadow to stile. Pass in front of thatched cottage to stile and track, opposite **Marsh Farm**.

3 Bear **L**, then **R** through gate. Keep to **L** through pasture to gate. Bear half **R** to gate in corner; proceed along field edge, eventually reaching stile and lane. To visit **Roman Villa**, turn **R** to T-junction, and turn **R** into entrance. Retrace steps.

4 Take track opposite. Enter copse; at junction of tracks, take arrowed path **L** up bank into field. Keep to **L-H** edge; head across field to track. Turn **R**, then **L** downhill through woodland edge. Pass house to lane.

5 Turn **R**, then **L** along bridleway; ascend through **Radnall Wood**. At fork of paths, bear **L** (blue arrow). Pass behind **Whitsbury House** to lane. Turn **L**, then **R** along track between properties to lane. Turn **R** then **R** (by fingerpost) on bridleway through **Whitsbury Wood**.

6 At junction with track, bear **L**; walk beside paddocks to bungalow. Turn **L** along track between paddocks towards **Whitsbury church**. Turn **L** at T-junction and shortly enter churchyard. Go through gate opposite church door to lane.

7 Turn **L** for **Cartwheel Inn**, otherwise turn **R**, then **L** along farm drive and keep ahead, bearing **L**, then **R** between paddocks, uphill to gate. Turn **L** along field edge then head across field to track.

8 Turn **R** and follow track **L** to junction of tracks. Cross stile opposite and walk back to Rockbourne church. Retrace steps back to village hall.

75 SUNNINGDALE
BERKSHIRE

4 MILES (6.4KM) 1hr 45min

PATHS: Enclosed woodland paths, estate drive, paths and tracks, path across golf course and polo ground, no stiles

SUGGESTED MAP: aqua3 OS Explorer 160 Windsor, Weybridge & Bracknell

GRID REFERENCE: SU 953676

PARKING: On-street parking in Sunningdale village

THE PUB: Nag's Head

1 From **Nags Head** turn **L**. Walk down High Street, keeping Anglican **church** on R and Baptist **church** on L. Pass Church Road and proceed along Bedford Lane. Cross brook. Turn **R** by bungalows to follow path cutting between hedgerows and fields. Look for large, shuttered house (R) just before **A30**. Bear **L**. Walk to sign on R for Shrubs Hill Lane and Onslow Road.

2 Follow path to junction by panel fence. Turn **R** by bridleway/footpath sign. Curve **L**, make for roundabout and swing **L**, looking for footpath by house (Highgate). Follow it through woodland and when you join wider path on bend, keep **L**. Skirt **golf course**, cutting between trees and bracken. Emerge from woodland and follow path across fairways, keeping **L** at junction by bunker. Veer **L** at 1st fork, into trees, and follow path to junction with tarmac drive.

3 Turn **L** and pass through **Wentworth Estate**, cutting between exclusive houses with secluded landscaped grounds and imposing entrances. On reaching **A30**, turn **L** and follow road west. Walk down to **Berkshire/Surrey border** and bear sharp **R** to join right of way. Follow shaded woodland path between beech trees and exposed roots. Beyond wood you reach buildings of **Coworth Park**.

4 Draw level with bridge, turn **L** and then follow well-defined footpath across broad expanse of parkland, part of which is used as a **polo ground**, crossing track on far side. Enter woodland, turn **L** at road and pass several houses. When you reach speed restriction sign, bear **R** to join byway by Sunningdale **Bowling Club**. Proceed ahead on tarmac drive and continue ahead. Turn **L** at road, swinging **L** just after fork. Pass Coworth Road and return to centre of **Sunningdale**.

76 WARGRAVE
BERKSHIRE

6 MILES (9.7KM) 2hrs 15min

PATHS: Stretches of road, field and woodland paths,13 stiles

SUGGESTED MAP: aqua3 OS Explorer 171 Chiltern Hills West

GRID REFERENCE: SU 786785

PARKING: Public car park in School Lane, just off A321

THE PUB: St George & Dragon

1 Turn **L**. Walk along School Lane, (**B477**). On 1st bend, bear **L** into Dark Lane, head up hill; turn **R** at T-junction. Follow road; turn **L** ('**Crazies Hill**'). Bear **R** by **East Lodge**, follow lane to bend; bear **L** over stile to join waymarked path. Keep alongside fence, and across fields towards trees. Cross stile; turn **R** at road, veering **L** opposite house, '**Crouch End**'.

2 Keep close to **L** boundary of field; look for stile in bottom corner. Descend steeply to 2 stiles and bridleway beyond. Cross stile almost opposite; climb hillside. Look for stile further up slope and keep ahead on higher ground, following path alongside fence. Descend to kissing gate at road; turn immediately **R**. Head uphill passing **Worley's Farm**.

3 Take next waymarked path on **R**, just before row of trees, and aim little to **L** as you cross field, lining up with white house in distance. Head towards stile in hedge and maintain direction, keeping to **L** of house. Look for stile; follow enclosed path to road. Turn **R**, then **L** beside village hall; after few paces, bear **L** by Old Clubhouse. Follow path by paddock to stile by road. Bear **R**, past entrance to **Thistle House** and bridleway into trees on R.

4 Continue for several paces to stile on **L**. Join woodland path (watch for white arrows on tree trunks) eventually reaching waymarked junction. Turn **R** here, avoid path on R and keep going to next waymarked junction, on edge of wood. Bear **L**; walk down to flight of steps and footbridge. Make for woodland perimeter; turn **R** along field edge.

5 Cross bridleway via 2 stiles. Proceed along woodland edge. Look for hedge gap on **R**; cross into adjoining field; maintain direction. Make for kissing gate and footbridge in field corner. Proceed to kissing gate. Follow path across field, heading towards trees. Make for kissing gate leading out to road. Turn **R**. Follow it to **A321**, turn **L.** Walk to School Lane.

77 BRIMPTON
BERKSHIRE

6 MILES (9.7KM) 2hrs 45min

PATHS: Field and woodland paths and tracks, parkland drives, meadow, road and riverside, 11 stiles

SUGGESTED MAP: aqua3 OS Explorer 159 Reading, Wokingham & Pangbourne

GRID REFERENCE: SU 567628

PARKING: Limited spaces in lay-by opposite Pineapple pub

THE PUB: Three Horseshoes

1 Follow path across 2 stiles to road. Cross to join byway, follow it **R** and across **common**. When it swings sharp L, keep ahead. Take path to **R** of Woodside; bear **L** at T-junction; follow path. Where it joins track, veer **L** at waymark, following field-edge path. Look for opening in trees ahead; cross bridge; turn **R** at track, following signs ('**Wasing Church**').

2 Take track, turn **L** at bend; cut through wood. Turn **R** and proceed to road. Bear **L** to junction, then **R** over **Enborne** to fork. Keep **L** and turn **R** at 'Wasing Estate' sign. Veer **L** along grassy track to junction; bear **L**.

3 Follow path to road; turn **R**, then **L** to join path. Keep to **L** edge of field, through kissing gate in top corner; veer **R**. Turn **R** to reach housing estate. Bear **R** at road; walk along to church, following path beside it. On reaching field corner, keep ahead, swinging **L** by power lines. Head south to Hyde End Lane.

4 Turn **L**, keeping **R** at fork. Look for stile to **L** of footbridge; go across meadow. Follow river bank to reach footbridge and stile. Cross over and take path to stile and bridge. Cross over road and follow track, taking path to **L** of it along woodland edge and making for bridge in far **R** corner. Follow line of trees to stile; cross next pasture towards buildings. Approaching gate and cottage veer **L** to stile. Cross to another stile by road.

5 Turn **R** over bridge; bear **L** to gate leading into Ashford Hill Meadows, veering **L** across pastures. After 75yds (68m) it becomes enclosed by trees, look for fork, and branch **L** to footbridge. Begin crossing field, after about 120yds (109m), make for gate on **L**. Swing **R** and keep **L** at fork after about 50yds (45m). Look for stile at fence corner and continue through trees. Head for stile, turn **L**. Cross over field to next stile. Proceed; when lane bends R, bear **L** and continue to road. Continue to return to lay-by.

78 FARNBOROUGH
BERKSHIRE

7.5 MILES (12.1KM) 3hrs

PATHS: Bridleways, field paths, tracks and quiet lanes, no stiles

SUGGESTED MAP: aqua3 OS Explorer 170 Abingdon & Wantage

GRID REFERENCE: SU 471825

PARKING: Room to park in West Ilsley's main street

THE PUB: Harrow, West Ilsley

1 Follow road out of **West Ilsley**, heading west. Take 1st bridleway on **L** and make for gate. Continue ahead with field boundary on R. Bear **L** at next junction, and then almost immediately **R** to follow path across large field. Look for boundary corner ahead and keep ahead in next field, with fence on R. Follow path across field to road by **Upper Farm**, veer **L** and walk along to **Farnborough church** and **Old Rectory**.

2 Walk along road to farm, rejoin track beside outbuildings and look for waymark and galvanised gates after about 60yds (55m). Field footpath and 2 tracks can be seen here. Keep **R**, alongside farm. Cut between trees, bushes and margins of vegetation and cross track further on. Continue ahead to junction with byway and bridleway. Keep going through woodland, following Ilsley Downs Riding Route. Make for next junction, where you can see field beyond the trees, bear **R** and follow clear path through woods.

3 Keep **R** at road and when it bends R, keep ahead along bridleway running across fields towards trees. At length, bridleway becomes byway. Keep ahead on reaching bend and walk along to on **L**. Take it into woodland and down slope. As you approach gap in hedge, with field ahead, veer **R** to follow path running through trees. Eventually it climbs gently to junction. Walk turns **L**, but it is worth stepping to R for several paces to admire timeless view of **Woolvers Barn** and Woolvers Down.

4 Follow byway, avoiding public footpath on R, and take next bridleway on **L**. Keep **R** at next junction and cut between hedges. When track bends **L**, there is memorable view of **West Ilsley** sitting snug in its downland setting. Keep **R** at next junction, following track alongside **West Ilsley Stables**. Walk down to and turn **L**. As it bends R by bridleway sign, go straight on by **Keeper's Stables**. Swing **L** as you reach centre of **West Ilsley** and pass **All Saints Church**.

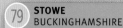

79 STOWE
BUCKINGHAMSHIRE

4.5 MILES (7.2KM) 2hrs

PATHS: Field paths, estate drives, stretches of road, 5 stiles

SUGGESTED MAP: aqua3 OS Explorer 192 Buckingham & Milton Keynes

GRID REFERENCE: SP 684357

PARKING: On-street parking in Chackmore

THE PUB: Queens Head, Chackmore

❶ Walk through **Chackmore**, pass **Queens Head** and continue through village. At speed derestriction signs, keep ahead for few paces and look for path on **L**. Aim diagonally **R** in field, passing under power lines. Make for stile beneath branches of oak in corner where waymarks indicate that path forks.

❷ Cross field towards 2 stiles, making for one on **L**, beyond which is plank bridge. Keep to **R** boundary of elongated field and when it widens, go diagonally **R** to far corner. **Stowe Castle** is visible to **R** and outline of **Corinthian Arch** to **L**. Join track, pass under telegraph

wires and look for gap and waymark as track curves **R** by hedge corner. Veer over to **R** in field and look for path ('Farey Oak'). Avoid this route and make for footbridge and stile few paces away.

❸ Cross into field and head up slope, keeping to **L** of 2 distant houses. Head for single-storey dwelling in top corner and as you climb slope, outline of **Gothic Temple** looms into view. Go through gate at **Lamport** and continue ahead on bridleway. The **Bourbon Tower** is clearly visible. Pass through gate and keep ahead towards monument commemorating Duke of Buckingham. Merge with another path and keep sports ground on **R**.

❹ Make for gate leading out to avenue of trees running down towards **Grecian Valley**. Cross over and follow grass track up to clump of trees. Bear **L** here and follow avenue (part of **Roman road**). Pass magnificent façade of **Stowe School** and keep along main drive. On reaching **Boycott Pavilions**, branch off half-**L** at stile and sign for **Corinthian Arch**. Down below lies **Oxford Water**, crossed by stone bridge.

❺ Follow drive through parkland. Drive eventually reaches **Corinthian Arch**. Line up with arch and enjoy views of **Stowe School**. Walk down avenue to road junction, swing **L** and return to **Chackmore**.

80 MENTMORE
BUCKINGHAMSHIRE

6.5 MILES (10.4KM) 2hrs 45min

PATHS: Field paths and tracks, roads and canal tow path, 2 stiles

SUGGESTED MAP: aqua3 OS Explorers 181 Chiltern Hills North; 192 Milton Keynes & Buckingham

GRID REFERENCE: Grid reference: SP 907196 (on Explorer 181)

PARKING: Limited parking in vicinity of Stag pub at Mentmore

THE PUB: Stag

❶ Walk back to junction by **Stag**, turn **R** and pass one of **Mentmore Towers'** entrances. Follow road round to **L**, then **R** by Church of St Mary the Virgin. Continue along road; bear **R** at stile, just beyond **Vicarage Cottage**. Go down field, keeping fence to **R**; look for stile in bottom boundary.

❷ Veer **R** briefly to plank bridge; swing **L** to skirt field, keeping ditch on **R**. On reaching next plank bridge and waymark, look for pond. Follow path alongside it into next

field and pass under telegraph wires to next plank bridge in boundary. Keep ahead and pass under electricity cables. Houses of **Ledburn** can be seen ahead. Make for footbridge; in next field aim slightly **L**, towards house. Keep to **L** of it, turning **R** at road.

❸ Walk through **Ledburn**, making for **L** bend. On **L** is **Cornfield Cottage**. Cross road to kissing gate and follow track running across farmland. As it curves **L**, keep ahead, following path across field. On reaching track, turn **R** and follow it to **Sears Crossing**. Cross **railway bridge**, follow track down to road. Turn **L**.

❹ Bear **R** at sign for Grove Church and Farm and down to **Grand Union Canal** at **Church Lock**. Pass Church Lock Cottage before turning **R** to join tow path. Follow **Grand Union** for about 1 mile (1.6km) and, about 140yds (128m) before bridge, with **weir** on the **L**, leave tow path at plank bridge and bear **R** for few paces to field corner.

❺ Swing **L** and keep boundary on **R**. Make for 2 gates leading out to road, turn **R**, then **L** at turning for Wing and **Ledburn**. Follow road to **Bridego Bridge**, pass beneath **railway**; keep ahead to **Rowden Farm**.

❻ Bear **L** at next junction for **Mentmore**. Pass Mentmore Courts and **Stud House** before turning **L** at end of stretch of pavement. Opposite junction are 2 wooden gates leading into field. Follow road round to **R** and return to playground and parking area.

81 BRILL
BUCKINGHAMSHIRE

4.5 MILES (7.2KM) 1hr 30min

PATHS: Field paths and tracks, several stretches of road, 8 stiles

SUGGESTED MAP: aqua3 OS Explorer 180 Oxford, Witney & Woodstock

GRID REFERENCE: SP 653141

PARKING: Room to park by windmill

THE PUB: Pheasant Inn

❶ From car park go down lane, South Hills, beside **Pheasant Inn**, keeping **windmill** visible on **R**. At lock-up garage and signpost ('Leyhill'), swing **L** to join track. Follow it round to **R** to pair of garages and cross low stile to **R**. On **R** is cottage. Keep to enclosed footpath and head for 2 more stiles before crossing rolling grassland. Head towards large house and stile to **L** of it. Cross over to road and turn **R**.

❷ Pass footpath, then look for bridleway and footpath sign further down on **R**. Cross into field at stile. Head diagonally **R** down field to plank bridge and stile. Aim broadly **L** at adjoining field, making for stile just to **R** of bottom corner.

Turn **L** and follow footpath through undergrowth to cottage. Keep **L** and bear **R** after few paces into **Oakley**. Walk along **Little London** Green to road; turn **R**.

❸ Take 1st path on **L**, opposite **Little London Farm**. Head diagonally **L** in field, pass under power lines and make for gateway. Cross next field to waymark and gate; then continue ahead across next pasture to stile and track. Bear **L** and walk up track towards **Leatherslade Farm**. As you approach farm gate, take bridlepath to **L** of it and skirt house and outbuildings. This is a modern house, built to replace the original farmhouse used by the gang after the robbery.

❹ Once clear of farmhouse buildings, keep climbing gently, passing public footpath on **R**. Cut between trees and banks of vegetation and make for next galvanised gate. Continue ahead, with field boundary on **R**. Pass several more footpaths on **R** and keep going until you reach gate in top boundary. Follow track ahead to road by entrance to house, '**Fairview**'.

❺ Keep **L** and keep ahead to **Brill**. Pass Wesleyan chapel, to **R**, across green is church. The **Red Lion** can also be seen. Pass turning on **L** to **Oakley** and look for barometer in wall. Bear **L** into Windmill Street and return to car park.

82 BURNHAM BEECHES
BUCKINGHAMSHIRE

4.5 MILES (7.2KM) 1hr 45min

PATHS: Woodland paths and drives, field paths, tracks and stretches of road, 9 stiles

SUGGESTED MAP: aqua3 OS Explorer 172 Chiltern Hills East

GRID REFERENCE: SU 957850

PARKING: Car park at Burnham Beeches

THE PUB: Blackwood Arms, Littleworth Common

❶ Follow drive away from **Farnham Common**, keeping car parking area on your **L**. Pass refreshment kiosk and veer **R** at fork just beyond. Soon reach gate where you enter National Nature Reserve's car-free zone. Follow **Halse Drive** as it curves **L** and down between trees. When you reach bottom of hill swing **L** into **Victoria Drive**.

❷ Follow broad stony drive between beeches, avoiding turnings either side of route; eventually reach major junction with wide path on **L** and **R**. On **R** is large beech tree with 'Andy 6.9.97' carved on trunk. If you miss path, you shortly reach road. Bear **R** and go up slope, keep **L** at fork and cross

several clearings to reach road at junction with Green Lane and **Park Lane**.

❸ Cross road to stile and waymark and go straight ahead, keeping boundary on **L**. Make for stile and descend into field dip, quickly climbing again to pass alongside grounds of **Dorney Wood**. Walk ahead to field corner, cross stile and turn **R** at road. Head for waymarked footpath on **L** and cross field to gap in trees and hedgerow. Turn **R** and skirt fields, making for belt of trees and banks of undergrowth. Path cuts between 2 oak trees in next field before reaching gap in hedgerow.

❹ Cross stile out to road; turn **L**. Pass Common Lane and Horseshoe Hill; turn **R** at next bridleway. Follow track through wood to next road at **Littleworth Common**. Cross stile to **R** of **Blackwood Arms** and follow Beeches Way. Beyond next stile continue ahead alongside wood, crossing 2 stiles before following fenced path. Go through gate and take path between trees of **Dorney Wood**.

❺ On reaching stile, cross over to road and continue on Beeches Way. Make for next major intersection and keep **R** along **Halse Drive**. Pass **Victoria Drive** and retrace your steps back to car park.

83 WINCHELSEA
EAST SUSSEX

4.5 MILES (7.2KM) 2hrs

Paths: Field paths and pavements, 19 stiles

Suggested map: aqua3 OS Explorer 124 Hastings & Bexhill or 125 Romney Marsh, Rye & Winchelsea

Grid reference: TQ 905173

Parking: Roadside parking near St Thomas's Church at Winchelsea

THE PUB: New Inn

❶ With **New Inn** on **L** and ruined **St Thomas's Church** on **R**, follow road round **R-H** bend. Head down to Strand Gate; then take road to junction with **A259**. Turn **R** and follow pavement.

❷ When road bends **L**, turn **R** at sign ('Winchelsea Beach'). Cross **Royal Military Canal** and bear immediately **R**. Follow tow path across empty landscape. Cross stile and avoid concrete footbridge. Eventually, canal begins to curve **L**. Here you will find a stile and galvanised gate.

❸ Bear **R** few paces beyond it at footbridge. Cross 2nd footbridge over ditch and make for stile. Pass birdwatching

hide and continue along path, making for next footbridge.

❹ Turn **R** here, veer **R** then follow path as it curves **L** through reedbeds. Begin moderate climb and head towards house. Keep to **L** of it and follow path through trees. Join drive, pass **Ashes Farm** and look for stile on **L**. Go diagonally across field to stile, then bear **R** briefly to 2 more stiles. Skirt field to next stile and exit to road. Keep **R** here ('**Winchelsea**') and soon pass below hilltop windmill, avoiding **1066 Country Walk**, which meets road at this point.

❺ Go straight ahead over stile when lane bends **L** and cross field. Look for stile and keep alongside some trees to next stile. Continue ahead, pass old pill box and head down gentle field slope to road.

❻ Turn **R** for few paces to stile on **L**. Bear **R**, still on **1066 Country Walk**, and cross next stile. Keep to **R** of **Wickham Manor** and look for stile in far boundary. Cross drive to stile and keep ahead across fields. Make for stile and gate in bottom **L** corner and follow **1066 Country Walk** waymarks. Path veers over to **R** to 2 stiles. Bear **L** and begin moderate ascent to stone stile. Turn **R** at road. Follow it round to **L** and return to centre of **Winchelsea**.

84 GODSTONE
SURREY

3.75 MILES (6KM) 1hr 45min

PATHS: Footpaths and bridleways can be muddy in places, 4 stiles

SUGGESTED MAP: aqua3 OS Explorer 146 Dorking, Box Hill & Reigate

GRID REFERENCE: TQ 350515

PARKING: Adjacent to village pond. Parking limited to 3 hours, should be plenty for this walk

THE PUB: White Hart

❶ Directly opposite pond in **Godstone**, take public footpath beside **White Hart** pub, signposted towards **church**. Cross Church Lane and follow path through churchyard. Keep **church** on **L**, and continue along winding path as it passes **Glebe Water** to yellow waymarker post at edge of open field. Turn **R** and drop down beside field to stile, then turn **L** here on to bridleway that leads under busy **A22**.

❷ Just beyond bridge, turn **R** at **Hop Garden Cottage** and follow waymarked bridleway out on to **Jackass Lane**.

Turn **R** here, opposite **Little Court Farm**, now converted into private houses. At top of hill, turn **L** for 100yds (91m) to visit **St Peter's Church**. Otherwise turn **R**, and follow Tandridge Lane to public footpath just 30yds (27m) short of **Barley Mow**.

❸ Turn **R** on to waymarked **Greensand Way**, and follow broad, sandy track between open fields to wicket gate beside **A22**. Cross main road on level, and take footpath directly opposite. Beyond small wood, 3-way wooden signpost guides you on to bridleway straight ahead. Jump tiny ford (or use footbridge) and walk up lane past **Leigh Place** pond as far as **B2236**.

❹ Leave **Greensand Way** here, and turn **R**. Follow pavement until just beyond Church Lane, then fork **L** at bus stop, up **Enterdent Road**. After 100yds (91m) turn **R** on to public footpath into woods. The waymarked path climbs, steeply in places, to stile near adventure playground on edge of **Godstone Farm**. Follow waymarked route through farm grounds, to stile just north of car park.

❺ Turn **R** on to **Tilburstow Hill** for 100yds (91m). Just beyond **Godstone Farm** delivery entrance, turn off **L** at wooden footpath signpost. Path runs briefly through farmland on edge of **Godstone** village, then leads out into **Ivy Mill Lane**. Turn **R** for short climb back to village green, then **R** again, back to car park

85 CHARLWOOD
SURREY

4.25 MILES (6.8KM) 1hr 45min

PATHS: Byways and woodland paths, short sections on village roads and farmland, 7 stiles

SUGGESTED MAP: aqua3 OS Explorer 146 Dorking, Box Hill & Reigate

GRID REFERENCE: TQ 243410

PARKING: On The Street, close to Rising Sun and post office

THE PUB: Rising Sun

❶ With recreation ground on your R, walk past **Pine Café** and turn **L** up Chapel Road. Continue on to byway and pass extraordinary **Providence Chapel**. Behind low picket fence, few tombstones lean drunkenly in front of small, weatherboarded chapel with a wooden verandah. The building, which dates from 1816, is straight out of an advert for Jack Daniels, and seems to have dropped in from Kentucky. Turn **L** at byway crossroads towards **Stan Hill**, and continue straight across **Norwoodhill Road**. At brow of hill, take signposted footpath on **L**, just at entrance to **Barfield Farm**.

❷ Path leads to corner of **Beggarshouse Lane**, where you turn **L**, and follow lane on to tree-lined byway. At woods beyond **Greenings Farm**, turn **L** over plank bridge and waymarked stile. Follow **L-H** edge of open field, then proceed to cross farm lane at pair of waymarked stiles. Continue over another pair of stiles until fence bears **L** at stile. Steer gently **R** here, towards stile in far corner of field then head across next field to stile into **Cidermill Road**.

❸ Turn **L**, and follow wide grass verge for 75yds (69m) before turning **L** again on to signposted bridleway. Soon path dodges into **Glover's Wood** and, 200yds (183m) further on, you'll come to pair of waymarker posts. Turn hard **L** at 1st one, follow waymarked footpath across **Welland Gill**, and carry on to far side of woods.

❹ Leave woods at wicket gate, and continue straight down Glovers Road. Cross Rectory Lane/Russ Hill Road, and keep ahead on footpath opposite. Path passes **St Nicholas Church** – but you must not. Inside this welcoming church are some of the finest medieval wall paintings in the country. Beyond churchyard, turn **R** past **Half Moon**, then **R** again for last 100yds (91m) back to recreation ground.

86 HEADLEY
SURREY

4.25 MILES (7.2KM) 2hrs 15min

PATHS: Mainly woodland tracks

SUGGESTED MAP: aqua3 OS Explorer 146 Dorking, Box Hill & Reigate

GRID REFERENCE: TQ 205538

PARKING: National Trust car park, Headley Heath

THE PUB: Cock Horse

❶ Face road, walk to far **R-H** corner of car park, and take bridleway on your **R**. Pass bench and follow track past **pond** to crossroads.

❷ Turn **R** here, and follow waymarked route down to parting of ways at foot of hill. Fork **R** along National Trust's waymarked route, and follow it over low rise and down to crossroads in valley bottom. Turn **L** along waymarked bridleway that climbs gently round to **L**. After 100yds (91m) turn **R**, following waymarked route that leaves track and climbs steeply up through woods to National Trust sign, half hidden in trees. If you reach road at **High Ashurst**, you've gone too far; turn back, and fork **L** after 50yds (46m).

❸ Double back to **R**, and wind your way down out of woods. Cross **Lodgebottom Road** at **Cockshot Cottage**, and climb steeply up narrow path to T-junction with good, level track.

❹ Turn **R**, and follow track as far as **Mill Way**. Just short of road, bear **R** on to horse margin and follow it until it leads you across road and then on to signposted byway.

❺ If you don't want to visit **Headley** village, turn **R** at end of byway, and rejoin route at Point ❻. Otherwise fork **L** here, into **Slough Lane**, and walk up to junction with **Church Lane**. Turn **R** on to permissive bridleway that runs beside road. Just past **Cock Horse**, fork **R** at bus stop on to signposted footpath. Follow it through to road junction, turn hard **R** into Leech Lane, and drop down to junction with Tumber Street.

❻ Turn **L** and cross **Mill Way** into Crabtree Lane. Follow waymarked horse track past **Broom House**, and up hill to pit on your **L-H** side. Bear **L** here, along blue waymarked track. Pass group of houses on your **L** and continue for 275yds (251m), until you see car park between trees on your **L-H** side. Turn **L** for short stroll back to your car.

87 BAYNARDS
SURREY

4.25 MILES (6.8KM) 2hrs

PATHS: Field and forest paths, section of old railway line

SUGGESTED MAP: aqua3 OS Explorer 134 Crawley & Horsham

GRID REFERENCE: TQ 078349

PARKING: Lay-by on Cox Green Road, Baynards, adjacent to railway bridge at start of walk

THE PUB: Thurlow Arms

❶ From lay-by, follow Downs Link signposts down on to old railway line and head north under **Cox Green Road** bridge. Soon reach wooden gate as old line approaches **Baynards Station**. Follow **Downs Link** as it zig-zags **L** and **R**, past station buildings, and back on to old line. There is small picnic area here, information panel, and **Thurlow Arms** is on **L**. Continue for 350yds (320m), until footpath crosses line at waymarker post.

❷ Turn **R** here, nip over stile and cross open field straight ahead. Keep just to **L** of corner of woodland jutting out into field, jump waymarked stile in front, and bear gently **L** along grassy track through **Massers Wood**. Leave woods at waymarked stile, and follow field boundary on your **R**.

❸ At top corner of field, turn **R** over stile on to bridleway. Continue along surfaced lane at foot of hill, towards massive buildings of **Home Farm**. Follow lane as it swings to **L** past farm, and continue for 80yds (73m) beyond entrance to **Brooklands Farm** on your **L**.

❹ Turn **L** here, on to gravelled track that passes back of farm and continues as grassy lane. At end of lane, carry on through 2 fields, following edge of woods on your **R** as far as buildings of **Vachery Farm**. Bear **R** here, and follow signposted bridleway until it meets farm drive at fork.

❺ Now bear **L**, signposted towards **Vachery Farm**; then, 20yds (18m) further on, fork **R** on to signposted bridleway. Bear **R** through small wood, cross wooden footbridge over **Cobbler's Brook**, and go though small gate. Now turn **R** and follow field edge as it bears around to **L** and comes to waymarked gate.

❻ Go through gate and continue straight ahead along waymarked bridleway. Follow it for 150yds (137m) then, as bridleway bears to **L**, dodge up to **R** and turn **L** on to **Downs Link**. Follow old railway back to **Thurlow Arms**. Retrace your steps to start.

88 PYRFORD
SURREY

3.5 MILES (5.7KM) 1hr 30min

PATHS: Riverside tow path, some field paths and roadside

SUGGESTED MAP: aqua3 OS Explorer 145 Guildford & Farnham

GRID REFERENCE: TQ 039573

PARKING: Unsurfaced car park at start

THE PUB: The Anchor

❶ Walk through car park, cross bridge at traffic lights and follow roadside pavement towards **Pyrford village**. Pavement begins on **R-H** side and crosses water-meadows on several small bridges. Enjoy views of **Newark Priory** and, in wet weather, flooded fields attract swans and other waterfowl. Now pavement switches to **L-H** side, and cross **Bourne stream** bridge; then, as road swings hard **R** at Church Hill, keep straight on up steep woodland path to **St Nicholas Church**.

❷ Bear **R** past **church**, cross road, and take stone-flagged path through churchyard. Nip over 2 stiles at far side and follow signposted path past **Lady Place**. Bear **L** under 1st set of power lines, following field edge on **R**. Carry straight on past footpath turnings, **R** and **L**, as you approach 2nd set of power lines. Cross 2 stiles, and continue for 60yds (55m) to public footpath signpost directly under wires. Turn **R** and head towards corner of garden that juts out into field. Bear slightly **L** here, keeping fence on **L-H** side. Continue over stile at Pyrford Green House and down gravelled drive to **Warren Lane**.

❸ Zig-zag **R** and then **L** across road, then take signposted public footpath up side of open field. Carry on over small footbridge straight ahead and follow waymarked route across Pyrford Golf Course. Watch out for flying golf balls. You'll come out on to Lock Lane, just by **Pyrford Lock**. Turn **R** here and walk across bridge by **Anchor** pub.

❹ Turn **R** again, to join easy-to-follow **River Wey** tow path. Just past **Walsham Lock**, tow path zig-zags **L** and **R** across weir. Continue walking with river on your **R**. Cross little footbridge at **Newark Lock**. From here continue along tow path; you're now on north side of river. Beyond lock, you'll come to **Newark Lane**, take **L** turn here, and cross over **Newark Bridge** to return to car park where walk began.

89 WAVERLEY ABBEY
SURREY

3 MILES (4.8KM) 1hr

PATHS: Sandy and easy to follow, two sections on minor roads

SUGGESTED MAP: aqua3 OS Explorer 145 Guildford & Farnham

GRID REFERENCE: SU 870455

PARKING: Waverley Lane between Farnham and Elstead

THE PUB: Barley Mow

❶ The ruins of Waverley Abbey are just at the start of the walk, a stone's throw across the fields from the car park. There was a monastic community at the abbey for over 400 years until it was suppressed by Henry VIII in 1536. Later, the buildings were quarried for stone, and many wagonloads found their way into the construction of nearby Loseley House. Turn **R** out of car park, taking care to watch out for traffic, and follow **Waverley Lane** (B3001) as it zig-zags **L** and **R** over **Waverleymill Bridge**. Continue for 200yds (183m) until road bears to **L**. Turn **R** here, on to public byway, and follow it through to metal gate and public byway signpost.

❷ Keep straight ahead and follow path past Friars Way Cottage until you come to **Sheephatch Lane**. Turn **L** briefly then **R** at junction with **Tilford Street** – there's no pavement for first 400yds (366m), so go carefully. Now follow road past school, over **River Wey** bridge and on to Tilford village green, where you'll find **Tilford Oak** and welcome refreshment at **Barley Mow**.

❸ To continue walk, retrace your steps across river bridge. Almost at once, turn **L** at public bridleway sign just before Post Office. Path climbs gently for 500yds (457m) and brings you to tarmac lane. Turn **L**, pass **Tilhill House**, and continue up narrow sandy track straight ahead. At top of short slope, fork **R** at public bridleway waymark for 400yds (366m) climb to **Sheephatch Farm**. Cross **Sheephatch Lane**, where public byway sign points your way up gravelled track directly opposite. Track leads you through Sheephatch Copse, and soon you'll be dropping down through ancient sunken way to rejoin your outward track at metal gate and public byway signpost.

❹ Turn **L** here for easy walk back to **Waverley Lane** (B3001). Watch out for traffic as you turn **L**, then retrace your outward route over **Waverleymill Bridge** and back to car park.

90 OSTERLEY
LONDON

5 MILES (8KM) 2hrs 30min

PATHS: Mixture of tow paths, tarmac paths and rough tracks

SUGGESTED MAP: aqua3 OS Explorer 161 London South

GRID REFERENCE: TQ 148779; Osterley tube 0.75 mile (1.2km)

PARKING: Car park in Osterley Park (free to National Trust members)

THE PUB: Hare and Hounds

❶ From car park in **Osterley Park** walk back along track heading towards entrance gates, passing **farm shop**.

❷ Just past **shop**, and opposite bungalow, turn **L** through gate and later another, to follow track between fields. When path ends bear **L** towards brick wall, cross track and continue to pub, **Hare and Hounds**.

❸ Turn **L** along road to pass under **M4**. After a further 440yds (402m), just past building on your **L**, turn **R** to go through kissing gate and follow enclosed path alongside playing field. At end of path go through metal gate to your **R**, then cross **railway line** and follow road ahead.

❹ Past bridge, go down steps on **R** to **Grand Union Canal**, then turn **R** under bridge, along tow path. During next mile (1.6km) you will pass **Hanwell Flight of 6 locks** and then Brunel's remarkable **Three Bridges** construction.

❺ Cross **white bridge** ahead of you and continue walking along Melbury Avenue. When you reach T-junction turn **L** and then **R** at mini-roundabout.

❻ Turn **L** along enclosed public footpath, signposted to St Mary's Avenue, beside **Plough pub**. Cross road and continue along footpath opposite, which crosses field. At far side of field climb the steps and follow road over **M4** motorway.

❼ Ignoring 1st metal gate along road, turn **R** through 2nd gate to re-enter **Osterley Park**. Keep going along this straight track, through farmland and avenue of small-leaved lime trees, to reach metal gate. Go past some stable buildings and main house, then take path around pond to reach car park where walk began. If you have time visit **Osterley Park House**, a neo-classical villa set in 140 acres (57ha) of park and ornamental lakes and home to some of the country's best collections of work by Scottish architect Robert Adam.

91 SANDWICH
KENT

3 MILES (4.8KM) 1hr 30min

PATHS: Easy town streets and field tracks, 9 stiles

SUGGESTED MAP: aqua3 OS Explorer 150 Canterbury & the Isle of Thanet

GRID REFERENCE: TR 351582

PARKING: Behind Guildhall in Sandwich

THE PUB: George & Dragon

❶ From **St Peter's Church** in town centre, walk down St Peter's Street to The Chain. Turn **R** into Galliard Street; walk to New Street. Continue to **Guildhall**. Go **L**, through car park and up to Rope Walk, where rope makers used this long, straight area to lay out their ropes.
❷ Turn **R** and, when you reach road, cross over and turn **R** down The Butts. At main road turn **L**, cross over and turn **R** up **Richborough Road**.
❸ Walk ahead, past scrapyard, and go through gate to join footpath on **R**. Follow track round, under main road and up to **railway line**. Cross stile and cross line with care, then go over 2 more stiles and on to road.
❹ Cross over, go over another stile, then walk across field to trees, heading for 3rd telegraph pole. Path now plunges into wood and up wide track. Where it splits, fork **R** and go through trees to stile. Now follow fence line and 2 more stiles over 2 fields to join road.
❺ Cross over and walk up track ahead. **Richborough Fort** is ahead. Path runs around fort with expansive views. At bottom of track turn **R** along end of garden. Nip over stile and back over railway, leaving it by another stile. Path now leads to **R**, over neglected-looking lock and back beside river. You will eventually rejoin road, and retrace your steps to end of **Richborough Road** where you turn **L**.
❻ Go **L** through kissing gate, pass **nature reserve** and go round edge of recreation ground. Turn **R** through gate, and on to Strand Street. Turn **L**. Then **L** again in front of **Bell Hotel** and **R** past Barbican. Walk along river bank, following line of old town wall. At bend in river, turn **R** to road. Cross over, continue along footpath, pass bowling green, then turn **R** down steps into Mill Wall Place. Cross over and go back along King Street to start.

92 CANTERBURY
KENT

3.5 MILES (5.7KM) 1hr 45min

PATHS: City streets and firm footpaths

SUGGESTED MAP: aqua3 OS Explorer 150 Canterbury & the Isle of Thanet

GRID REFERENCE: TR 145574

PARKING: Castle Street or one of several car parks in Canterbury

THE PUB: Simple Simon's

❶ Go **R** from **Castle Street** car park then **R** again past **castle**. At end turn **L** on Centenary Walk. Where this finishes go **R** and walk beside road. Cross bridge, turn **L**, go under another bridge and along river to other side of road.
❷ Cross some grassland, go over bridge and through children's play area. Walk across car park and turn **L** up road to join **Stour Valley Walk**.
❸ Go under bridge and continue to level crossing. Cross **railway**, then stroll up past **Whitehall Farm**. Walk under arch, through gate and over stream. Path bends round and main road is on your L. At junction turn **R** along **North Downs Way**.
❹ Go over bridge and up lane. To your L is **Golden Hill** – the point from which pilgrims traditionally had their first view of the city. When you come to track, turn **L** and follow it round. Go **R** along **Mill Lane** to main road. Take underpass to cross **Rheims Way**, walk down **London Road**, then turn **R** into **St Dunstans Street**.
❺ Walk down into Canterbury to **Westgate**, turn **L** along **Pound Lane** and into **St Radigund Street**, with **Simple Simon's pub** on R-H side.
❻ Continue into **Northgate**, go **L** then **R** down **Broad Street**. You're now walking around outside of the city walls. Turn **R** along Burgate, past tiny 16th-century building called Pilgrim's Shop. Soon come to pedestrianised area that brings you out at Butter Market and war memorial. On your R-H side is **cathedral** entrance.
❼ Turn **L** and walk down road, pass tourist information centre and then turn **R** to **Stour Street**. On R is city **museum**, set in ancient Poor Priests' Hospital and almost opposite, down Jewry Lane, is **Canterbury Wholefoods** where you can finish your walk with tea and cakes. To return to **Castle Street**, turn **L** on Rosemary Lane and then **R**.

93 ALDINGTON
KENT

3 MILES (4.8KM) 2hrs 30min

PATHS: Waymarked tracks and badly signposted field paths, 8 stiles

SUGGESTED MAP: aqua3 OS Explorer 137 Ashford

GRID REFERENCE: TQ 064355

PARKING: On street in Aldington

THE PUB: Walnut Tree Inn

❶ The **Walnut Tree Inn** at **Aldington Corner** at the start was once HQ to Aldington Gang of smugglers, probably formed by soldiers returning from the Napoleonic Wars. From pub, walk up Forge Road. At path on **L** cross stile to join **Saxon Shore Way**. Walk across field, hop over another stile, turn **L** and follow waymarker downhill. Cross stile into woods.
❷ Walk through woods, over stile and, still on **Saxon Shore Way**, follow fence line, then bear **L** and come up through pasture. Go through rusty gate on to road.
❸ Turn **R** and keep ahead. Go **L** up road, past Aldington **church**. Take track that leads to **R** past cottages. This was once the site of an **archbishop's palace**, which Henry VIII claimed for himself during the Reformation. Continue to gate, along vehicle track. Follow treeline down to stile. Follow fence line on **R**, cross stile and continue down to **Middle Park Farm**.
❹ Walk through farm where you might see some peacocks. Cross metal gate into field and continue ahead with hedgerow on L, walking under pylons. Continue walking along fence then take track round front of **Lower Park Farm**, over overgrown stile. Come on to shingle track and bear slightly **L** with hedgerows on R. Go over cattle grid and come on to road.
❺ Turn **L** down road, then turn **R** on to drive of **Hogben Farm**. Walk down drive then go **L** through wooden gate into paddock. Climb over wooden gate ahead, then walk straight across field, heading to bottom **L-H** corner. Go through gap in hedgerow and cross over field under pylons.
❻ Cross stream, then go diagonally across field to lone tree in corner. Climb stile then cut diagonally across field to top **L-H** corner. After going through another gap in hedge climb stile. Now go diagonally **R** across field and head down to main road. Go **L** then walk down main road and back into village.

94 GOUDHURST
KENT

3 MILES (4.8KM) 1hr 45min

PATHS: Well-marked field paths, short sections of road, 12 stiles

SUGGESTED MAP: aqua3 OS Explorer 136 The Weald, Royal Tunbridge Wells

GRID REFERENCE: TQ 723377

PARKING: Car park in Goudhurst behind duck pond

THE PUB: Star and Eagle Inn

❶ From car park turn **L**, cross over road and walk along opposite to duck pond. Just past bus shelter turn **L** and then follow public footpath, crossing stile and walking downhill. There are outstanding views from here – the whole countryside seems to be sprinkled with oasthouses. Keep going down, past 2 large trees and walk to the bottom **R** of field where you cross over stile and on to narrow, tree-lined path. Follow this to stile. Go over little bridge and on to tarmac minor road.
❷ Cross over to another stile and continue ahead over pasture to tennis court. Skirt round **L** of this and, after another stile, come on to road. Turn **R**. Turn **L** through gate ('Private Road') into **Trottenden Farm**. Follow track that winds to **R**, go past pond, over stile and walk ahead along fenced track and across pasture. Hop over stile by gate and continue ahead to another stile. At fencepost walk to **R**, round edge of meadow then cross wooden bridge, nip over another stile and into woodland. Walk uphill to another stile and continue ahead to road.
❸ Turn **R** and at corner turn **L** up public bridleway. Turn **R** at cottage and come down into field. At post by hedge turn **R** and go downhill. At bottom cross some water; then veer **L**, walking uphill towards farmhouse.
❹ Just before farm outbuildings turn **R** along track that runs by hedge. Eventually pass parkland of **Ladham House** on L then come to some concrete bollards. Continue walking to join road.
❺ At road turn **R**, and walk up to **B2084**. Cross over and walk along road immediately ahead. At junction keep to **R** and continue to reach main road. Turn **R** here. You can now see **St Mary's Church**. Follow road and walk back into village.

95 AYLESFORD
KENT

5 MILES (8KM) 2hrs 30min

PATHS: Field paths and ancient trackways, some road, 12 stiles

SUGGESTED MAP: aqua3 OS Explorer 148 Maidstone & the Medway Towns

GRID REFERENCE: TQ 729590

PARKING: Aylesford Friary

THE PUB: Little Gem

❶ From car park turn **R** towards village, cross road and join raised pathway. Ascend steps and go round by graveyard, then follow track to tarmac road. Go **L** here, then **L** again to follow **Centenary Walk**.
❷ At marker post take **L-H** track and walk **L** around field until you come to scrub. Walk through this, turn **R** and walk ahead to patch of woodland. Keep this on R and continue ahead, ignoring any tracks on R. Eventually path bends **L** into **Eccles**.
❸ Turn **L** along residential street then take public footpath opposite No 48. Cross stile and take **L-H** track around edge of the field. Cross 2nd stile and bear **R**, then cross 3rd stile just to L of electricity pylon. Keep ahead across fields, going over 5 more stiles until you reach Bull Lane.
❹ Turn **R** on to Pilgrims' Way (main road) then **L** until you reach cottages. Cross over and walk up **Centenary Walk** footpath. Follow this as it winds up to Blue Bell Hill, where there's final steep ascent. After crossing stile at top, route goes **R** along **North Downs Way**. (However, do take detour **L** to enjoy views from Blue Bell Hill.)
❺ Keep following **North Downs Way** until you join road. Don't cross bridge, but continue along road. Follow sign on **R** to **Kit's Coty House** (neolithic burial chamber, which dates back 5,000 years). Walk down to busy road junction, turn **L** and join Pilgrims' Way – it's on corner, by M20 sign. (**Little Kit's Coty House**, another neolithic burial chamber is on the main road further down to the R.)
❻ Follow lane, then take 1st track you see on **R** to reach road; follow ahead. Just past farmhouse take stile on **R** and walk diagonally across field. Cross another stile and bear **R** towards patch of woodland. Continue over another stile and find gate in bottom **R-H** corner. Go through and turn **R** along road. Turn **L** at junction, then **R** to return to start.

96 HEVER
KENT

3.5 MILES (5.7KM) 2hrs

PATHS: Paths, grassy tracks and field edges, some roads, 6 stiles

SUGGESTED MAP: aqua3 OS Explorer 147 Sevenoaks & Tonbridge

GRID REFERENCE: TQ 476448

PARKING: Car park by Hever Castle

THE PUB: King Henry VIII

❶ Walk under lychgate and go through churchyard following **Eden Valley Walk**. Path goes downhill, across bridge and soon becomes narrow lane parallel to road, offering occasional glimpses of lake at **Hever Castle**. The lake looks natural but was actually created by William Waldorf Astor when he bought the castle in 1903. Path now bends round, goes through woodland, across another bridge and finally opens out.
❷ When you come to house, climb gate following **Eden Valley Walk** (follow it all the way to Point ❹). Pass another house then take track on **R-H** side, which winds round edge of meadow to woodland. When you come to tarmac road, cross it and pop over stile.
❸ Continue along enclosed track, which can get very muddy, crossing 2 more stiles and gradually heading uphill. Another stile leads you past deer fencing and through gate on to tarmac road at **Hill Hoath**.
❹ Now turn back to **R** and go through large gate, so that you seem to be doubling back on yourself. This leads to broad, grassy track. Walk ahead (don't be tempted into crossing stile on L) and walk between trees, passing lake on your L-H side. Soon enter much thicker woodland and track becomes narrower, but is still clear to follow.
❺ At branching of footpaths, bear **R**. Be warned, this can be very muddy. Continue down track, passing another 2 areas of woodland until you reach road.
❻ Turn **R** here and walk to **Wilderness Farm**, then take road that leads to **L** opposite farm. At another road turn **R** and walk up, past road that leads to R. Continue ahead to take footpath on **R** that runs alongside **Greyhound pub**.
❼ When you come to fork by 2 stiles turn **L**, then walk around edge of field and past pond. Continue ahead to lane, where you turn **L** then take footpath on **R**. Follow this back into **Hever**.

Wales
& THE MARCHES

WALES & THE MARCHES

Contents

		page
97	St David's, Pembrokeshire	117
98	Stackpole, Pembrokeshire	119
99	Ogmore-by-Sea, Vale of Glamorgan	121
100	Castell Coch, Cardiff	123
101	Moelfre, Isle of Anglesey	125
102	Capel Curig, Conwy	127
103	Horseshoe Falls, Denbighshire	129
104	Welshpool, Powys	131
105	Teme Valley, Shropshire	133
106	Aymestry, Herefordshire	135
107	Wistanstow, Shropshire	137
108	Diddlebury, Shropshire	139
109	Coalbrookdale, Shropshire	141
110	Coalbrookdale, Shropshire	143
111	Swansea	145
112	Pembrokeshire	145
113	Powys	145
114 to 115 Gwynedd		145
116	Wrexham	145
117 to 119 Herefordshire		146
120 to 122 Shropshire		146

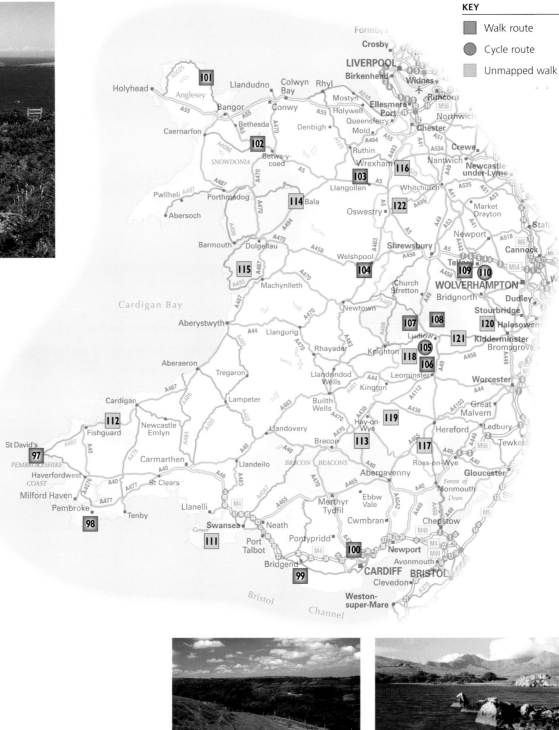

KEY

- Walk route
- Cycle route
- Unmapped walk

while you're there

The biggish island with rugged cliffs off St David's Head is Ramsey Island, an RSPB reserve. Birds that breed here include choughs, kittiwakes and razorbills, and it is also home to a colony of grey seals. Boats make the trip from from St Justinians, by the lifeboat station, from Easter to October.

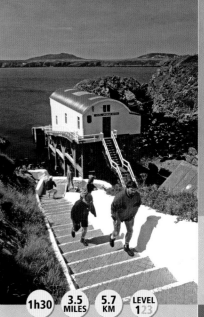

Left: Alpine chough (Pyrrhacorax graculus)

Right: The lifeboat station at St Justinians

St Non's Bay

Below left: Walkers in Pembrokshire Coastal National Park

Easy walking around the lovely coastline that gave birth to the patron saint.

St David's

This walk makes a great evening stroll. The paths from the city are pleasant and easy to follow but they're quickly forgotten as you step out into the glamorous surroundings of the coast. The all-too-short section of towering buttresses and jagged islets leads easily to the birthplace of St David.

Considering the immense influence he has had on Welsh culture, little is known about the patron saint. His mother is said to be St Non, who was married to a local chieftain. They settled near Trwyn Cynddeiriog, the rocky bluff that forms the western walls of the bay named after her.

Legend suggests that David was born in around AD 500, in the place where the ruined chapel stands today. Although a fierce storm raged throughout his birth, a calm light was said to have lit the scene. By the morning, a fresh spring had erupted near by, becoming the Holy Well of St Non.

Judging from his parentage, David would have been well educated and it is believed that he undertook a number of religious odysseys, including one to Jerusalem, before he finally returned around AD 550. He founded a church and monastery at Glyn Rhosyn, on the banks of the River Alun, on the site of the present cathedral, where he set about trying to spread the Christian word before his death in 589. St David's Day is celebrated on 1 March every year and St Non, who saw out her life in Brittany, is remembered on the following day.

St David's is little more than a pretty village, though it is a city due to its magnificent cathedral. It's a wonderful place and very popular. Known as Tyddewi – David's House – in Welsh, the city grew as a result of its coastal position at the western extreme of the British mainland. It would have been linked easily by sea with Ireland and Cornwall. As well as the cathedral and the ruins of the Bishop's Palace, it houses a plethora of gift shops and the National Park information centre, close to the car park, is one of the finest in the country.

the walk

1 Turn left out of the car park in **St David's** and walk down the road, as if you were heading for **Caerfai Bay**. As the houses thin out, you'll see a turning on the right that leads to more dwellings. Take this and then turn left on to a waymarked bridleway. Follow this bridleway between hedges, past the end of a road and on to a junction with another road.

2 Walk straight across and take the waymarked path down a pleasant track and pass through three gates. Keep to the left of the field to another gate, where you keep straight ahead again. Go through a gate, bear left then right through the farmyard into the **campsite**.

3 Keep the hedge on your right, where the drive swings off to the left. Continue across two fields and at the end drop down between gorse bushes to the road at **Porth Clais**. Before crossing the bridge, turn left on to the coast path.

Right: St David's Cathedral

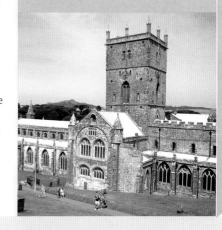

1h30 **3.5 MILES** **5.7 KM** **LEVEL 1 2 3**

MAP: OS Explorer OL35 North Pembrokeshire

START/FINISH: pay-and-display car park in St David's; grid ref: SM 757252

PATHS: coast path and clear footpaths over farmland

LANDSCAPE: leafy countryside and dramatic cliffs

PUBLIC TOILETS: next to tourist information centre

TOURIST INFORMATION: St David's, tel 01437 720392

THE PUB: The Glan-Y-Mor Inn, St David's

❶ One short climb; care to be taken on the cliff path

Getting to the start

St David's is located at the western tip of Pembrokeshire, 16 miles (25.8km) west of Haverfordwest on the A487. As you enter the town, turn left for the signed car park along Caerfai Road.

Researched & written by: David Hancock, Tom Hutton

More Islands

The waters flow fast and deep through Ramsey Sound, and boats must be careful to avoid the small islands there known as the Bitches. Off the western side of Ramsey Island spread the Bishops and Clerks, with a lighthouse on exposed South Bishop to ward off shipping.

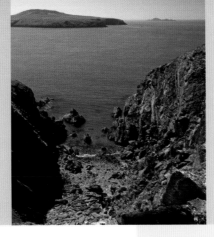

did you know?

Geoffrey of Monmouth, the 12th-century Welsh chronicler, largely made up his supposedly authoritative Historia Regium Britanniae, *which contains one of the earliest references to the legendary King Arthur – whom Geoffrey declared was the nephew of St David himself.*

97

WALK

4 Climb up steeply on to the cliff tops and bear around to the left to walk towards **Porth y Ffynnon**. The next small headland is **Trwyn Cynddeiriog**, where there's a lovely grassy platform above the cliffs if you fancy a rest. Continue walking into **St Non's Bay** and look for a footpath on the left that leads to the ruined chapel.

5 From the chapel, head up to a gate that leads to **St Non's Well** and then follow the path beneath the new chapel and back out on to the coast path. Turn left to climb easily on to **Pen y Cyfrwy**, continue around this and drop down towards **Caerfai Bay**.

6 You'll eventually come to a gate beneath the Caerfai Bay car park. Go through the gate and climb the steps on the left into the car park. Join the access and follow this past **The Glan-Y-Mor Inn** to St David's and the start of the walk.

what to look for

Shortly after the stiff climb out of Porth Clais, you'll round Trwyn Cynddeiriog, the headland that divides Porth y Ffynnon from St Non's Bay. This is where St Non and Sant, St David's parents, were said to have lived. A short distance further along the coast path, at the head of the bay, you'll see a footpath on the left that leads to the ruined chapel. This is thought to have been built in the 13th century on the spot where St David was born. A path then leads to a gate, behind which you'll see St Non's Well and a grotto. Further up the hill is the newer chapel, dedicated to Our Lady and St Non. This was actually built in the 1930s using stone from other principal local evangelical sites, including the original chapel.

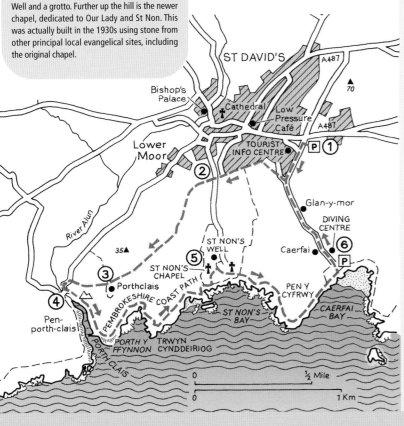

The Glan-Y-Mor Inn

Enjoying a rural setting close to town and just a short stroll from the Pembrokeshire Coast Path, the refurbished bar of this substantial old building looks out across St Bride's Bay towards the islands of Skomer and Skokholm. Modernised and open-plan, the bar is welcoming and informal, with leather settees, simple tables and chairs, and space for a pool table and television. There are separate raised dining areas and an adjoining restaurant with plants and access to a wooden platform for alfresco dining and savouring the sea views. There's also a campsite (tents only), rooms in the main building and a lodge in the garden.

Food

Menu choices range from sandwiches, paninis, lasagne, mixed bean chilli and steak, ale and mushroom pudding at lunchtime to Welsh leg of lamb with port, redcurrant and mint sauce, rump steak and fresh fish (sea bass, black bream) in the evenings. Puddings include sticky toffee pudding and apple and blackberry crumble. Curry menu on Sunday evening.

Family facilities

Children are welcome away from the bar until 9pm and kids' meals are available.

Alternative refreshment stops

Apart from the possibility of an ice-cream van in the car park at Porth Clais, the best bet for refreshment is St David's where there's plenty of choice. A favourite pub is the Farmers Arms on Goat Street, which has a good garden and serves up all the usual pub fare. For non-alcoholic refreshment, try the excellent Low Pressure Café.

about the pub

The Glan-Y-Mor Inn
Caerfai Road, St David's
Pembrokeshire SA62 6QT
Tel: 01437 721788
www.glan-y-mor.co.uk

DIRECTIONS: on entering St David's, turn left for Caerfai Bay, passing the main car park. Keep to the lane towards the sea; pub is on the left. At Point **6** of the walk

PARKING: 15

OPEN: daily; all day

FOOD: daily

BREWERY/COMPANY: free house

REAL ALE: Felinfoel Bitter

DOGS: allowed in the bar area

ROOMS: 10 bedrooms; 5 en suite

☛ Where to go from here

St David's Cathedral is both architecturally stunning and spiritually moving. In 1120 Pope Calixtus II decreed that two pilgrimages to St David's were the equivalent of one to Rome – an honour indeed. The cathedral and the nearby Bishop's Palace play host to a series of classical concerts every summer (www.stdavidscathedral.org.uk).

while you're there

East along the coast lies the magnificent 13th-century Manorbier Castle (open April–September). The medieval scholar Giraldus Cambrensis, famous for his accounts of everyday life and people in Wales, was born here in around 1146.

Huntsman's Leap

Just west of Bosherston village is a dramatic gap called Huntsman's Leap. Apparently a hunter jumped his horse over it, then died of fright when he realised how lucky he'd been.

Manorbier Castle's curtain wall and towers are largely intact

Beaches and Lakes at Stackpole

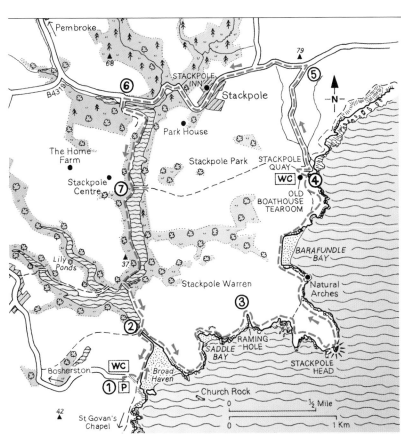

2h30 | **6 MILES** | **9.7 KM** | **LEVEL 1**23

MAP: OS Explorer OL36 South Pembrokeshire

START/FINISH: National Trust car park above Broad Haven Beach; grid ref: SR 976938

PATHS: easy coast path, quiet lanes and well trodden waterside walkways, 1 stile

LANDSCAPE: magnificent limestone headlands, secluded beaches and tranquil waterways

PUBLIC TOILETS: at start and at Stackpole Quay

TOURIST INFORMATION: Pembroke, tel 01646 622388

THE PUB: The Stackpole Inn, Stackpole

🛈 Take care with children on the cliff edge and beside the lake

Getting to the start

From the Pembroke one-way system take the B4319 south for Bosherton and Angle. Pass through St Petrox, ignore the lane left for Stackpole and take the next left for Bosherton. In the village follow the sign left for Broad Haven Beach. The car park (pay in summer) is at the end of the lane.

Researched & written by:
David Hancock, Tom Hutton

An undemanding tour of the cliff tops, beaches and lakes at the southernmost point of the Pembrokeshire Coast National Park.

Stackpole

The limestone headlands of St Govan's and Stackpole, some of the most impressive coastline in South Pembrokeshire, have grass-covered, plateau-like tops. The cliffs, however, make up only a short section of a varied walk that crosses two of the region's finest beaches and also explores some beautiful inland waters.

The beach is a broad gem of white sand, backed by rolling dunes and flanked by impressive headlands. Barafundle Bay is equally picturesque; a lack of road access keeps it relatively quiet for most of the year. The final attraction of this simple circuit is the three-fingered waterway that probes deeply inland from Broad Haven. The wooded shores and calm waters make a change from the wildness of the coast.

A series of interconnecting lakes was created at the turn of the 19th century by the then owner of the Stackpole Estate. A tidal creek was dammed which flooded the three tributary valleys. Subsequent sand drift has created a marram grass-covered dune system behind the beach. The lakes are abundant in wildlife, with herons prowling the shallows, swans, ducks, moorhens and coots all easily visible on the surface, and shyer creatures such as kingfishers often spotted. The Lily Ponds are managed as a National Nature Reserve, and the lilies themselves are at their best in June, while the woodland is a magnificent spectacle in spring and autumn.

The cliffs between Linney Head, closed to the public as part of the MOD firing range, and Stackpole Head comprise some of the best limestone coastal scenery in Britain. Exposed to the full force of the Atlantic at their feet, they are often overhanging and also contain many caves and blowholes. A few spectacular sea stacks have survived and now stud the coast just offshore – Church Rock, seen on this walk is one of the finest examples. The area is also popular for rock climbing.

the walk

1 From the car park, head back to the **National Trust building** at the top of the lane and bear right, down a set of steps, to the beach. Cross the beach and keep left to walk up the creek to a **footbridge**.

A fulmar (Fulmarus glacialis)

did you know?

The saint after whom St Govan's Head is named is thought to have been an Irish contemporary of St David. The story goes that he was hiding from pirates in the cleft of rock where his chapel is now wedged, when a crack miraculously opened in the floor. He entered the crack and it closed behind him, opening once more when the danger had passed.

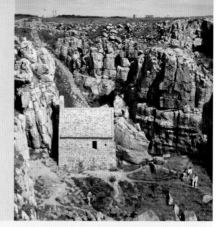

2 Go over this and bear right to walk above rocky outcrops, above the beach, to a gate. Follow the grassy path around the **headland** and back inland to a stile above Saddle Bay. Continue around a large blowhole and up to a gate above a deeply cloven zawn (cleft), known as the **Raming Hole**.

3 Go through the gate and hug the coastline on your right to walk around **Stackpole Head**. As you turn back inland, pass a blowhole and then go through a gate to drop down to **Barafundle Bay**. Cross the back of the beach and climb up the steps on the other side to an archway in the wall. Continue around to **Stackpole Quay**.

4 Turn left, above the tiny harbour, to pass the **Old Boathouse Tearoom** on your left before turning sharp right on to a road. (For a shorter walk, avoiding the road and pub, enter the car park at Stackpole Quay and go through the gate on the left.

what to look for

The views east from Stackpole Head stretch from Caldey Island – a religious enclave just off the coast of Tenby – to the Gower Peninsula in the distance. Beyond, to the south, you may be able to make out the lofty landform of Lundy Island and even the outline of the North Devon coast.

Follow this clear path across the centre of Stackpole Park to cross the bridge over the lake and pick up the route at Point 7). Follow this past some buildings on the right and up to a T-junction, where you turn left.

5 Drop down into Stackpole village, pass **The Stackpole Inn** on the right, and continue around a series of bends until you come to a road on the left, over a bridge.

6 Cross the bridge and bear left to follow a good path along the side of the **lake**. This leads through one kissing gate to a second, where you bear right, up a short steep section. At the top, bear left, on to a broad path with a wooden handrail. Follow this to a bridge.

7 Don't cross the bridge, but drop down on to a path and follow it with the lake on your left. Continue ahead to another bridge, cross it, then carry on with the lake now on your right. This path leads to the footbridge that you crossed at Point 2. Retrace your steps across the **beach** and up the steps back to the **car park**.

Left: Broad Haven bay

The Stackpole Inn

The inn is set in lovely landscaped gardens at the heart of the National Trust's Stackpole Estate, and its proximity to the coast makes this hostelry a popular venue for passing walkers. It was originally two 17th-century cottages, one of which subsequently became a post office, and the old King George postbox is still set in the wall. Inside is a warren-like series of interconnected rooms, with a Welsh slate bar, smart pine furniture, a wood-burning stove set within a stone fireplace, and some areas neatly laid up for dining.

Food

Local produce from the surrounding countryside and the nearby sea plays its full part on imaginative menus. Snacks range from baguettes and burgers to pasta meals and chilli. Main meals may include seafood risotto, sea bass with orange and ginger sauce, liver and bacon with bubble-and-squeak, and seared salmon with herb crust and red salsa. Good puddings and roast Sunday lunches.

Family facilities

Children are welcome indoors where youngsters have their own menu and

about the pub

The Stackpole Inn
Stackpole, Pembroke
Pembrokeshire SA71 5DF
Tel: 01646 672324
www.stackpoleinn.co.uk

DIRECTIONS: from the car park return through Bosherton to the B4319. Turn right, then next right to reach Stackpole. Pub is on the left in the village centre. See Point **5** on the walk.

PARKING: 25

OPEN: daily

FOOD: daily

BREWERY/COMPANY: free house

REAL ALES: Worthington, Brains Reverend James, Felinfoel Double Dragon

DOGS: allowed in the bar

smaller portions are readily available. Good safe garden.

Alternative refreshment stops

The Old Boathouse Tearoom at Stackpole Quay is an excellent National Trust café serving light lunches and tea and cakes. St Govan's Inn at Bosherston offers good food and a selection of real ales.

☛ Where to go from here

Providing the footpath is open, take a stroll to St Govan's Chapel, a humble but spiritually uplifting stone building tucked away in a deep cleft in the cliffs, west of St Govan's Head. The present chapel dates from the 13th century, but probably incorporates some much older stonework. Visit Pembroke Castle, a magnificent 12th-to 13th-century fortress with an impressive 80ft (24m) high round keep (www.pembrokecastle.co.uk).

Sands of Time

Shifting sands at the mouth of the Ogmore estuary, blown by the Atlantic gales, have hidden and revealed several interesting layers of history. The village of Merthyr-mawr-Warren has disappeared beneath the sands, but older prehistoric burial chambers and artefacts have been revealed in the area, including brooches of the La Tene period (now in Swansea Museum).

Kelp – close up

did you know?

Ewenny Priory, just east of Ogmore village, was founded by Maurice de Londres in 1141 as an outpost of the Benedictine abbey at Gloucester. Its defensive outer wall is an unusual survivor, and there's a solid, fortified tower on the Norman church (www.ewenny.org.uk).

A Stroll Along Glamorgan's Coast

A pleasant foray through sand dunes, returning along the impressive and little-known South Wales coast.

Glamorgan Heritage Coast

Granted Heritage Coast status in 1972, the 14-mile (22.5km) stretch of coastline that runs between Ogmore and Gileston stands defiant against progress. Sandy beaches, often punctuated by weathered strips of rock, break up an otherwise formidable barrier of limestone and shale cliffs that rise and dip gracefully above the turbulent grey waters. The unkempt wildness here has its own special appeal.

Dunraven Bay houses the Heritage Centre, with displays and information about the area. It's an appropriate starting point for a walk that gives a taste of this unique landscape. The early stages track inland, through woodland and farmland before heading coastwards, at the small village of St Bride's Major. From here, the path sneaks between dunes and drops to the Ogmore River. Following the estuary downstream through bracken which simply teems with wildlife, you'll meet the coast at Ogmore-by-Sea and pick up the coast path above one of many beaches here. With ocean views to your right and the dunes to your left, you'll now climb easily back up above Dunraven where, if you time it right, you'll witness the cliffs reflecting the pastel shades of sunset as you enjoy the final drop to the beach. It's a wonderful way to finish off an evening stroll.

The Glamorgan Heritage Coast was one of three pilot schemes set up in 1972 to protect the country's unique coastal landscapes and environments from development. There are now 43 such areas in England and Wales – in Wales they account for over 40 per cent of the total coastline. The aims of the scheme are fourfold; to maintain ecological diversity, to provide public access and encourage recreational use, to protect the needs of the local population, and to preserve the quality of the coastline. The Glamorgan Heritage Coast is managed by the Countryside Council for Wales and a ranger service takes care of the area.

the walk

1 Head up the lane at the back of the car park and pass the **Heritage Centre** on your right. Keep straight ahead on a narrow path that ducks into woodland and continue on this path to a stile. Cross the stile and walk along the edge of the field to

---

3h00 — **5.5 MILES** — **9.7 KM** — **LEVEL 1**23

MAP: OS Explorer 151 Cardiff & Bridgend

START/FINISH: large car park at Heritage Centre above Dunraven Beach at Southerndown; grid ref: SS 885731

PATHS: easy-to-follow across farmland and coastline, 5 stiles

LANDSCAPE: deciduous woodland, farmland, bracken-covered sand dunes and rocky coastline

PUBLIC TOILETS: at start and at Ogmore

TOURIST INFORMATION: Bridgend, tel 01656 654906

THE PUB: The Farmers Arms, St Bride's Major, Bridgend

⚠ One steep climb; keep children away from the cliff edge

Getting to the start

Ogmore-by-Sea is situated at the mouth of the Ogmore river south of Bridgend. Heading east on the M4 (J35) take the A473 towards Bridgend and Laleston. In 4 miles (6.8km) at the fourth roundabout turn left on the B4265 and continue to St Bride's Major. Turn right on to the B4524 for Ogmore, then at Southerndown follow signs left for Dunraven Beach.

Researched and written by: David Hancock, Tom Hutton

while you're there

Just to the northwest, the popular seaside resort of Porthcawl (left) has something for everybody, with two beaches, the Coney Beach amusement park, an esplanade and a famous golf course (tel 01659 786639 for tourist information).

Mediterrranean gull (Larus melanocephalus)

reach a **gate** on your left. Go through the gate, then cross a stile on your right to continue with the hedge to your right.

2 Cross into another field and keep to the left-hand side, following the hedgerow, which is now on your left. When you reach the next stile, continue ahead, go past a gate on the left, to reach another stile on the left. Cross this stile and head diagonally right to a stile between the house and the **farmyard**.

3 Turn left on to the road, pass **The Farmers Arms** and walk into the village. Keep left into Southerndown Road and then fork right into Heol-y-slough. Follow this road for 0.75 mile (1.2km) then, as the road bends to the left, keep straight across the common. Continue ahead where a bridleway crosses the track. As you join another track, maintain your direction along the valley floor.

what to look for

If the sea seems a long way out, it's worth remembering that the tidal flows in the Bristol Channel are the second largest in the world, with the differences between high and low water being well over 39ft (12m) on a high spring tide. The only larger tides are witnessed in Canada's Bay of Fundy.

4 The path winds its way down through sand dunes, passing a tributary valley on the left, and eventually emerges on the **B4524**. Cross the road and continue until you locate one of the many paths that lead left towards **Portobello House**. At the drive, keep right, then fork left by the house to continue through the bracken, parallel to the **estuary** of the Ogmore River.

5 Stay above the small cliffs near the mouth of estuary and you'll eventually arrive at a **car parking area** above the beach. From here, follow the obvious route along the coast to the left.

6 You'll come to a **dry-stone wall**, which will funnel you through a gate marked 'Coast Path – Emergency Vehicles Only'. Continue walking along the coast path until, about 1.25 miles (2km) from the gate, you meet with a **steep valley**. Turn left into this valley and then turn immediately right, on to a footpath that climbs steeply up the grassy hillside.

7 Stay with the footpath as it follows the line of a dry-stone wall around to **West Farm**. Keep to the right-hand side of the agricultural buildings and continue to reach the upper car park. A gap in the wall, at the back of this, leads you to a grassy track that follows the road down into **Dunraven**.

The Farmers Arms

Known locally as the 'Pub on the Pond', The Farmers Arms is a popular roadside pub that draws a good local trade for the fine choice of real ale and decent food on offer. The cosy, carpeted bar sports a warming wood-burning stove in the stone fireplace, dark wood furnishings, red plush chairs and numerous plates on high shelves. Dark beams are festooned with an assortment of ceramic and glass jugs, pans, bowls and brasses, and various rural artefacts. Straw boaters decorate the adjoining dining area. The small front verandah has benches overlooking the village pond.

Food

Blackboards in the bar list the lunchtime rolls (hot beef and onion) and the market fish (sea bass, black sea bream), while the printed menu lists the extensive range of traditional bar meals. Expect a good choice of steaks, lasagne, ham, egg and chips, steak and kidney pudding, authentic curries, and a good value two-course lunch selection.

Family facilities

Children are very welcome and there's a good 'small eaters' menu.

Alternative refreshment stops

A short detour into Ogmore-by-Sea offers plenty of typical beach-side eateries such as fish and chip shops and cafés.

☛ Where to go from here

Only a mile (1.6km) from Ogmore-by-Sea is Ogmore Castle, a 12th-century Norman fortification that lies in a pretty green valley and is reputed to be the place where King Arthur was fatally wounded. His body is said to be buried in a cave near by. True or not, the ruins, which are very basic but incredibly atmospheric, are well worth a visit (www.cadw.wales.gov.uk).

about the pub

The Farmers Arms
Wick Road, St Bride's Major, Bridgend
Vale of Glamorgan CF32 0SE
Tel: 01656 880224

DIRECTIONS: see Getting to the start. In St Bride's Major keep to B4265 towards Llantwit Major; pub on left opposite the pond

PARKING: 40

OPEN: daily; all day Sunday

FOOD: daily

BREWERY/COMPANY: free house

REAL ALES: Ushers Best, Courage Best, Greene King Old Speckled Hen, John Smith's Bitter, guest beers

DOGS: not allowed inside

did you know?

With its pepperpot towers, Castell Coch looks more like a French château than the battle-worn fortresses more usually associated with Wales. According to its architect, this romantic fantasy was never intended for more than 'occasional occupation in the summer'. Its name means 'red castle', from the colour of the sandstone used for its construction.

Living History

If all these castles seem static, then Caerphilly's Llancaiach Fawr Manor may be the answer (Tuesday–Sunday, November–February, tel 01443 412248). It's a living history museum, bringing to life the period of the Civil War.

Castell Coch

Right: The ceiling of the Octagonal Room at Castell Coch

| 2h30 | 5.5 MILES | 8.8 KM | LEVEL 123 |

MAP: OS Explorer 151 Cardiff & Bridgend

START/FINISH: Castell Coch; grid ref: ST 131826

PATHS: forest tracks, disused railway line and clear paths, short section of tarmac, 2 stiles

LANDSCAPE: mixed woodland and open hillside with views over residential and industrial developments

PUBLIC TOILETS: in castle and nearby Countryside Visitor Centre

TOURIST INFORMATION: Cardiff, tel: 029 2022 7281

THE PUB: Black Cock Inn, Caerphilly Mountain, Caerphilly

❶ Care to be taken on the steep, zig-zag path

Getting to the start

Castell Coch is located 6 miles (10.1km) northwest of Cardiff city centre, signposted off the A470/A4054 Merthyr Tydfil roads and the M4 (junction 32). Large free car park just below the castle.

Researched & written by: David Hancock, Tom Hutton

From a fairy-tale castle to a wild, windswept hillside – the new-look valleys

Castell Coch

At the bottom of the Taff Vale, a few miles north of Cardiff, is a fairy-tale castle that easily rivals those of Bavaria. Castell Coch is well worth a visit in its own right, but perched on a cliff top amid stunning woodland, it's also a great place to start a walk. Conveniently, two waymarked trails run close to the castle and these, together with a labyrinth of forest tracks, provide an invigorating circular route.

This majestic castle was built in the late 1870s, on the site of a 13th-century fortress, as a country retreat for the 3rd Marquess of Bute, who at the time was thought to be the richest man in the world.

Its design, by the architect William Burges, who also designed St Finbar's Cathedral in Cork, is pure fantasy, with a working drawbridge and portcullis, three circular towers and a boudoir that features a lavishly decorated domed ceiling.

The route away from the woods follows a section of the Taff Trail, a 55-mile (89km) waymarked route that leads from Cardiff Bay to Brecon via the Taff Valley, Llandaff, Pontypridd and Merthyr Tydfil. Most of the trail, including the lower section of this walk, is along disused railway lines, together with forest tracks and canal paths. From the Taff Trail, this walk follows an airy section of the 21 mile (33.8km) Ridgeway Walk (Ffordd-y-Bryniau). This trail traces a fascinating hill-top line across what was once the Borough of Taff Ely until the local government reorganisations of the mid-1990s. The section followed climbs steeply on to the narrow ridge of Craig yr Allt, a spectacular viewpoint which, on the one hand feels as wild as the mountains further north, but at the same time gives a raven's-eye view of the industrial side of the valleys.

the walk

1 From the car park, walk up to the castle entrance and keep right to locate an **information plaque** and a **waymarker** indicating a woodland walk. Take this path and climb steeply up to a junction of tracks.

2 Turn sharp left, signposted '**The Taff Trail**', by a picture of a viaduct, and follow this broad forest track around the hillside and then down, where it meets the **disused railway line**. Continue along this for over a mile (1.6km) until you pass a picnic area and come to a barrier.

3 Go through the barrier then, as you come to a disused bridge, turn right over a stile, signposted '**Ridgeway Walk**'. Take this up to a junction by a gate on the left and turn right. Turn sharp left to zig-zag back across the hillside, where you turn right again. Follow this around to the left again, aiming at the **mast** and then, as you reach the field edge, bear right once more. This leads up to a narrow ridge where you turn left.

4 Climb steeply up the ridge and continue, with high ground to your left, to a fork with a narrow track that leads to the ridge top. Ignore this turning and keep to the main path below the ridge. Eventually the path curves left to reach a gate and a **tarmac drive**.

5 Follow the drive past some houses on the right-hand side to reach a junction. Turn right and climb up to another junction, where you bear right. **The Black Cock Inn** is away to your left.

6 Carry on past the golf club, then fork right on to a narrow lane that drops and bears around to the left. Turn right here to walk past the **Forestry Commission sign**

Left: Castell Coch is of triangular construction, with a tower at each angle

while you're there

For a more traditional castle – and the biggest in Wales – visit nearby Caerphilly, a splendid pile dating from 1268, with gaunt towers, stern concentric walls and a system of defensive lakes and channels (open daily, tel 029 2088 3134).

Far left: Caerphilly Castle

and then left, on to a narrow footpath marked by a **yellow-ringed post**.

7 Follow this path, ignoring tracks on both the right and left, until the posts become blue and you come to a T-junction by a sign forbidding horse riding. Turn left here, where the posts are once again yellow, and continue downhill, past a turning on the left to the **Countryside Visitor Centre**.

8 The track swings around to the right and descends to meet the drive. Turn right to climb up the drive and back to the **castle**.

what to look for

Fforest Fawr is a great place to spot woodland birds and mammals. Grey squirrels are common and have become unpopular in some quarters due to their inquisitive nature, insatiable appetite and ability to destroy bird feeders – they are frequently referred to as bushy-tailed rats. Nevertheless, their acrobatic displays are spectacular enough to bring a smile to anybody's face. They are often blamed for the demise of the smaller red squirrel in this country, but recent research has shown that the smaller, tufty-eared relative has actually declined due to habitat loss, courtesy of development.

Black Cock Inn

Situated beside a rural lane halfway up Caerphilly Mountain, this old coaching house is named after a horse that had the title 'Black Cock' and whose job it was to take over leading a team of horses that pulled a quarry cart up the 'mountain'. Raised up from the road, it has a sunny patio and a side garden with play area. Inside, you'll find a wood-floored lounge/dining area with wood-burning stove, dark wood tables and chairs, attractive prints, fresh flowers and a relaxing atmosphere. The separate public bar is the venue for the popular quiz nights.

Food

Expect a varied choice of traditional pub food. Warm salads, baguettes and filled jacket potatoes at lunch while in the evening there are grills, lamb shank, specials such as coq au vin, venison casserole and black halibut with citrus butter sauce. Separate Sunday lunch menu.

Family facilities

Children are very welcome inside the pub. There's a children's menu, smaller portions of adult dishes, and high chairs are available. The garden has a safe play area.

about the pub

Black Cock Inn
Blackbrook Road,
Caerphilly Mountain
Caerphilly CF83 1NF
Tel: 029 2085 9031
www.theblackcockinn.co.uk

DIRECTIONS: just north of Castell Coch; head left out of the car park and bear around left at the top of the hill. At Point **5** on the walk

PARKING: 60

OPEN: daily; all day Friday to Sunday

FOOD: daily

BREWERY/COMPANY: free house

REAL ALES: Hancocks HB, Bass, guest beer

DOGS: welcome in the bar

Alternative refreshment stops
For tea, coffee and snacks, there's a decent tearoom within Castell Coch.

☛ Where to go from here
Head west along the M4 to junction 33 and follow the A4232 south to St Fagans and the Museum of Welsh Life (www.nmgw.ac.uk). A stroll around the indoor galleries and 100 acres (40.5ha) of beautiful grounds is guaranteed to give you a fascinating insight into how people in Wales have lived, worked and spent their leisure hours since Celtic times. Venture into Cardiff to view the city's impressive Norman castle (www.cardiffcastle.com), the fascinating National Museum of Wales in Cathays Park (www.nmgw.ac.uk), or the restored medieval Llandaff Cathedral (www.llandaffcathedral.org.uk).

while you're there

Nearby Traeth Bychan witnessed tragedy in 1939, when a submarine on sea trials from Birkenhead failed to surface in the bay. The vessel flooded and 99 men died. The submarine eventually washed onto the beach, and was recovered to serve another day.

Menai Bridge

Anglesey has long been seen as a stepping stone to (and from) Ireland. The handsome suspension bridge at Menai was built by Thomas Telford in 1826 as part of the A5 London–Holyhead link.

Moelfre and Anglesey's Coast

Menai Bridge, which links the Isle of Anglesey to the mainland

Walk along Anglesey's beautiful east coast and discover a remarkably intact ancient village.

Ancient Village and Tales of Shipwrecks

Being in Moelfre is like being in Cornwall: the pebble beach, rustic whitewashed cottages looking down from the cliff tops, small boats in a tiny harbour, and that same bracing quality of wave-wafted air. As you stroll along the rocky coastline above the low cliffs, past the two lifeboat stations and the Seawatch Centre, all thoughts are on ships and the ocean. If it's sunny and the breeze is slight, everything appears picturesque and peaceful, but the Royal Charter Memorial, tells a different story.

The monument remembers the night of 26 October 1859. A British cutter, the *Royal Charter* was on the last stretch of its journey from Melbourne to Liverpool. As night fell, a savage storm ensued; the captain signalled for a pilot, but none would come on such a night. He set anchor, but at 1.30am the chain parted. At daybreak two locals saw the wreck being pounded against the rocks.

To their horror they saw a man shimmy down a rope and into the furious sea. He had volunteered to try to swim with a hawser for shore, the only means to secure the ship. Twice he failed, but Joseph Rogers, an able seaman from Malta, finally made it and lashed the ship to a rock. The gallant seaman and the men of Moelfre made a human chain. They managed to rescue 41 people, but on that day 452 people, including 28 men from Moelfre, lost their lives.

Returning to Moelfre you follow country lanes through peaceful pastures. Through the hedges you'll spot a roofless 12th-century chapel, which you pass en route to Din Lligwy, an ancient village hidden in the woods. This is a wonderfully preserved Celtic settlement dating back to the 4th century AD. In a field further down the lane are the remains of a neolithic burial chamber. The Lligwy tomb has a massive capstone weighing 25 tons.

1h30	3 MILES	4.8 KM	LEVEL 1 2 3

MAP: OS Explorer 263 Anglesey East

START/FINISH: car park at entrance to village; grid ref: SH 511862

PATHS: well-defined coastal and field paths, 4 stiles

LANDSCAPE: sea cliffs and coastal pasture

PUBLIC TOILETS: by harbour at Moelfre and at Lligwy Beach

TOURIST INFORMATION: Llanfairpwllgwyngyll, tel: 01248 713177

THE PUB: The Kimmel Arms, Moelfre

Getting to the start

Moelfre is situated on the northeast coast of Anglesey and signposted off the A5025 between Menai Bridge and Amlwch, 6 miles (10.1km) south of Amlwch. Car park is on the right just before you descend to the harbour.

Researched & written by:
John Gillham, David Hancock

The remains of a 12th-century house at Capel Lligwy near Moelfre

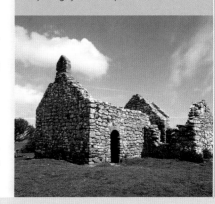

the walk

1 From the car park, follow the main road down to the shore. Here, where the road swings left and uphill for the village centre, leave it for the **shoreline path** on the right.

2 Pass the **Seawatch Centre** and the lifeboat station and ignore the footpath signs pointing inland. Instead follow a clear coast path that looks across to the island of **Ynys Moelfre**. After passing to the right of

did you know?

There's been a lighthouse on Point Lynas since 1835. Part of the keeper's duties was to wind the clockwork identification mechanism, which blocked the light for two seconds in every ten. This was achieved by pulling swiftly on an endless chain, and was required every four hours – an arduous labour described by one keeper as 'killing'. The light was electrified in 1952.

Left: Black guillemot (Cepphus grylle)

The Kinmel Arms

The homely, white-painted Kinmel Arms occupies a prime spot in this peaceful coastal village, overlooking the pebble beach with views across the harbour and out to sea. Arrive early to bag a seat in the pretty front patio garden. Inside there are memorabilia associated with the village lifeboats and rescues, as well as a display featuring ensigns from different parts of the world.

Food
There are bar snacks in the form of sandwiches, baps and ploughman's and more substantial dishes, including steaks, pies, curries and freshly caught fish, served at lunchtimes and in the evenings.

Family facilities
Children are very welcome inside. Youngsters have their own menu to choose from and high chairs are available.

Alternative refreshment stops
Ann's Pantry in the village is set in a pleasant whitewashed cottage with picnic tables in a lawned garden. There's also a café (Laura's Kitchen) beside the car park and beach, and a seasonal café at Lligwy Beach

☞ Where to go from here
Visit the Moelfre Seawatch Centre where you can climb aboard a real 20th-century lifeboat, learn about the marine wildlife found in these waters and discover Anglesey's fascinating maritime history (open Easter to September from 11am to 5pm). Head inland to Llangefni and visit Oriel Ynys Mon, a fascinating museum that tells the story about the history, wildlife and people of Anglesey.

about the pub

The Kinmel Arms
Moelfre Bay, Moelfre
Anglesey LL72 8HD
Tel: 01248 410231

DIRECTIONS: on the seafront; Point **1** of the walk
PARKING: use pay car park by quay or main village car park
OPEN: daily; all day
FOOD: daily
REAL ALE: Robinson's beers
BREWERY/COMPANY: Robinsons
DOGS: not allowed inside

A shingle beach at the edge of Moelfre village

some terraced cottages and going through a couple of kissing gates the path crosses a small caravan site. It then goes through another kissing gate and climbs past the **Royal Charter Memorial**.

3 After swinging left into **Porth Forllwyd**, go through another gate and then through a narrow ginnel that rounds the bay, past the cottage of Moryn into the large bay of **Traeth Lligwy**.

4 On reaching the **beach car park**, turn left along the narrow lane before going straight ahead at the crossroads with the main road.

5 Take the next path on the right, signposted to **Din Lligwy ancient village**. Before visiting the village you turn half right across the field to the old chapel, then half left towards the woods, where you'll find Din Lligwy. Return to the **lane** and turn right along it.

6 After 275yds (251m), turn left across a ladder stile and along a **signed footpath** which, after an initial dog-leg to the right to double stiles, follows a field edge to the roadside **quarry** at Aberstrecht.

7 Turn right along the lane, then left along a farm lane at **Caeau-gleision**. This brings you back to the shoreline **caravan site** met earlier in the walk.

8 Turn right beyond it and follow the back to the start.

what to look for
At Din Lligwy you enter the foundations of the old settlement through thick rubble walls, which would have been added as protection against the Romans who were, in those final years before retreat, quite quarrelsome. The circular huts inside were the living quarters, while the large rectangular hut in the top right-hand corner would have been the smelting workshop – the remains of a charcoal hearth were excavated here.

while you're there

A 7-mile (11.3km) loop south of Capel Curig takes in the rocky peak of Moel Siabod. It's an exhilarating climb, and the views to the Horseshoe and the major peaks of Snowdon are fabulous.

did you know?

Continue on the A5 towards Bangor and you'll pass the distinctive peak of Tryfan (3002m/9,847ft) on your left. The mountain is topped by Adam and Eve – not climbers but a pair of stone pillars.

Above the Llugwy Valley

Moel Siabod on a frosty morning

2h00 | **4 MILES** | **6.4 KM** | **LEVEL 1 2 3**

102

WALK

Capel Curig

CONWY

Discovering the valley where rocks and the mountains are still all important.

Capel Curig and the Llugwy Valley

Nowhere has one village been so strung out – Capel Curig's sparse cottages and inns stretch 6 miles (9.7km) between Pont-Cyfyng, beneath Moel Siabod, to the Pen y Gwryd, beneath Glyder Fawr. The well-spaced inns there first served quarrymen from the barracks of Siabod and the miners from the copper mines of Snowdon, and later walkers and climbers. These inns were a convenient meeting place for those pioneering new routes on the crags. Quickly, Capel Curig became the Zermatt of Wales, and Snowdon, the Matterhorn. In the 1950s the Pen y Gwryd Inn became a centre for planning Alpine and Himalayan expeditions. Here Lord Hunt and his team, who in 1953 were the first to reach the peak of Everest, met to make the final preparations before departing for Nepal.

This walk around the valley takes in views of the wide sweep of mountains that surround Capel Curig and the Llugwy Valley. There's an optional scramble to Capel's very own pinnacle, Y Pincin, where you can see the five distinctive peaks of Snowdon reflected beautifully below in the twin lakes of Mymbyr.

You continue through mature oak woods, before descending back down to the boisterous river. In front of the Ty'n y Coed Inn they have one of the old London to Holyhead stagecoaches on display. After crossing the river at Pont-Cyfyng you follow its delightful banks for a short while, then go over crag, across pasture and through woods. You come out by a footbridge on the shores of Llynnau Mymbyr, and again you see Snowdon, maybe still perfectly reflected in glass-like waters. On the other side of the bridge at the Plas y Brenin National Mountain Centre, they're training the next generation of mountaineers.

the walk

1 The path begins at a ladder stile by the **war memorial** on the A5 and climbs towards **Y Pincin**, a large craggy outcrop cloaked in wood and bracken. Go over another stile and keep to the north of the outcrop. Those who want to go to the top should do so from the northeast, where the gradients are easier. It's fun, but take care! You'll need to retrace your steps.

2 Continue east across woods and marshy ground, keeping to the south of the great crags of **Clogwyn Mawr**. On reaching a couple of ladder stiles, ignore the path back down to the road, but maintain your direction across the hillside.

3 Just beyond a footbridge over **Nant y Geuallt**, leave the main footpath and follow a less well-defined one across marshy ground. This veers south east to cross another stream before coming to a prominent track.

4 Turn right along the track, but leave it beyond a ladder stile and at a four-way meeting of paths. Go left here to reach a ladder stile and follow the path down into some woods. Take the right-hand fork descending to the road near **Ty'n y Coed Inn**.

Above left: Capel Curig in Snowdonia National Park

MAP: OS Explorer OL17 Snowdon

START/FINISH: free car park behind Joe Brown's shop at Capel Curig; grid ref: SJ 720582

PATHS: generally clear and surfaced, 9 stiles

LANDSCAPE: woodland, wetland and high pasture

PUBLIC TOILETS: by Joe Brown's shop

TOURIST INFORMATION: Betws-y-Coed, tel: 01690 710426

THE PUB: Bryn Trych, Capel Curig

❗ Care to taken if climbing the craggy outcrop (Y Pincin) and beside the River Llugwy

Getting to the start

Capel Curig is located at the junction of the A5 and A4086, 6 miles (10.1km) west of Betws-y-Coed. The car park is signed just north of the road junction, behind Joe Brown's outdoor shop.

Researched & written by:
John Gillham, David Hancock

The Ugly House

Midway between Capel Curig and Betws-y-coed, beside the A5, stands Ty Hyll – better known as the Ugly House. Built of lumpy, irregular stones, the cottage is said to be an example of a 15th-century dwelling built hastily in order to cash in on freehold rights to common land. It's now home to the Snowdonia Society (open Easter–October, tel 01690 720287).

Mount Tryfan in Snowdonia National Park

Bryn Trych

Appealing to walkers, climbers and holidaymakers, this homely, white-painted hostelry stands smack bang in the middle of Snowdonia National Park, 5 miles (8km) west of Betws-y-Coed. The draw is the well-worn interior, big winter fire and laid-back style. Picture windows run the length of the main bar with strategically placed tables taking in the view, or there are comfy sofas to sink into by the fire. The bare-bones hikers' bar sports a pool table and there's plenty of advice on climbs and walks. In the summer you can eat and drink outside.

Food
Lunch takes in ham and local Welsh cheese sandwiches, Welsh rarebit (made with Caerphilly and local real ale) and jacket potatoes. Evening blackboards add local lamb and leek sausages on mash, smoked haddock, prawn and mushroom pie, and confit of lamb with roasted winter vegetables. Desserts include such good things as lemon meringue pie and bread and butter pudding.

Family facilities
Children are made most welcome and smaller portions are available.

Alternative refreshment stops
The child-friendly Ty'n y Coed near Pont-Cyfyng is a popular free house serving very good food with a choice of tasty curries, steaks and fish dishes. The Pinnacle Café near the start of the walk is a lively place serving good café food, including all-day breakfasts and piping hot mugs of tea.

about the pub

Bryn Trych
Capel Curig, Betws-y-Coed
Gwynedd LL24 0EL
Tel: 01690 720223
www.bryntyrch-hotel.co.uk

DIRECTIONS: beside the A5 just east of the junction with the A4086 and the car park

PARKING: plenty

OPEN: closed Monday and Tuesday November–February

FOOD: daily, all day

BREWERY/COMPANY: free house

REAL ALE: Bass, Castle Eden Ale, Flowers IPA

DOGS: not allowed inside

ROOMS: 15 en suite

☞ Where to go from here
Visit the motor museum by the railway station at nearby Betws-y-coed. Based on the Houghton family's collection of vintage vehicles, exhibits include a Bugatti, Aston Martin, Bentley, Bullnose Morris, Model T Ford and MGs. There's also a land-speed-record jet engine and motoring memorabilia.

what to look for

The foxglove is one of Wales' most common plants. It's big, it's bold, and between June and August this biennial will be boasting columns of vivid pink bell-like flowers. It's deadly poisonous, but its leaves were the original source for the heart drug, digitalis. The word foxglove comes from 'folk's glove', probably a corruption of the Anglo-Saxon word 'gliew', the name of a musical instrument with bells just like the flower.

5 Turn left down the road, then right, along the lane over **Pont-Cyfyng**. Go right again beyond the bridge to follow a footpath that traces the Llugwy to another bridge opposite **Cobdens Hotel**. Don't cross this time, but scramble left over some rocks before continuing through the woods of **Coed Bryn-engan**, where the path soon becomes a wide track.

6 After passing the cottage of **Bryn-engan**, the track comes to the bridge at the head of the **Mymbyr lakes**. Turn right across it, then left along the road for a short way.

7 Go over the next ladder stile on the right-hand side of the road and take the higher of two tracks swinging round to the right. This hugs the foot of the southern **Glyder** slopes.

8 When you get beyond **Gelli farm** turn right to follow the cart track back to the **car park**.

Raven (Corvus corax)

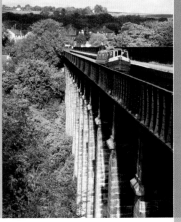

A barge on Telford's Pontcysyllte Aqueduct

Horseshoe Falls

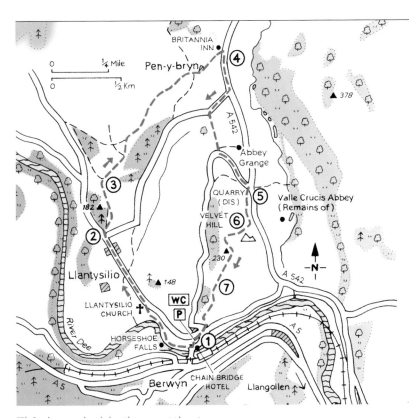

2h30 · **4 MILES** · **6.4 KM** · **LEVEL 1 2 3**

MAP: OS Explorer 255 Llangollen & Berwyn

START/FINISH: picnic site and car park at Llantysilio Green on minor road north of Berwyn Station; grid ref: SJ 198433

PATHS: field paths in valley and on hillside, 7 stiles

LANDSCAPE: rolling hillsides, woodland and riverside pastures

PUBLIC TOILETS: at car park

TOURIST INFORMATION: Llangollen, tel: 01978 860828

THE PUB: The Britannia Inn, Llangollen

❶ Care to be taken beside the canal and waterfall; 2 steep climbs

Getting to the start

The picnic area at Lantysilio can be accessed from the A5 or the A542, 2 miles (3.2km) northwest of Llangollen. From the A5 take the lane right by Berwyn Station, cross the River Dee and turn left for the car park, just past the Chain Bridge Hotel.

Researched & written by:
John Gillham, David Hancock

This is probably the prettiest walk in the Welsh section, aptly named the Velvet Hill.

Horseshoe Falls & Velvet Hill

At the picnic site at Llantysilio Green, there's an idyllic spot where the Dee, enshrouded by trees, squeezes between the beautifully named Velvet Hill and the wooded hillside of Bryniau-mawr Bank. Yet the moment descend to the banks of the Dee you realise you're not quite in the countryside yet. Through the trees you see the Chain Bridge Hotel, Llangollen Railway at Berwyn Station, and Llangollen Canal.

The canal ends after a short distance and you cross the meadows by the banks of the Dee. Just upstream are the Horseshoe Falls. Though they're an impressive piece of engineering, many visitors feel a bit let down that the falls are not nature's own creation. Set on a natural curve of the river, the weir was Thomas Telford's solution to harnessing the Dee to feed and control the levels of the Llangollen and Ellesmere canals. Beyond the falls, the walk climbs to Llantysilio's little church, dating from the 7th century, though much of the structure was added between the 18th and 19th centuries. There's a plaque in memory of poet, Robert Browning, who worshipped here in 1886. A tractor track takes you above the tree tops, then a sheep track leads you along the hillside of Pen-y-bryn, with views of both the Dee and its tributary the Eglwyseg opening up.

On Velvet Hill you should see wondrous landscapes in a hundred shades of green. The Dee meanders in crazy horseshoes. It's joined by the Afon Eglwyseg which flows beneath gleaming terraces of limestone. In the valley bottom beneath the crags, the Cistercian abbey of Valle Crucis seems diminutive in this big scene, as does the romantic castle-topped hill of Dinas Bran.

the walk

1 From the car park walk down to the road, turn right for a few paces then descend some steps to the back of the **Chain Bridge Hotel**. Turn right to follow the path between the river and the canal. Through a kissing gate at the end of the canal you traverse riverside fields past the **Horseshoe Falls** and climb to **Llantysilio church**. On reaching the road, turn left through Llantysilio to reach a junction.

2 Go through a five-bar gate a few paces along the side road and climb along a **rutted track**, which keeps a forest to the left, then climbs north on a high pastured hillside. Bear half-left at the **telegraph pole** to a reach a stile in the field corner.

while you're there

Try a taster of the Llangollen Canal. A narrow boat, the Thomas Telford, *takes 2-hour trips from the Wharf in Llangollen (Easter–October, tel 01978 860702), including the famous Pontcysyllte Aqueduct, or you can take a shorter, horse-drawn trip to the Canal Museum.*

In Passing

The walk passes the remains of the Cistercian Valle Crucis Abbey, founded in 1201 in this deep, narrow valley. It's open all year, with access to the church and some carved grave slabs.

Above: The ruins of Valle Crucis Abbey

parallel to the top edge of another wood. The now narrow path descends to cottages at **Pen-y-bryn**. After a stile and squeezing through a ginnel to the right of the first cottage the route follows a drive out to the Horseshoe Pass road at **The Britannia Inn**.

4 Turn right along the road, then right again when you get to the first junction. Go over a stile on the left to head south across two fields. Turn right along a **farm track** then left past a large stone-built house to arrive at a narrow lane. Go left along this to meet the **Horseshoe Pass road** again.

5 Go over a stile on the right-hand side of the road, signposted to the **Velvet Hill**, and ascend by **quarry workings**.

3 Turn right beside the fence, the path swings left uphill, then right, keeping

6 Turn right along a wide grassy track climbing steeply through the bracken to the ridge, there turning left for the **summit**.

7 Descend south on a narrow footpath to reach a fence above some woods. Do not cross (as many have done), but follow the fence down left to a **stile**. Descend to the lane, cross over and turn right along a path that leads back to the **car park**.

Above: A steam train crossing the viaduct at Berwyn Station on the Llangollen Railway

what to look for

On the hill slopes above Pen-y-bryn you pass the remains of a slate quarry incline. Quarrying has been carried out on the Llantysilio Mountains for many hundreds of years and the Berwyn Slate Quarry, over the hill near the Horseshoe Pass, still operates. You can see the remains of the old pulley houses and the ramps, which plummet straight as a die, all the way down to Abbey Grange.

The Britannia Inn

The location is an essential part of this pub's attraction. Set in the heart of the country at the foot of the famous hairpin ascent of Horseshoe Pass, tucked into the mountains, the 1462 building draws much of its custom from tourists, families and walkers, particularly during the summer months, when crowds attend the International Eisteddfod at Llangollen. You have the choice of two modern pine furnished bars and there's an award-winning garden with super rural views. This is a welcome half-way refreshment stop for Theakston ales and a good selection of bar meals.

Food

Bar food ranges from traditional snacks and the ever-popular Britannia steak pie to salmon with cucumber sauce and stuffed plaice Royal

Family facilities

Children are welcome in the bar and overnight. Young children have their own menu and smaller portions can be provided.

Alternative refreshment stops

Take the short drive into Llangollen to locate the Cornmill pub right beside the cascading River Dee. If you're looking for a cosy bistro for an evening meal, try Jonkers.

about the pub

The Britannia Inn
Horseshoe Pass, Llangollen
Denbighshire LL20 8DW
Tel: 01978 860144

DIRECTIONS: beside the A542 north of Llangollen at the foot of Horseshoe Pass; Point 4 on the walk

PARKING: 60

OPEN: daily

FOOD: daily

BREWERY/COMPANY: free house

REAL ALE: Theakston Best & Old Peculier

DOGS: allowed in the bar

ROOMS: 7 en suite

☛ Where to go from here

From the refurbished Llangollen Station you can take a ride on one of the vintage steam trains that operate along a beautiful 8 mile (13km) stretch of the Dee Valley to Carrog. Eventually the line will be extended to Corwen. You can plan a pub lunch or a picnic from any of the stations, which have been painstakingly restored to their early 1950s liveries. Berwyn Station lies close to the start of the walk.

Rochford's Revenge

The terraced gardens of Powis Castle owe their existence to the Earl of Rochford, a nephew of William III to whom the king granted the property in 1696. Unfortunately, when the property reverted to the Herbert family in 1722, Rochford stripped the house of 'all that he thought worth taking', including all the furniture.

Powis Castle

The statue of a piper on the terrace of Powis Castle

The terraced gardens of Powis Castle

See how the Earls of Powis lived as you walk through their deer park and past their huge red palace on the hill.

Powis Castle

A prosperous and bustling market town set amid rolling hills, woods and hedgerows, Welshpool has always been synonymous with the River Severn, which flows through it. The Severn brought trade to the town, for it was navigable by boat. The town was, until 1835, known as Pool and some of the old mileposts still refer to Pool. The 'Welsh' was added to distinguish the place from Poole in Dorset.

When you walk up the busy High Street today you'll notice the fine architecture, most of it Georgian, like the Royal Oak Hotel, but also many older half-timbered buildings. Almost every visitor to Welshpool comes to see the fine castle of Powis. On this route you turn through the impressive wrought-iron gates and stroll along the long drive through the estate's parklands. Oaks are scattered on the well-mown grasslands and a majestic scene is set when you see deer roaming among the trees.

Today, the castle is a grand red mansion, with castellated ramparts, tall chimneys, rows of fine leaded windows and 17th-century balustraded terraces looking over manicured lawns and neatly clipped yews. Lead statues of a shepherd and shepherdess keep watch over the colourful shrubs and perennial borders.

The scene would have been different in 1200, when the castle was built for the warring princes of Powys. The battlements would have been there, but there would have been no elegant windows or gardens, for this place was designed to repel enemies, both English and Welsh: more often than not Powis sided with the English, even against the Glyndwr rebellion. The fact that Powis has been continuously occupied

has meant that it has made a successful transition from fortress to a comfortable grand mansion.

In 1587 the powerful Herbert family, later Earls of Powis, took possession of the castle. They lived here until 1988, when the 6th Earl died.

On leaving the castle, you are in rural Wales and descend to the tow path of the Montgomery Canal. Today the canal is a quiet backwater and a pleasant return route to the wharf at Welshpool.

the walk

1 From the main car park, go past the tourist information centre then go left along **Church Street**. At the crossroads in the centre of town turn right to head up Broad Street, which later becomes High Street.

2 When you get to a point just beyond the **town hall**, turn left past a small car parking area and pass through the impressive wrought iron gates of the **Powis Castle Estate**. Now follow the tarmac drive through the park grounds and past **Llyn Du** (which means the black lake in English).

3 Take the right fork, the high road, which leads to the north side of the **castle**. You can detour from the walk here to visit the world-famous gardens and the castle with its fine paintings and furniture and works of Indian art collected by Robert Clive. Continue on the walk on the high road and follow it past two more pools on the left to reach a **country lane**.

2h00 · **4 MILES** · **6.4 KM** · **LEVEL 1 2 3**

MAP: OS Explorer 216 Welshpool & Montgomery

START/FINISH: large pay car park off Church Street, Welshpool; grid ref: SJ 226075

PATHS: tarmac drive, field path, canal tow path, 3 stiles

LANDSCAPE: country town, parkland and canal

TOILETS: by information centre in car park

TOURIST INFORMATION: Welshpool, tel: 01938 552043

THE PUB: The Royal Oak, Welshpool

❗ Care to be taken with children beside the canal

Getting to the start

Welshpool is located off the A483 between Newtown and Oswestry, 16 miles (25.8km) south of Oswestry and close to the Shropshire border. Church Street and the car park is just north of the High Street; follow signs for the Tourist Information Centre.

Researched & written by:
John Gillham, David Hancock

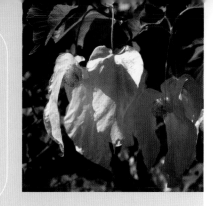

while you're there

The black-and-white cottage beside the church in Welshpool was the gift of Lady Nithsdale to her faithful servant, Grace Evans, for assisting in the escape of her husband from the Tower of London. Lord Nithsdale, a Catholic, was imprisoned and condemned for his support of the 1715 Jacobite uprising, but made his daring escape, disguised in his wife's clothes, on the eve of execution, before fleeing to exile in Rome.

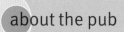

The Royal Oak

Far left: The view from the terrace of Powis Castle

Reputedly the manor house of the Earl of Powis, this substantial building in the heart of the town dates from the 17th century and later became a coaching inn. Named after the famous Montgomery Oak, which once stood at the crossroads by the inn, the former Oak Inn became Royal in the 19th century when Queen Victoria visited Powis Castle. Traditionally decorated inside, you have the choice of the Acorn Family Café and Restaurant for light meals or the Oak and Ostler Bars for good pub meals and cask ales.

Food

Lunchtime food is traditional pub fare, ranging from sandwiches and salads to fish and chips, curries, lasagne and pork escalope with fresh vegetables. Evening a la carte menu.

Family facilities

Children are made very welcome; there's a children's menu and high chairs are available in the Acorn Café. There are two family bedrooms.

about the pub

The Royal Oak
The Cross, Welshpool
Powys SY21 7DG
Tel: 01938 552217

DIRECTIONS: town centre at the junction of Church Street and Broad Street; Point **1** of the walk

PARKING: 25

OPEN: daily; all day

FOOD: daily

BREWERY/COMPANY: free house

REAL ALE: Woods Shropshire Lad, guest beer

DOGS: welcome in the bar outside meal times

ROOMS: 25 en suite

Alternative refreshment stops

At Peppers you'll find a wide variety of coffees and beverages to go with the home-made cakes and light meals. There are plenty of pubs in Welshpool and, if you are visiting Powis Castle, there's an excellent café/restaurant serving light lunches and afternoon teas.

☛ Where to go from here

You could take a trip on the Welshpool and Llanfair Railway, another one of those great little narrow-gauge steam railways of Wales. Pulled by engines from places as far afield as Sierra Leone and Austria, the train steams its way through the verdant valley of the Afon Banwy to Llanfair Caereinion. It's open at weekends between March and December and on most days in June, July and August.

what to look for

The lack of recent activity in the canal has allowed several interesting plant species to grow here such as floating water plantain with its white buttercup-like flowers with yellow spots – it blooms between May and August. The perennial plant's surface leaves are elliptical while those underwater are narrow and tapering. You may also see the scarce frogbit, another floating perennial with similar pearly white flowers and bronze-tinged green kidney shaped leaves.

4 Turn left along the country lane. Opposite the next **estate entrance** leave the lane for a path on the right which follows a dirt track across a field. The track turns left over a **bridge** and into another field. Here you follow a fence on the right and cut diagonally across the field to a step stile in the far corner. Over this a clear sunken grass track continues across another field to reach a country lane close to the **Montgomery Canal**. The canal, which runs for 33 miles (53km) from Welsh Frankton in Shropshire to Newtown in Powys, is gradually being restored. You may see narrowboats cruising this section.

5 Turn left along the lane before taking a path on the left which descends to the canal tow path at **Belan Locks**. Head north along the canal, passing close to some half-timbered cottages. Pass the **Powysland Museum** and Canal Centre to reach the wharf and aqueduct at **Welshpool**. Turn left here along the tarred path to return to the **car park**.

did you know?

The poet and scholar A E Housman (1859–1936) is buried in the churchyard of St Laurence's at Ludlow. He's best remembered for his book of poignant verse, A Shropshire Lad, *which evokes the countryside of this area (but written from a villa in north London).*

The Princes in the Tower

The boy king Edward V and his brother Richard, sons of Edward IV, were lodged in the 'safety' of Ludlow Castle before being removed to the Tower of London in 1483. They were never heard of again.

Through the Teme Valley

Above: Statue of A E Housman
Below: Time to check the map at a road junction

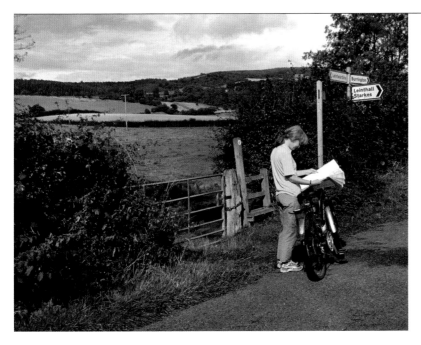

105

CYCLE

| 2h30 | 10.8 MILES | 17.4 KM | LEVEL 1 2 3 |

MAP: OS Explorer 203 Ludlow, Tenbury Wells & Cleobury Mortimer

START/FINISH: Petchfield Farm, Elton; grid ref: SO 454704 (small charge for parking)

TRAILS/TRACKS: quiet lanes throughout

LANDSCAPE: gentle valley amidst rolling hills

PUBLIC TOILETS: none on route

TOURIST INFORMATION: Ludlow, tel 01584 875053

CYCLE HIRE: Wheely Wonderful Cycling, Petchfield Farm, Elton, Ludlow, tel 01568 770755 (www.wheelywonderfulcycling.co.uk)

THE PUB: The Lion Hotel, Leintwardine

❗ Narrow country lanes, be aware of traffic and pedestrians

Getting to the start

Petchfield Farm, some 5 miles (8km) southwest of Ludlow, is most easily approached from the A4110 at Wigmore along a minor lane east through Leithnall Starkes. You will find the entrance to Petchfield Farm on the right after a mile (1.6km). Park in the yard beside 'Wheely Wonderful Cycle Hire'.

Why do this cycle ride?

The country lanes around Ludlow offer superb cycling, and although the general landscape is quite hilly, there are many easy routes that follow the base of the valleys. This one explores the valley of the River Teme between Elton and Leintwardine, and at one point follows the line of an important Roman road.

Researched & written by: Dennis Kelsall

Seeking out the valleys amongst the Shropshire Hills.

Leintwardine

The lane out of Leintwardine takes you below a prominent hill on the right, on which there are the earthbank remains of a large Iron Age stronghold. When the Romans arrived in the area around 50 AD, they too recognised its importance and, in addition to taking it over, established another camp, Bravonium, by the river where the village now stands. In fact the church actually straddles one of the ramparts. The camp lay on a Roman road, Welsh Watling Street, between Wroxeter (near Shrewsbury) and Caerleon (outside Newport), and was an important military route to help maintain order amongst the British tribes that still held strong in Wales. The road was also an imperial post road, and the camp was the equivalent of a stage post, supplying fresh horses and refreshment to speed the messengers on their way. During the calmer period of the 3rd century, the military presence declined, but by then, a civilian settlement had already sprung up, thriving on the trade that passed up and down the road.

Leintwardine's large church is known locally as the 'Cathedral of North Herefordshire'. It contains early 15th-century choir stalls with interestingly carved misericords, said to have come from the Augustinian Wigmore Abbey, which stood close to Paytoe Hall. In the churchyard of Burrington Church are a number of unusual cast-iron grave slabs, marking the burials of local iron-founding families. During the 17th and early 18th centuries, iron was smelted using charcoal, and the surrounding forests were managed to provide abundant supplies of fuel.

the ride

1 Leaving **Petchfield Farm**, go right towards the hamlet of Elton, shortly passing a narrow lane off on the right, **Killhorse Lane**. You will discover the appropriateness of its name if you turn up it, for it has just about the steepest gradient in the area. Thankfully your route bends left, signed to Ludlow, soon taking you past a splendid manor house, **Elton Hall**.

2 At the next junction, turn off left, signed 'Burrington and Leintwardine', along a narrower lane, where occasional breaks in the hedges allow views across the valley to a backdrop of rolling hills. Before long the road begins to lose height, soon passing a lane off to the right, some 150yds (137m) along which you will find the entrance to **Burrington Church**. The route, however, continues ahead, the lane by now a leafy tunnel formed by a profuse growth of hazels on either side. Keep ahead past a turning to Leinthall Starkes to cross a bridge over the **Teme**, ignoring successive turnings to Downton a little later on and eventually reaching a junction by **Nacklestone Farm**.

3 **Leintwardine** is signed to the right, the way falling easily and soon

while you're there

Croft Castle lies south of Leintwardine, and has provided a roof for the Croft family since records began with the Domesday Book (with just a 170-year blip from the mid-18th century). Now owned by the National Trust, it's open on selected days (tel 01568 780246), with a garden and tearoom to explore, and the Iron Age fort of Croft Ambrey accessible via a footpath.

The 14th-century clock tower of the Church of St Mary Magdalene at Leintwardine

affording a view to the village, the church with its sturdy tower an obvious feature. At a **T-junction**, sweep left with the main lane, and carry on to the end where there is a riverside green opposite **The Lion Hotel**.

4 Turn left over an arched bridge to re-cross the River Teme, and then go left again just beyond onto a narrow lane signed to **Paytoe**. After passing a couple

of **yards** on the outskirts of the village, the way continues in an almost dead-straight line along the flat valley floor following the line of a Roman road.

5 When you reach a junction, turn left in front of the splendid black-and-white **Paytoe Hall**, and pedal across the width of the valley, directed towards Ludlow. After crossing the Teme once more, go right and for a short while retrace your outward route. Just after the next bridge, turn off right to **Leinthall Starkes** and begin a short climb out of the valley that levels off to offer a view ahead to a **windmill** on the hillside above Leinthall. The lane then bends sharply right and later left to drop towards the village.

6 When you reach a T-junction at the end go left, the lane undulating gently downwards along the valley side to take you back to **Petchfield Farm**.

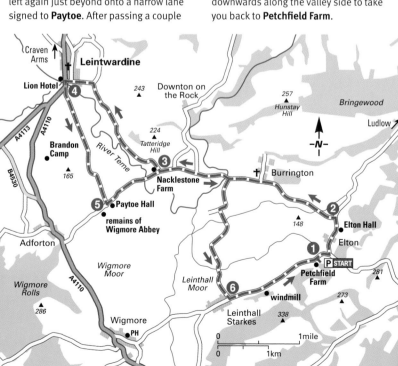

The Lion Hotel

The grounds of Croft Castle

The Lion enjoys an attractive riverside location by the bridge opposite the village green, and at the back has a peaceful, landscaped garden overlooking the River Teme and Brockley Meadow. It dates back to the 18th century when it was a thriving hotel and, although no longer residential, the building retains much of its character both in appearance and in the traditional hospitality offered by the hosts.

Food

Wide-ranging menus take in lunchtime sandwiches, baguettes and filled jacket potatoes, standard bar snacks, various pies and grills, and daily specials like lamb pie, Somerset pork and cauliflower cheese. On Sundays, you'll find a choice of roasts, and there is a regular barbecue on summer Friday evenings.

Family facilities

Children of all ages are welcomed inside and there's a children's menu and an area set aside for families.

about the pub

The Lion Hotel
High Street, Leintwardine, Ludlow
Shropshire SY7 0JZ
Tel: 01547 540203

DIRECTIONS: close to Leintwardine Bridge over the River Teme on the A4113 (see Point **3**)

PARKING: 40

OPEN: daily; all day Saturday

FOOD: no food Sunday evening

BREWERY/COMPANY: Enterprise Inns

REAL ALE: changing guest beers

Alternative refreshment stops

The Sun at Leintwardine (Rosemary Lane) is an unspoiled gem and worth a visit for Woods tapped from the barrel, but no food is available.

☛ Where to go from here

Spend some time exploring the extensive range of ruined buildings at Ludlow Castle (www.ludlowcastle.com), where audio guides bring the castle to life. Discover the secrets of the Shropshire Hills at the Discovery Centre in Craven Arms, where the history, nature and geography of the area is explored through a series of interactive displays and simulations, all housed in a striking building set in 25 acres (10ha) of meadows (www.shropshireonline.gov.uk/discover.nsf). Visit Stokesay Castle, a perfectly preserved 13th-century fortified manor house – stroll through the great hall and delightful cottage gardens.

did you know?

Mortimer's Cross, at a junction south of Aymestrey, was the scene of a decisive battle in 1461, towards the end of the Wars of the Roses. These battles for power were fought out between the houses of York and Lancaster, and made way for Yorkist Edward IV to take the throne of England from Lancastrian Henry VI.

Left: The millpond
at Eardisland

The Mortimer Trail around Aymestrey

What have 'Capability' Brown, Richard Payne Knight and Hanson Aggregates got in common? Find out on this brief walk through time.

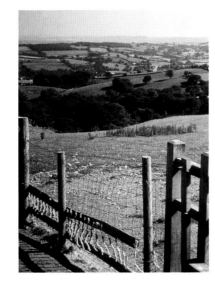

Natural and man-made landscapes
Shobdon Airfield was one of the many airfields built in 1940, as part of wartime preparations. The government compulsorily purchased the modest, privately owned quarry at Aymestrey, ensuring a local supply of stone for the airfield. In its latter years the quarry was run by Hanson Aggregates. The company may not expect to be remembered for its landscape architecture in the same way as Lancelot 'Capability' Brown, or Richard Payne Knight, but it should be commended for trying.

Towards the end of the walk, as you descend to the former quarry area, there is little to indicate that the landscape has been recently manufactured, although your curiosity may be alerted by the absence of any really substantial trees. Unlike many quarries, the plan here was to return the land to a mixture of agricultural use and woodland. People tend not to like quarries in their backyards, so quarries often get a bad press. The quarry companies will argue that 'restoration' and 'environmental sensitivity' were among their objectives a decade or two before their current fashionability.

West of Aymestrey the River Lugg runs in a small but spectacular gorge. This is a glacial overflow channel that exploited a fault in the rock, associated with the glacial Wigmore Lake. The paucity of contours on the map a few grid squares to the north shows the position of the former lake. At Mortimer's Cross, Richard of York's son, Edward, defeated the Lancastrian army in 1461 in one of the battles that changed the course of the Wars of the Roses (Edward was crowned king later that year). The battle site is 0.5 mile (800m) south of the road junction named Mortimer's Cross. The cross itself dates from 1799.

the walk

NOTE: You may experience some access problems with the path to the west of the A4110 (Point **2**). A major overhaul will be carried out at some stage but in the meantime the landowner has given permission to use the 'unofficial' parallel path a short distance to the south of the described route.

1 Walk up the access road for almost 0.5 mile (800m), until beyond the garden of a newish house and just before a **junction of tracks**. Note a stile on the right – your route returns over this.

2 Go 30yds (27m) further and turn left. Go left at a fork and walk along to a **T- junction**. Turn left to the A4110. Cross directly to a stile, walking along the left-hand field edge. Through a gate go forward then skirt round the right edge of an oak and ash embankment, to find a corner stile. Walk up the left edge of this field but, at the brow, where it bends for some 70yds (64m) to a corner, slip left through a gap in the hedge to walk along its other side. Within 60yds (55m) you will be on a clear path, steeply down through woodland, a ravine on your left. Join the driveway of **River Bow**, to a minor road. (The glacial overflow channel is directly ahead.)

3 Turn left here, joining the **Mortimer Trail**. Enjoy this wooded, riverside lane for nearly 0.75 mile (1.2km), to reach the A4110 again. Cross, then walk for just 25yds (23m) to the right. (**The Riverside Inn** is about 175yds/160m further.) Take a **raised green track**, heading for the hills. Then go diagonally across two fields, to a stile and wooden steps.

4 Ascend steeply through the trees. Leave by a stile, to cross two meadows diagonally. Take the stile on the right to walk along the left-hand edge of a field, still heading downhill. At the trees turn left. Soon reach a tarmac road. Turn left along

Open farmland by the Mortimer Trail

2h30 | **4.75 MILES** | **7.7 KM** | **LEVEL 123**

MAP: OS Explorer 203 Ludlow

START/FINISH: at old quarry entrance, on east side of A4110, 0.25 mile (400m) north of Aymestrey Bridge; grid ref: SO 426658

PATHS: excellent tracks, field paths, minor roads, steep woodland sections, 11 stiles

LANDSCAPE: wooded hills and undulating pastures

PUBLIC TOILETS: none on route

TOURIST INFORMATION: Ludlow, tel 01584 875053

THE PUB: The Riverside Inn, Aymestrey

❶ Several steep climbs, busy road crossing, lengthy section of quiet country lane. Not suitable for young children

Getting to the start

Aymestrey is on the A4110 road between Ludlow and Hereford. The layby/parking area where the walk starts is just to the north of the village, on the right coming from the south.

Researched & written by:
Nick Channer, Julie Royle

Right: Interior of Shobden church

Shobdon

Don't miss the church at Shobdon – it's a frothy rococo masterpiece of 1752, almost certainly by the same architects who created Horace Walpole's Gothic confection at Strawberry Hill. The interior decoration is white, picked out in blue, and has been likened to wedding cake.

while you're there

The village of Kingsland, off the A4110, is worth a detour – along with nearby Eardisland, it's one of the most attractive black-and-white villages in the area, with some good Georgian brickwork, too.

The Riverside Inn

An attractive half-timbered Welsh longhouse, dating from 1580, set on the banks of the River Lugg. An inn since 1700 it is perfectly placed midway along the Mortimer Trail and makes the ideal stop-off point for walkers. The interior, with its low beams and open fires, provides a relaxing atmosphere in which to sample local Wye Valley beers and some excellent food from an imaginative menu that utilises locally grown produce, notably fruit and vegetables from the pub garden. Lovely terraced and riverside gardens for summer sipping.

Food

Here you can eat anything from simple baguettes to proper country fare, including local black pudding and apple compôte, lamb's kidneys, saddle of rabbit with mustard and red wine jus, and roast venison on sweet and sour cabbage.

about the pub

The Riverside Inn
Aymestrey, Leominster
Herefordshire HR6 9ST
Tel: 01568 708440
www.theriversideinn.org

DIRECTIONS: see Getting to the start; pub just south of parking area by the River Lugg

PARKING: 40

OPEN: daily; closed Sunday & Monday evenings October to March

FOOD: daily

BREWERY/COMPANY: free house

REAL ALE: Woods & Wye Valley Brewery beers

DOGS: allowed inside

ROOMS: 7 en suite

Family facilities

Children are welcome in the dining areas of the pub. There are high chairs and two family bedrooms, and smaller portions of adult dishes can be provided.

Alternative refreshment stops

The Mortimer's Cross Inn, at the junction of that name, has a beer garden and a children's play area.

☛ Where to go from here

You'll have to do this walk on a Thursday if you want to visit Lucton Mill (also called Mortimer's Cross Water Mill), managed by English Heritage. Remarkably, this 18th-century mill was still grinding corn commercially in the 1940s. The wheel still turns today from time to time. You could spend the best part of a day on the Croft Estate. As well as viewing the castle, there are waymarked walks (www.nationaltrust.org.uk).

the road, now going back uphill. Beyond **Hill Farm**, enter the **Croft Estate**. Walk along this hard gravel track. After 110yds (100m) ignore a right fork but, 550yds (503m) further on, you must leave it. This spot is identified by an end to the deciduous trees on the left and a **Mortimer Trail marker post** on the wide ride between larches and evergreens on the right.

5 Turn left (there is no signpost). Within 110yds (100m) go half right and more steeply down. This aged access track gives expansive views over **felled forest**. Within 250yds (229m) look out for a **modern wooden gate**, waymarked, leading out of

the woods. Walk along its right-hand edge (and beside a recently appended small **plantation**). At the far corner, within the field, turn left to Point 2. Retrace your steps to the start of the walk.

what to look for

As you walk through Yatton there are stunning brick-arched barns on the right. These tall stone structures have brick apertures; one is filled in with attractive gridded brickwork. Later, look back from the other side of the A4110 to see more arches.

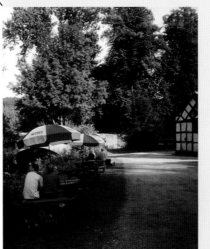

while you're there

Between Wistanstow and Bishop's Castle lies Walcott Hall, a country mansion commissioned by Robert Clive – better known as Clive of India – in 1763 from Scottish architect William Chambers. Clive was born in Market Drayton, in Shropshire, and no doubt saw this as returning to his roots, though he barely lived long enough to enjoy the house, committing suicide in 1774. The house is greatly changed inside, and now offers its ballroom as a wedding venue, but Clive memorabilia can be seen at Powis Castle (page 131).

Wistanstow and the Onny Trail

Great views from the hills, with reminders of the age of steam.

Left: The river Onny runs alongside the Onny Trail for part of the walk

107

2h00 | **4.5 MILES** | **7.2 KM** | **LEVEL 123**

WALK

MAP: OS Explorer 217 The Long Mynd & Wenlock Edge

START/FINISH: car park for Onny Trail, next to railway bridge on unclassified road from A49 to Cheney Longville; grid ref: SO 430843

PATHS: generally good, some muddy patches, steep out of Cheney Longville, sometimes slippery; 4 stiles

LANDSCAPE: wooded hills, pastureland and varied terrain by River Onny

PUBLIC TOILETS: none on route

TOURIST INFORMATION: Church Stretton, tel 01694 723133 (seasonal) or Ludlow 01584 875053

THE PUB: The Plough Inn, Wistanstow

⚠ Take care crossing busy road to and from the pub

Getting to the start

Follow the A49 between Craven Arms and Church Stretton and take the turning for Cheney Longville. The entrance to the car park where there is access to the Onny Trail, is on the right.

Researched & written by:
Nick Channer, Julie Royle

Craven Arms

Craven Arms is a young town, though possibly a very old settlement. It owes its present form to the coming of the railways, before which it was little more than a huddle of cottages at the hamlet of Newton, near the Craven Arms Hotel. The Shrewsbury and Hereford Railway was built through Craven Arms in the 1840s, followed by the Knighton line to Wales, the Buildwas line to the coalfields and the Bishop's Castle line, making The Arms, as it was known, a major railway junction. The cattle and sheep that had formerly travelled the drove roads now came by train, and other business opportunities were opened up. Local landowner Lord Craven recognised the potential and built a new town. For a while it seemed as though it might mushroom, but it never quite happened. Two of the railway lines have gone, but the Shrewsbury–Hereford line is still busy. The Knighton line is now part of the Heart of Wales line and runs through gloriously remote countryside to Swansea.

The line that inspired most affection has long gone. This was the Bishop's Castle line, authorised in 1861. The plan was for a link from the Shrewsbury and Hereford line to the Oswestry and Newtown (later Cambrian) line near Montgomery, with short branches to Montgomery and Bishop's Castle. Financial problems dogged the railway company from the start, but they went ahead with an official opening in 1865, using a borrowed locomotive hauling borrowed coaches. Regular traffic started the next year, but only from Craven Arms to Bishop's Castle, via a junction at Lydham Heath. The rest of the line was never finished. There was meant to be a double junction at Lydham, but they completed only part of it, and that faced in the wrong direction for trains from Craven Arms. Throughout the railway's life, it was necessary for locomotives to uncouple at Lydham and run around their carriages to recouple in reverse for the last few miles. Not surprisingly, the railway was never profitable. It is said it was so slow that people would get off to pick blackberries or mushrooms, then stroll along the line to reboard. When rural bus services started soon after 1900, the Bishop's Castle line was doomed, though it hung on until 1935.

The easternmost stretch of the line has now been turned into the Onny Trail, which is open for public access under the Countryside Stewardship scheme. It makes a delightful walk along the banks of the River Onny, giving an idea of what immensely scenic countryside was traversed by the old Bishop's Castle Railway. It also forms the return leg of this beautiful walk.

what to look for

The Onny Trail is notable for scenery and wildlife, but railway buffs will enjoy it too. The trail begins on the site of Strefford Junction, just north of Craven Arms, where the Bishop's Castle line left the Shrewsbury and Hereford main line. An interpretation board in the car park provides some useful information and access details.

the walk

1 Walk to the lane and turn right. Keep straight on at a junction and pass through **Cheney Longville**. Stay on the road, following it out of the village and up between fields with glorious views over the Welsh Marches. Pass alongside **woodland** and then turn right at a 'no through road' sign.

did you know?

The western spur of Roman Watling Street passed through Wistanstow. It was built as part of a defence programme against marauding Celts.

Left: Stokesay Castle

Stokesay Castle

This charming fortified manor house, south of Craven Arms, with its golden timber-framed gatehouse and lovely cottage gardens, is open all year and well worth a visit (tel 01588 672544).

107

WALK

2 Follow the lane beside **Longville Common** and at the end of the tarmac, continue on a stony and grass track between carpets of bracken. Cross the **disused railway** and then turn left at the waymark to join the **Onny Trail**.

3 Stay on the old trackbed, veering off half left at one point to cut through adjoining fields. On reaching a footbridge and an **Onny Trail sign**, turn left and follow the track to the A489. Cross it and take the lane to **The Plough** at Wistanstow.

4 Retrace your steps from the pub back to the A489, cross over and return to the Onny Trail. Turn left at the footbridge. When the path forks, keep right, moving away from the river to run alongside the **railway**. Return to the car park.

The Plough Inn

Next door to this village inn is Wood Brewery, a well-respected micro-brewery established in 1980, and The Plough is the brewery tap. The rough stone building dating from 1774 has been modernised over the years and the spacious and unpretentious carpeted lounge bar, with high ceilings, simple furnishings, and roaring winter log fire, is the place to come to sup some cracking beer – Parish Bitter, Plough Bitter, Shropshire Lad & Wonderful. Wine drinkers will find 15 wines available by the glass. Menus are listed on blackboards and draw on locally sourced produce.

Food

Seasonally changing menus may include hearty soups, filled baguettes, steak and kidney suet pudding, mixed game stew with celeriac mash, locally smoked organic salmon with honey mustard crust, and home-made puddings such as poached pears with hot chocolate sauce. Roast Sunday lunches.

Family facilities

Children are welcome in the family room and the eating areas of the bar. Smaller portions of main meals are served.

Alternative refreshment stops

Various pubs and cafés in nearby Craven Arms and cafés at both the Shropshire Hills Discovery Centre and the Acton Scott Working Farm Museum.

☛ Where to go from here

North off the A49 you'll find the Acton Scott Working Farm Museum, which provides a vivid introduction to traditional rural life, with plenty of rare breeds, period farm machinery, all work done by hand or horse power, and craft demonstrations (www.actonscottmuseum.co.uk). South of Craven Arms is Stokesay Castle, a magnificent 13th-century fortified castle (www.english-heritage.org.uk), and the fascinating Shropshire Hills Discovery Centre which explores the history, nature and geography of Shropshire through interactive displays and simulations (www.shropshire-cc.gov.uk/discover.nsf).

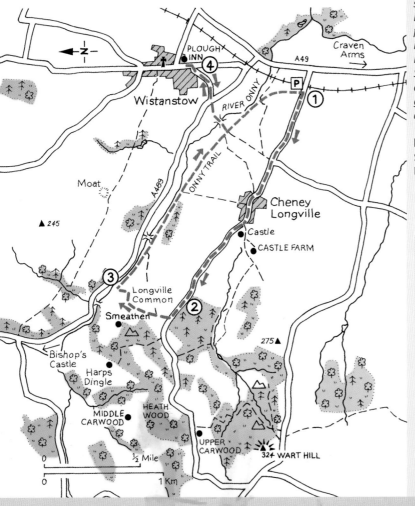

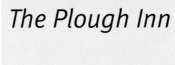

about the pub

The Plough Inn
Wistanstow, Craven Arms
Shropshire SY7 8DG
Tel: 01588 673251

DIRECTIONS: Wistanstow and the Plough are signposted off the A49; pub on the route at Point **4**

PARKING: 50

OPEN: closed Monday

FOOD: daily

BREWERY/COMPANY: Own Brew

REAL ALE: Wood Parish, Plough Bitter, Shropshire Lad, seasonal ales

DOGS: allowed in the bar

while you're there

An Elizabethan mansion near by is Wilderhope Manor. It contains a bigger surprise than most mansions – it's a youth hostel (tel 0870 7706090).

Left: Wilderthope Manor

Above: Elizabeth I

Diddlebury and Wenlock Edge

2h45 | **6 MILES** | **9.7 KM** | **LEVEL 1 2 3**

MAP: OS Explorer 217 The Long Mynd & Wenlock Edge

START/FINISH: car park/picnic site on east side of unclassified road between Middlehope and Westhope; grid ref: SO 479875

PATHS: mostly good but ford on Dunstan's Lane can be deep after rain, 10 stiles

LANDSCAPE: wooded ridge of Wenlock Edge, patchwork of Corve Dale

PUBLIC TOILETS: none on route

TOURIST INFORMATION: Church Stretton, tel 01694 723133 (seasonal), or Ludlow, tel 01568 770755

THE PUB: The Sun Inn, Corfton

⚠ Route crosses an often busy B-road twice. A stretch of track where there is a ford can be very wet

Getting to the start

Follow the B4368 and B4378 between Craven Arms and Much Wenlock. Take the minor unclassified road to the north (Middle Westhope and Upper Westhope). Keep left at the latter and follow the lane to the car park/picnic site.

Researched & written by:
Nick Channer, Julie Royle

Former drovers' roads link the crest of Wenlock Edge to the meadows of Corve Dale.

Wenlock Edge

Wenlock Edge needs a book to itself but this should whet your appetite for more. This great tree-clad escarpment is best seen from the west, appearing as an unbroken escarpment running from the Severn Gorge to Craven Arms. From the east it is elusive, rising almost imperceptibly. Within a basic ridge structure, it seems to form a series of waves or steps, and consists for part of its length of two parallel edges, divided by Hope Dale.

Wenlock Edge was formed of Silurian limestone about 420 million years ago. Developing as a barrier reef in a tropical sea on the edge of a continental shelf, it was built up from the accumulation of sediments and the skeletons of marine creatures. Earth movements and erosion then sculpted it into the escarpment we see today. Most of it is wooded, and much of this is ancient woodland, growing on steep slopes where there has been continuous tree cover since the end of the last ice age.

The ground flora is rich and varied, especially along the rides and in newly coppiced areas, where flowers respond to the increased light. In the past, the Edge was seen as a resource to be exploited. Timber provided building materials, tools and charcoal for iron smelting. Limestone was used for building, for making lime, for iron smelting and, more recently, as an aggregate. This latter use still continues and there are unsightly quarries between Presthope and Much Wenlock.

There's nothing like that on this walk, where the quarries you pass are small and long since abandoned and now transformed by nature into mossy, fern-filled caverns of green.

the walk

1 From the **car park** take the path to the south of the road, turn right at the point where it crosses the highway and follow the lane to a turning on the right for Westhope and Sefton. Walk along to **Burwood**. Turn left here, go up the track, passing **Burwood Court**, and skirt the field towards woods. Keep to the left of a house and enter trees.

2 Turn immediately left and cut through **woodland**, climbing quite steeply to a gate. Go straight ahead down the field, veer away from the wood and down to a galvanised gate. Head straight on to some **farm outbuildings** and turn right at the junction. On reaching **two gates**, where the track forks, keep left.

Wenlock Edge is a wooded escarpment running from Much Wenlock to Craven Arms

3 Keep left above **Corfton Bache**, a deep valley, until more blue arrows send you zig-zagging down into the valley. Follow it to the road at Corfton (**The Sun Inn** on your left) and cross to a lane opposite.

4 As the lane degenerates into a track, look on the left for a footpath starting at an **iron kissing gate**. Go diagonally left across cattle pasture to a prominent stile at the far side. Cross a farm track and walk to the far right corner of an arable field.

5 Go through a gate, then a little way along the left-hand edge of another field until a gate gives access to **parkland**. Head in the direction indicated by the waymarker. **St Peter's Church** at Diddlebury soon comes into view, providing an infallible guide.

6 Cross two stiles at the far side of the park and go straight on down a slope, to the right of a fence. A stile and footbridge give access to **Diddlebury**. Turn right, then left by the **church**. Join a footpath which passes to the right of the **village hall**, then goes diagonally right past the **school**. Cross two

did you know?

In 1909 composer Ralph Vaughan Williams took six of A E Housman's poems from his volume A Shropshire Lad, *and turned them into a song cycle for tenor and piano quintet. He named the piece 'On Wenlock Edge', after the first line of one of the poems.*

Wenlock Edge

Shipton Hall

When Elizabeth I got lost on her way from Shrewsbury to Ludlow, she was put up by the owners at Shipton Hall, and a bedroom now carries her name. The hall was very new then – it was built in 1587 – and its grey stone has mellowed over the centuries. The interior is an 18th-century rococo surprise (open Easter–October, Thursday pm only, tel 01746 785225).

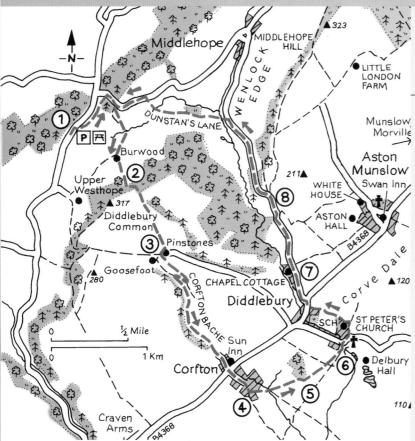

The Sun Inn

First licensed in 1613, The Sun is an unpretentious family-run pub tucked away in beautiful Corvedale beneath Wenlock Edge. The two homely bars are adorned with a mass of breweriana, which is appropriate as the pub brews its own award-winning Corvedale beers using local borehole water, and the ale is sold bottled or direct from the barrel in the pub. Hearty bar food is all home cooked using local produce and this friendly pub also acts as a useful tourist information point (a mini version of a tourist information centre).

Food

Tuck into home-made beef and ale pie, cottage pie, lamb Shrewsbury and faggots with mushy peas, all served with four to six vegetables, or opt for sandwiches, soups, baguettes, or the popular seafood platter.

Family facilities

The pub has a children's licence so youngsters of all ages are welcome inside. There are high chairs, a children's menu and an obstacle course for energetic children to explore in the large garden.

Alternative refreshment stops

Visit the Crown at nearby Munslow, or take your pick from some excellent pubs, tea rooms and quality restaurants if you visit Ludlow.

☛ Where to go from here

Within an easy drive are the Shropshire Discovery Centre and Stokesay Castle at Craven Arms. At Much Wenlock Priory a fascinating audio tour offers an insight into the history of the ruins of a large Cluniac

priory and the atmospheric remains of the 13th-century church and Norman chapter house. Head south through beautiful Corvedale to Ludlow and stroll through the historic streets, or explore the castle ruins (www.ludlowcastle.com) in the charming market town.

about the pub

The Sun Inn
Corfton, Craven Arms
Shropshire SY7 9DF
Tel: 01584 861239
www.suninncorfton.co.uk

DIRECTIONS: beside the B4368 north of Ludlow; Point **3**

PARKING: 30

OPEN: daily

FOOD: daily

BREWERY/COMPANY: Own Brew

REAL ALE: Corvedale Normans Pride, Secret Hop, Dark & Delicious

DOGS: allowed in the bar

---

stiles immediately to the left by the corner of the **school building** and then walk across several fields with a fence on the left to reach the road. Cross to the lane opposite, forking right after a few paces.

7 Continue up the lane. At a junction with a bridle track by a sign for **Aston Top** keep left, still on the lane. After a further 0.75 mile (1.2km), branch left on a byway, **Dunstan's Lane** (no signpost or waymarker). Follow it to the Middlehope road and turn left. Keep straight on at a **Y-junction**. When a footpath crosses the road, turn left into **woodland**. The path is signposted on the right, but not the left – the left branch is

a few paces further on. The path leads through the **woods** back to the **picnic site**.

what to look for

St Peter's Church at Diddlebury has a Saxon nave, its north wall constructed of herringbone masonry, which was the style favoured by the Saxons. The north doorway is typically Saxon, and there is a Saxon window. The tower also seems to be partly Saxon, though even the experts are unsure. Do go inside – very few churches of this kind survive in England.

did you know?

The Abraham Darby (1750–1791) who famously built the first iron bridge here, was the third generation of iron-masters in the family – all of the same name. Grandfather Abraham is credited with the realisation that coke was necessary for successful iron smelting back in 1709, and father Abraham produced cast-iron boilers for the emerging steam age.

Much Wenlock Priory

Escape the Industrial Age in Much Wenlock, where the remains of the 12th-century Cluniac priory provide peace in a dignified setting (open all year but limited in winter, tel 01952 727466).

Revolution at Coalbrookdale

An absorbing walk in the wooded hills and valleys where the Industrial Revolution began.

Coalbrookdale

At Coalbrookdale in 1709 Abraham Darby perfected a method of smelting iron with coke instead of charcoal and sparked a revolution that changed the world. By 1785 the Coalbrookdale district had become the foremost industrial area in the world. It was particularly celebrated for its innovations: the first iron bridge, the first iron boat, the first iron rails and the first steam locomotive. Decline eventually set in due to competition from the Black Country and South Wales and the area fell into decay.

Since the 1960s, the surviving industrial relics have been transformed into museums and the gorge has been designated a UNESCO World Heritage Site. Perhaps even more remarkable than the industrial heritage is the way nature has reclaimed sites of industrial despoilation and made them beautiful again.

The ironmasters built decent houses for their workers and took an interest in their well-being. When you walk through Dale Coppice and Lincoln Hill Woods you will be using the Sabbath Walks, designed by Richard Reynolds to provide healthy Sunday recreation for his workers.

the walk

1 Follow the River Severn upstream, using the **Severn Way**, and pass under two bridges. After the second one, bear away from the river towards **Buildwas Road**,

following a sometimes overgrown path. At the road, turn left for a few paces, then cross to a footpath that ascends through **woodland**. Keep close to the edge until a waymarker directs you obliquely right.

2 Cross a stile and continue in the same direction over pastureland. Pass under a **pylon**, then join a farm track and turn left through a gate. Follow the hawthorn hedge on your right to a junction, turn left on a **bridleway** and follow it along field edges, then across the middle of a meadow, avoiding a path on the right, to reach a lane at the top of the rise. Turn left.

3 Leave the lane when it bridges a road, turning right on a farm access track (**Shropshire Way**). Go through a white gate on the right, just before **Leasows Farm**, then downfield to enter **Lydebrook Dingle**. A path descends through the wood, beyond which you continue along a path called **Rope Walk**.

4 Descend some steps on the left into Loamhole Dingle. Cross **Loamhole Brook** at a footbridge and climb steps on

the other side to a T-junction. Turn right on what is mostly boardwalk and, when you reach **Upper Furnace Pool**, cross it on a footbridge to meet the road.

5 Your onward route is to the left, but a short detour right leads to the **Darby Houses**, Tea Kettle Row and the Quaker Burial Ground. Resuming the walk, go down to Darby Road and turn right beside the viaduct and the **Museum of Iron**. Turn left under the viaduct at a junction with Coach Road. Follow the road past the museum and **Coalbrookdale Works** to a junction.

6 Cross to Church Road, turn left after the Wesleyan chapel on the corner and take the stepped path (signposted **Woodside**) to enter **Dale Coppice**. Follow signs for **Church Road** at the first two junctions, but at the third ignore the Church Road sign and keep straight on. Leave the wood to enter grassland and go forward a few paces to meet a track. Turn left, then follow it as it bends right, passing a grassy path on the left. Keep left

The former warehouse building of 1843 in Coalbrookdale now houses the Museum of Iron

Left: The Museum of Iron beneath the bridge at Ironbridge

2h00 | **5 MILES** | **8 KM** | **LEVEL 123**

MAP: OS Explorer 242 Telford, Ironbridge & The Wrekin

START/FINISH: Dale End Riverside Park, just west of Museum of the Gorge; grid ref: SJ 664037

PATHS: woodland paths, lots of steps (mostly descending), may be fallen trees at Strethill, 2 stiles

LANDSCAPE: wooded hills of Severn Gorge

PUBLIC TOILETS: in Museum of the Gorge car park

TOURIST INFORMATION: Ironbridge, tel 01952 884391

THE PUB: The Malthouse, Ironbridge

⚠ Crosses a busy road, lots of up-and-down steps and several sections of boardwalk. Not suitable for very young children or inexperienced walkers

Getting to the start

Follow the A4169 south of Telford and look for the signs for Ironbridge and Coalbrookdale. The car park is signposted – by the river just west of the Museum of the Gorge.

Researched & written by:
Nick Channer, Julie Royle

Speckled wood butterfly

while you're there

A distinctive conical hill known as the Wrekin marks the northeast end of Wenlock Edge. According to one tale, a disagreeable pair of giants decided to build a new home here. They dug a trench – the River Severn – before mounding up the earth to create the Wrekin.

The Wrekin

at the next junction and then fork right, staying on the track. **Dale Coppice** is on your right, a cemetery on your left.

what to look for

Upper Furnace Pool in Loamhole Dingle is the pool that powered the bellows that blew the furnace where Abraham Darby first smelted iron with coke. The area of open water has been reduced by a profuse growth of marsh horsetail. This primeval-looking species is the evolutionary successor to the giant tree-like horsetails that were a major element in the swamp vegetation that 300 million years ago formed the coal measures.

7 A gateway accesses Dale Coppice. Turn right, avoid a left path after a few paces, and then further on swing sharp left, going downhill to a junction marked by a bench. Turn right, then left when a sign indicates **Church Road**, and left again beside the road.

8 Turn right into **Lincoln Hill Wood** and follow signs for the **Rotunda**, soon arriving at a viewpoint where the Rotunda formerly stood. Descend a very steep flight of steps to a junction. Turn right, then left down more steps and left again, signposted to **Lincoln Hill Road**. Cross the road to a footpath opposite, which descends through rather overgrown ground to the **Wharfage**. Turn right past **Lincoln Hill lime kilns** and the Swan to **Dale End Riverside Park**.

The Malthouse

Smartly converted and extensively refurbished this former malthouse has been an inn since the turn of the 20th century. It's set on the banks of the River Severn in the heart of this spectacular World Heritage Site, just 250yds (229m) from Ironbridge's main visitor centre. A successful combination of country pub/bar/restaurant-with-rooms, it is set around a cobbled courtyard and the bright and spacious Jazz Bar is the place for post-walk refreshment. Pine beams, scrubbed wooden tables, candles and an informal atmosphere set the scene for some contemporary bar food and, if you're here on Wednesday to Saturday evening, some live music. The rest of the pub is given over to dining and a more elaborate menu.

Food
Refuel on French bread pizzas, the Jazz Bar cheeseburger with salad and chips, various sandwiches and salad platters (steamed salmon), chicken and red wine casserole, and ribeye steak and chips.

Family facilities
Children are welcome in the eating area of the bar and in the restaurant. You'll find high chairs, baby-changing facilities, half-portions of main menu items, and two family bedrooms.

about the pub

The Malthouse
The Wharfage, Ironbridge
Telford, Shropshire TF8 7NH
Tel: 01952 433712
www.malthousepubs.co.uk

DIRECTIONS: see Getting to the start; pub is beside the river to east of the museum and car park

PARKING: 15

OPEN: daily; all day

FOOD: daily; all day Sunday

BREWERY/COMPANY: free house

REAL ALE: Flowers Original, Boddingtons

DOGS: not allowed inside

ROOMS: 9 en suite

Alternative refreshment stops
There is lots of choice, such as the Swan, a very attractive place, which is open all day.

☞ Where to go from here
The Museum of Iron brings the Darby family's achievements to life. It includes the Darby Furnace where it all began and it has much to say about the lives of those who lived and worked in the area during this period of momentous change. Equally fascinating are the ironmasters' homes near by (known as the Darby Houses) and the charming terrace of workers' houses at Tea Kettle Row. For information on all the museums and attractions at Ironbridge visit www.ironbridge.org.uk.

did you know?

The Darby family were Quakers, and Dale House, the home built by the first Abraham Darby in 1715, is now a study centre and meeting room. Learn more next door at Rosehill House, where a museum of local Quakers in the area lies at the back of the preserved house.

The Silkin Way to Ironbridge

Above left: Magpie (Pica pica)
Above: Dale House

Pedal back in time to discover what a 'Saggar-maker's Bottom Knocker' did.

The cast-iron bridge that spans the gorge and the River Severn at Coalbrookdale

Coalbrookdale

Although the gorge's natural resources had been exploited since medieval times, the industrial boom only began in 1709 with Abraham Darby's invention at Coalbrookdale that used coke rather than charcoal to produce large quantities of cast iron cheaply. It was his grandson who was responsible for the graceful cast-iron bridge that spans the gorge, erected between 1777 and 1779. Its 400 tons of castings represented nearly 4 months' output from a blast furnace and was the first structure of its kind to be erected.

But it was not only the blast of iron furnaces that lit up the gorge, for the abundant clay deposits in the area spawned a massive ceramic industry, with tile, pottery and china factories being set up beside the river. Indeed, Coalport was the new town of its day, established to house the families working in the potteries. To service the industries, a canal was built to Shrewsbury in 1793, with a link being built later to Norbury that gave access to the Shropshire Canal, some 18 miles (29km) away. In such hilly country, the use of locks was totally impractical, but William Reynolds, who owned ironworks here, invented the inclined plane whereby the tub-like boats could be lowered and raised on tracks between the different levels.

The most spectacular example is the Hay Inclined Plane, which moved the boats a vertical distance of over 200 feet (61m) in a matter of minutes, an operation that would otherwise have taken hours had the equivalent 27 locks been used.

The railways inevitably followed, the LNWR branch to Coalport (now the Silkin Way) being built in 1861 and the Severn Valley Railway the year after. A large goods yard grew up at Jackfield where coal, pottery, iron, tar and many other commodities were marshalled for transport to the various industrial centres and seaports around the country. Yet, even the railways lasted barely a century, for the decline had set in long before Beeching recommended his sweeping cuts to the rail system, as a result of under-investment after the War and competition from the greater flexibility offered by road transport.

the ride

1. Leaving the car park, cross the road and climb shallow steps to a tarmac track, the **Silkin Way**. Follow it left, passing **Station Road** and dropping to curve beneath the main road. Swing right as you emerge and carry on at the edge of a **park**, later joining the pavement to reach **Blists Hill Victorian Town**. Keep going down the hill, the cycleway shortly diverging from the road on a gradual tree-lined descent along the line of an old railway. Through a **short tunnel**, the way courses enjoyably down, later passing beneath the ingenious **Hay Inclined Plane**. The track eventually ends in front of the **Brewery Inn**.

2. Cross the road to a gated track left of the pub, that descends past **cottages** to the **riverbank**. Bear right as it forks, rising to meet a road. Follow that over the Severn, and then leave immediately down **steps** on the right to reach a riverside path. It skirts a **picnic area** and climbs around to a gate, there joining the line of another disused railway. The track continues above the river for just over half a mile (800m) before passing **Maws Craft Centre**, once the site of a booming tile industry. A little further on as the track ends, keep ahead on the right-most of two roads, which leads past more tile works at **Jackfield**. These were built by

2h00	7.5 MILES	12.1 KM	LEVEL 1 2 3

CYCLE 110

MAP: OS Explorer 242 Telford, Ironbridge & The Wreakin

START/FINISH: Legge Road car park, Madeley; grid ref: SJ 700043

TRAILS/TRACKS: off-road tracks (can be muddy) and lanes, gentle descents and gradual climbs

LANDSCAPE: wooded valley

PUBLIC TOILETS: main car park at Blists Hill, at Maws Craft Centre and in Ironbridge

TOURIST INFORMATION: Ironbridge, tel 01952 884391

CYCLE HIRE: None locally

THE PUB: The Swan, Ironbridge

🚴 Although an easy ride, there are long, but gentle gradients, an unlit tunnel, short stretches of loose pebbles, steps, and poorly surfaced roads

Getting to the start

Ironbridge Gorge lies south of Telford New Town. From the M54, follow the A442 south for 3 miles (4.8km), to its junction with the A4169. Turn right for Madeley, then at a roundabout as you approach the town, go left towards Blists Hill, Coalport and the Ironbridge Gorge Museums. The entrance to the car park is a short way along on the left.

Why do this cycle ride?

The gorge's tranquillity is deceptive, for here began a world-changing revolution. The ride takes you past the spectacular remains of its once-booming industry.

Researched & written by: Dennis Kelsall

For Children

Hoo Farm Animal Kingdom, north of Telford at Preston-on-the-Weald Moors (open mid-March to Christmas, tel 01952 677917) is a children's paradise. Join in with feeding lambs and pigs, watch the sheep racing, and wonder at the unusual livestock – which includes ostriches and llamas.

while you're there

Telford is a New Town, designed in the 1960s to make use of the land left despoiled and derelict by the abandoned Shropshire coalfield, and named after the great engineer Thomas Telford (among many other roles, he was appointed Shropshire's county surveyor in 1787).

The Swan

An 18th-century former malthouse set on the riverfront close to the heart of Ironbridge. This was an inn during Darby's time and it is rumoured that site meetings were held at The Swan from time to time. The inn has been developed in recent years by Malthouse Pubs to create a modern pub but with traditional home-cooked food, a buzzy all-day bar, a summer courtyard, and a warm welcome.

Food

Expect a varied menu of freshly prepared dishes ranging from home-made pork pie with chutney, smoked fish mousse with garlic toast, and confit chicken with salad. Substantial main meals take in braised lamb shank, bubble & squeak with port and redcurrant sauce, Cajun beefburger, and wild mushroom and basil risotto.

Family facilities

Children are welcome throughout the pub. There's a children's menu, smaller portions of adult dishes and crayons and colouring books to keep youngsters amused.

Alternative refreshment stops

Along the way you have the Foresters' Arms at Madeley, a café at the entrance to Blists Hill Victorian Town and at Maws Craft Centre and pubs and cafés in Ironbridge.

☛ Where to go from here

There is so much to see and do as the whole area here is a World Heritage Site with a remarkable series of nine museums relating the story of the bridge, re-creating Victorian times and featuring ceramics and social history displays. Explore Blists Hill Victorian Town, the Museum of the Gorge, Coalport China Museum, Jackfield Tile Museum, the Museum of Iron, and the Broseley Pipeworks, among others (www.ironbridge.org.uk).

Charles Lynam between 1871 and 1874 for Craven Dunnill & Co. and now house a fascinating museum.

3 Go forward at a **junction**, but as the road then bends to a reconstructed level crossing, turn off left to regain the line of the railway through **Jackfield Sidings**. Further on, beyond the Black Swan, pass beneath a skew bridge carrying the road to the **Jackfield suspension bridge**. It is then not far to the main car park at Ironbridge. Pedal through to the far side and dismount to cross the famous **Iron Bridge** into the town, where you will find the Malthouse a little way to the left.

4 The route from the bridge, however, is along the main street to the right. At a mini-roundabout, take the right fork ahead,

Right: A character in Blists Victorian Town

the B4373 to **Jackfield and Broseley**, leaving the town past the ruins of the **Bedlam Furnaces**. Where the road later bends to Jackfield Bridge, keep ahead on a narrow, bumpy lane, which undulates along the valley to **Coalport**. Keep going forward at a later junction, a bridge taking you over the **Hay Inclined Plane**, just beyond which, opposite the Shakespeare Inn, you will find the entrance to the **Tar Museum**. A little further on is the **Coalport China Museum**.

5 From the museum, go back along the lane a few yards/metres, turning off right onto a track that winds around **Coalport Village Hall** to an overflow car park. Pass through it right to find a track climbing to meet the **Silkin Way**. Turn left and retrace your outward route past **Blists Hill** to the car park from which you began. The way is steadily uphill, but the track is well-graded and the climb relatively easy.

about the pub

The Swan
The Wharfage, Ironbridge
Shropshire, TF8 7NH
Tel: 01952 432306

DIRECTIONS: just east of the Iron Bridge, see Point **4**

PARKING: 10

OPEN: daily; all day

FOOD: daily; all day Sunday

BREWERY/COMPANY: free house

REAL ALE: four changing guest beers

ROOMS: 8 en suite

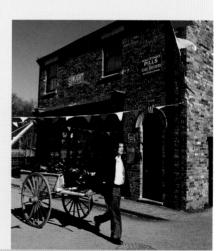

111 OXWICH
SWANSEA

4.5 MILES (7.2KM) 2hrs

PATHS: Clear paths through woodland, along coast and across farmland, quiet lane, 6 stiles

SUGGESTED MAP: aqua3 OS Explorer 164 Gower

GRID REFERENCE: SS 500864

PARKING: Oxwich Bay

THE PUB: Oxwich Bay Hotel

❶ **Oxwich** village was once a busy port that paid its way by shipping limestone from the local quarries, but it's now one of the prettiest and most unspoilt Gower villages, due in no small part to its distance from main roads. For maximum enjoyment it is best visited away from the main holiday season. Walk back out of the car park and turn **L** to crossroads. Turn **L** here (waymarked 'Eglwys') and pass Woodside Guesthouse and **Oxwich Bay Hotel**, on your R. This lane leads into woods and up to 6th-century **St Illtud's Church**, where gate marks end of road and start of path leading out on to **Oxwich Point**.

❷ Go through gate and bear **R**, going up some wooden steps to climb steeply up through wood. As footpath levels, bear **L** to drop back down through wood and around headland until it comes out into open above **Oxwich Point**.

❸ Path drops through gorse and bracken to become grassy coast path that runs easily above rocky beach. Keep sea on your L and ignore any tracks that run off to R. After approximately 1 mile (1.6km) you'll pass distinct valley that drops in from your R. Continue past this and cross succession of stiles, until you reach sandy beach of **The Sands**.

❹ Turn **R**, behind beach, and follow narrow footpath to stile. This leads on to broad farm track, where you turn **L**. Continue up and around to **R** until you come to galvanised kissing gate. Go through this and keep **R** to head up lane past some houses to crossroads.

❺ Turn **R** here and follow road along to fork where you keep **R**. Drop down to entrance of **Oxwich Castle** on **R**. This is a 16th-century mansion built by Sir Rhys Mansel on the site of a 14th-century castle, hence the name. After looking at or exploring the castle, turn **R**, back on to lane, and head down into **Oxwich** village. Keep straight ahead to car park.

112 NEWPORT
PEMBROKESHIRE

5.5 MILES (8.8KM) 3hrs 30min

PATHS: Coast footpaths, boggy tracks, rough paths over bracken and heather-covered hillsides, 2 stiles

SUGGESTED MAP: aqua3 OS Explorer OL35 North Pembrokeshire

GRID REFERENCE: SN 057392

PARKING: Free car park opposite information centre, Long Street

THE PUB: Llwyngwair Arms

❶ Turn **R** out of car park and **L** on to High Street. Fork **L** into Pen y Bont and continue to bridge, where waymarked footpath leads off to **L**. Follow this along banks of estuary to small road.

❷ Turn **R**; walk past toilets to its end, where path follows sea wall. Continue to another lane; turn **L** to follow it to **A487**. Turn **R** on to this road then **L** to continue up drive of **Hendre** farm.

❸ Go through gate, to L of buildings, and follow track across small stream. Path hugs L edge of field to reach another gate. Maintain direction along hedged section (boggy). Keep straight ahead at stile to climb up to road.

❹ Turn **R** on to road then fork **L** to continue past houses to pair of huge **stones** on **L**. Pass through these stones and follow faint track up to rocky tor. From here, head up towards larger tor of **Carn Ffoi**. From here you'll be able to pick up clearer path that leads on to broken wall.

❺ Pass through it and follow clear footpath across hillside, aiming towards obvious top of **Carn Ingli**, which rises ahead of you. Pass beneath highpoint of **Carningli** Common, where you'll see faint footpath on **R-H** side heading up towards shallow saddle. Take this footpath then, as ground levels off, bear **L** to follow any of faint tracks that lead up on to ridge.

❻ Follow ridge line northwards and drop down, again on faint footpaths, to join good, clear track that runs straight down hillside. Continue on this, keeping ahead at 2 crossroads. Turn **L** then **R** when you get to next junction. This drops down to gate in corner, which leads on to lane.

❼ Take lane to crossroads and keep ahead to walk past house to obvious sunken track. Follow this down to drive; turn **L**, then **R**, on to Church Street. Continue into centre and cross main road into Long Street.

113 Y GRIB
POWYS

8 MILES (12.9KM) 4hrs 30min

PATHS: Clear tracks over farmland, rolling moorland and narrow ridge, quiet lane, 3 stiles

SUGGESTED MAP: aqua3 OS Explorer OL13 Brecon Beacons National Park Eastern area

GRID REFERENCE: SO 175295

PARKING: Castle Inn, Pengenffordd, allows parking for small fee

THE PUB: Castle Inn

❶ Wooden steps go down from back of car park on eastern side of road. These lead on to rough track where you turn **R** then immediately **L** over stile. Follow permissive path down side of wood to stream, cross it and clamber over another stile.

❷ Keep to **L** edge of field, with wood on your L, and climb steeply to top of field. Leave wood behind and follow fence line upwards to another stile. This leads on to flanks of **Castell Dinas**.

❸ Keep ahead here to cross over ruins and descend steeply into deep saddle. Cross over broad track and then climb directly up steep spur ahead. You are now on **Y Grib** and it's possible to follow faint track all the way up to **cairn** then down to small notch where your route is crossed by bridleway.

❹ Climb steeply back out of this and hug crest up to another **cairn**, where ridge joins main escarpment. Don't be drawn off to L; instead keep ahead to climb short steep wall on to broad spur of **Pen y Manllwyn**, where you'll meet clear track.

❺ Turn **R** on to this track; follow it up to boggy plateau on top of **Waun Fach**. Summit is marked by concrete block that used to act as base for trig point. Turn **R**; follow obvious path down on to ever-narrowing spur of **Pen Trumau**.

❻ Cross narrow summit and, as ground steepens, follow path through rocky outcrops to broad saddle. Turn sharp **R** here; follow main track as it descends, easily at first. This steepens and becomes rocky for a while before it reaches gate above walled track.

❼ Follow track down to road; turn **R**, then immediately **L**. Drop to bottom of valley and climb out again on other side. As road turns sharply to L, bear **R** on to stony farm track that runs between hedgerows. Follow this track past stile you crossed earlier, on R-H side, then take steps on your **L**, back to car park.

114 BALA
GWYNEDD

5 MILES (8KM) 3hrs

PATHS: Woodland and field paths, 8 stiles

SUGGESTED MAP: aqua3 OS Explorer OL23 Cadair Idris & Llyn Tegid

GRID REFERENCE: SH 929361

PARKING: Car park at entrance to Bala town from east

THE PUB: Bala Lake Hotel

❶ Go to northeast side of car park in **Bala** to access riverside path, where you turn **R** to follow raised embankment along west bank of **Tryweryn**. After dog-leg to **R**, which passes through 2 kissing gates, footpath continues, first by banks of **Tryweryn**, then by north banks of **Dee**.

❷ At road by Bala's lake, **Llyn Tegid**, turn L then **R** along Llangower road. Go through kissing gate to cross small field to **Bala Station** on **Bala Lake Railway**. Footbridge allows you to cross track before traversing 2 small fields.

❸ Turn **R** along cart track, and pass behind **Bala Lake Hotel**. Waymarker points direction up grassy bank on **L**, and path continues southwest, accompanied by fence on R.

❹ After crossing stream, next to little cottage on R-H side, route comes upon area of rough pastureland interspersed with outcrops of rock, rushes and bracken. Here footpath on ground all but disappears. Ascend half **L** (roughly southwards) to reach fenceline at top, then aim for ladder stile in middle distance.

❺ Turn **L** along tarred lane just before that ladder stile. Where road ends take **R** fork track that ploughs through recently felled conifer plantation.

❻ At whitewashed house of **Encil y Coed**, turn **L** off track to climb **L-H** of 2 ladder stiles, then follow grooved grass track heading north across high pastures. Where track bends to R leave it to descend steeply to another ladder stile. Well-waymarked path continues north, with **Bala** town ahead.

❼ Go over partially hidden step stile into commercial forestry plantations of **Coed Pen-y-Bont**. Narrow footpath descends to bottom edge of woods (ignore forestry track you meet on way down).

❽ At bottom of woods turn **R** along track to road by **Pen-y-Bont Campsite**. Turn **L** along road, walking back towards town, then turn **L** again to follow lakeside footpath past **information centre**. At main road, turn **R** to explore town centre.

115 THE DYSYNNI VALLEY
GWYNEDD

5 MILES (8KM) 3hrs

PATHS: Field paths and tracks, 16 stiles

SUGGESTED MAP: aqua3 OS Explorer OL23 Cadair Idris & Llyn Tegid

GRID REFERENCE: SH 677069

PARKING: Car park in Pandy Square, Abergynolwyn village centre

THE PUB: Railway Inn

❶ Cross road to **Railway Inn** and take lane ('**Llanfihangel**'). At far side of bridge over **Dysynni river**, turn **R** through kissing gate and trace north banks. Beyond 2nd step stile, path turns **L** before climbing steps beside tall leylandii to reach lane.

❷ Turn **R** along lane which heads east through Dysynni Valley and beneath woodlands of **Coed Meriafel**. At junction with **B4405** turn **L**, over stile and climb northwest across field. Continue over 2 more stiles to woodland path. Climb along this to reach forestry track near top edge of woods.

❸ Turn **L** along track which climbs out of woods before veering **R** to gate and stile. Over stile, follow wall on L. Ignore faint grass track that goes ahead and across field. The route stays low and veers **L** through high grassy cwm with stream developing on L.

❹ After traversing several fields, path joins flinted track but leaves it after 200yds (183m) for streamside path on **L**. This descends into woods and stays close to stream. After passing several cascades it comes out of woods to reach track leading to road at **Llanfihangel-y-pennant** just opposite **chapel**.

❺ Turn **L** past chapel and **Castell y Bere** (detour through gates on R for closer look). Just beyond castle, take path on **L** that climbs to gate at top **R-H** corner of field. Beyond gate turn **R** along farm track passing **Caerberllan** farm to road. Turn **R** along road, **L** at crossroads and cross **Pont Ystumanner** (bridge).

❻ On other side, footpath signpost highlights track on **L** to pass **Rhiwlas farm** then continues as green path high above river. Path crosses slopes of **Gamallt** and swings gradually **L** with valley.

❼ Beyond river gorge, path approaches back of **Abergynolwyn** village and turns **L** to cross old iron bridge across river. Beyond it, turn **R** along unsurfaced street to return to village centre.

116 ERDDIG
WREXHAM

4 MILES (6.4 KM) 2hrs

PATHS: Waymarked field and woodland paths and tracks 3 stiles

SUGGESTED MAP: aqua3 OS Explorer 265 Clwydian Range

GRID REFERENCE: SJ 346491

PARKING: Small car park behind Kings Mill (on A525)

THE PUB: King's Mill

❶ From car park head west, following **River Clywedog** as it goes under road bridge. At other side turn **R** on grass path, then **L** alongside woods cloaking north slopes of valley. Go over stile and follow path into woods. This section is marked on maps as **Clywedog Trail**.

❷ Go through kissing gate and **L** along road. Turn **R** through gate at back of small car park and follow **L** of 2 paths to riverbank. Follow riverside path across fields, to south of bulrush-ringed lake.

❸ Go through gate to **R** of stone bridge, then turn **L** along track over bridge, keeping woods of Erddig to R. Near John Blakes Patent Hydraulic Ram go over stile on **L** and follow track south into woods. On reaching **Erddig Hall's** perimeter fence ignore path doubling back L, but follow path heading east by fence.

❹ Path ends at T-junction on far side of woods. Detour **R** for 50yds (46m) to get view of hall. This can be seen beyond some ornate wrought iron gates and long park-like gardens. (N.B. for those who want to pay to see the fine 17th-century hall continue to the south side entrance.) Return to T-junction. Head north along inside perimeter of woods then turn **R**. Go through kissing gate on to lane.

❺ Turn **L** along lane for a few paces and then cross over stile on **R-H** side of lane. Trace **L-H** field-edge to waymarker post and descend to another post at edge of woodland. Follow narrow path through woods, go over stile, down some steps to cross stream, then climb far banks to path overlooking bend in **River Clywedog**. Stay on path to continue above river, then, out of woods, turn **L** to cross over footbridge.

❻ Turn right along river banks to meet outward route at path going under road bridge and into grounds of Kings Mill.

117 KILPECK
HEREFORDSHIRE

4.75 MILES (7.7KM) 2hrs 45min

PATHS: Field paths, tracks and minor lanes, 21 stiles

SUGGESTED MAP: aqua3 OS Explorer 189 Hereford & Ross-on-Wye

GRID REFERENCE: SO 445304

PARKING: Spaces beside St Mary's and St David's Church, Kilpeck

THE PUB: Red Lion

❶ Walk down to **Red Lion**. Turn **R**. At junction follow 'Garway Hill'. Take 2nd fingerpost. Find another stile behind **The Knoll** (house). Strike diagonally across pasture. Cross another stile, now with field boundary on your R. Veer **L** to reach lane at bend. Turn **L**. Follow waymarkers through trees then go straight down field to near junction.
❷ Turn **L**, past **Two Brooks**. After 500yds (457m) turn **L**, through gate by **Grafton Oak**, tucked behind. Soon in meadow, follow fence until crossing stile. Now keep ahead but drift down, guided by gigantic oak. The stile you need is ahead, not another, further down, that crosses brook. Contour with trees on your L for 2 fields. In 3rd find footbridge down and **L**.
❸ Follow waymarkers, diagonally up field. Walk with wire fence on your R. Leave this long field at its top end (but, to observe rights of way, first cross and re-cross wire fence on your R, via wooded area). Go diagonally to opening beside hollow oak, not more easily seen, 3-bar stile. Move **L** to walk along **L-H** field edge. Ignore waymarker into L-H field – any way out has completely disappeared. Instead keep ahead, to tarmac road. Turn **L**. After 650yds (594m) fingerpost slants **L**.
❹ Take this path through bracken to track. Turn **R** for 25yds (23m), then **L**, to pass to **R** of **Saddlebow Farm**. Avenue below leads into field. Walk along this **R** edge, to just before gate. Join good track, following it for 650yds (594m), until 3 gates in corner.
❺ Take 2nd on **L**. Beyond **New House Farm** go over 0.25 mile (400m) to junction. Don't turn down to Kilpeck yet! Go 160yds (146m) further. Here go **L**, around old farm buildings. Descend to unseen gap not 50yds (46m) **L** of bottom R-H corner. Out of this copse, cross 2 fields to pass between buildings of **The Priory**. Avenue of horse chestnuts leads to **Red Lion**.

118 HARLEY'S MOUNTAIN
HEREFORDSHIRE

3.75 MILES (6KM) 2hrs 15min

PATHS: Meadows, field paths, woodland tracks with roots, 10 stiles

SUGGESTED MAP: aqua3 OS Explorer 201 Knighton & Presteigne

GRID REFERENCE: SO 364672

PARKING: At St Michael's Church, Lingen (tuck in well)

THE PUB: Royal George

❶ Walk away from **church**; cross to take minor road ('Willey'). At 1st bend, follow fingerpost directly ahead. Climb over difficult gate beside small corrugated shed; walk by paddock edge, reaching lane in trees.
❷ Strike up field, passing dead oak. Follow waymarker up and slightly **R**. In corner, negotiate rusty gate between better ones. At derelict **Mynde Farm** skirt **L**, around 2 collapsed buildings. Find gate on **R** behind low building.
❸ Go down and up meadow to stile. Veer **L**, passing beside **Mountain Buildings** on rutted, rocky track. After 160yds (146m) enter field. Take line diagonally across field (but if ridged with potatoes, or other crop, follow 2 field edges L) then keep that line, now with hedge L. Take track along ridge to gate with pool to R (dry in summer). Above and behind is trig point.
❹ Turn **L**, initially preferring L-H field edge to lane (overgrown). Descend for 650yds (594m). At bottom move **L**, to small gate. Through trees, shortly emerge close to **The Red House**. Keep ahead, finding narrow path within trees, **R** of garage and beside hedge. Within 40yds (37m) negotiate metal gate. Don't be tempted down; instead move **L**, beside wire fence for just a few paces, then, maintaining fence's line, proceed to walk below narrow ridge on faint tractor track for 100yds (91m). When ground ahead drops steeply into dell turn half **L**, to walk down woody edge of meadow. In 2nd meadow, where trees bulge out to L, dive back into woodland – (waymarker on oak).
❺ Go ahead, sometimes boggy, in woodland then pasture, for 0.5 mile (800m). At wobbly silver-grey gate drop **L** 10ft (3m) to waymarked stile into once pollarded, streamside lane. Reach road.
❻ Turn **L**. After 450yds (411m), on bend, go straight down field to hedge beside farm buildings. Find stile in **L** corner. Go ahead, to stile that gives on to village road – take care! Turn **R** to see **church** before reaching car.

119 GOLDEN VALLEY
HEREFORDSHIRE

6 MILES (9.7KM) 3hrs

PATHS: Minor lanes, good tracks, meadows, couple of short but severe descents over grass, 24 stiles

SUGGESTED MAP: aqua3 OS Explorer 201 Knighton & Presteigne or OL13 Brecon Beacons (East)

GRID REFERENCE: SO 313416 (on Explorer 201)

PARKING: Car park beside Dorstone Post Office

THE PUB: Pandy Inn, Dorstone

❶ Go down near side village green but turn **R** (not to church), passing houses. At lane end turn **L**, passing D'Or Produce Ltd. At **B4348** care is required. Continue, bridging **River Dore**. Be sure to switch sides before road bends severely **R**. Follow driveway towards **Fayre Way Stud Farm**. Clearly waymarked route across pastures leads up to **Arthur's Stone**.
❷ Beyond **Arthur's Stone** take route signed by fingerpost. Cross 2nd field diagonally. Follow **L** side of fence to stile **L** of the corner. After 2 fields descend very steeply on grass beside larches. Keep beside hedge to find awkward stile. Take lane but skirt **R** of **Finestreet Farm** using several stiles. In another steep meadow find stile below and **L** of massive oak with fallen one beside it. Cross field diagonally, to pass beside timber-framed house. Beyond is **Bredwardine**.
❸ Cross road carefully. In 80yds (73m) avenue leads to **St Andrew's Church**. At very end, stile and waymarkers lead to Bredwardine's bridge.
❹ Go back to Point ❸. Take '25%' gradient road beside **Red Lion Hotel**. Go 700yds (640m) up lane, including steepest section, to just before **Hill Cottage**. Fingerpost points R, and behind you is '1 in 4' sign.
❺ Keep ahead, ignoring R turn after 160yds (146m). When road rises sharply after stream, find gate **R**, just past house ('**Finestreet Dingle**'). Now ascend dell (also called Finestreet Dingle) guided by blue arrows. In front of house turn **L** then **L** again, to skirt plantation. Row of hawthorns points to stile near brow. Tackle awkward gate near scrawny pines, keeping this line to minor road. Turn **R**. In 325yds (297m) turn **L** ('20%'). After another 325yds (297m) find fingerpost, hidden behind holly tree.
❻ Soon join track visible ahead. Continue to and through **Llan Farm**. However, 220yds (201m) beyond it, take diagonal footpath (not old lane, R). Cross sunken lane, old **railway**, then village playing fields to reach road near church. Cross then skirt **R** of churchyard, along fenced path, to village green.

120 ALVELEY
SHROPSHIRE

5 MILES (8KM) 2hrs 30min

PATHS: Riverside paths, green lanes, can be slippery in places and shallow streams in winter, 12 stiles

SUGGESTED MAP: aqua3 OS Explorer 218 Wyre Forest & Kidderminster

GRID REFERENCE: SO 753840

PARKING: Visitor centre at Severn Valley Country Park, Alveley

THE PUB: River & Rail

❶ Walk to river from **visitor centre**, using whichever route you prefer (History Trail, waymarked by red arrows, takes you directly to Miners' Bridge). Don't cross bridge, but descend steps to river bank and walk upstream for nearly 2 miles (3.2km).
❷ Follow short track to car park of **Lion Inn**. Turn **L** past Old Forge Cottage to **Hampton Loade**, then turn **R** past house called The Haywain (just before **River and Rail** pub). Waymarked path leads up through garden into wood, then along edge of field bordering wood. Go along two sides of field to reach top **L** corner, cross stile, turn **R** and cross another stile in next corner. Proceed to track and turn **R**.
❸ After few paces, look for waymarker indicating path on **R**. It descends through woodland to **Lakehouse Dingle**. Pass **former watermill**, cross footbridge and keep going along pebbly track. When you meet concrete track, turn **R** to junction with lane.
❹ Turn left, staying on lane until you've passed **Yewtree Cottage** and its neighbour. Take **L** turn after 2nd cottage. There is no signpost or waymarker here, but it's well-defined field-edge bridleway. At bottom of field look for gap in hedge, where way descends through trees to dingle.
❺ Turn **R**, climb up to meet lane and turn **R** again. After 100yds (91m), join track on **R**. When it bends R, keep straight on instead, along tree-lined green lane. Before long it becomes narrower and deeply rutted as it descends to brook. Cross at stepping stones, or at nearby footbridge. Track then swings **L** beside brook for while before turning sharp **R**.
❻ Turn **L** when you meet lane and walk into **Alveley**. Go through village centre, passing cottages, **church**, pub, shop and bus stop, then turning **R** on footpath next to premises of IGM. Path descends to junction where you turn **L** until you reach field through which well-trodden paths descend to **country park**.

121 CLEE HILL
SHROPSHIRE

8.25 MILES (13.3KM) 3hrs 30min

PATHS: Good but rough, uneven and/or boggy in places, 2 stiles

SUGGESTED MAP: aqua3 OS Explorer 203 Ludlow

GRID REFERENCE: SO 595753

PARKING: Car park/picnic site opposite turning for Kremlin Inn on A4117 on eastern edge of Cleehill village

THE PUB: Kremlin Inn

❶ Walk up track opposite picnic area, towards **Kremlin Inn**. Before you **inn**, go through bridle gate on **L** and along track. After 220yds (201m), right of way to L of it can be difficult – most walkers use track.
❷ At **radar station** access road by Hedgehog House, go **R**. Walk to end of **Rouse Boughton Terrace**, go through gate (**L**) to track. Don't follow it but turn **R** along edge of pasture. Go along edge of next field and through gate in corner to **Shropshire Way**, which goes R. Ignore it and keep ahead, cutting corner of field, to meet then follow **L-H** boundary after 300yds (274m).
❸ Continue through next field to **L** corner. Follow track to cross **Benson's Brook** at bridge. Climb out of valley on track which passes abutments of old tramway bridge (**Bitterley Incline** is called Titterstone Incline on OS maps), before arriving at **Bedlam**.
❹ Turn **L** into hamlet, then fork **R** past Old Shop House and Hullabaloo House towards **Titterstone Clee Hill**. Gate gives access and path takes you **R**. After passing house, it cuts through bracken.
❺ Leave path when reach **Bitterley Incline** again. Climb embankment, joining **Shropshire Way**. Continue uphill towards ruined buildings ahead. Pass to **R** of main **quarry**, then go **L** to top.
❻ To north of trig pillar is cairn, **Giant's Chair**. Look north towards Brown Clee Hill to see **Callowgate**, red-roofed farm at edge of moorland. Aim for this, picking best way down slope then across moorland.
❼ At **Callowgate**, leave **Shropshire Way** and turn **R** by moorland edge. Joining lane at **Cleetongate**, turn **R** to **Cleeton St Mary**. Turn **R** past church, **R** past almshouses, **L** on to **Random bridleway** along moorland edge. Keep just to **R** of fence, except where you need to cut corner – obvious when you come to it.
❽ When fence makes sharp **L** turn, keep ahead to **radar station** access road. Turn **L** to **Rouse Boughton Terrace** then retrace your steps to start.

122 WHITTINGTON
SHROPSHIRE

6 MILES (9.7KM) 2hrs 30min

PATHS: Tow path, lanes and field paths, very overgrown, 19 stiles

SUGGESTED MAP: aqua3 OS Explorer 240 Oswestry

GRID REFERENCE: SJ 325312

PARKING: Car park next to Whittington Castle – honesty box

THE PUB: Jack Mytton Inn, Hindford

❶ Turn **R** by Shrewsbury road (B5009), using footway on left. After about 0.5 mile (800m), cross stile and follow waymarked path across 3 fields to far **R** corner of 3rd field.
❷ Walk along edge of next field, with wood on your L. Cross stile in corner, then go obliquely across another field as indicated by waymarker. prominent oak tree is useful guide. There is stile near tree, but you may have to wade through nettles to get to it. Continue in same direction across next field to lane and turn **L**.
❸ Keep **L** when you come to fork and continue to **A495**. Turn **R** for few paces, then cross to other side. Join footpath that runs along **L-H** edge of field to stile and footbridge. Beyond these, keep going along field edge until gap in hedge. Go through, but continue in same direction as before, soon going up bank.
❹ Meet canal at **Pollett's Bridge** (No 6). Don't cross it – go under to join tow path. Follow this to **Hindford Bridge** (No 11), then go up to lane. Turn **R** past **Jack Mytton Inn**, then **R** again, signposted 'Iron Mills and Gobowen'.
❺ Take footpath on left. Walk down long, narrow paddock to far end, then cross stile on right. Follow fence to footbridge, then continue across next pasture to another footbridge and keep straight on to stile ahead. Go up to far **R** corner of next field, through gate and then **L** by field edge.
❻ Join track that soon bends **R** beside course of **dismantled railway**. Look out for stile giving access to railway. Turn **R** on former trackbed for few paces, then up bank on **L** – watch out for steps concealed in undergrowth here. Cross stile to field, turn **R** to far side and cross another stile. Bear **L** to large oak tree, then continue to lane. Follow it to Top Street and turn right, then **L** to **Whittington Castle**.

Central
ENGLAND (SOUTH)

CENTRAL ENGLAND (SOUTH)

Contents

123 Forest of Dean, Gloucestershire — 149

124 Arlingham, Gloucestershire — 151

125 Ashleworth, Gloucestershire — 153

126 Sapperton, Gloucestershire — 155

127 Northleach, Gloucestershire — 157

128 The Slaughters, Gloucestershire — 159

129 Chipping Campden, Gloucestershire — 161

130 Bourton-on-the-Water, Gloucestershire — 163

131 Windrush Valley, Gloucestershire/Oxfordshire — 165

132 Chipping Norton, Oxfordshire — 167

133 Great Tew, Oxfordshire — 169

134 Kelmscott, Oxfordshire — 171

135 Oxford Canal, Oxfordshire — 173

136 Great Witley, Worcestershire — 175

137 Ombersley, Worcestershire — 177

138 Henley-in-Arden, Warwickshire — 179

139 King's Norton, Birmingham — 181

140 Wombourne, Staffordshire/West Midlands — 183

141 Kingsbury, Warwickshire — 185

142 Baddesley Clinton, Warwickshire — 187

143 Warwick, Warwickshire — 188

144 Stratford-upon-Avon, Warwickshire — 191

145 Edgehill, Warwickshire — 193

146 Napton on the Hill, Warwickshire — 195

147 to 152 Gloucestershire — 197

153 to 155 Gloucestershire — 198

156 to 158 Worcestershire — 198

159 to 164 Worcestershire — 199

165 to 170 Oxfordshire — 200

171 to 173 Oxfordshire — 201

174 to 175 West Midlands — 201

176 Warwickshire — 201

177 to 182 Warwickshire — 202

KEY

- ■ Walk route
- ● Cycle route
- ■ Unmapped walk

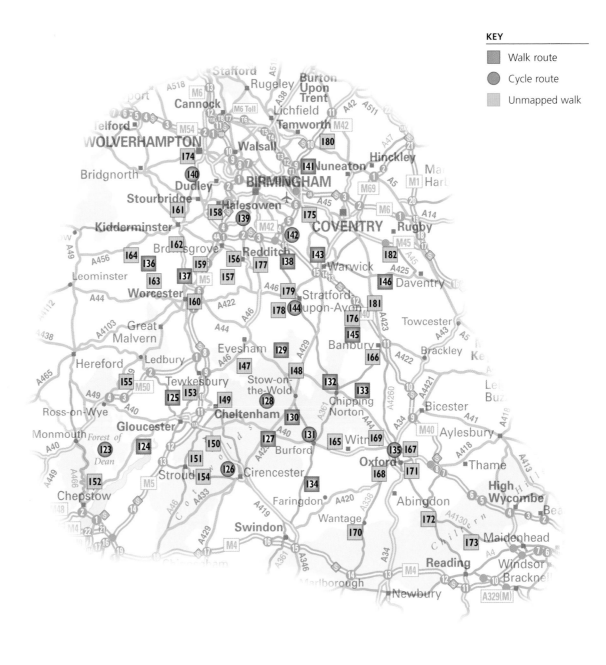

Norchard Station on the Dean Forest Railway

Forest of Dean family trail

Meander through an ancient forest, where Nelson ordered the planting of oaks to build British man-of-war ships.

Forest of Dean

In 1938, the Forest of Dean was designated England's first National Forest Park, and notwithstanding its wonderfully peaceful and unspoiled setting, it is a working forest from which hundreds of tonnes of timber are harvested annually. It has also been a source of coal, and almost everywhere within the forest bears some evidence of its industrial past.

The criss-crossing leisure paths often follow the network of rail- and tramways that serviced the collieries, while heaps of spoil mark the site of the deeper workings. Contrasting with the luxuriant growth of the surrounding forest, many of these are still uncolonised except by the hardiest plants, the barren shales providing little nutrient despite the weathering of 50 years or more since they were last worked. At one time there were more than ten large pits, with countless small drift and bell mines being worked from antiquity. Although large-scale mining came to an end in 1965, anyone born within the Hundred of St Briavels, over the age of 21, and who has worked for a year and a day in a mine is still entitled to work a 'gale' in the forest as a Free Miner. The privilege was bestowed by Edward I, after forest miners helped ensure his victory at the Siege of Berwick by undermining the castle walls.

A pretty bluebell wood in the Forest of Dean

the ride

1 The cycleway is signed from beside the hire shop along a track that drops steeply to the B4234. Opposite, there is a brief but steep pull to a junction. Go left and left again to join the cycleway in the direction of Drybrook Road Station, gently rising along the course of a disused mineral railway. At **Whitegates Junction**, fork left, dropping with the main track to another obvious junction at which, turn sharp right. Where the track then divides, bear right, still following signs for Drybrook Road Station. Keep going, passing beneath a graceful horseshoe-shaped bridge before shortly encountering a tarmac track at **Drybrook Road Station**.

2 Cross and carry on along the cycleway, which is now signed to **Dilke Bridge**, the earlier gradual climb rewarded with a gentle descent. Soon, the forest clears and the scars of former coal workings become evident. Hazard signs warn of a crossing track hidden in a dip, the way continuing beyond the former **Foxes Bridge Colliery**. After a moderate descent (watch for a bend at the bottom), carry on past a junction for Cinderford Linear Park and then the

outbuildings of Dilke Hospital to arrive at **Dilke Bridge**.

3 Beyond, more hazard signs announce a junction where a broad track joins from the left signed to Cannop Wharf. After a traffic barrier and the former **Lightmore Colliery**, a gate forces you to dismount. There follows a short but stiff pull, the track then bending sharply left before dropping once more past a couple of warned junctions, at the second of which, Spruce Ride to the right, offers a short-cut back via **Speech House**.

4 Otherwise, carry on to Central Bridge across **Blackpool Brook**, later reaching a crossing of tracks where Cannop Wharf and the Cycle Centre are signed right. After a turning to New Fancy picnic site, the track swings to a gate, a little distance beyond which is a road crossing.

5 Through another gate at Burnt Log, the track winds down to a fork. Keep ahead, before long coming to a notice warning of a steep descent. The main track drops through a sharply twisting 'S' bend, passing a massive ancient oak, the last survivor of The Three Brothers, where men from the nearby

---

2h30 | **9.25 MILES** | **14.9 KM** | **LEVEL 1 2 3**

MAP: OS Explorer OL14 Wye Valley & Forest of Dean

START/FINISH: Car park, Pedalabikeaway Cycle Centre; grid ref: SO 606124

TRAILS/TRACKS: good surfaced cycle trails

LANDSCAPE: forest and woodland

PUBLIC TOILETS: at Pedalabikeaway Cycle Centre (also showers & changing rooms)

TOURIST INFORMATION: Coleford, tel 01594 812388

CYCLE HIRE: Pedalabikeaway Cycle Centre, New Road, Forest of Dean, tel 01594 860065; www.pedalabikeaway.com

THE PUB: The Speech House Hotel, Coleford

❗ Gradual climbs and descents, one steep descent, 4 road crossings, overhanging twigs; route shared with pedestrians

Getting to the start

Pedalabikeaway Cycle Centre is in the Forest of Dean, 3 miles (4.8km) north east of Coleford beside the B4234.

Why do this cycle ride?

Decreed a royal hunting forest by King Canute in 1016, the Forest of Dean is steeped in a long history. Iron was smelted here before the Romans arrived and they valued not only the timber but also the abundant mineral reserves here – good-quality building stone, coal and iron ore – and began industries that continue to the present day.

Researched and written by: Dennis Kelsall

Clearwell Caves Ancient Iron Mines

The caves are a reminder that mining in this area dates back 7,000 years, when folk dug for ochre. Extraction of minerals continues here, mainly for artists' pigments, giving red, yellow, purple and brown (February–October, tel 01594 833362).

Clearwell Caves

Littledean village, east of Cinderford, is at a junction of ancient forest tracks. On its outskirts, Jacobean Littledean Hall is one of England's most haunted houses, claiming 16 ghosts. The remains of a Roman temple were discovered in the grounds, built over a Celtic water shrine.

collieries gathered on a Sunday morning for their union meetings. Beyond, the descent continues more easily, eventually ending at a T-junction beside **Cannop Wharf**.

6 The **Cycle Centre** is signed to the right beside a couple of **artificial lakes**, at the top of which a car park and picnic area are laid out. As the metalled drive bends towards a road, branch off right to a crossing point over the B4226. Speech House lies 0.5 mile (800m) to the right, although you may wish to return later in the car, whilst the way back is with the continuing track. Fork left when you reach a split, gently losing height to a second junction. There go left again, dropping steeply to the road. Go slowly for there is a sharp bend at the bottom. The **car park** is then at the top of the rise opposite.

The Speech House Hotel

In the heart of Forest of Dean, close to miles of woodland trails, The Speech House was built in 1676 as a hunting lodge for Charles II. Later it became the administrative centre of the forest. The largest room was the Verderer's Court where people went to talk or make a speech, hence the name of what is now a substantial hotel. The Verderer's Court still meets four times a year in what is Britain's oldest functioning courtroom and it retains much of its original decoration. Despite its hotel status, there's a good bar area with real ale on tap, notably a beer from Whittington's brewery in nearby Newent, a traditional bar menu, and a warm welcome for walkers and cyclists. To the rear there are extensive lawns and gardens for all to use.

Food
Hearty snacks in the bar include sandwiches (beef and horseradish) served with chips, various salads and traditional dishes such as ham, egg and chips, sausages and mash, and battered cod and chips. Separate restaurant menu and Sunday roast lunches.

Family facilities
Children are genuinely welcomed (extra beds and cots are provided if staying), and the welcome extends into the bar and dining area. Here there are high chairs and young children have a standard menu to choose from.

Alternative refreshment stops
Café at the Cycle Hire Centre at start and picnic areas in the forest.

☛ **Where to go from here**
Learn about the history and culture of the Forest of Dean at the Dean Heritage Centre at Soudley (www.deanheritagemuseum.com) where attractions include a forester's cottage, agricultural displays, blacksmiths and craft units. At Puzzlewood in Coleford, an unusual maze takes you through 24.5ha (14 acres) of pathways, deep ravines and passageways within pre-Roman open-cast iron ore mines.

about the pub

The Speech House Hotel
Coleford, Forest of Dean
Gloucestershire GL16 7EL
Tel: 01594 822607
www.thespeechhouse.co.uk

DIRECTIONS: beside the B4226 between Coleford and Cinderford, at the junction with a minor road for Lydney

PARKING: 60

OPEN: daily; all day

FOOD: daily

BREWERY/COMPANY: free house

REAL ALE: Bass, Whittington's Cat Whiskers

ROOMS: 37 en suite

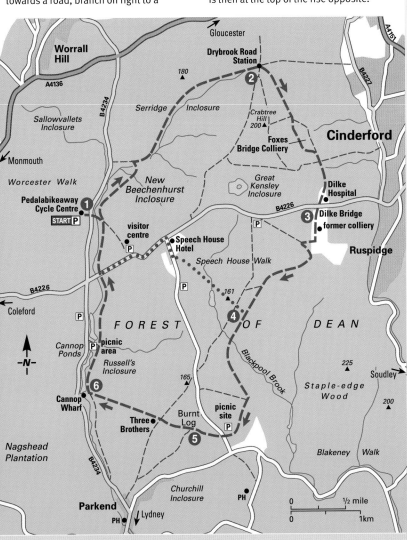

did you know?

Arlingham grew up as a ford on the River Severn, and has been used as such since prehistoric times. For Welsh cattle drovers, it was an important crossing point on their routes to the markets of the southwest. On the lane between Overton and the river, Wick Court is a medieval manor house surrounded by orchards – the last herd of rare Gloucestershire cattle was saved from extinction here.

Pied wagtail
(Motacilla
alba yarrellii)

The Severn Bore at Arlingham

A long but fairly level walk along the river where Britain's regular tidal wave rushes in.

Bore formula

The River Severn is at its most impressive around Arlingham – in its lower reaches before opening up to the Bristol Channel. Here Gloucestershire juts out into the river to form a large promontory, forcing the river into a huge sweeping loop, widening to well over half a mile (800m) at certain points. To the west it is overlooked by the Forest of Dean ridge, to the east by the Cotswold escarpment.

Shallow and placid though it might appear here, the River Severn has a capricious nature. The area has been devastated by floods in the past. The Severn Bore, for which the river is justly famous, is a tidal wave formed a little way downstream, where the river narrows at Sharpness. The fundamental cause behind the bore is the combination of a large volume of tidal water, funnelled into a quickly narrowing channel, hastening on to rock rising from the riverbed. A wave is created, which is then free to roll on to the Severn's middle reaches.

Flooding, however, is rarely a problem here now, because the flood control measures you see as you walk have succeeded in containing the river. It does, though, continue to create havoc every winter further upstream. Significant sea tides at the river's wide mouth make the Severn Bore such a spectacle. In fortnightly cycles over the course of each month the tides reach their highest and lowest points. Near the Severn Bridge the second highest rise and fall of tide in the world has been recorded (the first is in Canada, on the Petitcodiac River). Once a month, for a few days, the spring tides occur, reaching a height of 31ft (9.4m) at Sharpness. Whenever the tides reach 26ft (8m) or more, a bore will be unleashed.

the walk

1 Leave the crossroads at the centre of Arlingham along Church Lane, opposite the Red Lion. After 0.25 mile (400m), where the lane turns sharply right, keep ahead through a gate along a waymarked track that leads to the river. Climb onto the flood bank.

2 Turn left over a stile and, passing from field to field, follow the river downstream. Keep on for a mile (1.6km), eventually crossing a stile into the corner of a field that rises ahead to a wood on top of **Hock Cliff**.

Arlingham sits on a spur of land that is bounded by the Severn

3 At that point, turn from the river beside the hedge. Where it doglegs half-way along, pass over a stiled bridge to continue in the adjacent field. Emerging at the corner onto a track, go left towards a **barn** but before reaching it, look for a stile on the right. A hedged path leads away to meet a lane.

4 Cross to a drive opposite signed to **Colthill**. After winding right in front of one cottage the track ends before another. Slip through an opening on the left and walk at the garden edge to a stile in the corner. Keep ahead beside the field boundary, passing into the next field to climb past a couple of **houses**. Just beyond the second house, turn over a stile on the right into a small field. Bear left to a second stile half-way along the opposite hedge to reach a lane.

5 Follow it left through **Overton** for just over 0.5 mile (800m), leaving over a stile beside a gate on the left as the lane bends sharply right before a long house. Once more by the Severn, head downstream, shortly crossing a stile into a

---

3h15 **7.5 MILES** **12.1 KM** **LEVEL 123**

124

WALK

MAP: OS Explorer OL 14 Wye Valley & Forest of Dean

START/FINISH: Arlingham village; grid ref: ST 708109

PATHS: tracks, fields and lanes, 26 stiles

LANDSCAPE: river, meadows and distant hills

PUBLIC TOILETS: none on route

TOURIST INFORMATION: Gloucester, tel 01452 396572

THE PUB: The Red Lion, Arlingham

Although quite long the walk is suitable for all ages; no real hazards

Getting to the start

Arlingham occupies a promontory of the River Severn, 9 miles (14.5km) southwest of Gloucester and not far from Junction 13 on the M5. You will find roadside parking in the centre of the village near The Red Lion.

Researched and written by:
Dennis Kelsall, Christopher Knowles

while you're there

Pop into St Mary's Church at Arlingham – it's got some of the best stained glass in Gloucestershire.

Not Boring

In days gone by, when waterways were busy highways, boatmen would harness the power of the Severn Bore and use it to help carry them upstream towards Gloucester. Nowadays, it's left to thrill-seeking surfers and canoeists to ride the waves, which can reach up to 10ft (3m) and travel at 12mph (19kph).

The Severn Bore

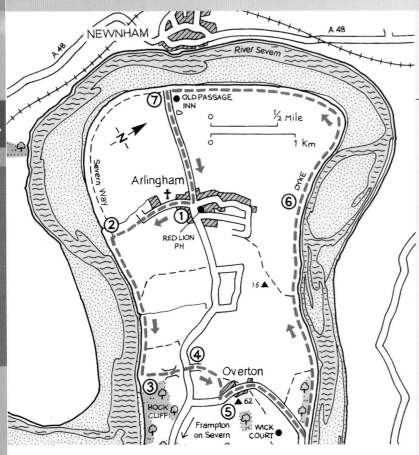

The Red Lion

Summer flower baskets add a splash of colour at this old stone pub on a crossroads in the heart of the village. Expect a cosy interior and a friendly atmosphere, typical of a well-managed community local, although the pub is fast making something of a name for itself locally for the quality of its food. Imaginative, restaurant-style menus draw discerning diners to the door but there remains a warm welcome for walkers and few will be disappointed with the lighter meals available at lunchtime, or the decent range of ales on tap. On warmer days you can sit outside in the small and sheltered patio garden or at pavement tables overlooking the village.

Food
From the 'lite bite' menu you could choose a ploughman's lunch, pasta carbonara, beer-battered haddock and chips, pork and chive sausages with mash and onion gravy or Thai-style salmon and cod fishcakes with lime and ginger mayonnaise. The separate à la carte menu includes fish soup, spiced monkfish with tomato and lemon sauce, warm almond and pear tart with clotted cream.

Family facilities
Although there are few special facilities for children they are welcome indoors and the patio garden is a safe and pleasant spot for families to retreat to on fine days.

Alternative refreshment stops
The Old Passage Inn (which specialises in fresh fish) is on the riverbank to the west of Arlingham and passed on the walk. It has a riverside terrace but is more restaurant than pub.

about the pub

The Red Lion
Arlingham, Gloucester
Gloucestershire GL2 7JN
Tel: 01452 740700

DIRECTIONS: see Getting to the start

PARKING: 8 (+ roadside parking)

OPEN: all day Saturday & Sunday; closed all Monday (except Bank Holidays) and Tuesday lunchtime

FOOD: no food Sunday evening

BREWERY/COMPANY: Enterprise Inns

REAL ALE: Fuller's London Pride, Caledonian Deuchars IPA, guest beers

DOGS: allowed in the bar area only

ROOMS: 3 en suite

☞ Where to go from here
The Wildfowl and Wetland Centre at Slimbridge (www.wwt.org.uk) is home to the world's largest collection of exotic wildfowl and up to 8,000 wild birds winter on the 200 acre (81ha) reserve of fields, marsh and mudflats on the River Severn. Berkeley Castle (www.berkeley-castle.com) is a rambling and romantic medieval fortress with terraced gardens and a beautiful butterfly house.

strip of scrubby woodland. At the far side, the path winds through tall reeds before crossing a stile into a crop field. Go right along the edge, turning the corner to find a **plank bridge** and stile about 15yds (14m) along. Carry on ahead, rejoining the riverbank to progress through successive fields.

6 Later climbing onto a flood dyke, the way continues ahead, eventually rounding a sharp bend in the river and then passing **Newnham** on the opposite bank. Keep going until you reach The Old Passage Inn.

7 Turn in beside it, following the lane for 0.75 mile (1.2km) across the flood plain back to **Arlingham**.

what to look for

Hock Cliff, composed of clay and limestone, is well-known for its fossils, including the so-called Devil's toenails, ammonites, belemnites and many others. Towards the walk's end, approaching the Old Passage Inn, you will see Newnham across the river. Tradition has it that the Romans crossed the river here by elephant to attack fugitive Britons.

Scandal at Haw Bridge

In the 1930s crowds of up to 5,000 on-lookers flocked to Haw Bridge as the grisly remains of a headless body were dredged from the bottom of the river. It was believed to be that of a Captain William Butt, murdered by his lover Brian Sullivan, who then committed suicide by gassing himself.

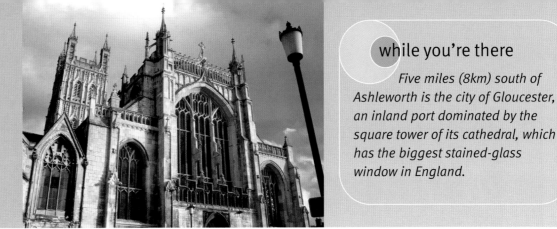

while you're there

Five miles (8km) south of Ashleworth is the city of Gloucester, an inland port dominated by the square tower of its cathedral, which has the biggest stained-glass window in England.

The west façade of Gloucester Cathedral

Severnside at Ashleworth and Hasfield

A fine walk along the banks of the River Severn, visiting a huge and beautifully preserved tithe barn.

Medieval taxes and tithe barns

Medieval tithe barns, such as the impressive example at Ashleworth, still survive around the country in surprisingly large numbers. They date back to the period before the 16th century, when the great monasteries owned much of the land that was not held by the Crown. Around Ashleworth the land belonged to Bristol Abbey. The local people who worked the land were tenants who, in return for working the land, were allowed access to common land and also to work some fields for themselves.

They were obliged to pay tithes, or taxes, to the abbey. This was most often in the form of produce, stored in the tithe barn, which usually stood close to the church and the abbot's residence. The presence of a huge tithe barn here, in what today is a comparatively remote village, has a geographical explanation. Ashleworth is situated at an easily fordable part of the river – an important consideration before the era of easy transportation. There had been a church at Ashleworth since before the compilation of the Domesday Book. A manor house certainly existed during the Norman period, and no doubt before. The barn, and Ashleworth Court next to it, date from the late 15th century.

The limestone barn is 125ft (38m) long, consisting of ten bays – a huge building by any standards. Had you wandered through the barn 500 years ago you would have seen different types of grain, honey, dairy produce and, of course, Cotswold wool, all of which would have been subsequently shipped downriver. Ashleworth Court, next door, is a fine example of a medieval stone building, barely changed since the time of its construction.

the walk

1 From the **Tithe Barn**, walk along the lane towards the River Severn, passing The Boat Inn on your left-hand side.

2h45	6.5 MILES	10.5 KM	LEVEL 123

MAP: OS Explorer 179 Gloucester, Cheltenham & Stroud

START/FINISH: Ashleworth Quay: Very limited parking on grass verges in the vicinity of the Tithe Barn; grid ref: SO 818251

PATHS: tracks, fields, lanes and riverbank, 21 stiles

LANDSCAPE: flat: river, meadows, woods, farms, villages and distant hills

PUBLIC TOILETS: none on route

TOURIST INFORMATION: Gloucester, tel 01452 396572

THE PUB: The Boat Inn, Ashleworth

Getting to the start

Ashleworth is 5 miles (8km) north of Gloucester close to the western bank of the River Severn. The village is signed from the A417 at Hartpury. There is parking for a small number of cars by the tithe barn (National Trust) on the lane leading to the Quay. Ensure you do not impede traffic or obstruct gateways.

Researched and written by: Dennis Kelsall, Christopher Knowles

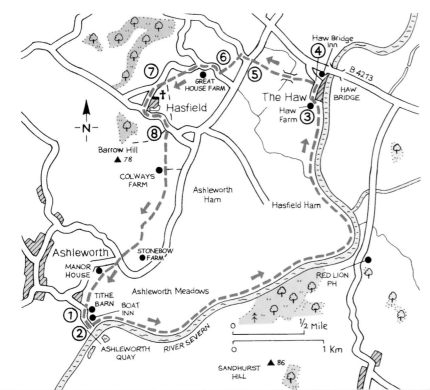

did you know?

As Charles I fled from the Siege of Gloucester in 1643, he hailed a boat at Ashleworth to carry him across the river. The boatman who obliged was a Mr Jelf, and the grateful monarch hastily granted him the rights to operate the ferry here. Jelf's descendants are now the landlords of The Boat Inn.

Above: The old Tithe Barn at Ashleworth
Previous page: Ashleworth Manor House

2 Turn left over a stile to walk along the riverbank. Follow it for a little over 3 miles (4.8km). In general the path is obvious, but where it sometimes appears to pass through gates that are locked, you should instead use a stile, usually found to the right. **Sandhurst Hill** will come and go across the river, followed by the Red Lion pub, sadly also out of reach.

3 Eventually you will pass a house, **Haw Farm**. Immediately after it follow a track that swings away from the river and then passes several half-timbered houses and cottages. It soon develops as a lane and **Haw Bridge** appears before you.

4 Approaching the pub, where the lane splits, leave over a stile on the left into a field. Walk straight on, but then as the field opens up, bear half left to a gate in the far corner. Through it, go forward a few paces, turn right to cross a bridge and then continue straight on across two more fields.

5 Emerging onto a junction of lanes, cross to walk down the one opposite, signed **Tirley Hill**. However, after 30yds (27m), turn over a plank bridge and stile concealed in the hedge on the left. Cross the field, aiming for a gateway about half-way along the right-hand hedge. Maintain the same line in the next field, exiting through a gateway onto a lane.

what to look for

The River Severn can flood quite badly and you will notice a number of damage limitation devices built in the vicinity of Ashleworth and elsewhere. In the past floods have reached as far as the church every two or three years. The worst flood, however, was in 1947. The level the water reached is recorded on the wall of the south aisle.

6 Walk right and pass **Great House Farm**, staying with the lane as it later winds left up the hill. After passing two houses, cross left into a field. Head downhill to the far-right corner and rejoin the lane.

7 Turn left and continue into **Hasfield**, keeping left for Ashleworth. **Hasfield Church** is then signed off left opposite a telephone box, and if you go to have a look, return to the main lane. Carry on through the village, keeping left again at the next junction, still heading towards Ashleworth.

8 After 0.25 mile (400m), look for a waymarked track into a field on the right beside a small post box and **flood depth marker**. Follow the perimeter track, but leave it over a stile on the left, just after entering the second field. Continue parallel with the track in the adjacent enclosure. Keep forward past **Colways Farm** to a kissing gate on the right just beyond the buildings. Pass through and go left beside the hedge. In the next field, strike a diagonal to the far corner and, over a bridge there, bear half left across. Over more stiles, cross an overgrown track and head towards the base of a pylon, passing **Stonebow Farm**, lying over to the left. Carry on to a last stile and escape onto a lane. In the corner of the junction, diagonally left, return to the fields over yet another stile. Make for a gap in the far corner and keep ahead at the field-edge, finally returning to the **tithe barn**.

The Boat Inn

Dandelions bordering the River Severn at Apperley near Ashleworth

With historic connections to King Charles who granted ferry rights to the pub, The Boat stands beside Ashleworth Quay and close by the medieval Tithe Barn and former Court House. In the same family since the pub was licensed by royal charter in the 17th century, it's a gem of a pub with its tiny front parlour, flagstone floors, old scrubbed tables, fireside chairs, ancient kitchen range and time-honoured pub games; a magnet to the many walkers exploring the nearby Severn or the village itself (leaflets available from the bar). Interesting real ales from local micro-breweries are dispensed direct from the cask and change daily. They are ideal to accompany perhaps a generously filled roll or ploughman's lunch with pickle. There is plenty of seating outside to enjoy the location. Come for the annual beer festival in late summer.

Food
Bar food is limited to excellent lunchtime ploughman's or rolls filled with home-cooked ham and mustard, cheese and pickle, salmon and cucumber, or egg and cress.

about the pub

The Boat Inn
The Quay, Ashleworth
Gloucester, Gloucestershire GL19 4HZ
Tel: 01452 700272

DIRECTIONS: beside the quay just south of the tithe barn

PARKING: 10

OPEN: closed Monday & Wednesday lunchtime in summer; all day Monday, and Wednesday & Thursday lunchtime in winter

FOOD: lunchtimes only

BREWERY/COMPANY: free house

REAL ALE: 4 changing micro-brewery beers

DOGS: allowed in garden only

Family facilities
Children are welcome until 8pm. Lovely courtyard garden for summer drinking.

Alternative refreshment stops
There is also a pub just off the route on the other side of the B4213 at Haw Bridge (unsurprisingly the Haw Bridge Inn), or you could try the Queen's Arms in Ashleworth village.

☞ Where to go from here
The Shambles Victorian Village in Newent has cobbled streets, alleyways and cottages set in over an acre (0.4ha) with display shops and trades. At the National Birds of Prey Centre near Newent, there are over 110 aviaries on view with 85 species, and birds are flown daily.

Sparrowhawk
(Accipiter nisus)

while you're there

There are four appealing Duntisbourne villages and hamlets in all – Abbots, Leer, Middle and Rouse – strung out along the Dunt Brook, and running parallel with the old Roman road, Ermine Street (now the A417).

The ford at Duntisbourne Leer

Around Sapperton

Above the valley of the River Frome and through the Earl of Bathurst's estate.

A steeply curving road through the Cotswold-stone Duntisbourne Abbots

Sapperton church

There are few churches dedicated to St Kenelm, an historical figure and mentioned in *The Canterbury Tales*, but Sapperton's is one. Heir to the throne of Mercia, Kenelm's kingdom was thrust upon him by the untimely death of his father in 819 when he was only eight years old. However, his elder sister wanted the crown for herself and persuaded the lad's guardian to murder him. The treachery was exposed in a parchment miraculously conveyed to the pope in Rome by a dove, and Kenelm's body was recovered and taken to Winchcombe Abbey for burial. Where his body was rested each night on its journey, a healing spring is said to have sprouted from the ground, and one of these is passed on the hillside during the walk from Winchcombe (see Route 18).

Go inside Sapperton's church and you might find it something of a surprise, for although of ancient foundation it was substantially rebuilt in the airy style of the 18th century by the Atkyns family of Sapperton Manor. Inside are several splendid features, including a funerary tableau depicting Sir Henry Pool with his wife Anne and their children. So fine is the work that even the half-turned pages

of their missals appear real. The tiny St Michael's Church at Duntisbourne Rouse is also not to be missed, for it has a beautiful Saxon doorway and striking herringbone work in its walls. Within are wall paintings from the 13th century and misericords that are believed to have been brought from the abbey at Cirencester.

the ride

1 Emerging from the cul-de-sac lane by **St Kenelm's Church**, turn left up the hill, passing The Bell. The gradient soon eases as the way approaches a junction, at which go left again. There follows a pleasant 3 miles (4.8km) along the high ground above the Frome valley, passing **Parkcorner Farm**, **Gloucester Lodge**, one of the gates into the Cirencester Park estate, and, later, **Jackbarrow Farm**.

2 There is an opportunity to shorten the ride at this point, by cutting right to **Duntisbourne Abbots** and turning right in the village at a sign to the church.

Otherwise, carry on ahead for a further 1.5 miles (2.4km), the road narrower and signed 'Winstone and Cheltenham'. Approaching **Winstone**, the lane bends sharply right into the village. After passing roadside farmhouses, bend left towards **Elkstone** and **Birdslip**, very soon reaching a crossroads beyond the village hall.

3 Now following a sign to Cirencester, keep ahead out of Winstone, where a fold in the open vista on the right conceals the head of the Duntisbourne valley. Before long, the lane turns abruptly right beside the **A417** trunk road, which follows the line of the Roman Ermine Way that ran between Corinium (Cirencester) and Calleva Atrebatum (Silchester). Cycle down to a junction by a bridge.

4 The onward route lies ahead, but to reach **The Five Mile House**, turn left through the underpass and then go right. Come back to this point to continue the ride, climbing in the direction of **Duntisbourne Abbots**. At the end go right, beyond a rise, the lane dropping into the village. However, control the speed of your descent, for there is a tight bend at the bottom of the hill. Climb to a junction and there go left to the church.

5 Follow the lane around **the church**, then turn sharp left to a second junction by a telephone box. The narrow lane to the right leads to a ford that follows the streambed a short distance, a causeway beside it offering a dry-shod crossing. Remounting beyond, carry on to a junction, go right and then left, leaving towards **Middle Duntisbourne** and **Daglingworth**. The way

---

2h45 | **14 MILES** | **22.5 KM** | **LEVEL 123**

(126)

🚲 **CYCLE**

MAP: OS Explorer 168 Stroud, Tetbury & Malmesbury & 179 Gloucester, Cheltenham & Stroud

START/FINISH: Sapperton: roadside parking beside the church; grid ref SO 947033

TRAILS/TRACKS: country lanes

LANDSCAPE: patterned fields and woodland

PUBLIC TOILETS: none on route

TOURIST INFORMATION: Cirencester, tel 01285 654180

CYCLE HIRE: none locally

THE PUB: The Five Mile House, Duntisbourne Abbots

❗ Care on narrow lanes; dismount to cross ford

Getting to the start

Perched on the brim of the River Frome's narrow valley, Sapperton lies some 7 miles (11.3km) east of Stroud. The A419 to Cirencester passes just south of the village, and entering via minor lanes, you will find roadside parking at the start of the ride in a cul-de-sac beside the church.

Why do this cycle ride?

It is difficult to go far in the Cotswolds without encountering steep hills, but at Sapperton, the rise and fall of the terrain is relatively gentle, offering for mostly easy cycling along quiet lanes. The route describes a loop through several attractive villages, returning across part of Cirencester Park.

Researched and written by: Dennis Kelsall

Gimson

Architect and craftsman Ernest Gimson (1864–1919), a member of the Arts and Crafts Movement, lies buried in Sapperton churchyard, along with brothers Ernest and Sidney Barnsley. Together they came to the village in 1895, to design and make distinctive furniture at nearby Daneway House – a venture that was doomed to fail during World War One.

Thames and Severn Canal

The Thames and Severn Canal of 1789 linked existing waterways at Lechlade and Stroud. A key part of the now derelict route was the 3,400 yard (3,109m) Sapperton Tunnel, and its entrance can still be seen south of the village.

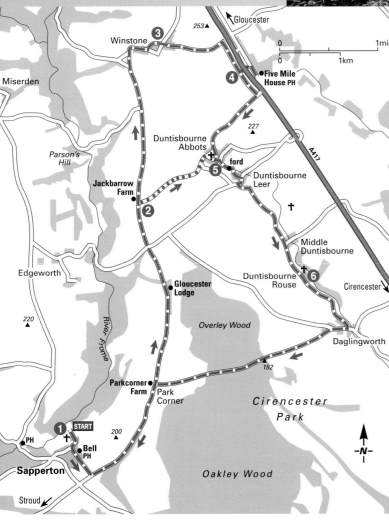

The Five Mile House

Despite undergoing some modernisation after remaining in a time warp for decades, this 300-year-old country tavern remains a classic, unspoiled gem and well worth lingering in over a pint or two of local Donnington BB. The tiny, bare-boarded bar and the simple tap room up the flagstoned hallway preserve an old-fashioned feel, the latter featuring two ancient high-backed settles, and a wood-burning stove in an old fireplace. Rightly, no food is served in these timeless rooms that are perfect for conversation and quaffing of ale. There is a smart dining room extension to the rear as well as a cellar bar and a family room. Escape to the lovely garden in summer and enjoy the country views.

about the pub

The Five Mile House
Lane's End
Duntisbourne Abbots
Cirencester, Gloucestershire GL7 7JR
Tel: 01285 821432

DIRECTIONS: off A417 north west of Cirencester, signposted Duntisbourne Abbots & Services, turn right, then right again and follow 'no through' road sign

PARKING: 30

OPEN: daily

FOOD: daily

BREWERY/COMPANY: free house

REAL ALE: Donnington BB, Timothy Taylor Landlord, Young's Bitter, guest beer

Food

The freshly prepared food includes lunchtime sandwiches, ham, egg and chips and deep-fried cod and chips. More imaginative evening dishes may feature pork glazed with honey and mustard and neck of lamb with rosemary jelly. Sunday roast lunches.

Family facilities

Well-behaved children are welcome in the family room. Smaller portions of some adult dishes can be prepared.

Alternative refreshment stops

Back in Sapperton, try The Bell at Sapperton.

☞ Where to go from here

Cirencester is not far away. As well as the Corinium Museum (www.cotswolds.gov.uk) and the largest parish church in England, you can explore Cirencester Park. This fine estate was partly designed by the poet Alexander Pope for Lord Bathurst and can be accessed from Sapperton.

soon becomes wooded and before long reaches Middle Duntisbourne. Keep right on the main lane and, just over the crest of the hill, look for the lych-gate entrance to **Duntisbourne Rouse**'s church on the left.

6 Carry on downhill, sticking with the main lane as it twists into Daglingworth. At a junction beside a telephone box, pedal right to **Park Corner** and **Sapperton**. Climb gently

away, keeping left when the lane forks at the edge of the village. There follows an undemanding 0.75 mile (1.2km) climb onto the high ground, entering the **woodland** of the Earl of Bathurst's estate towards the top of the hill. Beyond, the road falls gently to **Park Corner**, where you should go left towards Sapperton. Follow your outward route back to the start, not forgetting that you must turn right to drop back past The Bell.

Dutton Lands

Sherborne village and Sherborne Park, just east of Northleach, were bequeathed to the National Trust in 1982. They were originally the property of Winchcombe Abbey, and passed to the Dutton family after the Dissolution. The highlight of the estate is Lodge Park, a deer course – built in 1634 by the hunchback and gambler 'Crump' Dutton – with spectacular views from an ornate, restored grandstand (visit by arrangement, tel 01451 844794).

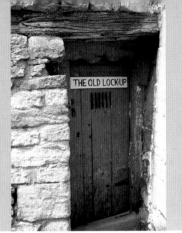

while you're there

Among the venerable houses in Northleach look out for the sinister Blind House. Built without windows, it later served as the village lock-up.

A loop walk from Northleach

Northleach's lock-up

1h45 · **4 MILES** · **6.4 KM** · **LEVEL 123**

A modest Cotswold village is home to an unusual museum.

Mechanical music museum

Northleach is a small country village with a fascinating and rather unusual museum, Keith Harding's World of Mechanical Music, which is one of those eccentricities that has, by happenstance, ended up here in Northleach.

The World of Mechanical Music is in the High Street at Oak House, a former wool house, pub and school. There are daily demonstrations of all manner of mechanical musical instruments, as well as musical boxes, clocks and automata. Some of the instruments, early examples of 'canned' music, date back more than 200 years. The presentation is simultaneously erudite and light-hearted. (You may also listen to early, live recordings of concerts given by some of the great composers including Gershwin and Grieg.) This is something more than a museum – both serious historical research and highly accomplished repairs are carried out here.

Northleach itself, like Cirencester and Chipping Campden, was one of the key medieval wool-trading centres of the Cotswolds and therefore also one of the most important towns in Europe. Though once on a crossroads of the A40 and the Fosse Way, neither now passes through the town. The completion of the A40 bypass in the mid-1980s left the town centre a quiet and very attractive place to visit. The main street is lined with houses, some half-timbered, dating from between the 16th and 19th centuries. Many of these retain their ancient 'burgage' plots at the rear that would originally have served as market gardens. Above the market square is a tiny maze of narrow lanes, overlooked by the Church of St Peter and St Paul, the town's impressive 15th-century Perpendicular 'wool church'. Its features include an array of brasses commemorating the wool merchants on whose wealth the church and town were founded.

the walk

1 From Northleach square, with the **church** behind you, turn left and walk along the main street past **The Wheatsheaf Inn** to traffic lights on the A429 by the former **Correction House**. Cross with care to the lane opposite, but then immediately after passing the austere old Police Station, turn through a gate on the right into a field.

2 Strike a diagonal line to the far corner, maintaining the same course across subsequent fields as you climb towards **Hampnett church**. Emerging onto a lane at the top, go left.

3 The route leaves the lane almost immediately along a concrete track that drops to the left. At a junction beyond a group of **farm buildings**, go left again, climbing towards a gate. Keep on to reach a road, crossing it to continue along the track facing you. It leads to a second road.

Right: Displays in Keith Harding's World of Mechanical Music in Northleach

Left: The 15th-century church of St Peter and St Paul in Northleach has a range of brasses commemorating the town's wool merchants

MAP: OS Explorer OL45 The Cotswolds

START/FINISH: Northleach village square; grid ref: SP 113145

PATHS: fields, tracks and pavement, muddy after rain, 3 stiles

LANDSCAPE: valley track, wolds and villages

PUBLIC TOILETS: in village square

TOURIST INFORMATION: Cirencester, tel 01285 654180

THE PUB: The Wheatsheaf Inn, Northleach

Getting to the start

Northleach lies beside the Fosse Way, the A429, near its junction with the A40; 10 miles (16.1km) north east of Cirencester and 12 miles (19.3km) southeast of Cheltenham. If the central car park in the square is full, you should have little difficulty in finding suitable roadside parking.

Researched and written by:
Dennis Kelsall, Christopher Knowles

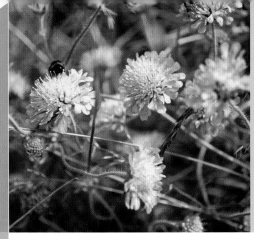

Charter Fair

On the last Saturday in June each year, the people of Northleach celebrate their Charter Fair. This recalls the granting by Henry III, in 1227, of a Market Charter, which permitted a weekly market to be held (sadly, no longer in existence) as well as this annual shindig.

The interior of an old vet's box from Northleach

4 Now turn left and walk over a crossroads to meet the busy A429. Cross with great care to a path opposite, which shortly takes you past **Winterwell Barn**. It then continues as a track to end at yet another road.

5 Cross to a field track, not the adjacent drive to Cats Abbey Farm, and follow this for a little over 0.33 mile (500m) to find a gap in the left hedge. Follow the left field margin down, **Northleach** soon coming into view. Cross a stile at the bottom corner and continue downhill leaving through a gate at the bottom, beside a playground.

what to look for

Leaving Northleach, look out for some interesting old houses. Walton House, for example, was formerly the King's Head, an important inn on the old London to Gloucester route. Further on, set back from the road, are the buildings of the old brewery.

6 Wind between it and a **tennis court**, leaving across a stream behind the court. Follow a passage up between houses, turning left at the top to return to the starting point.

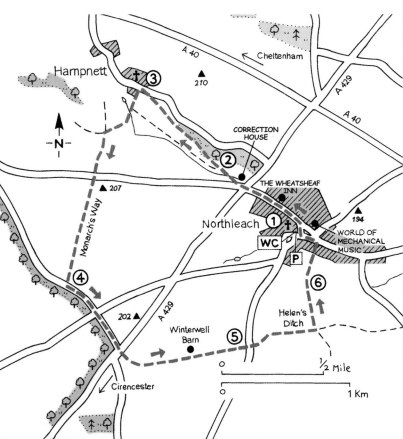

The Wheatsheaf Inn

Looking out across the main street to the famous parish church in this celebrated wool town, the mellow stone Wheatsheaf, built as a coaching inn during the 17th century, is a comfortable and civilised place to retreat to after this Cotswold ramble. In the friendly bar you'll find flagstones on the floor, a blazing log fire in the grate, lots of old wood and beams, and top-notch Hooky beer on handpump. The adjoining dining room is a little more formal, with large, neatly laid-up tables, prints and mirrors on the walls and a classy feel. There are excellent wines, smartly refurbished en suite bedrooms, and a fine terraced garden full of flowers for summer alfresco lunching.

Food

The short lunch menu lists home-made soup, smoked trout and horseradish sandwich (with chips and salad), beer-battered haddock and smoked chicken Caesar salad. There is a more elaborate evening menu and good blackboard specials, perhaps local sausages with mustard mash, and turbot fillet with watercress salad.

Family facilities

Children of all ages are welcome at the Wheatsheaf. Smaller portions of the main menu dishes are available and there are high chairs for younger family members.

Alternative refreshment stops

Although only fairly small Northleach has two other pubs, the Red Lion and the Sherborne Arms.

☞ Where to go from here

Visit Chedworth Roman Villa to view the remains of one of the finest Romano-British villas in Britain, replete with fine 4th-century mosaics, two bath houses and a temple with spring.

about the pub

The Wheatsheaf Inn
West End, Northleach
Cheltenham, Gloucestershire
GL54 3EZ
Tel: 01451 860244
www.wheatsheafatnorthleach.com

DIRECTIONS: on the main village street
PARKING: 15
OPEN: daily; all day March-October
FOOD: daily
BREWERY/COMPANY: free house
REAL ALE: Wadworth 6X, Hook Norton Bitter, guest beer
DOGS: welcome inside
ROOMS: 8 en suite

159

while you're there

The Cotswold Farm Park, near the village of Guiting Power, describes itself as 'a pageant of history on four legs' and is well worth a diversion. It's home to a rich variety of farm animals that would have been familiar to our ancestors but which, in this modern age, are preserved as rare breeds. You can join in at the petting and pets areas, or perhaps watch a seasonal demonstration of lambing, milking or shearing (open March–August and autumn weekends, tel 01451 850307).

Cotswold Farm Park

The Upper Windrush Valley and the Slaughters

3h00 | 9 MILES | 14.5 KM | LEVEL 123

Explore the countryside around two of the Cotswolds most famous villages.

The Slaughters

Bubbling from a spring in a secluded fold of the Cotswold hills, the River Eye embarks on a short but pretty journey past the Slaughters before becoming lost in the River Windrush, just a couple of miles further on below Bourton-on-the-Water. But for their unashamed loveliness, the two tiny villages would probably have escaped the notice of the modern world. Despite their popularity, they have remained unspoiled, resisting large car parks and commercial gift shops. At Lower Slaughter, you can visit a corn mill, which, although dating only from the 19th century, continues the tradition of a succession of earlier mills that have occupied the site since the Normans arrived on these shores. It houses a small shop, tea room, and museum which shows how grist milling has been carried out over the centuries.

Despite the proximity of the two villages, Upper Slaughter displays a completely different character to its neighbour. The cottages around The Square were reconstructed in 1906 by the great architect Sir Edward Lutyens, the designer

The River Eye passing through Upper Slaughter

of New Delhi, while a little earlier, the Victorian vicar of the Norman church, the Reverend Francis E Witts wrote *The Diary of a Cotswold Parson*.

Back in Naunton, the impressive dovecote is a rare survivor of its type, the roof sporting four gables and topped by a louvre to permit access by the birds. It is thought to date from around 1600 and was built to provide the lord of the manor with fresh meat during the winter months.

the ride

1 Starting with the pub on your left, follow the lane out of the village, as yet pedalling easily along the bottom of the **Windrush valley**. At a crossroads with the B4068, the honeymoon comes to an end as you take the leftmost of the two lanes opposite. Tunnelled in trees it climbs steeply away, but before long you can start changing up through the gears as the gradient levels past **Harfordhill Farm**. Your exertion is rewarded by a fine view across the wolds as you continue to a junction.

2 Go right past **Manor Farm**, and then left at the next turning, signed to Upper and Lower Slaughter. Free-wheeling down, watch your speed, for there is a T-junction at the bottom where you should go right to **Lower Slaughter**. Keep with the main lane as it shortly bends left in front of a junction and sweeps around beside the River Eye into the centre of the village.

MAP: OS Explorer OL 45 The Cotswolds

START/FINISH: The Black Horse Inn, Naunton (ask permission first); grid ref: SP 234119

TRAILS/TRACKS: country lanes

LANDSCAPE: rolling Cotswold countryside between the valleys of the Windrush and Eye

PUBLIC TOILETS: none on route

TOURIST INFORMATION: Stow-on-the-Wold, tel 01451 831082

CYCLE HIRE: none locally

THE PUB: The Black Horse Inn, Naunton

Several stiff and one steep ascent, and a long downhill stretch. Suitable for fitter, older family groups.

Getting to the start

Naunton is located just off the B4068, 4.5 miles (7.2km) west of Stow-on-the-Wold. Leaving the main road, follow a narrow lane through the village to find The Black Horse Inn, from which the ride begins.

Why do this cycle ride?

The twin villages of the Slaughters are the epitome of the Cotswold village, and although both can become unbearably crowded on a fine weekend during the summer, they display nothing but charm on a quieter day. Inevitably, the ride encounters a succession of hills, but take your time, and you will discover scenic beauty in this pastoral countryside that is often missed when travelling by car.

Researched and written by: Dennis Kelsall

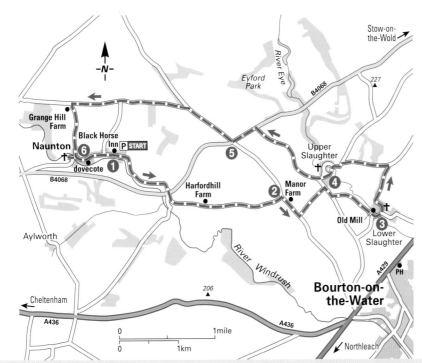

128

CYCLE

did you know?

Cotswold limestone is what gives the old houses of the area their distinctively mellow appearance. You'll see it also in the little footbridges that line the streets of nearby Bourton-on-the-Water. There were several quarries in the immediate area, including one at Naunton, and one east of Northleach (see page 157) at Farmington.

3 At a junction in front of **St Mary's Church**, go left, passing through the more recent part of the village and the cricket green before climbing steadily away.

After 0.33 mile (500m) at a bend, turn sharp left to **Upper Slaughter**, pedalling over a gentle rise before dropping to a junction. To the left the lane falls more steeply, winding sharply to a bridge at the bottom of the hill. Climb away on the far side to a small raised green at the heart of the village, above which to the right stands the **church**. Don't leave without having a look at the **ford**, which lies over the hill behind the church. The high ground opposite was the site of an early Norman stronghold.

4 The route continues with the main lane through the village to a junction. Go right towards Cheltenham. There follows a prolonged pull out of the valley, which eventually eases to a junction with the **B4068**. To the left the climb resumes for another 0.25 mile (400m) to a crossroads.

5 Turn right on a lane, signed to **Cotswold Farm Park**, enjoying a much easier 0.5 mile (800m). At a fork, bear left to Guiting Power and Winchcombe, the gently undulating road offering more expansive views to the south. Go past the first turning off left, signed to Naunton, continuing for a further 0.5 mile (800m) to a second turning, also on the left by **Grange Hill Farm**. An unmarked narrow lane, it drops steeply into the valley. Go carefully as it winds sharply to a junction at the edge of Naunton.

6 The way back to The Black Horse Inn is to the left, but first have a look at the **church**, which lies a short distance along to the right. As you return to the pub, another deviation is merited, this time, turning right just after the **Baptist church** to see Naunton's historic **dovecote**.

A cyclist passes through Lower Slaughter village without encountering other traffic

The Black Horse Inn

The setting is a typical Cotswold village sunk deep in the beautiful Windrush Valley, much beloved of ramblers, cyclists and locals alike. Original flagstones, blackened beams, open log fires, simple tables and chairs and fine oak pews exude rural charm in the main bar while the lounge offers a smaller, snugger retreat. Built of honey-coloured stone and dating from the 1870s, the pub is renowned for its home-cooked food, Donnington real ales and utterly peaceful bed and breakfast.

Food
Dishes range from ploughman's, filled baguettes and jacket potatoes to some accomplished main dishes: steak and kidney pudding, grilled trout, chicken breast with Stilton and bacon, salmon fillet in saffron sauce, and local game in season. There's also the day's selection of 'sinful sweets'!

Family facilities
Families are welcome inside the pub. There's a children's menu, smaller portions of adult meals and high chairs are available.

Alternative refreshment stops
Hotels for lunches and cream teas in both the Slaughters; café at The Mill in Lower Slaughter.

☞ Where to go from here
Spend some time in Bourton-on-the-Water. Children will enjoy the fabulous toy collection and the cars at the Cotswold Motoring Museum and Toy Collection (www.cotswold-motor-museum.com), the perfect replica of a Cotswold village at the Model Village, and a visit to Birdland Park and Gardens, a natural setting of woodland, river and gardens inhabited by more than 500 birds.

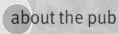

about the pub

The Black Horse Inn
Naunton, Stow-on-the-Wold
Gloucestershire GL54 3AD
Tel: 01451 850565
www.blackhorsenaunton.com

DIRECTIONS: see Getting to the start

PARKING: 12

OPEN: daily; all day Saturday & Sunday

FOOD: no food Monday evening

BREWERY/COMPANY: Donnington Brewery

REAL ALE: Donnington BB & SBA

ROOMS: 1 en suite

while you're there

North of Chipping Campden lie two great gardens: Hidcote Manor, created as a series of 'rooms' by Major Lawrence Johnston (National Trust, March–October, tel 01386 438333); and Kiftsgate Court (April–September, tel 01386 438777), developed by three generations of women gardeners and brought up to date with an ultra-modern water garden.

A fountain in the gardens at Kiftsgate Court

From Chipping Campden to Dover's Hill

Walk out from the Cotswolds' most beautiful wool town to Dover's Hill, the site of Whitsuntide festivities.

2h30 — **4.75 MILES** — **7.6 KM** — **LEVEL 1 2 3**

Cotswold Olimpicks

The Cotswold Olimpicks bear only a passing resemblance to their famous international counterpart. What they lack in grandeur and razzmatazz, however, they make up for in picturesqueness and local passion. Far from being a multi-million dollar shrine to technology which seems so vital to the modern Olympics, the stadium is a natural amphitheatre – the summit of Dover's Hill, on the edge of the Cotswold escarpment.

Dover's Hill is named after the founder of the Cotswold Olimpicks, Robert Dover. Established with the permission of James I, they were dubbed 'royal' games. Dover was born in Norfolk in 1582. His profession brought him to the Cotswolds but he had memories of the plays and spectacles that he had seen in the capital, for this was the era of Shakespeare.

It is generally accepted that the first games took place in 1612, but they may well have begun earlier. Initially the main events were horse-racing and hare-coursing. Other competitions were for running, jumping, throwing, wrestling and staff fighting. The area was festooned with yellow flags and ribbons and there were many dancing events as well as pavilions for chess and other similarly cerebral contests.

Nowadays, the games are a more like a cross between pantomime and carnival, but they have somehow retained their atmosphere of local showmanship. At the end of the events all the spectators, holding flaming torches, file down the road back into Chipping Campden, where the festivities continue with dancing and music along the main street and in the square.

Try to linger in Chipping Campden. A leisurely stroll along its curving High Street of handsome stone houses is essential. The church too is particularly fine and it's also worthwhile searching out the Ernest Wilson Memorial Garden, on the High Street.

MAP: OS Explorer OL45 The Cotswolds

START/FINISH: Chipping Campden High Street or main square; grid ref: SP 151391

PATHS: fields, roads and tracks, 7 stiles

LANDSCAPE: open hillside, woodland and village

PUBLIC TOILETS: a short way down Sheep Street

TOURIST INFORMATION: Chipping Campden, tel 01386 841206

THE PUB: The Eight Bells, Chipping Campden

Getting to the start

Chipping Campden, stands midway between Evesham and Moreton-in-Marsh, where the B4081 meets the B4035. Although there is no large car park, you will find plenty of roadside parking in and around the High Street. The walk begins by the medieval market hall on the High Street.

Researched and written by:
Dennis Kelsall, Christopher Knowles

the walk

1 From the medieval market hall in the middle of Chipping Campden, walk west along High Street past the Noel Arms Hotel. At **St Catharine's Catholic Church**, turn right into **West End Terrace**, keeping ahead into **Hoo Lane** when it shortly bends right. Carry on up to a farm, but where the track then swings into a field, go forward through a pinch stile on the climbing Cotswold Way, eventually meeting **Kingcomb Lane**.

2 Turn left, then after 50yds (46m), go right on a contained path leading to

did you know?

Chipping Campden owes part of its preservation to Arts and Crafts disciple Charles Ashbee, who moved here in 1902 with around 100 followers from London. All were involved in the Guild of Handicraft, which Ashbee had founded in 1888 to promote skilled practical training, especially in furniture design. Ashbee himself restored many of the houses on the main street.

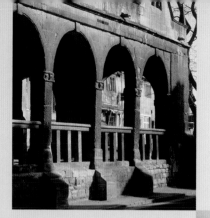

Broad Campden
Charles Ashbee also left his mark on nearby Broad Campden, where in 1905 he converted a Norman chapel into a dwelling for an Indian philosopher.

the top of **Dover's Hill**. Walk left along the escarpment, from which there is a splendid view to the west, passing the **trig point** to reach a **topograph**. Now swing right down the grassy slope, ignoring the first stile seen over to the left to find a second one onto a road, about 300yds (274m) from the top.

3 Over a stile opposite, walk away along the bottom of two fields to a kissing gate on the right, concealed in the corner just beyond a **horse shelter**. The way now lies straight down the hillside from field to field, eventually crossing a track to the right of a **cottage**. Carry on ahead to the bottom left corner of the field.

4 Cross the first of the two bridge and stiles that you find there and walk on with a hedge and then a stream to your right. Over another stile and bridge in the far corner, turn left onto a climbing **woodland path**. Entering a field higher up, the way develops as a track, ultimately ending at a country lane.

5 Turn left and then at a junction, go left again onto a busy road, **The Narrows**. Remaining alert to traffic, follow it down for 0.33 mile (500m). Rounding a left-hand bend, look for a waymarked gap on the right, through which you can continue

what to look for

On reaching Dover's Hill, the route almost doubles back on itself – this is necessary in order to observe legal rights of way. Spend a little time at the topograph – on a clear day there is much to try to identify. In Chipping Campden, look out for the 14th-century Grevel's House, opposite Church Lane. William Grevel, called 'the flower of the wool merchants of all England', is thought to have been the inspiration for the merchant in The Canterbury Tales.

on an accompanying field path. After some 400yds (366m), swing half right, cutting the field corner to exit at **Dyer's Lane**.

6 Keep going downhill, shortly passing a cottage on the right. Then, some 100yds (91m) beyond, turn left into a short field access track. Over a stile on the right, walk forward towards the buildings of **Chipping Campden**, emerging onto a street at the far side of the field. Cross to a footpath between the houses opposite, which takes you back onto **West End Terrace**. Turn right and retrace your footsteps to the town centre.

Postal deliveries in Chipping Campden

The Eight Bells

about the pub

The Eight Bells
Church Street, Chipping Campden
Gloucestershire GL55 6JG
Tel: 01386 840371
www.eightbellsinn.co.uk

DIRECTIONS: Church Street is off High Street, just beyond the old market hall

PARKING: roadside parking

OPEN: daily; all day Friday, Saturday & Sunday

FOOD: daily

BREWERY/COMPANY: free house

REAL ALE: Hook Norton Best & Old Hooky, guest beer

DOGS: welcome in the bar and garden

ROOMS: 4 en suite

Originally constructed in the 14th century to house the stonemasons and store the bells during construction of the nearby church, this tiny, low-built inn of Cotswold stone has two bars where the original oak beams, open fireplaces and even a priest's hole still survive. For centuries the pub has provided refreshment for the folk of this historic wool and silversmith town. Now, many of the customers are tourists, but traditions are upheld with a range of good local and guest ales and a seasonal menu reflecting a serious approach to food. During the summer the pub is hung with attractive flower baskets, and can be accessed through a cobbled entranceway where the bars lead on to the dining room. There is also an enclosed courtyard for drinking and dining in fine weather, plus terraced gardens overlooking the almshouses and the church.

Food
Freshly prepared local food is offered from a daily changing menu. Options range from salads and light dishes to full Sunday lunch. Typically, tuck into a starter of tomato and basil risotto, followed by seared tuna on niçoise salad with plum tomato oil and pesto, or confit loin of pork with five spice jus, and round off with raspberry Bakewell tart with lavender anglaise. Sandwiches, home-baked ham and chutney, and smoked salmon and scrambled egg are served at lunchtime only.

Family facilities
Children are welcome inside the pub. You'll find a kids menu (with colouring competition) and high chairs, and the rear courtyard and terrace is safe for children.

Alternative refreshment stops
Chipping Campden has plenty of pubs, tea rooms and restaurants. Badgers Hall, on the High Street, does a fine tea.

☛ Where to go from here
Broadway Tower, associated with William Morris, stands about 4 miles (6.4km) to the southwest of Chipping Campden. A Gothic folly, built of Portland stone in 1799, it glowers across the Vale of Evesham. There is an interesting small museum inside and fine views across the vale from the top.

while you're there

Little Rissington airfield, east of Bourton-on-the-Water, was the original home of the Red Arrows, the RAF's aerobatic display team, founded in 1965. Today they are based at RAF Scampton in Lincolnshire, but their nine bright red Hawk T. Mk.1s are a familiar sight at shows across the country.

Bourton-on-the-Water to Clapton-on-the-Hill

Walk on the wilder side of Bourton-on-the-Water to see its natural regeneration.

Bourton-on-the-Water

Despite Bourton-on-the-Water's popularity the throng is easily left behind by heading eastwards to a chain of redundant gravel pits. In the 1970s these were landscaped and filled with water and fish. Now they have bedded in, they seem to be an integral part of the landscape.

The fish and water acted as magnets for a range of wetland birds. During the spring and summer look out for the little grebe and the great crested grebe, as well as the more familiar moorhens and coots, and mallard and tufted ducks. Wagtails will strut about the water's edge, swans and geese prowl across the water and kingfishers, if you are lucky, streak from bush to reed. Come the autumn and there will be vast numbers of ducks – pintail, shoveler, widgeon and pochard among them – as well as occasional visitors like cormorants. Around the lakes or by the rivers you may also spy dippers and, in the hedgerows, members of the finch family.

In the village listen for birdsong and you will hear some improbable 'visitors'. Bourton-on-the-Water's bird sanctuary houses, among other birds, one of the largest collections of penguins in the world.

Penguins aside, Bourton-on-the-Water has a long history. The edge of the village is bounded by the Roman Fosse Way and many of its buildings are a pleasing mix of medieval, Georgian and Victorian. The village can become very crowded in summer so arrive early enough in the

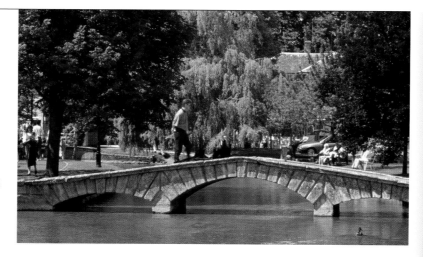

An elegant footbridge across the River Windrush

morning and you will find the bridges spanning the Windrush (one of which dates back to 1756) and the narrow streets beyond them highly picturesque. You'll see far fewer visitors in little Clapton-on-the-Hill, which overlooks Bourton. Make the brief detour just before Point 5 to see its handsome green and tiny church.

the walk

1 Opposite the entrance to the main pay-and-display coach and car park in Bourton-on-the-Water, a public footpath leads to a lane in front of the **cemetery**. Follow it right, then where it forks in front of **Cotswold Carp Farm**, bear right and pass through the rightmost of the two gates in front of you.

2 Walk along a grass track between lakes until it curves right. Leave there to go forward over a bridge and stile into a field, exiting onto a road at its far side.

3 Turn right and then left on to a track to Santhill Fishery. After 100yds (91m), in front of a gate, dog-leg over a stile into the field on the left, following the hedge on beside the track. Return to the track at the far end of the field, but where it later turns through a gate into the fishery, walk forward across a bridge and immediately swing left through a kissing gate onto a wooded path beside the **River Windrush**. Emerging into a field at the far end, turn left to a kissing gate and go over a bridge before turning right beside a lake.

4 About 100yds (91m) beyond a gate, where a second, smaller lake ends, bear right to a stile. Wind through trees, eventually crossing a bridge into a field. Follow the boundary right to meet a track at the far side of the next field. Walk forward along it, but at a junction of tracks by the entrance to a **house**, carry on ahead to the

---

2h15 · 5 MILES · 8 KM · LEVEL 123

MAP: OS Explorer OL45 The Cotswolds

START/FINISH: Bourton-on-the-Water: pay-and-display car park on Station Road; grid ref: SP 169208

PATHS: track and field, can be muddy and wet in places, 24 stiles

LANDSCAPE: sweeping valley views, lakes, streams, hills and village

PUBLIC TOILETS: at car park

TOURIST INFORMATION: Bourton-on-the-Water, tel 01451 820211

THE PUB: The Kingsbridge Inn, Bourton-on-the-Water

Getting to the start

Bourton-on-the-Water stands beside the A429, 15 miles (24.1km) north east of Cirencester. The walk begins from the well-signed main coach and car park on Station Road. Alternative parking is on Rissington Road on the eastern edge of the town.

Researched and written by:
Dennis Kelsall, Christopher Knowles

130 · WALK

The Penguin Millionaire

Pampered penguins at Birdland owe their presence to the zoo's founder, Leonard Hill. He bought the Jason Islands in the Falklands in 1970, as a private reserve, and papers of the day dubbed this successful builder the Penguin Millionaire. Some penguins came to Birdland, and some were traded with other zoos. Their glass-sided pool, allowing you to watch the birds transformed into sleek underwater torpedoes, was one of the first of its kind.

did you know?

The oldest of Bourton-on-the-Water's five bridges is Mill Bridge (1654). The Coronation Footbridge, opposite the Old New Inn, is the newest (1953).

WALK

130

The Kingsbridge Inn

about the pub

The Kingsbridge Inn
Riverside, Bourton-on-the-Water
Gloucestershire GL54 2BS
Tel: 01451 820286
www.roomattheinn.info

DIRECTIONS: beside the River Windrush in the village centre

PARKING: 15

OPEN: daily; all day

FOOD: no food Sunday evening

BREWERY/COMPANY: Eldridge Pope

REAL ALE: Caledonian Deuchars IPA, Bass, Courage Best

DOGS: allowed in the bar only

ROOMS: 24 en suite

The Kingsbridge Inn occupies a prime position in this honey-pot tourist village, famously known as the 'Venice of the Cotswolds', as it stands beside one of the many small bridges that span the tranquil River Windrush. Its bench-filled riverside garden and patio bustles with drinkers and diners on fine sunny days. If the weather's poor, the lively, open-plan, waterside bar is the place to be for good real ale and an extensive range of traditional pub food. Equally, the well-equipped en suite bedrooms are popular due to its central location.

Food

Diverse menu choices include cod in home-made beer batter, guinea fowl with chicken and cranberry mousse, daily pies, curries, steaks and roast lunches plus filled baguettes.

Family facilities

Expect a warm welcome towards children as well as a children's menu, high chairs, baby-changing facilities, and a courtyard garden for summer eating and drinking.

Alternative refreshment stops

Bourton-on-the-Water has many pubs, tea shops and restaurants, catering to most tastes. You could also try the Mousetrap on Lansdowne for reliable pub food and the Old Manse, also close to the river, serves a good lunch and dinner.

☞ Where to go from here

Bourton-on-the-Water has many and diverse attractions jostling for the contents of your wallet. The pick of these are probably Birdland Park and Gardens with their penguins, and the Cotswold Motor Museum (www.cotswold-motor-museum.com), which has lots of pre-1950 cars as well as a few novelty items to thrill children. The most popular activity is arguably just strolling around.

corner. In the next field, after 25yds (23m) dog-leg over a stile to continue on the opposite side of the hedge. Cross another stile and bear slightly left across the next two fields to a stile, then follow the right margin up to a junction of tracks.

5 To the left is the pretty village of **Clapton-on-the-Hill**. In the simple church is an intriguing Latin inscription beside the chancel arch describing an incantation for relief from purgatory. Return to this junction to follow the track in its opposite direction towards Bourton. Entering a field, the Right of Way initially hugs the left hedge then, half way along, crosses to the bottom corner. A grass track then takes you on past a wood before ending in a field at the bottom of the hill. Strike a shallow diagonal to a stile at the far side, maintaining the same course across successive fields until you approach a **wood**.

6 Do not follow the path ahead into the trees, instead, drop to the left, cross a stream and immediately turn right. Keep the same general line, crossing from field to field and eventually you will emerge onto a street at the edge of **Bourton**. Go to the end, turning left and then right into the town centre. After crossing the river beside **The Kingsbridge Inn**, turn right and then left to return to the car park.

what to look for

In the autumn, in particular, keep an eye out for swans. Mute swans – the most common type, with the orange bill – are present all the year round, but the whooper swan, with its erect neck and yellow bill, is only a winter visitor, flying in from northern Europe and Russia.

The 15th-century St John the Baptist Church in Burford

Orange-tip butterfly (Anthocharis cardamines)

Fettiplace Monument in Swinbrook's church

Burford and the Windrush Valley

Discover ancient village churches, built by master craftsmen from stone that was later used in Westminster Abbey.

Windrush Valley churches

The wealth generated by medieval sheep farming is evident in Burford's church, a magnificent edifice topped by a soaring spire, which is said to be one of the highest in Oxfordshire. Yet although the surrounding churches may be more modest in scale, they each have qualities worthy of investigation. At Little Barrington there is magnificent Norman stonework around the doorway, whilst Great Barrington's church contains an Elizabethan effigy of a Captain Bray, unusually depicting the sword on the right. Pardoned by his queen for killing a man in anger, Bray swore never again to draw his sword with his right hand. The church at Taynton has fine carving decorating the door and windows, with corbels fashioned into heads overlooking the nave. The font, too, is remarkable, adorned with angels, evangelists, and other figures including a mermaid.

At Swinbrook you will find two splendid Tudor-style monuments and the graves of Nancy, Unity and Pamela Mitford, whose family held Asthall Manor. Nancy is known for her novels, which included *Love in a Cold Climate* and Unity gained notoriety because of her association with leading Nazis. At St Nicholas's, Asthall, you can see one of the few surviving 'blacksmith' clocks. Widford's church is reached by a footpath off on the right after crossing the

river by Widford Mill. Isolated after the village was abandoned to escape the plague, its walls have sombre 14th-century frescoes, grimly reminding man of his mortality. The building occupies the site of a Roman villa, but a famous tessellated floor, discovered beneath the chancel, is sadly now covered to prevent vandalism.

the ride

1 Riding out of the car park, turn left up Guildenford and then, opposite the **Royal Oak**, go right along Witney Street. At the busy crossroads in the centre of town, cross diagonally into Sheep Street and head past the **hospital** out of the village. After 0.5 mile (800m), just as the road begins to climb, look for a very narrow, unsigned lane leaving on the right. It gently rises and falls along the side of the Windrush Valley, offering picturesque views over the low-lying meadows bordering the river. Although poorly surfaced initially, the lane improves towards **Little Barrington**, passing the village's tiny church along the way.

2 At the end of the lane, drop right beside the green, shortly going right again over the river towards Great Barrington. Beyond **The Fox Inn**, a second bridge heralds a short, but steepish pull into Great Barrington, passing the entrances to **Barrington Park** and the nearby church at the top on your left. Carry on into the village and keep right in front of the **war memorial** for Taynton, the way tracing long undulations along the valley side. The area is famed for its fine stone and the masons who worked it. **Taynton** provided stone for the repair of Westminster Abbey and the

Strong family from Barrington served as master masons for the building of Wren's St Paul's.

3 At Taynton, the **church** is set back from the lane on the right. It was once part of a small monastery belonging to the French abbey of St Denis, which was dissolved by Edward IV and given to the Abbot of Tewkesbury. Cycle through the hamlet and keep ahead towards Burford, eventually reaching a junction with the A424.

4 At this point you can shorten the ride by going forward and then right at a mini roundabout to return to Burford. Otherwise head left up the hill for 200yds (183m) before turning right on a narrow lane. It winds past **Manor Farm** over Westhall Hill, then falls beyond to join the A361. Follow it left through **Fulbrook**, very soon leaving at the second of two turnings on the right, a single track lane signed to Swinbrook. It climbs steadily away between fields and past woodland, later dipping to cross the head of **Dean Bottom** before descending to a junction. **Swinbrook** lies to the right, where another church on the right, St Mary's, merits a visit.

5 Carry on beyond the church for another 200yds (183m) before turning left uphill to leave the village. Keep right with the main lane, still gaining height along the valley side. Later levelling to a junction, go right to **Asthall**, dropping to cross the base of the flat valley where a sporadic line of pollarded willows marks the course of the river. Follow

3h00 · **13.5 MILES** · **21.7 KM** · **LEVEL 123**

MAP: OS Explorer OL45 The Cotswolds

START/FINISH: car park in Burford; grid ref: SP 253122

TRAILS/TRACKS: unclassified country roads and lanes, two short sections on main roads

LANDSCAPE: rolling countryside bordering the River Windrush

PUBLIC TOILETS: at car park

TOURIST INFORMATION: Burford, tel 01993 823558

CYCLE HIRE: none locally

THE PUB: The Fox Inn, Great Barrington

❗ Care to be taken crossing main road in Burford and on two stretches of main road later in ride. The ride is undulating.

Getting to the start

Burford stands by a crossroads of the A40 between Oxford – 23 miles (37km) and Cheltenham – 20 miles (32.2km) and the A361 north from Swindon. A car park, from which the ride begins, is signed along Church Lane from the A361 in the town centre.

Why do this cycle ride?

The ancient wool town of Burford is an attractive focal point for this exploration of the secluded Windrush Valley, presented here as an 'unclosed' figure-of-eight circuit that allows two shorter rides. Surrounded by the rolling Cotswold hills, the Valley is lined with pretty small villages.

Researched and written by: Dennis Kelsall

CENTRAL ENGLAND (SOUTH)

131

CYCLE

Windrush Valley

OXFORDSHIRE/GLOUCESTERSHIRE

166

Nell Gwyn's Favourite

Nell Gwynn (c1650–1687), the famous actress and notorious mistress of Charles II, had a particularly soft spot for Burford, where she and her royal lover would stay at the George Hotel while attending local race meetings. Their child became the Earl of Burford, and when Nell retired to Windsor, she named her house there after the town.

Burford's High Street

Burford Bait

In the days when Burford was an important coaching town, its inns competed fiercely for travellers' custom by providing extra-large meals – which became known as 'Burford Bait'.

the lane around right into the village, winding left in front of the church before turning right by the entrance of the **manor**.

6 Head away along the lane to a crossroads, where to the right, just across the river, you will find a welcoming pub, **The Swan Inn**. The onward way, however lies straight over, along the pretty valley, through the tiny hamlet of **Widford** and eventually back to Burford.

Great Barrington

The Fox Inn

about the pub

The Fox Inn
Great Barrington, Burford
Gloucestershire OX18 4TB
Tel: 01451 844385
www.foxinnbarrington.co.uk

DIRECTIONS: The village is signposted off the A40 3 miles (4.8km) west of Burford and the pub is located beside the River Windrush

PARKING: 60

OPEN: daily; all day

FOOD: daily

BREWERY/COMPANY: Donnington Brewery

REAL ALE: Donnington BB & SBA

ROOMS: 4 en suite

A genuinely unspoiled little Cotswold pub, built in the 17th century with the local honey-coloured stone and picturesquely set beside the gently meandering River Windrush. Its charm is of the simple alehouse sort, with low ceilings, stone walls, rustic furnishings, blazing winter log fires, and time-honoured pub games in the small main bar. Modern-day trends do exist here – the former skittle alley now houses a restaurant with river views and a splendid wall mural of the pretty valley, and four comfortable en suite rooms. Lovely river and lakeside gardens and a heated rear terrace make The Fox a great summer pub, in fact the best summer watering-hole for miles. Added attractions include the excellent local Donnington beer, heady farm ciders, and good, home-made food.

Food

Separate lunch and dinner menus offer a varied choice of meals. From lunchtime sandwiches and traditional dishes such as battered cod and chips, home-cooked ham, egg and chips, and beef and ale pie, blackboards may list Thai-style tuna, spinach, leek and chestnut pie, salmon fishcakes, and seasonal game, perhaps pigeon breast casseroled with mushrooms and red wine.

Family facilities

A genuine warm welcome awaits children who will enjoy the splendid lake and riverside gardens (care and supervision required). Inside, there are high chairs and smaller portions of adult dishes are served.

Alternative refreshment stops

You are spoilt for choice in Burford. Take your pick from hotel restaurants, pubs and tea rooms. Along the route there's the Carpenter's Arms and Mason's Arms in Fulbrook, The Swan at Swinbrook, and the Maytime Inn at Asthall.

☛ Where to go from here

The Cotswold Wildlife Park and Gardens (www.cotswoldwildlifepark.co.uk) is a great venue for gardeners and their children, with rare and endangered species in parkland and gardens, and there's a narrow gauge railway and an adventure playground. Learn more about the skills of spinning and weaving woollen fabric at the Cotswold Woollen Weavers in Filkins.

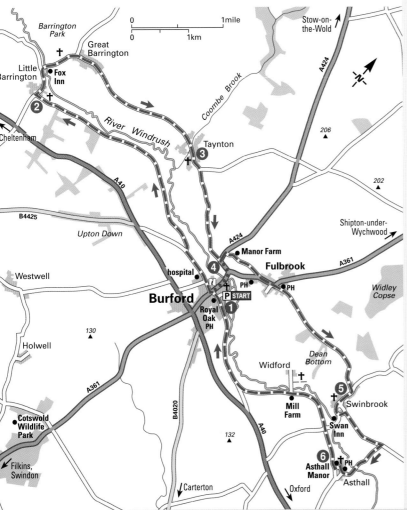

*Song sparrow
(Melospiza melodia)*

while you're there

Chastleton House, west of Chipping Norton, is a stately Jacobean mansion (National Trust, open April–October, tel 01608 674355). It was built between 1603 and 1612 by local wool merchant Walter Jones on land purchased from Robert Catesby, one of the Gunpowder Plotters.

Chastleton House

Beyond Chipping Norton

From Chipping Norton to an ancient site associated with a charming legend.

The 17th century church of St Philip, set in the lush green of the Oxfordshire countryside

Rollright Stones

Commanding a splendid position overlooking the rolling hills and valleys of the north east Cotswolds, the Rollright Stones comprise the Whispering Knights, the King's Men and the King Stone. These intriguing stones are steeped in myth and legend.

In reality the Rollright Stones form a group of prehistoric megalithic monuments created from large natural boulders found within about 600yds (549m) of the site. The stones are naturally pitted, giving them astonishing and highly unusual shapes. The Whispering Knights, of which there are five, are the remains of a Portal Dolmen burial chamber, probably constructed around 3800–3000 BC, long before the stone circle. It would have been very imposing in its day and it is the easternmost burial chamber of this kind in Britain. The King Stone stands alone and apart from the others, just across the county boundary in Warwickshire. The 8ft (2.4m) tall single standing stone was almost certainly erected to mark the site of a Bronze Age cemetery which was in use around 1800–1500 BC.

Finally you come to the King's Men Stone Circle – a ceremonial monument thought to have been built around 2500–2000 BC. There are more than 70 stones here but it has been said they are impossible to count.

No-one knows why this particular site was chosen to erect the stones. The origin of the stones remains a mystery. It is appropriate that the remote hilltop setting of these timeless stones has more than a hint of the supernatural about it.

the walk

1 Walk from the car park to the main A44 road and follow it downhill. Pass **Penhurst School** then veer right through a kissing gate. Skirt the left-hand edge of a recreation ground, aiming for another kissing gate. Descend to a bridge and, when the path forks, keep right. Go up the slope and stay straight ahead over successive stiles, crossing a drive and shortly arriving at a second one. Walk forward along the right-hand edge of the field opposite, continuing in the next field to a pair of gates in the bottom corner.

2 Emerging onto a track, follow it left for 0.75 mile (1.2km) towards **Salford**. Carry on into the village to a crossing of lanes, there turning right onto a track marked 'Trout Lakes' and '**Rectory Farm**'.

3 Follow the track for 0.5 mile (800m) to a right-hand bend. Go straight ahead through a gate, following the field edge to another gate and turn right in the next field. About 100yds (91m) before the field corner,

strike left across the field to an opening in the boundary. Veer left, then immediately right to skirt the field. Cross a little stream and maintain your direction in the next field to reach a road.

4 Turn left up the hill, and after 0.5 mile (800m) go left again for Little Rollright, keeping right at a fork to wind round to **St Philip's Church**. After seeing the church, retrace your steps to the edge of the hamlet and take the **D'Arcy Dalton Way**, signed off on the left. Follow the path straight up the field to the road. Cross over and continue on the D'Arcy Dalton Way, maintaining your direction across an open field to a stile beneath some trees at the far side. However, do not cross, instead turn left up the field edge, soon passing the **Whispering Knights**.

5 On reaching the road, go left, but be careful as traffic moves quickly. You will find the **King Stone** and the **King's Men** on either side, some 200yds (183m) along. There is a small charge to look around them. Return past the Whispering Knights to the stile, this time crossing it and an immediate second stile to walk ahead on a grassy swathe. Emerging over a stile onto a track, turn right towards **Brighthill Farm**, passing beside the buildings to a stile at the end. Head diagonally right down the field to the corner and, crossing consecutive stiles into the next field, keep going with the boundary on your right. After encountering another stile and then a gate, bear away from the hedge, leaving the far side of the field onto a lane. Go left.

4h30 | **9 MILES** | **14.5 KM** | **LEVEL 123**

MAP: OS Explorer 191 Banbury, Bicester & Chipping Norton

START/FINISH: Chipping Norton: free car park off A44, in town centre; grid ref: SP 312269

PATHS: field paths and tracks, country roads, 10 stiles

LANDSCAPE: rolling hills on the Oxfordshire/Warwickshire border

PUBLIC TOILETS: at car park

TOURIST INFORMATION: Chipping Norton, tel 01608 644379;

THE PUB: The Chequers, Chipping Norton

❶ Although this is a long walk there are no overly steep climbs. Suitable for fitter, older family groups.

Getting to the start

Chipping Norton stands 12 miles (19.3km) southwest of Banbury by the junction of the A361 and A44. The walk begins from a long-stay car park signed left off the A44 as it leaves the town centre for Moreton-in Marsh, opposite the entrance to the Somerfield supermarket car park.

Researched and written by:
Nick Channer, Dennis Kelsall

did you know?

Chipping Norton's most unusual landmark is clearly visible from the A44, just west of the town: the chimney (like a down-turned sink plunger) of the former Bliss Tweed Mill. This elegant building dates from 1872, and its preservation was assured after the closure of the works in the 1980s by its conversion into exclusive apartments.

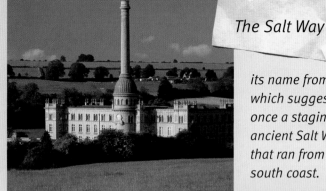

The former Bliss Tweed Mill, with its distinctive chimney

The Salt Way

The village of Salford gets its name from 'salt-ford', which suggests that this was once a staging post on the ancient Salt Way, a trade route that ran from Droitwich to the south coast.

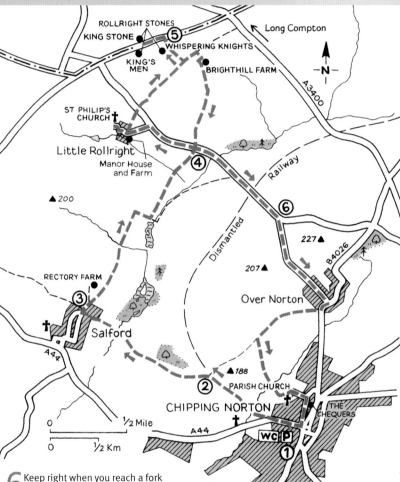

The Chequers

Standing next door to this bustling town's renowned theatre, The Chequers was built in the 16th century to provide lodgings for the stonemasons building St Mary's Church. An ale house ever since, it has a traditional look, with winter log fires, low ceilings, soft lighting and rug-strewn flagstone floors in the main bar, while the bright and airy conservatory-style restaurant has been created from the glassed over rear courtyard. A rural outpost for Fuller's Brewery, you'll find excellent beer, a global list of wine, a wide-ranging menu listing freshly prepared food, and a friendly welcome.

Food

For lunch tuck into honey-roast ham ploughman's, bacon and Brie sandwiches, or order beer battered cod and chips, spinach and mushroom lasagne, and specials like braised lamb shank with rosemary and redcurrant sauce. Evening additions may include roast cod fillet, duck breast and chargrilled steaks.

Family facilities

There are no special facilities but children are allowed in the bars, if eating, until 8pm; smaller portions of adult dishes are available.

Alternative refreshment stops

Chipping Norton offers a variety of pubs, hotels and tea rooms. The rambling old Blue Boar has views of the Market Place and the town's many historic buildings. The Black Horse at Salford offers the chance to stop off for refreshment during the walk.

☛ Where to go from here

Visit Woodstock and Blenheim Palace (www.blenheimpalace.com), the home of the 11th Duke of Marlborough and birthplace of Winston Churchill. See the magnificent state rooms, fine furniture, paintings and tapestries, view the sweeping lawns and stroll through the landscaped grounds.

about the pub

The Chequers
Goddards Lane, Chipping Norton
Oxfordshire OX7 5NP
Tel: 01608 644717
www.chequers-pub.co.uk

DIRECTIONS: town centre, next to the theatre

PARKING: use town centre car parks

OPEN: daily; all day

FOOD: no food Sunday evening

BREWERY/COMPANY: Fuller's Brewery

REAL ALE: Fuller's Chiswick, London Pride, ESB & seasonal ales

DOGS: well-behaved dogs are welcome in the public bar

6 Keep right when you reach a fork and head towards **Over Norton**. Walk through the village to a T-junction and turn right. When the road shortly swings left by **Cleeves Corner**, keep ahead on a tarmac track signposted to Salford. After 0.5 mile (800m), when the hedges give way, look for a waymark on the left. Follow a path down the slope with the hedge on your right, continuing through two kissing gates and then alongside a stone wall to the parish church. Join Church Lane, which leads to a T-junction. Turn right and return to the town centre, passing **The Chequers** on the way. The car park lies to the right off the A44.

what to look for

The manor house at Little Rollright was once important. It was the home of William Blower who gave St Philip's Church its pinnacled tower in 1617. The church, which dates mostly from the 15th century, has two 17th-century monuments to the local Dixon and Blower families.

Traditional transport at Hook Norton Brewery

The brewery at Hook Norton

The villages of Great Tew and Little Tew

Take a stroll through one of Oxfordshire's loveliest villages before exploring undulating countryside to the south.

The fall and rise of Great Tew

Arthur Mee, in his book *The King's England – Oxfordshire*, says that 'if our England is a garden, Great Tew is one of its rare plots.' Most would agree. The village is a gem of a place.

Designed as an estate village in the 19th century, with the intention of blending architectural beauty with utility and management, Great Tew went into decline in later years and virtually became derelict. However, the village has been given a new lease of life, with many of the thatched and ironstone cottages carefully restored, and it is now a designated Conservation Area.

The origin of its name is unclear, but Tew is thought to mean 'ridge', of which there are a great many in the area. The village has a long history and in later years became closely associated with Lucius Carey, 2nd Viscount Falkland, Secretary of State to Charles I. A later owner, G F Stratton, who inherited Great Tew in 1800, resided in a rather modest late 17th- or early 18th-century house which stood at the southern end of the village. During the early years of the 19th century, Stratton engaged in an ill-fated trial in estate management.

The estate changed hands several times before being acquired by Matthew Robinson Boulton. Outlying farms were rebuilt, cottages were re-thatched and other features such as mullioned windows and stone door heads were added. The estate

remained the home of the Boulton family for many years. Between 1914 and 1962 Great Tew was administered by trustees but by now the local workforce had decreased and the estate was all but abandoned.

It was Major Eustace Robb, an old Etonian and descendant of the Boulton family, who moved to the village with the aim of halting its steady decline. His efforts certainly paid off. A stroll through the village today is marked by a conspicuous air of affluence.

the walk

1 From the car park at the edge of Great Tew, walk left along the main lane and go past the turning into the village. Immediately beyond the junction, leave through a gate on the right, the path signposted to Little Tew. Climb diagonally across the field, heading for **Court Farm** on the brow of the hill. Enter the farmyard over a stile by a gate and bear right, skirting

Above: Little Tew is on the route of the walk

some silos to find another gate and stile behind them. Follow the right-hand field boundary to the top corner, emerging over a final stile at a junction.

2 Cross to a path at the left angle of the junction, again signposted to Little Tew. Head diagonally across the field, passing to the right of a **transmitter**. On reaching a lane, turn right and walk down the hill into **Little Tew**. At a junction by the church of St John the Evangelist turn left towards Enstone.

3 The lane climbs out of the village over a rise, dropping on the far side to a **bridge** bounded by white railings. Just beyond, go through an opening in the left-hand hedge into a field and follow the left boundary away. Through a gate in the corner, continue ahead in a meadow, shortly joining a track from a house, over to the left. Follow it out to the road.

133

WALK

1h45 | **3.75 MILES** | **6 KM** | **LEVEL 1**23

MAP: OS Explorer 191 Banbury, Bicester & Chipping Norton

START/FINISH: Free car park in Great Tew; grid ref: SP 395293

PATHS: field paths and tracks, stretches of quiet road, 3 stiles

LANDSCAPE: rolling parkland and farmland on edge of Cotswolds

PUBLIC TOILETS: none on route

TOURIST INFORMATION: Chipping Norton, tel 01608 644379

THE PUB: The Falkland Arms, Great Tew

❶ Paths at the edge of some crop fields may become overgrown in summer and may be difficult for young children

Getting to the start

Great Tew stands alongside the B4022, just south of its junction with the A361 and 7 miles (11.3km) southwest of Banbury. There is a small car park on the edge of the village beside the lane as it enters from the north.

Researched and written by:
Nick Channer, Dennis Kelsall

The Third Tew

Tiny Duns Tew lies 5 miles (8km) east of its Great and Little namesakes. It is recorded that in 1841 this village supported no less than four tailors, four shoemakers, three blacksmiths, two grocers, two bakers and a butcher, not to mention various carpenters, wheelwrights and roofers. Although still a thriving community, it can no longer support even a village shop.

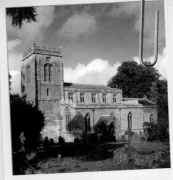
St Michael's Church in Great Tew

4 Be careful, for traffic moves quickly, as you cross to a track opposite, signed to Sandford. It eventually swings left over a bridge in front of **Tracey Barn Farm**. Immediately turn right and walk away at the field edge. Entering trees at the far side, a track leads on through a gate, but leave it after 50yds (46m) through a small waymarked gate on the left. Climb away at the edge of successive fields. Approaching a **lodge** at the top, leave the field through a gate and walk along its drive out to the road by a junction.

5 Cross to the lane opposite, signposted for Great Tew, and follow it down past the entrance to **St Michael's Church**, which lies peacefully amid the trees of the parkland on the right. Carry on, passing the school to

what to look for

Little Tew is worth close inspection. The church, built by George Street, dates back to 1835 and the Methodist chapel to 1871. The Grange, also by Street, was built as a vicarage about the same time as the church. The school and almshouses were constructed in the 1860s. Walk along the splendid avenue of laurels and traveller's joy leading to Great Tew's fine medieval church, which lies peacefully amid the trees of the parkland. The church walk was originally the carriage drive to the mansion of Lucius Carey, 2nd Viscount Falkland.

return to the **village green**, at the back of which, you will find The Falkland Arms.

The Falkland Arms

An unspoiled and historic village is the tranquil setting for this 500-year-old, creeper-clad, Cotswold-stone inn which takes its name from Lucius Carey, 2nd Viscount Falkland, who inherited the manor of Great Tew in 1629. Nestling at the end of a charming row of Cotswold-stone cottages – the quintessential English village scene – The Falkland Arms is a classic gem. The intimate bar features flagstone floors, high-backed settles, a huge inglenook fireplace with winter log fire, and a collection of jugs and mugs hangs from the old beams. A pretty garden is shaded by a large hornbeam tree, complete with dovecote.

Food

Home-made specials such as beef and ale pie or salmon and broccoli fishcakes supplement the basic lunchtime menu (baguettes & ploughman's), served in the bar or the pub garden. In the evening, booking is essential for dinner in the small, non-smoking dining room. Expect parsnip soup or grilled goat's cheese salad, followed by chicken breast with bacon and mushrooms in shallot sauce, or salmon and prawns with lemon and dill sauce.

Family facilities

Children are welcome in the separate dining area at lunchtimes only.

Alternative refreshment stops

Nearby Chipping Norton has a range of restaurants, pubs and cafés.

☞ Where to go from here

At North Leigh, near Woodstock, is the remains of a large and well-built Roman courtyard villa. In Woodstock you can visit the award-winning Oxfordshire Museum and learn more about the archaeology, landscape and wildlife of the county.

about the pub

The Falkland Arms
Great Tew, Chipping Norton
Oxfordshire OX7 4DB
Tel: 01608 683653
www.falklandarms.org.uk

DIRECTIONS: see Getting to the start; pub along dead-end lane by the village stores, opposite the church

PARKING: use village hall car park

OPEN: daily; all day Saturday & Sunday mid-July–September

FOOD: daily; restaurant only in evening; no food Sunday evening

BREWERY/COMPANY: Wadworth Brewery

REAL ALE: Wadworth 6X & Henry's IPA, 4 guest beers

DOGS: allowed on a lead

ROOMS: 5 en suite

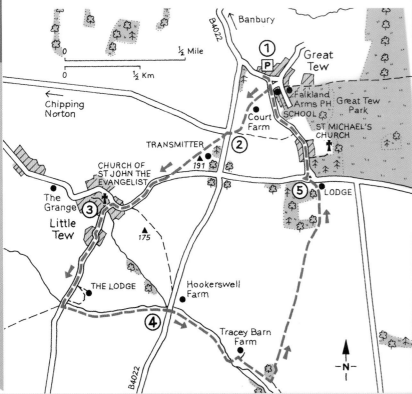

Banbury

Great Tew

Falkland Arms PH   Great Tew Park

SCHOOL

Chipping Norton

Court Farm

ST MICHAEL'S CHURCH

TRANSMITTER

CHURCH OF ST JOHN THE EVANGELIST

The Grange

Little Tew

LODGE

THE LODGE

Hookerswell Farm

Tracey Barn Farm

½ Mile
½ Km

-N-

Coxwell's Great Barn

West of nearby Faringdon at Great Coxwell stands the magnificent Great Barn (National Trust, open daily). It's a vast medieval, stone-built tithe barn with an intricate timber roof. William Morris so admired its workmanship that he loved to bring house-guests here to show them.

The Great Barn at Great Coxwell

did you know?

William Morris liked to travel to Kelmscott from his London home by river boat. He would hire a houseboat and row with friends and family – the journey took six days.

Buscot to Kelmscott

A quiet lane beside the Thames, heading towards Kelmscott

1h45 4.5 MILES 7.2 KM LEVEL 1 2 3

On the Thames Path to the home of William Morris.

Champion of Fine Craftsmanship

The village of Kelmscott is famous for its connections with William Morris (1834–96), founder of the Arts and Crafts Movement. Today he is best remembered for his furnishing designs, rich with flowers, leaves and birds.

Throughout his life Morris dedicated himself to a movement against what he saw as the vulgar tastes of his day, with its sentimentality, clutter and gaudy gewgaws. He put a new value on craftsmanship,

studying and experimenting with the techniques of ages past, and developing a style of apparent simplicity combined with functionality. He took it upon himself to educate too, with pronouncements such as 'Have nothing in your houses that you do not know to be useful, or believe to be beautiful' emphasising the place of good design in everyday life. His philosophy of design became hugely influential and Morris looked to medieval artists and architects for his inspiration.

Kelmscott Manor itself dates from 1570 and became Morris's country home in 1871. It's a mellow old place, built of the local

grey limestone, with mullioned windows and high pointed gables topped by ball finials. Morris loved the manor for its integrity and austerity, and for the harmony of the house in its setting. Now owned by the Society of Antiquaries of London, the house is open to the public on Wednesdays and some Saturdays through the summer.

As a memorial to the great man, several structures were designed to his principles and built in Kelmscott village, notably Memorial Cottages and next-door Manor Cottages. Reflecting traditional style but with a modern, practical twist, they blend effortlessly into the village and were overseen by his widow Jane and daughter May. On a wider scale, Morris's work did much for the emergence of a Cotswold identity in the 1920s. Morris is buried with his wife and daughters in the churchyard at Kelmscott, under a modest tombstone, its only adornment the elegant lettering designed by Philip Webb.

MAP: OS Explorer 170 Abingdon, Wantage & Vale of White Horse

START/FINISH: National Trust car park (free) in Buscot, signed 'Buscot Weir'; grid ref: SU 231976

PATHS: riverside paths, fields, village lanes, 5 stiles

LANDSCAPE: open, flat lands of the Thames floodplain

PUBLIC TOILETS: at the start

TOURIST INFORMATION: Witney, tel 01993 775802

THE PUB: The Plough Inn, Kelmscott

❶ An easy, level walk suitable for all ages; care to be taken with children on the riverside path.

Getting to the start

The tiny hamlet of Buscot stands beside the A417, 2 miles (3.2km) southeast of Lechlade on Thames. Turn off onto a lane to Buscot Locks, beside which you will find a tea room, toilets and a car park.

Researched and written by:
Dennis Kelsall, Ann F Stonehouse

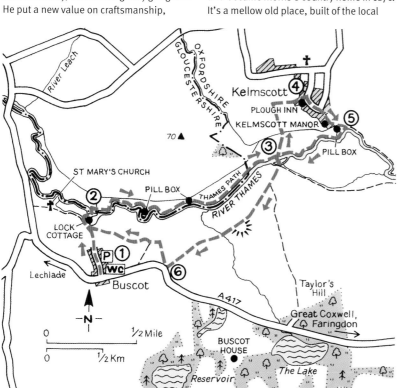

the walk

1 Before beginning the walk proper, stroll back from the car park to admire **Buscot's arcaded pump**. Retrace your steps and continue along the lane, signed to the weir. Bear right where it forks beside the village field, go across a bridge and then immediately turn right on a footpath past **Lock Cottage**. Follow the path over the weir and cross the lock gate.

2 Go right, over a stile and skirt the field edge to another bridge below the main weir. Turn right and follow the **Thames Path**

while you're there

St Mary's Church at Buscott has some good stained glass by Morris and Co, founded by William Morris in 1861. The colours are rich, the foliage sumptuous in its detail and the angels elegantly Pre-Raphaelite. Look out for the memorials to the first and second wives of Edward Loveden Loveden, who died within four years of each other.

A coot and chick
(Fulica atra)

William Morris plaque at Kelmscott

Kelmscott Manor

from field to field downstream beside the meandering river for 1.25 miles (2km), passing a couple of **wartime pill boxes** along the way. The roofs of Kelmscott eventually appear before you and then, entering trees, you will reach a bridge.

3 Walk past it to go through a gate just beyond and turn left up the field edge. At the far side cross a stile and two footbridges, then dog-leg left and right to continue at the edge of the next field with the hedge on your right. At the top, turn right along a sometimes overgrown path, which emerges onto a lane beside **The Plough Inn** at Kelmscott.

4 Go right in front of the pub and then bear left, following the lane past **Memorial Cottages** and **Manor Cottages**. Keep right to reach **Kelmscott Manor** and carry on along a track, passing another World War Two pill box before you come to the Thames.

what to look for

Look out for the charming relief carving of William Morris, set in the wall of the pair of Memorial Cottages at first floor height, between the windows. The great man is shown sitting under a tree, listening to the birds, with the old wool barn and summer house of the manor in the background.

5 Just before the river, turn right, cross a bridge and go through a gate to join the **Thames Path** once more. Over a stile, continue upriver through a gate, passing yet another pill box on your left. Go back through the gate by the footbridge, but now cross the river to a small **marina**. Bear left and right over a second bridge, climbing a stile to follow a track away. At the first bend, cross a ditch and then immediately leave the track, heading diagonally right across a field. At the corner cross a stile and footbridge by a fingerpost and turn right. Where the hedge then breaks, curve left to remain in the same field and climb along a track beside the continuing hedge, where there is a glimpse of **Buscot House** over to the left. Follow the track downhill and, as it then bends right, turn left over a footbridge. Continue on a path diagonally right across the next two fields.

6 Emerge through a gate by the main **A417** road, there turning right along an adjacent track. After 300yds (274m), look out for a **yellow waymark** and turn left through a gate. Over a stile veer left along the edge of the field, crossing another stile and a footbridge at the far end onto the village field. Return to the lane and retrace your steps to Buscot.

The Plough Inn

Built in 1631, the rambling Plough is situated along the dead-end village lane in sleepy Kelmscott, just a short stroll from the River Thames and Kelmscott Manor, once home to the artist and designer William Morris. Long a popular refreshment stop among the walking and boating fraternity, the pub has been sympathetically restored and refurbished inside, a new stylish and contemporary look mixing well with original flagstones, stone walls and the exposed beams and timbers of the 17th-century fabric of the building. Modern pub food is freshly prepared on the premises using local produce where possible. A peaceful overnight's rest is assured in well-equipped en suite bedrooms. Lovely garden and terrace for summer drinking.

Food

Beyond the extensive sandwich menu including pork and leek sausages with roast onion, local ham ploughman's and beef stir-fry with noodles on the bar menu, look out for slow-roasted belly pork with black pudding and apple mash and wide-ranging fish choices on the imaginative carte.

about the pub

The Plough Inn
Kelmscott, Lechlade
Oxfordshire GL7 3HG
Tel: 01367 253543
www.theploughatkelmscott.co.uk

DIRECTIONS: village signposted off the A416 1 mile (1.6km) east of Lechlade. Pub in the village centre near Kelmscott Manor

PARKING: roadside parking or use village car park

OPEN: daily; closed Monday in winter

FOOD: daily

BREWERY/COMPANY: free house

REAL ALE: Hook Norton Bitter, Timothy Taylor Landlord, guest beer

DOGS: welcome in the bar

ROOMS: 8 en suite

Family facilities

Children are welcome inside and there's a children's menu available as well as smaller portions of adult dishes. High chairs are also provided.

Alternative refreshment stops

Buscot Village Shop (closed Mondays) doubles as a tea room, also serving light lunches.

☛ Where to go from here

Make time to visit Kelmscott Manor (www.kelmscottmanor.co.uk), the country home of William Morris. Nearby is Buscot House, an 18th-century Adam-style house with a landscaped park, a splendid walled garden, and an extensive water garden designed by Harold Peto (www.nationaltrust.org.uk).

did you know?

In 1644, faced by the Parliamentarian advance, Charles I and 3,000 followers fled Oxford by night on an unguarded track via Port Meadow and lower Wolvercote to Yarnton and northwards.

Water rail
(Rallus aquaticus)

A Sheriff's Duty

Wolvercote village lies on the edge of Wolvercote Common and the open ground of Port Meadow. Geese were once grazed here, but their place has been taken by cattle and horses. The villagers still have the grazing rights, and the Sheriff of Oxford is required to impound beasts that are set there illegally.

The Oxford waterway

Follow a quiet canal to meet the Thames in Britain's most famous university city.

Oxford Canal

The Oxford Canal took over 30 years to build, its 91 miles (146km) running up £307,000 by the time it finally opened in 1790. Begun by James Brindley, it took a sinuous contour-hugging route to minimise the locks and aqueducts required. But the economy was double-edged, for although construction costs were reduced, passage time increased, and to stave off competition in the 1820s, Brunel was asked to straighten some of the bends. Financed by a consortium that included Oxford University, the City Corporation and the Duke of Marlborough, the canal brought coal from pits at Hawkesbury near Coventry. It quickly became profitable and managed to survive the steam revolution of the 19th century, carrying materials for the construction of the Midland railways and then reducing its tolls to maintain its share of traffic. Decline, however, was inevitable and by the early 1950s commercial traffic had all but ceased.

Oxford's university is thought to date from Henry II's reign, set up to accommodate English students thrown out of Paris by Louis VII. It comprises 41 separate colleges, many of them founded by rich monastic houses and bishops; Magdalen College was established by a Bishop of Winchester in 1458 and Queens College in 1540 by the chaplain of Queen Philippa, Edward III's wife. A tradition of museums stems from this great seat of learning, with collections on every possible theme. The Museum of History of Science has one of Einstein's blackboards – complete with equations – while the Ashmolean collection includes Guy Fawkes' lantern and Henry VIII's stirrups.

A houseboat on the Oxford Canal

the ride

1 Turning right from the car park, pedal back through the village to reach a pair of consecutive **bridges**. Leave the road immediately over the first, dismounting to negotiate a flight of downward **steps** on the left to the tow path .

2 Oxford lies to the right, the way shortly bridged by the railway and then running tree-lined past house gardens on the far bank. The residential suburbs of Oxford spill onto the canal itself, and many boats are permanently moored and serve as accommodation. Further on, wetland and marsh on the right, **Trap Grounds**, is managed as a **nature reserve**. Such marshy areas were once common around the old city where willows and osiers provided withies for basket-making. The reserve provides a last local refuge for the elusive water rail, where the timid bird finds secluded nest sites amongst the thick vegetation. Further on, although the surroundings become increasingly urban, the corridor of the canal retains a pleasant isolation.

3 Before long, a **cast-iron bridge** appears ahead where there is a choice of paths. Take the middle one crossing the bridge and continue on a narrow strip of land separating the canal from the **River Thames**. The path carries on for a little over 0.5 mile (800m) before reaching the canal's abrupt end at **Oxford**. Oxford's heart lies to the left, and there is much to see in this distinguished ancient city. However, as some of the streets are very busy, you may prefer to secure your bike and wander around on foot. Return along the canal to **Wolvercote** after your visit.

4 Following the canal in the other direction from Wolvercote takes you away from the city, passing beneath a couple of starkly functional bridges supporting the main roads. The tow path then crosses Duke's Cut, a short arm that connects to the River Thames. Keep ahead beside the main canal past **Duke's Lock**, pedalling beyond a disused railway bridge and another road bridge (where National Cycle Route 5 leaves for Woodstock), later reaching **Kidlington Green Lock**.

CYCLE

| 2h00 | 9.5 MILES | 15.3 KM | LEVEL 123 |

SHORTER ALTERNATIVE ROUTE

| 1h30 | 6 MILES | 9.5 KM | LEVEL 123 |

MAP: OS Explorer 180 Oxford

START/FINISH: car park in Wolvercote; grid ref: SP 487094

TRAILS/TRACKS: surfaced canal tow path , short road section

LANDSCAPE: canal through Oxford's fringes

PUBLIC TOILETS: at car park

TOURIST INFORMATION: Oxford, tel 01865 726871

CYCLE HIRE: Bee-Line, 61–63 Cowley Road, Oxford, tel 01865 246615

THE PUB: The Trout Inn, Lower Wolvercote

⚠ Steps down to tow path at start (unless you start at Thrupp); unguarded canal tow paths shared with pedestrians; low-arched bridges; busy roads in Oxford.

Getting to the start

The ride begins from Wolvercote, which lies just north of Oxford near the junction of the A40 and A44 roads. Follow a minor road from the roundabout through the village to find a car park at a bend on the left.

Why do this cycle ride?

Oxford is best approached by bike. This uncomplicated ride takes you along the canal from one of its quiet suburbs, where there is a splendid Morse pub on the very banks of the Thames, almost to its heart. For a rural ride, follow the canal in the other direction to the attractive canal-side hamlet of Thrupp.

Researched and written by: Dennis Kelsall

The village of Yarnton has a particularly interesting church. It combines Early English and Jacobean styles. The grandest memorials inside are to the Spencer family who remodelled it in the 17th century. Look out for the funeral of Reynard the Fox (an allegory for the Devil) portrayed in the chancel windows.

Taking a break on a sluice adjacent to the Oxford Canal

5 Another mile (1.6km) lies between you and **Roundham Lock** as the canal slowly climbs from the upper Thames valley towards Banbury and the Midlands. Later on a small **industrial area** unobtrusively stands away from the canal, beyond which is a handful of cottages. After passing beneath the A4260, the tow path briefly follows the main road to the **Jolly Boatman pub**. The waterway then swings away beside the tiny hamlet of Thrupp, where there is another pub and, opposite it, a much-weathered ancient cross. At the top end of the street, the tow path switches banks and the canal makes an abrupt turn in front of a maintenance yard. You can, of course continue north along the canal, but the hard surface later deteriorates making passage difficult. The way back to Wolvercote retraces your outward route.

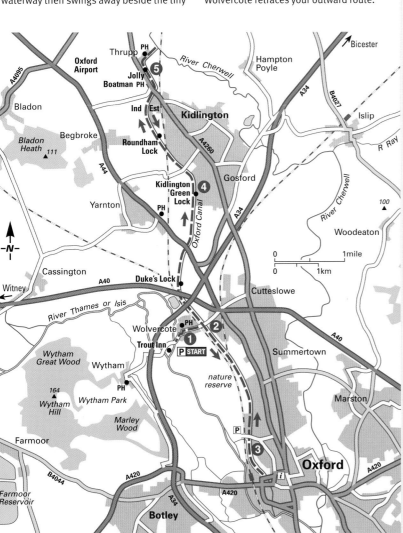

The Trout Inn

about the pub

The Trout Inn
Godstow Road, Lower Wolvercote
Oxford, Oxfordshire OX2 8PN
Tel: 01865 302071

DIRECTIONS: continue on from the car park to find the pub on the banks of the River Thames

PARKING: 95

OPEN: daily; all day

FOOD: daily; all day

BREWERY/COMPANY: Mitchells & Butler

REAL ALE: Bass, guest beer

Food
A good choice of food offers baked whole trout with garlic mushrooms and cheddar mash, lemon chicken, beef, mushroom and Bass pie, or Cumberland sausage wrapped in Yorkshire pudding, with liver and bacon. Sandwiches and specials are listed on the blackboard.

Family facilities
Children are welcome in the pub if eating and there are smaller portions of some adult dishes. Supervised children will love the peacocks on the terrace and looking for the fish in the river.

Alternative refreshment stops
Choice of pubs in both Wolvercote and Oxford (and cafés) and two pubs beside the tow path at Thrupp.

☛ Where to go from here
Linger longer in Oxford, for there's plenty to see and do. In particular, some fascinating museums to visit: the Museum of Oxford (www.oxford.gov.uk/museum); the Ashmolean Museum of Art and Archaeology (www.ashmol.ox.ac.uk); the Pitt Rivers Museum (www.prm.os.ac.uk); the Oxford University Museum of Natural History (www.oum.ox.ac.uk); and the Museum of the History of Science (www.mhs.os.ac.uk). Why not visit the university and its various colleges (www.visitoxford.org) or take in the oldest botanic garden in the country with its collection of more than 8,000 species of plant (www.botanic-garden.ox.ac.uk)?

Constructed in the 17th century from the ruins of Godstow Abbey, with a history that includes being torched by Parliamentarian troops, this famous medieval pub is serenely situated beside the River Thames and attracts thousands of visitors every year. In summer, the cobbled terrace beside the fast-running river with its weir makes a restful place for a quiet pint while watching the peacocks wandering round the terrace and catching a glimpse of the chub in the clear water. Inside, you'll find flagstones, beamed ceilings, bare boards and welcoming log fires throughout the several linked rooms, all adorned with hops, attractive pictures and country bric-a-brac. It has associations with Matthew Arnold, Lewis Carroll and Colin Dexter's Inspector Morse – numerous scenes from the TV series were filmed at the pub.

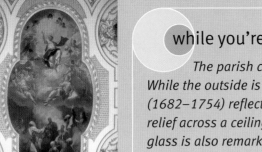

while you're there

The parish church of St Michael at Great Witley is a baroque wonder. While the outside is unremarkable, inside the decoration by James Gibbs (1682–1754) reflects exuberant Italianate tastes, with gilded papier-mâché relief across a ceiling inset with painted canvases. The 18th-century stained glass is also remarkable, bought at auction – like many furnishings for Witley Court – after the break up of the Duke of Chandos's Middlesex estate.

Great Witley Court

A circuit taking in Great Witley

WALK

136

2h45 **4.75 MILES** **7.7 KM** **LEVEL 123**

A mostly woodland walk up and down some of Worcestershire's hills.

Pollen research

What sort of walker are you – 'any weather' or 'fair weather'? Or are you a 'low pollen count walker', suffering from hay fever? Grasses are the most common cause, but allergy is by no means confined to these – just about any pollen can produce allergenic reactions. Between 10 per cent and 35 per cent of us suffer from 'pollinosis' (allergy to pollen), but these reactions may be species-specific. In addition, some species of tree seem to have more potent pollen, birch in particular. Pollen is typically released from grasses from May to August, oilseed rape from April to June, and stinging nettles from May to mid-September. These are all good reasons for walking in the winter, but if you are afflicted in January it could be pollen from alder or hazel, and in March it could be birch. Studies show that the season for birch pollen has shifted to five days earlier every decade over the past 30 years, a clear indication of global warming.

The National Pollen Research Unit (NPRU), at University College, Worcester, is at the forefront of the science of 'aerobiology'. Supplying pollen forecasts is just one of the NPRU's activities; others include studying changes in pollen seasons in relation to climate change, and studying asthma in relation to fungi and house-dust mites. The unit is undertaking a local 3-year study (2003–6) into chronic bronchitis (chronic obstructive pulmonary disease – COPD). It is caused primarily by smoking, but there

are other, secondary factors at work – this must be so, because in some southern European countries people smoke more but there is less COPD. Suspicion is aimed at Britain's higher humidity. The research is focused on whether this can increase the occurrence of this illness.

From early spring until mid-December the lane around Walsgrove Farm is awash with geese – about 3,500 of them. They are prepared for sale using an on-site 'low throughput processing unit'. Until then, these free-range birds wander very freely. Nearly all are destined for the Christmas table, mainly through retail outlets, but you can buy at the farm gate too.

the walk

1 From the pub cross the road and take the path waymarked **Wynniatts Way & Worcestershire Way**. Turn left at the entrance to a house, then swing right and climb steeply through fields, crossing four stiles. Go up through the woods to and up steps to the road. Turn right and then left to join the **Worcestershire Way North**.

2 In about 400yds (366m) reach a bright **trig point**. Walk along the ridge path a further 650yds (594m) to a Worcestershire Way sign at a path junction, just beyond which are four trees growing in a line across the path.

3 Take the path down to the right, initially quite steeply. Take a path on the left on a right-hand bend, emerge from the woods over a **stile** to walk down two large fields, meeting the road beside the **Hundred House Hotel**.

4 Cross the A451 with great care. Through an opening, strike half right, aiming for the **hedge end** beside the **last house**. Step over the fence then turn left on this lane. Walk for 0.5 mile (800m) along here, soon passing firstly **Walsgrove Farm** and secondly (most of the year) thousands of strutting, wailing geese. Do not turn right up a lane but go half right, taking the path that becomes a beautiful avenue of conifers, to the top of **Woodbury Hill**. At a **marker post** go straight over on a narrower track. In 130yds (119m) reach a farm track above **Lippetts Farm**. Shortly rejoin outward route, descending flight of steps on the left and return to Abberley.

5 Turn right, descending. At a hairpin bend, aim away from the farm to walk along the inside edge of a **wood**. Skirt to the left of the buildings at **Birch Berrow**, resuming on a service road. As this goes up, right, to an **exercise ring** for horses,

The Perseus Fountain in front of the 17th-century Witley Court

MAP: OS Explorer 204 Worcester & Droitwich Spa

START/FINISH: Adequate roadside parking by the church in Abberley; grid ref: SO 754679

PATHS: woodland paths, field paths, tracks, 9 stiles

LANDSCAPE: wooded hills and farmed valleys

PUBLIC TOILETS: none on route

TOURIST INFORMATION: Worcester, tel 01905 762311

THE PUB: The Manor Arms at Abberley

⚠ The route crosses several busy roads and involves some steep walking in places

Getting to the start

Follow the A443 between Droitwich and Tenbury. Go through Great Witley heading west, then turn off to follow signs for the pub which is near the church in Abberley.

Researched & written by:
Nick Channer, Nick Reynolds

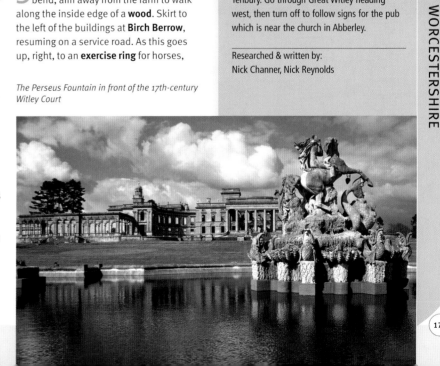

did you know?

The gardens at Witley Court were laid out by William Nesfield, and include the massive Poseidon fountain which shoots out 30 cascades around a central 100ft (31m) jet – it's said that crooner Bing Crosby was so impressed, he offered to buy it.

A pink peony rose

Worcestershire Way

The Worcestershire Way is a long-distance footpath throught the western part of the county to the Malvern hills. It stretches for 31 miles (50km) from Bewdley to Malvern.

take the right-hand of two gates ahead. Go steeply down, taking a stile into thick **pines**. Very soon, over another stile, turn right along the tarmac road for 100yds (91m), so that you are past **1 Hillside Cottages**, not before it.

6 Turn right again, back uphill. Continue north for nearly 1 mile (1.6km), over several **stiles**, walking mostly in trees but later enjoying fine views westwards. Then, on top of **Walsgrove Hill**, you'll see the elaborate and magnificent **clock tower** (1883) of Abberley Hall. Now go steeply down this meadow, to take a stile into a lane. Turn right for 80yds (73m) to the **B4203**.

7 Cross carefully. Turn left, along the verge. Take the driveway to **Abberley Hall School**. Keep ahead to some signs with a tarmac drive on the right. Maintain the same direction as before, following the track beside the clock tower to reach the A443. Take the road opposite, **'Wynniatts Way'**, up to the brow of the hill.

The Manor Arms at Abberley

Set just across the lane from the Norman church of St Michael in this delightful village high in the Abberley Hills, the exterior of this 300-year-old inn is emblazoned with fascinating coats of arms. Inside, original oak beams, log-burning fires and a fine collection of toby jugs in the two comfortable bars enhance the relaxing and welcoming atmosphere you can expect before or after your walk. There's a peaceful summer garden and a pretty patio for summer alfresco eating.

Food

In addition to home-made soups, beef and ale pie, battered cod, fish pie and Cajun chicken, you can expect a choice of grills and roasts and a blackboard listing daily specials and fresh fish dishes, perhaps poached haddock with chive and butter sauce.

Family facilities

Children under 5 are not allowed in the bars. There's a children's menu for younger appetites.

Alternative refreshment stops

The Hundred House Hotel in Great Witley has an enclosed beer garden to the side and an extensive menu.

☛ Where to go from here

Despite its size, Witley Court, 1.25 miles (2km) southeast of Great Witley, is unseen on the walk itself. No public footpaths go near Witley Court, and the road that serves it (and the church) is unadopted. But do make an effort to visit this spectacular building. The Court's spectacular architecture, mostly Victorian, is just stunning. Only the skeleton remains, since its flesh was burned by a fire in 1937. English Heritage describe it as their number one ruin (www.english-heritage.org.uk). Adjacent to Witley Court, St Michael's Church is also worth a visit.

about the pub

The Manor Arms at Abberley
Abberley, Worcester
Worcestershire WR6 6BN
Tel: 01299 896507
www.themanorarms.co.uk

DIRECTIONS: see Getting to the start

PARKING: 25

OPEN: daily; all day Saturday & Sunday; closed Monday lunchtime October to April

FOOD: daily

BREWERY/COMPANY: Enterprise Inns

REAL ALE: Hook Norton Bitter, Flowers IPA, Timothy Taylor Landlord, guest beer

DOGS: allowed in the back bar

ROOMS: 12 en suite

A Salty Tale

East of Ombersley is the quaint old market town of Droitwich Spa, famous for its remarkably salty water. Boasting ten times the salinity of seawater, it provided a source for local salt, and later the facilities of a curative spa. Learn more (and try your hand at brass-rubbing) at the town's Heritage Centre (Monday–Saturday, tel 01905 774312).

Raven Hotel in Droitwich dates from the 16th century

did you know?

Ombersley is a splendid village with many black and white, timbered houses. It's been the home of the Sandys family since 1560, and they lend their name to the unusually gabled Crown & Sandys Arms.

Ombersley and Holt Fleet

Explore an estate park and the banks of the River Severn.

Barn owls needed

A bypass here has made Ombersley quite tranquil. Ombersley Court was built in the 1720s but the nearest you'll get to even a reasonable view of it is at the far end of the churchyard. On the Ombersley Park Estate, St Andrew's Church was built 100 years after Ombersley Court, but in the decorated style of the early 14th century, presumably to reflect the fragment of the original church (now a mausoleum) behind it.

Along the river towards Holt Bridge is woodland adorning the steep slopes of the River Severn's flood plain. If you walked here at dusk you could hope to see an owl, but you probably wouldn't. A survey in Worcestershire in 1932 found 184 breeding pairs of barn owls, but a similar survey in 1985 found just 32. Part of the reason for this decline is believed to be the grubbing out of the hedgerows, thus removing a good habitat for small mammals. However, much blame is apportioned to pesticides moving along the food chain so that, by the time a barn owl has eaten 100 or so slightly contaminated mice, shrews or voles, the dosage of pesticide is fatal.

The goal of the Worcestershire Barn Owl Society (WBOS) is to reverse the trend. Barn owls are quite happy in tree hollows but they disapprove of barn conversions. The WBOS builds and erects nest boxes in strategic places to compensate for the loss – you can even buy or sponsor one. Like other owls, the barn owl flies silently, a useful trick, achieved by having soft tips to its wing feathers which deaden any noise.

The bridge at Holt Fleet replaced a ferry and it was the last bridge in Worcestershire to cease taking tolls. Mines were laid under the Holt Fleet Bridge during World War Two. The Holt Fleet Inn was built well before the bridge, and benefited greatly from the day-tripper business, being the northern terminus for paddle steamer trips from Worcester, about 7 miles (11.3km) to the south. These trips ran until the 1930s. In contrast, the Wharf Inn, on the east bank, marks the site of a coal wharf. Holt Lock, a little way upstream, was completed in 1844.

the walk

1 To the south of the village, and beyond the **cricket ground**, take a path on the right. This is the **Wychavon Way**. Briefly in trees, walk across a meadow to a stile beside a willow. Go along the left-hand field edge, and briefly by the water's edge. At the corner of the **fish pond** a waymarker leads out to a track. Turn left, following this track to the right and soon it becomes a **sunken path** through delicious woodland. Cross a meadow to the **river**.

2 Turn right. In a short mile (1.6km) you'll pass two fishing pools to reach **Holt**

Fleet Bridge. Go under this, continuing for about the same distance, passing the staffed **Holt Lock**. When opposite the **Letchford Inn** you'll come to a riverside stile.

3 Don't go over this stile; instead, turn right. In the field corner join the **access road**. At a junction go straight ahead on the public road. In 650yds (594m), at a right-hand bend, turn left, then immediately right on to a **farm track**. The large area on the right was formerly an orchard, but it has gone completely. It's over 0.25 mile (400m) to the top of this field. When you are 30yds (27m) before a **rusty shed**, turn right. Now, in about 75yds (69m), go left, through a **gate**.

4 What could be a golf course fairway turns out to be an enormous **garden**. Aim to pass to the right of the house, by a children's **wooden watchtower**. Cross the gravel in front of the house, **Greenfields**, to go down its private driveway. Turn right for 275yds (251m), passing several **black-and-white houses**, to a T-junction – **Uphampton House** is in front of you.

Right: Holt Fleet Bridge

2h30 | **5.75 MILES** | **9.2 KM** | **LEVEL 1** 2 3

MAP: OS Explorer 204 Worcester & Droitwich Spa

START/FINISH: towards southern end of road through Ombersley on eastern side (southbound exit from village); grid ref: SO 845630

PATHS: riverside paths, field paths and tracks, village street, 9 stiles

LANDSCAPE: estate parkland, riverside meadows and general farmland

PUBLIC TOILETS: none on route

TOURIST INFORMATION: Worcester, tel 01905 726311

THE PUB: The Crown & Sandys Arms, Ombersley

❶ Route can be busy in Ombersley at the start and finish of the walk

Getting to the start

Take the A449 Worcester to Kidderminster road. Coming from the north or south turn off at the sign for Ombersley and make for the southern end of the village. Parking in the vicinity of the Crown & Sandys Arms, which is located in the main street.

Researched & written by: Nick Channer, Nick Reynolds

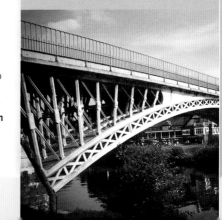

WALK

while you're there

Ombersley's village church is worth a look inside, to see the original box pews of 1830 which fill the nave. Look out for a private corner box pew with its own little fireplace, where the Sandys, lords of the manor, could warm themselves on chilly Sundays.

Barn owl (Tyto alba) and chicks

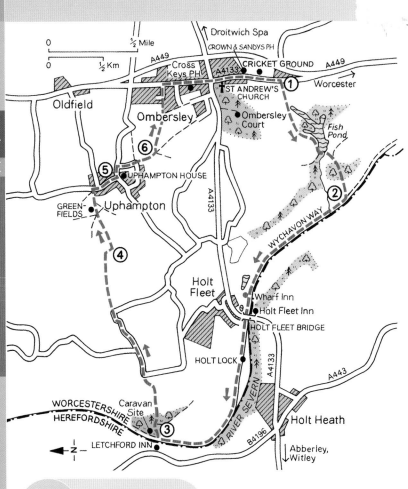

The Crown & Sandys Arms

A rambling and very distinctive Dutch-gabled, 17th-century former coaching inn that has been transformed from what was a basic and dated village local into a classy inn. Stylish and buzzing, it offers a striking mix of traditional and modern, with the bar featuring stone-flagged floors, low beams and huge fireplaces, and the smart bistro full of eye-catching zebra-print chairs and marble-topped tables. The attractions, other than the tip-top local ales, a superlative wine list, and the informal atmosphere, are the interesting modern menus, five tastefully kitted-out bedrooms, and the splendid summer garden and patio.

Food

Freshly made sandwiches, baguettes and hot meals such as braised steak and kidney with red wine and mushrooms or lamb shank with bubble & squeak feature at lunchtimes. The evening carte lists a wide choice of fresh market fish, seafood and seasonal game.

Family facilities

Families will find a genuine welcome towards children; all ages are accepted and there are high chairs, baby-changing facilities and smaller portions of main menu dishes are available.

Alternative refreshment stops

On the route, the substantial Wharf Inn has a riverside terrace and beer garden. Close by, across the bridge, is the Holt Fleet Inn. In Ombersley, there's the Cross Keys and the Kings Arms.

☞ Where to go from here

Take a look at a half-timbered 16th-century dovecote in nearby Hawford (www.nationaltrust.org.uk), step back in time with an audio tour and discover the history of the spectacular ruins of Witley Court, destroyed by fire in 1937 (www.english-heritage.org.uk), or explore the cathedral and museums in the historic city of Worcester (www.visitworcester.com).

about the pub

The Crown & Sandys Arms
Main Road, Ombersley
Worcestershire WR9 0EW
Tel: 01905 620252
www.crownandsandys.co.uk

DIRECTIONS:	see Getting to the start
PARKING:	100
OPEN:	daily; all day Sunday
FOOD:	daily; all day Sunday
BREWERY/COMPANY:	free house
REAL ALE:	Marston's Pedigree, Banks's Bitter, Wood's Quaff & Shropshire Lad
DOGS:	allowed in garden only
ROOMS:	5 en suite

what to look for

The very ordinary and workmanlike single arch bridge at Holt was built by Thomas Telford in 1828 – he was responsible for six others over the Severn. It is the only Severn crossing between Stourport and Worcester. Before you leave the river, you can see a camp site on the other side. The static caravans here are set on pillars as a flood limitation measure.

5 Turn left for 110yds (100m), then turn right, uphill. In 150yds (137m) don't bend right but go straight ahead, on a **shingly track**. About 220yds (201m) further, the main track bends right, a rough track goes ahead and a public footpath goes half left.

6 Take the **public footpath** option, along a field edge. Continue through a small area of **market garden**, reaching a cul-de-sac. Shortly turn right, along the village street. There are many houses to look at, the churches of St Andrew (current and former), and several points of refreshment to delay your return to your car.

As You Like It

The Forest of Arden, long since cut down for fuel, features largely in William Shakespeare's play, As You Like It *(1599). The forest provides a refuge first for hero Orlando, then for the heroine Rosalind, disguised as a boy and in company with her friend Cecilia and the jester, Touchstone. Orlando, believing Rosalind lost, writes love poems to her and sticks them on the trees, while she uses her diguise to further test his love. The comic ramifications continue before a satisfactorily happy ending can be found.*

William Shakespeare

Henley-in-Arden and the Stratford-upon-Avon Canal

A gentle walk around picturesque Henley-in-Arden, The Mount and the Stratford-upon-Avon Canal.

Henley-in-Arden

Henley-in-Arden has a mile-long (1.6km) street, lined with mostly 15th-, 16th- and 17th-century timber-walled buildings, with roofs at every level, ancient windows and a wide variety of old doors.

Peter de Montfort was Henley's Lord of the Manor until he fell in battle on Evesham Field in 1265. Following the battle, the town was burnt to the ground, but a new Henley rose from the ashes. The town maintains a Court Leet that has jurisdiction over petty offences and civil affairs. Each year the Burgesses elect ceremonial officials. These

roles were revived in 1915 by the then Lord of the Manor. The title was bought by Pittsburgh millionaire Joseph Hardy, who established a charitable trust which runs the heritage centre in the town.

Peter de Montfort lived at the castle that used to stand behind Beaudesert Church, and the hill is known locally as The Mount in his memory. In medieval days the horse ruled the world of transport and coaching inns became a feature of many towns. Three very old inns remain in Henley – the Three Tuns, the Blue Bell and the White Swan. The White Swan is opposite the Guildhall and was a haunt of local poets, possibly even Shakespeare. This fine walk takes you over the top of The Mount for a fine view over Henley-in-Arden and then descends on country lanes past Preston Bagot Manor House on the way to the Stratford-upon-Avon Canal.

Below: Stratford-upon-Avon Canal

the walk

1 From the car park follow the sign for the High Street, turn right and right again immediately before the church. Follow the **Heart of England Way** beyond Beaudesert Church, go through the kissing gate by the church wall and follow the waymarks for a steep but short ascent to the top of **The Mount**. Continue over the old earthworks of the former castle of the de Montfort family until you reach the corner of the top far field.

2 Go diagonally across the field in line with a row of power poles and look for a stile leading out to a lane in **Kite Green**. Go left along the lane for about 0.25 mile (400m), then turn right over a stile just beyond **Barn View**. Cross a stile and go down the field edge to another stile. Aim diagonally across the field towards **Church Farm**, passing to the right of the buildings.

3 Turn right and follow the lane, passing by **Manor Farm** to reach the **A4189** Henley to Warwick road. To visit **The Crabmill** turn right, to continue the walk go left along the road for about 220yds (201m), then cross it.

4 Join the tow path of the **Stratford-upon-Avon Canal** at **bridge 48** and take this back towards Henley-in-Arden, keeping the waterway on your left. Leave the towpath at the **second bridge** and turn right to follow the **tarmac lane**. In 180yds (165m), this bends sharp left, bringing you to a road near the **Pettiford Bridge**. Turn right over the bridge.

Some of the delightful houses in Henley-in-Arden

2h00	5 MILES	8 KM	LEVEL 1 2 3

MAP: OS Explorer 220 Birmingham

START/FINISH: Prince Harry Road car park, Henley-in-Arden; grid ref: SP 152658

PATHS: field paths, farm tracks and tow path, 11 stiles

LANDSCAPE: rolling countryside

PUBLIC TOILETS: Station Road, Henley-in-Arden

TOURIST INFORMATION: Stratford-upon-Avon, tel 0870 160 7930

THE PUB: The Crabmill, Preston Bagot

❶ Busy road crossings and town centre streets

Getting to the start

Henley-in-Arden is located at the junction of the A4300 and the A4189 between Redditch and Warwick, 9 miles (14.5km) west of the M40. Follow the signs for the car park in Prince Harry Road.

Researched & written by:
Nick Channer, Roger Noyce

180

while you're there

Head south along the canal to admire Edstone Aqueduct (1814). It carries the canal high above road, rivers and railway. In days gone by, steam engines would stop just below and refill with water.

A falcated teal

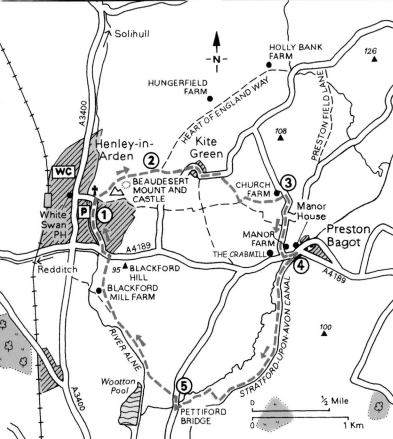

The Crabmill

Crab apple cider was once made at this 15th-century brick and timber hostelry, which is peacefully set on a leafy lane in beautiful rural surroundings. Restored to create an upmarket dining venue, the pub has a light, open feel with a range of individually themed and candlelit dining rooms, each divided by heavy beams and standing timbers, including a 'rude room' with risqué caricatures. Bustling bar area with wood floors and a steely bar leading to a cosy, split-level lounge area with an Italian-style decor. Super summer garden.

Food

The Italian influence extends to the imaginative, modern menu, with dishes such as Sicilian mutton pie, swordfish with herb and lemon polenta, chicken, Parma ham and wild mushroom pie, and fillet steak with confit garlic and olive oil mash. Lighter meals include ciabatta sandwiches and fresh-baked pizzas.

Family facilities

Children are welcome inside the pub and smaller portions of main meals can be prepared.

about the pub

The Crabmill
Preston Bagot, Henley-in-Arden
Warwickshire B95 5EE
Tel: 01926 843342
www.eatingpubs.co.uk

DIRECTIONS: off the A4189 west of Preston Bagot (near Point **3**)
PARKING: 40
OPEN: all day; closed Sunday evening
FOOD: daily
BREWERY/COMPANY: free house
REAL ALE: Wadworth 6X, Tetley, Greene King Old Speckled Hen
DOGS: allowed in the bar

Alternative refreshment stops

There are a number of good pubs in Henley-in-Arden. The White Swan, a restored 16th-century coaching inn opposite the Guildhall, is a regular stop-off for walkers completing the 100-mile (161km) Heart of England Way that passes through its archway.

☞ Where to go from here

Shakespeare enthusiasts should head for Stratford-upon-Avon and the surrounding villages of Wilmcote (Mary Arden's House and the Shakespeare Countryside Museum) and Shottery (Anne Hathaway's Cottage) (www.shakespeare.org.uk). National Trust properties within easy reach include Coughton Court, near Alcester, an Elizabethan house with exhibitions on the Gunpowder Plot and Children's Clothes; Packwood House, a much extended 16th-century house surrounded by stunning gardens; and Baddesley Clinton Hall, a romantically sited medieval moated house dating from the 14th century (www.nationaltrust.org.uk).

5 In 50yds (46m), go left into pastureland. The path arcs right, diagonally over a field. Cross the **stile** in the far left corner to reach the banks of the **River Alne**. Take the riverside path then, at a junction, bear right and proceed ahead. When you see **Blackford Mill Farm** across the field, leave the riverbank and follow the path directly to a modern house near the farm. Keep to the right of it, passing also to the right of Blackford Mill Farm buildings. Continue on field paths to the left of **Blackford Hill** to reach the A4189 road in Henley-in-Arden. Turn left, then right on to **Prince Harry Road** which leads back to the car park.

what to look for

Make a short detour to see the Norman All Saints Church in Preston Bagot. Enjoy the fine view from the seat by the church which carries the message 'Rest and be thankful'. On a summer's day the altar cross becomes ablaze with light as the sun sets behind the hills to the west.

Selly Manor Museum, Bournville

Selly Manor

To give their new village a focus, the Cadbury family imported a real, run-down Tudor manor house stone by stone, and restored it to medieval glory as it was rebuilt here in 1912. This was Selly Manor (closed Monday and winter weekends, tel 0121 472 0199), and among its attractions is a good collection of early vernacular furniture.

An advertisement of 1884

King's Norton to Birmingham Centre

Follow an 18th-century canal to the Venice of the Midlands.

Birmingham's Canals

Birmingham is at the centre of England's canal network with three major waterways meeting at Gas Street Basin. The Worcester & Birmingham Canal provided a route via the River Severn to Bristol, whilst the Birmingham & Fazeley Canal gave direct access to the Midlands coal fields as well as linking to the Trent & Mersey Canal, carrying traffic from the factories and ports of Lancashire, Cheshire and Yorkshire. The New Main Line brought the Shropshire Union into the city, a route from the north, but also giving access to the vast ironworks and potteries along the Ironbridge Gorge.

New interest and restoration has given them life, and there is a heritage of bridges, aqueducts and canalside buildings.

the ride

1 National Cycle Route 5 enters **King's Norton Park** beside the parking area and follows a red tarmac path through to Pershore Road, the A441. Cross at lights to continue across playing fields, beyond which the cycleway rises through an open tract to the Worcester & Birmingham Canal at **King's Norton Junction**. The tow path left is signed to Birmingham.

2 Passing through **old industrial areas**, the path soon rises to a road. Cross the canal using the **bridge** and double back beneath it to continue on the opposite bank. Later, after cycling under the railway and approaching another main road, the

tow path again swaps sides, but this time there is a short flight of **steps** to negotiate on the descent. Before long, the canal and railway run side by side, and it is then not far to **Bournville Station**.

3 With the aroma of chocolate in the air, the surroundings gradually improve and the way shortly passes the **university campus**. Further on, in leafy Edgbaston, is **Maple Bank Meadow**, a fine spot for a picnic on the edge of the city. A short distance past there is the 105yd (96m) long **Edgbaston Tunnel**. As it is unlit and has an uneven path, it is safer to dismount. Bridges then come thick and fast as you approach Birmingham centre, where the canal makes a sharp left turn in front of the **Mailbox development**. Gas Street Basin lies just around the corner, the hub of England's canal network and, where on the left, opposite the **marina**, you will find the **Canalside Café-Bar**.

4 A roundabout route is necessary to reach the far bank. Carry on through **Broad Street Tunnel** (again dismount) to the **National Sea Life Centre**. Cross a bridge over the **Soho Loop Canal**, but instead of rejoining the canal side, bear left and then veer right over a second bridge spanning the main canal. Carry on over a third bridge above the **Birmingham & Fazeley Canal** and swing round in front of the Malthouse, now heading back to **Gas Street Basin**. The tow path turns behind the marina to end on **Bridge Street** beside one of the many canalside bars, the James Brindley. There follows a winding route on pavements, along dedicated cycle tracks and back streets, which is well signed as **National**

Cycle Route 5. Main road crossings are all controlled, but you need to remain vigilant of traffic and pedestrians.

5 Turn right along Bridge Street and then go left into **Holliday Street**. Rising to a junction at the top, cross right to join a footpath below the elevated main road. At the bottom, bend left beneath a bridge, and on emerging, cross right to continue once more below the main road on another path to the foot of a large building, **Westside**. Now, go left along Lower Severn Street to a crossroads and turn right into **John Bright Street**. That then swings left into Station Street, at the end of which, turn right in front of **The Crown** onto a contra-flow cycleway along Hill Street. Keep ahead across two sets of traffic lights, through a short pedestrian precinct in front of the **Birmingham Hippodrome** and along Hurst Street. Carry on to the second set of lights, then turn right in front of the **White Swan** along Sherlock Street. At the next traffic lights, go left into **Gooch Street**, later crossing a mini-roundabout to reach a small **shopping area**. Follow the road as it bends right to more traffic lights at the main road.

6 Now following signs to **Rea Valley Park**, cross to Longmore Street opposite, pedalling along the pavement cycleway on the right as it later continues beside open grass to become Clevedon Road. Where that then bends left, leave right into **Cheddar Road**. Keep ahead over a crossroads into Harbury Road and at the end, go left into **Willows Crescent**. On reaching the next crossing, swing right into **Canon Hill Road**, which finishes at a junction with **Edgbaston Road**.

3h00	12.3 MILES	19.8 KM	LEVEL 123

MAP: OS Explorer 220 Birmingham, Walsall, Solihull & Redditch

START/FINISH: King's Norton Park; grid ref: SP 045792

TRAILS/TRACKS: canal tow paths and dedicated cycle tracks, city streets

LANDSCAPE: canal and park corridors through Birmingham's neglected industrial suburbs to the city-centre redevelopment

PUBLIC TOILETS: close to Gas Street Basin and Cannon Hill Park

THE PUB: The Canalside Café-Bar, Birmingham

TOURIST INFORMATION: Birmingham, tel 0905 1234000

CYCLE HIRE: none locally

! City-centre traffic, low bridges, unlit tunnels, barriers and mooring posts, steps, pedestrians. Suitable for older children only

Getting to the start

The ride begins from a parking area beside King's Norton Park. Leave the A441, just south of its double roundabout junction with the A4040, turning west into Camp Lane beside a garage and then left into Westhill Road. The car park is opposite the junction with Whychall Lane.

Why do this cycle ride?

The Worcester & Birmingham Canal goes to the heart of Birmingham. It is a traffic-free route where massive regeneration is creating bright new leisure and commercial centres.

Researched & written by: Dennis Kelsall

CENTRAL ENGLAND (SOUTH)

King's Norton

BIRMINGHAM

Chocolate Town

Bournville was a model village built by Cadbury's in the 1890s, to house its chocolate factory workers – and other families – in a hygienic setting beyond the slums of the inner city. The chief architect was Alexander Harvey, and the houses reflect the popular neo-Tudor style of the day.

139

🚲

CYCLE

did you know?

Edgbaston is the home of the Warwickshire County Cricket Club, whose nickname, The Bears, comes from their logo based on the chained bear of Warwick (for more information, see www.edgbaston.com).

Cricket at Edgbaston

7 Cross to enter **Canon Hill Park** and follow the marked cycle route along the main drive, passing the Information Centre and **Garden Tea Room**. Keep going beyond the floral beds through informal recreation areas, later joining a natural green corridor beside the River Rea. Swinging over a bridge, continue on the opposite bank, eventually emerging onto Kitchener Road. Go left into Cecil Road then, at the end, left again into Moor Green Lane. Immediately over the bridge, go right to rejoin the riverbank, later crossing Cartland Road and continuing on another track that ends beside a small industrial area. Cycle right over a bridge, and then left to resume your ride beside the river, crossing another road before finally emerging in Dagger Close. Go left and left again into a cul de sac, at the end of which a passage leads between houses onto the canal bank. Retrace your outward route left back to King's Norton Park.

The Canalside Café-Bar

An informal café-bar housed in one of the few original buildings dotted among the modern buildings in the smartened up and rejuvenated Gas Street Basin. In a prime position smack beside the canal, this white-painted old brick building was originally the lock-keepers cottage. It retains its small rooms, with the addition of a light and airy conservatory dining area overlooking the garden and canal, and you can expect a warm and friendly atmosphere. It is a popular refreshment stops among the many cyclists and walkers using the canal.

Food

Printed and blackboard menus list a host of home-made meals ranging from soups, pizzas, chilli, lasagne, beef stroganoff, and organic roasts. Good choice of ploughman's lunches, sandwiches, vegetarian meals and puddings.

Family facilities

Children are very welcome here. There's a children's menu for younger family members and smaller portions are readily available. Good canalside terrace but keep young children supervised.

Alternative refreshment stops

There is a choice of canalside and terrace bars around Gas Street Basin, and the Garden Tea Room in Canon Hill Park.

☛ Where to go from here

Visit Cadbury World in Bournville and learn more about the chocolate making process and how the chocolate is used to make famous confectionery (www.cadburyworld.co.uk). Take a tour of Birmingham's Botanical Gardens and Glasshouses in Edgbaston and see citrus fruits in the Mediterranean House and giant agaves and opuntias in the Arid House. There's a young children's discovery garden and sculpture trail (www.birminghambotanicalgardens.org.uk). You could also visit the National Sea Life Centre in Birmingham (www.sealifeeurope.com), or the Birmingham Nature Centre (www.birmingham.gov.uk).

about the pub

The Canalside Café-Bar
35 Worcester Bar, Gas Street
Birmingham, West Midlands B1 2JT
Tel: 0121 248 7979

DIRECTIONS:	on route see Point **3**
PARKING:	none
OPEN:	daily; all day until 8pm
FOOD:	daily; all day until 7pm
BREWERY/COMPANY:	free house
REAL ALE:	changing guest beers

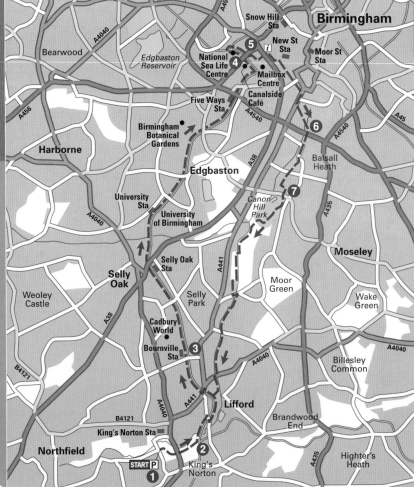

Take a Look

There's an unusual museum at Broadfield House at nearby Kingswinford. It centres on a magnificent collection of etched and coloured glass from the 19th and 20th centuries (open Tuesday–Sunday afternoons, tel 01384 812745).

while you're there

Wightwick (pronounced 'Wittik') Manor was the pseudo-Tudor creation of Theodore Mander, who made his fortune in paint. A fan of the Pre-Raphaelite artists and the Arts and Crafts Movement, he built his mansion in 1887 and filled it with treasures that remain today, including the famous Rossetti portrait of Janey Morris (National Trust, open March–December).

The Staffordshire & Worcestershire Canal

Above: Tiled fireplace in Wightwick Manor

Explore two transport systems that spurred Britain's Industrial Revolution.

Staffordshire & Worcestershire Canal

The Staffordshire & Worcester Canal was engineered by James Brindley, and runs for 46 miles (74km) from Great Heywood Junction on the Trent & Mersey Canal to the River Severn at Stourport. Construction took 6 years and the canal opened in the year that Brindley died, 1772. It followed contours wherever possible, but still had to descend over 360 feet (110m) through 43 locks, one for almost every mile (1.6km).

The three at Bratch lower the canal 30 feet (9m) and are overlooked by an unusual turret toll house. A major cargo was coal from Staffordshire, a trade that continued into the 1940s.

The canals declined because of the faster transport offered by the railways, but the line here was never the success that had been anticipated. A branch-line off the Worcester to Wolverhampton railway, it opened in 1925 and serviced local coal and ironworkings. Passenger trains were rarely busy, and by 1932 had been withdrawn, although freight traffic continued for another 30 years until final closure in 1966. Today, the trackside has become a wildlife corridor along which woodland has re-established, with birch, oak, alder and hawthorn forming a thick coppice. Many small birds find cover in the trees; redwings, redpolls, siskins, willow warblers and chiff chaffs, whilst hunting birds such as owls, kestrels and buzzards can sometimes be spotted. Small mammals such as voles and mice scurry about in the undergrowth, but there are foxes and badgers to be seen too.

the ride

1 Leave the car park at its far end to join the **disused railway track** and go along it to the right. After initial views across the fields the embankment becomes cloaked in trees and shrubs, the line passing beneath or over several bridges to reach the site of a former station, **Penn Halt**. Beneath more bridges, there is a long section through a wooded cutting, then a couple of barriers take the way across the end of a road connecting to a **housing estate**. Keep going, shortly passing the overgrown brickwork of a **platform** beside the path. Some 0.33 mile (500m) further on, and about 50yds (46m) before reaching a bridge at **Compton**, leave the embankment, dropping along a sloping path on the left to reach the main road at the foot of the bridge.

2 Turn left over the **canal** and cross the road to the towpath access. Double back beneath the bridge and follow the bank away from Compton. In contrast to the railway path that was largely shrouded in trees, the canal offers more **open views** across the surrounding countryside, whilst bordering the bank here on the opposite side is a small **nature reserve**. After passing a couple of locks the way arrives at **Wightwick Bridge**.

3 The charming pre-Raphaelite **Wightwick Manor** (National Trust) lies close by, and although its hours of opening are limited, is well worth a visit. To get there, leave the canal as you emerge from the bridge, doubling back up to the road above. Turn left and, at the **traffic lights**, continue ahead over the main road beside **The Mermaid**, climbing a steepish hill to the entrance, some 100yds (91m) along on the left. Return to the canal and carry on, passing beneath successive bridges and eventually reaching **Dimingsdale Lock**.

4 The tow path now switches to the other bank, running down to **Awbridge Lock**, which is overlooked by an unusual bridge, its parapets decorated with brick balustrades, apparently a novel attempt by Brindley to combine lock and bridge in a single entity. Carry on to **Bratch Locks**, where the tow path reverts to the west bank above an impressive flight of locks, overlooked by a striking **octagonal toll house**.

5 Dismounting, re-cross the canal and wheel your bike down beside the locks.

Left and above: Cycling on the tow path of the Staffordshire and Worcestershire Canal

2h00 · **9 MILES** · **14.5 KM** · **LEVEL 123**

140

MAP: OS Explorer 219 Wolverhampton & Dudley

START/FINISH: Kingswinford Railway Path car park, Wombourne; grid ref: SO 870940

TRAILS/TRACKS: well-surfaced track and tow path

LANDSCAPE: disused railway and canal through gentle countryside

PUBLIC TOILETS: none on route

TOURIST INFORMATION: Wolverhampton, tel 01902 556110

CYCLE HIRE: none locally

THE PUB: The Round Oak, Wombourne

⚠ Awkward barriers along railway track, low bridges and tow path occasionally narrow; children must be carefully supervised

Getting to the start

Wombourne lies 4 miles (6.4km) southwest of Wolverhampton. Leave the A449 at its roundabout junction with the A463 along an unclassified road to Wombourne and the Kingswinford Railway Walk. Go ahead at a crossroads and continue for 0.6 mile (1.1km) to a car park signed off on the right.

Why do this cycle ride?

Many disused railway lines have found new life as footpaths and cycle tracks; the one at Wombourne, beside a canal, is an easy, off-road circular route. The return passes not far from Wightwick Manor, a fine mansion whose design and furnishing was greatly influenced by the Arts and Crafts Movement.

Researched & written by: Dennis Kelsall

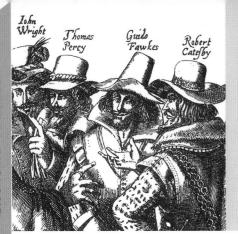

The Gunpowder Plotters

Remember, Remember

Robert Catesby and Thomas Percy, two of the notorious Gunpowder Plotters, died near Himley, southeast of Wombourne, in 1605. Traced to their hiding place at Holbeche House, the men were shot as they tried to leave – whether to surrender or to escape, we cannot know. The mansion (private) was burned to the ground, and later rebuilt.

Roufus bush robin (Cercotrichas galactotes)

If you want to return to the car park, leave onto the lane and go left. The entrance to the **car park** lies 0.25 mile (400m) along, on the left immediately after **Bratch railway bridge**. Otherwise, carry on beside the canal beneath the road. After the last of Bratch Locks you can remount, continuing for a further 0.5 mile (800m) past **Bumblehole Lock** to a canalside pub, **The Round Oak** at Ounsdale Bridge.

6 Return along the canal to Bratch Locks and, joining the road, go right back to the car park. Notice on the right, as you leave Bratch Locks, a splendid polychrome brick building, looking more like a minor French chateau than an industrial building. It is, in fact, a **Victorian waterworks**, opened in 1897 to coincide with the queen's silver jubilee, and housed two steam driven pumps named in royal honour, 'Victoria' and 'Alexandra'.

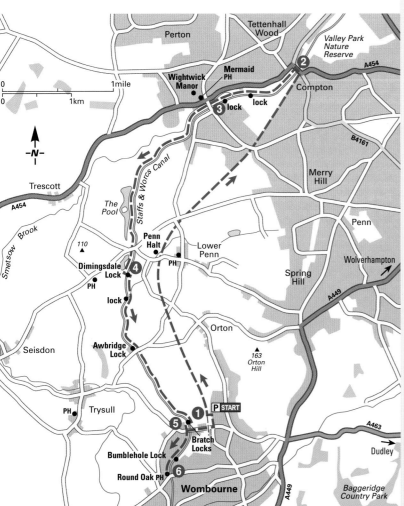

The Round Oak

about the pub

The Round Oak
100 Ounsdale Road, Wombourne
Wolverhampton, West Midlands
WV5 8BU
Tel: 01902 892083

DIRECTIONS: beside the canal at Ounsdale Bridge (see Point **5**)

PARKING: 45

OPEN: daily; all day

FOOD: daily; all day Saturday & Sunday; all day school holidays

BREWERY/COMPANY: Banks Brewery

REAL ALE: Banks Bitter & Original, Marston's Pedigree, guest beers

Big and busy family dining pub situated beside the Staffordshire and Worcester Canal and built to provide refreshment to the workers constructing the canal in the late 18th century. Extended in recent years it comprises several comfortably modernised dining areas, including a spacious bar area where locals congregate to sample pints of Marston's and Banks's beers. Expect a warm and friendly welcome, especially towards children.

Food
A standard pub food menu lists traditional bar snacks alongside a range of steaks, pies (cheese and potato, cottage pie), and a choice of fish dishes. Occasional theme food nights.

Family facilities
Very popular with families as it provides an indoor family room for dining, a children's menu and high chairs, while outside there's a play area and a bouncy castle.

Alternative refreshment stops
There's a café in the former station beside the car park at Wombourne, the Oddfellows at Compton, the Mermaid pub at Wightwick and a café if visiting Wightwick Manor.

☛ Where to go from here
Stop off at Wightwick Manor, one of the finest examples of 19th-century decorative style, where all aspects of William Morris's talents are shown in the house (www.nationaltrust.org.uk). Head for the Black Country Living Museum in Dudley, a re-created canalside village on a 26-acre (10.5ha) site. Meet the costumed guides and find out what life was like around 1900. Ride on a tramcar, take a trip down the underground mine, venture into the limestone caverns and visit the olde tyme fairground (www.bclm.co.uk).

Kingsbury Water Park

A lovely stroll through old Kingsbury and around the pools of its magnificent water park.

Kingsbury village and Water Park
The water park around Kingsbury was once 620 acres (251ha) of old sand and gravel pits, but today it has become a major leisure facility with more than 30 beautiful lakes and pools attracting around 200,000 visitors each year.

Raised planks lead into the water park where you can stroll around a number of the larger pools to enjoy watching a wide variety of contemporary activities taking place such as sailing, windsurfing, fishing and horse-riding. There are also several hides where you can do a spot of bird-watching.

The old village of Kingsbury sits on a small hill overlooking this wonderland of water. On this high ground is the Church of St Peter and St Paul from where you get a delightful view over the lakes. The church contains a 12th-century nave, a 14th-century tower and a 16th-century belfry. One of its old arches is incised by deep grooves in which it is believed the local bowmen used to sharpen their arrows.

Kingsbury village has been associated with many famous families over the years. In the Middle Ages the Bracebridge and Arden families were involved in a Romeo and Juliet-type feud when Alice Bracebridge married John Arden against the wishes of both families. John's brother's granddaughter was Mary Arden, the mother of William Shakespeare.

By the middle of the 19th century most of the land in the village was owned by Sir Robert Peel. The long-serving MP for Tamworth, one-time Prime Minister and founder of the modern police, lived at nearby Drayton Manor and was buried at Drayton Basset, a few miles up the Tame Valley. The main business of the area had been agriculture, but coal mining took over. Later sand and gravel was extracted from the land on the other side of the River Tame. Today the river divides a thriving village from the Kingsbury Water Park.

You leave the water park over Hemlingford Bridge which crosses the River Tame. This bridge was first built by public subscription in 1783 and takes its name from the Hundred of Hemlingford in which Kingsbury stands (a hundred was an old Saxon local administrative area). There used to be a toll house at one end of the original bridge, but this was demolished in 1937. On New Year's Day in 1982 the original bridge was destroyed by catastrophic floods. Flooding has been a regular feature of the area, with the water frequently rising and spreading over the flood plain between Kingsbury village and the nearby hamlet of Bodymoor Heath. Most people now live on the east side of the River Tame.

the walk

1 From the car park, go left along **Pear Tree Avenue** to reach the A51 road. The Royal Oak can be seen over to the left. Go straight over the road, pass the White Swan and at the corner of the road, take the path on the left. Pass the **churchyard**, keep to the right of the church and descend the steps to reach a footbridge over the **River Tame**. Cross the bridge and walk along the raised footway planks to enter **Kingsbury Water Park**. Follow the signs for the visitor centre, pass **Hemlingford Water** and **Bodymoor Heath Water** and keep right at the fork.

2 From the visitor centre make for the roundabout and go straight over following the signs for the **sailing club** and North Warwickshire Cycle Way. Pass by the entrance gate to **Tamworth Sailing Club** and continue on the right-hand side of **Bodymoor Heath Water**, along a mixture of tarmac lane and grass footpaths.

3 At the end of the stretch of water swing left, then right and follow the waymarks for the **Centenary Way**. Go diagonally across an access road, still following the waymarks, and take the path alongside

Below: Trees and lawns surround a lake in Kingsbury Water Park

1h00 **3 MILES** **4.8 KM** **LEVEL 123**

MAP: OS Explorer 232 Nuneaton & Tamworth

START/FINISH: Pear Tree Avenue car park (free, off the A51 near the White Swan in the centre of Kingsbury); grid ref: SP 217962

PATHS: reservoir paths and footpaths, 2 stiles

LANDSCAPE: reservoir and parkland

PUBLIC TOILETS: Visitor centre in Kingsbury Water Park

TOURIST INFORMATION: Tamworth, tel 01827 709581

THE PUB: The Royal Oak, Kingsbury

⚠ Two busy road crossings

Getting to the start
Kingsbury is on the A51 between junctions 9 & 10 of the M42, south of Tamworth.

Researched & written by:
Nick Channer, Roger Noyce

while you're there

Younger children will love petting the farm animals and rare breeds at Ash End House Farm Park, west of Kingsbury (open daily except January, tel 0121 329 3240).

Long-tailed tit
(Aegithalos
caudatus)

Drayton Manor Theme Park and Zoo

North of Kingsbury (open April–October, tel 01827 287979), this popular theme park has more than 100 rides, including the world's first stand-up tower drop, and a thrilling water ride, Stormforce 10.

Roller-coaster at Drayton Manor Theme Park

what to look for

Many wild birds visit the water park and you will certainly see plenty of ducks, swans, coots and moorhens, especially Canada geese. Look out for herons, kingfishers, common terns, great crested grebes, cormorants, little ringed plovers and lapwings. Some 200 species of bird have been recorded here and the park has one of the UK's largest inland breeding colonies of common terns.

4 Cross **Hemlingford Bridge** towards the busy A51, go left over a stile and cross the field to the next stile by the road, near the middle of the village of **Kingsbury**. Turn left for 100yds (91m), following the pavement to a path on the right, beside a detached house. There is a **Heart of England Way sign** here. Take the path, avoid the footbridge and carry on, keeping houses visible. Keep right at the fork just beyond the **bridge**, take the next left, then turn right. Turn left after a few paces into **Meadow Close**, then left again into Pear Tree Avenue to return to the car park.

lakes. Beyond **Swann Pool**, follow the path round to the left and then you can see **Mill Pool** on the right through the trees.

The Royal Oak

about the pub

The Royal Oak
Coventry Road, Kingsbury
Tamworth, Staffordshire B78 2LP
Tel: 01827 872339

DIRECTIONS: beside the A51 opposite the car park

PARKING: 40

OPEN: daily; all day

FOOD: no food Sunday evening and Monday lunchtime

BREWERY/COMPANY: Marston's

REAL ALE: Marston's Pedigree, Banks's Bitter & Original

DOGS: not allowed inside

The 'Oak' is handily placed for refreshment before or after this stroll around the Water Park as it's right opposite the car park. Expect a bustling and traditional town pub, with loyal local trade filling the split-level bar and dining area. It's a friendly place and is popular with walkers, birdwatchers and passing cyclists.

Food

A wide-ranging menu takes in sandwiches and traditional pub favourites such as steak and ale pie and cottage pie. There are roast lunches on Sundays.

Family facilities

The welcome towards children extends to smaller portions of adult meals, a menu for younger family members and a play area in the garden.

Alternative refreshment stops

The White Swan is a regular haunt of local rambling groups. You might like to try the Old Barn Coffee Shop at the visitor centre in the park.

☛ Where to go from here

Off the M42 (junction 11) is Twycross Zoo, set in 50 acres of parkland and home to around 1000 animals, most of which are endangered species. It specialises in primates, with a big range of apes, gibbons, orangutans and chimpanzees. There are other animals such as lions, elephants and giraffes, a pets' corner for younger children, a Penguin Pool with underwater viewing, and a children's adventure playground (www.twycrosszoo.com).

Map labels

Tamworth
Kingsbury
Bodymoor Heath
HEART OF ENGLAND WAY
M42
Hall (Remains)
KINGSBURY WATER PARK
THE ROYAL OAK PH
① ② ③ ④
P
VISITOR CENTRE WC
BODYMOOR HEATH WATER
HEMLINGFORD WATER
TAMWORTH SAILING CLUB
HEMLINGFORD BRIDGE
RIVER TAME
CENTENARY WAY
MILL POOL
SWANN POOL
A4097
B4098
Marston
—N—
0 ¼ Mile
0 ½ Km
Junc 9

The gates at the entrance to Packwood House

Baddesley Clinton and Packwood House

Ride along tow paths that connect two old houses.

Ancient houses

The Stratford-upon-Avon Canal created a route between the Worcester Canal at Kings Norton Junction, just south of Birmingham, and the River Avon at Stratford. Authorised by an Act of Parliament in 1793, the upper section to Hockley Heath was soon completed, but a shortage of funds delayed construction of the costly locks taking the canal downhill into the Avon valley. The waterway only reached Kingswood in 1802 and was not finally completed until 1816. A cut at Kingswood joined the Stratford to the Warwick and Birmingham Canal, which lay just to the east and was absorbed within the Grand Union system during the 1920s. Although commercial traffic continued on the Grand Union into the 1960s, the closure of the Avon Navigation in 1873 dealt a harsh blow to the Stratford Canal's fortunes and by the 1930s the section below Lapworth was derelict.

Centred like a jewel within its 13th-century moat, Baddesley Clinton has one of the most picturesque settings in the country. Slender Tudor chimneys of ornate brick rise above the roof, while below, the stonework of the inner sanctum gives way to half-timbering overlooking a delightful courtyard garden secluded from the world. Inside is no less a delight; elaborately carved chimney pieces and wood-panelled walls decorate rooms that are elegantly furnished to represent different periods in the life of the house, whilst shimmering reflections dance off the water through mullioned windows onto the ceilings.

Formerly held by the Benedictine priory of Coventry, Packwood passed into secular ownership following Henry VIII's Dissolution of the monasteries in the 1530s. The splendid many-gabled and chimneyed manor house was erected by the Fetherstones towards the end of the 16th century, originally a timber-frame building, but subsequently 'modernised' with a rendered brick façade. Inside, however, it is infused with the charm of its early period. Its last owner, Graham Ash, carefully restored the building and scoured the neighbourhood rescuing authentic furnishings and fittings from the break up or demolition of other ancient houses. He, too, is partly responsible for the yew garden, for which the house is famous, extending the mid-17th-century topiary towards the house in an arrangement that has since become known as 'The Sermon on the Mount'.

the ride

1 Join the Stratford-upon-Avon Canal behind the car park, turn right past a lock to a **bridge** where the canal splits. Cross to the spur, which drops through a second lock to another bridge, there dismounting to descend **four steps** on the far side. Follow the **tow path** away from the junction, passing a picnic site and going beneath a railway bridge to meet the **Grand Union Canal**.

2 Cycle along the tow path to the right for some 0.75 mile (1.2km) to the second **bridge (No. 63)**, leaving immediately beyond it for the lane above. Over the bridge, climb away past the Tom O' The Wood pub. At a **'Give Way'** crossroads, keep ahead over the **B4439**, enjoying easy pedalling for a little over 0.5 mile (800m) to the end of the lane.

3 To the left, the way leads past **Hay Wood**, eventually meeting another junction. Go left again towards Lapworth and **Baddesley Clinton**, the lane shortly falling to pass the entrance of Baddesley Clinton, which lies opposite Netherwood Lane. Turn in beside the **lodge** and follow the winding drive to a car park at its end. The National Trust has provided separate facilities for cycles, enabling you to explore the house and nearby church on foot.

4 Returning to the main lane, turn left towards **Hockley Heath**, soon dropping to a blind humpback bridge spanning the

Top right: The Stratford & Avon Canal
Left: Packwood House

CYCLE

2h00	9.75 MILES	15.7 KM	LEVEL 1 2 3

MAP: OS Explorer 220 Birmingham & Explorer 221 Coventry & Warwick

START/FINISH: Kingswood; car park in Brome Hall lane; grid ref: SP 185710

TRAILS/TRACKS: quiet lanes and canal tow paths with predominantly gravel surfaces

LANDSCAPE: hedged lanes and canals winding through rolling agricultural countryside

PUBLIC TOILETS: at the start

TOURIST INFORMATION: Solihull, tel 0121 704 6130

CYCLE HIRE: Clarkes Cycle Shop, Henley Street and Guild Street, Stratford-upon-Avon, tel 01789 205057, www.cycling-tours.org.uk

THE PUB: The Boot Inn, Lapworth

❶ Traffic on country lanes, one awkward right-hand turn, low bridges and overhanging branches along tow path

Getting to the start

From M42, junction 4, follow the A3400 south in the direction of Stratford. Passing through Hockley Heath, bear left onto the B4439, continuing for 2.5 miles (4km) to Kingswood. Shortly after passing The Boot Inn turn right into Brome Hall lane. The car park entrance is on the left.

Why do this cycle ride?

At Kingswood, two separate canals came within yards of each other. Their tow paths provide an off-road link in this enjoyable ride that visits two nearby ancient houses.

Researched & written by: Dennis Kelsall

The Baddesley Quartet

When Marmion Ferrers of Baddesley married the painter Rebecca Orphen in 1867, he soon learned that he had taken on her aunt and the aunt's younger husband as well – both writers of romantic novels. Together the couples made Baddesley a hive of literary and religious activity, and paintings of them all can be seen in the house.

Bracket fungus growing on a tree

while you're there

The clipped yews at Packwood bring this native evergreen neatly into focus. Yew trees, associated with immortality, have been known to grow to well over 2,000 years old, adding 1ft (30cm) to their girth for every 30 years.

The Boot Inn

Barely a stone's throw from the Grand Union Canal, the 16th-century Boot is a rustic and rambling brick building that became a pub when the canal was built some 200 years ago. Much of its early trade came from the canal, busy with cargo to Birmingham. Today it is a lively and convivial place, the smart refurbished bar with timbered ceilings, quarry-tiled floors and glowing fires, drawing diners from far and wide for modern brasserie-style food and interesting global wines. There's an attractive summer garden with a canopy and patio heaters for those cooler evenings. The inn sign depicts a caricature by renowned artist, Jim Bulmer, known for his humorous cartoons of local characters.

Food

Food is freshly prepared and both the main menu and blackboard specials take in 'first plates' like rustic breads with roast garlic and olive oil or onion tart with parmesan and rocket, with main dishes ranging from leek, spinach and smoked mozzarella risotto to haddock in tempura batter with pea purée. Sandwiches are served at lunchtime.

Family facilities

Children are most welcome inside the pub. There's a children's menu and both smaller portions of adult dishes and high chairs are available.

Alternative refreshment stops

The Punch Bowl and Tom O' The Wood pubs are along the route and there's a restaurant and tea room at Baddesley Clinton.

about the pub

The Boot Inn
Old Warwick Road, Lapworth, Warwickshire B94 6JU
Tel: 01564 782464
www.thebootatlapworth.co.uk

DIRECTIONS: See Getting to the start and point **7** of the ride

PARKING: 60

OPEN: daily; all day

FOOD: daily

BREWERY/COMPANY: Enterprise Inns

REAL ALE: Bass, Wadworth 6X, Greene King Old Speckled Hen

☞ Where to go from here

In addition to Packwood House and Baddesley Clinton (www.nationaltrust.org.uk), the area has two grand castles, Kenilworth and Warwick. The latter dominates the town and attractions include the gloomy dungeon and Torture Chamber, the grand State Rooms and Great Hall (www.warwick-castle.com). Shakespeare enthusiasts should head south to Stratford-upon-Avon and the surrounding villages – Mary Arden's house in Wilmcote and Anne Hathaway's Cottage in Shottery (www.shakespeare.org.uk).

Grand Union Canal. Beyond there, keep going over a railway bridge and later, ahead at a crossroads beside the **Punch Bowl**. About 0.5 mile (800m) further on, the road turns sharply left. Exercising caution, turn off right onto a narrow lane leading past **Packwood House**, which stands beside the road only a short distance along.

5 Resuming your ride, carry on for almost another 0.75 mile (1.2km) to the second lane leaving on the left, **Vicarage Road**. It is signed to Packwood and Hockley Heath. Follow that for 0.5 mile (800m) and then turn left at an unsigned junction. Winding past Packwood's church, **St Giles**, the lane eventually ends at a main road, the B4439.

6 Turn left towards **Lapworth and Warwick**, but after 200 yards (182m) and just before some **white cottages**, swing off right onto a gravel track, the entrance to **Drawbridge Farm**. Meeting the canal a few

yards/metres along, follow the tow path left to the first of a long series of **locks** (No 2) heralding the canal's descent to **Kingswood**. Prudent cyclists will then dismount to negotiate the sharp dip and low ridge immediately beyond the lock.

7 The path crosses to the opposite bank over a bridge below **lock No 4**, remaining on that side to pass beneath a road bridge and shortly reaching **lock No 6**. Beyond, locks then follow in quick succession, forming a staircase that drops the canal some 70ft (21m) in little over 0.5 mile (800m). The tow path reverts to the north bank below **lock No 7**, recrossing once more after lock No 14, where **The Boot Inn** lies, just along a track south of the canal. The final stretch continues along the tow path beneath a road bridge, bending past four more locks and under a final **bridge** to return you to the car park.

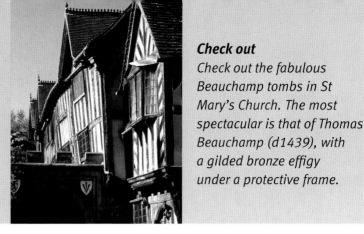

did you know?

The Lord Leycester Hospital was founded to provide a home for old soldiers – and still fulfils that role – with a resident population of eight. The so-called Brethren worship in the chapel every day, and fund themselves by opening their historic building to the public.

Check out

Check out the fabulous Beauchamp tombs in St Mary's Church. The most spectacular is that of Thomas Beauchamp (d1439), with a gilded bronze effigy under a protective frame.

The Lord Leycester Hospital

Warwick Castle

143

2h00 | **5 MILES** | **8 KM** | **LEVEL 1 23**

WALK

Stroll along the Grand Union Canal and visit magnificent Warwick Castle.

Warwick

This easy walk offers the opportunity to visit one of the most famous castles in England. Starting from the car park at Warwick Racecourse, a stroll along the tow path of the Grand Union Canal to the River Avon brings you to Castle Bridge. This is considered to be the classic view of Warwick's magnificent castle.

Built in the 14th century, Warwick Castle sits imperiously near the centre of the town. You can spend a whole day at the castle, there is so much to see: the Bailey, Guy's Tower (128ft/39m high), Caesar's Tower (147ft/ 45m high), the Gatehouse, the Clock Tower and the Old Bridge over the River Avon are all truly superb. Inside you can view a tapestry of the gardens of Versailles, Cromwell's helmet, Queen Anne's travelling trunk and Marie Antoinette's clock. Outside, wonderful gardens laid out by Lancelot 'Capability' Brown in the 18th century will beckon.

Tear yourself away from the castle to continue the walk, through the county town of 'Shakespeare Country'. It has a fascinating blend of Georgian and Tudor architecture. At St Mary's Church, you can climb its great 174ft (53m) tower for a fantastic view.

Before heading back to the racecourse you'll pass Lord Leycester's Hospital, at the West Gate of Warwick. This was originally the Guild House of St George which was transformed into the Almshouse in 1571 by Robert Dudley. Now it is probably the most famous of the medieval buildings in this fine town.

the walk

1 With your back to the main entrance, keep right to the end of the car park, then left towards the **golf clubhouse**. Pass to the left of it, curve to the right and follow the path between the golf course and the driving range.

2 In about 300yds (274m), cross over the **racetrack** and go over a stile on to a footpath. Keep right at the fork and, at the corner of common land, cross a stile and descend to the road. Go left along the pavement beneath the **railway bridge**, then left opposite a pub. Cross grassland to the tow path of the **Saltisford Canal**, pass a large narrowboat **mooring area** and climb the steps up to the canal bridge on to the pavement beside a road. Turn right to a junction with the A425, then left to the tow path of the **Grand Union Canal**.

Right: The cogs and wheels of Thwaite's Mill

MAP: OS Explorer 221 Coventry & Warwick

START/FINISH: Warwick racecourse car park; grid ref: SP 277647

PATHS: canal and riverside paths, street pavements, 2 stiles

LANDSCAPE: canalside and historic town

PUBLIC TOILETS: none on route

TOURIST INFORMATION: Warwick, tel 01926 492212

THE PUB: The Rose & Crown, Warwick

❶ Three busy road crossings, busy town centre and a footpath at the start which crosses the racetrack is closed on race days

Getting to the start

Warwick lies just off the A46, close to junction 15 of the M40. From the town centre follow the High Street to Bowling Green Street, then turn into Friars Street and make for Warwick Racecourse.

Researched & written by: Nick Channer, Roger Noyce

Beauchamp Chapel, St Mary's Church

while you're there

In Warwick Castle, keep an eye open for the ghost of Sir Fulke Greville, who haunts the tower where his bedroom is still preserved. Greville was an educated man, and a noted poet of his day. He took on all sorts of jobs at the court of Elizabeth I, including Secretary for Wales and even Chancellor of the Exchequer. He met an untimely end in 1628, murdered by a former servant.

A cuckoo
(Cuculus canorus)

3 Follow it for a lengthy stretch, passing by a lock gate with the **Cape of Good Hope pub** opposite and then going along the back of residential properties. Shortly after passing by a **Tesco** store and just before reaching the aqueduct over the River Avon, go left down steps to join the '**Waterside Walk**'.

4 Proceed right under the aqueduct and follow the **river bank footpath** for Warwick. At **Castle Bridge**, climb steps on to the pavement of the **A425** (Banbury) road and cross with care.

5 Stroll on to the bridge for the classic view of **Warwick Castle**, then turn around and follow the pavement towards Warwick town.

6 In 220yds (201m) go left and meander down picturesque **Mill Street** for the second classic view of the castle. Return to the main road and go left through the **entrance gate** to Warwick Castle grounds. Follow the drive, turn right up some steps by wrought iron gates and turn left at the '**Warwick Castle**' entrance sign. Cut through

Warwick Castle, built in the 14th century, stands proudly near the town centre

what to look for

As you walk up Castle Street you pass a very pretty timber-framed 15th-century house. This is Thomas Oken's House. Oken was a silk and luxury goods merchant who was a famous Warwick benefactor. He founded an almshouse for poor women, endowed a schoolmaster and provided money for bonfires for the young. Master of the Guild at the time of the 1545 town charter, he died, childless, in 1573.

the **courtyard** and swing right at the 'exit to town' sign. Go through the gate (locked at 6pm–5pm between November and March) and cross over into **Castle Street**. Walk ahead, passing by **Oken's House** until you reach the tourist information centre on the corner of the High Street. **St Mary's Church** is ahead if you wish to visit. Turn left here and then right into Swan Street, which leads to the **Rose & Crown** pub in the Market Place. Return to the junction, with the **Warwick Arms Hotel** opposite, turn right and follow the High Street. Turn right into Bowling Green Street, then left down Friars Street to reach **Warwick Racecourse**.

The Rose & Crown

Huge picture windows at this stylishly refurbished 18th-century inn overlook Warwick's main square. Escape the hustle and bustle and relax with the daily papers in one of the deep leather sofas that front low coffee tables in the smart bar area. Chunky wooden tables and chairs, bright paintwork and modern works of art set the scene in the dedicated dining area, and the atmosphere is relaxed and informal. Come for breakfast and enjoy coffee and bacon sandwiches before the walk, or call in for a decent post-walk lunch and a refreshing pint of Old Speckled Hen. The five en suite bedrooms are decorated in minimalist style.

Food
Nibble on a selection of cheeses, charcuterie, breads and antipasti from the deli board menu, or tuck into a Caesar salad, smoked chicken and chilli tagliatelle, or the risotto of the week. Other options include braised neck of lamb, smoked haddock and prawn fishcake with tomato salsa, or ribeye steak with béarnaise.

Family facilities
Children are very welcome inside and smaller portions of the main menu are available. Front terrace for summer alfresco meals.

Alternative refreshment stops
There are several good eating places in the town of Warwick. Along the walk route the Cape of Good Hope by the side of the Grand Union Canal is a popular pub with walkers.

☞ Where to go from here
No trip to Warwick is complete without a visit to fantastic Warwick Castle

about the pub

The Rose & Crown
30 Market Square, Warwick
Warwickshire CV34 4SH
Tel: 01926 411117
www.peachpubs.com

DIRECTIONS: town centre; in the Market Square (near Point **6**)

PARKING: street parking

OPEN: daily; all day

FOOD: daily; all day

BREWERY/COMPANY: Peach Pubs

REAL ALE: Fuller's London Pride, Greene King Old Speckled Hen

DOGS: allowed in the bar

ROOMS: 5 en suite

(www.warwick-castle.co.uk). Alternatively, visit the Doll Museum in Castle Street to view the fine collection of antique toys, games, dolls and bears, or head out of town to Kenilworth to explore the largest and most extensive castle ruin in England, with a past rich in famous names and events in history. National Trust properties in the area include Packwood House, Baddesley Clinton and Charlecote Park (www.nationaltrust.org.uk).

A huge teddy bear outside a shop in Stratford-upon-Avon

Teddy Bear Museum

Henry VIII once owned the house on Greenhill Street in Stratford which is now the Teddy Bear Museum (open daily, tel 01789 293160). Furry and much-loved occupants include some of the oldest teddies in the world, and Mr Bean's famous little button-eyed companion.

did you know?

According to legend, Charles II had ignominy piled upon his head at the King's Lodge at Long Marston, when, fleeing the Battle of Worcester in 1651 disguised as a lowly servant, he was roundly chastised for his incompetence in the kitchen.

Stratford Greenway

Explore the quiet countryside in which England's greatest bard grew up.

Stratford-upon-Avon

Whilst Stratford was already a prosperous town before Shakespeare's day, it is probably due to his association that so many of the town's splendid 16th-century buildings have survived. Some of the best line Church Street, along which the ride finishes. Buildings include a splendid row of almshouses, the early 15th-century Guild Hall and Grammar School (where Shakespeare is said to have been educated), some impressive inns and the site of New Place, where the poet died in 1616. Stop off too to look in Holy Trinity Church, where he was both baptised and buried.

The ride out follows the route of the Oxford, Worcester and Wolverhampton Railway, built in 1859 to link the Midlands with the southwest of England. A decade and a half later, another line was constructed to the town from the southeast, with junctions and sidings in the area now occupied by Swan Meadow car park and a separate station to service the racecourse. As the country's rail network developed, the smaller lines were absorbed, the Great Western buying up the Midlands line whilst the London, Midland and Scottish Railway took over the other. Bringing tourists to the town from the capital, the latter became known as the 'Shakespeare Route', but closed in 1965 as part of Beeching's rationalisation programme. The GWR, along which the Greenway now runs, was taken up in 1976, leaving only the route from the north into the town.

Safe family cycling on Stratford Railway Path

the ride

1 Leave Clopton Bridge along Waterside, passing the **Royal Shakespeare Theatre** and famous Dirty Duck pub. Turn left at the end to wind past Holy Trinity Church and then go left again into **Mill Lane**. It finishes in a narrow alley, usually busy with pedestrians, that leads to the river. The continuing path swings beneath a **bridge** to shadow the main road, shortly passing **Seven Meadows car park**.

2 If joining the **railway track** at Seven Meadows, turn right to **Milcote picnic area**. The way runs beside Stratford's **racecourse** where, on race days, horses gallop along the back straight. The track then crosses the Avon by a riverside picnic area and later, the River Stour. Pedal on beyond **Chambers Halt** and Pearces Crossing to the pine-grown platform of **Milcote Station**.

3 Through barriers and a parking area, cross a road to a **picnic site** where an old railway coach houses a café. The track continues for a further 2 miles (3.2km), passing crossings at **Knobbs Farm** and the **Airfield** before ultimately reaching **Wyre Lane Crossing**. Leave there, going right along Wyre Lane into **Long Marston**. The

Mason's Arms is just a short way along the main road to the right.

4 To return, either retrace your outward route, or alternatively, instead of going back along Wyre Lane, keep ahead on the road to the outskirts of the village. There, turn off right to **Dorsington**, passing the church of **St James the Great**. Carry on for 1.5 miles (2.4km) to a T-junction and go right, winding to another junction in the middle of Dorsington. Take the lane on the right to **Welford**, which snakes north between the fields, culminating in a short, stiff pull to give a view across the Avon valley. Drop to a road and follow that right into modern Welford. However, leave after just over 0.5 mile (800m) along **Headland Road** on the left, which ends in the old village opposite **St Peter's Church**.

5 The onward route lies to the right along **Church Street**, but first wander down Boat Lane to see its thatched black and white cottages. At the end of Church Street by the **Bell Inn**, take the main road right through the village, passing a small green where there stands a tall **maypole**. Leaving Welford, turn off left to **Weston and Clifford Chambers**, going left again after 0.5 mile (800m) on a narrow lane to **Weston-on-Avon**.

3h30 | 15.5 MILES | 25 KM | LEVEL 1 23

MAP: OS Explorer 205 Stratford-upon-Avon & Evesham

START/FINISH: Stratford: Clopton Bridge, grid ref SP 203549 or Seven Meadows car park, grid ref SP 195540

TRAILS/TRACKS: streets in Stratford and disused railway line with good gravel surface, country lanes and farm track

LANDSCAPE: patchwork fields of the Avon valley rising to a backdrop of low hills

PUBLIC TOILETS: in Stratford

TOURIST INFORMATION: Stratford, tel 0870 160 7930

CYCLE HIRE: Clarkes Cycle Shop, Henley Street and Guild Street, Stratford-upon-Avon; tel: 01789 205057; www.cycling-tours.org.uk

THE PUB: Masons Arms, Long Marston

⚠ Traffic on Stratford's busy streets and country lanes, pedestrians along the track

Getting to the start

Stratford-upon-Avon is close to junction 15 on the M40. If parking in the town, start the ride at Clopton Bridge, which brings the A422 into Stratford. Alternatively, begin from Seven Meadows car park on the A4390.

Why do this cycle ride?

Leaving Stratford-upon-Avon along the level track of a former railway line, the route leads to Long Marston, where the pub makes an excellent stop for lunch. Either return on the outward track or follow country lanes via the picturesque village of Welford-on-Avon.

Researched & written by: Dennis Kelsall

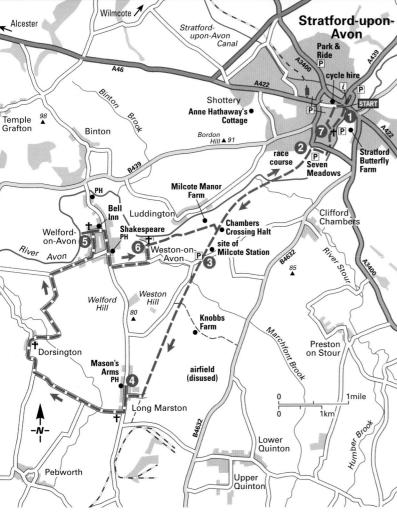

Masons Arms

Once part of the farm estate and a pub since 1861, this traditional pub may be small but it has bags of character, with cosy, low-beamed bars, a big inglenook with winter log fires, a worn stone-flagged floor, and a wealth of gleaming brasses for decoration. Add a popular skittle alley, summer barbecue evenings in the spacious garden, and weekly live music and you have a thriving village local.

Food

An extensive light snack menu lists a good range of sandwiches and baguettes, home-made pizzas, burgers and ploughman's lunches. Traditional main dishes include steak and ale pie, fish pie, lasagne and lamb's liver with mash and onion gravy. Specials take in ribeye steak, curries, and leek and potato bake.

Family facilities

Children are welcome inside the pub. Youngsters have their own menu and smaller portions of main menu meals are also available.

Alternative refreshment stops

There's a wide choice of pubs, cafés and restaurants in Stratford-upon-Avon, a café at Milcote picnic area, and you will also find the Bell Inn and the Shakespeare pub at Welford-on-Avon.

☛ Where to go from here

Associations with Shakespeare (www.shakespeare.org.uk) abound in and around Stratford. You can visit Mary Arden's House and the Shakespeare Countryside Museum at Wilmcote, the childhood home of the bard's wife, Anne Hathaway's

Cottage at Shottery, and in Stratford, Hall's Croft, Harvard House and Nash's House and New Place. Europe's largest live butterfly and insect exhibit can be seen at the Stratford Butterfly Farm (www.butterflyfarm.co.uk). Fine houses and parks in the area include Coughton Court, Alcester (www.coughtoncourt.co.uk), Ragley Hall, Alcester (www.ragleyhall.com), and Charlecote Park near Wellesbourne (www.nationaltrust.org.uk).

about the pub

Masons Arms

Welford Road, Long Marston
Stratford-upon-Avon, Warwickshire
CV37 8RG
Tel: 01789 720586

DIRECTIONS: village signposted off the B4632 south of Stratford-upon-Avon. On route at Point **3**

PARKING: 35

OPEN: daily; all day Saturday & Sunday

FOOD: no food Sunday evening, all Monday & Tuesday evening

BREWERY/COMPANY: Punch Taverns

REAL ALE: Boddingtons, Hook Norton Bitter

6 At the bottom turn right past the village **church**, the way deteriorating to a farm track as it continues between the fields beyond. Keep forward as it reverts to tarmac, later passing **Milcote Manor Farm** to a couple of **cottages**. The way disintegrates to dirt as it then swings right to meet the disused railway at **Chambers Crossing Halt**. Follow it left back to Seven Meadows car park and Stratford.

7 If you began from the town, after passing **Holy Trinity Church** you must now carry on past **Riverside** and instead turn right at the next crossroads into **Church Street**. Continue ahead along Chapel Street and **High Street** to a busy roundabout in the town centre, where you might wish to dismount to return to your car park.

An old Shell Oil box

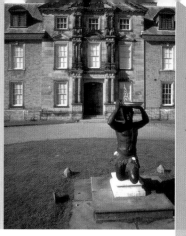

A statue in the grounds of Upton House

To Ratley and back by the Macmillan Way

A walk along Edgehill, scene of a major Civil War battle, with a visit to Upton House.

Battle of Edgehill
This hilly walk takes you along the escarpment of the famous Edgehill – a prominent sandstone ridge which runs north east to southwest at a height of around 600ft (183m) above sea level.

Below the ridge the first major battle of the Civil War took place in 1642. The site is hidden in a huge Ministry of Defence ammunition facility, but the Edgehill Battle Museum is in the grounds of Farnborough House, some 3 miles (4.8km) to the east. Radway Tower, passed near the end of the walk, was built to mark the battle's 100th anniversary, though it wasn't completed until 1750. This 70ft (21m) octagonal folly is now occupied by the popular Castle Inn.

From Ratley you descend to see an obelisk erected in 1854 to commemorate the Battle of Waterloo. At Nadbury Camp are the mounds of an 18-acre (7ha) Bronze Age camp. The walk passes close to the National Trust's Upton House before heading to the medieval village of Ratley.

You'll find Ratley is a peaceful village, largely unchanged since the turn of the 20th century. Its recognition in 1971 as a conservation area has helped ensure the survival of its oldest parts. Records show the manor was held by a Saxon named Ordic before the arrival of the Normans. Most of its houses are built of honey-brown Hornton stone from the Edgehill Quarry. The quarried land has been reclaimed, planted with trees and grass to encourage wild flowers and has become a nature reserve.

Ratley's 12th-century church has the unusual dedication of St Peter ad Vincula. Outside it is an ancient preaching cross but time has robbed it of its arms, and only the shaft remains.

the walk

1 Walk along Sugarswell Lane towards the junction with the A422. Turn right and in 40yds (37m) go right again through a **farm gate**, following a stone wall, then bearing left towards **Home Farm**. Pass to the left of the farm buildings, cross the grassy slopes with the farm on your right and make for a **gate** by some trees. Walk ahead to a stile leading out to the A422 road. Go right along the grass verge of the busy road past the entrance gates to **Upton House** (NT).

2 In about 600yds (549m) cross the **A422** with care and go left down the lane to **Hornton**.

3 In a further 300yds (274m) go left along a signed path. Keep a hedge and wall on the right and in the field corner follow the path ahead through **trees**, passing to the right of outbuildings at **Uplands Farm**. Continue into open countryside, swing right onto a track and go down to a **stile**. Keep alongside hedge and pass an old barn. Cross a series of stiles and use the **waymarks** to navigate your way across country, maintaining the same direction towards Ratley. At one point head diagonally down a steep field slope. Emerge in the village by **Manor Farm**.

4 At the main road go right to explore the old village, then retrace your steps past

2h30 | **5.5 MILES** | **8.8 KM** | **LEVEL 1 2 3**

145

WALK

MAP: OS Explorer 206 Edge Hill & Fenny Compton

START/FINISH: By roadside in Sugarswell Lane on Edgehill; grid ref: SP 362457

PATH: lanes and field paths, 6 stiles

LANDSCAPE: rolling countryside

PUBLIC TOILETS: none on route

TOURIST INFORMATION: Stratford-upon-Avon, tel 0870 160 7930

THE PUB: The Castle Inn, Edgehill

! Two busy road crossings, some hilly sections and several stretches of verge walking by a main road

Getting to the start
Follow the A422 between Stratford and Banbury. Turn into Sugarswell Lane which is situated just to the west of the entrance to Upton House. Roadside parking.

Researched & written by:
Nick Channer, Roger Noyce

Edgehill WARWICKSHIRE

 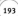

Upton House in Middle Tysoe standing in beautiful gardens

After the Battle

Warmington is a picture-postcard village with green, pond and 17th-century manor house. Soldiers killed in the battle at Edgehill (1642) were buried in the churchyard, but most graves are anonymous.

Ducks on the pond at Warmington

while you're there

Visit nearby Radway: the village war memorial carries the name of Field Marshal Earl Haig (1861–1928), who lived at the Grange. A World War One veteran, Haig's major legacy was the founding of the Royal British Legion, for the care of ex-servicemen and women, and the Haig Fund (renamed the Poppy Appeal) which raises money by selling poppies.

Manor Farm and continue along the road towards **Edgehill**.

5 Cross over the road at the T-junction and descend **Jacobs Ladder** into **Castle Wood** opposite, following the waymarkers

what to look for

While in Ratley take a look at the Church of St Peter ad Vincula – 'St Peter in Chains' (referring to his imprisonment in the Acts of the Apostles, Chapter 12). One of its brass memorial plates is of interest for it tells us that the heiress of Simon Bury died on the 14th February, Anno Domini 1696 aged 1697. Even in the 17th century typographical mistakes were made!

of the **MacMillan Way**. Follow the woodland path in a westerly direction. Keep left at the waymarked fork, following the obvious trail. Make a brief detour to visit the Castle Inn up by the road. From the inn rejoin the MacMillan Way, following it through the **woods**. Cross a lane at a **farm** and keep on the trail. Cross the A422 and follow the track ahead. Swing right by some **stables**, then left after a few paces, still following the MacMillan Way. Head for open land with a superb view of **Tysoe** and the surrounding countryside. Continue through a gate and follow a path on the edge of the woods for about 150yds (137m).

6 Go left through a **farm gate** and diagonally cross the field to arrive back in **Sugarswell Lane**.

The Castle Inn

Standing on the summit of a beech-clad ridge, this is one of the most unusual pubs in the country. Built as a gatehouse in the design of Guy's Tower at Warwick Castle in 1742 to commemorate the centenary of the Battle of Edgehill, it opened on the anniversary of Cromwell's death in 1750, was first licensed in 1822, and acquired by Hook Norton one hundred years later. Castellated and also known as Radway Tower, it is the place to come for views as they stretch out across several counties to the distant Malvern Hills and beyond on a really clear day. Enjoy your pint of Hook Norton ale and eat a hearty meal in the homely bars or in the splendid garden.

Food
Traditional, home-cooked dishes such as mixed grills, deep-fried cod and chips, liver and bacon casserole and lunchtime sandwiches and ploughman's appear on the straightforward menu.

Family facilities
Children are allowed in the eating area of the bar and there's a children's menu. The large and attractive garden is a super place for children in summer.

Alternative refreshment stops
The Rose and Crown in Ratley.

☛ Where to go from here
Visit Upton House (www.nationaltrust.org.uk). This 17th-century National Trust building was remodelled between 1927 and 1929 for the 2nd Viscount Bearsted. It contains fine collections of

about the pub

The Castle Inn
Edgehill, Banbury
Warwickshire OX15 6DJ
Tel: 01295 670255
www.thecastle-edgehill.co.uk

DIRECTIONS: see Getting to the start; turn right off the A422 for Edgehill and Ratley

PARKING: 40

OPEN: daily; all summer weekends; July & August

FOOD: daily

BREWERY/COMPANY: Hook Norton Brewery

REAL ALE: Hook Norton Bitter, Old Hooky, Hooky Dark & seasonal guest beers

DOGS: allowed inside

ROOMS: 3 en suite

paintings, including works by Stubbs, Canaletto and El Greco. The extensive gardens are outstanding. The Heritage Motor Centre at Gaydon is home to the largest collection of historic British cars and you can learn about Britain's motoring and social history. Children will love the go-kart tracks and children's electric roadway (www.heritage-motor-centre.co.uk).

Map

Radway
JACOBS LADDER
CASTLE WOOD
▲215
EDGE HILL
OBELISK
Ratley
5
CASTLE INN
Edgehill
4
MANOR FARM
Rose and Crown PH
MACMILLAN WAY
215 ▲
BARN
WARWICKS
OXON
Edgehill Farm
215 ▲
A422
UPLANDS FARM
UPLANDS HOUSE
A422
Hornton
SUN RISING HILL
1
HOME FARM
2
UPTON HOUSE
3
A422
Banbury

¼ Mile
0

1 Km
0

-N-

Male and female chaffinches (Fringilla coelebs)

did you know?

In Victorian times, J. Croft remodelled the old church at Napton, and went on to design a new one for Lower Shuckburgh, complete with painted bricks inside. Members of the Shuckburgh family fought in the battle at Edgehill (1642), but Shuckburgh Hall proved lamentably dreary when the enthusiastic traveller Celia Fiennes (1662–1741) passed through at the end of that century. The house (private) was extensively rebuilt in 1844.

From Napton on the Hill

A pleasant hilly walk passing by a famous windmill landmark, visible for much of the route.

Napton on the Hill

This walk takes you over Napton Hill and past its historic windmill. On a good day you can see seven counties from the windswept summit.

There has been a windmill at Napton on the Hill since 1543 – it is one of the great landmarks in Warwickshire. Next to the privately owned mill building is the former miller's stone cottage, which still houses parts of the original bread oven. The windmill is not open to the public.

The village of Napton on the Hill was a substantial settlement in 1086. It was granted a charter in 1321 to hold a weekly market and an annual fair and became a prosperous medieval village. Today, attractive mellowed brown and gold thatched houses contribute to a picturesque scene. You could be forgiven for thinking this was a timeless image, untouched by the revolutionary industrial changes which were taking place elsewhere in the West Midlands, but even Napton succumbed to 'canal mania' towards the end of the 18th century. In a two-year period in the 1790s, 37 separate Acts of Parliament were passed to enable the construction of a system of 4,250 miles (6,840km) of navigable rivers and canals. The Oxford Canal, completed in 1790, was part of this and it encouraged canalside businesses to develop.

the walk

1 From the car park, walk around the outside of the churchyard of **St Lawrence's Church** and pass by a smaller car park. From here take the track to **Church Leyes Farm**. At the lane junction, turn left and walk down to a fork. Keep left, then right at the next one and turn left opposite **Chapel Yard Cottage**. Follow the village main street, turning right into Godsons Lane, which leads into Dogs Lane and onto a residential housing development. Just before a **school** turn left to join a hedged bridleway. Go through three gates and then turn left, swinging right at the next gate. Make for the next single **galvanised gate** and turn right. Cross the fields to reach a final farm gate to the right of outbuildings at **Leys Farm**.

2 Go straight on along the road to the next junction. Head straight on towards **Napton**. Turn left on reaching a house called Eureka and follow the **waymarked path** to the right of it. Cross a stile into a field and head diagonally left to a footbridge. Make for the left corner of the pasture where the road can be seen, looking for a **galvanised gate**. Cross the Oxford Canal, turn left down to the towpath and pass under the **bridge (115)**.

3 Walk along to the next lock and pass a milepost before reaching **Napton Bottom Lock**. On reaching the Folly Inn cross the canal at the bridge into **Folly Lane** and turn left after about 60yds (55m) over a stile. Go diagonally right across a meadow to a footbridge in the corner and then walk along a short stretch of track to two stiles. Turn left in the field and head up the slope towards **houses**. Turn right at the stile, out to the road and right along **Poplar Road**. Turn left into Holloway Lane. To return to your car, turn right by **Church Leyes Farm**, to complete the full walk, keep ahead and follow the driveway towards the superb **windmill** which comes into view – the building and its land are private so please respect the 'Private' signs and keep off the property.

The Oxford Canal at Napton on the Hill

2h30 5.5 MILES 8.8 KM LEVEL 123

MAP: OS Explorer 206 Edge Hill & Fenny Compton & 222 Rugby & Daventry

START/FINISH: St Lawrence Church car park, Napton on the Hill; grid ref: SP 463612 (on Explorer 222)

PATHS: field paths, bridleways, towpath and country lanes, 8 stiles

LANDSCAPE: rolling Warwickshire countryside

PUBLIC TOILETS: none on route

TOURIST INFORMATION: Rugby, tel 01788 534970

THE PUB: The Folly Inn, Napton on the Hill

❶ Three relatively quiet road crossings, one busy road crossing and much of the walk is beside water

Getting to the start

Napton on the Hill is off the A425 between Warwick and Daventry. Drive into the village from the main road and turn right at the sign for the church.

Researched & written by:
Nick Channer, Roger Noyce

Lost Village

The medieval village of Wolfhampcote is long gone, but its large, low 14th-century church of St Peters survives, near Braunston, beside the waters of the Grand Union Canal.

while you're there

South of here are the twin villages of Priors Marston and Priors Hardwick. The stone houses of Priors Marston are particularly appealing, and the 17th-century Falcon Inn serves a good pint of real ale.

A toad hopping through grass

4 At the entrance by the 'private' sign, go right, along a **footpath** around the outside of the property, following the **waymarkers**. This leads to lovely open land and you now can go down the hill. Avoid turnings off and at the bottom follow the path as it bends left and out over open ground towards a house and some **industrial units**. Cross a stile to arrive on Brickyard Lane. Go right down the lane and cross **bridge No 112** over the Oxford Canal.

5 Descend right, on to the **tow path**, and then walk to the left. This is easy, pleasant walking with great views up to your right of Napton Hill with its windmill on top.

6 Leave the tow path at **bridge No 110** and walk up the lane back towards the village. At the road junction with **Butt Hill**, go right over a stile and cross the corner of a field to a further stile on to the **A425** road. Bear right and cross the main road to the

what to look for

Visit St Lawrence's Church whose squat tower has, like the windmill, withstood centuries of buffeting from the wind. The north door is called the Devil's Door and used to be opened during baptisms for the Devil to escape. At Christmas or other festivals you may hear the ringing of hand bells. Inside there is a slate portrait of John Shuckburgh of nearby Shuckburgh Hall.

junction with Hillside, then go through a **waymarked handgate** and begin to climb the hill up a clear hedged footpath. As you approach the top of the hill the path becomes less steep and you will go through three **metal kissing gates** to reach open land once again. To your right you will see **St Lawrence's Church**. Go right along the lane back to your car to complete the walk.

The Folly Inn

Built as a pub some 200 years ago, the attractive, brick-built Folly Inn stands isolated beside the canal and was formerly called the Bull & Butcher. Once popular with bargees, villagers and brickwork employees, the pub closed after World War Two following the decline of the canal trade. It became a farmhouse but re-opened as a pub in 1990 to serve the needs of the flourishing longboat business on the newly restored Midlands canal system. Walkers, cyclists, canal enthusiasts, and leisure boat users fill the two homely bars today. Both bars have open fires and there's a huge canalside garden.

Food

Hearty pub food ranges from ham, egg and chips, fresh-cut sandwiches and home-made soups, to their renowned pies (lamb and mint, sausage and bean), lasagne, and peppered steak with garlic potatoes.

Family facilities

The garden makes it a great summer pub for families. On inclement days children are welcomed inside and there are smaller portions of the main meals available.

Alternative refreshment stops

The walk route passes the Napton Bridge Inn as you reach the Oxford Canal.

about the pub

The Folly Inn
Folly Lane, Napton, Southam
Warwickshire CV47 8NZ
Tel: 01926 815185

DIRECTIONS: see Getting to the start; the pub is beside the canal and is well signposted east of the village (Point **3**)

PARKING: 30

OPEN: daily (check lunchtime opening times in winter)

FOOD: daily

BREWERY/COMPANY: free house

REAL ALE: Folly Bitter, Hook Norton Bitter & Old Hooky

DOGS: allowed inside

☞ Where to go from here

A visit to the Nickelodeon Museum is an amazing experience. It once occupied the old Methodist chapel in Napton, but the number of organs grew too large and it has been moved to Ashorne Hall, about 12 miles (19.3km) to the west of here. It's a remarkable working collection of vintage juke-boxes, symphoniums and many other exotic musical machines. At the James Gilbert Rugby Football Museum in Rugby there's a unique collection of Rugby football memorabilia, and you can watch a craftsman hand-stitching the footballs.

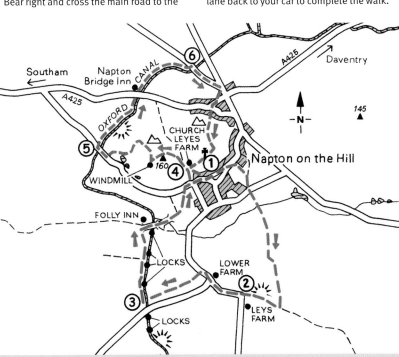

147 DUMBLETON HILL
GLOUCESTERSHIRE

8 MILES (12.9KM) 3hrs 15min

PATHS: Mostly good paths, field tracks and village roads, 6 stiles

SUGGESTED MAP: aqua3 OS Explorer OL45 The Cotswolds

GRID REFERENCE: SP 039363

PARKING: On street near church in Wormington

THE PUB: Pheasant Inn, Toddington

❶ Walk westwards to reach power lines. Just after, take footpath on **L**. Pass through gate, maintaining direction for 450yds (412m).
❷ Turn away from **Mill Farm**, to cross river. Cross field. Go diagonally across another field, under power lines, turning **R** beside fence that soon becomes hedgerow. In 120yds (110m) turn **L** through gate then along **R-H** field edge. Within 200yds (183m) turn **R**.
❸ Follow mud track – later green lane then tarmac – for nearly 1.25 miles (2km), to road junction. Turn **R**, passing entrance to **Toddington Manor**, to junction.
❹ Sign points to **Toddington's church**. Visit **church** and **Toddington House** ruin. Retrace your steps. Walk through **Toddington**. Turn **R**. Just after pavement ends (before **Buttermilk Farm**), cross to fingerpost and stile. Walk behind trees for 760yds (695m).
❺ Re-cross road. Take minor road past **Orchard Industrial Estate**. At T-junction turn **R**. Go **L**, before **farm shop**, up driveway, passing farmhouse (**Evergreen**). At next T-junction turn **L** along grassy tarmac way, contouring hill. Reach broken tree just before track bends **L** to **Frampton Farm**.
❻ Continue for about 30 paces, then turn hard **R**, uphill, heading for gate near trees. Once through, way soon steepens. On brow join stony track coming in from R. Now on level, continue for 600yds (549m) to signposts at junction of tracks. Follow 'Public Bridleway **Dumbleton** 1.25 miles', soon into big field. Good track now leads all the way down to minor road, then driveway to **Dumbleton Hall** (hotel).
❼ Cross to crucifix-style war memorial. Turn **L**. Visit **church**. About 30yds (27m) beyond Dairy Lane on L, turn **R** along residential cul-de-sac. Enter field to skirt 2 field edges. Cross B4078. When drive to **Lane Farm Cottages** bends L, continue to find field path, crossing 2 fields. Cross service road to **College Farm**. Cross river on bridge. Pass under power lines and over stile into pasture. Walk to end of breeze-block barn wall. Turn **R** to gate, rejoining road in **Wormington**.

148 SEZINCOTE
GLOUCESTERSHIRE

3 MILES (4.8KM) 1hr 15min

PATHS: Tracks, fields and lanes, 7 stiles

SUGGESTED MAP: aqua3 OS Explorer OL45 The Cotswolds

GRID REFERENCE: SP 175324

PARKING: Street below Bourton-on-the-Hill church, parallel with main road

THE PUB: Horse and Groom, Bourton-on-the-Hill

❶ Walk up road from **telephone box** with **church** to your R. Turn **L** down signposted track between walls. Go through gate into field and then continue forward to pass through 2 more gates.
❷ Cross stile, followed by 2 kissing gates among trees. This is the **Sezincote Estate**. Its architecture and design was inspired, like many other buildings in the early 19th century, by the colourful aqua-tints brought to England from India by returning artists, such as William and Thomas Daniell. Built on the plan of a typical large country house, in every other respect it is thoroughly unconventional and owes a lot to Eastern influence, not least the large copper onion dome that crowns the house and the garden buildings. Go straight ahead, following markers and crossing drive. Dip down to gate among trees, with ponds on either side. Go ahead into field, from where **Sezincote House** is visible to R.
❸ Walk into next field and go right to end, aiming for top, **R-H** corner. Pass through gate to reach narrow road and turn **L**. Walk down this road, passing **keepers' cottages** to your L, and through series of gates. Road will bottom out, curve **L** and **R** and then bring you to **Upper Rye Farm**. Pass to R of farmhouse, go through gate and, immediately before barn, turn **L** along track and road.
❹ After 2nd cattle grid, go **L** over stile. Follow edge of field to footbridge. Go over it and turn **R**. Now follow **R-H** margin of field to stile in far corner. Cross this to follow path through woodland until you come to stile and field and continue on same line to another stile.
❺ Cross track to another stile and walk on. After few paces, with **Bourton-on-the-Hill** plainly visible before you, turn **R** and follow path to next corner. Turn **L** and pass through 3 gates. After 3rd one, walk on for few paces and turn **R** through gate to return to start.

149 PRESTBURY
GLOUCESTERSHIRE

3.5 MILES (5.7KM) 1hr 30min

PATHS: Fields (could be muddy in places) and pavement, 10 stiles

SUGGESTED MAP: aqua3 OS Explorer 179 Gloucester, Cheltenham & Stroud

GRID REFERENCE: SO 972238

PARKING: Free car park near war memorial

THE PUB: The Plough

❶ Leave car park, turn **R** into The Bank and **R** into **Mill Street**. At main road turn **L**. After 100yds (91m) cross road to reach stile. Go into field then diagonally **L** to stile.
❷ Cross and follow track that is ahead and slightly to your L. Where it goes R, cross stile ahead. Cross field, heading slightly to **R**, to stile. Cross this into field and head for **Queen's Wood**.
❸ Stay to L of woods. Eventually cross track and enter another field. Where woods sweep uphill, continue through bushes to bridle gate. Go through on to woodland path. Turn **L** downhill, to reach main road.
❹ Ahead are medieval buildings of **De La Bere Hotel**. Cross road. Turn **R**. Follow pavement as it bears **L** into **Southam Lane**. After 200yds (183m) turn **L** along track to gate. Go through this and kissing gate to field.
❺ Head across, bearing slightly **R**, with **De La Bere** on L. Follow path across series of paddocks and fields via stiles and gates. At stile, amid bushes in corner, cross on to track. Follow this to bridge stile.
❻ Cross and continue ahead into field with hedge on R. Go over brow of slope and down to gate in hedge to your R. Go through to track. Follow this to road.
❼ Turn **L** along **Shaw Green Lane**. After 400yds (366m) turn **R** along footpath passing between houses. Eventually this brings you out on to **Mill Street**, opposite **church**. Turn **R**, to walk past **Priory** and brick wall (site of haunted Grotto) until you reach **The Burgage**. Turn **L**, passing **Royal Oak**, **Prestbury House** and Sundial Cottage.
❽ At junction with Tatchley Lane turn **L** then **L** again into **Deep Street**, passing Three Queens and stone cottages. Just before **Kings Arms** turn **L** on footpath leading to **church**. Turn **R** just before church and pass through churchyard to return to **Mill Street**, opposite **Plough Inn**. Turn **R** and return to car park.

150 BRIMPSFIELD
GLOUCESTERSHIRE

4 MILES (6.4KM) 2hrs

PATHS: Fields, tracks and pavement, 9 stiles

SUGGESTED MAP: aqua3 OS Explorer 179 Gloucester, Cheltenham & Stroud

GRID REFERENCE: SO 938124

PARKING: Brimpsfield village; lay-bys on Cranham road

THE PUB: Carpenters Arms. Miserden

❶ Go to end of road towards village centre. Turn **L**. Walk through village and, at corner, turn **R** through gate on to track towards **church**. Before church bear **L** across meadow (**site of castle**) to stile. In next field go half **R** to corner and road.
❷ Turn **R**. Follow road down to just before cottage near bottom. Turn **R** on to drive. After few paces drop down to **L** on to parallel path which will bring you back on to drive. Next, just before cottage, turn L and go down into woodland to follow path with stream on L. Follow this for 550yds (503m), ignoring bridge on L, to cross 2 stiles and emerge on to track.
❸ Turn **L**. Follow track as it rises to **R**. After 100yds (91m) go forward over stile into field with **Brimpsfield House** to R. Go half **R** to another stile, pass gate on R and cross another stile at next corner. Follow path to cross bridge. Bear **L** up to track. Follow this for 250yds (229m), until you reach crossways.
❹ Turn **R** to follow footpath along bottom of valley. After 0.75 mile (1.2km) track becomes grassy. Where houses appear above you to L you can go **L** up slope to visit church at **Syde**. Otherwise remain on valley floor and continue until you reach gates. Take one furthest to **R**. Go ahead to pass to L of cottage. Follow drive up to road.
❺ Turn **L**. Follow road as it turns sharp L. At this point turn **R** over stile into field and walk up steep bank to arrive in **Caudle Green**.
❻ Turn **R**. At green, just before large house ahead, bear **R** to stile. Follow winding path down to valley bottom. Turn **L**, through bridle gate. Follow path along valley bottom on same line for 0.75 mile (1.2km) until you reach stile at field.
❼ Once in field, continue up slope until you reach gate at road. Turn **L** to re-enter **Brimpsfield**.

151 SLAD VALLEY
GLOUCESTERSHIRE

4 MILES (6.4KM) 2hrs

PATHS: Tracks, fields and quiet lanes, 13 stiles

SUGGESTED MAP: aqua3 OS Explorer 179 Gloucester, Cheltenham & Stroud

GRID REFERENCE: SO 878087

PARKING: Lay-by at Bull's Cross

THE PUB: Woolpack

❶ From **Bull's Cross** walk to end of lay-by (going south). Turn **L** on to tarmac drive. Follow it down and, immediately before buildings, turn **L** over stile into field. Go half **R**, down field and up other side, to gate at top. Turn **L** along track. Where it joins another track stay **R** and continue to lane.
❷ Turn **R** and walk to bottom. Pass between **pond** and **Steanbridge Mill**. To visit Slad, follow lane into village. To continue, turn **L** immediately after **pond.** Continue to stile. Cross into field, with hedge on R. Continue to stile at top.
❸ Cross and follow path to another stile. Cross next field and another stile then continue as path curves **R** towards farm. Pass through gate on to track, stay to **R** of **Furners Farm** and curve **L**. About 30yds (27m) after curve turn **R** over stile on to wooded path then, after few paces, go **R** again over stile into field. Walk ahead, with farm above you to R. Cross another stile then keep to **R** of pond.
❹ At top of pond cross stile into field. Go half **L** across it to gate and stile. In next field, head straight across its lower part. At point where telegraph pole almost meets hedge, turn **R** over stile on to track. Turn **L** to reach lane.
❺ Turn **R**. Follow lane to valley bottom. Start to climb other side and at corner go over stile on **R**. Ascend steeply to another stile at road. Turn **R** along pavement. After 150yds (137m) cross to footpath and climb steeply. At junction of paths bear **L** and continue to field. Follow margin of field up then follow path as it weaves in and out of woodland.
❻ At top turn **R** on to **Folly Lane** and continue to junction. If you want to go into **Slad**, turn R otherwise continue on to path that will soon take you into woodland. Walk through woods, finally emerging at **Bull's Cross**.

152 BROCKWEIR
GLOUCESTERSHIRE

4.5 MILES (7.2KM) 2hrs 15min

PATHS: Tracks, fields, lanes, stony paths and riverbank, 5 stiles

SUGGESTED MAP: aqua3 OS Outdoor Leisure 14 Wye Valley & Forest of Dean

GRID REFERENCE: ST 540011

PARKING: Lay-by near telephone box in Brockweir; Tintern Old Railway Station, on other side of river (fee)

THE PUB: Brockweir Country Inn

❶ Walk uphill out of **Brockweir** until you reach junction on L ('Coldharbour'). Turn **L** along narrow lane for 160yds (146m). At corner beside **Rock Farm** turn **L** on to track ('**Offa's Dyke Path**'), which soon narrows markedly and climbs fairly steeply. Continue walking up to reach lane.
❷ Cross this. Continue ascent until you reach another lane. Turn **L**. Follow lane for 200yds (183m), to pass cottage on R, followed by ruined stone buildings. Turn **R** along lane.
❸ Keep to **R** of **Chapel Cottage** on to path, still ascending. When you reach wider track, fork **L**. This dwindles to path, continuing to climb, until it brings you to another track, beside stone stile. Turn **L** again.
❹ After few paces, before gate and house, fork **R** to stile at field. Cross this to another pair of stiles, to **L** of house. In next field, stay to **L** of farm and come to stile at lane. Turn **R** and follow gently climbing lane. It levels out then where it starts to climb again at corner, turn **L** on to **R-H** path, heading towards Oak Cottage, Bigs Weir and Monmouth. Descend until you arrive at lane before house.
❺ Turn **L** here to follow track that descends to R of another house. Track will continue down into woodland. Stay on main, obvious track, watching out for loose stones, as it meanders down hillside. This will bring you to cottage at corner. Go **L** with track, which later becomes narrow path. Stay on this. Follow it down hillside among trees, still keeping eye on loose pebbles. Soon **River Wye** will appear below you, to R. At bottom pass through gap in fence, and bear **R** towards grassy river bank, where you will meet stile.
❻ Turn **L** through stile. Follow river back to **Brockweir**, passing through gates and crossing bridges where they arise. As you approach the village keep close to river to enter path that will bring you on to lane leading up to road at Brockweir Bridge.

153 DEERHURST
GLOUCESTERSHIRE

3.25 MILES (5.3KM) 1hr 30min

PATHS: Fields, pavement and river bank, 11 stiles

SUGGESTED MAP: aqua3 OS Explorer 179 Gloucester, Cheltenham & Stroud

GRID REFERENCE: SO 868298

PARKING: Car park (small fee) outside Odda's Chapel

THE PUB: Coalhouse Inn, Apperley

❶ With **Odda's Chapel** behind you, turn **L** then **R** through gate to walk along track as far as river bank. Here, turn **L** to follow **Severn Way**. Continue through number of gates and over stiles, following obvious path (sometimes overgrown), with river always close by on R. Eventually you reach **Coalhouse Inn**, set back a little to L.

❷ Turn **L** after pub to follow road. Once behind pub turn **R** through kissing gate on to area of rough grass. Go half **R** to stile and cross into field. Continue to another stile. In following field go uphill to find another stile at top, beside gate. Go over and follow **R-H** margin of field to another gate. Go through, and continue to road in **Apperley**.

❸ Turn **L** to walk through village. Opposite **post office** (which will be on your L) turn **R** down road with houses on your L.

❹ Just before **village hall** turn **L** and then walk across playing fields to stile. Cross it, and stay on same line to arrive at another stile. Now follow **R-H** margin of field as it eventually curves **R** and brings you to stile to lane.

❺ Go over stile on to lane and then turn sharp **R** to gate. Once in field turn **L** to come swiftly to another stile. Cross this to enter another field then walk down, crossing another stile and passing to **R** of house. Cross another stile (if there is one – it may only be a temporary measure) and then go half **L** to stile in hedge, well before **farm** ahead. Go over to road and then turn **R**.

❻ Continue until you come to concrete block on your **L**. Go up this and walk along ridge alongside private garden. Cross stile into meadow and continue diagonally **R** heading for stile and gate beside **Odda's Chapel** and timbered building next to it. This will bring you to gate by your starting point.

154 CHALFORD
GLOUCESTERSHIRE

6 MILES (9.7KM) 3hrs

PATHS: Fields, lanes, canal path and tracks, 3 stiles

SUGGESTED MAP: aqua3 OS Explorer 168 Stroud, Tetbury and Malmesbury

GRID REFERENCE: SO 892025

PARKING: Lay-by east of Chalford church

THE PUB: Ship Inn, Brimscombe

❶ Walk towards **church**. Immediately before it, cross road and locate path going **R**, towards canal roundhouse. Note the **Belvedere Mill** on L. Follow tow path alongside **Thames and Severn Canal** (R).

❷ Cross road. Continue along tow path as it descends steps. Now follow path for about 2 miles (3.2km). It shortly disappears under railway line via culvert. Old mills and small factories line route.

❸ Shortly before reaching **Brimscombe**, path passes under railway again. Soon after, it becomes road into industrial estate. At road opposite mill turn **L**, to reach junction. Cross and turn **R**. Immediately after **Ship Inn** turn **L** along road among offices and workshops. Continue along path, with factory walls to R. Canal reappears (L). As you continue into country pass beneath 3 bridges and footbridge.

❹ At next bridge, with hamlet high on L, turn **R** to follow path to road. Cross this and turn **L**. After few paces turn **R** up short path to meet **Thrupp Lane**. Turn **R**. At top, turn **L** into **Claypits Lane**, turn **R** just before **Thrupp Farm** and climb steeply.

❺ After long climb, as road levels out, you will see **Nether Lypiatt Manor** ahead. Turn **R**, beside tree, over stile into field. Go half **L** to far corner. Cross stone stile. Follow narrow path beside trees to road. Descend lane opposite. Where it appears to fork, go ahead, to descend past a **house**. Enter woodland and fork **R** near bottom. Keep pond on L and cross road to climb **Bussage Hill**. After 100yds (91m) pass lane on L. At top fork **L**. Opposite **Ram Inn** turn **R**.

❻ After telephone box and bus shelter turn **L** to follow path among houses into woodland. Go ahead until you reach road. Turn **L** and immediately R down path beside **cemetery**. Descend to another road. Turn **R** for 50yds (46m); turn **L** down steep lane, leading back to **Chalford**. At bottom turn **L** to return to start.

155 DYMOCK
GLOUCESTERSHIRE

8 MILES (12.9KM) 3hrs 45min

PATHS: Fields and lanes, 27 stiles

SUGGESTED MAP: aqua3 OS Outdoor Leisure 14 Wye Valley & Forest of Dean; Explorers 189 Hereford & Ross-on-Wye; 190 Malvern Hills & Bredon Hill

GRID REFERENCE: SO 677288 (on Outdoor Leisure 14)

PARKING: Main road of Kempley Green; near its southeastern end

THE PUB: Beauchamp Arms

❶ Walk southeast out of **Kempley Green**. Turn **L** before **Knapp Cottage**. Take **R-H** of 2 paths. Cross stiles and pass barn. Go through gate into orchard. Enter **Dymock Wood** to follow path to road.

❷ Turn **R** then **L** before motorway bridge. Where road bears L, proceed through gate into fields. Follow route, alongside motorway, to reach stream. Turn **L** before it. Cross track and stiles, pass through gate and ahead along track, aiming to **R** of **Boyce Court**.

❸ Pass to **L** of lake. Go through woodland to lane. Turn **R** over bridge and **L** on to path by stream. Continue, staying first **R** then **L** of stream, to **Dymock**.

❹ Cross churchyard then go through gate into field. Turn half **L**; take 2nd bridge on **R**. Bear half **L** to stile. Turn **R** along disused road. Cross B4215. Follow track, leaving it to keep to **R** of **Allum's Farm**. Pass barn. Go half **L** across field to gate. Enter orchard, turn **R**. Follow its **L** margin then that of field, to road.

❺ Turn **R**. After 600yds (549m) turn **R** into field alongside woodland. After 120yds (110m) go half **R** over mound to enter woods. Turn **R**. Follow boundary to stile. Turn **L** and re-enter woodland. Follow obvious path, eventually emerging at stile. Cross field, keeping to **L** of chimney then **R** into field. Look for stile on **L**, cross into adjacent field; turn **R** to find bridge across stream. Go half **L** across fields to road.

❻ Turn **L**. Continue past **St Mary's Church**. At next T-junction, go into field ahead. Proceed into next field. Continue with stream on L across fields to lane. Turn **L** to junction at **Fishpool**.

❼ Turn **R**. After 50yds (46m), turn **L** over stile. Curve **R**; pass series of stiles to aim eventually just to **R** of cottage. Follow path through poultry enclosures. Bear **L** over stiles so that house is on R. Pass house; go **R** into field. Turn **L**. Follow same line to **Kempley Green**.

156 TARDEBIGGE
WORCESTERSHIRE

5.5 MILES (8.8KM) 2hrs 30min

PATHS: Tow path, pastures, field paths and minor lanes, 21 stiles

SUGGESTED MAP: aqua3 OS Explorer 204 Worcester & Droitwich Spa

GRID REFERENCE: SO 974682

PARKING: Limited space, so park tightly and considerately, on north and east side of road bridge

THE PUB: The Queens Head, Stoke Pound

❶ Cross bridge No 51 and turn **L**, taking tow path on south side. Follow this until about 15yds (14m) before next bridge – No 52.

❷ Turn **R** here, into trees, then down field. Cross double-stiled footbridge among trees then keep ahead, over driveway to **Patchetts Farm**. Skirt copse to L, then another stile and 2-plank bridge. Cross 2 fields, keeping hedge on your L. You will reach gate on your **L**, close to broken oak tree with substantial girth.

❸ Turn **R**. Within 110yds (100m) go through gate ahead (no waymarker), ignoring gate to L. Go a quarter **R** (or skirt crops) to find stile. Retain this diagonal line to cross footbridge of 3 planks, then find rickety, narrow stile in next field's corner. Walk with hedge on your L to reach minor road junction. Turn **R** for 55yds (50m). Turn **L** to walk across 3 more fields to dilapidated metal gate. Now take **R-H** field edge to reach minor road.

❹ Turn **R**. Follow this for 0.5 mile (800m) to **Lower Bentley Farm's** driveway. Go 140yds (128m) further, to fingerpost on **R**. Cross pastures by gaps in hedgerows, later with hedge on your L, but veer to stile in **R-H** corner at end. Cross this, then double stile, go three-quarters **L** to road.

❺ Turn **R**, and in 75yds (69m) turn **L**. Here, beyond awkward ditch, is new kissing gate with latch. Cross pastures easily towards **Orchard Farm**, but then turn **R**, away from it. Over corner stile go straight ahead. At double stile (across ditch) go half **L**, and at gap in hedge turn **R**. Now turn **L** without gaining height for 650yds (594m), aiming to **L** of black-and-white house, for stile and gate. In 80yds (73m) reach road.

❻ Turn **R**. At T-junction turn **L**. Join canal tow path this side of Stoke Pound Bridge. (The **Queen's Head** is on other side.) Now you have over 0.75 mile (1.2km) to return to your car at road bridge, approximately mid-way up **Tardebigge Flight**.

157 HANBURY HALL
WORCESTERSHIRE

4.75 MILES (7.7KM) 2hrs 15min

PATHS: Meadows, tracks and easy woodland paths, 17 stiles

SUGGESTED MAP: aqua3 OS Explorer 204 Worcester & Droitwich Spa

GRID REFERENCE: SO 957652

PARKING: Piper's Hill car park, on B4091 between Stoke Works and Hanbury (fast road and no sign)

THE PUB: Country Girl

❶ From bottom of car park, follow driveway to **Knotts Farm**. Go ahead on **L-H** (1 of 2 parallel paths). 350yds (320m) after farm reach track at fingerpost.

❷ Keep ahead, with field boundary on L. Ascending towards **church**, reach stake with 2 waymarkers.

❸ Fork **L**, soon passing spinney, then losing height across meadow. Take care as stile and steps here spill you straight on to minor but fast road. Cross then go beside **school**. Ahead, when 20yds (18m) before stile out of 3rd field, turn **R**, aiming just to L of young, fenced oak. Cross wobbly stile. In 70yds (64m) cross footbridge on **L**. Cross 2 stiles to Pumphouse Lane.

❹ Turn **R**. Take stile and gate close to black-and-white **Grumbleground Cottage**. In 40yds (37m) cross 3-plank footbridge. Ascend slightly, in line with electricity poles. After 2 fields turn **R**, alongside wire fence. Reach road.

❺ Cross road to footpath opposite. At stile go half **L**, guided by solitary, fenced conifer. Pass close to **Hanbury Hall's** entrance, easing away from perimeter wall to cross large field to corner.

❻ Ignore minor road, turning immediately **R**. Hug boundary fence of coppice. Continue down **R-H** field edge. At junction turn **R** at National Trust sign, into this former deer park. After just 50yds (46m), at small drainage ditch, edge **R**, along slight green hollow. After another 110yds (100m), where it curves **R**, leave hollow to keep line. Aim for stile about 300yds (274m) away, to **L** of clump of fenced trees, which hides round pond. Maintain this line going up incline – **Hanbury church** is seen on L – to reach tarmac driveway.

❼ Turn **L**. When it curves R go straight ahead to walk in oak avenue. Keep this line for 700yds (640m), to minor road. Turn **R**, then **L** up to church. In churchyard walk round perimeter, down to kissing gate. Shortly rejoin outward route at Point ❸. Remember to go **L**, into woods, at Point ❷.

158 CLENT HILLS
WORCESTERSHIRE

3.5 MILES (5.7KM) 2hrs

PATHS: Woodland paths (sometimes muddy), tracks, 8 stiles

SUGGESTED MAP: aqua3 OS Explorer 219 Wolverhampton & Dudley

GRID REFERENCE: SO 938808

PARKING: National Trust pay-and-display car park, Nimmings Wood

THE PUB: The Bell & Cross

❶ Return to car park entrance and turn **R** for few paces. Cross road to stile and take **L-H** of 2 options. Immediately you'll see striking urban panorama. Descend steadily but, at cylindrical wooden post, turn **R** (with waymarker). Continue across fields, probably populated with horses, until kissing gate. Here take forward option (not R fork), to reach churchyard of **St Kenelm's** in Romsley parish. It may appear to be 'overgrown' since it is managed like a traditional hay meadow.

❷ Leave by lychgate. Turn **L** along road for short distance, then **R** at T-junction. In about 125yds (114m) take waymarked path at driveway to **The Wesleys** to ascend gently. Turn **L** on to tarmac road. Ignore L turn but, just 30yds (27m) beyond it, take muddy, narrow path into woodland up on **R**, angled away from road and not signposted. Emerge from trees to trig point on **Walton Hill**. Turn **L**, taking **R-H** of 2 options. Follow this for 0.75 mile (1.2km) until just 10yds (9m) beyond National Trust marker post. Here take **R-H** fork to stile. Go steeply down 2 meadows to road beside **Church of St Leonard's** in **Clent**.

❸ Turn **R** then **R** again. At Church View Cottage, opposite church's driveway, turn **L**. In 125yds (114m) take upper, **L** fork. In 90yds (82m), at crossing, go **L**. After further 100yds (91m) ignore options to turn **R** or half **R**. Proceed for further 120yds (110m). Do not climb stile on your L but go straight on, soon ascending steeply up wooden steps. After another 100yds (91m) you'll emerge from trees. Now cross track then turn **R**.

❹ Keep on this broad, open path, passing close to (or viewing) a toposcope beside four standing stones. Maintain this line to descend in woodland to road. Just on L is car park.

159 DROITWICH SPA
WORCESTERSHIRE

5.75 MILES (9.2KM) 2hrs 30min

PATHS: Pavements, field paths, stony tracks, 6 stiles

SUGGESTED MAP: aqua3 OS Explorer 204 Worcester & Droitwich Spa

GRID REFERENCE: SO 898631

PARKING: Long-stay pay-and-display between Heritage Way and Saltway (follow signs for 'Brine Baths')

THE PUB: The Old Cock Inn

❶ From **TIC**, go along Victoria Square. Cross Heritage Way into Ombersley Street East. When it bends keep ahead, passing magistrates' court. After underpass proceed to St Nicholas's Church. Go round churchyard to take another underpass. Turn **L**. Take road over railway to mini-roundabout, filtering **R** to go through 3rd underpass. Walk for 65yds (60m) to fence corner, near lamppost. Turn **L**. In 30yds (27m) turn **R**. At bottom of this cul-de-sac, Westmead Close, turn **L**. Soon take Ledwych Close, on **R**. At **canal** you have left Droitwich Spa.

❷ Turn **L**. At bridge turn **R**; continue. Turn **L** just after A38 bridge. In 110yds (100m) reach **Westwood House** slip road. Facing allotments, take kissing gate to **L**. Beyond woodland go across several fields. Within 500yds (457m) of 2nd driveway is junction.

❸ Turn sharply **R**. Electric fencing leads between paddocks then veer **L** to walk briefly through **Nunnery Wood**. Aim for 2 gateposts beside tree. Keep ahead for 0.5 mile (800m), beside big **dairy** on L, then curving **L** past **industrial estate** to reach Doverdale Lane.

❹ Turn **R** on lane. Just before '30' speed-limit sign, fork **L**. Cross A442. Go through **Hampton Lovett** to **St Mary's Church**. Take meadow path under railway. In 140yds (128m), at footbridge, bear **R**, along field edge. Maintain direction for over 0.5 mile (800m), walking in trees beside **Highstank Pool** when fence allows. Track leads to evergreens shielding golf tee.

❺ Cross vast field, then aim slightly **L** to metal gate. Follow road under A38 into housing estate. Find path running between Nos 49 and 53. Go through 2 kissing gates flanking level crossing. Turn **L** to pass Gardeners Arms. In 20yds (18m) turn **R** over **River Salwarpe**, into Vines Park. Veer **L** to cross the Droitwich Canal. Over B4090, follow Gurney Lane to High Street – ahead is **Spats Coffee House**. Turn **R**, passing Tower Hill, then **L** into St Andrew's Street.

160 WORCESTER CITY
WORCESTERSHIRE

2.5 MILES (4KM) 1hr 30min

PATHS: City streets and tarmac riverside path

SUGGESTED MAP: aqua3 OS Explorer 204 Worcester & Droitwich Spa

GRID REFERENCE: SO 846548

PARKING: Long-stay pay-and-display car parks at New Road, Tybridge Street and Croft Road

THE PUB: The Salmon's Leap

❶ The described route begins at the city side of the road bridge, but you can pick it up anywhere – at The Commandery or the Guildhall, for example – depending on where you have parked. Turn **L**, along North Parade, passing **Old Rectifying House** (wine bar). Turn **R** up **Dolday**, then **L**, in front of **bus station**, along **The Butts**. Turn **L** along **Farrier Street**, **R** into **Castle Street**, reaching northern extremity of route at its junction with Foregate Street.

❷ Go **R** along **Foregate Street**, passing **Shire Hall** and **City Museum and Art Gallery**, continuing along The Cross and into pedestrianised area called **High Street**. Turn **L** into Pump Street. (Elgar's statue stands close to his father's piano shop, at the southern end of High Street.) Turn **L** again, into **The Shambles**. At junction turn **R** into Mealcheapen Street. Another **R** turn and you are in **New Street** (which later becomes **Friar Street**).

❸ Head down this street (look out for King Charles' House where he stayed during the battle of Worcester in 1651). At end of street is dual carriageway (College Street). Turn **R** then cross carefully, to visit **cathedral**.

❹ Leave cathedral along College Precincts to fortified gateway known as **Edgar Tower**. (It is named after the 10th-century King Edgar, but was actually built in the 14th century. Go through this gateway to see College Green.) Continue, along what is now **Severn Street**, which, unsurprisingly, leads to **River Severn**. Turn **R**, to complete your circuit, by following Kleve Walk, leafy waterside avenue; this section floods at some time most winters, and the **cricket ground** opposite was under several feet of water in 2000. For a more studied insight into the city's rich history, take a guided walk (on weekdays only) with a Green Badge Guide.

161 KINGSFORD
WORCESTERSHIRE

5.5 MILES (8.8KM) 2hrs 30min

PATHS: Forest rides, meadows, minor roads, village streets, canal tow path, 9 stiles

SUGGESTED MAP: aqua3 OS Explorer 218 Wyre Forest & Kidderminster or 219 Wolverhampton & Dudley

GRID REFERENCE: SO 835820 (on OS Explorer 218)

PARKING: Blakeshall Lane car park, Kingsford Country Park

THE PUB: Queens Head, Wolverley

❶ Take track inside northern edge of **country park** for 550yds (503m), to point about 50yds (46m) beyond end of extensive garden. To L is wide glade, falling gently; ahead rises woodland track.

❷ Turn **L**, down ride. In 275yds (251m), at 5-way junction, go ahead (not along slight R fork). Join farm track. At road turn **R**, through **Blakeshall**. After 300yds (274m), at R-H bend near power lines, take stile into muddy and brick-strewn field. Keep hedge on your R, following yellow waymarkers into small valley. Reach, but don't go through, 7-bar metal gate before **Debdale Farm**. Turn sharply to **R**, uphill, following vague track. Enter **Gloucester Coppice** at gate and broken stile. Follow this track, soon more defined, all the way to southern end of Blakeshall Lane.

❸ Turn **L**, descending through street, The Holloway, into **Wolverley**. After village stores take 2nd footbridge on **R**. Reach Church of St John the Baptist by zig-zagging up concreted footpath through deep cutting. Leave churchyard to **L**, by steps. Go down meadow opposite (with fingerpost) to minor road.

❹ Turn **R**. At B4189 turn **L**. In front of **The Lock** pub turn **L**, along tow path. After about 1.25 miles (2km) is Debdale Lock, partly hewn into rock. Some 220yds (201m) further, just before steel wheel factory, is stile.

❺ Turn **L** along track. At T-junction after coniferous avenue turn **R** on broad gravel track. After about 440yds (402m) turn **L** (waymarker), up new wooden steps surfaced with scalpings, into trees. Go up **L-H** edge of one field and centre of another to road. Turn **L** for just 15yds (14m), then **R**. Some 400yds (366m) along this hedged lane take yellow option to **R** (to reduce road walking). At next stile wiggle **L** then **R**. Proceed ahead at junction to road. Turn **R**. In 150yds (137m), walk round wooden barrier to re-enter **country park**. Here, 2 paths run parallel to road – both lead back to car park.

162 STOURPORT-ON-SEVERN
WORCESTERSHIRE

3.25 MILES (5.3KM) 1hr 30min

PATHS: Tow path, tracks, good paths, some streets

SUGGESTED MAP: aqua3 OS Explorer 218 Wyre Forest & Kidderminster or 219 Wolverhampton & Dudley

GRID REFERENCE: SO 820704 (on Explorer 218)

PARKING: Worcester Road car park on A4025 (poorly signed; height restriction bar spans narrow entrance)

THE PUB: Bird In Hand

❶ Cross A4025. Turn **L** for 25yds (23m) to take footpath. Strike across bottom part of **Hartlebury Common**: you'll see buildings in far distance. Veer **R**, through silver birches, to find sandy track at back of houses. At housing estate join tarmac briefly, aiming for dirt track beyond 2nd 'Britannia Gardens' sign and in front of Globe House. Shortly turn **L** down tarmac footpath, initially with wooden paling on L, to **river**.

❷ Turn **R**. In 650yds (594m) reach lock and Stourport's canal basins. Now, your route is neither across 2-plank walkway at upper lock gate, nor upper brick bridge with timber-and-metal railings; instead take neat brick-paved path to circumnavigate boarded-up **Tontine** public house. Now skirt Upper Basin, passing Severn Valley Boat Centre. Across York Street join tow path. Follow this for just under 0.75 mile (1.2km), leaving it at **Bird in Hand** pub, before defunct brick railway bridge.

❸ Go down Holly Road, then half **L** into Mill Road, going under railway then over **River Stour** to **B4193**. Cross and go to **L** of Myday Windows to take narrow, sandy, uphill path back on to common. Soon, at fork, go **L**, keeping direction as ground levels. Less than 50 paces after joining motor vehicle track reach trig point.

❹ Retrace your 50 paces and go another 30yds (27m), passing waymarker, to junction. Here turn **L**, away from car park. In just 40yds (37m) take **R** fork. In 100yds (91m) take **L** fork (not straight on). At corner of conifer plantation, 275yds further (251m), turn **R**. After 110yds (100m) turn **L**, then in 220yds (201m), just after far end of plantation, enjoy views. Now 65yds (60m) beyond this viewpoint take **R** option at subtle fork. Go forward for another 250yds (229m), until opening. Here step very carefully over pair of exposed and disused (and not actually hazardous) pipes. Follow sandy track slanting downhill for (110yds) 100m, then swing **R**, now head for car park.

163 MARTLEY
WORCESTERSHIRE

6.75 MILES (10.9KM) 3hrs

PATHS: Field paths, lanes, orchard paths, tracks, river meadows, minor roads, 20 stiles

SUGGESTED MAP: aqua3 OS Explorer 204 Worcester & Droitwich Spa

GRID REFERENCE: SO 766597

PARKING: St Peter's Church, Martley

THE PUB: Crown

❶ Go through churchyard to B4204. Cross to track. In 100yds (91m) enter **school's** grounds briefly then walk in trees, parallel. Turn **R** at stile, then another, to re-enter grounds. Briefly follow **L** edge of playing fields. Another stile gives on to field. At road turn **L**. Turn **R** ('Highfields'). Beside **Lingen Farm** go down track. At bend take stile, across field. Cross stream; ascend, taking **R-H** gates. Reach minor road.

❷ Turn **L**. At **Larkins** go ahead. At **The Peak** walk behind **Ross Green's** gardens. Cross fields to reach road. Go straight over, to partially concealed stile, not diagonally to fingerpost. Walk beside barn, then on, to another lane. Turn **L** to reach fingerpost pointing into apple orchard before **Pear Tree Cottage**.

❸ Follow waymarkers through trees. Emerge at bridge over ditch, beside apple-sorting equipment. Go 220yds (201m) up track, to gap in evergreens. Turn **L**, down orchard ride. At T-junction turn **R**, up to just before gate beside small house. Turn **L**, almost back on yourself. Go through orchard, following faded yellow splodges about 1.5ft (45cm) up on tree trunks. Leave by footbridge, crossing fields to B4197.

❹ Turn **R** for 60yds (55m). Take track for 0.5 mile (800m) to **Rodge Hill's** top. Turn sharp **L**, 'Worcs Way South'. Follow this for 1 mile (1.6km). Steps lead down to road's hairpin bend.

❺ Turn **R**. In 20yds (18m) turn **L**, but in 15yds (14m) turn **R** again, into conifers. Emerge to drop down steeply. At B4204 turn **R** for 200yds (183m). Turn **L**, skirt barn to L; go diagonally to **River Teme**. Follow riverside walk, later in **Kingswood Nature Reserve**, for over 0.5 mile (800m). Leave river when wire fence requires it. Ascend path, later driveway, to road.

❻ Turn **R**, uphill; this soon bends **L**. Near brow move **R** (waymarker) to walk in field, not on road. At end turn **L** but, in 275yds (251m), cross 2 stiles beside caravan. Beside fields and allotments, emerge between **Crown** and garage. Pass telephone box into village. Turn **R** to **church** and start.

164 MAMBLE
WORCESTERSHIRE

10.5 MILES (16.8KM) 5hrs

PATHS: Minor roads, field and woodland paths, tow path, 18 stiles

SUGGESTED MAP: aqua3 OS Explorer 203 Ludlow

GRID REFERENCE: SO 685712

PARKING: Lay-by (bend in old road) west of Mamble on A456

THE PUB: Sun and Slipper

❶ Towards Tenbury, take minor road. Down **High Point Farm's** driveway, gate marks indistinct green lane to **Tetstill**. Turn **R**. Soon cross railway bridge.

❷ Through 2 fields, reach stile. Follow **L** field edge. Turn **L**. Just before **Sturts'** private bridge go down and **R** – flagstones lead to footbridge. Ascend track **L** of Sturts. At brow move **R**, taking **L** of 2 gates. Go to **R** edge of conifers. In 220yds (201m), at next corner, turn **L**. Aim **L** of massive oak, to gate into conifers.

❸ Descend to cross footbridge. Continue (not over bridge) soon into pasture. In 325yds (297m) go **L**. Take stile via **The Great House's** gardens. Follow minor roads to **St Michael's Church**. Take waymarked route, following pylons. In 600yds (549m), when descending, cross 1 stile; turn **L** at 2nd (don't cross).

❹ Follow tow path for 275yds (251m). Cross canal bed via exposed earth. Find gate to **R**. Reach track, Tavern Lane. Where drive to **Oxnall Farm** bends, go ahead. Of 2 gates take lower, **R-H** one. In 60yds (55m) keep **L**. Leave plantation at stile;, take gate immediately **R**. Strike diagonally to opening. In 10yds (9m) turn **R** along track briefly then to corner stile into trees. Cross old railway. Ditch on L marks canal. Brick lining is evident at next stile (**Rea Aqueduct**).

❺ Follow canal for 1.25 miles (2km). At A456 turn **R**. Cross to old canal bend, taking public footpath. Leave driveway at **Broombank Farm's** gate. Walk along **L** edge of several fields. At corner strike half-**R** to pylon. Around dry valley head, keep on brow, by hedgerow. Move **L**, to trees shielding pond (possibly dry). Ease away from fencing (now R) to 2-bar stile through plantation. Go to woodland corner. Veer **R** for 75yds (69m); cross stile, go down to cross dam.

❻ Go up to gate in fence's **L** corner. Walk 80yds (73m) to 2nd (not 1st) stile. Go forward to road, turning **L** then **R** then **L**, into **Mamble**. Turn **R**, then **L**. Before **craft centre** take fingerpost, beside Tudor Cottage's garage. After 2-plank brook bridge go up and **L**, across fields to Neen Sollars road junction and lay-by.

165 MINSTER LOVELL
OXFORDSHIRE

4 MILES (6.4KM) 1hr 30min

PATHS: Meadows, tracks, pavement and lane, woodland, 17 stiles

SUGGESTED MAP: aqua3 OS Explorer 180 Oxford, Witney & Woodstock

GRID REFERENCE: SP 321114

PARKING: Car park (free) at eastern end of Minster Lovell, above church and hall

THE PUB: Old Swan Inn

❶ Walk up lane ('Crawley'). At end of village cross stile, **R**. Take footpath diagonally **L** across field ('Crawley'). Cross stile and keep ahead along path, with stone wall to L. Mill chimney on horizon belongs to **Crawley Mill**.

❷ Cross stile and ahead up slight incline. Cross another stile, go through gate and continue on path, walking up green tunnel of lane. Pass above **Crawley Mill**. At road turn **R**. Follow this down into **Crawley**. At bottom, Lamb Inn is on L.

❸ Turn **R**. Follow pavement past **Manor Farm**, with its huge pond. Cross humpback bridge over **Windrush**. At other side of bridge cross road. Turn **L** through gate ('Witney'). Follow bridleway beside stream, marked by line of willows.

❹ At junction of paths by gate look ahead and L to see **New Mill**. Turn **R** through gate and walk up field edge. Pass gate and cross road. Climb stile, go straight on to 2nd stile, and follow path down through woods.

❺ At bottom cross stile and follow path along fence. Wildflower meadows of **Maggots Grove** lie to R. Continue over 3 more stiles and bear **L** beside trees. Cross stile by meander of river.

❻ Cross further stile and enter woods. At gate bear **R**, following arrows, and cross 2 footbridges. After short distance cross bridge over river. Go through squeeze gate towards **Minster Lovell Hall**. Climb stile and go through gate to explore ruins.

❼ Leave by top entrance and walk through **churchyard**. Cross slab stile, continue along grassy path with village up to your R. Cross footbridge and stile and veer to **R**. Cross 1 stile then another into Wash Meadow recreation ground. Keep **R** and go through gate on to high street, with **Old Swan** pub to L. Turn **R**. Walk through village to car park.

166 BROUGHTON
OXFORDSHIRE

2.75 MILES (4.4KM) 1hr 30min

PATHS: Field and parkland paths and tracks, some roads, 6 stiles

SUGGESTED MAP: aqua3 OS Explorer 191 Banbury, Bicester & Chipping Norton

GRID REFERENCE: SP 421384

PARKING: Limited spaces in Broughton village

THE PUB: Saye and Sele Arms

❶ Keep **Wykeham Lane** R and parkland L and walk through **Broughton**. Pass Danvers Road on R-H side, followed by **Danvers Cottage** on L. When road curves R just beyond cottage, swing **L** over stile ('North Newington'). Keep ahead across field to reach stile in next boundary, then continue in next field to cross footbridge in trees (maybe obscured by foliage during summer). Continue ahead, keeping line of trees on your R-H side and, three-quarters of way along field boundary, look for footbridge on **R**.

❷ Cross footbridge, followed by concrete track, to reach stile. Head diagonally **R** across field to road. Take right of way on opposite side and follow stretch of **Macmillan Way** between fields to reach stile. Cross stile to lane; turn **L**. Walk towards **North Newington**, passing entrance to **Park Farm** on your R-H side. Pass **Blinking Owl** pub and Wheelwright Cottage then turn **L** into The Pound, opposite old village pump.

❸ Walk past **Pound Cottage** and look for footpath which starts about 30yds (27m) beyond it on **R-H** side. Follow footpath diagonally **R** across field to reach wide, obvious gap in hedgerow on far side. Turn **L** to reach another gap in hedge, then head obliquely **R** in field, making for top corner, which is defined by trees and hedgerow. Pass through gate and keep ahead, with field boundary on your immediate L. Walk along to next gate and then down field to road.

❹ Cross road to galvanised gate and follow track towards **barns**. Keep to **L** of barns and look for stile and footpath branching off to **L**, running hard by fence on R-H side. Follow path to reach stile in far boundary and cross over into parkland of **Broughton Castle**. Soon **Broughton church** spire and castle come into sight ahead. Continue across parkland and down to meet castle drive. Head for gate into churchyard then follow path to reach **B4035** on outskirts of **Broughton**. Turn **L** along road and return to start.

167 OXFORD
OXFORDSHIRE

2.25 MILES (3.6KM) 1hr 15min

PATHS: Pavements, field and riverside paths, 2 stiles

SUGGESTED MAP: aqua3 OS Explorer 180 Oxford

GRID REFERENCE: SP 513062

PARKING: Parking in city centre, or use park-and-ride, or travel by train

THE PUB: Turf Tavern

❶ Start at **Carfax**, where 4 streets converge. Charles II was proclaimed King at **Carfax Tower** in 1660. Walk ahead into St Aldates and head for entrance to **Christ Church**, Oxford's largest college, founded in 1525 by Cardinal Wolsey. When he was disgraced it was refounded as King Henry VIII's College. Later it became known as **Christ Church** when the college and the cathedral became one. Leave by south exit and walk ahead down tree-lined New Walk. On L is Christ Church Meadow.

❷ On reaching **Thames** tow path, swing **L** and follow river bank. Keep ahead until you reach confluence of Thames and **River Cherwell**. Avoid steeply arched footbridge and keep alongside Cherwell. River meanders between meadows and sports fields. Leave river bank and pass through wrought-iron gates to walk up Rose Lane.

❸ With Magdalen Bridge and **Magdalen College** bell tower on your R, turn **L** at **High Street** or 'the High', as it is known in Oxford. Cross Longwall Street and turn R into Queen's Lane. Continue into New College Lane and on **R**, beyond arch, is entrance to **New College**. Keep along New College Lane to Bridge of Sighs, a 1913 replica of its Venice namesake, and ahead of you now is **Sheldonian Theatre**, designed by Sir Christopher Wren and completed in 1669.

❹ Turn **L** here for Radcliffe Camera and cross Radcliffe Square towards Brasenose College, which probably took its name from a door-knocker in the shape of a nose. Turn **R** into Brasenose Lane, then **R** again into Turl Street, cutting between Jesus College and Exeter College. Make for Broad Street and on R is St Giles, where Charles I drilled his men during the Civil War. Turn **L** into Cornmarket Street, passing Church of St Michael at North Gate. Its Saxon tower is the oldest building in Oxford. Return to **Carfax**.

168 CUMNOR PLACE
OXFORDSHIRE

6 MILES (9.7KM) 2hrs 30min

PATHS: Field paths, quiet lanes and tracks, 1 stile

SUGGESTED MAP: aqua3 OS Explorer 180 Oxford

GRID REFERENCE: SP 458044

PARKING: Spaces by village hall in Cumnor

THE PUB: Bear and Ragged Staff, Cumnor

❶ Sadly, a stone fireplace set in a bank in the churchyard is all that remains of Cumnor Place. This is where Dudley's, the Earl of Leicester, estranged wife died of a broken neck. Dudley was believed to have been Elizabeth I's lover and apparently showed no outward sign of grief on hearing of his wife's mysterious death – suicide, accident or murder? Turn **R** from parking area and walk to mini-roundabout. Turn **R** into Appleton Road and pass **Bear and Ragged Staff** pub on R. Veer half **L** a few paces beyond and join footpath ('Bessels Leigh'). Pass **cricket club** on **L** then continue on track. When it peters out continue in field, keeping ditch R. Pass alongside line of trees on far side of field, turn **L**, then **R** and make for opening in corner, concealed by vegetation in summer. Continue to reach galvanised gate and keep houses over to L beyond pasture. Cross footbridge to galvanised gate, swing **L** and cross field towards road. Keep in line with telephone wires and make for waymark in field corner. Follow drive to road.

❷ To visit **Greyhound** pub, turn L. To continue turn **R** and follow road through **Bessels Leigh** and out into countryside, cutting between farmland. On reaching junction, keep **L** to next junction. Go straight on into **Eaton** and pass **Eight Bells** pub.

❸ Follow lane out of Eaton and through flat countryside. When lane becomes enclosed by trees, look for view of Thames on L. Continue to **Bablock Hythe**. Across river is **Ferryman Inn**. Walk back along lane for few paces and turn **L** at bridleway ('Cumnor').

❹ Pass through gate and when, some time later, path curves to **L**, look for **Physic Well** in trees to L. This is a muddy spring, once valued for its healing waters. Emerge from trees and cut between fields towards pylons. Go through gate, join drive and walk ahead. Ignore turning to **Upper Whitley Farm** and continue into Cumnor, passing **Leys Farm** on R. Look for United Reformed church and return to village hall and start.

169 BLADON
OXFORDSHIRE

5 MILES (8KM) 2hrs 15min

PATHS: Field and woodland paths and tracks, quiet roads, 7 stiles

SUGGESTED MAP: aqua3 OS Explorer 180 Oxford

GRID REFERENCE: SP 468138

PARKING: Limited spaces outside Begbroke church, St Michael's Lane

THE PUB: Royal Sun, Begbroke

❶ Keep **church** behind you, walk to Spring Hill Road. Turn **R**. Follow lane through 2 sharp bends, passing **Hall Farm**. Avoid path on R; continue to stile and galvanised gates. Follow track up gentle slope to next stile and cattle grid. Keep ahead, passing house on L, then swing **R** across field, passing under telegraph wires. Pass into next field; turn **R**.

❷ Follow obvious boundary across several fields, eventually turning **L** in corner. Continue for 50yds (46m) and look for stile and footbridge on **R**. Continue in next field, with hedge on L. At field corner, continue for few paces; turn **R** through opening in hedge into adjoining field. Maintain direction, with boundary L. Make for stile and oak in field corner. Continue across next field, keeping to **L** edge of woodland. With trees by you on R, follow path towards **Burleigh Lodge**. Swing **L** for few paces to stile leading out to road.

❸ Turn **R** by millennium stone, pass lodge and walk to footpath sign on **R** ('Bladon'). Cross stile and keep hedge on L. Make for footbridge in field corner, turn **L** and follow hedgerow. Look for hedge running diagonally R; keep it L and head towards Bladon. Make for stile on to road on bend. Go forward, keep entrance to **Lamb** pub car park on L, continue to next junction; cross to Church Street. Walk to **Church of St Martin**; head through churchyard to gate on far side.

❹ Turn **R**; follow tarmac lane to wooden gates. Continue on field path to corner; turn **R** at waymark. With hedgerow L, pass to **L** of woodland and head for white gate, with road beyond. Turn **L** by lock-up garages and follow path ('Begbroke').

❺ Cross rectangular pasture and, at far end, follow path into trees and through gate. Emerge at length from wood at another gate and continue ahead along field boundary towards **Begbroke**. Go through gate in corner; follow path alongside drive to road. Turn **L** and **L** again into St Michael's Lane, returning to church.

170 WANTAGE
OXFORDSHIRE

6 MILES (9.7KM) 2hrs 45min

PATHS: Pavements, tow path, field paths and tracks, 1 stile

SUGGESTED MAP: aqua3 OS Explorer 170 Abingdon, Wantage

GRID REFERENCE: SU 397881

PARKING: Long-stay car park off Mill Street

THE PUB: Greyhound, Letcombe Regis

❶ Keep to **R** edge of car park and look for pedestrian exit. Turn **L** into Mill Street and walk up into Market Place. Make for **statue of King Alfred** then follow signs for museum. Approach parish **Church of St Peter and St Paul**; turn **L** into Church Street. The **museum** is opposite you at next junction. Turn **R** here, avoid Locks Lane and follow Priory Road to **L**. Head for Portway and cross to footpath to **L** of The Croft.

❷ Follow clear tarmac path as it runs between fences and playing fields. At length you reach housing estate; continue ahead into **Letcombe Regis** and make for junction with Courthill Road. Keep it on your L and go straight ahead through village, passing **Greyhound** pub and thatched cottage dated 1698.

❸ Turn **R** by **church** ('Letcombe Bassett and Lambourn') and, when road bends sharp L, go straight ahead. After a few paces drive bends R. Keep ahead along path between banks of vegetation, following it as it curves **R**, then swings **L**. Pass **Antwicks Stud** over to R and climb gently between trees and bushes.

❹ Turn **R** at next intersection and follow tree-lined track to road. Turn **L** and make for junction. Cross, pass alongside house and follow **Cornhill Lane**. Begin gentle descent, cross track and continue down slope. Avoid R turning and keep ahead to footbridge crossing **Wilts and Berks Canal**. Turn **R** and follow tow path.

❺ Cross A417 road and then continue towards Wantage. Follow drive then take parallel path on **R**, running alongside section of restored canal. On reaching tarmac drive, turn **R** and walk along to row of houses. Turn **L** at path junction, pass **recreation ground** and follow path as it curves **R**. Turn **L** into Wasborough Avenue, then, after lock-up garages, **L** into St Mary's Way. Turn **R** and swing **L** into Belmont. Keep **R** at fork and make for Mill Street. Keep **L** and car park is on **L**.

171 GARSINGTON OXFORDSHIRE

3 MILES (4.8KM) 1hr 15min

PATHS: Field paths and roads (can be busy in Garsington), 11 stiles

SUGGESTED MAP: aqua3 OS Explorer 180 Oxford

GRID REFERENCE: SP 580024

PARKING: Spaces near Red Lion in Garsington village

THE PUB: Three Horseshoes

❶ Facing **Red Lion**, turn **L** and walk through **Garsington**. Veer half **L** at The Hill, leading to Sadlers Croft. Keep **R** and climb bank to bollards by war memorial. Cross over to The Green, keeping **Three Horseshoes** on L and historic cross on R.
❷ Continue along road to **St Mary's Church** and pass **Manor House.** Keep on road and, just as it descends quite steeply, branch **L** at sign ('**Denton**'). Strike out across field and pass between 2 trees. Ahead on horizon is hilltop church at Cuddesdon, with trees behind. Make for gap in boundary and continue in next field. Look for waymark in wide gap in next boundary and aim to **R** of copse. Pass through gap in field corner, avoid path on L and head diagonally **L** across field to far corner. Cross 2 stiles to reach road.
❸ Turn **R** and pass alongside stone wall on L. Walk along to R-H bend and bear **L** at sign ('Brookside only'). **Denton House** is on L and dovecote can be seen on R. Pass stile and footpath on R and keep along lane for few paces, turning **L** at public footpath.
❹ Head for stile and pass ornamental wall enclosing Denton House. Cross over paddock to next stile then go diagonally **R** across field to stile. Then head diagonally **L** in next field, keeping **farm** over to R. Cross 2 stiles and begin approaching houses of Garsington. Make for stile in **R-H** corner of field, keeping boundary on R in next pasture. Climb gently and look for stile on **R**. Cross it, turn **L** and make for 2 stiles in field corner. Join drive and follow it up to road.
❺ Turn **L** towards **Garsington**, pass houses of North Manor Estate and primary **school** before turning **R**, opposite **Denton Lane**, to join footpath. Follow it to lane, keep **R** and make for road. Turn **R** and return to parking area by **Red Lion**.

172 WALLINGFORD OXFORDSHIRE

3 MILES (4.8KM) 1hr 30min

PATHS: Bridleways, pavements, Thames Path, 11 stiles

SUGGESTED MAP: Aqua3 OS Explorer 70 Abingdon, Wantage

GRID REFERENCE: SU 604895

PARKING: Long-stay car park in St George's Road, Wallingford

THE PUB: Town Arms

❶ Turn **L** out of car park and walk along St George's Road. Turn **L** into High Street and head towards town centre. Wallingford is one of those towns that can hold your attention for hours. Its churches are well worth a look, its museum and Town Hall attract lots of visitors, and the grass-covered remains of its ruined castle serve as a reminder of the bitter struggle for supremacy during the Civil War. Continue past library and **Wallingford Museum** and keep ahead to junction with St Martin's Street and Castle Street. **Town Hall** is on R and remains of **castle** on L. Continue over junction and pass Lamb Arcade and **George Hotel**. On R is spire of St Peter's Church in Thames Street.
❷ Pass **Town Arms** and cross bridge over **Thames**. Continue along road and, about 80yds (73m) beyond traffic lights, turn **R** at bridleway ('Ridgeway and Grim's Ditch'). Follow enclosed track between fences, keeping river and adjacent meadows to your R. Keep **L** at waymark and stay on bridleway. Cross footpath and now woodland gives way to open fields.
❸ At junction with concrete farm track, turn **R** and head towards buildings of **Newnham Farm**. Keep **L** and walk along track to **St Mary's Church** at Newnham Murren. With church on your R, continue on tree-lined bridleway. Approaching **A4130**, veer **R** at sign ('cyclists dismount') then follow pavement along to bridge over Thames. Once over bridge, veer **R** and follow tarmac path down bank to riverside.
❹ Turn **L** and head upstream towards Wallingford, passing boathouse. Continue on Thames Path to tarmac drive running between houses. Just beyond property, '**The Boathouse**', turn **R** by flood marker (1894). Follow path to road by St Leonard's Church. Turn **R**; follow road along to St Peter's Street. Turn **L** then **L** again into Wood Street. After 70yds (64m) turn **R** into Mousey Lane and make for **Town Hall**. Retrace your steps along High Street to reach car park.

173 GREYS COURT OXFORDSHIRE

4 MILES (6.4KM) 1hr 45min

PATHS: Field and parkland paths, drives and tracks, stretches of road (can be busy), 12 stiles

SUGGESTED MAP: aqua3 OS Explorer 171 Chiltern Hills West

GRID REFERENCE: SU 726823

PARKING: Spaces by church at Rotherfield Greys

THE PUB: Maltsters Arms, Rotherfield Greys

❶ With church lychgate on L-H side, walk towards **Maltsters Arms** pub. Turn immediately **L** before William's Cottage to join gravel drive. Follow footpath alongside churchyard and make for stile ahead. Head obliquely **R**, across field to another stile, pass through gap in hedgerow then veer half-**R** in next field. Make for stile, cross and join path.
❷ Turn **R**; pass between trees, hedges and margins of bracken. Path graduates to a track and passes alongside **golf course** before crossing drive to gate. Continue ahead to road; turn **R**. Pass turning for **Shepherd's Green** on L and follow road along to **Greys Green**. Veer **L** on to green and aim to **R** of **pavilion**. Join footpath, cross stile and descend very steeply to next stile. Pass under power lines in pasture and keep fence on L. Make for stile, cross lane to footpath and after a few steps reach stile. Continue towards **Greys Court**.
❸ Walk to admission kiosk and swing **L**, following footpath to next boundary. Continue on path to pond and along section of boardwalk. Pass alongside fence and woodland, avoiding gate and steps to reach stile on **L** just beyond them by corrugated barn. Cross stile and keep to R-H side, with fence and field on R. Turn **R** at drive and make for road ahead. Turn R at this junction and continue, passing **Broadplat**.
❹ Keep **L** at next junction and continue along road to reach track on **R** ('Rotherfield Greys'). Continue ahead when track bends to L, and follow rough track ahead. Pass footpath sign and look for stile on **L**. Follow path down hillside, keeping belt of woodland on R. Beyond it, continue on grassy path with fence on R. Turn **R**, across stile in field corner and follow path alongside fencing. After 60yds (55m), look for stile on **L**. Cross it and maintain same direction. Make for stile ahead then swing **L** and follow path up slope and back to road opposite **church** at **Rotherfield Greys**.

174 WIGHTWICK WEST MIDLANDS

4.5 MILES (7.2KM) 1hr 30min

PATHS: Canal tow path, disused railway track and field paths, 1 stile

SUGGESTED MAP: aqua3 OS Explorer 219 Wolverhampton & Dudley

GRID REFERENCE: SP 870982

PARKING: Near Mermaid pub, Wightwick

THE PUB: Mermaid

❶ From car park, cross A454 at pedestrian crossing to enter Windmill Lane. Bear **R** and descend to tow path of **Staffordshire and Worcestershire Canal**, heading in southwesterly direction. Initially tow path leads along back of private residences. After passing Cee-Ders Club (on far side of canal), you reach open countryside, with ducks, coots and moorhens for company. This stretch of the canal is similar to a river and you are likely to see anglers fishing for perch, roach, chub, bream or carp. You may even see a colourful narrowboat pass by. Continue beneath bridge No 55 (**Castlecroft Bridge**) and along tow path until you come to bridge No 54 (**Mops Farm Bridge**).
❷ Leave tow path and cross bridge. Go **R** past Pool Hall Cottages and follow waymarkers of **Monarch's Way**, heading generally southeast. At first, path is to R of field hedge then, later, it crosses over to L-H side until you come to stile to reach Langley Road.
❸ Go **L** along road to junction and then bear **R** through small gateway to descend to dismantled railway. Head **L** and follow **Kingswinford (South Staffordshire) Railway Walk**. This is easy walking and you are likely to meet a number of other walkers and possibly cyclists. Continue for about 2 miles (3.2km). You will eventually pass beneath road bridge near **Castlecroft**; following this there are moments when the scene opens up to give lovely views. After passing **Wolverhampton Environment Centre** you come to **Compton**. Leave disused railway line and climb up to **A454**, going **L**.
❹ Go **L** again and descend by side of **Bridge No 59** restaurant on to tow path and take it back to bridge No 56, passing couple of lock gates and number of moored narrowboats. Go beneath Bridge No 56 and leave canal on to pavement of Windmill Lane. Continue towards main **A454** road and cross over to return to **Mermaid** pub in **Wightwick**.

175 BERKSWELL WEST MIDLANDS

4.5 MILES (7.2KM) 1hr 30min

PATHS: Field paths and parkland footpaths, 13 stiles

SUGGESTED MAP: aqua3 OS Explorer 221 Coventry & Warwick

GRID REFERENCE: SP 244791

PARKING: Free car park near church in Berkswell

THE PUB: Bear Inn

❶ From car park, near **church** in **Berkswell**, follow **Heart of England Way** to Meriden Road. Go **L** along this road for 300yds (274m), then cross over and go **R** up farm lane, passing **Blind Hall Farm**.
❷ At end of lane/track cross stile by farm gate, bear **L** and walk along field edge to its **L** corner. Go **L** over 2 stiles and continue ahead by hedge. Waymarked footpath weaves in and out of hedge. After going through wide hedge gap, walk to field corner and go **L** past small pond until you come to some houses in **Four Oaks**. Bear **L**, cross over large cultivated field diagonally and exit on to Meriden Road. Cross road and continue down driveway to **R** of **Wilmot Cottage** opposite, going through gateway on to farmland. Path goes to **R** of hedge, offering clear view of Home Farm to L, then crosses field diagonally. In about 625yds (571m) you will reach corner of Mercote Hall Lane.
❸ Go **L** along lane for about 0.5 mile (800m), passing Park Farm complex. Walk along lane past large enclosed **sand and gravel pits**.
❹ At end of pit area go **L** along footpath and over footbridges, ascending to **L** of hedge on approach to **Marsh Farm**.
❺ Just beyond farm, turn **L** and follow farm track towards **Sixteen Acre Wood**. Cross stile into wood and take track along wood edge for some 700yds (640m). Continue by hedge and go through strip of trees into parkland. Follow path for some 650yds (594m) and then enjoy a magnificent view of **Berkswell Hall Lake** before entering trees and going through kissing gate to rejoin **Heart of England Way**. Cross track and stile on to planked area with **Berkswell Hall** to your L. Continue through gates back into Berkswell. Just after going through church gate, bear **L** to return to car park.

176 EDGE HILL WARWICKSHIRE

3.5 MILES (5.7KM) 1hr 30min

PATHS: Field and woodland paths, country road, 6 stiles

SUGGESTED MAP: aqua3 OS Explorer 206 Edge Hill & Fenny Compton

GRID REFERENCE: SP 370481

PARKING: Radway village

THE PUB: Rose and Crown

❶ Walk through **Radway** to **church**. Veer **L** into West End and pass alongside grounds of **The Grange** on your L. Curve **L** by pond and thatched cottages. **Methodist chapel** can be seen here. Follow lane as it becomes stony track and go through kissing gate into field. Walk ahead to stile and continue ahead across sloping field towards Radway Tower, now **Castle Inn**. Look for gap in hedge by inspection cover and maintain direction, climbing steeply towards wooded escarpment.
❷ Make for stile and enter wood. Continue straight over junction and follow markers for Macmillan Way up slope to road. With Castle Inn on your R, turn **L** for several paces to **R-H** path running between Cavalier Cottage and Rupert House. Make for stile, turn **L** at road and walk along to **Ratley**. When road bends L by copper beech tree, turn **R** to fork. Veer **R** and follow High Street down and round to **L**. Pass **church** and keep **L** at triangular junction.
❸ With **Rose and Crown** to R, follow Chapel Lane and, when it bends L, keep ahead up steps to stile. Keep fence on L initially before striking out across field to stone stile in boundary hedge. Turn **R** and follow **Centenary Way** across field to line of trees. Swing **L** and now skirt field to gap in corner. Follow path down to galvanised kissing gate, cut across field to footbridge then head up slope to gap in field boundary.
❹ Turn **L** and follow road past bungalows. Pass **Battle Lodge** and make for junction. Cross over and join woodland path running along top of escarpment. On reaching steps on L, turn **R** and descend steeply via staircase known as **Jacobs Ladder**. Drop down to gate then follow path straight down field to a stile at bottom. Go through kissing gate beyond it then pass alongside private garden to reach drive. Follow it to road and turn **L** for centre of **Radway**.

177 STUDLEY
WARWICKSHIRE

4.75 MILES (7.7KM) 1hr 15min

PATHS: Field paths and parkland, 9 stiles

SUGGESTED MAP: aqua3 OS Explorer 220 Birmingham

GRID REFERENCE: SP 072637

PARKING: Atcheson Close car park, Studley

THE PUB: Barley Mow

❶ Walk down Needle Close to Alcester road; go **L** to traffic island. Cross and go to Priory Court on footpath to **L** of houses. Cross footbridge; bear **R** to stile into field, aiming towards 2nd stile at corner of field opposite. Head **L**; follow waymarker, going **L** alongside field hedge for about 0.5 mile (800m). Turn **R** at **The Dairy** and continue in northeasterly direction.
❷ Go **R** between buildings of **Field Farm** and walk along farm drive. In 100yds (91m), go **R** over stile crossing corner of field on to Hardwick Lane. Cross lane, walk between **Spinney Cottages**, then over parkland until you reach driveway near glasshouses. Cross over driveway, go through handgate and walk to **R** of cottage to enter wood. Follow footpath through trees and continue ahead by field edge until you reach end of woodland. Turn **L** and walk up farm track past duck pond and farm building.
❸ Go **R** to corner and cross next field diagonally to footbridge, then ascend to **L** of **Morton Common Farm**. Follow farm drive to road. Go **R** along road for 150yds (137m), then **R** again over footbridge and cross over cultivated field. At farm gate, bear **R** and walk by field hedge on to farm track.
❹ Continue **R** along track. In about 0.5 mile (800m), it arcs R; turn **L** here across middle of field towards Studley's **Church of the Nativity of the Blessed Virgin Mary**. Go through overflow graveyard and enter main churchyard, passing church and leaving via lychgate on to lane.
❺ Go **L** and cross lane and stile. Descend through pastureland, cross footbridge over **River Arrow**, then bear **R** and walk along river bank towards **Studley**. A handgate leads into end of Wickham Road. Head **L** along side of housing estate; bear **R** into Gunners Lane. Go **L** up Castle Road to Alcester road, cross and ascend Needle Close to car park.

178 WELFORD-ON-AVON
WARWICKSHIRE

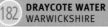

3 MILES (4.8KM) 1hr

PATHS: Village footpaths and field paths, 3 stiles

SUGGESTED MAP: aqua3 OS Explorer 205 Stratford-upon-Avon & Evesham

GRID REFERENCE: SP 148522

PARKING: Near Bell Inn, Welford-on-Avon

THE PUB: The Bell

❶ From your parking place, come out on to main road in Welford and go **L** down footpath at side of parking area. At end of path, near Daffodil Cottage, go **R** along footpath past back of houses until you come to end of Church Lane, by Applegarth House. Continue through gate and follow green path at back of more houses to reach main road once again, then go **L** along pavement for about 100yds (91m).
❷ Go **L** again into entrance gate of **Synder Meadow Sports Ground**. Walk along track then go over 2 stiles to continue along footpath down to **River Avon**. At river, go **L**; follow bank for 500yds (457m).
❸ Go over stile at end of field and **L** up Boat Lane, lined with beautiful old thatched black-and-white cottages. Look out for **Ten Penny Cottage**. Near top of lane is St Peter's Church; go **R** here along Headland Road. When you are opposite Mill Lane, turn **L** along footpath at back of houses. You will pass by extension to graveyard of St Peter's Church and in about 400yds (366m) come to junction of paths. Go **L** and walk up to High Street to emerge opposite Maypole Wine Stores, near the famous maypole. There has been a maypole on the village green since the 14th century and the village children still dance around it each year.
❹ Turn **R** along pavement for few paces, then cross and go down another waymarked footpath, past more thatched cottages. Walk through Pool Close to Chapel Street (chapel is on L). Go **R** along Chapel Street, then **R** again down Millers Close towards **Weston-on-Avon**.
❺ At crossroads bear **L** to descend bridlepath set just above **River Avon**. Follow it as it arcs **L** then on to Duck Lane by another thatched house, '**Pear Tree Close**'. At next residential drive, go **R** up hedged path and walk up to High Street, where you will emerge at junction with Church Street. **Bell Inn** is on R.

179 STRATFORD-ON-AVON
WARWICKSHIRE

2.5 MILES (4KM) 1hr

PATHS: Riverside paths and street pavements, no stiles

SUGGESTED MAP: aqua3 OS Explorer 205 Stratford-upon-Avon & Evesham

GRID REFERENCE: SP 205547

PARKING: Recreation Ground pay-and-display car park

THE PUB: Garrick Inn

❶ From car park, walk along banks of **River Avon** opposite the famous **Royal Shakespeare Theatre**. Pass weir until you come to footbridge over river, just in front of A4390 road bridge.
❷ Go **R** over footbridge and bear **R** past old mill building into Mill Lane. Continue up Mill Lane and go through churchyard of **Holy Trinity Church**, walking around church to see river view. Leave churchyard through main gate into Old Town and follow pavement. Just before reaching turn into Southern Lane, go **R** into New Place Gardens and walk up to **Brass Rubbing Centre**. Continue past ferry and stroll through attractive Theatre Gardens by side of Avon, exiting into Waterside and passing by frontage of old theatre building.
❸ Go **L** up Chapel Lane, taking time to wander through Knot Gardens on your way up to Chapel Street. At top of lane is Guild Chapel to Shakespeare's Grammar School, with New Place Gardens to your R.
❹ Go **R** along Chapel Street, passing Shakespeare Hotel and **Town Hall** into High Street. Harvard House is on L, near black-and-white **Garrick Inn**. At end of High Street, bear **L** around traffic island into Henley Street and walk along pedestrianised area that takes you past **Shakespeare's Birthplace** and the Museum. At top of Henley Street, bear **R** and then **L** into Birmingham Road. Cross road at pedestrian crossing and go **L** up to traffic-lights.
❺ Head **R** up Clopton Road for 100yds (91m), then descend to tow path of **Stratford-upon-Avon Canal**. Follow this, going southeast. Cross over canal at bridge No 68 and continue along tow path into Bancroft Gardens by canal basin where you will see an array of colourful narrowboats and the Royal **Shakespeare Theatre**. Cross old Tram Bridge to car park on R.

180 POLESWORTH
WARWICKSHIRE

4 MILES (6.4KM) 1hr 30min

PATHS: Canal tow paths, field paths and residential areas, 3 stiles

SUGGESTED MAP: aqua3 OS Explorer 232 Nuneaton & Tamworth

GRID REFERENCE: SK 262024

PARKING: Hall Court car park (free)

THE PUB: Fosters Yard

❶ From car park at Hall Court, walk into Bridge Street and bear **L** towards bridge. After walking 25yds (23m), turn **L** into alleyway that leads to public footpath ('River Anker'). Cross footbridge over river, then bear **L** through gardens by riverside on footpath that arcs gently **R** towards bridge No 51 over **Coventry Canal**. Descend to canal; turn **L** along tow path, which you follow for 1.5 miles (2.4km). Before walking beneath railway line look up to R and on far bank you will see **obelisk** on **Hoo Hill**. **Stiper's Hill** is to L. Continue beneath main electrified railway line.
❷ Leave Coventry Canal's tow path at bridge No 49 and ascend on to road going generally northwest past **Kitchens Bridge Cottage**. Soon after passing cottage look out for hedge gap on **L-H** side and proceed through this to cross footbridge over railway line. Now climb hill passing through farm gate close to buildings of **Dordon Hall** farm and continue up to road. Go **L** along road; turn **R** at junction, following signpost to Dordon. Continue along Dunne Lane into village.
❸ Immediately after passing house, '**Lyndon Lea**', turn to **R** down track that leads to stile on to footpath over open farmland. Follow this footpath, heading generally northwards, towards prominent trees of **The Hollies**. Continue past trees, crossing couple of stiles and soon you will find yourself walking along stone track that becomes Common Lane on approach to **Polesworth**. Take pavement of lane through residential estate until you reach B5000 Tamworth to Grendon road. Cross road (take care, it can be busy) and stroll down to park area by **River Anker**; cross back over footbridge. Public footpath now leads up to junction of paths where you go **R**, towards **abbey**. Bear **L** and leave through Old Nunnery Gateway on to High Street. Now turn **L** and continue along High Street, past **Nethersole Centre** and turn **L** again into Bridge Street to return to Hall Court car park.

181 DASSETT
WARWICKSHIRE

7.25 MILES (11.7KM) 2hrs 30min

PATHS: Field paths and farm tracks, 15 stiles Hilly countryside

SUGGESTED MAP: aqua3 OS Explorer 206 Edge Hill & Fenny Compton

GRID REFERENCE: SP 394523

PARKING: Burton Dassett Hills Country Park car park – small charge

THE PUB: Inn at Farnborough

❶ From car park in **country park** descend on footpath to **R** of **Bonfire Hill** into **Northend** to arrive at Hampden Court.
❷ Go **R** along main street for 300yds (274m), then **R** again through pair of kissing gates. Follow footpath heading generally eastwards towards Fenny Compton, crossing mixture of pastureland, fields and stiles.
❸ Enter **Fenny Compton** over stile, then head along Grant's Close into Avon Dassett road. Walk past Duckett Cottage and go through handgate to **R** of village church. Now bear **R** and cross over pastureland to road known as The Slade. Go **L** along road past large farm barn, then **R** over footbridge into large cultivated field. Follow footpath signs and cross this field to 2nd footbridge, then walk up next field, aiming for marker post in hedge ahead. Here go **L** and walk along field edge – from the top of the hill there is a fine view of the landmark four-sail windmill at Chesterton and the Post Office Communication towers near Daventry. Follow direction of waymarkers, climb **Windmill Hil**l, then descend over farm fields and hedged footpath into **Farnborough**, emerging on main street near **Butchers Arms** pub.
❹ Head **R**, along main street, and bear **R** past entrance gates to National Trust's **Farnborough Hall**. Continue up road to **L**, past lake, walking along footpath inside trees. At end of woodland continue along road for 500yds (457m) then go **R** over stile and cross 2 cultivated fields into pastureland. Descend to **L** of large barn, which brings you to **Avon Dassett**.
❺ Go **L** past church and in 75yds (69m) go **R** up track to **R** of **Avon Inn** into open countryside. Up to R is the impressive **Bitham Hall**. Waymarked footpath hugs top of fields until you arrive in **Burton Dassett**, passing by its lovely Norman church. Continue up road to return to car park near Beacon viewing point on **Magpie Hill** (630ft/192m).

182 DRAYCOTE WATER
WARWICKSHIRE

6.5 MILES (10.4KM) 2hrs

PATHS: Reservoir paths and field paths, 7 stiles

SUGGESTED MAP: aqua3 OS Explorer 222 Rugby & Daventry

GRID REFERENCE: SP 462690

PARKING: Pay-and-display car park at Draycote Water

THE PUB: Dun Cow, Dunchurch

❶ From **Draycote Water** car park proceed up to reservoir then bear **R** following tarmac lane along top of **Farnborough Dam** wall to reach **Toft Bay**.
❷ At end of Toft Bay go **R** and leave reservoir grounds via handgate. Continue ahead then go **R** and follow waymarker signs to footpath that climbs past llama pens up towards **Toft House**. Continue along hedged footpath to **L** of house. This bends **L** on to lane where you go **R** up to **A426** Rugby to Dunchurch road. Go **L** along road, cross road bridge and enter **Dunchurch**, passing thatched houses. Village Square and St Peter's Church are R of crossroads, with **Dun Cow**, an old coaching inn, immediately opposite.
❸ At crossroads, go **L** along pavement of B4429 past the Dunchurch & Thurlaston WMC. Bear **L** along School Street and follow footpath past more thatched houses and infant **school** down to Dunchurch Scout Group Hall. Here, go **R** then **L** along footpath to **R** of playing fields. Continue along hedged path and proceed to **R** of **Ryefield Farm**. Go ahead over pastureland then pass under M45 road bridge before diagonally crossing next field to 2 stiles to **Thurlaston**.
❹ Go to **L** by St Edmund's Church and down concrete farm track to handgate and footbridge to enter perimeter of **Draycote Water**.
❺ Go **R** along walkway by side of reservoir around **Biggin Bay**. To your R **Thurlaston Grange** can be seen, then you pass **golf course**. Continue around end of reservoir, passing by **treatment works**, and then stroll along **Draycote Bank**. To your R is spire of Bourton-on-Dunsmore church about 1 mile (1.6km) away; to its R is Bourton Hall. After passing by picnic area and just before reaching yachting area go **R** on footpath that leads up on to **Hensborough Hill** for a fine view. Meander past trig point, some 371ft (113m) above sea level, and return to car park.

Central
ENGLAND (NORTH)

Contents

		page
183	Shropshire Canal, Staffordshire	205
184	Brewood, Staffordshire	207
185	Cannock Chase, Staffordshire	209
186	Abbots Bromley, Staffordshire	211
187	Whittington, Staffordshire	213
188	Osmaston, Derbyshire	215
189	Calke Abbey, Derbyshire	217
190	Shipley, Derbyshire	219

		page
191	Tissington Trail, Derbyshire	221
192	Wolfscote Dale, Derbyshire	223
193	Hartington, Derbyshire/ Staffordshire	225
194	Matlock, Derbyshire	227
195	Hurdlow, Derbyshire	229
196	Lathkill Dale, Derbyshire	231
197	Bakewell, Derbyshire	233
198	Monsal Dale, Derbyshire	235

		page
199	Miller's Dale, Derbyshire	237
200	Castleton, Derbyshire	239
201	Stanage Edge, Derbyshire	241
202	Derwent Valley, Derbyshire	243
203	The Pennine Way, Derbyshire	245
204	Hayfield, Derbyshire	247
205	Longdendale, Derbyshire	249
206 to 211	Staffordshire	251
212 to 217	Derbyshire	252

CENTRAL ENGLAND (NORTH)

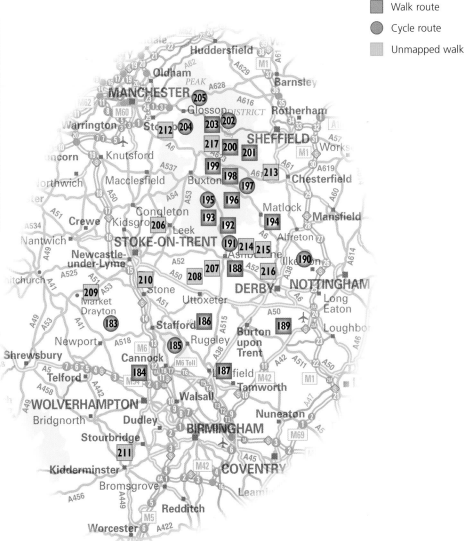

KEY

- Walk route
- Cycle route
- Unmapped walk

did you know?

Despite the increasing popularity of railways as a means of transporting raw materials and goods, the Shropshire Canal remained in use until World War One. At the beginning of the 20th century, for example, a chocolate maker by the name of Cadbury used it to pick up milk from farms between Norbury Junction and his factory at Knighton. Farmers left churns at collecting points along the tow path, and they were then collected and returned as empties at the end of the day.

Bluebells (Hyacinthoides nonscripta)

The Shropshire Canal

With more miles of canal than any other county, what better way to discover Staffordshire's countryside?

Shropshire Canal

The Shropshire Canal was built between 1830 and 1835 under the direction of Thomas Telford, creating a more direct link than hitherto between the industrial towns of England's heartland and the seaports along the Dee and Mersey rivers. A branch from Norbury ran to Wappenshall Junction on the edge of Telford where, via the Shrewsbury Canal and the Hay Inclined Plane, boats could reach the ironworks and potteries of the Ironbridge Gorge. From the very beginning, canals proved their worth in moving heavy and bulky cargoes cheaply and quickly, and the late 18th and early 19th centuries saw a period of spectacular industrial growth as the network spread across the country. All operated on a system

The Shropshire Canal at Gnosall Heath

of tolls to cover the cost of construction and maintenance and there was intense competition between rival routes to attract trade. Junctions like that here at Norbury would have been controlled with a toll bar, where charges were levied on the type of goods and weight carried. There would also have been a certain amount of reloading too, as cargoes were split or combined for the various destinations served by the separate branches. Alongside the canals, inns, stables and blacksmiths sprang up to provide sustenance for the bargees and the horses that pulled the boats. Workyards were also necessary to undertake repairs on the barges as well as to provide depots for the gangs maintaining the canal itself.

The branch to Wappenshall and Telford fell into disuse during the 1930s, the trade having been taken over by the railways. By the end of the war, it had been completely abandoned and much of it was filled in. You can still trace its ghostly course on the map, where odd short stretches are shown as pools. The main Shropshire Canal

survived and is today busy with leisure boats. Set against the backdrop of buildings at Norbury Junction, it takes little imagination to envisage how the waterway might have looked during its heyday.

the ride

1 Out of the car park go right and then left to pedal through the village, signed to **Oulton and Norbury Junction**. Keep with the main lane as it bends right past a track leading to the striking village **church**, a large building, dedicated to St Peter, of much weathered sandstone that nestles below a massive brick tower. Leaving the village, go left at a fork signed to **Norbury Junction and Gnosall**.

2 You will be passing through **Norbury Junction** on the way back, so for the time being, carry on over the canal bridge and continue along the lane behind the old canal offices and **workshops**. Beside the lane is a **millennium boulder**, similar to one beside the village hall, an erratic stranded as the vast ice sheets that covered this part of the country melted at the end of the last ice age, some 10,000 years ago. Beyond **cottages**, the lane falls towards a wood,

A barge on the Shropshire Canal

| 1h30 | 6.5 MILES | 10.6 KM | LEVEL 123 |

MAP: Explorer 243 Market Drayton, Loggerheads & Eccleshall

START/FINISH: Norbury Village Hall; grid ref: SJ 782235

TRAILS/TRACKS: canal towpath (one short grass section) and quiet lanes

LANDSCAPE: open countryside and woodland

PUBLIC TOILETS: none on route

TOURIST INFORMATION: Stafford, tel 01785 619619

CYCLE HIRE: none locally

THE PUB: The Navigation Inn, Gnosall

❗ One main road crossing, two dark bridges, tow paths (can be muddy after rain)

Getting to the start
Norbury lies 8.5 miles (13.7km) west of Stafford. An unclassified road off the A519 3 miles (4.8km) north of Newport leads into the village.

Why do this cycle ride?
An easy uncomplicated ride along quiet and gently undulating country lanes to the village of Gnosall Heath, where there is a splendid canalside pub. The return is along the canal, often busy with colourful boats plying their way through the Heart of England.

Researched and written by: Dennis Kelsall

183

🚲 CYCLE

Pheasant
(Phasianus colchicus)

what to look for

Along the edge of Shelmore Wood you might spot what look like street-lamp covers lining the path; these are in fact pheasant-feeders, designed to keep the seed dry for the hand-reared birds.

there bending sharply right to pass under a **bridge** (beware of traffic).

3 At the junction beyond, go left towards **Gnosall**, the lane rising gently along the base of a high **wooded embankment** upon which the canal runs. After a mile (1.6km), it twists beneath the canal once more (again watch out for traffic) and climbs to a bend beyond. Keep going with the undulating lane, eventually passing beneath a bridge that once carried the Stafford Newport Railway to a **T-junction** with the main road at the end.

4 Turn right, crossing the canal to find **The Navigation** on the right. If going to the pub, there are steps to the canal towpath from the car park, but an easier way lies down a **ramp** on the left-hand side of the road. Double back under the bridge and cycle away past the pub beside the canal, shortly going beneath the railway

again. The **bridge** here is very wide, the passage almost tunnel-like, not due to carrying several tracks, but because it is skewed across the canal. Such bridges were disproportionately expensive if built in brick or stone, and it was only the invention of the skew arch that allowed the bridge to be preserved within the width of the upper passage. Shortly emerging from a **cutting**, there are pleasing views across the open countryside. The way continues to **Shelmore Wood**, where there is a **stop lock**, a device inserted periodically along the canal for isolating individual sections so that they could be drained for maintenance. Carry on in trees for another 1.25 miles (2km) to **Norbury Junction**, there crossing a bridge over the abandoned Wappenshall Branch to reach **The Junction pub**.

5 Leave the canal for the lane, and retrace your outward route left back to the car park by the village hall in Norbury.

The Navigation Inn

Church of St Mary and St Barlock, Norbury

Constructed to serve the needs of the workers building the Shropshire Canal in the 1830s, the Navigation is a traditional, cream-painted pub smack beside the canal, with several cosy rooms adorned with brassware. There's also an airy conservatory dining area which overlooks the garden and passing canal boats.

Food
Standard pub food is available, the snack menu listing ploughman's lunches, a good range of sandwiches and various basket meals. The carte extends the choice to include steak and kidney pie, jumbo haddock and lamb shank, while the specials board may add wild boar, liver and bacon and fresh fish dishes.

Family facilities
Families can expect a good welcome here as children are allowed throughout the pub. Youngsters have a standard children's menu and they will love exploring the play area in a canal-side garden.

Alternative refreshment stops
The Junction pub at Norbury Junction.

☞ Where to go from here
At Weston-under-Lizard you'll find Weston Park (www.weston-park.com), a fine mansion built in 1671. It stands in elegant gardens and a vast park with three lakes, a miniature railway, a woodland adventure playground, an animal centre and deer park. The house contains a magnificent collection of pictures, furniture and tapestries. Take a self-guided tour of the Wedgwood Ceramic Factory at Barlaston (www.wedgwood.com) and learn about the story of Wedgwood. The visitor centre has a film theatre, exhibition area and a demonstration/hands-on area.

about the pub

The Navigation Inn
Newport Road, Gnosall
Staffordshire ST20 0BM
Tel: 01785 822327

DIRECTIONS: beside the canal and A518 Newport road just west of the village; Point 4 of the route

PARKING: 50

OPEN: daily; all day Sunday

FOOD: daily; all day Sunday

BREWERY/COMPANY: Banks Brewery

REAL ALE: Banks Bitter & Original, Greene King Old Speckled Hen, guest beer

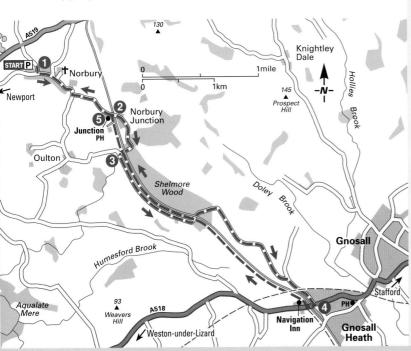

Royal Air Force Museum

More than 80 historic aircraft are displayed in three heated wartime hangars at the Royal Air Force Museum, Cosford. The Research and Development Collection includes the Notable TSR2, Fairey Delta, Bristol 188 and many more important aircraft.

At the RAF Cosford Air Show, an annual event usually held in June, you can see displays from a wide variety of aircraft, hundreds of exhibits on the ground, military demonstrations, stalls and children's entertainment. This is a great day out for all ages.

Brewood and the Shropshire Union Canal

A walk skirting a reservoir and taking in the intersection of two remarkable feats of engineering.

Romans at Brewood

The first thing you need to know about Brewood is that it's pronounced 'brood', and getting this right first time round will instantly endear you to locals. The name, cited as Breude in the Domesday Book (1086), is a hybrid word from the Celtic 'bre', or hill, and the Old English 'wuda', meaning wood.

It was during the Roman occupation of Britain that the area to the north of Brewood was first established as a main transport route, for it was here that Watling Street was built, stretching from London (Londinium) all the way to present-day Wroxeter, just to the west of Shrewsbury. It was just one of the dozens of major roads built by the Romans across Britain, the longest of which were Fosse Way (from Exeter to Lincoln), Ermine Street (from London to York) and of course Watling Street, built in the first years of the invasion (AD 100), and later extended to Chester.

Roman roads in Britain were an extension of a systematic network connecting Rome to the four corners of its vast empire, built principally as a means of moving its great armies quickly and efficiently across occupied countries. In order to do this they had to be exceptionally well constructed. They were usually built on a raised embankment (to allow adequate drainage) made out of rubble obtained from drainage ditches built on either side. Next came the layer of sand, or gravel and sand, sometimes mixed with clay; and finally the whole thing was metalled with flint, finer gravel or even the slag from the smelting of iron. The finished road was often several feet thick, cambered to allow water to run off it and with curb stones on each side to channel any excess water.

Given the complexity of the roads, the huge distances covered and the realisation that every single inch was laboriously built by hand, the fact that many Roman roads – or at least their foundations – still exist today provides mute testimony to the mind-boggling efforts of their builders. In addition to being well designed and well maintained, however, Roman roads also invariably followed straight lines. Today's A5 follows the route of Watling Street for much of its length, and you only have to glance at an atlas to see how much straighter it is than any modern road. This was achieved by lining up marker posts and the result meant both faster journey times and a much more efficient communications network.

It's worth noting that the Shropshire Union Canal, which bisects Watling Street just to the north of Brewood, was built along similar principles, raised on great embankments and built in a series of straight lines, ultimately to improve travel times.

the walk

1 From the Bridge Inn car park go straight across the main road and down some steps to the **canal**. Go right at the bottom of the steps and follow the canal **tow path** as far as the A5 and then through **Stretton Spoil Banks** to the bridge near **Lapley Wood Farm**.

2 Cross over the **bridge** and, at the wide sandy track, turn left for 75yds (69m). Just after the track bears right, go through the gate in the hedge to your right. Follow the **hedge** along the edge of the field and then along a **dirt trail** through a thin strip of woodland.

3 At the end of the trees go through a **gate**, avoid a path seen on the map running off to the left and cross the **pasture** to the corner. Go through another gate and continue in the same direction along the left-hand edge of the field. At the end of this long field go through the gate and across another small field to the courtyard of **White Gate Plantation**.

4 Skirt round the left-hand edge of the courtyard to reach the gate on to the **A5**. Take care crossing this busy main road and then head left for 50yds (46m) before turning right along the **metalled farm road**.

The Shropshire Union Canal

WALK

2h00 | **5.75 MILES** | **9.2 KM** | **LEVEL 123**

MAP: OS Explorer 242 Telford, Ironbridge & The Wrekin

START/FINISH: ample side-street parking in Brewood; grid ref: SK 880088

PATHS: tow paths, grass trails and roads, 2 stiles

LANDSCAPE: canal, farmland and reservoir

PUBLIC TOILETS: none on route

TOURIST INFORMATION: Stafford, tel 01785 619619

THE PUB: The Bridge Inn, Brewood

❶ Busy village centre and crossing the A5

Getting to the start

Brewood lies to the south of the A5 and the west of the A449, north of Wolverhampton. Follow the signs into Brewood and make for the Bridge Inn at the western end of the village by the bridge over the Shropshire Union Canal.

Researched and written by:
Nick Channer, Paul Grogan

The mid-19th century church of
St Mary, Brewood, close to the canal

The Royal Oak, frequently seen on pub signs throughout the country, commemorates the significant moment in British history when Charles II concealed himself in the spreading branches of an old oak tree in the grounds of Boscobel House before eventually fleeing to France.

Follow this as far as the **Hawkshutts** and, opposite the **farmhouse**, go left through a gate and head straight across the field, past the right-hand corner of the **wood** ahead, and cross the open pasture to a **gate** ahead.

5 After going through the gate, bear right along a path through bushes and trees as far as the gate into another field. Go straight across to a gravel-surfaced **farm track**. Turn right, along this track and then bear left along the road after **Birk's Barn**, following it as far as **Lea Fields Farm**.

6 Turn right through the **farm courtyard**, through a pair of gates. After the second gate go diagonally left across a field in the direction of the **church steeple** until you get to a stile. Cross the stile and

head right round the edge of the field to a **line of trees** down the middle. Head left here, following the line of trees as far as the **gravel track**. Go up the track as far as the canal and then turn right, back towards **St Mary's** and the start.

what to look for

Colonel Carless, a Brewood soldier who fought alongside Charles II at the Battle of Worcester in 1651 and hid with him in the oak tree, is buried in Brewood church cemetery. The church itself, dedicated to St Mary and St Chad, owes its surprising size to the fact that successive Bishops of Lichfield owned a medieval manor near Brewood.

The Bridge Inn

The Bridge was built as a pub during the 19th century to provide refreshment for the canal workers constructing the Shropshire Union Canal beside which it stands. It later served the bargees plying the waters and the horses that pulled the barges were stabled at the back of the pub. Today the welcoming bars bustle with locals and the walkers, fishermen and boating folk using the canal. Particularly popular is the canalside garden and heated patio, as are the Burtonwood beers and the regular entertainment – live jazz, comedy nights and theme evenings.

Food
Snack on sandwiches, filled baguettes and jacket potatoes, or opt for something more substantial, perhaps a suet pudding filled with lamb and mint or steak, ale and mushrooms, or fish and chips with mushy peas, home-made lasagne, or lamb shank with minted gravy.

Family facilities
Families can expect a genuine welcome and small children have their own menu to choose from.

Alternative refreshment stops
The Swan Hotel in Market Street serves food and changing guest beers.

☞ Where to go from here
Boscobel House, 3 miles (4.8km) to the west of Brewood, is famous for the part it played in the Civil War: Charles II fled from the Battle of Worcester and sought sanctuary at the hunting lodge of the royalist Giffard family, hiding himself in an oak tree.

Today, another oak grows on the same site, and the house is now a museum (www.english-heritage.org.uk). At Cosford Aerospace Museum you can see a spectacular collection of carefully arranged aircraft, including the Victor and Vulcan bombers, as well as missiles and engines (www.rafmuseum.org.uk).

about the pub

The Bridge Inn
22 High Green, Brewood
Cannock, Staffordshire ST19 9BD
Tel: 01902 851999

DIRECTIONS: see Getting to the start

PARKING: 40

OPEN: daily; all day April to December

FOOD: daily; all day April to December

BREWERY/COMPANY: Burtonwood Brewery

REAL ALE: Burtonwood Bitter, Mild & Top Hat, West beers

DOGS: allowed in the bar only

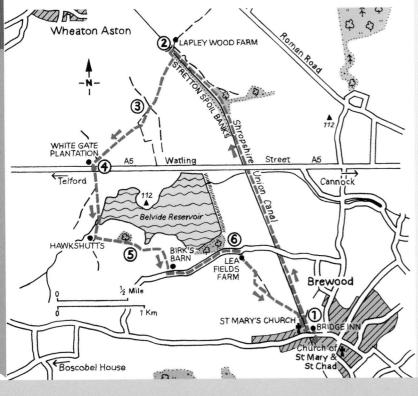

Cannock Chase

Shugborough Hall, built between 1693 and 1794

Woods in Sherbrook Valley, Cannock Chase

185

CYCLE

Cannock Chase   STAFFORDSHIRE

Explore Britain's smallest Area of Outstanding Natural Beauty.

Cannock Chase

Today covering some 26 square miles (6,734ha), Cannock Chase was once part of a vast Norman Royal Forest, where severe penalties were meted out for encroachment and poaching. By the end of the 13th century, the hunting rights had been granted to the Bishop and soon parts of the domain were being enclosed within private estates. By the 15th century, charcoal burners were coppicing the trees, producing fuel to smelt iron, and later large areas were cleared, with sheep being loosed onto the bare heaths. Coal mining began in the 17th century, developing rapidly as the canals arrived around the Chase's perimeter and continuing until the last century.

During World War One, two large infantry training camps were established on the Chase and later, a German prisoner of war camp was opened. There was also a hospital to treat the wounded brought back from France and which was inundated when an influenza epidemic struck the country just after the war ended in 1918. Many tragically died from the illness and are buried in the Commonwealth War Cemetery near Broadhurst Green, whilst next to it is the German War Cemetery, opened in 1967 and in which most of the Germans who died in this country during both wars are now buried.

The extensive forest area encourages a great diversity of wildlife, and amongst the animals you might see are 3 of the 6 species of deer to be found in Britain: fallow, red and the tiny muntjack. There are also foxes, badgers, hares and of course rabbits, with plenty of squirrels, both grey and red. On warm sunny days you may spot an adder or common lizard, whilst in the trees, are cuckoos, green woodpeckers and jays.

the ride

1 Leave the main car park at a large **signpost** to pass the District Office, turning left on a wide drive in front of Swinnerton's **cycle hire centre**. Immediately beyond, look for a track on the right marked '**Fairoak Walk**', which leads eventually to a T-junction. Go right, dropping around a left-hand bend to a second junction. Swing right again, the way still marked 'Fairoak Walk', passing a small **pond** to a fork at the edge of a clearing. Go left and then left again, a little further on, to skirt a **larger pool**. Meeting a broad track go right and then at its end, turn left.

2 Keep ahead past a track to **fishing lakes** on the right, soon reaching another junction. Turn right to climb through a **pine plantation**, meeting a cross-track after the gradient eases. To the right, another steep pull leads to a fork, where you should keep left, dropping sharply to another crossing. Go left, the way undulating more easily and eventually reaching a T-junction. Turn right onto **Marquis Drive**, passing the Park Rangers' depot and then emerging through a **gate**.

3 The **visitor centre** and toilets are off to the left, but the route continues ahead to a lane. Follow it right to a crossroads at **Flints Corner**, where the ongoing path marked '**Heart of England Way**' lies ahead, just to the right of the lane facing you. Go into the trees, soon reaching a crossing track. Turn right and then almost immediately left, doing the same at the next crossing, a little further on, to meet a road.

4 Cross to the continuing path opposite, which drops at the edge of **heather heath**. At a T-junction bear left to continue into the head of **Sherbrook Valley**. Go forward at the first crossing, but then immediately swing right onto a broad stony track, marked as the **cycleway**. A long descent hugs the base of the fold, loosely following the brook from which it takes its name. Part-way down, the track doglegs as another gully comes in from the left, resuming its course to pass a **small wood and pools**. Eventually, after a good 2 miles (3.2km) go right at a junction, crossing the stream at a **ford**. Pedal on along an undulating track, finally bearing left at a fork to arrive at **Beggar's Hill car park**.

5 Turn sharp right, doubling back onto a narrower path that rises gently into **Abraham's Valley**. Where it divides, keep right, climbing more steeply for a while until you reach a broad crossing track. Go right past an open area of younger trees and stay ahead across another wide track onto a narrower gravel way. Shortly, at a **5-way junction**, where just ahead is a **trig point**, turn left, now running easily along the high point of the ride. Continue forward at a later fork, eventually dropping to a T-junction near some **buildings**. Cycling left through a car park, then right, leave along a wide gravel road.

3h30 | 13.2 MILES | 21.2 KM | LEVEL 123

MAP: OS Explorer 6 Cannock Chase and Chasewater

START/FINISH: Birches Valley Forest Centre; grid ref: SK 018171

TRAILS/TRACKS: forest tracks throughout

LANDSCAPE: hilly woodland and heath

PUBLIC TOILETS: at Birches Valley Forest Centre and Cannock Chase Visitor Centre

TOURIST INFORMATION: Stafford, tel 01785 619619

CYCLE HIRE: at start – Swinnerton Cycles, Forest Enterprise, Birches Valley, Lady Hill, Rugeley, tel 01889 575170, www.swinnertoncycles.co.uk

THE PUB: The Horns Inn, Slitting Mill

Road crossings, loose gravel tracks, some overhanging branches, track shared with pedestrians and horses. Some hills with occasional attention to route finding – for older, more experienced children

Getting to the start

Birch Valley Forest Centre is 2 miles (3.2km) west of Rugeley. Take a minor road to Slitting Mill and bear right at a fork approaching the village onto Cannock Chase. The centre is signed to the left

Why do this cycle ride?

A route with plenty of ups and downs that will appeal to adventurous families. The ride reveals many different facets of the Chase, from plantations to natural woodland and open heath. The area abounds in wildlife.

Researched and written by: Dennis Kelsall

Cannock Chase, an area of heath and woodland, is used by thousands of visitors

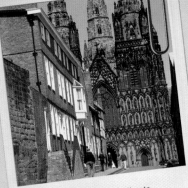

House-lined Westgate leading to Lichfield Cathedral

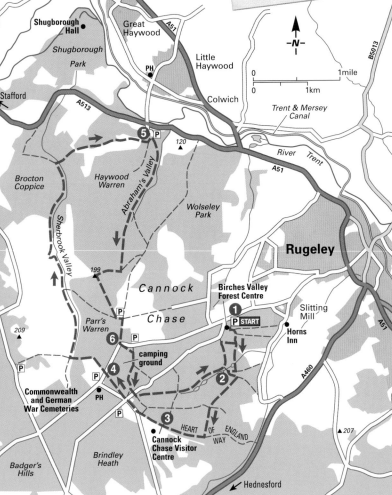

The Horns Inn

Slitting Mill village takes its name from the type of work the mills carried out along the stream, the process of splitting (slitting) wood and metal. Dating back around 200 years, the Horns is a brick-built pub that has been modernised and extended over the years, resulting in a large bar and open-plan dining areas. The atmosphere is bright and cheerful, there are some cosy corners tucked away by the bar, old pictures of the pub on the walls, and the staff are friendly and welcoming. Super summer patio adorned with colourful flower baskets.

Food

Home cooked meals on the printed menu range form pub favourites like chilli, lasagne, steak and kidney pie and fish and chips, to hearty snacks (ploughman's, filled jacket potatoes) and 'sizzle' boards with Thai, Cajun and steak meals.

Family facilities

Children are welcome in the pub and there is a children's menu for younger family members.

Alternative refreshment stops

Light refreshments at Birches Valley Forest Centre and a café at Cannock Chase Visitor Centre.

☞ Where to go from here

Head for Shugborough Hall (www.shugborough.org.uk) on the edge of Cannock Chase. A fine 18th-century mansion, set in 900 magnificent acres, containing collections of ceramics, silver, paintings and French furniture. At Whittington you can visit the Staffordshire Regiment Museum, where exhibits include vehicles, uniforms, weapons, medals and memorabilia relating to 300 years of regimental history, and visitors can also experience a World War One trench system with sound effects (www.staffordshireregimentmuseum.com).

about the pub

The Horns Inn
Slitting Mill Road, Slitting Mill
Rugeley, Staffordshire WS15 2UW
Tel: 01889 586000

DIRECTIONS: load up bikes, turn right out of the car park and right again to the village. At a junction there, go sharp right again to reach the pub.

PARKING: 50

OPEN: daily; all day Friday, Saturday & Sunday

FOOD: daily; all day Friday, Saturday & Sunday

BREWERY/COMPANY: Punch Taverns

REAL ALE: Wells Bombardier, Marston's Pedigree, Tetley, guest beer

6 Meeting the main road at **Rifle Range Corner**, carefully cross to a bridleway opposite. At the end bear right on a broad track, and then branch right again to pedal through a **camping area**. Keep ahead at the far side on a narrower path, gently descending through the trees. At a waymarked junction, go left, following **green and orange markers** out to another road. Cross to a barriered track opposite, almost immediately bearing left into a steadily steepening valley. Keep ahead over a bridleway past **Fairoak Pools**, then at the bottom, go left, climbing to the crest of the rise. Turn off right across a more open area to a crossing track at the far side and bear left and then left again past a **small pond**. The way back lies to the left, retracing your outward route to the Forest Centre.

Great crested grebe
(Podiceps cristatus)

did you know?

The shoreline at the north end of the causeway at Blithfield Reservoir makes a very pleasant spot for a picnic, and in the summer there is often a take-away food outlet selling snacks, hot and cold drinks and ice creams.

Around Abbots Bromley

A colourful and ancient tradition is alive and well in one of the county's most charming villages.

Abbots Bromley

The existence of Abbots Bromley can be traced back to long before the Norman Conquest of England in 1066, through a number of references in charters and wills dating from that time. The first market charter was granted in 1221 for a weekly market and an annual two-day fair to be held in the village, and this fair survives today in the form of a rare and slightly unusual ritual. One theory on the obscure origins of the horn dance is that it derived from an ancient fertility rite, another is that the dance celebrates the establishment of ancient hunting rites.

The horn dance was first performed at the Barthelmy Fair as long ago as 1226. It was originally held on the feast day of St Bartholomew, one of the apostles and the patron saint of tanners, but an alteration to the Gregorian calendar in 1752 changed this date to 4 September. Today it's held on the first weekend after the 4th, with the dance proper taking place on the Monday.

According to custom six pairs of ancient reindeer horns (or more accurately antlers) are collected from St Nicholas's Church just before 8am by a small entourage of dancers comprising – among others – a fool, a hobby horse, a bowman and Maid Marion. The first dance of the day is performed on the village green with music provided by a melodion (a small reed organ similar to an accordion). Then, a tour of the nearby villages, farms and pubs ensues with the final dance taking place back at the village green. In addition to the horn dance proper, this colourful procession also features displays of morris and clog dancing. Other attractions include exhibitions and craft stalls, plus the pleasures of no fewer than five pubs in Abbots Bromley alone. Each year the dance attracts hundreds of visitors from all over the world.

As well as the horn dance, Abbots Bromley also boasts a number of other notable legends. There is the story of the Bagot goats: these black-necked beasts used to roam Bagot Woods to the north of the village and were first given to Sir John Bagot by Richard II at the end of the 14th century. Legend has it that as long as the herd is maintained the Bagot family shall survive.

the walk

1 From the pub cross over to **Schoolhouse Lane**. At the top of the hill turn right along Swan Lane and when you get to the end head right along a path to a stile. Head diagonally left across the field to a gap in the hedge. Go through this gap and continue across the next field to a **footbridge**. After the footbridge keep following the faint grassy trail to a stile in the next boundary.

2 Go across the middle of the field to another stile. Carry on straight up the next field, keeping a hedge just to your left across a series of stiles and fields until you get to a road. Head straight across the road, following a footpath sign and, just as the track heads hard right, go straight on over a **concrete stile** and across the next field.

3 After another stile, follow the curve of a field to the right as far as a **metalled road**. Go left here, following the road and track as far as **Parkside farm gate**. Just before this gate, go through a gate on the right and then left through several **gates**.

4 Follow the hedge, keeping it and the **farmhouse** over to your left. Cross a stile into the wood and go diagonally right through trees to two footbridges and a stile. Leaving the wood behind, head for the far right-hand corner of the field.

5 At the road opposite **Park Lodge** turn left. Just after crossing **Story Brook** head left. At the far left-hand corner of the field, follow the hedge round to the right

A traditional horn-dancing ceremony in Abbots Bromley

2h00 · **5 MILES** · **8 KM** · **LEVEL 123**

MAP: OS Explorer 244 Cannock Chase

START/FINISH: ample street parking in Abbots Bromley; grid ref: SK 079245

PATHS: roads, grass trails and gravel tracks, 16 stiles

LANDSCAPE: farmland and village

PUBLIC TOILETS: none on route

TOURIST INFORMATION: Lichfield, tel 01543 308209

THE PUB: The Goats Head, Abbots Bromley

Getting to the start

Abbots Bromley lies to the south of Uttoxeter, between the A518 and the A515. Follow the B5013 from Uttoxeter or Rugeley, the B5017 and the B5234 from Burton-upon-Trent.

Researched and written by:
Nick Channer, Paul Grogan

Sudbury Hall

If you want to study the woodcarving by Grinling Gibbons and the superb plasterwork and painted ceilings at Sudbury Hall, it's best to avoid dull days and late afternoons towards the end of the season.

Various 'taster tours' held at Sudbury throughout the season include Glimpse of Sudbury, Behind the Scenes and Meet the Butler where visitors experience the hall through the eyes of a family butler in the 1880s.

186

WALK

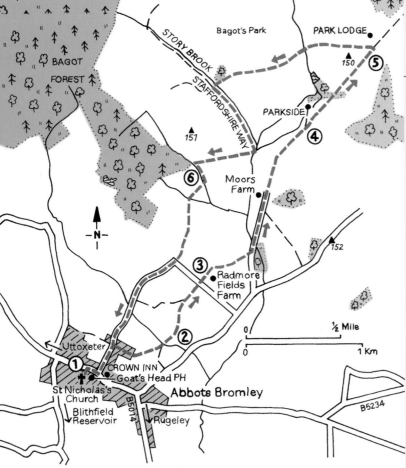

The Goats Head

Dating from the 16th century, this fine black-and-white timbered building overlooks the ancient market cross and village green. Highwayman Dick Turpin is believed to have lodged here after stealing a horse. Beyond the smart and well maintained exterior you'll find two modernised bars, although the carpeted lounge bar does retain some character, notably heavy Tudor beams, standing timbers, open fires and oak settles. There's also plenty of traditional brass, simple prints on the walls and a good mix of sturdy old dining tables. Pleasant rear lawn with views to the church.

Food

The main menus feature traditional meals (home-made steak and kidney pie and fresh cod in beer batter), and there is a light bite menu too. There's an Italian influence to the daily specials blackboard: perhaps Parma ham lasagne, mushroom porcini, steaks, or spaghetti with scallops, mussels and prawns among the choices.

Family facilities

Children are welcome in both bars and the lunchtime light bite menu has dishes and snacks to suit smaller appetites.

Alternative refreshment stops

There are five different pubs to choose from in Abbots Bromley alone.

☛ Where to go from here

Blithfield Reservoir, just to the west of Abbots Bromley, a Site of Special Scientific Interest (SSSI), plays a significant part as a refuge for wildfowl and immigrant waders. East of Uttoxeter is Sudbury Hall, a fine

country house with unusual diapered brickwork, tall chimneys and a Museum of Childhood with a Victorian schoolroom and a collections of toys (www.nationaltrust. org.uk). Head for Burton-upon-Trent and visit the Bass Museum with a unique collection of artefacts and memorabilia (www.bass-museum.com).

about the pub

The Goats Head
Abbots Bromley, Rugeley
Staffordshire WS15 3BP
Tel: 01283 840254

DIRECTIONS: see Getting to the start; pub by the market cross

PARKING: street parking

OPEN: closed Sunday evening/Monday lunch

FOOD: daily

BREWERY/COMPANY: Punch Taverns

REAL ALE: Marston's Pedigree, Greene King Abbot Ale

DOGS: not allowed inside

what to look for

The wooden Buttercross (opposite the Goat's Head pub and named after the produce once sold under it) would have been at the heart of the once-thriving market and is thought to have been built in 1339. However, architectural historian Nikolaus Pevsner, in The Buildings of England, Staffordshire, gives a more likely date of the 17th century.

and cross a small **copse**. Beyond it pass into the adjoining field on the left and maintain the same direction as before to the corner. Turn left here and follow the field boundary to a dilapidated stile and **waymark**.

6 Turn right and follow the field edge to a stile on the right. Cross it and swing left, following the **field track** beside crops, with hedging on the left. Carry on straight along the track as far as a **metalled road**. Go straight on to get back to the start.

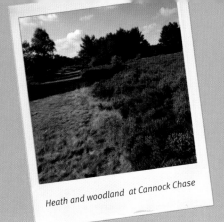

Heath and woodland at Cannock Chase

The Heart of England Way
Part of our route follows a stretch of the Heart of England Way, a walk of 100 miles (160km) from Milford, just south of Stafford, to Bourton-on-the-Water in Gloucestershire.

The Heart of England Way, part of the Trans-European E2 route, links the Staffordshire Way and the Cotswold Way with the Oxfordshire Way and other Long Distance Paths.

A statue of Dr Samuel Johnson in Lichfield

A walk to Whittington's Victoria Cross

A gentle walk taking in the history of Britain's most distinguished medal.

Whittington Barracks

Whittington Barracks, just south of the village of the same name, has been the home of the Staffordshire Regiment since 1881. The regiment's origins date back to 1705, when the 38th Foot was raised at the King's Head Hotel in Lichfield by Colonel Luke Lillingston. The raising of other regiments over the next 120 years led, through a complex process of change and amalgamation, to the formation of the Staffordshire Regiment after the end of World War Two. It was conferred the title of the Prince of Wales's in 1876, following the presentation of colours by the Prince of Wales (later King Edward VII). Today, its Colonel in Chief is HRH the Duke of York, Prince Andrew. All of this history, and much more besides, is told in the Staffordshire Regiment Museum at Whittington Barracks, with a chronological display of information and memorabilia from the regiment's many campaigns. The most interesting display, however, is arguably the one dedicated to the Victoria Cross, and to those in the regiment who have been awarded one.

The Victoria Cross was established by royal warrant in 1856, to recognise acts of uncommon valour during the Crimean War, 1854–56. Each VC is forged from the remains of two Russian cannon, captured at Sebastopol. The most recent issue of metal, sufficient to make 12 medals, was made in 1959. It's thought the remaining metal is enough to make a further 85 medals. Only 12 have been won since the end of World War Two.

In all, 1,355 Victoria Crosses have been won, and of these, 1,156 were awarded before the end of World War One. At least three witnesses are needed for recommendation. All medals require royal assent and are presented by the reigning monarch. The inscription on front of the VC states simply: 'For Valour'. It has been estimated that the chances of surviving a VC action is 1 in 10.

Among the 11 members of the Staffordshire Regiment who have been awarded the VC, is Lance Corporal William Coltman, a stretcher bearer at Mannequin Hill in France on 3 and 4 October 1918. Hearing that wounded men had been left behind during a retreat, Corporal Coltman went forward alone in the face of relentless enemy fire, found the casualties, dressed their wounds and carried some of them to safety on his back on three occasions. For the next two days and nights he looked after the wounded constantly. He later became the most decorated NCO of World War One.

Right: Whittington church

2h00 | **5.25 MILES** | **8.4 KM** | **LEVEL 123**

MAP: OS Explorer 232 Nuneaton & Tamworth

START/FINISH: ample roadside parking in Whittington; grid ref: SK 158083

PATHS: roads, gravel and sand tracks, dirt trails, may be muddy after rain, 3 stiles

LANDSCAPE: farmland and forest

PUBLIC TOILETS: none on route

TOURIST INFORMATION: Lichfield, tel 01543 308209

THE PUB: The Bell Inn, Whittington

❶ Hopwas Hays Lane is closed on live firing days. Open days listed in Tamworth Herald and at post offices at Whittington, the Barracks and Hints

Getting to the start
Whittington is just off the A51 between Tamworth and Lichfield. Turn left at the crossroads by the Dog Inn in the village centre.

Researched and written by:
Nick Channer, Paul Grogan

Map:
- 85
- BELL INN PH
- WHITTINGTON
- ST GILES'S CHURCH
- Hademore
- Lichfield
- Birmingham & Fazeley Canal
- STAFFORDSHIRE REGIMENT MUSEUM
- HOPWAS HAYS LANE
- Whittington Barracks
- THE BUNGALOW
- Danger Area
- River Tame
- HEART OF ENGLAND WAY
- A51
- HOPWAS HAYS WOOD
- 138
- Hopwas
- SAND AND GRAVEL PITS
- B5405
- Tamworth
- ½ Mile / ½ Km
- N

187

Lichfield Cathedral

The first cathedral on this site was founded in AD 700 to house the shrine of St Chad. The present building with its elaborate carvings has been much restored since it was attacked during the Civil War. Among its treasures are an 18th-century illuminated manuscript, the St Chad Gospels and a collection of modern silver.

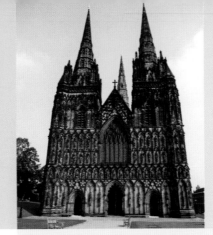

The soaring Gothic façade of Lichfield Cathedral

the walk

1 From St Giles's Church go right to the crossroads and then right for 250yds (229m) until you get to **Sandy Lane**. Follow this wide gravel track until it goes hard right, and here cross a stile to the left and continue in the same direction to a **wood**.

2 Keep left at a fork, then right after a few paces, walking through the heart of the wood. Keep left at the tarmac road, then right by the **estate office** to reach the **Staffordshire Regiment Museum**.

3 Turn left and follow the **A51**. Swing right into Jerry's Lane and walk along to the **Heart of England Way**. Turn left here. After about 300yds (274m) go past a small square of trees on the right and keep going straight until you reach a junction with **Knox's Grave Lane**, a clear track.

4 Cross it and turn immediately left to follow a parallel path. Keep right further on to reach the corner of the **sand and gravel pits**. Thread between the pits on either side and keep going along the surfaced road, down the dip and then up the other side. At the top of the rise, cross the stile on the left and head diagonally left across the field on the faint grass track.

At the far side of the field, cross a stile and the A51 and then go straight up the track to a **T-junction**. Go left and follow the edge of **Hopwas Hays Wood** for 0.5 mile (800m).

5 At the next major path junction go left down to the corner of the wood. From here follow the track of **Hopwas Hays Lane** for another 0.5 mile (800m). At the bridleway sign veer right, across the firing range and back to **Common Lane**. Go right here, back towards Whittington and, at the crossroads, turn left to return to the start.

what to look for

The Coltman Trench, named after Lance Corporal William Coltman, is certainly one of the highlights of the museum, and it goes some way to describing what conditions were like in the trenches. The figures mentioned, however, are incomprehensible. On 1 July 1916, the first day of the Battle of the Somme, 60,000 soldiers died in a single day. When the war finally ended on 11 November 1918, over 9 million people had been killed.

Staffordshire Regiment Museum at Whittington

The Bell Inn

Creeper-clad brick-built pub in the heart of the village, popular with walkers seeking refreshment after exploring the Birmingham & Fazeley Canal tow path and the nearby Heart of England Way. On sunny days savour a pint of Abbot Ale on the front patio or in the sheltered beer garden, which has a play area for adventurous kids. Open fires warm the traditional interior, where you can tuck into roast lunches on Sundays and enjoy live jazz on Monday evenings.

Food
The extensive menu choice ranges from 'lite bites' – baguettes, beanburger and a chicken and bacon panini, to scampi and chips, steak and ale pie, ham, egg and chips and beer-battered cod and chips.

about the pub

The Bell Inn
27 Main Street, Whittington
Lichfield, Staffordshire WS14 9JR
Tel: 01543 432377

DIRECTIONS: pub is along Main Street, straight ahead when you reach the crossroads coming from the A51

PARKING: 40

OPEN: daily; all day

FOOD: no food Saturday, Sunday & Monday evenings

BREWERY/COMPANY: Punch Pubs

REAL ALE: Bass, Marston's Pedigree, Greene King Abbot Ale

DOGS: allowed inside

Family facilities
Children are genuinely welcome in the pub and there's a children's menu for younger family members, smaller portions of the main menu are readily available, and on fine days kids can explore the play area in the garden.

Alternative refreshment stops
There are plenty of good pubs, cafés and restaurants in Lichfield.

☛ Where to go from here
Lichfield is worth a closer look, notably the fine cathedral whose three graceful spires, known as the Ladies of the Vale, dominate the surrounding landscape. Nearby, the Lichfield Heritage Centre gives a vivid account of the town's rich and varied history over 2000 years (www.lichfieldheritage.org.uk). In Breadmarket Street you'll find the birthplace and museum of Samuel Johnson, author of the famous English dictionary of 1755. One of Britain's greatest writers, he was born in the house in 1709 and now five floors are dedicated to his life, work and personality. Children will enjoy a visit to Drayton Manor Theme Park and Zoo near Tamworth, where there are more than 100 different rides and attractions (www.draytonmanor.co.uk).

A stone-carved fountain in the market place of Ashbourne

St John's Street in Ashbourne with the spire of St Oswald's Church in the background

while you're there

Why not have a look around Ashbourne, which proclaims itself to be the gateway to Dovedale. This bustling market town has many old buildings, including some fine old coaching inns. St Oswald's Church, with its 200ft (61m) spire and early 13th-century chancel was described by George Eliot as 'the finest mere parish church in the kingdom'.

From Osmaston to Shirley

Left: A secluded path in Osmaston Park
Right: The water mill at Osmaston Park

2h00 | **4.5 MILES** | **7.2 KM** | **LEVEL 1**2 3

WALK

MAP: OS Explorer 259 Derby

START/FINISH: Osmaston village hall car park; grid ref: SK 200435

PATHS: estate tracks and field paths, a number of stiles

LANDSCAPE: park, woodland and farm pasture

PUBLIC TOILETS: none on route

TOURIST INFORMATION: Ashbourne, tel 01335 343666

THE PUB: The Shoulder of Mutton, Osmaston

Getting to the start
Follow the A52 between Ashbourne and Derby. Follow the signs for the village of Osmaston and the car park is on the right in the centre of the village.

Researched and written by:
Nick Channer, John Gillham

the walk

1 Turn right out of the car park, and follow the road past The Shoulder of Mutton to the village green and **duck pond**. Turn left and take the middle of three rights of way – marked '**Bridleway to Shirley**'. The wide track descends among fields and through **woodland**.

2 Continue as the track reaches beyond **Home Farm**, which lies to the left, then follow it as it separates the two narrow **lakes**.

3 After passing the old Austrian-style **water mill** keep to the track ahead, which climbs up through the woodlands of Shirley Park. The track, part of the **Centenary Way**, eventually becomes a tarmac lane, continuing towards **Shirley**.

4 The return path to Osmaston, highlighted by a Centenary Way (CW) **waymarker**, begins on the right, just before the village, but most walkers will want to take a look around the centre, if only for refreshment at the **Saracens Head**.

5 Return to previously-mentioned footpath, which begins in some steps to a stile, then crosses a fenced off section of **lawn**. Beyond a second stile the path follows a **hedge** on the left round the edge of three fields. It then crosses a field, runs to the left and descends towards a wood, the southern extremity of **Shirley Park**. Maintain the same direction towards trees.

To the south of the Peak National Park, two aristocratic estates provide gentle parkland walking.

Osmaston
Osmaston is barely a few winding country lanes, but it's just the unspoiled tranquil village you'd hope to find on a country walk. The moment you leave the car you will experience the slow tick-over of the place.

Across the road from the car park is a terrace of four thatched cottages, built to celebrate the coronation of King George VI. As you walk down the lane you pass The Shoulder of Mutton, a fine pub with much promise for the end of the day. The walk enters the woodlands of Osmaston Park and threads between two of the estate's many lakes. On the other side there's an old mill, built in the style of an Austrian chalet and complete with a waterwheel. The path climbs through more woodland.

Shirley is another pretty village with its own aristocracy – Earl Ferrers and the Shirley family. Viscount Tamworth, the heir to Earl Ferrers, still lives in the village. From Shirley the walk turns back across fields and woods to Osmaston Park, reaching another of the estate's lakes. This one has the best setting, with a lush meadow surround and the occasional heron. As you continue along the track heading north and back into the woods now, you'll see a peculiar-looking tower peeping out from the canopy of trees. It's 150ft (45m) tall and all that remains of Osmaston Hall. The tower was designed to accommodate all the hall's various chimneys in one single stack. With this odd sight still lingering in your thoughts the walk ends in fine style as you walk down the hall's main drive, saluted by a fine avenue of lime trees.

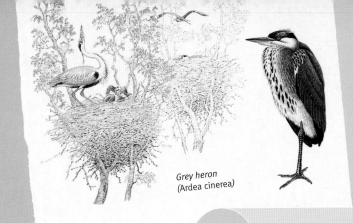

Grey heron
(Ardea cinerea)

what to look for

On the final part of the walk, heading north back into the woods, you'll see a peculiar-looking tower peeping out from the canopy of trees. It's 150ft (45m) tall and is all that remains of Osmaston Hall. The tower was designed to accommodate all of the hall's various chimneys in a single stack.

6 Cross the footbridge over **Shirley Brook** and turn right to follow a muddy streamside path to another footbridge. Go over this into the woods on a path with another **CW marker**.

7 Emerge at a track on a bend, keep left here and at the end of the wood, ignore the Centenary Way branching off right. Go straight on to pass alongside a pleasant **lake**, the southernmost of the Osmaston Park lakes.

8 You are now walking through the valley of **Wyaston Brook** and, although the path is invisible on the ground, the stiles in the cross-fences are all in place.

9 The bridleway from **Wyaston Grove**, seen in the distance, joins the route just

what to look for

The lakes are frequented by many birds, including grey herons, mallards, moorhens and many migratory wildfowl. The annual show of the Ashbourne Shire Horse Society is held in Osmaston Park in August.

beyond one of these stiles (grid ref 196423). Double back right along it, passing some **railings** on the right and entering the woods. The bridleway track now climbs north east out of the valley and back into the estate of **Osmaston Park**. Follow it through the park, ignoring private tracks to the lodge. Keep left at the junction and then left at an avenue of **lime trees**, following it to the village green. Turn left, by the **duck pond**, then right, back to the car park.

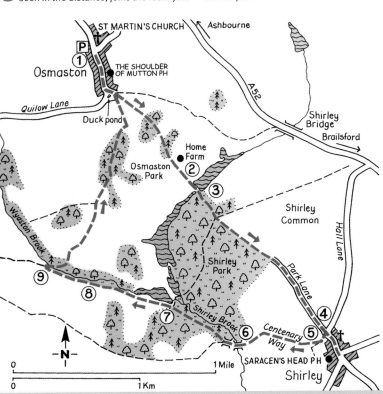

The Shoulder of Mutton

Like the timeless estate village in which it stands, The Shoulder of Mutton remains a traditional and unspoiled village pub, and like many of the pretty cottages in the village it is leased from the estate. Expect to find a homely, beamed public bar where locals congregate and a comfortable, carpeted lounge with dark wood furniture. The spacious and attractive rear garden with flower borders has picnic benches for summer alfresco meals.

Food

Extensive menus list traditional pub meals in the form of hot and cold sandwiches, filled baguettes, lasagne, vegetable Kiev, tuna and pasta bake, steak and kidney pie, and ploughman's lunches.

Family facilities

Children are welcome in the lounge where there's a pool table and a children's menu that offers smaller sized pies, omlettes and ploughman's.

Alternative refreshment stops

The Saracen's Head at Shirley serves tasty bar meals and Bass beer if you are looking for a meal or refreshment break in the middle of your walk.

☞ Where to go from here

South west of Ashbourne is Alton Towers, Britain's most famous theme park set in 200 acres (81ha) of landscaped gardens close to the majestic ruins of the Towers themselves. It offers an amazing range of rides, shows and attractions guaranteed to thrill every member of the family (www.alton-towers.com). Ilam Park (north of Ashbourne) runs along both banks of the River Manifold, with spectacular views towards Dovedale, and there's a Learning and Discovery Centre with information about the flora, fauna, geology and archaeology of the estate. Tea room and excellent walking opportunities (www.nationaltrust.org.uk).

about the pub

The Shoulder of Mutton
Osmaston, Ashbourne
Derbyshire DE6 1LW
Tel: 01335 342371

DIRECTIONS: see Getting to the start; pub on the left along the village street from the car park

PARKING: 20

OPEN: daily; all day Thursday to Sunday in summer

FOOD: daily

BREWERY/COMPANY: free house

REAL ALE: Marston's Pedigree, Bass, guest beer

DOGS: not allowed inside

A tree-lined avenue of trees at Ashby

Calke Abbey and Ticknall

Around Sir John Harpur's forgotten baroque mansion on Derbyshire's southern border.

Calke Abbey

Calke is not an abbey at all. The Augustinian order of monks did build one here in 1133 and dedicated it to St Giles, but since 1622 it has been the family home of the Harpurs and Harper-Crewes. In 1703 Sir John Harpur had the present baroque mansion built on the site of the abbey, keeping some of the old 6ft (2m) walls. This was a high society family, but things started to go wrong in the 1790s when Sir Henry Harpur married a lady's maid. Society shunned the couple and they, in turn, shunned society – the beginning of a tale of eccentricity and reclusiveness that would span two centuries.

Calke was a grand house with many rooms, and here was a family with money. When they tired of one room, they would just leave it the way it stood and move to another. For instance, when Sir Vauncey Harpur Crewe got married in 1876, he locked up his bachelor room, along with the heads of stuffed deer he had shot as a youth. When the National Trust bought the house in 1985 they found a dust-laden, neglected, but intriguing place, filled with treasures of centuries gone by.

Ticknall is an interesting village. Passing through it you see some pleasing timber-framed red brick cottages. When you reach the gates of the abbey, you are confronted with a horseshoe-shaped bridge, arching over the road. Built in 1800, it was part of an old tramway system, which included a 137yd (125m) tunnel under the

main drive to the abbey. Limestone from Ticknall's brickworks used to be carried by horse-drawn trams to the canal at Willesley. On the return journey the load would have been coal. The scheme was abandoned in 1915 and now just the bridge remains.

The magnificent tree-lined drive sets the scene for this trip round Calke. There are fallow deer in the woods, as well as barn and tawny owls. Betty's Pond is the first of the several lakes passed on the route. The house, in a dip, hides until the last moment. Its magnificent three-storey south front includes a four-column Ionic portico. If the place is open it is well worth a visit to see, among others, the resplendent Gold Drawing Room and the 18th-century Chinese silk state bed. The route heads north to Mere Pond, which is full of lilies and surrounded by attractive mature woods. It reaches its highest point on the fields of White Leys. Here you get glimpses of Staunton Harold Reservoir before you return to Ticknall.

the walk

1 Turn right out of the car park and follow the road to its junction with the A road through the village. Turn left by **The Wheel**

Inn, then right by the bridge to go through the gates of the **Calke Abbey Estate**. The tarmac estate road goes between an avenue of mature **lime trees** and through the Middle Lodge Gates. If you want to go inside the abbey itself you'll have to pay here.

2 Continue south east along the road, past **Betty's Pond** (left), then, as the road swings left, carry on along the grassy track ahead.

3 Take the left fork by trees and before a **white gate** and follow the track as it runs beneath the 18th century **deer shelter** enclosed by trees on the hilltop. Calke Abbey edges into view now. Veer left at the drive and follow the signs for the **car and coach park**. Cross the car park to a gap in the wall and descend north, down to the **Mere Pond**, a narrow strip of water surrounded by trees.

The early 18th-century stately home of Calke Abbey

2h00 | **3.75 MILES** | **6 KM** | **LEVEL 123**

MAP: OS Explorer 245 The National Forest

START/FINISH: village hall car park, Ticknall; grid ref: SK 352241

PATHS: estate roads and field paths, a few stiles

LANDSCAPE: parkland and crop fields

PUBLIC TOILETS: at car park

TOURIST INFORMATION: Ashby-de-la-Zouch, tel 01530 411767

THE PUB: The Wheel Inn, Ticknall

⚠ Lengthy stretch on the drive to Calke Abbey, which can be busy with cars; last section beside A514 (pavement)

Getting to the start

From the A42 and Ashby-de-la-Zouch take the B5006 road to Ticknall. Turn right onto the A514 at the T-junction in the village centre and then left at the signposted car park.

Researched and written by:
Nick Channer, John Gillham

Staunton Harold Reservoir

This 210 acre (85ha) reservoir has footpaths and nature walks linking it to nearby Calke Abbey. There is a visitor centre with exhibits and displays, and a picnic area and refreshment kiosk which is open in the summer.

Holy Trinity church in Staunton Harold

The goldeneye duck (Bucephala clangula)

The Wheel Inn

The three-storey Wheel Inn on Ticknall's main street used to be a basic Bass boozer until new owners arrived in 2003 and began transforming it beyond recognition. Now with a smart, cream-painted façade, this spruced-up village local sports a stylish bar with leather sofas and deep armchairs fronting an open fire, modern tables and chairs, a new wooden bar with Bass on tap, and a spacious upstairs restaurant. Expect a cosy atmosphere and interesting menus that utilise fresh ingredients from local suppliers. Small enclosed terraced garden for summer alfresco eating.

Food

Expect imaginatively cooked modern pub food cooked from fresh, with lunchtime choices ranging from sandwiches and baguettes to cod fillet in horseradish batter with chips and roasted loin of lamb with provencale risotto. Evening dishes may include fillet steak with black pudding.

Family facilities

Children are welcome inside the pub and smaller portions can be ordered from the main menu.

Alternative refreshment stops

There's a tea room at the back of The Wheel Inn.

☛ Where to go from here

Don't miss the Donington Grand Prix Collection at Castle Donington. View the largest collection of Mclaren racing cars on public display, every Williams F1 car from 1983 to 1999, Ferraris driven by Ascari and Ickx, Senna's winning Mclaren from the 1993

about the pub

The Wheel Inn
50 Main Street, Ticknall
Derby, Derbyshire DE73 1JZ
Tel: 01332 862966
www.thewheelinn.com

DIRECTIONS: see Getting to the start; pub is opposite the car park

PARKING: 20

OPEN: all day Sunday; closed Monday

FOOD: no food Sunday evening

BREWERY/COMPANY: free house

REAL ALE: Bass

DOGS: not allowed inside

European Grand Prix at Donington, a superb BRM display and more rare four-wheel drive racing cars than you'll see anywhere else (www.doningtoncollection.co.uk).

4 Turn right along a **water's-edge path**, then left between the end of the mere and the western extremities of another one, to follow a path running north.

5 On meeting a path at the top edge of the **woods**, turn left for a few paces, then right through a gate. After tracing the wall on the left, go over a stile in the hedge ahead to enter the next field. The path now heads diagonally across the field and down through the **pastures**.

6 On meeting a **flinted works road** turn left, following it through an area of woodland and old gravel pits (now transformed into pretty **wildlife ponds**). The winding track passes several **cottages** and meets the **A514** about 500yds (457m) to the east of the village.

7 Turn left along the road through the village, then right by the side of **The Wheel Inn** to get back to the car park.

Geese and swans at the edge of the Nutbrook Trail

Local History Museum

Ilkeston's museum has an Edwardian kitchen and wash-house and an exhibition of children's toys. Other displays tell the story of the local industries of coal mining, textile and iron manufacture.

Along the Nutbrook Trail

This gentle ride along a disused railway features a great picnic spot, an inviting pub and some fine views.

Shipley Country Park and the Nutbrook Trail

There has been a house on Shipley Hill since the 13th century, but the ruins of the hall that remain were once part of a grand mansion built by Edward Mundy in 1749. Some 50 years later it was renovated in a neo-classical style, and a hundred years after that it was enlarged by coal-mining magnate Alfred Miller-Mundy. In the end, however, the building's principal source of funding was to become its downfall: for generations a huge pillar of coal beneath the house had remained untouched, but after Godfrey Miller-Mundy sold the estate to Shipley Colliery in 1922, they tapped into these reserves, and the subsidence was so extensive that most of the hall had to be torn down in the early 1940s.

After decades of neglect, the estate was eventually purchased by Derbyshire County Council in the early 1970s, and in 1976 it became a Country Park. Today, it covers over 600 acres (242ha) of parkland and pond and boasts more than 18 miles of bridleways and footpaths. The remains of the hall can still be visited (access is via a public right of way through Derby Lodge).

the ride

1 At the southeast corner of the car park, take the track to the left of an **information board**, through or round a metal gate. Follow the tarmac and then a gravel track straight down the hill towards the **Country Park Inn**. Just before the inn, turn right on a wide dirt trail through the **woods** (the going's quite firm along here, but it may be slippery after rain). Follow this trail to the end of **Osborne's Pond** and then continue to the end of the next pond, keeping a tarmac road just to your right. When the trail you're on joins this road at an obvious junction, turn right following a sign for the **Nutbrook Trail**.

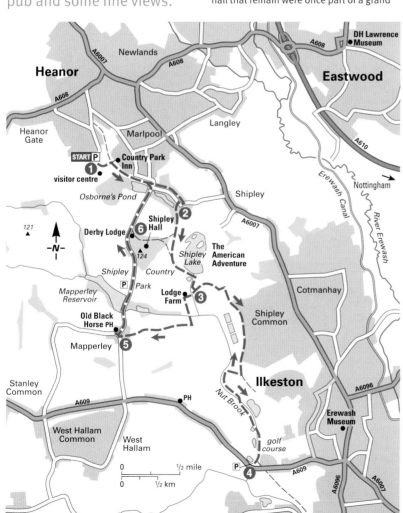

190

| 2h00 | 8.7 MILES | 14 KM | LEVEL 1 2 3 |

MAP: OS Explorer 260 Nottingham

START/FINISH: Shipley Country Park car park; grid ref: SK 431453

TRAILS/TRACKS: smooth gravel or tarmac all the way round

LANDSCAPE: railway cutting, woodland and village

PUBLIC TOILETS: at the start

TOURIST INFORMATION: Nottingham, tel 0115 915 5330

CYCLE HIRE: none locally

THE PUB: Old Black Horse, Mapperley

❗ One long hill towards the end, otherwise an easy ride

Getting to the start

The visitor centre at Shipley Country Park is tucked away in the suburbs of Heanor – take the Heanor turning off the A610 between Nottingham and Ripley and follow the signs from there. It can also be reached from both the A6007 and the A608, again following signs from the centre of Heanor.

Why do this cycle ride?

For the most part this meandering route follows tarmac trails, and as such is ideal for younger children. An alternative return loop towards the end provides an ideal opportunity to stop for a drink or snack at a cosy country pub, before taking in some wonderful views and some historic ruins at Shipley Hill.

Researched and written by: Paul Grogan

while you're there

The American Adventure theme park is one of Britain's few fully themed parks, based on the legend of a whole continent. The experiences here vary from the Missile Rollercoaster in Spaceport USA, to the wet and wild

excitement of the Rocky Mountain Rapids ride.

Fort Adventure is an action-packed challenge and the driving school is great for kids who want to know if they've got what it takes to be an advanced driver.

An unusual sculpture beside the Nutbrook Trail

2 After 400yds (366m) turn left off this road, again following a **sign** for the Nutbrook Trail. This will take you onto a **tarmac track** and up a short climb. Stay on this track as it levels off and eases back downhill to reach the corner of **Shipley Lake**. Turn right here, following the sign to **Long Eaton**. After 250yds (228m), turn left just before a building to your right, again following **Nutbrook Trail** signs.

3 Continue on the smooth tarmac track as it contours around the hill to reach a sharp chicane. Carry on as far as a junction with a **tarmac road**, where you'll find the first **information board** about the Nutbrook Trail. Stay on the trail as it skirts to the right of the **houses**. 200yds (182m) beyond the last of these houses, turn hard right, staying on the tarmac track. Follow this track as it bears around to the left and then passes under an **old railway bridge**. Pass a pond on your left and then right, before following the Nut Brook past the **golf course** on your right. Just after the golf course but just before an old railway bridge turn right through some **metal bars** to reach a pond and **picnic site**.

4 From the picnic site, return the way you came by turning left onto the Nutbrook

Trail. When you reach Point 3, turn left instead of right, towards **Lodge Farm**. Turn hard left after 150yds (137m) and then hard right after a further 400yds (364m) to follow this quiet tarmac road all the way into **Mapperley**.

5 From the junction in Mapperley, the **Old Black Horse** is straight ahead and on your right. To continue, return to the junction and turn left (assuming you're coming from the pub) towards Mapperley Reservoir. Look out for oncoming traffic when crossing the **dam**, before making the long but gradual climb up the side of **Shipley Hill**. Follow the road as it levels off and contours around the hill as far as **Derby Lodge**. From here the ruins of **Shipley Hall** are about 300yds (273m) to the southeast, along a public footpath.

6 Keep going past the lodge and down a long gentle hill to the east end of **Osborne's Pond**. Head left up a short trail just before the bridge to rejoin the main bridleway and then turn left to make your way back to the **Country Park Inn**. Opposite the inn, turn left up a steep gravel track to reach the start.

Old Black Horse

There's a homely, traditional feel to this friendly and inviting village pub, the spick-and-span and uncluttered bar and dining areas sporting red carpets, darkwood tables, soft, cosy lighting, open winter log fires, and some gleaming copper fittings. Small lawned garden overlooking the car park for summer drinking.

Food

Generous portions of freshly made food include a wide range of filled baguettes, burgers, ploughman's lunches, starters of mussels, home-made soups or pan-fried tiger prawns in garlic butter. Main dishes range from lasagne to braised lamb shank with red wine and mushroom sauce and monkfish with pea purée. There are roast lunches on a Sunday.

Family facilities

Children are welcome in the pub although there are no special facilities for them.

Alternative refreshment stops

A coffee shop at the start serves a wide range of snacks, lunches and afternoon teas.

☛ Where to go from here

The American Adventure amusement park is right next door to Shipley Country Park (www.americanadventure.co.uk). The DH Lawrence Museum is in nearby Eastwood, 2.5 miles (4km) to the northeast (www.lawrenceseastwood.co.uk). There's also a local history museum with a fascinating collection of children's toys on the High Street in Ilkeston, just 1 mile (1.6km) east of the picnic site at the end of the ride (www.erewash.gov.uk).

about the pub

Old Black Horse
Main Street, Mapperley
Ilkeston, Derbyshire DE7 6BY
Tel: 0115 932 3031

DIRECTIONS: Mapperley is signposted north off the A609 west of Ilkeston. Pub is in the village centre (see Point 5)

PARKING: 30

OPEN: daily; all day Saturday & Sunday

FOOD: daily

BREWERY/COMPANY: Hardys & Hansons Brewery

REAL ALE: Hardys & Hansons Kimberley Best, guest beers

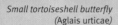

Tissington Estate Village

Take time to explore the pretty estate village of Tissington, either before or after your ride. Tissington has a village green with a stream running through it, a duck pond, several wells, old sandstone cottages set behind wide grass verges, a grand Jacobean hall and a Norman church.

Small tortoiseshell butterfly (Aglais urticae)

A canopy of trees on Tissington Estate

Along the Tissington Trail

An easy ride from the Tissington estate village along an old railway line above the secluded valley of the Bletch Brook.

Dew Ponds

Once beyond the old station at Alsop, one feature of the landscape you'll notice along the route are the occasional small ponds in the pastures – these are dew ponds. The name comes from the belief that morning dew would provide sufficient water for cattle and sheep to drink. In days gone by these would be hollows dug out and lined with clay to stop the water from draining away. As this is an area where the rock is predominantly porous limestone, rainwater seeps away and surface water is very rare. The modern-day versions are watertight and they don't rely on dew, either, as they are regularly topped up by the farmers.

Summertime on the Tissington Trail sees a profusion of butterflies. The Common Blue is one of the most noticeable. This very small insect feeds largely on clover flowers and the bright yellow flowers of bird's foot trefoil, a low-growing plant that flourishes in limestone areas. Another butterfly to look out for is the colourful Red Admiral which lays its eggs on nettles, the food plant of the caterpillar.

the ride

1 The Tissington car park is at the site of the old railway station. Take time to find the information board which has a fine picture of the place in its heyday. There's

also a village information board here; the village centre is only a short cycle away and it's well worth taking the loop before starting out. Turn left from the car park entrance, then right along **Chapel Lane**. This passes one of the five wells that are dressed in the village during the famous Well Dressing Ceremony held in May on Ascension Day. The lane rises gently to a junction at the top of the village. Turn left to drop down the main street, lined by greens and passing **Tissington Hall** and more wells. At the bottom keep left, passing the village pond before swinging right to return to the car park. Here turn left, passing beneath a bridge to join the old trackbed, which starts a long, easy climb.

2 This initial stretch is through a wooded cutting, soon shallowing to offer the occasional view through the trees across the glorious countryside here at the southern end of the National Park. The panorama sweeps across the peaceful valley of the **Bletch Brook** to take in the high ridge of rough pastures above **Ballidon** to the right.

3 The first natural place to turn around to return to Tissington is the car park and picnic area at the **former Alsop Station**. This would make a round trip of 6 miles (9.7km) and take perhaps 1.5 hours – and it's downhill virtually all the way back!

4 It's well worth continuing north, however, as once the old railway passes beneath the main road, the character of the Trail changes, and a more open terrain offers different views and experiences. The track continues its gentle climb, soon crossing the first of many embankments. There are grand views left (west) across the rolling pastureland of the **White Peak** towards the higher, darker hills that characterise the Staffordshire moorlands, forming the western horizon. Closer to hand are round-topped hills capped by crowns of trees.

5 Off to your left, the village of **Biggin-by-Hartington** soon appears – notice the old **army huts** down to the left, still put to good use as storerooms. In the distance and looking north, you may pick out the distinctive knolls of limestone near Longnor, Chrome Hill and Parkhouse Hill. The strand of cuttings and embankments continues towards the next logical turning point, **Hartington Old Station**. Here, the former signal box has been preserved; climb the steps to view the old points and levers.

6 This is the ideal place to turn round and retrace the route back to the car park at **Tissington**.

Top: The valley of Bletch Brook

3h30	16 MILES	25.7 KM	LEVEL 1 2 3

SHORTER ALTERNATIVE ROUTE

1h30	6 MILES	9.7 KM	LEVEL 1 2 3

MAP: OS Explorer OL24 White Peak

START/FINISH POINT: Tissington Old Station, grid ref SK 177520

TRAILS/TRACKS: old railway trackbed, lanes in Tissington village

LANDSCAPE: limestone plateau of the White Peak, extensive views

PUBLIC TOILETS: Tissington and Hartington old stations

TOURIST INFORMATION: Ashbourne, tel 01335 343666

CYCLE HIRE: Peak Cycle Hire, Mapleton Lane, Ashbourne, Derbyshire, tel 01335 343156, www.peakdistrict.org

THE PUB: Bluebell Inn, Tissington, see Directions to the pub, page 222

Getting to the start

Tissington is signposted off the A515 Ashbourne to Buxton road, a few miles north of Ashbourne. Pass the pond in the village and bear right to find the gated entrance to the Tissington Trail car park.

Why do this cycle ride?

This is one of England's most famous cycling trails and, as it is an old railway line, you can simply choose just when and where to turn round and return to the start. We've suggested heading north, but you could as easily head south to the pleasant market town of Ashbourne, with its antique shops and bookshops. Going north offers a short option along a wooded route followed by a contrasting, airy route through cuttings and along embankments. It's your choice!

Researched and written by: Neil Coates

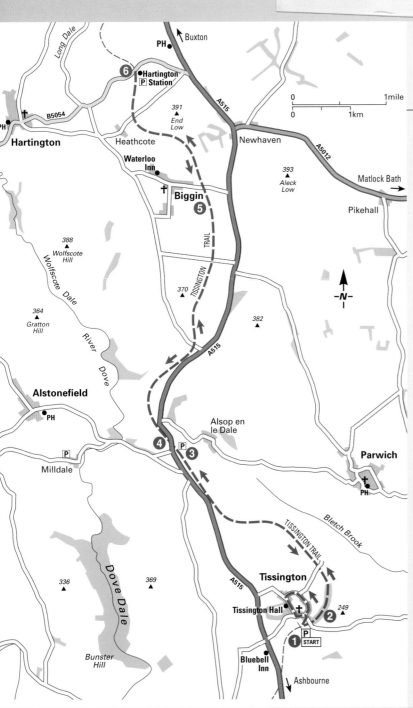

Bluebell Inn

A favourite watering hole for walkers and cyclists following a day on the Tissington Trail, the stone-built Bluebell Inn dates from 1777. In the long, beamed bar you can rest weary legs and savour a reviving pint of Hardys & Hansons bitter. Fires at either end add welcome winter warmth, while in summer vases of flowers on each table add a splash of colour to the narrow room. Prints of local scenes, framed advertisements and old photographs of the pub adorn the walls and high shelves are lined with traditional pub memorabilia. There is a light and airy dining room.

Food

The bar menu is very extensive and lists traditional pub fare. Tuck into wild mushroom lasagne, beef in ale pie, Hartington chicken, a ploughman's lunch or a decent round of sandwiches. Limited daily specials may take in beef and tomato casserole, a giant Yorkshire pudding filled with scrumpy pork casserole, and local trout.

Family facilities

Familes are welcome inside only if they plan to eat. There's a standard selection of children's meals, in addition to portions of lasagne and Yorkshire pudding filled with beef stew. Unfortunately the large garden is next to the busy road so keep an eye on children.

Alternative refreshment stops

There are two village tea rooms in Tissington, the Old Coach House and Bassett Wood Farm.

☛ Where to go from here

Ilam Country Park is a National Trust estate just west of Tissington. Ten miles (16.1km) south of Ashbourne is Sudbury Hall, home to the National Trust's Museum of Childhood (www.nationaltrust.org.uk).

about the pub

Bluebell Inn

Tissington, Ashbourne
Derbyshire DE6 1NH
Tel 01335 350317
www.bluebelltissington.co.uk

DIRECTIONS: from the Tissington Trail car park turn left back through the village to the A515 and turn right to locate the pub beside the main road

PARKING: 75

OPEN: daily, all day March–September

FOOD: daily, all day March–September

BREWERY/COMPANY: Hardys & Hansons Brewery

REAL ALE: Hardys & Hansons Best Bitter and Old Trip

did you know?

The pretty village of Tissington has given its name to the popular trail for walkers and cyclists. The Tissington Trail runs for 13 miles (20.9km) from Parsley Hey to Ashbourne along the old railway line which closed in 1963.

The pond in Tissington village

The Peak District has a thriving cheese industry

Wolfscote Dale and a Railway Trail

Left and below: Wolfscote Dale

Wolfscote Dale and Biggin Dale wind through the heart of the upland limestone country.

Compleat Angler
From its source, on Axe Edge, to Hartington the River Dove is little more than a stream, flowing past the dragon's back at Chrome Hill, and in an attractive but shallow valley south of Crowdecote. Once through the pretty woodlands of Beresford Dale it cuts a deep limestone canyon with with cliffs and tors almost equal to those of Dovedale. This canyon is Wolfscote Dale, and it is wilder and more unspoiled than Dovedale with narrower, less populated paths, and less woodland to hide the crags. Weirs have been constructed to create calm pools that attract trout and grayling to linger.

The river was a joy to Charles Cotton, a 17th-century poet born in nearby Beresford Hall. Cotton, an enthusiastic angler, introduced Izaak Walton to the area and taught him the art of fly-fishing. Together they built a fishing temple in the woods of Beresford Dale (in private grounds.) They wrote *The Compleat Angler*, a collection of fishing stories published in 1651.

The path up Wolfscote Dale begins at Lode Mill, which still has its waterwheel intact. The river, verged by lush vegetation, has cut a deep and twisting valley through the limestone. The slopes are wooded with ash, sycamore and alder. Further north this woodland thins out to reveal more of the crags, and a ravine opens out to the right of Coldeaton Bridge. The dale, like so many in Derbyshire, is rich in wildlife. Dipper, pied wagtails and grey wagtails often forage along the limestone banks, and if you're quick enough you may see a kingfisher diving for a fish. The dale divides again beneath the magnificent Peaseland Rocks. It's a shame to leave the Dove but Biggin Dale is a pleasing contrast. For most of the year it's a dry valley, but in winter the rocky path may be jostling for room with a newly surfaced stream. It's a narrow dale with limestone screes and scrub gorse.

Through a gate you enter a National Nature Reserve, known for its many species of limestone-loving plants and its butterflies. At the top of the dale you come to Biggin, a straggling village, from where the return route is an easy-paced one, using the Tissington Trail, which ambles over the high plains of Alsop Moor.

the walk

1 From the car park at **Alsop Old Station**, cross the busy A515 road and follow the **Milldale Road** immediately opposite. Bear right at the junction; in about 200yds (183m) the option of a parallel footpath, left, keeps you safe from the traffic.

2 On reaching the bottom of the dale by **Lode Mill**, turn right along the footpath,

tracing the river's east bank through a winding, partially wooded valley.

3 Ignore the footpath on the right at **Coldeaton Bridge**, but instead stay with **Wolfscote Dale** beneath thickly wooded slopes on the right. Beyond a stile the woods cease and the dale becomes bare and rock-fringed, with a cave on the right and the bold pinnacles of **Peaseland Rocks** ahead. Here the valley sides open out into the dry valley of **Biggin Dale**, where this route goes next.

4 The unsignposted path into **Biggin Dale** begins beyond a stile in a cross-wall and climbs by that wall. It continues through scrub woodland and beneath limestone screes. Beyond a gate you enter a nature reserve.

5 There's another gate at the far end of the nature reserve. Beyond it the dale curves left, then right, before dividing again beneath the hill pastures of **Biggin Grange**. We divert left here, over a stile to follow the footpath, signposted to **Hartington**. On the other side of the wall there's a concrete dewpond.

6 After 200yds (183m) there's another junction of paths. This time ignore the one signposted to **Hartington** and keep walking straight on up the shallowing dale, following the path to **Biggin**. It stays with the valley round to the right, passing a small sewage works (on the left) before

192

WALK

4h00 | **7.5 MILES** | **12.1 KM** | **LEVEL 123**

MAP: OS Explorer OL24 White Peak

START/FINISH: Tissington Trail pay car park at Alsop Old Station, grid ref SK 156549

PATHS: generally well-defined paths, about 20 stiles and gates

LANDSCAPE: partially wooded limestone dales and high pasture

PUBLIC TOILETS: none on route

TOURIST INFORMATION: Ashbourne, tel 01335 343666

THE PUB: The Waterloo Inn, Biggin-by-Hartington, see Point **7** on route

⚠ Limestone dale sides can be slippery after rain

Getting to the Start
The walk begins at Alsop Old Station, one of the former station sites on the Tissington Trail. It is signposted off the A515 about 6 miles (9.7km) north of Ashbourne.

Researched and written by:
Neil Coates, John Gillham

Wolfscote Dale

DERBYSHIRE

what to look for
In Biggin Dale, there are rampantly prickly gorse bushes as well as many limestone-loving plants including the purple-flowered meadow cranesbill, patches of delicate harebells, early purple orchids with their dark-spotted stems and leaves and the distinctive orangy-yellow cowslips.

while you're there

The delightful village of Hartington with its spacious market place, village green, duck pond, limestone houses, tea rooms and pubs is well worth a visit.

It can be very busy with walkers, especially at weekends, as it is at the northern end of the limestone dales on the River Dove and an excellent network of footpaths is centred on the village.

Hartington village with the medieval Church of St Giles

climbing out of the dale to reach the road at **Dale End**.

7 Turn right along the road for a few paces then left, following a road past the **Waterloo Inn** and through **Biggin** village.

8 Turn right again 500yds (457m) from the village centre on a path that climbs to the **Tissington Trail**. Follow this trackbed southwards across the pastures of **Biggin** and **Alsop** moors. After 2 miles (3.2km) you reach the car park at **Alsop Old Station**.

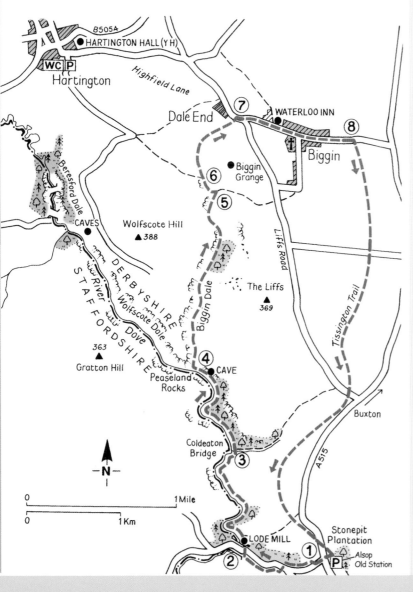

Waterloo Inn

Don't be put off by the grey pebble-dashed exterior of the Waterloo Inn – inside you'll find the atmosphere of a friendly and welcoming village pub. Well loved by locals and passing walkers alike, it comprises a quarry-tiled bar, wall-bench seating and traditional pub tables and chairs. There is a separate carpeted lounge area and a very popular pool room. It is a handy refuelling spot midway through this walk – a place to stop and savour a pint of Black Sheep Bitter in the garden on fine sunny days.

Food

As befits a homely village the local food is no-nonsense, good-value pub fare. Here you'll find an all-day breakfast, fish and chips, lasagne, a range of sandwiches and pizzas, and the occasional daily special such as lamb shank with mint gravy.

Family facilities

Children are welcome throughout the pub and have their own standard menu.

Alternative refreshment stops

The Blue Bell at Tissington Gate is a couple of miles south along the A515.

about the pub

Waterloo Inn
Biggin-by-Hartington, Buxton
Derbyshire SK17 0DH
Tel 01298 84284

DIRECTIONS: On Point **7** on the route. By car, Biggin is signposted left off the A515, north of Ashbourne

PARKING: 20

OPEN: daily, all day Friday, Saturday and Sunday

FOOD: daily

BREWERY/COMPANY: Enterprise Inns

REAL ALE: Black Sheep Bitter and Special, guest beers

DOGS: welcome throughout

☛ Where to go from here

Experience the atmosphere of a working 18th-century cotton mill at Masson Mills Working Textile Museum in Matlock Bath (www.massonmills.co.uk).

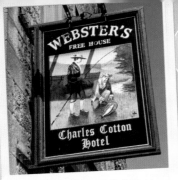

Anglers on the sign for Charles Cotton Hotel

did you know?

A pub in Hartington bears the name of Charles Cotton (1630–87) writer, angler and friend of Izaak Walton, who was born in Beresford, on the Staffordshire-Derbyshire border. His father died in 1658 leaving him estates at Beresford and Bentley. Cotton learned to fly fish on the River Dove which flows through Beresford Dale and it is likely that it was here that he met Izaak Walton. He is buried in London.

Pilsbury Castle and the Upper Dove Valley

The upper valley of the Dove is one of quiet villages and historic remains.

Hartington and Pilsbury Castle

Hartington, lying in the mid-regions of the Dove Valley, is a prosperous village with fine 18th-century houses and hotels built in local limestone and lined around spacious greens. The settlement's history can be traced back to the Normans, when it was recorded as Hartedun, the centre for the De Ferrier's estate. Hartington Hall, now the youth hostel, was first built in 1350 but was substantially rebuilt in 1611.

As you leave the village, the lane climbs past the church of St Giles, which has a splendid battlemented Perpendicular tower. It continues up the high valley sides of the Dove and on through an emerald landscape of high fields and valley.

Pilsbury Castle hides until the last moment, but then a grassy ramp swoops down to it from the hillsides. Only the earthworks are now visible, but you can imagine its impregnable position on a limestone knoll that juts out into the valley. You can see the motte, a man-made mound built to accommodate the wooden keep, and the bailey, a raised embankment that would have had a wooden stockade round it. The castle's exact history is disputed. It was probably built around 1100 by the Normans, on the site of an Iron-Age fort. It may have been a stronghold used earlier by William I to suppress a local rebellion in his 'Wasting of the North' campaign. Being in the middle of the De Ferrier estate it was probably their administrative centre. In the

what to look for

The Dairy Crest Creamery is one of only a few places which are licensed to make Stilton Cheese. There's a visitor centre in Hartington, where you can sample and buy. Look too for Hartington Hall, an impressive three-gabled manor house, now the youth hostel (see photo).

1200s this function would have been moved to Hartington.

Views up-valley are fascinating with the conical limestone peaks of Parkhouse and Chrome Hills in the distance. Now the route descends into Dovedale for the first time, crossing the river into Staffordshire. The lane climbs to a high lane running the length of the dale's east rim. Note the change in the rock – it's now the darker gritstone. The crags of Sheen Hill have been blocking the view east, but once past them you can see for miles, across the Manifold Valley to the Roaches and Hen Cloud. A field path takes the route on its finale, descending along a line of crags with lofty views of Hartington and the end of the walk.

the walk

1 Turn left out of the car park and follow the lane to the right beside the village green. Turn left up **Hide Lane** by the **church** and take the second path on the left in 600yds (549m), just past a large modern barn. This heads northwards across fields. Below a farm complex, the path swings left to follow a dry-stone wall on the left.

2 The path cuts down the concrete drive coming up the hill from **Bank Top Farm**. Waymarking posts highlight the continuing route along the high valley sides, about 50yds (45m) up from the break of slope.

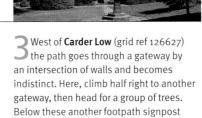

Hartington Hall dates from 1611 and is now a youth hostel

3 West of **Carder Low** (grid ref 126627) the path goes through a gateway by an intersection of walls and becomes indistinct. Here, climb half right to another gateway, then head for a group of trees. Below these another footpath signpost shows the way uphill and half right to a step stile in a ridge wall, where you look down into a small valley.

4 Descend into the valley and turn left at a fingerpost for **Pilsbury** and Crowdecote to reach a lane by a stone barn. A stile across the road allows you on to the continuing path, rounding the high slopes above Pilsbury. The footpath rakes left down the hill slopes to a farm track and wall alongside the ancient earthworks of **Pilsbury Castle**. Go through the stile here.

5 Turn right along the path, which takes a well-used course heading up the valley, gradually losing height to join the valley floor. Cross straight over a rough, walled field track. The path develops into a farm track; remain with this past **Bridge End Farm** to reach **Crowdecote** and the **Packhorse Inn**.

6 Retrace your steps to Bridge End Farm. Beside the barn look right for a footbridge across the **Dove** (there's a hidden fingerpost, left). Walk ahead up the field.

7 The path steepens up the valley side. After a walker's gate veer right, away from the wall, climbing up through scrub to reach the Longnor road. Turn left along the lane to reach **Harris Close Farm** in 2 miles (3.2km).

Right: The hamlet of Pilsbury

3h30 | **7.5 MILES** | **12.1 KM** | **LEVEL 123**

MAP: OS Explorer OL24 White Peak

START/FINISH: Hartington pay car park, grid ref SK 127603

PATHS: field paths and lanes, some steep climbs, about 32 stiles and gates

LANDSCAPE: pastures, limestone valley

PUBLIC TOILETS: at car park

TOURIST INFORMATION: Ashbourne, tel 01335 343666

THE PUB: The Packhorse Inn, Crowdecote, see Point 5 on route

! This is a long walk with several ascents and is best suited to older children

Getting to the start

From Buxton take the A515 south towards Ashbourne. Pass the Jug and Glass Inn and then look for the right turn on the B5054 for Hartington.

Researched and written by: Neil Coates, John Gillham

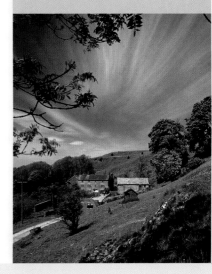

Pilsbury Road in the Upper Dove Valley

The main chamber in Poole's Cavern

while you're there

Poole's Cavern in Buxton Country Park is a natural limestone cave created by water over millions of years. A 45-minute guided tour leads visitors through easily accessible chambers used as a shelter by Bronze Age cave dwellers and Roman metal workers.

8 Turn into the drive and look immediately on the right for a narrow passage right of the low barn. This leads to a fieldside path. In all but one field there's a wall on the right for guidance. After going through a wood, in 50yds (45m) the path descends through scrub into the valley. It joins a farm track southwards towards **Bridge End Farm**.

9 At the fingerpost for **Hartington**, turn left through a gate and cross a field. Cross the **Dove** by a footbridge hidden by trees. The path gradually swings right (south east) across fields, aims for the woods to the left of the dairy and enters them via a stile. At the other side go into the forecourt of the dairy and turn left along the lane to return to **Hartington**.

The Packhorse Inn

Crowdecote consists of a huddle of cottages and farms clinging to a steep hillside above the juvenile River Dove. Tucked away in this hamlet is the 300-year-old Packhorse Inn, once frequented by trains of packhorses and their overseers, the jaggers. Although the little interconnecting rooms have been updated over the years they retain some of their original character, with solid beams, stone walls and open fires. With Timothy Taylor Landlord on tap, decent pies and sandwiches on the menu, and a terraced lawn rising up behind with views to the steep slopes of the Dove Valley, this homely, unassuming little pub makes a great halfway stop.

Food

From a weekly changing menu choose starters such as red mullet and cod fishcakes or a bowl of *moules* with crusty bread, or tuck into something more substantial like home-made steak and Guinness pie. Good sandwich menu.

Family facilities

On fine sunny days the terraced garden, with the added attractions of ducks and chickens, is the place to be. Inside, children can choose from their own menu, or order a small portion of many of the dishes featured on the main menu.

about the pub

The Packhorse Inn
Crowdecote, Buxton
Derbyshire SK17 0DB
Tel 01298 83618

DIRECTIONS: on Point 5 of the route, see Getting to the start, in the centre of Crowdecote off the A515 north west of Hartington

PARKING: 20

OPEN: all day Saturday and Sunday, Easter to September. Closed Monday, except Bank Holidays when it closes on Tuesday instead

FOOD: daily

BREWERY/COMPANY: free house

REAL ALE: Worthington Cask, Timothy Taylor Landlord, guest beer

DOGS: welcome throughout pub

ROOMS: 2 bedrooms

Alternative refreshment stops
The Charles Cotton Hotel in Hartington (free house).

☞ Where to go from here
Poole's Cavern in Buxton Country Park offers guided tours of the illuminated chambers and their amazing crystal formations (www.poolescavern.co.uk).

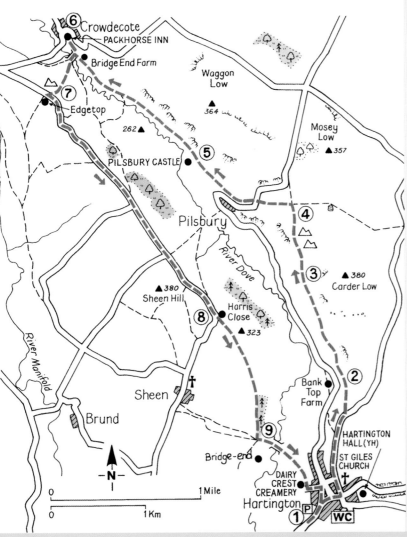

Matlock Bath's mining museum

while you're there

A large display at the Peak District Mining Museum in Matlock Bath explains the history of the Derbyshire lead industry from Roman times to the present day. The geology of the area, mining and smelting processes, the quarrying and the people who worked in the industry are all illustrated by a series of static and moving exhibits.

The Heights of Abraham

A steady climb raises you above the hurley burley of Matlock Bath to a more familiar Peakland landscape.

Matlock Bath and the Derwent Valley

Between Matlock and Cromford the River Derwent forges its way through a spectacular, thickly wooded limestone gorge. At Matlock Bath it jostles for space with the bustling A6 highway, the railway to Derby and a string of three-storey houses, shops and amusement parlours, built by the Victorians, who flocked here to take in the healing spa waters. On the hillside to the east lies the gaunt castle of Riber, while Alpine-type cable cars glide up the Heights of Abraham, above cliff tops to the west. The original Heights of Abraham rise above Quebec and the St Lawrence River in Canada. There, in 1759, British troops under General Wolfe fought a victorious battle with the French under General Montcalm.

Matlock Bath is Derbyshire's mini-Blackpool, yet there are peaceful corners, and this fine walk seeks them out. It climbs through the woods and out on to the hillside above the town. The Victoria Prospect Tower peeps over the trees. Built by unemployed miners a century ago it's now part of the Heights of Abraham complex. Above the complex, a little path leads you through woodland. In spring it's heavy with the scent of wild garlic and coloured by a carpet of bluebells. Out of the woods, an attractive hedge-lined unsurfaced lane weaves its way through high pastures, giving distant views of the White Peak plateau, Black Rocks and the cliffs of Crich Stand.

At the end of the lane is Bonsall, whose perpendicular church tower and spire has been beckoning you for some time. In the centre of this old lead mining village is a market square with a 17th-century cross. The lane out of Bonsall takes you to the edge of an area of old mine shafts and modern-day quarries. The route goes north, back into the woods of the Derwent Valley, passing the high hamlet of Upperwood, where fleeting views of Matlock and Matlock Bath appear through the trees.

Top: The River Derwent running through Matlock Bath

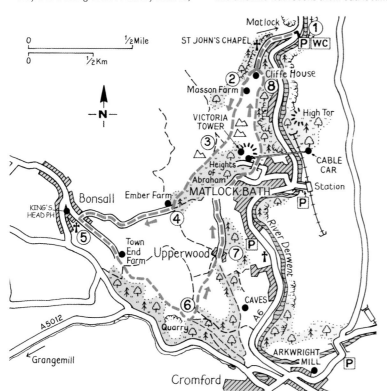

194

2h30 | **4.5 MILES** | **7 KM** | **LEVEL 1 2 3**

WALK

MAP: OS Explorer OL24 White Peak

START/FINISH: Matlock: pay car park at Artists Corner, grid ref SK 297595

PATHS: narrow woodland paths, field paths and unsurfaced lanes, 10 stiles and gates

LANDSCAPE: fields and wooded hillsides

PUBLIC TOILETS: at car park

TOURIST INFORMATION: Matlock Bath, tel 01629 55082

THE PUB: King's Head, Bonsall, see Point 4 on route

⚠ This walk has a long, and in some places, steep opening section before levelling out beside the Heights of Abraham leisure park

Getting to the start

Matlock is on the A6 between Buxton and Matlock. The car park at Artists Corner is well signed.

Researched and written by:
Neil Coates, John Gillham

Below: Cable cars heading up to the Heights of Abraham

Arkwright's Cromford Mill

Sir Richard Arkwright established the world's first working water-powered cotton spinning mill at Cromford in 1771. The Arkwright Society is involved in a major restoration to create a lasting monument to this extraordinary genius.

As you walk through the cobbled courtyard of the mill you are transported back to that austere world of the 18th century when mother, father and children all worked at the mills. Guided tours are available.

Masson/Arkwright Mill viewed across the river

the walk

1 Cross the A6, then take **St John's Road** up the wooded slopes opposite. It passes beneath **St John's Chapel** to reach the gates of **Cliffe House**. Take the path on the right signed 'To the Heights of Abraham'. The path climbs steeply beside the estate wall through the woodland edge; scramble over a high, broken stone step stile and veer left to another stile into the rough fields above **Masson Farm**.

2 The footpath continues to an old gateway and waymark post, with **Victoria Prospect Tower** directly ahead. Turn right beyond the gateway, and rise to a stile at the top of the field. Beyond this the footpath threads through hawthorn thickets before passing a small gated entry (left) into the **Heights of Abraham** complex.

3 Ignore this and continue uphill for about 30yds (27m), then turn left over a stile (waymarked **Derwent Valley Walk**). After crossing a tarred access road, the narrow footpath re-enters woodland.

4 At the far side of the woods turn right along a farm lane, passing well below **Ember Farm**. This pleasant walled lane winds down pastured hillslopes into Bonsall village. To find the **King's Head** turn right at the lane; it's about 200yds (183m) along here. Then return to this spot.

what to look for

St John's Chapel, seen early in the walk, was designed and built in 1897 by Sir Guy Dauber for Mrs Harris, who lived at Rock House, a short way down the hill. It was meant to serve the parishioners who found it difficult to reach St Giles at Matlock, but it was also a place for those who preferred a High Church service.

5 Turn left past the school along a lane that becomes unsurfaced when you get beyond **Town End Farm**. This track climbs gently as a wide track around the fenced perimeter of the quarry to reach an old gateway across the narrowing track at the edge of woods; there's also a waymark arrow ahead and an old stone gatepost here.

6 Don't go ahead, but look left for a squeeze stile into pasture. Follow the path straight across to another stile into woods. Drop down to an old lane at a ruinous barn. Take the lower track, past a rusty gate, and walk through to the stub-end of a tarred lane.

7 This is the hamlet of **Upperwood**. Walk ahead across the turning area and around the left bend, remaining with this narrow tarred lane between cottages for nearly 0.5 mile (800m) to pass the lodge-house entrance to the **Heights of Abraham** showcave. Just around the next bend, leave the lane for a stepped path through the woods on the left, signposted '**Public Footpath to Matlock**'. Climb some steps to a high wooden footbridge over the **Heights of Abraham** approach road, and then continue on the woodland path. You'll pass under the Heights of Abraham cable cars (not easily seen) before eventually joining a track that has come in from the left.

8 This track joins **St John's Lane** and the outward route at **Cliffe House**. Retrace your steps back to the start.

King's Head

Tiny, diamond-leaded windows, thick, weathered stone mullions and the mellowed stone structure to the cosy and homely King's Head indicate the pub's great age. Local word says that it was opened on the day King Charles I was executed in January 1649, although a more reliable date is the 1677 included in the structure. Outside, it is awash with colourful hanging baskets and flower tubs; inside are the Yeoman's Bar and the King's Lounge, both full of atmosphere. Expect darkwood panelling, glowing wood-burning stoves in winter, old benches and pews, a wealth of porcelain and china, and scrubbed tables topped with candles and fresh flowers. Don't forget tip-top ales from Bateman's and a good blackboard menu. It stands in the tiny market square next to the remarkable stepped Market Cross.

Food

Look to the chalkboard for steak and kidney pudding, parsnip and sweet potato bake, Caribbean lamb, Barnsley lamb chop, and a choice of fresh fish, perhaps including trout with prawn and garlic sauce. At lunchtime expect sandwiches and lighter meals.

Family facilities

Children will enjoy the pub's characterful interior – they are welcome throughout. They can choose from their own menu and eat al fresco in the sheltered courtyard on sunny days.

Alternative refreshment stops

The Barley Mow in the Dale just off the Via Gellia offers real ale and has a reputation for excellent food.

☛ **Where to go from here**

The Peak District Mining Museum at Matlock Bath Pavilion on the A6 alongside the River Derwent has reconstructed mines to explore and crawl through (www.peakmines.co.uk).

about the pub

King's Head
62 Yeoman Street, Bonsall
Derbyshire DE4 2AA
Tel 01629 822703

DIRECTIONS: in Bonsall village, near Point **5** on the route

PARKING: 10

OPEN: closed Monday lunch

FOOD: daily

BREWERY/COMPANY: Bateman's

REAL ALE: Bateman's XB, Dark Mild, seasonal beers

DOGS: welcome throughout

The White Peak Plateau

195

🚴 **CYCLE**

4h00 · 11.5 MILES · 18.4 KM · LEVEL 123

From the High Peak Trail and excellent by-roads to timeless villages and old churches.

Ancient Walls

One of the great characteristics of the White Peak are the miles of dry-stone walls that thread the landscape from valley bottom to the very tops of the plateau. You can pass them by without giving them a second thought, but they have a fascinating history that goes back to medieval times when the great monastic estates controlled huge tracts of land and boundaries were established between these religious holdings and the lands of the great families.

As the monasteries disappeared, their lands were gradually parcelled up, and a further phase of wall building occurred. These walls are often winding and uneven. Huge areas still remained open however. As well as the wealthy estates, poor villagers also were permitted to farm dispersed strips of land near their homes. These initially were separated by low earth embankments. From the early 1700s onwards land reform saw such holdings consolidated into larger areas, each separated by a stone wall. These small strip fields can be seen at Chelmorton.

The Enclosure Awards of, largely, the 18th century, saw the great, unwalled estates split up into regular 'Parliamentary' fields (each Enclosure Award needed an Act of Parliament); it is these regular, geometric walls that form the mosaic that dominate today's landscape. Some walls were even built by French prisoners during the Napoleonic Wars.

the ride

1 Ride north along the old railway, leaving the **Royal Oak** on your left. The current end of the High Peak Trail at **Dowlow** is soon reached; turn right here along a surfaced track for **Chee Dale** that heads for the A515. This is marked on the OS map as a footpath, but has been upgraded as part of the development of the **Pennine Bridleway** project and is open to pedal cycles. A fenced path beside the A515 then takes you right to a crossing point. Take great care crossing directly over here and join a lane heading north.

The small church at Chelmorton

2 This peaceful lane undulates across the limestone uplands, with grand vistas all around across a patchwork of old stone walls and hay meadows. Where the **Pennine Bridleway** joins a rough lane, you remain on the tarred road. A lengthy downhill freewheel brings you to a crossroads. Carefully cross straight over and continue along the lane, rising very gradually up the one street that makes up **Chelmorton**. Continue to the end to find the old **church**.

3 Drop back downhill again slightly to reach a left turn; take this and start a lengthy but shallow climb back up on to the breezy uplands. At the T-junction turn left, signposted '**Flagg and Taddington**', joining a largely flat road with excellent sight lines. Again, there are great views and there is little traffic to disturb your enjoyment. At the next junction turn right, signed **Flagg**, starting a good long descent into the village. Keep left at a bend, dropping along the straggling main street of the village and past the little **church**. Keep left to arrive at the **Plough Inn**, at the edge of the village.

4 Continue past the Plough for about 500yds (457m) to a right turn for **Monyash**, joining a rather bumpy surfaced lane and soon a long, easy descent to a T-junction. Here turn right, signed Monyash, to another long downhill cruise to the outskirts of **Monyash**. A short climb brings you to the village centre crossroads, village green and the **Bull's Head Inn.**

MAP: OS Explorer OL24 White Peak

START/FINISH POINT: Hurdlow car park, High Peak Trail, grid ref SK 128660

TRAILS/TRACKS: old railway track, back lanes with light traffic

LANDSCAPE: small walled fields, views across the White Peak plateau

PUBLIC TOILETS: Parsley Hay

TOURIST INFORMATION: Buxton, tel 01298 25106

CYCLE HIRE: Parsley Hay 01298 84493, www.derbyshire.gov.uk/countryside

THE PUB: The Plough Inn, Main Street, Flagg, see Point 4 on route

❗ Two direct crossings of an A road need care. Suitable for older children and/or fitter cyclists, one long climb of around 0.5 miles (800m) requires regular rest stops

Getting to the start

Hurdlow car park (named Sparklow on OS maps) on the High Peak Trail, is signposted off the A515 Buxton to Ashbourne road about 6 miles (9.7km) south of Buxton. At the crossroads signed for Monyash in one direction and Crowdecote/Longnor in the other, turn towards Longnor to the car park

Why do this cycle ride?

This is an easy, flowing route along quiet back roads and a section of the Pennine Bridleway. Largely level, quiet, minor roads skim between walled fields to charming villages. Rising gently to Monyash, lanes then rise steeply to the White Peak plateau before an exhilarating ride back to the start.

Researched and written by: Neil Coates

Lathkill Dale

Lathkill Dale runs east from the village of Monyash. It starts as a shallow dry riverbed and, about 1 mile (1.6km) down the valley, the River Lathkill springs from a cave and broadens out into a clear stream, the haunt of water voles and dippers.

what to look for

The area around Lathkill Dale, a National Nature Reserve, is rich in wild flowers in late spring and early summer, such as orchids, cowslips and the rare Jacob's ladder.

A common spotted orchid (Dactylorhiza fuchsii)

The Plough Inn

Flagg is no more than a strand of roadside farms and cottages surrounded by pastures, hay meadows and cornfields, so it's good to find that the pub in this secluded hamlet is thriving. Set well back from the lane, the Plough is a solid limestone building with a warren of little rooms radiating off the main bar room which features a splendid log fire, heavy beams, a few window seats and old local photos on the walls. Off to one end is a large pool and games room; at the other end is a light and airy luncheon room with light-blue walls, wicker-style chairs and pub dining tables. Upstairs there is a superb little restaurant, open to the rafters with an air of the East and a faint touch of Gothic decoration. An excellent pub, well worth passing the others on the route to find.

Food

You'll find an extensive printed bar menu offering Lancashire hotpot, lasagne, salmon en croute, steak and kidney pudding, a good range of steaks and a chalkboard listing several daily specials. The same menu serves the upstairs restaurant.

about the pub

The Plough Inn
Main Street, Flagg, Buxton
Derbyshire SK17 9QR
Tel 01298 85557

DIRECTIONS: the pub is on the route; alternatively it can be reached by following signs off the A515 south east of Buxton

PARKING: 40

OPEN: daily, all day Saturday and Sunday. Closed Monday lunchtime

FOOD: daily

BREWERY/COMPANY: free house

REAL ALE: Timothy Taylor Landlord, Marston's Pedigree, guest beers

ROOMS: 2 en suite

Family facilities

In summer, families should head for the hedged and lawned beer garden which enjoys rurals views. Children are most welcome indoors and youngsters have their own menu to choose from.

Alternative refreshment stops

There are pubs at Sparklow (Royal Oak), Chelmorton (Church Inn) and Monyash (The New Inn); tea rooms in Monyash; snacks at Parsley Hay.

5 Carefully cross directly over, taking **Rakes Road**, signposted '**Newhaven and Youlgreave**' and continue with a long ascent out of Monyash. Allow plenty of time to pause and take in the superb panorama across the southern stretches of the Peak District, easily visible over the low limestone walls. The road gradually levels out before dropping to the A515.

6 Take care crossing here, as the traffic can be fast despite restrictions on both speed and overtaking here. Go diagonally across to the lane signposted for the **Parsley Hay car park**. Just along the lane turn right along the access road to the car park. Pick up the **High Peak Trail** here and follow it north (signed as the Pennine Bridleway towards Peak Forest) to return to the car park at Hurdlow.

☛ Where to go from here

Buxton Spa Water is freely available from an ever-flowing tap in St Ann's Terrace, on The Crescent. On the southern edge of Buxton is Poole's Cavern, where you'll find Derbyshire's largest stalactite (www.poolescavern.co.uk).

Haddon Hall has proved a popular location with film-makers as a setting for period drama. Television productions and feature films shot here include: Franco Zeffirelli's Jane Eyre *(1996);* The Prince and the Pauper *for the BBC; Granada Television's* Moll Flanders; *and* Elizabeth *(1999).*

The hall has one of the most romantic English country gardens in Britain. The glorious terraced rose gardens and herbaceous borders are displayed against the backdrop of great stone buttresses and ancient walls of the house. Huge yew bushes by the gardener's cottage have been shaped into intricate topiary figures.

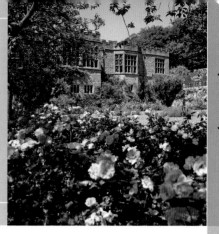

The colourful flower beds at Haddon Hall

Lathkill Dale

Lathkill Dale contrasts the wastes of a long-past lead-mining industry with the purity of its water.

Lead Mining and the Transparent Stream

Today, when you descend the winding lane into this beautiful limestone dale, you're confronted by ash trees growing beneath tiered limestone crags, tumbling screes, multi pastel-coloured grasslands swaying in the breeze and the crystal stream, full of darting trout.

Yet it was not always so. In the 18th and 19th century lead miners came here and stripped the valley of its trees. They drilled shafts and adits into the white rock, built pump houses, elaborate aqueducts, waterwheels and tramways; and when the old schemes failed to realise the intended profits, they came up with new, even bigger ones. Inevitably nobody made any real money, and by 1870 the price of lead had slumped from overseas competition and the pistons finally stopped.

On this walk you will see the fading but still fascinating remnants of this past, juxtaposed with a seemingly natural world that is gradually reclaiming the land. In reality it's English Nature, who are managing the grasslands and woods as part of the Derbyshire Dales National Nature Reserve. The walk starts with a narrow, winding lane from Over Haddon to a clapper bridge by Lathkill Lodge. A lush tangle of semi-aquatic plants surround the river and the valley sides are thick with ash and sycamore. In spring you're likely to see nesting moorhens and mallards. In the

Lathkill Stream flowing through reeds

midst of the trees are some mossy pillars, the remains of an aqueduct built to supply a head of water for the nearby Mandale Mine. The path leaves the woods and the character of the dale changes markedly once again. Here sparse ash trees grow out of the limestone screes, where herb Robert adds splashes of pink.

After climbing out of Cales Dale the walk crosses the fields of the White Peak plateau. If you haven't already seen them, look out for Jacob's ladder, a 3ft (1m) tall, increasingly rare plant with clusters of bell-like purple-blue flowers. By the time you have crossed the clapper bridge by Lathkill Lodge and climbed up that winding lane to the car park, you will have experienced one of Derbyshire's finest dales.

the walk

1 Turn right out of the car park, and descend the narrow tarmac lane, which winds down into **Lathkill Dale**.

2 Just before reaching **Lathkill Lodge** and the river, turn right along a concessionary track that runs parallel to the north bank. The path passes several caves and a mineshaft as it weaves its way through woodland and thick vegetation. South of **Haddon Grove**, beyond a gate and stile, the trees thin out to reveal the fine limestone crags and screes of the upper dale. The path now is rougher as it traverses an area of screes.

3 Go over the footbridge and follow a little path sneaking into **Cales Dale**. After 400yds (366m) take a left fork along a narrow path down to a stile. You now join the **Limestone Way** long-distance route on a steep, stepped path climbing eastwards out of the dale and on to the high pastures of **Calling Low**.

4 The path heads east of south east across the fields then, just before **Calling Low Farm**, diverts left (waymarked) through several small wooded enclosures. The path swings right beyond the farm, then half left across a pasture to its top left-hand corner and some woods.

5 Over steps in the wall the path cuts a corner through the woods before continuing through more fields to reach a junction of lanes; turn left along the near one.

The old mill in Lathkill Dale

3h00 / **5 MILES** / **8 KM** / **LEVEL 1 2 3**

MAP: OS Explorer OL24 White Peak

START/FINISH: Over Haddon pay car park, grid ref SK 203657

PATHS: generally well-defined paths, 24 stiles

LANDSCAPE: partially wooded limestone dales

PUBLIC TOILETS: at car park

TOURIST INFORMATION: Bakewell, tel 01629 813227

THE PUB: Lathkil Hotel, Over Haddon, see Directions to the pub, page 232

❗ Limestone dale sides can be slippery after rain. The ascent of the steps in Point 3 is particularly long and steep. The climb from the clapper bridge back to Over Haddon at the end of the route is also challenging

Getting to the start

Over Haddon is to the south of the B5055 road that links Bakewell and Monyash. The village is well signposted off this road; the car park is on Main Street.

Researched and written by:
Neil Coates, John Gillham

Short-eared owl
(Asio flammeus)

while you're there

In Over Haddon visit the Lathkill Dale Craft Centre built around a pleasant courtyard behind Manor Farm. You'll find an information centre, tea rooms, restaurant and craft and gift shops.

what to look for

In the dry periods of summer the river may disappear completely under its permeable bed of limestone. The sun-dried soils on the southern slopes are too thin to support the humus-loving plants of the valley bottom. Instead, here you'll see the pretty purple orchid, cowslips with their yellowy primrose-like flowers and clumps of the rock rose with its yellow flowers.

6 After about 500yds (457m), follow a signposted footpath that begins at a stile in a dry-stone wall on the left. This heads north east across fields to the huge farming complex of **Meadow Place Grange**. Waymarks show you the way across the cobbled courtyard, where the path continues between two stable blocks into another field.

7 After heading north across the field to the brow of **Lathkill Dale**, turn right through a gate on to a zig-zag track descending to the river. Cross the old clapper bridge to **Lathkill Lodge** and follow the outward route, a tarmac lane, back to the car park.

Lathkil Hotel

Formerly 'The Miners Arms', named from the old lead mines that date back to Roman times, an overnight stay at this unpretentious inn remains in the memory for its panoramic views from the Victorian-style bar down into Lathkill Dale and across the village to Youlgreave and Stanton Moor. Much beloved by walkers, who generally fill the two simply furnished rooms at lunchtime, the pub stocks up to five real ales and offers good quality bar meals. The large, airy main bar is warmed by a blazing log fire in winter.

Food

The home-cooked food has an enviable reputation locally with a lunchtime hot and cold buffet in summer and more extensive evening choices supplemented by cooked-to-order pizzas. Typically, tuck into tiger prawns in filo pastry, then follow with sea bass with garlic and rosemary or Wootton Farm venison steak with Stilton sauce. Good soups and filled rolls at lunchtime.

Family facilities

Children are welcome in the dining room where they have a children's menu to choose from. Smaller portions of main menu dishes are also available. There is patio seating with wonderful views.

Alternative refreshment stops

Geoff's Diner or the café in the craft centre.

☛ Where to go from here

Nearby Haddon Hall, home of the Dukes of Rutland, is well worth a visit. This impressive 14th-century country house has beautifully laid out gardens surrounding a Gothic style main building (www.haddonhall.co.uk).

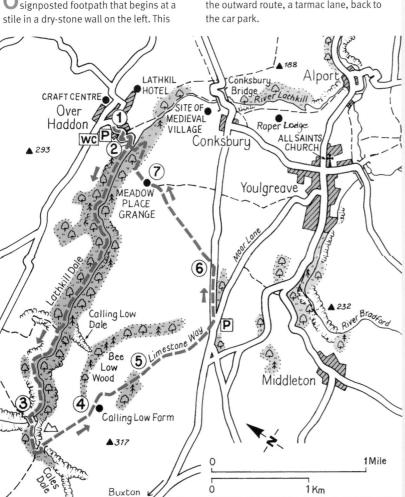

about the pub

Lathkil Hotel
Over Haddon, Bakewell
Derbyshire DE45 1JE
Tel 01629 812501
www.lathkil.co.uk

DIRECTIONS: 400yds (366m) from the village car park, along Main Street, then Wellgate Lane

PARKING: roadside parking

OPEN: daily, all day Saturday and Sunday

FOOD: daily

BREWERY/COMPANY: free house

REAL ALE: Marston's Pedigree, Hartington Bitter, guest beers

DOGS: welcome in the bar

ROOMS: 4 en suite

The place to go for authentic Bakewell Puddings

Bakewell and the Monsal Trail

An easy ride from the town of Bakewell, with its railway heritage, which loops through a picturesque limestone village and riverside hay meadows.

Bakewell and the Monsal Trail

The Monsal Trail is largely the trackbed of the former main line railway linking Manchester Central to Derby and London St Pancras. Opened in 1849 and built by the Midland Railway, it was latterly renowned for its comfortable Pullman carriages before closing in 1969. There

are ambitious plans to restore services through the Peak District, and a start has been made at nearby Rowsley, from where Peak Rail runs seasonal services through to Matlock and the surviving branch line to Derby. During the summer months the railway's banks (and the roadside verges) are bright with the vivid blue flower of the meadow cranesbill, that can often be seen in great drifts along with the ox-eye daisies and willowherb.

Bakewell is famed for its puddings, but there's much more to look out for here, including the Old House Museum and the lively market (Wednesdays are particularly busy and vibrant). Great Longstone was once a renowned centre for stocking manufacture, established by immigrant Flemish weavers who often traded their goods at the village market cross.

the ride

1 Access to the trackbed remains via the gap at the left side of the imposing structure. Turn left along the level track, a compacted and well-surfaced route that, beyond the industrial units that occupy the former goods yard, runs initially through thin woods. Passing beneath the main road, the buildings of Bakewell are left behind and soon **Hassop Old Station** comes into view.

2 The station buildings are largely gone, although an old warehouse has been converted to other uses. Beyond here, the trees become less constricting, and views to the hill slopes climbing towards **Longstone Edge** draw the eye. There's an

abundance of summer wild flowers along this section. The old trackbed passes under and over several roads and lanes before reaching the impressive buildings at Great Longstone's **old station**. The station partially retains its canopy, while next door is one of the buildings of the Thornbridge Estate.

3 A sign here warns that there is no exit for cycles beyond this point, but it is worth cycling the extra .25 mile (400m) to the end of the useable track for some great views across towards the hidden **River Wye** in its deep valley. You can choose here to simply retrace your route back to Bakewell, a total distance of 5.25 miles (8.4km). Another option, though, is to return to **Great Longstone Station** and take the steep flight of steps, left, to a minor road. Turn left along this, an easy, level ride to the village centre at **Great Longstone**.

4 At the market cross and village green, fork right along either of the lanes. Both wind down to the main street, lined with fine limestone cottages and houses, to reach the White Lion. Just beyond this, take **Church Lane**, left, to rise up a gentle hill to the parish **church**. The road bends right here, commencing an undulating, easy ride along this narrow road, **Beggarway Lane**, offering excellent views up to **Longstone Edge** and occasional glimpses back towards Bakewell.

5 In about 0.75 miles (1.2km), turn right along the lane that leaves at a left

Left: Medieval five-arch bridge spanning the River Wye in Bakewell

3h00	8 MILES	12.9 KM	LEVEL 123

SHORTER ALTERNATIVE ROUTE

1h15	5.25 MILES	8.4 KM	LEVEL 123

MAP: OS Explorer OL24 White Peak

START/FINISH: Bakewell Old Station, grid ref SK223690

TRAILS/TRACKS: old railway trackbed and back lanes

LANDSCAPE: woods and pastures below limestone edges, river valley, hay meadows

PUBLIC TOILETS: central Bakewell

TOURIST INFORMATION: Bakewell, tel 01629 813227

CYCLE HIRE: none near by

THE PUB: Monsal Head Hotel, Monsal Head, see Directions to the pub, page 234

❗ One short climb, one long downhill stretch

Getting to the start

The old railway station in Bakewell is on Station Road – the road that forks off to the right at the memorial as you take the A619 road for Baslow out of the town centre and cross the bridge over the Wye. There's ample parking at the old station.

Why do this cycle ride?

This is an easy, largely level ride from Bakewell into the folded, wooded countryside that characterises the eastern fringes of the national park. A couple of shorter add-ons include one of the Peak's charming little villages and a pleasant ride above the Wye Valley.

Researched and written by: Neil Coates

while you're there

Great Longstone, like many villages in the White Peak, owes its existence mainly to lead mining. The miners' families supplemented their income by keeping livestock and this is recorded in the carvings of a milkmaid and a miner in St Giles Church.

did you know?

You can enjoy Sunday lunch, a cream tea or an evening meal on the lovingly restored Palatine restaurant car on the Peak Rail line as you watch the scenery go by.

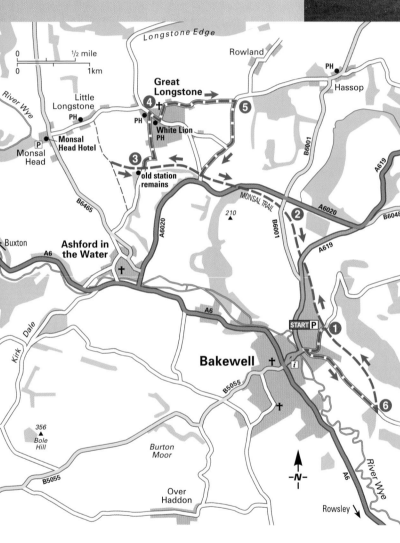

Monsal Head Hotel

Set against a spectacular backdrop of hills and dales, the disused viaduct at Monsal Head has long been a familiar landmark in the Peak District. In days gone by horses pulled guests and their luggage from the railway station up the steep incline to this imposing, ivy-covered hotel. However, the place for walkers, cyclists and passing trade is the Stables Pub to the rear of the building. The former stables, converted into a thriving bar, offer real ale and great food. Outside it's bare stone, two storeys with a steep pitched roof and wooden sash windows, while inside the fittings have been largely retained, with half-a-dozen stalls converted into individual drinking corners, each with cushioned wall benches. Add a huge solid fuel stove for cold winter days, eight real ales on handpump and a super courtyard garden for summer drinking and you have a great pub to retreat to after your ride.

Food

One menu operates throughout the restaurant, bar and eating area, with specials such as char-grilled wild boar, braised ham shank, and roast chump of lamb, as well as halibut, monkfish, salmon and scallops from a good fishy choice.

about the pub

Monsal Head Hotel
Monsal Head, Bakewell
Derbyshire DE45 1NL
Tel 01629 640250
www.monsalhead.com

DIRECTIONS: from Bakewell Old Station drop to the main road junction and turn right for Baslow. In 0.5 miles (800m) fork left (B6001) and continue to a traffic island. Turn left, then right after a mile (1.6km) to Great Longstone. Continue through the village to Monsal Head

PARKING: 15 (pay car park adjacent)

OPEN: daily, all day

FOOD: daily, all day

BREWERY/COMPANY: free house

REAL ALE: Caledonian Deuchars IPA, Theakston Best and Old Peculiar, Timothy Taylor Landlord, local guest beers

Small plates, grills, salads, omelettes and jacket potatoes extend the range.

Family facilities

Children are welcome away from the bar and small children have their own menu. There's good courtyard seating with plenty of tables and chairs.

Alternative refreshment stops

Pubs in Great Longstone (The Crispin Inn and The White Lion); choices in Bakewell.

☛ Where to go from here

The Peak Rail preserved railway (south of Rowsley) runs seasonal services, mostly steam operated (www.peakrail.co.uk). The spectacular medieval fortified manor of Haddon Hall has featured in many films and TV programmes (www.haddonhall.co.uk).

bend. **Longreave Lane**, is an easy downhill coast for nearly a mile (1.6km), eventually reaching a junction at a railway overbridge. Fork left here just before the bridge, up a gravelly ramp to regain the old railway. Turn left to return to **Bakewell**. To extend the route you can now cycle across the car park and take **Station Road** downhill (take care by the parked cars). At the junction at the bottom turn sharp left along **Coombs Road**, passing the car park entrance. This

peaceful, level lane runs for about a mile (1.6km), amid pastures and hay meadows to reach a high-arched viaduct crossing.

6 Immediately before the viaduct, look for the **Monsal Trail** board on the left, indicating a short, sharp incline up which you wheel your bicycle to gain the old railway. Turn left to return to **Bakewell**; there are some good views across the town from this elevated route.

while you're there

Bakewell, next door to Ashford, is well worth a visit. The spired church of All Saints looks down on this bustling town, which is built round a fine 14th-century bridge over the River Wye. The 13th-century church, refurbished in Victorian times, has many interesting monuments, including one in the Vernon Chapel dedicated to Sir George Vernon who was known as 'King of the Peak' because of his famed lavish hospitality. The Bakewell Show, held in August, is claimed to be the longest continuous running agricultural show in England.

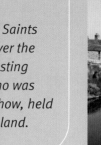

Through Monsal Dale

The River Wye flowing through a park in Bakewell

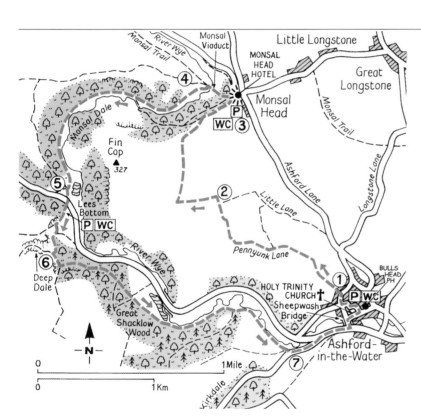

3h00 **5.5 MILES** **8.8 KM** **LEVEL 123**

MAP: OS Explorer OL24 White Peak

START/FINISH: Ashford-in-the-Water car park, grid ref SK 194696

PATHS: well-defined paths and tracks throughout, 17 stiles and gates

LANDSCAPE: limestone dales and high pasture

PUBLIC TOILETS: at car park

TOURIST INFORMATION: Bakewell, tel 01629 813227

THE PUB: The Bull's Head, Ashford-in-the-Water, see Getting to the start

❶ Parents should keep a close eye on children whilst in the vicinity of the Monsal Head Viaduct. There's a short, steady climb in Point 5. Take care crossing the A6

Getting to the start
Ashford-in-the-Water is signposted off the main A6 road a few miles north west of Bakewell. In the village pass the Bull's Head pub on your right and take Court Lane, the next narrow road on the right to the car park.

Researched and written by:
Neil Coates, John Gillham

Gods there morning and evening – Apollo and the sweet Muses of light – walking in fair procession on the lawns of it and to and fro among the pinnacles of its crags'.

It's just a short walk along the rim to reach one of Derbyshire's best-known viewpoints, where the Monsal Viaduct spans the gorge. Built in 1867 as part of the Midland Railway's line to Buxton, the five-arched, stone-built viaduct is nearly 80ft (25m) high. But the building of this railway angered Ruskin. He continued, 'you blasted its rocks away, heaped thousands of tons of shale into its lovely stream. The valley is gone and the Gods with it'.

The line closed in 1968 and the rails were ripped out, leaving only the trackbed and the bridges. Ironically, today's conservationists believe that those are worth saving and have put a conservation order on the viaduct. The trackbed is used as a recreational route for walkers and cyclists – the Monsal Trail. The walk continues over the viaduct, giving birds-eye views of the river and the lawn-like surrounding pastures. It then descends to the riverbank, following it westwards

Hilltop view of Monsal Dale and the disused railway viaduct

Following the ever-changing River Wye from Ashford-in-the-Water through lovely Monsal Dale.

The Valley of the Gods
The Wye is a chameleon among rivers. Rising as a peaty stream from Axe Edge, it rushes downhill, only to be confined by the concrete and tarmac of Buxton and the quarries to the east. Beyond Chee Dale it gets renewed vigour and cuts a deep gorge through beds of limestone, finally to calm

down again among the gentle fields and hillslopes of Bakewell. The finest stretch of the river valley must be around Monsal Head, and the best approach is that from Ashford-in-the-Water, one of Derbyshire's prettiest villages, just off the busy A6.

After passing through Ashford's streets the route climbs to high pastures that give no clue as to the whereabouts of Monsal Dale. But suddenly you reach the last wall and the ground falls away into a deep wooded gorge. John Ruskin was so taken with this beauty that he likened it to the Vale of Tempe; '...you might have seen the

Wild garlic (Allium ursinum)

The River Wye threading its way through Monsal Dale

what to look for

While away a few hours in Ashford-in-the Water by wandering along the banks of the River Wye. Stop at a bridge and look out for brown trout in the crystal clear waters below.

beneath the prominent peak of Fin Cop. The valley curves like a sickle, while the path weaves in and out of thickets, and by wetlands where tall bulrushes and irises grow. After crossing the A6 the route takes you into the mouth of Deep Dale then the shade of Great Shacklow Wood. Just past some pools filled with trout is an entrance to the Magpie Mine Sough. The tunnel was built in 1873 to drain the Magpie Lead Mines at nearby Sheldon. Magpie was worked intermittently for over 300 years before finally closing in the 1960s.

the walk

1 From the car park turn right up **Court Lane**, then right again along **Vicarage Lane**. A footpath on the left, signposted '**To Monsal Dale**', doubles back left, then swings sharp right to continue along a ginnel behind a row of houses. Beyond a stile the path enters a field. Head for a stile in the top right corner that drops you into **Pennyunk Lane**, where you turn left. This walled stony track winds among high pastures. Pass by a sign for Monsal Head, continuing to the end of the lane.

2 Turn left here past a squeeze stile and up along a field edge. In 400yds (366m) turn right through two handgates on to another track, heading north towards the rim of **Monsal Dale**. The path runs along the top edge of the deep wooded dale to reach the car park at **Monsal Head**.

3 Take the path marked 'Access to Viaduct' here. Descend steps and walk on to a fingerpost pointing left for '**Viaduct & Monsal Trail**'. Cross the viaduct; at the far end go through a stile on the left and take the middle of three paths, losing height gently through scrub woods down into the valley. This shouldn't be confused with the steep eroded path plummeting straight down to the foot of the viaduct.

what to look for

Ashford's Sheepwash Bridge, over the Wye was built on the original site of the ford that gave the village its name. On the far side of the bridge you can see the enclosures where the sheep were gathered for washing. The square-towered Norman Church of Holy Trinity, has an interesting 'black marble' tympanum over the door.

4 Now you walk down the pleasant valley. The right of way is well away from the river at first but most walkers trace the riverbank to emerge at **Lees Bottom** and a roadside stile.

5 Cross the A6 with care and go through the **White Lodge** car park where the path back to Ashford begins. Pass by the ticket machine and go through the wide gap in the fence and along a surfaced path. Take a stile and remain on the compacted path. At a fork go left; shortly climb a stile at a waymark post for **Ashford**, **Deepdale** and **Sheldon**. A braided path climbs steeply ahead to another low-waymarked fork, here go left for **Ashford** and **Sheldon**. The path continues to rise to a small gateway into **Great Shacklow Wood**.

6 The path now climbs more easily through the trees before levelling out as a ledged path along the steep wooded slopes. Ignore a path signed for Sheldon; eventually the path comes down to the river and shortly passes behind a ruined mill, its wheels still in place. Remain on the path (ignore the bridge) to reach a minor road at the bottom of **Kirkdale**.

7 Turn left along the road, down to the A6 and turn right towards **Ashford**. Leave the road to cross **Sheepwash Bridge**. Turn right along **Church Street**, then left along **Court Lane** to the car park.

The Bull's Head

There's a real buzz about this 17th-century coaching inn tucked away among charming old stone cottages close to the church. Locals in the know fill the place soon after opening, staking their claim to bar stools and favourite tables, as this is the place to eat in Ashford. But it's not just the food that draws folk in. The beamed bars are filled to the brim with antiques, lovely carved settles, cushions, clocks and country prints, and glowing coal fires burn in the grate on cold winter days. Peruse the day's newspapers over a pint of Robinson's Bitter, or tuck into some decent home-cooked food prepared from seasonal ingredients.

Food

You'll find no printed menus or chips here. Daily changing chalkboards may list a dozen dishes, perhaps baked plaice with lobster sauce, salmon and dill fishcakes with lemon sauce, chicken strips in white wine and lovage sauce, and sticky toffee pudding. The excellent lunchtime sandwiches are made with bread baked on the premises.

Feeding the ducks on the River Wye in the Peak District National Park

Family facilities

Children are welcome in the taproom where they can choose small portions of some of the dishes available, but note that this is a chip-free establishment. There is a peaceful rear garden overlooking the village recreation ground.

Alternative refreshment stops

Monsal Head Hotel in Monsal Head serves bar meals.

☞ Where to go from here

At Matlock Farm Park, near Matlock Bath, you'll find British farm animals alongside more exotic breeds. There is also a go-kart track (www.matlockfarmpark.co.uk).

about the pub

The Bull's Head
Church Street, Ashford-in-the-Water
Bakewell, Derbyshire DE45 1QB
Tel 01629 812931

DIRECTIONS: see Getting to the start

PARKING: 12

OPEN: daily

FOOD: no food Thursday evening in winter

BREWERY/COMPANY: Robinson's

REAL ALE: Robinson's Bitter, Old Stockport, seasonal ale

DOGS: welcome inside

while you're there

Make a detour to the tiny village of Litton with its cluster of 18th-century stone cottages beside a green, and a set of stocks close to the local pub.

Chimney Cottage at the 19th-century Litton Mill

Miller's Dale

*Left: The River Wye
Below: Looking over Hope Valley from the summit of Win Hill*

The rural serenity of modern Miller's Dale belies its early role in the Industrial Revolution.

Miller's Dale

It's all quiet in Miller's Dale these days, but it wasn't always so. Many early industrialists wanted to build their cotton mills in the countryside, far away from the marauding Luddites of the city. The Wye and its tributaries had the power to work these mills. The railway followed, and that brought more industry with it. And so little Miller's Dale and its neighbours joined the Industrial Revolution. The walk starts in Tideswell Dale. Nowadays it's choked with thickets and herbs but they hide a history of quarrying and mining. Here the miners wanted basalt, a dark, hard igneous rock that was used for road building.

Today's smart apartments belie the gruesome past at Litton Mill. The Memoirs of Robert Blincoe, written in 1863, tells of mill owner Ellis Needham's cruelty to child apprentices, who were often shipped in from the poorhouses of London. Many of the children died and were buried in the churchyards of Tideswell and Taddington. It is said that ghosts of some of the apprentices still appear in or around the mill. The walk emerges from the shadows of the mill into Water-cum-Jolly Dale. At first the river is lined by mudbanks thick with rushes and common horsetail. It's popular with wildfowl. The river widens out and, at the same time, impressive limestone cliffs squeeze the path. The river's widening is artificial, a result of it being forced to form a head of water for the downstream mill.

Round the next corner is Cressbrook Mill, built by Sir Richard Arkwright, but taken over by William Newton. Newton also employed child labour but was said to have treated them well. The rooftop bell tower would have peeled to beckon the apprentices, who lived next door, to the works. Like Litton, this impressive Georgian mill was allowed to moulder, but is now restored as flats. The walk leaves the banks of the Wye at Cressbrook to take in pretty Cressbrook Dale. In this nature reserve you'll see lily-of-the-valley, wild garlic, bee and fragrant orchids. Just as you think you've found your true rural retreat you'll climb to the rim of the dale. Look across it and see the grassed-over spoil heaps of lead mines. Finally, the ancient strip fields of Litton form a mosaic of pasture and dry-stone walls on the return to Tideswell Dale.

the walk

1 Follow the path southwards from beside the car park's toilet block into **Tideswell Dale**, taking the right-hand fork to cross over the little bridge.

2 On entering **Miller's Dale**, go left on the tarmac lane to **Litton Mill**. Go through the gateposts on to a concessionary path through the mill yard. Beyond the mill, the path follows the **River Wye** as it meanders through the tight, steep-sided dale.

3 The river widens out in **Water-cum-Jolly Dale** and the path, liable to flooding here, traces a wall of limestone cliffs before reaching Cressbrook. Do not cross the bridge on the right, but turn left to pass behind **Cressbrook Mill** to the road.

4 Turn left along the road, then take the right fork which climbs steadily into **Cressbrook Dale**. Where the road doubles back uphill leave it for a track going straight ahead into the woods. At a major fork keep right; the track degenerates into a narrow path that emerges in a clearing high above the stream. Follow it downhill to a footbridge over the stream, then take the right fork path, which climbs high up the valley side to a stile in the top wall. (To omit a very steep climb to a viewpoint here, follow the valley-bottom path at the fork past the footbridge to rejoin the route at the stepping stones in Point 5).

5 Do not cross the stile, but take the downhill path to the dale bottom, where there's a junction of paths. The one wanted here re-crosses the stream on stepping stones, and climbs into **Tansley Dale**.

6 The path turns right at the top of the dale, follows a tumbledown wall before crossing it on a step stile. Head for a wall corner in the next field, then veer right through a narrow enclosure to reach a walled track just south of **Litton village**.

7 Turn left along the track, which comes out on to a country lane at the crown of a sharp bend. Keep straight on along the lane but leave it at the next bend for a cross-field path to **Bottomhill Road**. Across the road, a field path descends to the lane at **Dale House Farm**. Turn left, then right on a lane marked unsuitable for motors. Follow this road into **Tideswell**.

3h00	6 MILES	9.7 KM	LEVEL 1 2 3

MAP: OS Explorer OL24 White Peak

START/FINISH: Tideswell Dale pay car park, grid ref SK 154743

PATHS: generally well-defined paths and tracks, path in Water-cum-Jolly Dale liable to flooding, 12 stiles and gates

LANDSCAPE: limestone dales

PUBLIC TOILETS: at car park

TOURIST INFORMATION: Buxton, tel 01298 25106

THE PUB: George Hotel, Commercial Road, see Point 8 on route

❗ There is a particularly steep section of the route at Point 4 which we recommend that families with young children avoid by remaining on the valley floor path. If the River Wye is running high and brown then the route will be impassable at Water-cum-Jolly Dale, Point 3

Getting to the start

Tideswell is just south of the A623 between Chapel-en-le-Frith and Baslow. Look for the 'Cathedral of the Peak' brown tourist signs. Pass through Tideswell and continue downhill, bending right into Tideswell Dale. The car park (well signed) is nearly a mile (1.6km) south.

Researched and written by:
Neil Coates, John Gillham

what to look for

In summer, in the dramatic twisting limestone gorges of Miller's Dale and Water-cum-Jolly Dale, look out for dippers and grey wagtails on the River Wye. The dipper is stubby and brown with a white bib, while the grey wagtail is slim and graceful with a long tail, blue-grey back and yellow breast

The grey wagtail (Motacilla cinerea)

8 After looking around the village head south down the main street, then right on to **Gordon Road** (in front of the **Horse and Jockey pub**), which then heads south.

9 Where this ends, continue down the stony track ahead, which runs parallel with the main road. At a gate keep left to find a waymarked handgate; the path then drops gradually to a stile on to the road just above the treatment works. Turn right along the road; in 150yds (137m) take a path off a rough pull-in, left, to join a path back to the car park.

what to look for

Cressbrook Dale is part of the Derbyshire Dales National Nature Reserve. On the limestone grassland you may see orchids, cranesbill, mountain pansy, globeflower and spring sandwort. One of the many limestone-loving plants is the Nottingham catchfly, which loves dry, stony places. The white flowers roll back in daytime, but are fragrant at night. Small insects are often caught on the sticky stalks but nature is being wasteful, for they're never devoured by the plant.

George Hotel

Locate Tideswell's famous parish church and you will find this unpretentious stone-built pub-hotel, its creeper-clad façade festooned with colourful hanging baskets and window boxes in season. A warm welcome awaits walkers in the traditional L-shaped bar lounge/dining area, with its comfortable upholstered wall benches, simple pub tables and chairs, and walls lined with old village photographs and local watercolours (for sale). The separate, quarry-tiled taproom is popular with local drinkers. The sheltered rear garden has been created from the old stabling yard; tables to the front overlook the village.

about the pub

George Hotel
Commercial Road, Tideswell
Buxton, Derbyshire SK17 8NU
Tel 01298 871382
www.george-hotel-tideswell.co.uk

DIRECTIONS: centre of Tideswell next to the church. See Getting to the start

PARKING: 20

OPEN: daily, all day Saturday and Sunday

FOOD: daily, all day Saturday and Sunday in summer

BREWERY/COMPANY: Hardy & Hanson

REAL ALE: Hardy & Hanson Best, Old Trip, seasonal ale

DOGS: welcome in the pub

ROOMS: 5 bedrooms

Family facilities

Children are made most welcome, as long as they keep away from the bar, and they have a standard children's menu to choose from. There is good outdoor seating.

Alternative refreshment stops

Angler's Rest at Miller's Dale, Hills and Dales Tea rooms in Tideswell.

☛ Where to go from here

Miller's Dale Railway Station (the line closed in 1967), just off the route, is a fascinating old site with a good deal of information on the railway, the wildlife and walks in the area.

Food

Reliable, traditional pub meals come in the form of steak and ale pie, seafood crumble, lasagne and a good range of sandwiches and filled jacket potatoes. Blackboard specials may include beef bourguignon and monkfish in Pernod on a bed of fennel.

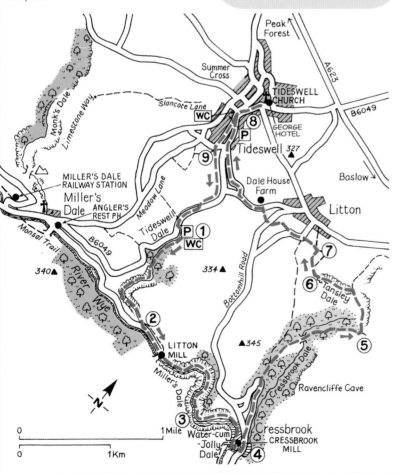

Mam Tor

Mam Tor, a famous viewpoint and landmark just under 2 miles (3.2km) northwest of Castleton, is known as the 'shivering mountain'. The east face is a dramatic and loose expanse of crumbling rock and the area below is constantly on the move as the loose shale slips further down the valley.

The fortifications of a large Iron Age fort can still be seen on the top of the hill and the trig point on the summit is placed on top of a tumulus which probably dates from the Bronze Age.

A wide-ranging view across the Peak District from Mam Tor

Castles and Caverns at Castleton

Castleton is where the limestone of the White Peak and the shales and gritstone of the Dark Peak collide.

Castleton and Cavedale

Castleton, a bustling tourist town, is the last settlement before the Hope Valley narrows and squeezes into the rocky ravine of Winnats. At Castleton the shales and gritstone of the Dark Peak meet the limestone plateaux of the White Peak. Here countless generations of miners have dug shafts and enlarged the natural caves that riddle the bedrock in search of ore. Here too, they built a road that eventually succumbed to the landslides of Mam Tor, 'the Shivering Mountain'. The castle keep is perched on an outcrop of limestone. It's one of the earliest stone-built castles in the country, built shortly after the Norman Conquest by William Peveril, William the Conqueror's illegitimate son.

The entrance to Cavedale is narrow and dramatic. From the village square you turn a corner and enter an awesome limestone ravine. Geologists used to think Cavedale was a collapsed cavern, but now believe it is a valley carved by glaciers of the last Ice Age. A little limestone path takes you through the ravine, climbing past cave entrances and over the tops of a system of subterranean passages, including those of the nearby Peak Cavern. The valley shallows and the next part of the journey is over high fields enclosed by dry-stone walls. Mam Tor, the Shivering Mountain, dominates the view ahead and soon you look down on the crumbling tarmac of the ill-fated road and huge shale landslides.

The first Castleton cavern of the day is the Blue John Cavern, high on the side of Mam Tor. It takes its name from the purple-blue fluorspar, unique to Castleton. The floodlights of the chambers show off the old river galleries with crystalline waterfalls, and an array of stalagmites and stalactites.

Winnat's Pass winding through the Peak District beyond Castleton

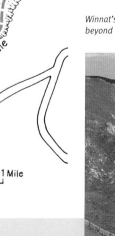

3h00 · **5 MILES** · **8 KM** · **LEVEL 1 2 3**

MAP: OS Explorer OL1 Dark Peak

START/FINISH: main Castleton pay car park, grid ref SK 149829

PATHS: mostly good limestone paths and old moorland roads, muddy in wet weather; around 16 stiles and gates

LANDSCAPE: limestone ravines and high pastureland

PUBLIC TOILETS: at car park

TOURIST INFORMATION: Castleton, tel 01433 620679

THE PUB: Castle Hotel in the centre of Castleton, set back off the main road

❗ Some steep slopes towards the end of the walk between the entrances to Blue John and Treak Cliff Caverns. The path below Blue John Cavern can be tricky in wintry conditions

Getting to the start

From Sheffield take the A625 south west and turn right on to the A6187 near Hathersage, following the brown tourist signs for the Caverns at Castleton. The main village car park is through the village on the right.

Researched and written by:
Neil Coates, John Gillham

200

WALK

what to look for

On a summer Sunday, the skies around the escarpments of Mam Tor, Lord's Seat and Rushup Edge are full of hang-gliders and paragliders making full use of the breezes and updraughts.

Beyond the Blue John Cavern, a path crosses the slopes past Treak Cliff Cavern to the Speedwell Cavern, at the foot of Winnats Pass. Here, lead miners excavated a level into the hill, through which they built a subterranean canal, 547yds (500m) long. This took them eleven years, but low yields and high costs forced the early closure of the mine. Take a boat trip down the canal to a landing stage just short of the 'Bottomless Pit', named because the spoil thrown in by miners made no impression on its depth.

The last stretch takes you across the National Trust's Longcliffe Estate. Before retreating to Castleton, take a look back up the valley, and across the limestone that was once a coral reef in a tropical lagoon.

the walk

1 From the car park turn left down the main street, then right along **Castle Street**, passing the **church** and the youth hostel.

2 On reaching the **Market Place**, turn left to **Bar Gate**, where a signpost points to **Cavedale**. Through a gate, the path enters the limestone gorge with the ruined keep of **Peveril Castle** perched on the cliffs, right.

3 As you gain height the gorge shallows. Go through a bridle gate in the dry-stone wall on the right, and follow the well-defined track across high pastureland. It passes through a gate in another wall before jioning a path that has descended the grassy hillside on the right. The track divides soon after the junction. Take the left fork, uphill, slightly away from the wall on the right to the top corner of the field. Go through the gate and follow a short stretch of walled track to a crossroads of routes near the old **Hazard Mine**.

4 Turn right through the gate here along a stony walled lane, which swings right to reach the B6061 near **Oxlow House Farm**.

Take the path beyond the right-hand gate across the road to pass the disused quarry on **Windy Knoll**.

5 Just before the road turn right on a grassy path parallel to the road. Join the road at a gate and turn left, then fork right down the lane for **Blue John Cavern**.

6 After 400yds (366m) turn right down the tarmac road to the **Blue John Cavern**, then left by the ticket office. Cross the stile in the fence and trace the path as it crosses several fields. Beyond a stile the path arcs right, traversing precipitous grassy hillslopes. Pass the **Treak Cliff Cavern** ticket office. Go left down concrete steps by the ticket office, then right on a concrete path with handrails.

7 Go through a gap in this handrail and follow a narrow cross-field path by a collapsed wall. On the approach to **Speedwell Cavern** the path becomes indistinct. Take an obvious gate straight ahead on to the **Winnats Pass Road**.

8 A path on the far side takes the route through **Longcliff Estate**. It roughly follows the line of a wall and veers left beneath the hillslopes of **Cow Low** to reach **Goosehill Hall**. Here, follow Goosehill (a lane), back into **Castleton**. Beyond **Goosehill Bridge**, turn left down a surfaced streamside path to the car park.

what to look for

Treak Cliff Cavern is one of the best places to see fossils. In the limestone you can study the remains of sea creatures that accumulated in the bed of a tropical sea 320 million years ago.

Castle Hotel

Unpretentious, yet full of character, this rambling, part 17th-century inn can be found tucked away from the main village road opposite the superb medieval church. Beyond the stone-built façade there's an inviting, stone-flagged bar with stone walls, carved beams, old pews and a magnificent open log fire. Equally comfortable adjoining rooms have open fires, a good mix of tables and chairs and walls lined with prints and old photographs of Castleton. Deep bay windows overlook the street and church, while outside there's a super heated terrace and a pretty garden with rural views.

Food

Good value bar food ranges from sausages and mustard mash with rich onion gravy, and chicken pie and Cajun salmon salad on the printed menu, to rump steak salad and chicken, bacon and avocado salad on the specials board. There is a separate sandwich menu.

about the pub

Castle Hotel
Castle Street, Castleton
Hope Valley, Derbyshire S33 8WG
Tel 01433 620578

DIRECTIONS: in the village centre, set back off the main road and opposite the church – see Getting to the start

PARKING: 20, or use main village car park

OPEN: daily, all day

FOOD: all day

BREWERY/COMPANY: Mitchells & Butler

REAL ALE: Bass, Tetley, John Smiths, guest beer

DOGS: on leads in garden only

ROOMS: 12 en suite

Family facilities
Children are welcome inside away from the bar and they have a good children's menu to choose from. There is a garden and terrace for fine days.

Alternative refreshment stops
There are plenty of tea shops, cafés, restaurants and pubs in Castleton

☞ Where to go from here
Besides the caverns seen on the route (Treak Cliff Cavern is one of the best places to see fossils), make time to visit Peveril Castle in the village. It has a Norman keep and enjoys spectacular views over the village and up Cavedale (www.english-heritage.org.uk).

while you're there

In Hathersage take a look round the parish Church of St Michael, which you pass on the hillsides above the village. It dates back to the 14th century, though the perpendicular tower and its spire are a hundred years younger.

The stained-glass east window came from the doomed church of Derwent before it was submerged beneath the rising waters of Ladybower Reservoir. In the churchyard a particularly long grave is claimed to be that of Robin Hood's henchman, Little John.

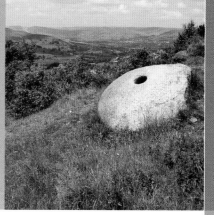

A 19th-century millstone on Millstone Edge above the Hope Valley

Stanage Edge

Skirting the gritstone cliffs which line Sheffield's moorland edge.

Hathersage and Stanage

From Moscar to Baslow a line of dark dramatic cliffs cap the heather moors east of the Derwent Valley. Stanage Edge, the highest of these cliffs, is a great place for walkers to stride out on firm skyline paths with Yorkshire on one side and Derbyshire on the other. High car parks mean that you can walk Stanage without much ascent, but it's more rewarding to work for your fun, so we'll start the route at Hathersage.

Hathersage is a neat village by the banks of the Derwent. The route starts on Baulk Lane and passes the cricket ground on its way through the little valley of Hood Brook. Gradients steepen and the route comes across the 16th-century castellated manor of North Lees Hall, the inspiration for Thornfield Hall, Mr Rochester's home in *Jane Eyre*. The remains of a chapel, built in 1685, only to be destroyed three years later, can still be seen in the grounds.

Above the hall the route climbs on to the moors and a paved causey track known as Jacob's Ladder takes it to the top of the cliffs. The cliff-edge path to High Neb and Crow Chin is a delight, the extensive views taking in a good deal of the Derwent and Hope valleys, Mam Tor and Kinder Scout. It may seem strange to descend to the foot of the cliffs, but the lost height doesn't amount to much and you can now view them from the perspective of the climber.

After rejoining the edge, the path passes above Robin Hood's Cave, where the legendary outlaw perhaps hid from the

Above: View south east along Stanage Edge
Below right: Grave of Little John

Sheriff of Nottingham, to reach the high road and climbers' car park. Now there's just Higger Tor to do. The rocky knoll surrounded by an ocean of heather makes a fine finale, one last lofty perch before the descent back to Hathersage.

the walk

1 From the car park in **Hathersage**, head up **Oddfellows Road** past the fire station. At the bend, go ahead into **Ibbotsons Croft** and along the ginnel through to the main road. Opposite, to the right of **The Square**, join **Baulk Lane**, soon passing the cricket ground. Beyond houses it becomes an unsurfaced track.

2 Just short of **Cowclose Farm** take the signposted left fork, which passes to the right of **Brookfield Manor** to reach **Birley Lane**. Turn right here, then left along a drive to **North Lees Hall**. After rounding the hall, turn right, climbing some steps that cut the corner to another track. This crosses hillside pastures before continuing through attractive mixed woodland.

3 A stepped path on the left makes a short cut to a roadside toilet block and mountain rescue post. Opposite this, a grassy path heads for the rocks of **Stanage**

Edge. After 200yds (183m) you join the path from the nearby car park. A paved path now climbs through **Stanage Plantation** before arcing left to the cliff top.

4 For the shorter option, turn right along the edge and pick up the route as detailed in Point 5, below. For the longer walk option, follow the firm edge path north westwards (left) to see the summit of **High Neb** and **Crow Chin**.

5 When you reach **Crow Chin**, where the edge veers north 200yds (183m) beyond the trig pillar, descend to a lower path that doubles back beneath the cliffs. Keeping within 100yds (91m) or so of the cliffs, this eventually joins a track coming up from the right, which returns the route to the top of the cliffs. (Shorter option goes on from here). Continue walking south east along the edge, soon keeping a broken wall on your left to eventually reach the trig pillar on the bouldery east summit (marked on OS maps by a spot height of 457m).

6 The track continues to the road at **Upper Burbage Bridge**. Go left along the road for 100yds (91m), then turn right to take the higher of the paths from the rear of the parking area before the bridges which head south to the top of **Higger Tor**.

7 From the rocky top, double back on a side path to the **Fiddler's Elbow Road** and two stiles opposite each other. Cross these and walk 30 paces to a wide cross-track. Turn left on this, and descend to **Callow Bank** to a walled track leading down to the **Dale Bottom Road**. Follow the road down for 300yds (274m) to a track on the

---

| 4h30 | 9 MILES | 14.5 KM | LEVEL 123 |

SHORTER ALTERNATIVE ROUTE

| 3h00 | 5.75 MILES | 9.2 KM | LEVEL 123 |

MAP: OS Explorer OL1 Dark Peak

START/FINISH: Hathersage car park, grid ref SK 232814

PATHS: well-defined paths and tracks, about 16 stiles and gates

LANDSCAPE: gritstone and heather moorland

PUBLIC TOILETS: at car park and on lane above North Lees

TOURIST INFORMATION: Castleton, tel 01433 620679

THE PUB: The Scotsman's Pack, Hathersage, see Point 8 on route

❗ Do not attempt this walk in misty weather. It is a very long, rewarding walk suitable for experienced family groups

Getting to the start

Hathersage is on the A6187 Hope Valley road. From Sheffield take the A625 and turn off right at the signs to Hope, Castleton and various caves. The pay car park in Hathersage is near the swimming pool and is signposted off the main street along Station Road (B6001).

Researched and written by: Neil Coates, John Gillham

201

241

WALK

what to look for

High Neb, the high point of Stanage Edge, is made of one of the finer gritstones which is ideal for rock-climbing, and on a summer weekend you will see plenty of evidence of this.

Old Millstone below Stanage Edge

right that traverses the hillslopes to **Toothill Farm**. Turn sharp left before the farmhouse on to a gated track that becomes a grassy field road. In 300yds (274m) look right for a stile into a sunken path leading to a tarred lane, taking the route through housing and down to Hathersage's impressively spired church and the Roman fort of **Camp Green**.

8 Turn right down **School Lane**, past the **Scotsman's Pack**, to reach **Main Road**, which descends into the centre of

what to look for

Beneath the cliffs of Stanage Edge you'll see piles of old millstones and grindstones, some intact and some incomplete. They are the abandoned relics of an industry that supplied the flourishing steelworks of Sheffield and local corn mills. French imports, which were both cheaper and better, and the coming of the roller mills saw the decline of the industry by the 1860s.

Hathersage. Then go left up the ginnel opposite **The Square** to return to the car park at **Hathersage**.

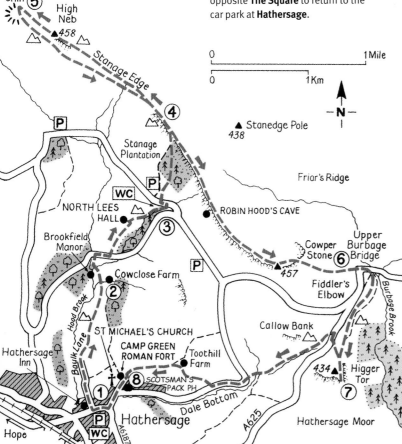

The Scotsman's Pack

Set into a hillside at the eastern edge of Hathersage, this imposing, gabled Edwardian inn borders a rushing trout stream and has long been a favoured watering hole among the local walking fraternity. The interior resembles a 'gentleman's parlour', with wood panelling and a huge copper fireplace at one end. The decorative beams are festooned with gleaming horsebrasses, and country prints and plates adorn the walls and display dressers. Comfortable wall-bench seating and an assortment of tables and darkwood chairs top the red carpet throughout the open-plan bar. Plush and modern it may be, but the welcome is warm and the huge selection of food is very popular.

about the pub

The Scotsman's Pack
School Lane, Hathersage
Hope Valley, Derbyshire S32 1BZ
Tel 01433 650253

DIRECTIONS: at the eastern edge of Hathersage on Point 8 of the route – see Getting to the start

PARKING: 14

OPEN: daily, all day Saturday and Sunday

FOOD: daily, all day Saturday and Sunday

BREWERY/COMPANY: Burtonwood

REAL ALE: Burtonwood Bitter and Top Hat, guest beer

DOGS: not allowed inside

ROOMS: 5 en suite

Family facilities
Well-behaved children are allowed in, if eating, at lunchtimes and early evenings. There is sheltered patio seating above the stream.

Alternative refreshment stops
There's generally a snack van on the car park at Upper Burbage Bridge.

☛ Where to go from here
See how everyday knives, forks, spoons and other tableware are made at the David Mellor Cutlery Factory at The Round Building just south of Hathersage off the B6001 (www.davidmellordesign.co.uk).

Food
Main menu dishes include smoked fish medley, pan-fried lambs' liver with bacon, and pork steak with apricot and ginger sauce. Daily specials may take in rack of lamb with mint gravy, beef fillet with Roquefort and brandy sauce, and a good selection of vegetarian meals. Book for Sunday lunch.

did you know?

Ashopton, which lay at the confluence of the rivers Derwent and Ashop, was a village of stone-built cottages, an inn and a blacksmith's shop. Its neighbouring village, Derwent, enjoyed an even quieter location.

After the completion of the dam in 1943, Ladybower Reservoir began to fill up and both villages were submerged. The reservoir holds soft water from the Bleaklow/Kinder watershed serving the cities of Sheffield, Nottingham, Derby and Leicester.

The Upper Derwent Valley reservoirs

A long and challenging route around the stunning chain of reservoirs in the Upper Derwent Valley.

Birds and bouncing bombs

Many of the high moorlands throughout the northern area of the Peak District are managed for grouse shooting, a long-established practice dating from Victorian times. In today's more conservation-minded days, the gamekeepers employed by the great estates and landowning companies are much more sympathetic to the natural predators of these game birds than were their predecessors.

Nonetheless, birds of prey such as the peregrine falcon are still targetted both by unscrupulous keepers and egg collectors, so defensive measures and management techniques are used to protect such raptors. You may see a peregrine 'stooping' (diving) at up to 150mph to kill its prey on the wing. A much more rare bird of prey is also regaining a toe-hold in the woods around the Upper Derwent reservoirs – the goshawk has recently been reintroduced, and is breeding successfully. During the nesting season (April to June), a remote-controlled camera sends back live pictures of a goshawk nest to the visitor centre at Fairholmes.

Paintings in the Yorkshire Bridge Inn are a reminder that the 617 Dambusters Squadron trained with their bouncing bombs here on Derwent and Howden reservoirs before their remarkable raid on the Ruhr dams in 1943. This was also the location of the film made in 1954 which tells the story of the raid.

the ride

1 Except on summer Sundays, the initial route is shared with cars, so take care. Head north from the **Fairholmes Centre**, rising to the level of the dam top of Derwent Reservoir. This dam was started in 1902, a year after the dam at Howden. Easy cycling with great views takes you past the memorial to Tip, a sheepdog who kept vigil beside his master's body, after the master perished on Howden Moors.

2 Dipping in and out of **Ouzelden Clough**, the road passes close to the site of **Birchinlee**, or 'Tin Town'. This village was created to house the workers who constructed the dams. Most of the buildings were of corrugated iron, hence the nickname. There's little evidence of the place today. Passing beside **Howden Dam**, the route now circuits a long arm of **Howden Reservoir** to arrive at the turning circle at Kings Tree, the end of the tarred road. This is a good place to turn around (9 mile/14.5km round trip) as the next section is more challenging.

3 Beyond the gate the route becomes a rough forest road that climbs gently through the woods above the narrowing tip of Howden Reservoir. At a fork keep right to drop to the old packhorse bridge at **Slippery Stones**. This bridge originally spanned the River Derwent at the hamlet of Derwent, now drowned beneath the waters of Ladybower Reservoir. The structure was rebuilt at this lonely spot on the Howden Moors in the 1940s. Just above the bridge swing sharp right to climb the roughening track along the eastern shore of the reservoir.

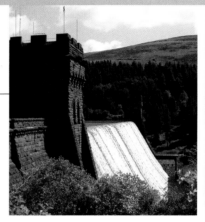

Howden Dam

4 The going is pretty rough for a mile (1.6km) or so before a well-graded service road heralds the approach to **Howden Dam**, particularly colourful in late spring and early summer when the rhododendrons are in full flower. A steep, rougher descent follows before the route comes close to the reservoir edge where steep, grassy banks drop straight into the water, so take care here. The track improves considerably as the route nears **Derwent Dam**. Passing close to one of the towers, the way develops into a tarred lane and passes the first of some isolated houses.

5 You can cut short the ride by turning right to pass the foot of **Derwent Dam** to return to **Fairholmes** (9.5 miles/15.2km). The main route continues south past **St Henry's Chapel**, becoming rougher again as it rounds an inlet to an interpretation board describing the now-lost village of Derwent which stood here until the 1940s.

6 Reaching a gateway, join the tarred lane and drop to the main road. Turn right along the wide cycle path across **Ashopton Viaduct**, and right again at the far end following the lane back to **Fairholmes**.

| 4h00 | 15 MILES | 24.2 KM | LEVEL 123 |

SHORTER ALTERNATIVE ROUTE

| 2h30 | 9 MILES | 14.5 KM | LEVEL 123 |

MAP: OS Explorer OL1 Dark Peak

START/FINISH: Fairholmes Visitor Centre, Upper Derwent Valley, grid ref SK176894

TRAILS/TRACKS: tarred lanes and rough mountain roads

LANDSCAPE: woodland and lakes amidst moorland and craggy valleys

PUBLIC TOILETS: at start

TOURIST INFORMATION: Fairholmes, tel 01433 650953

CYCLE HIRE: Fairholmes, tel 01433 651261

THE PUB: Yorkshire Bridge Inn, Ashopton Road, see Directions to the pub, page 244

❶ Take care at the start along a road shared by cars. There are rough tracks on the longer ride. The complete ride is suitable for older family groups using mountain or hybrid-style bikes

Getting to the start

Start at the Fairholmes Visitor Centre in the Upper Derwent Valley. This is signposted off the A57 Glossop to Sheffield road, immediately west of Ashopton Viaduct, which crosses the northern arm of Ladybower Reservoir. Fairholmes is 2 miles (3.2km) along this minor road.

Why do this cycle ride?

This route takes full advantage of the contrasting landscapes of the northern part of the National Park. It's a challenging family route of two halves: a gentle, forested, tarred lane replaced by rough upland tracks.

Researched and written by: Neil Coates

Slippery Stones

The packhorse bridge at the village of Derwent was moved before the construction of the reservoirs. It was rebuilt, stone by stone, at Slippery Stones at the head of Howden Reservoir.

The goshawk
(Accipiter gentilis)

Canada goose
(Branta canadensis)

202

CYCLE

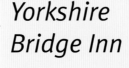

Yorkshire Bridge Inn

An armful of awards have been handed out to 'The Bridge' in recent years, not least third place in Pub Garden of the Year. The 200-year-old pub nestles in close to the famous Ladybower Reservoir, scene of the Dambusters' training exercises before their dramatic raid. In summer you'll want to make use of the courtyard and beer garden, while in more inclement weather the bars provide a cosy sanctuary and plenty of interest. Comfortable rooms sport open fires or wood-burning stoves and low beams hung with tankards and jars; one displays photographs of long-lost villages (now under the reservoirs), while another remembers the Dambusters raid.

Food

Food is available in the bar and dining room and starters can range from tandoori chicken strips to giant Yorkshire puddings. Main courses are equally varied with dishes such as chicken italiano, giant prawn cocktail or, from the specials menu, rack of lamb on a minted onion and honey sauce or fresh-dressed crab salad. An impressive selection of sandwiches, filled jacket potatoes and salad platters will more than satisfy those just popping in for a bite.

Family facilities

Children are made very welcome in the bars and the fascinating memorabilia should keep them entertained. On sunny days there's no better place to be than in the beautiful, award-winning gardens. Young children have their own menu and

there are cycle racks and secure overnight garaging for guests' use.

Alternative refreshment stops

There is a snack bar at Fairholmes Visitor Centre and the Ladybower Inn is near Ashopton Viaduct.

☛ Where to go from here

The various caverns at Castleton are a long-time favourite with visitors of all ages. The most unusual is Speedwell Cavern, where access is by an underground boat trip (www.speedwellcavern.co.uk).

about the pub

Yorkshire Bridge Inn
Ashopton Road, Bamford
Hope Valley, Derbyshire S33 0AZ
Tel 01433 651361
www.yorkshire-bridge.co.uk

DIRECTIONS: the Yorkshire Bridge Inn is about 3 miles (4.8km) from the Fairholmes car park. Return to the main road and turn left across the viaduct. At the traffic lights turn right towards Bamford; the pub is 1 mile (1.6km) on the right

PARKING: 60

OPEN: daily, all day

FOOD: daily, all day Sunday

BREWERY/COMPANY: free house

REAL ALE: Timothy Taylor Landlord, Black Sheep Bitter, Stones Bitter, Theakston Old Peculier

ROOMS: 14 en suite

Map labels

River Derwent
Ronksley Moor
Slippery Stones 4
Linch Clough
Upper Hey
Middle Moss
Ridge Nether Moor 3
545 ▲
Howden Reservoir
Howden Moors
River Westend
Howden Dam
Birchinlee Pasture
Little Howden Moor
Birchinlee 2
Derwent Reservoir
538 ▲ Black Tor
Ouzelden Clough
Rowlee Pasture
Glossop
Derwent Dam 5
Derwent Valley
A57
River Ashop
START P 1
Fairholmes Visitor Centre i
St Henry's Chapel ●
487 ▲
Derwent Edge
Derwent Moors
521 ▲
P
Ladybower Reservoir
P
Sheffield
Nether Moor
A57
Crook Hill 374 ▲
Ashopton PH
6
River Noe
476 ▲ Lose Hill
462 ▲ Win Hill
● Yorkshire Bridge Inn
Ladybower Reservoir
P
A6013

0 ——— 1mile
0 ——— 1km

Peak Cavern

Discover Peak Cavern, one of the spectacular natural limestone caves in the Peak District, on an underground walk of about 0.5 mile (800m). In the Grand Entrance Hall are the remains of an ancient village where a community lived and worked, making ropes for the local lead mines for more than 400 years.

Deeper in the cavern are chambers, illuminated by fibre-optic lighting systems, with names such as the Orchestra Gallery, Roger Rain's House and the Devil's Cellar where you can hear the source of the River Styx.

Pennine Ways on Kinder Scout

Left : A stone path at the start of the Pennine Way
Below right: Walking on the Pennine Way

One end of the famous long distance trail ascends to the craggy outcrops of the Kinder Plateau.

The Pennine Way

Edale sits peacefully in a paradise of pasture, riverside meadow and hedgerow, surrounded by high peaks, the crags of Kinder Scout, and the rounded hills of the Mam Tor ridge.

In Depression-torn 1930s England, Tom Stephenson, secretary of the Ramblers' Association told the readers of the *Daily Herald* of his dream to create a long, green trail across the roof of England. It took 30 years, a mass trespass and Acts of Parliament to achieve, but in 1965, the Pennine Way was opened. Spanning over 250 miles (405km) from Edale to Kirk Yetholm in Scotland, it was Britain's first official long distance trail. Go to Edale any Friday night and you'll see eager Pennine Wayfarers poring over maps or looking through Wainwright's green guidebook.

Unfortunately the popularity of the Way has led to the main route through Grindsbrook being diverted along the foul weather route up Jacob's Ladder. But as you leave Edale, or to be more strictly correct Grindsbrook Booth, you can look across to the old route, which delves deep into the rocky ravine. Your route climbs boldly to the top of Ringing Roger (echoing rocks), with an edge walk round the chasm of Grindsbrook, taking you past Nether Tor to the place where the old Pennine Way track comes to meet you. The Way didn't bother with the comforts of the edge, but got stuck into those peat hags to the right. Past weathered gritstone sculptures and the rocky peak of Grindslow Knoll you come to another ravine – Crowden Brook.

This route descends by the brook, passing several waterfalls. Beneath the open fell the path seeks the recently planted pine, larch, birch and oak. Wild flowers, including bluebells, daffodils and primroses, proliferate in this delightful spot, just above Upper Booth. Finally you meet again the Pennine Way, following the new route back across the fields of Edale.

the walk

1 Turn right out of the car park pedestrian entrance beside the toilet block and head north into **Edale** village, under the railway and past the **Old Nags Head**. Turn right by a path sign and follow the path across the footbridge over **Grinds Brook**.

2 Leave the main **Grindsbrook Clough** path by the side of a barn, taking the right fork that climbs up the lower hillslope to a gate on the edge of open country.

Beyond the gate the path zig-zags above **Fred Herdman's Plantation** then climbs up the nose of the Nab to the skyline rocks. Where the path divides, take the right fork to the summit rocks of **Ringing Roger**.

3 Head towards the edge, left of a hut, climbing rough steps to gain the path along the rim of the plateau. For a long way it is paved. Follow this path above the cavernous hollow of **Grindsbrook** and past **Nether Tor**. The old **Pennine Way** route is met on the east side by a large cairn.

4 Ignoring the left fork heading for the outlier of **Grindslow Knoll**, follow the paved footpath right (west) to the head of another deep hollow, the clough of **Crowden Brook**.

5 Cross Crowden Brook, then immediately leave the edge to follow a narrow level path traversing slopes on the left beneath the imposing outcrop of **Crowden Tower**. This meets a rough path from the Tower before descending the steep grassy hillslopes to the banks of the brook. This is a very steep, rough descent and requires great care. The path now follows the brook, fording it on several occasions.

3h00 | 5 MILES | 8 KM | LEVEL 123

MAP: OS Explorer OL1 Dark Peak

START/FINISH: Edale pay car park; grid ref SK 125853

PATHS: rock and peat paths, about 16 stiles and gates

LANDSCAPE: heather moor

PUBLIC TOILETS: at car park

TOURIST INFORMATION: Edale, tel 01433 670207

THE PUB: The Old Nags Head, Hope Valley, see Point 1 on route

❗ There is a long, steep climb near the start of this walk. The return from Crowden Tower is particularly steep and potentially slippery. Recommended for experienced family walking groups only

Getting to the start

From Sheffield take the A625 and follow the brown tourist signs for the caverns at Castleton. At Hope, turn right for Edale opposite the church; in 5 miles (8km) turn right into the car park at Edale. Edale Station is served by trains on the Sheffield to Manchester line.

Researched and written by:
Neil Coates, John Gillham

what to look for

You walk along the edge of Kinder Scout's summit peat bogs. Peat was formed by mosses such as the bright green sphagnum moss you'll see on wet patches. The moss cover is now restricted to small patches. It has been replaced by sedges, grasses, heather and bilberry in a vegetation cover riven by deep and numerous hags in which the naked peat comes to the surface.

Edale

6 Go through the stile at the edge of open country, then cross a footbridge shaded by tall rowans to change to the west bank. From here the path threads through woodland before descending in steps to the road at **Upper Booth**. You now need to follow the **Pennine Way** path back to **Edale**.

7 Turn left along the lane and left again into Upper Booth farmyard before crossing a stile at the top right corner, signposted for Edale. After following a track to a gateway, bear left uphill to a stile above an old barn. Here the way traverses fields at the foot of **Broadlee Bank** before joining a tree-lined track into the village at the Old Nags Head. Turn right down the road back to the car park.

Old Nags Head

about the pub

The Old Nags Head
Hope Valley, Edale
Derbyshire S33 7ZA
Tel 01433 670291

DIRECTIONS: see Getting to the start

PARKING: 10

OPEN: all day, closed Monday and Tuesday November–Easter

BAR MEALS: daily, all day Saturday and Sunday

BREWERY/COMPANY: free house

REAL ALE: Grays Best and Premium, guest beer

DOGS: welcome throughout the pub (drinking bowls)

Food
On the basic pub menu you'll find the Nags Head Special, a giant Yorkshire pudding filled with beef stew; steak, ale and mushroom pie; leek and potato bake, and a good range of sandwiches and filled jacket potatoes. Chalkboard offerings may include mushroom and nut fettucini.

Family facilities
To the rear of the pub (and with its own access) there is a popular family room. Here children have their own menu to choose from, while on warmer days they can use the front terrace or the garden and enjoy the views.

Alternative refreshment stops
The Rambler Inn, also in Edale, serves good bar meals and there's a snack bar in an old railway carriage by the railway station.

☛ Where to go from here
Peak Cavern, in nearby Castleton, offers tours of the cave and demonstrations of the old craft of ropemaking (www.peakcavern.co.uk).

The Old Nags Head, one of the most renowned ramblers' pubs in the land, stands at the start (or end!) of the Pennine Way National Trail, England's classic 256-mile (412km) long distance footpath. Its setting is dramatic, with the great scalloped edges of Kinder Scout looming above the sandstone tiles and its long, low gritstone façade broken by a couple of gables overlooking the village square. Climbing roses scale the front, whilst hanging baskets and raised beds brighten summer days. Booted walkers can choose from a series of flagstone rooms that radiate from the bar in the front room. The Hiker's Bar has an open log fire – great for warming the toes on cold days. This is a welcome retreat offering good beer and wholesome pub food.

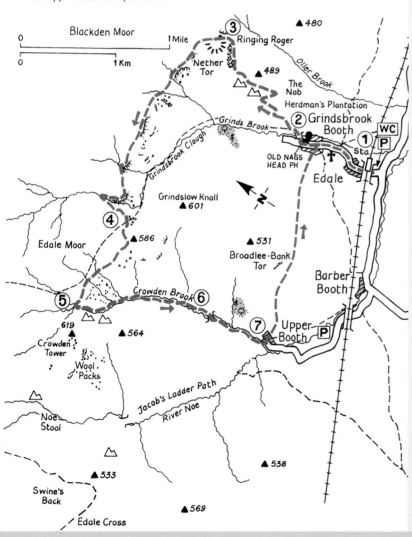

St Matthew's Church in Hayfield was rebuilt in 1818 after flooding

Town Bridge in Hayfield, known to locals as the Woolpack Bridge, was built in 1837. This is the third bridge to stand on this site, the first two were swept away by floods. When it was discovered that the bridge was partly built on quicksand, the problem was solved by using bags of wool as foundations.

Into the Dark Peak

Explore the Sett Valley Trail before branching off along well-graded back lanes and the Pennine bridleway to the foot of the forbidding Kinder Scout.

Bowden Bridge Quarry

On the extension to the route up the Sett Valley you'll pass by Bowden Bridge Quarry. This commands a special place in the hearts of many ramblers and those who seek open access to England's higher and wilder places. In the 1920s there was a growing demand from people who lived in the towns and cities adjoining what is now the Peak District National Park, for the fresh air and freedom that the hills offered. These areas, the property of the wealthy classes and the preserve of those shooting grouse for a few weeks a year, were fiercely guarded by gamekeepers and staff employed to keep interlopers off these great estates. Minor confrontations and court cases bubbled on until the early 1930s, when things came to a head. On 24th April 1932 several hundred supporters of the 'right to roam' assembled at Bowden Bridge Quarry and set off for the moorlands of Kinder Scout, to assert a right to roam freely. They were soon confronted by estate staff determined

Kinder Downfall at Kinder Scout

to keep them off. The protest leaders were arrested and jailed. This action, known as the Mass Trespass, led to improvements to access and to today's national parks' system. On a busy Sunday, maybe 3,000 people would take trains from Manchester to Hayfield Station to enjoy such hard-won freedoms. There's a plaque on the quarry wall recalling this seminal day.

the ride

1 The first stage is an easy ride along the trackbed of the former Hayfield to New Mills railway line that closed in the 1960s. Head away from the information and toilet block, following '**Sett Valley Trail**' signs past the cycle hire centre. Once through

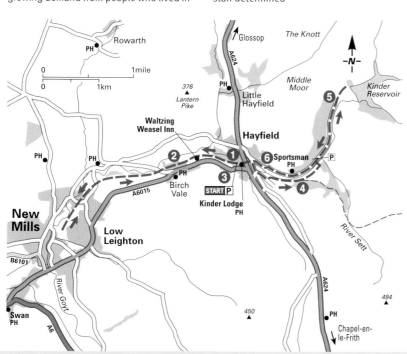

3h00 | **8.75 MILES** | **14.1 KM** | **LEVEL 1**23

SHORTER ALTERNATIVE ROUTE

1h45 | **5 MILES** | **8 KM** | **LEVEL 1**23

MAP: OS Explorer OL1 Dark Peak

START/FINISH: village car park at Hayfield Old Station, grid ref SK 037870

TRAILS/TRACKS: old railway trackbed, back lanes. One short footpath link where you walk your bicycle

LANDSCAPE: river valley woodlands with hill views; the extension has superb views to Kinder Scout plateau

PUBLIC TOILETS: Hayfield car park

TOURIST INFORMATION: Hayfield, tel 01663 746222

CYCLE HIRE: Old Station, Hayfield, tel 01663 746222

THE PUB: The Waltzing Weasel Inn, Hayfield, just off the route

Getting to the start

Start from the Hayfield village car park signposted off the A624 Glossop to Chapel-en-le-Frith road. Turn on to the A6015 road for New Mills and then turn immediately right just after the Kinder Lodge pub.

Why do this cycle ride?

This simple there-and-back route, ideal for families with young children, passes through the lower Sett Valley. An extension to the route heads towards Kinder Scout along bridlepaths and reservoir roads, revealing excellent views and passing a famous marker along the way.

Researched and written by: Neil Coates

A plaque marks the Mass Trespass on Kinder Scout by protesters claiming public right of access

Well Dressing

This ancient custom is celebrated in Hayfield in July, when for one week the wells are decorated with flowers and pictures made from petals, berries and leaves. The well in Bank Street is the first to be dressed. There is a Blessing Service on the first Sunday. For details contact www.visitpeakdistrict.com

did you know?

The road to Glossop passes Little Hayfield, just north of the main village. The mill here has been converted into flats, and there is a pub named The Lantern Pike after the hill that overshadows the hamlet. It's well worth the ascent for the excellent views.

a gateway a long, gentle descent takes the ride through the mature woodlands lining the old railway line. One section is a nature reserve; **Bluebell Wood** hints that a good time to visit is in May.

2 On the right, the mill lodge of one of countless local mills has been transformed into a fishery and is overshadowed by the hill of **Lantern Pike**. The trail bends to a roadside gate; don't take this but turn right to a lower gateway. Carefully cross the main road to the gateway opposite. The trail continues as an easy ride along a wooded course, crossing three more road crossings (all controlled by gates) to arrive abruptly at the end of the line, a gateway into **St George's Road** in **New Mills**. Turn here to retrace the route to the car park, a round trip of 5 miles (8km).

3 To extend the route along the **Sett Valley** and into the National Park, continue through the car park (signposted '**Kinder Trail**') and use the pedestrian-controlled lights to cross over the main road, keeping ahead to find the main village street. Turn right up this to reach the distinctively shaped old toll house near the hill crest. Fork left here, then immediately left again along **Valley Road**, signposted '**No Through Road**'. This quiet lane drops past cottages and houses to trace a course beside the lively **River Sett**. This is also the waymarked route of the new **Pennine Bridleway**.

4 Beyond the last cottages, you'll soon reach a parting of ways. The Pennine Bridleway is signed along a right fork, while a footpath is signed left along a wide path above the river. Dismount here and wheel your bicycle beside the water, shortly passing a footbridge to reach the **Peak Park Ranger Station** and a tarred access road. Pedal along this to **Bowden Bridge Quarry Car Park**. Turn right along the peaceful tarred lane. This undulates through woodland to arrive at a gateway into a service road to **Kinder Reservoir**. This is a concessionary bridleway, so pass through the gates and continue gently uphill to reach a turning area at the end of the road. It's well worth securing your bikes to rail fencing here and taking the very steep, cobbled bridlepath ahead-left a further 400yds (366m) to enjoy the views to **Kinder Downfall** (seasonal) waterfall and the surrounding hills.

5 Reclaim your bikes and return to **Bowden Bridge car park**. Remain on the lane here, soon passing by the **Sportsman** pub to reach the outskirts of **Hayfield**. The roads are narrow, so take care as you descend past cottages.

6 Ignore the first sharp left turn (**Spring Vale Road**); at the second a very short hill (**Bank Street**) drops you to the village centre. Turn left across the bridge, then right alongside the church to find the crossing back to the car park.

Birch Vale where you will find the Waltzing Weasel Inn

Waltzing Weasel Inn

Set within the heart of the Peak District, this traditional, 200-year-old country inn is popular with walkers and business people alike – no music or machines and no mobile phones permitted. Country antiques, carved oak pews and settles, stripped old tables, Victorian sporting prints, and a huge stone fireplace with roaring log fires in winter are impressive features of the cosy bar, while from the secluded terrace and garden and the mullion-windowed restaurant there are dramatic views of Kinder Scout. It's all very quiet, peaceful and homely, with the added attractions of good beer, decent wines and above average pub food.

Food
A solid English bar menu is supplemented by daily dishes inspired by the owners' love of Italy. You'll find sandwiches, home-made soups, freshly baked pizzas, Peak pie and fish of the day, and there's always a hearty stew or casserole. There is a good range of vegetarian meals plus a set evening menu in the restaurant and popular Sunday roast lunches.

about the pub

Waltzing Weasel Inn
New Mills Road, Birch Vale
High Peak, Derbyshire SK22 1BT
Tel 01663 743402
www.w-weasel.co.uk

DIRECTIONS: 0.5 miles (800m) from Hayfield along the A6015 towards New Mills

PARKING: 30

OPEN: daily

FOOD: daily

BREWERY/COMPANY: free house

REAL ALE: Marston's Best, Ruddles Best, guest beer

ROOMS: 5 en suite

Family facilities
Although there are no specific facilities for children they are welcome inside the pub and small portions of most main dishes are available. From the enclosed patio garden to the side there are good views for summer eating and drinking.

Alternative refreshment stops
There are plenty of pubs, cafés and restaurants in Hayfield.

☞ Where to go from here
The Chestnut Centre Wildlife Park near Chapel-en-le-Frith specialises in rare mammals and birds, such as otters and owls, from Britain, Europe and beyond (www.ottersandowls.co.uk).

There is a youth hostel in Crowden, just west of the Chapel of Ease, and this is where weary walkers head, weighed down with their heavy backpacks. More often than not they will have completed the first day of the Pennine Way over Kinder Scout and Bleaklow.

Longdendale Valley running through the rolling hills of the Peak District

The Jaws of Longdendale

The former Woodhead railway is the spine of a route that also includes reservoir roads amid the impressive scenery of Longdendale.

Torside Reservoir is popular with water sports enthusiasts as well as cyclists and walkers

Rare mammals and UFOs

During the winter you may be lucky enough to see one of Britain's rarest mammals near Crowden. Unlike its lowland cousin, the mountain hare changes the colour of its coat during the winter. Gone is the familiar brown, its place taken by a coat of white fur. With a white coat and potentially several weeks, if not months, of snow, it is difficult to spot these creatures, and thus they escape the attention of predators. In spring the fur gradually moults and is replaced by the familiar brown coat giving the hares an unusual mottled look.

If cycling at dusk, keep an eye on the sky for the 'Longdendale Lights'. Mysterious lights in the sky have been reported here for decades, and the area is a favourite with British UFO spotters.

The lights may be those of aircraft turning over a beacon en route to Manchester airport, or even will-o'-the-wisps – phosphorescent lights resulting from the combustion of natural gases.

the ride

1 From the car park, walk your bicycle the short distance up to the **Longdendale Trail** and turn left. At this initial stage you're passing through immature woodland, one of an innovative series of 'Life for a Life' plantations in the Greater Manchester area, where a departed loved one can be commemorated by the planting of a tree. The tree-lined route passes largely out of sight of **Torside Reservoir**, a popular venue for dinghy sailing, to reach the site of **Crowden Station**.

2 The two houses here are all that remain of the former railway, which was lifted amid great protest in the 1980s. Splendid views now open out up Longdendale, while above the far end of the dam is the little **Chapel of Ease, St James' Church**, where the victims of accidents and disease who died during the construction of the railway and reservoirs in the 1840s are buried in unmarked graves. The trackbed continues its easy, gentle climb eastwards just above the shoreline of **Woodhead Reservoir**.

3 This top reservoir narrows to a feeder stream, the infant **River Etherow**. Some miles downstream in **Stockport**, this combines with the rivers **Goyt** and **Tame** to form the **River Mersey**. The end of the line is reached at the **Woodhead Tunnels**. The latest, post-war bore was the last to be used by locomotives. Two earlier ones to the left are of a smaller diameter; one of them still has a narrow gauge railway disappearing into it. This allows engineers to service the power cables that have been routed beneath the **Pennines** here. High above, the notorious **Woodhead Pass Road** snakes across the hills. To your left are steep, heather-clad moors that are home to red grouse.

4 Returning to **Torside** you've completed 6 miles (9.7km). There's plenty more opportunity to the west however, so continue along the **Longdendale Trail** to a road crossing above the dam of **Torside Reservoir**. Take care crossing here. This is also where the **Pennine Way**, England's premier long-distance walk, is crossed. Pass high above **Rhodeswood Reservoir**, with views across to old hillside quarries now reclaimed by juniper woods. In about 0.75 mile (1.2km) reach a fingerpost giving a choice of routes. Turn right here (signed TPT West), go through a bridlegate and down a steep, gravelly path to a lane. Carefully cross this and take the even steeper rough track ahead (wheel your bikes here), leading to an undulating rough lane that eventually reaches the dam holding back **Valehouse Reservoir**. Cross this.

5 At the far side is a service road on the right. This is also a concessionary bridleway, so go through the gates and trace this level, tarred lane alongside the reservoir, the waters often obscured by pleasant woodlands. Beyond the lodge house the lane steepens around a series of bends to reach the next dam.

6 Cross this, **Rhodeswood Dam**, to a gate on the left signed for the **Longdendale Trail**. This steep track rises to an open gateway where you turn right up a narrower track to a bridlegate on the left. Take this to access the trackbed and turn left to return to the start.

3h30 | **11.5 MILES** | **18.5 KM** | **LEVEL 123**

SHORTER ALTERNATIVE ROUTE

1h30 | **6 MILES** | **9.7 KM** | **LEVEL 123**

MAP: OS Explorer OL1 Dark Peak

START/FINISH: Torside car parking, grid ref SK 068999

TRAILS/TRACKS: old railway trackbed, reservoir access roads and tracks

LANDSCAPE: moorland valley with reservoirs and industrial heritage

PUBLIC TOILETS: at start

TOURIST INFORMATION: Glossop, tel 01457 855920

CYCLE HIRE: Longdendale Valley Cycles, Hadfield tel 01457 854672

THE PUB: The Queen's Arms, 1 Shepley Street, see Directions to the pub, page 250

🛈 Don't do this ride on a cold, wet day with an easterly wind, as this will be funnelled down the valley making riding unpleasant and difficult

Getting to the start

Torside car park is on the B6105 south of Torside Reservoir to the east of Manchester. From the A628, turn right on to the B6105 just past Crowden.

Why do this cycle ride?

In this great trough-like valley that cuts through the Dark Peak, a string of reservoirs were developed during Victorian times to supply Manchester. The route follows a reclaimed railway along the shores of the reservoirs, while a branch crosses one of the dams to incorporate a pleasant wooded waterside stretch.

Researched and written by: Neil Coates

what to look for

The reservoirs attract a variety of wildfowl including mallard (the most common), teal, pochard, sandpipers, gulls and Canada geese. The moorland around Longdendale supports foxes and voles, and you may glimpse the mountain hare.

Birds such as the ring ouzel, wheatear, red grouse and golden plover may be seen, while predators such as kestrel, merlin and the short-eared owl also nest in the area. The grey heron may be seen anywhere in the valley.

The merlin (Falco columbarius)

205

CYCLE

Longdendale

DERBYSHIRE

Map labels:
Barnsley
Woodhead Tunnel entrances
Birchen Bank Moss
Bleaklow
633
Shining Clough Moss
Woodhead Reservoir
621
Sykes Moor
Shelf Moor
Shelf Brook
Hey Edge
Chapel of Ease
Harrop Moss
Crowden
START
Torside Reservoir
426
Cock Hill
Peaknaze Moor
A57
Shire Hill
500
Rhodeswood Reservoir
B6105
Swineshaw Reservoir
Queen's Arms PH
Valehouse Reservoir
Glossop
Arnfield Brook
Bottoms Reservoir
PH
Padfield
Arnfield Flats
Tintwistle
PH
Hadfield
Arnfield Reservoir
Gamesley

0   1mile
0   1km

The Queen's Arms

At the heart of a web of back lanes and passages that wind between the church, village cross and the nearby Manor Park, this is a splendid little pub in the picture-postcard village of Old Glossop. Hemmed in by fine old gritstone cottages, it's a solid street corner local with climbing roses and hanging baskets adding a splash of colour to the light stone exterior. The small taproom oozes character with darkwood panelling, deep upholstered wall benches, sporting prints on the walls, and eye-catching leaded glass windows. The low-beamed and carpeted L-shaped main bar is primarily laid up for dining, although drinkers are welcome here. There is a great range of real ales with changing guest beers.

Food
Expect to find a standard printed menu listing pub favourites – roast chicken, gammon, steak and kidney pie – and an ever-changing blackboard listing the likes of braised steak, lamb Henry and vegetable lasagne. Good value Sunday lunches; separate restaurant menu.

Family facilities
Although facilities are limited for children they are welcome away from the bar and a basic children's menu is available. Outdoor seating is limited to a few benches along the front of the pub.

about the pub

The Queen's Arms
1 Shepley Street, Old Glossop
Derbyshire SK13 7RZ
Tel 01457 862451

DIRECTIONS: The Queen's Arms is about 4 miles (6.4km) from Torside Car Park. Load the bikes on the car and turn left out of the car park on to the B6105 towards Glossop. In about 3 miles (4.8km), on a long downhill stretch into the outskirts of Glossop, pass the turn for the cemetery (right) and shortly turn left into Church Street. Pass the church, then bend right, and downhill, to find the pub on the left at a junction

PARKING: good on-street parking

OPEN: daily, all day

FOOD: daily, all day

BREWERY/COMPANY: Innspired

REAL ALE: Black Sheep Bitter, Worthington, 3 guest beers

Alternative refreshment stops
There is a part-time snack bar at Torside Visitor Centre.

☛ Where to go from here
In Stockport town centre are the fascinating Air Raid Shelters, a warren of tunnels hewn into the sandstone cliffs above the Mersey into which the townsfolk and millworkers could retreat during the Blitz (www.stockport.gov.uk and follow the links in Leisure and Culture).

206 ENDON
STAFFORDSHIRE

3.5 MILES (5.7KM) 1hr 30min

PATHS: Easy meadow paths and some roads, 11 stiles

SUGGESTED MAP: aqua3 OS Explorer 258 Stoke-on-Trent.

GRID REFERENCE: SJ 928537

PARKING: Ample parking in St Luke's Church car park

THE PUB: Plough

❶ From **St Luke's Church** car park turn **R** up hill. At top, go straight through farm to gate and slot in wall to **L**. Follow track round to **L** and, 50yds (46m) after **barn** on R, go through slot in wall. Cut off corner of field to reach stile, making straight for another stile. Bear **R** towards another double stile.
❷ Continue in same direction, keeping hedge just to your L. Cross stile at far side of field and proceed to another stile straight ahead. Keep following dry-stone wall to your L to reach well-hidden slot in top **L** corner of wall. After slot carry on up slope, now with hedge to your R.
❸ At top **R** corner of field, cross stile and continue along rough track to road. Go straight over and cross pair of stiles, following hedge on L. Cross next stile to small slot in far **L** corner of field.
❹ Turn **L** down road and, at junction with B5051, go **R** then 1st **L** along signed footpath, over residential road and up wide track to gate. After gate come to fork: head **L** to corner of wall then continue along bridleway that skirts bottom of **Tinster Wood**. As soon as path enters wood proper head sharp **L** down narrow track, following it to bottom **L-H** corner.
❺ Go through slot in wall to your **L**. Continue straight across field, keeping wall to your R, through pair of wall slots. Cross small footbridge beneath tree before cutting off corner of field. At gap in wall go **L** up muddy track and **L** along road. After 50yds (46m) go **R** following footpath sign.
❻ At bottom of this field cross stile to surfaced road, following it round to **L**. When you reach proper residential road, go hard **L** along rougher track to surfaced road. Head **R** and, shortly after, turn **L** along A53. Just before you get to **Plough** on R, head **L** up road signed to St Luke's Church.

207 ELLASTONE
STAFFORDSHIRE

3.5 MILES (5.7KM) 1hr 30min

PATHS: Gravel tracks, roads and grass trails, 11 stiles

SUGGESTED MAP: aqua3 OS Explorer 259 Derby

GRID REFERENCE: SK 118426

PARKING: Ample parking along roads

THE PUB: Duncombe Arms

❶ Ellastone, the start of the walk, inspired the setting of *Adam Bede*. From **post office** go **L** and then take 1st **L** down obvious gravel track. At junction of 2 bridleways, keep going straight to **Calwich Abbey**, where Handel composed *The Messiah* while staying with friends. Follow track **L** of abbey and along metalled road as far as **Calwich Home Farm**.
❷ Pass farm and follow track round to **L** of **The Grove** and through gate. At fork follow yellow footpath arrows to your **L** and, after 50yds (46m), veer **L** off track up short hill to stile in front of **Cockley** farm. Cross stile and head just to **R** of **Cockley**, following dirt and grass track all way to B5032.
❸ At road go **L** and then 1st **R**, through **Calwichbank Farm** and up gravel track. When track bears round to R, keep going straight into field, making for gap in hedge at top **R-H** corner. Shortly after this gap, go through gate on **R** and then follow hedge **L**, down field.
❹ At bottom follow hedge round to **L** and cut diagonally **R** across field to stile. After crossing stile, skirt round top of wood to another stile and continue as far as **Hutts Farm**. After stile take gravel track up hill to gate into farmyard and head straight on to another stile into field.
❺ Continue straight across this field making for corner of **Aldercarr Wood**. Keep going to stile in bottom **R-H** corner of field and carry on along **R**-H edge of next field. At far end is another stile, cross this and continue straight to B5032. Turn **R** along road and, after 100yds (91m), take path to **L**. Head diagonally **R** across field to double stile and then **L** round bottom of small mound with trees. Keep going as far as junction of 2 bridleways, at Point ❶, and from here retrace your steps back to post office.

208 ALTON
STAFFORDSHIRE

4.75 MILES (7.7KM) 1hr 30min

PATHS: Roads, gravel tracks and dirt trails

SUGGESTED MAP: aqua3 OS Explorer 259 Derby

GRID REFERENCE: SK 072423

PARKING: Ample parking on Alton village roads

THE PUB: Bulls Head Inn

❶ At **castle** gate, head straight down track to **R** of **St Peter's Church**. At main road, head **R**, down hill to river and **Alton Bridge Hotel**. Head **L** along metalled road, past hotel, going straight ahead where road goes round to L, along base of **Toothill Wood**. Just after road goes round an obvious hairpin bend, follow wide track into woods on **L** ('Smelting Mill and **Dimmings Dale**'). After 400yds (366m) go **R** off track down less obvious trail which will bring you out at Dimmings Dale car park and **Rambler's Rest** pub.
❷ Go through car park to **R** of pub and then continue straight on following signs for **Staffordshire Way**. Pass the **smelting mill,** now a private residence and although it's hard to see any detail the original waterwheel is still there and you can't miss the necklace of pools that stretches up the valley. The mill was built in 1741 and was used for forging lead ore. Next pass lake on your L, and continue straight on at end of lake, staying to **R** of impressive stone house.
❸ When you climb up to path coming in from **R**, go briefly **L**. Where path turns back on itself, carry straight on. At top of hill go **R** along metalled road, over cattle grid and follow this road all way to T-junction.
❹ Go **L** at junction and, after 400yds (366m), go **L** again just before **Old Furnace House**. When you get to fork in track, head **R**, close to stream and past series of pools, until you get to picnic table and causeway between 2 **pools**.
❺ Continue to **L** of stream after final pool, staying on **L** at 1st wooden footbridge. When you get to dry-stone wall barring way straight ahead, go **R** over wooden footbridge and continue to follow river **L**. This path will shortly bring you back to smelting mill and Rambler's Rest. From there head along road back to hotel and then retrace your steps back to St Peter's Church.

209 LOGGERHEADS
STAFFORDSHIRE

5.5 MILES (8.8KM) 2hrs

PATHS: Gravel tracks, roads and grass trails, 8 stiles

SUGGESTED MAP: aqua3 OS Explorer 243 Market Drayton

GRID REFERENCE: SJ 738359

PARKING: Ample parking in Loggerheads village

THE PUB: Loggerheads Inn

❶ Head along A53 towards Market Drayton and take 1st **L** along Kestrel Drive. Just after The Robins head **L** along gravel track down back of houses. Follow this to end of fence then go **L** along metalled track. This becomes gravel track leading to clearing; bear **R** past iron bar across wide track and, at fork, go **R** to clearing.
❷ From clearing take 3rd path on **L**. When this runs out, after 400yds (366m), veer slightly **R** on to narrower track to join gravel track. Turn **R** and continue for 0.5 mile (800m), until main track goes R.
❸ Head straight through gate and along footpath, hedge to **R-H** side. At bottom of field bear **R** towards **R-H** corner of trees. Go through gate and head up towards **Knowleswood** farm (derelict) and gate.
❹ Continue straight ahead and, at bottom of field, go **R** over stile and descend through small dip. At bottom of dip go through gate and head **R** along concrete track. At fork go **L** to **The Nook Farm** and, after 1 mile (1.6km), to **Home Farm**. Turn **R** along **Flash Lane** and up hill to **Blore Farm**. At junction keep going straight ahead and, after 200yds (183m), head **L** through hedge over stile. Follow hedge **R** to stile in **R-H** corner of field – a vantage point from which to view the main battlefield, now private farm land. At time of writing it was overun by pigs.
❺ Continue to bottom **R-H** corner of next field before bearing diagonally **R** across another field to **R-H** end of trees. Cross stile and follow faint track across middle of next field to stile.
❻ Follow path to fence ahead then cross stile to **L**. Keep following faint track alongside wood to your R and, at clearing, head diagonally across field to **L-H** end of trees. At corner of this field cross stile and footbridge to wide dirt track, which you follow **R** and up hill to large oak at top. Turn **L** to cross stile back on to **A53**.

210 BARLASTON
STAFFORDSHIRE

3.25 MILES (5.3KM) 1hr 15min

PATHS: Roads, gravel tracks and tow paths,1 stile

SUGGESTED MAP: aqua3 OS Explorer 258 Stoke-on-Trent

GRID REFERENCE: SJ 889395

PARKING: Ample parking along road at starting point

THE PUB: Plume of Feathers

❶ From **visitors' centre** drive head **L** across river and then **R** up drive towards **Barlaston Hall**. Go past this hall and continue along metalled road as far as crossroads in **Barlaston**. Josiah set up his first pottery factory in Burslem in 1759 and revolutionised what up until that point had been a cottage industry. Rather than rely on family members he paid people to work in the factory. A decade later and with business booming Josiah built a bigger factory in Burslem and this became a model for other pottery manufacturers. At crossroads turn **R** and after 250yds (229m), just past St John's Church on your L, head **L** along wide gravel track. This track passes through broad expanse of open farmland, with sweeping (if not altogether dramatic) views of Trent and Mersey canal to R and, beyond, flood plain of Trent Valley.
❷ After about 800yds (732m), you get to gate ahead of you: from here follow less obvious track **R**, around to stile where another track comes in on L. After crossing stile head **R** along track, straight over railway, before bearing **R** to bridge over canal. Go over bridge and take steps down to **L**.
❸ At bottom of steps head **L** and then follow canal all way to 1st bridge (at Barlaston) and then 2nd (at Wedgwood Station). The **Trent and Mersey Canal**, completed in 1777, linked the River Trent at Derwent Mouth near Derby with the Bridgewater Canal at Preston Brook, near the mouth of the Mersey. This effectively meant that the country could be navigated all the way from the west coast to the east and that fine clay from the West Country could be shipped to the doorstep of Josiah Wedgwood's factories. Head **L** here, up to metalled road, and then **R**, back towards visitors' centre. To find out more about Wedgwood, visit The Wedgwood Story **visitors' centre**.

211 KINVER
STAFFORDSHIRE

2.75 MILES (4.4KM) 1hr

PATHS: Wide gravel tracks

SUGGESTED MAP: aqua3 OS Explorer 219 Wolverhampton & Dudley

GRID REFERENCE: SJ 835836

PARKING: Ample parking in car park at start

THE PUB: The Red Bull, High Street, Killerton

❶ From National Trust car park, head back along road towards **Kinver** village. Within 100yds (91m), after going **R** at fork in road, follow public footpath signs to **R**, up into woods. Once you're in woods proper, take obvious stepped path **L** to small clearing and then turn 90 degrees to **R** to follow short, steep path to viewpoint.
❷ Enjoy the lovely views before continuing along top of escarpment, following wide, gravel track running more or less alongside western edge of ancient rectangular earthworks to your **L**, with glimpsed views across Severn Valley through trees to your R. After 400yds (366m) you will come to end of clearing. Take fork to your **L** here, up slight rise at corner of earthworks, before carrying on along escarpment top and past trig point.
❸ Staying on highest path, continue as far as National Trust boundary gate and then continue straight along main track avoiding smaller trails off to L and R. Path descends gradually to picnic spot with benches, an information board and signs for **Staffordshire Way** and **Worcestershire Way**. Narrow track to **R** leads back down to road and public toilet if required, although it criss-crosses other paths and it's very easy to lose your bearings!
❹ For this reason, it's easiest to return way you came. From path junction, head back along escarpment to viewpoint. At end, head **R** and then **L**, back down to clearing, and then **L** again down wooden steps, through trees to road. Follow road **L** as far as car park. For those armed with relevant OS map, there is suitable alternative which returns via forested slopes to west of ridge top, but because of number of little tracks that cross back and forth, it's difficult to give adequate directions here.

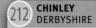
212 CHINLEY
DERBYSHIRE

5 MILES (8KM) 3hrs

PATHS: Field paths, quarry and farm tracks

SUGGESTED MAP: aqua3 OS Outdoor Leisure 1 Dark Peak

GRID REFERENCE: SK 041827

PARKING: Roadside parking by Chinley War Memorial, Maynestone Road, or village car park

THE PUB: Navigation Inn, Whaley Bridge

1 From **war memorial**, head northeast up **Maynestone Road**. Leave it for signposted path (grid ref 042828) through narrow ginnel on **L**. Go over stile; climb northwest across fields towards **Cracken Edge**. At cart track turn **R**, then **L** on path passing between 2 hillside farmhouses. Go through gate, past farm on **R** before climbing to lower edge of quarry.

2 Swing **R** on sketchy path, passing hawthorn tree at base of hillslope. Join quarry track that zig-zags up slope before heading beneath quarry cliffs. Go over stile in fence over track; climb by this fence to clifftop.

3 Turn **R** along narrow edge path, then **R** again on grassy ramp bridging 2 quarried pits. Now descend **L** to prominent grassy track running beneath brow of hill and past **Whiterakes** cottage.

4 Turn **R** on track from **Hills Farm** then descend to tarred lane which passes **Peep-O-Day** to A624.

5 Turn **L** on pavement. After 150yds (137m) cart track (**R**) takes your route past quarry crater. Turn **R** at T-junction of tracks to traverse lower slopes of **Mount Famine** to reach col beneath **South Head** peak.

6 To detour to **South Head** take obvious route which leaves track to climb to summit. Back at col, go through gate by more easterly of 2 access notices. Go over stile by pole and descend southwestwards to walled track.

7 Follow this down to crossroads of routes north of **Andrews Farm**. Keep ahead into muddy field. Path soon develops into track and joins descending cart track from **Andrews Farm**.

8 On reaching A624 turn **R** for 50yds (46m) then cross to signposted footpath, which cuts diagonally to **R** corner of 1st field before following wall towards **Otter Brook**. As old field boundary comes in from R, path turns half-**L** to cross brook on slabbed bridge.

9 Muddy path climbs out through scrubby woodland to **Maynestone Road**. Turn **L**; follow it to **Chinley**.

213 CHESTERFIELD
DERBYSHIRE

5 MILES (8KM) 3hrs

PATHS: Generally good paths and farm lanes. Field paths can be muddy at times of high rainfall

SUGGESTED MAP: aqua3 OS Outdoor Leisure 24 White Peak

GRID REFERENCE: SK 336727

PARKING: Linacre Woods car park

THE PUB: George & Dragon, Old Brampton

1 From bottom of lowest car park go down steps into woods. After about 100yds (91m) turn **R** along waymarked bridleway heading westwards, high above lower reservoir. Ignore path going off to L, which goes to dam of middle reservoir, but continue on wide bridleway along north shore of middle reservoir.

2 Take **R** fork on footpath raking up to top end of woods, high above upper reservoir's dam. Path continues westwards, dipping to one of reservoir's inlets. Cross bridge; follow well-defined concessionary footpath along shoreline.

3 At end of reservoir, ignore L turn over **Birley Brook**, but head west on waymarked footpath. Shortly exit wood via stile and enter first scrub woodland then fields with woods to L of wall and gorse bushes to R.

4 Cross stone slab across brook (grid ref 317727), then stile beyond it. Muddy path now climbs through more woods before emerging in fields north of **Wigley Hall Farm**. It passes to **R** of farm to tarmac lane in **Wigley**. Follow lane to crossroads.

5 Turn **L** towards **Old Brampton**. Just beyond **Royal Oak** pub turn **R** down tarmac bridleway, **Bagthorpe Lane**, following it past **Bagthorpe Farm**. Lane, now unsurfaced, descends into valley of **River Hipper**, passing through farmyard of **Frith Hall**, down to river bridge. Winding surfaced track climbs to **Westwick Lane**, where you should turn **L**.

6 Just before **Broomhall Farm**, descend **L** on another track down to river, then up other side of valley into **Old Brampton**.

7 Turn **L** on lane, passing **George and Dragon** pub and **church**. Turn **R** by telephone box. Track descends to top edge of **Linacre Wood**, and swings **R**.

8 At junction of paths turn **L** through gate before descending to dam. At far side of dam turn **L** on metalled lane, passing toilets and ranger's office; climb back to car park.

214 TISSINGTON
DERBYSHIRE

4.25 MILES (7KM) 2hrs 30min

PATHS: Field paths, lanes and an old railway trackbed, lots of stiles

SUGGESTED MAP: aqua3 OS Outdoor Leisure 24 White Peak

GRID REFERENCE: SK 177522

PARKING: The Tissington Trail pay car and coach park

THE PUB: Bluebell Inn

1 From car park follow trackbed of northeast bound **Tissington Trail**. After 800yds (732m) leave trail and turn **R**, over bridge and along cart track.

2 Just past 1st bend descend on waymarked but trackless path into valley of **Bletch Brook**, going through several stiles at field boundaries and across footbridge spanning brook itself. More definite path establishes itself on climb out of valley. It reaches top of pastured spur, well to **R** of small cottage.

3 In next high field, path follows hedge on **L** to stile in field corner. It then descends to footpath signpost, which points short way across last field to western edge of village.

4 To explore village of Parwich turn **R**, otherwise turn **L** down lane to Brook Close Farm. A signposted footpath on your **L** follows tractor tracks climbing to ruined stone barn, beyond which lies stile into next field. Path now heads southwestwards to top **R-H** corner of field then follows muddy tree-lined track for few paces.

5 On entering next field turn **L**. This first follows hedge on **L**, then descends to recross **Bletch Brook** footbridge. It climbs up middle of next long field before zig-zagging up steep upper slopes to reach bridge over **Tissington Trail**. Go down to trail and follow it northwestwards through Crakelow cutting.

6 After 500yds (457m) turn **L**, following Tissington footpath over stile to **R-H** corner of field. Now follow wall on **R** to **Rakes Lane** at edge of Tissington.

7 Maintain your direction along lane to reach **Chapel Lane**. You can walk either way around village square. Hall and church are straight ahead, while Methodist **chapel** and **Coffin Well** are on Chapel Lane to L. Car park lies to southeast of square; take **L** turn just beyond **Coffin Well**.

215 CARSINGTON RESERVOIR
DERBYSHIRE

5.5 MILES (8.8KM) 3hrs 30min

PATHS: Hill paths, some hard to follow and railway trackbed, numerous stiles

SUGGESTED MAP: aqua3 OS Outdoor Leisure 24 White Peak

GRID REFERENCE: SK 249528

PARKING: Sheepwash pay car park by Carsington Reservoir

THE PUB: Miner's Arms, Carsington

1 Take signposted path northwards towards **Carsington**. It winds through scrub woods and rounds finger of lake before reaching B5035. Path continues on other side, meeting lane by **Wash Farm**; follow it to enter village by Miners Arms pub.

2 Turn **L** on lane to reach Hopton road. Where road turns **L** keep ahead along lane, passing cottages. Beyond gate lane becomes fine green track beneath limestone-studded slopes of **Carsington Pasture**.

3 Where track swings L, leave it for path climbing slopes to west. At top, aim **R** of copse; go through gap in broken wall before descending into little valley.

4 Go over 2 stiles to cross country lane, then follow miners' track for 200yds (183m) towards old mine workings. Here footpath sign directs you around limestone outcrops before arcing **R** towards **Brassington**. Turn **L** at footpath signpost; follow waymarked route across fields into village.

5 Turn **L**, then **R** up Miners Hill. Go **R** up Jasper Lane, **L** up Red Lion Hill, and **L** along Hillside Lane. After 200yds (183m) leave lane for footpath on **R**, which climbs past outcrops. Faint waymarked path gradually veers **R**, and passes head of green lane.

6 Climb **R** to waymarking post. Through next 3 fields path climbs parallel to, and to **R** of, line of electricity pylons. In 4th field bear half **R** above outcrops; go through top gate. Aim for buildings of **Longcliffe Dale Farm**. Cross next stile; turn **L** up road, passing farm. Footpath on **R** cuts corner to High Peak Trail, passing electricity sub station and Peak Quarry Farm.

7 Turn **R** along trackbed of **High Peak Trail** passing **Harborough Rocks**.

8 Go **R** at footpath ('Carsington'). Go down field to cross **Manystones Lane**. Follow wall over **Carsington Pasture**; descend by woods to gate by cottage.

9 Turn **L** down little ginnel leading to road and **L** again to retrace earlier route to Sheepwash car park.

216 MACKWORTH
DERBYSHIRE

6 MILES (9.7KM) 4hrs

PATHS: Farm tracks and field paths (can be muddy after rain), quite a few stiles

SUGGESTED MAP: aqua3 OS Explorer 259 Derby

GRID REFERENCE: SK 333379

PARKING: Markeaton Park car park

THE PUB: Mackworth Hotel

1 Leave car park at **Markeaton Park**; cross road to follow surfaced lane to **Markeaton Stones Farm**. Once past farm, track becomes stony, climbing gently up crop fields towards stand of trees on hilltop.

2 At trees turn **L** at T-junction; follow crumbling tarmac lane alongside trees until you reach buildings of **Upper Vicarwood Farm**.

3 At farm buildings continue through gate on **L-H** side of stable block; follow grassy hilltop track.

4 Through gate, track reaches **Lodge Lane**. Turn **L** along lane to gardens of **Meynell Langley**, then **L** into field next

to drive. Path heads southeast, following hedge on R. Through small, wooded enclosure lake appears in hollow to R. Beyond next stile, route enters large field and hedge wanders off to R.

5 Aim for large lime tree at far side of field to locate next stile. Cross footbridge spanning **Mackworth Brook**. Path now goes parallel to hedge on R, aiming for large barn on hillside ahead.

6 At gateway, path divides. Take path on R, whose direction is highlighted by waymarking arrow. Go through next gate; follow R field edge, passing to L of red-bricked **Bowbridge Fields Farm**. Now head south across fields following hedge on L.

7 Cross stile in tall hedge; turn **L** along pavement of busy A52 (take care), passing garage and Little Chef. After 600yds (549m) go **L** along **Jarveys Lane**, passing through **Mackworth** village.

8 Where lane turns sharp R, leave it for path passing in front of **church**. Bonnie Prince Charlie waymarks show well-defined route eastwards across fields to **Markeaton**.

9 At road you can either turn **L** to car park or continue through **Markeaton Park**. For latter go through gateway, turn **L** over twin-arched bridge, **L** by children's playground, and **L** again past boating lake.

217 EDALE
DERBYSHIRE

6 MILES (9.7KM) 3hrs 30min

PATHS: Mainly good but can be boggy in wet weather

SUGGESTED MAP: aqua3 OS Explorer OL24 White Peak

GRID REFERENCE: SK 124853

PARKING: Good public car park at Edale

THE PUB: Old Nag's Head, Irby

1 Exit car park at **Edale** and turn **R** on to road. Look out for public footpath sign on your **L** and turn on to farm road. Just before this road turns sharply L, take public footpath that forks off to **R** and goes uphill through wood.

2 At end of wooded area, cross over stile and continue uphill. Near top of hill, follow path across open hillside and then cross yet another stile and turn **L** on to road. Just before road bends sharply L, cross over road, go over stile and then follow this path towards hill.

3 Near foot of hill, cross over stile to **L** and then turn **R** on to road. Continue to find some steps on **L** leading through ramparts of Iron-Age fort to summit of **Mam Tor**, enjoy the views. From here retrace your steps back to road.

4 Cross road, go over stile and continue on this footpath uphill and on to **Rushup Edge**. Follow this well-defined path along ridge, crossing 5 stiles. Where another path intersects, turn **R**. This is **Chapel Gate** track, badly eroded by off-road motorbikes. Go through kissing gate then head downhill.

5 Near bottom of hill go through gap stile on **L**. Go across another stile, pass through gate, then across another stile on **L**. This leads to some tumbledown buildings. Cross over stile by corner of one building then veer **R** and cross another stile on to farm road.

6 Cross road, go over stile and follow path until it joins road. Turn **R** then **L** at junction and continue towards **Barber Booth**. Take 2nd road on **L** then, near outskirts of village, go **L** on road ('Edale Station').

7 Follow path across series of meadows, going through several gates and 3 stiles to join road to **Edale Station** next to **Champion House**. Turn **R** on to road then, near junction, turn **L** into car park.

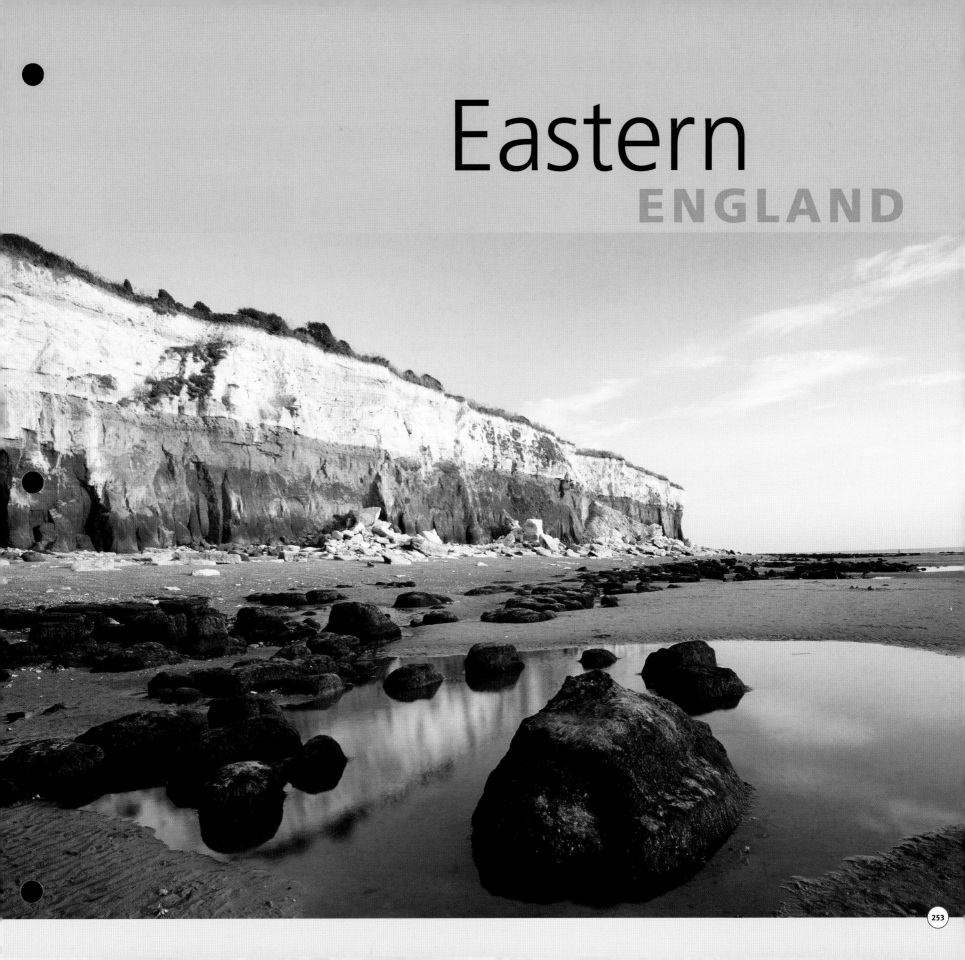

Eastern

ENGLAND

EASTERN ENGLAND

Contents

		page
218	Badby, Northamptonshire	255
219	Sulgrave, Northamptonshire	257
220	Pitsford Water, Northants	259
221	Brampton, Northamptonshire	261
222	Medbourne, Leicestershire	263
223	Foxton Locks, Leicestershire	265
224	Exton, Rutland	267
225	Rutland Water, Rutland	269
226	Measham, Leicestershire	271
227	Waltham Abbey, Essex	273
228	Paglesham, Essex	275
229	Laxfield, Suffolk	277
230	Southwold, Suffolk	279
231	Aylsham, Norfolk	281
232	Brancaster, Norfolk	283
233	Blakeney, Norfolk	285
234 to 237	Hertfordshire	287
238	Bedfordshire	287
239	Northamptonshire	287
240	Cambridgeshire	288
241	Rutland	288
242 to 243	Leicestershire	288
244 to 245	Nottinghamshire	288
246 to 247	Lincolnshire	289
248 to 251	Essex	289
252 to 254	Suffolk	290
255 to 257	Norfolk	290

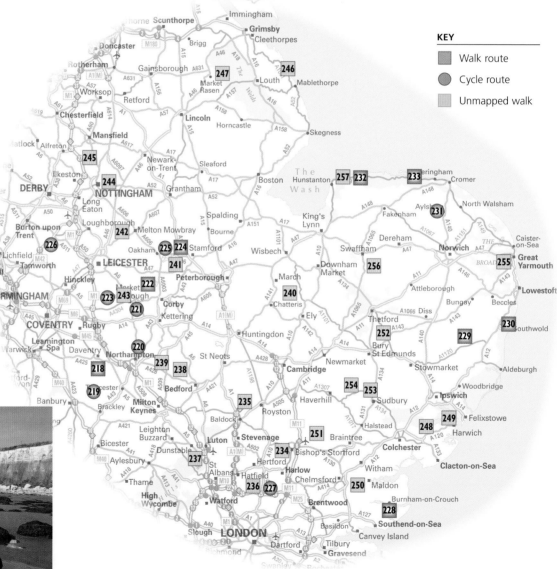

KEY

- Walk route
- Cycle route
- Unmapped walk

*Wood warbler
(Phylloscopus
sibilatrix)*

while you're there

The Elizabethan Canons Ashby House is set in formal gardens with colourful herbaceous borders, topiary yew, apple and pear orchards dating from the 16th century, and a wildflower meadow. An avenue of limes leads to the Church of St Mary, one of few privately owned churches in England. This impressive church is all that remains of an Augustinian priory.

A village trail from Badby

3h00 | **6.75 MILES** | **10.9 KM** | **LEVEL 123**

This route links three delightful villages west of Northampton.

Fawsley Hall and Park

Between Badby and Fawsley you will be following the Knightley Way, a handily waymarked trail that stretches 12 miles (19.4km) from Badby to Greens Norton, near Towcester, and which is named after the family that lived at Fawsley Hall for 500 years. The Knightleys moved to Fawsley from Staffordshire in the 1600s and, although considerably refashioned several hundred years later, the original vaulted Great Hall of their Tudor mansion is retained in what is now a country hotel, complete with Georgian and Victorian wings. It also boasts the Queen Elizabeth I Chamber, named after the monarch who apparently stayed there on a visit in 1575. In addition to the new house the Knightleys created their own private parkland, turning local arable land into pasture for their animals and in the process evicting most of the village. This is why only the 14th-century Church of St Mary is left, standing isolated before the hall. It contains the tomb of Sir Richard Fawsley, knighted by Henry VIII.

The English Midlands have a high proportion of deserted villages; the gentry in Northamptonshire was quite adept at turfing out the commoners without a moment's notice. Enclosure was at its height in the late 15th and early 16th centuries. When the fashion for grand landscaped parks was reaching its height 200 years later, whole communities were sometimes moved so that the view from the

The church at Badby

MAP: OS Explorer 207 Newport Pagnell & Northampton South

START/FINISH: on Main Street (roadside parking), Badby; grid ref: SP 560590

PATHS: mostly pasture, muddy where cows congregate, 22 stiles

LANDSCAPE: undulating hills covered with fields, woods and parkland

PUBLIC TOILETS: none on route

TOURIST INFORMATION: Daventry, tel 01327 300277

THE PUB: The Windmill, Badby

Getting to the start

Badby lies just to the east of the A361 between Banbury and Daventry. Follow the signs into the village. Roadside parking on Main Street.

Researched & written by:
Nick Channer, Andrew McCloy

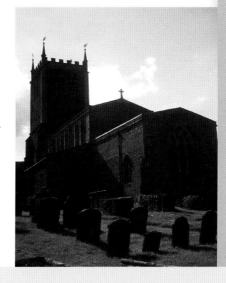

Map showing the village trail route with numbered waypoints 1–7, featuring Everdon Hall, Little Everdon, Everdon, Plough PH, Weedon Bec, Nene Way, Newnham, Romer Arms PH, Everdon Hill 186, Westcombe Farm, Canons Ashby, Badby Wood ▲174, Temple Hill ▲169, Fawsley Park, Fawsley Hall, Youth Hostel, Badby, Maltsters PH, Windmill PH, Daventry, Fawsley, Knightley Way, River Nene, B 4037, Badby Road, A 361.

Badby Wood

The ancient trees of Badby Wood, designated as a Site of Special Scientific Interest, include native hazel and oak trees as well as ash, birch, elder, honeysuckle, holly and rowan.

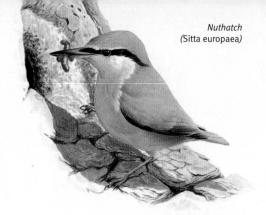

Nuthatch
(Sitta europaea)

what to look for

As you make your gentle descent through fields towards the River Nene, between Everdon and Newnham, you'll notice that one in particular is characterised by a series of long undulating ripples, like grassy waves. This is a legacy of the medieval farming practice of ridge and furrow, when the land was ploughed in long, narrow strips, which over time left a pattern of parallel ridges that endures to this day. It's a bit like walking on oversized corduroy.

main house or hall across the parkland could be 'improved' and uninterrupted. The term 'park' originally meant simply a piece of ground used for hunting, and enclosure through imparking ultimately led to the creation of the numerous stately parks that you see scattered across the Midlands today.

Other notable estates include the Marquess of Northampton's Castle Ashby and Althorp, seat of the Spencer family, while across the Bedfordshire border is the Duke of Bedford's 3,000-acre (1,215ha) Woburn Abbey.

the walk

1 Walk up to Badby church via Vicarage Hill (off which is Britain's only thatched youth hostel). Take the **alleyway path** signposted '**Fawsley**', opposite the south side of the church and follow it through woodland to a sign for the **Knightley Way**. Veer right up a sloping field and then follow a path around the western edge of **Badby Wood**, famous for its springtime bluebells.

2 After about 0.25 mile (400m) take the right fork (upper path), and follow waymarks for the **Knightley Way** out across the open hilltop of Fawsley Park and down towards the lakes near the hall.

3 Go ahead along the lane at the bottom to inspect the church, otherwise turn left, and soon (before the cattle grid) you come to a **footpath** on the left, heading up and across a large sloping field. The **lakes at Fawsley** are seen from here. Go through a gate and down a track to the road, then resume opposite climbing steadily through fields, passing **Westcombe Farm** on the left. Continue across Everdon Hill and down to the village of **Everdon** below, joining a lane via a stile to the right as you near the bottom.

4 Walk left through the village, following the road as it bends left by the **church** and pub, and turn left for the lane to reach **Little Everdon**. When the road appears to split go ahead/left for a path via stiles to the left of the **farm buildings**. This path, part of the Nene Way, continues out across parkland and open fields, with **Everdon Hall** to your right. Maintain your north westerly direction to reach the river **Nene**.

5 Cross the river via a **footbridge** (aim just to the right of Newnham's **church spire** when it comes into view) and follow the **Nene Way** across the fields to a concrete and tarmac farm drive which, beyond a gate and stile, becomes **Manor Lane**. Walk on to join the main street.

6 Avoid the church on the right and drop down past the pub by the green, continuing along **Badby Road** out of the village. In 150yds (137m) go left to follow field-edge paths alongside the infant **River Nene**.

7 Follow the **Nene Way** over two footbridges and along a path and arrive into Badby. Veer left by the green, pass **The Windmill** pub and head back to the centre of the village.

The Windmill

A friendly and relaxed atmosphere prevails in the two beamed and flagstoned bars of this 17th-century thatched inn. It is set in the heart of this pretty ironstone village, overlooking the green. Sensitively enlarged over the years, it now operates as a small hotel with comfortable en suite rooms housed in a modern extension. Both bars have warming winter fires – one being a wood-burning stove in a big inglenook – and feature scrubbed wooden furnishings, rug-strewn floors and a wealth of sporting memorabilia.

about the pub

The Windmill
Main Street, Badby
Daventry, Northamptonshire
NN11 3AN
Tel: 01327 702363
www.windmillinn-badby.com

DIRECTIONS: see Getting to the start
PARKING: 25
OPEN: daily; all day Saturday & Sunday
FOOD: daily; all day Saturday & Sunday
BREWERY/COMPANY: free house
REAL ALE: Wadworth 6X, Flowers IPA, Fuller's London Pride, Bass
DOGS: allowed in the bar
ROOMS: 10 en suite

Food

A varied menu includes steak and kidney pie, lambs' liver and onions, venison burgers with creamy peppercorn sauce, and loin of lamb wrapped in bacon with orange, redcurrant and port sauce.

Family facilities

Children are welcome; there's a children's menu, two family bedrooms and a safe front garden overlooking the village street.

Alternative refreshment stops

The Maltsters in Badby, the Plough at Everdon, an attractive, family-friendly village pub which serves food Wednesday to Sunday, and in Newnham the food-serving pub is the Romer Arms.

☛ Where to go from here

Nearby Canons Ashby House is an exceptional small manor house, with Elizabethan wall paintings, Jacobean plasterwork and fine restored gardens (www.nationaltrust.org.uk). Althorp House has been home to the Spencer family since 1508 and today houses the award-winning exhibition 'Diana, A Celebration' in six rooms and depicts the life and work of Diana, Princess of Wales (www.althorp.com).

did you know?

At the Battle of Edgecote, the two armies camped on either side of a small stream or river the night before the battle. It is most likely that this was the Cherwell, and they fought to take control of the crossing at Trafford Bridge before the main event on the plain to the south.

A 15th-century soldier on display at Sulgrave Manor

A circuit from Sulgrave

This scenic ride on smooth and quiet country lanes encircles a major battlefield from the War of the Roses.

Battle of Edgecote Moor

The Battle of Edgecote Moor (1469) was one of the many skirmishes fought during the so-called Wars of the Roses (1455–1487). This involved an on-going struggle for the throne of England between rival royal families: at the time of the battle Edward IV (represented by the white rose of York), was king, having successfully ousted Henry VI (represented by the red rose of Lancaster), some eight years previously. The battle itself centred on control of a ford over the River Cherwell and was fought between the Earls of Pembroke and Devon (loyal to Edward), and Robin of Redesdale (loyal to Henry). Although heavily outnumbered, Pembroke and Devon appeared to win the first round of fighting, but the late arrival of some 15,000 Lancastrian soldiers (led by the Earl of Warwick) proved to be decisive.

Devon panicked and his men were duly routed, and although Pembroke continued to put up a spirited fight, he too was eventually defeated and executed. Devon was later captured by commoners and murdered for his cowardice. Despite the outcome of the battle, Edward IV remained on the throne for more than a year, before being forced to seek exile in Burgundy by an overwhelming tide of Lancastrian support. After rallying his own allies from abroad, however, he returned in 1471 to defeat the Lancastrians at Barnet and Tewkesbury, and had Henry VI executed. He continued to reign until his death in 1483.

the ride

1 From the Star Inn car park, turn left and continue past **Sulgrave Manor**. At the end of this road bear slightly left and continue along a narrow country lane. After a couple of gentle rises and then a steeper hill, follow the road round to the left to reach a T-junction. Turn left here along **Banbury Lane**, and at the next crossroads continue straight on towards **Culworth**.

2 Just after you enter the village of Culworth you come to a T-junction. Bear right here to continue through the village. Take care on the long, fast descent as you leave the village. Carry on along this winding road until you get to **Trafford Bridge**, the scene of a bloody battle during the War of the Roses. Go straight on here, ignoring the lane going over a little bridge to your right. Stay on this rolling section of the route as far as the **Hare & Hounds** pub.

3 Cross the road directly opposite the pub to reach the pavement on the far side, and walk your bikes right, towards the **A361**. At this busy A-road turn left, continuing to wheel your bikes along a pavement for the next 440yds (402m). At the next left turn, into the village proper, wheel your bikes up to the top of a short rise and remount. Cycle as far as a **T-junction** and turn left to continue through the picturesque village of **Upper Wardington**, with its thatched roofs and its Cotswold stone buildings.

4 Beyond Upper Wardington, follow a quiet **country lane** for around 1.25 miles (2km) to reach a short but **steep hill**. At the brow of this hill, turn left along another narrow country road, which is initially paved with concrete (there are no signs here, so it's easy to miss – if you find yourself going downhill, you've gone too far). From this hilltop road you get some superb views out to your left. There are one or two little pot-holes to look out for towards the end of this section, but these are easily avoided.

5 At an obvious track crossroads continue straight across, following signs to **Thorpe**

A quiet lane around Sulgrave

2h00 | **11.5 MILES** | **18.5 KM** | **LEVEL 123**

MAP: OS Explorer 206 Edge Hill & Fenny Compton

START/FINISH: on-street parking in Sulgrave grid ref: SP 558455

TRAILS/TRACKS: tarmac roads all the way

LANDSCAPE: country lanes and villages

PUBLIC TOILETS: none on route

TOURIST INFORMATION: Banbury, tel 01295 259855

CYCLE HIRE: none locally

THE PUB: The Star Inn, Sulgrave

! A fairly long ride on country lanes, with some steep hills. Section where bikes have to be walked along a pavement to avoid a short stretch of busy A-road. Unsuitable for young, inexperienced children

Getting to the start

Sulgrave is signed off the B4525 between Banbury and the A43. To get to the start from Magpie Farm junction (see map), follow the main road into Sulgrave and at an obvious fork in the centre of the village, bear left, following signs to Sulgrave Manor. Park in the village street. The Star Inn is along this road on your left.

Why do this cycle ride?

This long and scenic circular route provides some superb road riding on smooth and quiet country lanes and takes in some charming villages. It avoids the worst of the region's hills, but there are still one or two steep climbs to negotiate.

Researched & written by: Paul Grogan

while you're there

Visit Sulgrave Manor, home to George Washington's ancestors until 1656 when his great-grandfather, John, emigrated to Virginia. Though much of the house is a 20th-century restoration, original parts include the porch (with a carving of the first American flag), a screens passage, the great hall and the great chamber. Many events are held here.

Living history groups stage re-enactments at Sulgrave Manor

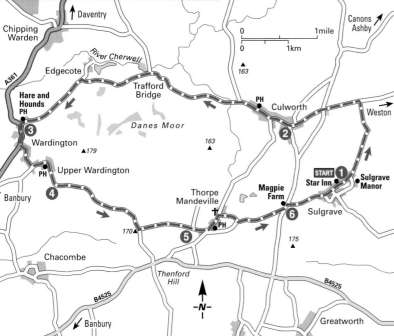

The Star Inn

A cosy, creeper-clad pub, created out of a 300-year-old former farmhouse a short stroll from Sulgrave Manor, where locally brewed Hook Norton ales and imaginative pub food are served in a smartly rustic and civilised bar and dining room. In the cosy bar you'll find a warm red and cream décor, a worn flagstone floor and a big inglenook with a blazing winter log fire. Separate, equally inviting dining room, a vine-covered patio and a secluded, well maintained garden for enjoying summer alfresco meals.

Food

Blackboard menus change daily and list above average pub food in the form of wild mushroom and foie gras terrine with onion marmalade and Tuscan bean soup for starters, with mains like smoked haddock fishcakes with ginger and lime mayonnaise and roast pheasant with mash, chestnuts, cranberries and game jus. Good range of sandwiches and specials and lighter meals at lunchtime.

Family facilities

Children are welcome in the dining areas. Here they can order smaller portions or opt for the children's menu choice. There are high chairs available.

Alternative refreshment stops

Pubs at Wardington (half-way) and in Thorpe Mandeville.

☛ Where to go from here

Sulgrave Manor, a short stroll to the northeast of the Star Inn, is the ancestral home of George Washington. You can take a guided tour and walk around the formal garden (www.sulgravemanor.org.uk). Nearby is Canons Ashby House, an exceptional small manor house with Elizabethan wall paintings and Jacobean plasterwork. Stowe Landscape Gardens, near Buckingham, has one of the finest Georgian landscape gardens in the country (both www.nationaltrust.org.uk). For some of the best views to be found in the area, look no further than the Burton Dassett Hills, about 10 miles to the northwest of Wardington.

about the pub

The Star Inn
Manor Road, Sulgrave
Banbury, Northamptonshire OX17 2SA
Tel: 01295 760389
www.starinnsulgrave.com

DIRECTIONS: see Getting to the start

PARKING: 20

OPEN: closed Sunday evenings

FOOD: no food Monday

BREWERY/COMPANY: Hook Norton Brewery

REAL ALE: Hook Norton Best & Old Hooky, guest beer

ROOMS: 3 en suite

Mandeville. At the first T-junction in Thorpe Mandeville, turn left and continue as far as a squat Gothic **church** on your left (note the massive yew tree to the east of the church, which is thought to be over a thousand years old). Turn right at the church, down a long steep hill on an uneven road, to reach a wider road; turn left here to go up a short **steep hill** and continue as far as the junction at **Magpie Farm**.

6 At this junction, take care turning right towards **Sulgrave** and Sulgrave Manor. Finish on a long, gradual downhill into the village. At a fork in the centre of Sulgrave, bear left to get back to the start.

The porch of Sulgrave Manor, the ancestral home of George Washington

Canada geese

did you know?

With a day or annual permit you can visit the nature reserve at the northern end of Pitsford. The water is also popular with anglers fly fishing for trout. If you visit after the harvest, look in the local fields for a huge flock of Canada geese feeding on the left over grain. If disturbed their heads go up, and with loud honking, they are airborne in seconds.

Around Pitsford Water

Watersports on Pitsford Water

Look out for the abundant birdlife along this purpose-built, waterfront cycle track.

1h30 | **7.5 MILES** | **12 KM** | **LEVEL 123**

MAP: OS Explorer 223 Northampton & Market Harborough

START/FINISH: Brixworth Country Park car park; grid ref: SP 752695

TRAILS/TRACKS: smooth gravel or tarmac all the way round

LANDSCAPE: woodland, waterside and causeway

PUBLIC TOILETS: at the start

TOURIST INFORMATION: Northampton, tel 01604 622677

CYCLE HIRE: Pitsford Water Cycle Hire, tel 01604 881777

THE PUB: The White Horse, Old Northampton

❶ Care needs to be taken when exiting the car park at the west end of the causeway

The Reservoir

Established in 1997 with the help of a substantial grant from the Millennium Fund, Brixworth is the newest country park in Northamptonshire, while Pitsford Water was designated as a Site of Special Scientific Interest (or SSSI) in 1971. The latter is home to numerous species of wading birds, is the site of the county's largest winter gull roost, and is regularly visited by ospreys on their spring migrations. In the winter, wildfowl numbers have been known to reach 10,000, with ducks, grebes, geese and swans being the most common residents. The wide variety of habitats around the reservoir also provides food and shelter for migrant birds in spring – surveys show a breeding population of 55 species.

In the summer, meanwhile, the reserve comes alive with dragonflies and damselflies. Common blue and emerald damselflies are probably the most abundant species,

with each numbering many hundreds of thousands on a good day. Butterflies add to the colour with 23 different species recorded. Other attractions at the park include a brand new playground, a sensory garden, a boules area (balls are available for hire), three wheel-chair accessible nature trails and a human sundial. Sailing, windsurfing and canoeing lessons are available from the Marina (April to October) and fly fishing can be arranged at the Lodge on Holcot Causeway (the reservoir is stocked with 35,000 trout each year).

the ride

1 From the main exit of the car park, turn left on a **gravel track**, following the obvious cycle path signs. Take this track down towards the water's edge, heading to the right of the **playground**, until you reach the **main cycle track** around the reservoir, with the marina off to your right.

2 Turn left here, along the wide and smooth gravel track, following the water's edge. You shortly pass through a sequence of gates

and continue to follow the shore around a series of **shallow bays**. As the reservoir starts to narrow, you come to the first gradual rise of the ride, followed by the option of a quick up-and-down single track for the more adventurous. This whole stretch is dotted with little coves, benches and **picnic tables**, while signs along the water's edge warn of back-casting by anglers.

3 Within sight of the causeway, proceed through another **swing gate**, and then just before you reach the causeway, go through another gate and over a **cattle grid** to reach a car park and picnic area (during the summer, there may be an ice-cream van here, providing the perfect excuse for a rest). This is also a good place for a spot of bird watching.

4 Take care when exiting the car park to reach the cycle path across the **causeway** (this path, which is marked with a bike symbol, is on the car park side of the causeway, so you don't need to cross the main road). Continue to the end of the causeway and up a short rise.

Getting to the start

Brixworth Country park is signed from the A508 between Market Harborough and Northampton. The route starts at the visitor centre on the reservoir's western shore just to the south of Brixworth.

Why do this cycle ride?

This is a gentle and enjoyable ride on smooth gravel tracks. With great views of the reservoir and little in the way of hills or other challenges to contend with, it's ideal for families with younger children.

Researched & written by: Paul Grogan

259

Falconry at Holdenby House

Nearby Holdenby House has a long history with falconry, which dates from the times of James I who stayed here and hunted his birds over the estate. There are 50 birds of prey at the falconry centre ranging from the little owl to black eagles.

Little owl (Athene noctua)

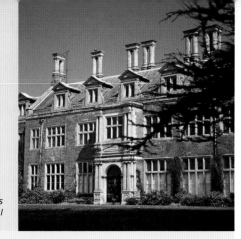

Holdenby House, once England's largest house, was built by Sir Christopher Hatton, Chancellor to Elizabeth I

An orientation sign at Pitsford Water

6 Continue to skirt around the reservoir until you come to a corridor through some **trees**. Go through a gate and follow the track along the left-hand edge of a wood until you reach a pair of gates and a tarmac road (to the left is **Moulton Grange**). Turn right on the road, over a miniature causeway. Immediately after the causeway, turn right again, back onto the **cycle track** (this is not well signed) and follow it around to the **dam**. Continue across the dam, taking a moment to soak in the expansive views of the reservoir. At the end of the dam, go through a gate and then turn right onto the wooded cycle track just past the **sailing club entrance**. At the end of the woods, you reach the point where you first joined the **main trail**. Turn left here to get back to the car park and the start.

5 Just before the top of this gradual rise, turn right, through a gate and into some **woods**. Enjoy the ride's first little stretch of downhill through the trees, before negotiating a sweeping left-hand turn. Proceed through a gate and follow the water's edge into a long, narrow **inlet**. Go through a gate just before the end of the inlet. A tight turn at the end of the inlet will take you back along the other side.

The White Horse

Small, friendly village local in a superb village setting overlooking the 13th-century St Andrew's church, a view best appreciated from the lovely enclosed garden which also features a fine restored red-brick chimney. Inside, the character bar and comfortable lounge areas, are spotlessly maintained, with hunting prints and collections of china decorating the walls, and splendid log fires to cosy-up to on cold winter days.

Food
Traditional home-cooked meals range from good-value sandwiches and filled baguettes to lamb and mint suet pudding, spinach and ricotta cannelloni, grilled tuna steak, and beef Wellington. Regular theme nights.

Family facilities
Children are welcome in the bars.

Alternative refreshment stops
A wide selection of hot and cold snacks and meals are available from the Willow Tree Café at the start. Ice creams may be available at the causeway car park during the summer, and snacks and hot and cold refreshments are available from the nature reserve lodge, near the eastern end of the causeway.

☛ Where to go from here
Holdenby House, about 4 miles (6.4km) to the west of the reservoir, boasts a splendid Elizabethan garden and a falconry centre (www.holdenby.com). Also nearby, about the same distance to the south, is the Northampton and Lampton Railway, on the Brampton Valley Way, just to the east of Chapel Brampton (www.nlr.org.uk). About five miles (8km) to the southwest is Althorp, the final resting place of Diana Princess of Wales (www.althorp.com).

about the pub

The White Horse
Walgrave Road, Old
Northampton, Northamptonshire
NN6 9QX
Tel: 01604 781297

DIRECTIONS: Old is located north of Northampton between the A508 and A43; pub is in the village centre next to the church

PARKING: 10

OPEN: closed Monday & Tuesday lunchtime

FOOD: daily

BREWERY/COMPANY: Banks Brewery

REAL ALE: Banks's Bitter, two guest beers

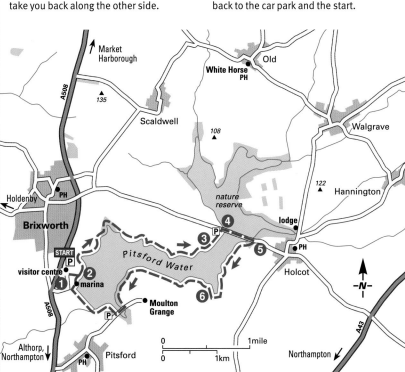

did you know?

Although the Brampton Valley Railway line officially closed in August 1981, the Royal Train stopped overnight, on several occasions, at the former Lamport Station.

Along the Brampton Valley Way

Younger kids will love the tunnels along this disused railway, while older children will enjoy the challenge of the optional route back.

Brampton Valley Railway

The Brampton Valley Railway was originally built in the 1850s to transport iron ore and coal from Northamptonshire and Nottinghamshire to London, although it later became an important passenger link between Northampton and Market Harborough. After decades of neglect following the Second World War, it was eventually closed in 1981, and in 1987 work began to develop it as a linear country park. The Brampton Valley Way, a 14-mile (22.5km) stretch of reclaimed track set aside for walkers and cyclists, was officially opened in the spring of 1993. Today, it is part of Route 6 of the National Cycle Network, which goes all the way from Sheffield to London. The Northampton and Lamport Railway Society continues to operate a short section of the line (www.nlr.org.uk).

The Brampton Valley Way

Its quiet and secluded location makes it the perfect place for wild flowers to thrive: look out for white oxeye daisies in May and June and yellow St John's wort or purple knapweed later in the summer. Not surprisingly, this abundance of flowering plants provides a continuous supply of nectar and butterflies thrive along this route too. Green and lesser-spotted woodpeckers are also common.

the ride

1 Walk your bikes along the pavement in the direction of Market Harborough. After just 55yds (50m), turn right along a wide **gravel drive**, following a sign to the tunnel's end. Follow this drive past some **sheds** to a gate at the end, and continue across a small meadow to a stile on the edge of the **woods**. Cross the stile and fork left, down through the woods. Walk your

This cycle ride passes through cooling tunnels

bikes along this narrow dirt trail and down a short series of **shallow steps** to reach the **Brampton Valley Way.**

2 Turn right along this wide gravel track to reach the entrance to **Oxendon Tunnel,** which is 1,371ft (418m) long. It's very dark in the tunnel, although if you remember to take your sunglasses off (!) you should be able to make out the floor and walls, and the light at the end of the tunnel is visible the whole time. It also feels mercifully cool down here on a hot day. Good bike lights are needed to ride through the tunnel, but if it's busy it's probably a good idea to walk. About two-thirds of the way along the tunnel is a **vent,** which was originally built to provide an outlet for steam from the trains.

3 Two miles (3km) beyond the tunnel the path splits into two – a sign indicates that cyclists should stay left, but if you want to continue, it's better to stay right to avoid

---

| 2h00 | 8 MILES | 12.8 KM | LEVEL 1 2 3 |

MAP: OS Explorer 223 Northampton & Market Harborough

START/FINISH: Great Oxendon; on-street parking in the village; grid ref: SP 736835

TRAILS/TRACKS: smooth gravel or tarmac all the way round

LANDSCAPE: railway cutting, tunnel and farmland/villages

PUBLIC TOILETS: none on route

TOURIST INFORMATION: Market Harborough, tel 01858 821270

CYCLE HIRE: none locally

THE PUB: The George, Great Oxendon

❶ Good lights are needed to cycle through the tunnels, and when it's busy it's safer to walk through them. The optional return route takes in some steep hills, although these are on very quiet lanes and can be walked

Getting to the start

Great Oxendon is on the A508 with plenty of on-street parking in the village. The start of the ride itself can only be accessed on foot, so you'll need to walk your bikes to reach the Brampton Valley Way (see below).

Why do this cycle ride?

This secluded cycle path is wide, smooth and well maintained and its verges are brimming with colourful wild flowers in the summer. Cycling (or walking) the route's two tunnels is an experience to remember, and the optional return journey takes in some superb views on smooth, traffic-free roads.

Researched & written by: Paul Grogan

while you're there

The Northampton and Lamport Railway Society operate steam and heritage diesel trips on a section of line through the countryside from the Pitsford and Brampton Station. Trains operate on weekends and bank holidays from March to October, and December. Children will enjoy Days Out with Thomas and Percy, Easter egg themed trips and the Santa specials.

Lesser spotted woodpecker (Dendrocopos minor)

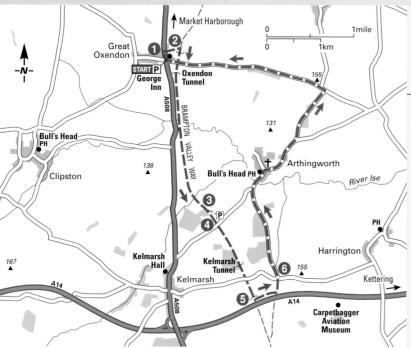

The George

Menus state that the George is a 'pub by name, restaurant by nature', yet although dining is the main emphasis, a relaxed and friendly atmosphere prevails throughout the cosy and club-like bar, with its beamed ceilings, part-panelled walls, leatherette chairs, crackling log fire and daily newspapers. In fact, the whole place is comfortably furnished throughout, and there's a smart conservatory dining area overlooking a large, formal garden.

separate restaurant menu and popular roast lunches on Sundays.

Family facilities
Children of all ages are welcome in the pub. There are high chairs and smaller portions of main menu meals are available, and colouring/drawing materials can be provided for children on request.

Alternative refreshment stops
The Bull's Head in Arthingworth is en route for those who choose to do the full circuit.

☞ Where to go from here
Pitsford Reservoir, about 10 miles (1.6km) to the south of Great Oxendon on the A508, boasts a wealth of attractions for kids and adults alike. Also nearby is an aviation museum in Harrington, commemorating the so-called Carpetbagger missions of World War II (www.harringtonmuseum.org.uk), and Kelmarsh Hall in Kelmarsh (www.kelmarsh.com) which has fabulous landscaped gardens.

about the pub

The George
Great Oxendon, Market Harborough
Leicestershire LE16 8NA
Tel: 01858 465205

DIRECTIONS:	see Getting to the start
PARKING:	34
OPEN:	daily
FOOD:	no food Sunday evening
BREWERY/COMPANY:	free house
REAL ALE:	Bass, Adnams Bitter
ROOMS:	3 en suite

Food
Good quality, reasonably priced bar food includes lunchtime 'light bites', perhaps sandwiches and rolls, salmon and smoked haddock fishcakes, home-made soups, pork and leek sausages with mash and onion gravy and beef and Guinness pie. There's a

having to carry your bikes up some **steep wooden steps** a little further along. At the bottom of these steps is a car park and **picnic site** which might make a good spot for a break on the return journey, if you're planning on coming back this way.

4 Just beyond the steps the track crosses over the top of the B-road to **Arthingworth**, and after a further 0.5 mile (800m) it reaches the entrance to **Kelmarsh Tunnel** (1574ft/ 480m). Emerging from the tunnel the route then proceeds through a cool, shaded tree-lined glade to reach a **short tunnel** under the A14.

5 This is a good place to turn around if you're feeling low on energy, but if you're after some good views and don't mind a few hills, turn left just before the **A14**, following a **bridleway sign** up a grassy track to the top of a field. The noise of the traffic here is distracting, but it does

provide a timely reminder of how quiet and peaceful the rest of the route is! At the brow of this small hill, turn left, again following a wooden **bridleway sign**, and skirt the edge of a field to reach a tarmac road.

6 Cross this road with care and then follow the narrow country lane to **Arthingworth**, down a long, fast descent. At the first T-junction (after about a mile/ 1.6km), turn right into Arthingworth and then right again at the fork in the village, past the **church** on your left. After leaving Arthingworth, take the left fork up a **long steep hill** (signed to Braybrooke). There's a **bench** at the bottom. The first hill is closely followed by a second. They may look tiring, but at the next left turn you'll soon be losing all the height you've gained on a long, fun descent down into **Great Oxendon** (the views to the right here are superb). At the **A508**, turn right along the pavement to get back to the start.

while you're there

Just to the west of Hallaton village is a motte and bailey castle, visible from the nearby lane or public footpath. Introduced by the Normans, the 'motte' was a flat-topped conical mound of earth, usually topped by a wooden palisade and tower, either inside or next to an embanked enclosure known as the 'bailey'.

A medieval stone bridge in Medbourne

From Medbourne to Hallaton

3h50 | **7.5 MILES** | **12.1 KM** | **LEVEL 123**

MAP: OS Explorer 233 Leicester & Hinckley (224 Corby, Kettering & Wellingborough, also useful)

START/FINISH: roadside parking near village hall, Main Street, Medbourne; grid ref: SP 799929

PATHS: farm paths, tracks, some rough and muddy, about 15 stiles

LANDSCAPE: rolling pastoral scene of fields and woodland

PUBLIC TOILETS: none on route

TOURIST INFORMATION: Market Harborough, tel 01858 821270

THE PUB: The Nevill Arms, Medbourne

Getting to the start
Medbourne is situated on the B664 between Market Harborough and Uppingham, south east of Leicester.

Researched & written by:
Nick Channer, Andrew McCloy

Below: The Church of St Giles in Blaston dates from the 13th century

Discover some very unusual Eastertide goings-on in two picturesque South Leicestershire villages.

Bizarre traditions
Bottle-kicking, they claim hereabouts, is a sport older than football, cricket and even so-called real tennis, but is it a 'sport'? Every Easter Monday hundreds of people gather in Hallaton to try to propel a tiny barrel (known confusingly as a bottle) towards the village of Medbourne. The villagers of Medbourne, meanwhile, try to stop them by any means possible. And as far as rules go that's about it.

But bottle-kicking is just one part of the ancient day-long celebrations. The beer inside the actual barrels plays an important part in the day's proceedings as does the hare pie scrambling. The hare has long been a symbol of Easter and used to be paraded ahead of Hallaton's procession each year. Home-made hare pie is as important as the bottle-kicking, although the traditional dish has variously been made with beef, veal and bacon over the

years. To the south of the village the walk passes Hare Pie Bank. This is where Easter's mayhem truly begins.

The events of Easter Monday follow a set order in Hallaton. A children's parade is led by a marching band, after which comes the bottle-kicking service in St Michael's Church. The bottles and hare pie are then paraded through the village and the pie is cut up and 'distributed' (often thrown at the assembled mob), who move on to Hare Pie Bank to begin the contest. Bottle-kicking is a rough and unruly affair, usually conducted by scrums of young men who get covered in mud and bruises. There are no set rules, no team kits, and no limits on numbers. The result is usually decided from the best of three games.

For more information on this fascinating and bizarre custom, read John Morison and Peter Daisley's book, on sale at Hallaton Village Museum.

the walk

1 Walk up Rectory Road, opposite the **church**, which becomes a path. Go over the road at the end and up through the

fields opposite. Cross a stile and a private garden to a drive. Go forward and up the field to exit in the top left corner. Turn right and walk along the road to **Nevill Holt**.

2 Turn left at the end and where the brick wall finishes go left through a **gate** to cross a wide arable field. Follow the direction of the **finger sign** and aim to the left of **Hallaton** (in the middle distance). Go through a gate and drop down through two fields, separated by Uppingham Road. Beyond a **woodland strip** go left, then up the right-hand side of the next field along before veering half left across the top one – aim for the solitary **tree** on the skyline. At the far corner drop down ahead to join a track. Turn right and walk the farm track into **Blaston**.

3 At the lovely **Church of St Giles** turn left and follow Hallaton Road to the junction at the end. Go straight over and after the second stile turn right to walk through open pasture towards **Hallaton**. Follow the **yellow-topped waymark posts**, aiming for

Above: A conical butter cross on the village green at Hallaton

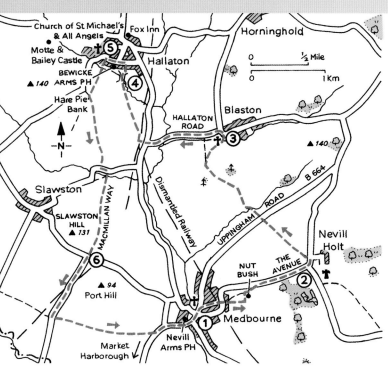

The Nevill Arms

A handsome old coaching inn built of warm golden stone with latticed mullioned windows, enjoying a truly picturesque riverside setting by the village green. As its name suggests, it once belonged to local landowners – the Nevill family – and was rebuilt in 1863 following a disastrous fire. The interior is delightfully unpretentious and welcoming, the inviting bar features two log fires, lofty beamed ceilings and some ancient wall settles. The popular pub garden has a dovecote and is a great attraction for children who like to feed the ducks.

Food
Home-made food is hearty and appetising, ranging from soups and sandwiches to chicken with Stilton and leeks, steak and kidney pie, smoked haddock bake and lamb shank with redcurrant and mint gravy.

Family facilities
There's a spacious room at the back where children are welcome. Here they will find a Lego table and a box of toys to keep themselves amused. High chairs, smaller portions and a children's menu are also available.

about the pub

The Nevill Arms
12 Waterfall Way, Medbourne
Market Harborough, Leicestershire
LE16 8EE
Tel: 01858 565288

DIRECTIONS: see Getting to the start; pub beside the green and river in the village centre

PARKING: 30

OPEN: daily

FOOD: daily

BREWERY/COMPANY: free house

REAL ALE: Fuller's London Pride, Adnams Bitter, Greene King Abbot Ale, guest beers

DOGS: allowed in the bar

ROOMS: 8 en suite

Alternative refreshment stops
There are two further excellent pubs, which all serve food daily: the Bewicke Arms and Fox Inn at Hallaton. The Bewicke Gift Shop and Tea Room at Hallaton is open daily, and the well-stocked village store near the church makes filled rolls to order.

☛ Where to go from here
Set on a hill overlooking five counties just north of Corby is Rockingham Castle, built by William the Conqueror. You'll see the site of the original keep (now a rose garden), the outline of the curtain wall, the foundations of the Norman hall and the twin towers of the gatehouse (www.rockinghamcastle.gov.uk). Bede House in Lyddington was once a prominent medieval palace before being converted into an almshouse. An evocative audio tour brings its history to life (www.english-heritage.org.uk).

---

the spire of Hallaton church, then veer to the right of an isolated clump of **trees** in the middle of the field, and cross a **footbridge**.

4 Go left then sharply right beyond a stile and follow the signs through a small, **modern housing** development. Eventually turn left on to Medbourne Road and straight on to reach the centre of **Hallaton**.

what to look for
The parish Church of St Michael's and All Angels at Hallaton has a display about St Morrell, a French monk (St Maurille) who became the Bishop of Angers in the Loire Valley. It's thought that Norman settlers at Hallaton may have established a chapel dedicated to the saint, and over the centuries a local cult developed in the area.

5 Leave the village via a **passageway** underneath a house, almost opposite the **butter cross**. Cross a footbridge and go directly up a gently sloping field, aiming just to the right of a wooden fence beneath trees. Go through a gate and turn left for a wide track waymarked '**Macmillan Way**', a route running from Lincolnshire to Dorset which was specially created to raise funds for the Macmillan Cancer Relief charity. Continue along the edge of two gated fields, then left into a lane. Turn right at the first bend and follow this long, pleasant semi-surfaced lane below **Slawston Hill**.

6 At a road junction go straight over and down a lane, and 500yds (457m) beyond the **former railway bridge** turn left for a bridleway along the foot of successive fields. When you reach the far end, turn left to follow the road back into **Medbourne**.

*Tufted duck
(Aythya fuligula)*

what to look for

The brightly painted narrowboats that make the canal such a spectacle today should not be confused with barges. These are much larger craft, usually over 14ft (4m) wide and primarily involved in commercial use. Because of their size they tend to be found on rivers and a handful of wider canals.

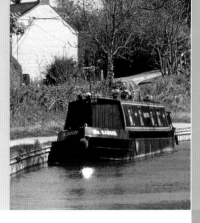

A narrowboat on the Grand Union Canal

Foxton Locks and the Grand Union Canal

2h00 **9.6 MILES** **15.5 KM** **LEVEL 123**

Enjoy varied and challenging traffic-free riding along one of England's most famous canal systems.

Foxton Locks and the Grand Union Canal

The Grand Union Canal actually started its life as lots of separate canals, which were joined to provide a navigable waterway from Birmingham to London (the name 'Grand Union' comes from the amalgamation of a number of different companies in 1926). In 1793, long before this name was coined, a canal was begun in Leicester to link up with the Grand Junction Canal, which had started north from the Thames a year earlier. In 1814, the two were finally joined by the ten locks at Foxton, which raised the level of the Leicester canal by some 75ft (22.8m). It takes about 50 minutes for a boat to negotiate all ten locks, and each boat requires about 25,000 gallons of water. The history of the locks is explained in more detail at the Foxton Locks Museum (www.fipt.org.uk), near the start of the ride.

Also worth exploring is Millfield Wood, one of 200 woods created around the country as part of the Woods on Your Doorstep Project to celebrate the Millennium. The 18.8-acre (7.6ha) site was acquired by the Woodland Trust after a successful fund-raising appeal by Fleckney Village. Oak, ash, silver birch and small numbers of field maple are the dominant species.

the ride

1 From the car park exit, turn left along a gravel track to get to the **bridge** over the canal. Cross the bridge and turn right to reach the **canal** and, after about 300m (330 yards), the **locks** themselves. Cycling isn't permitted on this section, so you'll have to walk your bikes down the side of the locks (the Foxton Locks Museum is situated on the far side of the passing pond about half-way down this long, steep slope, and can be reached on foot). Stay to the left at the bottom to reach the shop and **café**.

2 Continue past the shop to cross a **cobbled bridge**. On the far side, keep going in the same direction. The shingle track along this part of the canal is wide and smooth, although there are one or two places where the left hand edge has collapsed a little, so it's a good idea to stay right. After 1.5 miles (2km), you come to **Debdale Wharf**. Beyond Debdale Wharf, the path becomes narrow and grassy, and on dry days it may be quite bumpy. In the summer, this section may also be quite overgrown with reeds and bull-rushes, but it should still be passable. At **Gumley Road**, the track becomes smoother and wider again, before continuing on to **Saddington Road**.

The tow path of the Grand Union Canal

MAP: OS Explorer 223 Northampton & Market Harborough

START/FINISH: Foxton Locks car park; grid ref: SP 692892

TRAILS/TRACKS: smooth gravel, narrow grassy track, road and rutted farm track

LANDSCAPE: towpath, village and farmland

PUBLIC TOILETS: at the start

TOURIST INFORMATION: Market Harborough, tel 01858 821270

CYCLE HIRE: none locally

THE PUB: The Bell Inn, Gumley

❶ A fairly challenging ride along an often bumpy tow path and some rough tracks – mountain bikes recommended. One short, steep descent to a railing over the canal (can easily be walked). Care is required crossing Kibworth Road. Suitable for older, more experienced and adventurous children

Getting to the start

Foxton is well signed off the A6 between Leicester and Market Harborough, off the A4304 to the west of Market Harborough, and off the B6047 to the north of Market Harborough. From Foxton, follow signs for the Foxton Locks car park, which is at the top end of the locks.

Why do this cycle ride?

This ride provides the perfect challenge to budding young mountain bikers, combining easy gravel towpath, flat grassy single tracks, a few gentle climbs, and some rough farm roads at the end of an alternative return route. The wonderfully preserved locks at the start are merely an added bonus.

Researched & written by: Paul Grogan

did you know?

At the basin below the locks, a 6-mile (9.7km) arm leads to Market Harborough, although most craft head up and down the main Grand Union route. Boats can be hired, or else you can just enjoy a short afternoon cruise up and down the waterway on board The Vagabond.

A flight of ten locks at Foxtgon, on the Grand Union Canal

3 Just beyond Saddington Road, a short sharp climb takes you up to the right of **Saddington Tunnel**. A longer but more gentle rise, still on a wide gravel track, then takes you along the top of the tunnel, before an equally gentle descent carries you back down to **Kibworth Road**. From here it's possible to return the way you came, but what follows is an alternative for those who are still feeling energetic.

4 If the gate is locked here, you'll have to carry your bikes over a **narrow stile**, before crossing the road with care to reach another, wider stile. Another gradual downhill then takes you to a short, steep slope down to a **fence** above the canal. This can be ridden, but you may prefer to walk it. At the fence turn left to continue along the canal. The path is quite narrow, and can be slippery in wet weather, so take great care here. At the next **bridge**, continue past it for

about 30 yards to reach a gate – go through this gate to reach the bridge.

5 Cross the bridge and continue to the top of the field ahead, where you'll find an enormous slab of granite welcoming you to **Millfield Wood**. Go through a gate and continue along a wide bridleway across a field. Follow the track as it bears left to reach **Kibworth Road** and then cross the road to continue in the same direction along another **gravel track**.

6 After 1.5 miles (2km) of gentle downhill riding on a wide, occasionally pot-holed **track**, turn right at the road in **Smeeton**, and then first left along Debdale Lane. This rough **farm track** rises gently and then more steeply to reach the canal. At the top of the track, bear left towards **Debdale Wharf Farm** and then turn right at the farm to regain the **towpath**. From here, turn left to retrace your tracks back to the start.

The Bell Inn

Note the collection of miniature cricket bats in a case in the lobby as you enter this early 19th-century village pub. Beyond lies an L-shaped bar furnished with dark wood tables and chairs and decorated by more cricket bats and cricketing prints and cartoons, china jugs and mugs, hunting prints, and gleaming horse brasses on black beams. You'll also find a good range of beers, a warming log fire and a small no-smoking dining room. Pretty summer garden for alfresco eating and drinking.

Food
Good value bar meals take in sandwiches, ploughman's lunches, home-made soups, salmon mornay, steaks and home-made puddings like sherry trifle. Popular three-course Sunday roast lunches.

Family facilities
Children over 5 are welcome in the restaurant but not in the terraced garden to the rear of the pub.

Alternative refreshment stops
Cold drinks, ice-creams and hot and cold snacks are available from the shop at Foxton Locks.

☞ Where to go from here
Market Harborough is a very picturesque medieval town with an interesting local museum and is well worth a visit if you have an hour or two to spare. Further afield, up the A6 to Leicester and a must if you have kids in tow, is the National Space

about the pub

The Bell Inn
2 Main Street, Gumley
Market Harborough, Leicestershire
LE16 7RU
Tel: 0116 279 2476

DIRECTIONS: signposted off the A6 north west of Market Harborough

PARKING: 20

OPEN: closed Sunday evening

FOOD: no food Monday evening

BREWERY/COMPANY: free house

REAL ALE: Bass, Batemans XB, Greene King IPA, guest beer

Museum (www.nssc.co.uk), which offers five themed galleries, cutting-edge audio-visual technology and glimpses into genuine space research. More great cycling and walking can also be found on the Brampton Valley Way, which starts behind the Bell pub, on the A508 near the southern edge of Market Harborough.

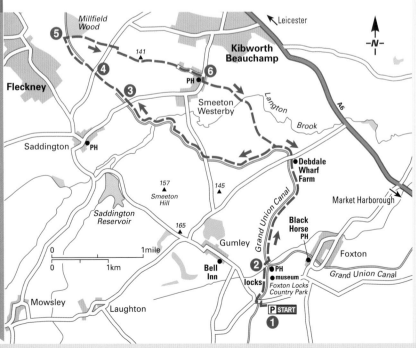

Barnsdale Gardens

These gardens, a mile (1.6km) west of Exton, will be familiar to TV gardeners as the home of the late Geoff Hamilton. Open daily, there are 37 gardens within the south-facing 8-acre (3.2ha) site, including walks, terraces, formal lawns, ancient meadows, a lily pond, an ornamental vegetable garden and knot gardens. You'll also find an arboretum, tea rooms and a nursery with plants initially propagated from the gardens.

A loop from Exton

A row of 18th-century thatched cottages

3h00 6.5 MILES 10.4 KM LEVEL 123

224

WALK

Explore the open countryside and parkland around Exton, a thatched village north of Rutland Water.

Exton

A couple of miles north of Rutland Water, Exton is a picturesque village of ironstone and thatched cottages laid out around a green, ringed by mature sycamore trees and overlooked by the tall, creeper-covered village pub.

There has been a community here since Norman times, and the manor once belonged to King David of Scotland. Since then it has changed hands a number of times, finally passing to the Noels, Viscounts Campden, Earls of Gainsborough, in the 1620s. The family still owns neighbouring Exton Hall, which was built to replace the Old Hall after it was largely destroyed by a fire in 1810.

The ruins of the Old Hall are inside the grounds (accessible to the public from the road to the south) close to the Church of St Peter and St Paul, which itself was struck by lightning in 1843, causing the spire to collapse. Although some of the original work was lost, most of the fine monuments survived, including some medieval sculptures and various tombs. Also look out for the giant statue by the master carver Grinling Gibbons of the 3rd Viscount Campden, his wife and 19 children, which is considered something of a rarity since Gibbons is far better known for working in wood rather than stone. The film *Little Lord Fauntleroy* (1980) was shot on location in Exton and featured, among other places, the village church.

The grounds and parkland were mainly developed in the late 17th century by the 6th Earl of Gainsborough, when water features such as cascades, artificial ponds and streams were created. Among the ornamental follies on the estate is an elaborate Gothic summer house known as Fort Henry, overlooking Fort Henry Lake, which you will see half-way round the walk. Behind it stood the even more bizarre Bark Temple, an elaborate wooden structure that not surprisingly has rotted away over time.

Measuring less than 20 miles (32.4km) across, Rutland has a resident population of around 37,000, and apart from Oakham and Uppingham most of its inhabitants live in tiny villages and hamlets. The county's name may derive from the 11th-century word 'Roteland', denoting the red colour of the soil in the east of the region; or it could have been part of the estate belonging to an early landowner called Rota. For many years this tiny place was in the hands of either the Crown or the Church, but in 1974 local government reorganisation ended its independence and relegated it to a mere district of Leicestershire.

That decision was reversed in 1997, and Rutland is once more England's smallest county, whose Latin motto 'Multum in Parvo' means 'so much in so little'.

the walk

1 With your back to the pub leave the Green on the far right-hand side on **Stamford Road** and, at the end, turn right. This becomes Empingham Road and, when the houses finish, continue over the stream and turn left to follow a **public footpath**.

2 Just before the fence ahead veer off half right onto a lower **grassy path** and follow the wide track along the shallow valley for just under 1 mile (1.6km), at one point climbing into a field on the left to avoid Cuckoo Farm. Look for a stile and **footbridge** and clamber up through the fields on the right to reach a lane.

3 Turn left and walk the verge until just beyond the bend, then go left on a footpath indicated '**Fort Henry and Greetham**'. Follow this route above the trout hatchery, then head diagonally right via a small concrete bridge to reach the fence at the top. Turn left and walk along to **Lower Lake**, then go ahead/right on the surfaced drive for a few paces, keeping to the left of the bar gate, and out across open pasture above the water.

Pretty gardens in a Rutland village

MAP: OS Explorer 234 Rutland Water

START/FINISH: roadside parking in centre of Exton; grid ref: SK 924112

PATHS: mainly field paths and firm farm tracks, 12 stiles

LANDSCAPE: open and undulating fields and parkland, mixed woodland

PUBLIC TOILETS: none on route

TOURIST INFORMATION: Oakham, tel 01572 724329

THE PUB: The Fox & Hounds, Exton

Getting to the start

Follow the A606 between Oakham and Stamford. Turn off at Rutland Water at the sign for Exton and drive to the village. There are spaces in the vicinity of The Fox & Hounds.

Researched & written by:
Nick Channer, Andrew McCloy

Since medieval times the shallow quarries in the area have provided stone for local buildings and, although long exhausted, they have resulted in a series of peculiarly low or uneven fields.

The Fox & Hounds

about the pub

The Fox & Hounds
Exton, Oakham
Rutland LE15 8AP
Tel: 01572 812403
www.foxandhoundsrutland.com

DIRECTIONS: see Getting to the start

PARKING: 20

OPEN: daily

FOOD: no food Sunday evening in winter

BREWERY/COMPANY: free house

REAL ALE: Greene King IPA, Grainstore Ales, guest beer

DOGS: allowed in the bar

ROOMS: 4 bedrooms

Rutland Water is only 2 miles (3.2km) away from this rather proud-looking and ivy-covered 17th-century coaching inn overlooking the picturesque village green. It is also a handy refreshment stop for ramblers on the Viking Way. The attraction in summer is the fine walled garden for alfresco dining, as well as pints of local Grainstore ales and imaginative pub food with an Italian twist, served in the civilised high-ceilinged lounge. Here you'll find sturdy pine tables, hunting prints on the walls, fresh flowers, and a crackling winter log fire in the large stone fireplace.

Food
From the 'casual lunch' menu order soup and sandwiches or filled jacket potatoes, or look to the main menu for interesting pasta meals, starters of asparagus and gruyère cheese tart or seared scallops with salad and dill dressing, and main dishes such as halibut with Mediterranean vegetables, or marinated lamb shank. Separate pizza menu.

Family facilities
Children of all ages are welcome. High chairs and half-portions of main meals are available and there's a children's menu and a play area in the garden.

Alternative refreshment stops
Nearby Greetham also has three thriving pubs. Alternatively visit the coffee shop at Barnsdale Gardens, which is open daily all year round (weekends from November to February).

☛ Where to go from here
Rutland County Museum in Oakham has displays of farming equipment, machinery and wagons, rural tradesmen's tools, domestic collections and local archaeology, all housed in a splendid 18th-century cavalry riding school. Don't miss Oakham Castle, a fine Norman Great Hall of a 12th-century fortified manor house (www.rutland.gov.uk). At the Rutland Railway Museum in Cottesmore there are over 40 industrial steam and diesel locomotives and other wagons and vehicles used in the ironstone quarries and industry.

4 At the far side turn right on to another lane then, in a few paces, left for the footpath indicated 'Greetham'. Follow this beside **Fort Henry Lake**, then on along a corridor between lovely mixed woodland. At the far end climb the **stairs** to reach the lane.

5 Turn left and walk up through more **woods** and, when the semi-surfaced drive bears left, go straight on through an area of newly planted **trees**. The wide, unmade track now heads directly out across the **open fields** for a mile (1.6km).

6 When you reach the **trees** on the far side turn left on to a track that drops down and bears left. Here go straight on via a stile and **wooden plank footbridge** and head up diagonally left towards the top of the field. Go over the stile and turn left on to the **farm track** once more.

7 At the junction turn right on to the straight, metalled **lane**. Bear left at a fork before woods and follow this back to Exton. Follow signs around **Home Farm**, then turn left at the end of West End and right by the stone shelter into High Street and return to the Green.

what to look for
Although the gentle farmland of Rutland and South Lincolnshire is by and large a peaceful place, every now and then you may be aware of a distant roar and a fast-moving object zooming through the sky. A few miles to the north lies the busy airfield at Cottesmore, which opened in 1938 and was a base for American bombers throughout World War Two. Today Tornado pilots train there.

Upper Hambleton

It's said that there's no higher land between Upper Hambleton on the peninsula and the Wash and, although modest in height, the hilltop position of the village spared it from the fate that claimed its neighbours, now under Rutland Water. Among the views from the peninsula is Burley on the Hill, a striking mansion on a densely wooded ridge to the north which was built for David Finch, Earl of Nottingham, between 1694 and 1705.

Left: Walking beside Rutland Water

Around Rutland Water

Ride around Europe's largest man-made reservoir at the heart of England's smallest county.

Rutland Water

Rutland Water was rubber-stamped in 1970 to provide drinking water to the surrounding area. Completed seven years later, it flooded an area of 3,100 acres (equivalent to around 3000 football pitches). The dam itself is 1,312yds (1,200m) long, and the maximum depth of the reservoir is 34 metres (111ft). One of the few local landmarks to survive the flooding was Normanton Church, which had to be raised above the level of the water and joined to the shore by a causeway to protect it from ruin. Originally built in 1826, it today houses a local history museum. Other attractions include a climbing wall and marina (at Whitwell car park), a butterfly centre (at the north end of the dam), and a nature reserve (at the southwest corner of the reservoir).

The nature reserve is one of the most important bird-watching centres in the UK. Depending on the time of year, Rutland Water is home to as many as 20,000 waterfowl. Equally important are the reserve's ospreys. These impressive raptors have brown plumage, white bodies and wingspans of up to 5.6ft (1.7m). They were introduced to the region in 1996 in an attempt to encourage them to start breeding, and in 2003, after a few false starts, they were successfully bred in England for the first time since 1847. The reserve also boasts an environmental display, a viewing gallery, 22 hides and a nature trail.

An undulating path near Rutland Water

3h00 · 17 MILES · 27.4 KM · LEVEL 123

225

CYCLE

MAP: OS Explorer 234 Rutland Water

START/FINISH: Whitwell car park; grid ref: SK 923082

TRAILS/TRACKS: largely smooth tarmac and compacted gravel and tarmac

LANDSCAPE: woodland and waterside, with the occasional village

PUBLIC TOILETS: at the start and at Edith Weston car park

TOURIST INFORMATION: Oakham, tel 01572 724329

CYCLE HIRE: Rutland Cycling (at the start), tel 01780 460705 (www.rutlandcycling.co.uk)

THE PUB: The White Horse, Empingham

❶ There's one short, steep descent with a tight turn at the bottom (well signposted). Take care crossing the main road when you make the right turn towards Manton

the ride

1 From the car park exit opposite the bike shop and **climbing tower**, turn right and then immediately left into the **marina**. Follow the road round to the left, away from the marina buildings, and drop down to the water's edge as it becomes a **cycle track**. Turn right at the tip of the inlet and continue around the **water's edge** until you reach another car park. Continue through this car park to reach the dam.

2 After crossing the **dam**, turn right at the end, through a pair of swing gates, and continue along the obvious tarmac track as far as **Normanton Church**. Beyond the church, cross a narrow tarmac road and continue straight through an uneven gravel parking area to reach the main **Edith Weston car park**, with public toilets, snack bar and bike shop. Proceed to the far end of the car park and turn right to continue around the water's edge, past the **sailing club** and marina.

3 A mile (1.6km) past the sailing club, the track delves into a small **wood** before dropping down a steep hill to a **tight bend** at the bottom; a sign near the top gives riders plenty of warning that this hill is coming up.

4 At the next road turn left up a steep hill to reach the B-road between **Edith Weston and Manton**. Cross the main road with care and then turn right towards Manton, following the **cycle lane**. At the first junction continue straight on into Manton. Soon after passing a **phone box** on your left, turn right, following a **Rutland Water cycling sign**. Bear left past the **Horse & Jockey** pub to reach a wide gravel track down to the A6003. Follow a narrow pavement at the bottom beneath the **railway bridge** (a sign advises riders to dismount for this bit) and stay on this pavement for a further 440yds (402m).

5 Turn right through a **swing gate** here, following the cycle track around the water's edge until it cuts across the Lax-Hill

Getting to the start

The north and south shores of Rutland Water are signed from the A606 between Oakham and Stamford. This route starts at Whitwell car park on the north shore. Coming from Stamford, drive through Whitwell and turn left at the top of the hill to the car park.

Why do this cycle ride?

This is a long but gentle circuit that mostly follows the water's edge. The first few miles of tarmac are ideal for younger children, while the tracks on the western half are great for older, more adventurous kids. You can walk the one or two short sharp ascents.

Researched & written by: Paul Grogan

Goosander
(Mergus merganser)

while you're there

Just to the south of Rutland Water is the picturesque village of Wing, where there is a most unusual and historic maze. Cut into the roadside turf near the recreation ground, Wing Maze is based on an 11-ringed design often found on the floors of medieval French cathedrals.

Wing Maze is 40ft (12m) in diameter

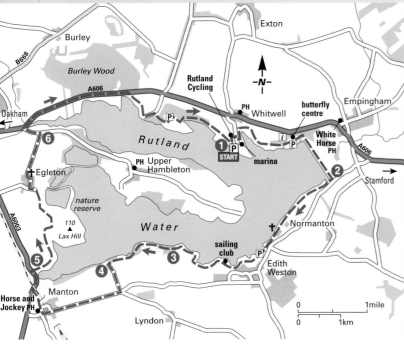

The White Horse

A stone's throw from the serene Rutland Water, the stone-built, 17th-century White Horse is the centre of village life and a meeting place for the walkers, cyclists, anglers and watersport enthusiasts exploring Europe's largest man-made lake. Originally a court house, it is now a popular inn with smart accommodation, a restaurant and a genteel, country-style bar, the latter full of traditional character, with low, beamed ceilings, dark wooden furniture and a large open log fire for cold winter days. In attempting to be all things to most callers its day stretches from morning coffee and croissants through lunches and cream teas to late evening suppers.

Food
Daily blackboard and printed menus provide plenty of choice and typically include giant Yorkshire pudding filled with sautéed liver of lamb, bacon and onions, beef, ale and mushroom pie, and trout with prawns, mixed pepper and spring onion sauce. Lighter meals include soups, moules and pasta dishes.

Family facilities
Children of all ages are welcome. There's a children's menu and smaller portions are also available. Small sheltered garden and two family bedrooms.

Alternative refreshment stops
Drinks, ice-creams and hot and cold snacks are available from the café at the Edith Weston Car Park. Another pub on route is the Horse & Jockey in Manton.

☛ Where to go from here
About 10 miles (16.1km) to the east of Rutland Water, on the B1443 out of Stamford, is Burghley House, a great Elizabethan palace surrounded by a fine country park landscaped by Capability Brown (www.burghley.co.uk). Head east to Oakham to view the town's castle, an exceptionally fine Norman Great Hall of a 12th century fortified manor house. Earthworks, walls and remains of an earlier motte can be seen along with medieval sculptures. Learn more about England's smallest county by visiting the Rutland County Museum in Catmos Street.

peninsula. This track eventually leads to **Egleton**. Turn left into the village and then right again after around 200yds (182m). Continue past the **church** and stay on the road to the main road into Hambleton.

6 Turn left, and then right after 300yds (273m) along a short **cycle track** to reach the A606. From here, stay on the rolling pavement for 1.5 miles (2km), before heading right, back onto a gravel track and around the water's edge. At the bottom of the next tarmac road, turn left up the short, sharp hill before turning right towards **Barnsdale Wood car park**. After going down and then steeply uphill to reach the car park, continue downhill again to the bottom, far right-hand corner of the car park; delve into **Barnsdale Wood** here and follow the track all the way back to the start point.

Modern sculpture above Rutland Water

about the pub

The White Horse
2 Main Street, Empingham
Stamford, Rutland LE15 8PS
Tel: 01780 460221
www.whitehorserutland.co.uk

DIRECTIONS: load up bikes, return to Whitwell and turn right along the A606 for 2 miles (3.2km) to Empingham. The pub is at the junction with the main village street

PARKING: 60

OPEN: daily; all day

FOOD: daily; all day

BREWERY/COMPANY: Unique

REAL ALE: Ruddles Best, Adnams Bitter, Greene King Abbot Ale

ROOMS: 13 en suite

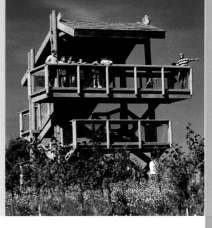

Conkers

Take time on the route to visit Conkers. Children will enjoy the indoor adventure play area and discovery zones, where they can get close to the forest and discover its secrets. Outside is an adventure playground and an assault course, or ride on a steam train and explore woodland trails. There are shops, craft units plus snack kiosks and restaurants. Find out more on www.visitconkers.com

The play area at Conkers visitor centre

A lookout at Conkers

Along the Ashby Woulds Heritage Trail

Celebrate Leicestershire's rich industrial heritage on this short linear ride along a disused railway.

Ashby Woulds Heritage Trail

The Ashby Woulds Heritage Trail follows the route of the old Ashby to Nuneaton railway, and runs right through the heart of what was once an important coal-mining area. When pits were closed across the region in the mid 1980s, the landscape was left derelict and decaying, but in 1992 a forum was formed to help regenerate the local environment and boost the region's economy. The trail is a part of this initiative. It starts at the old railway station in Measham before crossing Donisthorpe Woodland Park, which was planted on the site of a reclaimed colliery. Further along is Conkers, a state-of-the-art visitor centre built on the site of Rawdon Colliery, one of the last deep mines in the Midlands to close. It finishes at Overseal sidings, where a short length of track and an abandoned signal box can still be seen. The trail also falls within the so-called National Forest, a government-backed initiative instigated in 1995 to help improve some 200 sq miles (518sq km) of land in Leicestershire, Derbyshire and Staffordshire which have been scarred by hundreds of years of coal mining. It is hoped that 30 million trees will eventually be planted, and that 33 per cent of the total area will be wooded.

Right: A pond on the Ashby Woulds Trail

the ride

1 From the south west corner of the car park, proceed up a narrow path to reach the main bridleway, past a **heritage trail information board**. Bear right along the gravel bridleway, past a **picnic bench** at the top of the rise. After 750yds (686m), the bridleway veers to the left and goes through some **wooden bike stiles** to reach a main road. At the main road turn right along the pavement and go under the **A42**.

2 Straight after the A42, turn right to regain the **main bridleway** (there is another right turn just before this which also looks like a bridleway, but this is clearly a dead end). Continue under a pair of **road bridges**. Much of this section, and indeed the whole trail, is raised up above the surrounding landscape, but because it's enclosed by trees and bushes, it feels quite secluded and peaceful. There are numerous **signposts** and **picnic benches** along the route.

3 Just beyond the next bridge, bear left up the first short climb of the ride to reach a **main road**. Turn right along the pavement and then cross the road with care to continue along the **heritage trail** (signed). Here the trail is wider and more open as it crosses **Donisthorpe Woodland Park**. On the way it drops down a long gentle hill to a bridge and a small stream before heading back up the far side.

4 At the northern corner of the park, keep going in the same direction (frustratingly enough, you may have to dismount here to negotiate a pair of **wooden bike stiles**). The trail becomes enclosed and shaded again

 1h30 **6.8 MILES** **11 KM** **LEVEL 123**

MAP: OS Explorer 245 The National Forest

START/FINISH: Measham Country Park car park; grid ref SK 332119

TRAILS/TRACKS: mostly gravel, with a short section of pavement

LANDSCAPE: railway embankment

PUBLIC TOILETS: at the start

TOURIST INFORMATION: Ashby-de-la-Zouch, tel 01530 411767

CYCLE HIRE: none locally

THE PUB: Navigation Inn, Overseal

⚠ Take care when riding along the pavement under the A42, and also when crossing the road in Donisthorpe. Keep an eye on young children when approaching the road at the Navigation Inn

Getting to the start

Park at a free car park just off the B5006 in the middle of Measham, which is signposted off the A42 1.5 miles (2km) south west of Ashby-de-la-Zouch. Go to the left-hand parking area, where the public toilets are situated

Why do this cycle ride?

This gentle ride is almost completely flat, and what it lacks in terms of views it more than makes up for in terms of peace and solitude. The family-friendly pub at the halfway point is an ideal spot for a rest, and kids will love the attractions at Conkers visitor centre, a short detour off the main route.

Researched & written by: Paul Grogan

did you know?

Nearby Ashby-de-la-Zouch Castle was used as the setting for the famous jousting scene in Sir Walter Scott's novel Ivanhoe. *Today these impressive ruins are in the hands of English Heritage.*

On the Ashby Woulds Trail

as you pass over a number of roads before eventually getting to a string of **ponds** at the end of the trail; just beyond these ponds is the B5004 and, off to your left, **the Navigation Inn**.

5 To reach the **National Forest Visitor Centre (Conkers)**, go back along the trail and at the far end of the **ponds** turn left, following a sign to the **Bath Yard**. When you come to another **sign** and information board turn right, into a field, and cross it on

a well-trodden track. Turn right at the far end of this track, under a bridge, and continue as far as a **railway crossing**. Just beyond this crossing is the visitor centre.

6 To get back to the start, retrace your tracks from the Navigation Inn or the visitor centre. At the main road in Donisthorpe turn right and then left to stay on route, and at the main road into **Measham**, turn left along the pavement to go under the A42 and then left again, back into the woods.

Navigation Inn

Interesting black and white prints of the local area adorn the walls of this big, family orientated pub in Overseal village. Bar and dining areas are open-plan in layout, light, spacious and immaculately maintained, and decorated in traditional style with dark wood tables and chairs laid out on bright red carpets. In summer the big garden is very popular with families and kids can let off steam in the huge adventure play area.

Food
An extensive menu offers light meals like sandwiches, wraps and paninis, standard pub main courses, and dishes like Mediterranean trout, Hawaiian chicken, salmon salad and a daily carvery.

Family facilities
Children of all ages are welcome throughout the pub and there's a safe, enclosed adventure play area in the large lawned garden. The 'young adults' menu includes lasagne, burgers and ice creams.

Alternative refreshment stops
There's a café at Conkers that serves hot and cold drinks, snacks and main meals throughout the day.

☛ Where to go from here
Aside from Conkers, other local attractions worth visiting include the superb Moira Furnace Museum, just off the route, which boasts a host of displays and interactive exhibits on the history of the furnace, and Ashby Castle in Ashby-de-la-Zouch, which offers great views of the surrounding countryside. There's also a dry-slope ski centre in nearby Swadlincote just 3km (2 miles) to the north of the Navigation Inn (www.jnll.co.uk).

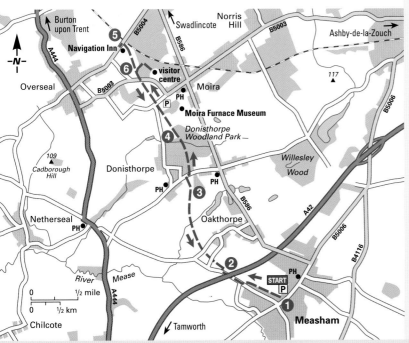

about the pub

Navigation Inn
166 Spring Cottage Road, Overseal
Swadlincote, Derbyshire DE12 6ND
Tel: 01283 760493

DIRECTIONS: on B5004 east of Overseal (Point 5 on the route)

PARKING: 50

OPEN: daily; all day

FOOD: daily; all day

BREWERY/COMPANY: Hardy & Hanson's

REAL ALE: Hardy & Hanson's Bitter, Marston's Pedigree

ROOMS: 3 bedrooms

Map labels: Burton upon Trent, Swadlincote, Norris Hill, Navigation Inn, Overseal, Moira, Ashby-de-la-Zouch, visitor centre, Moira Furnace Museum, Donisthorpe Woodland Park, Cadborough Hill 109, Donisthorpe, Willesley Wood, Netherseal, Oakthorpe, River Mease, Chilcote, Tamworth, START, Measham, 117
0   ½ mile
0   ½ km
–N–

while you're there

Visit the Royal Gunpowder Mills at Waltham Abbey for an explosive day out. Create your own explosion through interactive computer displays, find out what it was like to work here or join a guided tour which includes wildlife watching and a visit to the largest heronry in Essex. The renovated site here is a must-see for those interested in industrial archaeology.

From Waltham Abbey to Tottenham

Discover hidden wildlife and London's industrial history.

Waltham Abbey

In 1540 Waltham was the last abbey in the country to be dissolved by Henry VIII. A settlement since Saxon times, Waltham came to prominence when Tovi the Proud, a member of King Canute's court, brought a stone crucifix (the Holy Rood or Holy Cross) from his estate in Somerset to the Lee Valley in the 11th century. According to legend the cross was supposed to be taken to Glastonbury Abbey (15 miles/24km from where it was discovered), but the oxen refused to go in that direction and instead travelled across the country until they reached Waltham. The town prospered from pilgrims flocking to the shrine of the Holy Rood. Waltham Abbey is also notable as the

Stonebridge Lock

burial place of King Harold II after his death at the Battle of Hastings in 1066. From the 1600s Waltham's gunpowder mills became the town's major employers. It is reputed that both the gunpowder used by Guy Fawkes and the explosives used in the Dam Busters raids were manufactured here.

the ride

1 From the pub head south along the gravel tow path past **Hazlemere Marina**, which has toilets and a café. Shortly before reaching the M25 you will see the Sea Scout base on **Rammey Island** to the left.

2 Rammey Marsh Lock is the first on this ride; Rammey Marsh is the open expanse to the right. On this section part of a **dismantled bridge** has been converted into a good vantage point. A 1998 bridge

carries Ordnance Road over the navigation and tow path. The Greyhound pub is immediately to the south.

3 At **Enfield Lock** the path moves to the east bank. Take care crossing the road here on the sharp bend. You will soon reach the **Swan and Pike Pool**, once a place for bathing but now a picnic area. It takes its name from a pub that used to stand here. The tow path passes under a disused railway bridge. The high bank of **King George's Reservoir** soon looms on the left, marking the start of almost 4 miles (6.4km) of reservoirs. Look out for the **sculptures** on the right past the blue footbridge.

4 The double lock at **Ponders End** is preceded by the huge timber-framed bulk of the Navigation Inn. At the locks the path plunges under the bridge carrying Lea Valley Road, which runs between **King George's Reservoir** and William Girling Reservoir.

5 At the North Circular Road the tow path joins a concrete road alongside the **Lea Valley Trading Estate**. Take care on this section, which is shared with out-of-service buses heading to the Arriva garage. Past the bus depot the route goes under the footbridge and the path is once again traffic-free, wide and well surfaced.

6 The tow path returns to the west bank at **Stonebridge Lock** for the final run to Tottenham Lock. Those tired out by the southbound ride may wish to return north by train from Tottenham Hale to Waltham Cross, about a mile (1.6km) from the Old English Gentleman pub.

4h00   **14 MILES**   **22.8 KM**   **LEVEL 123**

MAP: OS Explorer 174 Epping Forest & Lee Valley

START/FINISH: The Old English Gentleman, Waltham Abbey; grid ref: TL 375006

TRAILS/TRACKS: largely compacted gravel tow path, some tarmac and paved sections

LANDSCAPE: industrial and waterside

PUBLIC TOILETS: Hazlemere Marina, Waltham Abbey

TOURIST INFORMATION: Waltham Abbey, tel 01992 652295

CYCLE HIRE: Abbey Cross Discount Cycle Centre, Waltham Cross, tel 01992 651135

THE PUB: Old English Gentleman, Waltham Abbey, EN9

! Some narrow gaps at locks. A free permit is necessary to cycle along the Lee Navigation – see www.waterscape.com

Getting to to the start

Waltham Abbey is just outside the M25 and is accessible from junction 26 via the A121. The Old English Gentleman is west of the town centre on the road to Waltham Cross. Please ask permission before parking at the pub. The alternative is to use the pay-and-display in Waltham Abbey town centre.

Why do this cycle ride?

This is a totally off-road ride from the north-eastern edge of Greater London to the urban bustle of Tottenham through the green corridor of the Lee Valley. It is also linear, so you can turn round at any time if you get tired.

Researched and written by: James Hatts

Male and female
goldeneye
(Bucephala clangula)

did you know?

The gunpowder factory sprawled across the Lee Valley provided employment for many local women during World War One before closing its doors to become an explosives research and development establishment.

Old English Gentleman

This small, two-bar pub is just south of Waltham Lock and minutes away from the abbey church and the shops and facilities of Waltham Abbey. The cosy, compact interior is complemented by a large riverside terrace. The pub is run in a traditional way, with the emphasis on quality beer and good food, and holds regular real ale festivals and events. It's busy at weekends, but surprisingly quiet, even on sunny summer weekdays.

Food

Expect a modest menu of well-priced and well-presented dishes from fish and chips to lamb rogan josh, as well as lighter options such as jacket potatoes and a range of ploughman's meals.

Family facilities

Children are welcome inside and there's a small play area at the rear of the pub.

Alternative refreshment stops

There's a café at Hazlemere Marina and several waterside pubs along the Lee Navigation.

☛ Where to go from here

Visit the great Norman church and the remains of the abbey buildings at Waltham Abbey, just a few hundred yards from the start of the ride (www.walthamabbeychurch.co.uk). Also at Waltham Abbey are the Royal Gunpowder Mills, which are open every weekend during the summer (www.royalgunpowdermills.com). You can view many types of farm animals, including a variety of rare breeds in a traditional-style farmyard at Lee Valley Park Farm at Crooked Mile. Children will also enjoy the pet centre and summer tractor rides (www.leevalleypark.com).

about the pub

Old English Gentleman
Highbridge Street,
Waltham Abbey
Essex EN9 1BA
Tel: 01992 713222

DIRECTIONS: see Getting to the start

PARKING: Ample parking is available for patrons at the pub. Others are welcome to park here, but please inform the landlord on arrival

OPEN: daily; all day

FOOD: daily; all day

BREWERY/COMPANY: free house

REAL ALE: Everard's Tiger, Tetley Imperial, Fuller's London Pride

Hadleigh Country Park

Hadleigh Country Park, near by, has been an important conservation area since the 1950s due to its variety of habitats, from grassland and woodland to salt marsh and mudflat. The park covers 472 acres (191ha) and overlooks Canvey Island, the River Thames and the Kent Downs. This a delightful place to visit: in spring you can see shaded woodlands of bluebells, yellow calandine and plenty of butterflies; in summer you may hear the sound of a cuckoo.

Hadleigh Country Park

A stroll near Paglesham Creek

Below: Paglesham Creek

Walking in the footsteps of smugglers, 'wife-farmers' and oyster fishermen.

Paglesham

Just a few miles from Southend-on-Sea, Paglesham is bordered to the north by the River Crouch and to the south by the River Roach. Its origins go back to Saxon times and its population survived mainly by rearing sheep which grazed on the flat marshlands. But its remote position on Essex's east coast, and its proximity to waterways, attracted smugglers.

Smuggling was such big business that at one time the entire population of Paglesham was involved. In the 18th century William Blyth – known as Hard-Apple Blyth – was considered to be one of the most notorious smugglers Paglesham ever produced. He started out as the village grocer and progressed to churchwarden. Blyth would not only evade customs officials, but his party piece was spending evenings at the Punch Bowl pub drinking kegs of brandy and crunching wine glasses. This diet and lifestyle clearly did him no harm – he died in 1830, aged 74, and was buried at Paglesham church.

'Wife-farming' seems to have been another local activity. Daniel Defoe, in his travels around Paglesham, noted that some men boasted that they had fifteen or more wives. It was said that the women who couldn't stand the rigorous lifestyle and bad weather, either died from the cold or abandoned their more robust husbands and the men simply chose a replacement.

Another lucrative local business was oyster farming. In the 19th century oysters were a popular, inexpensive food for Londoners who couldn't get enough of them.

On this walk you will see sheep grazing along the grassy sea wall and marshland, just as they have done for centuries. Oysters are still farmed locally and an annual oyster festival brings a flurry of foodies to the pubs.

The Walk

1 Walk to the left of the **Plough and Sail Inn** along a driveable track, and after 100yds (91m) follow the fingerpost straight ahead to the left of the house called **Cobblers Row**. Maintain direction along a good field-edge path until the path narrows and you approach houses. Keeping the red brick wall on your left go through the white wicket gate, with the brook on your right, and along the lawn of **Well House**. Go through another wicket gate and follow the metalled lane left, ignoring arrowed path right.

2 At the corrugated barn of **East Hall**, follow the Roach Valley Way waymark, right and then left behind the barn. Join a track along the field edge, bear right, then left through a gate to join a good, grassy field edge path. Walk by paddock fencing, with Church Hall on your right and the pond on your left, to **St Peter's Church** at Paglesham Churchend.

3 Keeping the church on your right, continue along Churchend High Street to **The Punch Bowl Inn**. Maintain direction for 50yds (46m), take the concrete path to your right and after a few paces follow the **Roach Valley Way** waymark, left, which soon becomes a grassy field-edge path running parallel with a waterway on your left.

4 Take a short clamber up the grassy embankment and, leaving the Roach

2h45 | **6.25 MILES** | **10.1 KM** | **LEVEL 123**

WALK

MAP: OS Explorer 176 Blackwater Estuary, Maldon

START/FINISH: informal street parking at Paglesham Eastend beside Plough and Sail Inn; grid ref: TQ 943922

PATHS: grassy sea wall, field edge, unmade tracks, 5 stiles

LANDSCAPE: river estuary, salt marsh, mudflats, grazing and arable farmland

PUBLIC TOILETS: none on route

TOURIST INFORMATION: Southend-on-Sea, tel 01702 215120

THE PUB: The Plough and Sail, Paglesham

❶ Keep children away from tidal creeks/marshes

Getting to the start

Paglesham is located north east of Southend-on-Sea. Take B1013 north from A217 for Hockley. Follow signs right for Rochford, then Stambridge and Paglesham. Adequate roadside parking opposite The Plough & Sail.

Researched & written by:
David Hancock, Katerina and Eric Roberts

while you're there

Near by you'll find Southend-on-Sea, one of the first seaside resorts, and the attractive coastal towns of Burnham-on-Crouch, Bradwell-on-Sea and the small town of Maldon which offers river trips on restored Thames barges.

A funfair by the pier in Southend-on-Sea

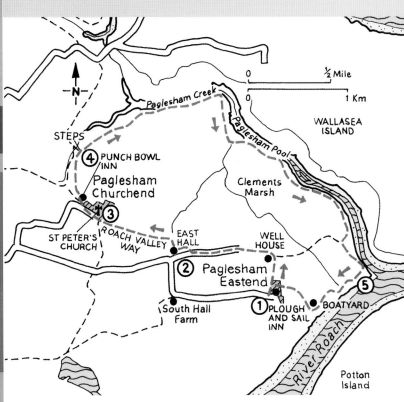

The Plough & Sail

Charming, weather-boarded, 17th-century dining pub on the bracing Essex marshes, within easy reach of the rivers Crouch and Roach. For over 300 years this has been a meeting place for the farming, fishing and sailing communities. Inside are pine tables, brasses and low beams, giving the place a quaint, traditional feel. You'll find local Mighty Oak and Ridley's ales among the four beers on handpump. The splendid, well-maintained garden has an aviary and is a popular spot during the summer months.

Food
Renowned for its good quality food, such as home-made steak and Stilton pie and fresh local fish, perhaps including skate, tuna and Dover sole. Traditional bar snacks are also available.

Family facilities
Children are very welcome inside the pub. There's a menu for youngsters and children can let off steam in the large garden, and watch the birds in the aviary.

about the pub

The Plough & Sail
East End, Paglesham
Essex SS4 2EQ
Tel: 01702 258242

DIRECTIONS: see Getting to the start

PARKING: 30

OPEN: daily

FOOD: daily

BREWERY/COMPANY: free house

REAL ALE: Greene King IPA, Ridley's, Mighty Oak, Fuller's London Pride

DOGS: allowed in the bar

Alternative refreshment stops
Another pub providing great food and a smugglers' inn atmosphere is the Punch Bowl Inn at Paglesham Church End. Crews of smugglers once played cricket in the nearby field, but would keep their cutlasses and loaded pistols within arm's reach just in case the law caught up with them!

☛ Where to go from here
Rayleigh Mount, 6 miles (9.7km) north west of Southend, is a motte and bailey earthwork with a fascinating history and dates back to the period following the Norman invasion of 1066. Southend Pier is over a mile long (1.6km) and you can learn about its history in the Pier Museum. Children will also enjoy the Southend Museum, Planetarium and Discovery Centre which houses displays of archaeology, natural history and local history, telling the story of man in the south east Essex area.

Valley Way, turn right on to the sea wall of **Paglesham Creek**. Keep to the path as it meanders by Paglesham Creek, which widens as you approach the River Roach. To your left the salt marshes stretch towards the River Crouch where you have views of the marinas of Burnham-on-Crouch and the warehouses and timber yards of **Wallasea Island**. Much of the landward side of the embankment is given over to sheep grazing which makes this walk somewhat difficult for larger dogs as enclosures are often divided by wooden stiles and low voltage electric fencing.

5 As the path bears right, with the river on your left, maintain direction past **oyster beds** until you reach the boatyard. Go down the steps from the sea wall and pick your way through boats and machinery to the

gate. Squeeze through the gate and follow the unmade track until you pass a row of cottages on your left, followed by **Cobblers Row** and the fingerpost on your right that was the direction for the outward journey. Turn left and return to **The Plough and Sail**.

what to look for

Paglesham Creek is the habitat of a host of visiting wildfowl. Look for brent geese, black-tailed godwits and shelduck and in winter you may see short-eared owls. You may be lucky and spot insects such as the rare Scarce Emerald damselfly or the Roesel's bush-cricket. In the sea wall look for rare plants such as sea barley and beaked tassel-weed.

Framlingham Castle

Framlingham Castle (English Heritage), to the south, was built in the 12th century by Hugh Bigod, whose ancestors had been granted the manor of Framlingham in return for their support during the Norman Conquest. You can walk the full length of the castle's parapet walls and climb some of the 13 towers. The entry price includes an audio tour and also a museum of local history.

Nightingale (Luscinia megarhynchos)

A circuit from Laxfield

Below left: The Guildhall in Laxfield

What better way to enjoy a summer evening than a country stroll to a Victorian pub?

Laxfield and the Low House

This walk is really just an excuse to work up a good thirst before a visit to one of Suffolk's most charming pubs. The King's Head at Laxfield is usually known as the Low House because of its situation below the church and the village centre. This thatched pub, which actually dates from Tudor times, has changed little since the Victorian era when Arthur Fellgate, the village blacksmith, was landlord for 61 years before handing over the pub to two of his 14 children. A grainy black-and-white photo of Arthur and his long-suffering wife Anna hangs in the front parlour. The pub sign on the street is eccentric, featuring the head of Charles I on one side and Henry VIII on the other.

This much-loved old local was threatened with closure in the 1990s but the villagers formed a consortium and bought the pub to secure its future. Adnams, the respected Southwold brewery, now owns the pub. Musicians play here on Tuesday afternoons and on summer evenings the gardens are the setting for Shakespearean plays. This really is the perfect place to end a walk.

Laxfield is a historic village whose former market square is edged on three sides by All Saints Church, the Guildhall and the 15th-century Royal Oak pub. The church is unusual in being some 36ft (11m) wide yet having a single nave and no aisles. The most impressive building is the timber-framed Guildhall, which dates from the 16th century and has since seen service as a schoolroom, a wholesale shop, a poorhouse, a reading room, a billiard room and a working men's club. These days it houses the parish office, a doctor's surgery and a museum on the upper floor.

The walk takes you out into the countryside around Laxfield, with views of All Saints Church across the fields. Although much of the walk is on tarmac lanes rather than footpaths, there is little traffic and, in this part of Suffolk, this is often preferable to fighting your way along the edge of a large arable field, beating back long ears of overgrown barley, rape and wheat.

The Walk

1 Start on **Church Plain** with the Royal Oak behind you and walk along the High Street. After passing a Baptist chapel on your right, look for a footpath on the same side of the street which runs between a hedge and a cemetery. Stay on this path as it passes beneath a green canopy and crosses a **footbridge** over the River Blyth. The river rises just outside Laxfield and is little more than a stream at this point.

2 Keep straight ahead to enter a field and take the right-hand field-edge path. Ignore all paths leading off and stay on this path to climb around the field towards a distant farmhouse. Eventually the path turns left beside a ditch and then right to reach a road to right of a **farmhouse**.

3 Turn right and stay on this road for 1 mile (1.6km), keeping to the right when the road divides. This is a lovely quiet country lane and there are good views towards Laxfield across the huge fields to your right.

what to look for

As you walk past the Baptist chapel, notice the plaque to John Noyes, who was burned at the stake on this spot in 1557. A firm Protestant, he was charged with heresy after he refused to accept the Catholic doctrine of transubstantiation, which states that the bread and wine at the Eucharist become Christ's actual body and blood.

| 1h30 | 3.5 MILES | 5.7 KM | LEVEL 1**2**3 |

MAP: OS Explorer 231 Southwold & Bungay

START/FINISH: Church Plain, Laxfield; grid ref: TM 296724

PATHS: field-edge paths and country lanes

LANDSCAPE: farmland and village

PUBLIC TOILETS: none on route

TOURIST INFORMATION: Aldeburgh, tel 01728 453637

THE PUB: The King's Head, Laxfield

Getting to the start

Laxfield is located on the B1117 between Halesworth and Eye, 7 miles (11.3km) south west of Halesworth. Parking at the church.

Researched & written by:
David Hancock, Tony Kelly

Below: The plaque to John Noyes, martyred in 1557

did you know?

Saxtead Green Post Mill, 2.5 miles (4km) north west of Framlingham, is the best-preserved 18th-century windmill in Suffolk. It is open during the summer months for tours and you can climb up the stairs to watch the mill turn on its post to face the wind.

Left: Saxtead Green Post Mill

4 Turn left at **Corner Farm** and fork right along the lane, signposted 'Ubbeston'. After passing a stud farm, the road bends right, then narrows and starts to descend into the valley. When you see a cream-coloured cottage ahead, turn right on to a footpath. As you pass through the hedge you will once again see the tower of **All Saints Church** up ahead. Keep left and walk along a line of willow trees and continue along the edge of the field. Turn right then left to join a farm track that leads to a tarmac lane, where you should keep straight ahead.

5 When you reach a road, turn left to return to Laxfield. Take the first right to arrive at the **Low House** (The King's Head pub) and that well-earned pint. When you are ready, turn right outside the pub and left along Church Walk, or walk through the churchyard to return to **Church Plain**.

The Kings Head

about the pub

The Kings Head
Gorams Mill Lane, Laxfield
Suffolk IP13 8DW
Tel: 01986 798395

DIRECTIONS: see Getting to the start; pub behind the church, off the road to Banyards Green. Point **5** of the walk.

PARKING: 30

OPEN: daily

FOOD: no food Monday evening

BREWERY/COMPANY: Adnams

REAL ALE: Adnams Best, Broadside, seasonal ales, guest beer

DOGS: allowed in the bar

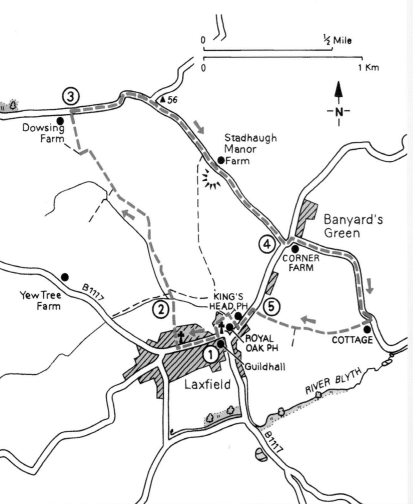

Virtually unchanged since Victorian times, this quintessential thatched Tudor pub is known locally as the Low House because it is secreted away down a lane below the village centre. An open fire burns in the parlour on winter evenings, and drinkers warm themselves while seated on a three-sided Victorian settle or high-backed wooden bench. To either side of the parlour are more cosy little rooms, filled with wooden tables, cushions and pews. There is no bar – pints of Adnams bitter come straight from the barrel in a tap room out the back. In summer, you can sit out of doors around a historic bowling green or take a seat inside the summer house.

Food
Home-cooked food is hearty and traditional, ranging from soup, sandwiches and ploughman's to cottage pie, sausages and mash, ham with mustard sauce and whole grilled plaice. Puddings include apple and rhubarb crumble.

Family facilities
Children are welcome in certain areas of the bar and in the restaurant. Smaller portions are available and the secluded rear garden is ideal for families.

Alternative refreshment stops
The Royal Oak, at the start of the walk, is another good village pub with parasols out on the square in summer.

☛ Where to go from here
The Laxfield and District Museum, in the Guildhall, is open on weekend afternoons from May to September and features rural and domestic bygones, a restored Victorian kitchen and village shop, and displays of local history and archaeology. A popular outing in summer is a horse-drawn carriage ride from nearby Tannington Hall, an Elizabethan manor house and hotel. Details are available at The King's Head.

Marsh harrier
(Circus aeruginosus)

Benacre Broad

Visit Benacre Broad, just north, a nationally important birdwatching site. What you see will obviously depend on the season and on migration patterns but among the species frequently observed here are avocet and marsh harriers. There is a small hide overlooking the lagoon which can be reached by a permissive path.

Avocet

A walk around Southwold

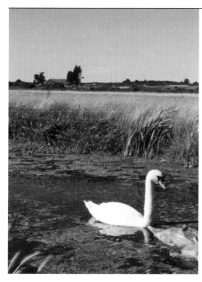

Walk around this old-fashioned holiday resort on an island surrounded by river, creek and sea.

Southwold Pier

The arrival of the first steamboats for more than 70 years marked a return to the glory days for Southwold Pier in the summer of 2002. The pier was originally built in 1899, when Southwold was a flourishing holiday resort. Mixed bathing had just been introduced on the beach, on condition that men and women were kept at least 20yds (18m) apart and changed in separate 'bathing machines' into costumes that covered their bodies from neck to knees. The *Belle* steamer brought holidaymakers on its daily voyage from London and the pier was a hive of activity as porters carried cases to their lodgings.

The T-end, where the boats docked, was swept away in a storm in 1934. During World War Two, the pier was split in two as a precaution against a German invasion. By the time Chris and Helen Iredale bought the pier in 1987, storms and neglect had reduced it to a rotting hulk. Years later, the couple have realised their dream of rebuilding and reopening the pier, so that visitors can once again stroll along the boardwalk with the sea spray in their faces and watch the boats unloading their passengers at a new landing stage.

An exhibition on the pier tells the history of the seaside holiday, complete with saucy postcards, kitsch teapots, palm readers, end-of-the-pier shows, high-diving 'professors' and old-style arcade machines, such as the 'kiss-meter' where you can find out whether you are flirtatious, amorous, frigid or sexy. A separate pavilion contains modern machines by local inventor Tim Hunkin, who also designed the ingenious water clock, with chimes and special effects every half-hour. You can eat ice cream or fish and chips, drink a pint of the local beer, play pool in the amusement arcade or watch the fishermen while taking in the sea air. Especially in summer, the pier provides a focus for good old-fashioned fun.

Southwold, situated on an island between the River Blyth and the sea, is one of those genteel, low-key seaside resorts where, in spite of the pier, everything is done in good taste. Make no mistake, this is a popular spot but it has none of the brashness of kiss-me-quick Felixstowe or Lowestoft. The character of Southwold seems to be summed up by the rows of brightly coloured beach huts on the

what to look for

It's worth a visit to the cathedral-like St Edmund's Church, whose 100ft (30m) flint tower stands guard over the town. The greatest treasure here is the 15th-century rood screen which spans the width of the church, a riot of colour as vivid as when it was painted, with angels in glory and a set of panels depicting the twelve apostles.

seafront promenade – some of which have been sold for the price of a three-bedroom cottage elsewhere – and the peaceful greens with their Georgian and Edwardian houses. Adnams brewery dominates the town and it is no surprise to discover that the beer is still delivered to pubs on horse-drawn drays. Southwold is that sort of place.

The Walk

1 Leave the **pier** and turn left along the seafront, either following the promenade past the beach huts and climbing some steps or walking along the clifftop path with views over the beach. After passing **St James' Green**, where a pair of cannon stand either side of a mast, continue along the clifftop path to **Gun Hill**, where six more cannon, captured at the Battle of Culloden near Inverness in 1746, can be seen facing out to sea.

2 From Gun Hill, head inland alongside the large South Green, then turn left along Queen's Road to the junction with Gardner Road and Ferry Road. Cross the road and take the footpath ahead, that

1h45 · **4 MILES** · **6.4 KM** · **LEVEL 1**23

MAP: OS Explorer 231 Southwold & Bungay

START/FINISH: beach car park (pay-and-display) or free in nearby streets; grid ref: TM 512767

PATHS: riverside paths, seaside promenade, town streets, 2 stiles

LANDSCAPE: Southwold and its surroundings – river, marshes, coast

PUBLIC TOILETS: beside pier, near beach and car park at Southwold Harbour

TOURIST INFORMATION: Southwold, tel 01502 724729

THE PUB: The Harbour Inn, Southwold

Getting to the start

Southwold is signposted off the A12 between Woodbridge and Lowestoft. Take the A1095 north of Blythburgh and head east for 4 miles (6.4km). Pass through Reydon and turn left just before Southwold town centre, signed to the beach and pier. A car park is at the pier.

Researched & written by:
David Hancock, Tony Kelly

Herring gull
(Larus argentatus)

did you know?

Nowhere else in Suffolk do you feel the power of the sea so much as along the cliffs at Covehithe, north of Southwold. Coastal erosion is threatening much of East Anglia, but here the sea is advancing at the rate of almost 10yds (9m) a year. The ground is being swallowed up from under your feet and the beach is littered with the debris of collapsed trees.

230

WALK

passes a hut and follows a stream beside the marshes as it heads towards the river. Alternatively, stay on the clifftop path and walk across the dunes until you reach the mouth of the **River Blyth**.

3 Turn right and walk beside the river, passing the **Walberswick ferry**, a group of fishing huts where fresh fish is sold, and **The Harbour Inn**. After about 0.75 mile (1.2km) you reach an iron bridge on the site of the old Southwold-to-Halesworth railway line.

4 Keep straight ahead at the bridge, crossing a stile and following the path round to the right alongside **Buss Creek** to

make a complete circuit of the island. There are good views across the common to Southwold, dominated by the lighthouse and the tower of **St Edmund's Church**. Horses and cattle can often be seen grazing on the marshes. Keep straight ahead at a four-finger signpost and stay on the raised path to reach a white-painted bridge.

5 Climb up to the road and cross the bridge, then continue on the path beside Buss Creek with views of beach huts in the distance. The path skirts a **boating lake** on its way down to the sea. Turn right and walk across the car park to return to the pier.

The Harbour Inn

Nautical memorabilia adorn the rambling bars of this appealing old Adnams pub situated away from the town on the bustling quay close to the working boatyard and fishing sheds beside the tidal River Blyth. There is a classic wood-panelled front bar with tiled floor, low beams and old settles. Local ship and boat photographs, model ships and flags fill the charactered back bar. It's the place to sup pints of superb Adnams ale, brewed just up the lane. Good summer alfresco tables on the front gravel overlooking the river and boats, or in the rear garden. Note the 1953 flood level mark on the pub wall.

Food
Expect a good range of freshly prepared food ranging from soups, baguettes, pint of prawns, ploughman's, lasagne and steaks. Draws a good crowd for first-rate fish – beer-battered haddock and daily specials.

Family facilities
Children are welcome in the bottom bar and restaurant until 9pm. There's a children's menu and high chairs are available.

Alternative refreshment stops
There are numerous cafés and restaurants in Southwold, many of them specialising in fresh local fish. Among the pubs serving Adnams beer are the Sole Bay Inn, a Victorian pub opposite the brewery on East Green, and the Red Lion on South Green.

☞ Where to go from here
The Southwold Sailors' Reading Room on East Cliff was opened in 1864 in memory of Captain Rayley, a naval officer at the time of the Battle of Trafalgar. Although it still retains its original purpose as a library and meeting place, it is now a small museum containing model boats, figureheads and portraits of local sailors and fishermen. Near by, on Gun Hill, a former coastguard look-out houses the tiny Lifeboat Museum, open on summer afternoons, with exhibits on the history of the Southwold lifeboats. Among the items to look for is a hand-operated foghorn, similar in appearance to a set of bellows.

about the pub

The Harbour Inn
Blackshore, Southwold
Suffolk IP18 6TA
Tel: 01502 722381

DIRECTIONS: in Southwold turn right at the Kings Head and follow the road to Blackshore Quay. At Point **3** of walk

PARKING: 50

OPEN: daily; all day

FOOD: daily

BREWERY/COMPANY: Adnams Brewery

REAL ALE: Adnams Best, Broadside, Fisherman & seasonal ale

DOGS: allowed in the bar

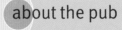

Reydon

BOATING LAKE

A1095

BUSS CREEK

SOUTHWOLD PIER

Reydon Marshes

SOUTHWOLD
▲10

ST EDMUND'S CHURCH

Southwold Common

ST JAMES' GREEN

Sailors' Reading Room

RIVER BLYTH

Lifeboat Museum

HARBOUR INN

▲1

GUN HILL

Town Marshes

WALBERSWICK COMMON

FERRY

ST ANDREW'S CHURCH

B1387

HERITAGE CENTRE

BELL INN

Walberswick

½ Mile

1 Km

N

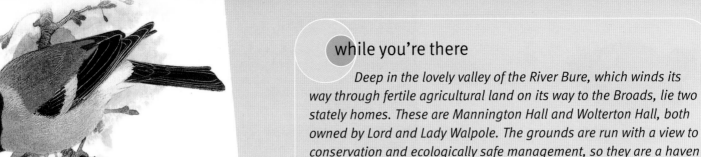

A female bullfinch
(Pyrrhula pyrrhula)

while you're there

Deep in the lovely valley of the River Bure, which winds its way through fertile agricultural land on its way to the Broads, lie two stately homes. These are Mannington Hall and Wolterton Hall, both owned by Lord and Lady Walpole. The grounds are run with a view to conservation and ecologically safe management, so they are a haven for many species of birds, small mammals and plants.

Blickling Hall and The Marriott Way

Cycle peaceful country lanes and a former railway track from Blickling Hall

Blickling Hall

Flanked by 17ft (5m) dark yew hedges planted in the 17th century, Blickling Hall (NT) is a magnificent Jacobean brick-fronted hall and one of the great houses of East Anglia. Dutch gabling, mullioned windows and domed turrets characterise the exterior. Inside there are fine collections of furniture, pictures and tapestries, and a spectacular Jacobean plaster ceiling in the 123ft (37.5m) Long Gallery (moulded in the 1620s) is very impressive. The gardens are also well worth exploring.

Salle

The tiny village of Salle is the unlikely setting for a 15th-century cathedral-like church full of rich treasures, apparently totally out of proportion to the tiny parish it serves. It was built by three wealthy families – the Briggs, the Fontaynes and

the Boleyns – who made their fortunes from the weaving industry. Of particular note is the unusual seven-sacrament font, of which only 39 are said to exist. Well worth looking at are the 26 carved oak stalls. Some have good carvings of human heads, others boast birds and animals; note the swan, squirrel, dragon and ape.

The Ride

1 From the car park follow the path to the information board and sign stating 'Park Only'. Turn left along the estate road, bearing right at a fork to enter **Blickling Park**. In a few yards, at a fork, take the

bridleway left across the park (Weavers Way). Proceed for 1 mile (1.6km), passing a track to the Mausoleum, and keeping to the left of **Great Wood** to reach a parking area and lane.

2 Turn left, then turn left at the junction in **Itteringham Common**, following the lane uphill to a T-junction. Turn right, then left for Oulton and shortly reach the B1354. Turn right and then left in 100m, signposted Oulton. Pass **Oulton Hall**, turn left at a crossroads and pass Oulton church. Keep to the lane for a mile (1.6km) to a T-junction and turn right into Oulton Street.

3 The road crosses a **disused airfield** to reach the busy B1149. Cross straight over and follow the lane for 0.75 mile

Top: Blickling Hall fronted by its gardens
Left: Cyclists pause to look across to the church in Salle village

| 3h00 | 19 MILES | 30.6 KM | LEVEL 123 |

SHORTER ALTERNATIVE ROUTE

| 2h00 | 13.5 MILES | 21.8 KM | LEVEL 123 |

MAP: OS Explorer 252 Norfolk Coast East

START/FINISH: National Trust car park at Blickling Hall; grid ref: TG176285

TRAILS/TRACKS: parkland tracks, narrow country lanes, old railway track

LANDSCAPE: open and gently rolling agricultural countryside and parkland

PUBLIC TOILETS: Blickling Hall and Aylsham

TOURIST INFORMATION: Aylsham, tel 01263 733903

CYCLE HIRE: Blickling Hall (mid-March to October), tel 01263 738015 www.nationaltrust.org.uk/blickling

THE PUB: The Buckinghamshire Arms, Bllickling

🛈 Puddles after rain along the Marriott Way, care to be taken crossing B1354 and through Aylsham

Getting to the start

Blickling Hall is located on the B1354 Aylsham to Holt road, 1.5 miles (2.4km) north-west of Aylsham and 15 miles (24.1km) north of Norwich.

Why do this cycle ride?

A level and easy-going ride, this enjoyable route begins at the splendid National Trust property of Blickling Hall, and incorporates a variety of parkland tracks, peaceful country lanes and a 6-mile (9.7km) section of disused railway track, the Marriott Way. Diversions along the way include a fascinating church and the little market town of Aylsham.

Researched and written by: David Hancock

The Royal National Lifeboat Institute's Henry Blogg was an old man when he died in 1954. He was awarded more medals and commendations than any other lifeboatman in the British Isles, and hundreds of sailors owed him their lives. You can learn more at the boathouse museum on the promenade.

Henry Blogg Memorial at Cromer

(1.2km) to a crossroads by cottages (Southgate). (For the short ride, continue towards Cawston and at an old railway crossing turn left to join the **Marriott Way**, signed 'Aylsham 4', Point 6). Turn right at the crossroads, signposted Heydon, and continue to a T-junction (unsigned).

4 Turn right, then in 0.5 mile (800m) turn left for Salle. Pass **Cherry Tree Farm** and keep left at the next junction. Take the next right turning and soon pass the impressive church at **Salle**. Pass through the hamlet to a junction and follow the road left, signposted to Reepham. Continue to **Reepham** and a T-junction on the outskirts of the village.

5 For refreshments at the old Reepham Station turn right, then right again (Kerri's). Turn left, then cross the road and pass through a gate to join the Marriott Way, a good, surfaced cycling trail along the former railway track. In 2 miles (3km) pass under a bridge and immediately fork left to climb an **embankment** (former platform of Cawston Station). Continue to a level crossing and cross a by-road.

6 Proceed for a further 4 miles (6.4km) through open country to the end of the trail in **Aylsham**, almost opposite the Bure Valley Railway (toilets). Turn left towards the town centre. Pass Budgens and follow the road left, signed to **Blickling Hall**. Pass the square and remain on the road for 0.5 mile (800m) before forking left on to a lane, signposted Abel Heath.

7 In 1 mile (1.6km) at **Abel Heath**, fork right and pass through the hamlet of Silvergate to reach the B1354, opposite Blickling Church. Turn left to return to the National Trust car park and **The Buckinghamshire Arms.**

The Buckinghamshire Arms

'The Bucks', a rather stately late 17th-century coaching inn, stands by the gates of the magnificent Blickling Hall. Once the estate builder's house and later servants quarters for the fine Jacobean mansion, it has three charming and well-furnished bars with open log fires and a typically National Trust-style of décor and taste. The Victorian cellar houses ales from Norfolk, Suffolk and Kent and the spacious courtyard and gardens are popular on summer days. Bedrooms have four-posters and en suite bathrooms, and two have dramatic evening views across to the floodlit hall.

Food
Menus offer fresh local food served in both traditional and modern ways. Typically, tuck into lasagne, salmon and prawn tagliatelle, sautéed lambs' kidneys with Marsala, steak and kidney pie, Morston mussels, or local game in season. The usual bar snacks include sandwiches and ploughman's lunches

Family facilities
Well-behaved children are welcome in the dining area. No children overnight.

Alternative refreshment stops
The National Trust tea room at Blickling Hall offers good lunches and teas and a children's menu. Along the way, stop off at the café in the Old Reepham Station, or at one of the pubs in Aylsham.

☛ Where to go from here
Allow time to visit Blickling Hall (www.nationaltrust.org.uk) and its beautiful gardens. Take a trip on the Bure

The Buckinghamshire Arms
Blickling, Aylsham
Norfolk NR11 6NF
Tel: 01263 732133

DIRECTIONS: see Getting to the start; pub beside the National Trust car park

PARKING: 60

OPEN: daily; all day in summer if busy

FOOD: daily

BREWERY/COMPANY: free house

REAL ALE: Woodforde's Wherry & Nelson's Revenge, Adnams Bitter, guest beer

ROOMS: 4 en suite

Valley Railway between Aylsham and Wroxham on the Norfolk Broads (www.bvrw.co.uk), visit the outstanding gardens that surround Mannington Hall (www.manningtongardens.co.uk), or explore the timeless estate village of Heydon. The church has some remarkable 14th-century wall paintings and the village is often used at a film set.

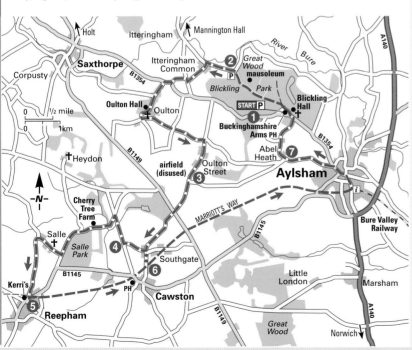

what to look for

Hunstanton's striped cliffs, the only hard rocky cliffs on the East Anglian coast are formed of white chalk over red chalk and carstone – a rust-brown sandstone. Look out for churches with round towers, nationally rare but common in east Anglia, as at Sedgeford.

Crumbling striped cliffs at Hunstanton

A round-towered church

From Brancaster to Branodunum

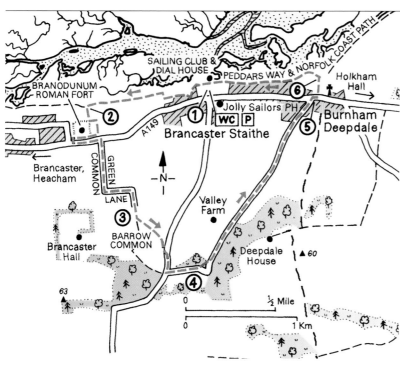

2h15 · **4.5 MILES** · **7.2 KM** · **LEVEL 1**23

MAP: OS Explorer 250 Norfolk Coast West; grid ref: TF 792443

START/FINISH: near National Trust's Dial House or in lay-by on A149 on edge of Brancaster Staithe

PATHS: winding paths and tracks, with some paved lanes, 2 stiles

LANDSCAPE: salt marshes, mudflats, farmland and common

PUBLIC TOILETS: none on route

TOURIST INFORMATION: Burnham Deepdale, tel 01485 210256

THE PUB: The White Horse, Brancaster Staithe

Getting to the start
Brancaster Staithe is on the A149 between Hunstanton and Wells-next-the-Sea. Lay-by parking is on the west side of Brancaster, a short distance from Harbour Way where there's limited parking.

Researched & written by:
Liz Cruwys, David Hancock, Beau Riffenburgh

The air is rich with the scent of the sea as you walk from Brancaster to its Roman fort.

The Roman Fort of Branodunum
Some time around AD 240–250 the Romans came to Brancaster and built a fort. It was square with a sturdy tower to protect each corner. Running between the towers was a curtain wall about 10ft (3m) thick, and there was a gate halfway along each of the four walls. In addition to the walls, gates and towers, they dug a wide ditch, so that any attackers would have to climb down it and up the other side – all the while bombarded with arrows and stones from the defenders above. They reinforced the walls by adding a rampart inside.

The fort was quite extensive – about 6.5 acres (2.6ha), and was probably built over a site levelled by previous occupants. Although it lies in a field that is about a mile (1.6km) from the sea today, when the Romans built it, Branodunum was right on the estuary. It was a fabulous location, because not only did it provide good access to the sea, but it was near the Peddars Way, an important line of communication in Roman times. When you walk it today, think of the men who were sent to protect and patrol this remote outpost.

By the 4th century AD, the civilian population that relied on the fort's protection had moved from Branodunum. The military settlement survived for a while but eventually it was abandoned. Only earthworks covered in vegetation remain.

The fort is now in the care of the National Trust, which owns around 2,000 acres (810ha) of the coast, of which Branodunum is a part, comprising some 4 miles (6.4km) of tidal foreshore. The entire region, with its salt marshes, mudflats and sand dunes, is a haven for wildlife and you might expect to see redshank, greenshank, sharp-eyed gannets with their dazzling white plumage, and the delicate common and Sandwich terns. Watching and waiting for a chance to grab a sick, weak or careless bird is the Arctic skua, a fierce scavenger-predator, which is a summer visitor here.

When you are out in the marshes take the opportunity to stop, close your eyes and listen – to the hiss of wind in long grass, the muted roar of distant waves and the piping whistles of birds. The countryside is never completely silent and it is always restful to hear the many sounds of nature.

The Walk

1 Walk towards the harbour and into the area owned by the Sailing Club and, just before the slipway, you will see the **National Trail** marker on your left. Shortly, go through the kissing gate and stroll along the boardwalk edging the marshes. Continue walking for 0.75 mile (1.2km).

2 Turn left and leave the coastal path, passing through a kissing gate to enter

Wells and Walsingham Light Railway

The Wells and Walsingham Light Railway covers 4 miles (6.4km) between Wells and Walsingham, and is the longest ten-and-a-quarter-inch gauge track in the world. The line passes through attractive countryside, which is particularly noted for its wild flowers and butterflies. This is the home of the unique Garratt Steam Locomotive which was specially built for this line.

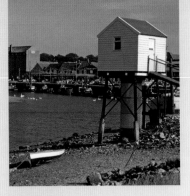

The harbour area of Wells-next-the-Sea

Above: Wind-swept sand dunes at Brancaster

a large field. This is **Rack Hill**, the area that houses the Roman fort. Follow the left-hand side of the field until you reach the top, then turn right and continue to the first five-bar gate and kissing gate on your left. Cross the gravel drive, go through another gate and continue ahead through the field. At the top, turn left parallel with the A149, exiting the field via a kissing gate in the field corner. Cross the A149 and walk up **Green Common Lane**, passing the felled tree stumps blocking vehicular access. The track bends left, then sharp right at a field entrance, heading uphill between the hedges.

3 At a waymarked gate further up the hill, enter **Barrow Common nature reserve**. Follow the main path ahead, then at a junction of three paths take the middle path and remain on this to a peaceful paved lane. Turn right, and follow the lane down a fairly steep (for Norfolk!) hill. Turn left at the junction and continue straight on until you reach a wood.

4 Head left at the footpath that cuts through a copse to emerge back on the paved lane. When you reach the lane, turn left along it. Just past **Valley Farm**, enter the field

on your left and walk parallel with road along the permissive path. Rejoin the lane at **Burnham Deepdale** and continue to the A149.

5 Cross over the A149 and turn right. After a few paces turn left along **The Drove**, opposite the garage and post office. At the end of the lane is a sign for the coast path. Follow it down a narrow, tree-lined track until it emerges on to the marshes and the main **Norfolk Coast Path**.

6 Turn left and walk along the path, soon to pass the garden and car park (access) of **The White Horse**. Continue to a small boatyard and follow the trail through some wooden huts, remaining on the coast path to the **Sailing Club** and the car park.

what to look for

Scolt Head Island nature reserve and bird sanctuary lies about 1 mile (1.6km) north. It is about 3.5 miles (5.7km) long, and is made up of shingle banks, salt marshes and sand dunes. You can visit the island by boat from Brancaster Staithe – do not attempt to reach it on foot across the marshes. There is a nature trail for visitors, but the ternery is closed during the breeding season.

The White Horse

The White Horse is smack on the North Norfolk coast path and enjoys wonderful views across wild and unspoilt tidal marshes to Scolt Head Island from its sun terrace and conservatory restaurant. The pub is truly special, especially for the birdwatchers, walkers and sailors who flock to this beautiful coastline. Scrubbed pine tables, high-backed settles and a warming wood-burning fire contribute to the bright, welcoming atmosphere in the bustling bar. Expect tip-top Norfolk ales, impressive wines by the glass and super accommodation in tastefully decorated bedrooms, some with memorable salt marsh views.

Food

At lunch there may be dressed Cromer crab, local mussels and oysters, deep-fried cod in beer batter or Caesar salad. Seafood dominates the inventive evening menus, perhaps black bream with shrimp sauce or cod with colcannon and red wine jus. Meat-eaters can opt for steak with chips and aioli.

Family facilities

Children are most welcome at the inn. There's a children's menu and smaller portions and high chairs are available. The inn also has five family bedrooms.

Alternative refreshment stops

The Jolly Sailors in Brancaster Staithe has a pleasant beer garden and families are welcome. There is a refreshment hut in Harbour Way, near the car park, which sells baguettes filled with local seafood, and the Lazy Lounge Café in Burnham Deepdale.

☛ Where to go from here

Norfolk Lavender in nearby Heacham is one of England's finest lavender farms. It is open all year and there is a shop and a tea room. In the opposite direction is Holkham Hall and its Bygones Museum, while closer to Brancaster is Wells-next-the-Sea with its charming narrow streets and Georgian houses. Next to it is Warham St Mary, which has handsome Renaissance glass in its church.

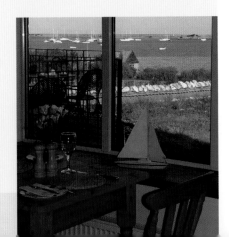

Norfolk Seafood

Norfolk is well known for a variety of regional seafoods including King's Lynn for shrimps; Cromer, world famous for its crabs; Wells-next-the-Sea for whelks and cockles and Yarmouth for bloaters – whole unsplit herrings, slightly salted and smoked, and kippers – herrings split, slightly salted and smoked.

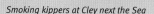

Smoking kippers at Cley next the Sea

Blakeney Eye's Marshes

Walk along the sea defences to some of the finest bird reserves in the country

Blakeney and Birds

Blakeney was a prosperous port in medieval times, but went into decline when its sea channels began to silt up. However, although the merchants decried the slow accumulation of salt marsh and sand bars, birds began to flock here in their thousands. By the Victorian era it had become such a favoured spot with feathered migrants that it became known as the place to go shooting and collecting. Some sportsmen just wanted to kill the many waterfowl, while others were more interested in trophy collecting – looking for species that were rare or little-known. The maxim 'what's hit is history; what's missed is mystery' was very characteristic of the Victorians' attitude to biological science. Many of these hapless birds ended up stuffed in museums or private collections.

In 1912, after many years of slaughter, the National Trust purchased the area from Cley Beach to the tip of Blakeney Point. It became one of Britian's first nature reserves. It is a fabulous place for a walk, regardless of whether you are interested in ornithology. A bright summer's day will show you glittering streams, salt-scented grasses waving gently in the breeze and pretty-sailed yachts bobbing in the distance. By contrast, a wet and windy winter's day will reveal the stark beauty, with the distant roar of white-capped waves pounding the beach, rain-drenched vegetation and a menacing sky filled with scudding clouds.

Although we regard the Victorians' wholesale slaughter with distaste, they left a legacy of valuable information. It was 19th-century trophy hunters who saw the Pallas' warbler and the yellow-breasted bunting in Britain for the first time – at Blakeney. Later, when the Cley Bird Observatory operated here between 1949 and 1963, the first sub-alpine warbler in Norfolk was captured and ringed.

Victorian records tell us that a good many red-spotted bluethroats appeared in September and October, and any collector who happened to visit then was almost certain to bag one. In the 1950s the observatory discovered that these were becoming rare at this time of year.

Today, bluethroats are regular spring visitors but are seldom seen in the autumn. It is thought that this change over time is related to different weather patterns and indicates how climate change, even on this small scale, can dramatically effect the behaviour of birds.

what to look for

Blakeney Point and its marshes comprise one of the best birdwatching areas in Norfolk. What you see depends on the time of year, but in the winter you can expect a huge variety of waterfowl, along with curlews, rock pipets and hen harriers. In early summer, plovers and terns arrive, while high summer and autumn are the best seasons, with the potential for spotting hundreds of different species of birds.

2h00 | **4.25 MILES** | **6.8 KM** | **LEVEL 1**23

MAP: OS Explorer 251 Norfolk Coast Central; grid ref: TG 028441

PATHS: footpaths with some paved lanes, can flood in winter

LANDSCAPE: salt marshes, scrubby meadows and farmland

PUBLIC TOILETS: Carnser (pay) car park, on seafront opposite Blakeney Guildhall

TOURIST INFORMATION: Holt, tel 0870 225 48551

THE PUB: The White Horse, Blakeney

❶ The lane from Wiveton to Blakeney can be busy

Getting to the start

Blakeney is situated off the A149 coast road between Wells-next-the-Sea and Cromer. Turn left down the High Street to locate the car park on the Quay.

Researched & written by:
Liz Cruwys, David Hancock, Beau Riffenburgh

Little tern
(Sterna albifrons)

did you know?

Cley next the Sea is not next to the sea any more, and has not been since the reclaiming of the marshland for pasture in the 17th century left it a mile (1.6km) or so inland. In earlier days Cley was an important port at the mouth of the River Gleven, ranking second only to King's Lynn on this coast.

The Walk

1 From the car park head for the **wildfowl conservation project**, a fenced-off area teeming with ducks, geese and widgeon, located on the east side of the car park. A species list has been mounted on one side, so you can see how many you can spot. Take the path marked **Norfolk Coast Path** out towards the marshes. This raised bank is part of the sea defences, and is managed by the Environment Agency. Eventually, you have salt marshes on both sides.

2 At the turning, head east. Carmelite friars once lived around here, although there is little to see of their chapel, the remains of which are located just after you turn by the **wooden staithe** (landing stage) to head south again. This part of the walk is excellent for spotting kittiwakes and terns in late summer. Also, look for Sabine's gull, manx and sooty shearwaters, godwits, turnstones and curlews. The path leads you past **Cley Windmill**, built in 1810 and which last operated in 1919. It is open to visitors and you can climb to the top to enjoy the view across the marshes. Follow signs for the Norfolk Coast Path until you reach the A149.

3 Keen birdwatchers may wish to turn around here and return along the embankment, or you can cross the A149 and turn left along the pavement to visit **Cley-next-the-Sea** and its windmill. To return via the inland route, cross the A149 to and turn right. Take the first left after crossing the little creek. Eventually you reach the cobblestone houses of **Wiveton** and a crossroads; go straight ahead.

4 Take the grassy track opposite **Primrose Farm** and follow it to a road. This is the Blakeney Road, and you turn right along it. (For the Wiveton Bell pub turn left.) The lane is wide and ahead you will see **St Nicholas' Church** nestling among trees. This dates from the 13th century, but was extended in the 14th. Its two towers served as navigation beacons for sailors, and the narrower, east one is floodlit at night.

5 At the A149 there are two lanes opposite you. Take the High Street fork on the left to walk through the centre of Blakeney village, passing **The White Horse**. Don't miss the 14th-century Guildhall undercroft at the bottom of Mariner's Hill. Then continue straight ahead into the car park.

Boats in Blakeney's harbour

The White Horse

At the heart of this delightful fishing village of narrow streets lined with flint-brick cottages stands The White Horse, a 17th-century coaching inn located just 100 yards (90m) from the tidal quay. The rambling bars, covered courtyard conservatory and the restaurant, located in the converted stable block, are tastefully decorated in creams and darkwood with soft lighting and attractive works of art. There are quay and salt-marsh views from the bar and the best of the upstairs bedrooms. Walled garden and courtyard.

Food
The food is good and the bar menu takes in regular dishes such as cockle chowder and deep-fried cod in beer batter, alongside lamb hotpot, wild boar sausages and daily specials like crabcake with tomato dressing and grey mullet on spring greens with chips. Separate evening restaurant menu.

Family facilities
Children are welcome in the top bar and the Garden Room conservatory to the rear of the pub. You will find a short children's menu, including fresh fish and chips.

Alternative refreshment stops
In Blakeney the Kabin sandwich bar in the car park operates between Easter and October. The Blakeney Hotel, Manor Hotel and King's Arms all have restaurants and bar food. The Moorings Bistro serves tea and coffee as well as meals. On the walk itself you can try the Wiveton Bell.

☛ Where to go from here
Langham Glass at nearby Morston, has

about the pub

The White Horse
4 High Street, Blakeney
Norfolk NR25 7AL
Tel: 01263 740574
www.blakeneywhitehorse.co.uk

DIRECTIONS: see Getting to the start
PARKING: 10. Use car park on the Quay
OPEN: daily
FOOD: daily
BREWERY/COMPANY: free house
REAL ALE: Adnam's ales, Woodfordes ales
DOGS: allowed in the bar
ROOMS: 10 en suite

restored 18th-century workshops, demonstrations and a shop. Morston Marshes are in the care of the National Trust and are an important site for migrating wrynecks, icterine and barred warblers. If you have time, a boat trip out to see the seals is a rewarding experience. These endearing creatures breed and bask on the isolated sandbars to the north.

234 MUCH HADHAM
HERTFORDSHIRE

4.5 MILES (7.2KM) 2hrs 30min

PATHS: Field paths and tracks, 4 stiles

SUGGESTED MAP: aqua3 OS Explorer 194 Hertford & Bishop's Stortford

GRID REFERENCE: TL 428197

PARKING: North end of High Street, just south of B1004 L turn

THE PUB: Jolly Waggoners

1 Walk along High Street into village, going **R** just before **war memorial**, over stile beside ball-finialled gate piers. Follow drive, then go **L** to stile at corner of tennis courts. Now in parkland of **Moor Place**, head diagonally to skirt to **L** of farm buildings. Go to **R-H** corner of wood and join farm access track. Cross drive on to metalled track, bear **L** along granite slabway to kissing gate beside **Dell Cottage**.

2 Cross road to footpath ('Windmill Way') and cross arable field, heading **L** of rendered cottage. Follow track behind gardens to road which bears **R** past telephone box, becoming metalled lane and later hedgeless track in cultivated land. Where this swings L, carry straight on to valley floor, bearing **R** at cottages, still along field edge. Head towards **Camwell Hall**, attractive 15th-century house.

3 At farm bear **L** on to its access drive, which becomes lane, passing **Wynches** on L. Turn **R** on to **B1004** to descend to **Hadham Mill**. Turn **L** at lane after crossing bridge over **River Ash**.

4 Follow lane and go **L** through gate with bridleway and **Hertfordshire Way** signs. Turn **R** along track and then bear **L**, not uphill to R. Follow delightful, waymarked path, with steeply sloping woods to R and river to L. Eventually reach lane.

5 Go **L** here and follow it to turn **L** at T-junction by **Sidehill House**. At kissing gate go **R** ('**Hertfordshire Way**'), to walk along floor of valley, **River Ash** to L. At lane go straight on, then go **R** ('Public Footpath 21') over **River Ash.** Climb steeply through copse. Turn **L** on to metalled lane, wooded river cliff now on L.

6 Just before road junction go **L** at public footpath sign. Bear **L** (not straight on) to descend steeply on hollow way track through woods down to river. Cross footbridge and follow path to churchyard.

7 Visit **St Andrew's Church**. Continue westwards, back to High Street.

235 ASHWELL
HERTFORDSHIRE

6.5 MILES (10.4KM) 2hrs 30min

PATHS: Tracks and paths, some lanes around Ashwell, 1 stile

SUGGESTED MAP: aqua3 OS Explorers 193 Luton & Stevenage; 208 Bedford & St Neots

GRID REFERENCE: TL 268396 (on Explorer 193)

PARKING: East end of High Street, outside United Reformed church

THE PUB: Three Tuns

1 Walk west down **Ashwell** High Street, curving **L** to ascend to junction. Turn **R** into **Hinxworth Road**. Shortly after passing gates to **West Point**, go straight on to track at bridleway sign, road bearing **R**.

2 Ascend **Newnham Hill** with views back to **Ashwell church** tower. Descend to bridleway junction. Turn **R** alongside hedge, turn **L** at footpath post to go through hedge and continue westward.

3 Beyond former farm cottages turn **R** on to road to walk past **Caldecote Manor** and **St Mary's Church** (not open). Follow road until just before **Meadow Cottages**. Here go **L** to skirt copse, then keep along track between fields. At deep ditch, go **L** few paces to cross it. Continue ahead, aiming for **L** end of hedge, turning **R** to walk beside it, and then through pasture.

4 At lane keep ahead past medieval **Hinxworth Place** to skirt to **R** of scrub. Go diagonally over arable land, heading for **Hinxworth** church. Go through hedge, beside deep ditch, then **L** over footbridge. Go along field edge before turning **R** into churchyard via kissing gate.

5 Leave churchyard along short lime avenue, turning **L** up High Street, past war memorial clock tower. Turn **R** into **Chapel Street**. At footpath sign go **R** on to cinder track which curves **L** to pass between 2 cottages, then through arable fields. At crossroads pass farm buildings to descend over arable land. Cross footbridge over **River Rhee**, go diagonally **L** in pasture to cross 2nd bridge. Turn **L** along field edge.

6 At lane go **L** past cottage and opposite go **R**, with **moat** in field on L. Turn **R** on to lane and, where this turns R, go **L**, path curving **R** through farmland to stile. Over stile turn **R**; stay on lane into Rollys Lane.

7 At T-junction go **R** into Mill Street, visit **church**. Cross Swan Street to path beside **Ashwell Village Museum**, and back to High Street.

236 CHESHUNT
HERTFORDSHIRE

6 MILES (9.7KM) 2hrs 45min

PATHS: Lanes, footpaths, field and river paths, 7 stiles

SUGGESTED MAP: aqua3 OS Explorer 174 Epping Forest & Lee Valley

GRID REFERENCE: TL 349023

PARKING: Churchgate, Cheshunt, east of church near Green Dragon pub

THE PUB: Green Dragon

1 From **Churchgate** cross over churchyard; leave by its far corner. Pass to **R** of **St Mary's School**, on path initially between fences, then playing fields. At road go **L**, then **L** again into **Dark Lane**. Beyond Cromwell Avenue, pass between cemeteries into **Bury Green Road**.

2 Just past No 104 turn **R**, on to footpath. Go along cul-de-sac and turn **L** at T-junction, almost immediately turning **R**, on footpath ('Barrow Lane'). At bypass path goes **R**, to road bridge.

3 Over bridge turn **L** by footpath ('Whitewebbs') along **Broadfield Farm's** access road. Turn **L** at farmyard gate, skirt some farm buildings and descend to cross Theobalds Brook. Now ascend **R** side of paddock. Once over stile go **R**, along edge of fields towards woods. Skirt these, **L** then **R**, to join track by **Theobalds Estate Yard** and turn **L** to lane.

4 Turn **L** and, just before **Theobalds Manor**, go **R** ('Whitewebbs Road'). At some woods path goes along their L side and crosses **M25**. Descending to stile and footbridge, follow line of oaks to climb another stile into pasture. At its corner go **R** over bridge, path then skirting stables towards **King and Tinker pub**.

5 Turn **L** along **Whitewebbs Lane** and turn **L** opposite **White Webbs Centre** on to Bulls Cross Ride ('**Theobalds College**').

6 Across **M25** follow lane past Western Cemetery, bearing **L** at gates to **Theobalds**. At T-junction go **R**, on to bridleway, initially alongside walls of Theobalds' kitchen gardens, then along green lane curving **L**.

7 Past **Temple Bar**, continue to **Cheshunt** bypass. Across it, go **R** over stile into wood. Continue into paddocks, then through gate by bridge over New River.

8 Turn **L** along tow path. Walk past housing estates and leave **New River** at road bridge. Turn **L** then **R** into **Churchgate**, passing borough offices to church.

237 MARKYATE
HERTFORDSHIRE

7 MILES (11.3KM) 3hrs

PATHS: Chalk ridges on either side of young Ver's valley

SUGGESTED MAP: aqua3 OS Explorer 182 St Albans & Hatfield

GRID REFERENCE: TL 059166

PARKING: On Markyate High Street

THE PUB: Three Blackbirds, Flamstead

1 From north end of **Markyate** High Street walk southwards. Turn **L** into **Hicks Road**, crossing **A5** on footbridge. Past **Lotus Lodge** turn **R**. Where lane turns L, go straight on along green lane which shortly turns **R** to descend, through mud, to valley road.

2 Turn **L** on to course of **Watling Street (Roman road).** Continue for over 1 mile (1.6km), at **garage** turn **R** to cross **A5**.

3 Over stile head diagonally **R**, across stream to stile. Follow field edge before heading into copse that climbs valley side. From copse, climb stile to go **L** alongside hedge. Cross stile and head to lane, River Hill, which leads into **Flamstead**.

4 At junction turn **L** along High Street, **R** into Church Lane and then **R** again, into parish churchyard. Leave via gate by war memorial cross. Turn **L** along High Street and then **L** into Trowley Hill Road. Beyond number 30, **Pound Farm**, turn **R** on to tarmac path ('The Chiltern Way'). At footpath post turn **L** and descend along edge of arable field. At bottom of field go **L** between gardens to lane and turn **R**.

5 At **Trowley Bottom** go straight on, then immediately **R** on to bridleway, behind cottages then along valley. At lane turn **R** to climb out of valley. At crest turn **L**. At footpath ('**Cheverells Green**'), bear **L** into **Friendless Wood**. Out of wood go **R** and follow ridge along edge of this and another wood before heading through kissing gates and sheep pasture to rejoin lane.

6 Go **L** to junction, turn **R**, then **L** to footpath ('**Buckwood Road**'). At footpath junction turn **R** and walk alongside arable field and gardens to road. Across it path climbs between gardens. Go along Cowper Road to Cavendish Road junction. Turn **R**, descending to **Markyate** High Street. Turn **L** and, just before White Hart Inn, go **R** to subway under **A5**. Turn **L** to visit church. Retrace your steps to High Street.

238 HARROLD ODELL
BEDFORDSHIRE

4.25 MILES (6.8KM) 2hrs

PATHS: Park tracks, field edges and woodland paths, can get boggy

SUGGESTED MAP: aqua3 OS Explorer 208 Bedford & St Neots

GRID REFERENCE: SP 956566

PARKING: Country park car park, near Harrold

THE PUB: The Bell, Odell

1 Leave car park by **visitor centre** and walk to far end of park beyond main lake – either along semi-surfaced path between 2 lakes or across long meadow by side of **River Great Ouse** (this may be difficult after heavy rain). Go through gate at far end of main track and along lane to **pub** at **Odell**, with its riverside garden. Beyond this join pavement of main road on rising bend and cross over at top, before you reach church.

2 Go through double gate on **L** for public bridleway – not footpath further on beside church. Follow wide grassy track uphill between fields, ignoring all paths and tracks off L and R, and follow this broad and direct route into **Odell Great Wood**. After ¼ mile (400m) of woodland walking you reach major junction of routes.

3 Turn 1st **L**, almost back on yourself, for public footpath (indicated on nearby waymarked post) through trees to southwest edge of wood. Turn **L** and walk along perimeter to end, then don't go through inviting gap in hedge but turn **R** to follow field-edge to far corner.

4 Go over high stile. Turn **L** to follow series of field edges gradually downhill to road at bottom – admire views over country park and river valley. **St Nicholas's Church**, isolated on the hilltop on the far side of river, is prominent, and to the west is the 14th-century tower of St Peter's Church at **Harrold**. Final field is narrow, enclosed grassy strip used by local stables.

5 Cross road and turn **L** to walk along pavement. In 150yds (137m) go **R**, down through wide field opening, and follow **R-H** side of field as it zig-zags around to far corner.

6 Re-enter **country park** and turn **R** on to semi-surfaced path that skirts northern side of main lake. At far end either walk along grassy strip back to **visitor centre** or follow path into woodland by road, and turn **L** for short and shady track back to start.

239 CASTLE ASHBY
NORTHAMPTONSHIRE

6.5 MILES (10.4KM) 3hrs 15min

PATHS: Field paths, farm tracks and river bank, potentially muddy

SUGGESTED MAP: aqua3 OS Explorer 207 Newport Pagnell & Northampton South

GRID REFERENCE: SP 860594

PARKING: Roadside in Castle Ashby; car park for visitors to gardens and farm shops

THE PUB: Falcon Inn

1 Walk out of **Castle Ashby** along road heading southwestwards, with house (and visitors' car park) over to L. Where pavement ends turn **R** for hamlet of **Chadstone**. Descend lane past cottages and converted barns to farm of **Chadstone Lodge**.

2 Turn **L** for bridleway alongside hedge and, at end, go on through trees to continue route alongside next field and down to road. Cross over for footpath down to **Whiston Spinney**, then via footbridge in shady dell to junction of tracks on far side. Here go straight on ('Footpath via Jerusalem Steps'), and cross field to trees on far side.

3 Follow path up steps and out along field edge with woodland (**The Firs**) on your R. Beyond gate go down sharp flight of steps to **R** and across field to turn **L** on far side and descend to road below.

4 Route continues up through field opposite. Head half-**L**, then follow bridleway waymarks to **R**, through long narrow field with houses of Cogenhoe on your L. At far side join lane and descend to **Cogenhoe Mill**.

5 Just before old mill buildings and sluice, with caravan park beyond, turn **R** for path alongside River Nene ('Nene Way'). Follow this waterside walk for 1 mile (1.6km) as far as **Whiston Lock**, then turn **R** for straight farm track across fields to main road, heading towards **Whiston church** sitting astride hilltop.

6 Go across junction and walk along lane into **Whiston**, branching **L** at triangular green. Take gated passageway beside outbuildings of **Manor Farm** up to church. There are good views over Nene Valley.

7 Walk past **church** to far side of churchyard, go over metal rung in wall and turn **R** on to an obvious field-edge path. This continues along grassy strip between further fields and emerges on to bend of lane. Go straight on/**L** and continue all the way back to **Castle Ashby**.

240 MANEA
CAMBRIDGESHIRE

6.25 MILES (10.1KM) 3hrs

PATHS: Lanes and hard farm tracks

SUGGESTED MAP: aqua3 OS Explorer 228 March & Ely

GRID REFERENCE: TL 478893

PARKING: Roadside parking in centre of Manea

THE PUB: Rose & Crown

1 Walk eastwards along High Street (which becomes Station Road), past **post office** and fish and chip shop, then turn **R** for public footpath alongside primary **school**. At football pitch at far end turn **R** and go past **Manea Wood**. Continue along path as it bears **R** and approaches **Bearts Farm**.

2 Turn **L** by old barns and sheds for wide track out into fields, with farm on your R, to reach attractive reedy lake known locally as '**The Pit**'. This was originally dug for clay, which was then transported across fields on a light railway to shore up the banks of nearby **Old and New Bedford rivers**. **The Pit** is now a popular place for fishermen and wildlife.

3 At end of track turn **R** on to lane, with lake still on your R, then when you reach junction at corner of road turn **L**, on to **Straight Road**, and follow this through fields to end.

4 Turn **L** on to **Purl's Bridge Drove** ('Welches Dam and RSPB reserve'). Follow this open lane to **Purl's Bridge**, by **Old Bedford River**. Continue along bank to reach **Ouse Washes Nature Reserve** (**visitor centre** and public toilets).

5 Return along lane for 440yds (402m) and turn **L** for signposted public bridleway by dark wooden sheds. Known as **Old Mill Drove**, this runs directly across open fields as far as rusting farm machinery and outbuildings of **Boon's Farm**. Turn **R** and walk along dead-straight **Barnes's Drove** for 1.25 miles (2km) to road at far end.

6 Turn **L** and after 80yds (73m) turn off **R** over stile for public footpath across fields back into **Manea** (aim for **fire station** tower). Route veers one way then other as it skirts series of pig enclosures – just follow clear yellow waymarks past enormous porkers. At far side cross successive stiles and turn **R**, past village stores, to follow main road back to centre.

241 RUTLAND WATER
RUTLAND

4.5 MILES (7.2KM) 2hrs 30min

PATHS: Wide and firm the whole distance

SUGGESTED MAP: aqua3 OS Explorer 234 Rutland Water

GRID REFERENCE: SK 900075

PARKING: Roadside parking in Upper Hambleton

THE PUB: Finch's Arms, Upper Hambleton

1 From **St Andrew's Church** in centre of **Upper Hambleton**, walk east on long and level main street as far as red pillar box. Turn **L** through gate for grassy lane ('public footpath') that leads straight through gate and down middle of sloping field.

2 Go through gate at bottom and turn **R** on to wide track that runs just above shore. This popular and peaceful route around Hambleton peninsula is also shared by cyclists, so be alert. Follow it from field to field, and through **Armley Wood,** with views across **Rutland Water**. You gradually swing around tip of Hambleton peninsula with views towards dam at eastern end.

3 When you arrive at tarmac lane (gated to traffic at this point, as it simply disappears into water a little further on!), go straight across to continue on same unmade track. It turns **R** and for short distance runs parallel with road before heading **L** and back towards water's edge and mixed woodland.

4 Approaching **Old Hall**, handsome building perched just above shore, turn **L** to reach its surfaced drive, then go **R** and walk along it for 160yds (146m) to reach cattle grid.

5 At this point you can return directly to **Upper Hambleton** by following lane back uphill; otherwise veer **L** to continue along waterside track, with views across to Egleton Bay and corner of **Rutland Water** reserved for wildlife (out of bounds to sailing boats).

6 After 500yds (457m) look for easily missed stile in hedge on your **R**, and public footpath that heads straight up field. (If you overshoot, or want to extend walk by ½ mile/800m, carry on along track to far end and return along lane to village.) Aim for apex of field, where successive stiles lead to narrow passageway between hedge and fence that eventually brings you out in churchyard in centre of village.

242 FRISBY ON THE WREAKE
LEICESTERSHIRE

3.75 MILES (6KM) 1hr 45min

PATHS: Pasture, ploughed fields heavy if wet, around 20 stiles

SUGGESTED MAP: aqua3 OS Explorer 246 Loughborough

GRID REFERENCE: SK 694176

PARKING: Roadside parking on Main Street or Water Street, Frisby

THE PUB: Blue Bell Inn

1 Go along **Frisby's** Main Street, past **post office**. Turn **L** into Mill Lane. After 50yds (46m) turn **R** between houses on public footpath (fingerpost bearing footprint). Walk over field, dropping slightly downhill. Cross double stile and ahead through 2nd field.

2 Ignore turning down to railway (L), instead continue across further wide fields, with **Ash Tree Farm** away to your R. Despite lack of well-walked path, route is clearly indicated by yellow-topped signposts. Continue to road.

3 Go across and continue through 2 smaller fields, 2nd in which horses are usually kept, and via kissing gate in corner to reach houses of **Kirby Bellars**. Turn **L** and walk down lane to **church**.

4 Continue down narrowing lane, which twists **L** and then **R**, past **nursery**. Track emerges into open field where you turn **L** and walk beside top fence. Where fence juts out before The Hollies go **R**, across pasture, and over stile by lifebuoy for leafy path along causeway across **Priory Water** (nature reserve). At end go ahead over more stiles, as path veers **L** and follows bank of **River Wreake**. It then winds through copse to end at road bridge into **Asfordby**.

5 To visit **Asfordby** turn **R** and take surfaced pathway off to **R** on far side of bridge. Otherwise cross road (but not bridge) for path opposite, which initially shadows river then strikes out diagonally **L** across 2 fields. Aim for far corner of 2nd, with spire of Frisby church just in view above treetops ahead.

6 Turn **R** and walk along narrow, grassy field parallel with railway, then cross railway via pedestrian crossing ('stop, look and listen', as sign directs). Follow lane on far side until it bends L. Here go **R** into Carrfields Lane, then **L** via short alleyway and another quiet back street to reach Church Lane. Turn **L** and follow this back to Main Street. Entrance to church is via side of old school building on Church Street.

243 FOXTON LOCKS
LEICESTERSHIRE

5 MILES (8KM) 2hrs 30min

PATHS: Canal tow path and open fields (mostly pasture), 12 stiles

SUGGESTED MAP: aqua3 OS Explorer 223 Northampton & Market Harborough

GRID REFERENCE: SP 691891

PARKING: Foxton Locks Country Park (pay-and-display)

THE PUB: The Bell Inn, Gumley

1 Turn **L** out of car park and along signposted path parallel with road to reach canal. Go **R**, under road bridge, then over footbridge, in order to turn **R** on far bank and along tow path to **Foxton Locks**. Descend lock staircase to basin at bottom.

2 Go ahead past former lock-keepers' cottages and switch banks via high-arched brick footbridge (**Rainbow Bridge**). Walk along tow path beyond. Continue along this route for 1.75 miles (2.8km), following **Grand Union Canal** as it swings **L** beyond **Debdale Wharf**. Notice the boats moored in the marina, some for repairs and renovation, others are kept here permanently. There are lovely views towards **Kibworth Beauchamp** to the north.

3 At **bridge No 68** go over stile on **R** to cross metal footbridge via 2 more stiles. On far side go up **L-H** edge of wide, sloping field to pass **Debdale Grange**. Continue through top field to lane on far side.

4 Turn **R** and walk along road for ¼ mile (400m) then, approaching road junction, cross stile on **L** for signposted public footpath across field, aiming for far edge of **Gumley Wood**. Follow path around side of plantation until 2nd stile, by section of fence used as horse jump.

5 From here strike out across deeply undulating grassy field towards stile below trees on far side. To visit pub in village of **Gumley**, go **R** before stile for short uphill path, otherwise aim half-**L** through next field. Go over stile and directly out across more fields, separated by farm drive, to return to canal on very far side. Cross high, thin footbridge and turn **R** to return to basin and locks. Walk back up beside staircase, crossing over half-way up to visit **museum**.

6 From **museum** follow path along its side (don't recross main canal again) and on along canal arm through trees. Go over lock and continue back to road bridge. Go under this. Turn **L** to return to car park.

244 LAMBLEY
NOTTINGHAMSHIRE

6.25 MILES (10.1KM) 3hrs 30min

PATHS: Undulating paths and green lanes, over 20 stiles

SUGGESTED MAP: aqua3 OS Explorer 260 Nottingham

GRID REFERENCE: SK 627452

PARKING: Recreation ground car park behind school (opposite Nags Head, on Catfoot Lane)

THE PUB: Nag's Head

1 From **Nags Head pub** walk down Main Street into village. In 220yds (210m) go **R** for public footpath between houses and around edge of fenced field. Turn **L** at end. Cross successive stiles (at 2nd take **L-H** choice of 2) for path behind houses. Turn **L**, via gate, to descend, cross road, and enter **nature reserve**.

2 Veer **L** to gate in far L corner. Turn **R** and out along bottom of several large fields, cutting across lower part of 2nd. At opening to large field (straight ahead) by copse, turn **L**.

3 Follow wide track uphill to **L** of hedge. In far corner of 3rd field, with grassy airstrip along its middle, turn **L** (not footpath straight on) and walk along field edge.

4 Just before it ends go **R** and, following direction of footpath post (not bridleway), aim half-**L** across next field then bear **L** across pasture. Drop down hillside, to stile beyond wooden enclosure in far corner by road.

5 Turn **R** and walk along verge past **Wood Barn Farm** to sharp R-H bend. Go **L** across top of fields to reach wooded track on far side, here turn **L** and follow it back to junction with **Lingwood Lane**.

6 Turn **R**, cross field (aiming half-**L**), then follow waymarks down through 3 fields into woodland at bottom. Go straight on via footbridge, **L** into field on far side, then almost immediately **R** and walk up through field to top. Turn **L** on to road for 100yds (91m), then go **R** beside bungalow to descend diagonally **R** across ridged fields to football pitch.

7 At far corner continue on path to walk through newly planted woodland area, **Bonney Doles**. Go over footbridge, turn **L**, and follow field edge to corner.

8 Here path with handrail leads into wooded dell for short way. Ignore this. Continue to cross footbridge. Turn **L**. Follow path through woods then field bottom along south side of **Lambley Dumble**. Eventually turn **L** on to Spring Lane to return to car park.

245 NEWSTEAD ABBEY
NOTTINGHAMSHIRE

5.75 MILES (9.2KM) 3hrs

PATHS: Firm, uncomplicated paths and tracks, well-signposted

SUGGESTED MAP: aqua3 OS Explorer 270 Sherwood Forest

GRID REFERENCE: SK 541540

PARKING: Newstead Abbey car park (small charge), access from A60

THE PUB: Horse and Groom, Linby

1 From main car park walk down drive short distance to **abbey**, then on along tarmac lane below large **Upper Lake**. Follow this route for 1.25 miles (2km) until you exit perimeter of park after 2nd lodge.

2 Immediately turn **L** and go through gate to reach small hill with young trees (**Freckland Wood**). Quite easy path runs up and across its panoramic top, or else skirt its R-H foot on waymarked **National Cycle Network Route 6**. Both routes meet up on far corner for direct 1.25-mile (2km) track all way to **Linby**.

3 Turn **L** when you emerge close to roundabout, and **L** again to walk through **Linby** as far as **pub**. Cross over to read notice board by bus stop detailing village's history. Continue out of village on pavement opposite 2nd of 2 medieval road-side crosses.

4 When pavement ends cross over once more and take popular local footpath on **L** across **Church Plantation**. Continue across **River Leen**, then half-way up next field go through archway in hedge on **L** to reach tiny Papplewick church. Leave churchyard via main gate and go down surfaced drive to main road. Turn **L** and walk along pavement for 550yds (503m) until entrance for **Papplewick Hall**.

5 Turn **L**, not to enter hall's gated driveway but for wide, semi-surfaced Hall Lane that runs via green gate past **Top Farm**. Where lane bends sharply L, around brick wall, go straight on via gate along hedged farm track across fields. Where farm track turns R to **Newstead Grange**, go straight on along main grassy track towards wooded perimeter of park.

6 Follow waymarks around lodge and continue along surfaced drive through trees – look out for ancient beech and oak along way. About 0.75 mile (1.2km) beyond lodge, lane bends **L** and path branches off ahead/R, clearly indicated. Soon it drops down to reach main drive to **abbey**.

7 Turn **L** and walk along road to car park.

246 SALTFLEET
LINCOLNSHIRE

4.75 MILES (7.7KM) 2hrs 30min

PATHS: Coastal tracks and field paths, some muddy after rain

SUGGESTED MAP: aqua3 OS Explorer 283 Louth & Mablethorpe

GRID REFERENCE: TF 467917

PARKING: Nature reserve car park at Rimac, off corner of A1031

THE PUB: New Inn

❶ From **RAF memorial** opposite **Bardney** post office, walk along adjacent Church Lane. Just beyond **St Lawrence Church** take public footpath indicated on **L**, which squeezes between two fences and turns **R** along end of gardens. (This path can be overgrown in summer, in which case follow road around to **R**, past Methodist chapel, and then **L** on to main road, turning off **L** at sign for **Viking Way**.)
❷ At end of path turn **L** on to wide track through fields, with huge sugar **factory** away to your R. Ignore permissive bridleways into **Southrey Wood** (L).
❸ When wood ends proceed on main track, which despite kink maintains its southeasterly direction. When it reaches buildings of **Southrey** it swings L past **Poplars Farm**. Take 1st road on **R**. At end of road go **R** again to reach **pub** at far end of **Ferry Road**.
❹ Turn **L** on to raised river bank. The overgrown platforms and signs of the former waterside railway station make a strange spectacle. Follow old trackbed alongside anglers by river for 650yds (594m).
❺ Go **L** at public footpath sign and across footbridge over drainage dyke for track across field. Continue straight on as it turns into firmer track and then surfaced **Campney Lane**.
❻ At road junction at end turn **L**. After sharp **L** bend, turn **R** on to signposted public bridleway. Follow this wide grassy ride between hedges. Go through gate and past **farm** to reach **remains of Tupholme Abbey**.
❼ Beyond **abbey** turn **R** on to road and then almost immediately **L** on to lane. About 750yds (686m) after **Low Road Farm** take public footpath indicated between two fields on **L**. Fence is first on your R, but when small dividing dyke appears keep both it and fence on your L. Go across small wooden bridge and then through another field to turn **R** on to cross track all way to road.
❽ Turn **L** for verge then pavement back to **Bardney**.

247 TEALBY
LINCOLNSHIRE

4.25 MILES (6.8KM) 2hrs

PATHS: Field paths, some steep and others muddy, 16 stiles

SUGGESTED MAP: aqua3 OS Explorer 282 Lincolnshire Wolds North

GRID REFERENCE: TF 157907

PARKING: Front Street, Tealby, near tea rooms

THE PUB: King's Head

❶ From **Tealby** Tea Rooms walk down Front Street as far as B Leaning & Sons, butchers. Turn **R** into Church Lane, which becomes walkway. At top, turn **L** and cross over **Rasen Road** to follow public footpath that runs between houses on opposite side. As far as **Walesby** you will be following Norse helmet waymarks of **Viking Way**.
❷ Cross rough pasture, aiming for stile in far bottom corner. Go over this and along path ahead, ignoring footbridge to L. Walk up hillside ahead to reach corner of **Bedlam Plantation** above **Castle Farm**.
❸ Turn **R**. Cross stile for fenced path beside woods. At far end strike out diagonally **L** and down undulating grassy field to pass below **Risby Manor Farm**. Keep ahead, crossing deep valley, to reach **R-H** edge of **Walesby Top Wood**. Beyond stile path leads out across field to **All Saints Church, Walesby**.
❹ From church, continue along **Viking Way** as it drops down wide track then lane into village. At Rasen Road at bottom go straight on, past **St Mary's Church**, to junction with **Catskin Lane**.
❺ If you need refreshment, cross road to **Walesby House**. Otherwise turn **L** and walk along **Catskin Lane** for 0.75 mile (1.2km) until just past R-H curve, then turn **L** at entrance of farm drive and go over cattle grid. This public bridleway leads back up to hilltop, but you should turn **R** in few paces and join footpath route (not defined) across rough pasture, initially parallel with road. At large ploughed field go along its **L-H** side to meet drive to **Castle Farm**.
❻ Public footpath continues east over field beyond. Path is waymarked at either end (at time of writing it had been ploughed; line of path indicated by sticks). At far side of field, cross stile and descend to cross footbridge. Turn **R** to rejoin route back to **Tealby**. This time turn **L** up **Rasen Road** to visit **All Saints Church**.

248 MANNINGTREE
ESSEX

7 MILES (11.3KM) 3hrs 30min

PATHS: Field paths, footpaths, tracks and sections of road, may be boggy, 5 stiles

SUGGESTED MAP: aqua3 OS Explorer 184 Colchester, Harwich & Clacton-on-Sea

GRID REFERENCE: TM 093322

PARKING: Pay-and-display at Manningtree Station; free at weekends

THE PUB: Mistley Thorn Hotel, Mistley

❶ From car park turn **R** at Dedham following fingerpost (**'Lawford'**) on steep, grassy path to **St Mary's Church**. Go through black gate, keep church on your R, cross stile over church wall. Turn **L** and, at wooden post, follow yellow waymark half **R** across meadow. Cross earth bridge over Wignell Brook, go **L** uphill keeping line of trees on your R. Just before house at top of hill, cross stile and bear **L** to **Cox's Hill**, on to **A137**.
❷ Cross **Cox's Hill**, turn **L** and after 40yds (37m), at fingerpost ('Essex Way'), turn **R**. Walk downhill with trees on L and pond on R. Pass housing estate on L and cross plank bridge over stream. Follow gravel path through Owl Conservation Area. Ignoring concrete path on L, turn half **R** on to cross-field path towards playing fields. Cross **Colchester Road**, and at T-junction turn **R** into Trinity Road, ignoring signs for Essex Way. At Evangelical church turn **L** between houses to New Road, **Wagon and Horses pub** is on L.
❸ Cross **New Road** and follow yellow waymarked footpath between backs of houses. At T-junction turn **L** on to wide bridleway. After 70yds (64m) follow waymark half **R** and rejoin Essex Way. Continue, crossing earth bridge over brook and 2 stiles. Just after 2nd stile, follow track between 2 concrete posts into wooded slopes of **Furze Hill**. Emerge from woods, go ahead keeping to field-edge path to **Church Farm**. Turn **L** on to Heath Road.
❹ Cross road to low wall to **remains of St Mary's Church**. Continue north and turn **L** on to B1352 and into **Shrubland Road** which becomes green lane. Cross 1st stile on **R** and walk under railway. Turn **L** into Mistley Green which joins **High Street**.
❺ Turn **L** at **High Street**; follow The Walls by **River Stour** to **Manningtree**. Turn **L** into **High Street**. Walk 1 mile (1.6km) along **Station Road** to car park.

249 BRADWELL ON SEA
ESSEX

6 MILES (9.7KM) 3hrs

PATHS: Stony and grassy paths with some road walking

SUGGESTED MAP: aqua3 OS Explorer 176 Blackwater Estuary, Maldon

GRID REFERENCE: TM 024078

PARKING: Informal parking at the footpath at East Hall Farm entrance; free car park at Bradwell Nuclear Power Station

THE PUB: Cricketers

❶ Take wide grassy path from car park towards sea. In 0.25 mile (800m) reach **Chapel of St Peter's-on-the-Wall**. Continue walking towards sea for another 30yds (27m) and turn **L** at T-junction. After 100yds (91m) climb wooden steps to sea defence wall.
❷ At fingerpost (**'Othona Community'**) turn **R**. Walk along wall with sea on your R. For next 2 miles (3.2km) stay on top of sea wall, mainly firm, grassy path punctuated with areas of concrete. On your L is private farmland. On your R, salt marsh gives way to white sand and shingle and mudflats at low tide. The seashore makes a lovely detour but at high tide you must remain on the concrete path. On seaward side there are concrete pill boxes. The 2nd pill box marks **Sales Point**, from where there are views of the mooring area used by Thames sailing barges. Follow path for 1 mile (1.6km).
❸ In 1.5 miles (2.4km) reach **Bradwell Nuclear Power Station**. Either continue on the route by the coast or make a detour to the nature trail around the station and Visitor Centre. Route continues along sea wall to **Bradwell Waterside**.
❹ At jetty, turn **L** on to Waterside Road keeping yacht club and **Green Man pub** on your R. Continue along Waterside Road with marina on your R. Continue past marina and turn **L** into Trusses Road. At T-junction, turn **R** towards **Bradwell-on-Sea** (turn **L** here towards **Bradwell Nuclear Power Station** to **RAF memorial** at Bradwell Bay Airfield).
❺ At **Bradwell-on-Sea** follow High Street to its junction with East End Road where, on corner, is **St Thomas' Church** opposite **Kings Head pub**. Pass Caidge Cottages on L, village school on R and continue for about 1 mile (1.6km) along **Roman Road**, past **Cricketers pub**, before reaching car park.

250 DANBURY
ESSEX

4 MILES (6.4KM) 2hrs

PATHS: Grass and woodland paths, field paths, some road

SUGGESTED MAP: aqua3 OS Explorer 183 Chelmsford & The Rodings, Maldon & Witham

GRID REFERENCE: TL 781050

PARKING: Free car park off Main Road opposite library and inside Danbury Country Park

THE PUB: Cricketers Arms

❶ Leave car park via grassy path to **R** of leisure centre. Walk downhill, with playing fields L and hedgerows R. In 100yds (91m) after **Armada beacon**, turn **L** at cross path for panoramic views.
❷ Turn **R** into Pennyroyal Road past **Cricketers Arms pub**. Cross Bicknacre Road into Sporehams Lane. Follow path ('Butts Green'). At signpost, take track through oaks and gorse, to cross bridge. After 25yds (23m), turn **R**, past houses in Fitzwalter Lane.
❸ At last house, called Dane View, keep **L** and follow footpath through woodland to Woodhill Road, and turn **L** to sign marking entrance to **Danbury Country Park** on R. In car park take kissing gate on L and go **L** again on to path just before information board.
❹ Maintain direction past another car park and 2nd lake, until you reach toilets. Turn **R** between lakes, and continue ahead to red-brick perimeter wall of Danbury Conference Centre and Palace.
❺ Turn **R** through formal gardens and, with lake on your R, follow path half-**L** through woods. Maintain direction uphill, diagonally across meadow and through kissing gate. From kissing gate, walk half-**L** uphill towards copse. Follow boardwalk around small water-filled gravel pit, then take path uphill between red-and-white painted posts and continue ahead, passing yellow waymark. Cross meadow towards oak trees, keeping white metal posts to your R.
❻ At last white post, turn **L** and cross over stile carefully on to busy **A414**. Cross road into Riffhams Lane, and walk uphill to Elm Green Lane. Turn **R**, uphill, to A414 by **war memorial** on green. Cross **A414**, turn **L** along verge and **R** along footpath beside **Rectory Farmhouse**.
❼ At T-junction turn **L** for views of **St John the Baptist Church**. At 2nd T-junction, turn **L** to visit church. Turn **R** to rejoin outward path past radio mast and return to car park.

251 THAXTED
ESSEX

3 MILES (4.8KM) 1hr 30min

PATHS: Field-edge paths, bridleway prone to muddiness, river bank and some town streets

SUGGESTED MAP: aqua3 OS Explorer 195 Braintree & Saffron Walden

GRID REFERENCE: TL 610311

PARKING: Free car park at Margaret Street

THE PUB: Swan Hotel

❶ From car park turn **L** into Margaret Street, **R** into Weaverhead Lane and **L** into **Copthall Lane**, passing cottages called **Bridgefoot**. After houses on L, pass through gap between trees by gate ('Walnut Tree Meadow'). Turn **R** along grassy path and keep parallel with **Copthall Lane** on your R. After 400yds (366m) bear **L** at yellow waymark through trees, cross 2 footbridges at R angles, in quick succession, and turn **R** keeping stream and hedgerows on your R.
❷ Continue along field-edge path through 2 fields. After line of trees on your L, turn **L** at waymark over footbridge and follow another field-edge path keeping hedgerow on your L to **B1051**, Sampford road. In distance, to your L, spire of **St John the Baptist Church** dominates skyline. Turn **R**, cross road with care, and take 1st turning **L** along farm track (**'Boynton End'**). The track zig-zags **L** and **R** past **Sorrel's Farm House** and **Golden's Farm**. At the farm bear **R** on to canopied bridleway between buildings, keeping paddock fence on L. Proceed downhill to waymarks outside **Goddard's Farm**, turn **L** then **R**; follow path uphill with farm on R-H side.
❸ Descend short steep embankment and cross farm track to follow fingerpost through hedge. Turn half-**L** across field and follow path with **River Chelmer** on your R to **Walden Road**.
❹ At **Walden Road** turn **R** across **Armitage Bridge** and immediately **L** at fingerpost. Follow field-edge path with river on your L passing conifers and, after 300yds (274m) where river veers away, turn **L** at waymark concealed in hedgerows. You are now on **Harcamlow Way**. Turn **L** downhill past house called **Haslemere**, over bridge across river. Ignore paths L and R and keep on tarmac road, past modern housing.
❺ Continue along Watling Lane passing cottages and Piggots Mill to emerge opposite **Swan Hotel**. Turn **L** and **R** into Margaret Street and return to car park.

252 PAKENHAM
SUFFOLK

4.5 MILES (7.2KM) 1hr 45min

PATHS: Bridleways, field-edge paths and quiet country lanes

SUGGESTED MAP: aqua3 OS Explorers 211 Bury St Edmunds & Stowmarket; 229 Thetford Forest in the Brecks

GRID REFERENCE: TL 932703 (on Explorer 229)

PARKING: Ixworth village hall free car park

THE PUB: Pykkerell Inn

❶ Leaving village hall car park, cross High Street and take path that leads through churchyard around R of parish church. Turn **L** on to Commister Lane and follow road as it bends round to **R**.

❷ Turn **L** on to bridlepath opposite Abbey Close. Looking L there are good views of **Ixworth Abbey**, a Georgian manor built around the ruins of a 12th-century Augustinian priory. Stay on this path as it crosses Black Bourn and continues towards small wood, where it swings **R**. A footpath on your **L** after 600yds (549m) is a short cut across fields. For full walk, keep straight on towards Point ❸.

❸ Turn **L** at end of hedgerow and follow field-edge path to metal gate ahead. Turn **L** here on to farm track that passes around wood. Soon after wood, short cut rejoins main walk from your L and you glimpse **Pakenham Windmill** ahead. Stay on this track to reach main road, **A143**.

❹ Cross road carefully and go ahead to another crossroads, where you keep straight ahead to **windmill**. Stay on this narrow road, Thieves Lane, as it descends to **Fulmer Bridge**, bucolic spot of meadows and streams. Continue towards T-junction, then turn **L** along **Fen Road**, passing council houses and bungalows before reaching junction at foot of hill.

❺ Stay on **Fen Road** as it bends round to **L** into small hamlet of **Grimstone End** and soon reach **Pakenham Watermill**. Just beyond **watermill**, there are views of Mickle Mere, a popular birdwatching spot, to your R. Stay on this road to return to **A143,** turn **L** along pavement before crossing main road at white post to quiet lane on far side. Turn **L** where you see house with dovecote in garden. At end of lane, turn **R**. Follow road into **Ixworth** to return to car park.

253 LONG MELFORD
SUFFOLK

6 MILES (9.7KM) 2hrs 45min

PATHS: Farm tracks, field and woodland paths, 8 stiles

SUGGESTED MAP: aqua3 OS Explorer 196 Sudbury, Hadleigh & Dedham Vale

GRID REFERENCE: TL 864465

PARKING: Church Walk, Long Melford

THE PUB: Crown Hotel

❶ Starting from **Black Lion Hotel**, walk up west side of green towards church, passing almshouses of Trinity Hospital on way. Bear **L** around church and walk through rectory garden. Cross stile, then turn **R** across paddock and head for corner behind stables. Cross 2 more stiles to reach meadow and continue straight ahead until you reach long drive to **Kentwell Hall**.

❷ Turn **L** and walk beside avenue of lime trees towards **Kentwell Hall**. At main gate, turn **L** to walk through grounds with good views of hall. Follow waymarks to turn **R** beside hedge and continue straight ahead on wide track that crosses farmland with sweeping views to both sides. Ignore tracks leading off to R and L; continue towards **Kiln Farm**.

❸ Just before derelict farm buildings, turn **R** on to track running between fields and woods. At 2nd wood, **Ashen Grove**, turn **L** on to shady woodland path that crosses 2 areas of grassland and swings **R** through trees to emerge on to field-edge path. Continue ahead on cross-field path, that cuts through hedge and makes its way across fields towards **Bridge Street**. Cross lane and walk past recreation ground, go over pair of stiles to reach **A134** by **Rose and Crown pub**.

❹ Cross main road carefully and take **L** fork opposite. Almost immediately, turn **R** on to path alongside **Chad Brook**. Stay on path for about 1.75 miles (2.8km) as it crosses footbridge to west side of brook, then clings to stream between farmland to R and woodland to L. Ignore 1st path off to R. At end of woods, path suddenly swings **R** to climb around edge of field and return to **A134.**

❺ Cross road again and keep straight ahead along **Hare Drift**, now tarmac lane. Reach **Long Melford** between garden centre and pub, directly opposite entrance to **Kentwell Hall**. Cross road, turn **L** and walk back down towards green.

254 CAVENDISH
SUFFOLK

6 MILES (9.7KM) 2hrs 30min

PATHS: Field paths, bridleways, short stretches of road, 3 stiles

SUGGESTED MAP: aqua3 OS Explorers 196 Sudbury, Hadleigh & Dedham Vale; 210 Newmarket & Haverhill

GRID REFERENCE: TL 805464 (on Explorer 196)

PARKING: Cavendish High Street, opposite Sue Ryder Museum

THE PUB: Bull Inn

❶ Take path on far side of **Cavendish** village green past **Five Bells pub** and school, then cross stile by cemetery to join **Stour Valley Path**. Continue around meadow and through hedge, then turn **L** along field-edge path that crosses plank bridge and swings round to **R** between fields and hedgerows to road.

❷ Turn **L**. Walk uphill for 0.25 mile (400m). Pass single house, turn **L** on to path along edge of field path. Path descends, then bends **R** and crosses wooden bridge to huge field. Turn **R** beside hedge, then **L** between fields, following **Stour Valley Path** waymarks to **Houghton Hall**. Keep ahead and stay on path as it turns **L** and then half-**R** to drop to **Hermitage Farm**.

❸ Keep to **Stour Valley Path** as it bends **L**, entering trees before reaching lane and passing playing field on its way to **A0192**.

❹ Cross road carefully, walk across bridge and turn **L** on narrow path beside small graveyard ('**Clare Castle Country Park**'). Enter park and keep **L**, beside stream to old railway bridge. Cross bridge and immediately ascend path to your **L** to housing estate. Turn **R** and cross old bridge over railway to **Mill House** and footbridge by old mill.

❺ Cross bridge and walk diagonally **L** across field, taking footbridge over **River Stour**. Keep ahead across field. At road, go **L** for 200yds (183m) before turning **L** on wide bridleway leading back down to river. At T-junction of paths, turn **R** across field. The track swings **L**, passes poplar grove and enters muddy section of woodland as it meets river.

❻ At lane, turn **L** passing half-timbered **Bower Hall**. Keep on public bridleway for 1 mile (1.6km) as it crosses farmland towards **Pentlow Hall.**

❼ Turn **L** on to road and cross bridge. Cross stile on **L-H** side to walk beside river. Climb bank on **R**, cross stile and walk through gardens to main road by **Sue Ryder Museum**.

255 BREYDON WATER
NORFOLK

8.5 MILES (13.7KM) 3hrs

PATHS: Riverside paths, footpaths, some roads, several steps, 1 stile

SUGGESTED MAP: aqua3 OS Explorer OL40 The Broads

GRID REFERENCE: TG 476050

PARKING: Car park near Church Farm Freehouse

THE PUB: Queen's Head

❶ Follow drive away from **Farnham Common**, keeping car parking area on your L. Pass refreshment kiosk and veer **R** at fork just beyond. Soon reach gate where you enter National Nature Reserve's car-free zone. Follow **Halse Drive** as it curves **L** and down between trees. When you reach bottom of hill swing **L** into **Victoria Drive**.

❷ Follow broad stony drive between beeches, avoiding turnings either side of route; eventually reach major junction with wide path on L and R. On R is large beech tree with 'Andy 6.9.97' carved on trunk. If you miss path, you shortly reach road. Bear **R** and go up slope, keep **L** at fork and cross several clearings to reach road at junction with Green Lane and **Park Lane**.

❸ Cross road to stile and waymark and go straight ahead, keeping boundary on L. Make for stile and descend into field dip, quickly climbing again to pass alongside grounds of **Dorney Wood**. Walk ahead to field corner, cross stile and turn **R** at road. Head for waymarked footpath on **L** and cross field to gap in trees and hedgerow. Turn **R** and skirt fields, making for belt of trees and banks of undergrowth. Path cuts between 2 oak trees in next field before reaching gap in hedgerow.

❹ Cross stile out to road; turn **L**. Pass Common Lane and Horseshoe Hill; turn **R** at next bridleway. Follow track through wood to next road at **Littleworth Common**. Cross stile to **R** of **Blackwood Arms** and follow Beeches Way. Beyond next stile continue ahead alongside wood, crossing 2 stiles before following fenced path. Go through gate and take path between trees of **Dorney Wood**.

❺ On reaching stile, cross over to road and continue on Beeches Way. Make for next major intersection and keep **R** along **Halse Drive**. Pass **Victoria Drive** and retrace your steps back to car park.

256 GREAT CRESSINGHAM
NORFOLK

5.75 MILES (9.2KM) 2hrs 30min

PATHS: Paved country lanes

SUGGESTED MAP: aqua3 OS Explorer 236 King's Lynn, Downham Market & Swaffham

GRID REFERENCE: TF 845018

PARKING: Car park opposite Windmill pub, Great Cressingham

THE PUB: Windmill

❶ Park opposite **Windmill pub** in **Great Cressingham**. Turn **L** along peaceful country lane. The grassy verges and hawthorn hedges here are a joy in spring, with nesting thrushes, wrens, blackbirds and robins. After 350yds (320m) reach crossroads.

❷ Turn **R** along lane ('**South Pickenham**') that runs parallel to **River Wissey**. Some of trees on this lane – oaks, chestnuts and beeches – were planted in 19th century. There is marshy meadow to **R** then lane plunges into shady wood where pheasants nest. After woods look for meadow with mature trees on your R. Due to modern agricultural methods trees are seldom tolerated in the middle of fields, so when you see them, it means the landscape must be fairly ancient.

❸ Turn **R** at crossroads, and join **Peddars Way** bridle route towards Ashill. This is another wooded lane, with sturdy walls of **Pickenham Hall** estate to R. The Hall, which you may glimpse through trees, is known for its shooting – hence the number of pheasants in the surrounding fields. Before long, you will see distinctive round tower of **South Pickenham's All Saints' Church**. Go straight over next junction towards Ashill. Lane can be plagued by fast cars, so walk with care. Cross brick bridge over **River Wissey** and continue to next junction.

❹ Turn **R** along narrow track, part of long distance National Trail, **Peddars Way and Norfolk Coast Path**, and continue along it for about 2 miles (3.2km), to junction with main road.

❺ Turn **R** and continue to **Great Cressingham**. You pass **St Michael's Church**, which has flint walls and large Gothic windows. There are interesting carvings above the tower door – each shield is crowned with the letter 'M', standing for **St Michael's**. Inside, you'll see 15th-century stained glass and brasses.

❻ Leave church and follow main road as it bears **L** into village. Turn **R** at T-junction to return to car park.

257 OLD HUNSTANTON
NORFOLK

8 MILES (12.9KM) 3hrs 15min

PATHS: Country tracks, lanes, muddy paths and sand dunes, 1 stile

SUGGESTED MAP: aqua3 OS Explorer 250 Norfolk Coast West

GRID REFERENCE: TF 697438

PARKING: Beach car park at Holme next the Sea

THE PUB: Gin Trap inn

❶ Walk towards sea and turn **L** to head across **dunes**. This is Norfolk at its best, with miles of flat sandy beaches, and **dunes**. You may find some areas fenced off to protect breeding birds. After about 1 mile (1.6km) you will see a notice board and outskirts of **Old Hunstanton.**

❷ Take path that leads past **golf course** and into Smugglers' Lane, to a T-junction. Turn **R** and walk past **Caley Hall Motel**. Cross **A149** and aim for road ('To **St Mary's Church**'), where you can see grave of William Green.

❸ Turn **R** up Chapel Bank Green, through a tunnel of shade before reaching open farmland. When road forks, go down a grassy track with views of Norfolk's countryside. At **Lodge Farm**, follow track around farm buildings to T-junction.

❹ Turn **R** along route ('Norfolk County Council Ringstead Rides') along avenue of mature oaks and ashes. In the field to your R are the stark ruins of 13th-century St Andrew's Chapel.

❺ Bear **L** at **Downs Farm**; head for gate and notice telling you what to expect in **Ringstead Downs Nature Reserve**. It belongs to the Norfolk Wildlife Trust and the area is grazed by traditional hill sheep. This is one of the most beautiful parts of the walk. Follow path **R** through reserve until you reach lane.

❻ Turn **L** into **Ringstead**. Pass **Gin Trap Inn**, continue through village, then take **R** fork. This is part of Peddars Way. It jigs **L** again after a few paces, but is clearly marked. Follow it along towards sail-less windmill.

❼ At last house, look for waymarked path to **L**. This cuts across field, then turns **R** into tunnel of hedges. Note **Norfolk Songline sculpture** halfway along path.

❽ Cross **A149**. Walk through **Holme**, with its long village green until you reach car park.

Northwest
ENGLAND

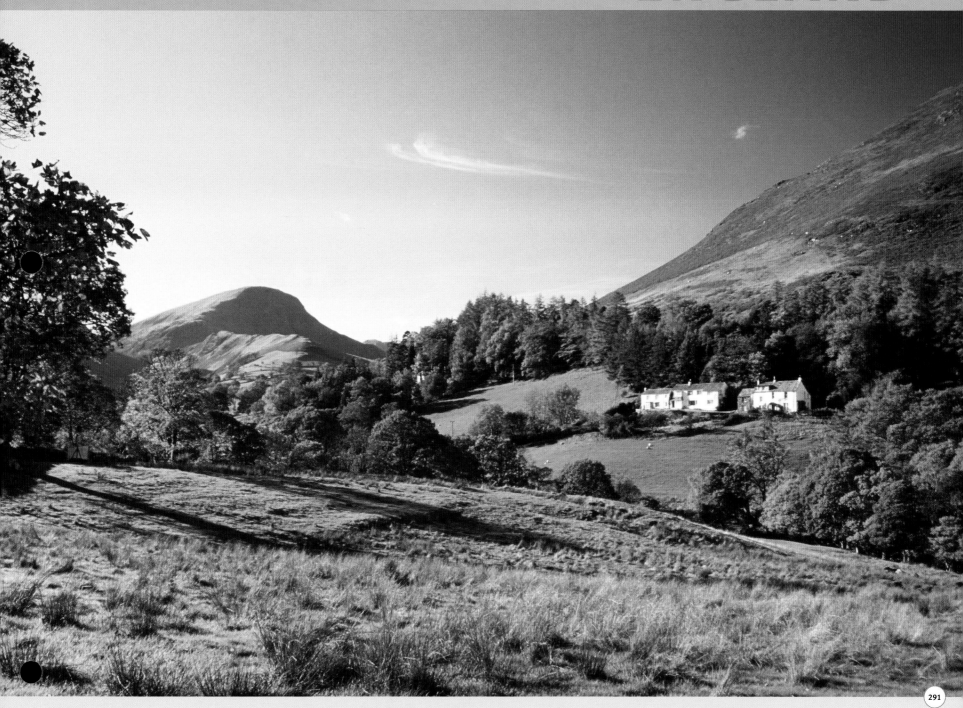

NORTHWEST ENGLAND

Contents

		page
258	Wrenbury, Cheshire	293
259	Little Budworth, Cheshire	295
260	Chester, Cheshire	297
261	Frodsham, Cheshire	299
262	Tatton Park, Cheshire	301
263	Lyme Park, Cheshire	303
264	Darwen Moors, Lancashire	305
265	Knott End, Lancashire	307
266	Hurst Green, Lancashire	309
267	Lancaster, Lancashire	311
268	Gisburn Forest, Lancashire	313
269	Silverdale, Lancashire	315
270	Cartmel, Cumbria	317
271	Seathwaite, Cumbria	319
272	Coniston, Cumbria	321
273	Brant Fell, Cumbria	323
274	Patterdale, Cumbria	325
275	Wast Water, Cumbria	327
276	Buttermere, Cumbria	329
277	Keswick, Cumbria	331
278	Pooley Bridge, Cumbria	333
279	Eden Valley, Cumbria	335
280	Castle Carrock, Cumbria	337
281	Garrigill, Cumbria	339
282 to 286	Cheshire	341
287	Merseyside	341
288	Manchester	342
289 to 293	Lancashire	342
294 to 299	Cumbria	343
300 to 305	Cumbria	344

KEY

- ▧ Walk route
- ⬤ Cycle route
- ▧ Unmapped walk

Colourful rhododendrons

From Wrenbury to Marbury

Visit ancient villages and explore rural Cheshire at its best.

Wrenbury Church

The church of St Margaret's in Wrenbury is dedicated to St Margaret of Antioch, a popular figure in the Middle Ages, a third-century martyr and the patron saint of expectant mothers. Today's church dates from around 1500, built from fine red Cheshire sandstone brought from the nearby Bickerton Hills. There was a chapel on this site, dating from the twelfth century. Just inside the south door is a single pew, which used to be occupied by a colourful character in village life. He was the Dog Whipper, a title which changed into a more dignified 'Beadle' in 1826. His duties were not necessarily to keep dogs out of the church – the Squire's dog, for example, was always welcome – but to evict dogs that interrupted the service. His duties also included prodding any worshippers who may have nodded off during the long sermons.

The church is particularly well-endowed with grotesque gargoyles, which took the water off the tower and aisle roofs, and other carvings may also be found, many with amusing faces, depicting the sense of humour, and sometimes sense of mischief, of medieval masons.

the ride

1 Start from the **village green** and ride left into Cholmondeley Road, gently downhill to reach and cross the **Shropshire Union Canal**. Immediately over the canal, go left alongside it. The road soon moves

A canal boat passing through the bridge at Wrenbury

away from the canal, and undulates gently through lush farmland. At a side-road junction, bear left for **Norbury** following the main road, and at the next junction, turn left into **Gauntons Bank**, heading for Marbury. The road climbs gently, and then steeply for a while, to meet **School Lane**.

2 Turn left onto a descending narrow lane flanked by hedgerows, which runs on to re-cross the Shropshire Union Canal, and continues into the village of Marbury. At the end of **School Lane**, at a junction with **Wirswall Road**, turn right, soon descending around a bend.

3 Take the next turning on the left (signed for **Wirswall**), the road once again undulating. Keep following the narrow main road, ignoring joining lanes right and left, and gradually the road begins to climb into Wirswall, a long climb up towards a **radio mast**. Go past **Wood Farm** and **Wicksted Hall**, still climbing, and continue through a section with very high hedgerows. Eventually, you reach a long descent, steep in places, which leads down to a **T-junction**, not far from the centre of Whitchurch (though this is not obvious).

4 Turn left, climbing once more on a broad road to pass a small **industrial estate** before levelling and running on between mainly hawthorn hedgerows, with the road starting to narrow and descend.

The parish church in Wrenbury

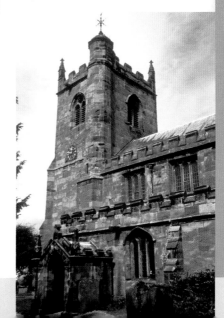

2h30	12 MILES	19 KM	LEVEL 123

MAP: OS Explorer 257 Crewe and Nantwich

START/FINISH: roadside parking beside Wrenbury village green; grid ref: SJ 595477

TRAILS/TRACKS: entirely on roads and country lanes, potholed in places

LANDSCAPE: rural Cheshire farmland

PUBLIC TOILETS: none on route

TOURIST INFORMATION: Nantwich, tel 01270 610983

CYCLE HIRE: none locally

THE PUB: The Dusty Miller, Wrenbury

! Numerous undulations and some long steady ascents and descents

Getting to the start

Wrenbury is a small village between Nantwich and Whitchurch. It is most easily reached from the A49, leaving it at Cholmondeley for minor roads to Chorley and Wrenbury. On reaching Wrenbury, continue over the canal bridge and keep forward to the village green.

Why do this cycle ride?

The villages of Wrenbury and Marbury which feature in this ride, are splendidly typical of ancient, rural Cheshire, both having pedigrees extending back to Norman times. The ride travels numerous country lanes, many flanked by neatly managed hedgerows of some antiquity.

Researched and written by: Terry Marsh

Dominated by a romantic Gothic castle started in 1801 and built of local sandstone, Cholmondley Castle Gardens are laid out with fine trees, rhododendrons and azaleas. Other attractions include water gardens, lakeside and woodland walks and rare breeds of farm animals.

Cholmondley Castle, built between 1801 and 1830

5 At a road junction, bear right for **Wrenbury**, along a narrow, undulating road, to cross a railway bridge. At the next junction, bear left into **Ossmere Lane**, onto a long gentle climb past a sizeable stand of Scots pine on the right, and then climbing past a small broad-leaved woodland to another junction. Bear right for Wrenbury with distant views now appearing on the left of the **Peckforton Hills**. Follow the road

(**Hollyhurst Road**), out to a T-junction just beyond a railway bridge.

6 Turn right into Wrenbury Road. At **Pinsley Green**, keep forward into New Road, a long straight road descending gently and flanked by low hedgerows and oak trees. This leads directly back to the **village green** in Wrenbury.

The Dusty Miller

A black-and-white lift bridge, designed by Thomas Telford, completes the picture-postcard setting for this beautifully converted 16th-century mill beside the Shropshire Union Canal. The current landlord is the great-grandson of Arthur Summer, who ran the mill up until World War Two. There's a light and airy interior with high-arched windows facing the canal, a mixture of furnishings – rustic tables, banquette seating, church pews – and hunting prints on terracotta walls. Super summer alfresco seating on a raised gravel terrace beside the River Weaver and canal.

Food
The menu, which increasingly uses

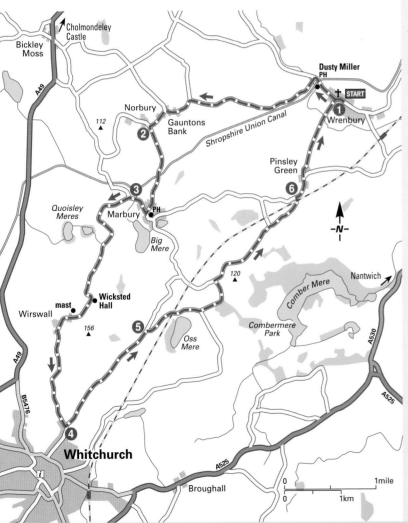

ingredients sourced from the north west, might offer smoked fresh haddock and prawns baked in a Staffordshire oatcake, slow-roasted duck breast with Cumberland sauce and garlic mash, jugged beef, home-made soups and a good selection of sandwiches.

Family facilities
Children of all ages are allowed in the pub. Youngsters have their own menu and older children can order small portions from the main menu. There are also high chairs.

Alternative refreshment stops
Restaurants and pubs in Whitchurch near Point 4 on the route and a pub at Marbury.

☞ Where to go from here
Hack Green Secret Nuclear Bunker, for 50 years Cheshire's nuclear headquarters, was a secret known only to Civil Service emergency planners. Now preserved, tou can explore the blast-proof HQ, war rooms, TV studios and see film footage of the day (www.hackgreen.co.uk). The bunker is south of Nantwich, just off the A530.

about the pub

The Dusty Miller
Cholmondeley Road, Wrenbury
Nantwich, Cheshire CW5 8HG
Tel: 01270 780537
www.dustymiller-wrenbury.com

DIRECTIONS: by the canal (on the route), 500 yds (460m) from the village and start point of the ride

PARKING: 50

OPEN: daily; all day

FOOD: daily; no food Mondays in winter

BREWERY/COMPANY: Robinsons Brewery

REAL ALE: Robinsons Best, Old Stockport Bitter, Hatters Mild, Frederics Bitter, XB & Old Tom

while you're there

In nearby Nantwich, Churche's Mansion is a wonderful Elizabethan manor house built by Richard Churche in the 1570s. It survived a fire which consumed much of the town in 1583.

did you know?

Great spotted woodpeckers prefer a habitat of mature deciduous woods where they excavate a new nest hole every year. The picture shows a male, distinguished from the female by his crimson nape patch. Syrian woodpeckers are very similar but lack the black moustache linking to the nape.

Great spotted woodpecker (Dendrocopos major)

Woods and heaths of Little Budworth

Far left: Fountains in Stapeley Water Gardens
Left: Preparations for a celebration in the village of Little Budworth

259

WALK

1h30 · **3.5 MILES** · **5.7 KM** · **LEVEL 123**

MAP: OS Explorer 267 Northwich & Delamere Forest

START/FINISH: main car park for Little Budworth Country Park; grid ref: SJ 590654

PATHS: easy tracks at first, field paths and some (usually quiet) road walking, 9 stiles

LANDSCAPE: mature woodland, open heath, farmland and mere

PUBLIC TOILETS: at start

TOURIST INFORMATION: Northwich, tel 01606 353534

THE PUB: Red Lion Inn, Little Budworth

Getting to the start

Little Budworth is a small village 2.5 miles (4km) west of Winsford and 3 miles (4.8km) north east of Tarporley in the area of Cheshire known as Vale Royal.

Researched and written by:
Terry Marsh, Jon Sparks

An easy walk centred around the distinctive heathland of Little Budworth Country Park.

Budworth Country Park

In the middle of all the rich green farmland of lowland Cheshire is an island of a rougher, older landscape. Usually it's peaceful, but a word of warning – it is very close to the Oulton Park motor-racing circuit. On race days the traffic and noise are abominable.

The area now called Little Budworth Country Park is a fragment of lowland heath. Britain now has only 18 per cent of the area of lowland heath recorded in 1800.

The essence of heath is an open landscape, with a mix of heather, gorse, bracken and grasses and with only scattered, if any, trees. There are two characteristic species of heather: ling (*Calluna vulgaris*) and bell heather (*Erica cinerea*). They often grow together and look quite similar, but ling has slightly paler and more open flowers. Heathland typically developed in areas cleared of trees from Neolithic times onward, as the poor soil made it unsuitable for cultivation. The land was, however, used for grazing. Gorse was traditionally used as fuel and for animal fodder, while bracken provided animal bedding and was also a valuable source of potash. These activities, and the occasional natural fire, prevented the heath reverting to woodland. Much of today's country park is wooded, but you will also see large areas of heath.

The majority of the heathland at Little Budworth is dry, but there are some low-lying wetter areas. The pool passed on the walk is a breeding ground for dragonflies and damselflies. The second half of the walk crosses farmland and skirts Budworth Mere. Many of Cheshire's meres were created by subsidence resulting from salt mining. Others, like this one, are natural, formed in hollows left by retreating ice at the end of the last ice age.

Finally the walk visits Little Budworth village. It is peaceful and attractive but has not become a tourist magnet. You'll probably agree that this is to its benefit.

the walk

1 Go straight across the **Coach Road** to a path then turn right on a wider path. Fork left and follow the main path, keeping straight on at a cross-path with a **Heathland Trail sign**, and again at the next crossing. When a field appears ahead, follow the path alongside to its right. This veers away right. Go back left just before a cleared area, by another Heathland Trail marker.

2 Go right on a wide track to the Coach Road and straight across into **Beech Road**. After 100yds (91m) go right on a path near a **metal barrier** to a former car park. Near its far end is a signboard with a map. Go through a gap in the fence beside this. The path skirts a depression with a **boggy pool**, then curves round a larger pool.

3 Cross a **causeway** by the pool and gently climb a sunken track beyond.

As it levels out, fork left by a **Heathland Trail sign** then turn left, with an open field not far away to the left. Bear left on a wider surfaced track, swinging down past an **ornamental pool** in a dip. Immediately after this turn right on a sandy track beside a stream.

4 Where another path crosses, most people evidently go through a gate ahead into the corner of a field. Strictly speaking, however, the right of way goes over a **stile** to its right then across the very wet corner of a wood to a second stile close by. Over this, bear right under power lines, to a stile in the far corner. Follow a narrow path (beware nettles), then go over a stile on the right and straight across a large field. Aim just left of the **farm** to a gate and stile. Go left on a lane for 30yds (27m) then right down a track. This becomes narrower, then descends slightly.

5 As it levels out, there's a stile on the right, with a sign for **Budworth Mere**.

The countryside surrounding Little Budworth

while you're there

The Salt Museum in Northwich was established in 1889. It has displays and artefacts from an industry that stretches back over 2,000 years in this area. The museum has been in its present premises, a former workhouse, since the 1970s. A short film sets the scene for visitors before they visit the galleries.

259

WALK

Go down towards the water then left on a path skirting the mere. At the end go right up a road, swinging further right into the centre of **Little Budworth**, passing the Red Lion pub.

6 Keep straight on along the road, through the village then past open fields, and passing **Park Road**. Opposite the main entrance gates of **Oulton Park** is the start of the **Coach Road**. Follow this, or the parallel footpath to its left for 125yds (114m), to the car park.

what to look for

The Heathland Trail signs show a great spotted woodpecker, though ironically this is (as you'd imagine) a woodland bird. A characteristic bird of the true heath is the stonechat. The males are easily recognised with black heads, white collars and orange breasts. Both sexes make a distinctive sound, like two pebbles being knocked together.

Red Lion Inn

An exhibit at Northwich's Salt Museum

Formerly a coaching inn dating from 1797, the Red Lion is a small, friendly village pub in an unspoiled rural spot, with original oak beams, ancient settles, winter log fires, and gleaming copper and brassware. You'll also find Robinson's ales on tap and good bar food at very reasonable prices. There's outside seating at the front, close to the road – but the traffic's light – and more benches and umbrellas at the back, overlooking the bowling green.

Food

As well as the usual bar snacks like soup, sandwiches and pub favourites, there's pork fillet, pan-fried chicken, salmon Provence, and grilled gammon steak.

Family facilities

Children are welcome in the family dining area if eating. There's a simple children's menu and smaller portions of the menu are available.

about the pub

Red Lion Inn
Vicarage Lane, Little Budworth
Tarporley, Cheshire CW6 9BY
Tel: 01829 760275

DIRECTIONS: see Getting to the start; pub in the village centre opposite the church

PARKING: 30

OPEN: all day; closed Monday

FOOD: daily

BREWERY/COMPANY: Robinsons Brewery

REAL ALE: Robinsons beers, guest beers

DOGS: allowed in the garden only

ROOMS: 4 en suite

Alternative refreshment stops

The Egerton Arms in Budworth, or the Abbey Arms near Delamere.

☞ Where to go from here

Nearby Northwich, like Middlewich and Nantwich, prospered on salt and Britain's only Salt Museum tells the story of Cheshire's oldest industry. Much of Nantwich was rebuilt after a catastrophic fire in 1583 though 14th-century St Mary's Church, one of the finest in Cheshire, survived. Churche's Mansion is an impressive Tudor house. Just outside Nantwich, Stapeley Water Gardens is the world's largest Water Garden Centre and the Palms Tropical Oasis is home to exotic flowers and a zoo collection (www.stapeleywg.com).

Map labels: A 54, Winsford, Beech Road, Polo Ground, Poolhead Farm, Budworth Mere, Little Budworth Country Park, Coach Road, Little Budworth, Red Lion PH, Motor Racing Circuit, Oulton Park, Nantwich, ¼ Mile, ½ Km, N, 75, 76

The remains of a Roman hypocaust (underfloor heating) and colonnade in Chester

Roman history

You can learn all about Chester's past from the hands-on re-creations of The Deva Roman Experience, where you can stroll along reconstructed streets experiencing the sights, sounds and smells of Roman Chester. Then return to the present day on an extensive archaeological dig.

Chester to Connah's Quay

The cycle way on Hawarden Bridge across the River Dee

 2h30 | **16.25 MILES** | **26 KM** | **LEVEL 123**

Make the most of an enjoyable and easy ride along an old railway trackbed.

Trees on the trail

Along the old track are many plant species of the hardy type capable of thriving in the harsh conditions alongside railways. On this ride, keep an eye open for two types of tree: the elder and the willow. The elder produces lovely white flowers in summertime, and then supports huge clusters of lush black berries, which, although insipid when raw, produce a distinctly flavoured wine. The tree is also believed to hold mystical powers and many ancient superstitions are associated with it. In some English counties, it is considered unwise to cut the wood of elder without first securing permission by bowing three times before it, or by making an apology. It is also claimed that elder is a safe shelter in a storm, because the cross on which Jesus was crucified was made of elder, and so lightning never strikes it.

Willow is another tree that grows alongside this route, and it grows well on fertile riverside land. Cricket bats are traditionally made from willow, but it is thought unlucky to burn the wood, and few fenmen in the east of England will take willow into the house to burn, while there is a tradition in Lancashire that willow should not be burned on Bonfire Night. Have a look for the graceful weeping willow, which is found along the route; it is a tree that originated in China.

the ride

1 Leave the Northgate Car Park, and turn right along **Northgate Avenue**, soon riding through a modern housing estate. At the far end of Northgate Avenue, go through a barrier into a small **park**, riding left on a surfaced track to emerge on the **former railway trackbed**, now surfaced. Turn left.

2 You soon cross the **Shropshire Union Canal**, and gradually the houses of Chester fall away, and the route enters a long stretch flanked by light **woodland**. Eventually, it passes into **Wales**, and open countryside with far-reaching views.

3 The A55 at **Sealand** is crossed by a new bridge, beyond which the route gradually starts to bend towards the River Dee and **Hawarden Bridge**.

4 Ramps lead up to a **cycle way** alongside the railway, and down the other side. Loop back left (animal grid to cross), and pass under the **bridge**, then continue once more on a broad surfaced track, which gradually veers right (after a barrier, and another grid) towards the long wharf and car park at **Connah's Quay**.

5 The return route is simply back the way you came.

Uninterrupted riding along a cycle way near Chester

MAP: OS Explorer 266 Wirral and Chester

START/FINISH: Northgate Car Park (pay), Northgate Avenue, at the rear of the Northgate Arena; grid ref: SJ 406672

TRAILS/TRACKS: easy, surfaced track all the way, with two bridge crossings; a few barriers to contend with

LANDSCAPE: mainly farmland, but with some industrial sites

PUBLIC TOILETS: none on route

TOURIST INFORMATION: Chester, tel 01244 402111

CYCLE HIRE: Eureka Cyclists Cycle Hire, Woodbank, Chester, tel 0151 339 5629; www.eurekacyclists.co.uk

THE PUB: Northgate Arms, Chester

Getting to the start

The Northgate Car Park, is located at the rear of the Northgate Arena, a prominent building near the centre of Chester. Access is from a dual carriageway, the A5268 (eastbound).

Why do this cycle ride?

Although linear, the route is delightful in either direction. It offers very easy riding from the heart of Chester, out along a smooth-surfaced track all the way to the wharf at Connah's Quay. The route is being developed as a linear park and woodland, and crosses attractive countryside. Crossing the Dee at Hawarden Bridge is a highlight, with the end of the outward section then only a few minutes away.

Researched and written by: Terry Marsh

260

CYCLE

Chester's walls

Parts of Chester's ancient red sandstone city walls date back to Roman times, when the city was known as Deva, but most of the towers and gates that you see today were constructed in the Middle Ages. The 2-mile (3.2km) stroll around the walls is one of the finest ways to admire this bustling Deeside city, famous for its two-storey galleried medieval shops known as The Rows.

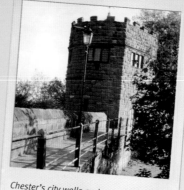

Chester's city walls and King Charles' Tower

Northgate Arms

Despite its busy position beside the main dual carriageway through the city, the Northgate is relaxing and quiet inside, offering a haven away from the traffic, with soft sofas to sink into and warming log fires to warm your toes. Sporting memorabilia adorns the interior, including a pool table, which is fixed upside down to the ceiling – it's time to worry when you think you can pot any of the balls on it!

Food

The menu lists a wide range of pub food, from Cajun chicken salad, vegetable bake and scampi and chips to steak pie, lasagne, chilli, and locally made sausages with mash. Snacks take in sandwiches, baguettes and filled jacket potatoes.

Family facilities

Children are welcome inside the pub. There's a children's menu for youngsters and smaller portions are available. Small beer garden for summer drinking.

Alternative refreshment stops

If exploring Chester you'll find plenty of good pubs and cafés – seek out the Albion on Park Street.

☞ Where to go from here

Take a trip to Chester Zoo (www.chesterzoo.org), famous for its large enclosures and attractively landscaped gardens. With over 7,000 animals and over 500 species there's much to see, notably the Tsavo Black Rhino Experience, the Spirit of the Jaguar and the children's Fun Ark Adventure playground. At the Blue Planet Aquarium (www.blueplanetaquarium.com), near Ellesmere Port, you can take a voyage of discovery along a 230ft (70m) underwater tunnel through the waters of the world and see giant rays and menacing sharks.

about the pub

Northgate Arms
Delamere Street, Chester
Cheshire CH2 2AY
Tel: 01244 372074

DIRECTIONS: beside the A5268 near the start of the ride. Best reached on foot from the Northgate Car Park, via subways beneath the dual carriageway

PARKING: limited (use Northgate Car Park)

OPEN: all day; closed Monday

FOOD: all day

BREWERY/COMPANY: Punch Taverns

REAL ALE: Courage Directors, guest beer

A circuit outside Frodsham

Far left: Buildings lining Manchester's canal basin
Left: Frodsham's war memorial

A short and simple walk on the crest and along the flanks of a prominent red sandstone escarpment.

Sandstone Trail

Frodsham is at the northern end of the Sandstone Trail. The sandstone ridge that bounds the western edge of the Cheshire Plain is not continuous but does dominate the lowlands along much of its length. In a few places it breaks out into real crags, notably at Beeston, Frodsham and Helsby.

On Woodhouse Hill, near the southern end of the circuit, there was once a hill fort, probably dating back to the Iron Age. It can be hard to discern the remains now, though it's easier if you go in the winter when they're less obscured by vegetation. After a steep descent the walk returns along the base of the scarp then climbs up through Dunsdale Hollow to the base of the crags. Here you can return to the crest by a flight of steps, though there's an alternative for the adventurous in the steep scramble known to generations of Frodsham people

as Jacob's Ladder. Above this the path passes more small crags, before emerging into the open at Mersey View, crowned by the village war memorial. As the name suggests, the grand curve of the Mersey is unmistakable. Hugging the nearer shore is the Manchester Ship Canal, joined almost directly below by the Weaver Navigation. Beyond it you can pick out Liverpool's airport and the city's two cathedrals.

the walk

1 Go right along the lane for 100yds (91m), then left down a sunken footpath and over a stile on to a **golf course**. The path is much older than the golf course and officially walkers have priority, but don't take it for granted! Head straight across and you'll arrive at the **17th tee**, where there's an arrow on a post. Drop down slightly to the right, to a footpath into the trees right of a green. Bear left at a sign for Woodhouse Hill, down a few steps. Keep to the left, passing above crags, then go down steps into **Dunsdale Hollow**.

2 Go left, rising gently, below more **crags**. Pass a stile on the right then go up scratched steps on the corner of the rocks ahead. Follow a level path through trees, near the edge of the golf course. Soon after this ends, the path rises slightly and passes a **bench** and after another 20yds (18m), the path forks. Keep straight on along the level path, soon passing a **Woodland Trust sign**, to a wider clearing with a signpost on the left near the corner of a field beyond.

3 Just before the corner of the field there's a break in a very overgrown **low wall** on the right, from which a narrow path slants steeply down the slope. There's some bare rock and it can be slippery when wet, so it needs a little care. Near the bottom it turns directly downhill to the bottom of the wood. From a **gate**, go right along the base of the hill. After 800yds (732m) the path twists and descends a little into the bottom of **Dunsdale Hollow**. Cross this and go up the other side alongside a stone wall and up a flight of steps. Go right on a **sandy track**, climbing steadily then passing below a **steep rock face**.

The view across Frodsham golf course towards Helsby

WALK

1h30	3 MILES	4.8 KM	LEVEL 123

MAP: OS Explorer 267 Northwich & Delamere Forest

START/FINISH: small car park on Beacon Hill, near Mersey View; grid ref: SJ 518766

PATHS: clear woodland paths, golf course, 4 stiles

LANDSCAPE: largely wooded steep slopes and gentler crest with a few open sections

PUBLIC TOILETS: in Frodsham village and at Castle Park

TOURIST INFORMATION: Runcorn, tel 01928 576776

THE PUB: The Ring O'Bells, Frodsham

❶ Generally suitable for all ages; a steep descent at Jacob's Ladder means that children will need to be closely controlled on this section

Getting to the start

Frodsham, 2.5 miles (4km) south of Runcorn, and overlooking the Mersey Estuary, is easily reached from the M56 motorway and by rail (though it's quite a climb from the station to the start of the walk). The car park lies up a convoluted series of minor lanes, but it's easily figured out with the aid of a map.

Researched and written by:
Terry Marsh, Jon Sparks

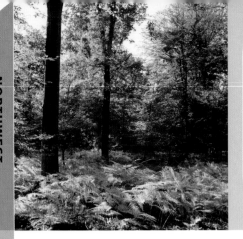

Halton Castle, near Frodsham, was originally a timber castle, dating from the 11th century. It was given stonework in the 12th century at about the time it passed into the control of the powerful Lacy family. It was then owned by the Earls, later Dukes, of Lancaster in the 14th century, one of whom became King Henry IV. It was severely damaged during the Civil War. Events are staged in the summer, for details visit the website, www.haltoncastle.org

4 Go left up steps, briefly rejoining the outward route. **Jacob's Ladder** is just to the left here, up the right-hand edge of the crags. When you reach the top, follow a sandy track, and then bear left at a signpost for **Mersey View**, with occasional Sandstone Trail markers, along the brink of the steeper slope. This passes below some small steep crags before emerging near the **war memorial**.

5 Turn right just at the memorial on a grassy footpath, aiming for **elecommunications towers** ahead. Go through the ornate **iron gates** on to the lane and turn right, back to the car park at the start of the walk.

what to look for

New red sandstone is about 200 million years old which is fairly new in geological terms! It's a relatively soft rock, as you can see from the worn footholds of Jacob's Ladder. Curious knobbly shapes in some of the crags often result from wind erosion. Despite strenuous efforts at clearance, rhododendrons remain abundant in parts of the woods. Originating in the Himalayas, they are very hardy plants which frequently crowd out native species.

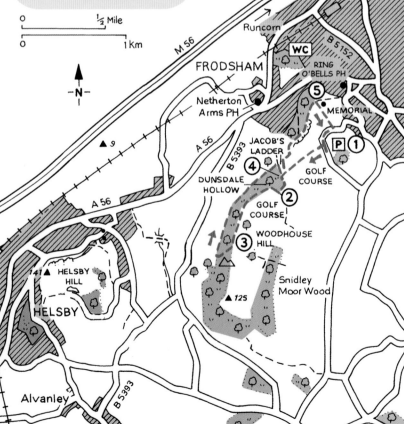

The Ring O'Bells

Rustic, white-painted 17th-century pub, festooned in summer with colourful hanging baskets, and pleasantly situated opposite the parish church. Three small, rambling rooms have antique settles, beams, dark oak panelling and stained glass, logs fires and lovely views over the church and the Mersey Plain. From a hatchway bar you can order pints of Black Sheep or the guest brew, and blackboard menus list some good-value lunchtime food. The secluded rear garden has a pond and plenty of shady trees for summer eating and drinking.

Food
Blackboards list sandwiches and filled baked potatoes and hearty walking fare such as steak and mushroom pie, Cumberland sausage and mash, and apple and blackberry crumble.

Family facilities
Children are welcome in the eating area of the bar only, where young children can choose from a standard children's menu.

Alternative refreshment stops
Also near the church in Frodsham is the Helter Skelter pub or you could try the Netherton Arms on the A56 between Frodsham and Helsby.

☛ Where to go from here
You can hardly ignore the chemical industry, especially from Mersey View, and you can find out a lot more about it at the Catalyst Science Discovery Centre near Widnes. Science and technology come alive through 100 interactive exhibits and hands-on displays (www.catalyst.org.uk). Just across the unmistakable Runcorn Bridge is Norton Priory Museum and Gardens (www.nortonpriory.org), where 38 acres (15.4ha) of peaceful woodland gardens provide the setting for the medieval priory remains, museum galleries and walled garden.

about the pub

The Ring O'Bells
Bellemont Road, Overton
Frodsham, Cheshire WA6 6BS
Tel: 01928 732068

DIRECTIONS: off B5152 at parish church sign; pub opposite Overton church

PARKING: 20

OPEN: daily

FOOD: daily; lunchtime only

BREWERY/COMPANY: Punch Taverns

REAL ALE: two changing guest beers

DOGS: allowed in the bar

An avenue of trees in Tatton Park

Tatton Hall has a beautiful dining room, and library, family portraits, fine glass, silver and porcelain. More than 200 pieces of furniture were designed especially for Tatton by renowned cabinet makers, Gillow of Lancaster and London.

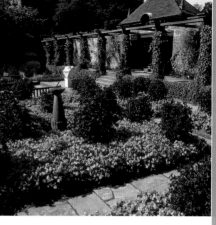

Tatton Park to Dunham Park

Link two great estates – Tatton and Dunham – and get the best of both worlds.

Left and above: The award-winning gardens in the grounds of Tatton Park

A pub and two parks

It is always fascinating to research pub names. They invariably tell a great deal about the surrounding communities and countryside. This route passes the Swan with Two Nicks (corrupted in some parts of England as the Swan with Two Necks, an improbable likelihood). The name comes from an association with the Vintners Company, founded in 1357 by importers of wine from Bordeaux. The company was incorporated by Henry VI (1422–1461) into one of the oldest of the Trade Guilds of London. Its symbol is a swan with two nicks on its beak. Then, as now, swans were the exclusive property of the Crown, but a Royal Gift was made to the Vintners, and each year the Vintners would put a nick on each side of the beak of cygnets to identify them as Vintner's swans.

The ride also links two of Britain's old estates, which offer a wealth of exploration and learning for all ages.

Tatton Park: the Mansion and Tudor Old Hall are set in 1,000 acres (405ha) of beautiful rolling parkland with lakes, tree-lined avenues and herds of deer. There are award-winning gardens, a working farm, play area, speciality shops and a superb programme of special events. There is plenty here to entertain the family, but there are extra charges for admission to the mansion, garden, farm or Tudor Old Hall.

Dunham Park: An early Georgian house built around a Tudor core, Dunham Massey was reworked in the early 20th century, to produce one of Britain's most sumptuous Edwardian interiors. It houses collections of 18th-century walnut furniture, paintings and Huguenot silver, as well as extensive servants' quarters. Here is one of the North West's great plantsman's gardens with richly planted borders and ancient trees, as well as an orangery, Victorian bark-house and well-house. The deer park contains beautiful avenues and ponds and a Tudor mill, originally used for grinding corn but refitted as a sawmill c.1860 and now restored to working order.

the ride

1 Leave the car park and ride out along the driveway to the **Rostherne Entrance** – keep an eye open for deer roaming in the park. Cross the road onto the **Cheshire Cycle Way West**, and ride on towards the village of Rostherne. Just on entering the village, turn left into **New Road**, climbing steeply for a short while, and then descending as it becomes **Cicely Mill Lane**, and leads out to a junction of two A-roads, near the **Swan Hotel** at Bucklow Hill. The easiest thing to do here is dismount and cross the two roads (at traffic lights) as a pedestrian.

2 Cross into **Chapel Lane**, initially a long, straight road, leading to Hulseheath. Keep on, riding round bends, and then turn right into **Back Lane**. At a junction, go left into Thowler Lane, and at the next junction, bear right for Bollington, along **Boothbank Lane**.

3 On reaching **Booth Bank**, keep forward into **Reddy Lane** (signed for Bollington and Dunham Massey). Descend a little to pass beneath the M56 motorway, and then climbing around bends. The road eventually straightens and leads out to meet the A56, opposite a pub.

4 Cross the road with care, going left and then immediately right into **Park Lane**. Continue past the **Swan with Two Nicks** pub, to the end of the surfaced lane, where a narrow bridge crosses the **River Bollin**.

2h30   **12.5 MILES**   **20 KM**   **LEVEL 123**

MAP: OS Explorer 267 Northwich and Delamere Forest and 276 Bolton, Wigan and Warrington

START/FINISH: Tatton Park (charge for admission); grid ref: SJ 741815

TRAILS/TRACKS: Outside Tatton Park, the route is entirely on minor roads, with a major A-road crossing (at lights)

LANDSCAPE: Cheshire farmland and two major estate parks

PUBLIC TOILETS: at Tatton Hall

TOURIST INFORMATION: Knutsford, tel 01565 632611

CYCLE HIRE: none locally

THE PUB: Swan with Two Nicks, Little Bollington

⚠ Two major A-road crossings, one using traffic lights

Getting to the start

The main entrance is at Rostherne. You can take the A50 from Knutsford, then branch onto the A5034 and then on to a minor road (signed for Tatton Park).

Why do this cycle ride?

The opportunity to link two of Cheshire's important estates should not be missed. The ride follows quiet lanes across farmland landscape and reaches a mill and weir on the edge of Dunham Park. Both parks have family attractions. The nearby village of Rostherne is a lovely community of brick houses with a few thatched cottages.

Researched and written by: Terry Marsh

Tatton Park

Tatton's open park has trails, fishing and horse-riding, and a play area. It is the perfect place to take a picnic and enjoy the abundant wildlife. Deer have been a feature of the park for centuries – herds of fallow deer roam freely across the park – while flocks of sheep can be seen grazing in summer. Rare species of birds spotted in the park and on the meres are often highlighted by the park rangers on a wildlife notice board.

Fallow deer

5 At **Bollington Mill**, go forward, but as the road bends left leave it by branching right onto a fenced and tree-lined path into **Dunham Park**.

6 Retrace the outward route. Avoid tempting alternative routes, as **Bucklow Hill** is the safest place to cross the Chester Road (A556).

The 18th-century Dunham Massey Hall

262

CYCLE

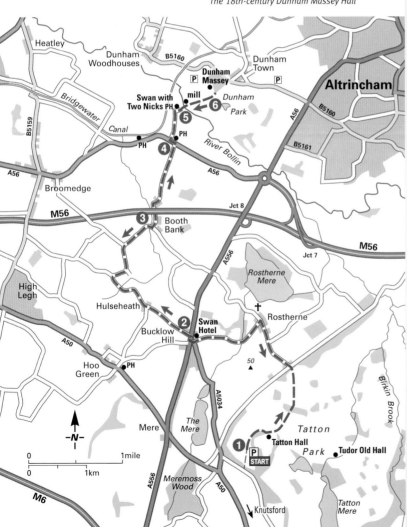

Swan with Two Nicks

Tucked away in a tiny hamlet close to Dunham Hall deer park, this distinctive, smartly refurbished pub is a real find and a super place for refreshments on this ride. Welcoming features include heavy ceiling beams, lovely antique settles, roaring winter log fires, while gleaming brass and copper artefacts and a wealth of bric-a-brac decorate the bars. There's also good seating in the patio garden, freshly prepared pub food, decent wines and three real ales on handpump.

Food

Typically, tuck into filled baguettes, various omelettes, sandwiches and salads at lunchtime, with main menu dishes including a hearty steak and ale pie, sausages and mash, grilled gammon and egg, and a range of pasta dishes.

Family facilities

A good welcome awaits families as children are allowed throughout the pub. Half portions of main meals are provided and there's a children's menu for younger family members.

Alternative refreshment stops

Stables Restaurant at Tatton Park serves hot meals, snacks and hot or cold drinks.

☛ Where to go from here

Take a closer look at Tatton Park, one of England's most complete historic estates (www.nationaltrust.org.uk), or visit nearby Tabley House, west of Knutsford, (www.tableyhouse.co.uk), the finest Palladian house in the North West, which holds the first great collection of English

pictures ever made, and furniture by Chippendale, Gillow and Bullock. Further afield is Jodrell Bank Visitor Centre (www.jb.man.ac.uk), where a pathway leads you 180 degrees around the massive Lovell radio telescope as it surveys the Universe. There's also an arboretum, and a 3-D theatre explores the solar system.

about the pub

Swan with Two Nicks
Little Bollington, Altrincham
Cheshire WA14 4TJ
Tel: 0161 928 2914

DIRECTIONS: Little Bollington is signposted off the A56 between Lymm and the M56. The pub is in the village centre at the halfway point of the ride

PARKING: 80

OPEN: daily; all day

FOOD: daily; all day Sunday

BREWERY/COMPANY: free house

REAL ALE: Timothy Taylor Landlord, Greene King Old Speckled Hen, Swan with Two Nicks Bitter

did you know?

In 1946 Lyme Park and its mansion were donated to the National Trust who now receive financial support from Stockport Metropolitan Borough Council to manage the estate. The grounds are open all year and the lovely rolling parkland and moorland tracks, with their fabulous views over Cheshire and the Dark Peak, are well worth exploring.

Around Lyme Park

Above: A tiered fountain in the orangery at Lyme Park

A circuit of the attractive grounds of Lyme Park, a fine country house.

Lyme Park

It's the classic English stately home: a medieval manor house that was gradually transformed into a large elegant Palladian mansion, full of antique furniture, tapestries, carvings and clocks. Outside, there are formal gardens (including an Edwardian Rose Garden and an Orangery), plus open moorland and parkland that is home to red and fallow deer. In 1946 the house and park were donated to the National Trust.

Lyme Park and its mansion was the location for the BBC production of Pride and Prejudice *in 1994*

This circular walk offers ever-changing views of Lyme Park. From tree-lined avenues and open meadows to the tiny reservoirs of the Bollinhurst Valley. The rough moors to the south and east offer the best vantage points – it is said you can see seven counties from the top of Sponds Hill – but don't forget to examine things closer to hand. Near Bowstonegate is a small enclosure containing the Bow Stones, thought to be the middle sections of late-Saxon crosses which may have been ancient boundary markers. The sole surviving cross head is now to be found in the courtyard at Lyme Park.

the walk

1 With the lake on your right and the house on your left leave the car park by the **drive** and, as it begins to bend away to the right, turn left for a wide track through a gate signposted 'Gritstone Trail'. Follow this through **Knightslow Wood**, negotiating several ladder stiles, until you emerge on **moorland**.

2 Go straight ahead/left on the main track as it climbs the moorland, aiming for the small **TV masts** on the skyline. At the top cross another stile and a short field to emerge at the end of a surfaced lane by the **Bow Stones**.

3 Turn left and follow the lane downhill until you reach its junction with another road, opposite the driveway to a **hotel**. Turn left and walk up the drive of **Cock Knoll Farm**. When you get to the buildings head right, across the farmyard, as indicated by footpath signs. At the far side, go through a gate and down the left-hand side of a field.

4 As you draw level with a small thicket in the shallow valley on the left, go over a **stile** and through the trees. Out on the other side, head right across the bottom of a field. Clear **waymark posts** now point you through several rough fields to a walled lane on the far side.

5 Once you are on the lane turn right and continue over **Bollinhurst Bridge**. (If you turn left you can take a short cut back to the house from here via **East Lodge**.) Beyond **Millennium Wood** you reach a junction of tracks. Go through the gate on the left and

3h30	5.5 MILES	8.8 KM	LEVEL 1 2 3

MAP: OS Explorer OL1 Dark Peak

START/FINISH: Lyme Park, off A6 (free to National Trust members); grid ref: SJ 964823

PATHS: generally firm, field tracks can be slippery if wet, 12 stiles

LANDSCAPE: rolling parkland and fields, some moorland

PUBLIC TOILETS: by Old Workshop Tea Room, near main car park

TOURIST INFORMATION: Macclesfield, tel 01625 504114

THE PUB: The Ram's Head, Buxton Road West

❗ The undulations and cumulative ascent would be tiring for very young children

Getting to the start

Access to the park is from the A6 (Stockport–Disley) road, just 0.5 mile (800m) west of Disley.

Researched and written by:
Terry Marsh, Andrew McCloy

263

WALK

while you're there

Near Pursefield Wood is the 300-year-old Paddock Cottage, which was built partly to enhance the radiating views visitors enjoyed to and from the main house. A few of these so-called vista lines, all carefully plotted so that the house can be admired from surrounding locations, are still visible today, including one impressive corridor through the trees of Knightslow Wood to the south of the house.

take a grassy track, half left, signposted to **North Lodge.**

6 Descend the right-hand side of a rough field to the woodlands at the bottom. The path now goes over several stiles as it skirts round **Bollinhurst Reservoir** – keep close to the wall on your left. A newly laid, gated gravel path takes you around the side of **Cockhead Farm,** and then continues across another field and down a shaded grassy lane. At the end of the lane turn right, on to a surfaced drive, to reach **North Lodge.**

7 Go through the **pedestrian gate** at the lodge, then turn left and walk along the main drive for about 250yds (229m). Take the obvious footpath up the hillside on your left, between a short avenue of trees, to

what to look for

The curious hilltop folly known as The Cage is one of Lyme Park's most visible landmarks. An elegant three-floored structure, it was built around 1735 as a banqueting house, but since then has been variously used as an observation tower for watching the stag hunt, as a lodging for the park's gamekeepers, and even as a temporary prison for poachers. After falling derelict, it has undergone restoration and is occasionally open to visitors.

reach the top of the open, grassy ridge. Head for the unmistakable hilltop folly known as **The Cage,** then continue straight on to return to the house and car park.

The Ram's Head

Far left: Lyme Park mansion seen across the lake

Located at an important highway junction on the A6 in the village of Disley, the Ram's Head is a bright, friendly and bustling pub, with elegant Georgian fireplaces and neo-contemporary chandeliers hang from the ceiling. A popular refreshment stop for A6 travellers, it is also a convenient post-walk destination as it is close to Lyme Park. Refresh and refuel at all times of the day with good cask ales and enjoyable, traditional bar food that includes Sunday roast lunches.

Food

From an extensive menu choose lasagne, Cajun salmon salad, lamb cutlets, chicken pie or a mixed grill, or something lighter such as freshly made sandwiches.

Family facilities

Children are welcome inside and young children have their own menu. The large enclosed rear garden and patio are perfect for summer sipping.

Alternative refreshment stops

The Ale Cellar Restaurant inside the house serves a range of 'traditional meals and historic menus' and is licensed, while the

Old Workshop Tea Room, located near the car park by the large millpond and open daily in season, operates on a self-service basis and has a decent range of snacks and light refreshments.

☛ Where to go from here

It would be a shame not to visit the house itself, with its splendid gardens (www.nationaltrust.org.uk). Otherwise the nearby Macclesfield Canal provides a pleasant corridor for recreation, and not just for water-borne users. It forms part of the Cheshire Ring Canal Walk, a 97-mile (156km) circular route around Greater Manchester incorporating the tow paths of six historic canals, including the Peak Forest and the Trent & Mersey. The stretch past Lyme Park, between Macclesfield and Marple, is particularly rural and peaceful.

about the pub

The Ram's Head
Buxton Road West, Disley
Stockport, Cheshire, SK12 2AE
Tel: 01663 767909

DIRECTIONS: turn left out of the gates to the park, follow the main road to Disley to locate the pub at a road junction, near traffic lights

PARKING: 80

OPEN: daily; all day

FOOD: daily; all day

BREWERY/COMPANY: Tetley

REAL ALE: Boddingtons, Bass, John Smiths

DOGS: not allowed inside

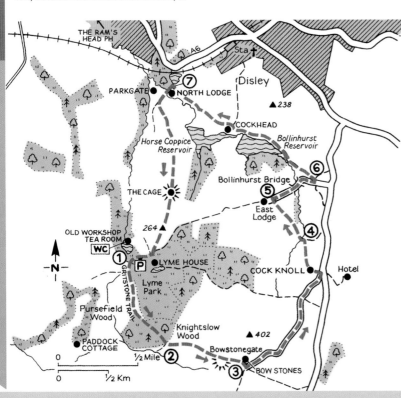

Construction on Darwen Tower began in 1897, the year after the achievement of access to the moor, which also happened to be Queen Victoria's Diamond Jubilee. The building was opened in 1898. There are 65 wide stone steps, and then 16 iron ones leading to the small glasshouse on the top. The tower did fall into some decay during the middle of the 20th century but was restored, with funds from a public appeal, in the 1970s.

*Whinchat
(Saxicola rubetra)*

Darwen Tower and moors

Square-shaped Sunnyhurst Hey Reservoir seen from Darwen Tower

A simple walk, if moderately steep in parts, to a great physical and historical landmark on the moors.

Darwen Moors

The opening stages of the walk are a pleasant preamble, through the woods around Upper Roddlesworth Reservoir and over a shoulder by some old tracks to Earnsdale Reservoir. Here you are just above Sunnyhurst Wood, Darwen's main park, which provides a direct link from the town on to the moors. Above the reservoirs you climb in stages. After the old quarry you begin the final, longest stage, on a corner of the moors overlooking the town. The dominant feature is India Mill dating from the 1860s. The chimney is 302ft (92m) high and its style is not Indian but Italianate. The

mill closed in 1991 but now houses new light industry and office space.

Construction of Darwen Tower began in 1897, the year after achievement of the right to roam on the moor. There are 65 wide stone steps, and 16 iron ones leading to the small glasshouse on the top. The tower fell into some decay but has been restored, with funds from a public appeal.

Naturally the view is extensive, especially in the northern half. Some of it has changed totally since the tower was built; the new industrial areas alongside the M65 above Blackburn are the most obvious example. But the skylines of Bowland and Pendle are the same. The descent takes you past some old mine workings and a waterworks channel. Just before the end, the row of houses (Hollinshead Terrace) was built as workers' accommodation for a nearby mill that no longer exists.

the walk

1 From the car park cross a bus turning area and then the road. Go through some gates and reach a footpath sign in 30yds (27m). Go right, following the sign for **'Woods and Water Trail'**. The path descends steadily to a cross-path. Turn right here on a broad path – still the 'Woods and Water Trail' – then after 200yds (183m) go right at a fork on a gently rising path. Gradually curve to the right and climb a little more steeply, with open fields on the left, out to the road. Go left for 200yds (183m).

2 Go right up a walled track, part of the **Witton Weavers' Way**. Go straight on at a crossroads then descend steeply, with a section of old paving, towards **Earnsdale Reservoir**. Cross the dam and swing left at its end then follow the lane up right until it swings left once more, over a cattle grid. Go straight up the steep grass slope on the right to meet a track.

3 Go left on the track then, just after a **house**, bear right up a concrete track. As the track bends right, go through a gap in the aluminium barrier and bear left on a level path towards an **old quarry**. As this is reached, go up right on a stony track. Above a gate, keep left where it forks. A gate on the left, flanked by fine flagstones, gives a good view of the town of Darwen, dominated by the **India Mill chimney**. Continue up the main track for another 100yds (91m). As the gradient eases and

Darwen Tower was started in 1897, a year after the hard-won right to roam on the moor

264

2h00	4 MILES	6.4 KM	LEVEL 123

WALK

MAP: OS Explorer 287 West Pennine Moors

START/FINISH: car park near Royal Arms; grid ref: SD 665215

PATHS: well-defined tracks throughout, 3 stiles

LANDSCAPE: reservoir and wooded surroundings, farmland, open moors

PUBLIC TOILETS: at car park

TOURIST INFORMATION: Blackburn, tel 01254 53277

THE PUB: Royal Arms, Tockholes

❶ Some fairly steep sections

Getting to the start

Tockholes lies within the West Pennine Moors, only 2 miles (3.2km) west of Darwen, but is most easily accessible from the A666 and A6062 south of Blackburn to the north. Car park and toilets just south of the Royal Arms.

Researched and written by:
Terry Marsh, Jon Sparks

Darwen Moors

LANCASHIRE

while you're there

Astley Hall near Chorley is a museum and art gallery set in an historic house. Archaeological evidence shows that a medieval structure stood on the site, but the earliest standing remains date from the reign of Elizabeth I. The displays here include glassware, ceramics and textiles.

Meadow brown butterfly

the tower comes into view bear right, past a **marker stone** on which there's a likeness of the tower, and straight up to the real thing.

4 From the tower bear left past the **trig point** and along a broad path above the steeper slope that falls to **Sunnyhurst Hey Reservoir**. The path swings left past a bench. Go over the second stile on the right overlooking the valley of **Stepback Brook** and down a path. Don't cross the next stile but go down left, to a stile beside a gate. Go left on a track.

5 The track swings right and up through a wood. As it levels out pass to the

right of a pair of gates and continue down towards a row of **houses**. A lane just left of these leads to the road. Go back past the bus turning area to the car park.

what to look for

You can look, with care, for old coal-mine shafts on the moor, in the area where you begin to descend. Usually there's little left to see but a conical pit, with scattered spoil heaps near by forming good markers, but one or two still have open shafts. The deepest of the shafts went down around 200ft (61m).

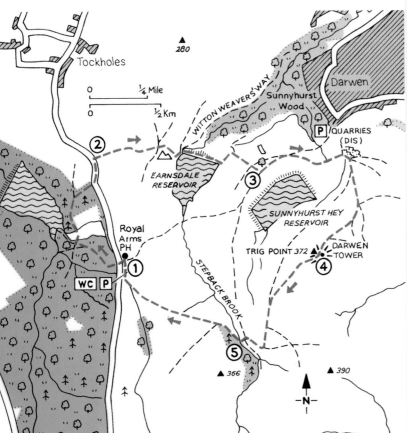

Royal Arms

Set high on the moors above Blackburn, the Royal Arms has an old-fashioned feel inside, with its several small and unpretentious rooms featuring open log fires, cracking ales from Isle of Man micro-breweries, and a traditional decor, though in a welcome modern development one room is no smoking. Bustling and very friendly, it is particularly popular with walkers – there's a nature trail opposite – and the big garden is a real a sun trap with fine views of Darwen Tower.

Food

The menu is also fairly traditional but still provides a reasonable choice of good home cooked meals. It constantly changes with the seasons, often listing summer fish and lobster specials and local game in winter. Good bar snacks.

Family facilities

Children are allowed inside the pub but there are no special facilities, although the garden does have a play area to keep them amused on fine days.

Alternative refreshment stops

There's nothing along the route, but the nearby Victoria Hotel in Tockholes is also a popular destination for walkers.

☛ Where to go from here

Tockholes village, which lies below the main road, is best explored on foot as its streets are narrow in places. There are several fine 17th-century houses and the village school, dating from 1854, has an external pulpit which allowed open-air preaching. West of Blackburn is Samlesbury Hall, a well restored half-timbered manor

house, built during the 14th and 15th centuries, and set in 2 hectares (5 acres) of beautiful grounds (www.samlesburyhall.co.uk). South of Darwen you will find Turton Tower, an historic house incorporating a 15th-century tower house and Elizabethan half-timbered buildings, and displaying a major collection of carved wood furniture (www.bolton.org.uk).

about the pub

Royal Arms
Tockholes Road, Tockholes
Darwen, Lancashire BB3 0PA
Tel: 01254 705373

DIRECTIONS: see Getting to the start

PARKING: 50

OPEN: all day; closed Monday

FOOD: all day; no food Tuesday evening

BREWERY/COMPANY: free house

REAL ALE: O'Kells Bitter, Bushy's beers, guest beers

DOGS: allowed in the bar

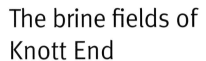

while you're there

Fleetwood, a short ferry ride across the River Wyre, is a seaside town and port. In the summer, mingle with holidaymakers visiting the pier and traditional seaside attractions along the promenade.

Marsh harrier (Circus aeruginosus)

The brine fields of Knott End

An easy walk exploring an unexpected and curiously salty corner of Lancashire's coastal plain.

Fields of brine

The salt industry here is not as ancient as that in Cheshire and has not had the same impact on the landscape, but it still had a significant role in the present scene.

Extensive deposits of rock salt lie below the surface around Knott End and Preesall and it is extracted by pumping fresh water down bore holes to dissolve the rock salt. The first such wells in this area were drilled in the 1890s and many of the well-heads remain.

Knott End today is a mixture of modest resort and commuter village. At low tide the sands are exposed for miles, far out into Morecambe Bay, and when it's clear the Lakeland skyline is a wonderful backdrop.

As you leave the built-up area, you meet the trackbed of the railway line that once linked Knott End to the main line at Garstang. The line was affectionately known as 'The Pilling Pig', a name derived from the note of the whistle of an early engine. The line closed in 1963. When you leave the old trackbed you climb a small rise – almost the only one you'll encounter on the whole walk – and from the far side, beyond New Heys Farm, you get your first sighting of the brine fields. To begin with they may look like nothing more than ordinary farmland, but then you will notice several pools – the walk soon passes close by one – left by subsidence.

As the walk continues, you'll see more reminders of the salt industry, especially

Walking the dog at the edge of a field, Knott End

along the track from the lane out to the sea wall. You follow this northward, with extensive creeks and salt marsh off to the left. Flying golf balls add spice to the next part of the walk. There's an interlude as you pass Hackensall Hall. The present building was erected in 1656 and was extensively renovated in the 19th century. There's more golf course to cross before returning to the sea wall for the last short stretch.

the walk

1 Go out to the **sea wall**, turn right past the ferry, along the road past the Bourne Arms and then along the **Esplanade**. Where the main road swings away, keep on along the seafront, down a private road then a short stretch of footpath. Where this ends, before a grassy stretch of seafront, go right down a short side street then straight across the main road into **Hackensall Road**. Go down this almost to its end.

2 Just before the last house on the left there's a **footpath** (sign high up on lamp-post) which wriggles round and then becomes a clear straight track. Follow this through a narrow belt of **woodland**, across open fields and then alongside a wooded

slope. Where the wood ends, go through an iron kissing gate on the right, then up the edge of the wood and over a stile into a **farmyard**. Go straight through this and down a stony track, which swings left between pools. It then becomes a surfaced lane past some **cottages**.

3 Join a wider road (**Back Lane**) and go right. It becomes narrow again. Follow this lane for about a mile (1.6km), over a slight rise and down again, to **Corcas Farm**.

4 Turn right on **Corcas Lane**, signed 'Private Road Bridle Path Only'. Follow the lane through the brine fields. After 0.5 mile (800m) it swings left by a **caravan site**.

5 Go right, past a **Wyre Way sign** and over a stile on to the embankment. Follow its winding course for about a mile (1.6km) to a stile with a signpost just beyond.

6 Go straight ahead on a **tractor track**, signed 'Public Footpath to Hackensall Hall 1m'. When it meets the **golf course**, the track first follows its left side then angles across – heed the danger signs! Follow the track to the right of **Hackensall Hall**. At a T-junction go left on a track with a Wyre

Right: A rutted pathway at Knott End

2h45 | **6 MILES** | **9.7 KM** | **LEVEL 123**

MAP: OS Explorer 296 Lancaster, Morecambe & Fleetwood

START/FINISH: free car park by end of B5270 at Knott End; grid ref: SD 347485

PATHS: quiet streets and lanes, farm tracks and sea wall, 3 stiles

LANDSCAPE: short built-up section, seashore, farmland and golf course

PUBLIC TOILETS: at side of coastguard building adjacent to car park

TOURIST INFORMATION: Fleetwood, tel 01253 773953

THE PUB: Bourne Arms, Knott End

Getting to the start

Knott End lies at the northern tip of the River Wyre, just a short easterly ferry ride from Fleetwood. Getting there is a lovely convoluted drive across low-lying farmland from Poulton-le-Fylde or from the direction of Lancaster via Cockerham and Preesall. Free parking at the end of the Esplanade.

Researched and written by:
Terry Marsh, Jon Sparks

did you know?

It is easiest to see shovelers in winter, when small groups gather to feed in the shallows, moving slowly forward, sieving food from the mud with their broad, flattened bills. Male shovelers (illustrated right) are brightly coloured.

Above: A shoveler (Anas clypeata)

Way sign. This skirts round behind the **outlying buildings**.

7 The path swings to the right and then crosses the **golf course** again. Aim for a green shelter on the skyline then bear right along the edge of the course. Skirt round some **white cottages**, then go left to the sea wall. Turn right along it, and it's just a drive and a chip back to the car park.

what to look for

The well-heads, pools, and one small extraction plant all bear witness to the salt industry. The fields provide good grazing for dairy cattle and also for a large number of brown hares, which are larger than rabbits, with longer legs and ears. Hares don't burrow but rear their young in shallow scrapes in the ground.

Bourne Arms

☞ Where to go from here

For most of the year, a small passenger ferry regularly makes the short crossing to Fleetwood. The town was planned as an integrated whole in the 1830s and 40s by the architect Decimus Burton, at the instigation of Sir Peter Hesketh-Fleetwood from nearby Rossall Estate. The Fleetwood Museum tells much more about the salt industry. Britain's oldest surviving tram system links Fleetwood with Blackpool.

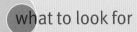

Close to the start of the walk and smack on the Esplanade with views across Morecambe Bay, the Bourne Arms is a large and rambling pub with cosy nooks and crannies inside and an airy conservatory dining room. Like the big, south-facing terrace, it makes the most of the wide sea views.

Food

Expect a wide range of traditional Lancashire dishes plus gammon, egg and chips, Cumberland sausage, lamb cutlets, grilled halibut, and salmon with horseradish sauce. There's also a choice of sandwiches and Sunday roast lunches.

Family facilities

Families are welcome in the eating areas of the bar and in the conservatory. Bargain children's menu.

Alternative refreshment stops

There's a café adjacent to the car park and a couple of others in the village.

about the pub

Bourne Arms
Bourne May Road, Knott End
Lancashire FY6 0AB
Tel: 01253 810256

DIRECTIONS: see Getting to the start; pub is on the Esplanade (Point 1)

PARKING: 20

OPEN: daily; all day

FOOD: daily; all day Sunday; no food Monday & Tuesday evening

BREWERY/COMPANY: free house

REAL ALE: Flowers Original, Boddingtons, Greene King Abbot Ale, Timothy Taylor Landlord

DOGS: allowed in tap room

ROOMS: 3 en suite

266

WALK

while you're there

Stonyhurst College was originally the home of the Shireburn family and much of the original Elizabethan house still exists, although almost enveloped by vast 19th-century additions. It was taken over in 1794 by Jesuits fleeing the French Revolution and is now a leading Catholic boarding school. It's open to visitors during the summer holidays.

The remains of baths at Ribchester Roman Fort

Hurst Green and the Three Rivers

A fisherman standing in the waters of the Ribble

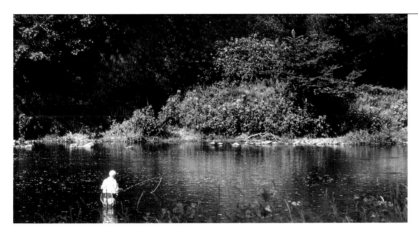

Did these rivers, fields and woods inspire Tolkien's creation of The Shire?

Tolkien connection

J R R Tolkien, author of *The Lord of the Rings*, knew this area well and he spent long periods here while writing the trilogy. In the hobbits' Shire there's a River Shirebourn and the Shireburn family once owned Stonyhurst. But does that mean that Hurst Green is Hobbiton? A locally available leaflet gives more detail.

Just after reaching the Ribble, you pass an aqueduct, then an easy 0.75 mile (1.2km) brings you to Jumbles Rock, outcrops of limestone, which form natural weirs and a ford. The isolated Boat House was a ferryman's home. In the fields near by are two obvious mounds. The lower one was excavated in 1894 and dated to around 1250. The larger, though known to be artificial, has yet to be properly examined. As the Ribble swings round, the River Calder enters opposite, close to 17th-century Hacking Hall. Less than 0.75 mile (1.2km) further on is the confluence of the Ribble and the Hodder, which you follow briefly, leaving it near Winckley Hall. You return to the river at Low Hodder Bridge.

You follow the Hodder for almost another mile (1.6km) before climbing steeply away to Woodfields. Tolkien stayed in one of these houses. The track passes St Mary's Hall and then reaches Hall Barn Farm. Near by, on the edge of Stoneyhurst's precincts is a small observatory, one of a network.

the walk

1 Walk down the road to the centre of Hurst Green village. Cross the main road and go down left of the **Shireburn Arms** to a stile below the main car park. Go down the edge of a field, when possible move to the right of a small **stream** and follow it to some duckboards and a footbridge. After a slight rise, **wooden steps** wind down to another footbridge just before the **River Ribble**. Bear left just above the river.

2 Skirt the aqueduct and return to the river bank. A gravel track swings right past **Jumbles**. Stay on the track towards the **Boat House**, and there bear right to the river bank.

3 After rounding the big bend, go up slightly to a **track**. Follow this for about 0.5 mile (800m). Opposite the confluence of the Ribble and the Hodder, keep forward through a **gate**.

4 Continue along the track to **Winckley Hall Farm**. There go left to the houses, right between barns then left past a pond and out into a lane. This climbs steadily, then levels out, swinging left past **Winckley Hall**. Go through a kissing gate on the right and across the field to another. Keep straight on across a large field, just left of a wood, then down past a **pond** and across to a road.

5 Turn right down a pavement to the river. Immediately before the **bridge**, turn left along a track. Follow the river round, climb up past **Hodder Place** then descend again to a bridge over a stream.

6 Go left along a track, cross a footbridge then climb a long flight of wooden steps. Follow the top edge of a **plantation** then cross a stile into a field. Keep to its edge and at the end cross a stile into a stony track. Keep left, to pass **Woodfields** and out to the road. Go down the track by the post-box to **Hall Barn Farm** and along the right side of the buildings.

A run-down barn with vegetation starting to encroach upon it, Ribbleside

| 2h30 | 6.5 MILES | 10.4 KM | LEVEL 123 |

MAP: OS Explorer 287 West Pennine Moors

START/FINISH: car park at Hurst Green village hall or on roadside adjacent; grid ref: SD 684382

PATHS: grassy riverside paths, woodland and farm tracks, 12 stiles

LANDSCAPE: pastoral scenery, scattered woodlands, backdrop of moors

PUBLIC TOILETS: centre of Hurst Green

TOURIST INFORMATION: Clitheroe, tel 01200 425566

THE PUB: The Shireburn Arms, Hurst Green

Getting to the start

Hurst Green is a quiet but popular village north of the River Ribble, and about 5 miles (8km) south west of Clitheroe on the B6243 to Longridge. Parking at the village hall.

Researched and written by:
Terry Marsh, Jon Sparks

266

WALK

Blue tit
(Parus caeruleus)

Downstream from Low Hodder Bridge is the ancient Cromwell's Bridge – a misplaced name. The bridge was actually built for one of the Shireburn dynasty in 1562. Legend has it that Cromwell vandalised it, destroying the parapets that impeded the progress of his troops.

7 Turn right on a tarmac track for 200yds (183m). Go left through a gate by the end of a wall and along the left-hand side of a narrow field. Follow a grassy path bearing right to a path alongside a wood, then up to a kissing gate. Follow the field edge to another kissing gate. At the top of the final field, through a gate, a narrow path leads to a short lane. At its end turn left back to the start.

what to look for

One plant to look out for, especially along the riversides, is butterbur. This is another name that will ring bells with Tolkien devotees; there's an innkeeper in The Lord of the Rings called Barliman Butterbur. The flower spikes, which appear in early spring, look superficially like dull pinkish hyacinths, but the individual flowers are daisy-like. Later in the year huge leaves develop, which were traditionally used to wrap butter.

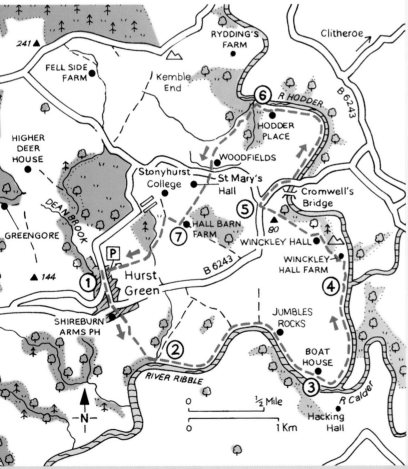

The Shireburn Arms

In the absence of a Green Dragon or Prancing Pony, the Shireburn Arms has the most Tolkeinesque name, and it's a very comfortable place, if a little bit upmarket for hobbits – you'll probably want to change out of muddy boots first. A focal point of the village since it was built in the 17th-century, this civilised small hotel enjoys an idyllic setting with fine views over the Ribble Valley to the Pennines. The lovely beamed lounge bar serves locally brewed Bowland ales on handpump, and there's a smart restaurant as well as a good range of bar food. The neat rear terrace and gardens are perfect for peaceful post-walk refreshment on warm sunny days.

Food
From the bar menu, order sandwiches, ham and eggs, shepherd's pie, vegetable lasagne, liver and onions, pork Stroganoff or steak and kidney pudding.

Family facilities
Like many good hotels, children are warmly welcomed here and you'll find a children's menu, high chairs, toys to keep little ones amused, a play area in the garden and three family bedrooms.

Alternative refreshment stops
The Bayley Arms in Hurst Green and there's a tea room at Stonyhurst College (if visiting).

☛ Where to go from here
Ribchester Roman Museum (www.ribchestermuseum.org) contains many impressive artefacts excavated from the area including urns, coins, jewellery and a ceremonial helmet. Visit the ruins

about the pub

The Shireburn Arms
Whalley Road, Hurst Green
Clitheroe, Lancashire BB7 9QJ
Tel: 01254 826518
www.shireburnarms.fsnet.co.uk

DIRECTIONS: see Getting to the Start; inn beside the B6243 in the village centre

PARKING: 120

OPEN: daily; all day

FOOD: daily; all day Sunday

BREWERY/COMPANY: free house

REAL ALE: Bowland Brewery beers

DOGS: allowed in the bar

ROOMS: 18 en suite

of 14th-century Whalley Abbey (south of Clitheroe), set in the delightful gardens of a retreat and conference centre, or explore Clitheroe Castle's 12th-century Norman keep and fascinating museum, which houses exhibits relating to the history and geology of the local area (www.ribblevalley.gov.uk).

Lancaster Castle

Large parts of Lancaster Castle are still used as a prison, while the remainder also houses law courts. When these are not in session tours take in the courtrooms, the ancient dungeons, the magnificent Shire Hall and the Drop Room, where the condemned awaited execution

Of the many alleged witches brought to Lancaster to be tried, the most famous were from Pendle. At the end of the three-day assize in 1612, a total of ten people were found guilty of witchcraft and hanged.

Glasson Dock to Lancaster

Follow the River Lune to explore Lancaster, and share the delights of its canal towpath on the way back.

Wildlife along the way

Aldcliffe Marsh is a Site of Special Scientific Interest because of its importance for waders such as redshank and lapwing. At one time the lapwing was a common sight on ploughed fields, but the use of insecticides and farming machinery has driven it to meadows and marshes in summer. Keep an eye open for the bright yellow ragwort, a plant that attracts the cinnabar moth, which lays its eggs on the stems and produces gaudy black-and-yellow caterpillars. In Freeman's Wood is a black poplar (*Populus nigra*), a native tree of lowland marshes and of this area, but not all that common. There are thought to be fewer than 3,000 black poplars in Britain today. The tree in Freeman's Wood is one of only two in Lancashire.

the ride

1 Begin from the large car park near the dock by crossing the road onto a cycleway along the edge of the **Lune Estuary**. A gravel track leads on to cross the River Conder before turning north through the **Conder Green car park**. (Follow the road right for The Stork pub.) Beyond the car park, ride onto a tree-lined track, and keep following this until it reaches a surfaced lane end, not far from the village of Aldcliffe.

2 Turn left into a **gravel area**, and then immediately, just before a footpath

Looking across the Lune to Lancaster

stile, onto a broad vehicle track. At a cross-track, keep forward along a bridleway for **New Quay Road**, and going into **Freeman's Wood**. The track, now surfaced, crosses a section of **Aldcliffe Marsh**, and eventually comes out to meet a much wider road near a small light industrial complex. Keep forward until you reach an old arched bridge with the modern, **Millennium** (foot) **Bridge** near by.

3 Turn onto the footbridge, and then immediately right to leave it, without crossing the river. Go left on a surfaced **cycle lane** (signed for Halton and Caton). Follow the lane until it rises, to run briefly alongside the main road. Almost immediately turn right to perform a loop to the left into an **underpass** – you may need to dismount here. On the other side, go forward on a **signed cycle route**, which passes beneath a bridge and goes forward on a surfaced track down an avenue of trees. When it forks, keep left, and carry on to reach the stone **Lune Aqueduct**. Just before it, turn right onto a narrow path that leads to the foot of a flight of steps. Here you will need to dismount and carry your cycle up the steps to reach the tow path – a breathless few minutes, but well worth the effort.

4 Turn right along the tow path. At **Whitecross**, dismount again to change to the other side of the canal. At a couple of places now you may need to dismount again as you pass canalside pubs, but eventually a **bridge** leads back over the canal. Over the bridge, turn immediately right down steps (dismount again) to rejoin the **tow path**.

5 Continue until you pass **Bridge 95**, following which the canal has a road on the right, and bends to the left. A short way on, leave the tow path and go onto the road (near a **lodge** on the right, dated 1827). Go forward, climbing steadily into the village of **Aldcliffe**. At the top of the climb, on a bend, take care, and turn right into the first lane on the right, descending quite steeply, and continuing down past **houses**, to ride along a narrow country lane to rejoin the outward near the gravel area.

6 Turn left onto the **trackbed**, and follow this back to Conder Green, turning left into the village for **The Stork**, or continue round the coast to **Glasson Dock**.

Top left: Lancaster Castle's gate house

<table>
<tr><td>2h30</td><td>14 MILES</td><td>22 KM</td><td>LEVEL 123</td></tr>
</table>

CYCLE

MAP: OS Explorer 296 Lancaster, Morecambe and Fleetwood

START/FINISH: Quayside, Glasson Dock; grid ref: SD 446561

TRAILS/TRACKS: good route, though cyclists will need to dismount at a few points on the canal while passing waterfront pubs

LANDSCAPE: mainly old railway trackbed or canal towpaths

PUBLIC TOILETS: at the start

TOURIST INFORMATION: Lancaster, tel 01524 32878

CYCLE HIRE: none locally

THE PUB: The Stork, Conder Green

❶ Cycles will need to be carried up and down steps to reach the canal tow path

Getting to the start

Glasson Dock is on the Lune Estuary, 4 miles (6.4km) south west of Lancaster. It is best reached from Lancaster, or Cockerham to the south, along the A588, but may also be reached from Junction 33 on the M6 via Galgate – turn left at the traffic lights in the village centre and follow signs.

Why do this cycle ride?

A superb introduction to coastal Lancashire. The old trackbed and the return along the Lancaster Canal makes for easy riding, while the traffic-free cycle route through riverside Lancaster is ingenious. You can opt out at the Millennium Bridge and explore Lancashire's ancient capital.

Researched and written by: Terry Marsh

267

CYCLE

while you're there

Glasson itself is worth a little more time: there's usually something going on in the outer harbour or the inner yacht basin. There's also a gallery/craft shop and, round the corner, the Smokehouse offers a wide range of delicacies.

*Redshank
(Tringa totanus)*

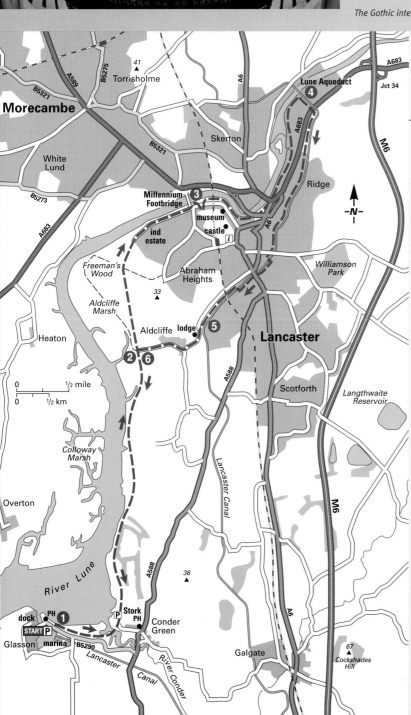

The Stork

about the pub

The Stork
Conder Green, Lancaster
Lancashire LA2 0AN
Tel: 01524 751234

DIRECTIONS: just off the A558 (west), a mile (1.6km) from Glasson and the start of the ride

PARKING: 40

OPEN: daily; all day

FOOD: daily; all day Saturday & Sunday

BREWERY/COMPANY: free house

REAL ALE: Theakston Best, Black Sheep Best, Timothy Taylor Landlord, Marston's Pedigree, guest beers

ROOMS: 10 en suite

A white-painted coaching inn spread along the banks of the estuary, where the River Conder joins the Lune estuary and just a short stroll along the Lancashire Coastal Way from the quaint seaport of Glasson Dock. The inn has a colourful 300-year history that includes several name changes. It's a friendly, bustling and ever-popular place, the draw being the location, the range of real ales, and the rambling, dark-panelled rooms, each with warming open fires. The south-facing terrace and patio look across the marshes.

Food

Seasonal specialities join home-cooked food such as steak pie, locally smoked haddock, salmon fillet with bonne femme sauce, Cumberland sausage with onion gravy and mash.

Family facilities

Children of all ages are welcome and well catered for. There are family dining areas, family en suite accommodation, a children's menu, and a play area outside.

Alternative refreshment stops

There are plenty of cafés, restaurants and pubs in Lancaster.

☛ Where to go from here

A trip to Lancaster will be rewarded with a visit to the Maritime Museum, where the histories of the 18th-century transatlantic maritime trade of Lancaster, the Lancaster Canal and the fishing industry of Morecambe Bay are well illustrated (www.lancsmuseums.gov.uk). Take time to view Morecambe Bay or visit the Edwardian Butterfly House in Williamson Park (www.williamsonpark.com), or take a look at Lancaster Castle which dominates Castle Hill, above the River Lune. The Shire Hall contains a splendid display of heraldry (www.lancastercastle.com).

Whalley Abbey

The delightful ruins of this 14th-century Cistercian abbey are set in the gardens of the Blackburn Diocesan Retreat and Conference House, a 17th-century manor house with gardens leading down to the River Calder. The abbey remains include two gateways, a chapter house and the abbot's lodgings and kitchens. Whalley Abbey is situated just off the A59, 4 miles (6.4km) south of Clitheroe

Remains of Whalley Abbey, with its well-preserved gateway

Gisburn Forest

Explore Lancashire's biggest forest and discover its flora and fauna.

Gisburn Forest

Gisburn Forest is Lancashire's biggest, covering 3,000 acres (1,215ha). It was opened in 1932, around the same time as Stocks Reservoir, alongside it. The reservoir is huge, formed by damming the River Hodder and submerging the village of Stocks in the process of providing drinking water for the towns of central Lancashire. When it's full it can hold 2.6 billion gallons. Gisburn Forest and Stocks Reservoir are favoured places for birdwatchers. In springtime, keep an eye open for visiting osprey, which quite often use the reservoir for on-the-wing food supplies on their way northwards to Scotland at breeding time.

You will almost certainly spot members of the tit family, notably great, blue and coal tits, and may be lucky to see a great-spotted woodpecker. This is a good time, too, to look for orchids: Gisburn is renowned for its common spotted orchid, which flourishes in the damp conditions.

the ride

1 Set off along a narrow path from the car park, to a sharp left-hand bend, then descend, before climbing gently to pass a barrier, and reach a **broad forest trail**. Turn right, and about 100 yards (110m) later, when the track forks, keep forward. Before reaching a group of buildings (**Stephen Park**), leave the broad trail and turn right at a waymark onto a very narrow path that follows the edge of an open area, and finally heads back towards the buildings.

2 On reaching **Stephen Park**, turn right on a broad trail, which immediately forks. Keep left, climbing gently, and then heading downhill. Continue following the main trail as it weaves a way through the forest to a **barrier** coming up to a T-junction, where the three main forest cycle trails divide. Here turn left, pursuing the **Purple Trail**.

3 Continue to the access to **Hesbert Hall Farm**, and there branch right, passing a barrier into a short stretch of dense woodland with a clearing ahead. Now make a long descent to cross a **stream**, beyond which the track rises to a T-junction, where the Red and Green route rejoin. Turn left.

Top: Picnic tables in Gisburn Forest
Below: A view from the Gisburn Forest Trail

1h00 · **6 MILES** · **9.7 KM** · **LEVEL 1 2 3**

MAP: OS Explorer OL41 Forest of Bowland and Ribblesdale

START/FINISH: Cocklet Hill car park; grid ref: SD 746550

TRAILS/TRACKS: mainly broad forest trails, some narrow paths and stony, bumpy trails

LANDSCAPE: forest

PUBLIC TOILETS: none on route

TOURIST INFORMATION: Clitheroe, tel 01200 425566

CYCLE HIRE: Pedal Power, Waddington Road, Clitheroe, Lancashire BB7 2HJ, tel 01200 422066

THE PUB: The Hark to Bounty, Slaidburn

! Maps are useless in Gisburn – follow the Purple Trail. Stony trails and overhanging vegetation

Getting to the start

Gisburn Forest is well signed across the surrounding countryside, but the start is best reached along the B6478 from Slaidburn (south west) or Long Preston (north east).

Why do this cycle ride?

Forests like Gisburn are known for mile after mile of conifers with scarcely a decent view. But at Gisburn, more and more broadleaved trees are being planted, and areas are being cleared to allow for good views. The trails in Gisburn are waymarked; this route follows the shortest, the Purple Trail. Maps can't keep up-to-date with what is happening on the ground, so waymark chasing is the best way.

Researched and written by: Terry Marsh

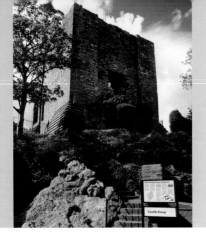

Steps leading to the Norman keep at Clitheroe Castle

Clitheroe Castle Museum

The museum has a good collection of carboniferous fossils, and items of local interest. Displays include local history and the industrial archaeology of the Ribble Valley, while special features include printer's and clogger's shops, an Edwardian kitchen and the restored Hacking ferry boat believed to be the inspiration for Buckleberry Ferry featured in JRR Tolkein's Fellowship of the Ring. *The area is renowned for its early 17th-century witches, and the museum has a small display on witchcraft.*

4 The broad trail eventually leads on, after winding through the forest, to another T-junction. Here, turn left, descending, and following a bumpy route that brings **Stocks Reservoir** into view. Eventually, just before reaching a road, turn left at a **waymark post** onto a narrow path through mixed woodland to reach the **road**, which now crosses an arm of the reservoir.

5 On the other side, leave the road by turning left up a steep and narrow path – you may have to dismount here. Follow this through **woodland**, steep in places, and finally emerge at a broad forest track at a bend. Keep left and then forward, and climb to another **barrier** giving on to a T-junction. Turn right, and 100yds (110m) later turn left, having now rejoined the outward route, which is retraced to the start.

The Hark to Bounty

The setting – a beautiful village on the moors above Clitheroe – is one of the attractions of this historic stone pub. It dates from the 13th century and was known as the The Dog until 1875 when Bounty, the local squire's favourite hound, disturbed a post-inn drinking session with its loud baying. View the original first floor courtroom, for many years the main court between Lancaster and York, and still in use until 1937. It's now a function room, complete with old jury benches and a witness box. Downstairs, the atmospheric old bar has old-fashioned settles, exposed beams, a roaring log fire, plenty of brass ornaments and old pictures on the walls.

area. South of Clitheroe are the 14th-century ruins of Whalley Abbey, originally a medieval monastery, set in the grounds of a 17th-century manor house, now a retreat and conference centre. Guided tours, visitor centre and coffee shop.

Food

Traditional favourites include home-made fish, steak and kidney pies, vegetable and cheese crumble, and grilled haddock topped with tomatoes and Lancashire cheese, supplemented by pasta and curries from the chalkboards. Snacks take in filled jacket potatoes and ploughman's lunches.

Family facilities

Children are very welcome throughout and there's a children's menu, high chairs, smaller portions and changing facilities.

Alternative refreshment stops

None on the route. Refreshments in Slaidburn and Clitheroe.

☛ Where to go from here

Developed on the site of former 17th-century cottages, Slaidburn Heritage Centre provides a site for exhibitions and information relating to the history of this fascinating

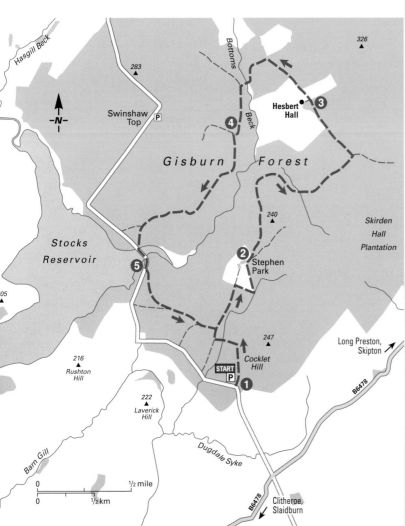

Hasgill Beck

Bottoms

283 ▲

Swinshaw Top **P**

-N-

4

Beck

Hesbert ● **3**
Hall

326 ▲

Gisburn   Forest

Skirden
Hall
Plantation

240 ▲

*Stocks
Reservoir*

5

2
Stephen
Park

205 ▲

247 ▲

216 ▲
Rushton
Hill

START **P**
1

Cocklet
Hill

Long Preston,
Skipton

222 ▲
Laverick
Hill

B6478

Barn Gill

Dugdale Syke

0   ½ mile
0   ½km

B6478

Clitheroe,
Slaidburn

about the pub

The Hark to Bounty
Slaidburn, Clitheroe
Lancashire BB7 3EP
Tel: 01200 446246
www.harktobounty.co.uk

DIRECTIONS: from Gisburn Forest return to the B6478 and turn right for 3 miles (4.8km) to reach Slaidburn. Cross the river and take the second turning right for the pub

OPEN: daily; all day

FOOD: daily; all day Sunday

BREWERY/COMPANY: free house

REAL ALE: Courage Directors, Theakston Old Peculier, guest ales

ROOMS: 9 en suite

Leighton Hall

Early Gillow furniture is displayed among other treasures in the fine interior of this neo-Gothic mansion where entertaining guides reveal the history of the house and its occupants. Outside, a large collection of birds of prey can be seen, and flying displays are given each afternoon. There is landscaped parkland as well as a pretty 19th-century walled garden, a maze and woodland walks.

The grand façade of Leighton Hall, overlooking the grounds and lake

Around Silverdale

An easy-going walk, yet fascinating with its continuous changes of scenery.

A mosaic of habitats

The Arnside-Silverdale Area of Outstanding Natural Beauty (AONB) is intricate and exquisite. This walk tries the impossible, to sample all of its delights in one go.

The AONB covers a mere 29sq miles (75sq km) yet includes rocky coastline, salt marsh, wetland, pasture, woodland, heathland, crags and quarries, and some attractive villages, principally Silverdale in Lancashire and Arnside in Cumbria. With such a mosaic of habitats, it's no surprise that the area is rich in wildlife – more than half of all British flowering plant species are found here. There's a fine start, through Eaves Wood, then the route sidles through the back lanes of Silverdale before reaching the coast. The channels of Morecambe Bay shift over time and so does the shoreline. Changes to the course of the river now makes it impossible to follow the shore, at least at high tide. (Fortunately the footpath across The Lots, just above, offers a ready-made alternative.)

The route here avoids a tricky section of the coast south of Silverdale, returning to the shore near Jenny Brown's Point. After Heald Brow comes Woodwell, the first of three 'wells' (actually springs) on the walk. At Woodwell the water issues from the crag above the square pool. This was used for watering cattle but now you're more likely to see dragonflies. Woodwell and the other 'wells' around Silverdale occur where the water-permeable limestone is interrupted by a band of impermeable material, such as

clay. Rainfall generally sinks quickly into limestone and there are no surface streams over most of the area, so the springs were of vital importance. This rapid drainage also means that few of the footpaths are persistently muddy, even after heavy rain. Lambert's Meadow, however, is damp. It sits in a hollow where fine wind-blown silt (loess) accumulated after the last Ice Age. The soil is dark and acidic, very different from that formed on the limestone, and the plant community is different too.

the walk

1 From the end of the National Trust car park at **Eaves Wood**, follow the footpath to a T-junction. Go right a few paces then left between **old gate pillars**, climbing gently. At a fork, keep left to a ring of beech trees, then straight on. At the next junction, go forward, then bear left, down to a high wall and continue on this line to a lane.

2 Cross on to a track signed '**Cove Road**'. Keep ahead down a narrow path, a drive, another track and another narrow path to a wider road. After 200yds (183m) go left down a road leading to The Cove.

3 At **The Cove**, go left to white gate, and onto path for **The Lots**, climbing above cliffs to a gate. Cross a field (**Bank House Farm**) on grassy path to a gate in a wall. Then cross another field to **Stankelt Road**. Turn right to reach **The Silverdale Hotel**, just a short way further on round the corner.

Jenny Brown's Point is near the walk route

4 Return to the corner and go into Lindeth Road. Follow this as far as the turning at **Gibraltar Farm**. Go along this lane for 350yds (320m). Enter the National Trust property of **Jack Scout**.

5 Descend left to a **lime kiln** then follow a narrowing path bearing right. This swings left and later passes above a steep drop. Follow a clear path to a gate. After 100yds (91m), another gate leads into the lane. At its end bear right to pass below **Brown's Houses**. Follow the edge of the salt marsh to a stile, go forward to a **signpost**.

6 Turn left, climbing steeply to a gate at **Heald Brow**. Climb over rock and through a lightly wooded area into the open. Go left to cross a stile then alongside a wall to a **small wood**. From a gate, follow a walled path down right. Cross the road to a squeeze stile in a wall, descend, then walk below the crags to **Woodwell**.

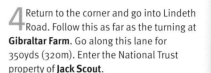

2h30 | **5.5 MILES** | **8.8 KM** | **LEVEL 123**

MAP: OS Explorer OL7 The English Lakes (SE)

START/FINISH: small National Trust car park for Eaves Wood; grid ref: SD 471759

PATHS: little bit of everything, 6 stiles

LANDSCAPE: pot-pourri of woodland, pasture, village lanes and shoreline

PUBLIC TOILETS: in Silverdale village

TOURIST INFORMATION: Lancaster, tel 01524 32878

THE PUB: The Silverdale Hotel, Silverdale

Getting to the start

Silverdale clings to the northern edge of Lancashire, a few miles north of Carnforth off the A6 and the M6 (junction 35), and looks across the great expanse of Morecambe Bay to the Furness peninsula.

Researched and written by:
Terry Marsh, Jon Sparks

A peregrine falcon with its handler. Falconry was the preserve of the lords of the manor in medieval times, when hunting was retricted to landowners

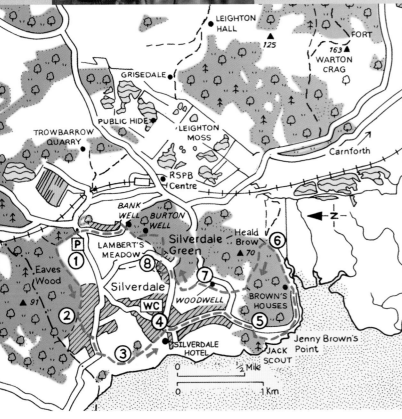

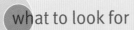

The Silverdale Hotel

A listed coaching inn, built in 1836, and run by the Carney family since 1987, the Silverdale Hotel is a very popular pub with a warm and welcoming interior decorated with paintings of local and country scenes, ornaments and bric-a-brac, and a small conservatory where food is served overlooking the garden. The pub stands just a few minutes' stroll from the shore and has far-reaching views across Morecambe Bay. This is the ideal retreat for walkers on wild winter days.

Food

Wide-ranging menus offer a traditional choice of meals, including hot steak and onion sandwiches, filled jacket potatoes and salads, Cumberland sausage and mash, steak, ale and mushroom pies and a roast of the day. Puddings include sticky toffee pudding and speciality ice creams.

Family facilities

Children are welcome and the pub offers a children's menu as well as two family bedrooms.

Alternative refreshment stops

The tea room at Wolf House Gallery is a great spot for mid-walk refreshments, as long as you can find a table. For post-walk celebrations, you could also head for the New Inn in the nearby village of Yealand Conyers. There's good food and beer, a small cosy bar, a non-smoking dining room and a walled beer garden that's delightful on summer evenings.

about the pub

The Silverdale Hotel
Shore Road, Silverdale
Carnforth, Lancashire LA5 0TP
Tel: 01524 701206

DIRECTIONS: village centre, along Shore Road; see Point 3

PARKING: 30

OPEN: daily; all day

FOOD: daily

BREWERY/COMPANY: free house

REAL ALE: Bass, guest beers

DOGS: allowed in the bars

ROOMS: 7 en suite

☛ Where to go from here

The Leighton Moss RSPB reserve (www.rspb.org.uk) and nearby Leighton Hall (www.leightonhall.co.uk) are obvious attractions, but for something different (and free) pop in to Trowbarrow Quarry. Last worked in 1959, the quarry is now a Local Nature Reserve, and it's also a Site of Special Scientific Interest (SSSI) for its geology. Most striking is the near-vertical Main Wall, basically an upturned slice of fossil seabed.

7 The path signed 'The Green via cliff path' leads to a rocky staircase. At the top go straight ahead to join a broader path. Follow it left to a gate, slant right, then continue left into woodland. Follow a **woodland path** to a stile on the right and a narrow section leads to a road. Go right 100yds (91m), then left into **The Green**. Keep right at a junction, then join a wider road.

8 Go left for 75yds (69m) then right, signposted 'Burton Well Lambert's Meadow'. The track soon descends then swings left, passing **Burton Well** on the right. Go through a gate into **Lambert's Meadow**, then go right, over a footbridge to a gate. Climb up, with some steps, and continue more easily to a fork. Go left

what to look for

If you do this walk in winter, you'll see huge flocks of wading birds around the shoreline. Morecambe Bay is an internationally important site for migrants and over-wintering birds. In spring listen, rather than look, for the rare bittern. This relative of the heron is rarely seen but its booming courtship call – like someone blowing across the top of a milk bottle – can be heard up to a mile (1.6km) away.

alongside a pool (**Bank Well**) into a lane. Go left and at the end the car park is virtually opposite.

Gardens with tropical trees and an ornamental lake at Grange-over-Sands

A circuit around Cartmel

Explore a handsome valley between the fells and the sea.

Cartmel

There have been buildings on the site of Cartmel Priory for more than 800 years, though only the church and the gatehouse remain standing today. One of the most striking features of the notably beautiful church is the number of memorials to travellers who lost their lives crossing Morecambe Bay. In the days before railways and modern roads, the sands of the bay were in regular use by travellers of all kinds, and an official Queen's Guide was charged with ensuring their safety.

Those who dispensed with his services risked blundering into quicksand or being caught by the fast-advancing tides – hazards which are still very real. The office of Queen's Guide survives to this day, and visitors are still guided safely across these treacherous sands every year.

Horse racing at Cartmel also has a long tradition behind it, and the meetings around the late May and August bank holidays draw horses, jockeys and punters from far and wide for an exciting day out. However, busy roads on race days mean these times are best avoided by cyclists.

The church at Cartmel Priory with its square tower set diagonally

the ride

1 From the **racecourse** ride back into **Cartmel village square** and turn sharp left (round the village shop). This quickly takes you out of the village again and alongside the racecourse. Keep left at a junction, following signs for Haverthwaite and Ulverston, and begin a steady climb (never really steep). The road forks again at **Beck Side**.

2 Keep on to the right, still climbing steadily. The limestone arch on the right just above the fork is the remains of a **lime kiln**. There's a brief dip at **High Gateside**, another short rise, then turn right and begin an excellent swooping descent, with no tricky bends.

3 A turn on the right at a triangle of grass offers the option of a short return back to Cartmel. Otherwise, keep straight on here, and at a second junction. Cross the tiny river of **Ayside Pool** (pool as the word for a river occurs several places hereabouts), then up slightly to reach a T-junction. Turn left on a broader road and continue for about 0.5 mile (800m), passing **Field Broughton church**, whose spire dominates the upper part of the valley just as Cartmel Priory does the lower.

4 At the next junction fork right, signed to **Barber Green**, and keep left where the road splits again. At a tiny crossroads under a spreading beech tree turn right, following signs for Barber Green. Ascend gently through the village of **Barber Green**, then

1h00 **8 MILES** **12.9 KM** **LEVEL 1 2 3**

MAP: OS Explorer OL 7 The English Lakes (SE)

START/FINISH: Cartmel racecourse; grid ref: SD 375791

TRAILS/TRACKS: country lanes, some wider roads. Avoid doing this ride when race meetings are on

LANDSCAPE: wide valley flanked by ridges, with views to the higher fells and to Morecambe Bay

PUBLIC TOILETS: Cartmel

TOURIST INFORMATION: Ulverston, tel: 01229 587120

CYCLE HIRE: South Lakeland Mountain Bike Sales and Hire, Lowick Bridge, Ulverston, tel: 01229 885210

THE PUB: Cavendish Arms, Cartmel, see Point 6 on route

! Railway path section is suitable for all ages. If continuing into Threlkeld, suitability: children 6+; if returning via stone circle there's a short section (walk on pavement) alongside busy A road, and crossing another. Suitability: children 10+

Getting to the start

Cartmel is 2 miles (3.2km) west of Grange-over-Sands. The racecourse is west of the village square, and there's an honesty-box at the car park there.

Why do this cycle ride?

The Vale of Cartmel is a classic English landscape, its skylines punctuated by nothing more obtrusive than a church tower. Add views of the high Lakeland fells and the shining expanse of Morecambe Bay, and there are few better rides for scenic variety.

Researched and written by: Jon Sparks

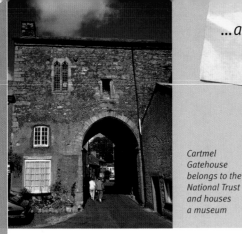

...and present

Cartmel Gatehouse belongs to the National Trust and houses a museum

Grange has many fine and interesting buildings and its ornamental gardens, complete with ponds, provide suitable solitude in which to relax and enjoy a picnic. The gardens rise to the open spaces of Hampsfell via the charming mixed woods of Eggerslack.

the road climbs more seriously again. Keep straight on at the crossroads just beyond the village. The next bit is steeper, but as you near the top there's a great view to the right down the valley, with the **tower** of the priory standing out and the sweep of Morecambe Bay beyond. Finally, the climb levels off. Just beyond this, reach a T-junction on the outskirts of **High Newton**.

5 Turn right and shortly keep right at a fork by the aptly named **Valley View**. Descend (another fine run) past **Head House**. Keep straight on at the crossroads of **Four Lane Ends**. After 0.5 mile (800m) reach an angled junction with a wider road. Keep left (almost straight ahead) for an easy run back to **Cartmel**.

6 About 200yds (183m) past the 30mph sign on the edge of Cartmel, turn right at an 'Unsuitable for heavy goods vehicles' sign. Follow the narrowing lane between cottages and past the back of the **Priory**, then loop round and past the **Cavendish Arms**. Go under the gatehouse arch into the village square. Take the lane left of the village shop back to the **racecourse**.

Bust of Sir William Lowther, Cartmel Priory

Cavendish Arms

Cartmel's oldest hostelry dates from the 15th century and stands tucked away from the village square. It is built within the old village walls and was once a thriving coaching stop, with stables where the bar is now. Note the mounting block dated 1837 outside the main door. The civilised main bar has low oak beams, a comfortable mixture of furnishings, Jennings ale on tap, a good selection of wines by glass or bottle, and welcoming log fires burn on cooler days. There is a separate non-smoking restaurant, and ten well appointed bedrooms.

about the pub

Cavendish Arms
Cavendish Street, Cartmel
Grange-over-Sands,
Cumbria LA11 6QA
Tel 015395 36240
www.thecavendisharms.co.uk

DIRECTIONS: off the main square

PARKING: 15

OPEN: daily, all day

FOOD: daily, all day Saturday and Sunday; no food Sunday evening in winter

BREWERY/COMPANY: free house

REAL ALE: Jennings Bitter, Wells Bombardier, guest beer

ROOMS: 10 en suite

Food
Bar food ranges from soup and sandwiches to lamb Henry, Cumberland sausages in a rich onion gravy and smoked haddock on black pudding mash. The dessert menu includes Cartmel's speciality, sticky toffee pudding. Typical restaurant dishes might be fillet steak, sea bass and ostrich.

Family facilities
Children are genuinely welcome. Children's menu is available, and the rear garden has small play area and a viewpoint from which to feed the ducks.

Alternative refreshment stops
Try the King's Arms, Royal Oak, Market Cross Cottage Tea Rooms or the Pig and Whistle Bistro in Cartmel. Close to the midpoint is the Crown Inn at High Newton.

☞ Where to go from here
There's plenty to see at Holker Hall, west of Cartmel at Cark, including magnificent gardens and the Lakeland Motor Museum (tel: 015395 58328; www.holker-hall.co.uk).

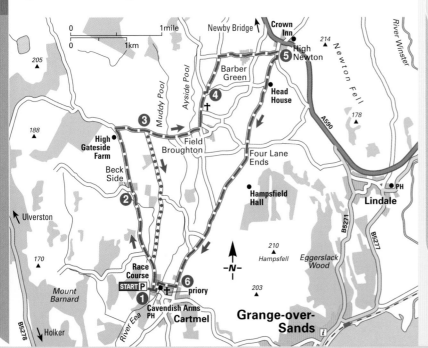

did you know?

Hardknott Castle Roman Fort, to the north of Seathwaite, is one of the most dramatic Roman sites in Britain, with stunning views of the Lakeland fells. The fort, built between AD 120 and AD 138, controlled the road from the port at Ravenglass to the fort at Ambleside. The remains include the headquarters building and commandant's house, with a bathhouse and parade ground opposite the fort.

Seathwaite and the Duddon Valley

Top left: Roman fort ruins, Hardknott Pass
Left: The valley of Tarn Beck
Next page: Houses in Seathwaite, built of rocks from the surrounding area

Follow in the footsteps of the Romantic poet, William Wordsworth.

Wordsworth and the Duddon Valley
William Wordsworth loved the Duddon Valley so much that he wrote many sonnets about it, including 'Hints for the Fancy from the River Duddon' (1820). And little has changed since his day. There's tarmac on the winding walled lanes, but the byres and woods and the lively stream that so enthralled the poet are still there, untouched for all to see.

The walk begins in Seathwaite, a remote village with a rustic pub, a little church and a handful of farms, set beneath the crags of Wallowbarrow. A reservoir service road takes the route easily up into the Coniston Fells to the dam of Seathwaite Tarn. The hushed waters of the large reservoir are dwarfed by the rocks of Great Blake Rigg and Buzzard Crag towering above.

Look the other way, and the jagged cone of Harter Fell dominates the skyline high above the forests, streams and farmhouses. The route descends through the heather and the bracken, and by a chattering beck to the Duddon. Over the

road, it comes to the Fickle Steps across the river. Wordsworth remembers them in a fanciful sonnet:

Not so that Pair whose youthful spirits dance
With Prompt emotion urging them to pass;
A sweet confusion checks the Shepherd lass;
Blushing she eyes the dizzy flood askance;
Too ashamed – too timid to advance

There's a wire across the river to steady your progress these days. It's an exciting prelude to a wonderful walk through the Wallowbarrow Gorge. From a lofty path you look down on the river and its bounding cataracts, then descend for a riverside stroll back into Seathwaite.

the walk

1 From **The Newfield Inn** at Seathwaite follow the road past the little church. In about 400yds (366m) turn right on the tarmac lane towards **Turner Hall Farm**, then take a track on the left signposted 'High Moss'. Keep left at a junction and follow the track to the isolated houses of **High Moss**. Skirt them on the left, go through a gate behind and follow the field path, ahead and then bearing left, out to the **Walna Scar Road**.

2 Turn right up the road. Where the tarmac ends turn left onto the utility company's access road to **Seathwaite Tarn**. This pleasant green track climbs steadily up the fellsides to the reservoir dam.

3h00 · **5 MILES** · **8 KM** · **LEVEL 1 2 3**

WALK

MAP: OS Explorer OL 6 The English Lakes (SW)

START/FINISH: Seathwaite: roadside pull-off; grid ref: SD 231975, limited roadside parking near pub and church; grid ref: SD 228960

PATHS: paths, tracks, can be muddy below Seathwaite Tarn, 9 stiles

LANDSCAPE: craggy mountainside and wooded gorge

PUBLIC TOILETS: none on route

TOURIST INFORMATION: Broughton-in-Furness, tel 01229 716115

THE PUB: The Newfield Inn, Seathwaite, see Point **1** on route

⚠ River crossing by stepping stones, too far apart for younger children; also rough slopes above river. If river is low it may be possible for children to paddle, otherwise return to Seathwaite along road. Suitability: children 11+ in typical conditions but very dependent on water level

Getting to the start

Seathwaite is on a minor road, 3 miles (4.8km) north of Ulpha and south of the Hardknott Pass. There are a few roadside parking spaces before the village (do not use those directly outside the pub), and a small lay-by opposite the church. If all these are full, continue for almost 1 mile (1.6km) to larger grassy spaces where the road reaches open fellside (Point 5 on the walk).

Researched and written by:
Dennis Kelsall, Jon Sparks

271

👫
WALK

did you know?

Visitors to the Lake District are encouraged to help the environment by parking their cars and using the waymarked walks, cycling, taking local trains and buses, and launches on the lakes. One of the best ways to see the high passes is on a minibus tour.

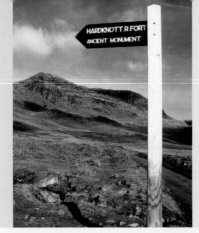

Far left: Buzzard (Buteo buteo)

The Newfield Inn

Located in Wordsworth's favourite – Duddon Valley – this unassuming 17th-century inn is understandably popular with walkers and climbers, with many good walks starting close to its door. 'Tardis-like' inside, the bar area has a magnificent slate floor, rustic wooden tables, a real fire, tip-top real ales, and a small collection of historic photographs. Slate floors are common enough in Cumbrian pubs but this is one of the best – it's still polite to get the worst of the mud off your boots first, though! On a good day the garden, tucked away at the back, is idyllic. Bask in the sun and gaze up at the Coniston Fells while the kids let off steam in the adjacent paddock. If the weather's less clement, a blazing fire will warm the cockles – helped along, perhaps, by a glass or two of Theakston's legendary Old Peculier ale.

Food
The menu encompasses home-made steak pie, large gammon steaks, local beef, lasagne, spicy bean casserole and an ever-changing specials board.

Family facilities
Children are welcome indoors.

☞ Where to go from here
Take a look around Broughton-in-Furness, a pleasant village near the Duddon Estuary. Chestnut trees surround the village square, where there is an obelisk erected to commemorate the jubilee of George III, and a set of stocks. Broughton's oldest building is the Church of St Mary Magdalene, which has Saxon walls and a Norman archway.

about the pub

The Newfield Inn
Seathwaite, Duddon Valley
Broughton-in-Furness
Cumbria LA20 6ED
Tel 01229 716208
www.newfieldinn.co.uk

DIRECTIONS: in Newfield, south west of the church

PARKING: 30

OPEN: daily, all day

FOOD: daily, all day

BREWERY/COMPANY: free house

REAL ALE: Daleside Bitter, Jennings Cumberland Ale, Theakston Old Peculier, guest beer

DOGS: well-behaved dogs on leads welcome inside

3 Retrace your steps for 400yds (366m) to a waymarked post highlighting a downhill path, faint at first, that weaves through rock and rough pasture and steeply down beside a mountain stream. Cross a gate/stile, continue to another gate, and then cross a ladder stile to the banks of **Tarn Beck**.

4 Cross the footbridge and turn left. Follow a footpath along the lower edge of a wood. Pass behind a cottage and continue along to a ladder stile. Skirt a very wet area, then go through a gap in the wall and climb up to the **Duddon Valley road**.

5 Across the road follow the signed bridleway to the **Fickle Steps**, huge boulders which enable you to cross the River Duddon. Caution: if the river is high and the steps are awash, do not cross. The steps are too far apart for younger children to negotiate safely but it may be possible to paddle if the river is low. If there is any doubt, return by the road. (A footpath which starts opposite the church allows you to visit Wallowbarrow Gorge from the other end.)

6 Assuming you have crossed safely, turn left on the riverside path. Cross a footbridge over **Grassguards Gill**. The path gradually pulls away from the river, then traverses steep slopes above the tight wooded **Wallowbarrow Gorge**, before descending again to cross boulder-strewn terrain on the bank of the **River Duddon**, eventually reaching an arched stone footbridge.

7 Cross the bridge and turn right, following the east bank of the Duddon, to meet a tributary, **Tarn Beck**. Go up to a footbridge and cross to a short track out to the road. Turn left to return to **Seathwaite**.

what to look for

You will see clumps of bog myrtle in the peat meadows of the Duddon Valley, especially near the end of the walk. It's a low aromatic shrub with woody stems and oval leaves and it thrives in this marshy terrain. The branches have been used in past centuries, both for flavouring beer and for discouraging flies and midges, which apparently don't appreciate its eucalyptus-like scent.

272

WALK

while you're there

Visit the Ruskin Museum in Coniston village, opposite the fire station, set up by his private secretary WG Collingwood, both as a memorial to Ruskin (1819–1900) and as a guide to the area's heritage. The museum contains many of his watercolours, drawings, letters, sketchbooks and other items. There are exhibits about the geology of Coniston and its copper mines. The museum also has an extensive collection of Campbell family memorabilia.

IN MEMORY OF
DONALD CAMPBELL, C.B.E.
QUEEN'S COMMENDATION FOR BRAVE CONDUCT
WHO DIED ON
JANUARY 4th 1967
WHILE ATTEMPTING TO RAISE
HIS OWN WORLD WATER SPEED RECORD
ON CONISTON WATER

From Coniston to Tarn Hows

3h30 **6.75 MILES** **10.9 KM** **LEVEL 1 2 3**

PATHS: OS Explorer OL 7 The English Lakes (SE)

START/FINISH: Coniston car park; grid ref: SD 303975

PATHS: road, grassy paths and tracks, 4 stiles

LANDSCAPE: woods, field, fell, tarn and lake

PUBLIC TOILETS: at car park

TOURIST INFORMATION: Ambleside, tel 015394 32582

THE PUB: Black Bull Inn, Coniston, see Point **1** on route

❶ Suitability: children 8+

Getting to the start

Coniston is just off the B593 between Broughton-in-Furness and Ambleside. Approaching from Ambleside, go down the short main street and turn left just after the Black Bull Inn, before the bridge. The main car park is obvious, on the right, a short way past the church.

Researched and written by:
Bill Birkett, Jon Sparks

Explore the wooded intricacies of Yewdale before reaching the scenic favourite of Tarn Hows.

Coniston

This long route of great variety, much interest and heart-stopping beauty contrasts the quiet mixed woods in and around the fringes of forgotten Yewdale, with the popular Tarn Hows, and views back over Coniston Water or west to the mountains of Coniston Old Man and Wetherlam.

Copper mining started in the bowels of the mountain, Coniston Old Man, during the Bronze Age. So extensive were these early workings that when a group of German miners, brought over in Elizabethan times to kickstart 'modern mineral mining' in Britain, started work, they were shocked to find that the mountain was already riddled with workings. They referred to these earlier sites as 'the old men workings', which is possibly one derivation of the modern name Coniston Old Man.

Coniston Water is some 5 miles (8km) long and reaches a maximum depth of 184ft (56m). It is the third largest of the Lakeland lakes. It once provided an important fish source for the monks of Furness Abbey, who owned the lake and much of the surrounding land in the 13th and 14th centuries. Many of their iron bloomery and charcoal burning sites remain intact around the shores of the lake. The copper mines were revitalised around 1859, and at the height of production some 800 men worked in Coppermines Valley above the village.

Speed ace Donald Campbell was killed on Coniston Water in 1967, attempting to beat his own water speed record. His boat became airborne and crashed, but in 2001 was raised from the bed of the lake. He is buried in St Andrew's Church.

the walk

1 Exit the **car park** on to the main road (**Tilberthwaite Avenue**) and turn right. In a few hundred paces a road leads off left, signposted to Ambleside. Follow this beyond the football field to a stone bridge on the right, over **Yewdale Beck**. Cross and go immediately left over the low stone stile. Go through a kissing gate into a field. Follow the path curving right and gently uphill beside a stone wall. The path leads to a recently renovated **stone building**.

did you know?

The Coniston area has two distinct rock groups. The older Borrowdale volcanic group was laid down around 460 million years ago. The area was then submerged beneath a subtropical sea and the sediments from it formed the impure Coniston limestone. In a collision of landmasses the rocks were intensely heated, and uplifted over 90 degrees. The volcanic rocks now form the high peaks with the sedimentary layer underlying the lusciously wooded valleys.

Brantwood House was the home of poet, artist and social reformer John Ruskin from 1872 until 1900

Tarn Hows, now in the care of the National Trust

2 Pass the building on the left and ascend through a gate. Go up a little further, then take a branch path right below the mass of gorse. Go up to a little gate through the stone wall enclosing **High Guards Wood**. Climb steeply through the Scots pine. Cross a ruined stone wall and follow the waymarked path to descend through **Guards Wood**. Leave the wood and continue down a stony track, muddy in places, to a gate and stile leading on to a **stony lane**.

3 Go left up the lane. In a few hundred paces go right through a gate. Follow the track winding up through fields, through one gate and then a gate/stile. The grassy track meets a fence beside **Tarn Hows Wood**. Keep right along the track and continue to a steep, surfaced track. **Tarn Hows Cottage** is below to the left. Go right along the track to a road. Go left, ascending the road and passing a **car park**. Take the track opposite the car park entrance, then bear off right, across the slope overlooking **Tarn Hows**.

4 Several tracks come together to form one clear track. Follow this to make an anticlockwise circuit of the tarn. At the end of the circuit is a little **dam**.

5 Turn right immediately before the dam and descend the path to the right of the beck. This is steep and rocky in places. At the bottom go left over the footbridge, then out on to the **Coniston road**. Cross and go left. Turn right towards **Yewtree Farm** and right again before the farmyard. Follow the track up to another gate, then go left above the fence. Keep along this grassy track, ignoring branches to the right, to pass above **High Yewdale Farm**. A final gate leads out to a narrow road. Turn left over **Shepherd's Bridge** and meet the **Coniston road**.

6 Cross and go left until, opposite **High Yewdale Farm**, a path leads right along a line of yew trees. Around 200yds (183m) beyond the last of the trees, bear right across the fields and straight ahead through the farmyard of **Low Yewdale**. Go left along a track, over a bridge, and continue alongside the beck. The track curves away from the stream. At a sharp bend go right, signposted '**Cumbria Way**', through the field. Beyond a wall the track is indistinct: keep parallel to the walled wood on the left. The track becomes clear again and enters **Back Guards Plantation**. Follow the track through the wood. Pass through yew trees and descend to join the outward route back into **Coniston village**.

what to look for

The Victorian philosopher and art critic John Ruskin lived at Brantwood, across the lake, from 1871 until 1901. He was buried at St Andrew's Church in Coniston. His grave is marked with a large cross carved from local green slate. Designed by his secretary, Lakeland authority W G Collingwood, it depicts aspects of Ruskin's work and life.

Black Bull Inn

The Black Bull sits just above Church Beck and in the shadow of the Old Man, and has been at the heart of Coniston village for nearly 400 years. Walls in the black-beamed bar are adorned with many photos celebrating the history of the village and the pub, and in particular the late Donald Campbell, who stayed here while preparing for the attempt on the world water speed record which cost him his life. Both the painter J M W Turner and the poet Samuel Taylor Coleridge also enjoyed the hospitality of this old coaching inn. The Coniston Brewery behind the pub supplies the beer, so sample a pint of Bluebird and see just why it won the title Champion Beer of Britain.

Food
The wide-ranging menu caters for all tastes, from sandwiches, ploughman's lunches and salads to freshly battered haddock and chips, local Esthwaite trout, half a shoulder of local lamb and generous Cumbrian grills. Separate evening restaurant menu.

about the pub

Black Bull Inn
1 Yewdale Road, Coniston
Cumbria LA21 8DU
Tel 015394 41335
www.conistonbrewery.com

DIRECTIONS: just west of St Andrew's Church in Coniston

PARKING: 12

OPEN: daily, all day

FOOD: daily, all day

BREWERY/COMPANY: free house

REAL ALE: Coniston Bluebird, XB, Old Man – all brewed at the pub

DOGS: welcome in the the pub

ROOMS: 15 en suite

Family facilities
The pub has a children's licence, so kids are welcome throughout the pub and young children have their own menu. Summer seating on the riverside patio.

Alternative refreshment stops
There is plenty of choice in Coniston. The Crown Inn also does bar meals, and there is a good café at Bridge End.

☞ Where to go from here
The restored steam yacht *Gondola*, built in 1859, was relaunched in 1980 and plies Coniston Water every summer. The trip starts at Coniston Pier, passing Coniston Hall and stopping at Brantwood, before returning.

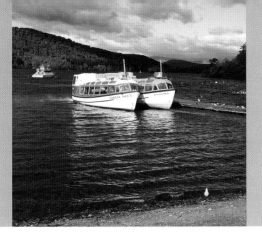

Overlooked by this walk, the privately owned Belle Isle is said to have been used since Roman times. Today, this island is supplied by a little boat that serves the 38-acre (15ha) estate. Belle Isle's interesting circular house was originally built by a Mr English in 1774. Apparently William Wordsworth accredited Mr English with the honour of being the first man to settle in the Lake District for the sake of the scenery. There have been many more since.

Brant Fell at Bowness-on-Windermere

From Windermere's shores to high ground above the bustling town.

Bowness-on-Windermere

Fed by the high rainfall of the Lake District fells, via the rivers Brathay, Rothay and Troutbeck, Windermere is England's largest natural lake. It stretches some 12 miles (19km) in length, is up to 1 mile (1.6km) wide in places, and reaches a depth of 220 feet (67m).

Bowness-on-Windermere is the main gateway and access point to the lake, and the most popular holiday destination in the Lake District. Over 10,000 boats for recreation are registered on the lake. The town developed rapidly after the Oxenholme and Kendal-to-Windermere railway line opened in 1847, growing up around the station from the nucleus of what was once a small village. Indeed it was the railway company that named the station Windermere to attract a trade, although it is sited some distance from the lake. In the late 19th century wealthy businessmen, principally from the industrial towns of Lancashire, built large and luxurious residences overlooking the lake. Many of these private houses have been converted into hotels, such as the Langdale Chase, and Brockhole has been the National Park Visitor Centre since the late 1960s.

The Belsfield Hotel, overlooking Bowness Bay, was bought in 1860 by Henry Schneider, the chairman of the Barrow Steelworks and Shipworks. Reputedly he would leave his luxurious home and board his steam yacht SL *Esperance*, where he breakfasted while travelling across the lake to Lakeside. He would continue his journey to Barrow by steam train – he owned the railway and had his own private carriage.

the walk

1 Walk up **Glebe Road** (against the traffic) to the steamer pier. Cross the main road here and follow it left. Opposite the impressive **Church of St Martin** turn right to ascend the little street of **St Martin's Hill**. Cross the Kendal road to climb **Brantfell Road** directly above and pass the **Royal Oak Inn**. At the head of the road an iron gate leads on to the **Dales Way**, a stony path climbing directly up the hillside. Continue to a kissing gate by a wood.

A wet dock at the Steamboat Museum, Bowness-on-Windermere

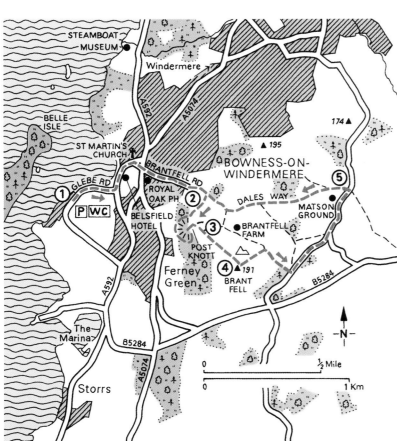

1h30 · **3.5 MILES** · **5.7 KM** · **LEVEL 123**

MAP: OS Explorer OL 7 The English Lakes (SE)

START/FINISH: pay-and-display car park on Glebe Road above lake, Bowness-on-Windermere; grid ref: SD 398966

PATHS: pavement, road, stony tracks, grassy paths, 2 stiles

LANDSCAPE: town, mixed woodland, open fell, lake and fell views

PUBLIC TOILETS: at car park and above information centre

TOURIST INFORMATION: Windermere, tel 015394 46499

THE PUB: Royal Oak Inn, Bowness-on-Windermere, see Point 1 on route

❶ Care needed with traffic on busy streets at the start and finish. Suitability: children 6+

Getting to the start

Bowness-on-Windermere is located on the A592 just south of Windermere town, and the A591 Kendal-to-Ambleside road. In Bowness, turn left just before the steamer terminal into Glebe Road, where the main car parks are located.

Researched and written by:
Bill Birkett, Jon Sparks

while you're there

Blackwell, in Bowness-on-Windermere, was designed by MH Baillie Scott (1865–1945) and completed in 1900. Part of the late 19th-century Arts and Crafts Movement, it houses changing exhibitions of high-quality applied arts and crafts.

Dipper (Cinclus cinclus)

273

WALK

2 Pass through the kissing gate and turn right on a stony lane, signposted 'Post Knott'. Follow this up through the woods until it crests a rise near the flat, circular top of **Post Knott**. Bear left and make the final short ascent to the summit. The view from here was once exceptional but is now mainly obscured by trees. Retrace a few steps back to the track to find a **kissing gate** leading out of the wood on to the open hillside.

3 Take the path beyond the kissing gate, rising to a rocky shoulder. Cross the shoulder and bear left to a ladder stile near the top corner of the field between birch and holly trees. Immediately over the stile the path forks. Bear right to ascend directly up the open grassy flanks of **Brant Fell** to its rocky summit.

4 Bear left (north) from the highest point. The path is very indistinct but there are cairns, and the prominent white buildings of **Matson Ground** are a good guide. Go through a kissing gate into a new plantation. Emerge onto a stony track. Turn right and follow the track to a stone stile and gate, which lead on to the road. Turn left and continue left at the junction, to pass the stone buildings and entrance drive to Matson Ground. Just beyond is a kissing gate on the left, waymarked for the Dales Way.

Rowing boats beside a jetty onto Lake Windermere

what to look for

St Martin's Church, an impressive building surrounded by ancient yew trees, is the parish church of Bowness, built in 1483 and restored and enlarged in 1870. It is well worth taking a look inside. Behind the church is the oldest area of Bowness, known as Lowside, where an intriguing web of narrow streets thread between buildings of dark slate.

5 Go through the kissing gate. Then continue down the field to cross a track. Pass through another kissing gate. Follow the path, under the trees, to the left of a new **pond**, until it swings left to emerge through a kissing gate onto a surfaced drive. Go right along the drive for 30yds (27m) until the path veers off left through the trees to follow the fence. An **iron kissing gate** leads into a field. Follow the grassy path, first descending and then rising to an **iron gate** in the corner of the field. Go through it and follow the wall on the left to a kissing gate leading to a walled track. Cross the surfaced drive of **Brantfell Farm**. Keep straight on to another kissing gate leading to a field. Follow the path downhill, alongside the wall, to another kissing gate, with the stony lane of Point 2 just beyond. Retrace your steps back to **Glebe Road**.

Royal Oak Inn

The Royal Oak is the official finishing pub for the Dales Way, so it seems fitting to make it the unofficial finishing pub for our much shorter walk. It's a tall slate building set back from the road, just off the bustling main street in slightly quieter surroundings, and a stone's throw from Bowness Bay piers and Windermere. As befits a pub that sets out to serve hungry walkers, it serves an extensive range of food throughout the day and quenches thirsts with handpumped ales, including the award-winning and locally brewed Coniston Bluebird.

Food
The pub specialises in griddled steaks with a choice of sauces, but also offers traditional fish and chips, chilli nachos, sandwiches and light snacks such as blue cheese and asparagus tart with red onion and tomato chutney.

about the pub

Royal Oak Inn
Brantfell Road,
Bowness-on-Windermere
Cumbria LA23 3EE
Tel 015394 43970

DIRECTIONS: close to St Martin's Church at the start of the walk

PARKING: very limited, so use walk car park

OPEN: daily, all day

FOOD: daily, all day

BREWERY/COMPANY: free house

REAL ALE: Coniston Bluebird, Tetley, Greene King Old Speckled Hen, guest beers

DOGS: not allowed indoors

ROOMS: 9 bedrooms

Family facilities
Children are welcome in the left-hand side of the pub. There's a children's menu and on fine days the small garden at the front (away from the road) is the place to sit and eat.

Alternative refreshment stops
Bowness-on-Windermere is inundated with cafés, inns, shops and restaurants. Santameras Bakery Café is conveniently located near the start and finish of the route, at the foot of Brantfell Road.

☛ Where to go from here
The Windermere Steamboat Centre, 0.5 mile (800m) north of Bowness on the A592, has many working exhibits and provides a chance to chug across the lake on a genuine steam yacht, weather permitting (tel 015394 45565).

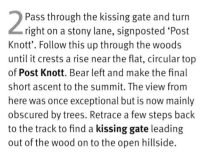

Lady of the Lake *takes day trippers along the length of Ullswater*

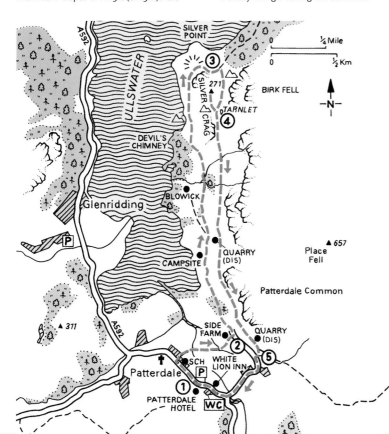

did you know?

The elongated hamlet of Patterdale has a rugged, mountain quality. Sited below the mighty Helvellyn massif its straggle of houses, inn, hotel, mountain rescue base, church and school have a certain bleakness about them. A perfect contrast to the splendour that is Ullswater, whose southern shore lies hardly a stone's throw away.

From Patterdale by Ullswater

Along the shores of Ullswater silver point, a spectacular viewpoint.

Ullswater

Ullswater is undoubtedly one of the loveliest of the lakes. Its three arms add up to a total length of 7.5 miles (12.1km) with an average width of 0.5 mile (800m) and a maximum depth of 205ft (62.5m). It is Lakeland's second largest lake, not quite measuring up to Windermere. Its waters are exceptionally clear and in the deepest part of the lake, off Howtown, lives a curious fish called the schelly – a creature akin to a freshwater herring.

Apart from rescue and Park Ranger launches, you won't see many power boats here, but Ullswater 'Steamers' have three boats operating between Glenridding and Pooley Bridge during the summer.

Alfred Wainwright (1907–91), known for his seven *Pictorial Guides to the Lakeland Fells*, regarded this to be a part of one of the most beautiful walks in the Lakes – a sentiment with which many would agree. Preservation of the lake in its present form is due to a concerted campaign, led in Parliament by Lord Birkett, against the proposed Manchester Corporation Water Act in 1965. Although the act was passed, and water is extracted from the lake, the workings are hidden underground and designed in such a way as to make it impossible to lower the water level beyond the agreed limit.

It was the sight of golden daffodils amongst the trees and beside the shore of this lake that inspired William Wordsworth's most widely known poem, 'I wandered lonely as a cloud' (1807). Wordsworth's sister Dorothy recorded the occasion vividly in her diary: 'I never saw daffodils so beautiful. They grew among the mossy stones about and around them, some rested their heads upon these stones as on a pillar for weariness and the rest tossed and reeled and danced and seemed as if they verily laughed with the wind that blew them over the lake.'

1h45   **4 MILES**   **6.4 KM**   **LEVEL 123**

PATHS: OS Explorer OL 5 The English Lakes (NE)

START/FINISH: pay-and-display car park, Patterdale; grid ref: NY 396159

PATHS: stony tracks and paths, no stiles

LANDSCAPE: lake and fell views, mixed woodland

PUBLIC TOILETS: opposite White Lion in Patterdale village centre

TOURIST INFORMATION: Ullswater (Glenridding), tel: 017684 82414

THE PUB: Patterdale Hotel, Patterdale, see Point **1** on route

❶ Rough tracks with some steep sections. Suitability: children 8+

Getting to the start

Patterdale village lies at the southern tip of Ullswater, stretched along the A592. The car park is opposite the Patterdale Hotel.

Researched and written by:
Bill Birkett, Jon Sparks

Aira Force in the Lake District

while you're there

After reaching the famed viewpoint of Silver Point, the adventurous may also wish to make the scramble to the top of Silver Crag, as did the horsedrawn coach parties of old, for an even better view over the lake.

the walk

1 Walk out to the **main road**. Cross to gain the pavement and turn right. Opposite a sign for Side Farm cross back to a stony track, signed to Howtown and Boardale. Follow the track over a bridge and up between the buildings of **Side Farm**. Turn left on another roughly surfaced track.

2 Follow the undulating track, with a stone wall on your left. The lake head and **Glenridding** appear away to the left, with the lead mine remains prominent in the valley beyond. Continue on above the campsite and through further undulations before the path ascends again to crest a craggy knoll above the woods of **Devil's Chimney**. Make a steep rocky descent (care required) before the path levels to traverse beneath the craggy heights of Silver Crag. In places the steep ground falls directly to the lake below. A slight ascent, passing some fine holly trees, gains the shoulder of **Silver Point** and an outstanding view of **Ullswater**.

3 Follow the path, which sweeps round beneath the end of **Silver Crag**, until a steep stony path, eroded in places, breaks off to the right. Ascend this, climbing steeply through the juniper bushes, into

The small 19th-century Church of St Patrick in Patterdale with Helvellyn in the background

the narrow gap which separates Silver Crag to the right from the main hillside of **Birk Fell** to the left. This little valley is quite boggy and holds a small tarn.

4 The path ahead soon begins a gradual descent back towards **Patterdale**. (If you have energy to spare, a short steep ascent leads to the top of Silver Crag – the view is not that much better than from Silver Point, but you are more likely to enjoy it in solitude. Where the main path levels out, climb steeply through a grassy gap between the crags. Bear right at the top on a narrow path through the prickly juniper, to the top. Descend by the same route to the main path.) The path traversing the open fell is easy, though it may be boggy in places. Pass above an old quarry, tree-filled and unfenced, and then descend across the slate spoil from another quarry. An artificial **cave** here usually has a waterfall spilling over its lip. Continue along the hillside above **Side Farm**, passing through more quarry workings. Descend to meet a wider track and follow it down to the right to a gate.

5 Go through the gate and bear left on a lane. Bear right at the next junction and through the meadows back to the main road. Turn right back into **Patterdale**.

what to look for

The distinctive golden yellow and white of the indigenous daffodil still abounds in the woods by the lakeshore and may be seen at its best from mid-March to mid-April. This wild variety is smaller than the cultivated version and, many would say, even more lovely. There has been concern recently that the introduction of cultivated daffodils to this area is actually damaging the survival prospects of its smaller relative and jeopardising the view Wordsworth loved.

Patterdale Hotel

This roadside hotel stands at the southern edge of Ullswater, with magnificent views of the valley and fells. Although it is a large hotel catering mainly for the tourist trade, its location also makes it a popular base for walkers, who are most welcome in the spacious and very comfortable main bar. Not only is it open all day, with food available throughout the day, but you'll find Jennings beer on tap and an extensive garden with super views across to Place Fell, along whose slopes this walk runs.

Food

Expect a wide range of traditional pub dishes, including local Cumberland sausage, pasta meals, ploughman's lunches and decent sandwiches. There's a separate restaurant menu – rack of lamb with herb crust and a redcurrant and port sauce or baked salmon supreme with lemon butter sauce, for example.

Family facilities

In keeping with most Lakeland hotels, families are made very welcome. Children are allowed in the bar, youngsters have their own menu to choose from, and the secluded and safe garden is great for kids to relax in.

Alternative refreshment stops

Side Farm sometimes offers teas and ice creams. In the centre of Patterdale, the White Lion Inn serves bar meals throughout the year, but its outdoor seating is very close to the road.

about the pub

Patterdale Hotel
Patterdale, Ullswater
Cumbria CA11 0NN
Tel 017684 82231
www.patterdalehotel.co.uk

DIRECTIONS: in the centre of Patterdale village

PARKING: 40

OPEN: daily, all day

FOOD: daily, all day

BREWERY/COMPANY: Chace Hotels

REAL ALE: Jennings

DOGS: welcome in the garden only

☛ Where to go from here

North along the A592 via a scenic 0.25 mile (400m) walk through National Trust woodland is Aira Force. This impressive waterfall is best seen just after rain or on a misty morning. Further along the A592, Dalemain House is set in stunning parkland. Its attractions include the Westmorland and Cumberland Yeomanry Museum, and a countryside collection in the 16th-century barn. The house has beautiful gardens and there's an adventure playground for children.

Affectionately known as La'al Ratty, the Ravenglass and Eskdale Railway opened in 1875 to serve a granite quarry. After a period of closure it was bought by enthusiasts in 1960, overhauled and reopened. The line runs from Ravenglass via Eskdale Green to Dalegarth Station, near Boot. The railway runs almost all year, but there are times in the winter when there are no services. Few Lakeland journeys compare with a trip both ways.

A circuit from Wast Water to Stanton Bridge

Restocking coal on the miniature Northern Rock *on Ravenglass and Eskdale Railway*

A pleasant rural ride with a short option and a magnificent scenic finale.

Wast Water

Wast Water is England's deepest lake, reaching a maximum depth of almost 260ft (79m), which means that its bed is well below sea level. The steep slope of The Screes, which face you across the lake, is continued deep underwater. The Screes, below the two summits of Whin Rigg and Illgill Head, are composed of decaying crags and masses of loose rock and boulders. This is landscape that is still evolving. There is a path, which you may be able to make out, running along the base of The Screes just above the level of the lake. It is no surprise to find that it is extremely rough going in places.

Looking up to the head of the lake and at the centre of the view (and of the National Park logo) is the pyramidal peak of Great Gable, 2,949ft (899m) high. High on its slopes facing you are the Napes Crags,

Left: Cyclists on the route above Wast Water
Page 43: Scafell and Great Gable

beloved of the earliest rock-climbers and of generations since. But only with very sharp eyes, or binoculars, and even then only in favourable light, are you likely to discern the natural obelisk called Napes Needle. Its first ascent in 1886 is often regarded as the birth of rock-climbing. It features in a memorial window in the lovely little church at Wasdale Head.

the ride

1 Head west along the road towards **Gosforth**, climbing slightly and passing close under the craggy slopes of **Buckbarrow**. Climb a little more and then descend to a junction.

2 For the shorter loop, go left here, signed for Nether Wasdale. Follow the narrow lane and descend to a junction. Keep left and descend quite steeply into **Nether Wasdale**, levelling out at the village green, with **The Screes Inn** on the left and the **Strands Hotel** on the right (Point 5). For the longer ride, continue straight ahead at Point 2 and go straight on at the next junction. The road is fairly level, with views over the valley of the **River Irt** to the left and wooded slopes on the right. A little over 1 mile (1.6km) from the last junction, look for a bridleway on the left, signed for Hall Bolton.

3 Turn left onto the bridleway. The initial descent from the road is as rough as it gets. Keep right where the track forks and go straight ahead between the buildings at **Rainors**. Wind down to an attractive bridge over the **River Bleng**. Beyond this there's a

short grassy section, then join the surfaced drive to **Hall Bolton**. Turn right and follow the drive out to a road. Turn left. Note, this track is rarely very muddy, but after wet weather you risk a soaking on the grassy section beyond the bridge. To avoid this, continue along the road at Point 3 over a small climb and then down steeply to **Wellington Bridge** and the outskirts of **Gosforth**. Bear left on a farm lane (bridleway) through **Row Farm** and on to **Rowend Bridge**. Turn left to follow the road to Santon Bridge. This adds about 1 mile (1.6km) to the total distance. Follow the road easily to **Santon Bridge**, past the pub and over the bridge.

4 Turn left on a narrow road past a campsite and soon begin a steeper climb at **Greengate Wood**. The gradient eases and the views ahead start to include the craggy outline of **The Screes**. Descend gently to **Forest Bridge**, then keep left, over **Cinderdale Bridge**, into **Nether Wasdale**. Follow the level road into the village and its twin pubs.

5 Retrace to **Cinderdale Bridge**, then keep left on the lane, signed to Wasdale Head. There are glimpses of The Screes and then of the lake, but trees screen them as you pass the youth hostel at **Wasdale Hall** and it's only when you cross a cattle grid to open fellside that the full panorama hits you. Follow the road down and then up a short climb to near a **cross-wall shelter** on the right, which commands a great view.

6 Continue down to cross **Countess Beck** and turn left. It's now little more than 0.25 mile (400m) back to the start.

2h00	11.25 MILES	18.1 KM	LEVEL 1**2**3

SHORTER ALTERNATIVE ROUTE

1h00	5 MILES	8 KM	LEVEL 1**2**3

MAP: OS Explorer OL 6 The English Lakes (SW)

START/FINISH: by Wast Water, roadside parking at Greendale; grid ref: NY 144057

TRAILS/TRACKS: lanes; longer route has a short section of grassy bridleway

LANDSCAPE: wooded farmland then open fellside with view of lake and high fells

PUBLIC TOILETS: Gosforth

TOURIST INFORMATION: Ravenglass, tel 01229 717278; Sellafield, tel 019467 76510

CYCLE HIRE: Ainfield Cycle Centre, Cleator, tel 01946 812427; Mark Taylor Cycles, Whitehaven, tel 01946 692252

THE PUB: The Screes Inn, Nether Wasdale, see Point 5 on route

❶ Some ascents and descents on both routes. Shorter loop, suitability: children 8+. Longer loop, suitability: children 11+

Getting to the start

Head east from Gosforth, pass a car park, then keep left on the Wasdale road. Follow this for 3 miles (4.8km) then keep left, signed to Wasdale Head for 2.5 miles (4km). Park in a grassy area on the left just past Greendale.

Why do this cycle ride?

The magnificent view of high fells around the head of Wast Water inspired the Lake District National Park logo, and would win many votes for the finest view in England. The ride saves this until near the end, first exploring the gentler scenery around Nether Wasdale.

Researched and written by: Jon Sparks

275

CYCLE

while you're there

Explore the little village of Ravenglass. It's essentially a fishing village at the confluence of the rivers Irt, Mite and Esk. Apart from being a Roman port, by 1280 it had charters for a weekly market and annual fair.

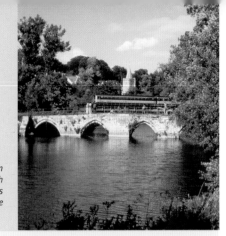

A train passing through Ravenglass village

Map labels

Wasdale Head ↑
Nether Beck
West Water
The Screes
Whillan Beck
Tongue Moor
604 ▲ Illgill Head
582 ▲ Middle Fell
Long Crag
0 — 1mile
0 — 1km
535 ▲ Whinn Rigg
Blea Tarn
River Mite
Miterdale
START P ① ⑥
Greendale
Wasdale Hall
Buckbarrow
395 ▲
329 ▲ Great Bank
Great Bank
Nether Wasdale
Screes Inn
Forest Bridge
PH ⑤
Strands Hotel
Miterdale Forest
Eskdale Green
200 ▲ Latterbarrow
②
Hollow Moor
River Irt
Bowerhouse Inn
Bolton Wood
229 ▲ Irton Pike
Irton Park
Greengate Wood
④ Santon Bridge
campsite
PH
③
Rainors
Hall Bolton
River Bleng
Row Farm
Wellington
Gosforth
P
PH
A595
B5344
River Irt
River Mite
A595
PH
Holmbrook
← Cleator Moor, Egremont
↓ Seascale
N

The Screes Inn

Two pubs face each other across the lane through Nether Wasdale, but both are owned by the same people. To pick one over the other may be invidious, but the 300-year-old Screes Inn does have one or two advantages: it's easy to park your bikes in sight of the outdoor tables, and it's open all day. Outside seating is separated from the road by an expanse of grass – a sort of village green – with a sunny aspect and glimpses of the fells lining Wasdale. Inside, it's a typically rambling Lakeland pub. The bars are partly slate-floored, and there's usually a log fire crackling in the grate – the perfect spot to savour a pint of Yates's bitter. Bike storage for overnight visitors.

Food

Specials from the blackboard might include smoked haddock, leek and potato pasties or Mexican wraps. Alternatively, try Woodall's Cumberland sausage with apple sauce, lasagne or home-baked steak and kidney pie. Vegetarians will always be well looked after as The Screes has a vegetarian chef.

Family facilities

Families will find a separate family room for the children to relax in. Small portions of main menu dishes are available (young children have their own menu), and there is plenty of good outdoor seating.

Alternative refreshment stops

The Strands Hotel in Nether Wasdale and, on the longer ride, the Bridge Inn at Stanton Bridge.

☞ Where to go from here

St Olaf's Church at Wasdale Head is one of England's smallest, and in its cemetery are the graves of several rock-climbers; this village became known as the birthplace of rock-climbing in Britain in the 1880s.

about the pub

The Screes Inn
Nether Wasdale, Seascale
Cumbria CA20 1ET
Tel 01946 726262
www.thescreesinnwasdale.com

DIRECTIONS: on the main road through the village, west of the church

PARKING: 20

OPEN: daily, all day

FOOD: daily

BREWERY/COMPANY: free house

REAL ALE: Black Sheep Bitter, Coniston Bluebird, Yates's Bitter, guest beer

ROOMS: 5 en suite

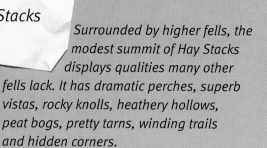

Hay Stacks

Surrounded by higher fells, the modest summit of Hay Stacks displays qualities many other fells lack. It has dramatic perches, superb vistas, rocky knolls, heathery hollows, peat bogs, pretty tarns, winding trails and hidden corners.

A family walk around Buttermere

Around Buttermere

A relaxing walk in one of Lakeland's most attractive valleys.

Buttermere

Much has been written about lovely Buttermere – the dale, the village and the lake. The area achieved considerable notoriety at the pen of Joseph Budworth, who stayed here in 1792 and encountered Mary, the daughter of the landlord of the Fish Inn. In his guidebook *Fortnight's Ramble to the Lakes*, he described Mary as 'the reigning Lily of the Valley', and the unfortunate woman became a tourist attraction.

In 1802 the tale brought to Buttermere one John Hadfield, a man posing as the Honourable Anthony Augustus Hope, MP. Hadfield wooed and won Mary, and they were married at Lorton church on 2 October 1802 (coincidentally just two days before William Wordsworth married Mary Hutchinson). With the honeymoon scarcely begun, however, Hadfield was exposed as an impostor and arrested on a charge of forgery – a more serious offence than that of bigamy, of which he was also guilty. He was later tried and hanged at Carlisle. The whole saga was dramatised and found its way on to the stages of some London theatres. Accounts of the episode are given by Thomas de Quincey in *Recollections of the Lakes and the Lake Poets* and by Melvyn Bragg in his 1987 novel *The Maid of Buttermere*, and a description used by Wordsworth in 'The Prelude'. As for Mary, she later remarried, had a large family and by all accounts a subsequently happy life.

the walk

1 Leave the car park and turn right, passing the **Fish Hotel** to follow a broad track through gates. Ignore the signposted route to Scale Force and continue along the track towards the edge of the lake. Then follow the line of a hedgerow to a bridge at **Buttermere Dubs**. Cross over and bear left, passing just below the foot of the cascade of **Sourmilk Gill**. Cross a smaller footbridge and go through a gate into **Burtness Wood**. Bear left on a track through the woods that roughly parallels the lakeshore, finally emerging from the trees near **Horse Close**, where a bridge spans **Comb Beck**.

2 Keep on along the path to reach a wall leading to a sheepfold and a gate. Go left through the gate, cross **Warnscale Beck** and walk out to **Gatesgarth Farm**. At the farm, follow signs to reach the valley

Left: Hikers gazing across Buttermere
Below: Ducks on the shore of Crummock Water

road (the **B5289**). Turn left on the road for about 500yds (457m) until it meets the **lakeshore**. For much of this distance there are no pathways: take care against approaching traffic.

3 As the road leaves the lakeshore again, leave it for a **footpath** on the left signposted 'Buttermere via Lakeshore Path'. The path leads into a field, beyond which it never strays far from the shoreline and continues to a stand of Scots pine, near **Crag Wood**.

4 Beyond **Hassnesshow Beck bridge**, the path enters the grounds of Hassness, where a rocky path, enclosed by trees, leads to a gate. Here a path has been cut across a crag dropping into the lake below, and shortly disappears into a brief, low and damp **tunnel**, unique in the Lake District. The tunnel was cut by employees of George Benson, a 19th-century Manchester mill owner who then owned the Hassness Estate, to enable him to walk around the lake without straying too far from its shore. After you emerge from the tunnel a gate gives access to a gravel path across the wooded pasture of **Pike Rigg**. Where a permitted path goes left to stay by the lakeshore, the main path keeps straight ahead, crossing a traditional Lakeland bridge of slate slabs.

276

 WALK

2h00 | **4.5 MILES** | **7.2 KM** | **LEVEL 1 2 3**

MAP: OS Explorer OL 4 The English Lakes (NW)

START/FINISH: Buttermere, National Park car park beyond Fish Hotel (fee); grid ref: NY 173169

PATHS: good paths, some road walking, 2 stiles

LANDSCAPE: lakeside, fells, woodland and farmland

PUBLIC TOILETS: at start

TOURIST INFORMATION: Keswick, tel 017687 72645

THE PUB: Bridge Hotel, Buttermere, see Point **5** on route

! Suitability: children 5+

Getting to the start

Buttermere village lies between the lakes of Buttermere and Crummock Water, on the B5289. Approaching from the south, pass Buttermere church and turn left before the Bridge Hotel. The car park is to the right of the Fish Hotel.

Researched and written by:
Terry Marsh, Jon Sparks

Scots pine trees reflected in snow-tinged water at Buttermere in spring

5 A short way on, through another gate, the path leads on to **Wilkinsyke Farm**, and an easy walk out to the road, just a short way above the **Bridge Hotel**. Turn left to return to the car park.

what to look for

While walking out to Gatesgarth Farm, have a look at the craggy sides of Fleetwith Pike. On the lower slopes a white cross can be seen clearly. This was erected by the friends of Fanny Mercer, a luckless visitor to Lakeland who, in 1887, while out walking, tripped over her long walking pole and fell to her death.

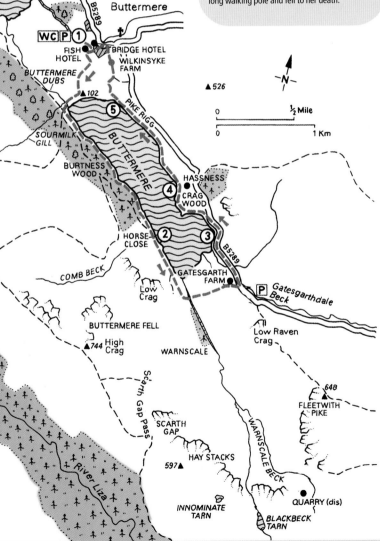

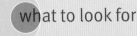

Bridge Hotel

Spend a weekend at this 18th-century former coaching inn and enjoy its stunning location in an area of outstanding natural beauty between Buttermere and Crummock Water. You can round off spectacular walks with afternoon tea, excellent ales or a hearty meal. On a fine day there can be fierce competition for tables in the small garden, a sheltered suntrap surrounded by climbing roses, with jaw-dropping views to High Crag, High Stile and Red Pike. What better place to enjoy a pint of Old Faithful from the (Cumbrian) Tirril Brewery? If the seats are all taken or the weather forces you indoors, there are two bar areas, one with oak beams, a flagstone floor and traditional Lakeland character. There's also a plush lounge with deep sofas and an open fire. Individually designed bedrooms.

Food
Main courses include Cumberland hotpot, home-made steak and kidney pie, vegetable stirfry, and deep-fried haddock in crisp beer batter. For smaller appetites there's a good selection of salads, sandwiches and toasties. Separate five-course dinner menu in the restaurant.

Family facilities
Children are welcome in the eating area of the bar; children's menu.

Alternative refreshment stops
There is a café at Buttermere and, like the Bridge Hotel, the Fish Inn serves teas, coffee, snacks and bar meals throughout the day. Wilkinsyke Farm does home-made ice cream and there's often a tea-wagon at Gatescarth.

☛ Where to go from here
Buttermere's attractive church of 1841 is in a superb position on a rocky knoll. It is tiny, with a bellcote and a lower chancel. From it there is a lovely view of the valley and the high fells on the south side, all the way to Hay Stacks.

about the pub

Bridge Hotel

Buttermere
Cumbria CA13 9UZ
Tel 017687 70252
www.bridge-hotel.com

DIRECTIONS: in the centre of Buttermere village

PARKING: 26

OPEN: daily, all day

FOOD: daily, all day (restaurant evenings only)

BREWERY/COMPANY: free house

REAL ALE: Black Sheep Bitter, Theakston Old Peculier, Tirril Old Faithful

DOGS: welcome in garden only

ROOMS: 21 en suite

From Keswick to Threlkeld

Visitors aboard a launch on Derwent Water

1h30 · **9 MILES** · **14.5 KM** · **LEVEL 123**

SHORTER ALTERNATIVE ROUTE

1h00 · **8 MILES** · **12.9 KM** · **LEVEL 123**

CYCLE

MAP: OS Explorer OL 4 The English Lakes (NW) and OL 5 The English Lakes (NE)

START/FINISH: Keswick Leisure Centre; grid ref: NY 269238

TRAILS/TRACKS: old railway track, short section of cycle track beside main road, minor road; optional return on minor roads with short section of busy A road (or walk down pavement alongside)

LANDSCAPE: woodland and river valley; open farmland with views to fells on return via stone circle

PUBLIC TOILETS: Keswick

TOURIST INFORMATION: Keswick, tel 017687 72645

CYCLE HIRE: Keswick Mountain Bikes, Keswick, tel 017687 75202

THE PUB: Horse & Farrier Inn, Threlkeld, see Point **3** on route

ⓘ Railway path section suitable for all ages. If continuing into Threlkeld, suitability: children 6+; if returning via stone circle, suitability: children 10+

Getting to the start
Follow the A66 to a roundabout north west of Keswick. Take the A5271 towards the town. After 300yds (274m) turn left , signposted 'Leisure Pool' and roadside parking.

Why do this cycle ride?
This route crosses and recrosses the river, running through woodland. Return the same way take the climb to Castlerigg Stone Circle.

Researched and written by: Jon Sparks

Keswick CUMBRIA

A linear ride along an old railway, with an optional return via Lakeland's greatest ancient site.

Castlerigg Stone Circle in winter

The Greta Valley
The railway to Keswick was completed in 1864, having taken just 18 months to build, at a total cost of £267,000 for 31 miles (50km), and with 135 bridges. Goods traffic declined quite early in its life. Passenger numbers peaked in 1913 at 182,000, but never really recovered after World War One, though the line struggled on until it finally closed in 1972.

The railway route passes the bobbin mill site at Low Briery. The Lake District once produced half of all the wooden bobbins used by the world's textile industry, and Low Briery alone exported 40 million of these every year.

Whether you cycle there, drive there or take the bus, Castlerigg Stone Circle is a 'must-see' site. It may not be the most impressive such circle in Britain, but it's hard to think of one that has a finer location. Best of all, come early in the morning or late in the evening when there are few others around and your imagination can have free rein. It was probably built around 3000 BC, and no one today knows exactly what it was for, although significant astronomical alignments have been identified.

the ride

1 Ride down towards the **Leisure Centre** and bear left, signed Keswick Railway Footpath, past the former railway station, now a smart hotel. The old trackbed leads on to a bridge over the river and then over the **A5271**. Pass a housing estate on the left, then climb – more steeply than you'd expect from a railway track (the route here was disrupted by the construction of the A66 bypass and bridge). There's a **National Cycle Network/C2C sign** just before the route goes under **Greta Bridge**. At the end of an unusual elevated boardwalk section, look right and you can just see the top of a stone arch, once the mouth of a tunnel, indicating the original line of the railway. Continue with views of the river then past the caravans of **Low Briery**. Go under a bridge and pass an information board about the former **bobbin mill**.

2 Continue across a bridge over the **River Greta**, seemingly a simple flat span but actually supported by an inverted ironwork arch. There's a second, similar bridge, and then a third with its arch 'right side up'. Just

277

CYCLE

A stunning view across Derwent Water

before the fourth bridge an **old railway hut** is now a shelter and information point. The bridge overlooks the junction of the river with **Glenderaterra Beck**. Cross another inverted bridge, then go through a short **tunnel** (no need for lights). There's another bridge, another information shelter and then a cutting. Cross another bridge and make a short climb, where the original line of the railway has again been obliterated by the **A66**. Emerge alongside the busy road on a separate cycle track. After about 200yds (183m) swing left on the minor road to **Threlkeld**, and follow it into the village, past the church, to the **Horse and Farrier**.

3 Retrace the route as far as the last bridge you crossed, and go over. (You can, of course, return all the way along the railway track from this point.)

4 About 30yds (27m) past the bridge, turn sharp left through a small gate. A steep

drop down and a bumpy path take you under the A66 and soon lead out to a road. Turn right and climb, with good views of **St John's in the Vale** and **Helvellyn**. Make a sweeping descent and turn left just before it levels out.

5 Swing round through a little valley, then turn left again and climb steadily, now looking down the **Naddle Valley**. The climb is quite long, levelling out just as the **stone circle** appears in a field on the left. Almost at once the road sweeps down again. Drop down to a T-junction on the outskirts of **Keswick**.

6 Families may feel safer walking the next short section. Follow the road left to another T-junction, then turn right down the hill. Round the first bend and just before a **bridge** with slate parapets go left round a barrier onto a gravel path leading down onto the **railway track** and so back to the start.

Horse & Farrier Inn

For over 300 years this stone inn has stood in an idyllic position below Blencathra. Ever popular with fell walkers, it provides imaginative home cooking, and real ales from the host brewer, Jennings. It has recently been refurbished, but original features have been retained and restored to their former glory, including slate floors, some fine panelling and oak beams. Hunting prints hang on the walls and warming log fires burn in the grate to create a cosy, welcoming atmosphere. It is noted locally for imaginative, rather restauranty food, although there is plenty of space for drinkers, and walkers are welcome in the bar. Garden seating has views up to the scarred face of Blencathra.

Food

An adventurous menu offers plenty of choice including fresh fish and local produce. Starters like stir-fried king prawns and giant mussels with green chillies, and smoked haddock and sea trout terrine might precede fillet of red mullet with egg noodles and a Thai green curry sauce or pan-fried venison steak in a juniper marinade. Additional lunchtime fare includes cold and hot open sandwiches, and seasonal salads.

Family facilities

Children are welcome in the bars and overnight. 'Lakeside Larry's' menu offers a standard selection of children's meals, and various puzzles and drawings to colour in.

Alternative refreshment stops

Excellent choice of pubs, cafés and restaurants in Keswick and the Salutation pub in Threlkeld.

☛ Where to go from here

The Cars of the Stars Motor Museum in Keswick houses an unusual collection of cars from film and TV, including Chitty Chitty Bang Bang, the Batmobile and the James Bond cars. North of Keswick on the A591 is Mirehouse, a 17th-century house in a spectacular lakeside setting, near where Tennyson wrote much of *Morte d'Arthur*.

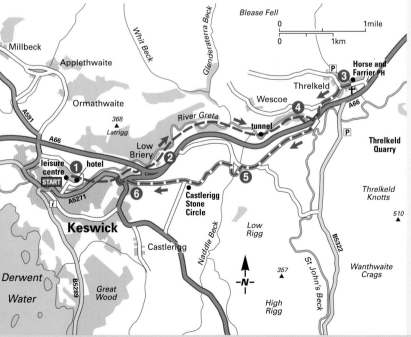

Millbeck
Applethwaite
Ormathwaite
Whit Beck
Glenderaterra Beck
Blease Fell

0 —— 1mile
0 —— 1km

P Horse and Farrier PH
3
Threlkeld
Wescoe
A66
368 Latrigg
River Greta
tunnel
4
P
Threlkeld Quarry
Low Briery
2
5
A591
A66
leisure centre hotel
1
START
A5271
6
Castlerigg Stone Circle
Keswick
Castlerigg
Naddle Beck
Low Rigg
Threlkeld Knotts
510 ▲
B5322
B5289
Great Wood
High Rigg
St John's Beck
Wanthwaite Crags
357 ▲
–N–
Derwent Water

about the pub

Horse & Farrier Inn
Threlkeld, Keswick
Cumbria CA12 4SQ
Tel 01687 79688
www.horseandfarrier.com

DIRECTIONS: on the village main street, east of the church

PARKING: 60

OPEN: daily, all day

FOOD: daily, all day in summer

BREWERY/COMPANY: Jennings Brewery

REAL ALE: Jennings Bitter, Cocker Hoop and Sneck Lifter, guest beer

ROOMS: 9 en suite

did you know?

Although the name given on the map to the steeply wooded hill rising directly above Pooley Bridge is Dunmallard, it is known locally as Dunmallet. This is a striking defensive site, which looks directly down on the river crossing at Pooley Bridge. Unseen from below, and now lost in a thick canopy of trees, the top is adorned by the earthworks of a hill fort dating from the Iron Age.

Cruising across Ullswater

Across Heughscar Hill from Pooley Bridge

This walk leads to views over the second largest lake in the region, crosses a Roman road and takes in prehistoric sites.

Romans and ancients

The walk takes in a short section of the High Street, a Roman road. This leads directly to the Cockpit stone circle which, although not a circle of upright standing stones, is quite distinct and unmistakable. Two concentric stone circles, some standing, some fallen, contain a circular bank of earth and stones up to 3ft (1m) high. It has an internal radius of around 85ft (26m) and, as it is thought to be of Bronze Age origin, c2000 BC, it predates the Roman road. In more recent times, it was used as an arena for cockfighting, a once-popular sport that was outlawed in 1849.

Extending south east from here is desolate Moor Divock where many prehistoric burial mounds and cairns are hidden in the landscape of coarse hill grass, bracken, heather and bog. A mound known as White Raise, presumably because of the white quartz which marks its rocks, was partially excavated in the 19th century. A crouched skeleton was revealed in one of its cists (a coffin or burial chamber of stone or wood). Near by, the Cop Stone, a gnarled standing stone some 5ft (1.6m) high, tops a low hill and provides a direction indicator in this otherwise rather featureless landscape. Local sports were held by this stone up until 1800, and tradition claims that an avenue of standing stones known as the Shap Avenue once

led to it. Two further Bronze Age stone circles close by, referred to as Moor Divock 4 and Moor Divock 5, have been partially excavated to reveal urns and ashes.

the walk

1 From the bridge crossing the **River Eamont** follow the main street **(B5320)** through the centre of Pooley Bridge. Pass **The Sun Inn** and the **church**, then turn right to follow the pavement along the Howtown road.

2 At the junction continue over the crossroads. The road (**Roe Head Lane**) rises pleasantly through trees, ending at an unsurfaced track beneath **Roehead**. A gate and kissing gate lead out on to the open moor.

3 Climb the broad track beyond the gate. Just before it levels out, at a **cairn**, a recently resurfaced track bears off to the right.

A wintery view over Ullswater from Hallin Fell

4 Follow the clear track, on the line of the **High Street** Roman road, to reach an ancient, low circular wall of earth and stone. This is **the Cockpit**, the largest of the many prehistoric antiquities found on **Moor Divock**.

5 Turn left on another reconstructed track, curving to the left at a marshy dip. Pass some shallow shake holes (sinkholes) before crossing the original track at **Ketley Gate** (there's no actual gate here). A little to the right is **White Raise** burial cairn. Follow the track ahead towards a walled wood high on the hillside. As the track begins to level, bear left to the top corner of the wood. Turn left on a grassy track and then bear right on a narrower track parting the bracken, to the cairn on the highest point of **Heughscar Hill**. This is in a commanding position offering extensive views.

2h00   **4.5 MILES**   **7.2 KM**   **LEVEL 123**

WALK

MAP: OS Explorer OL 5 The English Lakes (NE)

START/FINISH: pay-and-display car parks either side of the bridge, Pooley Bridge; grid ref: NY 470244

PATHS: surfaced roads, stony tracks, grassy tracks and hillside

LANDSCAPE: village, dale and open fell

PUBLIC TOILETS: centre of Pooley Bridge

TOURIST INFORMATION: Pooley Bridge, tel 017684 86530

THE PUB: The Sun Inn, Pooley Bridge, see Point **1** on route

❶ Navigation can be tricky on upper reaches of Heughscar Hill in poor visibility. Suitability: children 6+

Getting to the start

Pooley Bridge lies at the top of Ullswater. From the M6, junction 40, head west on the A66 for 1 mile (1.6km). Turn left on the A592 for 3.5 miles (5.7km), then turn left on the B5320 into the village. There are car parks both before and after the bridge.

Researched and written by:
Bill Birkett, Jon Sparks

did you know?

Cumbria is home to 10 per cent of England's sheep, and the white-faced Herdwick is the distinctive Cumbrian breed that produces a hardy wool used in carpets. The fleece is black when young, turning grey as the sheep matures.

The Sun Inn

The 18th-century Sun Inn presents a classic Lakeland pub frontage, white with black trim, and brightened with plenty of colourful hanging baskets in summer. The interior retains much of its original character, with some fine wood panelling, open log fires, and low-beamed ceilings throughout the rambling and intimate bars and dining room. Real ales are from the Jennings Brewery in Cockermouth – relax by the crackling log fire and sup a pint of the strong and dark Sneck Lifter after walking this route on a bracing winter's day.

Food

At lunchtime tuck into a range of sandwiches, filled jacket potatoes and traditional pub snacks. For something more substantial, order braised lamb Jennings, home-made chilli, vegetable Kiev, or the hearty fellman's salad.

Family facilities

The welcome and provision for families is good, with children allowed inside. Smaller portions of certain main dishes are available and there are baby-changing facilities in the toilets. The large garden is backed by mature trees with great views over fields to the surrounding fells.

Alternative refreshment stops

Numerous cafés and inns in the village of Pooley Bridge cater for a wide range of tastes.

☛ Where to go from here

Take a boat trip on Ullswater. Two beautifully preserved 19th-century boats, *Lady of the Lake* and *Raven*, run regular trips from the jetty at Pooley Bridge, stopping at the landing stages at Howtown and Glenridding.

about the pub

The Sun Inn
Pooley Bridge, Penrith
Cumbria CA10 2NN
Tel 017684 86205
www.suninnpooleybridge.co.uk

DIRECTIONS: in the village centre, diagonally opposite the church

PARKING: 50

OPEN: daily, all day

FOOD: daily

BREWERY/COMPANY: Jennings Brewery

REAL ALE: Jennings Bitter, Cumberland Ale and Sneck Lifter

DOGS: welcome inside

ROOMS: 9 en suite

what to look for

The High Street Roman road is followed for two short sections of this walk. In its full length, the road traverses the eastern Lakeland fells, exceeding a height of 2,500ft (762m) in several places. It stretches from the Troutbeck Valley near Ambleside to Brougham by the River Eamont, where it intercepts the main south east/north west Roman arterial road. Even today, though heavily eroded in places, it remains a remarkable testament to the ambition of Roman engineering.

6 Bear right on a broad green track, to pass the broken limestone crag of **Heugh Scar** below to the left. At the end of the scar a faint path descends the steep hillside to the well-worn **High Street**. Turn left on this for 300yds (274m), then bear right on a green track towards the corner of a stone wall at the top of a line of trees. Just before reaching this, pass a small quarry and the remains of a lime kiln. From the wall corner descend steeply alongside the wall until the track of the outward leg comes into view. Bear left to regain it and turn right. Retrace the outward route back to **Pooley Bridge**.

while you're there

Hutton-in-the-Forest 6 miles (9.6km) northwest of Penrith is a beautiful house set in woods that were once part of the medieval forest of Inglewood. The house consists of a 14th-century pele-tower with later additions, and contains a fine collection of furniture, portraits, tapestries and china, a 17th-century gallery and cupid staircase. The walled garden has a large collection of herbaceous plants, topiary terraces and a woodland walk with impressive specimen trees.

Top left: Hutton-in-the-Forest

The Eden Valley from Armathwaite

Discover an unsung but lovely corner, with exciting off-road options.

The Eden Valley

The route offers great views of both the Lake District and the Pennines, the latter being particularly well seen on the final descent. The highest peak is Cross Fell. At 2,930ft (893m) it is the highest peak in the Pennines and indeed the highest in England outside the Lake District, but is merely part of a massive mountain wall that hems in the Eden Valley to the east. It has a major influence on local weather and has its very own wind, the notorious Helm wind, possibly so called because it is accompanied by a helmet-like cap of cloud on the ridge.

The railway line which is crossed several times on the right – at track level if you take the first off-road option – is the Settle to Carlisle line, one of Britain's most scenic rail routes. It runs for 72 miles (116km) between Settle in North Yorkshire and Carlisle. Completed in 1876, the line was a major engineering challenge, with 20 viaducts and 14 tunnels. Its highest point is at Ais Gill summit, 1,169ft (356m) above sea level, and its most famous feature is probably the great Ribblehead viaduct, a few miles further south. It was the expense of restoring this, as well as general maintenance of the route, that led to a threat of closure in the 1990s, but a vigorous public campaign and the promotion of the line as a tourist attraction ensured its survival.

Top right: Railway viaduct near Armathwaite
Right: A cyclist using an unmanned crossing over the Settle to Carlisle rail line

the ride

1 Head north through the village and past the church, ignoring all turnings to right and left. Continue along this lane, with a few minor undulations before a dip alongside a railway viaduct. Now climb, in two stages, to the level crossing at **Lowhouse Crossing**. Bump across the line and continue less steeply to a junction near **Froddle Crook**. The old, rusty signpost has lost one arm.

2 For the shorter ride, turn left here and follow the lane beside **High Stand Plantation**, with fine views, to the crossroads at **Blackmoss Pool**. Go straight across to rejoin the longer route. For the longer route, go straight ahead at Froddle Crook for 1.5 miles (2.4km) to a turning on the left signed to Cotehill.

3 To stay on tarmac turn left here and follow the road for 1 mile (1.6km) to the crossroads in **Cotehill village**, then turn left. For the off-road alternative, continue straight ahead to a bridge over the railway

and then past a small **wood** on the left. At the end of the wood follow a bridleway sign left through a gate and down a short track. Where this bends left into a farmyard go straight ahead, through an awkward gate, and follow field edges, with no real track but no great difficulty unless the grass is high. At the bottom of the second field, just below the railway line, bear right on a short track to a gate and out onto the tracks. Cross with care – there is good visibility both ways. Go through the gate on the other side and straight out along a green track, rounding a bend to reach a clearer track. Follow this more easily, to emerge onto a road. Turn left for a short climb into **Cotehill**. Be alert where the road squeezes between two houses. At a crossroads, go straight across to rejoin the road alternative.

4 Carry straight on, signed to Armathwaite. Climb to **Stand End**, then on beside **High Stand Plantation** to the crossroads at **Blackmoss Pool** (more marsh than open water).

5 Turn right, signed to Aiketgate and Low Hesket. The tree-lined lane runs dead straight, first down, then up. A view of the fells opens up as the road dips to a T-junction. Turn left, signed to Nunclose and Armathwaite, and make a short climb into the hamlet of **Aiketgate**. A fork in the road, opposite the phone box, offers another off-road option.

6 To stay on tarmac, keep right here, and then bear left at the next fork. The lane begins a fine sweeping descent and the off-road alternative rejoins halfway down,

CYCLE

1h30	10 MILES	16.1 KM	LEVEL 1 2 3

LONGER ROUTE (OFF ROAD)

2h00	11 MILES	17.7 KM	LEVEL 1 2 3

SHORTER ALTERNATIVE ROUTE

1h00	6.5 MILES	10.4 KM	LEVEL 1 2 3

MAP: OS Explorer OL5 The English Lakes (NE) and OL315 Carlisle

START/FINISH: Armathwaite village; grid ref: NY 504461

TRAILS/TRACKS: lanes, with two optional off-road sections

LANDSCAPE: rolling farmland, woodland and river valley, views to distant fells

PUBLIC TOILETS: none on route

TOURIST INFORMATION: Carlisle, tel 01228 625600

CYCLE HIRE: Scotby Cycles, Carlisle, tel 01228 546931

THE PUB: The Duke's Head, Armathwaite

❗ Crosses rail tracks twice. The shorter road route is suitable for children 8+; the longer loop is for children 10+. Two optional off-road sections: the first is suitable for most abilities, the second is rougher and steeper, for experienced children 12+ only, mountain bike recommended.

How to get to the start

Armathwaite east of Low Heskett and High Heskett, off the A6. There is no car park, so park considerately on verges.

Why do this cycle ride?

One of the unsung jewels of England, the Eden Valley retains a peaceful atmosphere that can be missing in the Lake District.

Researched and written by: Jon Sparks

279

CYCLE

while you're there

Visit the Eden Valley Woollen Mill in Armathwaite where you will find two restored 19th-century looms manufacturing woven products from jackets and skirts to ties and scarves. There is also a shop with knitwear and yarns for sale.

Top left: Tortoiseshell butterfly

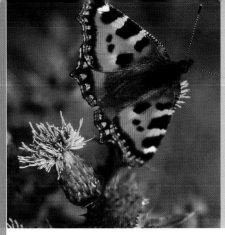

at **Windy Nook**. For the off-road adventure, take the left fork at Point 6. The tarmac lane leads into a stonier track, climbing steeply at first. The gradient eases, but the track continues stony all the way to the crest. The descent ahead is on a much greener track. This isn't difficult, just a little bumpy, but in summer the vegetation makes it hard to see where your wheels are going. Go through a gate and continue downhill, gradually curving right. The undergrowth

diminishes as the descent steepens. The final 100yds (91m) before the road are steep and tricky, with large stones and no soft landings: consider walking here. Rejoin the road at **Windy Nook** and turn left.

Continue on this road past the turning for Nunclose. The road swings round towards another railway viaduct. Keep left at another junction, go under the railway, and follow the road back into **Armathwaite**.

The Duke's Head

A long-standing favourite in the area, the comfortable, stone-built Duke's Head stays firmly traditional. Its fishing connections are well documented in the Last Cast Lounge, from where it's only a few paces into a glorious garden with flower beds and beech trees disappearing down the banks of the River Eden below. Fishing can be arranged for guests, who come here in search of the finest trout and salmon in the north of England. Expect stone walls, open log fires, oak tables and settles in the civilised lounge bar, a lively locals' bar dispensing tip-top Jennings bitter, and simply furnished bedrooms. The inn's bold claim to be the 'home of probably the best roast duck in Cumbria' is one which many will feel obliged to put to the test. Cyclists exploring the valley are made very welcome, and the pub even has some bikes for hire.

Food

Fresh local produce features on the wide-ranging menu. If you don't fancy roast duck, try hot potted Solway shrimps, venison steak with red wine, mushroom and redcurrant sauce, locally smoked salmon or prime steaks from a local farm. Or there are sandwiches and a 3-cheese platter.

about the pub

The Duke's Head
Armathwaite, Carlisle
Cumbria CA4 9PB
Tel 016974 72226

DIRECTIONS: From the A6 take the Armathwaite turning

PARKING: 40

OPEN: daily, all day

FOOD: daily

BREWERY/COMPANY: Punch Taverns

REAL ALE: Jennings Cumberland Ale, guest beers

ROOMS: 5 bedrooms (3 en suite)

Family facilities

Small portions from the main menu are available to children, who are welcome inside the pub. It's a super garden for summer alfresco eating and drinking, but beware the river.

Alternative refreshment stops

None on route but you'll also find the Fox and Pheasant by the river in Armathwaite.

☛ Where to go from here

Long Meg and Her Daughters is a Bronze Age stone circle at Little Salkeld, south of Kirkoswald (open access).

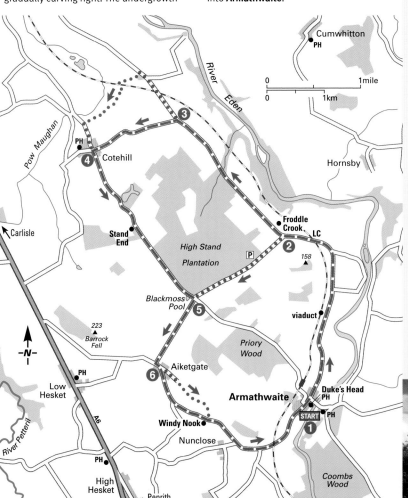

while you're there

You'll find the Augustinian priory at Lanercost, just 2 miles (3.2km) northeast of Brampton, close to Hadrian's Wall. Set in a delightful wooded valley, much of it is in ruins, although the nave of the church survives and is today the local parish church.

The ruins of monastic quarters at Lanercost Priory

Castle Carrock lime kilns

Through a once-industrial landscape, now peaceful and green.

Castle Carrock

The landscape around Castle Carrock has undergone many changes. Perhaps the most obvious is the reservoir, seen from above in the middle stages and at closer quarters near the end of the walk. This was completed in 1906 to provide water for the growing city of Carlisle. An army of workers was employed in the excavation and construction, and a quarry on the hillside provided stone for the dam. The local population increased by a factor of five during this period and no fewer than 12 pubs were apparently needed to quench the workers' thirsts. As you follow the route higher up the hills, the route passes the overgrown remains of several quarries.

It is perhaps less obvious that coal was also mined on these hillsides. But the most obvious sign of industrial activity is the succession of lime kilns straggling along the hillside, all at a similar level. Lime (calcium oxide) has long been valuable both as a major component of mortar (the Romans used lime mortar in Hadrian's Wall) and as a soil improver. Lime was produced by burning limestone (which is basically calcium carbonate). Originally the crushed limestone was mixed with wood, later with coal.

The lime kilns on this walk are in varying states of repair but common design features can be seen in all of them. Lime kilns were almost always built into a steep slope, allowing horses to bring the stone and fuel to the top of the kiln, from which the raw ingredients were fed in. The finest example

is seen between Points 3 and 4, where the walk crosses Totter Gill. This is an unusual double kiln in a good state of preservation.

the walk

1 Continue down past the **church** and then turn right past the **school**, on to a footpath signposted 'Garth Head'. Cross a bridge into a field, ascend left of a hedge and where it ends maintain direction through some trees. Bear slightly left on rising ground to a gate. Go up the small rise beyond, then keep the hedge on your right, up to a stile almost hidden behind a bush.

2 Bear slightly left up the bank, then cross the field to a gate in the top corner. Follow the track up through **Garth Marr** farmyard. It swings right and then continues straight on up, past **Garth Head** farmyard, and out to a lane.

3 Go left for 20yds (18m), then turn right (signposted '**Brackenthwaite**'). Follow the track ahead to a stile and continue on a more defined track, over a rise to a sudden view of the Lakeland fells. Keep following the wall down into the corner and go left through a gateway. Follow a vague track uphill, with a **wall** now on your right. Keep following this

wall to the crest of a rise, then descend a more obvious track ahead. Cross a small stream (**Totter Gill**), with a fine double lime kiln up on the left, and continue along the hillside above the wall until the track skirts a fenced-off bog. Cross a stile just beyond, go ahead to reach drier ground, then bear right and down to find a **fingerpost**.

4 Turn left and up to an obvious gate. Turn right along a narrow path above the **fence** (beware – the fence may be electrified). Pass another lime kiln on the left. Soon the path has to skirt a boggy area: keep to the base of the steeper slope for the best footing. Cross a beck and pass another lime kiln. Continue in the same vein, following a fence and then a wall on the right. Cross the wall at a stile but keep alongside it until the track bears right to pass directly in front of another **lime kiln** with trees growing out of it.

5 Follow the track down, through a gap in a wall, and then pass just left of a low tin-roofed structure – note the oven door, which suggests this is the remains

Above: Looking towards the Lake District from above Tottergill
Right: The view above Brackenthwaite with a lime kiln to the left

---

280

WALK

| 2h00 | 4.5 MILES | 7.2 KM | LEVEL 123 |

MAP: OS Explorer 315 Carlisle

START/FINISH: on street between parish church and Watson Institute, Castle Carrock; grid ref: NY 543553

PATHS: field paths, farm tracks, metalled lanes, 7 stiles

LANDSCAPE: fields, moorland with extensive views, waterside and woodland

PUBLIC TOILETS: the nearest are at Talkin Tarn

TOURIST INFORMATION: Brampton, tel 016977 3433

THE PUB: Weary Sportsman, Castle Carrock

⚠ Suitability: children 7+

Getting to the start

Castle Carrock is a small village on the B6413, about 4 miles (6.4km) south of Brampton. Go to the top of the main street, by the Weary Sportsman pub, then off the main road, and shortly left into a narrow road which runs down past the church. Park here.

Researched and written by:
Chris Bagshaw, Jon Sparks

Brampton, one of Cumbria's many attractive market towns (chartered since 1252), is well worth a visit. Wednesday is market day when the cobbled square around the Moot Hall is particularly lively. Pop into the hall and you'll find the tourist information centre with lots of suggestions on where to go and what to do. Look out for St Martin's Church which has fine stained-glass windows designed by Edward Burne-Jones and made by William Morris.

of a furnace. Continue down a walled track to a tarmac lane by the large farm of **Brackenthwaite**. Turn right, and go through several gates to a detached **barn**. Go right again, through a gate and up the field for 20yds (18m) to a **waymark** and boulder. Turn left and then follow a straight course through successive gates to a tarmac lane, just past a green shed.

6 Turn left. Follow the lane for 0.5 mile (800m) to an obvious track on the right, signed 'Tottergill'. Go a few paces further to a footpath sign and go right, soon joining the surfaced track alongside the **reservoir**. Half-way along, it becomes grassy. Pass the

what to look for

Half-way along the reservoir, the surfaced track swings away to Tottergill. Look up towards the farm and you should see an exceptionally large oak tree. Known as the Champion Oak of Cumbria, its girth has been measured at 24 feet 9 inches (approximately 7.5m). Its age is less certain but may be as much as 800 years.

dam and continue through woods to a road. Turn left, back into Castle Carrock.

Weary Sportsman

about the pub

Weary Sportsman
Castle Carrock, Brampton
Cumbria CA8 9LU
Tel 01228 670230
www.theweary.com

DIRECTIONS:	in the centre of the village
PARKING:	4
OPEN:	daily, closed Monday lunchtime
FOOD:	daily
BREWERY/COMPANY:	free house
REAL ALE:	bottled Jennings Cumberland Ale and Sneck Lifter only
DOGS:	welcome in the garden only
ROOMS:	5 en suite

From the outside the Weary Sportsman looks like a typical Cumbrian village pub. But step inside and you're in for a big surprise. If you read the sign carefully you might get a clue, as it says 'Bar and Brasserie with Rooms', but you're still likely to be surprised by the striking contemporary décor that greets you. It's what you might expect in a converted warehouse in Leeds or Manchester, not an out-of-the-way Cumbrian village. But clearly people do go out of their way to come here. The main attraction is the menu, which is as contemporary and stylish as the surroundings. Beer lovers will be disappointed that there is no real ale, although you can get Jennings Cumberland Ale or Sneck Lifter in bottled

form, and traditional pub enthusiasts will still find original beams in the bar. Walkers and families are made very welcome, and there's a small sheltered patio for summer eating and drinking.

Food

The wide-ranging menu offers a cosmopolitan choice, taking in light snacks (sandwiches, baguettes and salads) and more imaginative dishes like lamb fillet (cooked to order) with wild mushroom charlotte, grape chutney and red wine jus, pheasant breast on lemon and thyme potato rosti with pepper sauce, or wild mushroom stroganoff.

Family facilities

There is no problem with children venturing into the bar. Although there is no special children's menu, small portions are available from the main menu.

Alternative refreshment stops

In Brampton, the Abbey Bridge Inn welcomes walkers, both it and the Blacksmiths Arms welcome children.

☛ Where to go from here

Take a short walk through Gelt Woods, south west of Brampton, where ancient woodland has survived in a rocky gorge above the Gelt ('mad') river. The woodland is part of an RSPB nature reserve and also the home of the Written Rock of Gelt, a vertical sandstone face bearing an inscription believed to have been carved by a Roman legionary in the 3rd century AD.

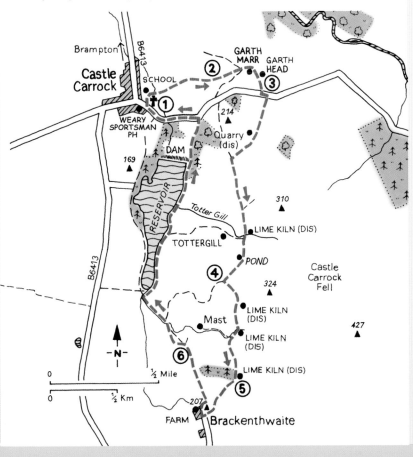

while you're there

North of Garrigill is the pretty town of Alston which has a reputation for local delicacies such as cheese and mustard. The town grew up around the lead-mining industry on Alston Moor, and although that industry is long gone, visitors can take an underground trip through the Nenthead Mines, last worked for lead in 1915. The mines are part of the Nenthead Mines Heritage Centre, 5 miles (8km) east of Alston. This hands-on centre contains exhibitions and displays on geology, local wildlife and social history.

Grey wagtail
(Motacilla cinerea)

From Garrigill to Ashgill Force

A broad valley hides exciting waterfalls and ravines.

Garrigill

As you approach the village, with the long ascent over Hartside, on one of the highest main roads in the country, you cross the main watershed of England. Below is the valley of the South Tyne, its waters feeding not west to the Irish Sea but east to the North Sea. The landscape is different from the Lake District, the hills big, bare and simple in their outlines.

It might appear that this landscape has changed little for centuries. The truth is, of course, that few English landscapes are static, and this is no exception. Today's generally pastoral scene conceals the scars of an industrial past. Garrigill's population in the mid-19th century was five or six times what it is today. Two main trends lie behind this decline, one being that fewer people work on the land today, while the second factor

View across Garrigill and the South Tyne Valley

has been the disappearance of the once-dominant lead-mining industry. Mining developed rapidly from the mid-18th century onwards, largely under the control of the Quaker-owned London Lead Mining Company, which built houses, schools and reading rooms for its workers and their families. Garrigill was virtually a 'company town'. Sharp eyes will be able to spot traces of this industry on the upper slopes. Look out, in particular, for sharp V-shaped valleys cut into the moorland, many of which are artificial. Known as hushes, they were created by damming a stream and then allowing the water to escape in a flash flood. This was a relatively quick and easy way of stripping off the topsoil to expose the rocks beneath.

the walk

1 Walk down the road in front of the **post office** and the **George & Dragon Inn** (signposted 'Alston, Nenthead') to a bridge high above the river **South Tyne**. The road bends left but a track continues straight ahead. Follow this track, very steep at first, to reach a tarmac lane at a bend.

2 Turn right immediately, signed to **Pasture Houses**, go through a gate and straight across a field. Cross a stile and continue to a gate below some new and restored buildings, and then to a stile. Bear right, descending slightly, towards a **farm** and trees. Go through a gate in the field corner and then along the left (upper) side of the **barn**. Cross the yard diagonally to a track which leads out to a road.

1h30 | 3 MILES | 4.8 KM | LEVEL 1 2 3

MAP: OS Explorer OL31 North Pennines

START/FINISH: parking on green in front of post office, Garrigill; grid ref: NY 7444150

PATHS: field paths, tracks and a quiet lane, 17 stiles

LANDSCAPE: open fields, wooded river valley with cascades and waterfalls

PUBLIC TOILETS: beside village hall, just before bridge at start of walk

TOURIST INFORMATION: Alston Moor, tel 01434 382244

THE PUB: George & Dragon Inn, Garrigill, see Point 1 on route

! Path runs above steep drops to river. Suitability: children 7+

Getting to the start

Garrigill lies south east of the village of Alston, which is at the junction of the A686 and the A689, due south of Haltwhistle. From Alston take the B6277 and turn off right. In Garrigill, park considerately around the village green.

Researched and written by:
Chris Bagshaw, Jon Sparks

while you're there

Running along the beautiful South Tyne valley, the narrow-gauge South Tynedale Railway follows the route of the former Alston to Haltwhistle branch. At present the line runs between Alston and Kirkhaugh.

Steam locomotive Helen Kathryn at Alston station

3 Cross directly to a stile. Follow the wall below gardens on the left, then continue straight ahead to a stile. Keep straight ahead and level to another stile, then aim for another **farm** ahead. Go left of the first building and into the yard, then go left and right between the houses to a stile where the lane bends left again. Cross a short field and emerge onto a track. Cross this, and the **paddock** beyond, to a stile. Turn right, along the back of a house and through a gateway into a field.

4 Turn left and follow a green track, initially parallel to the wall and then descending to a **footbridge** and four-way fingerpost.

5 Don't cross the bridge but turn left (signposted 'Ashgill Force') and follow a path left of **Ashgill Beck**. Follow this, passing some small cataracts, to a footbridge with the main falls visible ahead. Cross the bridge and continue to the **falls**, passing **old mine workings** on the right. It's possible to walk right behind the falls, but be careful as the surface is loose, and often wet and slippery too.

6 Retrace your steps, crossing the first footbridge, to the lower footbridge by the four-way **fingerpost**. Now continue downhill, still following **Ashgill Beck**.

7 Where Ashgill Beck meets the River South Tyne, cross a stile on to the riverside path (**South Tyne Trail** waymarks). Follow the path, paved with flagstones in places, above a wooded gorge-like section. Where the river curves away to the left, it's possible to continue straight ahead across a rushy field. Go past a bridge (to **Mid Crossgill**) and continue along the river, under tall pines (watch for red squirrels here), to reach another four-way fingerpost.

Looking from behind Ashgill Force waterfall with the river running down the valley

8 Turn left across the **bridge**; walk up the track to a gate opposite **Low Crossgill** farm. Turn right along the road into **Garrigill**.

what to look for

Ashgill Force waterfall is the most striking sight on the walk. The stream has carved itself a significant gorge. A harder band of limestone has resisted its efforts while the softer shales below have been cut back, creating an overhang which allows you to walk right behind the fall, which is approximately 50ft (15m) high. There are several smaller but still lovely cascades lower down the course of the beck before it joins the South Tyne.

George & Dragon Inn

The 17th-century George & Dragon Inn occupies a unique position, where the best-known of Britain's long-distance walks, the Pennine Way, crosses perhaps its most popular major cycle route, the C2C. Needless to say, walkers and cyclists are big business here, and the owners know exactly what their priorities are. On bleak Pennine days, getting warm and dry is often the first priority and a blazing fire in the homely, stone-flagged bar helps. There's also an attractive stone and panelled dining room and four new bedrooms. Robust appetites and hearty thirsts are well looked after, the latter with foaming pints of Black Sheep or local micro-brewery ales. The pub is also a mini information centre with maps, leaflets and advice all on hand.

Food

The menu concentrates on traditional pub favourites, done well: the Cumberland sausage is from a butcher in nearby Alston, the game pie home-made. Non-carnivores are recommended to try the vegetarian moussaka. Snacks include sandwiches, filled jacket potatoes and a giant Yorkshire pudding filled with steak and gravy.

Family facilities

Children are welcome in the lounge and dining room until 9.30pm. In summer there's alfresco seating on the village green.

☛ Where to go from here

Visit Alston, England's highest market town, 1,000 feet (305m) above sea level, with steep cobbled streets and many 17th-century buildings. It's also home to the narrow-gauge South Tynedale

about the pub

George & Dragon Inn
Garrigill, Alston
Cumbria CA9 3DS
Tel 01434 381293
www.garrigill-pub.com

DIRECTIONS: centre of Garrigill, at the start of the walk

PARKING: village green

OPEN: daily, and all day Saturday and Sunday from Easter to October. Closed Monday to Thursday lunchtime in winter

FOOD: daily

BREWERY/COMPANY: free house

REAL ALE: Black Sheep Bitter, 3 guest beers

DOGS: welcome inside

ROOMS: 4 bedrooms

Railway running on part of the route of the (standard-gauge) Haltwhistle-to-Alston branch line. A few miles away, the Nenthead Mines Heritage Centre gives a real insight into the area's lead-mining past, and you can even venture underground to see exactly what a mine was like.

282 MOW COP
CHESHIRE

5.25 MILES (8.4KM) 2hrs

PATHS: Open fields and woodland paths, canal tow path, quiet lanes, short sections where path indistinct, 10 stiles

SUGGESTED MAP: aqua3 OS Explorer 268 Wilmslow, Macclesfield & Congleton

GRID REFERENCE: SJ 857573

PARKING: National Trust car park directly below Mow Cop castle

THE PUB: Mow Cop Inn

❶ Head towards castle. Before reaching it take narrower path **L**, to road. Go **R**, then **L** ('**Old Man**' and '**South Cheshire Way**'). Swing **L**, then **R**, then fork **R** on narrow path past Old Man. Rejoin wider track, heading towards communications mast.

❷ At junction of footpaths go **L**. Follow field edges downhill into wood. Where footpath splits at holly bushes go **L** and into field; bear **R**. Skirt farm then join rough track. Keep descending to join surfaced lane. Bear **L**; cross railway at Ackers Crossing.

❸ Follow lane to wider road and turn **R**. Cross canal bridge, then go down steps and **L**, along tow path. At bridge No 81 go up to lane and turn **L**, over bridge.

❹ Follow lane to crossroads by **Baytree Farm** and continue up track to **Limekiln Farm**. Take track on **L** just beyond buildings. Keep low, along edge of wood, until track bends **R** by post marked with yellow arrows.

❺ Go **L**, through undergrowth to duckboards and stile. Turn **R** along field edge. After 100yds (91m) there's another post. Descend sharp **R**; cross several, sometimes slippery, plank bridges. Narrow path heads uphill to wider track, then tarmac near house. Before track starts to descend, go **R** to stile. Follow **L** edge of field alongside wood. After another stile go up narrower field until it opens out. Above signpost, go **R** on green track to stile amid holly trees. Continue to another boundary; beyond is rougher ground with rushes and gorse. Firm track curves across this, though last bit to stile remains rough and rushy. Bear **L** up drive to road, then follow it **R** for 300yds (274m).

❻ By gateway on R-H side **Gritstone Trail** sign under tree points way into wood. Footpath roughly follows its upper margin and emerges on level floor of old quarry workings. Bear **L**, below communications **tower**, to rejoin outward route near **Old Man of Mow**.

283 THE CLOUD
CHESHIRE

7 MILES (11.3KM) 2hrs 30min

PATHS: Field paths, canal tow path, some lanes, rougher and steeper on The Cloud, 11 stiles. Meadows and fields along canal, craggy summit

SUGGESTED MAP: aqua3 OS Explorer 268 Wilmslow, Macclesfield & Congleton

GRID REFERENCE: SJ 894627

PARKING: Car park on outskirts of small village of Timbersbrook

THE PUB: Waggon and Horses (Rainbow Hill Road)

❶ From car park, turn **R** on road for 500yds (457m). Just past houses, go **L** over stile and down track. After 600yds (549m) go **R** over stile. Follow trodden line to cross stream in dip. Continue diagonally across meadow. A short embankment leads to a canal bridge.

❷ Cross and loop round **L**, under bridge and along tow path. Follow this for 0.75 miles (5.3km) to bridge 57. Go up steps and over bridge. Vague track bears **L** then **R** through gorse along edge of hollow. Descend to stile under sycamore then down slope (muddy) to footbridge.

Cross stile, go down to **River Dane** and step round tree on its edge. Turn **R** up edge of field.

❸ Cross stile to road. Turn **R** and climb steadily. As it levels out, go **L** on narrower lane. Opposite house, cross stile on **R**, then up fields over series of stiles, bearing slightly **L**. Join lane and go **L**, past **Hillside Farm**, then right, up track to stile.

❹ Here is National Trust sign ('The Cloud'). Path is narrow but clear, directly uphill then slanting **R**. It passes below crags then levels out and dips slightly to start of broad shelf. Path now goes straight up hillside, through highest band of crags, to summit ridge. Trig point is about 100yds (91m) to **L**.

❺ Retrace this short section of summit ridge then follow edge down, gently descending and swinging slowly **L**. Lower down path runs through pine plantations. Below gap in wall, broader track runs through more open woods. As track starts to curve **L**, clear path continues straight ahead. Stick to crest of ridge until you rejoin gravel track near sharp bend. Just below bend is footpath sign and steeply descending line of steps. Turn **L** on road, into edge of **Timbersbrook**. Just after 1st house on R go through gap in fence, down few more steps and across field with picnic tables. Car park is at its far end.

284 ALDERLEY EDGE
CHESHIRE

3 MILES (4.8KM) 1hr

PATHS: Woodland tracks and paths, some field paths, 7 stiles

SUGGESTED MAP: aqua3 OS Explorer 268 Wilmslow, Macclesfield & Congleton

GRID REFERENCE: SJ 860772

PARKING: Large National Trust car park off B5087

THE PUB: Royal Oak

❶ From large National Trust car park, off B5087, walk towards tea room and information room. Go **R** on wide track past **National Trust works yard**, then **L**. Cross open area past **Engine Vein**. At crossroads of paths turn **L** and come out by Beacon Lodge.

❷ Go straight across road into **Windmill Wood**. Follow descending track to clearing, bear **L** and continue. About 140yds (128m) beyond National Trust sign, in more open terrain, with bare sand hills ahead, bear **R** across grass to crossroads with field ahead. Turn **R**, skirting damp ground then pool. Just before another open field, go **R**, along edge

of wood. Continue in strip of trees, with fields either side. Cross road again and follow track to crest of **Castle Rock**.

❸ Descend steps to level path. Go **L** 120yds (110m) to **Wizard's Well**. Return to steps and continue below crags on terrace path, then up steps to join higher path. Go **L** and almost immediately start descending, with more steps in places. At bottom cross footbridge and climb, levelling out briefly by **Holy Well**. Few paces to **L** of well go up over tree roots to where path resumes. Climb shallow steps to wider path, go **L** then turn **R** on to crest of **Stormy Point**.

❹ Follow wide level track to crossroads; go **L**. Follow signs ('Hare Hill'), descend with small ravine at bottom. Turn **R** and ascend. Climb steps past beech trees, then descend through **Clock House Wood**. Climb again to National Trust sign and out into open.

❺ Go **R**, over stile, across waist of field to stile near pond. Go **L** along hedge to stile hidden in curve, then up fenced path. Join wider track and at top go over stile on **R**. Go **L** over next stile and up to stile and grassy track. Cross gravel track into narrow fenced path and at end turn **L**. Opposite **National Trust works yard** go **L** through gate for short cut to car park or continue straight on to tea room.

285 SHUTLINGSLOE
CHESHIRE

5 MILES (8KM) 2hrs

PATHS: Farm and forest tracks, field paths, lane, moorland, 11 stiles

SUGGESTED MAP: aqua3 OS Explorer OL24 White Peak. **GRID REFERENCE:** SJ 984706

PARKING: Car park at Vicarage Quarry, Wildboarclough (alternative at Clough House, lower down valley)

THE PUB: Crag Inn

❶ From car park at **Vicarage Quarry**, turn **L** up road, away from **Wildboarclough** village. Just past **Dingers Hollow Farm**, go over stile on **L** and up to iron gate. Go **R** through another gate and follow green track across hillside to 3rd gate. Cross field near power line, down to stream then up **L** to stile by gate. Cross lane and walk few paces to stile. Narrow path rises gently, but our route rises steeply, above large trees. Continue on this line to stile into another lane. Go **R** to junction.

❷ Turn **L**, on lane ('Macc Forest Chapel'), over top and down, past chapel. Follow road for 250yds (229m) to dip. At corner of wood go **L** on footpath, down hill. At bottom, near small dam, take newly made permissive footpath on **R**, over bridge. When gate blocks way, drop to **L**, down steps to stile and road.

❸ Cross to gap in wall almost opposite. Continuation path parallels road; when it rejoins it by gate, bear **L** on wider path, swinging back **R**. Go up flight of steps on **L** and sharply back **L** on path climbing alongside stone wall. When gradient eases near kissing gate, bear **L** on established footpath. At next junction, after 300yds (274m), go **R**, with sign ('**Shutlingsloe**'), and up to kissing gate.

❹ Footpath, partly surfaced with large gritstone flags, crosses open moorland. At shoulder, path levels out and **Shutlingsloe** rears up ahead. Descend slightly, cross duckboards to stile and then follow obvious, flagged path alongside wall. Final steep staircase leads to trig point.

❺ Descend ahead, winding down steeply between low outcrops. Keep ahead as gradient eases. After 2 stiles follow wall to tarmac track. Go **R** on track to cattle grid. Take another track sharply back to **L**. This runs more or less level along hillside, then gently descending green track interrupted by stile and small stream leads down to road. Go **L** up this back to start.

286 MACCLESFIELD FOREST
CHESHIRE

7 MILES (11.3KM) 3hrs 30min

PATHS: Sloping field paths, lanes and easy forest tracks, steep hillside, 20 stiles

SUGGESTED MAP: aqua3 OS Explorer OL24 White Peak

GRID REFERENCE: SJ 980681

PARKING: Lay-by at Brookside, on lane 1 mile (1.6km) south of Wildboarclough

THE PUB: Hanging Gate

❶ Walk along road for 440yds (402m) to **Crag Inn**, then at foot of its drive cross stile on **L** for path across sloping field. This maintains its direction through successive fields (each with ladder stile) until finally you reach farm drive at very top. Turn **L** and then walk along to lane.

❷ Turn **R**; walk along lane as far as **Greenway Bridge**. Go over stile on **R**; follow path beside stream, until it crosses it to veer **L**, up **Oaken Clough**. Keep to bottom of little valley, past ruined stone shelter, and as it rises continue to its far head, near small **pond**. Turn **R** on to

private drive; then go almost immediately **L** for wall-side path uphill.

❸ At top, go over stile and across moorland on clear grassy track. Keep ahead until you reach stile on far side. Cross, and descend sunken, fenced track to emerge opposite **Hanging Gate pub**.

❹ Turn **R**; follow road for 1 mile (1.6km), keeping ahead at junction where road bends sharply **L**. Ignore another turning on **L**, until finally lane turns **R**, into **Macclesfield Forest**, where there is wide gate on **R**.

❺ Don't go through main gate, but cross stile to **L** ('**Shutlingsloe/Trentabank**'); follow footpath, which runs parallel with lane. Drop down to newly planted area; cross footbridge; at junction of tracks, near wood sculpture, keep ahead ('**Shutlingsloe**'). At far end turn **R**, or for **visitor centre**/toilets at Trentabank turn **L**.

❻ Walk up wide forest drive; go **L** at fork; at far end turn **R** for long but quite easy gravel track through trees. At top go through gate, then continue ahead; turn **R** to leave forest for stone-flagged path across open moorland to distinctive top of **Shutlingsloe**.

❼ From summit descend eroded track down steep eastern slope of hill, until eventually turn **R** on to open farm drive. Follow this all the way down to road at bottom; turn **R** to return to car park.

287 FORMBY POINT
MERSEYSIDE

3.5 MILES (5.7KM) 1hr 30min

PATHS: Well-worn paths through woods and salt marsh, plus long stretch of sand

SUGGESTED MAP: aqua3 OS Explorer 285 Southport & Chorley

GRID REFERENCE: SD 278082

PARKING: Either side of access road just beyond kiosk

THE PUB: The Grapes

❶ Start just **L** of large notice-board. Follow 'Squirrel Walk', with its wooden fencing, to **L** and then round to **R**. Keep straight on at crossroads, where there's sign for **Blundell Avenue**. There are many subsidiary paths but the main line runs virtually straight ahead to **Blundell Avenue**. Cross avenue to fainter path almost opposite, with 'No Cycling' sign and traces of bricks in its surface. Follow this, skirting around edge of field (brick traces still useful guide). Go up slight rise then across more open sand hills to line of pines on rise ahead. Skirt **L** round

hollow and see houses ahead.

❷ Just before houses turn **R** on straight track. This swings **L** slightly then forks. Go **R**, down steps, then straight on down side of reed-fringed pool. Beyond this keep fairly straight on, towards sand hills. When you reach them swing **L** then **R**, picking up boardwalk, to skirt highest dunes and out to beach.

❸ Turn **R** along open and virtually level sand. The firmest walking surface is usually some way out from the base of the dunes. Walk parallel to these (north) for over 1.25 miles (2km). The shoreline curves very gently to **R** but there are few distinctive landmarks apart from signs to various approach paths. Watch for sign for Gipsy Wood Path.

❹ Distinct track winds through sand hills then swings more decisively to **R** near **pools**, where there's sign board about natterjack toads. Follow track back into woods and, at junction, go **R**. The track curves round between woods and sand hills then joins wider track by Sefton Coastal Footpath sign. Go through patch of willows then bear **L** to line of pines on rise. From these drop down to broad path with gravelly surface and follow it **L** into woods again. Stay on main path, with timber edgings and white-topped posts, bear **R** by large 'xylophone', and it leads quickly back to the start.

288 BLACKSTONE EDGE
MANCHESTER

6.5 MILES (10.4KM) 2hrs 30min

PATHS: Field paths, rough tracks and faint paths across open moorland, 2 stiles

SUGGESTED MAP: aqua3 OS Explorer OL21 South Pennines

GRID REFERENCE: SD 939153

PARKING: Hollingworth Lake Visitor Centre

THE PUB: White Horse Inn

❶ From far end of car park well-made path runs past picnic tables then crosses and follows small beck. At track go **L** 200yds (183m) then up **R** with yellow arrows. Zig-zag up slope then **L** and down to stream and footbridge. Where path forks keep to lower one, just above stream, through birch woods then up to wider path and round to **Owlet Hall**.
❷ Go through lychgate and **L** alongside house to stile. Cross stream, then another stile. Ignore path on L and keep **R**, just above stream, along line of thorn trees. Cross decrepit fence and follow neglected path alongside wall. Go up to trees flanking drive to **Shore Lane Farm**. Turn **L**, then **L** again on lane.
❸ Just before road, turn **R** on track past houses. Continue on narrower but clear path. Meet farm track just below A58, go **R** few paces, then **L** up well-worn path ('**Roman Road**'). Cross water-cut and keep climbing. Slope eases near **Aggin Stone**.
❹ Turn **R**, through kissing gate; follow path across rock-strewn moor to trig point. Follow main edge south for 400yds (366m) to break in line of rocks.
❺ Slant down **R** across rough moor to old water-cut. Go **L** alongside this until path veers off **R**. It soon rises again, across shoulder of moor, then levels off by small cairn. Keep **R**, along edge, descend more steeply then swing **R**, joining old grooved track. Continue down green track, past **cairn**, then back **L** descending towards **Dry Mere**.
❻ Where ground steepens, just beyond tarn, path splits. Take lower path, towards pylon. Go straight across well-used track to another track just below. Go **L**, fording small stream, then swing **R**. Drop down to shale track in small valley and go **R** down it.
❼ At **Syke** farm join old lane. At **Hollingworth Fold**, with its multicoloured signpost, keep straight on down lane to join road along lake side. Entrance to **visitor centre** is just across 1st embankment.

289 RIVER DOUGLAS
LANCASHIRE

4 MILES (6.4KM) 1hr 45min

PATHS: Field paths and canal tow path, 7 stiles

SUGGESTED MAP: aqua3 OS Explorer 285 Southport & Chorley

GRID REFERENCE: SD 517109 Parking: Large lay-by on A5209

THE PUB: Rigbye Arms

❶ At end of lay-by there's stile into corner of field. Go up side of field and **L** along top, then into wood. Cross small footbridge and continue up footpath, then alongside tiny stream. Follow side of conifer plantation until it bends away, then bear **R** to L-H side of trees enclosing pool. Continue up to **R** into enclosed track below power lines and up to meet junction with tarmac track.
❷ Go **L**, then bear **L** again down earthy track. (If you want to visit **Rigbye Arms** pub first, go **R** at this point, then **L** along **High Moor Lane**.) At end of earthy track go slightly **R**, across field, to corner of wood then down its **L-H** edge. Keep following this, which eventually becomes narrow strip of woodland, to stile in bottom corner of field. Follow footpath down through wood then up to A5209.
❸ Cross road and go **L** to stile where pavement ends. Go straight down field and over another stile into lane. Go **R** on this then immediately **L** down another lane. Cross railway at level crossing and continue to bridge over canal. Drop down to tow path and follow it eastwards for about 0.5 mile (800m) to next canal bridge (No 40).
❹ Cross bridge and follow obvious track, taking you back over railway and up to gate and stile. Turn **R** on another track. In places there's separate footpath alongside, but it's always obvious. Where track finally parts company, go ahead over stile and along bottom edge of field beside area of new plantings. Cross next field to post and then stile.
❺ Descend steep steps down into wood and bear **L** into **Fairy Glen**. Cross footbridge, climb some steps, then go **L** up good track. Cross another footbridge below waterfall and ascend steps. Keep to principal footpath, straight on up glen as it becomes shallower, until path crosses tiny footbridge. Soon after this footpath leaves side of brook and briefly joins track before it emerges on to **A5209**. Cross and go **R**, back to lay-by.

290 ANGLEZARKE
LANCASHIRE

7 MILES (11.3KM) 2hrs 30min

PATHS: Mostly good tracks with some field paths, 20 stiles

SUGGESTED MAP: aqua3 OS Explorer 287 West Pennine Moors

GRID REFERENCE: SD 621161

PARKING: Large car park at Anglezarke

THE PUB: Yew Tree Inn

❶ Leave car park by kissing gate and follow track near water. Fork **R**, via Lester Mill **Quarry**; go **R**, and straight on at next junction. Track climbs steep rise.
❷ Go through gap on **L**, on bend. Path traverses wooded slope. Descend steps, join wider track and go **L**. Beyond stile follow narrower path to road.
❸ Go **L** 50yds (46m) to kissing gate. Follow track up valley below **Stronstrey Bank**. Cross bridge then go through kissing gate and over another bridge to **White Coppice cricket ground**.
❹ Bear **L** up lane, then follow tarmac into White Coppice hamlet. Cross bridge by post-box. Follow stream then go up **L** by reservoir. Bear **L** to stile. Cross next field to top **R** corner and go **R** on lane. Where it bends R go **L** up track.
❺ Skirt **Higher Healey**, follow field edges, then angle up **L** into dark plantations. Fork **L** just inside, and ascend to an old **quarry**. Follow its rim for three-quarters of way round then bear away **L** through larch plantation.
❻ Go **L** on clear path then **R** to large cairn on **Grey Heights**. Descend slightly **R**, winding down past small plantation, and join wider green track. Bear **L** over small rise; follow track to lane by **White House farm**.
❼ Cross stile on **L**, below farmyard wall; bear **L** to corner of field. Cross stile on **L** then go up field edge and join confined path. From stile on **R** follow trees along field edge to rough track. Go **R** and ahead to **Kays Farm**.
❽ Go **R** down track then **L** on lane below reservoir wall. As lane angles away, go **L** over stile then skirt reservoir until pushed away from water by wood. Join road across dam. Go through gap and up steep track. Go **L** at top round **Yarrow Reservoir** to road.
❾ Go L, passing entrance to **Anglezarke Quarry**, to junction. Go R, and car park entrance is on 1st bend.

291 RENDLE HILL
LANCASHIRE

4.75 MILES (7.7KM) 2hrs

PATHS: Field paths and rough moorland, surfaced track, 10 stiles

SUGGESTED MAP: aqua3 OS Explorer OL21 South Pennines or OL41 Forest of Bowland & Ribblesdale

GRID REFERENCE: SD 823403 Parking: Public car park in Barley village

THE PUB: Pendle Inn

❶ From toilets follow path **R** across green then over footbridge. Go **R** then up street. Just past Meadow Bank Farm go **L** up footpath alongside stream.
❷ Keep straight on up then cross footbridge and join lane. Follow this, with signs, to kissing gate and well-marked path that leads to **Brown House**. Go into yard, **R** on track for 60yds (55m) then **L** through kissing gate. Go down and **R**, then up through new plantings and up to gate **L** of **Pendle House**.
❸ Go **L** to meet path just above wall. After another gate, climb away from wall. Path undulates, then dips more definitely and meets wall again. From stile (don't cross it) just above **Under Pendle**, bear **R** and follow fence. Cross stream then go straight on up clearer track to rejoin wall.
❹ Bear **R** on trackway climbing alongside obvious groove. Pass old wooden gateposts. There's another gate and stile just ahead, go **L** through gate and straight down by wall. Cross track and descend to gate just below **Upper Ogden Reservoir**.
❺ Follow reservoir road until just above Lower **Ogden Reservoir**. Go **R** over bridge, down steps then round **R** to footbridge. Climb steps; go **L** and climb steps through plantation. At its end go up **R** to ridge.
❻ Turn **L** following fence then wall. At signpost bear **R**, keeping roughly level until rooftops of **Newchurch** appear. Aim for water trough, then stile and signpost. Descend short path to road.
❼ Go down road opposite ('Roughlee'). After 100yds (91m) cross stile on **L-H** side; follow rising footpath. Fork **L** just inside plantation. At far end of plantation keep ahead, gradually converging with wall on **L-H** side. Follow wall, changing sides halfway along, to join sunken track. Cross it and descend to road.
❽ Go down tarmac track opposite, cross Pendle Water then go **L** alongside it. Continue on stonier track past cottages and old mill. Finally short path on **R** leads back to car park.

292 HODDER VALLEY
LANCASHIRE

7 MILES (11.3KM) 2hrs 30min

PATHS: Field paths, farm tracks and quiet lane, 8 stiles

SUGGESTED MAP: aqua3 OS Explorer OL41 Forest of Bowland & Ribblesdale

GRID REFERENCE: SD 658468

PARKING: Roadside parking near Inn at Whitewell or below church

THE PUB: Inn at Whitewall

❶ From lower parking area follow river bank **L** to stepping stones. Climb just **R** of woods and straight through farmyard of **New Laund**. By old cheese press go **L** on curving track below slopes, then up field. Bear **L** to gate into lane. Go few paces **L** to stile on **R**.
❷ Cross rough pasture, aiming just **L** of house, then go **R** on surfaced track, swinging round into another little valley. Go **L** to **farm**, then **R**, through farmyard and down to footbridge.
❸ Turn **L**, past chicken coops, to stile on **R**. Cross field corner to 2nd stile thenahead to **Dinkling Green Farm**. Gap to **R** of cow shed leads into farmyard.
❹ Halfway down yard go **R**, between buildings, to ford. Keep **L** past plantation, follow next field edge then go through gate in dip. Follow hedge round then cross it and go over rise. Bear **R**, down to beck, then up lane to **Lickhurst Farm**.
❺ Turn **L** into farmyard then bear **R** and straight on down track. When it swings R, go **L** before next gate then straight ahead on intermittent track.
❻ Just before **Knot Hill Quarry**, turn **L**, past limekiln, to junction. Go **R** and down to lane. Go **L** then **L** again, round bend and down. Cross bridge on **R** and head towards **Stakes** farm, crossing river on stepping stones.
❼ Turn **L** and climb above river. At next junction go **L**, descend steeply, then swing **R**, slightly above **River Hodder**, to stile. Follow fence to stile, then bear **L** to ford. Go up rough track and keep climbing past **R** edge of plantation. Keep straight on across open field to stile in furthest corner.
❽ Across road, few paces **L**, is gate. Bear **L** to iron gates. Contour round hill, just above fence, to more gates. After 100yds (91m) go down through aluminium gate. Track swings **R**. Just past Seed Hill turn **L** and descend steps by graveyard. Short steep lane descends back to start.

293 BROCK BOTTOM
LANCASHIRE

6 MILES (9.7KM) 2hrs

PATHS: Field paths, in places indistinct, clear tracks, 19 stiles

SUGGESTED MAP: aqua3 OS Explorer OL41 Forest of Bowland & Ribblesdale

GRID REFERENCE: SD 565426

PARKING: By Beacon Fell visitor centre

THE PUB: Horns (nr Goosnargh)

❶ Look for public footpath sign in **L-H** corner of car park by **visitor centre**. Go down broad track, then through field. Bear **L** towards **Crombleholme Fold**. Walk, via farmyard, to country lane. Turn **R** to bend.
❷ Go **L**, cross stream then up track swinging **R**. After 50yds (46m) go **L**, down to stile just before field ends. From stile, 15yds (14m) further on, go down field then angle **R** to low bridge and straight up track beyond.
❸ Go through **Cross Keys** car park, through farmyard and into field. Go **R** to stile then straight on to corner of hedge. Follow it to tree then **L** to stile. Go **R** then straight ahead to lane and go **L**.
❹ Go **R** to **Lower Trotter Hill**. Cross cattle grid, go **L**, then round to **R** and past house. Go through **L-H** gate and up to stile. Follow field edge, eventually bending **L**. Go down stony track and **R** on road.
❺ As road bears R keep ahead. Descend on sunken track through woods; cross footbridge. Go up few paces then **R**. Follow path near river to **Brock Mill**.
❻ Cross bridge then go through gateway on **L**. Bear **R** up track then go **R**, through rhododendrons. Follow edge of wood, then go **R**, crossing stream. Go up field edge and straight on towards **Lower Lickhurst**. Go round into drive and up to road. Go **L** few paces, then go **R**, up drive. Keep straight on as it bends L, up fields to lane. Go **R** for 140yds (128m).
❼ Go **L** over stile and diagonally to isolated thorn tree. Continue to gateway and then to stile and footbridge. Follow old boundary, now muddy depression, then bear **L** to power lines. Follow these to marker post. Go **R**, directly uphill. Cross road to track rising through forest. At junction go **L** for 200m (183m) then **R** up narrow path to summit trig point.
❽ Bear **R** along edge of forest then **L** across boardwalk. Keep straight on to **visitor centre**.

294 KENDAL
CUMBRIA

3 MILES (4.8KM) 1hr 30min

PATHS: Pavements, surfaced and grassy paths with steps, no stiles

SUGGESTED MAP: aqua3 OS Explorer OL7 The English Lakes (SE).

GRID REFERENCE: SD 518928

PARKING: Free parking area by river, plenty of pay car parks near by

THE PUB: Castle Inn/Ring O'Bells

❶ From end of National Trust car park at **Eaves Wood**, follow footpath to T-junction. Go **R** few paces then **L**, climbing gently. Keep **L** to beech ring, then straight on. Descend through complex junction to high wall and continue on this line to lane.
❷ Cross on to track ('Cove Road'). Keep ahead down narrow path (Wallings Lane), drive, another track and another narrow path to wider road. After 200yds (183m) go **L** down Cove Road.
❸ From Cove walk **L**, below cliffs, to shore. Walk up road to Beach Garage then take footpath alongside.
❹ At next road turn **R** for 600yds (549m) then bear **R** down Gibraltar Lane for 350yds (320m). Enter National Trust property of **Jack Scout**.
❺ Descend **L** to limekiln then follow narrowing path directly away from it. This swings **L** above steep drop and descends. Follow broad green path to gate. After 100yds (91m), another gate leads into lane. At end bear **L** below **Brown's Houses**. Follow edge of salt marsh to stile, go up slightly, then along to signpost.
❻ Turn **L**. Climb steeply to awkward squeeze stile. Gradient eases, over rock and through lightly wooded area into open. Go **L** to stile; follow wall down and into small wood. Follow track down **R**. Cross road to gap in wall, descend then walk below crags to **Woodwell**.
❼ Path ('The Green via cliff path') leads to rocky staircase. At top go ahead to join broader path. Follow it **L**, slant **R**; continue into woodland. Stile on **R** and narrow section lead to road. Go **R** 100yds (91m), then **L** into The Green. Keep **R** at junction; join wider road.
❽ Go **L** for 75yds (69m) then **R** ('**Burton Well Lambert's Meadow**'). Track soon descends then swings **L**, passing Burton Well on R. Cross stile into **Lambert's Meadow**, then go **R**, over footbridge to gate. Climb up, with steps, and continue more easily to fork. Go **L** alongside pool (**Bank Well**) into lane. Go **L** and at end car park is virtually opposite.

295 GRANGE OVER SANDS
CUMBRIA

4 MILES (6.4KM) 2hrs

PATHS: Paths and tracks, can be muddy in places, 7 stiles

SUGGESTED MAP: aqua3 OS Explorer OL7 The English Lakes (SE)

GRID REFERENCE: SD 410780 Parking: Car park below road and tourist office in central Grange

THE PUB: Commodore Inn

❶ Join main road through Grange; go **R** (north), to pass **ornamental gardens**. Cross road; continue to roundabout. Go **L** along **Windermere Road** rising to round bend; find steps up to squeeze stile on **L** ('Routen Well/Hampsfield').
❷ Take path rising through Eggerslack Wood. Cross over surfaced track; keep ahead, passing house on L. Steps lead to track. Cross this diagonally to follow track ('Hampsfell'). Track zig-zags to **R** (house to L) and ascends through woods to stile over wall.
❸ Cross stile to leave wood; follow path directly up hillside. Pass sections of limestone pavement and little craggy outcrops until path levels and bears **L** to stile over stone wall. Cross stile; go **R** along wall. Continue ahead, following grassy track, to pass stone cairns and up to square tower of **Hospice of Hampsfell**.
❹ Leave tower heading south and following path over edge of limestone escarpment (take care). Continue over 2nd escarpment. Descend to stile over wall, then to bottom of dip; rise directly up hill beyond. Cross over top; descend to find stile over wall. Path bears diagonally **L** but it is usual to continue to cairn marking **Fell End**. Go down **L**, picking up grassy track, which leads **L** round valley to gate leading on to road.
❺ Cross road, take squeeze stile; descend diagonally **L** across field to gate on to road by **Springbank Cottage**. Descend surfaced track to enter farmyard; continue **L** over stone stile. Go over hill, following path (parallel to wall); take stile into narrow ginnel. Follow this down, with high wall to **R**, round corner; descend to junction of roads. Go **L** on private road/public footpath; bear **R** at fork. At next junction, turn **R** to descend track. At following junction go **L** down **Charney Well Lane**. At next junction, turn **L** below woods of **Eden Mount** to junction with Hampsfell Road near bottom of hill. At junction with larger road go **L** (toilets to R); pass church before descending past clock tower and junction with road (**B5277**). Go **L** then **R** to car park.

296 AMBLESIDE
CUMBRIA

3.25 MILES (5.3KM) 1hr 45min

PATHS: Road, paths and tracks, can be muddy in places, 3 stiles

SUGGESTED MAP: aqua3 OS Explorer OL7 The English Lakes (SE)

GRID REFERENCE: NY 375047

PARKING: Ambleside central car park

THE PUB: Golden Rule Inn

❶ Take wooden footbridge from car park; go **R** along Rydal road to pass waterwheel and Bridge House. At junction bear **R** along Compston Road. Continue to next junction (cinema on corner); bear **R** to cross side road and enter Vicarage Road alongside chip shop. Pass school; enter Rothay Park. Follow main path through park to emerge by flat bridge over **Stock Ghyll Beck**. Cross beck, then go **L** to cross over stone arched **Miller Bridge** spanning **River Rothay**.
❷ Bear **R** along road over cattle grid until, in few paces, steep surfaced road rises to L. Climb road, which becomes unsurfaced, by buildings of **Brow Head**. At S-bend, beyond buildings, stone stile leads up and off **L**. Pass through trees to find, in few dozen paces, stone squeeze stile. Pass through; climb open hillside above. Paths are well worn and there are various possible routes. For best views keep diagonally **L**. Rising steeply at first, path levels before rising again to ascend 1st rocky knoll. Higher, larger knoll follows and offers good views.
❸ Beyond this, way descends to **R**, dropping to well-defined path. Follow path to pass little pond before cresting rise and falling to little pocket-handkerchief **Lily Tarn** (flowers bloom late June to September). Path skirts **R** edge of tarn, roughly following crest of **Loughrigg Fell**. Gate/stile leads to base of further knoll and this is ascended to another viewpoint.
❹ Take path descending **R** to track below. Bear **R** to gate, which leads through stone wall boundary of open fell and into field. Continue to descend track, passing **old golf clubhouse** on L. Intercept original route just above buildings of Brow Head.
❺ Continue to cross **Miller Bridge** then, before flat bridge, bear **L** to follow track by side of **Stock Ghyll Beck**. Beyond meadows, lane through houses leads to main Rydal road. Bear **R** along road to car park beyond fire station.

297 SOUTHER FELL
CUMBRIA

6 MILES (9.7KM) 3hrs

PATHS: Grassy and stony paths, open fellside, 4 stiles

SUGGESTED MAP: aqua3 OS Explorer OL5 The English Lakes (NE)

GRID REFERENCE: NY 364300

PARKING: Wide verge above river in Mungrisdale

THE PUB: The Mill Inn, Mungrisdale

❶ Head north on road, following **Glenderamackin** upstream. Bear **R** where road crosses bridge and continue to hairpin bend. Go **L** to leave road, pass telephone box; follow lane between cottages. Go through gate; continue on track above north bank of river. Bear **L**; cross little **Bullfell Beck** by footbridge.
❷ Bear **L** off steeply ascending track; follow lesser stony track, which traces route along R bank (true L) of **River Glenderamackin**. Route is straightforward although path is eroded in places and there is steep drop into little river. Continue along track (very boggy in places) to ford **Bannerdale Beck**. Quite easy if you keep dry by balancing on stones. Round shoulder of **Bannerdale Fell** (**White Horse Bent**). Continue ascent until path falls **L** to wooden footbridge to cross **River Glenderamackin**.
❸ Path ascends hillside striking diagonally **L** to climb to top of high grassy shoulder. **Mousthwaite Comb** lies down below to R. Bear **L** following path; ascend long shoulder of **Souther Fell**. Pass large circular cairn and continue along level shoulder, heading north to summit (little rocky knoll).
❹ Keep north and continue to descend grassy nose of fell. Easy at first, angle steepens progressively until nearing base. Little craggy outcrops are best avoided by following path to their L. Path is well defined and soon leads to stone wall near bottom of fell. Go **R** alongside wall. Path is extremely boggy in places. Continue along by wall until it bends L and steep short descent leads to surfaced road.
❺ Go **L** on road, through gate until, at bottom of hill, grassy lane continues to **River Glenderamackin**, just upstream of buildings of **Beckside**. Before reaching ford that crosses river, stone steps over wall on **R** give access to footbridge. Cross bridge; go **L** to exit field via squeeze stile. Turn **R**, climb grassy bank to road. Head **L**; go upstream to return to parking area.

298 SATTERTHWAITE
CUMBRIA

4.75 MILES (7.7KM) 2hrs

PATHS: Mainly good paths and tracks throughout, 3 stiles

SUGGESTED MAP: aqua3 OS Explorer OL7 The English Lakes (SE)

GRID REFERENCE: SD 344912

PARKING: Forest car park at Blind Lane

THE PUB: Eagles Head

❶ Path from back of car park, marked by green-and-white-topped posts, heads **R**, over rise to forest trail. Walk **L** and, after 400yds (366m), turn **L** on to path through birch wood. Go ahead over junction at top and descend to join metalled track into **Satterthwaite**.
❷ Turn **L** by church; walk through village. After 0.25 mile (400m), at L-H bend, go **R** on to track, **Moor Lane**, and then at marker post, head **L** on to rising path into trees. Bear **L** in front of reconstructed charcoal burner's **hut** and then shortly drop down on to broader track.
❸ Go **R**, over another hill and **R** again where you eventually reach broad forest trail. Pass **waterfall**. Beyond, track bends across stream before rising to junction. Turn **L** for 220yds (201m) and branch **L** again on to unmarked, descending grass track.
❹ Emerging on to lane at bottom, go **R**, then turn in between cottages at **Force Forge**. Through gate on **R**, go **L** by tall beech hedge and across **Force Beck**. Continue along winding path into **Brewer Wood**, bearing **R** when you shortly reach crossing path.
❺ After about 0.25 mile (400m), at fork, bear **L** to gap in wall and continue through trees. Reach indistinct fork beyond crest of the hill and take **R-H** branch, which descends to **Rusland** Reading Rooms. Cross out to lane in front of church and walk **L**.
❻ After little way along, leave lane for byway opposite junction. Climb over top of **Stricely** beside wooded pastures and eventually drop to lane at **Force Mills**. Go **R** and then **L** to ascend beside **Force Falls**.
❼ At green-and-white post, part-way up hill, turn **R** on to path climbing steeply into larch plantation. Keep **R** where path forks, shortly passing through gap in wall. Go through another gap few paces on; descend through trees back to car park.

299 ELTERWATER
CUMBRIA

4 MILES (6.4KM) 2hrs

PATHS: Grassy and stony paths and tracks, surfaced lane, 4 stiles

SUGGESTED MAP: aqua3 OS Explorer OL7 The English Lakes (SE)

GRID REFERENCE: NY 328048

PARKING: National Trust pay-and-display car park at Elterwater village

THE PUB: Britannia Inn

❶ Pass through small gate to walk downsteam above **Great Langdale Beck**. Continue to enter mixed woods of **Rob Rash**. Gate leads through stone wall (open foot of **Elter Water** lies to R). Continue through meadows above river. (Lane can be wet and is prone to flooding.) Pass through gate and enter mixed woods. Keep along path to pass **Skelwith Force** waterfall down to R. A little bridge leads across channel to viewing point above falls. Keep along path to pass through buildings (Kirkstone Quarry).
❷ **Kirkstone Gallery** is on R, as path becomes surfaced road. Continue to intercept **A593** by bridge over river. Turn **L** to pass **hotel**. At road junction cross over Great Langdale road to lane, which passes by end of cottages. Follow lane, ascending to intercept another road. Turn **R** for short distance, then **L** towards **Tarn Foot farm**. Bear **R** along track, in front of cottages. Where track splits, bear **L**. Through gate continue on track to overlook **Loughrigg Tarn**. At point halfway along tarn cross stile over iron railings on **L**.
❸ Follow footpath down meadow to traverse **R**, just above tarn. Footpath swings **R** to climb ladder stile over stone wall. Follow grassy track leading **R**, up hill, to gate and stile on to road. Turn **L** along road, until surfaced drive leads up to **R** ('Public Footpath Skelwith Bridge'). Pass small cottage and keep on track to pass higher cottage, **Crag Head**. Little way above this, narrow grassy footpath leads off **R**, up hillside, to gain level shoulder between outcrops of **Little Loughrigg**.
❹ Cross shoulder and descend path, passing little tarnlet to R, to intercept stone wall. Keep **L** along wall descending to find, in a few hundred paces, ladder stile leading over wall into upper woods of **Rob Rash**. Steep descent leads to road. Cross this, and go over little stone stile/broken wall next to large double gates. Descend track to meet with outward route. Bear **R** to return to **Elterwater**.

300 BARDSEA CUMBRIA

8 MILES (12.9KM) 3hrs

PATHS: Paths and tracks, some field paths may be muddy, 10 stiles

SUGGESTED MAP: aqua3 OS Explorer OL6 The English Lakes (SW); OL7 The English Lakes (SE)

GRID REFERENCE: SD 301742 (on Explorer OL7)

PARKING: Small car parks between coast road and shore at Bardsea

THE PUB: Ship Inn

1 Follow shore to **Sea Wood**. Path runs parallel, turning **R** on inside edge of wood to reach road. Turn **L**, then **R** at gate into another part of wood.
2 Turn **L** to follow path around top edge of wood, then **L** again to leave wood at gate. Cross road; follow grassy path across **Birkrigg Common**. Turn **L** to reach wall corner; walk few paces to **stone circle**. Follow any grassy path to skyline and trig point.
3 Pass bench; take path to **R** to reach road. Cross then walk parallel to another road – common tapers out to cattle grid. Proceed on road; make sharp **R** along walled track.
4 Cross stile at end; bear **R** past stone trough (ancient **homestead**). Keep **L** of wall to cross stile at gate. Bear **L** to take path down valley to gate. Turn **R** before gate; cross stile; follow hedgerow across slope to house. Cross stile leading down to road; turn **L** to pass farm buildings at **Holme Bank**.
5 Turn **R** ('Public Footpath Church Road'). Cross ladder stile and footbridge; take path to **village hall** and road. Cross road; turn **R** to pass school. Pass church and shop.
6 Turn **R** at **Coot on Tarn** to follow another road. At Clint Cottage on L and Tarn House on R, turn **L** up steep track. At 2 gates go through gate on **L**; proceed ahead, keeping R of low hill.
7 Wall leads to gate, then keep straight on. Cross stile on **R**, other side of gate; cross stile on **L**. Walk ahead, crossing 2 stiles to reach road junction. Turn **R** to walk through crossroads to farm.
8 Turn **R** at **Far Mount Barrow** ('Bardsea Green'). Cross stile by gate; keep **L** to cross road on **Birkrigg Common**. Turn **L** for **Bardsea Green**, along path parallel to road, then parallel to wall.
9 At corner of wall, go through gate; follow track to road and cross dip. Turn **L** at junction into **Bardsea** then **R** at **Braddylls Arms** pub. Follow road to shore.

301 ESKDALE CUMBRIA

6.75 MILES (10.9KM) 4hrs

PATHS: Good paths in valleys, but often indistinct on hills, 4 stiles (Not advised in poor visibility)

SUGGESTED MAP: aqua3 OS Explorer OL6 The English Lakes (SW)

GRID REFERENCE: NY 173007

PARKING: Car park beside Dalegarth Station (pay-and-display)

THE PUB: The Boot, Boot

1 Follow lane down valley towards **Beckfoot Bridge**. Immediately before railway halt, cross line to gate from where zig-zag path to **Blea Tarn** is signed up hillside. Approaching tarn, go **L**, crossing stream emanating from its foot.
2 Vague path maintains firm ground **R** of **Blind and Siney tarns**; at fork, bear **L**. Beyond lone tree, go **L** again. Although way is marshy, old sleepers span worst patch around Sineytarn Moss. Eventually, route joins wall, dropping beside it to level grass.
3 Bear **R** to fence stile by forest and continue along its edge below **Fell End**. Keep going near wall, eventually reaching its corner before another plantation. Short track on **R** descends to junction, and another **R** turn takes you into Miterdale.
4 Emerge on to tarmac lane at bottom; go through gate opposite into Miterdale Forest. Drop over river and then bear **R** on undulating, weaving path above its far bank. Lateral wall shortly forces you uphill on to forest track. Turn **R** and follow it out of trees, joining track from R to continue up valley to **Low Place farm**.
5 Walk past farmhouse and through 2nd yard, leaving by **R-H** gates ('Wasdale'). Follow river upstream before crossing bridge to track that continues along its opposite bank. Keep ahead for nearly 0.75 mile (1.2km) until you cross stile at far end of plantation. Here, leave track and climb hill beside trees to another stile at top.
6 Bear **L** above **Black Gill** and continue parallel to wall towards higher ground of **Low Longrigg**. After 400yds (366m) strike **R** on barely visible path, making for stone circles, which briefly break horizon.
7 Bear **R** at 2nd circle; after passing beneath rocky outcrop, fork **L**. Way is still vague, but drops towards stone huts where clear path descends by them to **R**.
8 Follow it down **Boot Bank** and into **Boot**, and cross Whillan Beck by **Eskdale Mill** to continue through village. At end turn **R** to **Dalegarth Station**.

302 BUTTERMERE CUMBRIA

4.5 MILES (7.2KM) 2hrs

PATHS: Good path, some road walking, 2 stiles

SUGGESTED MAP: aqua3 OS Explorer OL4 The English Lakes (NW)

GRID REFERENCE: NY 173169

PARKING: National Park car park beyond Fish Hotel (fee)

THE PUB: Bridge Hotel

1 Leave car park and turn **R**, passing **Fish Hotel** to follow broad track through gates. Ignore signposted route to Scale Force; continue along track towards edge of lake. Then follow line of hedgerow to bridge at **Buttermere Dubs**. Cross small footbridge; go through nearby gate in wall at foot of **Burtness Wood** and cascade of **Sourmilk Gill**. Turn **L** on track through woodland that roughly parallels lakeshore, finally emerging from woodland near **Horse Close**, where bridge spans **Comb Beck**.
2 Continue along path to reach wall leading to sheepfold and gate. Go **L** through gate, cross **Warnscale Beck** and walk out to **Gatesgarth Farm**. At farm, follow signs to reach valley road. Short stretch of road walking, **L** on **B5289**, now follows, along which there are no pathways. Take care against approaching traffic.
3 As road bends L, leave it for footpath on **L** ('Buttermere via Lakeshore Path'). Path leads into field, beyond which it never strays far from shoreline; continue to stand of Scots pine, near **Crag Wood**.
4 Beyond Hassnesshow Beck bridge, path enters grounds of **Hassness**, where rocky path, enclosed by trees, leads to gate. Here path has been cut across crag where it plunges into lake below, and shortly disappears into brief, low and damp tunnel. The tunnel was cut by employees of George Benson – 19th-century Manchester mill owner – so that he could walk around the lake without straying too far from its shore. After you emerge from tunnel, gate gives access to gravel path across wooded pasture of **Pike Rigg**, beyond which clear path leads to traditional Lakeland bridge of slate slabs.
5 Short way on, through gate, path leads to **Wilkinsyke Farm**, and easy walk out to road, just short way above **Bridge Hotel**. Turn **L** to return to car park.

303 SEDBERGH CUMBRIA

4.5 MILES (7.2KM) 1hr 30min

PATHS: Mostly on field and riverside paths, 7 stiles

SUGGESTED MAP: aqua3 OS Explorer OL19 Howgill Fells & Upper Eden Valley

GRID REFERENCE: SD 659921

PARKING: Pay-and-display car park just off Sedbergh main street (which is one-way, from west)

THE PUB: The Dalesman

1 From car park, turn **R** along main street, continue to junction with main road; turn **L**. At churchyard turn **R** ('Cattle Market or Busk Lane'). At next signpost, go **L** behind pavilion; straight ahead through 2 kissing gates and out on to road. Cross and go through another metal kissing gate ('**Birks**'). Follow path through another gate to **Birks House**.
2 Go through kissing gate beyond house; turn **L** along lane. Opposite Old Barn go **R**, through metal kissing gate. Follow **Brigflatts** sign roughly half **L** to waymarker. Go through 4 gates and under gated railway arch. Continue ahead and go through, in turn, gate in crossing wall, metal kissing gate and farm gate on to lane opposite Quaker Burial Ground.
3 Turn **L** to visit **Meeting House**, then return to gate, continuing up lane to main road. Turn **L**. Just beyond bend sign, go through signed kissing gate in hedge on **L**. Follow riverside path through 2 gates to another gate, to **L** of large railway bridge over river.
4 Go through gate; over embankment to another gate. Continue along riverside, passing through gate near confluence of 2 rivers, then 2 more gates to reach metalled lane by old **mill.**
5 Follow lane back into **Birks**. Go **R**, though kissing gate ('Rawthey Way') (you went through this gate on outward route). By hedge around **Birks House**, bear **R** towards river and over stile. Follow river to another stile; climb slightly **L** to stile by gateway; past **folly**, to **L** of wood, through kissing gate. Walk through wood to stile. Go across field to metal gate then stile on to road by bridge. Turn **L**. By ('30') sign, go **R**, though stile. Go across field to another stile; bear **L** alongside building to another kissing gate.
6 Cross drive to another kissing gate. Continue downhill to another, and go straight on along lane to main road. Cross over road. Walk behind row of houses, along **Sedbergh's** main street to car park.

304 DENT CUMBRIA

6 MILES (9.7KM) 2hrs 15min

PATHS: Tracks, field and riverside paths, some roads, 13 stiles

SUGGESTED MAP: aqua3 OS Explorer OL2 Yorkshire Dales – Southern & Western

GRID REFERENCE: SD 70487 Parking: Pay-and-display car park at west end of Dent

THE PUB: The Sun

1 Leave car park; turn **R**, then **L** by **Memorial Hall**. Pass green; keep ahead at signpost ('Flinter Gill'). Metalled lane becomes stony track that climbs steeply. Cross stile by gate. Continue uphill, through gate, to another gate by seat. Go through gate to T-junction of tracks.
2 Turn **R** ('**Keldishaw**'). Follow walled track for 1.5 miles (2.4km), through gate and over bridge, then downhill to metalled road. Turn **R**; follow road for 0.25 mile (400m) to signpost to Underwood on **L**.
3 Go through gate. Follow grassy track, to ladder stile. Continue with wall on L to reach track. It bends **R** and becomes path on ridge above valley, eventually descending through yard of **ruined farmhouse**.
4 Bend **R** at end of farm buildings to follow track to **R** of ruined stone wall. Go through gap in wall, then downhill, bending **R** to another gateway. After gateway keep ahead, away from track, to waymarked post. Turn **L** along stream bank for few paces, then go downhill to cross simple bridge of 2 stones. Climb other side of bank; go through 2 gates by buildings.
5 Continue down track, until just before telephone lines, then cross it. Turn **L** by tree; go through waymarked gate. Walk ahead across field, around **R** of ruined farmhouse. Continue downhill to gate with handgate beside it, after which track bends **R**, descending to metalled lane by barn.
6 Turn **L** along lane for few paces; keep ahead along track to **Dillicar** farm. In farmyard, bear **L** then **R** to gate; turn **R** to ladder stile by barn. Turn **L** along lane; turn **R** to plank bridge and stile ('**Dales Way**'). Cross field to river bank; follow river upstream through 7 gates and over 3 footbridges to arrive at gated stone steps up to squeeze stile and on to stone bridge.
7 Cross bridge, go through stile and down steps, to continue on riverside path. Cross 4 stiles, plank bridge, then 3 more stiles to emerge to road. Turn **L**. Follow road to **Dent**.

305 KIRKBY LONSDALE CUMBRIA

4.75 MILES (7.7KM) 2hrs 30min

PATHS: A little overgrown and indistinct in patches, quiet lanes and tracks, plenty of stiles

SUGGESTED MAP: aqua3 OS Explorer OL2 Yorkshire Dales – Southern & Western

GRID REFERENCE: SD 615782

PARKING: Devil's Bridge car park, Kirkby Lonsdale (free of charge)

THE PUB: Dragon's Head, Whittington

1 From west bank of river, downstream from **Devil's Bridge**, take path ('**Whittington**') across park to **A65**. Cross road, go through meadow and between houses; cross B6254. At meadow head uphill, keeping walled wooded area on L. Yellow markers and sign to **Wood End** help find route. Proceed over brow of hill and through 2 stiles. Turn **L** at gap stile into Wood End farmyard.
2 Turn **R** on track towards **Wood End Cottage**. Go **L** in front of cottage along walled path to **Sellet Mill**. Stream comes in L, but drier ground approaches. Path opens out by mill race.
3 Turn **R** by homesteads; walk up field, keeping fence L, until level with end of garden. Go **L** through yellow-marked gate; cross field to gate followed by stream. Bear **R** around **Sellet Bank**, aiming initially for corner of hedge under pylons. Continue with hedge R.
4 Go through yellow-marked stile on **R**; bear **L** round wooded area. Facing **Sellet Hall**, turn **R** next to driveway following marker arrows; cross over corner of field to cross stile; descend steps to road at T-junction. Turn **L** on **Hosticle Lane** towards **Whittington**.
5 Follow lane to Whittington with **Hagg Wood** on R, beech and hawthorn hedges beside you.
6 Go **L** at T-junction for few paces; cross road; turn **R** over mosaic at **Church of St Michael the Archangel**. Keep bell tower on L before descending steps to go through stile and graveyard. Proceed through gate in **L** corner. Cross over 2 fields to stone stile leading to walled lane leading to Main Street. Turn **R**, in front of building (1875). Continue past village hall and **pub**.
7 At sharp R bend on village edge turn **L** along sandy track, passing farm and tennis courts. Follow lane between fields to reach pair of gates. Go through gates on **L**. Bear **L** to reach riverside walk – **Lune Valley Ramble** – back to **A65** bridge at **Kirkby Lonsdale**. Go through gate, up steps to L of parapet. Cross road then drop down other side to cross park.

Northeast
ENGLAND

Contents   page

306   Wharncliffe Woods,
South Yorkshire   347

307   High Ackworth,
West Yorkshire   349

308   Calderdale, West Yorkshire   351

309   Harewood Estate,
West Yorkshire   353

310   Bolton Abbey,
North Yorkshire   355

311   Malham Cove,
North Yorkshire   357

312   Hubberholme,
North Yorkshire   359

313   West Burton,
North Yorkshire   361

314   Hawes & Hardraw,
North Yorkshire   363

315   Wensleydale,
North Yorkshire   365

316   Horsehouse, North Yorkshire   367

317   Lofthouse, North Yorkshire   369

318   Harland Way,
North Yorkshire   371

319   Bardsey, West Yorkshire   373

320   York, North Yorkshire   375

321   Lastingham, North Yorkshire   377

322   Goathland, North Yorkshire   379

323   Terrington, North Yorkshire   381

324   Hambleton Hills,
North Yorkshire   383

325   Byland Abbey,
North Yorkshire   385

326   Dalby Forest,
North Yorkshire   387

327   Thixendale, North Yorkshire   389

328   Robin Hood's Bay,
North Yorkshire   391

329   Robin Hood's Bay,
North Yorkshire   393

330   East Riding   395

331   South Yorkshire   395

332   to 335   West Yorkshire   395

336   West Yorkshire   396

337   to 341   North Yorkshire   396

342   to 344   North Yorkshire   397

345   to 346   Durham   397

347   Tyne & Wear   397

348   to 353   Northumberland   398

NORTHEAST ENGLAND

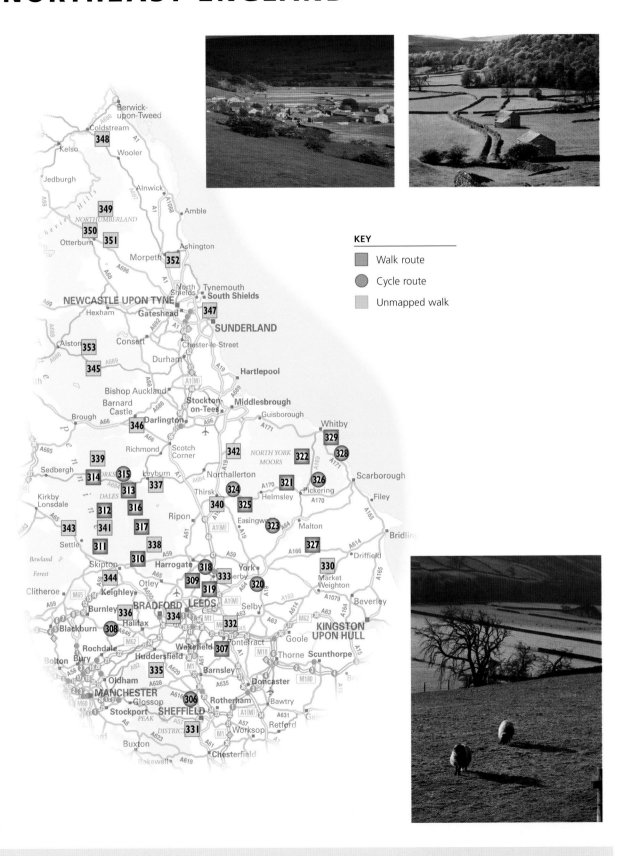

KEY

- Walk route
- Cycle route
- Unmapped walk

Sheffield's Kelham Island Museum stands on a man-made island more than 900 years old. At this 'living' museum you can see the most powerful working steam engine in Europe, reconstructed workshops, and craftspeople demonstrating traditional 'made in Sheffield' skills. Find out about the growth of the city, the people, and processes of industrial Sheffield, from the Victorian era through both world wars. Younger visitors will enjoy the activity trails.

Wharncliffe Woods

The Don River steam engine at Kelham Island Museum

1h30 · **7 MILES** · **11.3 KM** · **LEVEL 123**

Below: Wharncliffe Woods

A taste of mountain biking in a hotbed of the sport.

Wharncliffe Woods

Mountain biking is a relatively young sport, its origins usually traced to California in the late 1970s, but has grown hugely in popularity and cross-country racing has been an Olympic discipline since 1996. But it's the downhill variety for which Wharncliffe Woods is most notable. Double World Cup downhill champion Steve Peat learned his trade in this area and has subsequently been among those responsible for the construction of some fearsome routes here. Serious downhillers require some highly specialised gear, including body protection and full-face helmets. The bikes, too, are specialised, with beefed-up suspension front and rear and powerful disc brakes. There is also a sub-sport known as freeride, which involves tackling the biggest possible jumps and drop-offs.

The Wharncliffe Woods area has been subject to quarrying for millennia, with evidence of Iron Age activity on Wharncliffe Crags; in fact the name Wharncliffe derives from the word 'quern', which is a small hand-operated grindstone mostly used in grinding grain for flour. The rock is, of course, millstone grit. The crags are now popular with rock-climbers. Later the woods were managed to provide fuel for the iron industry that flourished in the Don Valley from the 16th century onwards. Today Forest Enterprise continues to extract some timber commercially but the woods are increasingly managed for amenity and conservation and areas have been planted with broad-leaved native trees such as oak and birch.

the ride

1 From the car park turn left along the broad trail. At a collection of **signposts** turn right and then duck under a barrier on the left on to a narrower path. After

another barrier the trail becomes broader again, descending gently through attractive **woods** of oak and birch. Negotiate another barrier and turn right on a track that descends more steeply. At the bottom of a particularly steep section is a **3-way bridleway sign**.

2 Turn right, and continue through more downhill sections. Cross a small wooden bridge, and duck under a barrier, back into **Wharncliffe Woods** proper.

3 Turn left and continue downhill, swinging right on to a more gently descending section of track. At a fork bear left, emerge on to a broad track, and immediately fork right, passing a Trans Pennine Trail sign for **Wortley**. Continue downhill, taking great care on a section with a very loose surface where another track joins from the left. As a second track comes in from the left, look up to the right and you can see the first of the **MTB downhill routes** emerging on to the main track.

4 Now there's a slight climb followed by some gentle undulations, bringing you into a densely wooded section and coming close to a **railway line** on the left. After more level riding there's a fork, with a **Trans**

Pennine Trail sign. Follow this down the broader left branch, swinging back right and rising where a narrower track forks off to the left. Now begin a long gentle ascent, which dips under power lines. Look out for **Wharncliffe Crags** on the right through the trees before a slight dip. The track levels out for a short way. When it begins to climb again look for a sharp right turn just beyond another Trans Pennine Trail sign. There are also signs for **Wharncliffe Heath nature reserve**.

5 The climb isn't excessively steep anywhere, but some sections are made really tricky by the surface, which is either loose sand, loose stones or a mixture. Anyone who completes the ascent without dismounting can claim to have passed the entry exam to real mountain biking. Keep straight on through a gap in a wall and along a more level sandy track, now with open **moorland** on the right and some fine mature **oak woods** on the left. After another short ascent, meet a slightly wider track and continue straight ahead. Just beyond this the path levels out, with the most expansive views of the entire ride. As you come back into woods, the track dips down, with quite a tricky section over rocks and mud, to a road.

306

CYCLE

MAP: OS Explorer 278 Sheffield & Barnsley

START/FINISH: Wharncliffe Woods car park; grid ref: SK 325951

TRAILS/TRACKS: mostly good forest tracks with a few narrower and/or rougher sections

LANDSCAPE: mature woodland, mostly coniferous plantations, with occasional views of farmland, heathland and crags

PUBLIC TOILETS: none on route

TOURIST INFORMATION: Sheffield, tel 01142 211900

CYCLE HIRE: Cycosport, Barnsley, tel 01226 204020

THE PUB: The Wortley Arms Hotel, Wortley

❶ Some steep climbs and descents; beware some loose surfaces. For older, experienced children; mountain bike essential

Getting to the start

From M1 junction 36, follow the A61 towards Sheffield for 1.5 miles (2.4km), over a roundabout. Take the next right turn to Howbrook. Go left at the crossroads in the village. Follow this lane for about 0.5 mile (800m), crossing the A629, to reach a T-junction. Go left and in about 2 miles (3.2km) reach the main parking area for Wharncliffe Woods (on the right).

Why do this cycle ride?

Wharncliffe Woods is a name that dedicated mountain bikers recognise. Competitions are regularly held here. Our route doesn't involve anything extreme, but it does give a little of the flavour, with some fairly steep but well-surfaced descents, and a challenging climb. For a more straightforward ride, follow the green waymarked route from the car park.

Researched and written by: Jon Sparks

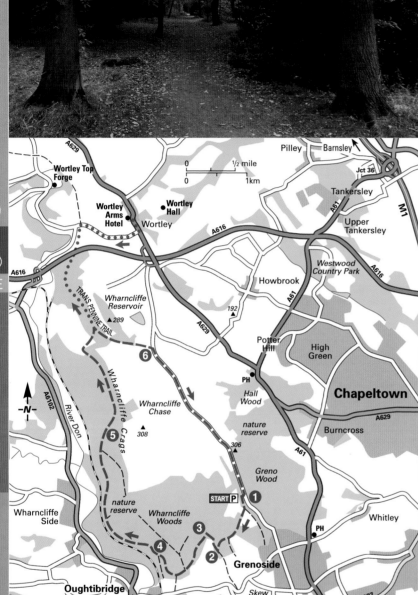

The small car park at the start of the cycle ride is also the starting point for forest walks and horse-riding trails. You'll also find a picnic site and an information point.

A quiet, shady path in Wharncliffe Woods

The Wortley Arms Hotel

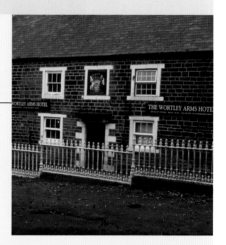

The landlord of this rambling old village pub is well used to cyclists and walkers. The pub is an official Trans Pennine Trail Stamping Point (anyone riding or walking the full coast-to-coast route can obtain a card and get it stamped at various points along the route). Also, since it was formerly known as The Wharncliffe Arms, there couldn't be a much more appropriate choice for this ride. It's a solid stone building that was built on the site of an earlier hostelry in 1754, with the arms of the Earls of Wharncliffe carved in stone over the door. Many of the old materials were used in the construction and inside you can see some fine wood panelling, exposed stonework, wooden floors and low beams, while in the lounge bar there's a huge inglenook fireplace with a log fire in winter.

Food

The lounge bar menu lists good traditional pub food. Choices include an extensive list of sandwiches and baguettes, various salads and filled jacket potatoes, and main dishes such as cod and chips, steak and ale pie and a roast of the day.

Family facilities

Children are welcome in the bars. There are no play facilities but young children do have their own menu.

Alternative refreshment stops

None on the route. Plenty of hotels, cafés, pubs and restaurants in Sheffield.

☞ Where to go from here

Sheffield has much to offer the family. Visit Kelham Island Museum for the story of Sheffield, its industry and life (www.simt.co.uk), the Fire and Police Museum or the Sheffield Bus Museum. Nearer Wharncliffe and Wortley is Wortley Top Forge (www.topforge.co.uk), the last example of a working water-powered drop forge. You can also look round Wortley Hall Gardens.

about the pub

The Wortley Arms Hotel
Halifax Road, Wortley
Sheffield, South Yorkshire S35 7DB
Tel: 01142 882245

DIRECTIONS: turn left from Wharncliffe Woods car park. At the junction of the A616 and A629, follow the A629 north for 0.5 mile (800m) to Wortley. Pub in village centre

PARKING: 30

OPEN: daily; all day

FOOD: daily; all day Saturday, Sunday until 6.30pm

BREWERY/COMPANY: free house

REAL ALE: Wortley Golden Best, Oakwell Barnsley Bitter, Black Sheep Bitter, Timothy Taylor Landlord, guest beers

ROOMS: 3 en suite

6 Turn right and follow the road up a long gentle ascent. At the crest of the climb, coming back to **woods** on the right, another **Trans Pennine Trail sign** indicates a track that leads back to the car park.

There's no pub right on the ride route, though it could fairly easily be extended by continuing along the Trans Pennine Trail for about another mile (1.6km); pass under the A616 then soon after drop down to a minor road and follow it east to the A629. Turn left into Wortley.

Nostell Priory is now cared for by the National Trust

High Ackworth and East Hardwick

Below left: Walkers near High Ackworth

An undemanding stroll through history in rolling, pastoral countryside to the east of Wakefield.

Ackworth

With its village green acting as the centrepiece for some fine old houses, High Ackworth has a pleasantly old-fashioned air and is now a designated conservation area. Today the village is best known for its school, founded by a prominent Quaker, John Fothergil, to teach the children of 'Friends not in affluence', in October 1779. Opposite the village green are almshouses, built in 1741 to house 'a schoolmaster and six poor women'. Nearby Ackworth Old Hall, dating from the early 17th century, is said to be haunted by John Nevison, a notorious robber and highwayman. His most famous act of daring was in 1676 when he rode from Rochester to York in just 15 hours. The story goes that he committed a robbery and was afraid he had been recognised. Fleeing the scene, he covered the 230 miles (370km) in record time. When he arrived in York, he asked the

Lord Mayor the time. After his arrest he used the Mayor as his alibi and he was acquitted. No one believed the journey could be made in so short a time.

Until the Reformation, the stone plinth on the village green was topped by a cross. It was knocked off by Cromwell's troops. The cross had been erected in memory of Father Thomas Balne of nearby Nostell Priory, who once preached from here. On a pilgrimage to Rome, he succumbed to the plague. When his body was being brought back to the priory, mourners insisted on opening the coffin here in High Ackworth. As a result, the plague devasted the community. The Plague Stone, by the Pontefract Road, dates from a second outbreak in 1645.

the walk

1 From the top of the village green, take a narrow ginnel immediately to the right of **Manor House**. Beyond a stile made of stone slabs (not the last you'll see today), keep to the right-hand edge of a small field, to another stile. A ginnel brings you out into **Woodland Grove**; go left here, then first

right, to meet the A628, Pontefract Road. Go left, but for just 100yds (91m). Look out on the right for a gap in the hedgerow and a footpath sign (opposite a house called **Tall Trees**). Walk straight across a field (follow the direction of the sign), to a tiny footbridge over a beck. Continue along the right-hand edge of the next field, over another tiny bridge. Keep ahead between fields – going sharp left, then sharp right, over another footbridge – to follow a hedgerow. When you come to a gap in the hedge, head straight across the next two fields (towards the **houses** you see ahead).

2 Take a bridge over a railway line, and continue between fields towards **Hundhill Farm**. Keep right at the farm's boundary wall, to a stile. Bear left along the lane; after just 75yds (69m), and after a left-hand bend, take a gap stile in the wall on your right, on to an enclosed path. Beyond the next stile, bear right along a minor road that soon meets the A639. Cross the road, passing the **old village pump**, and walk into the village of **East Hardwick**. Beyond the **church**, where the road bears left, look out for a sign ('Public Bridleway') on your right, just before a house called **Bridleways**.

3 Go right here, along a track between hedgerows. Soon after the track goes left, take a gap in the hedge to your right. Follow a field path uphill, keeping a hedgerow to your right. At the top of this narrow field, keep straight ahead on a footpath between fields. Follow a drainage channel to meet a crossing track. Go right here, to cross over the A639 again. Take the road ahead (this is Rigg Lane) and, at **White Gates Farm**, go left, between farm buildings, on to a concrete track.

2h30 | **5 MILES** | **8 KM** | **LEVEL 123**

MAP: OS Explorer 278 Sheffield & Barnsley

START/FINISH: High Ackworth, park near church and village green; grid ref: SE 441180

PATHS: mostly field paths; care should be taken with route finding, on the first section to East Hardwick, 11 stiles

LANDSCAPE: gently rolling, arable country

PUBLIC TOILETS: none on route

TOURIST INFORMATION: Wakefield, tel 01924 305000

THE PUB: The Brown Cow, High Ackworth

❶ Busy and fast roads to cross at High Ackworth and East Hardwick

Getting to the start

High Ackworth is on the A628 road 3 miles south of Pontefract. The village green, where there is parking, can be found to the west of The Brown Cow pub. Coming from the west it is on the left, just beyond the junction with the 'Featherstone' B road.

Researched and written by: John Gillham, John Morrison

The National Trust

For over a hundred years, the National Trust has been acquiring and protecting threatened coastline, countryside and buildings. To find out more about the organisation, its sites and policies, visit their website at www.nationaltrust.org.uk

A green country lane at High Ackworth

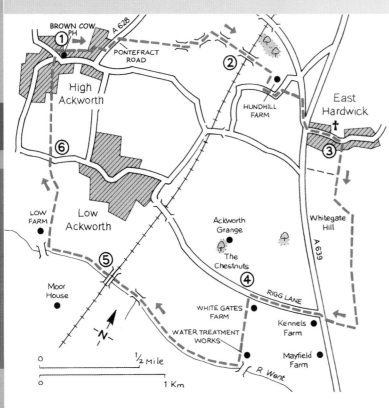

The Brown Cow

On the main road near the triangular village green, this Victorian pub was once a coaching inn. There are a couple of tables in front of the pub and a few more to the rear. A large carpeted bar area with a deep sofa and a combination of upholstered bench seats and wooden cottage-style chairs characterise the plushly refurbished interior.

Food

From the standard menu you can order sandwiches, jacket potatoes, omelettes, lasagne, gammon and chips and a choice of steaks. Daily home-made specials may include spinach and ricotta cannelloni, salmon and broccoli mornay, a roast joint of beef (also used for sandwiches), and chilli with rice.

Family facilities

Children are very welcome in the dining areas if they are eating. There's a kiddies menu and half-portions of some main meals are available.

Alternative refreshment stops

There are restaurants in Ackworth.

about the pub

The Brown Cow
Pontefract Road, Ackworth
Pontefract, West Yorkshire WF7 7EL
Tel: 01977 704735

DIRECTIONS: beside the A628 and village green in High Ackworth

PARKING: 30

OPEN: daily; all day Friday, Saturday and Sunday

FOOD: daily at lunchtime; Thursday, Friday and Saturday evenings only

BREWERY/COMPANY: Enterprise Inns

REAL ALE: John Smiths, guest beer

DOGS: not allowed inside the pub

☛ Where to go from here

Spend some time at Nostell Priory, built in the mid 18th century and extended in 1766 and containing a notable saloon, a tapestry room, pictures and Chippendale furniture (www.nationaltrust.org.uk). Take the children to the National Coal Mining Museum near Wakefield and travel 460ft (140m) underground for a tour with an ex-miner. Discover the fascinating galleries and exhibitions, explore the colliery site and meet the pit ponies (www.ncm.org.uk). South of Wakefield, off the M1, is the Yorkshire Sculpture Park at West Bretton (www.ysp.co.uk). Set in 500 acres (202ha) of 18th century designed landscape, it is an international centre for modern and contemporary sculpture.

4 Follow this track past a **water treatment works**, to a concrete bridge over the River Went (notice the old packhorse bridge next to it). Without crossing either bridge, bear right, on a field-edge path, to accompany the river. A little **plank bridge** takes you across a side-beck, before you walk beneath the six arches of a railway viaduct.

5 Continue by the riverside, passing (not crossing) a stone bridge over the river. Bear right here, across the corner of a field, in front of the barns of **Low Farm**, to join a field-edge path. Follow a hedge towards houses, to a stile and a road. This is **Low Ackworth**.

6 Cross the road and take a ginnel between houses. Beyond a stile at the far end, bear half left across a field to a stile and across another field. A stile gives access to another ginnel. Continue along Hill Drive, soon bearing right, down into a **cul-de-sac**. At the bottom, take a narrow ginnel on the left, to arrive back in High Ackworth near the village green and **The Brown Cow**.

what to look for

Village greens are uncommon features in West Yorkshire, a county in which even the smallest community can feel like a town. But the Industrial Revolution passed Ackworth by; no mill chimneys ever disturbed the symmetry. Surrounded by buildings of character – including the parish church, Manor House and a row of almshouses – Ackworth has managed to retain its village atmosphere.

The fieldfare
(Turdus pilaris)

while you're there

North east of Hebden Bridge is the National Trust's Hardcastle Crags. Here waymarked walks lead through a beautiful wooded valley with deep rocky ravines, streams and woodland to Gibson Mill.

Hardcastle Crags

Calderdale and the Rochdale Canal

The Rochdale Canal flowing through the mill town of Hebden Bridge

Take an easy tow-path ride through West Yorkshire's industrial heritage.

The Rochdale Canal

Like most northern valleys, Calderdale used to be a swamp, choked with scrub alder trees. For centuries packhorse trains carried by Galloway ponies had tramped the Pennine high roads, linking the mill villages like Mankinholes, Heptonstall, and Sowerby. The Industrial Revolution changed all that. Fast transportation became the watchword as new heavy industries flourished. The valleys were cleared and drained, with new roads and towns built. The idea for the Rochdale Canal was first mooted in 1766 when James Brindley was asked to undertake a survey. It wasn't until 1794, 22 years after Brindley's death, that the necessary Act of Parliament was passed. The 33 mile (53km) canal, designed by William Jessop, would extend the existing Calder and Hebble Navigation through Todmorden and Rochdale to link with the Bridgewater Canal at Castlefield in Manchester. Upland reservoirs had to be constructed to feed the 92 locks before the first trans-Pennine canal opened in 1804.

The railways came. In 1841 George Stephenson surveyed and built a line parallel to the canal. Initially, the combination worked well and the annual goods passing through by barge had reached 686,000 tons. By the 20th century, however, the tonnage had declined. In 1952 the canal closed. Happily, that was not the end of the story, for the 1980s and 90s saw the restoration of the canal – this time for leisure activities.

the ride

1 There's access to the canal at the back of the car park where you turn left along the tow path, past old mill buildings. On the initial stages the shapely hill of **Stoodley Pike** and its obelisk monument looms large on the horizon. You'll see many houseboats moored on Veever's Wharf just outside the town – many have their own canalside gardens. Take care when rounding the canal locks hereabouts for the gates protrude across the tow path. High on a hillside to the left the gaunt soot-stained church at **Cross Stone** offers a stark contrast to the stone-built canalside terraces with their pretty cottage gardens. The River Calder closes in on the canal, and before long you find yourself cycling on a narrow tree-lined island between the two watercourses.

2 Just beyond **Holmcoat Lock No 14** the tow path joins a tarred lane for a short stretch before descending back to the canalside. Take care here. At **Charlestown** pass the sewage works as quickly as possible! Just beyond the works the route is crossed by the Pennine Way long-distance path. For those in need of early refreshment, the tow path goes right by the **Stubbing Wharf pub**, which has tables outside in the summer, then the canal café. Next to the latter there's the Hebden Bridge Alternative Technology Centre.

3 On reaching Hebden Bridge proper you climb to and cross a **humpback bridge**, beyond which the tow path continues on the opposite bank, between the canal and a park (with toilets). However, you will probably wish to take a look around this

pleasant mill town. This is also a good turning point for cyclists with limited time or with young children. The wharf here has been restored and is usually highlighted by smart, brightly coloured longboats.

4 A mile (1.6km) beyond the town the tow path climbs out to the busy Halifax road to avoid a short tunnel. It's best to get off here and cross carefully. There's a short track leading back to the canalside, which leads into **Mytholmroyd**. To get to the pub, leave the tow path and turn right along the road to the A road. Turn right again here, then left down New Road, signed 'to Cragg'.

5 Return to the tow path and continue past the **cricket club**. Beyond this there's a short but steady climb to reach a road near the apex of a bend. Cross with care and descend back to the tow path. You're back into the country again until **Luddenden Foot** where you'll need to get off to go down some steps in the tow path.

6 The tow path goes through the short **Hollins Mill Tunnel** where it's single file only. Give way to riders and walkers already in the tunnel. Beyond this you arrive at Sowerby Bridge. The **Tuel Lock** here is the deepest inland water lock in the UK. **Wainhouse Tower** is on the distant hill. Turn round and retrace your route back to the start or go back by train.

4h00 | 18 MILES | 29 KM | LEVEL 123

MAP: OS Explorer OL21 South Pennines

START/FINISH: Lever Street car park, Todmorden; grid ref: SD 938241

TRAILS/TRACKS: narrow canal tow path

LANDSCAPE: mill towns, woodland and a semi-rural valley

PUBLIC TOILETS: the park at Hebden Bridge, and car park at Tuel Lock, Sowerby Bridge

TOURIST INFORMATION: Hebden Bridge, tel 01422 843831

CYCLE HIRE: none locally

THE PUB: Shoulder of Mutton, Mytholmroyd

❶ Unsuitable for small children. Take care under bridges: dismount if not confident. Permit needed to cycle tow paths (download from www.waterscape.com/cycling)

Getting to the start

Todmorden is at the junction of the A646 Burnley to Halifax Road and the A6033 to Rochdale. The car park is just east of the town centre along the Halifax Road. With your back to the town centre, turn right (south) along Union Street South, which leads to Lever Street Car Park. The railway runs parallel, with stations at Todmorden, Hebden Bridge, Mytholmroyd and Sowerby Bridge, so it is possible to cycle one way and get the train back.

Why do this cycle ride?

Ride through the history of the Industrial Revolution and transportation, past and present.

Researched and written by: John Gillham

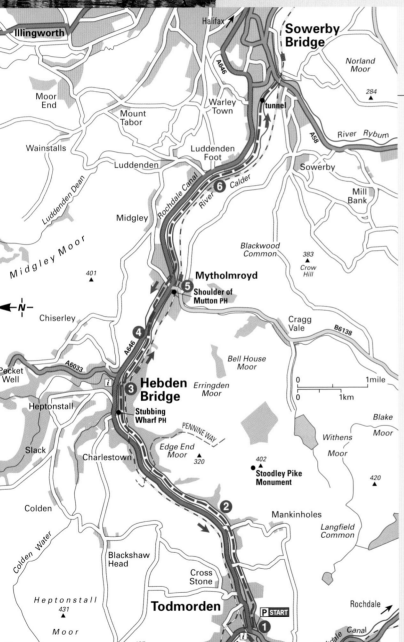

did you know?

The visitor centre on the Rochdale Canal is situated in a converted barge at the Marina in Hebden Bridge. From here there are motorboat and horse-drawn cruises on the canal. Visitors can travel up and down the locks and be legged through a tunnel by crew in traditional dress. The cruises vary from 30 minutes to 2 hours.

A daily summer water bus operates to Walkleys Clog Factory, Britain's last remaining such factory, where visitors can see traditional clogs being made and talk to master clog-makers.

Shoulder of Mutton

A typical Pennines pub, next to a trout stream, well situated for local walks and the popular Calderdale Way. It was associated with the infamous Crag Coiners, 18th-century forgers who made their own golden guineas. There's a display of memorabilia (coins and tools) relating to the Coiners above the fireplace in the spacious bar, which also features a rustic board and black-and-red tiled floor. There's a cosy, cottage-style dining room with low beams and dark wood furnishings, and a secure back yard for bikes.

Food

A menu featuring home-cooked dishes from fresh ingredients includes good-value snacks like sandwiches (served with chips), filled jacket potatoes and burger and chips. Main meals include beef in ale pie, Cumberland sausages, steak and onion pie, a daily roast from the carvery, and up to ten vegetarian dishes.

Family facilities

Children are welcome inside and smaller portions of dishes are readily available. Sheltered garden beside the trout stream.

Alternative refreshment stops

The Stubbing Wharf pub beside the canal near Hebden Bridge and the Canal Café at Hebden Bridge.

☛ Where to go from here

Drive up to see the attractive old weaving village of Heptonstall, above Hebden Bridge. Take the children to Eureka! The Museum for Children in Halifax, a fully interactive museum with over 400 'must touch' exhibits inviting you to take a journey of discovery through four main gallery spaces: Me and My Body, Living and Working Together, Our Global Garden and Invent, Create and Communicate (www.eureka.org.uk).

about the pub

Shoulder of Mutton

New Road, Mytholmroyd
Halifax, West Yorkshire HX7 5DZ
Tel: 01422 883165

DIRECTIONS: On B6138 in Mytholmroyd, opposite the railway station

PARKING: 16

OPEN: daily; all day Saturday and Sunday

FOOD: no food Tuesday evening

BREWERY/COMPANY: Enterprise Inns

REAL ALE: Caledonian Deuchars IPA, Timothy Taylor Landlord, Flowers IPA, Black Sheep Bitter, guest beers

A statue near the steps at Harewood House

did you know?

You can learn more about Harewood by attending the daily free talks. In the house, experts give talks covering key elements of the collections and tours of the house take place twice a day. There are daily talks in the gardens and guided tours on Thursdays.

Harewood House and estate

A stately home with parkland by 'Capability' Brown, a few miles from Leeds.

Harewood Estate

The Harewood Estate passed through a number of hands during the 16th and 17th centuries, eventually being bought by the Lascelles family who still own the house. Edwin Lascelles left the 12th-century castle in its ruinous state but demolished the old hall. He wanted to create something special and hired the best architects and designers.

John Carr of York created a veritable palace of a house in an imposing neo-classical style, and laid out the estate village of Harewood too. The interior of the building was designed by Robert Adam. Thomas Chippendale made furniture for every room. The foundations were laid in 1759; 12 years later the house was finished. Inside are paintings by J M W Turner and Thomas Girtin. Turner was particularly taken with the area, producing pictures of many local landmarks. The sumptuous interior, full of portraits, ornate plasterwork and silk hangings, is in sharp contrast to life below stairs, in the kitchen and scullery.

The house sits in extensive grounds, which were groomed to be every bit as magnificent as the house. They were shaped by Lancelot 'Capability' Brown, the most renowned designer of the English landscape. In addition to the formal gardens, he created the lake and the woodland paths you will take on this walk.

Harewood House has had to earn its keep in recent years. The bird garden was the first commercial venture, but now the house hosts many events.

the walk

1 From the lay-by walk 50yds (46m) away from the village of Harewood, cross the busy road with care, and walk right, down the access track to **New Laithe Farm**. Keep to the left of the farm buildings, on a rutted track heading into the valley bottom. Go through two gates and bear half left up a field, towards **Hollin Hall**. Keep left of the buildings to pass **Hollin Hall Pond**.

2 Beyond the pond take a gate and follow a track to the left, uphill, skirting **woodland** before climbing half right by **gorse bushes** to a gate in the top corner of the field. Beyond this an enclosed track now continues the climb to the top of the hill.

3 Here it is joined by a grass track from the left and bends right (you are now joining the **Leeds Country Way**). Keep straight ahead when the track forks, through a gate. Skirt woodland to emerge at a road; bear right here to arrive at the main **A61**.

4 Cross the road to enter the **Harewood Estate** (via the right-hand gate, between imposing gate-posts). Follow the broad track ahead, through landscaped parkland, soon getting views of Harewood House to the right. Enter **woodland** through a gate, bearing immediately left after a stone bridge.

5 Bear right after 100yds (91m), as the track forks. At a crossing of tracks, bear half right, downhill on a track signed **Ebor Way**. Turn right at the next junction, then take a left fork to pass in front of **Carr House**. Follow a good track down towards the lake. Go through a gate, keep left of a high **brick wall** and walk uphill to join a metalled access road to the left. Walk down past a **house** and keep straight ahead at crossroads. Cross a bridge and follow the lane up to a gate, soon passing **Home Farm** (now converted to business units).

6 Follow the road through pastureland, turning right at the T-junction. Continue through woodland and pasture until you come to the few **houses** that comprise the estate village of Harewood.

The south façade of Harewood House overlooks a flower-covered parterre

3h00 · **6.5 MILES** · **10.5 KM** · **LEVEL 123**

MAP: OS Explorer 289 Leeds

START/FINISH: lay-by parking in Harewood; grid ref: SE 332450

PATHS: good paths and parkland tracks all the way, 2 stiles

LANDSCAPE: arable and parkland

PUBLIC TOILETS: none on route; in Harewood House if visiting

TOURIST INFORMATION: Wetherby, tel 01937 582151

THE PUB: The Harewood Arms, Harewood

🛈 Path passes deep water at Hollin Hill Pond. Very busy and fast roads to cross (A61 and A659)

Getting to the start

Harewood is 8 miles due north of Leeds on the junction of the A61 and the A659. The lay-by car parking lies on the north side of the A659, about a mile (1.6km) to the east of the village. When arriving from the east, the lay-by is the same distance past the fourth and last turn-off to East Hardwick.

Researched and written by:
John Gillham, John Morrison

while you're there

Harewood Bird Garden, one of the country's premier avian collections, houses more than 100 species of threatened and exotic birds. The garden promotes conservation and education, and participates in captive breeding programmes. The small colony of Humboldt penguins can be seen swimming underwater through the window into their pool. Penguin-feeding takes place every day at 2pm.

The Aysgarth Falls are in the Dales National Park

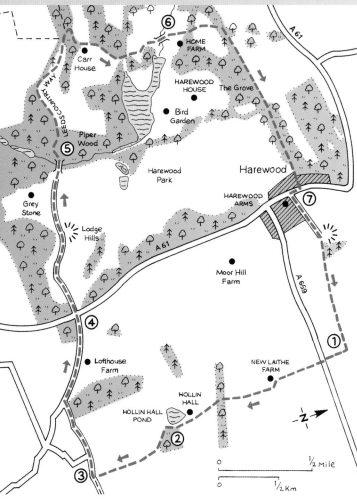

The Harewood Arms

about the pub

The Harewood Arms
Harrogate Road, Harewood
Leeds, West Yorkshire LS17 9LH
Tel: 0113 288 6566
www.harewoodarms.co.uk

DIRECTIONS: opposite the main gates to Harewood House in the village centre

PARKING: 100

OPEN: daily; all day

FOOD: daily; all day Saturday and Sunday

BREWERY/COMPANY: Samuel Smiths

REAL ALE: Samuel Smith's OBB

DOGS: allowed in the bar and garden

ROOMS: 23 en suite

Behind the rather foreboding stone façade of this Georgian hall lies a friendly pub serving excellent food. The carpeted lounge bar is extremely comfortable with many easy chairs, and Sam Smith's Old Brewery Bitter is hand-pulled from wooden casks. The restaurant serves à la carte and table d'hôte menus. Its Georgian windows look out on to the pleasant leafy back garden.

Food

In the bar tuck into various salads, sandwiches, filled baguettes, grilled Yorkshire gammon, omelettes, and local sausages and mash. In the restaurant, roast rack of lamb with redcurrant jus and sea bass with cream, white wine, prawn and fennel sauce show the style of cooking. Afternoon teas are also served.

Family facilties

Although there are no specific facilities for children, there is a family area in the bar and children are welcome overnight.

Alternative refreshment stops

If visiting Harewood House you will find a licensed café/restaurant.

☞ Where to go from here

While the walk described here uses rights of way through the grounds of Harewood House, you need to pay if you want to investigate the house itself, or the bird gardens, or the many other attractions that include an adventure playground. Make a day of it: do the walk in the morning, have lunch at the Harewood Arms and investigate the unrivalled splendour of Harewood House in the afternoon (www.harewood.org).

7 Cross the main A61 road with care and walk right, for just 50yds (46m), to take a metalled drive immediately before the Harewood Arms. Pass **Maltkiln House**, keeping straight on, through a gate, as the road becomes a track. Enjoy great views over Lower Wharfedale. Ignore the stile in the fence to your right and and stay with the pleasant track to a junction south of **Stockton Grange Farm**, where you turn right. This permissive bridleway takes you back to the A659 a few paces away from the lay-by.

what to look for

The red kite, a beautiful fork-tailed bird of prey, used to be a familiar sight. But the numbers had dwindled to just a few pairs, mostly in Wales, due to centuries of persecution. There is now a new initiative to reintroduce the red kite to Yorkshire, and a number of birds have been released at Harewood House. You may be lucky enough to spot one.

Built in 1815, this former coaching inn stands opposite the gates to Harewood House and provides a smart and comfortable base for those visiting Harrogate, Leeds, York and the Dales.

Romantic Setting

Augustinian canons built Bolton Priory in 1154. The ruins make one of the most romantic scenes in the country, and many great English artists, from Girtin and Turner onwards, have painted it.

The view across the River Wharf to the ruins of Bolton Abbey

River and woodland at Bolton Abbey

2h30 **6.75 MILES** **10.9 KM** **LEVEL 123**

MAP: OS Explorer OL2 Yorkshire Dales – Southern & Western

START/FINISH: main pay car park at Bolton Abbey; grid ref: SE 071539

PATHS: field and moorland paths, then riverside paths, 4 stiles

LANDSCAPE: moorland with wide views and riverside woodland

PUBLIC TOILETS: by car park and at Cavendish Pavilion

TOURIST INFORMATION: Skipton, tel 01756 792809

THE PUB: Devonshire Arms Hotel (Brasserie), Bolton Abbey

❗ Navigaton over moors would be difficult in poor weather. Dangerous river and currents around the Strid – read warning notices

Getting to the start

Bolton Abbey lies just to the north of the A59 between Skipton and Harrogate. Follow the B road past the Devonshire Arms. The main car park is on the left by the abbey and just before the village store.

Researched and written by:
John Gillham, David Winpenny

Over moorland and alongside the Strid to the romantic priory.

Bolton Abbey

Bolton Abbey has always been one of the showpieces of the Yorkshire Dales. The priory was built for Augustinian canons who founded their house here in 1154. This walk takes you a little further afield, and has the priory – it was never an abbey – as its climax. After passing under the archway you reach Bolton Hall, a hunting lodge for the Earls of Cumberland and their successors the Dukes of Devonshire. The walk then passes westwards through woodland to the top of a hill offering excellent views.

At the entrance to the woodland around the Strid, information boards explain the birds and plants here, including the sessile oak. Characteristic of the area, it is distinguished from the pedunculate oak by

the fact that its acorns have no stalks. At the Strid itself the River Wharfe thunders through a narrow gorge between rocks.

The underlying geology is gritstone, with large white quartz pebbles embedded in it. The flow is fast and the river is 30ft (9m) deep here, so don't be tempted to cross; there have been many drownings.

A little further on is the Cavendish Pavilion. A survivor from the early 20th century, it has been restored and is still reminiscent of leisurely days in the 1920s.

the walk

1 Leave the car park at its north end, past the Village Store and the telephone box. Turn right, walk down the left side of the green, then turn left. Pass under an archway. Opposite the battlemented **Bolton Hall**, turn left on to a track through a signed gate. Where the track bends left, go through a

gate on the right with a bridleway sign. Cross the next field, aiming slightly left for a fingerpost to the right of some trees, then pass to the right of some **pools**. Continue through the gate beyond, and then turn right towards another gate into the wood.

2 Go through the gate and follow the clear track through the wood to the top gate out into a field. A **signpost** highlights the direction of the faint grass path across fields and towards some rounded **grassy hills**. In the second large field the path crosses a well-defined track to reach a gate in the wall corner. Beyond this turn right to follow a wall then climb a small hill, with wide views to the **Lower Barden Reservoir**

and the heather hills of **Barden Moor**. A prominent green path now descends gradually to the road.

3 Turn right along the road. After about 0.75 mile (1.2km) go right through a gate by a sign '**FP to B6160**'. Follow the path across sodden fields. The path meets and follows a wall on the left, then a

Top left: The white waters of the Strid, as the River Wharfe tumbles through rocks near Bolton Abbey
Left: The ruins of Bolton Abbey

White water at the Strid on the River Wharf

6 Immediately at the end of the bridge turn right signed **'Bolton Abbey'**. Follow the path parallel with the river, eventually descending to a bridge beside stepping-stones and the **priory**.

7 Cross the bridge and walk straight ahead up the slope and the steps to a gateway – known as the **Hole in the Wall**. Go through the gateway then straight ahead beside the green to reach the car park.

footpath diversion sign points the way left over a stone stile. Descend by a wall on the left to a roadside stile directly opposite to the **Strid car park**.

4 Cross the road, go through the car park and pass beside the **Strid Wood Nature Trails Kiosk**. Follow the most prominent path, signed 'The Strid'. Turn left just before **Lady Harriot's Seat** and descend to the riverbank where you turn right to reach the narrowest part of the river at the Strid.

5 From the Strid, continue on the riverside path until you reach an **information board** and gateway. Ignore the minor path signed Lud Stream and continue along the main track slanting away from the river to the **Cavendish Pavilion**. Go through a gate, turn left by the café and go over the **footbridge**.

while you're there

If you're interested in steam trains, it's best to visit the Embsay and Bolton Abbey Steam Railway at weekends, and most days in August, too when enthusiasts run steam trains. At other times an historic diesel service operates.

what to look for

Bolton Priory church is worth exploring. It is a mix of Norman and later styles – look out for the tell-tale round Norman arches and the pointed arches of the later work. The west front is very complicated – mainly because the tower was added just before the priory was shut. It has a huge, decorative window, but masks an even better 13th-century west front. The eastern end of the church – where the canons worshipped – is in ruins. The remains of the huge east window are one of the most memorable things about Bolton Priory. The nave, now the parish church, still gives an impression of the building's original grandeur. Notice the stained-glass windows on the right-hand side as you enter. They date from the first half of the 19th century and were designed, in convincing medieval style, by Augustus Pugin, whose decorative work is found in the Houses of Parliament.

Devonshire Arms Hotel (Brasserie)

about the pub

Devonshire Arms Hotel (Brasserie)
Bolton Abbey, Skipton
North Yorkshire BD23 6AJ
Tel: 01756 710441
www.thedevonshirearms.co.uk

DIRECTIONS: see Getting to the Start

PARKING: 150

OPEN: daily; all day; closed afternoons Monday to Wednesday between October and March

FOOD: daily; all day Sunday

BREWERY/COMPANY: free house

REAL ALE: Black Sheep Bitter, Wharfedale Folly Ale

DOGS: allowed inside outside food times

ROOMS: 41 en suite

Set in the Wharfe valley close to Bolton Abbey, this former 17th-century coaching house is a stylish country house hotel with impressive bedrooms and a smart leisure club. Less formal, however, is the brasserie, with its polished wooden floorings, colourful modern art paintings on the walls, and a warm and friendly welcome to walkers and families. The bar is rather elegant, with comfortable easy chairs for those in need of a rest after their walk. There are many wooden tables on the patio to the rear of the Brasserie, for those who wish to dine outside or just relax with a cool drink. Besides the excellent (but quite expensive) main meals, sandwiches are available.

Food
Imaginative meals take in starter/main-course options like salmon fishcakes with lemon and lime mayonnaise and Moroccan chicken, lunchtime ploughman's and a smoked chicken, bacon and guacamole sandwich. Main dishes and specials may include saddle of rabbit with langoustines and capers and seared tuna on tomato, red onion and basil salad.

Family facilities
Families can expect a genuine welcome in the brasserie. There are high chairs and baby-changing facilities available, a small children's menu, and a cupboard full of games to keep children amused.

Alternative refreshment stops
Bolton Abbey is well supplied with places for a drink, a snack or a full meal. The Cavendish Pavilion has snacks, light meals and afternoon teas. The Priest's House at Barden Tower, about a mile (1.6km) north of the entrance to Strid Woods, has a restaurant and tea terrace.

☛ Where to go from here
Take a trip on the Embsay and Bolton Abbey Steam Railway, which has a station 1.5 miles (2.4km) south of the priory (www.embsayboltonabbeyrailway.org.uk). Explore Skipton and its medieval castle (www.skiptoncastle.co.uk), or view stalactites and stalagmites at Stump Cross Caverns at Greenhow near Pateley Bridge.

Gordale Scar in the Yorkshire Dales

while you're there

Visit Gordale Scar (a short walk beyond Janet's Foss). The route takes you along a valley that rapidly narrows and twists beneath overhanging rocks, until a final bend brings you to the waterfall in the narrowest part of the gorge.

Once thought to be a collapsed cave system, it is now believed to have been formed by erosion from the stream, which has carved this spectacular gash through the limestone.

A circuit taking in Malham Cove

Left: the New Bridge crossing Malham Beck is also known as the Monk's Bridge

The noble Malham Cove is the majestic highlight of this quintessential limestone Dales walk.

Malham Water Sinks and Cove

As you begin this walk, the stream from Malham Tarn suddenly disappears in a tumble of rocks. This is the aptly named Water Sinks. In spectacular limestone country like this, it is not unusual for streams to plunge underground – it was subterranean watercourses that sculpted the cave systems beneath your feet. You will see as you continue that this particular stream has not always been so secretive. The now-dry valley of Watlowes just beyond Water Sinks was formed by water action.

It was this stream, in fact, that produced Malham Cove, and once fell over its spectacular cliff in a waterfall 230ft (70m) high. Although in very wet weather the stream goes a little further than Water Sinks, it is 200 years since water reached the cove.

Beyond Watlowes valley you reach a stretch of limestone pavement – not the biggest, but probably the best-known example of this unusual phenomenon in the Dales. The natural fissures in the rock have been enlarged by millennia of rain and frost, forming the characteristic blocks, called clints, and the deep clefts, called grikes.

the walk

1 From the car parking space, walk right along the lane and through the gate, before turning left through a kissing gate at the **Malham Raikes**, Langscar Gate sign. Walk down to the dry-stone wall on your left and follow a deepening dry valley. Beyond a cave in crags to the left, an engineered path doubles back right into a second dry valley.

2 Turn left and follow the footpath down the valley to reach the limestone pavement at the top of **Malham Cove**. Turn right and walk along the pavement to reach steps, which begin by an opening in a wall. Over 400 steps descend in zig-zags to the foot of the Cove.

3 When you reach the bottom, turn right along the path beside the river to reach

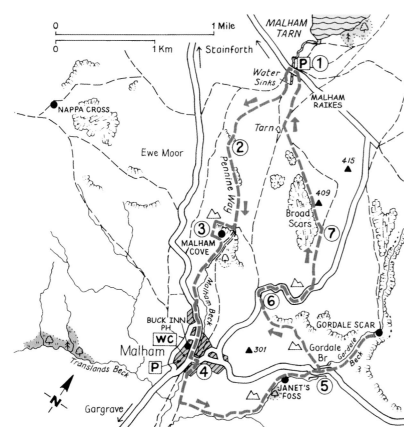

3h00 · **6.25 MILES** · **10.1 KM** · **LEVEL 1 2 3**

MAP: OS Explorer OL30 Yorkshire Dales – Northern & Central

START/FINISH: At Water Sinks, Malham Tarn, near gateway across road; grid ref: SD 894658

PATHS: well-marked field and moorland paths, more than 400 steps in descent from Malham Cove, 5 stiles

LANDSCAPE: spectacular limestone country, including Malham Cove

PUBLIC TOILETS: car park in Malham village

TOURIST INFORMATION: Malham, tel 01729 830363

THE PUB: The Buck Inn, Malham

❗ Some slippery sections on the limestone in the dry valley preceding Malham Cove. Steep drops from Cove's edge

Getting to the start

Malham nestles at the head of the Aire Valley, 8 miles (13km) east of Settle. It is accessed by narrow lanes from Settle and from the A65 Leeds to Kendal road, between Gargrave and Hellifield. Drive through the village on the Malham Cove road, then turn right at the crossroads. The car park and start of the walk are on the left side of the road immediately south of Malham Tarn.

Researched and written by:
John Gillham, David Winpenny

311

WALK

did you know?

It's worth looking closely into the grikes on the limestone pavement; their sheltered environment provides a home to spleenworts and ferns, and you will sometimes find rare primulas flowering in their shade. Take care as you explore the pavement, as the edge is not fenced.

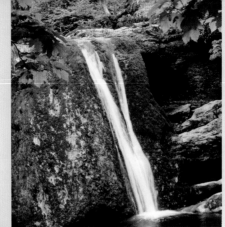
Janet's Foss, where a stream runs over moss-covered rock

the road. Turn left and follow the road into the centre of **Malham** village.

The path that leads to the natural amphitheatre at Malham Cove

4 **The Buck Inn** lies on the right side of the road, just beyond the little bridge. Go over the bridge, then turn right along an unsurfaced lane between the river and a row of cottages. At the end a gravelled footpath signed 'Janet's Foss' heads south across fields. At a junction with the Pennine Way, turn left across more fields, then into woodland. At **Janet's Foss** the path climbs left to the Goredale road. Turn right along the road, towards **Gordale Scar**.

5 At the bridge go through a gate to the left. (To visit Gordale Scar, continue straight ahead here. Take a signed gate to the left and follow the path up through a field into the gorge. Keep going on the obvious route as far as the **waterfall,** then follow the same route back to the previously mentioned bridge.) On the main route, follow the signed public footpath uphill through two stiles and out on to a lane.

6 Turn right and walk uphill on the winding lane for 0.25 mile (400m), to a ladder stile over the wall on your left. Follow the track, going left at a fork to reach another **footpath fingerpost**.

7 Turn left along the edge of the limestone clints of **Broad Scars** to reach some **small pools**. Turn right at the sign for Malham Tarn, go over a ladder stile in a cross-wall, then take the left fork path and follow it back to the car park.

what to look for

Nothing is what is seems in the Alice-in-Wonderland world around Malham. The logical among us would assume that if water disappears underground, heading in the direction of Malham Cove, just a mile (1.6km) ahead, it will reappear at the base of the Cove. But logic is wrong. The stream that bubbles up from under Malham Cove actually comes from Smelt Mill Sink, 0.75 mile (1.2km) to the west of Water Sinks. The stream from Water Sinks, on the other hand, reappears at Aire Head Springs to become the infant River Aire. All this is known from experiments first undertaken at the end of the 19th century and still continuing today. Several methods are used. One involves creating surges of water by opening and closing the sluice gates at the stream's exit from Malham Tarn. A more modern method dyes club-moss that can be collected in plankton nets and scanned with a fluorometer.

The Buck Inn

A rather grand hall-like stone building with mullioned windows, The Buck Inn was built in 1874 and is set in the heart of the village, near to the village green and the little packhorse bridge over the Aire (just a stream hereabouts). You can eat in style in the elegant restaurant and in the open-plan, carpeted lounge bar, or in the Hikers Bar, a simply furnished flag-floored room with scrubbed tables and local Copper Dragon beers on tap – perfect for booted walkers. There are benches outside for those who just want to watch the ducks glide along the nearby stream.

Food
An extensive menu lists a wide range of home-made pub food. For a snack there are filled baguettes (home-cooked ham and mustard mayonnaise) and jacket potatoes filled with chilli or cheese. For something more substantial there's home-battered fresh haddock and chips, pork and leek sausages, leek and macaroni cheese, and the famous Malham & Masham pie (beef and Old Peculier ale).

Family facilities
Children are welcome in the pub and there's a separate menu for younger family members. Pool table in the Hikers Bar.

Alternative refreshment stops
As one of the most visited villages of the Yorkshire Dales, Malham is well supplied with eating places. The Malham Café offers meals and snacks, while the Lister Arms Hotel provides good food, real ale and, in summer, real cider.

☛ Where to go from here
Head for Settle and enjoy a ride on the Carlisle to Settle Railway (www.settle-carlisle.co.uk), or visit the Museum of North Craven Life. South to Skipton offers the chance to visit Skipton Castle, one of England's most complete medieval castles (www.skiptoncastle.co.uk), and the children will love a steam ride on the Embsay and Bolton Abbey Steam Railway (www.embsayboltonabbeyrailway.org.uk).

about the pub

The Buck Inn
Malham, Skipton
North Yorkshire BD23 4DA
Tel: 01729 830317
www.buckinnmalham.co.uk

DIRECTIONS: see Getting to the Start; pub is close to the river bridge in Malham village

PARKING: 20

OPEN: daily; all day May to October

FOOD: daily

BREWERY/COMPANY: free house

REAL ALE: Theakston Best, Timothy Taylor Landlord, Copper Dragon beers

DOGS: welcome in Hikers Bar and garden

ROOMS: 10 en suite

did you know?

Parcevall Hall Gardens, near Appletreewick, lie on a steep hillside in the Yorkshire Dales National Park. They were laid out by the late Sir William Milner from 1927 onwards, and are planted with specimen trees and shrubs collected from Western China and the Himalayas.

The peregrine falcon (Falco peregrinus)

Along Langstrothdale from Hubberholme

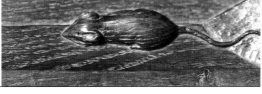

From J B Priestley's favourite Dales village, along Langstrothdale and back via a limestone terrace.

Hubberholme and Langstrothdale

Literary pilgrims visit Hubberholme to see The George Inn, where J B Priestley could often be found enjoying the local ale, and the churchyard, the last resting place for his ashes, as he requested. He chose an idyllic spot. Set at the foot of Langstrothdale, Hubberholme is a cluster of old farmhouses and cottages surrounding the church. Norman in origin, St Michael's was once flooded so badly that fish were seen swimming in the nave. One vicar of Hubberholme is said to have carelessly baptised a child Amorous instead of Ambrose, a mistake that, once entered in the parish register, couldn't be altered. Amorous Stanley used his memorable name later in life as part of his stock-in-trade as a hawker.

The interior of St Michael's church in the Yorkshire Dales

Hubberholme church's best treasures are of wood. The rood loft above the screen is one of only two surviving in Yorkshire, (the other is at Flamborough, far away on the east coast). Master-carver Robert Thompson provided almost all the rest of the furniture in 1934 – look for his mouse trademark on each piece.

Yockenthwaite's name, said to have been derived from an ancient Irish name, Eogan, conjures up images of the ancient past. Norse settlers were here more than 1,000 years ago – and even earlier settlers have left their mark, a Bronze Age stone circle a little further up the valley. The hamlet now consists of a few farm buildings beside the bridge over the Wharfe at the end of Langstrothdale Chase, a Norman hunting ground which once had its own forest laws and punishments. You walk along a typical Dales limestone terrace to reach Cray, on the road over from Bishopdale joining Wharfedale to Wensleydale. Here is another huddle of farmhouses, around the White Lion Inn.

You then follow the Cray Gill downstream, past a series of small cascades. For a more spectacular waterfall, head up the road a little way to Cray High Bridge.

Back in Hubberholme, the George Inn was once the vicarage and each New Year's Day is the scene of an ancient auction. It begins with the lighting of a candle, after which the auctioneer asks for bids for the year's tenancy of the 'Poor Pasture', a 16 acre (6.5ha) field behind the inn. All bids must be completed before the candle burns out.

The Mouse Man's signature from Hubberholme's 15th-century Church of St Michael

the walk

1 Go through a Dales Way signed gate near the east end of the church, bend left and then take the lower path, signed 'Yockenthwaite'. Walk beside the **river** for 1.75 miles (2.8km) through three stiles, a gate and two more stiles. The path eventually rises to another stone stile into **Yockenthwaite**.

2 Go through the stile and bend left to a wooden gate. Continue through a farm gate by a sign to Deepdale and Beckermonds. Before the track reaches a bridge go right and swing round to a sign to **Cray**.

3 Go up the hill and, as the track curves right, continue it to follow a slightly higher grass track highlighted by a **Cray and Hubberholme sign**. Part-way up the hill go right at a footpath sign through a wooden gate in a fence.

4 Go through a second gate to a footpath sign and ascend the hillside. Go through a gap in a wall by another signpost and follow the obvious path through several gaps in crossing walls. The path climbs left to reach a stile at the edge of **woodland**.

5 Cross the bridge beyond and continue through the woodland, back on to high pasture. The high path follows a line of limestone crags with Buckden in the valley below before arcing left into the hollow of **Crook Gill**. Go over a footbridge spanning

2h00 | **5 MILES** | **8 KM** | **LEVEL 123**

MAP: OS Explorer OL30 Yorkshire Dales – Northern & Central

START/FINISH: Beside river in Hubberholme, opposite church (not church parking); grid ref: SD 927782

PATHS: field paths and tracks, steep after Yockenthwaite, 11 stiles

LANDSCAPE: streamside paths and limestone terrace

PUBLIC TOILETS: none on route

TOURIST INFORMATION: Grassington, tel 01756 752774

THE PUB: The George Inn, Hubberholme

Getting to the start

The tiny village of Hubberholme is situated in Upper Wharfedale 18 miles (29km) north of Skipton. From the A59 Skipton bypass, follow the B6160 north. In Buckden turn off left along a narrow country lane for Hubberholme. Cross the bridge by the George Inn, where there is roadside parking by the river.

Researched and written by:
John Gillham, David Winpenny

while you're there

If you have the energy, a walk to the summit of nearby Buckden Pike will reward you with fine views and a memorial to five Polish airmen whose plane crashed there in November, 1942. One man survived the crash, following a fox's footprints through the snow down to safety at a farm. The cross he erected has a fox's head set in the base as thanksgiving. Buckden Pike is best climbed up the track called Walden Road from Starbottom.

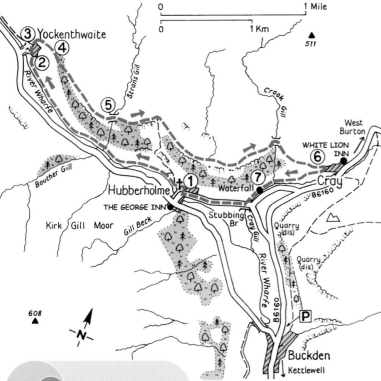

The pretty 16th-century St Michael's Church in Wharfedale

The George Inn

Ruggedly beautiful countryside, much loved by walkers, surrounds The George, a rough whitewashed stone building formerly owned by the church opposite and dating from 1600. It stands in a wonderfully peaceful setting on the banks of the Wharfe. Inside, it's a haven of unspoilt character, with splendid flagstone floors, thick, stripped stone walls, blackened beams and mullioned windows featuring throughout the homely bars. An open kitchen-range fireplace adds warmth in inclement weather, and a candle burns continuously on the bar, a reminder of the annual letting of the Poor Pasture. Sheltered patio for summer drinking.

Food
Home-cooked meals are prepared from local produce, with sandwiches, quiche, gammon, egg and chips and beefburgers served at lunchtimes. Evening dishes include Black Sheep casserole, Dales lamb chops with red wine gravy and steak and ale pie.

Family facilities
Children are welcome in part of the bar and youngsters have a standard menu to choose from. No under-14s overnight.

about the pub

The George Inn
Kirk Gill, Hubberholme
Skipton, North Yorkshire BD23 5JE
Tel: 01756 760223
www.thegeorge-inn.co.uk

DIRECTIONS: see Getting to the Start; pub opposite the bridge and lane leading to the church

PARKING: 20

OPEN: daily; closed one weekday November to Easter

FOOD: daily

BREWERY/COMPANY: free house

REAL ALE: Black Sheep Bitter, Copper Dragon Beers

DOGS: welcome in the garden only

ROOMS: 6 en suite

Alternative refreshment stops
The White Lion at Cray – slightly off the route – is worth a detour.

☛ Where to go from here
Head for Malham Cove to experience and explore some magnificent limestone scenery. Near Grassington at Greenhow is the Stump Cross Cavern, a 500-year-old cave with a superb collection of stalactites and stalagmites. Visit Parcevall Hall Gardens near Applewick (www.parcevallhallgardens.co.uk).

what to look for

A number of barns in the area have been converted to become holiday accommodation bunk barns. An initiative set up by the Yorkshire Dales National Park Authority and the Countryside Commission in 1979, the aim is to solve two problems – how to preserve the now-redundant barns that are so vital a part of the Dales landscape, and a lack of simple accommodation for walkers. Also known as stone tents, these bunkhouse barns offer farmers an alternative to letting the barns decay. They add basic amenities for cooking, washing and sleeping (and sometimes extras like comfortable chairs!) and let them to families or groups at a realistic nightly rate. They help to keep the farms viable, and both walkers and farmers benefit in other ways, too; meeting each other helps each to appreciate the needs and hopes of the other. As one farmer's wife said, 'We've made a lot of friends though the barn'.

the gill, then climb the far banks to pass to the right of a barn. The footpath winds its way down the valley side. Go through a gate and straight ahead across meadowland to a gateway on to a track, and on to a **stone barn**.

6 Bend to the right beyond the barn, down to a public footpath sign to **Stubbing Bridge**. Go down the path between stone walls and through a wooden gate and on to the grassy hillside. Continue downhill to meet the stream by a **waterfall**.

7 Continue along the streamside path through woodland. Go over a wooden stile and on past a barn to a stone stile on to the road. Turn right along the road back to the parking place in **Hubberholme**.

while you're there

On the return leg of the walk, you pass two follies in the parkland behind the house at Sorrellsykes Park. One is a round tower, with narrowing waist like a diabolo, the other, sitting like Thunderbird 3 ready for lift off, is known to local people as the 'Rocket Ship'.

A folly in the shape of a rocket ship on the grassy hills at Aysgarth

From West Burton to Aysgarth

From West Burton to Aysgarth and back, via the famous Aysgarth Falls and some unusual farm buildings.

Aysgarth Village and Falls

Many regard West Burton as the prettiest village in the Dales. It is at the entrance to Bishopdale, with its road link to Wharfedale. South is the road to Walden Head, now a dead end for motorists, but for walkers an alternative route to Starbotton and Kettlewell. At the end of the walk you'll travel for a short time, near Flanders Hall, along Morpeth Gate, the old packhorse route to Middleham.

After crossing the wide flood plain of Bishopdale Beck, and crossing Eshington Bridge, you climb across the hill to descend into Aysgarth. A village of two halves, the larger part – which you come to first – is set along the A684 road. The walk takes you along the field path to Aysgarth's other half, around the church. Look inside at the spectacular choir screen from Jervaulx Abbey. Like the elaborate stall beside it, it was carved by the renowned Ripon workshops.

Beyond the church, the path follows the river beside Aysgarth's Middle and Lower Falls. They are now one of the most popular tourist sights in the Yorkshire Dales National Park.

On your return, you pass two oddities in the parkland behind the house at Sorrellsykes Park. These two follies were built in the 18th century by Mrs Sykes and no one seems to know why.

the walk

1 With your back to the Fox and Hounds turn left along the lane, past the Village Shop. Opposite 'Meadowcroft' go left through a ginnel, signed '**Eshington Bridge**'. Cross the road, turn right then left, through a gate and down steps. Pass the barn, go through a gateway and across the field. Go through a gap in the wall with a stile beyond, then bend right to a stile on to the road.

2 Turn left, go over the bridge and ahead up the narrow lane. As it bends left go ahead through a stile, signed '**Aysgarth**',

then on through a gated stile. Go ahead to a gap in the fence near a **barn**, then through a gate. Bend left to a gate in the field corner, go through a gateway and on to a stile with a **footpath signpost**. Turn right and descend to another signpost, which points half right into a grassy hollow.

3 Go ahead to a stile in the field corner. Follow the signpost direction 'to Aysgarth' uphill to a gateway and go through a stile on the right. Cross the field half left to go through a gated stile on to a lane. Turn left, then almost immediately right through a stile, signed '**Aysgarth**'. Go through three stiles to a road.

4 Turn right into the village, past **The George & Dragon**. At the left bend, go ahead toward the Methodist church, then right at the green, and follow the lane. Go through a gate by **Field House** and to another stile, turning left along the track. Follow the path through eight stiles to the road.

5 Go ahead into the **churchyard**, pass right of the church and go through two stiles, through woodland, then over another stile. Follow the path downhill towards the river, descending steps to a gate, then a stile. When the footpath reaches the **river bank**, take a signed stile right.

6 Follow the path over two stiles to a signpost, bending right across the field to a road. Turn left over the bridge, turning right into **woodland** a few paces beyond,

Above: The Aysgarth Falls are a major attraction in the Yorkshire Dales National Park

313

WALK

2h00   4.25 MILES   6.8 KM   LEVEL 123

MAP: OS Explorer OL30 Yorkshire Dales – Northern & Central

START/FINISH: centre of West Burton, by (but not on) the Green; grid ref: SE 017867

PATHS: field and riverside paths and tracks, 35 stiles

LANDSCAPE: two typical Dales villages, fields and falls on the River Ure

PUBLIC TOILETS: none on route; Aysgarth Falls National Park visitor centre is close

TOURIST INFORMATION: Leyburn, tel 01969 623069

THE PUB: The George & Dragon, Aysgarth

❶ The main road at Aysgarth can be very busy at the weekend

Getting to the start

West Burton lies at the convergence of Bishopdale and the Walden Valley. It's a mile south of the A684 Wensleydale road and can be accessed by taking the B6160 between West Witton and Aysgarth. There's no car park but there's plenty of space around the huge village green.

Researched and written by:
John Gillham, David Winpenny

313

WALK

did you know?

Upper Falls, by the bridge, featured in the film Robin Hood, Prince of Thieves. *Robin (Kevin Costner) fought Little John here with long staves.*

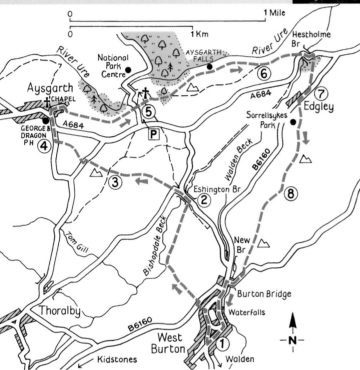

what to look for

The woods around Aysgarth have long been used for the production of hazel poles, and there is evidence of this trade on the walk, with the now-overgrown stumps of the hazel trees sprouting many branches, some of them of considerable age. In Freeholders' Wood beside the Middle and Lower Falls, on the opposite side of the River Ure from the route of the walk, the National Park Authority has restarted this ancient craft of coppicing. The name comes from the French couper, meaning to cut. Each year the hazel trees are cut back to a stump – called a stool – from which new shoots are allowed to grow. As long as they are protected from grazing cattle, the shoots develop into poles, and can be harvested after around seven years' growth. Hazel poles are traditionally used for making woven hurdles, and the thinner stems for basket-weaving.

signed '**Edgley**'. Go over a stile and cross the field to a gate on to the road.

7 Turn right. About 150yds (137m) along, go left over a stile, signed '**Flanders Hall**'. Walk below the follies to a footpath sign, beyond which the route crosses two tracks from the farming complex of **Sorrellsykes Park**. Past the last house, waymarking posts highlight the route which crosses a dyke, then passes above a copse of trees.

8 Opposite a **stone barn** on the hillside to the left, go right, through a gate, and go downhill through two more gates, then over three stiles to a lane. Turn right and go over a bridge to join the village road. Turn left, back to the Green.

The George & Dragon

Beautifully situated near the Aysgarth Falls in the heart of Herriot country, this attractive and very popular 17th-century coaching inn has a long tradition of offering warm Yorkshire hospitality. The small and cosy bar sports beams hung with tankards, jugs and copper pots, wood-panelled walls, built-in cushioned wall seats, and a warming winter log fire. Separate, plush lounge filled with antique china, and seven comfortable en suite bedrooms. Paved beer garden with lovely views of Upper Wensleydale.

Food

On the light lunch menu you will find sandwiches, ploughman's and popular snacks. More substantial dishes take in lamb chump with fondant potato, spring greens and lamb jus, loin of pork with caramelised apple and black pudding with mash, steamed monkfish, and battered haddock. Fresh fish dishes and Sunday roast lunches.

Family facilities

Smaller portions of the main menu dishes can be ordered and youngsters have a children's menu to choose from. There are two family bedrooms upstairs.

Alternative refreshment stops

Up the road from the church in Aysgarth, just off the route of the walk, the Palmer Flatt Hotel has bar meals and a restaurant, as well as a beer garden with views. In West Burton, the Fox and Hounds is a traditional village pub serving meals. Aysgarth Falls National Park Centre, across the river from the church, has a good coffee shop.

about the pub

The George & Dragon
Aysgarth, Leyburn
North Yorkshire DL8 3AD
Tel: 01969 663358
www.georgeanddragonaysgarth.co.uk

DIRECTIONS: beside the A68 in the centre of the village

PARKING: 35

OPEN: daily; all day

FOOD: daily

BREWERY/COMPANY: free house

REAL ALE: Black Sheep Best & Special, John Smiths, Theakston Bitter

DOGS: allowed in the bar

ROOMS: 7 en suite

☞ Where to go from here

Visit the Yorkshire Carriage Museum by the bridge below the church in Aysgarth. Housed in a former cotton mill that wove cloth for Garibaldi's 'Red Shirts', the revolutionary army of 19th-century Italy, the museum has a fascinating display of old-time transport, from carriages and carts to hearses and fire engines. The Dales Countryside Museum in Hawes (www.destinationdales.org) tells the story of the landscape and people of the Dales past and present, with hands-on exhibits for children.

while you're there

From the tiny village of Sedbusk, near the end of the walk, came the area's first-known rope-maker, John Brenkley, who died in 1725. The tradition is continued today in Hawes by W R Outhwaite and Son in their Hawes Ropeworks.

Widgeon (Anas penelope)

A rope-maker checks progress at the works in Hawes

Hawes and Hardraw

From busy Hawes to Hardraw, with a visit to the famous waterfall.

Hardraw Force

For many people, Hawes means two things – Wensleydale cheese and motorcyclists. The bikers use the town as a base at summer weekends and bank holidays, enjoying a friendly drink in the pubs and spectacular rides on the surrounding roads. However, it is the Wensleydale Creamery that attracts other visitors. Just above the car park in Gayle Lane, the Creamery offers tours and tastings, as well as the chance to buy a traditional Wensleydale.

Cheese has been made in Wensleydale since French monks brought the skill here in 1150. After centuries of farm production, a factory was started in Hawes in 1897. It was saved from closure in the 1930s by local man Kit Calvert, and again in 1992, when the local managers bought the creamery from Dairy Crest. It is now a thriving business and a vital part of the Hawes economy.

The walk gives you the chance – which you should take – to visit the famous Hardraw Force, a 90ft (27m) waterfall in a deep and narrow valley. There is a modest entrance charge, payable in The Green Dragon Inn in Hardraw village, and a short, pleasant walk to the fall. Despite appearances, what you see isn't entirely natural. On 12 July 1889 an unprecedented deluge on the hill above caused a wall of water to descend Hardraw Beck and through the valley, destroying buildings in the village and washing away bridges. It also devastated the waterfall, reducing it

The spectacular waterfall of Hardraw Force in the Yorkshire Dales National Park

to a mudslide. After seeing to the clearing up in the village and the welfare of his tenants, the local landowner, Lord Wharncliffe, arranged for his workmen to reconstruct the lip of the fall, pinning together the blocks of shattered stone. This he did so successfully that today's visitors have no idea of the disaster that happened more than a century ago.

the walk

1 From the top end of the car park turn left, then go right over a stile signed 'Youth Hostel'. The path flirts with a track, which soon ends by a **stone outbuilding**, then climbs uphill to a stile. Continue west across several fields passing a barn and crossing a lane, to reach the B road. Turn left, then right through a gate signed **'Thorney Mire House'**. Follow the path for 0.5 mile (800m) to a gate on to a lane. Turn right. Follow this for 0.75 mile (1.2km), passing under the viaduct to the road at **Appersett**.

2 Turn left across the bridge. Follow the road and cross the next bridge, then bend left to the junction. Go through a stile, signed **'Bluebell Hill'**. Cross the field, go through a gate and over a bridge, then bear half left uphill. Go through a gate and continue to a crossroads signpost.

3 Turn right and follow the valley to a stile (**Bob's Stile**). Cross the field beyond, go over a stile, then turn left to a ladder stile over a wall. Cross the field towards Hardraw, going over a wooden stile, then over a ladder stile into a lane.

4 Turn right, then left at the main road and cross the bridge. Hardraw Force entrance is through **The Green Dragon Inn**, so you can see it before or after refreshment. Immediately beyond the pub, turn left and go right through a signed gate in the wall, through a courtyard and over a stile. Follow the flagged path over another stile, steeply uphill, over a stile and up steps. By the house, go through a stile and right of the

2h30 **6 MILES** **9.7 KM** **LEVEL 123**

MAP: OS Explorer OL30 Yorkshire Dales – Northern & Central

START/FINISH: pay car park off Gayle Lane at west side of Hawes; grid ref: SD 870898

PATHS: field and moorland paths, may be muddy, 44 stiles

LANDSCAPE: moorland and farmland

PUBLIC TOILETS: at car park

TOURIST INFORMATION: Hawes, tel 01969 667450

THE PUB: The Green Dragon Inn, Hardraw

❗ Take care on bustling Hawes streets

Getting to the start

Hawes is on the main A684 road, which links the M6 near Sedbergh with the A1 near Northallerton. This bustling market town has two car parks. The one used here is at the west side of the town, just off the minor road to Gayle.

Researched and written by:
John Gillham, David Winpenny

did you know?

On the way to Hardraw Force you will pass the circular bandstand used for the annual Hardraw Scar Brass Band Contest, usually held in September. It was founded in 1881, and is reputed to be the second oldest brass band competition in the world. Bands from throughout the North of England and beyond compete, cheered on by supporters who crowd the valley floor and hillsides of this natural amphitheatre.

Redshank
(Tringa totanus)

what to look for

Redshank and widgeon are among the birds that you may see on the walk, especially around the pond by the New Bridge near Appersett (the second one you cross here). The wading redshank, with its long legs, has a characteristic alarm call and nests in grass, laying four eggs during the breeding season from April to July. Look out for the characteristic white bar across its wings. Widgeon, members of the duck family, graze on wet meadowland, often in huge flocks. The male has a rusty-red head with an orange crown, while the female is plainer, though of a distinctive dull orange colour.

stables, then through two more stiles on to a lane by the **Simonstone Hall Hotel**.

5 Turn right, then left along the road. Almost immediately turn right through a stile signed '**Sedbusk**'. Follow the track through a metal gate and over two ladder stiles and another gateway, then through 14 stiles into Sedbusk.

6 Turn right along the road, bend left near the post-box and go downhill. Go right, over a stile signed '**Haylands Bridge**'. Cross the field, bend right to a stile in a crossing wall, then down to a stile on to a road. Cross to another stile and follow the path, cross a stream, go over a stile, then bear right over a humpback bridge. Go through a gated stile on to a road.

7 Turn left. Cross Haylands Bridge and beyond go right through a kissing gate signed '**Hawes**'. Follow the path, go over a stile, then turn left, then right on to the main road. At the junction cross and turn right past the post office. Follow the main road through Hawes, turning left after the school to the car park.

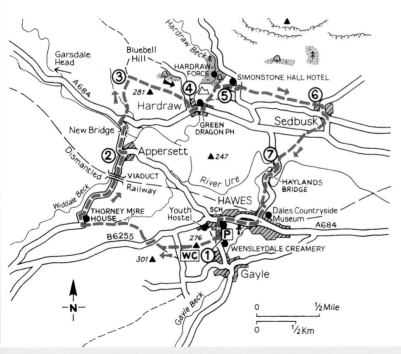

The Green Dragon Inn

The Green Dragon is a legendary old Dales pub with a history dating back to the 16th century when it was an outpost for Cistercian monks from Jervaulx Abbey. Today, it's a great walkers' pub, with its own footpath to Hardraw Force, England's highest unbroken waterfall, beginning from its back door. Little has changed inside over the years, with a big panelled public bar and a cosy, beamed snug bar with a glowing coal fire in a fine old range, traditional benches, tables and chairs, and cracking real ales from Yorkshire micro-breweries on hand-pump. Lovely rear garden and 15 acres (6ha) of woodland with superb views.

Expect a warm welcome and, if you're lucky, you may arrive when the Hardraw Gathering (Folk Festival) is in full swing.

Food

Food is hearty and traditional pub fare. The popular menu takes in filled baguettes, gammon and egg, lasagne and good home-made dishes like game casserole, rabbit pie, pheasant in red wine and chicken and leek pie, with vegetarian options. Home-made apple pie for pudding.

Family facilities

Children are very welcome inside. The pub has a family room and a large garden.

Alternative refreshment stops

There is plenty of choice in Hawes with its pubs, cafés and tea rooms, as well as a fish and chip shop. More upmarket is the Simonstone Hall Hotel, on the walk between Hardraw and Sedbusk.

☛ Where to go from here

To find out more about life in the Dales, visit the Dales Countryside Museum (www.destinationdales.org) in the Station Yard at Hawes. Here you can walk through a Time Tunnel that takes you back through 10,000 years of Dales' history, and see how life has changed over the centuries. Also included in the admission charge is a trip 'down' a lead mine, a visit to an old doctor's surgery, and the nostalgia of a kitchen in the Dales from the last century.

about the pub

The Green Dragon Inn
Hardraw, Hawes
North Yorkshire DL8 3LZ
Tel: 01969 667392
www.greendragonhardraw.com

DIRECTIONS: Hardraw is signposted north off the A684 in Hawes. Pub is beside the river bridge

PARKING: 50

OPEN: daily; all day

FOOD: daily; all day

BREWERY/COMPANY: free house

REAL ALE: Theakston Bitter & Old Peculier, Black Sheep Bitter, Timothy Taylor Landlord, York Bitter, guest beers

DOGS: allowed in bars and garden

ROOMS: 17 en suite

The tower of Bolton Castle above shops

did you know?

Mary, Queen of Scots arrived with her retinue at Bolton Castle on 13 July 1568 and was imprisoned here for six months. During her time at the castle she took over the solar, a warm and sunny family sitting room, where she spent time at her needlework, gazing out of the window and writing long letters to people she hoped would help her.

Mary, Queen of Scots

Green ways of Wensleydale

A glorious green terrace above one of the grandest of the Dales.

Bolton Castle

You hardly need to look for Bolton Castle. It dominates the landscape as you follow the road east of Carperby and towers over you as you toil up the lane of the main climb. The bulk of the castle dates back to 1399; it was established by Richard le Scrope, 1st Lord Scrope of Bolton and Lord Chancellor of England, and is still owned by his descendants. Much of the fabric is intact and there are rooms on five floors with furnishings and tableaux that give a vivid impression of what life in the castle was like. Mary Queen of Scots was imprisoned here for a time, though she was probably not too uncomfortable as she is said to have had 51 servants at her disposal! The castle grounds include a medieval garden, a herb garden and England's highest vineyard.

14th-century Castle Bolton is visible on parts of the route

The old lead-mine site that is so conspicuous near the end of the off-road section is only one of many in the area, with the highest concentration being in nearby Swaledale. There is little to see in the way of buildings, shafts or levels here, just the large areas of bare spoil. The lack of vegetation colonising the ground indicates that there are significant residual concentrations of lead.

the ride

1 Cross the footbridge and follow a narrow tarmac path out to a wider, roughly surfaced lane. Bear right, cycle up to a road and turn right. About 2 miles (3.2km) beyond Carperby is a left turn signed for **Castle Bolton**, and the main climb of the route. Pass close under the corner of one of the **towers** and then at the top turn left, following signs for the car park and toilets.

2 Where the lane swings up into the car park, keep straight ahead through a gate and along an easy track. Follow the track through several gates and skirt to the left of some large **wooden farm sheds**; there can be muddy splashes here. After the next gate, the track becomes a little rougher, wiggling left through another gate and then right again. The track beyond is distinctly rougher, especially where it

dips at a small **ford**; many people may prefer to walk this short section.

3 At the next gate bear left above the wall, on easy grassy going with some wheel ruts and a few avoidable rocky patches. After some perfect, almost lawn-like grass, dip to a ford, sometimes dry but still quite rough. More good grassy going follows. At the next gate bear half left on a smooth green track, following signs to Askrigg and Carperby, which gives delightful easy riding for the next 0.5 mile (800m) to **Low Gate**.

4 At Low Gate go straight ahead up the hill on more smooth green track, signed for Askrigg. Level out and descend to a gate where a rougher track (**Peatmoor Lane**) crosses. Follow the green track ahead, across a level grassy plateau, until it descends to **Oxclose Gate**. From here the track skirts to the left of the conspicuous bare ground and spoil heaps on the site of the **old lead mine**.

5 Opposite this the track acquires a good gritty surface, and soon swings down to a gate, with a **ford** just beyond. Wheel the bikes across this and beware the drop just below. Follow the stony track through another gate. Beyond this a short section is sometimes wet but can be avoided by skirting to the right, crossing ruined walls. Go up to another gate, swing left through it and down 50yds (45.7m) to a signpost.

6 For the shorter loop, descend the steep, twisting track to the little village of **Woodhall**. The surface is loose in places, and inexperienced riders should walk

---

2h00 | 12.5 MILES | 20.1 KM | LEVEL 1 2 3

SHORTER ALTERNATIVE ROUTE

1h30 | 9.75 MILES | 15.7 KM | LEVEL 1 2 3

MAP: OS Explorer OL30 Yorkshire Dales – Northern & Central

START/FINISH: small car park on A684 at Aysgarth; grid ref: SD 995889

TRAILS/TRACKS: good grassy tracks; a few short rough sections to be walked; return on lanes which are muddy after rain

LANDSCAPE: high pasture and moorland with views of broad pastoral dale

PUBLIC TOILETS: at Bolton Castle car park

TOURIST INFORMATION: Aysgarth Falls National Park Centre, tel 01969 663424

CYCLE HIRE: none locally

THE PUB: The Wheatsheaf Hotel, Carperby

❗ Basic loop: steep climb on road, short sections of rough track, steep descent – mountain bike recommended. Off-road sections on longer loop are considerably rougher and only for older, experienced children – mountain bike essential

Getting to the start

Aysgarth is on the main A684 road through Wensleydale. Parking by arched footbridge about 0.5 mile (800m) west of the village.

Why do this cycle ride?

Persevere as far as Low Gate and the real worth of this ride becomes apparent. From here on, you follow a magical green ribbon of a bridleway along a broad terrace high above the valley. Then you crest another slight rise and more smooth grassy trails unfurl ahead. When you get back to tarmac, it's downhill nearly all the way.

Researched and written by: Jon Sparks

315

CYCLE

Cheeses on sale at Hawes Creamery Shop

while you're there

Climb to the top of the turrets for splendid views over Wensleydale and imagine the area covered in forest as it would have been in medieval times.

Wensleydale cheese is checked at the curd stage

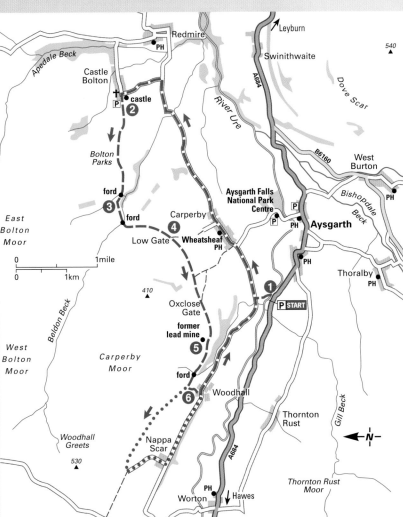

The Wheatsheaf Hotel

The Wheatsheaf is quietly proud of a couple of its more famous guests. In 1941 it was the honeymoon location for Alf Wight – rather better known as 'James Herriot' of All Creatures Great and Small fame. The following year it played host to an even more famous visitor in the shape of Greta Garbo, then performing a few miles away at Catterick Garrison. Garbo's legendary wish of 'I want to be alone' might be satisfied on the expansive moors above rather than in the sociable bar or the adjoining snug – which truly lives up to its name.

There is also a panelled dining room, and while you're there, do take a peek into the residents' lounge with its magnificent 17th-century fireplace. When the weather permits, there is outside seating at the front (south-facing) and there are more tables tucked in among shrubs and conifers behind the car park.

Food

Home-made dishes on the bar menu include giant Yorkshire puddings with various fillings, leek and parsnip hotpot, steak and bacon pie, Kilnsey trout with almonds, in addition to sandwiches and ploughman's lunches.

about the pub

The Wheatsheaf Hotel
Carperby, Leyburn
North Yorkshire DL8 4DF
Tel: 01969 663216
www.wheatsheafinwensleydale.co.uk

DIRECTIONS: village signposted off the A684 at Aysgarth

PARKING: 20

OPEN: daily; all day Saturday and Sunday; closed Monday lunchtime in winter

FOOD: daily

BREWERY/COMPANY: Black Sheep Brewery

REAL ALE: Black Sheep Best & Special, Websters Yorkshire Bitter

ROOMS: 8 en suite

Family facilities

Children are welcome in the pub and overnight (one family room), and there's a children's menu.

Alternative refreshment stops

The George & Dragon in Aysgarth village and a café at Aysgarth Falls National Park Visitor Centre.

☞ Where to go from here

Stop off at Bolton Castle (www.boltoncastle.co.uk); head for Hawes to visit the fascinating Dales Countryside Museum (www.destinationdales.org.uk); watch traditional ropemaking at the Hawes Ropemaker (www.ropemakers.co.uk); or learn about cheese-making at the Wensleydale Cheese Experience (www.wensleydale-creamery.co.uk).

down. Turn left on the wider road for an easy run, almost entirely downhill, back to the start.

For the optional extension, turn right and climb the steep rough track. After two gates the gradient eases and the track winds through hummocks. Go through a gate alongside a **small plantation**. Beyond is the final climb, very tricky in places with bare rock and large loose stones; only experts will ride it all. Over the top there's

smooth friendly grass, then a final section of rutted track leads to a gate by a barn. The track beyond soon begins to descend, getting steeper and rougher. At a junction turn sharp left, almost immediately meeting tarmac. Follow the steep lane, which can have an overlay of loose grit in places, down into the hamlet of **Nappa Scar** and turn left on to the wider road.

The River Cover gently rolling through Coverdale

Horsehouse and Coverdale

A moorside and riverside walk in one of the loveliest valleys in the Dales.

Horsehouse and Coverdale

It is hard to believe that the quiet village of Horsehouse was once bustling with traffic, as stagecoaches and packhorse trains passed through it on one of the main coaching routes from London to the North. Two inns served the travellers on their way to and from Richmond, a principal coaching centre. Beyond Horsehouse, to the south west, Coverdale grows steeper and wilder before the sharp drop down Park Rash into Kettlewell in Wharfedale – a descent that must have scared 17th- and 18th-century travellers. Pack-horses also used the route, bringing goods to the valley and taking lead and minerals from the mines on the moors.

Pedlars, too, followed the routes, and some met a gruesome end; three headless corpses were found by a side road into Nidderdale. Evidence suggested that they were Scottish pedlars, killed for their money and goods. Their heads were not found – nor were their murderers.

West Scrafton, a tiny village set beside Great Gill as it tumbles towards the River Cover below, is dominated by the heights of Great Roova Crags (1549ft/472m). Before the dissolution of the monasteries in the 1530s, the village was owned by the monks of Jervaulx Abbey. Much of the land was later owned by the Earl of Lennox; West Scrafton Manor House is said to have been the birthplace of his son Lord Darnley, murdered second husband of Mary, Queen of Scots and father of King James VI and I.

Carlton-in-Coverdale, the next village on the walk is the largest settlement in the

Harvesting the hay in Coverdale

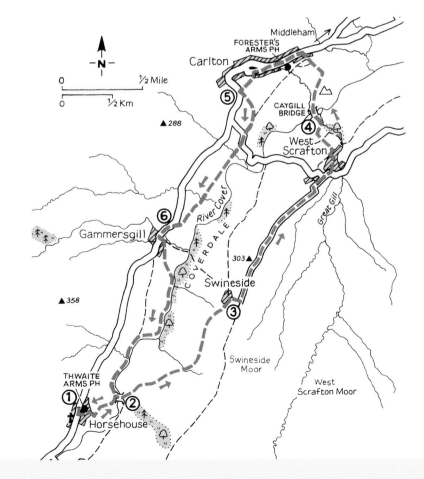

2h30 | **6.5 MILES** | **10.4 KM** | **LEVEL 1 2 3**

MAP: OS Explorer OL30 Yorkshire Dales – Northern & Central

START/FINISH: roadside parking below former school in Horsehouse; grid ref: SE 047813

PATHS: field, moorland and riverside paths and tracks, 31 stiles

LANDSCAPE: farmed valley and moorland, with River Cover

PUBLIC TOILETS: none on route

TOURIST INFORMATION: Leyburn, tel 01969 623069

THE PUB: The Forester's Arms, Carlton

Getting to the start

Horsehouse in Coverdale lies on a remote and narrow road linking Kettlewell in Wharfedale with Middleham in Wensleydale. It's advisable and much easier to access the village from Wensleydale, where you should head south along a country lane just to the east of Wensley village.

Researched and written by:
John Gillham, David Winpenny

while you're there

Carlton-in-Coverdale, on the route, is the largest of the dale's settlements, with some pretty houses lining the main street and the motte of a small castle visible to the south of the main street.

Coverham Bridge crosses the River Cover

dale. Flatts Farm at the west end of the village has an inscription to Henry Constantine, 'The Coverdale Poet'.

Miles Coverdale, the first to translate the whole Bible into English, was born in the valley – no one knows exactly where – in 1488. The first edition of his Bible was published in Paris in 1535, and a revised version, known as the Great Bible, in 1538.

the walk

1 Walk past the **Thwaite Arms**, then curve behind it on a track. Turn right down a signed track, go through two gates, then bend left to a third gate. Beyond it bear half right to a gate and **footbridge**.

2 Cross the bridge and bear left. Go over a stile signed **'Swineside'**, cross a small field to another stile then bear half right. Cross a track and follow a wall to a stile. Bear left, eventually on a path, through two stiles, then go half left to a signed stile. Climb the grassy path to a gap in the wall, then take the lower path, levelling out across **Rampshaw Bank**. Go through a stile and a gateway, then bend right to a gate, to the right of **Swineside Farm**.

3 After the gate, follow the track past the farmhouse then right, uphill. At the top,

what to look for

Like Middleham at the end of the valley, Coverdale is much given over to horses, with riding schools and livery stables throughout the dale. This is not a recent phenomenon – in Daniel Defoe's day the whole area was geared to the horse; in the third volume of his Tour through the Whole Island of Great Britain published in 1726, he wrote that 'all this country is full of jockeys, that is to say, dealers in horses, and breeders of horses…'

go over a cattle grid and follow the tarred lane for 1.5 miles (2.4km) into **West Scrafton**. In the village take a track to the left signed 'No Through Road'. Turn left signed 'Carlton', then turn right. After a gate and a walled section, turn left down the field. Go through a kissing gate and right of a **barn**, towards Caygill Bridge. Bear right, following the wooded valley, through a gate and down to two **footbridges**.

4 After the bridges, go through a gate and ascend steeply, past a signpost. At the top bear right alongside a wall and on to a gate. Follow the footpath sign left, eventually reaching **Carlton**. Turn left along the road passing the **Forester's Arms**. Where it widens, bear left between cottages following a footpath sign to a stile. Continue through six more stiles to a road.

5 Turn left and go immediately through a gate. Descend to a stile, bear right above a **barn** to another stile and follow a wall to a stile on to a road. Turn left. At a left bend, go right, over a stile signed 'Gammersgill'. Go over two more stiles and cross a stream (sometimes dry) and maintain direction across another field, passing to the left of a 5-bar gate then through a small waymarked gate. Cross the fields, going over a stile and a **wooden footbridge**, then follow an enclosed path. At the end of this turn half right across a field to a stile on to the road.

6 Turn left into **Gammersgill**, cross the bridge, then turn left through a gate signed 'Swineside'. Bear right to another gate, then cross to a stile beside a gate. Bear half left to the field corner and go over a stile. Now follow the river over five more stiles and past a **stone bridge**. After another stile reach the footbridge crossed near the start of the walk. Retrace your steps back to **Horsehouse**.

The Forester's Arms

Stone-flagged floors, solid wooden furniture and a large, farmhouse-style fireplace add to the appeal of this fine old Dales pub hidden away in sleepy Coverdale. Built in 1630 of typical York stone, it has changed little over the years with its chunky oak beams and low ceilings, and careful refurbishment has successfully retained the historic and traditional atmosphere. Pretty, en suite bedrooms are available, with good views of the Dales, and there are lovely rural views from benches at the front of the inn.

Food
An imaginative menu lists such starters as Greek salad and garlic, chilli and parsley scallops and prawns, served with home-made bread, with main dishes ranging from roast belly pork with mash and cider gravy, rabbit stew and home-made fish cakes with dill *buerre blanc*, to battered haddock and chips, whole roast sea bass with dill hollandaise, and roast duck with marmalade sauce and sauté potatoes. Sandwiches available at lunchtime.

Family facilities
Children are welcome inside. Smaller portions of adult dishes are available.

about the pub

The Forester's Arms
Carlton, Leyburn
North Yorkshire DL8 4BB
Tel: 01969 640272

DIRECTIONS: see Getting to the Start; Carlton is 4.5 miles (7.2km) south west of Middleham and the A6108; pub is in the village centre

PARKING: 15

OPEN: all day Sunday; closed Mondays

FOOD: no food Sunday evening

BREWERY/COMPANY: free house

REAL ALE: Wensleydale Brewery beers

DOGS: allowed inside

ROOMS: 2 en suite

Alternative refreshment stops
The Thwaite Arms in Horsehouse serves meals and has a reputation for its friendly atmosphere.

☞ Where to go from here
Visit the Forbidden Corner at Tupgill, 3 miles (4.8km) east of Carlton, a fantasy garden full of follies, tunnels, secret chambers and passages offering intrigue and unexpected discoveries for children. Open by timed ticket in advance only – call in at the tourist information centre in Leyburn. Take a look at Aysgarth Falls, the ruins of Jervaulx Abbey near East Witton, or enjoy a fascinating tour of the Black Sheep Brewery in Masham (www.blacksheep.co.uk).

Golden plover
(Pluvialis apricaria)

A pub fronted by a well on the green at Ramsgill

A circuit from Lofthouse

Below right: A shady cobbled path in Middlesmoor village

3h00	7 MILES	11.3 KM	LEVEL 1 2 3

From Lofthouse to Ramsgill and Middlesmoor in the valley of the River Nidd.

Nidderdale

Nidderdale is a designated Area of Outstanding Natural Beauty. It is an area of moorland wildness and deep, farmed valleys. In the late 19th and 20th centuries parts of the dale were dammed as a chain of reservoirs was constructed to supply water to the city of Bradford.

Throughout Nidderdale are small, stone-built settlements like those visited on the walk – many of them of great antiquity. The monks of Fountains Abbey, near Ripon, founded the attractive village of Lofthouse as a grange in the Middle Ages. It was one of the bases from which they controlled their vast farming interests. Lofthouse now consists mainly of 19th-century cottages. Ramsgill, at the southern end of the route, is at the head of Gouthwaite Reservoir, which was opened in 1899 and is renowned for its spectacular bird life. The village was the birthplace, in

Left: Hilltop Middlesmoor village

1704, of Eugene Aram, scholar and murderer, who arranged for the slaughter of his wife's lover and was hanged for the crime.

In the third village, Middlesmoor, with its spectacular hilltop setting, the head of an Anglo-Saxon cross with its inscription to St Cedd in the church again indicates the age of the settlement.

It was once possible to travel from Pateley Bridge up the dale on the Nidd Valley Light Railway. It closed to passengers in 1929, but the track is still visible on much of the route.

the walk

1 Walk downhill past the Crown Hotel to the main road and turn left. Just beyond the drive for the **Old Vicarage**, go right, through a stile, signed the Nidderdale Way (the first of many waymarkers you'll see on this route). The path joins a short track to a gate, but instead of going through turn left, following a wall at first, then maintaining direction across a field. Over a stile at the far end turn half right to join the causeway of an **old railway**, which leads out to a roadside stile.

2 Cross the road and go through a gate. Follow the wire fence to a stile, then maintain direction across the field ahead. Before the next gateway, go left over a stile, avoiding the railway trackbed (private). Bear left and ascend, to a gate where a **Nidderdale Way** signpost highlights your direction towards the woods on the skyline. Through a kissing gate the path follows the lower edge of the woods. The narrow path passes above **Longsight House**. Take the right fork track

towards **Longsight Farm** to go left of the farmhouse. Follow the waymarkers to a wooden gate and ladder stile. Over the stile descend by a hedge on the left and go over a wooden bridge, where a gravel track leads past the buildings of **Bouthwaite** and out onto the road.

3 Turn right down the road to a T-junction. Turn left, over the bridge. Take the next track right, by the **triangular green**, then bear right again signed 'Stean'.

4 On reaching **West House Farm** go over a stile between the farm and a bungalow, cross the farm road and follow the waymarked posts, heading slightly left to join a track by **metal outbuildings**. The track heads up valley before raking down to a two-storey **barn**. From here a gravel track descends into a wooded valley and over a small bridge.

5 At a T-junction of tracks, turn left, uphill, and follow the walled track as it bends right. Beyond the approach road to **Moor House** the track becomes grassy. At a T-junction of tracks turn right. At the bottom, bend left above the **houses** and descend to the road at **Stean**.

MAP: OS Explorer OL30 Yorkshire Dales – Northern & Central

START/FINISH: car park by Memorial Hall in Lofthouse; grid ref: SE 101734

PATHS: mostly field paths and tracks; may be muddy, 20 stiles

LANDSCAPE: rich farmland and moorland, wide views from Middlesmoor

PUBLIC TOILETS: on main valley road at Lofthouse

TOURIST INFORMATION: Pateley Bridge, tel 01423 711147

THE PUB: Crown Hotel, Middlesmoor

❶ A long walk for young children

Getting to the start

Lofthouse lies near the end of the Nidderdale road, 6 miles (9.7km) north west of Pateley Bridge. The best road heads north from the west side of Pateley Bridge. Turn right, uphill, in Lofthouse village to reach the car park, which is on the left. If that's full there is roadside parking on the moorland fringes above the village.

Researched and written by:
John Gillham, David Winpenny

317

WALK

did you know?

You used to be able to ride up the dale from Pateley Bridge on Britain's only corporation-run light railway. The Nidd Valley Light Railway, originally laid down as a narrow-gauge line by the builders of Angram Reservoir, was taken over by Bradford Corporation in 1907 and re-laid as standard gauge. Regular services ran from Pateley Bridge to Lofthouse with stations at Wath and what was called Ramsgill, but was really Bouthwaite. It closed to passengers in 1929.

6 Beyond the **telephone box**, take a stile on the left signed 'Middlesmoor'. This descends to cross a bridge over **How Stean Gorge** then climbs the far banks to a gate. Beyond this go diagonally right across the field and over a stile. Now follow the wall uphill to the road. Turn left towards **Middlesmoor** where you'll find the Crown Hotel. Retrace your steps and turn left beside the **Wesleyan chapel** to the gateway of the parish church.

7 Turn right before the gate, through a stile signed 'Lofthouse'. Go down steps then through a stile and two gateways by **Halfway House**. Continue through a small gate then go diagonally left to a gate in the corner. In the lay-by go left on the nearside of the **cricket ground** to a laneside gate. Cross the lane and go over a bridge, then bear right to the centre of Lofthouse. Turn right to the car park.

Crown Hotel

A tranquil view across Gouthwaite Reservoir

This remote and popular 17th-century stone-built pub at the top of the village has fine views over the rooftops towards the valley pastures and hills of Nidderdale and the distant Gouthwaite Reservoir. Ideal for those potholing or following the Nidderdale Way, it offers the chance to savour a refreshing pint of Black Sheep ale by roaring log fires in cosy and welcoming bars, or in the sunny garden in summer. Good value simple bedrooms.

Food

Good pub food ranges from decent sandwiches (home-cooked ham or beef) and cheese ploughman's to starters of black pudding, bacon and mash, home-made soups and garlic mushrooms. Main meals include lasagne, steak and ale pie, giant Yorkshire puddings filled with beef and vegetables, Nidderdale lamb chops, and salmon and broccoli pasta bake.

Family facilities

Children of all ages are welcome in the pub. There's a children's menu, smaller portions of adult dishes, and high chairs for younger family members.

about the pub

Crown Hotel
Middlesmoor, Pateley Bridge
North Yorkshire HG3 5ST
Tel: 01423 755204

DIRECTIONS: see Getting to the Start and continue up valley to Middlesmoor for the Crown Hotel

PARKING: 10

OPEN: closed Monday lunchtime

FOOD: daily

BREWERY/COMPANY: free house

REAL ALE: Black Sheep Bitter, Special & Emmerdale Ale, guest beer

DOGS: allowed in the bar and garden

ROOMS: 7 bedrooms (4 en suite)

Alternative refreshment stops

The Yorke Arms in Ramsgill serves top-of-the-range meals and enjoys an enviable reputation.

☛ Where to go from here

A visit to the attractive town of Pateley Bridge will prove rewarding. There are many fascinating small shops, as well as walks by the River Nidd and the interesting Nidderdale Museum in King Street, housed in a former workhouse, which illustrates the life and background of the Dales folk. Towards Ripon are the spectacular 12th-century remains of Fountains Abbey, the most complete Cistercian abbey in Britain (www.fountainsabbey.org.uk).

Map:

0 — 1 Mile
0 — 1 Km

Gouthwaite Reservoir
Bouthwaite
③
Yorke Arms PH
▲ 399
Dismantled Railway
Ramsgill
④
Pateley Bridge
GRINDSTONE HILL HOUSE
②
River Nidd
Nidderdale Way
WEST HOUSE FARM
Ramsgill Beck
HIGH LOFTHOUSE
Leighton
Ramsgill Bents
Memorial Hall **P**
①
Lofthouse
HALFWAY HOUSE
⑤
Middlesmoor
How Stean Gorge
⑦
CROWN HOTEL
⑥
How Stean Beck
Stean

what to look for

Oil beetles have been sighted at Middlesmoor. Thought to be the most common of the seven species of oil beetle in Britain, this was meloë proscarabaeus. Unlike other beetles, their wing cases do not overlap, making them look as if they are wearing waistcoats. They also have kinked antennae – the male beetle's end with blobs. Oil beetles get their name from an oily fluid they secrete from their leg joints if they're disturbed. It deters predators and can cause blistering on human skin.

did you know?

Gardens through Time, the most recent project at RHS Garden Harlow Carr, consists of seven themed gardens reflecting trends in horticulture from the Regency period through to a 21st-century garden designed by Diarmuid Gavin. Each garden displays the most popular and influential features and techniques of that period, many of which are still used. The gardens also reflect national events such as Queen Victoria's Golden Jubilee and the Festival of Britain.

Pretty white scabious

The Harland Way

2h00 · **8 MILES** · **12.9 KM** · **LEVEL 123**

Follow a picturesque railway line to discover Yorkshire's forgotten fortress.

Around Spofforth

Lying among the peaceful pastures of the Crimple Valley, Spofforth is an idyllic backwater for a Sunday afternoon ride. Go back in time to the medieval era and things were very different. A year after the Battle of Hastings, William the Conqueror's friend, William de Percy, made Spofforth his headquarters. The original dwelling would have been a fortified hall, of which nothing remains, but by the 13th century the castle was taking shape, built into the rock on which it stood. Subsequent alterations of the 14th and 15th centuries gave the castle its powerful walls and that strong Gothic look.

In 1309 Henry de Percy bought the Manor of Alnwick in Northumberland and made that his main residence, but the family's alliances were to land them in trouble on several occasions – after their rebellion against King Henry IV in 1408, and their support in the Wars of the Roses. On both occasions the Crown confiscated Spofforth Castle. The castle lay waste for around a hundred years until Henry, Lord Percy restored it in 1559. Within another hundred years, however, it was sacked by Oliver Cromwell's forces during fierce fighting of the Civil War. Stand on the green today, and you can still feel the presence and imagine the times of turmoil endured by this rugged historic building.

the ride

1 With your back to the car park entrance, turn right along the railway trackbed, highlighted by a **Harland Way fingerpost**. The line has been exploded through the bedrock to reveal limestone crags, now hung with pleasant woodland that offers excellent shade on hot summer days.

2 Take the left fork at the junction that used to be known as the **Wetherby Triangle**. You're soon joined from the right by another branch of the line and together the routes head west towards Spofforth. Halfway along the track you have to dismount to get through a **metal gateway**, then again almost immediately at another gate. The trackbed forges through an avenue of beech, hawthorn, ash, and rowan before coming out into the open. Now you'll see thickets of wild roses and bramble, with scabious and purple vetch among the numerous wild flowers of the verges. There are wide views across cornfields, and soon the tower of **Spofforth church** comes into view ahead.

3 The Harland Way ends beyond a gate just short of the village. A gravel path veers right across a green on to **East Park Road**. This threads through **modern housing** to come to the main road where you should turn right. If you have young

The grounds of ruined Spofforth Castle

318

MAP: OS Explorer 289 Leeds

START/FINISH: Sicklinghall Road, Wetherby; grid ref: SE 397483

TRAILS/TRACKS: well compacted gravel railway trackbed, lanes and smooth bridleways

LANDSCAPE: pastureland and village

PUBLIC TOILETS: none on route

TOURIST INFORMATION: Wetherby, tel 01937 582151

CYCLE HIRE: none locally

THE PUB: The Castle, Spofforth

❶ A short section of main road through Spofforth village

Getting to the start

From the A661 Wetherby to Harrogate road turn off on the westbound Sicklinghall Road then after 300yds (274m) a blue cycleway sign points to the car park on the right.

Why do this cycle ride?

The Harland Way forms the basis of a delightful rural ride following in the tracks of the steam trains and visiting one of Yorkshire's most fascinating Norman castles.

Researched and written by: John Gillham

371

The Harland Way, the Spofforth to Wetherby cycle/ footpath route, lies on part of the York and West Midland Railway Company's Church Fenton to Harrogate line and the former Leeds to Scarborough route from Crossgates to Wetherby. The railway was closed to passengers in 1964.

Willow warbler (Phylloscopus trochilus)

Cycling through the grounds of Spofforth Castle

children it might be better to dismount to cross the road, and use the pavements to get to **The Castle** inn.

4 Just beyond the pub, where the road bends right, take the lane on the left, which heads for the **castle**. When you've seen the castle retrace your route past the pub then turn right along Park Road. Beyond the **houses** this becomes a stony bridleway, rising gently across the fields.

5 Ignore turn-offs until you come to **Fox Heads Farm**. Turn left along the track here, passing left of the farmhouse. The dirt and stone track descends to a bridge over a stream, then climbs again past an **old quarry**. Though there are a few climbs the track is still quite easy, being

smooth-surfaced and fairly well drained. Often it's lined with bramble, ferns and foxgloves, with the odd tree. Just beyond the summit of the hill the track bends right. After being joined from the right by another farm track it comes to the road, just to the west of **Sicklinghall village**.

6 Turn left along the road into the village. On the right there's a pond with lilies and coots, then on the left there's another pub, the **Scott Arms**. The winding road makes a long but gradual descent towards Wetherby, passing the upmarket **Linton Springs Hotel**. Beyond the hotel, ignore the right turn 'to Linton'. After passing through housing in the Wetherby suburbs watch out for the **blue cyclists' sign**. This marks the access road back to the car park.

The Castle

Sited on Spofforth's main street, the Castle Inn has old red sandstone walls clad with a little creeping ivy and, in summer, with colourful hanging baskets. There's a courtyard in the back for outdoor dining.

garden, peaceful woodland and arboretum, and a Museum of Gardening (www.rhs.org.uk). In Harrogate, the Royal Pump Room Museum tells the story of Harrogate's heyday as England's European spa (www.harrogate.gov.uk).

Food
Home-cooked traditional pub food includes ciabatta sandwiches (roast peppers and goat's cheese), omelettes and pasta meals, alongside cod in beer batter, steak and kidney pie, Castle mixed grill and a range of vegetarian dishes.

Family facilities
Children are allowed in the eating areas of the bar. Smaller portions of any main course dishes on the menu are available.

Alternative refreshment stops
The Scott Arms at Sicklinghall.

☛ Where to go from here
The 58-acre (23.5ha) RHS Harlow Carr Botanical Gardens west of Harrogate includes a breathtaking streamside

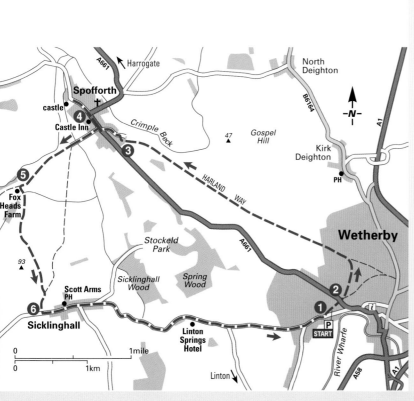

about the pub

The Castle
35 High Street, Spofforth
Harrogate, North Yorkshire HG3 1BQ
Tel: 01937 590200

DIRECTIONS: The Castle in Spofforth is on the route and lies on the corner at the top end of High Street, near the junction with Castle Street

PARKING: 24

OPEN: daily; all day

FOOD: no food Monday

BREWERY/COMPANY: Punch Taverns

REAL ALE: Black Sheep Bitter, Ruddles County, Timothy Taylor Landlord

Purple foxglove (Digitalis purpurea)

what to look for

Some of the stonework from the castle, which stood on the mound near Bardsey's church, was incorporated into the fabric of Bardsey Grange, whose most notable inhabitant was William Congreve. Born here in 1670, Congreve went on to write a number of Restoration comedies for the stage, such as The Way of the World.

Bardsey and Pompocali

| 2h00 | 3.5 MILES | 5.7 KM | LEVEL 123 |

MAP: OS Explorer 289 Leeds

START/FINISH: Roadside parking on Church Lane in Bardsey; grid ref: SE 369430

PATHS: good paths and tracks (though some, being bridleways, may be muddy), 8 stiles

LANDSCAPE: arable and woodland

PUBLIC TOILETS: none on route

TOURIST INFORMATION: Leeds, tel 0113 242 5242

THE PUB: The Bingley Arms, Bardsey

⚠ Busy road through Bardsey and a dangerous road crossing at point 5. Unattended young children could wander off the slippery river bank in a couple of places between Points 2 and 3.

Getting to the start

Bardsey is located just west of the A58 between Leeds and Wetherby. From Wetherby, turn right into the village along Church Lane, where there is parking and The Bingley Arms.

Researched and written by:
John Gillham, John Morrison

A rolling landscape with Roman echoes.

Roman connections

The Romans built a network of important roads across Yorkshire linking their most important forts. One of these roads passed close to Bardsey village and you walk a short stretch of the old Roman road when you take the track from Hetchell Wood. Adjacent to these woods – and marked on the Ordnance Survey map as Pompocali – are a set of intriguing earthworks. Though rather overgrown, they are unencumbered by signs and information panels. Roman finds have been unearthed here. A couple of miles away, at Dalton Parlours, the site of a large Roman villa has been discovered.

Once the Romans had abandoned this outpost, Bardsey became part of the kingdom of Elmet, and was later mentioned in the Domesday Book. By the 13th century, the village had been given to the monks of Kirkstall Abbey. After the dissolution of the monasteries, in 1539, Bardsey came under the control of powerful local families. The Parish Church of All Hallows, visited near the end of this walk, is another antiquity – the core of the building is Anglo Saxon.

Above the church is a grassy mound, where a castle once stood. From pottery found on the site, archaeologists can tell it was occupied during the 12th and 13th centuries, after which it was abandoned.

Close to the city, yet retaining its own identity, Bardsey has expanded beyond its ancient centre and is a commuter village for people who work in Leeds. The Bingley Arms pub can claim a long existence; there is documentary evidence of brewers and innkeepers going back a thousand years. Bardsey is, in short, a historic little spot.

A rural view beyond the commuter village of Bardsey

the walk

1 With your back to the Bingley Arms turn right along **Church Lane** to the T-junction with the A58 Wetherby Road. Turn right here, then after about 200yds (183m) turn left past some **metal bollards** into the woods. Join the old **railway trackbed**, going right, for just a few paces, before bearing left, over a stile, to continue on a woodland path. After passing through a narrow meadow on a field-edge path, continue with a fence to your left and the woods to your right. Keep straight ahead when the fence ends to enter a huge field. Ignore the path across the field ahead but instead turn right, following a hedge and **Bardsey Beck**, downhill.

Scarcroft

BINGLEY ARMS

Wayside Gardens

CHURCH LANE

P

Bardsey

WAYSIDE MOUNT

A 58

Rowley Grange

LEEDS COUNTRY WAY

MOAT HALL

DISMANTLED RAILWAY

BARDSEY BECK

HETCHELL WOOD

HETCHELL CRAGS

Spring Wood

OAKLANDS MANOR

RUINED MILL BUILDINGS

POMPOCALI

½ Mile

1 Km

CARR LANE

VICTORY HALL

Thorner

KENNELS LANE

what to look for

Bardsey's church is like a time capsule of architectural styles. The original Anglo-Saxon building was small – just the nave we see today. The old Saxon porch was extended into a bell tower, aisles were added in Norman times and in the 19th century the nave walls were heightened to support a new roof.

The formal garden of Bramham Park

Walking near Bardsey

2 Through an opening, you enter **Hetchell Wood**. Keep right, on a good path through the woods, soon passing beneath **Hetchell Crags**, whose soft gritstone façade offers a challenge to local climbers. You soon come to a meeting of paths, close to a wooden footbridge over the beck. Don't cross the beck, but go left for a few paces and along a track (of Roman origin) going uphill.

3 Go right, almost immediately, over a stile. The path goes right, around the **earthworks** (marked on the map as Pompocali), but first you should take five minutes to investigate these intriguing remains. Pass between a stream and an over-hanging rock; take a stile next to a gate. Walk uphill to pass **ruinous mill buildings**, take another stile, and join a good track that takes you under the old railway line. Immediately after crossing a stream, go through a small gate on the right and walk diagonally left across a small field to another gate where you turn right along a lane. Beyond the main gate to **Moat Hall**, follow a track for just 20yds (18m), and take a step stile in the wall on your right.

4 Take a field-edge path, with a hedge to the right (from here back to Bardsey you are walking the Leeds Country Way). Towards the far end of the field your path bears right into a copse. Cross a stile and a

beck on a little wooden footbridge. Go left, as you leave the copse, and immediately left again on to a hollow way hemmed in by hedgerows. Follow this path through scrubland, past a couple of small **fishing lakes**, to emerge at a field. Continue up a field-edge path, keeping a hedge to your right. At the top of the hill, walk downhill for 75yds (69m). Where the hedge ends you meet a cross-track. Ignore the good track ahead and go left here on a track that follows a wall to meet the A58 road.

5 Walk left for just 20yds (18m) and bear right on to **Wayside Mount**, an unsurfaced access road that serves a collection of detached houses. Beyond the last **house** go through a gate and follow the track ahead, with a tall hedge on your left. When the track bears left walk ahead down a field-edge path, following a hedge on the left. Bear half right, near the bottom of the field, to join a narrow path through scrubland, over a little beck, and up to a gate into the **churchyard**. Keep right of the church to meet a road.

6 Go right on Church Lane back to your car, or left if you're going straight to The Bingley Arms.

The Bingley Arms

The Guinness Book of Records *lists the Bingley Arms as the oldest inhabited inn and brewhouse in England with records dating back to AD 905. Formerly known as the Priests Inn, it was once connected with Kirkstall Abbey and was used as a rest house for travelling monks. The impressive stone building is partially clad with ivy and shaded by a fine willow tree. Inside it is crammed with historical interest with an old-world atmosphere created by exposed wooden beams, wood-panelled walls hung with hunting prints, cushioned settles and open log fires. Don't miss a glimpse of the beautiful upstairs dining hall. A lovely terraced garden filled with flowers makes a delightful place to sit on warm summer days.*

Food
Expect a good choice of interesting bar meals ranging from the traditional – steak and mushroom pie, lambs' liver and bacon and pork sausages on creamy mash – to home-made curries, Chinese dishes and pasta meals. Good steaks, daily specials and a popular sandwich menu.

Family facilities
Children are welcome in all areas of the pub and half portions of all the dishes on the bar menu are available.

Alternative refreshment stops
None on route. There are other refreshment opportunities in Bardsey.

about the pub

The Bingley Arms
37 Church Lane
Bardsey, Leeds,
West Yorkshire LS17 9DR
Tel: 01937 572462

DIRECTIONS: see Getting to the Start; the pub is on Church Lane

PARKING: 70

OPEN: daily; all day

FOOD: all day Sunday; no food Sunday evening and Monday

BREWERY/COMPANY: Honeycombe Leisure

REAL ALE: Timothy Taylor Landlord, Moorhouses Black Cat, Black Sheep Bitter, Tetley

DOGS: allowed in taproom and garden on leads

☞ Where to go from here
At nearby Bramham Park you will find a splendid Queen Anne mansion built in 1698. The beautiful gardens were laid out by Robert Benson, 1st Lord Bingley, with cascades, ponds and grand vistas in the manner of Versailles (www.bramhampark.co.uk). In Roundhay Park on the northern edge of Leeds you will find Tropical World. Here the atmosphere of the tropics is recreated with exotic trees, waterfall cascades, a Nocturnal House, a South American rainforest, and a Desert House (www.vrleeds.co.uk).

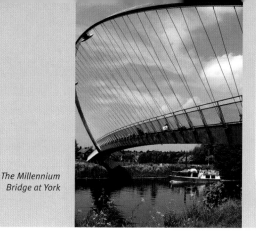

The Millennium Bridge at York

did you know?

York's stunning Millennium Bridge, spanning the River Ouse at Fulford, was opened on April 10, 2001. A slender arch of stainless steel, strung with fine cables suspends the deck of the bridge, which is for the use of pedestrians and cyclists.

Wheeling along the York to Selby cycle track

York's solar cycle path

A railway track with space in mind and a visit to one of England's most historic cities.

The Railway

York is a railway city so what better way to approach it than on an old railway line. And this old railway line was a famous one – part of the London King's Cross to Edinburgh East Coast Line. Here the *Flying Scotsman* and the world's fastest steam engine, the *Mallard*, thundered along the tracks carrying long trains of dark-red carriages.

So why did they close this stretch? Well, in the early 1980s an ultramodern coalfield at Selby was developed, necessitating a diversion of the railway to avoid the risk of subsidence. Sustrans bought the old line and set about their first major project – a new cycle track, from Riccall to York.

For budding astronomers the line includes a 6.4-mile (10km) scale model of the Solar System, with the Sun being closest to York and Pluto sited near Riccall. Perhaps one of the most fascinating aspects is the Naburn Swing Bridge spanning the River Ouse. Sad and dowdy, its old grey metal structure is showing its age, but there's a fascinating sculpture set across the top. 'The Fisher of Dreams' by Pete Rogers shows an angler sitting peacefully astride the bridge-top with his faithful dog. As you pass below, look closer at that naughty hound, for he is waiting to pee on your bike.

the ride

1 Follow the narrow dirt path leading down to the main trackbed where you turn right. The cycling is easy on a fairly level firm surface. After passing beneath the bridge at **Maude Ridding** and **Naburn Wood** you come to the first planet en route – Uranus. The **church spire** you can see at ten to the hour is that of Naburn village, and soon you pass under the bridge carrying Moor Lane, the Naburn road. Some woods largely obscure the village as you get closer but if you want to visit the village it can be accessed on the left by the **Howden Bridge**, where you see the ringed Saturn model.

2 Just a short way further along the track you reach **Naburn Bridge,** a huge steel structure that carries the track over the River Ouse and its marina. The bridge looks a little neglected, except for the **sculptures** topping it (see 'The Railway'), but it does offer fine views of the tree-lined Ouse, its boats and the vast plains of York. Over the bridge the track continues into the suburb of **Bishopsthorpe** where planet Jupiter awaits.

3 Suddenly there's a sign saying end of the railway track and you find yourself on a **housing estate** without having seen Earth. Don't worry – follow the blue and white cycleway signs first to the right, then left, and you'll soon be back on a tarred track passing Mars, Earth, Venus and Mercury in quick succession.

4 The track passes under the **York Ring Road**. On the other side there's a huge golden globe representing the Sun. Here the path splits. This is a logical finishing point for those with young children, who will retrace their route back to Escrick. Otherwise, turn right following the tarred track running parallel to the ring road before skirting several fields. The main stand of **York Racecourse** comes into view and the path rounds it to the right, crossing two straights before turning left towards the right side of the **stand**.

5 The path comes to a road just south of the famous **Terry's chocolate factory**, which is about to be shut down. Cross the road at the nearby crossing, turn left along the cycle/walkway, then right on a tarred track descending to the banks of the River Ouse. Turn left along the **riverside promenade**. You'll soon see the ultramodern **Millennium Bridge**. Past **Rowntree Park** and a campsite you follow a quiet back street, Terry Avenue, which still follows the riverside towards the centre of York. Now you'll see the large red and white **pleasure boats** cruising the river.

6 A block of buildings now separates the road from the river. Shortly, at the **Cock and Bottle pub**, turn right back to the riverside, where you should turn left. There are some **cycle racks** by the Ouse Bridge. On the opposite side of the river you'll see the whitewashed **Kings Arms**. To get to it just climb the steps ahead, turn right over the bridge and down the other side; or you could look around the city first. The Railway Museum, the Minster and the Shambles are a must. Retrace your route back along the railway path to Escrick.

4h00 | **14 MILES** | **22.6 KM** | **LEVEL 1**23

MAP: OS Explorer 290 York

START/FINISH: Escrick; grid ref: SE 616419

TRAILS/TRACKS: easy-riding former rail track plus back roads

LANDSCAPE: field, suburb and city

PUBLIC TOILETS: none on route

TOURIST INFORMATION: York, tel 01904 621756

CYCLE HIRE: Europcar Cycle Hire, Platform 1, York Station, tel 01904 656161

THE PUB: Kings Arms, Kings Staithe, York

❶ The route crosses a road and mixes with light traffic from Point 5 (Terry's factory) to the centre of York

Getting to the start

Escrick is just off the A19, 7 miles (11.3km) south east of York. From the north take the A19 turn-off from the A64 ring road, then half a mile (800m) beyond Escrick take the first turn on the right. Turn left at the nearside of the brick-built railway bridge following a rough stone track down to the car park. From the south follow the A19 to York (junction 34 from the M62) and turn left just short of Escrick.

Why do this cycle ride?

If you're new to cycling this is one of the easier routes with smooth surfaces and little traffic, even in the centre of York. The railway verges are flower-filled in spring and summer and the views are superb for most of the way.

Researched and written by: John Gillham

while you're there

York has the world's largest railway museum and families can spend all day exploring the halls that house this impressive collection. Among the exhibits are the Chinese Locomotive (built in 1935 and weighing in at 193 tons with tender), the Mallard, which holds the world speed record for steam traction on rail, and the famous Stephenson's Rocket.

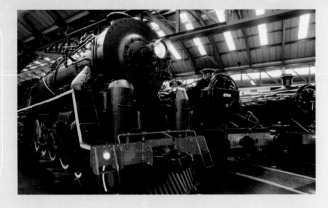

Steam engines at York's railway museum

Map labels:
A59, Heworth, York, York Minster, National Railway Museum, Jorvik, Kings Arms PH, A1079, Acomb, campsite, A1036, factory, Heslington, York Race Course, A19, Fulford, Woodthorpe, Heslington Common, A64, shopping centre, B1222, A64, PH, Copmanthorpe, Bishopthorpe, A19, Naburn Bridge, Crockey Hill, marina, Acaster Malbis, PH, Naburn, Naburn Moor, Deighton, airfield (dis), Naburn Wood, Maude Ridding, hotel, Escrick, PH, Escrick Park, Acaster Selby, B1222, River Ouse, P START, A19, Stillingfleet, PH, Selby

0 —— 1mile
0 —— 1km

Kings Arms

York's most famous pub, is sited right by the river. Each time the Ouse bursts its banks TV cameramen flock to the Kings Arms to capture the floodwaters flowing through the bar – there's a marker by the door that shows the level of famous floods of the past. For that reason, the pub's interior furnishings are spartan. It's a joy, however, to dine on their outside tables, which are laid across a cobbled area, right by the river. The food is simple, but oh-so-tasty alfresco style!

about the pub

Kings Arms
Kings Staithe, York,
North Yorkshire Yo1 9SN
Tel 01904 659435

DIRECTIONS: Kings Staithe is on the opposite bank of the river to the ride's finishing point

PARKING: none

OPEN: daily; all day

FOOD: no food Sunday evening

BREWERY/COMPANY: Samuel Smiths

REAL ALE: none

Food

Traditional pub food comes in the form of giant Yorkshire puddings filled with tuna or chilli, home-made steak pie, burgers, cheese ploughman's lunch, haddock and chips, a daily roast, and chalkboard specials.

Family facilities

Children are welcome and the pub provides a simple menu for youngsters to choose from. The cobbled riverside area offers a most attractive venue for alfresco dining but children need to be supervised at all times.

Alternative refreshment stops

Though there's nothing en route, there's a wide choice of cafés and pubs in the city.

☛ Where to go from here

While you're in York a visit to the fine minster is a must, as is Jorvik (www.vikingjorvik.com) where you discover what life was like in Viking-age Yorkshire. At the National Railway Museum (www.nrm.org.uk), you will see trains that steamed along the track you've just been on, including the pale-blue streamlined Mallard.

while you're there

Reckoned by many people to be one of North Yorkshire's prettiest villages, Hutton-le-Hole has a long been associated with the Society of Friends.

One Quaker inhabitant, John Richard, was a friend of William Penn, founder of Pennsylvania. He spent much time preaching in America; it is said he rode more than 3,726 miles (6,000km) and acted as a mediator between the white settlers and the Native Americans. He finally retired to the village, where he died in 1753.

Lastingham and Hutton-le-Hole

*Ryedale Folk Museum
at Hutton-le-Hole*

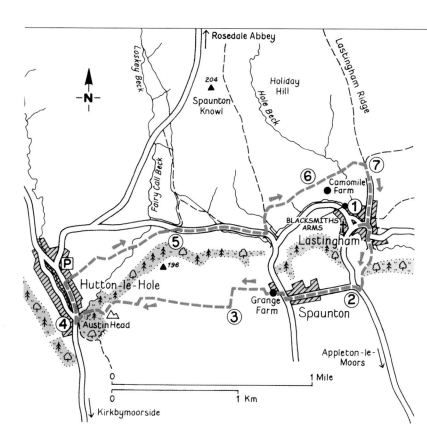

2h00 | 4.5 MILES | 7.2 KM | LEVEL 1 2 3

MAP: OS Explorer OL26 North York Moors – Western

START/FINISH: village street in Lastingham; grid ref: SE 729905

PATHS: farm tracks and field paths, 8 stiles

LANDSCAPE: moorland and woodland, with views

PUBLIC TOILETS: Hutton-le-Hole

TOURIST INFORMATION: Pickering, tel 01751 473791

THE PUB: The Blacksmiths Arms, Lastingham

Getting to the start

Lastingham is reached by turning north from the A170 Thirsk to Scarborough road between Kirkby Mills and Sinnington. Park sympathetically on the village street. Turn left by the church for the Blacksmith Arms.

Researched and written by:
John Gillham, David Winpenny

across a new local landmark. Marking the year 2000, the people of Lastingham placed a boulder carved with a cross on the hillside above the village. On it are two dates – AD 2000 and AD 654, the year in which St Cedd founded the original Lastingham monastery.

the walk

1 From the Blacksmiths Arms walk back down to the **green** and turn left, following signs to Cropton, Pickering and Rosedale. Where the road swings left, go right along a lane to wind over a small bridge and beside a **stream**. Ascend to a footpath sign, and go right, uphill, through a gate and through woodland to a handgate on to a road. Take the upper right fork lane, signed '**Spaunton**'.

2 Follow the road through Spaunton, and bend right at the end of the village, then turn left by the **public footpath sign** over the cattle grid into the **farmyard**. The waymarked track curves through the farm to reach another footpath sign, where the track bends left. At a large **outbuilding** the track bends left again.

3 After about 200yds (183m), follow a public footpath sign right and walk on to another sign as the track bends left. After 100yds (91m) take a footpath to the right, down the hill into **woodland**. Where the path divides, take the left fork down to a stile on your right, going off the track and down a steep grassy path into the valley. Descend

From St Cedd's monastery to the attractive village of Hutton-le-Hole.

Lastingham & Spaunton

St Cedd founded his monastery at Lastingham in 654. Nothing survives of his church but a Norman church was built in 1078 when the monastery was refounded after destruction in Danish raids in the 9th century.

Leaving Lastingham, the walk quickly reaches the only street in Spaunton. The village has hidden secrets; the fields here are set out on a Roman pattern, and at the beginning of the 19th century a Roman burial site was found near the village.

Pretty Hutton-le-Hole clusters around an irregular green and along the banks of the Hutton Beck. The village has an old Meeting House and a long association with the Society of Friends. Away from the village, near the end of the walk you'll come

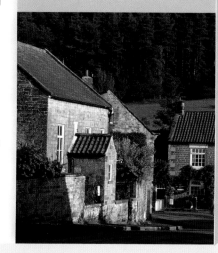

Pretty cottages line a quiet lane in Lastingham

did you know?

Excavations near Spaunton indicated that it was once an important village, owned by St Mary's Abbey in York. When the estate was sold in the 16th century, the new landowners constituted a special court, which still meets to consider the rights of those whose animals graze on the commons.

The view to the Church of St Mary in Lastingham

beside a stream to a stile by a gate, which takes you on to the road in **Hutton-le-Hole**.

4 Turn right up the main street. After passing the **Barn Hotel** and the Wychwood Gifts shop turn right, following a route signed to Lastingham. Beyond a gate, pass through a garden and to the right of some **sheds** to reach a stile, which gives entry to a large field that is sometimes used as a campsite. Turn left and follow the edge of the field and over two more stiles to a kissing gate before a **footbridge**. Follow the path through woodland to a gate and follow the grassy track to the road.

5 Turn right and follow the road for 0.5 mile (800m) and turn left at a footpath sign just before the road descends to a stone bridge. A rutted track bends right between farmland on the right and **Spaunton Moor**.

6 Just before **Camomile Farm**, leave the track on the left and follow the footpath sign and waymarker posts to round a **copse** of sycamores, beyond which you descend

into a valley. Cross over the stream to a stile and a kissing gate. Continue walking with the wall on your right-hand side to another kissing gate and stile, which will lead you to a **carved stone** with a cross and a three-pointed sign.

7 Turn right, downhill, through a gate and on to the metalled road that descends to the village of **Lastingham**.

what to look for

There is a full range of activities at the Ryedale Folk Museum in Hutton-le-Hole (www.ryedalefolkmuseum.co.uk), where old structures from around the North York Moors have been reconstructed as a hamlet. As well as an authentic Elizabethan manor house with a massive oak cruck frame, farm buildings, cottages and traditional long houses, you can see an early photographer's studio, a medieval glass kiln and a variety of agricultural tools and transport. There's also a fire engine and a hearse. Maypole dancing, rare breeds days and quilting are just some of the activities that take place during the year and you may catch the historic farm machinery working, or have the chance to try your hand at some of the almost-forgotten crafts.

Visitors examining the shop fronts in the Ryedale Folk Museum, Hutton-le-Hole

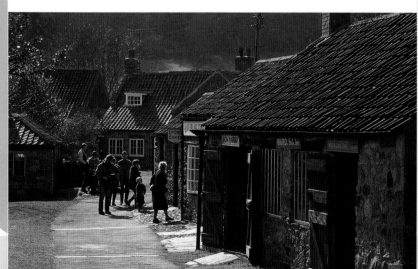

The Blacksmiths Arms

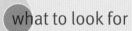

A charming stone-built inn dating from 1693 and unspoilt by progress, situated in a beautiful village that is part of a conservation area. Antiquity is evident everywhere, from the pretty York-stone building to the flagged and beamed bar, and the range that houses the open log fire is 200 years old. Even the furnishings are in keeping with the pub's great age. There are excellent changing real ales from micro-breweries and a wide-ranging pub food menu, as well as three cosy, cottagey bedrooms.

Food

Bar snacks include sandwiches, filled Yorkshire puddings and home-made soups, while the main menu and specials board offer beer-battered cod, steak and ale pie, lamb and mint pie, crispy roast duck with orange sauce, Yorkshire hotpot and a roast of the day. Good vegetarian options. Afternoon teas.

Family facilities

Children are welcome inside the pub. No children's menu but smaller portions are available, as are high chairs.

Alternative refreshment stops

There is a range of cafés, tea rooms, restaurants and pubs in Hutton-le-Hole – the Barn Hotel Tea Rooms and the Crown Hotel are recommended. In Lastingham, the excellent Lastingham Grange offers dinner and light lunches, as well as a full Sunday lunch, but is closed from mid-November to March.

☞ Where to go from here

If you're a real ale enthusiast, the Cropton Brewery and Visitor Centre (www.croptonbrewery.co.uk), 1.5 miles (2.4km) east of Lastingham, is the place to head for. Visit the Beck Isle Museum of Rural Life in Pickering (www.beckislemuseum.co.uk) or visit the Ryedale Folk Museum in Hutton-le-Hole.

about the pub

The Blacksmiths Arms
Front Street, Lastingham
North Yorkshire YO62 6TL
Tel: 01751 417247

DIRECTIONS: see Getting to the Start

PARKING: roadside parking

OPEN: daily; all day May to October; closed Tuesday lunchtime November to April

FOOD: daily; all day May to October

BREWERY/COMPANY: free house

REAL ALE: Lastingham Ale, two micro-brewery guest beers

DOGS: in garden only

ROOMS: 3 en suite

Red grouse (*Lagopus lagopus scoticus*)

did you know?

Visitors in late summer will see the moors covered in the purple of ling heather. Patches of the rarer bell heather with flowers of a deeper purple, and the pink cross-leaved heather, flower earlier.

Above: Purple heather moorland in North Yorkshire
Left: Water splashing down rocks at Mallyan Spout

Moorland around Goathland and Mallyan Spout

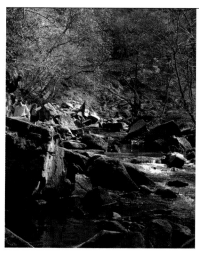

From the popular moorland village with its television links, through woodland and over the moor.

Heartbeat country

Goathland is one of the most popular destinations for visitors to the North York Moors National Park. Its situation, around a large open common, criss-crossed by tracks and closely cropped by grazing sheep, has always been attractive. Today many tourists are drawn to Goathland because it is used as the fictitious village of Aidensfield for the popular television series *Heartbeat*. The Goathland Story exhibition tells the village's history from the time it was an Iron Age centre for making stone querns to grind corn, to today – and there's a special *Heartbeat* collection. The walk begins with a visit to the 70ft (21m) Mallyan Spout waterfall into the West Beck. In dry weather

only a trickle of water may fall from the side of the gorge into the stream below but after rain it can become an impressive torrent. Take care at all times: sometimes it may be impossible to pass the waterfall on the streamside path.

After you have crossed the ford and turned on to the moorland by Hunt House, you might find yourself accompanied by the sudden flutter of red grouse rising from their nest sites on the heather moorland.

If you visit in late summer, the moors will be clothed in the colours of heather. Sheep grazing has for centuries been the traditional way of managing the moors as the animals help keep the heather short and encourage the new shoots. To regenerate the heather, landowners regularly use carefully controlled burning in the early spring or the autumn when the ground is wet. The fire burns away the old heather stems, but does not damage the roots, nor the peat. New growth quickly springs up to feed the young grouse.

what to look for

In the valley of the West Beck, and especially near Mallyan Spout, you will see lots of ferns. Among the sorts you might spot are the male fern, with its pale green stems, the buckler fern, which has scales with a dark central stripe and paler edges, and the hartstongue fern, with its distinctive strap-like fronds. They are all typical of damp, humid areas, and like every fern, they are flowerless. Instead, they reproduce by means of spores – look under the leaves to find the characteristic dots that are the spore sacs or sporangia. The spores are dispersed by wind or by animals.

the walk

1 Opposite the church go through the kissing gate to the right of the **Mallyan Spout Hotel**, signed 'Mallyan Spout'. Follow the path to a streamside signpost and turn left. Continue past the waterfall (take care after heavy rain). Follow the footpath signs, over two footbridges, over a stile and up steps. Continue by the stream, then ascend to a stile on to a road beside a **bridge**.

2 Turn left along the road and climb the hill. Where the road bends left, go right along a **bridleway** through a gate. Turn left down a path to go over a bridge, then ahead by the **buildings**, through a gate and across the field.

3 Part-way across the field, go through a gate to the right into **woodland**.

| 2h00 | 4.5 MILES | 7.2 KM | LEVEL 123 |

MAP: OS Explorer OL27 North York Moors – Eastern

START/FINISH: west end of Goathland village, near church; grid ref: NZ 827007

PATHS: streamside tracks, field and moorland paths, 2 stiles

LANDSCAPE: deep, wooded valley, farmland and open moorland

PUBLIC TOILETS: Goathland village

TOURIST INFORMATION: Whitby, tel 01947 602674

THE PUB: The Goathland Hotel, Goathland

❗ The initial riverside path to Mallyan Spout is slippery

Getting to the start

Goathland is situated 8 miles (12.9km) southwest of Whitby. It lies just 2 miles (3.2km) west of the A169 Whitby to Malton road and can also be reached using the North Yorkshire Moors Railway from Grosmont or Pickering. The easiest parking is at the west end of the village near the church.

Researched and written by:
John Gillham, David Winpenny

did you know?

The red grouse is a medium-sized game bird. It has a plump body, a short tail, a lightly hook-tipped bill and is a reddish brown colour. Its feet and legs are covered with pale feathers. Red grouse breed in the uplands of the north and west and are resident all year round. The population is in decline due to the loss of its natural habitat, heather moorland.

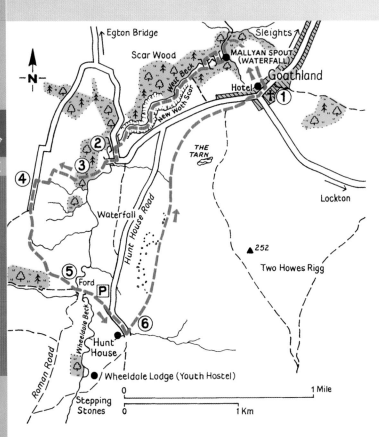

The Goathland Hotel

Conveniently sited on Goathland's main street, just 500 yards (457m) from the North Yorkshire Moors Railway, this stone-built Victorian building draws the crowds despite its off-the-beaten-track moorland village location. It is the Aidensfield Arms in the TV series Heartbeat and can get very busy with 'location' enthusiasts, so arrive early! Traditionally furnished, it has a spacious main bar with tiled floor, ceiling beams and winter log fires, a plush, carpeted lounge bar, and a wood-panelled restaurant. Comfortable bedrooms have moorland views.

Food

Food is simple but well prepared. At lunchtime expect open sandwiches (home-cooked ham) and salads, ploughman's lunches and traditional bar meals like filled giant Yorkshire puddings (roast beef and onion gravy), home-made steak and kidney pie, and Whitby scampi and chips.

Family facilities

There are two family areas in the bars and smaller portions of adult dishes are available. Good-sized rear garden and three bedrooms with extra beds or cots for families.

Alternative refreshment stops

As you would expect from a popular village, there are cafés and snack bars dotted around Goathland, as well as ice-cream vans on the green. The restaurant at the Mallyan Spout Hotel has a fine reputation.

☛ Where to go from here

Take a nostalgic trip on the North Yorkshire Moors Railway, which has a station in the valley below the village. It runs through Newtondale between Pickering and Grosmont and ran steam trains from 1847 until it was closed in 1957. It reopened in 1973 and most of its trains are steam-hauled (www.northyorkshiremoors railway .com).

about the pub

The Goathland Hotel
Goathland, Whitby
North Yorkshire YO22 5LY
Tel: 01947 896203

DIRECTIONS: on main village street

PARKING: 20

OPEN: daily; all day in high summer

FOOD: daily

BREWERY/COMPANY: Punch Taverns

REAL ALE: Flowers IPA, Camerons Strongarm

DOGS: welcome on leads

ROOMS: 9 bedrooms (8 en suite)

Ascend a stony track, go through a wooden gate then left to another gate on the edge of the wood. Ignoring the gate, turn right up the field, before going left at the top through a **gateway**. Continue with a wall on your right and go through a waymarked gateway in the wall and up the field, to emerge through a gate on to a **metalled lane**.

4 Turn left along the lane, go through a gate and follow the '**Roman Road**' sign. Go through another gate, still following the public bridleway signs as you join a green lane. Continue through a small handgate, to descend to another gate and then on until you reach a **ford**.

5 Cross the ford and go straight ahead along the track, eventually to reach a road by a **bungalow**. Turn right up the road and left by a **wooden garage** to continue along a green track up the hillside.

6 Go straight ahead at a crossing track, passing a small **cairn** and bending left along the heathery ridge. The obvious path is marked by a series of **little cairns**. Eventually, take a left fork to go down a shallow gill and join a clear track. **Goathland church** soon comes into sight. Pass a bridleway sign and descend to the road near the church. The **Goathland Hotel** can be found on the right-hand side at the far end of the main street.

323

while you're there

Visit Yorkshire Lavender at Terrington where you can see row upon row of different varieties of lavender in a fantastic array of colours ranging from white through to blues, lilacs and a magnificent deep purple.

The gardens at Yorkshire Lavender

Terrington and Castle Howard

Castle Howard is set amongst 1,000 acres (405ha) of grounds and gardens

A ride through Yorkshire's most magnificent estate.

Castle Howard

Six years after Henderskelfe Castle burned down in 1693, Charles Howard, the 3rd Earl of Carlisle, asked his friend, Sir John Vanbrugh, to design its replacement, Castle Howard. Vanbrugh at this time was a complete novice, though he would later design Blenheim Palace. However, he formed a successful team with Christopher Wren's clerk, Nicholas Hawksmoor. The building programme would last 100 years, the lifetime of three earls, but the legacy left Yorkshire with one of Britain's most elegant palaces, set among magnificent and colourful gardens, complete with lakes, fountains, classical statues and temples.

In the house itself, the marble entrance hall is lit subtly by a dome. Explore further and you'll see treasures built up over centuries, including antique sculptures, fine porcelain, and paintings by Rubens, Reynolds and Gainsborough. In 1940 fire came to haunt the Howards once more. A devastating blaze destroyed the dome and twenty of the rooms, leaving the palace open to the elements and in need of extremely costly renovation. That it was done so successfully is all down to George Howard, who inherited the estate after the death of his two brothers in World War Two.

the ride

1 Terrington is a peaceful little village with fine sloping greens either side of the main street, giving the place a spacious feel. The cottages, which are largely Victorian, are built with local limestone. Above them, just off the main street, stands the church, a square-towered building that dates back to Saxon times – there's an Anglo-Saxon window in the south aisle. Much of the structure is 13th-century but was modernised around 1860.

Heading east past the ivy-clad **Bay Horse Inn** towards Castle Howard is slightly downhill, a nice start – the tea rooms tempt you straight away. If it's hot, a splendid avenue of trees on the way out of the village will offer some welcome shade.

2 Take the right fork, signed 'to Ganthorpe, York', 0.5 mile (800m) out of the village. Now you pay for your downhill as the road climbs to the top of **Cross Hill**, where there's a good view back to Terrington. The lane levels out as it passes through the stone cottages and farms of **Ganthorpe**. This hamlet was the birthplace of the historian, Arthur Toynbee (1886–1975) and the botanist, Richard Spruce (1817–93), who travelled to places like the Andes and the Amazon in search of specimens for scientific research. There's another short downhill section as the lane bends right by **Sata Wood**, then it's uphill again.

3 Turn left at the T-junction, where you get glimpses of a couple of the **Castle Howard domes**, then left at the crossroads following the directions to Slingsby and Castle Howard. The road, known as the **Stray**, is straight and madly undulating like a Roman road, with wide verges and avenues of trees lining the way. Some of the traffic is speedy so take care! Soon you pass beneath the extremely narrow stone arch of the Castle Howard estate's **Carrmire Gate**, which is flanked by castellated walls, then you come upon the gate house with its pyramidal roof. There's a roundabout next to a 100ft (91m) **obelisk** of 1714 dedicated

2h00 | **9.3 MILES** | **15 KM** | **LEVEL 123**

MAP: OS Explorer 300 Howardian Hills and Malton

START/FINISH: roadside parking in the main street, Terrington; grid ref: SE 670706

TRAILS/TRACKS: country lanes with some hills

LANDSCAPE: rolling pastoral hills and parkland

PUBLIC TOILETS: at Castle Howard

TOURIST INFORMATION: Malton, tel: 01653 600048

CYCLE HIRE: none locally

THE PUB: Bay Horse Inn, Terrington

🛈 The hilly terrain might be a little tiring for younger children. Take care on the Stray (Point 3) – some of the traffic here is faster than it should be

Getting to the start

From the A64 north east of York, follow the signs for Castle Howard and take the first left after the castle entrance. Alternatively, from Helmsley follow the B1257 signed 'Malton' to Slingsby and turn right for Castle Howard. Turn right by the castle's Great Lake.

Why do this cycle ride?

This pleasant ride combines the sophistication of the Castle Howard Estate and the simple beauty and rural charm of the Howardian Hills.

Researched and written by: John Gillham

did you know?

Not everything at Castle Howard is 18th century. The largest piece of garden sculpture is the grandiose Atlas Fountain, with Titan holding up the globe and surrounded by Tritons spouting water from their shells. This was put in place when the Victorian garden designer W E Nesfield laid out a new parterre at Castle Howard's south front. The fountain was sculpted by John Thomas and came to Castle Howard in 1851 after being displayed at the Great Exhibition of that year.

Castle Howard's Atlas Fountain

to Lady Cecilia Howard. Here you need to decide whether or not to visit the palace (highly recommended).

4 Continuing down the Stray you'll pass the **Obelisk Ponds**, which are enshrouded by woodland, then the **Great Lake**, across which you get a great view of the palace and its many domes.

5 Turn left for 'Terrington' at the crossroads just beyond the lake. The lane soon swings right and climbs through the trees of **Shaw Wood**. If you have mountain bikes and

Neatly lawned houses at Terrington at the end of your ride

are experienced riders you could take the bridleway at the next bend (**South Bell Bottom**) then double back on the track over Husket and Ling Hills to meet the lane further west. If not, continue with the lane, which winds downhill across **Ganthorpe Moor** to meet the outward route by the first T-junction east of Terrington. Though you've still got the trees for shade, the downhill is now an uphill so you'll probably deserve that refreshment at the **Bay Horse Inn**.

Bay Horse Inn

about the pub

Bay Horse Inn
Main Street, Terrington
Malton, North Yorkshire YO60 6PP
Tel: 01653 648416

DIRECTIONS: see Getting to the Start; pub in the village centre

PARKING: 30

OPEN: daily; all day

FOOD: daily; all day

BREWERY/COMPANY: free house

REAL ALE: Theakston Best, Black Sheep Riggwelter, John Smith's Cask, guest beers

ROOMS: 4 en suite

substantial offerings like lambs' liver and onions, loin of pork in cider and apple cream sauce, steak and ale pie, and lamb shank with mash and fresh vegetables.

Family facilities
Families are very welcome inside the pub, especially in the conservatory. There's a typical children's menu and the garden is sheltered and safe for children.

Alternative refreshment stops
Tea Rooms, Terrington (by the post office); Hayloft and Lakeside Cafés at Castle Howard; The Malt Shovel, Hovingham – a fine pub just north of Terrington.

Terrington is an idyllic peaceful little village with stone cottages and greens, surrounded by the rolling Howardian Hills. The homely and friendly 400-year-old Bay Horse Inn, formerly a tailor's shop, reflects this rural charm from the outside to the interior. An archway of ivy surrounds the door of this whitewashed stone-built pub. Inside there's a welcoming log fire in the cosy lounge, while the public bar offers time-honoured pub games in the form of darts, dominoes, shove ha'penny and cribbage. At the back there's a conservatory adorned with old farm tools, and a small but attractively planted garden.

Food
Well-liked bar food takes in sandwiches, salads and sausage and mash and more

☞ Where to go from here
Don't miss out on exploring Castle Howard and its wonderful gardens and landscaped grounds (www.castlehoward.co.uk). Near Malton is the Eden Camp Modern History Theme Museum (www.edencamp.co.uk) which tells the story of civilian life in World War Two. Within reach is Nunnington Hall (www.nationaltrust.org.uk), Sherriff Hutton Castle and Yorkshire Lavender in Terrington.

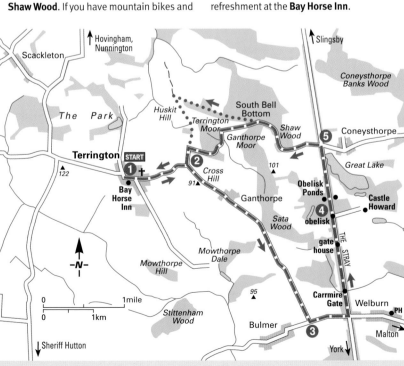

Sutton Bank is excellent for gliding

did you know?

Dialstone, a former drovers' inn and today a farm passed on this route, was once the site of the Hambleton Race Ground, where jockeys would compete for cups donated by wealthy patrons including Queen Anne and George I.

Sutton Bank near Helmsley

The Hambleton Hills

An exciting ride on the top of the moors.

Hambleton Hills

The long tarmac lane that takes you north from Sutton Bank seems unremarkable in itself, but there's a history, dating back to the Iron Age tribes who settled here around 400BC. They would have used this road long before the Romans followed in their footsteps. Evidence of the tribes' existence is all around you, from the burial tumuli near the escarpment's edge to a 60 acre (24.3ha) fort on Roulston Scar. Strangely, there are no traces of any hut circles within the fort's huge ramparts. It is possible that this was a temporary bastion in times of war, but it could also have been a huge cattle corral for neighbouring settlements.

Hambleton has many connections with beasts of burden. When the Great North Road became a turnpike the Scottish cattle drovers turned to the hills to avoid the tolls. The previously mentioned road became

known as the Hambleton Drove Road, a busy highway with several drovers' inns along the way. Hereabouts there were two – one, Dialstone House, is now a farm, but the other, the Hambleton Hotel, remains an inn.

Hambleton has long been associated with racehorses. In 1740 an Act of Parliament decreed that racing could only take place at Hambleton, York and Newmarket. Fifteen years later, however, the racecourse was closed, but nearby Hambleton House is to this day a well-known training stable for thoroughbreds.

the ride

1 Before you leave the centre, take a look at the panoramas to the south and west, for you can see for miles across the flat fields of the Vales of Mowbray and York. Alf Wight, alias the fictional vet James Herriot, believed this view to be the finest in England. Apparently, both York Minster and Lincoln Cathedral are discernible on a clear day. From the visitor centre car park, turn left up

the lane signed to Cold Kirby and Old Byland. Take the left fork past **Dialstone Farm** and its tall **communications mast**, before heading north on an ever-so-straight lane through cornfields and pastures.

2 The lane comes to a T-junction by a triangular wood, the **Snack Yate Plantation**. This is a popular starting point for serious mountain bikers who will swoop down on rough tracks through Boltby Forest. Your route turns left down the lane. It's a gentle downhill for a short distance. Just before the road dives off the edge, turn left through a gate on to a grassy bridleway along the escarpment's edge. You're riding on the Hambleton Hills. The first stretch is slightly uphill, but the track is firm and the views wide-sweeping. You'll see a small **reservoir** surrounded by forestry and the village of **Boltby** huddled under a pastured hill.

3 The bridleway climbs to the top of the hill at **High Barn**, an old stone ruin shaded by a fine stand of sycamore. The going eases and the cliffs of an **old quarry** appear ahead. Here the bridleway goes through a gate on to a walled track for a short way. Ignore the bridleway on the left, which goes back to the Hambleton Road, and stay with the edge path to the hill above the rocks of **Boltby Scar**. This is the highest point of the ride. Note the wind-warped larch trees around here – they add to the views over the edge and across the expansive Vale of Mowbray.

4 The trees of the **Boltby Forest** now cover the west slopes, almost to the summit.

A view near Boltby Forest

2h00 | **7.4 MILES** | **12 KM** | **LEVEL 123**

MAP: OS Explorer OL26 North York Moors – Western

START/FINISH: Sutton Bank Visitor Centre; grid ref: SE 516831

TRAILS/TRACKS: good level lanes followed by undulating bridleways on the escarpment's edge

LANDSCAPE: pastoral plateau and moorland ridge

PUBLIC TOILETS: Sutton Bank Visitor Centre

TOURIST INFORMATION: Sutton Bank Visitor Centre, tel 01845 597426 (weekends only Jan–Feb)

CYCLE HIRE: none locally

THE PUB: The Hambleton Inn, Sutton Bank

❶ A short section near Point 5 becomes narrower and with a few rocks in places. Inexperienced cyclists should dismount

Getting to the start

Sutton Bank is 6 miles (9.7km) east of Thirsk. Take the A170 Scarborough turn-off from the A19 at Thirsk. This climbs the difficult road to Sutton Bank (caravans prohibited). The centre and car park are on the left at the top.

Why do this cycle ride?

You can enjoy some of the north of England's best views and experience a bit of adventure with a ride on the 'edge'.

Researched and written by: John Gillham

324

CYCLE

while you're there

Sutton Bank is home to the Yorkshire Gliding Club and on summer weekends, as powered planes tow the gliders over the edge, the sky is filled with these silent aircraft using invisible rising air currents to gain height and soar away. The highest ground for miles, Sutton Bank is also a mecca for hang-gliders and microlight aircraft and the skies here can be very busy indeed.

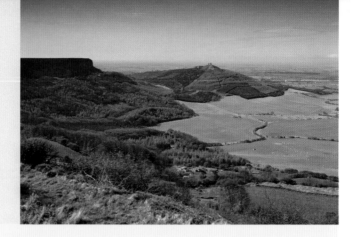

The view from Sutton Bank across the Vale of York

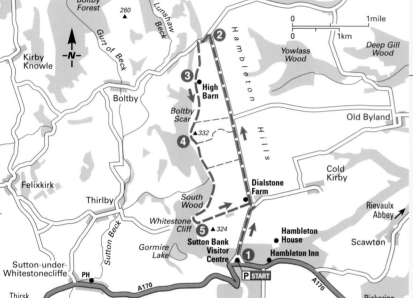

The Hambleton Inn

about the pub

The Hambleton Inn
Sutton Bank, Thirsk
North Yorkshire YO7 2HA
Tel: 01845 597202

DIRECTIONS: beside the A170 Thirsk to Scarborough road, at the top of Sutton Bank

PARKING: 50

OPEN: all day Sunday; closed Monday except Bank Holidays

FOOD: daily; all day Sunday

BREWERY/COMPANY: free house

REAL ALE: local Hambleton ales

meals range from beef burger and chips and deep-fried Whitby haddock and chips to liver and bacon with onion gravy, and pasta with poached salmon and lemon and watercress sauce. Separate evening menu.

Family facilities
The pub is really geared up for families. Children are very welcome inside the pub where an above-average children's menu is available for younger family members, as well as smaller portions of adult dishes. When the weather's fine there's good patio seating and a large lawned area with play area to keep children amused.

Alternative refreshment stops
Café at Sutton Bank Visitor Centre.

☛ Where to go from here
Visit nearby Rievaulx Abbey (www.english-heritage.org.uk), once the most important Cistercian abbey in Britain; the soaring ruins are powerfully atmospheric in the beautiful Rye valley. Another evocative ruin to explore is Byland Abbey at the base of the Hambleton Hills, or head east to Pickering to take a steam railway journey through stunning scenery on the North Yorkshire Moors Railway (www.northyorkshiremoorsrailway.com).

Beyond the next offshoot bridleway, which you should ignore, the path becomes narrower with a few embedded rocks in places. The difficulties are short-lived, but the younger and less experienced riders might prefer to dismount. The riding gets easier again as the bridleway arcs right above **South Wood**. At the end of this arc you turn left to a sign that tells you that the continuing edge path is for walkers only. This is a fine spot to linger and admire the views. To the south the half-moon-shaped **Gormire Lake** lies in a nest of broad-leaved woodland and beneath the sandy-coloured **Whitestone Cliff**.

5 When you've rested, turn left on a bridleway to **Dialstone Farm**. This heads east across large prairie-like fields. Beyond a wood, the **High Quarry Plantation**, you'll see the hurdles of the **equestrian centre**.

A cyclist takes a track near Boltby Forest

Past the large **farm** turn right along the tarred lane, then right again, back to the visitor centre car park.

Just a few hundred yards from the Sutton Bank edge and those famous James Herriot views, The Hambleton Inn is backed up by sprucewoods. It's an extremely popular pub with walkers and cyclists. The whitewashed Georgian building was once frequented by cattle drovers, who herded their beasts across the high Hambleton Drove Road. The inn has a large lawned garden to the rear, and flagged patios to the front and sides. Expect an enthusiastic and extremely friendly service, imaginative pub food, summer hog roasts and live entertainment.

Food
Food is freshly prepared and a cut above the pub norm. Snacks include a traditional ploughman's lunch and baked baguettes (crab and lemon mayonnaise, roast ham and pickle), while more substantial bar

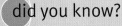
The monks at Byland Abbey, like all of their Cistercian brethren, rose at about 2am for the first service, Vigil. Two more services and a meeting followed before they dined at midday. They spent the afternoon working at their alloted tasks, and there were three more services, after which they went to bed at round 8.30pm. The choir monks did some of the manual work on the estate and in the abbey but the Cistercians also had lay brothers to work for them. They too took vows (though simpler ones) and had their own church services.

A craftsman at Robert Thompson's workshop

Byland Abbey and Oldstead Observatory

From the romantic ruins of Byland Abbey to an old observatory – and back through the fish pond.

Byland Abbey

In 1134 a party of Savigniac monks set out from their English mother house in Furness on the west coast of Cumbria to found a new monastery. Six moves and 43 years later, Byland was founded as their permanent home, and by then they had become part of the Cistercian Order. The final move was from nearby Stocking, where they had settled in 1147. The relocation to Byland in 1177 must have been long planned, for Byland's earliest buildings, the lay brothers' quarters, were complete by 1165; everything had to be in order for the arrival of the monks themselves.

The most impressive parts of the ruins remaining today are in the church – and especially the remnants of the fine rose window in the west front. Beneath it the main door leads into the nave, the lay brothers' portion of the church. Although the walls of the south transept collapsed in 1822, that area of the church still retains one of Byland's greatest treasures – the geometrically tiled floors, with their delicate patterns in red, cream and black.

At the highest point of the walk is Oldstead Observatory, built on the splendidly named Mount Snever by John Wormald, who lived at Oldstead Hall in the valley below. At just over 40ft (12m) high, 1,146ft (349m) above sea level, it is high enough to scan the heavens. History does not record if Mr Wormald made any startling astronomical discoveries.

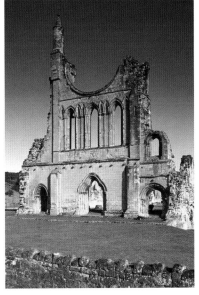

The ruins of Byland Abbey, dating from 1177

the walk

1 From the car park, walk towards the abbey ruins, then turn left along the lane at the abbey's north side. At a public footpath sign, go left up the drive of **Abbey House**, then right through a waymarked gate just before the house. After a second gateway bear slightly left, skirting a grassy bank towards the top left-hand corner of the field. Here you go though a waymarked gate behind a **bench seat**. Go through two more gates and on to a tarred lane just to the left of the buildings of **Wass** village.

2 Turn left. At a T-junction go through a gate signed '**Cam Farm, Observatory**'. The path climbs then leaves the wood edge

to rise to a terrace. After a stile take the left-hand path, signed **Cam Farm**, to join a track climbing uphill to reach a **forestry vehicle turning circle**.

3 Turn right and, just before a waymarked metal gate at the edge of the forest, turn left along the inside wood edge (not waymarked). Follow the path, which soon bends left over wet ground to **Oldstead Observatory**. Pass to the left of the observatory and go down a slope to a track running steeply downhill. The path can be slippery – take care!

4 Turn right along a track, signed '**Oldstead**', then take a left turn at the next junction, over a stream where it is joined by another track and becomes a tarred country lane. Turn left at the T-junction to pass through Olstead village. Just before the 'road narrows' sign, turn left.

5 Go through some gateposts and over a **cattle grid**. Then, as the avenue of trees ends, take a waymarked footpath to the

Walkers taking a road near Byland Abbey

2h30 **5 MILES** **8 KM** **LEVEL 1 2 3**

MAP: OS Explorer OL26 North York Moors – Western

START/FINISH: car park behind Abbey Inn in Byland Abbey; grid ref: SE 548789

PATHS: woodland tracks, field paths, 11 stiles

LANDSCAPE: undulating pasture and woodland on slopes of Hambleton Hills

PUBLIC TOILETS: at Byland Abbey

TOURIST INFORMATION: Sutton Bank Visitor Centre, tel 01845 597426 (weekends only Jan–Feb)

THE PUB: The Abbey Inn, Byland Abbey

❶ In summer some paths may be choked with nettles and giant hogweed, so unsuitable for small children

Getting to the start

Byland Abbey is 2 miles (3.2km) south of the A170 road halfway between Thirsk and Helmsley. It is best reached by turning south off the A170 3 miles (4.8km) east of Sutton Bank. In the village turn right by the inn to access the signed car park.

Researched and written by:
John Gillham, David Winpenny

while you're there

Take a trip to nearby Kilburn to the Mouseman Visitor Centre. This is where Robert Thompson, born in 1867, created his renowned furniture, each piece carved with his characteristic mouse. Oak furniture is still made by his successors, and the centre demonstrates the history of the firm and its work.

The nightjar (Caprimulgus europaeus) roosts on the ground in the daytime and hunts moths at night

The Abbey Inn

Do seek out this isolated rural pub – it's worth it for the modern British-based food it serves and, if you're looking for somewhere to stay, its superior accommodation. A well-proportioned, creeper-clad façade conceals a highly distinctive interior. The four splendid dining areas have, variously, bare boards, rug-strewn flagstones, open fireplaces, huge settles with scatter cushions, Jacobean-style chairs, and oak and stripped deal tables. Fine tapestries, stuffed birds and unusual objets d'art complete the picture. The abbey ruins are floodlit at night and look amazing from two of the three superb en suite bedrooms. The third overlooks the gardens and surrounding countryside.

Food

Expect a changing menu and daily specials board. At lunchtime your meal could be Brie and red onion tart, chicken and mushroom pie, deep-fried cod with minted pea puree, sweet potato and watercress cakes with chilli dressing, sandwiches, or ploughman's terrine with honey and sunflower bread. Excellent, more elaborate evening menu.

about the pub

The Abbey Inn
Byland Abbey, Coxwold
Thirsk, North Yorkshire YO61 4BD
Tel: 01347 868204
www.bylandabbeyinn.com

DIRECTIONS: see Getting to the Start; pub opposite the abbey ruins

PARKING: 40

OPEN: closed Sunday evening and Monday lunchtime

FOOD: daily

BREWERY/COMPANY: free house

REAL ALE: Black Sheep Bitter, Tetley

DOGS: not allowed inside

ROOMS: 3 en suite

Family facilities

Children of all ages are welcome inside and smaller portions of the main menu dishes are available. Safe large garden for summer eating and drinking. No children overnight.

Alternative refreshment stops

The Wombwell Arms at Wass has bistro-style food, with sandwiches and ploughman's at lunchtime.

☞ Where to go from here

Take a trip to nearby Kilburn to visit the Mouseman Visitor Centre. Here Robert Thompson worked at his now-famous furniture (www.robertthompsons.co.uk). Visit Newburgh Priory, Shandy Hall in Coxwold or the World of James Herriot Museum and Visitor Centre in Thirsk.

right, uphill to a stile, before climbing a steep grassy bank. Note: this path can become overgrown with nettles, bramble and giant hogweed.

what to look for

The lumps and bumps of the final field you cross on the walk are the remains of the monks' ponds. It is difficult to visualise the abbey in the Middle Ages almost surrounded by water. There was a large pond that stretched almost 0.5 mile (800m) from east to west, to the north of the abbey buildings, which was used to flush the drains, and two more south and south east. To the south west, where this walk passes through, was a roughly triangular pond, bounded by a bank supporting the abbey's mill. The ponds were also used for breeding fish, one of the most important staples of the monks' diet. They practised large-scale fish farming at nearby Oldstead Grange.

6 On reaching a tarred lane turn right, then take a track to the left by the **Oldstead Grange sign**. As you near the house, turn left towards some barns and wind your way through the **farmyard** to a stile by a metal gate. Bear half-right downhill on the track, then bend slightly right to a waymarked stile.

7 Ten yards/metres beyond the stile turn left and go through a wood to a **Byland Abbey signpost**. Follow the path as it leaves the woods and bends left beyond **Cams Head Farm**. Follow the hedge on the left, before going through a large gap. Now keep the hedge to the right.

8 The path crosses more fields with **Byland Abbey** directly ahead. In the last field veer left to follow the fence to a roadside stile. Turn left along the lane, then left again past the Abbey Inn to the car park.

while you're there

The Dalby Forest Visitor Centre is situated adjacent to the forest village of Low Dalby. This is where you'll get information about Dalby and other forests in the area, plus maps and booklets about the various walking and cycle trails. Refreshments are available and there are picnic tables and toilets. The visitor centre is open daily from Easter to the end of October.

Dalby Forest

A duck and her ducklings on Staindale Lake

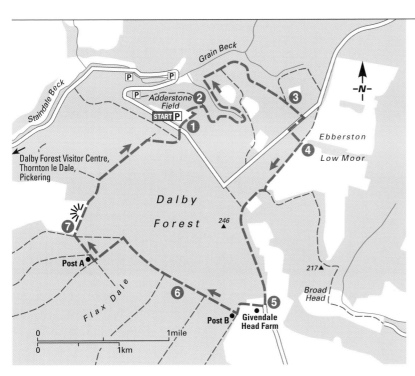

A short ride through the forest where you seek the wildlife that's watching you.

The Forest

In 1919, when the Forestry Commission was founded, Britain's woodland cover had shrunk to around 5 per cent, which meant we had to import large quantities of timber to meet the increasing needs of industry. In Yorkshire they turned to Dalby on the south east corner of the North York Moors. The area, once part of the Royal Hunting Forest of Pickering, had degenerated into boggy heathland, poverty-stricken upland farms and a huge rabbit warren that provided fur for a felt hat industry. Several streams drained the moorland plateau and flowed south west into Dalby Beck, forming a rigg and dale landscape. Scrub oak and birch clustered around these streams, but in general the ground was only suitable for conifers. By 1921 the planting began and within years over 8,500 acres (3,442ha) of Sitka Spruce and Scots Pine had covered the ground.

Conservationists hated these new forests, complaining that wildlife had been decimated, but today, if you stay quiet and look hard enough, you'll see that it's really quite abundant. In quieter corners you may stumble upon the Bambi-like roe deer. Many of the mammals, such as the pygmy shrew and the otter, stay clear of humans and it's bird-life you're more likely to spot. Besides the common blue tits, you're quite likely to see a wading heron, or a tiny warbler such as that summer visitor, the chiffchaf, so called because of its birdsong.

the ride

1 The **green cycle route** begins beyond the trees at the south east end of the large **Adderstone Field** (the furthest from the visitor centre). Here you turn left along a narrow slightly downhill track. Though still easy, it's the most difficult section of the route – use gentle braking if you're a little unsure. Ignore two lesser, unsigned left fork tracks.

2 Turn right along a much wider forestry track which takes a winding course round the afforested valley of **Worry Gill**. Where the more demanding red route goes off on a rough track to the right, your green route goes straight on, still using a well-graded track.

3 Where a track doubles back, go straight on up a steady hill before meeting the **forest drive** again. Cross this with care – it can be quite busy on summer weekends – before turning right along it for 200yds (183m). Turn left along a narrow path signed with red and green waymarkers and just before a 30 mile per hour speed limit sign (hope you were not speeding!). If you're early and it's summer, you may be able to dally and eat some of the bilberries that grow beside the path.

2h00	6 MILES	9.7 KM	LEVEL 1 2 3

MAP: OS Explorer OL27 North York Moors Eastern Area

START/FINISH: car park at Adderstone Field, Dalby Forest; grid ref: SE 883897

TRAILS/TRACKS: forestry roads and a few narrow paths, mostly well graded

LANDSCAPE: conifer forest

PUBLIC TOILETS: Visitor Centre, Lower Dalby (not on route)

TOURIST INFORMATION: Dalby Forest Visitor Centre, tel 01751 460295

CYCLE HIRE: Cycle Hire Kiosk next to Visitor Centre, Low Dalby, tel 01751 460400

THE PUB: New Inn, Thornton le Dale, off the route

! There's a short, rough and slightly downhill section of track at the start. The forest drive road needs to be crossed with care twice

Getting to the start

From the A170 at Thornton le Dale head north on a minor road signed the Dalby Forest, then turn off right on the Dalby Forest Drive, where you'll come to the tollbooths. Adderstone Field, the start of the ride, lies about 5 miles (8km) beyond the visitor centre.

Why do this cycle ride?

It's a good introduction to forest tracks, with just a few hilly bits to get your pulse racing, but nothing frightening to put off the inexperienced. There's lots of wildlife for the observant cyclist.

Researched and written by: John Gillham

326

Dalby Forest

NORTH YORKSHIRE

did you know?

If you cycle this route in summer you're likely to hear the distinctive song of the chiffchaff. Seen in open woodland, copses and hedgerows, the adults are a dull brownish-olive above with pale yellow below merging into buff on the flanks, and with dark legs. The sexes are similar and juveniles resemble adults but are a little browner above with warmer yellow underparts. They have a persistent hweet hweet call and chiffchaff song.

*A first winter chiffchaff
(Phylloscopus collybita)*

A track in Dalby Forest

4 The path reaches a **flinted road** at the south east edge of the forest. Turn right along this then left at the next junction. Looking left, you'll see the rougher high pastures of **Ebberston Low Moor** decline to the greener, more fertile fields of the **Vale of Pickering**.

5 Turn right just before reaching **Givendale Head Farm** along a rutted farm track with a grassy island in the middle. Turn right at the next junction (**Post B**) on a downhill section, followed by an uphill one where you're joined by a **farm track** from the left.

6 A long hill follows to a wide junction where you go straight on along a tarred lane. A sign tells you that you're now at the head of **Flaxdale**. Stay with the tarred lane at the next bend and junction. Turn right at the crossroads along a long sandy track (**Post A**), then right again at the next

junction. Note the **linear earthwork** to both left and right – nobody seems to know the exact origins of these.

7 After going straight on at the next junction past a fine stand of **Scots pines**, you get fine views over the farm pastures of High Rigg to **Levisham Moor**. There's another downhill section followed by an uphill one. Take a right fork at **Newclose Rigg**. Where the red route goes straight on, your green route veers right along the main track. There's a downhill left curve beyond which you take the **upper right fork**, which brings the route back to the forest drive opposite Adderstone Field.

New Inn

A Georgian coaching inn in the centre of a picturesque village complete with beck running beside the main street, and village stocks and market cross. The inn retains its old-world charm, with log fires, low beamed ceiling, traditional furniture and hand-pulled ales.

Food
Freshly cooked food is one of the pub's attractions, with many tempting choices on the interesting menu and specials board: medallions of beef fillet, pan-fried chicken supreme, grilled halibut steak, rack of lamb, and salmon fillet with baby cucumber show the range of main courses.

Family facilities
Children are welcome in the dining area if eating and they have their own menu.

about the pub

New Inn
Maltongate, Thornton le Dale
Pickering, North Yorkshire YO18 7LF
Tel: 01751 474226

DIRECTIONS: beside the A170 in the centre of the village

PARKING: 15

OPEN: daily; all day in summer

FOOD: daily

BREWERY/COMPANY: Scottish & Newcastle

REAL ALE: Theakston Black Bull, John Smith's, Greene King Old Speckled Hen

ROOMS: 6 en suite

Alternative refreshment stops
There's a café and kiosk at the Dalby Forest Visitor Centre.

☛ Where to go from here
The Beck Isle Museum at Pickering houses many photos and artefacts that will show you the local customs. The museum follows the historical developments in social and domestic life of the last two centuries (www.beckislemuseum.co.uk). Re-live the golden age of steam with a ride on the North Yorkshire Moors Railway, Britain's most popular heritage railway, through 18 miles (29km) of stunning scenery (www.northyorkshiremoorsrailway.com).

did you know?

Whenever you visit the Wolds you are likely to come across a wide variety of earthworks from large circular barrows to simple ditches. Between Points 4 and 5 on this walk is a typical example, a ridge of earth beside a deep cut. The date and origin of these linear earthworks is not conclusively proved, though it is likely that some of them were built during the Bronze Age between 2000 and 600 BC.

Walking a path above the houses of Thixendale

A walk on the Wolds from Thixendale

A valley close to Thixendale

From the hidden village of Thixendale over chalk hills and through dry valleys.

Going the Wolds Way

Chalk underlies the Yorkshire Wolds. Unlike the harder rocks of the dales and the moors, the Wolds chalk is soft and permeable, so the landscape around here is one of rounded hills and deep dry valleys. Our walk is through rich farming land – indeed, these slopes have been cultivated since Neolithic people set up home here more than 5,000 years ago.

More than half the walk follows the Wolds Way, a 79 mile (127km) National Trail that runs from the bridge over the Humber Estuary to Filey Brigg. Much of the walk follows the Centenary Way, established by North Yorkshire County Council in 1989 to mark 100 years of local government.

Some say that Thixendale is named from the six dry valleys that meet here. The more imaginative reckon to count 16 converging dales. Place-name dictionaries, more prosaically, derive it from a Viking called Sigstein. Whatever its origin, Thixendale is one of the most remote of the Wolds villages, approached by deep, winding dry valleys between steep chalk escarpments. It has a number of old cottages, but much of its character is due to local landowner Sir Tatton Sykes in the later part of the 19th century. As well as building estate cottages, he contributed the church, the school and the former vicarage. Do visit the church – the stained glass by Clayton and Bell, showing the Days of Creation, is great fun, especially the flamingos and the fearsome waterspout.

Sir Tatton Sykes was a great church-builder and philanthropist – and an even greater eccentric. He insisted that his body needed to maintain an even temperature, and was known to stick his bare feet out of the windows of railway carriages to make sure. As he warmed up on his walks he would shed clothing, paying local boys to return it to the house. He even wore two pairs of trousers to preserve decency as he divested himself. Flowers were a great hate; he had the estate gardens ploughed up and told his tenants that the only kind of flowers they could grow were cauliflowers.

the walk

1 Leave the Cross Keys and turn right down Thixendale's village street, passing the church and the Old Post Office. Just beyond the last house on the right, go up a track, following the **Wolds Way/Centenary Way** sign. Cross over a ladder stile in a wire fence on your right and continue walking up the track as it curves right around the hillside.

2 As you approach the top of the hill, watch out on the left for a **Wolds Way sign**, which takes you left along a grassy track. Go over a ladder stile then along the field side to join the track again.

3 At the next **Wolds Way sign** leave the track to go over a stile where you continue with the **wire fence** on your left. At the top of the field go right by the sign. The path descends to reach a stile and descends steeply into a dry valley. Halfway along the descent, go over a stile, partially hidden by bushes to the left. Descend further to another **waymarked stile**, then to a stile by a gate at the bottom.

2h00 · **4 MILES** · **6.4 KM** · **LEVEL 123**

MAP: OS Explorer 300 Howardian Hills & Malton

START/FINISH: Thixendale village street near the church; grid ref: SE 842611

PATHS: clear tracks and field paths, 9 stiles

LANDSCAPE: deep, dry valleys and undulating farm land

PUBLIC TOILETS: none on route

TOURIST INFORMATION: Malton, tel 01653 600048

THE PUB: Cross Keys, Thixendale

⊘ Under 14s not allowed inside pub

Getting to the start

Thixendale lies secluded in a little valley 3 miles (4.8km) north of the A166 York to Bridlington road, 9 miles (14.5km) south of Malton. From the south, leave the A166 at Fridaythorpe and take the left fork at the end of the village, or from the north, take the B1248, then the second left at Wharram le Street. Park in the village street near the Cross Keys.

Researched and written by:
John Gillham, David Winpenny

Visit nearby Castle Howard, one of Britain's finest historic houses set in a dramatic landscape featuring temples, lakes, statues and fountains. Historical character guides are located inside the house. Visitors can join outdoor tours.

A silhouetted Castle Howard reflected in the ornamental pond

4 Follow the blue **public bridleway sign** to the right, winding left up the side valley. Near the top of the valley is a deep **earthwork ditch**; cross over a stile and continue along the edge of the field. Where the footpath divides go right through the patch of **woodland** on to a track by a signpost.

5 Turn right and follow the **Wolds Way sign**. Follow this clear field-edge path for 0.75 mile (1.2km). At the end of the woodland on your right, look out for a signpost. Turn right here, now following the **Centenary Way**, going down the edge of the field and passing a ruined building with a **tall chimney**. Follow the winding footpath past a signpost.

6 At the next signpost turn right off the track, signed **'Centenary Way'**. Walk down the field side on a grassy track. At the field end leave the track and go through a **waymarked gate**. The path goes left and passes along the hillside to descend to a stile beside a gate.

7 Follow the **yellow waymark** straight ahead across the field (pathless on ground), then pass to the left of a row of trees. A path develops and descends to the right of the village **cricket field** to reach a lane by some houses. This leads back to the **Cross Keys** and out onto the village street.

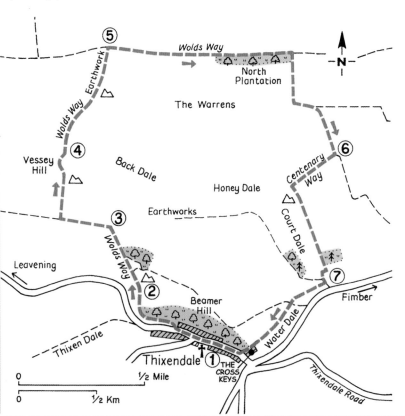

Cross Keys

Although this former 18th-century farmhouse has an unassuming appearance – plain whitewashed exterior with green and blue paintwork – it is one of the hidden gems in the Wolds. Simple, unspoilt and a very traditional village local, popular with walkers and cyclists, you'll find a single, welcoming and very cosy L-shaped bar with fitted wall benches, a relaxing atmosphere, well-kept beer and good value home-cooked food. Blissfully free of intrusive piped music and gaming machines, but there is a juke box that only plays old songs. Bedrooms are housed within a converted stable and provide a peaceful base from which to explore the surrounding rolling countryside.

Food
The short menu offers home-made soups, ploughman's lunches, roast beef sandwiches, steak buns, home-made pasties, sausage, egg and chips, and local game dishes in season. Good nursery puddings like treacle tart, sticky toffee pudding and toffee apple crumble.

Family facilities
Facilities are limited as children under 14 years are not allowed inside the pub. However, there is a super, sun-trap rear garden for fine weather eating and drinking.

Alternative refreshment stops
Behind Thixendale Store and Post Office is a café (closed Fridays), offering breakfast, lunch, teas and snacks.

☞ Where to go from here
Visit Sir Tatton Syke's home, Sledmere House. An elegant Georgian mansion, largely designed by Sir Christopher Sykes in 1751, it has superb plasterwork, an elegant staircase and attractive grounds. At the Eden Camp Modern History Theme Museum (www.edencamp.co.uk) near Malton, relive the civilian way of life during World War II through the sights, sounds and smells of those dangerous years. Castle Howard of Brideshead Revisited fame is just a short drive away (www.castlehoward.co.uk).

about the pub

Cross Keys
Thixendale, Malton
North Yorkshire YO17 9TG
Tel: 01377 288272

DIRECTIONS:	see Getting to the start
PARKING:	village street
OPEN:	daily
FOOD:	daily
BREWERY/COMPANY:	free house
REAL ALE:	Tetley, Jennings Bitter, guest beer
DOGS:	in garden only
ROOMS:	3 en suite

Ravenscar's Coastal Centre

while you're there

Visit the Captain Cook Memorial Museum by the harbour in Whitby. James Cook came here in 1746 when he was apprenticed to Captain John Walker. The museum's exhibits chart Cook's years in Whitby and his later achievements.

The ruins of Whitby Abbey

From Ravenscar to Robin Hood's Bay

A collection of red-roofed stone cottages stand on the cliffs above Robin Hood's Bay

Fabulous views and a unique industrial heritage.

Alum Quarries

Just after the start of the railway track proper, you pass through an area of partly overgrown spoil heaps with quarried faces above. For around two centuries, up to the Victorian era, this was an internationally important source of alum (potassium aluminium sulphate). This chemical, known since at least Roman times, had many uses, notably in the fixing of dyes. The shale rock in the cliffs was rich in aluminium sulphate and it is reckoned that over a million tons of rock were removed. The manufacturing process was centred on the alum works. The best source of potassium was seaweed; however, to complete the reaction, ammonia was required, and the best source of this was human urine! Much of this was shipped all the way from London and off-loaded on the rocky shores directly below – a trade with some unique hazards. It is said that proud sea-captains were reluctant to admit that they carried this undignified cargo, but if they were found out the cry would go up, 'You're taking the piss!' It's as good an explanation as any for the origins of the phrase. You can find out more about the alum industry at the Coastal Centre in Ravenscar.

the ride

1 Descend the road until it bends sharply right. Turn left, past the **National Trust Coastal Centre**, on to an obvious descending concrete track. A rougher section needs care, but lasts less than 100yds (91m). Swing left through a gate on to the old **railway trackbed** and a much easier surface.

2 The track now runs below the scarred face of the **alum workings**, with some ups and downs that clearly don't match the original rail contours exactly. After this, take care crossing a **steep concrete track** that runs down to a farm.

3 Pass under an **arched bridge**. Note more quarried cliffs up on the left, while looking down to the right – if the tide is not too high – there are extensive rocky platforms in the bay, with conspicuous parallel strata. There's a short cutting and the sea views are blocked by tall gorse and broom, then it becomes more open again as the track swings gradually inland. A tall embankment

2h00 | **11.25 MILES** | **18.1 KM** | **LEVEL 123**

328

CYCLE

MAP: OS Explorer OL27 North York Moors – Eastern

START/FINISH: roadside parking on way into Ravenscar; grid ref: NZ 980015

TRAILS/TRACKS: almost entirely on well-surfaced old railway track; short street sections at Ravenscar and Robin Hood's Bay

LANDSCAPE: steep cliffs and coastal slopes, woodland and farmland, sea views

PUBLIC TOILETS: at start

TOURIST INFORMATION: Whitby, tel 01947 602674

CYCLE HIRE: Trailways, Hawsker (about 3 miles from Robin Hood's Bay, on the railway route), tel 01947 820207

THE PUB: The Laurel Inn, Robin Hood's Bay

❶ Busy roads and car park in Robin Hood's Bay village (possible to turn round before this)

How to get to the start

Turn off the A171 about midway between Whitby and Scarborough – signed for Ravenscar. Turn left at a T-junction, then right near an old windmill. The road descends into Ravenscar and there is extensive roadside parking as the descent gets steeper.

Why do this cycle ride?

The former railway line between Whitby and Scarborough can now be followed, in its entirety, on two wheels. The full distance is 20 miles (32.2km) one way, so this ride picks out probably the finest section, looping around Robin Hood's Bay. It is a little confusing that the name of the bay and the much-photographed village are exactly the same, but the ride gives great views of the former and a chance to visit the latter.

Researched and written by: Jon Sparks

NORTH EAST ENGLAND

328

CYCLE

Robin Hood's Bay

NORTH YORKSHIRE

392

Despite strong claims that Robin Hood was a Yorkshireman, no one has yet put forward a convincing reason why this remote fishing village should bear his name – as it has since at least the start of the 16th century. Legend is quick to step in; two of the stories say that either Robin was offered a pardon by the Abbot of Whitby if he rid the east coast of pirates, or that, fleeing the authorities, he escaped arrest here disguised as a local sailor.

The curve of Robin Hood's Bay

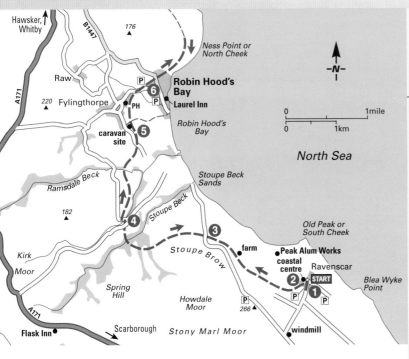

The Laurel Inn

The picturesque fishing village of Robin Hood's Bay is the setting for this delightful little pub. Tucked away in a row of fishermen's cottages at the bottom of the village overlooking the sea, the pub retains lots of character features, including beams and an open fire. The traditional bar is decorated with old photographs of the area, Victorian prints and brasses and an international collection of lager bottles. This coastal village was once the haunt of smugglers who used a network of underground tunnels and secret passages to bring the booty ashore.

Food
Bar food is limited to a simple and straightforward menu offering wholesome sandwiches and soups.

Family facilities
Due to its size there are few facilities for family groups although children are very welcome in the snug bar until 9pm.

Alternative refreshment stops
Various pubs and cafés in Robin Hood's Bay including The Victoria Hotel at the top of the village.

☛ Where to go from here
Locally, learn more about alum mining at the Peak Alum Works in Ravenscar and this fascinating coastline at the Ravenscar Coastal Centre. Children will enjoy visiting the Old Coastguard Station in Robin Hood's Bay. Head north to Whitby to see the moody and magnificent ruins of Whitby Abbey (www.english-heritage.org.uk) and visit the Captain Cook Memorial Museum

about the pub

The Laurel Inn
New Road, Robin Hood's Bay
North Yorkshire YO22 4SE
Tel: 01947 880400

DIRECTIONS: bottom of the village
PARKING: use village car park
OPEN: daily; all day (2pm–11pm Monday to Friday November to February)
FOOD: daily
BREWERY/COMPANY: free house
REAL ALE: Adnams Broadside, Tetley, Jennings Cumberland

(www.cookmuseumwhitby.co.uk). High on the list for children may be the Sea Life and Marine Sanctuary in Scarborough, home to seahorses, otters, sharks, a seal hospital and convalescing sea turtles.

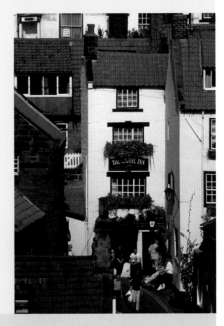

crosses a **steep wooded valley**. Go under a bridge and make a sharp left turn on to a lane.

4 Go up 20yds (18m) and then sharp right to the continuation of the track. Keep right at a fork and the track resumes its steady gentle descent, then starts to turn uphill for the first time. As you come into the open after a **tunnel of trees**, the direct way ahead is again blocked (unless you're Evel Knievel!). Slant down left, cross a lane, and then climb back up on to the continuing trackbed.

5 Pass a **cricket ground**, the back of a caravan site, then a farm. Cross the rough farm track and keep straight on, through a gate where the surface changes to tarmac, on the outskirts of Robin Hood's Bay. Go through another gate and drop down to a road. Turn right down this for 100yds (91m) then left on a lane signposted to **Station Workshops**. At the top of the rise is the old

station building and just beyond it a large car park. (It is, of course, possible to descend the road all the way into the village of Robin Hood's Bay, but it's a very steep climb back. An alternative is to lock the bikes at the car park and go down on foot.)

6 Continue alongside the car park, drop down to a road, turn left and almost instantly right (very nearly straight across) on to **Mount Pleasant**. Follow this to its end then bear left up a short gravelled ride to regain the railway path. Continue for about 0.5 mile (800m). There are good views back now over Robin Hood's Bay to the cliffs near Ravenscar. Look for a National Trust sign for **Ness Bay**. There is open access on foot so you could leave the bikes and walk down to the headland, a great picnic spot. This makes as good a turn-round point as any, though the track continues into Hawsker and on to Whitby.

Walking on a path near Robin Hood's Bay

A Cleveland Way sign to Ravenscar

while you're there

Explore further along the coast to Ravenscar, a headland where the Romans built a signal station. In the middle of the 19th century a new resort, a rival to Scarborough, was begun here, then abandoned. The streets are still there, but only one row of houses was constructed.

Walking on a path near Robin Hood's Bay

Cleveland Way and Robin Hood's Bay

Through fields from this obscurely named village and back along part of the Cleveland Way.

Robin Hood's Bay

Walking the coastal path north of Robin Hood's Bay, you will notice how the sea is encroaching on the land. The route of the Cleveland Way has frequently to be redefined as sections slip into the sea. Around Robin Hood's Bay, the loss is said to be around 6 inches (15cm) every 2 years.

For countless visitors, Robin Hood's Bay is perhaps the most picturesque of the Yorkshire coast's fishing villages – a tumble of pantiled cottages that stagger down the narrow gully cut by the King's Beck. Narrow courtyards give access to tiny cottages, whose front doors look over their neighbours' roofs. Vertiginous stone steps link the different levels. Down at the shore, boats are still drawn up on the Landing, though they are more likely to be pleasure craft than working vessels.

There was a settlement where the King's Beck reaches the coast at least as far back as the 6th century. No one has yet put forward a convincing reason why this remote fishing village should bear Robin Hood's name – as it has since at least the start of the 16th century. Stories say that either Robin was offered a pardon by the Abbot of Whitby if he rid the east coast of pirates, or that, fleeing the authorities, he escaped arrest here disguised as a sailor.

the walk

1 From the lower car park opposite the **Victoria Hotel**, turn left up the hill and, where the road bends round to the left, take a signed footpath to the right over a stile. Walk up the fields over three stiles to a metalled lane.

2 Turn right. Go left through a **signed metal gate**. At the end of the field the path bends right to a gate in the hedge on your left. Continue down the next field with a stone wall on your left. Again, go right at the end of the field and over a stile into a green lane.

3 Cross to another waymarked stile and continue along the field edge with a wall

on your right. At the field end go over a stile on your right, then make for a **waymarked gate** diagonally left.

4 Walk towards the **Bottom House Farm**, through a gate and take the waymarked track round the right of the buildings to another gate, then to a waymarked opening beside a metal gate. Continue with a stone wall on your right, through another gate and on to a track that eventually bends left to a **waymarked stile**.

5 Continue to another stile, which leads to a **derelict footbridge** over a narrow beck. At a T-junction by a wooden electricity pylon, veer right and take a path to the right of the bank. After 50yds (46m), look for a signpost for **Hawsker** in woodland. Walk to the signpost then follow it right. As the hedge to your right curves left, go through a gap on the right and over a **signed stile**, walking straight ahead through the field to an opening by the main road.

6 Go right and right again, following the footpath sign, up the metalled lane towards two holiday parks. Pass **Seaview Caravan Park**, cross the former railway track and continue along the metalled lane, which bends right, goes downhill,

Large stones are strewn across the beach around Robin Hood's Bay

| 2h30 | 5.5 MILES | 8.8 KM | LEVEL 1 2 3 |

MAP: OS Explorer OL27 North York Moors – Eastern

START/FINISH: Car park at top of hill by the old railway station, Robin Hood's Bay; grid ref: NZ 950055

PATHS: field and coastal paths, a little road walking, 14 stiles

LANDSCAPE: farmland and fine coastline

PUBLIC TOILETS: at car park

TOURIST INFORMATION: Whitby, tel 01947 602674

THE PUB: The Victoria Hotel, Robin Hood's Bay

⚠ Take care on the road at the beginning of the walk. Keep well away from the friable cliff edges

Getting to the start

The old smugglers' village at Robin Hood's Bay huddles in a coastal hollow at the end of the B1447. It can be accessed from High Hawsker on the A171 Whitby to Scarborough road. There are two main car parks, both off to the right of the B road in the upper part of the village. The lower streets are access only.

Researched and written by:
John Gillham, David Winpenny

Far left: Narrow streets and alleys in Robin Hood's Bay are fronted by a jumble of houses

did you know?

In 1800 everyone who lived in the Bay was, supposedly, involved with smuggling. The geography of the village gave it several advantages. The approach by sea was, usually, the easiest way to the village; landward, it was defended by bleak moorland and a steep approach. The villagers linked their cellars, so that (it is said) contraband could be landed on shore and passed from house to house before being spirited away.

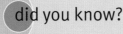

The panoramic view across Robin Hood's Bay from the grounds of Raven Hall hotel

329

WALK

crosses a stream and ascends to the **Northcliffe holiday park**.

7 Follow the footpath sign right, then go left and follow the metalled track down through the **caravans**, eventually leaving the track to go left to a waymarked path. Follow the path towards the **coastline**, to reach a signpost.

8 Turn right along the **Cleveland Way** for 2.5 miles (4km) alongside eroded shaly cliffs. At **Rocket Post Field** there's a minor waymarked **diversion** across fields to the right, caused by the cliff path collapsing into the sea. On the approach to Robin Hood's Bay go left through a gate and past

what to look for

At low tide, the bay reveals concentric arcs of rocks, the remains of a large rock dome that has, over the millennia, been eroded by the action of the sea. The ridges are bands of hard limestone and ironstone that have eroded less quickly than the softer lias between them. Where the lias is exposed fossil hunters search for shells (among them the characteristic whirls of the ammonites) and larger sea creatures.

houses to reach the main road. Turn left for the lower car park and hotel.

The Victoria Hotel

Sited at the top of the village with fine views over the bay, this Victorian 'Gothic-style' building delivers more than first impressions promise, with fine food, hand-pulled Camerons beers and helpful courteous service. There is a family 'no smoking' room, simply but attractively furnished with bright warm colours – also an airy dining room with wood-panelled floor and huge panoramic windows overlooking the bay. Add ten pine-furnished en suite bedrooms, most with sea views, and you have a comfortable coastal retreat.

Food

Traditional food ranges from cold platters (cheese ploughman's with salad and pickles) and burgers to freshly battered Whitby haddock and chips, sausages and mash, steak pie, garlic chicken, sirloin steak with Stilton and white sauce, and home-made curries.

Family facilities

Families are made very welcome at this friendly inn. There's a family area downstairs and children have a good menu to choose from. Bedrooms include en suite family rooms.

Alternative refreshment stops

Stoke up in Robin Hood's Bay before the walk, as there is nowhere else on the route. In the village there are several pubs and cafés, including the Laurel Inn on New Road.

☞ Where to go from here

Travel south along the coast to Ravenscar, a headland where the Romans built a signal

station. Alum shale, used in fixing, was mined here in the 17th and 18th centuries; you can see the scars of the industry and the Peak Alum Works explains more about the activity. Head north to Whitby and visit the town's fascinating museum (www.whitby-museum.org.uk) or enjoy a trip around Whitby harbour on board an authentic replica of Captain Cook's HMS *Endeavour*.

about the pub

The Victoria Hotel
Robin Hood's Bay, Whitby
North Yorkshire YO22 4RL
Tel: 01947 880205

DIRECTIONS: see Getting to the Start; pub opposite the car park

PARKING: use village car park

OPEN: daily; all day July and August

FOOD: daily

BREWERY/COMPANY: free house

REAL ALE: Camerons Bitter & Strongarm, guest beer

DOGS: in garden only

ROOMS: 10 en suite

330 HUGGATE
EAST RIDING

6.5 MILES (10.4KM) 3hrs

PATHS: Field path, farm tracks, 1 stile

SUGGESTED MAP: aqua3 OS Explorer 294 Market Weighton & Yorkshire Wolds Central

GRID REFERENCE: SE 882551

PARKING: On street around village green

THE PUB: Wolds Inn

❶ From green, walk past play area and duck pond. Continue past cottages to junction. Turn **R**, down lane. Past last house, fork **L** ('**Wolds Way**'). Follow access road for 0.5 mile (800m) until it bends **R** into farmyard. Take path **L** between fences. Emerge on road on other side of farm. Continue up to fingerpost on horizon.
❷ Turn **R** along field-edge path ('**Chalkland Way**'). At end of field, go through gate and turn **L** along top of **Horse Dale**. Track descends to valley floor and gate. Go through gate and up side valley. Aim for **R-H** fence corner and go through **L-H** gate. Continue up enclosed track ignoring gate to R. After 300yds (274m) track continues along edge of open field. Eventually reach crossing track to **Wold House Farm**.
❸ Turn **R** along track into farmyard. Bear **L** across yard, through gate diagonally opposite. Bear **R**; continue on track across 3 fields. At end of 3rd field, turn **L** (don't follow right of way); turn **R** down side of field to gate. Bear **L** with rising track above **Holm Dale**; then dip to collection of fingerposts at gate.
❹ Go through gate. Cross to enclosed track ('**Wolds Way**'). Follow this to Huggate Lane into **Fridaythorpe**. Turn **R** along main road then **L** by **Manor House Inn** to the green and **St Mary's Church**.
❺ Return to Huggate Lane; follow lane back to gate by collection of fingerposts. Go through gate and follow **Wolds Way** down dale. Keep to **L** of fence as **Horse Dale** joins from **R**.
❻ Go through gate, ignore Wolds Way going off to R, but turn **L** over stile and continue down **Harper Dale**. Pass game breeding area on L then bear **R** with rising path to meet track on hill. Bear **R** to cattle grid. Turn **L** and follow track round to **R**. Turn **L** at end and follow track to **Northfield House**.
❼ Walk through yards; follow access road back towards **Huggate**. Continue up lane; turn **L** across green to return to car park.

331 CARL WARK
SOUTH YORKSHIRE

5.5 MILES (8.8KM) 3hrs

PATHS: Generally good paths

SUGGESTED MAP: aqua3 OS Explorer OL1 Dark Peak

GRID REFERENCE: SK 252801

PARKING: Surprise View car park on A6187 beyond Hathersage

THE PUB: Millstone Inn (road to Hathersage)

❶ From car park at Surprise View go through kissing gate and uphill on well-worn path. At large group of stones path veers **L** and continues uphill towards **Over Owler Tor**. Just before this, go **L** on smaller track, head downhill towards fence. Turn **R** at fence.
❷ Continue following track until it meets with dry-stone wall that has been running parallel with track. Follow path **R** towards sheepfold. At end of sheepfold, path veers slightly **R** across moorland. Rocky outcrop of **Higger Tor** is on L and **Carl Wark** in front. The fort is probably of Iron- or Bronze-Age construction and was re-fortified at the end of the Roman occupation.
❸ When path intersects another, turn **R**. Continue past Carl Wark, keeping it to R. Go downhill towards far **R** corner of wood. Cross stone bridge then wooden bridge, head uphill on well-worn path to join old green road; turn **L**.
❹ Continue along road with **Burbage Rocks** above you and to R. At **Upper Burbage Bridge** cross 2 streams via large stones, head uphill and follow upper of 2 paths to **L** and uphill. Continue across moorland then ascend **Higger Tor** on stone stepped path. Cross tor then descend other side near southeast corner.
❺ Follow track across moor towards **Carl Wark**. Ascend and turn **L** to reach summit then return to top of path and, keeping stone ramparts on L, continue past cairn and descend via path to southwest.
❻ From here, path heads across boggy section of moor, curves round small, rocky hill then heads downhill towards **A6187**. Cross on to this via stile, cross road and turn **R** on to pavement. Follow this to next stile on **L**, cross it and continue on path that runs parallel to road.
❼ When track nears car park go through kissing gate, cross road then continue on grass track back into car park

332 FAIRBURN INGS
WEST YORKSHIRE

5 MILES (8KM) 2hrs 30min

PATHS: Good paths and tracks (some newly created from spoil heaps), 7 stiles

SUGGESTED MAP: aqua3 OS Explorer 289 Leeds

GRID REFERENCE: SE 472278

PARKING: Free parking in Cut Road, Fairburn. From A1, drive into village, turn L 100yds (91m) past Three Horseshoes pub

THE PUB: Chequers Inn

❶ Walk down Cut Road as it narrows to track. Soon you have main lake to R, and smaller stretch of water to L. When track forks, keep **R** (unless you want to visit 1st of bird hides, in which case detour to L). Path finishes at end of lake, on approaching **River Aire**.
❷ Go **R** here to join path along top of ridge (old spoil heap), with river to L and lake R. Look out for couple of other bird hides, before you lose sight of lake. Path crosses broader expanse of spoil heap, through scrubland, following river in broad arc to **R**, before descending to stile above another small mere. Bear **R** on broad track and drop down into car park of **Fairburn Ings visitor centre**.
❸ Meet road. Go **R** for 100yds (91m), then go L ('Ledston and Kippax') for just 100yds (91m), and pick up path on **R** that hugs **R-H** fringe of wood. Beyond wood, take path between fields; it broadens to track as you approach **Ledsham**. At new housing estate, turn **R**, along Manor Garth.
❹ You arrive in village by **ancient church**. Walk **R**, along road (or, for refreshments, go **L** to **Chequers Inn**). Beyond village, where road bears L, take gate on **R**, leading to good track uphill. Where main track goes R, into fields, continue along track ahead, into woodland. Leave wood by stile, crossing pasture on grassy track. Cross 2 stiles taking you across narrow spur of woodland.
❺ Head slightly **L**, uphill, across next field, to follow fence and hedgerow. Continue – soon on better track – across stile. Beyond next stile track bears L, towards farm buildings: but keep straight on, with fence on R, along field path. Go through metal gate then join access track downhill. When you meet road, go **L** and back into **Fairburn**.

333 WETHERBY
WEST YORKSHIRE

3.5 MILES (5.7KM) 2hrs

PATHS: Field paths and good tracks, a little road walking, 1 stile

SUGGESTED MAP: aqua3 OS Outdoor Leisure 289 Leeds

GRID REFERENCE: SE 405479

PARKING: Free car parking in Wilderness car park, close to river, just over bridge as you drive into Wetherby from south

THE PUB: The Angel

❶ Walk to far end of car park, to follow path with River Wharfe on your R and cliffs to your L. You pass in quick succession beneath shallow arches of 2 modern bridges, carrying **A58** and A1 roads across **River Wharfe**. Go through kissing gate to continue on riverside path, soon with open fields on L. Take another kissing gate to arrive at Wetherby's **water treatment works**.
❷ Go **L** here, up track around perimeter fence. After 150yds (138m) you meet metalled track at works' main entrance; go **L** here. At top of incline, where track bears slightly to **R**, you have choice of routes. Your path is sharp **R**, along grassy track between fields. You soon approach wooded slope that overlooks River Wharfe. Take stile, and follow line of trees to farm, **Flint Mill Grange**. It was here where flints were ground for use in the pottery industry of Leeds. Enter farmyard and take farm access road to **L**.
❸ Meet **Walton Road** and walk **L** for 75yds (68m), then go **R**, along metalled drive (this is signed as a bridleway and the entrance to **Wetherby Racecourse**). After gate you have a choice of routes. Bear **L** here, downhill, to join the trackbed of the old Church **Fenton–to–Harrogate** railway line, which carried its last train in 1964.
❹ Go **L**, to enjoy level walking along railway trackbed, until you approach A1 road, raised up on embankment as it skirts around Wetherby. Take underpass beneath road, and bear **R** along Freemans Way, until you meet Hallfield Lane.
❺ Walk **L**, along Hallfield Lane, which bears **R** around **playing fields** of Wetherby **High School** and back into centre of Wetherby and start.

334 FULNECK
WEST YORKSHIRE

4 MILES (6.4KM) 2hrs

PATHS: Ancient causeways, hollow ways and field paths, 12 stiles

SUGGESTED MAP: aqua3 OS Explorer 288 Bradford & Huddersfield

GRID REFERENCE: SE 222306

PARKING: Lay-by in Tong village, near church, or on edge of village

THE PUB: Greyhound Inn

❶ From **Tong** village walk up **Keeper Lane** which, beyond gate, becomes sandy track. Walk steadily downhill, following line of old causey stones, into woodland. Cross **Pudsey Beck** on footbridge.
❷ After bridge you have choice of tracks. As you approach waymarker post, continue ahead between stone posts ('**Leeds Country Way**'). Follow beck with **golf course** on **R**. Beyond stile follow field path to another stile, footbridge and meeting of paths. Don't cross bridge, but turn sharp **R** instead, up farm track. Meet road by **Bankhouse Inn**.
❸ Follow road to **R** to see Georgian buildings that make up **Fulneck Moravian settlement**, on ridge with good valley views. 50yds (46m) beyond Fulneck Restaurant go **R**, down lane that soon bends to **R**. At bottom of large brick building look out for steps and footpath downhill. Follow delightful sunken path with hedgerows – and golf fairways – to either side. Come out on to **golf course**, keeping half **L** across fairway, to rejoin path accompanying **Pudsey Beck**.
❹ After 3 stiles reach ruined **mill**; bear **R** to continue on beckside path. You have easy walking, through fields and scrubland, punctuated by stiles. Leave beck via walled path out on to road.
❺ Go **R** here, passing another mill, to T-junction. Cross over road and take waymarked footpath between gateposts into Sykes Wood. Go **R** through gate ('Leeds Countryside Way'). Follow path downhill, soon with **Tong Beck**. After walking about 0.5 mile (800m) through woodland, take footbridge over beck and walk across field, bearing **L** to stile. Follow path along field edge, then through woodland. Keep **L**, when track forks, to stile. Keep following track – ignoring bridges and side-paths – until you reach stile next to gate and broader track.
❻ Go **R**, uphill, on good track. When you meet road go **L** to arrive back in **Tong** village.

335 HOLMFIRTH
WEST YORKSHIRE

4.5 MILES (7.2KM) 2hrs

PATHS: Good paths and tracks, 8 stiles

SUGGESTED MAP: aqua3 OS Explorer 288 Bradford & Huddersfield

GRID REFERENCE: SE 143084

PARKING: Park in Crown Bottom car park (pay-and-display) on Huddersfield Road

THE PUB: Rose & Crown

❶ From car park, walk to **R** along **Huddersfield Road** for 100yds (91m) then turn **L**, up **Wood Lane**. Road soon narrows to steep track. Keep **L** of house, through gate, to continue on walled path. At top of hill, by bench, follow track to **R** and into valley. Shortly after nearing woodland, there's several tracks: keep **L** on walled path, uphill. Join farm track and, 100yds (91m) before cottage, look for wall stile on **L**. Follow field path to emerge, between houses, in **Upperthong**. Turn **R** into village, past pub to T-junction.
❷ Bear **L** along road, which wheels round to **R**. Walk downhill. After 150yds (138m), take cinder track on **R**. Descend past **Newlands Farm** to road. Cross and take lane ahead, down into valley and up other side. When road forks at top go **R** uphill. Immediately after 1st house, go **L** on sandy track. Follow track to **Lower Hogley Farm**; keep **R**, past houses, to gate and on to field path (wall to L). Cross stile and next field (wall to R). Past next wall stile, veer half **L** across next field (aim for mast). After another field, descend to road.
❸ Go **R** for 50yds (46m) to bear **L** around **schoolhouse**. Follow walled path downhill, through gate. As path opens out into grassy area, bear **L** on track into valley. Follow high wall on **R**, over stile, on to enclosed path. On approaching houses, take stile and join metalled track at fork. Bear **R**, then immediately **L**, on path between houses. Follow field path through gate, pass houses and mill to meet **A6024**.
❹ Cross road; by cottages take **Old Road** to **L**. Keep ahead at junction down **Water Street**. Beyond **mill**, cross **River Holme** on footbridge; follow riverside path. Soon path veers **R** through pasture; when path forks, keep **R**, uphill, to enter woodland. Continue in same direction, uphill, emerging from wood on to field path. After 2 stiles join track by house. Pass more cottages to meet road.
❺ Go **L** on road to make long descent to **Holmfirth**.

336 OXENHOPE
WEST YORKSHIRE

6 MILES (9.7KM) 3hrs

PATHS: Good paths and tracks, 6 stiles

SUGGESTED MAP: aqua3 OS Outdoor Leisure 21 South Pennines

GRID REFERENCE: SE 033354

PARKING: Street parking in Oxenhope, near Keighley and Worth Valley Railway station

THE PUB: Dog and Gun

❶ From **station** entrance take minor road to **L**, to **A6033**. Cross and take **Dark Lane** ahead, sunken lane that ascends steeply. Follow track to road. Go **R**, downhill, to join Denholme Road (**B6141**). Walk **L** to reach **Dog and Gun** pub then **R** on to Sawood Lane.

❷ At **Coblin Farm**, route becomes rough track. Go through gate to join metalled road to **R**, uphill (**'Brontë Way'**). After 100yds (91m), when road accesses **Thornton Moor Reservoir**, keep ahead on unmade track. Go through gate into rough pasture, ignoring **Brontë Way** sign to R.

❸ At fork, just 50yds (46m) further on, keep **R** as track goes downhill towards **transmission mast** on mid-horizon. Pass clump of trees, and cross watercourse before descending to minor road.

❹ Go **R** here to pass cattle grid and **mast**. 150yds (138m) beyond **mast**, as road begins steep descent, take wall stile on **L**. Go through another wall stile, to walk **L**, uphill, on broad, walled track to **Waggon and Horses** pub.

❺ Cross road. Take track between gateposts, which bears **R**, steeply downhill. Where it bears sharp **R** again, after 300yds (274m), take stile to **L**, by gate. Follow wall downhill to take 3 stiles; at bottom meet walled path. Go **L** here; cross stream, and continue uphill to arrive at entrance to **Lower Fold Farm**.

❻ Follow farm track to **R**; turn **R** again, 20yds (18m) further on, at end of cottage, to join metalled track. Track soon bears **R** above **Leeshaw Reservoir** and makes gradual descent. Pass mill to meet road.

❼ Cross road and take track ahead ('Marsh'). Keep **R** of 1st house, on narrow walled path, then paved path. Pass through courtyard of house as path goes **L**, then **R** and through kissing gate. Follow path between wall and fence to meet walled lane. Go **R** here, passing houses, then on field path to meet road. Go **R** here and back down into **Oxenhope**.

337 MIDDLEHAM
NORTH YORKSHIRE

7 MILES (11.3KM) 2hrs 30min

PATHS: Field paths and tracks, with some road walking, 18 stiles

SUGGESTED MAP: aqua3 OS Outdoor Leisure 30 Yorkshire Dales – Northern & Central

GRID REFERENCE: SE 127877

PARKING: In square in centre of Middleham

THE PUB: Black Swan Hotel

❶ From cross in Square, walk uphill past Black Swan Hotel. Just beyond, turn **L** up passage beside tea rooms. Continue over road and **L** of **castle** to gate.

❷ Go half **L** across field, following sign towards stepping stones. Cross next 3 fields, over waymarked stiles. After 3rd field, turn along side of field, ignoring track to R. Turn **R** at waymarked crossing wall down to bank of **River Cover** by stepping stones.

❸ Turn **R** (don't cross stepping stones); follow riverside path, going through gate and up steps. After returning to river bank, go **R** where path forks. Cross 2 more stiles, turning immediately **R** after 2nd stile. Follow waymark uphill to marker post.

❹ Turn **L**; follow line of wood. At end of field go **L** through waymarked stile, through trees to 2nd stile, then straight down field back to river bank. Cross waymarked stile and onward to bridge.

❺ Go through gate over bridge. Follow track as it winds **R** and uphill through 2 gates on to road, opposite **Braithwaite Hall**. Turn **R** and follow road for 1 mile (1.6km) to **Coverham Bridge**. Turn **R** over bridge, then **R** again.

❻ Before gates, turn **L** through gate, walk beside waterfall nto churchyard. Leave by lychgate; turn **L** along road. After 0.25 mile (400m) go through gate on **R**, opposite disused factory, bearing slightly **L.** Cross 3 stiles. Go through gate, pass between buildings, cross 3 stiles through woodland.

❼ Cross field to gateway **R** of wood. After passing house, bend **L** to gate on to track. Turn **R**; go through gate; turn **R** again. Don't follow track, but go half **L** to meet bridleway across moor. Follow it for 1.5 miles (2.4km) to road.

❽ Turn **L**. Just before sign (**'Middleham'**) take signposted path on **R**. Turn **L** over stile. Follow path parallel to road. Go through 2 more stiles, then take another towards **Middleham Castle** (favourite home of King Richard III), passing through gate on to lane. Turn **L**. Return to square.

338 GREENHOWE
NORTH YORKSHIRE

6 MILES (9.7KM) 2hrs 45min

PATHS: Field and moorland paths and tracks, 5 stiles

SUGGESTED MAP: aqua3 OS Explorer 298 Nidderdale

GRID REFERENCE: SE 128643

PARKING: Car park at Toft Gate Lime Kiln

THE PUB: Miners Arms

❶ Cross road from car park; go over stile opposite into field. Follow faint path downhill, over gate in wall and to **R** of barn. Cross another stile; descend to track. Turn **L**; walk up hill through 2 gates to road. Turn **L**; walk up to main road. Turn **R**; follow this past burial ground and **Miners Arms** pub. About 100yds (91m) after pub, just past converted chapel, take lane to **R**. At junction go **L**; follow lane to cattle grid and through gate. Curve **R**, round behind farmhouse.

❷ Follow track downhill into valley of **Gill Beck** and then **Brandstone Beck**. Where track swings L, go ahead down valley to reach main track near concrete building. Go **R** of building. Just beyond, proceed down valley to **ford**.

❸ Cross, then follow obvious track up hill. Cross stile beside gate by trees then, 100yds (91m) beyond, take another stile on **R**. Follow track towards farm, going **L** between stone walls. Descend to stile on to track.

❹ Turn **L**, through waymarked gateway. By spoil heap follow track to **R** and downhill. Veer slightly **L**, past iron cogwheel, to cross **Ashfold Side Beck** on concrete causeway to gate.

❺ Follow bridleway sign **R**. Climb hill, to **Nidderdale Way** sign. Turn **R** along track to gate. Wind round valley head, via 2 gateways and 3 cattle grids. Just beyond 3rd, go through gate to **R**. Cross bridge.

❻ Go ahead; bear **L** to gate; follow track uphill and **L** to wall. Turn **R** at end of wall along lane between walls. Continue on track to gate; cross footbridge.

❼ Turn **R** through gate; follow track uphill, passing through another gate. Turn **L** at track, making towards farmhouse, but bear **R** across grass to meet metalled lane. Turn **R**; follow lane over cattle grid.

❽ About 100yds (91m) beyond farm on R, turn **L** up path. After cattle grid go **R**; follow track through gate. At **Coldstonesfold Farm** turn **R**; follow track uphill through gate. Go **L** over stile to retrace outward route.

339 KELD
NORTH YORKSHIRE

6 MILES (9.7KM) 2hrs 30min

PATHS: Field and riverside paths and tracks, 10 stiles

SUGGESTED MAP: aqua3 OS Outdoor Leisure 30 Yorkshire Dales – Northern & Central

GRID REFERENCE: NY 892012

PARKING: Signed car park at west end of village near Park Lodge

THE PUB: Farmers Arms, Muker

❶ Walk back down car park entrance road, and straight ahead down gravel track (**'Muker'**). Around **Muker**, you will see traditional hay meadows. They are an important part of the farmer's regime and help maintain the wide variety of wild flowers that grow in them, which is why signs ask you to keep to single file as you walk through them. Continue along at upper level, ignoring path downhill to **L**. Go through gate, pass sign to **Kisdon Force**, and continue along track to signpost.

❷ Turn **R**, following **Pennine Way** National Trail. Path goes through gated stone stile, then through gap in wall to continue with wall on your L. Go on through gate and over 4 stiles to descend towards **Muker** to reach signpost where **Pennine Way** goes R.

❸ Go straight on down track (**'Muker'**), between stone walls. Go through wooden gate, still following bridleway to **Muker**. Track becomes metalled, as it descends through 2 gates and into walled lane in village to T-junction.

❹ Turn **L** and **L** again by sign to **Gunnerside** and **Keld**. Follow paved path through 5 stiles to reach river. Turn **R** and go over stile to footbridge.

❺ Walk up steps beyond footbridge and turn **L** (**'Keld'**). Follow course of river along clear track, until it curves **R** around **Swinner Gill**, over footbridge by remains of lead workings, and through wooden gate.

❻ Go straight ahead up hill and into woodland. Track eventually winds **L** then **R** round stone barn, then downhill through wooden gate to reach another gate above **Kisdon Force**.

❼ Go **L** by wooden seat, at sign to **Keld**. Follow stream down to footbridge. Go through gate and turn **R**, walk uphill to T-junction, where you turn **R** and proceed to follow path back to car park.

340 THIRSK
NORTH YORKSHIRE

5 MILES (8KM) 2hrs

PATHS: Town paths, field paths and tracks, 6 stiles

SUGGESTED MAP: aqua3 OS Explorer 302 Northallerton & Thirsk

GRID REFERENCE: SE 430813

PARKING: Roadside parking in the main street of Sowerby village

THE PUB: Three Tuns

❶ Walk down street, away from **Thirsk**. Just past Methodist Church on L, go **L** down Blakey Lane. After **bridge** turn **L** through kissing gate. Go through 4 kissing gates to reach footbridge.

❷ Continue along path, with stream on L, to stile. Go through 2 gates to car park, keeping ahead to road. Cross it and take path that curves **L** then **R** by bridge. At paved area turn **R**, to go alongside green to road.

❸ Cross and continue beside houses, going **L** at top of green. Cross metal bridge and continue beside **beck** opposite east end of church. Before reaching road take path to **R**, beside bench, to footbridge on **R**.

❹ Cross bridge, go through 2 gates and curve **L** to follow **beck** to gate by bridge. Go ahead (not over bridge). Go over fields, veering slightly **R** to stile on **R**.

❺ Go over stile; follow stream, crossing another 2 stiles to pass beside houses. Continue **L** over footbridge by mill buildings. Path winds **R** to 2nd footbridge. Follow bridleway sign across field through 2 more gates to reach main road.

❻ Cross road; go through signed gate opposite, to another gate beside wood. At open space, past wood, turn **L** through gap in hedge, opposite waymark to R.

❼ Walk down field with hedge on L. In 2nd field, go **L** over stile. Continue with hedge on R to another stile. Bear **L** to meet path that crosses field and becomes grassy lane between hedges, then track.

❽ At metalled road keep ahead, bearing **L** then **R** past church tower. Turn **R**; walk into town centre. In Market Place head half **L** towards Three Tuns Inn then down signed passageway by drycleaners.

❾ Cross road diagonally **R**; go towards **swimming pool** entrance. Turn **L**; bend round pool building to gate. Proceed to gate and alongside **beck**. At bridge turn **R** across field on grassy track to gate on to lane. Keep ahead to return to **Sowerby**.

341 ARNCLIFFE
NORTH YORKSHIRE

6.5 MILES (10.4KM) 3hrs 30min

PATHS: Mostly clear, some rocky sections; may be muddy, 23 stiles

SUGGESTED MAP: aqua3 OS Explorer OL30 Yorkshire Dales – Northern & Central

GRID REFERENCE: SD 932719

PARKING: In Arncliffe, near church

THE PUB: Falcon Inn

❶ From car park, cross bridge. Turn **R** at its end, over gated stile. Walk parallel with river then ascend steps to cross road via 2 stiles. Bear **R**. Follow footpath steeply uphill over stile and through gate. Bear **R**. Climb through woods up **Park Scar** to stile.

❷ Beyond, follow footpath to **R** to another ladder stile. Pass signpost; go through gap in tumbled wall to another signpost. Continue to ladder stile then cross corner of field to another ladder stile at summit.

❸ Beyond stile, bear half **R**; descend to ladder stile. Follow path beyond towards **Kettlewell**, descending steeply to signpost. Cross track to reach limestone scar. Descend through narrow cleft (**The Slit**) then walk down to stile and, beyond it, footpath sign. Turn **R**; go through gate and on to road.

❹ Turn **R** for 300yds (274m); go **R** through gate (**'Hawkswick'**), bending **R** at another sign. Climb through woodland, through waymarked gate; bear **L** through gap in wall. Continue uphill, winding steeply to gap in wall by stile. Bear **L** to another stile then ascend grassy path, bearing **R** where path forks, to another stile. Beyond, continue downhill bending **R** by **cairn**.

❺ At junction of tracks proceed with wall L. Go through gated stile into **Hawkswick**. Bear **L** at junction, curve **R** between buildings; go through gate to bridge.

❻ Cross and follow road, bending **R**. Just before farm buildings on L, turn **R** towards footbridge. Don't cross but turn **L** at sign (**'Arncliffe'**). Follow river, cross 3 stiles, then footbridge and another ladder stile. Path leaves riverside and reaches gate. Go across field beyond to ladder stile, then another footbridge.

❼ Walk to **R** of barn; go through gate. Bear **L** to squeeze stile in crossing wall. Cross track. Go through 3 stiles, following river then through gate near house. Follow waymarked posts to kissing gate, past churchyard, to start.

342 SWAINBY
NORTH YORKSHIRE

6 MILES (9.7KM) 2hrs 30min

PATHS: Tracks and moorland paths, lots of bracken, 11 stiles

SUGGESTED MAP: aqua3 OS Outdoor Leisure 26 North York Moors – Western

GRID REFERENCE: NZ 477020

PARKING: Roadside parking in Swainby village

THE PUB: Blacksmiths Arms

1 With church on L, walk down village street to R of stream. Continue past sign 'Unsuitable for Coaches' and proceed uphill. As road bends to R, follow bridleway sign to Scugdale, up track ahead.

2 Go through 2 gates, turning **L** after 2nd to join waymarks for Cleveland Way National Trail. Walk through woodland, turning **L**, just after bench, down to stile. Footpath goes downhill across fields to another gate. Cross over stream on footbridge to reach lane, with another footbridge, over **Scugdale Beck**.

3 Follow lane past **Hollin Hill Farm** to T-junction with telephone and post boxes. Cross lane and go through Cleveland Way signed gate. Walk up path beside woodland to gate with stile beside it.

4 Path turns **R** to stile and goes on to paved track in wood. Keep ahead at crossing track to another stile, Continue to follow paved path on to heather moorland. After 1st summit, path descends beyond cairn into dip. After paved path ends, look out for narrow path off to **L**, down through heather.

5 After about 100yds (91m) you reach concrete post where path forks. Take **L** fork; follow path down gully to fence beside wall. Turn **L**, forking **L** again down another gully to signpost by wall and fence. Follow sign **L** and go over spoil heap to reach gate on **R**.

6 Through gate, go down hill via woodland. At bottom cross stile by gate; go down lane. Just past drive, where wood begins, take footpath over 2 stiles.

7 Walk through woodland on to grassy track. Turn **L**, and L again at another track. At T-junction, turn **L** again; follow track downhill to stile. Keep ahead through waymarked gateway.

8 Cross stile beside gate; follow track along hillside. Over stile with steps beyond, turn **L** at bottom; follow field edge. Go over waymarked stile by gate and along field. At gate at end of field, follow metalled lane past **Whorlton church** and **castle** back to **Swainby**

343 AUSTWICK
NORTH YORKSHIRE

5.5 MILES (8.8KM) 2hrs 30min

PATHS: Field and moorland paths, tracks, lanes on return, 10 stiles

SUGGESTED MAP: aqua3 OS Outdoor Leisure 2 Yorkshire Dales – Southern & Central

GRID REFERENCE: SD 767684

PARKING: Roadside parking in Austwick village

THE PUB: The Game Cock Inn

1 From green in centre of **Austwick**, walk northwards out of village ('Horton in Ribblesdale'). Pass Gamecock Inn and, just past cottage, 'Hob's Gate', turn **L** up Town Head Lane. Just after road bends round to R, go **L** over waymarked ladder stile.

2 Walk through field to another stile and on to another stile on to lane. Turn **R**. Just before reaching metalled road turn **L** over ladder stile. Follow line of track. As track veers L, go straight on, following line of stone wall to stone stile by gate.

3 Go through gate; continue along rocky track. Where stone wall on L bends L, by very large boulder across path, go **R** on track to pass R-H edge of **scar**. At signpost, go **L** ('**Norber**').

4 Follow path uphill, to plateau; explore **Norber Erratics**. Return same way, back to signpost. Turn **L** ('Crummack'). Follow track as it winds downhill then up beside wall by scar to stone stile on **R**.

5 Descend to another stile; follow path beneath rocky outcrop, which goes downhill with wall to L to reach ladder stile on to metalled lane. Cross lane; go over another ladder stile opposite.

6 Turn **L** across field. Go over 2 ladder stiles then cross farm track and ridge of rock to stone stile then ladder stile. Cross stile and on to track. Turn **R**. Cross **ford** on clapper bridge.

7 Follow track between walls for 0.5 mile (800m) into **Wharfe**. Turn **L** by bridleway sign in village; follow road round to R and down village approach road to reach metalled road. Turn **R**. After 100yds (91m) turn **L** at bridleway sign to **Wood Lane**, down road to **Wood End Farm**.

8 By farm buildings track goes **R**. Follow it, as it bends **L** and **R** to crossroads of tracks. Go straight ahead, following line of telegraph poles. Track winds to reach metalled lane into village. Turn **R** over bridge to village centre.

344 LOTHERSDALE
NORTH YORKSHIRE

4 MILES (6.4KM) 2hrs

PATHS: Tracks and field paths, some steep sections. 8 stiles

SUGGESTED MAP: aqua3 OS Explorer OL21 South Pennines

GRID REFERENCE: SD 939472

PARKING: Roadside parking on Carleton to Colne road, north of Clogger Lane

THE PUB: Hare and Hounds

1 From car park walk downhill towards mast on hillside. Just before cattle grid turn **L** up signed track. At next signpost turn **R**, off track. Follow wall; bend **L** to go over stile in wall on **R**. Bear **L**, past small plantation, then go diagonally **R**. Go over stile and continue downhill with wall on R, which bends L to signed stile on to metalled drive.

2 Turn **L** along drive. After cattle grid bear **R** along concrete road and over another cattle grid. Emerge on to metalled lane; turn **L**. Follow lane as it bends downwards over small stream then starts to rise again. Turn **R** over cattle grid by house sign '**The Knott**'.

3 Follow concrete road, which bends **L** round building, then **R** on to track. Follow track with wall on L and, at end, descend towards pool in valley. At bottom of field go across stile in crossing wall; over another stile; then across dam at end of small pool and on to road. Turn **L**. Just beyond **Hare and Hounds**, turn **L** at **Pennine Way** sign.

4 Follow track uphill. Leave track to go **R** of large farm building. Follow wire fence on **R** above wooded valley and continue straight ahead at top of valley, now with stone wall on L. Pass broken wall, then take stile in wall on **L**, signed with acorn. Go straight across field to stone stile on to lane.

5 Cross lane and continue up track ahead ('**Pennine Way**'). Where concrete farm track bends L, keep ahead over stone stile on to walled track. Follow wall on L to stile; continue to follow wall on L to where it bends sharply **L**.

6 Follow wall **L**, go over plank bridge; continue to **trig point** on hilltop. Follow either of 2 downhill paths, which converge, and continue past signpost (passed near start). Continue downhill to road; turn to **R** to car parking place.

345 WESTGATE
DURHAM

6.75 MILES (10.9KM) 4hrs

PATHS: Field paths, tracks and country lanes, 5 stiles

SUGGESTED MAP: aqua3 OS Explorer OL31 North Pennines

GRID REFERENCE: NY 909380

PARKING: By river at Westgate

THE PUB: Hare and Hounds

1 From car park walk out to road bridge that crosses over **River Wear**. Don't cross but follow path ahead, which goes across fields alongside river's south bank. This path crosses minor road close to ford and footbridge, then continues by some cottages and across riverside meadows, passing more cottages at Windyside.

2 On reaching main road at **Daddry Shield** turn **R**, then **L**, over crash barrier and down to Wear's south bank again. This new path stays closer to river than before. Turn **L** on meeting country lane and follow it into village of **St John's Chapel**. Turn **R** along its main street and pass through village.

3 At far side of village, turn **R** along signed footpath that tucks under old railway bridge and crosses footbridge over river. Beyond crossing turn **L** through gap stile to follow path close to north bank. Ignore next footbridge, but instead head for farmhouse, which should be rounded on **L**.

4 Follow grassy enclosed path raking diagonally across hillside pasture to reach high country lane above hamlet of **New House**.

5 Turn **R** along lane then, after about 0.75 mile (1.2km), take higher **L-H** fork which traverses southern side of **Carr Brow Moor** with its disused quarries and mine shafts.

6 At its terminus turn **L** up walled **Seeingsike Road** (track). Turn **R** at junction of tracks and descend into Middlehope Cleugh. Conveniently placed stones allow you to cross over river.

7 Turn **R** again to follow **Middlehope Burn's** east bank, past series of lead mines. The path enters **Slit Woods** and comes out by mill and some cottages on outskirts of **Westgate**.

8 The lane leads to main road where you turn **L**, then **R** past **Hare and Hounds** pub, back to car park.

346 BARNARD CASTLE
DURHAM

4.25 MILES (6.8KM) 2hrs 30min

PATHS: Town streets and good paths, 6 stiles

SUGGESTED MAP: aqua3 OS Explorer OL31 North Pennines

GRID REFERENCE: NZ 051163

PARKING: Pay-and-display car park at end of Queen Street between Galgate and Newgate

THE PUB: The Morritt Arms Hotel, Greta Bridge

1 From car park go through passageway signposted for river. Go across Newgate Street and continue through little ginnel, which leads through churchyard of **St Mary's**, founded in the 12th century, then out on to riverside parkland of **Demesnes**.

2 Here turn **L** along stony path, which angles down to river. It passes **Demesnes Mill** and then follows north bank of **Tees**, with river on your R.

3 You pass (quickly if the wind is in the wrong direction) local sewage works. Ignore upper L fork of 2 paths and stay by river to enter pretty woodland, which allows glimpses of remains of **Egglestone Abbey** on far banks. Go through gate on to road and turn **R** over **Abbey Bridge**.

4 Turn **R** at junction on far side of bridge, then go **L** up access track to view the 12th-century **abbey**. Return to road and follow it **L**, to pass **Bow Bridge**. Squeeze stile in hedge on **R** marks start of path along south bank of Tees. On approach to **caravan park** path crosses fields and veers slightly away from river.

5 Turn **R** along surfaced track, down to **caravan park** and take 2nd drive on **L**, which eventually leads to continuation of riverside path.

6 Turn **R** to cross over footbridge back into **Barnard Castle** and then go straight ahead into Thorngate. Turn **L** along Bridgegate. Where road crosses County Bridge go straight ahead, on to follow path that rounds **castle** walls to entrance. The **castle** was built in 1112 for Bernard de Balliol, whose father fought side by side with William the Conqueror at the Battle of Hastings. After visiting castle continue past Methodist church to start of Galgate.

7 Turn **R** along Market Street and continue to Market Cross. Carry on down The Bank then, at top of Thorngate, go **L** to **Demesnes**. Retrace earlier footsteps back to car park.

347 MARSEDN BAY
TYNE & WEAR

5.5 MILES (8.8KM) 2hrs

PATHS: Roads, tracks, field and coastal paths

SUGGESTED MAP: aqua3 OS Explorer 316 Newcastle upon Tyne

GRID REFERENCE: NZ 412635

PARKING: Whitburn Coastal Park car park, signed off A183 (southern end)

THE PUB: Marsden Grotto

1 Leave car park at its southern end, following gravel track toward houses. Path winds and goes past sign for Whitburn Point Nature Reserve. Follow track ahead to go through gap in wall. Turn **R**. Path bends **R**, **L** and **R** again to join road into houses. Keep ahead to join main road.

2 Cross road; turn **L**. Walk until you reach **windmill**. Turn **R** to enter grounds. Go up slope on path then between houses. Bear **L** then **R** to T-junction.

3 Keep ahead on path that goes to **R** of house No 99. When you reach another road turn **L**. Just after 1st bungalow on R, turn **R** along signed track. Follow track towards farm. Go through farmyard over 2 stiles and follow lane beyond, with hedge to your R; where it ends, turn **R** over stile.

4 Follow path along field edge. Cross another stile, gradually ascending. Path bends **L** then **R**, still following field edge. Go over another 2 stiles. Path will bring you to tower of **Cleadon Windmill**.

5 Go to **R** of windmill, following wall on your R. Go **R** through kissing gate, then bear slightly **R** (brick tower to L). Go parallel with wall on your R. Cross track and go through wire mesh fence at R angles to wall. Follow path through scrubland to emerge by yellow post by **golf course**.

6 Cross course, following yellow posts (watch out for golfers). Go over stone stile; turn **R** along signed footpath, following wall on your R. Path eventually descends beside houses to road.

7 Cross and take footpath almost opposite, to **R** of **caravan site**, heading towards sea. Carefully cross busy **A183** then turn **R**, following sea edge. **Marsden Rock** is near by, and **Marsden Grotto** to your L as you cross road. Follow coast as it bends **L** to **Lizard Point**. After visit to **Souter Lighthouse**, continue ahead on path slightly inland from coast, which returns you to car park.

348 ETAL
NORTHUMBERLAND

6 MILES (9.7KM) 2hrs

PATHS: Lanes, tracks and field paths

SUGGESTED MAP: aqua3 OS Explorer 339 Kelso & Coldstream

GRID REFERENCE: NT 925392

PARKING: Free car park by Etal Castle

THE PUB: Black Bull

❶ Walk to main road. Turn **R** towards **Ford**, shortly leaving along lane on **L-H** side to **Leathamhill**. At cottages, go **R** on track beside sawmill ('Heatherslaw and Hay Farm'), and keep on across fields beyond.
❷ At bottom, by **Shipton Dean**, go through gate on **R** into strip of wood. Beyond, head down edge of successive fields to main road opposite **Heatherslaw Station**. Cross to lane opposite, following it over bridge and around past **Heatherslaw Mill**.
❸ Keep going to **Heatherslaw** farm but, after R-H bend, leave through 5-bar gate on **L** ('Ford Bridge'). Pass shed and go through 2nd gate. Bear **R**, crossing to gate in far corner of field by river. Continue above **Till** to Ford Bridge, there following field edge away from river to gate leading out to lane. Head back along it, crossing bridge to junction.
❹ To **R**, road winds up to **Ford**. Go past entrance to church and **Ford Castle** before turning **L** into village. At bottom, opposite **Lady Waterford Gallery**, turn **R** to ascend to junction opposite Jubilee Cottage.
❺ Now go **L** but, where lane later bends sharply R beyond former stables, leave through gate on **L** into wood ('**Hay Farm**'). Ignore obvious track ahead; instead, bear **L** on path through trees to stream. Continue over bridge to emerge in field and follow its perimeter to **L** above wood.
❻ Don't go through corner gate, turn **R** up field edge to top of hill. There, pass **L** through gate and cross small field to track in front of **Hay Farm** cottages.
❼ Walk as far as another track on **R**, which leads past barns to junction. Turn **R** to enter gate 20yds (18m) along on **L** ('Heatherslaw and Leathamhill'). Follow field edge to power cable post; go **R**, following boundary and eventually pass wood to reach bottom corner. Drop through gate into trees to bridge over stream. Through 2nd gate, turn **L** along field edge to return to Point ❷. Retrace outward steps to **Etal**.

349 ALWINTON
NORTHUMBERLAND

4.5 MILES (7.2KM) 3hrs

PATHS: Mostly hill footpaths, 8 stiles

SUGGESTED MAP: aqua3 OS Explorer OL16 The Cheviot Hills

GRID REFERENCE: NT 919063

PARKING: Car park at Alwinton

NOTE: Close to MOD artillery range over Barrow Scar. When red flags flying, walk may be inadvisable. Contact Range Control Officer on 01830 520569 or 0191 239 4261 prior to setting off

THE PUB: Rose and Thistle

❶ Turn **R** out of car park and follow road for 700yds (640m) to gate on **L** leading to **Barrow Mill**. Go through gate and down to farm, passing remains of a corn-drying kiln (1812). Go through another gate into field, cross this and go through gate to river bank. Ford river. After rain, this will involve getting your feet wet.
❷ Enter field and follow fence to **R** to gate. Go through this or over stile about 20yds (18m) away to **L** and continue to derelict farm buildings. Follow track up hillside to **R-H** corner of conifer forest.
❸ About 50yds (46m) before reaching signpost marking edge of military firing range, follow less well-defined track across heather-covered hillside to **R**, rising slightly, until you come to wire fence. Follow this over top of **Barrow Scar**, keeping fence on your R. When you meet 2nd fence, follow this to stile. Cross stile and go down to obvious loop in river. In late summer, bracken may obscure track.
❹ At river bend, cross stile, then another after 100yds (91m). Cross field and stile into farmyard at **Linshiels**. Go through farmyard, across 2 bridges and join road. Turn **L** and follow road until just past farm buildings, to signpost ('Shillmoor').
❺ Go up hillside, over stile and follow track overlooking gorge and its waterfalls. For short distance, slopes below are quite precipitous and care is needed, though track is good. When track splits, keep to higher branch and go round hillside to join more prominent track leading up from L. Turn **R** and follow this track uphill.
❻ At top continue over level ground then descend to stile. Cross and follow track, over 2nd stile and down to road. Follow road for 1 mile (1.6km) back to **Alwinton**.

WALK

NORTHUMBERLAND

350 OTTERBURN
NORTHUMBERLAND

4.5 MILES (7.2KM) 2hrs

PATHS: Bridleway, moorland track and metalled road.

SUGGESTED MAP: aqua3 OS Explorer OL42 Kielder Water & Forest

GRID REFERENCE: NY 889929 **Parking:** Roadside car park at eastern end of Otterburn village

NOTE: Close to MOD danger area. When red flags flying, walk may be inadvisable. Contact Range Control Officer on 01830 520569 or 0191 239 4261 before setting off

THE PUB: Percy Arms

❶ From car park, walk through **Otterburn**. About 100yds (91m) after passing Church of St John the Evangelist, turn **R** on to road to **Otterburn Hall**. At top of incline, go on to public bridleway on **L**, past farm buildings and into field. Follow bridleway alongside wall and through gate into next field. Continue, this time with wall, which gives way to wire fence on R.
❷ Go through next gate and, keeping in same direction, cross field to gate through opposite wall. Go through gate and across marshy ground past small plantation, now mostly cut down, to junction with metalled road. Follow this to **R**, across cattle grid and around bend to **L**, up gentle incline.
❸ About 100yds (91m) after bend, follow grassy track across hillside to **R**, past **sheep pen**. This leads to gate, beyond which there is military warning notice. Go through gate and continue across moorland, downhill. The ground is boggy and track indefinite in places, but it leads to better track, which follows fence on your R to join metalled road at **Hopefoot** farm.
❹ Follow road to **R**, crossing bridge over stream, then through woods, to join main army camp to Otterburn road at **Hopefoot Cottages**. Turn **R** and follow road past **Doe Crag** cottages and across bridge to entrance to **Otterburn Hall**. Go through gate opposite this on to footpath, signposted to Otterburn and leading across field.
❺ Follow track, passing **sports centre** on your R. At bend in wire fence, track forks. Follow **L** fork downhill, across 2 small footbridges, through kissing gate and along river bank. The track may be muddy and overgrown at times. After crossing stile, track brings you into Otterburn, just opposite **Percy Arms**. Turn **L** and return to car park.

351 ELSDON
NORTHUMBERLAND

4 MILES (6.4KM) 1hr 45min

PATHS: Field paths and tracks

SUGGESTED MAP: aqua3 OS Explorer OL42 Keilder Water & Forest

GRID REFERENCE: NY 937932

PARKING: Signed car park in Elsdon, by bridge on Rothbury road

THE PUB: Bird In Bush Inn

❶ Follow 'Toilets' sign past village hall and through gateway. Climb lane past **Mote Hills**, pass house and cross gravel to gate. Cross small field and go through next gate, then head half **R** to go through gate near trees. Follow path up sunken lane then along field edge to gate.
❷ Go through gate and turn **L** over cattle grid. Follow metalled lane through farm buildings and down to row of cottages. Opposite them, turn **R** in front of barn, cross stream and go through gate.
❸ Walk ahead through field with bank on L and, at top of rise, bear **L** across bank, making for gate in crossing wire fence. After gate, bear half **L** again, towards **L-H** end of crossing wall.
❹ Turn **R** and follow wall downhill. Go through gate in crossing wall and continue to follow wall on your L to reach waymarked post. Turn **R**, cross small bridge, then go uphill to gate beside barn. Go straight on then take metal gate on your **L**. Curve **R** to another gate on to road. Turn **L** along road, crossing cattle grid and bridge, to 2nd cattle grid.
❺ Cross it, then turn immediately **R** ('**East Todholes**'). Cross stream and go through gate, then cross 2nd stream. Follow wall on your L-H side to reach ladder stile by pine trees. After stile bear half **L** to go round **R-H** side of **East Todholes** farm and cross over stile on to lane.
❻ Follow lane past next farm and up hill to join road. Turn **R**. Opposite 'bend' sign go **R** over stile. Follow old wall downhill towards **Elsdon**, bending **R**, then **L**, at fence to cross stile. After another stile bear **R** to footbridge, then **L** to another. Path eventually brings you to larger footbridge near village.
❼ Cross footbridge, then turn **R** to stile beside gate. Go up track between houses to road that takes you to green. Bear **R**, along edge of green. Go over bridge and back to start.

352 MORPETH
NORTHUMBERLAND

8.5 MILES (13.7KM) 2hrs 45min

PATHS: Woodland paths (muddy after rain) and field paths, 9 stiles

SUGGESTED MAP: aqua3 OS Explorer 325 Morpeth & Blyth

GRID REFERENCE: NZ 198859 **Parking:** Car parks within town

THE PUB: Old Red Bull Inn

❶ From **Town Hall**, walk east along Bridge Street to end, continuing around to **L** along main road towards **Pegswood**. Immediately after **Old Red Bull Inn**, take enclosed path on **R** that later rejoins main road. Cross to footpath rising through woodland opposite ('Whorral Bank and Cottingwood Common'). Bear **R** when you get to fork, past residential home, then go **R** at next junction to again meet main road.
❷ On far side, path ('**Bothal**') descends into lushly wooded valley through which flows **River Wansbeck**. There follows delightful, undulating walk for 2.25 miles (3.6km), eventually ending over stile by sawmill. Walk to lane beyond and turn **R** across river.
❸ After climbing from valley, lane continues above wood. Where it later bends sharply **L** at **Shadfen Cottage**, go ahead over stile into field corner, and continue at edge of series fields beside **R-H** boundary. Eventually pass **R** of deep excavation, before dropping to stile into woodland. Go through to bridge; cross.
❹ Re-emerging into fields above far bank, follow path ahead between cultivation to gain track past **Parkhouse Banks**. After 120yds (110m), immediately beyond drive, turn through gap in **R-H** hedge ('Whorral Bank'), and walk away beside field edge. At corner, slip **R** through another gap and carry on along track past cottage and through fields to railway bridge.
❺ Keep going over field beyond to stile, there dropping across rough pasture back into wood. Soon joined by track, continue down to junction by river and turn **L** above bank. Emerging from trees, bear **L** along field path that leads past cottage, ongoing track returning to river.
❻ Over bridge, street leads around past ambulance station into town. Go ahead to St George's Church then turn **L** over Telford Bridge to Castle Square. Cross into **Carlisle Park** and, beyond flowerbeds, bear **R** following main drive to riverside promenade. Walk upstream past Elliott Bridge to top of park then turn **R** over Oldgate Bridge to return to town centre.

353 ALLENHEADS
NORTHUMBERLAND

5 MILES (8KM) 3hrs

PATHS: Stony tracks and generally well-defined paths, 3 stiles

SUGGESTED MAP: aqua3 OS Explorer OL31 North Pennines

GRID REFERENCE: NY 860453

PARKING: In Allenheads village centre

THE PUB: Allenheads Inn

❶ From front of **heritage centre** head east to B6295. Cross to follow lane ('Rookhope'). This climbs steeply out of valley between spruce plantations. At sharp L-H bend beyond **Eastend Reservoir**, leave road and go over step stile on path ('Rookhope Road'). Trackless, but guided by wall on **R**, path climbs westwards across 2 fields of pasture and over 2 stiles.
❷ After cutting corner, path rejoins road and arrives at an old quarry high on moors. Turn **L** along road for a few paces, then follow stony track at **R-H** side. This traces moorland rim above **Allenheads**.
❸ After passing quarry and huge cairn, track turns **R** then meanders around **Middle Rigg** before turning sharp **L** to pass old ruins of **Byerhope** hamlet.
❹ Beyond **Byerhope Farm**, at **High Haddock Stones**, track swings R again, away from valley. Here you leave it. A waymarker post, 1st of many, signs your bridleway. This clear grooved grassy path makes circuitous descent into Allendale, where you'll see quarries of Swinhope and **Coatenhill Reservoir**. After passing old quarry workings, bridleway descends to gate by terraced cottages on main valley road.
❺ Across road go ahead, down minor lane, which fords **River East Allen**; use footbridge on **R** to cross.
❻ Where road bends R uphill at **Peasmeadows**, leave it and go down cottage's drive, beyond which riverside path begins. Ignore 1st bridge across river and stay with path past **Burnfoot**. Go across footbridge over **Middlehope Burn**, then continue though pleasing little ravine of heather and bilberry. As it approaches lead mining spoil heaps, path gets sketchy. The easiest course is to climb to brow of bank on **R** and follow this to road near **Slag Hill**.
❽ Turn **L** down road to recross East Allen, then turn **R** at T-junction. This quiet lane leads back into **Allenheads**, past hamlet of **Dirt Pot** and old Presbyterian chapel.

Scotland

Contents

		page
354	Loch Ard, Stirling	401
355	Pentlands, City of Edinburgh	403
356	New Town, City of Edinburgh	405
357	Roslin, City of Edinburgh	407
358	St Abb's Head, Scottish Borders	409
359	Pitlochry, Perth & Kinross	411

			page
360	to 361	Dumfries & Galloway	413
362		Scottish Borders	413
363		City of Edinburgh	413
364	to 365	Highlands	413

SCOTLAND

KEY

■ Walk route

● Cycle route

■ Unmapped walk

Inchmahome Priory

Walter Comyn founded Augustinian Inchmahome Priory in 1238, and it became famous as the retreat of the infant Mary, Queen of Scots in 1547. The ruins of the church and cloisters are situated on an island in the Lake of Monteith.

*Great snipe
(Gallinago media)*

*The crumbling ruins of
the Augustinian priory*

The Great Forest of Loch Ard

Below left: Stirling Achray Forest in Queen Elizabeth Forest Park

One of Scotland's great woodlands, hiding place of the Stone of Destiny and birthplace of the Scottish Parliament.

Lying between Aberfoyle and the foothills of Ben Lomond, this area of woodland is part of the Queen Elizabeth Forest Park.

Most of the forested land was purchased by the Forestry Commission in the 1930s. It was planted straight away and by the closing years of the century consisted of mature woodland. On-going thinning started in the 1950s and areas were felled towards the end of the 20th century. Some 60,000 tons of timber are extracted each year from the park as a whole. The area south of Lochan Spling was initially planted with Norway spruce, Sitka spruce, larch and Scots pine. Most of the

spruce, together with some of the larch and pine, was felled in the 1980s and replaced with Douglas fir, larch and Sitka spruce. But native broadleaves have been planted too, including 10,000 oak trees to augment the remains of the ancient oak woods that once covered most of the area. Birch and rowan have been regenerating naturally. Part of this area has been left to mature to provide magnificent specimens that are the equal of anything in European forests.

Wildlife is abundant, including red squirrels and capercaillie. Decaying pines, which have been uprooted in gales or just collapsed, support wood-boring insects and provide a ready food supply for a whole host of birds. There are peat bogs and wilderness areas like the one just south of Duchray water in the old wood of Drumore. Here there are no trails, but amid this jungle-like habitat are blueberry, chickweed, wintergreen, cow-wheat and

cowberry. You will probably see some evidence of red and roe deer and if you are really quiet may see rare birds like blackcock and woodpecker. Changing attitudes to conservation and forestry management have brought a gradual reshaping of the forest to provide a more diverse range of tree species, a wider range of habitat.

The Covenanters Inn is where the Nationalists met in 1949 to launch a petition, which they called the Second Covenant. The signatories called on the government of the day to give Scotland a devolved parliament. Over 2 million people signed the petition but it was not until the closing years of the 20th century, and after much argument, campaigning and voting, that their wishes were granted.

the walk

1 Leave from the west end of the car park and turn left into **Manse Road**. Cross a narrow bridge over the River Forth (the river has its source near here although it is more usually associated with Edinburgh) and continue along the road past a terrace of houses named Craigmore View. Turn right here and head uphill, passing the **Covenanters Inn**. A short distance past here is open countryside and the start of the Great Forest of Loch Ard.

2 Head straight on along the forest road, keeping an ear open for heavy timber lorries. During the week this can get fairly busy, as this is a main forestry extraction route, so keep well into the side. After about 0.5 mile (800m) you will reach a

2h00 · **3.5 MILES** · **5.6 KM** · **LEVEL 1 2 3**

MAP: aqua3 OS Explorer 365 The Trossachs

START/FINISH: tourist information centre; grid ref: NS 521009

PATHS: roads, forest roads and trails

LANDSCAPE: fields, hills, forest and loch

PUBLIC TOILETS: beside tourist office

TOURIST INFORMATION: Aberfoyle, tel 01877 382352

THE PUB: The Forth Inn, Aberfoyle

❶ Keep dogs under control or on lead to avoid disturbing wildlife

Getting to the start

The small town of Aberfoyle lies on the A821, 20 miles (32.2km) to the west of Stirling. The visitor centre and car park are on the south side of the Main Street.

Researched and written by:
Moira McCrossan, Hamish Scott, Hugh Taylor

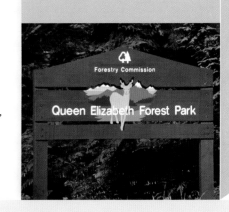

while you're there

On the Doune–Stirling road, Blair Drummond Safari Park, the only wildlife park in Scotland, is a credible day out for the family. Here you can drive through the reserves and see animals from lions and elephants to camels and bison roaming free. Other attractions include a pet farm, pedal boats, an adventure playground and a waterfowl cruise.

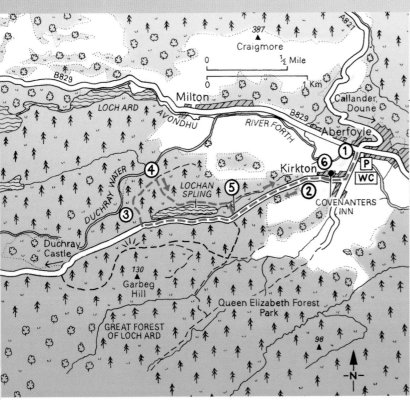

The Forth Inn

'Modernised' in period style six years ago, there is a large public bar with a pool table and walls are decorated with old photos of Aberfoyle. Food is available in the bar, and there is a separate restaurant. There are also outside tables. The pub is for sale at the time of writing.

Food
Lunchtime choices range from baked potatoes, sandwiches and baguettes to hot specials such as ribeye steak with pepper sauce. The full lunch menu includes a wide a range of dishes and desserts. Children have their own small menu including lasagne, stewed steak with vegetables, scampi and other favourites. The dinner menu has a Scottish flavour – beef olives filled with haggis, roast peppers filled with Scottish cheeses – alongside offerings such as lasagne, noisette of lamb and veal escalope.

Family facilities
Children are welcome and the inn has toys and colouring books to keep them amused.

Alternative refreshment stops
Aberfoyle has a good range of restaurants.

about the pub

The Forth Inn
Main Street
Aberfoyle
FK8 3UQ
Tel: 0177 382372
www.ghd35.dial.pipex.com

DIRECTIONS: on Main Street near the information centre.

PARKING: large public car-park behind pub.

OPEN: daily, all day.

FOOD: daily, all day.

BREWERY: free house

REAL ALE: Belhaven Best.

DOGS: allowed in bar.

ROOMS: 6 en suite.

☛ Where to go from here
Visit 14th-century Doune Castle, 13 miles (21km) east of Aberfoyle. It was a ruin by the 18th century but has been restored and now offers a look at life in a medieval royal household. It featured in the film *Monty Python and the Holy Grail* (1974) and in the BBC dramatisation of *Ivanhoe*. Although usually associated with the City of Edinburgh, the River Forth actually rises near here where the Duchray Water meets the Avondhu River.

staggered crossroads. Continue straight ahead along the forest road until you come to a turning on the right with a **waymarker**. Turn right here.

3 Follow this waymarked trail through the forest almost to the banks of **Duchray Water**. This rises on the north face of Ben Lomond and joins with the Avondhu from Loch Ard to create the River Forth near Aberfoyle. The path curves right, continues to descend slightly and then reaches a junction.

4 Turn right and follow the path uphill through the trees to the north banks of **Lochan Spling**. The path then swings left and, at the end of the Lochan, turns right at a waymarker pole, crosses a small stream and heads slightly uphill.

5 When the path reaches the T-junction, turn left and rejoin the **main forest access road** continuing along it to the Covenanters Inn. This takes its name not from the activities of the 17th-century Scottish Presbyterians, who were persecuted by the Stuart monarchy for refusing to give up their faith, but from the activities of 20th-century Scottish Nationalists.

6 Continue past the inn, where a later group of Nationalists temporarily hid Scotland's Stone of Destiny when it was liberated from Westminster Abbey in 1950, then turn left on to **Manse Road** at the junction and return to the start.

The Pentlands

Top left: Edinburgh's Malleny Garden

Below: A peaceful woodland walk

A lovely, bracing walk across the hills.

Although this walk starts from Edinburgh's busy city bypass, you'll soon feel that you're miles from the city. The Pentlands are an uncompromising range of hills which clasp the city in their craggy, green arms.

Their peaks rise up to 1,898ft (579m) above sea level and offer many great walks.

This route takes you past several reservoirs, which keep Scotland's capital supplied with water. The first you pass is Torduff Reservoir, which was built in 1851 and is 72ft (22m) deep. Later on you come down to Glencorse Reservoir. Beneath its waters lie the remains of the Chapel of St Katherine's (or Catherine's) in the Hopes dating to the 13th century and the reign of Robert the Bruce. If it's been very dry (unlikely, I know) and the waters are shallow, you might just see it.

The Pentlands are full of such historic monuments and memories. In prehistoric times, the hills were far more populated than they are today. On a low hill above Flotterstone, Castlelaw is a well-preserved hill fort dating from around the time of the Roman invasions. Its most intriguing feature is a souterrain, a long underground passage with a small side-chamber. The purpose that such structures served remains unclear.

The hills are criss-crossed with ancient routes and, near Farmilehead, the Camus Stone commemorates a battle fought against the Danes. In 1666, General Dalyell of The Binns (an ancestor of the former MP, Tam Dalyell) beat a ragged army of insurgents fighting for the Covenant at Rullion Green. These days there are army firing ranges near Castlelaw, while recruits from barracks at Glencorse and Redford are put through their paces on the hills.

In the final stages of this walk you'll pass Bonaly Tower, once the home of Lord Cockburn (1779–1854), a writer and judge who is remembered for the sketches that he penned of Edinburgh society. He was a conservationist who loved traditional Scots architecture. Cockburn employed architect William Playfair to rebuild an old farmhouse as a castle. The tower, for all its battlements and turrets, is a fake. All the same, Cockburn loved the castle he created. 'Human nature is incapable of enjoying more happiness than has been my lot here,' he wrote.

4h00	10 MILES	16 KM	LEVEL 123

MAP: aqua 3 OS Explorer 344 Pentland Hills

START/FINISH: Bonaly Tower, grid ref: NT 212679

PATHS: wide firm tracks, short stretches can be muddy, 3 stiles

LANDSCAPE: reservoirs, fields and hills

PUBLIC TOILETS: at Flotterstone Information Centre

TOURIST INFORMATION: Edinburgh, tel 0131 473 3800

THE PUB: The Flotterstone Inn, Milton Bridge

❶ Obey signs to keep dogs on leads near livestock.

Getting to the start

Bonaly Country Park is 4 miles (6.4km) southwest of Edinburgh city centre and 1 mile (1.6km) south of Colinton. The car park is in Torduff Road, a turning to the right off Bonaly Road just across a bridge over the bypass.

Researched and written by:
Rebecca Ford, Hamish Scott

Edinburgh Crystal

You can watch skilled craftspeople as they take molten crystal and turn it into intricately decorated glassware at the Edinburgh Crystal Centre at Penicuik on the A701. Not only can you talk to the craft workers themselves but there are also artefacts, storyboards, video footage and audio listening posts to help you understand the 300-year-old history of glassmaking. The shop includes the largest collection of Edinburgh crystal and seconds at bargain prices.

Edinburgh Crystal Centre

the walk

1 From the car park by the bypass, follow the signs pointing in the direction of Easter Kinleith and walk along the metalled track. You will reach the **water treatment works** on your left-hand side. Continue on past the works to reach the gate by the East of Scotland Water sign.

2 Go through the gate and continue walking ahead, keeping **Torduff Reservoir** on your left-hand side. When you reach the top of the reservoir, walk over the little bridge and follow the metalled track as it bends round to the right. Walk under a line of electricity pylons, and go over a small bridge, passing an artificial cataract on your left-hand side, and continue past **Clubbiedean Reservoir**.

3 Your path now bears left and then immediately right, with fields on either side. Pass under another line of pylons and walk to **Easter Kinleith farm**. Now follow the path as it bends back to the left to become a metalled track signposted 'Harlaw'. Pass a sign for Poets' Glen and continue ahead, over a bridge and on to a large white house on the left-hand side called **Crossroads**, where the track meets a public road.

Below: A boat bobs on Glencorse Reservoir

4 Turn left and follow the sign for **Glencorse Reservoir**. Follow this track, past a conifer plantation on your left-hand side, then cross a stile next to a metal gate. Continue ahead until you reach a T junction. Turn left through a wooden gate next to larger metal gate.

5 Follow the track, which runs beside a dry stone wall before crossing open moorland. Continue in the same direction until you come to a copse of conifers on the right-hand side, with Glencorse Reservoir ahead. You will see a sign indicating the route by foot to **The Flotterstone Inn** (1 mile/1.6km). You could head for the inn now, or continue to the car park, and drive there later

6 Turn left here and follow the sign to **Colinton by Bonaly**. Walk up hill and maintain direction to go through a gap in a wire fence. The track now narrows and takes you through the hills; until it eventually opens out. Continue in the same direction to reach a fence encircling conifers. Keep the fence on your left and walk down to cross a stile on the left-hand side.

7 Walk past **Bonaly Reservoir**, then through a kissing gate and on downhill, getting good views over Edinburgh as you descend. When you reach a wooden gate, go through and continue ahead, walking downhill, with trees on either side. Go through another kissing gate and follow the tarmac path ahead, passing a **Scout Centre** on the right-hand side followed by **Bonaly Tower**. Turn left at the bridge over the bypass and return to the car park at the start of the walk.

The Flotterstone Inn

Just 7 miles (11.3km) from the city centre, yet backing onto wild, unspoilt countryside, The Flotterstone Inn has long been a mecca both for hill-walkers and for families on weekend outings. The long established pub, which would once have been a farm, is an attractive whitewashed building several miles from the nearest village. Inside, there is a spacious bar with comfortable seating, whilst the garden is equally beguiling on hot summer afternoons, with a backdrop of trees and the gurgle of a woodland burn to complement the rustic ambience.

Food
The food on offer will satisfy the most ravenous of appetites. Steaks – prime Scottish beef – have been properly hung and marinated before being chargrilled on hot coals, whilst the blackboard menu may include a 'roast trio' of beef, turkey and gammon. For those in search of lighter fare there are half a dozen different salads, Ploughman's lunch, club sandwiches or a

about the pub

The Flotterstone Inn
Milton Bridge
Near Penicuik
EH26 0RD
Tel: 01968 673717

DIRECTIONS: on A702 (Biggar Road) 2 miles (1.2km) south west of Easter Howgate.

PARKING: 30

OPEN: daily, all day

FOOD: daily, all day from 12 noon.

BREWERY: free house.

REAL ALES: varying selection of cask ales.

DOGS: allowed in bar

range of vegetarian specialities. There is always a selection of real ales, although the choice varies week to week.

Family facilities
Children are permitted in the bar and high chairs are available. Dogs are always welcome, as long as they are polite to Toby, the resident Old English Sheepdog.

Alternative refreshment stops
The Spylaw Tavern in Colinton serves light lunches, and they have a beer garden.

☞ Where to go from here
If you're feeling fit then make for Hillend Ski Centre on the Pentlands. This is a dry-ski slope, suitable for ski and snowboarding practice. A chairlift takes you to the top if you don't fancy the climb. You're also close to the Gilmerton Cove, a mysterious complex of underground chambers that have yet to be properly explained (for details of tours contact tourist information office).

Greenfinch
(Carduelis chloris)

what to look for

It's well worth stopping to explore St Giles Cathedral, where the Reformation in Scotland was launched by John Knox. Look out for the plaque to Jenny Geddes, who threw a stool during a service at the minister who tried to introduce the English prayer book into Scottish services.

Edinburgh's New Town

Top right: St Giles Cathedral in Edinburgh

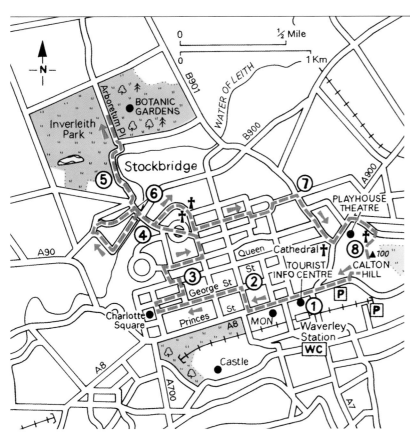

1h30 · **3 MILES** · **4.8 KM** · **LEVEL 123**

WALK

MAP: AA Street by Street Edinburgh

START/FINISH: tourist information centre; grid ref: NT 257739

PATHS: busy city streets

LANDSCAPE: elegant Georgian townscape

PUBLIC TOILETS: Waverley Station

TOURIST INFORMATION: Waverley Market, Princes Street, tel 0131 557 1700

THE PUB: The Cumberland

⚠ Keep dogs on a lead; they are not allowed in the Botanic Gardens

Getting to the start

There are several large car parks in central Edinburgh, including one in Princes Street along from the tourist information centre, which is in Waverley Market on Princes Street and close to the main railway station.

Researched and written by:
Rebecca Ford, Hamish Scott

Walking by the Water of Leith, Stockbridge

Edinburgh's most opulent architectural creations. From then on, the New Town kept expanding. It was only in the 1830s that the New Town project foundered, when a rise in interest rates slashed house values, leaving elegant new streets and crescents half built.

This walk will take you through the first New Town, from Princes Street to Charlotte Square, before exploring neighbourhoods developed in the early 19th century. The site of Princes Street is still magnificent. It was once entirely residential but in later years, it became Edinburgh's premier shopping street. Now, the crown of fashion has passed on to George Street, whilst Charlotte Square houses the official residence of Scotland's First Minister. Stockbridge combines exclusive residential streets with a faintly bohemian air. Further on along the route, Great King Street and Drummond Place exemplify the later New Town at its best, with blocks of tenements and houses unified within a single grand

A walk in the footsteps of literary giants

Edinburgh's New Town was laid out in the mid-18th century and built over a period of more than 70 years. It is the finest example of Georgian town planning in Britain, if not in the world. New Town was deliberately intended to encourage Edinburgh's elite to adopt a more modern way of life that would bring prestige and prosperity to Scotland.

The first phase of the development was planned by James Craig, a young architect who won a competition for the design in 1766. His plan was simple, consisting of a grid laid out along a ridge, taking full advantage of stupendous views. At first developers were reluctant to invest and it was not until the 1790s that society abandoned the old city centre. By then Robert Adam had been commissioned to design Charlotte Square, one of

Edinburgh Castle

Edinburgh Castle dominates the city. Built on a volcano plug, it dates back to the 12th century, although there was a hill fort there long before that. Here, you can see the Honours of Scotland – the name given to the Scottish Crown Jewels – as well as the Stone of Destiny. The castle was the birthplace of Mary, Queen of Scots' son, who became James VI of Scotland and later James I of England.

design. At Broughton Street, you will see where the New Town met its end. Look right and you will see Georgian facades. Look left and, just across the road, you will see a bizarre Gothic church with a 1920s school behind. Finally, when you reach the top of Calton Hill, you will see the city as a whole.

the walk

1 From the tourist information centre, turn left and walk along **Princes Street**, passing the Scott Monument on your left. Cross the road at the **Royal Scottish Academy** and turn right up Hanover Street.

2 Take the second turning on your left and walk along George Street to **Charlotte Square**. Then turn right and right again to go along Young Street. At the end, turn left and walk down North Castle Street to reach Queen Street.

3 Cross the road, turn left, then right down Wemyss Place and right into Heriot Row. When you reach Howe Street turn left and, before you reach the church, turn left and walk along South East Circus Place. Walk past the sweep of Royal Circus and down into **Stockbridge**.

4 Cross the bridge, then turn left along Dean Terrace. At the end, turn right into Ann Street. When you reach **Dean Park Crescent**, follow road through into St Bernard's Crescent and on into Leslie Place to reach Stockbridge again. Cross the road to walk down St Bernard's Row (it's slightly to the left but almost opposite). Follow this, then bear left into **Arboretum Avenue**.

5 Follow this road as it leads you past the **Water of Leith** and down to Inverleith Terrace. Cross over and walk up Arboretum Place until you reach the entrance to the **Botanic Gardens** on the right. Turn left after

exploring the gardens and retrace your steps to reach Stockbridge again.

6 Turn left at Hectors bar, cross the river and walk uphill, then turn left along St Stephen Street. When you reach the church follow the road uphill to the right, then turn left along **Great King Street**. At the end, turn right, then immediately left to walk along Drummond Place, past Dublin Street and continue ahead into London Street.

7 At the roundabout turn right and walk up Broughton Street to Picardy Place. Go left, pass the statue of **Sherlock Holmes**, then bear left towards the **Playhouse Theatre**. Cross, continue left, then turn right into Blenheim Place. At Greenside church turn right up a steep tarmac path, continue uphill and turn left at the meeting of paths.

8 Go up the steps on the right, walk over **Calton Hill**, turn right to pass the cannon. Go downhill, take the steps to the left, walk into Regent Road. Turn right and walk back into **Princes Street** and the start.

Below: The Sir Walter Scott Monument

The Cumberland

It can be hard to find a pub in Edinburgh that welcomes children and harder still to find one with a garden. The Cumberland scores on both these counts, aside from being one of the New Town's most appealing bars. Set in a quiet residential street where houses can sell for over a million pounds, it is very much a local pub for one of Britain's smartest inner-city areas so don't expect a juke-box and sing-songs. Nonetheless the atmosphere is friendly, with a mixed clientele of executives, students and bohemian 'creatives'. For real ale enthusiasts, the pub has an ever-changing range of up to eight different beers from breweries across Britain. If the names of some are unfamiliar, you can ask for a taster before you buy a pint. The Cumberland has a superb garden. But be warned: the pub is quiet on weekdays but on weekends, if the sun is shining, you should get there early to secure an outside table.

Food

Cumberland sausage is inevitably on the menu, along with other traditional pub fare such as haggis, home-made burgers and deep-fried haddock. Portions are generous, although there are also lighter options including salads, wraps and paninis. At weekends, a huge Scottish breakfast or the mixed grill may prove appealing.

Family facilities

Children are welcome, although families are encouraged to use either the garden or the cosy panelled room at the back of the pub. There are no special facilities for children, nor is there a children's menu.

Alternative refreshment stops

George Street is home to some of Edinburgh's trendiest bars and cafes. In Stockbridge there's Pizza Express, whilst Broughton Street is lined with eateries.

☛ Where to go from here

Edinburgh has diversions for all ages. Ann Street in Stockbridge is said to have been the inspiration for J M Barrie's novel *Quality Street* (1901). The Royal Botanic Gardens contain many plant species that were discovered by early Scottish botanists. Our Dynamic Earth is a top attraction and will please children and adults alike.

about the pub

The Cumberland.
1–3 Cumberland Street
Edinburgh EH3 6RT
Tel: 0131 558 3134
www.cumberlandbar.co.uk

DIRECTIONS: on corner of Cumberland Street and Drummond Place.

PARKING. on street.

OPEN: daily all day.

FOOD: daily 12–3 and evenings.

BREWERY: free house.

REAL ALE: Deuchars and many others, changing weekly.

DOGS: allowed in bar if well behaved.

while you're there

Kailzie Gardens, set on the River Tweed, provide a rich variety of colour and charm throughout the seasons – visit the wild garden with its snowdrops in February. There is a walled garden with herbaceous borders and fountain, a laburnum arch and a formal rose garden.

Osprey
(Pandion haliaetus)

A new CCTV osprey viewing centre at Kailzie is part of the Tweed Valley Osprey Project which aims to educate the public about these birds of prey. There is also a similar blue tit watch site.

The Romance of Rosslyn Glen

Right: The richly carved interior of Rosslyn Chapel
Below left: The river flowing through Rosslyn Glen

357

2h30	5 MILES	8 KM	LEVEL 1 2 3

WALK

Tree-lined paths take you to a very special ancient chapel in this glorious glen.

Despite the splendour of its lush woodland, gurgling waters and delicate wild flowers, the most striking feature of romantic Rosslyn Glen is man-made. The beautiful, mysterious Rosslyn Chapel is now world famous due to the best-selling book *The Da Vinci Code* by Dan Brown. Founded in 1446 by Sir William St Clair, the richly decorated little church took 40 years to build.

The interior is full of intricate stone carvings, created by foreign masons commissioned and supervised by Sir William. The carvings are not just rich in biblical imagery, but also depict masonic and pagan symbols. There are over one hundred images of the 'green man', the pagan figure that once symbolised great goodness – as .well as great evil. There is also a depiction of a *danse macabre*, an allegorical representation of death's

supremacy over mankind. There are some surprising images too, notably the New World corn carved into a window arch. Just think – this was several decades before Columbus discovered America. So how did they know what corn looked like? Well, Sir William's grandfather, Prince Henry of Orkney, is thought to have discovered the New World long before Columbus, sailing from Nova Scotia in the 14th century. And there is a Native American tribe, the Micmac, who still pass on the tale that a great lord once sailed from the east and taught them to fish with nets.

Perhaps the most stunning carving in the chapel is the Apprentice Pillar, an extraordinarily ornate piece of work. It is said that the pillar was carved by a talented apprentice in his master's absence. When the master returned he was so jealous of the work that he killed the boy.

Rosslyn's greatest mysteries come from its associations with the Knights Templar, the medieval order of warrior monks. They were originally formed to protect pilgrims travelling to the Holy Land – and one of their founders was married to a relative of Sir William. The Templars became immensely wealthy and powerful and were eventually persecuted. Many fled to Scotland, with help from the freemasons, taking their treasures with them.

The St Clairs have strong masonic links and Rosslyn Chapel is

said to have been built as a memorial to the Templars. For centuries there have been stories of a secret vault, guarded by long-dead knights in rusting armour. It is said to hold some kind of treasure; jewels looted from Jerusalem, scrolls that tell the true story of Christ's life, or perhaps the Holy Grail itself.

the walk

1 From the **country park car park**, walk north east on to the track until you reach the river. Go up the metal stairs, cross the footbridge, then walk ahead, following the path uphill. In summer, the smell of wild garlic will soon waft over you. At the bottom of a flight of steps, turn right, walk under the **old castle arch**, down some stone steps, then turn to your left.

2 Your path now crosses a wild meadow of grass and hawthorn before climbing a set of **timber steps**. Continue through the woodland to an intersection by a small muddy spring. Ignore downhill path to right and continue uphill. As the path levels out, you pass a bench carved from a log. Shortly after this, bear right at fork, following the course of the river, to pass beneath **ancient yews** growing from a ruined wall. At intersection, turn right and follow the path that runs steeply downhill. Keep going down until you reach the river.

3 Walk to your left, then follow the path as it climbs again, ignoring minor paths to either side and following the course of the river. As you climb out of the gorge

MAP: aqua3 OS Explorer 344 Pentland Hills

START/FINISH: Roslin Glen Country Park car park; grid ref: NT 272627 (car park closes 8pm in summer, 5pm in winter)

PATHS: generally good, but can be muddy and slippery

LANDSCAPE: woodland and fields, short sections of road

PUBLIC TOILETS: Rosslyn Chapel Visitor Centre

TOURIST INFORMATION: Princes Street Edinburgh, tel 0131 473 3800

THE PUB: The Original Rosslyn Hotel

❶ Dogs must be kept on leads near livestock.

Getting to the start

The village of Roslin lies 7 miles (11.2km) south of Edinburgh and is signposted off the A701 to Penicuik. The country park is 0.5 mile (800m) from the village, on the B7003 to Rosewell.

Researched and written by:
Rebecca Ford, Hamish Scott

Neidpath Castle

Neidpath Castle, occupying a spectacular position on the River Tweed, is a 14th-century stronghold which was adapted to 17th-century living. It contains a rock-hewn well, a pit prison, a small museum and a tartan display.

The ruins of Neidpath Castle stand on a promontory west of Peebles

there are dramatic views of **Hawthorndean Castle** on the far bank. Beyond a broken fence the view opens out to fields on your left, then takes you closer to the river again. Cross a burn and another stile to the point where the river goes back on itself.

4 The path continues through a wooden gate, then immediately turns left to climb a **steep flight of steps** up the hill. You now get great views over the river valley as you cross the ridge then keep walking to reach a metal gate.

5 Turn left and follow the wide path. You eventually walk past estate offices and the **Roslin BioCentre**, then pass a memorial to the Battle of Rosslyn on your right-hand side. Keep walking straight ahead, through the outskirts of **Roslin** and up to the crossroads at the village centre.

6 Turn left here and walk ahead. After a short distance you see **Rosslyn Chapel** on the right-hand side. If you don't intend to visit the chapel, turn right just beyond the car-park. When you reach the cemetery turn left, following the signpost for '**Polton**', and walk between the cemeteries to the metal gate for **Rosslyn Castle**. Go down the steps on the right-hand side, over the bridge again and return to the car park.

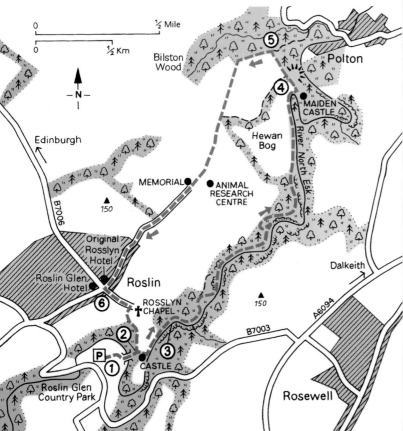

The Original Rosslyn Hotel

Graham Harris has been the landlord of this delightful pub for 33 years and would be happy to stand Dan Brown a pint if the best-selling author happened to stop by. Thanks to The Da Vinci Code, visitors from across the world now call in on the pub, where they can at least enjoy good food even if they haven't found an answer to the mysteries they have come to solve. In medieval times, Roslin's inn was by the chapel, in a building that still stands, but it moved to the present site when its landlord fell out with the St Clairs. The main bar is both spacious and cosy, with comfy armchairs that are much appreciated by tired walkers. Stone walls, a beamed ceiling, shelves of books, pictures and assorted knick-knacks add further to the home-like character, whereas the public bar is more traditional and down-to-earth; a plainly furnished room in which even the muddiest of dogs and boots need not prove embarrassing. There is an elegant conservatory and also outside tables for sunny afternoons.

Food

The blackboard may feature grilled swordfish or a roast. Soups are home-made and served with crusty bread, whilst the menu offers favourites such as steak pie, haggis and pork and apple sausages, and grills. For vegetarians there is nut roast, pizzas, or a vegetable pie. Desserts include sticky toffee pudding and crème brulée.

Family facilities

Children are welcome everywhere except in the public bar.

Alternative refreshment stops

The Roslin Glen Hotel, and the visitor centre at Rosslyn Chapel also has a café.

☞ Where to go from here

Butterfly and Insect World, at Lasswade, near Dalkeith is a great place to bring kids as the enclosures contain loads of beautiful and exotic butterflies in a tropical setting.

about the pub

The Original Rosslyn Hotel
Main Street
Rosslyn EH25 9LE
Tel: 0131 440 2384
Web site: www.originalrosslyn.co.uk

DIRECTION: on crossroads in centre of village.

PARKING: in street (ample).

OPEN: daily, all day.

FOOD: daily, lunches to 3pm weekdays, all day weekends.

BREWERY: free house.

REAL ALES: Belhaven Best.

DOGS: allowed in public bar, but not in main bar when food is being served.

ROOMS: 7 en suite.

Southern Upland Way

Covering a distance of 212 miles (341km) Britain's first coast-to-coast footpath runs from Portpatrick to Cockburnspath passing through the rolling hills and farmland of southern Scotland. Highlights along the route include the industrial history at Wanlockhead, and Traquair House and Melrose.

Lead-mining remains at Wanlockhead

A Walk to St Abb's Head

A refreshing wildlife walk along the cliffs

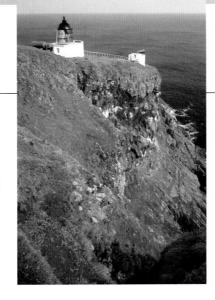

Left: The lighthouse at St Abb's Head

St Abb's Head is one of those places that people forget to visit. You only ever seem to hear it mentioned on the shipping forecast – and its name is generally followed by a rather chilly outlook – along the lines of 'north easterly five, continuous light drizzle, poor'. In fact you could be forgiven for wondering if it even exists or is simply a mysterious expanse of sea – like Dogger, Fisher or German Bight.

But St Abb's Head does exist, as you'll find out on this lovely windswept walk which will rumple your hair and leave the salty tang of the sea lingering on your lips. The dramatic cliffs, along which you walk to reach the lonely lighthouse, form an ideal home for thousands of nesting seabirds as they provide superb protection from mammalian predators. Birds you might spot on this walk include guillemots, razorbills, kittiwakes, herring gulls, shags and fulmars – as well as a few puffins. Guillemots and razorbills are difficult to differentiate, as they're both black and white, and have an upright stance – rather like small, perky penguins. However, you should be able to spot the difference if you've got binoculars as razorbills have distinctive blunt beaks. Both birds belong to the auk family, the most famous member of which is probably the great auk, which went the way of the dodo and became extinct in 1844 – a victim of the contemporary passion for egg collecting.

Luckily no egg collector could scale these cliffs, which are precipitous and surrounded by treacherous seas. Do this walk in the nesting season (May to July) and you may well see young birds jumping off the high cliff ledge into the open sea below. Even though they can't yet fly, as their wings are little more than stubs, the baby birds are nevertheless excellent swimmers and have a better chance of survival in the water than in their nests – where they could fall prey to marauding gulls. Neither razorbills nor guillemots are particularly agile in the air, but they swim with the ease of seals, using their wings and feet to propel and steer their sleek little bodies as they fish beneath the waves.

While the steep cliffs are home to most of the seabirds round St Abb's Head, the low, flat rocks below are also used by wildlife, as they are the favoured nesting site of shags. These large black birds are almost indistinguishable from cormorants – except for the distinctive crest on their heads that gives them a quizzical appearance. They tend to fly low over the water, in contrast to the graceful fulmars that frequently soar along the cliff tops as you walk, hitching a ride on convenient currents of air.

the walk

1 From the car park, take the path that runs past the information board and the play area. Walk past the **visitor centre**, then take the footpath on the left, parallel to the main road. The path turns left beside a garden wall before emerging through a gate out onto the cliffs.

2 Follow the path, ignoring the sign to Starney Bay and continue, passing fields on your left-hand side. Your track now winds around the edge of the bay – to your right is the little **harbour at St Abbs**. The track then winds around the cliff edge, past dramatic rock formations and eventually to some steps.

3 Walk down the **steps**, then follow the grassy track as it bears left, with a fence on the left. Go up a slope, over a stile and maintain direction on the obvious grassy track. The path soon veers away from the cliff edge to run between two fences. Where fence to left ends, continue straight ahead up a short, steep slope to a crossing of tracks.

4 Maintain direction by taking the left-hand track which runs up a slope above the sea. You'll soon get great views of the St Abb's Head **lighthouse** ahead, dramatically situated on the cliff's edge. Continue to the lighthouse and walk past the lighthouse buildings and down to join a tarmac road.

5 Follow this road which takes you away from the cliff edge. Continue to an obvious bend, from where you get your first views of the **Mire Loch** below. Continue to

358

1h30	4 MILES	6.4 KM	LEVEL 1 2 3

WALK

MAP: aqua3 OS Explorer 346 Berwick-upon-Tweed

START/FINISH: visitor centre, grid ref: NT 913674

PATHS: clear footpaths and established tracks

LANDSCAPE: dramatic cliff tops and lonely lighthouse

PUBLIC TOILETS: at visitor centre

TOURIST INFORMATION: St Abbs Visitor Centre, tel: 018907 71443

THE PUB: The Anchor Inn, Coldingham

 Keep dogs on a lead

Getting to the start

The St Abb's Wildlife reserve is 1 mile (1.6km) to the north of Coldingham on the B6438. The visitor centre car park is to the left of the road, half a mile before the village of St Abbs.

Researched and written by:
Rebecca Ford, Hamish Scottt

A fishing vessel moored in the harbour at St Abbs

Common tern
(Sterna hirundo)

while you're there

St Abbs is a working fishing village and you can take a boat trip from here to get a closer look at the large colonies of birds which nest on the surrounding rocks and cliffs. The area is also a good base for divers wishing to explore the St Abbs and Eyemouth Voluntary Marine Reserve.

follow the lane downhill to the right, to within 50yds (45m) of a cattle grid.

6 Turn left here to pick up a faint path across the grass towards the Mire Loch. Cross a style and continue along loch side. At a footpath sign keep straight ahead, following the path as it emerges from the trees to run between gorse bushes and a stone wall. Continue to end of loch where the path meets a broad track.

7 Turn right along the track and walk up to the road. Go left now and continue to cross a **cattle grid**. When you reach a bend in the road, continue along the tarmac track as it bears left. You'll soon go through a gate, then pass some **cottages** before reaching the car park on the left-hand side.

The Anchor Inn

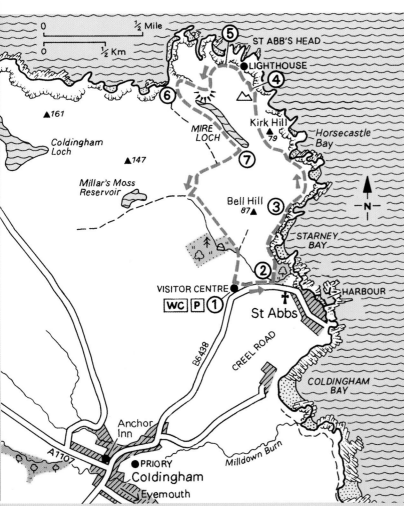

As befits a pub beside a wildlife reserve, The Anchor Inn belongs to an endangered species. It is a traditional village pub with a plain and simple public bar, a dining room and garden. The bar, with its scrubbed wooden floor and coal fire, is both a meeting place for local fishermen and farmers and a favourite refreshment stop for the bird-watchers, divers and walkers who pass through Coldingham on their way down to St Abbs. The atmosphere is friendly and the small bar encourages strangers to converse, so you may well find yourself drawn into a discussion. Food can be eaten in the bar, but those in search of greater privacy might prefer the dining room – a cosy space with panelled walls and a small cast-iron stove. There is also an attractive garden where, depending on the weather, barbecues are sometimes held.

Food

The breaded haddock has the sweetness of fish that is truly fresh. Perhaps even more appealing is the seafood platter, which is likely to include squid, king prawns, scampi. For carnivores there is a choice of steaks and chops, while vegetarians are also generously catered for with nine choices, including pastas, curry and a hazelnut and mushroom roast. There is also

about the pub

The Anchor Inn
School Road
Coldingham
Berwickshire TD14 5NS.
Tel: 01890 71243.

DIRECTIONS: on crossroads in village centre.

PARKING: 20 spaces in public car park across road.

OPEN: daily; all day.

FOOD: daily; last lunch orders 4pm in summer, 2.30 in winter.

BREWERY: free house.

REAL ALE: Wadworth 6X. Belhaven Best. Morlands Old Speckled Hen.

DOGS: only in garden.

a variety of bar-snacks such as toasted sandwiches and baked potatoes.

Family Facilities

Children are not permitted in the bar, but are welcome in the dining room and garden, which is within parental sight of a council-owned playground. There is an extensive children's menu.

Alternative refreshment stops

Lunches at St Abbs' Springbank Cottage Tea Room may include fresh crab, and St Abbs Visitor Centre has a café serving snacks.

☛ Where to go from here

Just along the coast from St Abbs is the little village of Eyemouth – the haunt of smugglers in the 18th and 19th centuries. If you go into the little museum you can see the Eyemouth Tapestry, which was made by local people to mark the centenary of the Great Disaster of 1881, when 189 fishermen died during a terrible storm.

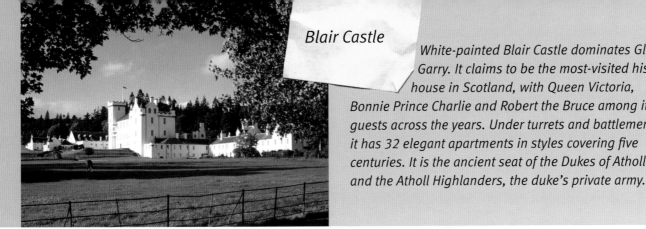

Blair Castle

White-painted Blair Castle dominates Glen Garry. It claims to be the most-visited historic house in Scotland, with Queen Victoria, Bonnie Prince Charlie and Robert the Bruce among its guests across the years. Under turrets and battlements, it has 32 elegant apartments in styles covering five centuries. It is the ancient seat of the Dukes of Atholl and the Atholl Highlanders, the duke's private army.

The Braes o' Killiecrankie

Queen Victoria

Below left: The tree-shaded paths of the Pass of Killiekrankie
Below right: Fishing at Soldiers Leap

4h30 | **8.75 MILES** | **14.1 KM** | **LEVEL 123**

WALK

MAP: aqua3 OS Explorer 386 Pitlochry & Loch Tummel

START/FINISH: Killiecrankie visitor centre, grid ref: NN 917626

PATHS: wide riverside paths, minor road, no stiles

LANDSCAPE: oak woods on banks of two rivers

PUBLIC TOILETS: at start

TOURIST INFORMATION: Killiecrankie Visitor Centre, tel 01350 728641

THE PUB: The Old Mill Inn, Pitlochry

Getting to the start

Killiecrankie Visitor Centre is on the B8019, 3 miles (4.8km) north west of Pitlochry. Car parking is available at the visitor centre.

Researched and written by:
Hamish Scott, Ronald Turnbull

A deeply wooded riverside leads from the famous battlefield to Loch Faskally

'If ye'd hae been where I hae been
Ye wouldna been sae swanky o
If ye'd hae seen where I hae seen
On the braes o Killiecrankie o'

The song commemorating the victory of the Battle of Killiecrankie in July 1689 is still sung wherever anyone with an accordion sits down in a pub full of patriotic tourists. In fact, both sides in the battle were Scots. When James II was ousted from England in a bloodless coup in 1688, the Scots Parliament (the Estates) voted to replace him with William of Orange.

John Claverhouse, 'Bonnie Dundee', raised a small army of Highlanders in support of King James. The Estates sent a larger army under another Highlander, General Hugh Mackay, to sort things out. Dundee, outnumbered two to one, was urged to ambush Mackay in the Pass of Killiecrankie. He refused, on the grounds of chivalry. The path above the river was steep, muddy and wide enough for only two soldiers; a surprise attack on such difficult ground would give his broadsword-wielding Highlanders too great an advantage. The battle actually took place on open ground, north of the pass.

Killiecrankie was the last time the claymore conquered the musket in open battle, due to a deficiency in the musket. Some 900 of the 2,500 Highlanders were shot down as they charged, but then the troopers had to stop to fix their bayonets, which plugged into the muzzle of the musket. The Highlanders were upon them, and they fled. The battle lasted just three minutes. Half of Mackay's army was killed, wounded, captured or drowned in the Garry. One escaped by leaping 18ft (5.5m) across the river; the 'Soldier's Leap'. Dundee died in battle.

Today, it is hard to believe that such bloody events occurred along the route of this peaceful riverside walk. Mature mixed woodland cloaks the steep slopes of the pass above the tumbling waters of the River Garry, trout rise in the rock pools of the Linn of Tummel and red squirrels may sometimes be seen in the branches of old pines. Loch Dunmore is an idyllic spot: a placid pond with an oriental bridge set in the wooded grounds of Faskally House.

the walk

1 Cross the front of the visitor centre to steps, signed 'Soldier's Leap', leading down into the wooded gorge. A footbridge crosses the waterfall of Troopers' Den. At the next junction, turn left (**'Soldier's Leap'**). Ten steps down, a spur path on the right leads to the viewpoint above the Soldier's Leap.

2 Return to the main path, signed **'Linn of Tummel'**, which runs down to join the River Garry below the railway viaduct. After a mile (1.6km) it reaches a footbridge.

3 Don't cross this footbridge, but continue ahead, signed 'Pitlochry', along the riverside under the tall **South Garry road bridge**. The path runs around a huge river pool to a tarred lane; turn right here, passing the **Fisheries Research laboratories**. The lane leaves the lochside, then passes a track on the right, blocked by a vehicle barrier. Ignore this; shortly turn right at a signpost, **'Pitlochry'**.

4 Immediately bear left to pass along the right-hand side of **Loch Dunmore**, following red-top posts. A footbridge crosses the loch, but turn away from it, half right, leaving the main path to follow a much fainter path across a grassy glade.

Hen harrier
(Circus cyaneus)

did you know?

Robert the Bruce marched down Glen Tilt, north of Killiecrankie, in 1306 on his way to a minor defeat near Tyndrum. James V attended a deer drive in 1529, and Mary, Queen of Scots was there in 1564. The next monarch to complete the route was Queen Victoria with Prince Albert on one of their 'great expeditions' from Balmoral.

Robert the Bruce statue

The path soon becomes more distinct and after 110yds (100m) it reaches a wider track. Turn left, with a white/yellow waymarker. After 220yds (201m) the track starts to climb; a short distance up the slope the white/yellow markers indicate a smaller path on the right, which follows the lochside. Where it rejoins the wider path, bear right at a **green waymarker** and cross a footbridge to the A9 road bridge.

5 Cross Loch Faskally on the **Clunie footbridge** below the road bridge, turn left up the path and then immediately right, on to a quiet road around the loch. In 1 mile (1.6km), at the top of the grass bank on the left, is the **Priest Stone**, an early Christian monolith. After the **Clunie power station**, you reach a car park on the left. Here a sign indicates a steep little path down to the **Linn of Tummel**.

6 Return to the road above for 0.5 mile (800m), to cross a grey suspension bridge on the right. Turn right, downstream, to pass above the Linn. A spur path back right returns to the falls at a lower level, but the main path continues along the riverside (signed 'Killiecrankie'). It bends left and goes down wooden steps to the Garry, then runs upstream and under the high road bridge. Take the side-path up on to the bridge for the view of the river, then return to follow the descending path signed **'Pitlochry via Faskally'**. This runs down to the bridge, Point 3. Return upstream to the start.

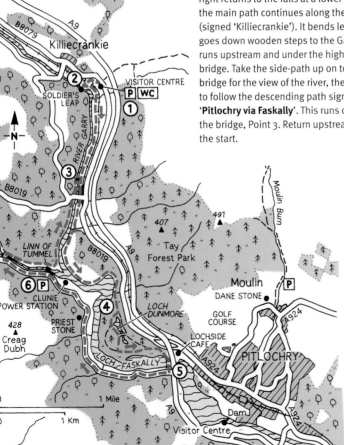

about the pub

The Old Mill Inn
Mill Lane
Pitlochry
Perthshire PH16 5BH
Tel: 01796 474020
www.old-mill-inn.com

DIRECTIONS: just off the north side of the High Street, behind the Royal Bank of Scotland.

PARKING: 30

OPEN: daily, all day.

FOOD: daily, all day until 10pm.

BREWERY: free house

REAL ALE: Jennings Cumberland Ale, Tetley Bitter and changing range of other beers.

DOGS. only in garden.

The building was a working watermill until the 1950s and still retains a fine undershot water-wheel and mill-stream flowing through its grounds, which include an outside seating area. A range of around 150 malt whiskies is on offer, including rarities such as a 1955 Strathisla at £30 a dram!

Food
The menu includes Aberdeen Angus steak and locally caught fresh fish. Barbecues are a regular feature in the summer, while the upstairs restaurant serves the best Scottish produce and dishes: the menu offers soups, haggis, venison casserole, black pudding and steak and ale pie.

The Old Mill Inn

Family facilities
Children are welcome. The pub garden features an attractive play area beside the water-wheel.

Alternative refreshment stops
Pitlochry is well provided with pubs, restaurants and cafes. Killiecrankie Visitor Centre has a small cafeteria for light snacks.

☞ Where to go from here
At the Pitlochry dam, which forms Loch Faskally, Scottish and Southern Energy has a small visitor centre celebrating its hydro-electric schemes. It also has a window into the salmon ladder beside the dam. From March to October you can watch the fish battle their way up towards Killiecrankie.

360 WIGTOWN
DUMFRIES & GALLOWAY

4 MILES (6.4KM) 3hrs

PATHS: Roads, old railway tracks and pavements

SUGGESTED MAP: aqua3 OS Explorer 311 Wigtown, Whithorn & The Machars

GRID REFERENCE: NX 439547

PARKING: At Wigtown harbour

THE PUB: Wigtown Ploughman

1 Leave car park, turn **R** and head uphill on narrow country lane, Harbour Road. House on **L** near top of road was former station house for **Wigtown**. Just before it is farm gate on **L**. Go through it and on to farm track.

2 Follow track to where it goes through another gate then veer **R** and climb up old railway embankment. This has a good grassy surface. Proceed along embankment and through gate.

3 Wall across track will stop you where former railway bridge carried track across **River Bladnoch**. Turn **R** and go down side of embankment and cross fence into field. Veer **R** and head across field to far corner then go through gate on to main road.

4 Turn **L** and walk through **Bladnoch**. At junction by roundabout, cross road to enter **Bladnoch Distillery** car park. After visiting distillery head back out of car park and turn **L** at roundabout. Continue along this road (B7005) for 1 mile (1.6km) to crossroads.

5 Turn **R** on to B733 and walk along it to **Wigtown**. At centre of town bear **L** round square and head towards large and impressive former county buildings. Pass them on your **R**, then church and war memorial on your **L** and continue downhill. Eventually turn **R** into car park for **Martyrs' Memorial**.

6 Walk through car park; turn **L** and make your way to bird hide at end of path. From here retrace your steps to car park and continue on path leading to **Martyrs' Memorial**. Turn **L;** walk over sands on wooden causeway to reach the memorial erected to mark the spot where the two women were drowned.

7 Return to path and turn **L**. Go through kissing gate then another gate, which is slightly below level you are walking on and to **L**. At end of path go through another gate in front of old station house, turn **L** on to Harbour Road and return to car park.

361 PORT LOGAN
DUMFRIES & GALLOWAY

3 MILES (4.8KM) 2hrs

PATHS: Shoreline, country lanes and hill tracks, 1 stile

SUGGESTED MAP: aqua3 OS Explorer 309 Stranraer & The Rhins

GRID REFERENCE: NX 097411

PARKING: Public car park on road to Logan Fish Pond

THE PUB: Port Logan Inn

1 From car park go across wooden walkway, down some steps on to beach and turn **L** to walk along beach. When you reach start of village climb on to road in front of **Port Logan Inn**. Turn **R** and then continue along main street, passing war memorial to reach **village hall**. In the television series, *Two Thousand Acres of Sky*, the village hall features as a school, and has a school sign fixed to the front. There's also a timetable for Caledonian MacBrayne ferries displayed on the notice-board on the wall. Opposite the village hall is a small but picturesque harbour with a

rather unusual lighthouse. Nowadays, when it is not in use as a film location, **Port Logan** harbour is used only by a few pleasure craft.

2 This was a thriving fishing port in the past and the **pier** once again looks as though it is busy, festooned with fishing gear, gas bottles and sacks of coal. Although they are all real, they are only there as props. Move away from harbour area and go along road to farm of **Muldaddie**.

3 Just before farm turn **L** on to old hill track and head uphill. Near the top look back downhill for a magnificent view back to the village and across **Port Logan Bay** to the Mull of Logan. Track is heavily overgrown here, and is blocked by barrier made from gates, but this can easily be crossed by stile at side.

4 Continue along track to T-junction. Turn **L**, go through gate and head along farm road to **Cowans farm**. Continue through farm steading and reach end of road at T-junction. Turn **L** on to B7065 and then head downhill.

5 Follow this winding road back to Port Logan then go back on to beach, turn **R** and retrace your steps to car park. From here you can continue along rough road to **Logan Fish Pond**. It's right at end on **L** and is by only building there.

362 DUNS
SCOTTISH BORDERS

4.5 MILES (7.2KM) 2hrs 30min

PATHS: Quiet roads and firm tracks

SUGGESTED MAP: aqua3 OS Explorer 346 Berwick-upon-Tweed

GRID REFERENCE: NT 785539

PARKING: Long-stay car park near Duns Market Square

THE PUB: Whip and Saddle

1 From Market Square walk northeast, and turn **R** along Currie Street and then **L** at main road **(A6105)** and continue ahead for about 1.5 miles (2km). Take care walking along this road as it can be busy. When the **A6105** bears off **R** continue ahead following signs for **Manderston House**.

2 After a short distance, you pass entrance to **Manderston House** on your R-H side. Continue walking ahead until your reach fork in road.

3 Take **L-H** fork and follow road downhill, then take track on **L** just after **Howdens Plantation**. Follow path, passing

in front of **Broomhill** on R. Continue ahead to cross cattle grid and join another road.

4 Turn **R**; take track on **L** that runs between cottages. Follow it between fields and under pylons. At main road turn **L**, then take turning to **R** ('Abbey St Bathans, Cranshaw and Gifford').

5 Follow road, take turning on **L** that leads into wildlife reserve. Follow track ('**Hen Poo**', lake). Pass pond on R and come to head of **Hen Poo**. Turn **L**.

6 Keeping lake on your **R**, follow track as it bears to **R**, around water. Continue, to cross cattle grid and, after short distance, enjoy great view of **Duns Castle**. Continue to castle entrance on your **R**.

7 Turn **L**, walk past **memorial** to John Duns Scotus and continue. When you reach a signpost on your **L**, you can follow this to climb **Duns Law**. Otherwise just follow road, go through arch, walk down Castle Street and continue ahead to reach start of walk in Market Square in **Duns**.

363 LEITH
CITY OF EDINBURGH

3.5 MILES (5.7KM) 1hr 30min

PATHS: Wide riverside paths and city streets

SUGGESTED MAP: aqua3 OS Explorer 350 Edinburgh

GRID REFERENCE: start NT 243739; finish NT 271766

PARKING: Scottish National Gallery of Modern Art, Belford Road

THE PUB: The Shore

1 From junction of Dean Bridge and Queensferry Street, turn **L** to walk down Bell's Brae. You are now in **Dean Village**, which dates back to 1128. It was once a milling centre and had 11 water mills producing meal for Edinburgh. At bottom, turn **R** into Miller Row.

2 Follow this to walk under impressive arches of Dean Bridge, designed by Thomas Telford and opened in 1832. Your path then runs along bottom of steeply sided gorge, beside **Water of Leith**, and feels extremely rural. Pass old well on your **L**, followed by impressive **St Bernard's Well**.

3 **St Bernard's Well** was discovered by schoolboys in 1760. The mineral water was said to have healing properties and, in 1789, the present Roman Temple was built. From here continue along main path, then go up steps. Turn **L**, and go **R** on to Dean Terrace to reach **Stockbridge**.

4 Cross road; go down steps ahead, immediately to R of building with clock tower. Continue to follow path beside river. Where path ends, climb on to road, turn **L** and then **R** to go down Arboretum Avenue.

5 Walk along this road, then turn **R** along path marked Rocheid Path. This runs beside river and is popular cycleway and jogging path. Follow this, passing backs of Colonies – low-cost housing built by Edinburgh Co-operative for artisans in the late 19th century. Walk to Tanfield Bridge.

6 Go **R**, over bridge, up steps, then turn **L**, walking towards clock tower. At end turn **L** along Warriston Place, cross road. Turn **R** down Warriston Crescent, lined with elegant town houses. Continue to **park**.

7 Bear **R**, around edge of park, then follow path uphill between trees. Turn **L** at top and follow cycle track ('Leith 1¼'). Follow it into **Leith**, where it brings you out near old Custom House. Bear **R** then **L** to walk along **The Shore**, before returning to town by bus.

364 CORPATCH
HIGHLANDS

4.5 MILES (7.2KM) 1hr 45min

PATHS: Wide tow paths, no stiles

SUGGESTED MAP: aqua3 OS Explorer 392 Ben Nevis & Fort William

GRID REFERENCE: NN 097768

PARKING: Kilmallie Hall, Corpach

THE PUB: Moorings Inn

1 Go down past **Corpach** Station to **canal** and cross sea lock that separates salt water from fresh water. Follow **canal** (on L) up past another lock, where path on **R** has blue footpath sign and **Great Glen Way** marker. It passes under sycamores to shore. Follow shoreline path past football pitch. Turn **L**, across grass to road sign warning motorists of nearby playground. Path ahead leads up wooded bank to tow path.

2 Turn **R** along tow path, for 0.5 mile (800m). Just before **Banavie** swing bridge, path down to **R** has **Great Glen Way** marker. Follow waymarkers on street signs to level crossing then turn **L** towards other swing bridge, one with road on it.

3 Just before bridge, turn **R** at signs for **Great Glen Way** and the Great Glen Cycle Route and continue along tow path to **Neptune's Staircase**. The 60ft (18m) of ascent alongside 8 locks is the serious uphill part of this walk, but more serious for boats. It takes about 90 minutes to work through the system.

4 Gate marks top of locks. About 200yds (183m) later, grey gate on R leads to dump for dead cars; ignore this one. Over next 100yds (91m) **canal** crosses little wooded valley, with black fence on R. Now comes 2nd grey gate. Go through, to track turning back sharp **R** and descending to cross stream.

5 On R, stream passes right under **canal** in arched tunnel, and alongside is 2nd tunnel which provides a walkers' way to other side. Water from the **canal** drips into the tunnel (it's a bit spooky) – try not to think of the large boats sailing directly over your head! At end, track runs up to join **canal's** northern tow path. Turn **R**, back down tow path. After passing **Neptune's Staircase**, cross A830 to level crossing without warning lights. Continue ahead along **R-H** tow path. After 1 mile (1.6km) tow path track leads back to **Corpach** double lock.

365 GAIRLOCH
HIGHLANDS

5.25 MILES (8.4KM) 2hrs 45min

PATHS: Tracks and smooth paths, mostly waymarked, no stiles

SUGGESTED MAP: aqua3 OS Explorer 433 Torridon – Beinn Eighe & Liathach or 434 Gairloch & Loch Ewe

GRID REFERENCE: NG 807756 on OS Explorer 433

PARKING: Beach car park, southern end of Gairloch

THE PUB: Old Inn

1 Cross road and head up to **R** of cemetery. Turn **L** at corner, into trees to track above. Turn **R** until footbridge leads on to wide path that descends. With wall corner ahead, turn **R** ('**Flowerdale Waterfall**'). Track descends to tarred driveway.

2 Turn **L** to pass **Flowerdale House**. Way is marked with red-topped poles. Track passes to L of old barn and turns **R** at sign for **waterfall** to pass **Flowerdale Mains**. In 0.25 mile (400m) pass concrete bridge on R.

3 Follow main path, still to L of stream to footbridge, just before you get to **Flowerdale Waterfall**.

4 Path leads up past **waterfall** to cross footbridge above. It runs up into pine clump, then turns back down valley. After another footbridge it joins rough track, to meet forest road beside Point **3**. Turn **L**, away from concrete bridge, through felled forest.

5 Look for blue-topped pole marking path on **R** with footbridge. It leads through meadowland and bracken with blue waymarker poles. Path bends **R** at old fence cornerpost and descends through bracken and birch to pass above and to L of enclosed field. Turn **R** under 2 large oak trees and cross stream to earth track.

6 Turn **L** for few steps, until small bracken path runs up to **R** past waymarked power pole. Path bends **L** under oaks, then drops to rejoin earth track. This soon meets larger track, old road from Loch Maree to Gairloch. Turn **R** along this, through couple of gates, to **Old Inn** at **Charlestown**.

7 Cross old bridge, and main road, to **pier**. Turn **R** at sign for Gairloch Chandlery, to tarmac path ('beach'). This passes to **L** of pinewood, then turns **R** into trees. It bends **L** and emerges to run along spine of small headland. Just before being carried out to sea it turns sharp **R**, and crosses above rocky bay to fort (An Dun). Duckboard path runs along back of beach, then turns **R** to car park.

Pub index

Here we list, by chapter, the pubs we suggest. The numbers in bold are the route numbers, not page numbers.

SOUTHWEST ENGLAND

Anchor, Shapwick,	Dorset	**37**
The Anchor Inn, Seatown,	Dorset	**19**
Bird in Hand, Saltford,	Bath & NE Somerset	**22**
Blackmoor Vale, Marnhull,	Dorset	**40**
The Brentor Inn, North Brentor,	Devon	**12**
The Bridford Inn, Bridford,	Devon	**16**
Cadgwith Cove Inn,		
Cadgwith Cove,	Cornwall	**3**
Castlebrook Inn,		
Compton Dundon,	Somerset	**35**
Cross Guns, Bradford-on-Avon,	Wiltshire	**48**
Crown Inn, Ibberton,	Devon	**39**
The Drewe Arms, Broadhembury,	Devon	**18**
Driftwood Spars Hotel,		
Trevaunance Cove,	Cornwall	**4**
Dumb Post Inn, Bremhill,	Wiltshire	**46**
Edgcumbe Arms, Cremyll,	Cornwall	**11**
The Flemish Weaver, Corsham,	Wiltshire	**24**
Fox & Hounds, East Knoyle,	Wiltshire	**47**
The George, Bathampton,	Bath & NE Somerset	**23**
The Godolphin Arms, Marazion,	Cornwall	**2**
Golden Lion, Port Isaac,	Cornwall	**25**
The Greyhound Inn, Corfe Castle,	Dorset	**21**
The Grove, Exmouth,	Devon	**17**
Hart Inn, Hartland Quay,	Devon	**30**
Hood Arms, Kilve,	Somerset	**33**
Hunter's Inn, Heddon Gate,	Devon	**29**
The Inn on the Green, Bude,	Cornwall	**8**
Lamorna Wink, Lamorna,	Cornwall	**1**
Logan Rock, Treen,	Cornwall	**27**
The New Inn, Veryan,	Cornwall	**5**
Pilchard Inn, Burgh Island,	Devon	**14**
The Puffing Billy,		
Great Torrington,	Devon	**10**
The Quarryman Inn, Edmonton,	Cornwall	**7**
Red Lion Inn, Avebury,	Wiltshire	**45**
Royal Oak, Meavy,	Devon	**28**
Royal Oak, Withypool,	Somerset	**31**
Rusty Ax, Stembridge,	Somerset	**34**
Saxon Inn, Child Okeford,	Dorset	**38**
The Sea Trout Inn, Staverton,	Devon	**15**
The Ship, Pentewan,	Cornwall	**6**
Ship Inn, Porlock,	Somerset	**32**
The Skylark Inn, Clearbrook,	Devon	**13**
The Springhead, Sutton Poyntz,	Dorset	**20**
Star Inn, St Just,	Cornwall	**26**
Three Elms, North Wootton,	Dorset	**41**
Three Tuns, Great Bedwyn,	Wiltshire	**43**
Wheatsheaf, Lower Woodford,	Wiltshire	**44**
The Williams Arms, Wrafton,	Devon	**9**
Winyard's Gap Inn,		
Winyard's Gap,	Dorset	**42**
Wookey Hole Inn, Wookey Hole,	Somerset	**36**

SOUTHEAST ENGLAND

The Anchor, Pyrford,	Surrey	**88**
The Bargeman's Rest, Newport,	Isle of Wight	**53**
Barley Mow, Waverley Abbey,	Surrey	**89**
The Black Horse, Amberley,	West Sussex	**60**
Blackwood Arms,		
Littleworth Common,	Buckinghamshire	**82**
The Boater's Inn,		
Kingston-upon-Thames,	Surrey	**67**
The Bridge Inn,		
Houghton Bridge,	West Sussex	**59**
The Bull, Ditchling,	East Sussex	**62**
The Bull's Head, Barnes,	London	**90**
Cittie of York, High Holborn,	London	**70**
Cock Horse, Headley,	Surrey	**72**
The Fox Goes Free, Goodwood,	West Sussex	**58**
George & Dragon, Sandwich,	Kent	**91**
The Giants Rest, Wilmington,	East Sussex	**65**
Golden Galleon, Seaford,	East Sussex	**64**
Hare and Hounds, Osterley,	London	**90**
Hare and Hounds, Stoughton,	West Sussex	**56**
Harrow, West Ilsley,	Berkshire	**78**
The High Corner Inn, Linwood,	Hampshire	**49**
King Henry VIII, Hever,	Kent	**96**
Lass O'Richmond Hill,		
Richmond,	Surrey	**69**
Little Gem, Aylesford,	Kent	**95**
Nag's Head, Sunningdale,	Berkshire	**75**
New Inn, Winchelsea,	East Sussex	**83**
The Oak Inn, Bank,	Hampshire	**51**
Pheasant Inn, Brill,	Buckinghamshire	**81**
The Plough and Harrow,		
Litlington,	East Sussex	**66**
Queens Head, Chackmore,	Buckinghamshire	**79**
The Queens Head, Burley,	Hampshire	**50**
The Ram Inn, Firle,	East Sussex	**63**
The Red Lion, Freshwater,	Isle of Wight	**52**
The Red Lion, Southwick,	Hampshire	**54**
Rising Sun, Charlwood,	Surrey	**85**
Rose & Thistle, Rockbourne,	Hampshire	**74**
Royal Oak, Poynings,	East Sussex	**61**
St George & Dragon, Wargrave,	Berkshire	**76**
The Shoe, Exton,	Hampshire	**55**
Simple Simon's, Canterbury,	Kent	**92**
The Spotted Cow, Hunston,	West Sussex	**57**
Stag, Mentmore,	Buckinghamshire	**80**
Star and Eagle Inn, Goudhurst,	Kent	**94**
Three Horsehoes, Brimpton,	Berkshire	**77**
Thurlow Arms, Baynards,	Surrey	**87**
Walnut Tree Inn, Aldington,	Kent	**93**
The White Cross, Richmond,	Surrey	**68**
White Hart, Godstone,	Surrey	**84**
The Wilton Arms, Kinnerton Street,	London	**71**
Wykeham Arms, Winchester,	Hampshire	**73**

WALES & THE MARCHES

Bala Lake Hotel, Bala,	Gwynedd	**114**
Black Cock Inn,		
Caerphilly Mountain,	Caerphilly	**100**
The Britannia Inn, Llangollen,	Denbighshire	**103**
Bryn Trych, Capel Curig,	Conwy	**102**
Castle Inn, Y Grib,	Powys	**113**
The Farmers Arms,		
St Bride's Major,	Vale of Glamorgan	**99**
The Glan-Y-Mor Inn, St David's,	Pembrokeshire	**97**
Jack Mytton Inn, Whittington,	Shropshire	**122**
King's Mill, Erddig,	Wrexham	**116**
The Kinmel Arms, Moelfre,	Isle of Anglesey	**101**
Kremlin Inn, Clee Hill,	Shropshire	**121**
The Lion Hotel, Leintwardine,	Shropshire	**105**
Llwyngwair Arms, Newport,	Pembrokeshire	**112**
The Malthouse, Ironbridge,	Shropshire	**109**
Oxwich Bay Hotel, Oxwich,	Swansea	**111**
Pandy Inn, Dorstone,	Herefordshire	**119**
The Plough Inn, Wistanstow,	Shropshire	**107**
Railway Inn, the Dysynni Valley,	Gwynedd	**115**
Red Lion, Kilpeck,	Herefordshire	**117**
River & Rail, Alveley,	Shropshire	**120**
The Riverside Inn, Aymestrey,	Herefordshire	**106**
Royal George,		
Harley's Mountain,	Herefordshire	**118**
The Royal Oak, Welshpool,	Powys	**104**
The Stackpole Inn, Stackpole,	Pembrokeshire	**98**
The Sun Inn, Corfton,	Shropshire	**108**
The Swan, ironbridge,	Shropshire	**110**

CENTRAL ENGLAND SOUTH

Barley Mow, Studley,	Warwickshire	**177**
Bear and Ragged Staff, Cumnor,	Oxfordshire	**168**
Bear Inn, Berkswell,	West Midlands	**175**
Beauchamp Arms, Dymock,	Gloucestershire	**155**
The Bell, Welford-on-Avon,	Warwickshire	**178**
The Bell & Cross, Clent Hills,	Worcestershire	**158**
Bird in Hand,		
Stourport-on-Severn,	Worcestershire	**162**
The Black Horse Inn, Naunton,	Gloucestershire	**128**
The Boat Inn, Ashleworth,	Gloucestershire	**125**
The Boot inn, Lapworth,	Warwickshire	**142**
Brockweir Country Inn, Brockweir,	Gloucestershire	**152**
The Canalside Café-Bar,	Birmingham	**139**
Carpenters Arms, Miserden,	Gloucestershire	**150**
The Castle Inn, Edgehill,	Warwickshire	**145**
The Chequers, Chipping Norton,	Oxfordshire	**132**
Coalhouse Inn, Apperley,	Gloucestershire	**153**
Country Girl, Hanbury Hall,	Worcestershire	**157**
The Crabmill, Preston Bagot,	Warwickshire	**138**
The Crown & Sandys Arms,		
Ombersley,	Worcestershire	**137**
Crown, Martley,	Worcestershire	**163**
Dun Cow, Dunchurch,	Warwickshire	**182**
The Eight Bells,		
Chipping Campden,	Gloucestershire	**129**
The Falkland Arms, Great Tew,	Oxfordshire	**133**
The Five Mile House,		
Duntisbourne Abbots,	Gloucestershire	**126**
The Folly Inn, Napton on the Hill,	Warwickshire,	**146**
Fosters Yard, Polesworth,	Warwickshire	**180**
The Fox Inn, Great Barrington,	Gloucestershire	**131**
Garrick Inn, Stratford-on-Avon,	Warwickshire	**179**

INDEX

Greyhound, Letcombe Regis, Oxfordshire 170
Horse and Groom,
   Bourton-on-the-Hill, Gloucestershire 148
Inn at Farnborough, Dasset, Warwickshire 181
The Kingsbridge Inn,
   Bourton-on-the-Water, Gloucestershire 130
Maltsters Arms,
   Rotherfield Greys, Oxfordshire 173
The Manor Arms at Abberley, Worcestershire 136
Masons Arms, Long Marston, Warwickshire 144
Mermaid, Wightwick, West Midlands 174
The Old Cock Inn, Droitwich Spa, Worcestershire 159
Old Swan Inn, Minster Lovell, Oxfordshire 165
Pheasant Inn, Toddington, Gloucestershire 147
The Plough, Prestbury, Gloucestershire 149
The Plough Inn, Kelmscott, Oxfordshire 134
Queens Head, Wolverley, Worcestershire 161
The Queens Head, Stoke Pound, Worcestershire 156
The Red Lion, Arlingham, Gloucestershire 124
Rose and Crown, Edge Hill, Warwickshire 176
The Rose & Crown, Warwick, Warwickshire 143
The Round Oak, Wombourne, West Midlands 140
The Royal Oak, Kingsbury, Warwickshire 141
Royal Sun, Begbroke, Oxfordshire 169
The Salmon's Leap, Worcester, Worcestershire 160
Saye and Sele Arms, Broughton, Oxfordshire 166
Ship Inn, Brimscombe, Gloucestershire 154
The Speech House Hotel,
   Coleford, Gloucestershire 123
Sun and Slipper, Mamble, Worcestershire 164
Three Horseshoes, Garsington, Oxfordshire 171
Town Arms, Wallingford, Oxfordshire 172
The Trout Inn, Lower Wolvercote, Oxfordshire 135
Turf Tavern, Oxford, Oxfordshire 167
The Wheatsheaf Inn, Northleach, Gloucestershire 127
Woolpack, Slad Valley, Gloucestershire 151

CENTRAL ENGLAND NORTH

The Bell Inn, Whittington, Staffordshire 187
Bluebell Inn, Tissington, Derbyshire 181, 214
The Bridge Inn, Brewood, Staffordshire 184
The Bull's Head,
   Ashford-in-the-Water, Derbyshire 198
Bulls Head Inn, Alton, Staffordshire 208
Castle Hotel, Castleton, Derbyshire 200
Duncombe Arms, Ellastone, Staffordshire 207
George & Dragon, Old Brampton, Derbyshire 213
George Hotel, Tideswell, Derbyshire 199
The Goats Head, Abbots Bromley, Staffordshire 186
The Horns Inn, Slitting Mill, Staffordshire 185
King's Head, Bonsall, Derbyshire 194
Lathkil Hotel, Over Haddon, Derbyshire 196
Loggerheads Inn, Loggerheads, Staffordshire 209
Mackworth Hotel, Mackworth, Derbyshire 216
Miner's Arms, Carsington, Derbyshire 215
Monsal Head Hotel, Monsal Head, Derbyshire 197
Navigation Inn, Chinley, Derbyshire 212
The Navigation Inn, Gnosall, Staffordshire 183
Old Black Horse, Mapperley, Derbyshire 190
Old Nags Head, Irby, Derbyshire 217

The Old Nags Head, Edale, Derbyshire 203
The Packhorse Inn, Crowdecote, Derbyshire 193
Plough, Endon, Staffordshire 206
The Plough Inn, Flagg, Derbyshire 195
Plume of Feathers, Barlaston, Staffordshire 210
The Queen's Arms, Old Glossop, Derbyshire 205
The Red Bull, Killerton, Staffordshire 211
The Scotman's Pack, Hathersage, Derbyshire 201
The Shoulder of Mutton,
   Osmaston, Derbyshire 188
The Waltzing Weasel, Hayfield, Derbyshire 204
Waterloo Inn,
   Biggin-by-Hartington, Derbyshire 192
The Wheel Inn, Ticknell, Derbyshire 189
Yorkshire Bridge Inn, Bamford, Derbyshire 202

EASTERN ENGLAND

The Bell, Odell, Bedfordshire 238
The Bell Inn, Gumley, Leicestershire 223, 243
Blue Bell Inn,
   Frisby on the Wreake, Leicestershire 242
The Buckinghamshire Arms,
   Blickling, Norfolk 231
Bull Inn, Cavendish, Suffolk 254
Cricketers, Bradwell on Sea, Essex 249
Cricketers Arms, Danbury, Essex 250
Crown Hotel, Long Melford, Suffolk 253
Falcon Inn, Castle Ashby, Northamptonshire 239
Finch's Arms, Upper Hambleton, Rutland 241
The Fox & Hounds, Exton, Rutland 224
The George, Great Oxendon, Leicestershire 221
Gin Trap Inn, Old Hunstanton, Norfolk 257
Green Dragon, Cheshunt, Hertfordshire 236
The Harbour Inn, Southwold, Suffolk 230
Horse and Groom, Linby, Nottinghamshire 245
Jolly Waggoners, Much Hadham, Norfolk 234
King's Head, Tealby, Lincolnshire 247
The King's Head, Laxfield, Suffolk 229
Mistley Thorn Hotel, Mistley, Essex 248
Nags Head, Lambley, Nottinghamshire 244
Navigation Inn, Overseal, Leicestershire 226
The Nevill Arms, Medbourne, Leicestershire 222
New Inn, Saltfleet, Lincolnshire 246
Old English Gentleman,
   Waltham Abbey, Essex 227
The Plough and Sail,
   Paglesham, Essex 228
Pykkerell Inn, Pakenham, Suffolk 252
Queen's Head, Breydon Water, Norfolk 255
Rose & Crown, Manea, Cambridgeshire 240
The Star Inn, Sulgrave, Northamptonshire 219
Swan Hotel, Thaxted, Essex 251
Three Blackbirds, Flamstead, Hertfordshire 237
Three Tuns, Ashwell, Hertfordshire 235
The White Horse, Blakeney, Norfolk 233
The White Horse,
   Brancaster Staithe, Norfolk 232
The White Horse, Empingham, Rutland 225
The White Horse,
   Old Northampton, Northamptonshire 220

Windmill, Great Cressingham, Norfolk 256
The Windmill, Badby, Northamptonshire 218

NORTHWEST ENGLAND

Black Bull Inn, Coniston, Cumbria 272
The Boot Inn, Boot, Cumbria 301
Bourne Arms, Knott End, Lancashire 265
Bridge Hotel, Buttermere, Cumbria 276, 302
Britannia Inn, Etterwater, Cumbria 299
Castle Inn, Kendal, Cumbria 294
Cavendish Arms, Cartmel, Cumbria 270
Commodore Inn,
   Grange over Sands, Cumbria 295
Crag Inn, Shutlingsloe, Cheshire 285
The Dalesman, Sedbergh, Cumbria 303
Dragon's Head, Whittington, Cumbria 305
The Duke's Head, Armathwaite, Cumbria 279
The Dusty Miller, Wrenbury, Cheshire 258
Eagles Head, Satterthwaite, Cumbria 298
George & Dragon Inn, Garrigill, Cumbria 281
Golden Rule Inn, Ambleside, Cumbria 296
The Grapes, Formby Point, Merseyside 287
Hanging Gate,
   Macclesfield Forest, Cheshire 286
The Hark to Bounty, Slaidburn, Lancashire 268
Horns, nr Goosnargh, Lancashire 293
Horse & Farrier Inn, Threlkeld, Cumbria 277
Inn at Whitewall, Hodder Valley, Lancashire 292
The Mill Inn, Mungrisdale, Cumbria 297
Mow Cop Inn, Mow Cop, Cheshire 282
The Newfield Inn, Seathwaite, Cumbria 271
Northgate Arms, Chester, Cheshire 260
Patterdale Hotel, Patterdale, Cumbria 274
Pendle Inn, Pendle Hill, Lancashire 291
The Ram's Head, Disley, Cheshire 263
Red Lion Inn, Little Budworth, Cheshire 259
Rigbye Arms, River Douglas, Lancashire 289
The Ring O'Bells, Frodsham, Cheshire 261
Ring O'Bells, Kendal, Cumbria 294
Royal Arms, Tockholes, Lancashire 264
Royal Oak, Alderley Edge, Cheshire 284
Royal Oak Inn,
   Bowness on Windermere, Cumbria 273
The Screes Inn, Nether Wasdale, Cumbria 275
Ship Inn, Bardsea, Cumbria 300
The Shireburn Arms, Hurst Green, Lancashire 266
The Silverdale Hotel, Silverdale, Lancashire 269
The Stork, Conder Green, Lancashire 267
The Sun, Dent, Cumbria 304
The Sun Inn, Pooley Bridge, Cumbria 278
Swan with Two Nicks,
   Litle Bolllington, Cheshire 262
Twa Dogs Inn, Keswick, Cumbria 302
Waggon and Horses, The Cloud, Cheshire 283
Weary Sportsman, Castle
   Carrock, Cumbria 280
White Horse Inn, Blackstone Edge, Manchester 288
Yew Tree Inn, Anglezarke, Lancashire 290

NORTHEAST ENGLAND

The Abbey Inn, Byland Abbey,	North Yorkshire	325
Allenheads Inn, Allenheads,	Northumberland	353
The Angel, Wetherby,	West Yorkshire	333
Bay Horse Inn, Terrington,	North Yorkshire	323
The Bingley Arms, Bardsey.	West Yorkshire	319
Bird in Bush Inn, Elsdon,	Northumberland	351
Black Bull, Etal,	Northumberland	348
The Blacksmiths Arms, Lastingham,	North Yorkshire	321
Blacksmiths Arms, Swainby,	North Yorkshire	342
Black Swan Hotel, Middleham,	North Yorkshire	337
The Brown Cow, High Ackworth,	West Yorkshire	307
The Buck Inn, Malham,	North Yorkshire	311
The Castle, Spofforth,	North Yorkshire	318
Chequers Inn, Fairburn Ings,	West Yorkshire	332
Cross Keys, Thixendale,	North Yorkshire	327
Crown Hotel, Middlesmoor,	North Yorkshire	317
Devonshire Arms Hotel, Bolton Abbey,	North Yorkshire	310
Dog and Gun, Oxenhope,	West Yorkshire	336
Falcon Inn, Arncliffe,	North Yorkshire	341
Farmers Arms, Muker,	North Yorkshire	339
The Forester's Arms, Carlton,	North Yorkshire	316
The Game Cock Inn, Austwick,	North Yorkshire	343
The George & Dragon, Aysgarth,	North Yorkshire	313
The George Inn, Hubberholme,	North Yorkshire	312
The Goathland Hotel, Goathland,	North Yorkshire	322
The Green Dragon Inn, Hardraw,	North Yorkshire	314
Greyhound Inn, Fulneck,	West Yorkshire	334
The Hambleton Inn, Sutton Bank,	North Yorkshire	324
Hare and Hounds, Lothersdale,	North Yorkshire	344
Hare and Hounds, Westgate,	Durham	345
The Harewood Arms, Harewood,	West Yorkshire	309
Kings Arms, York,	North Yorkshire	320
The Laurel Inn, Robin Hood's Bay,	North Yorkshire	328
Marsden Grotto, Marsden Bay,	Tyne & Wear	347
Millstone Inn, Carl Wark,	South Yorkshire	331
Miners Arms, Greenhowe,	North Yorkshire	338
The Morritt Arms Hotel, Greta Bridge,	Durham	346
New Inn, Thornton-le-Dale,	North Yorkshire	326
Old Red Bull Inn, Morpeth,	Northumberland	352
Percy Arms, Otterburn,	Northumberland	350
Rose & Crown, Holmfirth,	West Yorkshire	335
Rose and Thistle, Alwinton,	Northumberland	349
Shoulder of Mutton, Mytholmroyd,	West Yorkshire	308
Three Tuns, Thirsk,	North Yorkshire	340
The Wheatsheaf Hotel, Carperby,	North Yorkshire	315
Wolds Inn, Huggate,	East Riding	330
The Victoria Hotel, Robin Hood's Bay,	North Yorkshire	329
The Wortley Arms Hotel, Wortley,	South Yorkshire	306

SCOTLAND

The Anchor Inn, Coldingham,	Scottish Borders	358
The Cumberland, New Town,	Edinburgh	356
The Flotterstone Inn, Milton Bridge,	Edinburgh	355
The Forth Inn, Aberfoyle,	Stirling	354
Moorings Inn, Corpatch,	Highlands	364
Old Inn, Gairloch,	Highlands	365
The Old Mill Inn, Pitlochry,	Perth & Kinross	359
The Original Rosslyn Hotel, Roslin,	Edinburgh	357
Port Logan Inn, Port Logan,	Dumfries & Galloway	361
The Shore, Leith,	Edinburgh	363
Whip and Saddle, Duns,	Scottish Borders	362
Wigtown Ploughman, Wigtown,	Dumfries & Galloway	360

Acknowledgements

The Automobile Association wishes to thank the following photographer, photo libraries and establishments for their assistance in the preparation of this book.

Barnstaple Town Council 25tc; Black Bull Inn, Coniston 322c; The Blacksmith's Arms, Lastingham 378c; Blair Drummond Safari Park 402t; Cavendish Arms, Carmel 318tc; Clearwell Caves 150tc; Drayton Manor 186tr; Driftwood Spars Hotel 16c; Edinburgh Crystal 404t; Environment Agency 152tc; Glan-y-Mor Inn 118br; Goathland Hotel 380br; Hallaton Bottle Kicking 264t; Hoo Farm 144tc; Horse & Farrier Inn, Loweswater 332cr; Horseshoe Falls Pub 130br; E J van Koningsveld 163t; Illustrated London News 97tr, 105t, 181tr, 411tr; Imagestate 128br; Isle of Wight Tourism 70tr, 72t; Matchtight Events Ltd 106t (Phil Searle); Peak District Mining Museum 227t; Photodisc 64t, 121tc, 182tc, 185tl, 242tc, 244tr, 259tl, 302tr; Planning Solutions Ltd 271tl 271tr; Poole's Cavern, Buxton 226tc; RAF Museum, Cosford 207tc; Royal Gunpowder Mills 373t; The Royal Oak, Kingsbury 186br; Seven Sisters Sheep Centre 98t; Stapeley Water Gardens 295tc; Sulgrave Manor 257tr, 258t; Sun Inn, Corvdale 140cr; Tradesman Pub front cover r, 5b; The White Horse, Brancaster 284b; Yorkshire Lavender 381tr; York Tourism Bureau 375tl.

The remaining photographs are held in the Association's own photo library (AA World Travel Library) and were taken by the following photographers:

Martyn Adelman 212br, 263c, 270b, 383tl; Pat Aithie 129br, 130cl; Marius Alexander 409b; Norman Arlott 36tr, 77tl, 96tr, 122tr, 151tc, 167tl, 190tr, 206tl, 238t, 262t, 312tr, 324tr, 339tl, 364tr, 372tr, 379tl, 386tr, 388tr, 401tl; Adrian Baker 55tr, 135tl, 141c, 155c, 283tr, 309tr, 324bl, 369tr, 400tr; Peter Baker 3, 31tl, 35tr, 39br, 40tr, 42tl, 44tr, 47c, 48tr, 49tc, 61, 89t, 91c, 95b, 153br, 154cl, 154b, 192tl, 210tl, 213tl, 231tr, 235tr, 235b, 236tc, 300tl; Stewart Bates 117cl; Vic Bates 87t, 261tr, 373tl; Jeff Beazley 5t, 118t, 213tr, 225br, 226tl, 226br, 315tl, 337tr, 338tl, 409t, 409c; Pete Bennett 381cl, 382tr; Malc Birkitt front cover cr, 62bc, 229tr, 233tl, 234t, 245tr, 245b, 246c, 247t, 247c, 248t, 255tr, 258tl, 259tr, 260tr, 263t, 263b, 265tr, 266t, 267cr, 268t, 269t, 276t, 281b, 303tr, 303bl; P & G Bowater 312tl; Ted Bowness 317bl, 318tl, 318c, 320br, 321tr, 321br, 324c, 325tc, 326br, 328tr, 328br, 330cr, 331br, 334tr, 334br, 335t; Trevor Boyer 126tc, 129tl, 178tc, 181tr, 260tl, 265tl, 270tl, 274t, 277tr, 305tr, 351tl; Peter Brown 77br, 79bl, 83tr, 243t; Ian Burgum 116t, 117tr, 117br, 122tl, 123cr, 123bl, 124tl, 125br, 126cl, 144br, 149tr; Hilary Burn 9tc, 42tl, 66tr, 69t, 369tl; Michael Busselle 208tr; Nick Channer 135cl, 135br, 136bc, 137c, 138cr, 176cr, 177c, 177br, 178cr, 179bl, 179br, 180b, 190br, 195bl, 196c, 207c, 208cr, 213br, 214cr, 214bl, 215cr, 215cl, 216c, 218br, 255b, 256cr; Neil Coates 221c, 222cr, 222c, 222br, 226c, 228cr, 229bc, 230bc, 231br, 232cr, 234b, 236cr, 238c, 240b, 241c, 242t, 242b, 243cr, 244b, 248b, 249c, 250c; Douglas Corrance 403t, 406b; John Cox 23tc, 295tr, 308tr, 363tr; Derek Croucher 3, 73b, 75c, 115; Richard Czaja 45bl; Peter Davies 279c, 284t; Steve Day 3, 53tc, 55br, 56tr, 148bc, 155tr, 157bl, 157br, 159cr, 160cl, 161b, 162tc, 162bl, 163c, 165tl, 165c, 166c, 167tr, 167c, 168tc, 189br, 193tr, 291, 292tr, 292bl, 301tl, 301c, 302c, 322tr, 324tr, 326tc, 329br, 347tl, 400cl, 401cl, 401br, 411b; Kenya Doran 159tl, 161tl, 172tr, 173c, 191tl; Robert Eames 127cl; Eric Ellington 310tr; Richard Elliott 407cr; Robin Fletcher 68t; Derek Forss 62cl, 65c, 65b, 66c, 77cl, 100tl, 277tl; David Foster 72c; John Gillham 352tr, 354c, 356cr, 358cr, 360br, 368c, 369cl, 370c, 372cr, 374br, 384br, 386c, 388cr, 394cr; Robert Gillmor 84t, 86tl, 216tl; Joan Gravell 119tc, 120tr; Van Greaves 170tc, 194tc, 209tr, 211br; S Gregory 379l, 393c, 394tl; Tony Griffiths 311tl, 313tc; Paul Grogan 219tl, 220cl, 220cr, 257c, 258cr, 259c, 260cl, 260cr, 261c, 261b, 265b, 269c, 270cr, 271b, 272cl, 272cr; David Halford 74cr, 74bl, 74br, 80c, 83b, 84b, 88b, 92c, 96tl, 96b; David Hancock 10c, 14bc, 18cr, 18bc, 23tr, 24cr, 48cr, 120bl, 120bc, 122c, 122bl, 124c, 126br, 131tr, 132tl, 132c, 277c, 277b, 278cr, 280cr, 282b, 286br; Rebecca Harris 102c, 105c, 106c; James Hatts 99l, 99r, 100br, 103c, 103b, 104b, 107c, 108c, 273b, 274c; Peter Hayman 186tl, 195tl, 281t, 310t, 405tl; Mike Hayward 143tr, 143c; Anthony Hopkins front cover l, 3, 203, 204b, 222tl, 222tr, 224tl, 225tl, 225c, 227c, 228bl, 229tc, 230tr, 231c, 233cl, 236b, 237tc, 237tr, 237b, 238b, 239b, 241tr, 241b, 245c, 249t; Debbie Ireland 51tl, 52cr; Richard Ireland 15tl, 50tl, 81t, 151br, 152br, 156tc, 158tl, 224cr, 224cb, 262t, 262b; Nick Jenkins 116br; Caroline Jones 8br, 11bc, 19cr, 21cr, 29cr, 29bl, 32tc, 39tc, 54tl, 56cl, 129tr, 133tr, 134cl, 138tc, 142tr, 175tl, 175tr, 175br, 177tl, 298tr; Max Jourdan 47cr, 49br, 50tr, 107tr, 108t; Dennis Kelsall 51bl, 52bc, 53c, 54cl, 54cr, 56cr, 56bl, 133cl, 134bc, 142bc, 150cr, 151tr, 156bc, 160br, 162cr, 166cr, 168cr, 172bc, 181c, 182c, 183cr, 183bl, 184br, 187cr, 187bc, 188cr, 188br, 191c, 192cr, 205c, 205bl, 205bc, 210cr; Paul Kenward 109t, 110t; S King 326c, 333tr; Ian Knapp 264c, 266b, 268c; Alex Kouprianoff 371tr; Andrew Lawson 3, 7, 17tr, 23br, 29tl, 31br, 86tr, 126tr, 193bl, 258b; Cameron Lees 320cl, 327tr, 340tr; Ian Lewington 184tr; Tim Locke 86cr, 89c, 90cr, 97tl; Tom Mackie 4, 253, 254tc, 254tr, 254b, 279b, 282tr, 285tr, 286bl, 292cr, 293c, 293bc, 294cr, 295c, 295br, 296bc, 297c, 297cl, 298br, 299c, 299bl, 300bc, 302br, 304c, 305cl, 305br, 306cr, 307c, 307br, 308c, 309cl, 309br, 310br, 311c, 312br, 313tr, 313bl, 314cr, 315br, 316cr, 329c, 330tl, 331cl, 332tc, 333c, 336tr; S&O Mathews 30tc, 69c, 70tl, 79br, 88t, 92tl, 101tc, 101c, 102t, 158tr, 171tl, 278tr, 279tr, 281c, 283tl, 284c, 285tl, 286tr, 358tc, 360tl, 362tc, 363tl, 363c, 367tr, 368tl, 385tr, 386tl; Simon McBride 71b, 108b; Chris Mellor 208tl, 217tr; Andrew Midgeley 204ct, 204cb, 225tr, 227br, 239t, 240tl, 240tr; John Miller 77tr, 79tr, 86cl, 87b, 101b, 103t, 104t; Colin Molyneux 125tc; John Morrison 219tr, 347cr, 348tl, 348cr, 348bc, 349bl, 349br, 350tr, 350c, 354tr, 355tr, 358cl, 361c, 364tl, 364cr, 365tl, 367br, 369br, 370tr, 373cr, 374cl, 374tr, 375tr, 376cr, 377tc, 378bl, 382cl, 382cr, 383tr, 383bl, 384bc, 385c, 385br, 387tr, 388cl, 389tr, 389cr, 390tl, 390cr, 391tl, 391c, 392tr, 393tl, 393tr, 393bl; Robert Mort 105b; Roger Moss 8cl, 8bc, 9bl, 10tl, 11tl, 13br, 14cl, 14tr, 15c, 15cr, 16t, 18tl, 20tc, 24tl, 27tl, 27bl, 36tc, 37tl; John Mottershaw 294tl, 296tl, 299tl, 304tl, 314tc; Rich Newton 95t, 130tc, 131tc, 183tc, 270tr, 376tr, 379tr; C Nicholls 116bc; John O'Carroll 37c, 37br, 38br, 64cl, 164tc; Chris Orr 137tr, 246tc, 280tr, 282tl, 308tl; Hugh Palmer 153tlc, 189tlc, 190bl; Ken Paterson 3, 40tl, 196tl, 205tr, 256tl, 303tl, 399, 401tr, 403b, 404bl, 405tr, 405b, 406t, 412tl; Brian Pearce 30c, 32c, 32bl, 35c, 36br, 40cr; David Quinn 18tr, 280tl; Roy Rainford 171cr, 172tcl; Neil Ray 41tc; Darren Rees 117tc, 143tl; Eon Roberts 127tc; Chris Rose 12tr, 37tr, 45tr, 64tl, 94tl, 94tr, 155tl, 172tc, 173tc, 211tr, 232tl, 244tl, 250tl, 255tl, 256tr, 279tl, 286tl, 307tr, 320tl, 359tl 40tl, 410t, 412tr; Graham Rowatt 392br; Hamish Scott 402br, 404br, 406cr, 407b, 408cr, 410c, 412br; Peter Sharpe 317tr, 319tl, 322cl, 323tl, 323br, 325br, 329tr; Michael Short 134tr, 140tc, 141tr, 154tr, 160tr, 174tl, 196tr, 236tl, 316tc, 318tr; Jonathan Smith 400bl; Tony Souter front cover cl, 6, 62br, 65tr, 75t, 78tr, 81c, 85t, 85c, 90t; Jon Sparks 319c, 327cl, 328c, 335c, 335bc, 336br, 337c, 337br, 338cr, 339tr, 340c, 340br, 366c; Forbes Stephenson 3, 147, 166tc; Rick Strange 107tl; Nick Sumner 52tc; Richard Surman 120tl, 139tl, 141br, 214tc, 218tc; David Tarn 3, 345, 355cl, 357tl, 357c, 359bl, 359c, 366tl; Michael Taylor 408t; Rupert Tenison 11c, 19tl, 21tc, 22tc; Peter Toms 50cr, 68b, 70b, 78br, 82c, 82b, 98c; Martyn Trelawny 80tr, 82t, 91t, 92tr, 100tr, 110cl; Andy Tryner 215tcl, 215tcr, 221tr, 222tc, 228tc, 261tl, 272t; Sue Viccars 12bc, 19bl, 20c, 21bl, 22cr, 25bl, 26bc, 27tr, 28cr, 33t, 34cr, 41bc, 42cr; Wyn Voysey 26tc, 31tr, 43tr, 44cl, 44b, 46tc, 55tl, 63t, 64br, 66tl, 67tl, 67tr, 67c, 71t, 73t, 74t, 75br, 76t, 76b, 80tl, 81b, 93t, 93c, 94c, 110cr, 123tc, 132tr, 136tc, 142tl, 148br, 157tc, 164cr, 164br, 165tr, 169tl, 169tr, 169c, 170bc, 176tc, 180tl, 193tl, 275t, 275tb, 276b, 293tr, 306t, 336tl; Ronnie Weir 28tl, 411tl; Jonathan Welsh 139bl, 181tl, 185br, 187tl, 209c, 210tc; John White 83tl; Linda Whitwam 2, 13tl, 346b, 351cl, 352tl, 353bl, 361tc, 371bl, 372tl, 391tr; Harry Williams 34t, 149tl, 149c; Peter Wilson 349tr, 351tr, 361tr, 380tr; Trevor Woodcock 217br.

INDEX